COMPARISON OF TWO OR MORE POPULATIONS	ANALYSIS OF THE RELATIONSHIP BETWEEN TWO VARIABLES	ANALYSIS OF THE RELATIONSHIP AMONG TWO OR MORE VARIABLES
χ^2-test of a contingency table Section **13.3**	χ^2-test of a contingency table Section **13.3**	
Kruskal–Wallis test Section **14.5** Friedman test Section **14.6**	Spearman rank correlation Section **15.10**	
Analysis of variance: completely randomized design Section **12.2** Analysis of variance: randomized block design Section **12.3** Kruskal–Wallis test Section **14.5** Friedman test Section **14.6**	Simple linear regression and correlation Chapter **15**	Multiple regression Chapters **16** and **17**

STATISTICS

FOR MANAGEMENT AND ECONOMICS

Second Edition

STATISTICS

FOR MANAGEMENT AND ECONOMICS
A SYSTEMATIC APPROACH
Second Edition

Gerald Keller
Wilfrid Laurier University

Brian Warrack
Wilfrid Laurier University

Henry Bartel
York University

Wadsworth Publishing Company
Belmont, California
A Division of Wadsworth, Inc.

Acquisition Editor: Kristine M. Clerkin
Editorial Assistants: Nancy Spellman, Cathie Fields
Production Editor: Hal Lockwood, Bookman Productions
Associate Production Editor: Kristen Coston, Bookman Productions
Print Buyer: Martha Branch
Designer: Vargas/Williams/Design
Copy Editor: Steven Gray
Technical Illustrator: Alexander Teshin Associates
Compositor: Polyglot Compositors Pte., Ltd.
Cover: Vargas/Williams/Design
Signing Representative: Peter Jackson
Cover Illustration: Pauline Phung

Printed in the United States of America
2 3 4 5 6 7 8 9 10—94 93 92 91 90

Library of Congress Cataloging-in-Publication Data

Keller, Gerald.
    Statistics for management and economics.

    1. Management—Statistical methods.   2. Economics—
Statistical methods.   I. Warrack, Brian.   II. Bartel,
Henry.   III. Title.
HD30.215.K45   1990   658.4′033   89-70687
ISBN 0-534-12678-2

BRIEF CONTENTS

DETAILED CONTENTS

CHAPTER 15 **Simple Linear Regression and Correlation 660**

CHAPTER 16 **Multiple Regression 744**

KEY TO EXERCISE CODES

The exercises and cases illustrate how statistics can be used in a wide range of applications. The areas of applications of the cases and many of the exercises are identified using the following codes:

Application	Code
Accounting	ACC
Economics	ECON
Education	EDUC
Finance	FIN
General	GEN
Management	MNG
Marketing	MKT
Production/Operations Management	POM
Politics and Government	PG
Real Estate	RE
Retailing	RET
Science/Health	SCI
Tourism	TOUR

P R E F A C E

The second edition of this textbook is a further attempt to make the basic business and economic statistics course a more effective and enjoyable learning experience for both instructors and students. In preparing this edition we have been influenced by the overwhelmingly positive response to the first edition, in which we formalized an approach to teaching that many instructors found to be consistent with their own pedagogy. Our approach derived from a general disenchantment with the existing teaching material. We believed that there was far too much emphasis on number crunching and too little on meaningful practical applications. The results were unhappy, fearful students who were unable to satisfactorily perform statistical techniques. We believe that our systematic approach addresses this problem in the following ways.

STATISTICS CAN BE TAUGHT SYSTEMATICALLY

In general, students have little difficulty in understanding the central concepts of statistics or in performing the calculations. Where students face their greatest difficulty is in recognizing which technique to use to solve a specific problem. Students can practice their arithmetic skills solving exercises at the end of chapters. However, since these exercises must inevitably employ the methods described in those chapters, students are not challenged to identify the correct technique. That is, they're not challenged until they write exams, or must use statistical methods in other courses or in a practical application once they enter the real world of business. This book attempts to prepare students to successfully overcome the key challenge of statistics.

Our philosophy in this book can be expressed quite clearly. We regard the calculation of the statistical procedure as the least important element of an application. Far more important is the ability to set up the problem properly, which includes recognizing which technique to use. Equally important is the ability to interpret the results and incorporate the statistics into the larger decision problem. This philosophy is made operational in several ways.

In Chapter 5 we introduce the system by describing the critical factors that determine the appropriate statistical technique. These are the problem objective and the data scale. We teach that fundamentally all statistical techniques are alike in that (except for nonparametric methods) we start by identifying a parameter of interest, the parameter's estimator, the estimator's sampling distribution, which leads to the confidence interval estimate, and the test statistic. Changing a factor merely changes one or more of the elements. Review Chapters 11 and 18, placed at the midpoint and conclusion of statistical inference, allow students to practice recognizing the correct method.

STATISTICS MUST BE PERCEIVED AS USEFUL TO BUSINESS AND ECONOMICS

Recent academic conferences devoted to improving the teaching of applied statistics have advocated the use of cases to help motivate students. A large proportion of business and economics students are required to analyze case studies in other courses (e.g., marketing, finance, operations management and policy), but seldom if ever must they analyze statistics cases. The lack of exposure to realistic applications in their statistics courses fosters the impression that there are no useful applications of statistics. Our approach relies heavily on cases adapted from actual business studies published in journals, magazines, and our own consulting experience. Most provide extensive real data sets drawn from the studies. Twenty-six of the 52 cases can be analyzed by computer software, and for these the data have been stored on a disk available from Wadsworth Publishing Company. We have also added many new sections showing computer output accompanied by guidance for student interpretation and analysis.

STATISTICS MUST MAKE USE OF THE COMPUTER

In the first edition of our book we included a number of teaching aids to help instructors proceed with computerizing the course: Minitab and SAS instructions in appendixes, a few cases with large data sets stored on disk, and tutorial software. The reaction to these aids was quite overwhelming: there is no doubt that the movement to bring computers into the statistics course will grow in strength and numbers. For example, the American Academy of Colleges and Schools of Business has made computerized curricula an absolutely essential element of its accreditation requirements.

We have continued these aids and added many more (as described below), but what's most important about this movement is how it can favorably change the teaching and learning style of the course. Teachers can now focus on interesting problems, examples, and cases rather than calculations. As they move away from calculation, students begin to see the course as necessary and applicable while learning important microcomputer skills. The course becomes more interactive: instead of listening to a lecture, students can be called upon to reason through problems and interpret results. We continue to believe that students benefit from doing some calculations manually, particularly when a new technique is introduced. The key concepts of statistical reasoning are reinforced in this way. Consequently, most examples in this second edition are solved in three ways: manually, using Minitab, and using SAS. Instructors can emphasize any one of the three or, as we do, briefly describe the manual calculations and then discuss how to interpret the Minitab printout.

Our experiences with the first edition taught us that though nearly all of our colleagues are committed in the long term to having students use the computer for analytical work, some do not yet have the actual resources to do so. As an interim step, these instructors often decide to rely extensively on analysis and interpretation of computer output—the scenario business students are most likely to encounter.

Our much more extensive presentation of computer output in this second edition was designed to be of use in these classes.

In summary, through the features and teaching aids described above, we have attempted in this text to make teaching and learning business and economic statistics a more positive and useful experience. We try to make our business statistics classrooms minimodels of the business world—to help students step into the shoes of the business managers and executives they hope to be someday. To do this, we've developed a logical system that allows students to recognize easily the appropriate technique to use in a given situation. Once they've mastered this easy-to-use system, they can concentrate on analyzing data and interpreting the results—the real guts of the course, which computers now allow us to emphasize. We give them many exercises and cases to solve using real data, so they can put what they have learned to use. We even ask them to work in teams to solve problems and present case reports, as they might be required to do in business situations. We've tried to take the "math anxiety" out of the course and out of this textbook. During our almost ten years' experience, we've found that our students like this approach: they say it gives them more confidence and makes learning statistics more fun. We hope that your students have the same reaction to this textbook.

LEARNING AIDS

Though we have mentioned several of the book's learning aids above, it may be useful to summarize them here:

Cases. There are 52 cases scattered throughout the book. These have been adapted from real studies and provide real data. Students are expected to analyze the cases and draw conclusions in the same way as the authors of the studies. These cases are marked with a logo identifying the discipline most closely associated with the subject (accounting, finance, marketing, etc.).

Computer Output. For most of the worked examples throughout the text, we provide both the Minitab and SAS output. This exposes students to how statistics is actually applied in the real world. Whenever possible, we guide students in the interpretation of the output.

Minitab and SAS Instructions and Exercises. We provide instructions and commands for the actual use of these two popular packages in the appendixes of many chapters where they might actually be used. We have also included exercises in those appendixes permitting students to practice using the software.

Review Chapters. There are two review chapters in the text to help students identify the correct techniques. Chapter 11 appears midway through our discussion of statistical inference, and Chapter 18 reviews all of the statistical methods covered. Both feature flowcharts that summarize the systematic approach, as well as exercises and cases that require the use of *several, different* statistical procedures.

Exercises.   There are approximately 1,300 exercises of varying levels of difficulty in this book:

• *Learning the Techniques* exercises appear at the end of most sections. These were developed to help students learn the arithmetic involved in a specific procedure.

• *Applying the Techniques* exercises follow. These stress when and why the technique is used and show how the results assist in the decision-making process.

• *Supplementary Exercises* appear at the end of each chapter. Because they cover all the topics presented in that chapter, they offer students practice in identifying which of the techniques encountered in that chapter should be employed. They also tend to be more realistic and are considered somewhat more difficult than the other two types of exercises.

NEW IN THIS EDITION

This second edition features a number of improvements suggested by reviewers and users of the first edition that we hope will make the task of teaching and learning statistics more enjoyable. The major changes are as follows:

1. We now treat the analysis of variance (Chapter 12) much as we do multiple regression—as a technique involving too much calculation to be done by hand. Aside from two examples, which are computed the "long way," all examples and many exercises deal with interpreting computer output. Some exercises require students to complete the calculation of the relevant statistics in situations where most of the preliminary calculations have already been provided. For instructors and students who prefer to perform the analysis of variance by hand, Appendix 12.A provides the shortcut computations.

2. Chapters 19 (Time Series Analysis and Forecasting) and 20 (Index Numbers) have been rewritten to emphasize understanding the concepts as well as calculating the statistics.

3. Most sections now have *Self-Correcting Exercises*. These are exercises for which complete solutions have been provided in the chapter appendix. Students can work on these exercises and correct any mistakes themselves.

4. We've added about 500 new exercises and improved some of the others. Many exercises now have codes identifying the particular area of business and economics to which they apply.

5. New cases have been created, many of which require the use of a computer software package. The term *minicase* has been eliminated, and some former minicases are now called *cases.*

6. We now refer to the *required conditions* of statistical techniques, as opposed to the *assumptions.*

7. The overall appearance and readability of the text has been improved in a variety of ways, including the creation of many additional summary boxes for easy student reference.

8. Two new sections—describing the exponential distribution (Section 4.8) and the sign test (Section 14.3) have been created. The description of the *p*-value of a test (Section 7.6) appears earlier in Chapter 7. We now explain more fully what this statistic measures and how it is interpreted. In addition, we show how to calculate the *p*-value only when the test statistic is normally distributed.

9. New *computer output exercises* appear in many sections. These require students to analyze and interpret computer output. There are also new *software practice* exercises in the Minitab and SAS appendixes of many chapters. These exercises provide drill and practice in the use of the software.

TEACHING AIDS

To assist professors, we have provided a number of teaching aids. All of these aids are available from Wadsworth Publishing.

An *Instructor's Resource Book with Test Bank* includes the following elements:

1. Suggestions about teaching statistics using the systematic approach.

2. Transparency masters keyed to the teaching suggestions.

3. Teaching notes for each case, detailing goals of the case, assignment questions, analysis and solution, teaching strategy, and (where necessary) Minitab computer instructions.

4. A write-up of supplemental topics that have been omitted from the text but that some instructors may wish to cover (these have been formatted for easy reproduction and distribution to students):
   a. Joint probability distributions and covariance
   b. Continuous probability distributions with calculus
   c. Deriving the normal equations

5. SPSS instructions which can be used instead of Minitab and SAS (these too can be copied and distributed).

6. A test bank containing about 600 problems and answers, and a description of our approach to testing.

A *Solutions Manual* is also available. It furnishes detailed solutions to almost all of the textbook's exercises. These were produced by the authors with independent assistance from teaching assistants.

A *Data Disk* is available that stores the data from 26 of the cases as well as data for exercises requiring computer use.

For students, we have written a *Study Guide* that contains overviews of each chapter in the text, examples illustrating specific techniques, and exercises and their solutions. For use with the *Study Guide,* we offer the *Study Guide Tutorial Software,* which enables students to practice using appropriate statistical techniques as they work through 35 problems from the two review chapters (Chapters 11 and 18).

Interested instructors are advised to contact Wadsworth Publishing for the *Study Guide Tutorial Software*, which can be copied for student or computer laboratory use as they wish.

Wadsworth Publishing has made available an *option* to purchase this text packaged with the *Student Edition of Microstat II,* a powerful and easy-to-use statistical package. For less than the price of a study guide, students can have a personal copy of this software for use in the business and economic statistics course as well as other courses throughout their academic career. For further information on this option, please contact Wadsworth Publishing Company.

This book was developed from several courses we've taught in business and economics programs in a total of ten universities over a combined 45 years of teaching. We are most grateful to our colleagues, our teaching assistants, and especially our students, whose helpful suggestions, comments, and criticisms have benefited this text. We also acknowledge the excellent work of our word processor, Elsie Grogan.

The following reviewers also provided valuable suggestions and comments: Bruce Bowerman, Miami University; Maggie Capen, East Carolina University; Henry Crouch, Pittsburg State University (Kansas); Tim Daciuk, Ryerson Polytechnic Institute; Paul Eaton, Northern Illinois University; David Eldredge, Murray State University; Myron Golin, Widener University; Bhisham Gupta, University of Southern Maine; Robert C. Hannum, University of Denver; Iris B. Ibrahim, Clemson University; J. Morgan Jones, University of North Carolina; Howard Kaplon, Towson State University (Maryland); John Lawrence, California State University, Fullerton; Charles Lienert, Metropolitan State College (Denver); Yih-Wu Liu, Youngstown State University; Alan Neebe, University of North Carolina at Chapel Hill; Dennis Oberhelman, University of South Carolina; Nancy V. Phillips, University of Texas at Austin; Carl Quitmeyer, George Mason University; Farhad Raiszadeh, University of Tennessee at Chattanooga; Andrew Russakoff, St. John's University; Mike Ryan, University of South Carolina; Sunil Sapra, State University of New York, Buffalo; Stanley Schultz, Cleveland State University; Edwin Sexton, Wichita State University; Dale Shafer, Indiana University of Pennsylvania; Michael Sklar, Emory University; Craig Slinkman, University of Texas at Arlington; Jae H. Song, St. Cloud State University; William Stein, Texas A & M University; Jeffrey Strieter, State University of New York, Brockport; Will Terpening, Gonzaga University; Martin T. Wells, Cornell, University; Jim Willis, Louisiana State University; Marvin Wolfmeyer, Winona State University; Chin Yang, Clarion University; and Ben Zirkle, Virginia Western Community College.

WHAT IS STATISTICS?

INTRODUCTION TO STATISTICS

To some people, statistics means summarized numerical data, such as unemployment figures or the number of runs, hits, and errors in a baseball game. To others, it means an unpleasant course on the way to a business or economics degree. Neither description is adequate. In presenting our subject as a method of getting information from data to help managers make decisions, we will show that statistics comprises various techniques with a wide range of applications to practical problems. Managers today have access to more data than ever, through the ever-increasing use of computers, and they risk confusion unless they can effectively screen the data for useful information.

Examples from different areas of business and economics will provide illustrations of various applications of statistical methods. Statistical techniques will be applied to problems in production (such as quality control), finance (investment analysis and forecasting), marketing (analysis of market surveys), and accounting (statistical auditing).

Statistics is a body of principles and methods concerned with extracting useful information from a set of numerical data. It can be subdivided into two basic areas: descriptive statistics, and inferential statistics. **Descriptive statistics** deals with methods of organizing, summarizing, and presenting numerical data in a convenient form. For example, a fast-food franchiser may wish to compare the weekly sales levels over the past year at two particular outlets. Descriptive statistical methods could be used to summarize the actual sales levels (perhaps broken down by food item) in terms of a few numerical measures, such as the average weekly sales level and the degree of variation from this average that weekly sales may undergo. Tables and charts could be used to enhance the presentation of the data so that a manager could quickly focus on the essential differences in sales performance at the two outlets.

There is much more to statistics, however, than these descriptive methods. Decision makers are frequently forced to make decisions based on a set of numerical data that is only a small subset (sample) of the total set of relevant data (population). **Inferential statistics** is a body of methods for drawing conclusions (that is, making inferences) about characteristics of a population, based on information available in a sample taken from the population. The following example illustrates the basic concepts involved in inferential statistics.

A cable television company is contemplating extending its selection of pay-TV offerings by adding a business channel, whose programming is devoted to stock-market quotations, news reports, and commentaries from the world of business.

After some careful financial analysis, the company has determined that the proposed channel would break even if at least 10% of all households subscribing to the company's basic service also signed up for the new channel. This collection of all households of interest is called the **population**. To obtain additional information before reaching a decision on whether or not to proceed with the new business channel, the cable company has decided to conduct a survey of 500 of the households subscribing to its basic service. These 500 households are referred to as a **sample** of households, selected from the entire population. Each household in the sample is asked if it would subscribe to the proposed channel if it were offered at some specified price. Suppose that 60 of the households in the sample reply positively. While the positive response by 60 out of 500 households (12%) is encouraging, it does not assure the cable company that the proposed channel will be profitable.

If the cable company concludes, based on the sample information, that at least 10% of *all* households in the population would subscribe to the proposed channel, the company is relying on inferential statistics. The company is drawing a conclusion, or making a **statistical inference**, about the entire population of households on the basis of information provided by only a sample taken from the population. The available data tell us that 12% of this particular sample of households would subscribe; the inference that at least 10% of all households would subscribe to the new channel may or may not be correct. It may be that, by chance, the company selected a particularly agreeable sample and that, in fact, no more than 5% of the entire population would subscribe.

Whenever an inference is made about an entire population on the basis of evidence provided by a sample taken from the population, there is a chance of drawing an incorrect conclusion. Fortunately, other statistical methods allow us to determine how **reliable** the statistical inference is. They enable us to establish the **degree of confidence** we can place in the inference, assuming the sample has been properly chosen. These methods would enable the cable company to determine, for example, the likelihood that less than 10% of the population of households would subscribe, given that 12% of the households sampled said they would subscribe. If this likelihood is deemed small enough, the cable company will probably proceed with its new venture.

SECTION 1.2
THREE KEY STATISTICAL CONCEPTS

The foregoing example introduced three key considerations present in the solution to any statistical problem: the population, the sample, and the statistical inference. We will now elaborate more fully on each of these.

POPULATION

A **population** is the set of all items of interest in a statistical problem. It is frequently very large and may, in fact, be infinitely large. Unlike its meaning in everyday usage, the word *population* in statistics does not necessarily refer to a group of people. It may, for example, refer to the population of diameters of ball bearings produced at a large plant. In another case, it may refer to the population of owners of cars, where the measurement of interest is the make of car. Although, technically speaking, a population consists of a set of observations or measurements, we will not attempt to make the fine distinction between the observations per se and the objects about which the observations are made. Thus, for practical purposes, the population in our preceding example may be taken either as the set of all households subscribing to the basic cable service or as the set of all responses given by these households.

A descriptive measure of a population is called a **parameter**. The parameter of interest in the pay-TV example was the proportion of all households that would subscribe to the new business channel. If the population under consideration is a collection of ball bearings, two possible parameters would be the *average* of the ball bearing diameters and the *proportion* of diameters in the population that exceed a specified size.

SAMPLE

A **sample** is a set of data drawn from the population. For example, if we observe the diameters of 100 ball bearings, that set of observations would represent a sample from the population described earlier. Other examples of samples include the daily sales by a department store for the past month, the annual dividends paid last year by 50 companies listed on the New York Stock Exchange, and the annual salaries of 100 doctors in Albuquerque.

A descriptive measure of a sample is called a **statistic**. In the sample of 100 ball bearings mentioned above, the proportion of these 100 whose diameters exceed a specified size would be a sample statistic that could be used to estimate the corresponding population parameter. Unlike a parameter, which is a constant, a statistic is a variable whose value varies from sample to sample. The variability of statistics is what we study in this book.

STATISTICAL INFERENCE

Statistical inference—the process of making an estimate, forecast, or decision about a population, based on the sample information—is the primary purpose of statistics. Because populations are very large, it is impractical and expensive to investigate or survey every member of a population. (Such a survey is called a **census**.) It is far cheaper and easier to take a sample from the population of interest and to draw conclusions about the population based on information provided by the sample.

For instance, the Nielsen ratings provide television network executives with estimates of the number of television viewers who are tuned into each network. Despite the fact that the number of potential viewers is more than 200 million in the United States and 20 million in Canada, the inference is based on a sample of only 2,000 viewers. Likewise, political pollsters predict, on the basis of a sample of about

1,500 voters, how the entire population of voters will cast their ballots; and quality-control supervisors estimate the proportion of defective units being produced in a production process from a sample of several hundred units.

Because a statistical inference is based on a relatively small subset of a large population, statistical methods can never decide or estimate with certainty. Since decisions involving large amounts of money often hinge on statistical inferences (millions of dollars of advertising revenue depend on the Nielsen ratings, for example), the reliability of the inferences is very important. As a result, each statistical technique includes a measure of the reliability of the inference. For example, if a political pollster predicts that a candidate will receive 40% of the vote, the measure of reliability might be that the true proportion (determined on election day) will be within 3% of the estimate on 95% of the occasions when such a prediction is made.

You will find, as we progress through this text, that the appropriate technique to choose depends on the population involved and the type of information you want. In turn, the measure of reliability depends on the technique you select.

SECTION 1.3   ## PRACTICAL APPLICATIONS

Throughout the text, you will find cases that describe actual situations from the business world in which statistical procedures have been used to help make decisions. For each case, you will be asked to choose and apply the appropriate statistical technique to the given data and to reach a conclusion. Following are summaries of a few of these cases, without the data, to illustrate additional applications of inferential statistics. But you'll have to wait until you work through these cases yourself to find out the conclusions and results.

CASE 1.1*

When consumers shop outside their local trading area, the phenomenon is called *outshopping*. Small communities are much affected by outshopping: the prosperity of the area declines if outshopping becomes too prevalent. If local retailers can figure out what factors cause outshopping, they may be able to curtail it. In a study to learn more about this phenomenon, three researchers (Samli, Riecken, and Yavas) examined a small locality where everyone outshops to some extent.

The study involved a survey of a sample of 113 residents, some of whom outshopped frequently and some of whom did not. The survey solicited information concerning the residents' demographic characteristics, the number of outshopping trips they made each year, and the types of products they purchased. After using descriptive statistical methods to summarize the data collected from the survey, the

* Adapted from A. C. Samli, A. Riecken, and G. Yavas, "Intermarket Shopping Behavior and the Small Community: Problems and Prospects of a Widespread Phenomenon," *Journal of the Academy of Marketing Science* 11 (1, 2) (1983): 1–14.

researchers used techniques from inferential statistics to determine whether differences existed between frequent outshoppers and infrequent outshoppers with respect to such demographic characteristics as age and income. Statistical tests were also conducted to determine which (if any) types of products (groceries, jewelry, furniture, and so on) were more likely to be purchased out of town than in town. The results of such tests could assist local retailers in determining where they should concentrate their efforts to curtail outshopping.

CASE 1.2

Investors frequently entrust their funds to an "active" investment manager, who seeks to invest the funds in a portfolio of stocks that will earn a rate of return higher than the market average, as measured (for example) by the Dow Jones Industrial Average. Because investors often select investment managers on the basis of their past performance, an important question is whether or not past performance is a reliable indicator of future performance. This question was addressed by Dunn and Theisen,* who collected annual returns for 201 institutional portfolios covering the period from 1973 through 1982.

The stock portfolios were then ranked—first according to how well they performed over the period from 1979 through 1981, and second according to how well they performed in 1982. It would be too much to expect the two rankings to coincide; however, statistical techniques can be used to determine if the disparity that does appear between the two rankings is too great for an investor to reasonably conclude that portfolio managers who perform well in one period will continue to perform well over the next period. Based on a statistical investigation of the portfolio performance rankings for several pairs of consecutive periods, the study drew conclusions about the predictive ability and consistency of active portfolio managers.

CASE 1.3[†]

Bonanza International is one of the top 15 fast-food franchisers in the United States. Like McDonald's, Burger King, and most others, Bonanza uses a menu board to inform customers about its products. One of Bonanza's bright young executives believes that not all positions on the board are equal. That is, he feels that the position of the menu item on the board influences sales. This is an important concept because, if true, Bonanza should place its high-profit items in the positions that produce the highest sales. After watching the eye movements of several people, the executive noticed that customers first looked at the upper right-hand corner,

---

* Patricia C. Dunn and Rolf D. Theisen, "How Consistently Do Active Managers Win?" *Journal of Portfolio Management* 9 (1983): 47–50.

† Adapted from M. G. Sobol and T. E. Barry, "Item Positioning for Profits: Menu Boards at Bonanza International," *Interfaces* (February 1980): 55–60.

FIGURE 1.1   *DIRECTION OF EYE MOVEMENT ACROSS MENU BOARD*

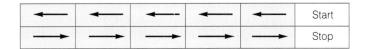

then across the top row to the left-hand side, then down to the lower left-corner, and finally across the bottom toward the right (see Figure 1.1).

This analysis suggested that items placed in the upper right-hand corner are likely to produce higher sales than items placed in the lower left-hand corner. In order to test this hypothesis, 10 Bonanza stores with similar characteristics were chosen as sites for the test, and two moderately popular items were selected as variables. During weeks 1 and 3 (of a 4-week study), item *A* was placed in the upper right-hand corner and item *B* was placed in the lower left-hand corner. In weeks 2 and 4, the positions were switched. The number of sales of each item was recorded for each week and for each store. Statistical procedures were then applied to this sample of data to determine whether the young executive was correct in thinking that menu position influences sales.

CASE 1.4*

A successful television advertisement must attract and hold the attention of the viewer. Numerous techniques are used for this purpose, but one of the most popular is to use ads with sexual content. At the same time, it is possible that some viewers will be offended by such an advertisement. In an investigation of the effectiveness of advertisements with sexual content, two groups of university students were selected as the sample. The 53 students in Group *A* were shown 10 ads with sexual content, while the 60 students in Group *B* were shown similar ads without sexual content. Immediately after viewing each ad, the students in both groups were asked to rate the ad (on a scale from 1 to 5) on its power to attract and hold attention.

A second phase of the investigation attempted to measure the effect of an advertisement's sexual content on the viewer's ability to recall the product advertised. Two days after viewing the advertisements, each student was asked to name the specific brands mentioned in the ads. The responses from both phases of the study were then summarized and used as a basis for making statistical inferences regarding the effectiveness of sexual content in advertisements in attracting attention, holding attention, and increasing product recall. As always, the statistical inferences were made on the assumption that the responses of the sample of students fairly represented the responses of the entire population of viewers.

* Adapted from L. T. Patterson and J. K. Ross, "A Study of Sex in Advertising," *Developments in Marketing Science* 7 (1984): 244–48.

The National Patent Development Corporation (NPD) has recently acquired a new product that can be used to replace the dentist's drill. The product, called Caridex, is a solution that dissolves decayed matter in cavities, without drilling. NPD would like to forecast its first-year profits from the solution and the solution's dispensing unit, which is approximately the size of a large radio.

NPD has learned that about 100,000 dentists in the United States treat cavities. (An additional 35,000 do work that does not involve cavities.) The dispensing unit costs NPD $200; and the company intends to sell the unit for $800. The solution costs $0.50 per cavity and will be sold to dentists for $2.50 per cavity. Fixed annual costs are expected to be $4 million.

To complete the collection of information necessary to forecast profits, NPD might undertake a survey of several hundred dentists. Armed with relevant survey results—such as the proportion of dentists in the sample who would purchase the dispensing unit and the average number of cavities filled each week by these dentists—NPD could use statistical procedures to make inferences about its expected share of the entire market. NPD could then combine these results with its other information to estimate its expected profits in the first year of operation.

SECTION 1.4 **STATISTICS AND THE COMPUTER**

In many practical applications of statistics, the statistician must deal with large amounts of data. For example, in Case 1.1 the data would include (among other variables) the ages and incomes of the 113 people who were surveyed. As part of the statistical analysis, the statistician would have to perform various calculations using the data; and although the calculations do not require any great mathematical skills, the sheer number of computations involved makes this aspect of the statistical method time-consuming and tedious. Fortunately, numerous commercially prepared computer programs are available to perform some or all of the arithmetic work involved.

An introduction to two of the most commonly used packages of computer programs—Minitab and SAS—can be found in Appendix 1.A (see page 10). Instructions for using them appear in appendixes to chapters involving applications for which the computer can be used.

If you have access to either of these computer packages, we advise you to become acquainted with it, for several reasons. Using a computer will save you a great deal of time and frustration (particularly if, like most human beings, you are prone to making arithmetic errors). It will also allow you to concentrate on the more important aspects of statistical analysis: recognizing which technique to use, and understanding the computations. In addition, since the computer is almost always used in real-life statistical applications, learning how to use it effectively will help you in applying statistical techniques to problems in actual business and economic settings. Even if you do not anticipate being employed in a job that requires you to perform statistical calculations, you will very likely have to read and interpret computer output at some point. Therefore, at the very least, you should become familiar with the format of the output.

The approach we prefer to take is to minimize the time spent on manual computations and to focus instead on selecting the appropriate technique to deal with a problem and on interpreting the output after the computer has performed the necessary computations. To this end, many of the examples in this book have been solved using computer packages. Wherever possible, immediately following these examples, we provide the output that was generated by one or both of the computer packages (Minitab and SAS).

EXERCISES

UNDERSTANDING THE CONCEPTS

1.1 In your own words, define and give an example of each of the following statistical terms:

a. population

b. sample

c. parameter

d. statistic

e. statistical inference

1.2 Briefly describe the difference between descriptive statistics and inferential statistics.

1.3 In each of the five real cases outlined in this chapter, more than one statistical inference is required. For Cases 1.1, 1.3, and 1.5, describe one of these statistical inferences. Your answer should briefly describe the population and its parameter, the sample and its statistic, and the type of inference that is required.

INTRODUCTION TO STATISTICAL APPLICATION PACKAGES

This textbook will describe how to use approximately 40 different statistical techniques. All of the exercises and examples that require these methods can be performed with the assistance of an inexpensive calculator, since they have relatively small data bases. In real-life applications of statistics, however, the sample sizes are quite large, and solving a problem often requires the application of several techniques. The amount of calculation involved in solving the problem can be formidable. As a result, in practice the computer is almost always employed for statistical problem solving. Fortunately, statisticians do not have to create their own programs for this use. Previously prepared programs—often referred to as **"canned" computer programs** or, in modern terminology, **statistical application packages**—are quite readily available.

In this book we will provide instructions for using two of the most popular statistical application packages: Minitab and SAS. Minitab is quite popular with students because it is extremely user-friendly, and the commands it operates on are quite short. The statistical application package, SAS, is designed for larger data bases and is capable of very powerful statistical computations.

Instructions for both Minitab and SAS are provided in the appendixes of the chapters for which the system performs the statistical techniques there described. For example, Appendix 2.A and Appendix 2.B give instructions for commanding the computer to produce various descriptive statistics presented in Chapter 2. Ways of inputting, editing, and printing data are also discussed in these appendixes. The other chapters that have appendixes containing computer instructions are Chapters 7, 9, 11, 12, 13, 14, 15, 16, and 19.

DESCRIPTIVE MEASURES AND PROBABILITY

The first part of this book lays the foundation for the explanations of the statistical techniques that follow. Chapter 2 discusses graphical and numerical methods used to summarize and describe sets of data. Chapters 3 and 4 develop the concepts and techniques of probability that form the basis of all statistical methods.

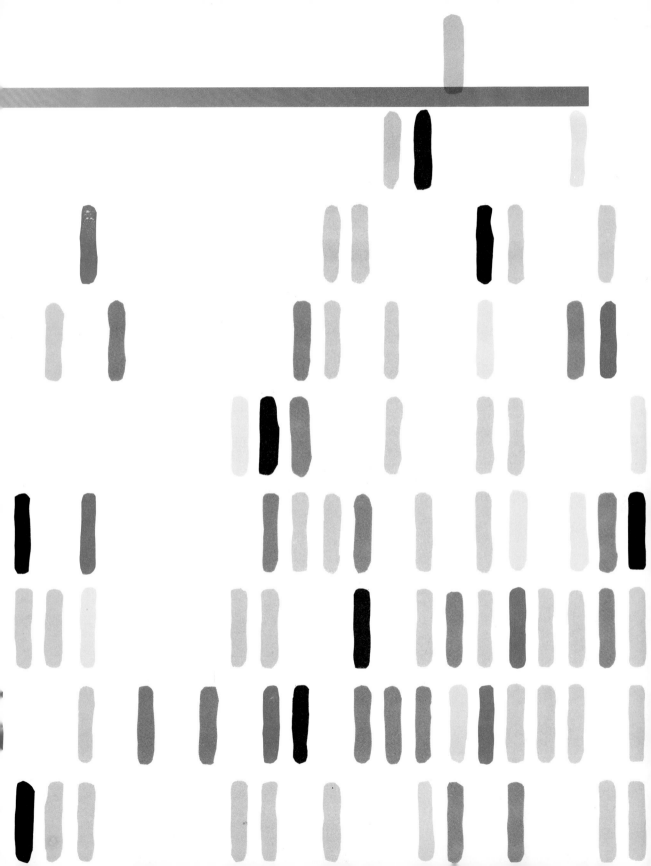

DESCRIPTIVE STATISTICS

INTRODUCTION

In Chapter 1, we pointed out that statistics is divided into two basic areas: descriptive statistics and inferential statistics. The purpose of this chapter is to describe the principal methods that fall under the heading of descriptive statistics.

The term **data** refers to the actual observations that result from an experiment or investigation. They may be either quantitative (numerical) or qualitative (categorical). Examples of quantitative data include the wages of a company's employees, the daily closing prices of gold bullion over the last year, and the number of beers consumed weekly by students on a particular campus. Although qualitative data, such as the brands of toothpaste preferred by a group of shoppers, cannot be measured in a purely numerical way, they can be categorized according to some qualitative criterion (such as brand of toothpaste), followed by a numerical count of the observations in each category.

Managers frequently have access to large masses of potentially useful data. But before the data can be used to support a decision, they must be organized and summarized. Consider, for example, a video store manager who has just received a detailed record of the thousands of purchases made at her store during the past year. In its present form, the data set is simply too voluminous to give the manager a clear picture of the store's operations. But by using descriptive statistical methods, the manager can determine average weekly sales levels, peak periods of activity, the relative success of various products, and so on.

Descriptive statistics, then, involves arranging, summarizing, and presenting a set of data in such a way that the meaningful essentials of the data can be extracted and grasped easily. Its methods make use of graphical techniques and of numerical descriptive measures to summarize and present the data in a meaningful way. Although descriptive statistical methods are relatively straightforward, their importance should not be underestimated. Most students of business and economics will encounter numerous opportunities to make valuable use of descriptive statistics when preparing reports and presentations in the workplace.

Recall, from Chapter 1, that a **population** is the entire set of observations or measurements under study, while a **sample** is a set of observations selected from the population and is therefore only a part of the entire population. The descriptive methods presented in this chapter apply equally well to data consisting of an entire population and to data consisting of a sample drawn from a population.

SECTION 2.2   ## *FREQUENCY DISTRIBUTIONS*

The first step to take in making sense of a mass of numerical data is to form what is known as a *frequency distribution*. This is a simple, effective method of organizing and presenting data so that one can get an overall picture of where measurements are concentrated and how spread out the measurements are.

Consider a Dallas firm that is interested in the duration of long-distance telephone calls placed by its employees. Controlling the cost of these calls is important because, for many large companies (such as national accounting firms), costs may run into the hundreds of thousands of dollars per month. Suppose that, three months ago, our Dallas firm instituted a program to encourage employees to reduce the cost of long-distance calls. Employees were urged to reduce the duration of their longer calls by minimizing the amount of small talk and the amount of file searching during each call. At the same time, employees were urged to reduce the number of their shorter calls. Several short calls were placed daily to the Houston office for purposes of checking customers' credit. Cost savings would result if fewer such calls were placed, with more than one credit check requested per call, since the long-distance charge per minute falls dramatically after the first few minutes.

Suppose that, given the job of collecting and summarizing relevant data on the firm's calls, you record the duration of a sample of 30 long-distance calls placed in a given week. The results are shown in Table 2.1.

Once you have collected this set of 30 measurements, your next task is to extract some meaningful information from the data. You might begin by noting the smallest and largest measurements. In this case, the shortest call was 2.3 minutes, while the longest one was 19.5 minutes. Aside from these two extreme values, we are less interested in each particular observation than in how the observations are distributed between the smallest and largest values. That is, we wish to determine the proportions of all observations that lie within various intervals between the two extreme observations. For example, did about 75% of all long-distance calls in the sample last more than 14 minutes, with only a small percentage lasting less than 5 minutes? Or did most calls last about 10 minutes, give or take a few minutes, with only a small proportion of phone-call durations approaching either of the two extremes?

This information is easily obtained by forming a **frequency distribution**—an arrangement or table that groups data into intervals called **classes** and records the number of observations in each class. One possible frequency distribution for the data in Table 2.1 is given in Table 2.2.

As can be seen from Table 2.2, a set of data presented in the form of a frequency distribution is more manageable than the original set of raw data, although some of the detailed information is lost. For example, the information in the frequency distribution does not allow us to say anything about the actual values within each class.

Before constructing a frequency distribution, we must decide on the appropriate number, size, and limits of classes to use. The choices of these are intertwined, and it is usually best to experiment with a few different choices in order to find the

TABLE 2.1	*DURATION OF LONG-DISTANCE CALLS (in minutes)*

11.8	3.6	16.6	13.5	4.8	8.3
8.9	9.1	7.7	2.3	12.1	6.1
10.2	8.0	11.4	6.8	9.6	19.5
15.3	12.3	8.5	15.9	18.7	11.7
6.2	11.2	10.4	7.2	5.5	14.5

TABLE 2.2	*FREQUENCY DISTRIBUTION OF TELEPHONE-CALL DURATIONS*

Class Limits	Tally	Frequency
2 up to 5*	|||	3
5 up to 8	⊬		6
8 up to 11	⊬ |||	8	*a lot of activity*
11 up to 14	⊬ ||	7
14 up to 17	||||	4
17 up to 20	||	2
Total		30

* Class contains all measurements from 2 up to (but not including) 5.

most useful frequency distribution. Despite the arbitrariness of the choice of classes, a few guidelines can be given. The classes must be nonoverlapping and must contain all observations; that is, each observation must fall into exactly one class. The number of classes used normally ranges between 5 and 20, with fewer classes used for smaller data sets. If the number of classes chosen is too large, detecting the major clusterings of observations (which helps to reveal the shape of the distribution) becomes difficult. An example of this is shown in Table 2.3(a). On the other hand, if the number of classes chosen is too small, too much detail is lost. This is evident from Table 2.3(b). While the appropriate number of classes to use is ultimately a subjective decision, a rough guide is provided in Table 2.4.*

---

* A rough guide to the number of classes k required to accommodate n measurements is given by Sturge's formula: $k = 1 + 3.3 \log n$.

TABLE 2.3   FREQUENCY DISTRIBUTIONS WITH DIFFERENT NUMBERS OF CLASSES

a. Twelve Classes		b. Three Classes		c. Five Classes	
Class	Frequency	Class	Frequency	Class	Frequency
2 to 3.5*	1	2 to 8*	9	2 to 5.5*	3
3.5 to 5	2	8 to 14	15	5.5 to 9	10
5 to 6.5	3	14 to 20	6	9 to 12.5	10
6.5 to 8	3			12.5 to 16	4
8 to 9.5	5			16 to 19.5	3
9.5 to 11	3				
11 to 12.5	6				
12.5 to 14	1				
14 to 15.5	2				
15.5 to 17	2				
17 to 18.5	0				
18.5 to 20	2				
Total	30		30		30

* Class contains all measurements from 2 up to (but not including) upper limit.

TABLE 2.4   APPROXIMATE NUMBER OF CLASSES IN FREQUENCY DISTRIBUTION

Number of Measurements	Number of Classes
Less than 50	5–7
50–200	7–9
200–500	9–10
500–1,000	10–11
1,000–5,000	11–13
5,000–50,000	13–17
More than 50,000	17–20

Once the number of classes to be used has been chosen, the approximate size (or width) of each class is given by

$$\text{Approximate class width} = \frac{\text{Largest value} - \text{Smallest value}}{\text{Number of classes}}$$

It is usually recommended that all classes be given the same width, to facilitate interpretation of the frequency distribution. Finally, the actual class intervals, defined by the class limits, are defined. Whenever possible, simple (preferably integral) values should be chosen as the class limits (which depend on the class width). For example, "2 up to 5" is a better choice for a class than is "2.2 up to 5.2."

With the preceding considerations in mind, let's look at how the frequency distribution was constructed for the data in Table 2.1. Since the largest and smallest measurements are 19.5 and 2.3 minutes, respectively, the range of values for our data is $19.5 - 2.3 = 17.2$ minutes. We must now choose how many classes to use in subdividing the entire range of values. If we use 5 classes, the width of each class will be about $17.2 \div 5 = 3.4$ minutes; if we use 6 classes, the width of each will be about $17.2 \div 6 = 2.9$ minutes. For ease of reading, let's round these approximate class widths off to 3.5 and 3.0, respectively. By employing 5 classes with a width of 3.5 minutes each, we would obtain the frequency distribution shown in Table 2.3(c). We felt that using 6 classes with a width of 3 minutes each produced a frequency distribution (Table 2.2) that offers somewhat better insight into the pattern of telephone-call durations. The lower limit of the first class has been set at 2, so that the smallest measurement will fall into that class. The remainder of the class limits are obtained by successively adding increments of 3.

The class limits must be defined carefully to ensure that each measurement falls into exactly one class. The first class, "2 up to 5," contains all measurements from 2 up to (but not including) 5. Alternatively, we could have used "2–5" to denote the first class, with the understanding that measurements equal to the upper-limit value are not included in the class. A third way of identifying this class would be to use "2–4.99," whereby upper-limit values are used that have more significant digits than do the measurements themselves, to ensure that no ambiguity arises in determining the class to which any measurement belongs. Ultimately, the choices about the number, size, and description of the classes represent the analyst's subjective view of what produces the most readable table.

Having decided upon the classes, we next count and record the number or **frequency** of measurements belonging to each class. The frequency distribution is then complete, as shown in Table 2.2. The column of tally marks, of course, is created only to facilitate counting the measurements; it is omitted when a frequency distribution is presented in final form.

Often, the information in a frequency distribution can be grasped more easily—and the presentation can be made more visually appealing—if the distribution is graphed. One very common graphical presentation is the **histogram,**

FIGURE 2.1  *HISTOGRAM OF TELEPHONE-CALL DURATIONS*

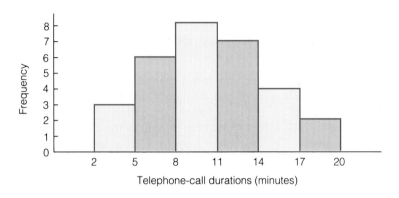

---

which is constructed by marking off the class limits along the horizontal axis and then erecting over each class interval a rectangle, the height of which equals the frequency of that class. The histogram corresponding to the frequency distribution in Table 2.2 is shown in Figure 2.1. Casual inspection of the histogram quickly reveals the general pattern or distribution of values: the distribution is reasonably symmetrical, with the majority of calls lasting between 5 and 14 minutes. As the Dallas firm had hoped, the proportion of calls of very short or very long duration is relatively small.

COMPUTER OUTPUT FOR TELEPHONE-CALL DURATIONS*

Minitab

```
Histogram of Durations    N=30
  Midpoint            Count
    3.50              3***
    6.50              6******
    9.50              8********
   12.50              7*******
   15.50              4****
   18.50              2**
```

Notice that Minitab produces a histogram lying on its side.

---

* Appendixes 2A and 2B provide the Minitab and SAS instructions that produced these outputs.

SAS

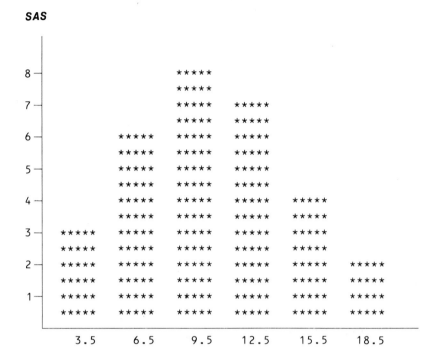

Rather than showing the absolute frequency of measurements in each class, we might prefer to show the proportion (or percentage) of measurements falling into the various classes.* To do this, we replace the class frequency with the class **relative frequency,** defined by

$$\text{Class relative frequency} = \frac{\text{Class frequency}}{\text{Total number of measurements}}$$

Having done so, we can talk about a **relative frequency distribution** (Table 2.5) and a **relative frequency histogram** (Figure 2.2). Notice that, in Figure 2.2, the area of any rectangle is proportional to the relative frequency (or proportion) of measurements falling into that class. These relative frequencies are useful when dealing with a sample of data because they provide insights into the corresponding relative frequencies for the population from which the sample was taken. Relative frequencies should also be used in comparing histograms or other graphical

---

* Over the course of this book, we express relative frequencies (and later, probabilities) variously as decimals, fractions, and percentages.

| TABLE 2.5 | RELATIVE FREQUENCY DISTRIBUTION OF TELEPHONE-CALL DURATIONS |

Class Limits	Relative Frequency
2 up to 5	3/30 = .100
5 up to 8	6/30 = .200
8 up to 11	8/30 = .267
11 up to 14	7/30 = .233
14 up to 17	4/30 = .133
17 up to 20	2/30 = .067
Total	30/30 = 1.000

| FIGURE 2.2 | RELATIVE FREQUENCY HISTOGRAM OF TELEPHONE-CALL DURATIONS |

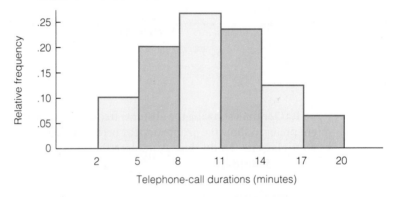

descriptions of two or more data sets. Even when the total numbers of measurements in the data sets differ, relative frequencies permit a meaningful comparison of these sets.

As was previously mentioned, it is best to use equal class widths whenever possible; but in some cases, unequal class widths are necessary to avoid having to include several classes with low relative frequencies. Suppose that, instead of having 6.7% of the telephone-call durations fall between 17 and 20 minutes, 6.7% of the durations were sparsely scattered between 17 and 29 minutes. This new situation might be best represented by the relative frequency histogram shown in Figure 2.3, where the upper four classes have been combined. It is important, however, that the height of the corresponding rectangle be adjusted (from 0.067 to 0.067/4) so that the area of the rectangle remains proportional to the relative frequency of measurements falling between 17 and 29 minutes.

FIGURE 2.3 *RELATIVE FREQUENCY HISTOGRAM WITH UNEQUAL CLASS WIDTHS*

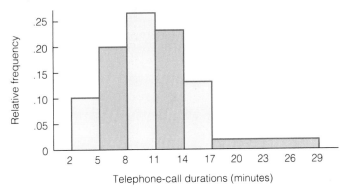

Telephone-call durations (minutes)

TABLE 2.6 *PERCENTAGE DISTRIBUTION OF AMERICAN FAMILY INCOME FOR 1982*

Class Limits ($1,000s)	Percentage
Under 5	6.0
5 up to 10	10.6
10 up to 15	12.5
15 up to 20	12.1
20 up to 25	12.3
25 up to 30	10.7
30 up to 40	15.8
40 up to 50	9.1
50 and over	10.9

The measurements in the preceding example all fall within a fairly compact range. In some cases, however, the measurements may be sparsely scattered over a large range of values at either end of the distribution. When this situation arises, it may be necessary to use an *open-ended class* to account for these measurements, as shown in the relative frequency distribution in Table 2.6.

Another common way of presenting a frequency distribution graphically is to use a **frequency polygon** (Figure 2.4), which is obtained by plotting the frequency of each class above the midpoint of that class and then joining the points with straight lines. The frequency polygon is usually closed by considering one additional class (with zero frequency) at each end of the distribution and then extending a straight

FIGURE 2.4   FREQUENCY POLYGON OF TELEPHONE-CALL DURATIONS

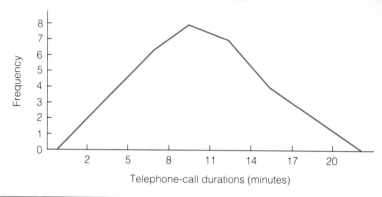

FIGURE 2.5   COMPARING TWO RELATIVE FREQUENCY POLYGONS

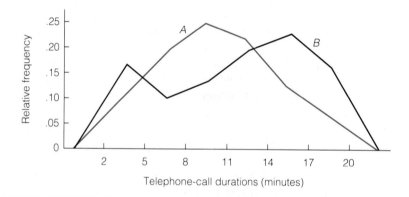

line to the midpoint of each of these classes. Notice that the frequency polygon is generated from the same data as is the histogram. Frequency polygons are useful for obtaining a general idea of the shape of the distribution.

Just as with histograms, we can plot relative frequencies in place of frequencies, thereby obtaining a **relative frequency polygon.** Polygon *A* in Figure 2.5 is the relative frequency counterpart of the frequency polygon in Figure 2.4. Relative frequency polygons allow visual comparison of two distributions, by superimposing one frequency polygon over another as in Figure 2.5. The second frequency polygon (*B*) in Figure 2.5 might represent, for example, the distribution of telephone-call durations before the Dallas firm instituted the cost-cutting program. The difference

TABLE 2.7   *CUMULATIVE RELATIVE FREQUENCY DISTRIBUTION OF TELEPHONE-CALL DURATIONS*

Class Limits	Relative Frequency	Cumulative Relative Frequency
2 up to 5	3/30 = .100	3/30 = .100
5 up to 8	6/30 = .200	9/30 = .300
8 up to 11	8/30 = .267	17/30 = .567
11 up to 14	7/30 = .233	24/30 = .800
14 up to 17	4/30 = .133	28/30 = .933
17 up to 20	2/30 = .067	30/30 = 1.000

in the distribution of durations before and after the program is readily apparent from the two polygons.

If we are given a set of measurements that has been subdivided into classes, the relative frequency distribution identifies the proportion of measurements falling into each of the classes. In some instances, however, our needs may be served better by working with a *cumulative* relative frequency distribution. The **cumulative relative frequency** of a particular class is the proportion of measurements that fall below the upper limit of that class. The cumulative relative frequency of a class is therefore obtained by adding the relative frequency of that class to the relative frequencies of all prior classes.* Table 2.7 displays the cumulative relative frequency distribution for the telephone-call durations.

From the cumulative relative frequency distribution shown in Table 2.7, we can state, for example, that 30% of the telephone calls lasted less than 8 minutes. Likewise, 80% of the calls were shorter than 14 minutes; so 20% of the calls were longer than 14 minutes. This type of information can also be read from the graph of a cumulative relative frequency distribution, which is called an **ogive.** The ogive for the telephone-call durations is shown in Figure 2.6.

Notice how the construction of an ogive differs from that of a relative frequency polygon. The cumulative relative frequency of each class is plotted above the *upper limit* of the corresponding class, and the points representing the cumulative relative frequencies are then joined by straight lines. The ogive is closed at the lower end by extending a straight line to the lower limit of the first class. Once an ogive such as the one shown in Figure 2.6 has been constructed, the approximate proportion of measurements that are less than any given value on the abscissa can be read from the graph.

---

* We assume here that the classes have been ordered, from smallest to largest, according to the magnitude of the measurements they contain.

FIGURE 2.6   *OGIVE OF TELEPHONE-CALL DURATIONS*

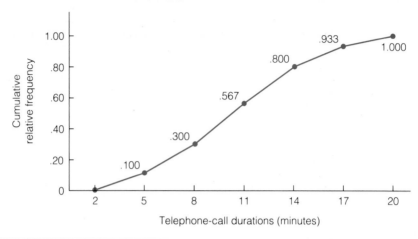

STEM AND LEAF DISPLAY

A statistician named John Tukey has introduced a relatively new method of organizing quantitative data, called the *stem and leaf display*. This display, which may be viewed as an alternative to the histogram, is most useful in preliminary analysis. In particular, it provides a useful first step toward constructing a frequency distribution and a histogram. The histogram remains preferable for formal presentations.

Suppose that we wish to organize the data shown in Table 2.8 into a more usable form. These data represent the annual incomes, in thousands of dollars, of a sample of 30 factory workers. A stem and leaf display for these data is shown in Table 2.9. The first step in developing the display is to decide how to split each observation (income) into two parts: a **stem,** and a **leaf.** In this example, we have defined the stem as the digits to the left of the decimal and the leaf as the digit to the right of the decimal. The first two incomes in Table 2.8 are therefore split into stems and leaves as follows:

Income	Stem	Leaf
19.1	19	1
20.0	20	0

The remaining observations are split into their stem and leaf components in a similar manner.

TABLE 2.8   SAMPLE OF 30 ANNUAL INCOMES (in $1,000s)

19.1	19.8	18.0	19.2	19.5	17.3
20.0	20.3	19.6	18.5	18.1	19.7
18.4	17.6	21.2	19.7	22.2	19.1
21.1	19.3	20.8	21.2	21.0	18.7
19.9	18.7	22.1	17.2	18.4	21.4

TABLE 2.9   STEM AND LEAF DISPLAY FOR 30 ANNUAL INCOMES (in $1,000s)

Stem	Leaf
17	623
18	4705147
19	1983627571
20	038
21	12204
22	12

Having determined what constitutes the stem and the leaf of an observation, we next list the stems in a column from smallest to largest, as shown in Table 2.9. Once this is done, we consider each observation in turn and place its leaf in the same row as its stem, to the right of the vertical line. The resulting stem and leaf display (Table 2.9) now presents the original 30 observations in a more organized fashion. The first line in Table 2.9, describing stem 17, has three leaves: 6, 2, and 3. The three observations represented in the first row are therefore 17.6, 17.2, and 17.3. Similarly, seven observations are presented in the second row. Whether to arrange the leaves in each row from smallest to largest (as is done in the next example) is largely a matter of personal preference.

From the stem and leaf display in Table 2.9, we can quickly determine that the incomes range from $17,200 to $22,200, that most incomes fall between $18,000 and $20,000, and that the shape of the income distribution is not symmetrical. A stem and leaf display is similar to a histogram turned on its side, but the display holds the advantage of retaining the original observations. Moreover, because the stems are listed in order of size, the middle observation(s) can be determined fairly easily. In this example, the two middle incomes are $19,500 and $19,600; splitting the

TABLE 2.10   *STEM AND LEAF DISPLAY FOR TELEPHONE-CALL DURATIONS*

Stem	Leaf
2	3
3	6
4	8
5	5
6	128
7	27
8	0359
9	16
10	24
11	2478
12	13
13	5
14	5
15	39
16	6
17	
18	7
19	5

difference, we can assert that half the incomes are below $19,550 and half are above it. On the other hand, a histogram can readily accommodate a large number of observations, can display relative frequencies, and can be adapted more easily to changes in the classes used.

The appropriate definitions of the stem and the leaf depend, in part, on the range of the observations. Suppose that the incomes in the preceding example had ranged from $17,200 to $55,500; in such a case, it would be reasonable to define the stem as the first digit and the leaf as the remaining two digits. The income 19.1 ($19,100) would then have stem 1 and leaf 9.1, and there would be five stems or classes in all. Since each leaf would consist of more than a single digit, the leaves in any row should be separated by commas for clarity.

As well as serving an end in itself, a stem and leaf display can form the first step in the construction of a frequency distribution and histogram. Table 2.10 shows the stem and leaf display for the original data on telephone-call durations given in Table 2.1 (page 17), where the stem is defined as the digits to the left of the decimal and the leaf as the digit to the right of the decimal. This display can be created fairly quickly, but you may feel that it is insufficiently compact for your needs. Even so, it will be helpful when you undertake to choose the classes to use in grouping the data into a frequency distribution.

SAMPLE OR POPULATION?

Before proceeding, we should note that the descriptive methods presented in this chapter apply equally well to samples and to populations of data. If you are interested only in the durations of telephone calls for some particular week, and if all of the calls for that week are accounted for in the data set given in Table 2.1, then those 30 observations can be considered a population, and your task is simply to summarize the durations of those 30 calls. On the other hand, if your primary interest is to obtain information concerning the distribution of the population of durations of all long-distance calls placed by employees at any time, the 30 durations represented in Table 2.1 may be treated as a sample, and you will want to make sure that the sample has been properly selected so that it may be used as a basis for statistical inference about the population.

EXERCISES

2.1   The grades on a statistics exam are as follows:

75	79	58	73	82	94
61	77	54	77	65	67
62	61	64	45	58	86
66	83	70	91	48	78
86	66	52	80	59	55

a. Construct a stem and leaf display for these data.

b. Construct a frequency distribution for these data, using six class intervals.

c. Construct a relative frequency histogram for these data.

2.2   Refer to Exercise 2.1.

a. Construct a cumulative relative frequency distribution for the grades.

b. What proportion of the grades are less than 70? Greater than 70?

2.3   The real estate board in a wealthy suburb wishes to investigate the distribution of prices of homes sold during the past year. The following sample of prices (in $1,000s) was collected:

274	429	229	435	260
222	292	419	242	202
235	215	390	359	409
375	209	265	440	365
319	338	414	249	279

a. Construct a stem and leaf display for these prices.

b. Construct a frequency distribution for the prices, using five class intervals and the value 200 as the lower limit of the first class.

c. Construct a relative frequency histogram for the prices.

2.4   Refer to Exercise 2.3.

a. Construct an ogive for the house prices.

b. What proportion of the prices are less than $300,000? Greater than $300,000?

2.5   Table 2.9 shows a stem and leaf display for the annual incomes listed in Table 2.8.

a. Use the stem and leaf display to construct a frequency distribution.

b. Draw a histogram for the incomes.

c. Draw a frequency polygon for the incomes.

2.6   The percentage distribution of American family incomes for 1982 is shown in Table 2.6.

a. Use this table to construct a cumulative relative frequency distribution.

b. Graph the cumulative relative frequency distribution.

c. What percentage of family incomes were less than $20,000 in 1982?

d. Use the graph in part (b) to estimate the income below which the incomes of 50% of American families fell.

2.7   The president of a local consumer-advocacy group is concerned about reports that similar generic drugs are being sold at widely differing prices at local drugstores. Upon surveying 30 stores, she collected the following set of prices at which one drug was being sold:

6.49	10.75	10.29	7.69	5.61
5.25	7.15	9.20	6.89	9.49
8.34	7.60	7.99	8.65	7.19
7.75	6.29	5.99	7.69	7.90
8.75	6.09	7.20	10.99	8.09
7.15	9.89	8.35	7.35	6.25

a. Construct a stem and leaf display for these data.

b. Construct a frequency distribution for these data. Use six class intervals, with $5.00 as the lower boundary of the first class.

c. Construct a relative frequency histogram for these data.

d. The consumer advocate discovers that all of the drug stores buy the product from the same wholesaler at $4.50. Given that the president considers a markup of more than 100% to be unfair to consumers, what fraction of the stores sampled will not meet with her approval?

2.8   A guard sitting beside the main door to a large office building decided to count the number of people entering the building during a 30-minute period. Using a system by which, for example, all times in the minute beginning at 7:45 sharp were recorded as 7:45, he obtained the following data:

Time	No.	Time	No.	Time	No.
7:45	1	7:48	0	7:51	10
7:46	4	7:49	4	7:52	8
7:47	2	7:50	7	7:53	4

Time	No.	Time	No.	Time	No.
7:54	9	8:01	10	8:08	0
7:55	15	8:02	2	8:09	1
7:56	21	8:03	0	8:10	1
7:57	9	8:04	3	8:11	0
7:58	12	8:05	0	8:12	0
7:59	6	8:06	0	8:13	1
8:00	4	8:07	4	8:14	0

a. Construct a relative frequency distribution for the arrival times, using six classes.

b. Construct a cumulative relative frequency distribution for the arrival times.

c. Assume that everyone working in the building starts work at 8:00 sharp. What fraction of the employees sampled were late? (Those arriving at 8:00 are considered late.)

d. What assumption(s) must you make if you want to use these sample data to estimate the fraction of employees who arrive late on any given day?

2.9   A compilation of the number of sales calls made during the past week by a sample of 20 salesmen for a large computer firm produced the following data:

10	12	8	15
7	12	9	14
10	6	8	9
9	8	11	4
13	10	8	8

a. How might you improve upon the data presentation?

b. The sales manager feels that any salesman worth his salt can make at least eight calls per week. Estimate the fraction of salesmen in the firm who are not worth their salt.

SECTION 2.3   ## *OTHER GRAPHICAL PRESENTATIONS*

Several types of commonly used graphical presentations are available besides histograms and frequency polygons. The increasing availability of desktop computers that can produce color graphics enables managers to summon (almost instantaneously) a bar chart showing sales in various regions, a pie chart displaying major causes of accidents within their firm, or a line chart depicting the trend in productivity over time. Numerous types of graphical presentations are possible, although only a few of the more popular ones will be discussed here.

Before proceeding, we should say a few words about the measurement scale for the data that are to be summarized graphically. The topic of data scales will receive a more detailed treatment in Chapter 5, but here we should at least note that attributes of items in a population are sometimes measured on a quantitative basis and sometimes on a qualitative basis. When you hear the word *measurement*, you probably think of it in a quantitative sense, as it would be used when applied to such attributes as height, weight, income, or distance traveled. The data in these examples are numerical measurements and are said to have an **interval scale.** On the other hand, measurement on a qualitative basis is used whenever items are sorted into categories on the basis of qualitative attributes such as sex, occupation, or type of dwelling inhabited. The data in these examples are simply the names of possible classifications and are said to have a **nominal scale.**

Nominal data (or count data) generally arise whenever we wish to consider the number or percentage of members of a population that belong to each of the possible categories. *If the categories defining a nominal scale can be ordered or ranked, the data are said to have an* **ordinal scale.** This would be the situation, for example, if each of the hotels in a given city had been classified as excellent, good, fair, or poor, depending on the quality of accommodation provided. The level of measurement for an ordinal scale is somewhat higher (that is, more refined) than the level for a nominal scale, but it is not as high as the level for an interval scale.

If the raw data to be summarized have an interval scale and come from a single population (as was the case with the telephone data in Table 2.1), the descriptive methods presented in the previous section—frequency distributions, histograms, stem and leaf displays, and so on—are useful and appropriate. These methods basically group the raw data into categories, which we call *classes,* and record the number of measurements falling into each category. Recall that the categories are defined in a rather arbitrary manner, with the objective of obtaining some idea as to how the data are distributed. We next consider a situation in which the raw data can be naturally categorized in a more meaningful and less arbitrary manner.

The student placement office at a small Ontario university conducted a survey of last year's business school graduates to determine the general areas in which the graduates found jobs. The placement office intended to use the data to help it decide where to concentrate its efforts in attracting companies to the campus to hold job interviews. The data collected are given in Table 2.11.

The data in this example have a nominal scale, defined by the five employment areas. The student placement office would likely find the percentages more useful

TABLE 2.11   *AREAS OF EMPLOYMENT FOR BUSINESS GRADUATES*

Area	Number of Graduates	Percentage of Graduates
Accounting	75	30%
Marketing	62	25%
Finance	50	20%
General Management	38	15%
Other	25	10%
Total	250	100%

FIGURE 2.7   *PIE CHART OF EMPLOYMENT AREAS*

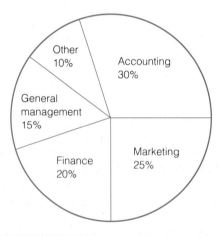

than the absolute numbers of graduates in each category—particularly if the results are to be compared with those from other years or other schools. For one thing, percentages permit a more meaningful comparison of data from graduating classes of different sizes.

A more visually appealing presentation of the employment data may be obtained by using a pie chart. A **pie chart** is simply a circle subdivided into a number of slices that represent the various categories. It should be drawn so that the size of each slice is proportional to the percentage corresponding to that category, as shown in Figure 2.7. Since the entire circle corresponds to 360°, every 1% of the observations should correspond to $(0.01)(360) = 3.6°$. The angle between the lines demarcating the accounting sector in Figure 2.7 is therefore $(30)(3.6) = 108°$.

FIGURE 2.8   *PIE CHARTS OF GULF + WESTERN'S SOURCES OF REVENUE*

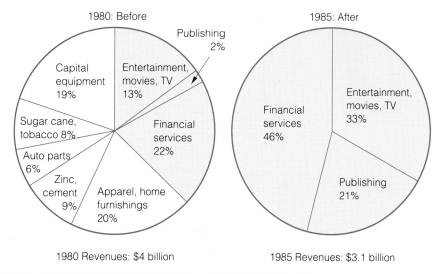

1980 Revenues: $4 billion   1985 Revenues: $3.1 billion

SOURCE: *New York Times,* 23 February 1986, p. 8F.

Pie charts are effective whenever the objective is to display the components of a whole entity in a manner that indicates their relative sizes. Because of their eye-catching appearance, they are used extensively by newspapers and magazines—especially to show breakdowns of budgets. Similarly, a treasurer may use a pie chart to show the breakdown of a firm's revenues by department, or a marketing analyst may use one to display the market shares of various brands of beer. In all of these examples, the raw data have a nominal scale, and the categories are defined in a natural rather than an arbitrary way.

Pie charts can also be used to compare two breakdowns. Figure 2.8 shows the sources of revenue for the conglomerate Gulf + Western Inc. before and after it sold off a large portion of its operations.

If, in a situation involving *nominal* data, we wish to develop a pictorial representation of the frequency (rather than the percentage) of each category, we can use a bar chart. A **bar chart** represents the frequency of each of the categories as a bar rising vertically from the horizontal axis; the height of each bar is proportional to the frequency of the corresponding category. Since the bars correspond to categories or points, rather than to class intervals (as the rectangles of a histogram do), the widths of the bars are arbitrary, although all must be equal. The bar chart illustrated in Figure 2.9 shows the total value of all mergers and acquisitions of firms in the United States from 1979 to 1985. The number of billions of dollars corresponding to each category (year) is indicated on the bars—a laudable practice that removes any uncertainty as to the exact heights of the bars.

FIGURE 2.9   *BAR CHART SHOWING TOTAL VALUE OF MERGERS AND ACQUISITIONS*

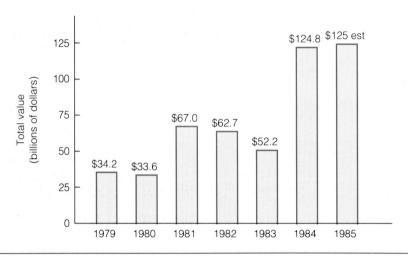

SOURCE: *New York Times,* 29 December 1985, p. 1F.

Instead of producing a separate bar for each category, we could make use of a **component bar chart.** In this case, all categories are represented within a single bar, which is partitioned into components whose heights are proportional to the frequency of the categories they represent. Component bar charts offer a good alternative to using two pie charts, when a comparison of two breakdowns is desired. Component bar charts usually enable the reader to detect the magnitude of the changes in the category sizes more easily than do pie charts. Figure 2.10, for example, shows different breakdowns of the price of a liter of gasoline in Toronto.

The last graphical technique to be considered here is the line chart. A **line chart** is obtained by plotting the frequency of a category above the point on the horizontal axis representing that category, and then joining the points by straight lines. Since a line chart is normally used when the categories are points in time, it is known alternatively as a *time-series chart.* Suppose that we wish to graph the total value of all mergers and acquisitions of firms in the United States from 1979 to 1985. A bar chart for these data is given in Figure 2.9, but if the objective of the graph is to focus on the trend in the value over the years—rather than on the relative sizes of the total amounts in different years—then a line chart is appropriate, as shown in Figure 2.11.

Line charts have the added advantage of clearly depicting the trend in the components of the total over time. When mergers and acquisitions are opposed by the management of the firm being taken over, they are referred to as *hostile.* Assuming that the breakdown of all takeovers into hostile and nonhostile ones was known, this breakdown could be plotted in the same style shown in Figure 2.11.

Pie charts, bar charts, and line charts are used extensively in reports compiled

FIGURE 2.10   COMPONENT BAR CHARTS SHOWING BREAKDOWNS OF GASOLINE PRICE

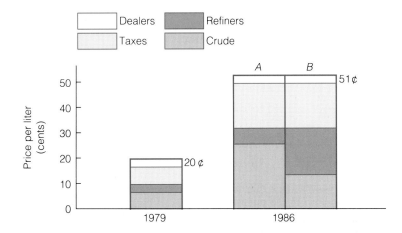

A: Industry's view of price per liter
B: Critics' view

SOURCE: *Globe and Mail*, 21 February 1986, p. 1.

FIGURE 2.11   LINE CHART SHOWING TREND IN TOTAL VALUE OF TAKEOVERS

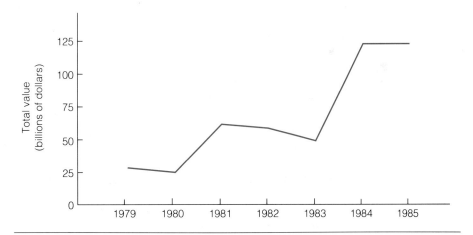

by business, government, and the media. Variations on these and other pictorial representations of data abound, and their possibilities are limited only by their creators' imaginations. The objective of all such charts is to present a summary of the data clearly and in a form that allows the reader to grasp the relevant comparisons of trends quickly.

▬▬▬▬▬▬ **EXERCISES**

2.10 For each of the following examples of data, determine whether the data scale is interval, nominal, or ordinal.

a. The starting salary of graduates from an MBA program. *int*

b. The month in which a firm's employees take their vacation. *nom*

c. The final letter grade received by students in a statistics course. *ord*

d. The number of miles driven annually by employees using a company car. *int*

2.11 Information concerning a magazine's readership is of interest both to the publisher and to the magazine's advertisers. A survey of 20 subscribers to a magazine included the following questions. For each question, determine whether the possible responses have an interval, nominal, or ordinal scale.

a. What is your age? *n*

b. What is your sex? *n*

c. What is your marital status? *n*

d. Is your annual income less than $20,000, between $20,000 and $40,000, or over $40,000? *in*

e. How many other magazines do you subscribe to? *in*

2.12 A variety store's monthly sales (in $1,000s) for the previous year were as follows:

Month	Sales	Month	Sales
January	65	July	88
February	61	August	93
March	70	September	91
April	74	October	78
May	72	November	68
June	80	December	84

a. Construct a relative frequency bar chart for these data.

b. Construct a line chart to depict these data.

2.13 The United States is Canada's most important trading partner, as is evidenced by the table showing the percentage distribution of exports from and imports to Canada in 1985. Use a graphical technique to depict the information given in the table.

Region	Exports (1985)	Imports (1985)
United States	78%	69%
Asia/Pacific	9%	13%
Western Europe	8%	13%
Latin America	3%	4%
Other	2%	1%

SOURCE: *Financial Post,* 6 April 1987, p. 34.

2.14 Inco Limited is the (noncommunist) world's major producer of nickel, which is used in the production of such alloy products as stainless steel. The annual demand for nickel in the noncommunist world and the amount supplied by Inco are shown in the table. Use a component bar chart to display the data.

Year	World Demand (Millions of lb.)	Inco Deliveries (Millions of lb.)
1980	1,150	345
1981	1,095	342
1982	985	251
1983	1,145	314
1984	1,260	356

SOURCE: Inco Limited, *Annual Report,* 1984, p. 5.

2.15 The cover story for the February 6, 1989, edition of *Time* magazine was entitled "The Other

Arms Race." It reported the purchase by American citizens of more and deadlier guns. To dramatize the extent of the problem, the magazine used a bar chart to compare the number of people killed by handguns in different countries. Reconstruct the bar chart from the data in the table.

PEOPLE KILLED BY HANDGUNS IN 1985

Country	(Population)	Number
Canada	(25 million)	5
Britain	(57 million)	8
Japan	(121 million)	46
U.S.	(239 million)	8,092

SOURCE: *Time,* 6 February 1989, p. 18.

2.16 Americans today are waiting longer before getting married for the first time. A major contributing factor to this trend is the sharp increase in the percentage of women who now wish to become established in a career before taking on family responsibilities. Use a graphical technique to compare the 1970 and 1987 percentages of people who have never married, broken down by age.

PERCENTAGE WHO HAVE NEVER MARRIED

Age	Men 1970	Men 1987	Women 1970	Women 1987
20–24	55%	78%	36%	61%
25–29	19%	42%	11%	29%

SOURCE: *Wall Street Journal,* 14 October 1987, p. 33.

2.17 Nestlé S.A., the international food giant, had worldwide sales in 1987 amounting to $23 billion. The percentage distribution of sales according to geographic region is shown in the table. Show how this information could be conveyed to shareholders by using a graphical technique.

1987 SALES FOR NESTLÉ

Region	Sales
Europe	43%
North America	29%
Asia	13%
Latin America and Caribbean	10%
Africa	3%
Australia, New Zealand, and Pacific Islands	2%

SOURCE: *New York Times,* 1 January 1989, p. F1.

2.18 Unlike the banking system in the United States, which consists of thousands of regional banks of varying sizes, the Canadian banking system is dominated by a handful of national banks that have branches throughout the country. Use both a bar chart and a pie chart to depict the information in the following table of bank deposits.

Bank	Millions of Dollars*	Market Share (%)*
1. The Royal Bank	81,787.6	22.3
2. Bank of Montreal	67,347.7	18.9
3. Bank of Commerce	64,242.7	17.5
4. Bank of Nova Scotia	53,533.0	14.6
5. Toronto-Dominion Bank	42,535.3	11.6
6. National Bank	18,051.8	4.9
7. Foreign Bank Subsidiaries	21,479.4	5.9
8. Others	17,337.9	4.3
Total Market	366,315.4	100.0

* As of April 1985.

SOURCE: *Financial Times of Canada,* 23 September 1985.

DECEPTION WITH GRAPHS

The use of graphs and charts is pervasive in newspapers, magazines, business and economic reports, and seminars. This is in large part due to the increasing accessibility of computers and software that allow large masses of raw data to be stored, retrieved, manipulated, and summarized. It is therefore more important than ever to be capable of critically evaluating information presented by means of graphical techniques. In the final analysis, graphical techniques merely create a visual impression, and it is easy to create a distorted one. Although the heading for the section mentions deception, it is quite possible for an inexperienced user of graphs to create distorted impressions inadvertently. In any event, you should be aware of possible methods of distortion. This section illustrates a few of them.

The first thing to watch for is a graph without a scale on one axis. The time-series graph of a firm's sales shown in Figure 2.12 might represent a growth rate of 100% or of 1% over the five years marked on the horizontal scale—depending on the vertical scale. It is best simply to ignore such graphs.

A second trap to avoid is to be unduly influenced by the caption appearing on a graph. Your impression of the trend in interest rates may be different, depending on whether you read a newspaper carrying caption (a) or caption (b) in Figure 2.13.

Perspective is often distorted when only absolute changes in value, rather than percentage changes, are reported. A $1 drop in the price of your $2 stock is relatively more distressing than is a $1 drop in the price of your $100 stock. On January 9, 1986, newspapers throughout North America displayed graphs similar to the one shown in Figure 2.14 and reported that the stock market, as measured by the Dow Jones Industrial Average (DJIA), had suffered its worst one-day loss ever, on the previous day. The loss was 39 points, exceeding even the loss on Black Tuesday—October 29, 1929. While the loss was indeed a large one, many news reports failed to mention that the 1986 level of the DJIA was much higher than the 1929 level. A better perspective of the situation could be had by noticing that the loss on January 8, 1986, represented a 2.5% decline, while the decline in 1929 was 12.8%. As a point of interest, we note that the stock market was 12% higher within two months of this historic drop, and 40% higher one year later. A dramatic crash was to follow, however. On October 19, 1987, the DJIA did suffer its worst one-day loss ever—a decline of 508 points, or 22.6%.

We now turn to some rather subtle methods of creating distorted impressions with graphs. Consider the graph in Figure 2.15, which depicts the growth in a firm's quarterly sales over the past year, from $100 million to $110 million. This 10% growth in quarterly sales can be made to appear more dramatic by *stretching the vertical axis*—changing the scale on the vertical axis so that a given dollar amount is represented by a greater height than before. As a result, the rise in sales appears to be greater, since the slope of the graph is visually (but not numerically) steeper. The expanded scale is usually accommodated by employing a break in the vertical axis (Figure 2.16(a)) or by truncating the vertical axis (Figure 2.16(b)) so that the vertical scale begins at a point greater than zero. The effect of making slopes appear

FIGURE 2.12   *GRAPH WITHOUT A VERTICAL SCALE*

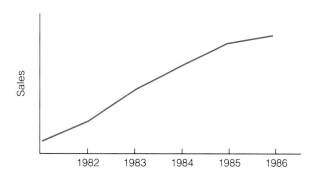

FIGURE 2.13   *DIFFERENT CAPTIONS FOR THE SAME GRAPH*

(a) Interest rates have finally
begun to turn downward

(b) Last week provided temporary relief
from the upward trend in interest rates

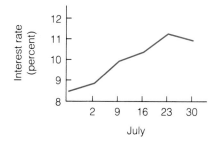 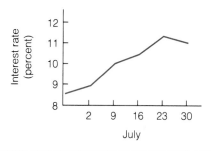

FIGURE 2.14   *HISTORIC DROP IN THE DJIA, 1986*

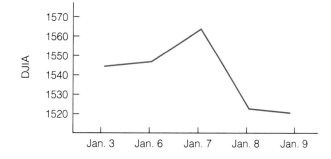

FIGURE 2.15   *QUARTERLY SALES FOR THE PAST YEAR*

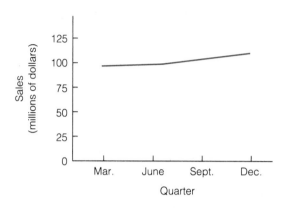

FIGURE 2.16   *STRETCHING THE VERTICAL AXIS*

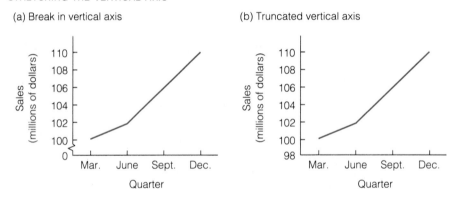

steeper can also be created by shrinking the horizontal axis, in which case points on the horizontal axis are moved closer together.

Exactly the opposite effect is obtained by *stretching the horizontal axis*— spreading out the points on the horizontal axis to increase the distance between them, thereby causing slopes and trends to appear less steep. The graph of a firm's profits shown in Figure 2.17(a) shows considerable swings, both upward and downward, in the profits from one quarter to the next. The firm could convey the impression of reasonable stability in profits from quarter to quarter, however, by stretching the horizontal axis, as in Figure 2.17(b).

Similar illusions can be created with bar charts by stretching or shrinking the vertical or horizontal axis. Another popular method of creating distorted impressions with bar charts is to construct the bars so that their widths are

FIGURE 2.17   *QUARTERLY PROFITS OVER TWO YEARS*

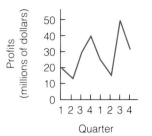
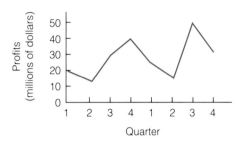

(a) Compressed horizontal axis   (b) Stretched horizontal axis

FIGURE 2.18   *AVERAGE WEEKLY FOOD EXPENDITURES BY CANADIAN FAMILIES*

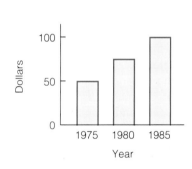
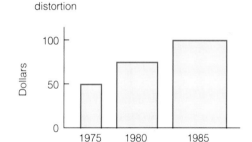

(a) Correct bar chart   (b) Increasing bar widths create
                                             distortion

proportional to their heights. The bar chart in Figure 2.18(a) correctly depicts the average weekly amount spent on food by Canadian families in three particular years. This chart correctly uses bars of equal widths, so that both the height and the area of each of the bars are proportional to the expenditures they represent. The growth in food expenditures is exaggerated in Figure 2.18(b), in which the widths of the bars increase with their heights. A quick glance at this bar chart may leave the viewer with the mistaken impression that food expenditures increased fourfold over the decade, since the 1985 bar is four times the size of the 1975 bar. This type of distortion should be watched for particularly in pictograms, where bars are replaced by pictures of objects (such as bags of money, people, or animals) to enhance the visual appeal.

The preceding examples of deceptive graphs are not exhaustive, but they include some of the more popular methods. They should also serve to make the point that graphical techniques are used to create a strictly visual impression: the impression you obtain may be a distorted one, unless you examine the graph with care. You are less likely to be misled if you focus your attention on the numerical values that the graph represents. Begin by carefully noting the scales on both axes; graphs with unmarked axes should be ignored completely.

MEASURES OF CENTRAL LOCATION

Our overall objective in this chapter is to see how a large set of raw data can be summarized so that the meaningful essentials can be extracted from it. Thus far, we have seen how to group the data set into a more manageable form and how to make various graphical representations of it. Faced with a set of measurements like the telephone data, we begin by finding the smallest and largest value, and then we form a frequency distribution and histogram that reveal the approximate shape of the distribution and indicate where the measurements are concentrated.

As useful as a frequency distribution is in providing a general idea of how the data are distributed between the two extreme values, we can usually improve our summary of the data even further by computing a few numerical descriptive measures. Numerical descriptive measures provide precise, objectively determined values that are easy to manipulate, interpret, and compare with one another. In short, they permit a more careful analysis of the data than can be developed from the general impressions conveyed by tabular and graphical summaries. This is especially important when the data represent a sample from which inferences will be made concerning the entire population.

The next step, then, is to compute some numerical descriptive measures of the data. Interest usually focuses on computing two such measures: a measure of the central or average value of the data, and a measure of the degree to which the observations are spread out about this average value. Measures of central location (averages) are discussed in this section, while measures of dispersion are discussed in Section 2.6. Of the various types of averages, we will consider only three: the arithmetic mean, the median, and the mode.

ARITHMETIC MEAN

By far the most popular and useful measure of central location is the **arithmetic mean,** which we will simply refer to as the *mean*. Widely referred to in everyday usage as the *average,* the mean of a set of measurements is defined as

$$\text{Mean} = \frac{\text{Sum of measurements}}{\text{Number of measurements}}$$

Before expressing this algebraically, we should introduce some notation.* If we are dealing with a population of measurements, the total number of measurements is denoted by N, and the mean is represented by μ (the lower-case Greek letter

---

* Students unfamiliar with summation notation should read Appendix 2.D for further background.

mu). If the set of measurements is a sample, the total number of measurements is denoted by n, and the sample mean is represented by $\bar{x}$ (referred to as *x-bar*). Since the measurements in a sample are a subset of the measurements in the parent population, $n \leq N$ if the parent population consists of N measurements. In actual practice, you won't normally have access to all of the measurements in a population, so you will most often calculate the sample mean. As we'll see in Chapter 7, the sample mean $\bar{x}$ is used to make inferences about μ (the mean of the population from which the sample was taken). In particular, the value of $\bar{x}$ will frequently be used as an estimate of μ.

Sample Mean

The mean of a sample of n measurements $x_1, x_2, \ldots, x_n$ is defined as

$$\bar{x} = \frac{\sum_{i=1}^{n} x_i}{n}$$

EXAMPLE 2.1

The mean of the sample of six measurements, 7, 3, 9, -2, 4, and 6, is given by

$$\bar{x} = \frac{\sum_{i=1}^{n} x_i}{n} = \frac{7 + 3 + 9 - 2 + 4 + 6}{6} = 4.5$$

The formula for calculating the mean of a population is the same as that for calculating the mean of a sample, differing only in notation.

Population Mean

The mean of a population of N measurements $x_1, x_2, \ldots, x_N$ is defined as

$$\mu = \frac{\sum_{i=1}^{N} x_i}{N}$$

EXAMPLE 2.2

Suppose that the telephone-call durations in Table 2.1 (page 17) represent a population of measurements. Then the population mean is

$$\mu = \frac{\sum_{i=1}^{N} x_i}{N} = \frac{11.8 + 3.6 + \cdots + 14.5}{30} = 10.26$$

Referring to the histogram of telephone-call durations in Figure 2.1 (page 20), we see that the value 10.26 is located approximately at the center of the distribution.

The sum of deviations of individual measurements from the arithmetic mean is zero, or

$$\sum_{i=1}^{N} (x_i - \bar{x}) = 0$$

This special property has an interesting physical interpretation. Imagine that the individual measurements are marked off along a weightless bar and that a 1-lb weight is placed at each such mark, as depicted in the accompanying diagram (based on measurements from Example 2.1). The bar will be in perfect balance if a support is placed at the mean; therefore, the arithmetic mean may be interpreted as the center of gravity or the balance point.

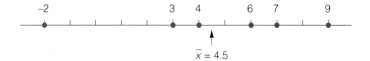

The mean is a popular measure because it is easy to compute and interpret and because it lends itself to mathematical manipulation. More importantly for statisticians, it is generally the best measure of central location for purposes of statistical inference. *Its one serious drawback, however, is that it is unduly influenced by extreme observations.* For example, if the sample of six measurements in Example 2.1 is enlarged to include a seventh measurement that has a value of 22, the mean of the resulting sample of seven measurements is $49/7 = 7$. Adding this single, relatively large value to the original sample of measurements substantially increases the value of the mean. This is one reason why we sometimes resort to another measure of central location, the median.

THE MEDIAN

Median

The median of a set of measurements is the value that falls in the middle when the measurements are arranged in order of magnitude.

When an even number of measurements are involved, any number between the two middle values would satisfy the foregoing definition of *median*. In such a case, however, it is conventional to take the midpoint between the two middle values as the median.

Calculating the Median

Given n measurements arranged in order of magnitude,

$$\ast \quad \text{Median} = \begin{cases} \text{The middle value, if } n \text{ is odd} \\ \text{The mean of the two middle values, if } n \text{ is even} \end{cases}$$

In the examples that follow, we have arbitrarily chosen to arrange the measurements in ascending order (from smallest to largest) as a preliminary step to locating the median. Arranging them in descending order would, of course, yield identical results. The median has intuitive appeal as a measure of central location: at most, half of the measurements fall below the median; and at most, half fall above. Because of the distorting effect of extreme observations on the mean, the median is often preferred in such situations as salary negotiations.

EXAMPLE 2.3

The annual salaries (in $1,000s) of the seven employees working in a small government department are as follows:

28, 60, 26, 32, 30, 26, 29

To find the median salary, first arrange the salaries in ascending order: 26, 26, 28, 29, 30, 32, 60. The median salary is therefore $29,000, which is clearly more representative of a typical salary than is the mean value ($33,000).

EXAMPLE 2.4

Suppose that we wish to find the median of the following values:

28, 60, 26, 32, 30, 26, 29, 31

Arranging the values in ascending order, we have 26, 26, 28, 29, 30, 31, 32, 60. For an even number of measurements, the convention is to locate the median at the midpoint between the two middle values. The median in this case is 29.5—the midpoint between 29 and 30.

The median is the most appropriate measure of central location to use when the data under consideration have an ordinal (rather than interval) scale. Such a situation arises whenever items are simply ranked—perhaps according to preference, degree of ability, or degree of difficulty. For example, if eleven statistical problems are ranked from 1 to 11 according to their degree of difficulty, problem 6 is the problem of median difficulty.

MODE

A third measure of central location is the mode, which indicates the most frequently occurring value. The mode doesn't necessarily lie in the middle of the set of measurements, although it often does. The mode's being characterized as a measure of central location in this context simply means that it indicates the location of the greatest clustering or concentration of values (just as a population *center* refers to a location of concentrated population).

> **Mode**
>
> The mode of a set of measurements is the value that occurs most frequently.

EXAMPLE 2.5

The manager of a men's store observes that the ten pairs of trousers sold yesterday had the following waist sizes (in inches):

31, 34, 36, 33, 28, 34, 30, 34, 32, 40

The mode of these waist sizes is 34 inches, and this fact is undoubtedly of more interest to the manager than are the facts that the mean waist size is 33.2 inches and the median waist size is 33.5 inches.

The mode is useful when demand for an item is of interest—perhaps for the purpose of making purchasing or production decisions—and the item is produced in a variety of standard sizes. But when the number of possible data values is very large, the mode is usually not useful as a measure of central location. In such situations, it may happen that no single value occurs more than once, making all of the measurements modes and providing no useful information. This, in fact, is the situation with the telephone data in Table 2.1. In a case such as this, it is more useful to group the data into classes and refer to the class with the largest frequency as the *modal class*. A distribution is then said to be **unimodal** if there is only one such class, and **bimodal** if there are two such classes. While the *midpoint of the modal class* is sometimes referred to as the mode, it does not identify the measurement occurring most frequently (as the true mode does) but the measurement about which there is the greatest clustering of values; thus, it corresponds graphically to the highest point on the frequency polygon.

If the data have a nominal scale, as do the employment areas in Table 2.11 (page 32), it is senseless to use the mean or the median; the mode must be used. The modal value in that example is accounting, since that category contains the most students. On the other hand, if the measurement data have an interval scale, all

FIGURE 2.19   *RELATIONSHIPS BETWEEN MEAN, MEDIAN, AND MODE*

(a) Symmetric distribution

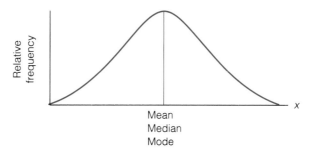

(b) Distribution skewed to the right (positively skewed)

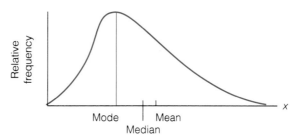

(c) Distribution skewed to the left (negatively skewed)

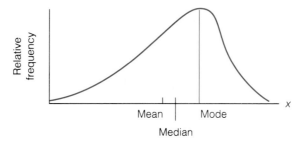

three measures of central tendency are meaningful. The mean is the best measure of central location for the purpose of statistical inference and thus will be used extensively from Chapter 6 onward. But for descriptive purposes, it is usually best to report the values of all three measures, since the three values usually differ and since each conveys somewhat different information. Moreover, the relative positions of the mean and the median provide some information about the shape of the distribution of the measurements.

The relationship among the three measures of central location can be observed from the smoothed relative frequency polygons in Figure 2.19.* If the distribution is symmetrical and unimodal, the three measures coincide, as shown in Figure 2.19(a). If a distribution is not symmetrical, it is said to be **skewed.** The distribution in Figure 2.19(b) is **skewed to the right,** or **positively skewed,** since it has a long tail extending to the right (indicating the presence of a small proportion of relatively large extreme values) but only a short tail extending to the left. Distributions of incomes commonly exhibit such positive skewness. As mentioned earlier, these extreme values pull the mean to the right of the median; a mean value greater than the median therefore provides some evidence of positive skewness.

The distribution in Figure 2.19(c) is **skewed to the left,** or **negatively skewed,** since it has a long tail to the left but a short tail to the right. Once again, the extreme values affect the mean more than they do the median, pulling the mean to the left of the median; a mean value less than the median is an indication of negative skewness.

EXERCISES

LEARNING THE TECHNIQUES

2.19 The number of days that each of 15 office workers was absent during a one-month period is as follows:

0, 1, 1, 3, 0, 0, 2, 5, 0, 1, 1, 2, 0, 1, 1

Compute the mean, the median, and the mode of the number of days absent.

2.20 The following data represent the number of product defects found during each 8-hour shift of each day for a week:

	M	T	W	Th	F
Shift 1:	24	17	35	15	19
Shift 2:	21	13	15	20	18

Find the mean number of defects found per shift.

2.21 What are the characteristics of a set of data for which the mean, the median, and the mode are identical?

2.22 Given a set of nominal data, what is the only appropriate measure of central location?

APPLYING THE TECHNIQUES

Self-Correcting Exercise (See Appendix 2.C for the solution.)

2.23 The ages of the employees of a fast-food outlet are as follows:

19, 19, 65, 20, 21, 18, 20

a. Compute the mean, the median, and the mode of the ages.

b. How would these three measures of central location be affected if the oldest employee retires?

2.24 When a certain professor left one university to teach at another, a student was heard to remark, "That move will surely raise the average IQ at both universities." Explain the meaning of the remark.

2.25 The cash compensation (excluding such benefits as stock options) received in 1986 by the highest-paid executives of Canadian companies having shares listed on U.S. stock exchanges is

---

* Relative frequency polygons tend to look more and more like smooth curves as the underlying data sets get larger.

shown in the accompanying table. (Other Canadian companies needn't disclose executive compensation, since disclosure laws in Canada are less strict than those in the United States.)

Executive	Company	Compensation (in $1,000s)
Frank Stronach	Magna International	$2,215
E. M. Bronfman	Seagram	1,888
P. E. Beekman	Seagram	1.477
E. B. Fitzgerald	Northern Telecom	1,059
A. J. de Grandpré	Bell Canada Enterprises	977
Manfred Gingl	Magna International	956
G. H. Drabinsky	Cineplex Odeon	947
M. I. Gottlieb	Cineplex Odeon	924
C. R. Bronfman	Seagram	899
J. R. McAlpine	Magna International	856
M. R. Hottinger	Magna International	856
J. V. R. Cyr	Bell Canada Enterprises	803

SOURCE: *Financial Post*, 13 April 1987, p. 16.

a. Find the mean and the median compensation of the executives.

b. Comment on the skewness of the distribution of the executives' compensations.

c. Repeat part (a), ignoring the highest compensation. Is the mean or the median more affected by dropping the highest compensation?

2.26 Twenty families were asked how many cars they owned. Their responses are summarized in the table.

Number of Cars	Number of Families
0	3
1	10
2	4
3	2
4	1

Determine the mean, the median, and the mode of the number of cars owned per family.

2.27 Some observers claim that, while smaller companies are the most important source of new jobs for Americans, large companies are best able to compete in international markets. Shown in the table are the 20 largest American companies ranked according to their market value in 1986.

Company	Market Value (in $billions)
1. IBM	$91.7
2. Exxon	40.1
3. General Electric	34.7
4. General Motors	26.5
5. AT & T	24.3
6. DuPont	17.4
7. Sears Roebuck	16.7
8. Bell South	15.7
9. Amoco	15.6
10. Ford	15.1
11. American Express	14.6
12. Philip Morris	14.2
13. Eastman Kodak	13.5
14. Coca Cola	13.3
15. Chevron	12.9
16. Procter & Gamble	12.4

Company	Market Value (in $billions)
17. Bell Atlantic	12.3
18. Mobil	12.1
19. 3M	12.0
20. Nynex	11.9

SOURCE: *Business Week,* 18 April 1986, p. 50.

a. Compute the mean market value of the 20 largest companies.

b. Find the median market value.

c. Repeat parts (a) and (b) after eliminating IBM from the data set. How have the mean and median been affected by this change?

2.28 Canada's third most important crop is rapeseed, almost half of which is grown in the province of Alberta. The accompanying table gives the number of acres planted in rapeseed and the average yield per acre, broken down by agricultural reporting area (ARA), for 1974 and 1984.

ALBERTA RAPESEED PRODUCTION

	1974	
ARA	Yield (bushels/acre)	Area (thousands of acres)
1–3	18.2	177.3
4–6	17.1	476.3
7	14.8	496.4

	1984	
ARA	Yield (bushels/acre)	Area (thousands of acres)
1	16.3	18.0
2	18.4	246.1

ARA	Yield (bushels/acre)	Area (thousands of acres)
3	11.4	216.0
4	21.8	1,070.8
5	26.2	351.4
6	22.9	229.4
7	15.4	768.3

SOURCE: Alberta Agriculture (Statistics Branch), *Agricultural Statistics,* December 1978 and January 1985.

a. Find the number of bushels of rapeseed grown in ARA 1 in 1984.

b. Find the average rapeseed yield (bushels per acre) for the entire province in 1974 and in 1984.

c. If you were asked to compare the 1974 and 1984 rapeseed yields for each ARA, you would be unable to do so, since the only data available for 1974 is somewhat aggregated. The only comparisons that can be made, aside from those involving ARA 7, require that you compute the average 1984 yields for the combined areas 1–3 and 4–6. What values do you obtain?

2.29 Sporting competitions that use judges' scores to determine a competitor's performance often drop the lowest and highest scores before computing the mean score, in order to diminish the effect of extreme values on the mean. Suppose that competitors *A* and *B* receive the following scores:

A: 6.0, 7.0, 7.25, 7.25, 7.5, 7.5, 7.5
B: 7.0, 7.0, 7.0, 7.25, 7.5, 7.5, 8.5

a. Compare the performances of competitors *A* and *B* based on the mean of their scores, both before and after dropping the two extreme scores.

b. Repeat part (a), using the median instead of the mean.

SECTION 2.6   **MEASURES OF DISPERSION**

We are now able to compute three measures of central location. But these measures fail to tell the whole story about a distribution of measurements. For example, if you were told only that the average maximum temperature is 83.2°F in Honolulu and 79.4°F in Las Vegas, you might ask why Honolulu attracts significantly more sunseekers in the winter months than does Las Vegas. A contributing factor may be that Honolulu's climate is much more temperate year-round. Honolulu's monthly average maximum temperatures vary only from 79°F to 87°F, while those of Las Vegas vary from 56°F to 104°F. Clearly, the average maximum temperature of 83.2°F for Honolulu is far closer to the maximum monthly temperatures likely to be encountered than is Las Vegas' average maximum temperature to its maximum monthly temperatures.

Once we know the average value of a set of measurements, our next question should be: how typical is the average value of all the measurements in the data set? Or in other words, how spread out are the measurements about their average value? Are the measurements highly variable and widely dispersed about the average value, as depicted by the smoothed relative frequency polygon in Figure 2.20(a), or do they exhibit low variability and cluster about the average value, as in Figure 2.20(b)?

The importance of looking beyond the average value is borne out by the fact that many individuals make use of the concept of variability in everyday decision making, whether or not they compute a numerical measure of the dispersion. Consider the case of Tuffy Rocknee, the college football coach, agonizing over which player should handle the punting in Saturday's big game. Tuffy has decided to base his decision on the results of ten practice kicks by each player. The recorded yardages are as follows:

A: 41, 55, 30, 38, 50, 42, 39, 25, 28, 52

B: 39, 42, 38, 42, 44, 40, 41, 38, 36, 40

FIGURE 2.20   *SMOOTHED RELATIVE FREQUENCY POLYGONS*

(a) High variability

(b) Low variability

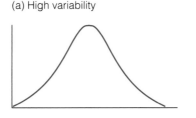
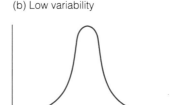

The mean number of yards punted by each player is 40 (as you should verify); but if Tuffy is looking for consistency, he will select player *B*. Without actually computing a measure of dispersion (and probably not caring to know how to), Tuffy will choose the player whose punts exhibit the lowest variability.

The concept of variability is of fundamental importance in statistical inference. It is therefore important that we, unlike Tuffy, be able to measure the degree of variability in a set of measurements.

RANGE

The first and simplest measure of dispersion is the range, which we already encountered when forming frequency distributions.

> **Range**
>
> The range of a set of measurements is the numerical difference between the largest and smallest measurements.

The usefulness of the range stems from the ease with which it can be computed and interpreted. The first observation we made in connection with the telephone data in Table 2.1 was that the shortest and longest telephone calls were 2.3 and 19.5 minutes, respectively, which established that the range was $19.5 - 2.3 = 17.2$ minutes. We later computed the mean duration of the telephone calls to be 10.26 minutes.

A major shortcoming of the range is that it provides no information about the dispersion of the values falling between the smallest and largest measurements. These intermediate values might all be clustered very closely about the mean value of 10.26, or they might be dispersed fairly evenly across the range between the two extreme values, or they might be clumped in two groups near each extreme (resulting in a barbell-shaped distribution). Information concerning the location, and hence the dispersion, of these intermediate values can be conveyed by means of percentiles.

PERCENTILES

> **Percentiles**
>
> The pth percentile of a set of measurements is the value for which *at most* $p\%$ of the measurements are less than that value and *at most* $(100 - p)\%$ of the measurements are greater than that value.

The pth percentile is defined in much the same manner as is the median—the value for which at most 50% of the measurements are smaller and at most 50% of the measurements are greater. In fact, the median is simply the 50th percentile. Just as we have a special name for the percentile that divides the ordered set of measurements in half, we have special names for the percentiles that divide the ordered set of measurements into quarters and into tenths: *quartiles* and *deciles*.* The following list identifies some of the more commonly used percentiles, together with notation for the quartiles:

$$
\begin{aligned}
\text{First (lower) decile} &= \text{10th percentile} \\
Q_1 = \text{First (lower) quartile} &= \text{25th percentile} \\
Q_2 = \text{Second (middle) quartile} &= \text{Median (50th percentile)} \\
Q_3 = \text{Third (upper) quartile} &= \text{75th percentile} \\
\text{Ninth (upper) decile} &= \text{90th percentile}
\end{aligned}
$$

EXAMPLE 2.6

To find the quartiles for the set of measurements

7, 18, 12, 5, 17, 29, 8, 18, 4, 27, 30, 2, 4, 10, 21

we must first arrange the measurements in ascending order:

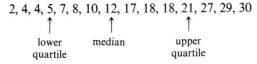

2, 4, 4, 5, 7, 8, 10, 12, 17, 18, 18, 21, 27, 29, 30

      ↑   ↑   ↑

   lower   median   upper
  quartile   quartile

The lower quartile is the value for which at most $0.25 \times 15 = 3.75$ of the measurements are smaller and at most $0.75 \times 15 = 11.25$ of the measurements are larger. The only measurement satisfying these criteria is 5, so 5 is the first quartile. Similarly, we can establish that the median is 12 and that the third quartile is 21.

Occasionally, you will find that the percentile you are seeking falls between two of the measurements in the data set. In such circumstances we suggest that, to avoid becoming unnecessarily pedantic, you simply choose the midpoint between the two measurements involved. This will usually provide an adequate approximation of the required percentile. To illustrate this convention, suppose that we wish to find the 20th percentile of the 15 measurements in Example 2.6. The 20th percentile would be the value for which at most 3 of the measurements are smaller and at most 12 of the measurements are larger. Since any number between the

---

* Quartiles are dividers—that is, values that divide the entire range of measurements into four equal quarters. In practice, however, the word *quartile* is sometimes used to refer to one of these quarters. A measurement "in the first quartile" is in the bottom 25% of the measurements, whereas a measurement "in the upper quartile" is among the top 25%.

measurements 4 and 5 (inclusive) satisfies this criterion, we choose 4.5—the midpoint between 4 and 5—as the 20th percentile.

Percentiles per se are measures of location, and they are widely used as measures of relative position because they are so easy to interpret. For example, they are frequently used to indicate the relative scores of applicants on admissions tests. Percentiles are also a popular means of conveying information about the relative performances of pension fund investment portfolios over the most recent year. To provide a good indication of the dispersion of a set of measurements, however, a number of percentiles must be computed.* With ordinal data, such a procedure is necessary to convey the dispersion, or variability, of a data set. In contrast, the next measure of dispersion to be considered can summarize the variability of the measurements in a single number, but it is only appropriate if the measurements have an interval scale.

VARIANCE

We now come to variance, one of the two most widely accepted measures of the variability of a set of data (the other is standard deviation). Closely related to one another, variance and standard deviation take all of the data into account and (as we will see in Chapter 6) are of fundamental importance in statistical inference.

Consider two very small populations, each consisting of only five measurements:

A: 8, 9, 10, 11, 12

B: 4, 7, 10, 13, 16

The mean of both population A and population B is 10, as you can easily verify. The population values are plotted along the horizontal x-axis in Figure 2.21. Visual inspection of these graphs indicates that the measurements in population B are more widely dispersed than those in A. We are searching for a measure of dispersion that confirms this notion and takes into account each measurement in the population.

Consider the five measurements in population A. To obtain a measure of their dispersion, we might begin by calculating the deviation of each value from the mean:

$$(8 - 10), (9 - 10), (10 - 10), (11 - 10), (12 - 10)$$

The four nonzero deviations are represented by the double-pointed arrows above the x-axis in Figure 2.21. It might at first seem reasonable to take the sum of these deviations as a measure of dispersion, but the sum of deviations from the mean is always zero. While this difficulty could be overcome by summing the absolute values

---

* The number of percentiles that must be computed can be limited to two if the statistician is content to report only the *interquartile range*—the difference between the third and first quartiles. While it is helpful to know this range, within which the middle 50% of measurements fall, it (like the range) is based on two measurements only.

FIGURE 2.21   DEVIATIONS OF MEASUREMENTS FROM THE MEAN

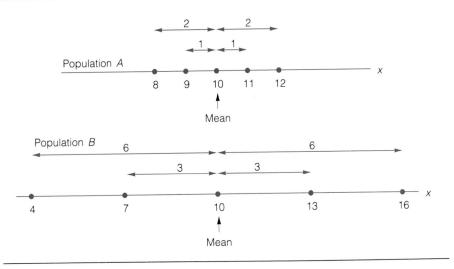

of the deviations from the mean, absolute values are somewhat difficult to work with mathematically. More mathematically tractable and more useful in statistical inference are the squares of the deviations from the mean. Thus, we might consider

$$(8 - 10)^2 + (9 - 10)^2 + (10 - 10)^2 + (11 - 10)^2 + (12 - 10)^2 = 10$$

as a measure of the variability of our measurements in population A. The corresponding expression for a population of measurements $x_1, x_2, \ldots, x_N$ would be

$$\sum_{i=1}^{N} (x_i - \mu)^2$$

Unfortunately, although this sum of squared deviations has the desirable property of being larger for sets of measurements that have greater dispersion, it also increases in magnitude simply from an increase in the number of measurements in the data set—even though the larger data set may have less dispersion than a smaller one. This is remedied by taking the average of the squared deviations as the required measure of dispersion. This measure of the dispersion, or variability, of a population of measurements is called the **variance;** it is denoted by σ^2, where σ is the lower-case Greek letter *sigma.*

Letting σ_A^2 denote the variance of population A, we obtain

$$\sigma_A^2 = \frac{(8 - 10)^2 + (9 - 10)^2 + (10 - 10)^2 + (11 - 10)^2 + (12 - 10)^2}{5}$$

$$= \frac{(-2)^2 + (-1)^2 + 0^2 + 1^2 + 2^2}{5} = \frac{10}{5} = 2$$

Proceeding in an analogous manner for population B, we obtain

$$\sigma_B^2 = \frac{(4-10)^2 + (7-10)^2 + (10-10)^2 + (13-10)^2 + (16-10)^2}{5} = 18$$

The variance of B therefore exceeds the variance of A, consistent with our initial visual impression that the values in population B were more dispersed than those in population A.

Variance of a Population

The variance of a population of N measurements $x_1, x_2, \ldots, x_N$ having mean μ is defined by

$$\sigma^2 = \frac{\sum_{i=1}^{N}(x_i - \mu)^2}{N}$$

We suggest that, rather than blindly memorizing this formula, you think of the variance as being the mean squared deviation—the mean of the squared deviations of the measurements from their mean μ. This should help you to remember and to interpret the formula for variance.

Now suppose that you are working with a sample, rather than with a population. Given a sample of n measurements, your interest in computing the variance of the sample (denoted by s^2) lies in obtaining a good estimate of the population variance (σ^2). While it would seem reasonable to define the sample variance s^2 as the average of the squared deviations of the sample measurements from their mean $\bar{x}$, defining s^2 in this way tends to underestimate the population variance σ^2. This problem is rectified, however, if the sample variance s^2 is defined as the sum of the squared deviations divided by $n - 1$, rather than by n. Further discussion of this point is provided in Chapter 7.

Variance of a Sample

The variance of a sample of n measurements $x_1, x_2, \ldots, x_n$ having mean $\bar{x}$ is defined as

$$s^2 = \frac{\sum_{i=1}^{n}(x_i - \bar{x})^2}{n - 1}$$

Computing the variance of a large sample can be made less tedious by means of a shortcut formula derivable through simple algebraic manipulation of the formula just presented. The sample mean is usually calculated before the sample variance, in which case the value of the second summation in the shortcut formula is already known.

Shortcut Formula

The shortcut formula for the sample variance is

$$s^2 = \frac{1}{n-1}\left[\sum_{i=1}^{n} x_i^2 - \frac{\left(\sum_{i=1}^{n} x_i\right)^2}{n}\right]$$

EXAMPLE 2.7

Find the mean and the variance of the following sample of measurements:

3.4, 2.5, 4.1, 1.2, 2.8, 3.7

Solution.   The mean of this sample of six measurements is

$$\bar{x} = \frac{\sum_{i=1}^{6} x_i}{6} = \frac{3.4 + 2.5 + 4.1 + 1.2 + 2.8 + 3.7}{6}$$

$$= \frac{17.7}{6} = 2.95$$

To find the sample variance by means of the shortcut formula, we first compute

$$\sum_{i=1}^{6} x_i^2 = (3.4)^2 + (2.5)^2 + (4.1)^2 + (1.2)^2 + (2.8)^2 + (3.7)^2 = 57.59$$

From the computation of the mean, we already know that

$$\sum_{i=1}^{6} x_i = 17.7$$

So

$$s^2 = \frac{1}{5}\left[\sum_{i=1}^{6} x_i^2 - \frac{\left(\sum_{i=1}^{6} x_i\right)^2}{6}\right] = \frac{1}{5}\left[57.59 - \frac{(17.7)^2}{6}\right] = 1.075$$

Alternatively, we could compute s^2 directly, using the definition of *sample variance:*

$$s^2 = \frac{(3.4 - 2.95)^2 + (2.5 - 2.95)^2 + (4.1 - 2.95)^2 + (1.2 - 2.95)^2 + (2.8 - 2.95)^2 + (3.7 - 2.95)^2}{5}$$

$$= 1.075$$

One important application of variance arises in finance, where variance is the most popular numerical measure of risk. In this context we might refer to the variance of a firm's sales, profits, or return on investment. In all cases, the underlying assumption is that a larger variance corresponds to a higher level of risk. The next example illustrates this important application of variance.

▬▬▬▬▬▬ **EXAMPLE 2.8**

Mutual funds are becoming an increasingly popular investment alternative among small investors. To help investors decide on the particular fund to invest in, the *Financial Times of Canada* regularly reports the average annual rate of return achieved by each of more than 100 mutual funds over the past 10 years.* The publication also indicates each fund's level of risk, by classifying the historical variability of each fund's rate of return as high, intermediate, or low.

If the annual (percentage) rates of return over the past 10 years for two mutual funds are as follows, which fund would you classify as having the higher level of risk?

Fund *A*: 8.3, -6.2, 20.9, -2.7, 33.6, 42.9, 24.4, 5.2, 3.1, 30.5

Fund *B*: 12.1, -2.8, 6.4, 12.2, 27.8, 25.3, 18.2, 10.7, -1.3, 11.4

Solution. For each fund, we must find the variance of the sample of rates of return. To avoid having to compute several squared deviations of returns from their mean, we'll use the shortcut formula for calculating a sample variance. For Fund *A*, we have

$$\sum_{i=1}^{10} x_i = 8.3 - 6.2 + \cdots + 30.5 = 160.0$$

$$\sum_{i=1}^{10} x_i^2 = (8.3)^2 + (-6.2)^2 + \cdots + (30.5)^2 = 5{,}083.06$$

The variance for Fund *A* is therefore

$$s_A^2 = \frac{1}{9}\left[\sum_{i=1}^{10} x_i^2 - \frac{(\sum_{i=1}^{10} x_i)^2}{10}\right] = \frac{1}{9}\left[5{,}083.06 - \frac{(160.0)^2}{10}\right] = 280.34(\%)^2$$

For Fund *B* we have

$$\sum_{i=1}^{10} x_i = 12.1 - 2.8 + \cdots + 11.4 = 120.0$$

$$\sum_{i=1}^{10} x_i^2 = (12.1)^2 + (-2.8)^2 + \cdots + (11.4)^2 = 2{,}334.36$$

The variance for Fund *B* is therefore

$$s_B^2 = \frac{1}{9}\left[\sum_{i=1}^{10} x_i^2 - \frac{(\sum_{i=1}^{10} x_i)^2}{10}\right] = \frac{1}{9}\left[2{,}334.36 - \frac{(120.0)^2}{10}\right] = 99.38(\%)^2$$

Notice that, since the calculation of s^2 involves squaring the original measurements, the sample variance is expressed in (percent)^2, or $(\%)^2$, which is the square of the unit used to express the original measurements of rate of return.

---

* The annual rate of return of a mutual fund is given by $(P_1 - P_0)/P_0$, where P_0 and P_1 are the prices of the fund's shares at the beginning and end of the year, respectively. This definition assumes that no dividends are paid by the fund during the year.

On the basis of the sample data, Fund A has the higher level of risk as measured by variance, since the variance of its rates of return exceeds that of Fund B's rates of return. Notice that Fund A has also enjoyed a higher average rate of return over the past 10 years. Specifically, the mean rates of return for Funds A and B were

$$\bar{x}_A = \frac{160.0}{10} = 16\%$$

and

$$\bar{x}_B = \frac{120.0}{10} = 12\%$$

This is in keeping with our intuitive notion that an investment with a higher level of risk should have a higher average rate of return.*

STANDARD DEVIATION

As was mentioned previously, calculating variance involves squaring the original measurements, and as a result the unit attached to a variance is the square of the unit attached to the original measurements. For example, if our original measurements are expressed in minutes, the variance is expressed in minutes squared. While variance is a useful measure of the relative variability of two sets of measurements, statisticians often want a measure of variability that is expressed in the same units as the original measurements, just as the mean is. Such a measure can be obtained by taking the square root of the variance.

Standard Deviation

The standard deviation of a set of measurements is the positive square root of the variance of the measurements.

Sample standard deviation: $s = \sqrt{s^2}$

Population standard deviation: $\sigma = \sqrt{\sigma^2}$

For instance, the standard deviations of the samples of rates of return for Funds A and B in Example 2.8 are

$$s_A = \sqrt{s_A^2} = \sqrt{280.34} = 16.74\%$$

---

* Students of finance will realize that, strictly speaking, the mutual funds must be well-diversified for this statement to hold when variance is used as the measure of risk.

and

$$s_B = \sqrt{s_B^2} = \sqrt{99.38} = 9.97\%$$

As you can see, the measurements in sample A are more variable than those in sample B, whether we use variance or standard deviation as our measure of variability. But standard deviation is the more useful measure of variability in situations where the measure is to be used in conjunction with the mean to make a statement about a single population, as we shall see in the next section.

COEFFICIENT OF VARIATION

The coefficient of variation, CV, of a data set is the set's standard deviation divided by its mean. Thus, we have

$$CV = \frac{s}{\overline{x}} \qquad \text{or} \qquad CV = \frac{\sigma}{\mu}$$

depending on whether the data set represents a sample or a population. Rather than comparing two variances, we can often obtain a more accurate assessment of the relative variability of two data sets by comparing their coefficients of variations, which adjust for differences in the magnitudes of the means of the data sets.

For instance, the coefficients of variation of the samples of rates of return from Funds A and B in Example 2.8 are

$$CV_A = \frac{s_A}{\overline{x}_A} = \frac{16.74}{16} = 1.05$$

and

$$CV_B = \frac{s_B}{\overline{x}_B} = \frac{9.97}{12} = .83$$

In this particular case, comparing coefficients of variation and comparing standard deviations lead to the same conclusion about which measurements are more variable: those in sample A.

The coefficient of variation is sometimes multiplied by 100 and reported as a percentage, which effectively expresses the standard deviation as a percentage of the mean. Thus, for the Fund A returns in Example 2.8, the coefficient of variation is 105%.

COMPUTER OUTPUT FOR EXAMPLE 2.8 (FUND A)*

Minitab

	N	MEAN	MEDIAN	TRMEAN	STDEV	SEMEAN
C1	10	16.00	14.60	15.41	16.74	5.29

---

* Appendixes 2A and 2B provide the Minitab and SAS instructions that produced these outputs.

```
         MIN      MAX      Q1        Q3
C1      -6.20    42.90    1.65     31.27
```

The output includes the following statistics:

N (the sample size)

MEAN

MEDIAN

TRMEAN (the mean of the observations after the largest and smallest 5% are trimmed or omitted)

STDEV (the sample standard deviation)

SEMEAN (the standard error of the mean, which equals $STDEV/\sqrt{N}$; this statistic is discussed in Chapter 7)

MIN (minimum observation)

MAX (maximum observation)

Q1 (first or lower quartile)

Q3 (third or upper quartile)

SAS

```
Variable=X
                          Moments
N                10    Sum           160
Mean             16    Variance      280.34
Std Dev     16.7433
```

Much of the actual output has been omitted. Some of the missing statistics will be discussed in later chapters. Our current objectives are satisfied with the following printout:

```
n=10
x̄=16
∑ xᵢ=160
s=16.7433
s²=280.34
```

───── **EXERCISES**

LEARNING THE TECHNIQUES

2.30   Compute the range, variance, and standard deviation for the following sample of data:

   5, 7, 12, 14, 15, 15, 17, 20, 21, 24

2.31   Calculate $\bar{x}$, s^2, and s for the following sample of data:

   $3, -2, -4, 1, 0, -1, 2$

2.32   Calculate $\bar{x}$, s^2, and s for each of the following samples of data:

a. 14, 7, 8, 11, 5

b. −3, −2, −1, 0, 1, 2, 3

c. 4, 4, 8, 8

d. 5, 5, 5, 5

2.33 Treating each of the four sets of data in Exercise 2.32 as populations, calculate μ, σ^2, and σ for each of the four populations.

2.34 What are the special names for the 25th, 50th, and 75th percentiles?

2.35 The numbers of hours a student spent studying over the past 7 days were recorded as follows:

2, 5, 6, 1, 4, 0, 3

Compute the range, $\bar{x}$, s, and s^2 for these data. Express each answer in appropriate units.

2.36 Given a set of ordinal data, what is the most appropriate measure of central location? What would be an appropriate measure of dispersion?

2.37 Given a set of interval data, what is the most popular measure of central location? What is the best measure of variability? Explain both answers.

APPLYING THE TECHNIQUES

Self-Correcting Exercise (See Appendix 2.C for the solution.)

2.38 The 15 stocks in your portfolio had the following percentage changes in value over the last year:

3	0	6	−5	−2
5	−18	20	14	18
10	10	50	−20	14

a. Compute μ, σ^2, and σ for this population of data. Express each answer in appropriate units.

b. Compute the range, median, 20th percentile, and 60 percentile for these data.

2.39 The owner of a hardware store that sells electrical wire by the meter is considering selling the wire in precut lengths in order to cut down on labor costs. A sample of lengths of wire sold one day produced the following data:

3, 7, 4, 2.5, 3, 20, 5, 5, 15, 3.5, 3

a. Find the mean, the median, and the mode of the lengths of wire sold on the given day.

b. For each of the three measures of central location, indicate its weakness in providing useful information to the store owner.

c. Find the upper and lower quartiles of the lengths of wire sold.

d. How might the store owner decide upon the appropriate precut lengths to sell?

2.40 Consider once again the two mutual funds, A and B, in Example 2.8. For convenience, their annual percentage rates of return over the past 10 years are repeated here. Suppose that, 10 years ago, you formed a portfolio by investing equal amounts of money in each of the two funds. The rate of return you would have earned on the portfolio in the first year would then have been $0.5(8.3) + 0.5(12.1) = 10.2\%$.

Fund A: 8.3, −6.2, 20.9, −2.7, 33.6,
            42.9, 24.4, 5.2, 3.1, 30.5
Fund B: 12.1, −2.8, 6.4, 12.2, 27.8, 25.3,
            18.2, 10.7, −1.3, 11.4

a. Compute the rate of return earned on the portfolio in each of the 10 years.

b. Find the mean return on the portfolio over the past 10 years.

c. Find the standard deviation of the portfolio returns over the past 10 years.

d. Rank the three possible investments (Fund A, Fund B, and the portfolio) according to their average returns and according to their riskiness (as measured by standard deviation) over the past 10 years.

2.41 The annual total rates of return on Canadian common stocks and long-term government bonds, for each of 25 years, are shown in the accompanying table. To understand the meaning of these returns, consider the 15.56% return that was realized on common stocks in 1963. This means that $100 invested in common stocks at the beginning of 1963 would have yielded a profit of $15.56 over the year, leaving you with a total of $115.56 at year's end.

ANNUAL TOTAL RATES OF RETURN (IN %)

Years	Common Stocks					Long-Term Government Bonds				
1960–64	1.66	32.54	−7.25	15.56	25.30	7.10	9.78	3.05	4.60	6.59
1965–69	6.54	−7.10	18.00	22.36	−0.96	0.96	1.55	−2.20	−0.52	−2.31
1970–74	−3.60	8.07	27.31	−0.42	−26.61	−21.98	11.55	1.11	1.71	−1.69
1975–79	19.70	10.94	9.93	29.22	44.38	2.82	19.02	5.97	1.29	−2.62
1980–84	29.93	−10.29	5.51	34.84	−2.44	2.06	−3.02	42.98	9.60	15.09

SOURCE: *Report on Canadian Economic Statistics: 1924–1984* (Canadian Institute of Actuaries, May 1985), pp. 22, 32.

a. Find the mean, the median, the range, and the standard deviation of this sample of common-stock returns.

b. Find the upper and lower quartiles of the common-stock returns.

c. Repeat parts (a) and (b) for the bond returns.

d. Which type of investment (common stocks or bonds) appears to have the higher level of risk? The higher average return?

e. Compute the mean stock return for each of the five 5-year periods.

f. Compute the mean and the standard deviation of the five mean returns in part (e). Compare these values with the mean and the standard deviation calculated in part (a), and explain any differences observed.

2.42   Individual firms in the toy industry find that their annual growth rates in sales tend to fluctuate substantially from year to year, because of chang-

ing fads. In comparison, the growth rate in total industry sales is relatively stable.

a. Determine whether or not this statement is supported by the data in the accompanying table, by comparing the variances of the growth rates in sales for Mattel, Tonka, and the entire toy industry.

b. Answer part (a) of this exercise by comparing coefficients of variation rather than variances.

PERCENTAGE GROWTH RATES IN SALES

	1980	1981	1982	1983	1984
Mattel	13.7	23.9	18.3	−52.8	39.1
Tonka	−21.7	4.1	−22.9	8.3	58.3
Industry	8.4	14.0	28.9	−19.9	50.0

SECTION 2.7   *CHEBYSHEV'S THEOREM AND THE EMPIRICAL RULE*

CHEBYSHEV'S THEOREM

By now, you probably understand how variance and standard deviation can be used as relative measures of dispersion. Given the standard deviation of a single set of measurements, however, you would likely have difficulty interpreting that value intuitively. The standard deviation would be more useful if it could be used to make a statement about the proportion of measurements that fall into various intervals of values. For example, suppose you are told that the average daily maximum temperature in Honolulu is 82°F, with a standard deviation of 1.5 Fahrenheit degrees. You would probably find it helpful to be able to say something about the proportion of days on which the maximum temperature falls within a specified range—between 79°F and 85°F, for example. Fortunately, someone has developed a theorem that enables you to do just that. We now consider this theorem, which was first proved by Russian mathematician Pavroty Chebyshev.

> **Chebyshev's Theorem**
>
> Given any set of measurements and a number $k \geq 1$, the fraction of these measurements that lie within k standard deviations of their mean is at least $1 - 1/k^2$.

To see how Chebyshev's theorem can be applied to the descriptive measures of Honolulu temperatures, first notice that all temperatures between 79°F and 85°F are within two standard deviations of the mean maximum temperature. That is,

$$(79, 85) = (82 - 2[1.5], 82 + 2[1.5])$$

Therefore, setting $k = 2$ in Chebyshev's theorem, we determine that at least $1 - 1/2^2 = \frac{3}{4}$ of the maximum temperatures fall between 79°F and 85°F.

Because this famous theorem is valid for any set of measurements, it holds both for a sample and for a population. Although we have chosen to use the notation for a sample in the discussion that follows, population notation would serve equally well. The thrust of the theorem is to provide a minimum value for the fraction of measurements falling within an interval of the form $(\bar{x} - ks, \bar{x} + ks)$. This interval of values, which is centered at the mean, contains an increasingly large fraction of the measurements as we choose an increasingly large number to be k, since the interval widens as k increases. For example, the interval $(\bar{x} - 3s, \bar{x} + 3s)$ contains a larger fraction of the measurements than does the interval $(\bar{x} - 2s, \bar{x} + 2s)$. According to Chebyshev's theorem, that increasingly large fraction of measurements lying within the interval $(\bar{x} - ks, \bar{x} + ks)$ is at least $1 - 1/k^2$.

Let's now look at what the theorem asserts for some specific values of k. The theorem provides no useful information for $k = 1$, as it simply states that the fraction of measurements lying in the interval $(\bar{x} - s, \bar{x} + s)$ is at least 0. But if we select $k = 2$, we find that at least $1 - 1/2^2 = \frac{3}{4}$ of the measurements lie in the interval $(\bar{x} - 2s, \bar{x} + 2s)$, as observed earlier. These and other examples are listed in Table 2.12. Figure 2.22 illustrates Chebyshev's theorem graphically for $k = 2$, where $\bar{x}$ and s are the mean and the standard deviation of a sample of measurements x_i.

The importance of Chebyshev's theorem stems from the fact that it applies to *any* set of measurements, regardless of their distribution. Consequently, $1 - 1/k^2$ is

TABLE 2.12   *CHEBYSCHEV'S THEOREM FOR VARIOUS VALUES OF k*

k	Interval	Fraction (Percentage) of Measurements in Interval	
1	$(\bar{x} - s, \bar{x} + s)$	at least 0	(at least 0%)
2	$(\bar{x} - 2s, \bar{x} + 2s)$	at least $\frac{3}{4}$	(at least 75%)
2.5	$(\bar{x} - 2.5s, \bar{x} + 2.5s)$	at least $\frac{21}{25}$	(at least 84%)
3	$(\bar{x} - 3s, \bar{x} + 3s)$	at least $\frac{8}{9}$	(at least 89%)

FIGURE 2.22   *CHEBYSHEV'S THEOREM FOR k = 2*

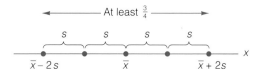

necessarily a conservative lower bound on the fraction of measurements in the interval $(\bar{x} - ks, \bar{x} + ks)$. In other words, since the fraction of measurements in the interval $(\bar{x} - ks, \bar{x} + ks)$ varies from one set of data to another, the best we can do is to specify a minimum value for this fraction—a value that is correct for any set of measurements. For a particular set of data, the actual fraction of measurements lying in the interval may in fact be much larger.

EXAMPLE 2.9

The telephone-call durations in Table 2.1 have a mean of $\bar{x} = 10.26$ and a standard deviation of $s = 4.29$. Given nothing else about the distribution of the durations, Chebyshev's theorem asserts that at least $\frac{3}{4}$ or 75% of the durations lie in the interval

$$(\bar{x} - 2s, \bar{x} + 2s) = (10.26 - 2[4.29], 10.26 + 2[4.29])$$
$$= (1.68, 18.84)$$

In fact, all but the largest of the 30 durations fall into this interval; that is, the interval actually contains 96.7% of the telephone-call durations—a percentage well above the lower bound asserted by Chebyshev's theorem.

EMPIRICAL RULE

In many real-world applications, the sample of data is so large that determining the percentage of measurements lying within a particular interval by counting them would be impractical. A very good estimate of this percentage is available, however, if the distribution of the data is mound-shaped (or bell-shaped). An example of a mound-shaped distribution is shown in Figure 2.23, which reproduces the relative frequency histogram of the telephone-call durations. (A smoothed outline of the histogram would resemble a mound.)

A rule of thumb, called the *Empirical Rule*, has evolved from empirical studies that have produced samples possessing mound-shaped distributions. For a sample of measurements with a mound-shaped distribution, the Empirical Rule gives the approximate percentage of the measurements that fall within one, two, or three standard deviations of the mean.

Empirical Rule

If a sample of measurements has a mound-shaped distribution, the interval

$(\bar{x} - s, \bar{x} + s)$ contains approximately 68% of the measurements

$(\bar{x} - 2s, \bar{x} + 2s)$ contains approximately 95% of the measurements

$(\bar{x} - 3s, \bar{x} + 3s)$ contains virtually all of the measurements

For purposes of comparison, Table 2.13 provides both the Empirical Rule percentages and the corresponding Chebyshev percentages (which apply to any distribution of measurements) of measurements falling within one, two, and three standard deviations of the mean.

Consider once again the sample of telephone-call durations, which has an approximately mound-shaped distribution (Figure 2.23) and for which $\bar{x} = 10.26$ and $s = 4.29$. The interval $(\bar{x} - s, \bar{x} + s) = (5.97, 14.55)$ actually contains 70% of the durations, while the interval $(\bar{x} - 2s, \bar{x} + 2s) = (1.68, 18.84)$ actually contains 96.7% of the durations. The percentages comport well with the Empirical Rule's assertion that approximately 68% and 95% of the durations will fall within the named intervals.

This example may also be used to anticipate an idea that will be elaborated in Chapter 4, when we deal with a particular mound-shaped distribution called the *normal distribution*. We noted in Section 2.2 that the area of any rectangle erected as part of a histogram is proportional to the percentage of the measurements that fall into the class it describes. As we've just observed, the Empirical Rule states that about 95% of the telephone-call durations fall in the interval between 1.68 and 18.84 minutes. Therefore, approximately 95% of the area under the mound-shaped histogram in Figure 2.23 lies between 1.68 and 18.84. More generally, approximately

FIGURE 2.23   *MOUND-SHAPED HISTOGRAM*

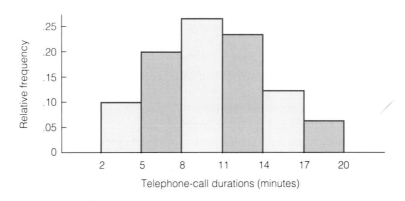

TABLE 2.13   *EMPIRICAL RULE PERCENTAGES*

Interval	Approximate Percentage of Measurements in Interval	Chebyshev Percentage
$(\bar{x} - s, \bar{x} + s)$	68%	at least 0%
$(\bar{x} - 2s, \bar{x} + 2s)$	95%	at least 75%
$(\bar{x} - 3s, \bar{x} + 3s)$	100%	at least 89%

95% of the area under any mound-shaped histogram lies between $\bar{x} - 2s$ and $\bar{x} + 2s$.

As a final point, we note that the Empirical Rule forms the basis for a crude method of approximating the standard deviation of a sample of measurements that has a mound-shaped distribution. Since most of the sample measurements (about 95%) fall within two standard deviations of the mean, the range of the measurements is approximately equal to 4s. Once we have found the range of the measurements, we can approximate the sample standard deviation by

$$s \cong \text{Range}/4$$

This **range approximation of** *s* is useful as a quick check to ensure that our computed value of *s* is reasonable, or "in the ballpark." For example, the range of the telephone-call durations is 17.2, so 17.2/4 = 4.3 is an approximation of *s*. In this case, the range approximation is very close to 4.29, our computed value of *s*. Such accuracy isn't generally to be expected. More will be said about this approximation in Chapter 7.

![EXERCISES]

LEARNING THE TECHNIQUES

2.43 The mean and standard deviation of the grades of 500 students who took an economics exam were 69 and 7, respectively.

a. At least how many of these students received a grade in the intervals $\bar{x} \pm 2s$, $\bar{x} \pm 2.5s$, and $\bar{x} \pm 3s$?

b. How many of these students, at most, did not receive a grade in the intervals $\bar{x} \pm 3.5s$ and $\bar{x} \pm 4s$?

2.44 Refer to Exercise 2.43. If the grades have a mound-shaped distribution, how many students received a grade in the intervals $\bar{x} \pm s$, $\bar{x} \pm 2s$, and $\bar{x} \pm 3s$?

2.45 The mean and standard deviation of the wages of 1,000 factory workers are \$25,600 and \$2,200, respectively.

a. At least how many of these workers receive wages of between \$21,200 and \$30,000? Between \$20,100 and \$31,100? Between \$19,000 and \$32,200?

b. How many of these workers, at most, receive wages that are not between \$17,900 and \$33,300? Not between \$16,800 and \$34,400?

2.46 Refer to Exercise 2.45. If the wages have a mound-shaped distribution, how many workers receive wages of between \$23,400 and \$27,800? Between \$21,200 and \$30,000? Between \$19,000 and \$32,200?

APPLYING THE TECHNIQUES

2.47 The following 20 values represent the number of seconds required to complete one spot-weld by a sample of 20 automated welders on a company's production line:

2.1, 2.7, 2.6, 2.8, 2.3, 2.5, 2.6, 2.4, 2.6, 2.7
2.4, 2.6, 2.8, 2.5, 2.6, 2.4, 2.9, 2.4, 2.7, 2.3

a. Calculate the variance and the standard deviation for this sample of 20 measurements.

b. Use the range approximation of s to check your calculations in part (a). What assumption must you make in order to use this approximation?

c. Using Chebyshev's theorem, what can you say about the fraction of measurements falling within 1.5 standard deviations of the mean of the 20 measurements?

d. How does your answer to part (c) compare with the actual fraction of measurements falling within 1.5 standard deviations of the mean?

Self-Correcting Exercise (See Appendix 2.C for the solution.)

2.48 A bookstore has determined that weekly sales of *Newsweek* have an approximately mound-shaped distribution, with a mean of 85 and a standard deviation of 6.

a. For what percentage of the time can we expect weekly sales to fall in the intervals $\bar{x} \pm s$ and $\bar{x} \pm 3s$?

b. For what percentage of the time can we expect weekly sales to have a value that is more than 2 standard deviations from the mean?

c. If the bookstore stocks 97 copies of *Newsweek* each week, for what percentage of weeks will there be an insufficient number of copies to meet the demand? (HINT: A mound-shaped distribution is symmetrical.)

2.49 Last year, the rates of return on the common stocks in a large portfolio had an approximately mound-shaped distribution, with a mean of 20% and a standard deviation of 10%.

a. What proportion of the stocks had a return of between 10% and 30%? Between -10% and 50%?

b. What proportion of the stocks had a return that was either less than 10% or more than 30%?

c. What proportion of the stocks had a positive return? (HINT: A mound-shaped distribution is symmetrical.)

2.50 Refer to Exercise 2.41, which deals with stock and bond returns.

a. Compute the standard deviation of both the common-stock returns and the bond returns.

b. Use the range approximation of s to check your answers to part (a).

2.51   In Exercise 2.3, you were asked to depict graphically the distribution of the following sample of house prices (in $1,000s):

274	429	229	435	260
222	292	419	242	202
235	215	390	359	409
375	209	265	440	365
319	338	414	249	279

a. Calculate the variance and the standard deviation of this sample of prices.

b. Compare the range approximation of s to the true value of s. Explain why you would or would not expect the approximation to be a good one for this sample.

c. Using Chebyshev's theorem, what can you say about the fraction of measurements falling within 1.2 standard deviations of the mean of the 25 prices?

d. How does your answer to part (c) compare with the actual fraction of measurements falling within 1.2 standard deviations of the mean?

SECTION 2.8   *APPROXIMATING DESCRIPTIVE MEASURES FOR GROUPED DATA*

The two most important descriptive measures are the mean and the variance (or alternatively, the standard deviation). This section looks briefly at how to approximate these two measures for data that have been grouped into a frequency distribution.

You will find that the approximations given here are useful in two types of situations. The first is when you are confronted with a large set of ungrouped data. Although you could calculate the mean and the variance precisely with the aid of a computer, you may decide that approximations of these measures suffice to meet your needs. In this case, you may find it faster and cheaper simply to group the data into a frequency distribution and use the methods described here. The second situation, which arises frequently in practice, is when you rely on secondary data sources such as government publications. Data collected by others is usually presented in the form of a frequency distribution, and you do not have access to the ungrouped data. In this case, you have no choice but to approximate the descriptive measures.

Consider a sample of n measurements that have been grouped into k classes. If f_i denotes the frequency of class i (for $i = 1, 2, \ldots, k$), then $n = f_1 + f_2 + \cdots + f_k$. A good approximation of the sample mean $\bar{x}$ can be obtained by making the assumption that the midpoint m_i of each class i closely approximates the mean of the measurements in class i. This assumption is reasonable whenever the measurements in a class are dispersed fairly symmetrically about the midpoint. The sum of the measurements in class i is then approximately equal to $f_i m_i$.

The approximation of the sample variance is obtained by approximating the shortcut formula for the sample variance of ungrouped data, which was given in Section 2.6. The approximation of the sample variance actually requires a stronger assumption than the assumption of symmetry mentioned above: each measurement in a class is assumed to be equal to the midpoint of that class. The more accurate this

TABLE 2.14   EXTENDED FREQUENCY DISTRIBUTION OF TELEPHONE-CALL DURATIONS

Class i	Class Limits	Frequency f_i	Midpoint m_i	$f_i m_i$	$f_i m_i^2$
1	2 up to 5	3	3.5	10.5	36.75
2	5 up to 8	6	6.5	39.0	253.50
3	8 up to 11	8	9.5	76.0	722.00
4	11 up to 14	7	12.5	87.5	1,093.75
5	14 up to 17	4	15.5	62.0	961.00
6	17 up to 20	2	18.5	37.0	684.50
Total		$n = 30$		312.0	3,751.50

assumption is, the better the approximation to the sample variance will be. If the grouped data represent a *population* of n measurements, the formula for approximating σ^2 is $(n - 1)/n$ times the formula used to approximate s^2.

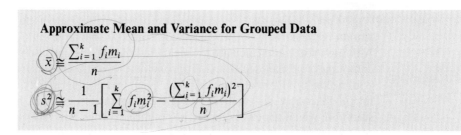

Approximate Mean and Variance for Grouped Data

$$\bar{x} \cong \frac{\sum_{i=1}^{k} f_i m_i}{n}$$

$$s^2 \cong \frac{1}{n-1} \left[\sum_{i=1}^{k} f_i m_i^2 - \frac{\left(\sum_{i=1}^{k} f_i m_i \right)^2}{n} \right]$$

EXAMPLE 2.10

The frequency distribution for the telephone-call durations, introduced in Section 2.2, is reproduced in Table 2.14. Three additional columns have been included in the table to record the information required by the formulas for approximating the mean and the variance of the durations from these grouped data. We are now considering the 30 telephone-call durations to be a sample, and the sample mean and variance are approximated as follows:

$$\bar{x} \cong \frac{\sum_{i=1}^{6} f_i m_i}{30} = \frac{312.0}{30} = 10.4$$

$$s^2 \cong \frac{1}{29} \left[\sum_{i=1}^{6} f_i m_i^2 - \frac{\left(\sum_{i=1}^{6} f_i m_i \right)^2}{30} \right] = \frac{1}{29} \left[3,751.5 - \frac{(312)^2}{30} \right] = 17.47$$

These approximations match the true values of $\bar{x} = 10.26$ and $s^2 = 18.40$ reasonably well.

███████████   **EXERCISES**

Self-Correcting Exercise (See Appendix 2.C for the solution.)

2.52   a. Approximate the mean and the variance of the sample of data presented in the accompanying frequency distribution.

Class	Frequency
0 up to 16	50
16 up to 32	160
32 up to 48	110
48 up to 64	80

b. Use the range approximation of s to check your approximation of the variance in part (a).

2.53   a. Approximate the mean and the variance of the sample of data presented in the accompanying frequency distribution.

Class	Frequency
−20 up to −10	8
−10 up to 0	21
0 up to 10	43
10 up to 20	48
20 up to 30	25
30 up to 40	15

b. Use the range approximation of s to check your approximation of the variance in part (a).

2.54   a. Approximate the mean and the variance of the sample of data presented in the accompanying frequency distribution.

Class	Frequency
0 up to 10	90
10 up to 20	50

Class	Frequency
20 up to 30	40
30 up to 40	120

b. Use the range approximation of s to check your approximation of the variance in part (a). Comment on the degree to which these two approximations differ from each other.

2.55   The gross hourly earnings of a group of workers randomly selected from the payroll list of a large industrial concern were organized into the following frequency distribution:

Hourly Earnings	Number of Workers
$8 up to $10	11
$10 up to $12	17
$12 up to $14	32
$14 up to $16	27
$16 up to $18	13

a. Approximate the mean and the standard deviation of hourly earnings for this sample of workers.

b. Your answers to part (a) only approximate the true values of $\bar{x}$ and s for this group's earnings. Explain why this is so.

2.56   A national car-rental agency recently bought 1,000 identical new compact cars from a major car manufacturer. After the customary 1,000-mile break-in period, it selected 100 cars randomly and obtained the following mileage data on them:

Gasoline Mileage (miles per gallon)	Numbers of Cars
24 up to 28	9
28 up to 32	13
32 up to 36	24
36 up to 40	38
40 up to 44	16

Approximate the average gasoline consumption and the standard deviation of consumption for this sample.

2.57 The ages of Americans who were classified as having work disabilities in 1988 are summarized in the following frequency distribution:

Ages	Number of Americans (in 1,000s)
16 up to 25	1,177
25 up to 35	2,292

Ages	Number of Americans (in 1,000s)
35 up to 45	2,508
45 up to 55	2,522
55 up to 65	4,854

SOURCE: *Statistical Abstract of the United States: 1988.*

Approximate the mean and standard deviation of the ages of the *population* of Americans with work disabilities. (Notice that the width of the first class differs from that of the others.)

SECTION 2.9   **SUMMARY**

Descriptive statistics is concerned with methods of summarizing and presenting the essential information contained in a set of data, whether the set be a population or a sample taken from a population. A collection of **interval (quantitative) data** can be usefully summarized by grouping the measurements to form a **frequency distribution.** Constructing a **stem and leaf display** is often helpful during preliminary analysis of the data. Either a **histogram** or a **frequency polygon** can then be used to convey the shape of the distribution of the measurement data graphically. On the other hand, in a set of **nominal** (qualitative) **data,** the relative frequencies of the categories can be graphically displayed by means of **pie charts** or **bar charts.**

Once the statistician has obtained a general idea about the distribution of the data, numerical measures can be used to describe the central location and the dispersion of the data. Three popular measures of central location, or averages, are the **mean,** the **median,** and the **mode.** These averages, taken by themselves, provide an inadequate description of the data because they say nothing about the extent to which the data are dispersed about their central value. Information regarding the dispersion, or variability, of the data is conveyed by such numerical measures as **range, percentiles, variance,** and **standard deviation.**

Chebyshev's theorem describes how the mean and the standard deviation of a set of measurements can be combined to determine the minimum proportion of measurements that lie within various intervals centered at the mean. For the special case in which a sample of measurements has a mound-shaped distribution, the **Empirical Rule** provides a good approximation of the percentages of measurements that fall within one, two, or three standard deviations of the mean. Beginning in Chapter 7, you will learn how these two important descriptive measures (mean and standard deviation), computed for a sample of measurements, can be combined to support inferences about the mean and the standard deviation of the population from which the sample was taken.

■■■■■■■ **SUPPLEMENTARY EXERCISES**

2.58 Determine the mean, median, and standard deviation for the following sample of data:

43	46	44	55	59	48
44	50	40	54	52	42

2.59 Consider the following population of measurements:

11	-1	5	2	8	7
12	4	-6	-10	1	5

a. Find the mean, median, and standard deviation of this population of measurements.

b. Find the upper and lower quartiles of these measurements.

2.60 The number of items rejected daily by a manufacturer because of defects was recorded for the last 25 days. The results are as follows:

21	8	17	22	19
18	19	14	17	11
6	21	25	19	9
12	16	16	10	29
24	6	21	20	25

a. Construct a frequency distribution for these data. Use five class intervals, with the lower boundary of the first class being 5 days.

b. Construct a relative frequency histogram for these data.

c. What is the relationship between the areas under the histogram you have constructed and the relative frequencies of observations?

2.61 Find the median, the mode, $\bar{x}$, s^2, and s for the data in Exercise 2.60. Do not approximate these values, but use the shortcut formula for s^2.

2.62 Refer to Exercises 2.60 and 2.61.

a. What proportion of items fall into the interval $\bar{x} \pm 2s$?

b. Is your answer to part (a) consistent with the claim made by Chebyshev's theorem?

c. Does it appear that the population from which this sample was taken has a mound-shaped distribution?

d. Compare the actual proportion of items falling into the intervals $\bar{x} \pm s$ and $\bar{x} \pm 2s$ with the proportions suggested by the Empirical Rule.

2.63 The American airline industry has changed considerably since its deregulation in 1979. There have been numerous mergers and bankruptcies of airlines, and most major airports are now dominated by one of the eight major carriers. The table shows, for a sample of seven airports, the market share of the dominant carrier in 1979 and in 1987.

Airport	Dominant Carrier	Market Share of Dominant Carrier	
		1987	1979
Cincinnati	Delta	68%	37%
Detroit	Northwest	65	20
Houston	Continental	72	17
Minneapolis	Northwest	82	40
Pittsburgh	U.S. Air	83	48
St. Louis	TWA	82	43
Salt Lake City	Western	71	42

Source: *New York Times,* 20 November 1988, p. 1F.

a. On the basis of inspection only (without performing any calculations), which year would you guess had the higher mean market share of the dominant carrier? The higher standard deviation?

b. Check your answers to part (a) by computing the mean and the standard deviation of the market shares for each of 1979 and 1987.

2.64 A large investment firm on Wall Street wants to review the distribution of the ages of its stockbrokers. The firm feels that this information will be useful in the development of plans relating to recruitment and retirement options. The ages of a sample of 25 brokers are as follows:

50	64	32	55	41
44	24	46	58	47
36	52	54	44	66
47	59	51	61	57

49   28   42   38   45

Construct a stem and leaf display for the ages.

2.65   Refer to Exercise 2.64.

a. Find the median age.

b. Find the lower quartile of the ages.

c. Find the upper quartile of the ages.

d. Find the 80th percentile of the ages.

e. Do you think this firm has reason to be concerned about the distribution of ages of its brokers?

2.66   Refer to Exercise 2.64.

a. Compute the mean of the sample of data.

b. Compute the variance of the sample of data.

c. Compute the standard deviation of the sample of data.

2.67   Refer to Exercise 2.64.

a. Compute the range of the data.

b. Compute the range approximation to the standard deviation of the data.

2.68   Refer to Exercise 2.64.

a. Construct a frequency distribution for the data, using five class intervals and the value 20 as the lower limit of the first class.

b. Approximate the mean and variance of the ages, based on the frequency distribution constructed in part (a).

2.69   Refer to Exercise 2.64.

a. Construct a relative frequency histogram for the data, using five class intervals and the value 20 as the lower limit of the first class.

b. Construct an ogive for the data.

c. What proportion of the total area under the histogram constructed in part (a) falls between 20 and 40?

2.70   A financial analyst is preparing to give a talk on stock market activity in North America. Following is one of the tables she intends to show to her audience.

a. Use a graphical technique to depict the information given in the table.

b. In what way is your graphical display superior to the tabular presentation?

1988 TRADING ACTIVITY ON NORTH AMERICAN STOCK EXCHANGES

Rank	Exchange	Value (in $billions)
1	New York	1,643.2
2	Midwest	101.7
3	Toronto	68.1
4	American	55.7
5	Pacific	49.0
6	Philadelphia	32.4
7	Boston	25.4
8	Montreal	15.1
9	Cincinnati	8.5
10	Vancouver	3.3
Total		2,002.4

SOURCE: *Globe & Mail*, 4 April 1989, p. B10.

2.71   According to the *Statistical Abstract of the United States: 1989*, the percentage of households with video cassette recorders has increased over the years, as shown in the accompanying table. Use a graphical technique to depict the information given in the table.

Year	Households with VCRs (in %)
1980	1.1%
1982	3.1
1983	5.5
1984	10.6
1985	20.8
1986	36.0
1987	48.7
1988	58.1

2.72 Dun & Bradstreet regularly publishes the medians (Q_2), upper quartiles (Q_3), and lower quartiles (Q_1) of the distributions of selected financial ratios for over 100 industries. The accompanying table gives these three percentiles for the profit-to-net-worth ratio (expressed in %) for four industrial categories. Insight into the skewness of a distribution can be obtained by comparing $(Q_3 - Q_2)$ and $(Q_2 - Q_1)$.

a. Why is symmetry indicated if these two differences are approximately equal?

b. Why is a positive skewness indicated if $(Q_3 - Q_2) > (Q_2 - Q_1)$?

c. For each industrial category in the table, determine if there is evidence that the distribution of this ratio is symmetrical, positively skewed, or negatively skewed.

d. Is the mean profit-to-net-worth ratio for soft-drinks firms greater than or less than 17.31%?

Industry	Lower Quartile	Median	Upper Quartile
Soft Drinks	10.25%	17.31%	29.34%
Manufactured Ice	5.42%	17.75%	23.87%
Cutlery	− 5.60%	17.79%	29.21%
Mobile Homes	11.52%	22.70%	39.80%
Business Forms	13.00%	20.88%	28.88%
Pottery Products	7.51%	26.08%	38.91%

SOURCE: Dun & Bradstreet's *1980 Key Business Ratios*.

2.73 Refer to Exercise 2.72.

a. Suppose that both a soft-drinks firm and an ice manufacturer have a profit-to-net-worth ratio of 10.25%. Which firm is performing better relative to other firms in the same industry?

b. Suppose that the profit-to-net-worth ratio is 20% for a cutlery manufacturer and 25% for a pottery producer. Which firm is performing better relative to other firms in the same industry?

2.74 Referring to Exercise 2.72, suppose that the profit-to-net-worth ratios for the business-forms

industry have a mean of 20.9% and a standard deviation of 6%.

a. Use Chebyshev's theorem to find an interval containing at least 75% of the ratios. Is this consistent with the data given in Exercise 2.72?

b. If the distribution of the profit-to-net-worth ratios is normal for the business-forms industry, what interval contains about 68% of the ratios?

c. From parts (a) and (b) of this exercise, does it appear that the distribution of the profit-to-net-worth ratios for the business-forms industry is mound-shaped? Explain.

2.75 The price–earnings ratio of a stock is of interest to investment analysts because it provides information about both the risk and the growth opportunities of the stock. The price–earnings ratios for 30 bank stocks (as of August 30, 1985) are given in the accompanying table.

a. Compute the mean and the standard deviation of the sample of 30 price–earnings ratios.

b. Construct a relative frequency histogram for the price–earnings ratios.

c. Determine the median price–earnings ratio, and locate the mean and median on your histogram.

d. Use your relative frequency distribution to estimate the mean and standard deviation of the 30 price–earnings ratios, and compare your estimates with the values obtained in part (a).

6.3	9.6	10.6	8.0	8.6	9.2
6.1	4.8	9.9	8.0	6.4	9.7
7.7	5.3	7.6	6.9	8.4	8.1
6.9	6.2	9.4	8.6	11.0	8.9
8.4	7.9	9.0	8.1	10.0	7.0

SOURCE: Value Line, *Selection & Opinion,* 30 August 1985.

2.76 The price–earnings ratios (as of August 30, 1985) of the stocks of 25 firms engaged in food processing or wholesaling are shown in the accompanying table.

a. Compute the mean and the standard deviation of the sample of 25 price–earnings ratios.

b. Construct a relative frequency histogram for the price–earnings ratios.

c. Determine the median price–earnings ratio, and locate the mean and median on your histogram.

d. Use your relative frequency distribution to estimate the mean and the standard deviation of the 25 price–earnings ratios, and compare your estimates with the values obtained in part (a).

11.4	11.6	12.5	13.4	12.4
14.0	13.0	10.8	9.5	15.2
17.0	12.1	10.3	12.8	15.4
15.5	10.3	15.2	12.3	12.7
13.4	12.8	11.5	12.5	11.3

SOURCE: Value Line, *Selection & Opinion,* 30 August 1985.

2.77 The yield of a common stock is obtained by dividing its annual dividend by its price. The yields for the next 12 months (following August 30, 1985) were estimated for 30 bank stocks. They are expressed as percentages in the accompanying table.

a. Compute the mean and the standard deviation of the sample of 30 yields.

b. Construct a relative frequency histogram for the yields.

c. Find the median of the 30 stock yields, and locate the mean and median on your histogram..

4.0	2.9	4.3	3.1	3.5	3.4
5.2	6.8	4.5	3.3	4.9	3.4
4.3	6.4	3.0	4.7	4.4	4.1
5.0	4.9	3.6	3.7	1.9	3.1
4.0	4.0	3.7	4.4	6.3	4.4

SOURCE: Value Line, *Selection & Opinion,* 30 August 1985.

2.78 The yields for the next 12 months (following August 30, 1985) were estimated for the common stocks of 25 firms engaged in food processing or wholesaling. They are expressed as percentages in the accompanying table.

a. Compute the mean and the standard deviation of the sample of 25 yields.

b. Construct a relative frequency histogram for the yields.

c. Find the median of the 25 stock yields, and locate the mean and median on your histogram.

d. Refer to Exercise 2.77. Determine whether the yields of bank stocks or of food processing stocks are more concentrated about their mean value, by inspecting their respective histograms.

e. Answer part (d) by comparing their respective standard deviations.

0	3.2	2.6	0.2	1.5
2.6	3.3	0	0	2.0
1.4	3.3	4.1	3.9	1.1
2.6	2.7	1.6	2.8	1.8
3.2	2.8	1.0	2.2	3.2

SOURCE: Value Line, *Selection & Opinion,* 30 August 1985.

2.79 As a result of experiencing a prolonged economic boom, Toronto is undergoing several changes that are referred to by some observers as the "Manhattanization" of Toronto. One serious problem is the lack of affordable housing for young people. Use a graphical technique to depict the information in the following table.

1988 MEDIAN HOUSE PRICES IN METRO TORONTO

Month	Price	Month	Price
January	$174,000	July	$198,842
February	179,250	August	204,729
March	187,000	September	208,135
April	198,207	October	215,807
May	203,044	November	215,475
June	200,115	December	219,464

SOURCE: *Toronto Star,* 11 January 1989, p. A29.

MINITAB
INSTRUCTIONS

INTRODUCTION

Minitab is most often accessed on a mainframe computer terminal equipped with a screen or printer. Instructions are input from a keyboard. When you complete a line of instruction, you simply press the carriage return key. Before doing so, however, you should make sure that the line is correctly typed. Any errors you discover at this point can easily be corrected by backspacing and retyping; but once the carriage return is pushed, the error may be more difficult to correct. A second way to use Minitab is through a microcomputer. The instructions here should be valid for the microcomputer; they assume that you are in interactive mode on the mainframe computer or that you are using a microcomputer.

LOGGING

To log on, you will likely need an account number, an identification number, and a password. These should be provided to you by your computer center. Once you have logged-on, in order to access the Minitab package, you generally have to type the word MINITAB. Once again, your computer center will provide you with guidance.

At this point, we assume that you are in the Minitab system. When the computer is ready to accept a command from you, it will prompt you with MTB⟩.

DATA INPUT

In order for the Minitab program to perform the statistical computations, data must first be input. The following command can be used:

⟨READ C1⟩

where C1 represents ⟨*column 1.*⟩After typing this line, press the RETURN or ENTER key on your keyboard. Then type in (and enter) the data, one number per line. The computer will prompt you after each entered line with

DATA⟩

When all of the data have been input, type

END

For example, suppose that you have the following five observations: 12, 15, 8, 16, and 9. These data would be input as follows, where the underlined terms are the ⟨computer promptings:⟩

```
MTB⟩ READ C1
DATA⟩ 12
DATA⟩ 15
DATA⟩  8
DATA⟩ 16
DATA⟩  9
DATA⟩ END
```

In all further illustrations of the instructions, we will not show the computer prompts.

If two or more groups of data are to be read, you could type

READ C1 C2

or

READ C1 C2 C3

or

READ C1-C3

Another way of inputting data is by using the SET command. This command allows you to type numbers consecutively on one or more lines. For example,

```
⟨SET C1⟩
12    15    8   16    9
END
SET C2
17    25   13   15   32
26    20    5    3
END
```

CORRECTIONS

Suppose that, after inputting the data, you discover an error. The following three instructions allow you to correct errors:

1. To replace an erroneous entry, use the LET instruction. For example,

   ```
   LET C1(2)=5
   ```

   changes the second value in column 1 to 5.
2. To delete rows 2 through 5 from column 1, type

   ```
   DELETE 2:5 C1
   ```
3. To insert a new row of data between rows 3 and 4, type

   ```
   INSERT BETWEEN ROWS 3 AND 4 OF C1, C2
           7     15
   END
   ```

OUTPUT

To check to see if entered data have been input correctly, type

```
PRINT C1
```

or

```
PRINT C1 C2 C3
```

or

```
PRINT C1-C3
```

SAVING DATA

If you intend to use a set of data another time in the future, you can save (and later retrieve) it. To save a data set, type

```
SAVE  '[name of data set]'
```

Once the data set has been saved, you can retrieve it at any time with the following command:

```
RETRIEVE  '[name of data set]'
```

You can use any file name you like, although the rules governing the use of SAVE and RETRIEVE commands may vary among computer centers. If you have difficulty with these two commands, seek advice from your computer center.

If your data base is quite large, we suggest that you periodically save your data to avoid problems associated with accidental erasure of columns.

OTHER COMMANDS

To create new variables from existing ones, use the LET command. For example,

```
LET C3=C1+C2
```

creates a variable that is the sum of the first two and stores the values of this variable in column 3. Some useful arithmetic operations, identified by their Minitab symbols, are

+   addition

−   subtraction

∗   multiplication

/   division

∗∗   exponentiation (raise to a power)

In some situations it is useful to name the variables. To do so, type

```
NAME C1='[name of variable 1]',  C2='[name of variable 2]'
```

Commands such as PRINT and DELETE can then use the variable name instead of the column number. For example, after the command

```
NAME C1='INCOME', C2='AGE'
```

has been entered, the command

```
PRINT C1 C2
```

is equivalent to the command

```
PRINT INCOME AGE
```

To erase columns, type

```
ERASE C1
```

or

```
ERASE C1 C2 C3
```

or

```
ERASE C1-C3
```

When you have completed your work in Minitab, type

```
STOP
```

This restores you to the computer operating system, from which you can sign off.
At any time, you may receive help by typing

```
HELP '[command]'
```

in order to get help regarding that command. For example,

```
HELP READ
```

will produce a brief explanation of READ. Typing

```
HELP HELP
```

will give you a summary of other help that you can get from Minitab.

CHAPTER 2 INSTRUCTIONS

The instructions that follow will allow you to perform some of the techniques described in Chapter 2.

To create a histogram when the data are stored in column 1, type

```
HISTOGRAM C1 K1 K2
```

where K1 is the first midpoint, and K2 is the interval size. For example, to create a histogram of the data in Table 2.1 of Chapter 2, use the following commands:

```
SET C1
11.8 8.9 10.2 15.3 6.2 3.6 9.1 8.0 12.3 11.2 16.6 7.7 11.4 8.5 10.
13.5 2.3 6.8 15.9 7.2 4.8 12.1 9.6 18.7 5.5 8.3 6.1 19.5 11.7 14.5
END
HISTOGRAM C1 3.5 3
```

These commands would produce the following output:

```
Histogram of C1   N=30
Midpoint   Count
   3.50     3***
   6.50     6******
   9.50     8********
  12.50     7*******
  15.50     4****
  18.50     2**
```

DESCRIPTIVE STATISTICS: NUMERICAL TECHNIQUES

The command

```
DESCRIBE C1
```

causes Minitab to print a number of useful statistics. To illustrate, we produce the descriptive statistics for Fund A in Example 2.8 as follows:

```
SET C1
8.3 -6.2 20.9 -2.7 33.6 42.9 24.4 5.2 3.1 30.5
END
DESCRIBE C1
```

The output is

	N	MEAN	MEDIAN	TRMEAN	STDEV	SEMEAN
C1	10	16.00	14.60	15.41	16.74	5.29

MIN	MAX	Q1	Q3
-6.20	42.90	1.65	31.27

If you wanted to know the number of times each value of the variable occurred, you would use the TABLE command. For example, typing in

```
SET C1
1 2 2 2 3 1 3 3 1 2 2 1
END
TABLE C1
```

would produce the output

```
ROWS: C1
          COUNT
1          4
2          5
3          3
ALL       12
```

If there were two variables, the TABLE command would produce a cross-classification table (which counts the number of times each combination occurred), list the totals for each variable, and print them in the margins of the table. For instance, suppose that the following data are input:

```
READ C1 C2
1 2
1 1
1 1
1 2
1 1
1 1
1 1
1 2
1 1
2 2
2 2
2 1
2 2
END
```

In this situation, the command

```
TABLE C1 C2
```

would create the following output:

```
ROWS: C1       COLUMNS: C2
             1        2      ALL
1            6        3       9
2            1        3       4
ALL          7        6      13
CELL CONTENTS-
                      COUNT
```

Other output can be generated by means of several possible subcommands. To use a subcommand, you must be careful to end the preceding commands in semicolons; the last subcommand must end in a period. The following subcommands can be used with the TABLE command:

TOTPERCENTS   (outputs the percentage instead of the actual count)

ROWPERCENTS   (prints the row percentage)

COLPERCENTS   (outputs the column percentage)

For example, the commands

```
TABLE C1 C2;
ROWPERCENTS;
COLPERCENTS.
```

would print both the row and the column percentages.

SAS INSTRUCTIONS

INTRODUCTION

The statistical application package, SAS, is a powerful computer package for manipulating data, performing varied statistical analyses, and generating high-resolution graphics. Despite its broad capabilities, it is quite simple to use.

SAS is normally run in batch mode, rather than interactively. This means that you first put all of your command statements into a file (or program) and then submit the entire file to SAS for processing. SAS performs the requested analyses and returns two items: a log of your program (the SASLOG), with notes and any error messages; and a listing of the results from the analyses.

The instructions that follow assume that you know how to create a file in the computer and how to edit its contents. Before proceeding, we should draw your attention to an important point: every statement in SAS must end with a semicolon. The most common error in SAS programs is omission of a semicolon.

DATA INPUT

In order to obtain any statistical computations, you must first input the data. The first command in any SAS program is the DATA command. The command

```
DATA ANYNAME;
```

will create a data set called ANYNAME. It is not necessary to name the data set, but you must have the DATA command at the beginning.

To read-in the data, you must issue an INPUT command. Next comes the CARDS statement, which tells SAS where to start reading, followed by the data to be read. Let's first deal with the INPUT command. The command

```
INPUT ID 1-8 AGE 10-11;
```

informs SAS that you are going to read-in two variables, called ID and AGE, and that their values are found in columns 1 through 8 and 10 through 11, respectively.

It is often convenient to omit the column numbers (which is what we will do in our illustrative examples). If the column numbers are omitted for a variable, SAS simply takes the next set of nonblank columns on the data card to be the value of that variable. In some cases, you may have a variable with nonnumerical values. To indicate to SAS that you want to input a nonnumerical variable, place a $ after the variable name. For example,

```
INPUT   ID   NAME   $   SCORE;
```

indicates that the (numerical) values of the variable I D appear first, followed by the nonnumerical values of the variable NAME. The next entries are the (numerical) values of the variable SCORE.

For example, suppose that we have six student identification numbers, together with their names and their statistics exam marks. These would be input as follows:

```
DATA;
INPUT ID   NAME $    SCORE;
CARDS;
573612  GREEN 83
639258  COLLINS 75
586351  BLACKWOOD 92
694112  JONES 56
735614  JOHNSON 71
712556  BRANTSFORD 88
```

Data can be read from other sources (files, tapes, and so on) by using the INFILE command in combination with a few system-dependent commands. See your computer center for help with the details of using INFILE.

MODIFYING DATA

To create new variables from existing ones, you simply specify the appropriate formula, using the following symbols for the standard arithmetic operations:

- \+ addition
- \- subtraction
- * multiplication
- / division
- ** exponentiation (raise to a power)

Here are some examples:

```
TOTAL=SCORE1+SCORE2+SCORE3+SCORE4+SCORE5;
AVG  =TOTAL/5;
DIFF =X1-X2;
```

The DROP command is used to delete variables. For example,

```
DROP SCORE;
```

would delete the SCORE variable from the data set. Commands to create and delete variables should appear after the INPUT statement but prior to the CARDS statement.

PRINTING DATA

A listing of all the data can be obtained by using the PRINT procedure. To print all of the data, type

```
PROC PRINT;
```

On the other hand, if you only want to look at some of the variables, you can do so by adding the VAR statement:

```
PROC PRINT;
VAR  NAME  TOTAL  AVG;
```

The print procedure lists the values of the requested variables, printing one observation per line, with the variable names identified at the tops of the appropriate columns.

CHAPTER 2 INSTRUCTIONS

The instructions that follow will allow you to perform some of the techniques described in Chapter 2.

DESCRIPTIVE STATISTICS

Once the data have been specified in the data step, you can produce descriptive statistics for variables by using the UNIVARIATE procedure. The command

```
PROC UNIVARIATE;
```

will produce output including the mean, median, mode, standard deviation, variance, and quartiles for each numerical variable in the data set. To obtain this information for specific variables, you can add a VAR statement (like the one for the PRINT procedure). For example, the following set of commands will produce a separate page of descriptive statistics for each of the variables SCORE 1, SCORE 2, . . . , SCORE 5:

```
DATA SCORES;
INPUT ID SCORE1-SCORE5;
CARDS;
   .
   .
   .
PROC UNIVARIATE;
VAR SCORE1-SCORE5;
```

Suppose we want to calculate the descriptive statistics for Fund A in Example 2.8. We proceed as follows:

```
DATA;
INPUT X;
CARDS;
8.3
-6.2
20.9
-2.7
33.6
42.9
24.4
5.2
3.1
30.5
PROC UNIVARIATE;
VAR X;
```

The partial output is

```
Variable=X
                        Moments
N             10   Sum           160
Mean          16
Std Dev  16.7433   Variance  280.34
```

If you wanted to know the number of times each value of the variable occurs, you would use the **FREQ** procedure. This produces frequencies, percentages, cumulative frequencies, and cumulative percentages for each variable in the **TABLES** statement. For example, suppose that the following statements were input:

```
DATA;
INPUT X1 X2;
CARDS;
1    2
1    1
1    1
1    2
1    1
1    1
1    1
1    2
1    1
2    2
2    2
2    1
2    2
PROC FREQ;
TABLES X1 X2;
```

As a result, the following output would be created:

```
SAS
X1  FREQUENCIES  PERCENT  CUMULATIVE  CUMULATIVE
                          FREQUENCY   PERCENT
1       9          69.2       9         69.2
2       4          30.8      13        100.0
X2  FREQUENCY     PERCENT  CUMULATIVE  CUMULATIVE
                          FREQUENCY   PERCENT
1       7          53.8       7         53.8
2       6          46.2      13        100.0
```

To produce a cross-classification table (which counts the number of times each combination occurred), you would type the statement

```
TABLES X1*X2;
```

after the procedure statement. The output that would be produced is

```
          TABLE OF X1 BY X2

     X1            X2
 Frequency |
 Percent   |
 Row Pct   |
 Col Pct   |      1 |      2 | Total
 ----------+--------+--------+
        1 |     6  |     3  |      9
          | 46.15  | 23.08  |  69.23
          | 66.67  | 33.33  |
          | 85.17  | 50.00  |
 ----------+--------+--------+
        2 |     1  |     3  |      4
          |  7.69  | 23.08  |  30.77
          | 25.00  | 75.00  |
          | 14.29  | 50.00  |
 ----------+--------+--------+
    Total       7        6        13
             53.85    46.15   100.00
```

■■■■■■■■   **COMPUTER EXERCISES**

2.80 Consider the following sample of measurements:

183	193	172	178	164
175	187	189	168	190
181	170	155	196	174
185	161	181	192	176
198	179	185	172	167

a. Construct a histogram for the data, using 150 as the lower limit of the first class and 10 as the class width.

b. Find the mean and the standard deviation of the measurements.

2.81 Consider the following sample of measurements:

306	331	280	325	208	274	365	267
275	298	340	230	350	250	295	254
223	313	276	215	302	472	334	282
315	265	241	289	348	276	270	310
258	210	225	384	278	261	229	404

a. Construct a histogram for these measurements, using 200 as the lower limit of the first class and 50 as the class width.

b. Find the mean and the standard deviation of the measurements.

SOLUTIONS TO SELF-CORRECTING EXERCISES

2.23 a. The mean age is

$$\mu = \frac{\sum_{i=1}^{7} x_i}{7}$$

$$= \frac{19 + 19 + 65 + 20 + 21 + 18 + 20}{7}$$

$$= \frac{182}{7} = 26$$

To find the median, first arrange the ages in ascending order:

$$18, 19, 19, 20, 20, 21, 65$$

The median is the middle age, which is 20. There are two modes: 19 and 20; these are the ages that occur most frequently.

b. Suppose that the highest age, 65, is removed from the data set. The new mean age is

$$\mu = \frac{\sum_{i=1}^{6} x_i}{6}$$

$$= \frac{19 + 19 + 20 + 21 + 18 + 20}{6}$$

$$= 19.5$$

The ages, arranged in ascending order, are now

$$18, 19, 19, 20, 20, 21$$

The median is now 19.5, the mean of the two middle ages. There are still two modes: 19 and 20. Notice that the mean has decreased substantially, the median has decreased only slightly, and the modes haven't changed at all.

2.38 a.

$$\mu = \frac{\sum_{i=1}^{15} x_i}{15} = \frac{3 + 5 + \cdots + 18 + 14}{15}$$

$$= 5.67\%$$

$$\sigma^2 = \frac{\sum_{i=1}^{15} (x_i - \mu)^2}{15}$$

$$= \frac{(3 - 5.67)^2 + (5 - 5.67)^2 + \cdots + (18 - 5.67)^2 + (14 - 5.67)^2}{15}$$

$$= 277.16(\%)^2$$

$$\sigma = \sqrt{277.16} = 16.65\%$$

b. Range = Largest value − Smallest value
$$= 50 - (-20)$$
$$= 70\%$$

Arranging the 15 measurements in ascending order, we obtain

$$-20, -18, -10, -5, -2, 0, 3, 5, 6, 10,$$
$$14, 14, 18, 20, 50$$

The median is the middle value, which is 5%.

The 20th percentile is the value for which at most $.2 \times 15 = 3$ measurements are smaller and at most $.8 \times 15 = 12$ measurements are larger. Since these conditions are satisfied by both -10 and -5, we take the 20th percentile to be their mean: -7.5%.

The 60th percentile is the value for which at most $.6 \times 15 = 9$ measurements are smaller and at most $.4 \times 15 = 6$ measurements are larger. Since these conditions are satisfied by both 6 and 10, we take the 60th percentile to be their mean: 8%.

2.48 a. Weekly sales will fall, 68% of the time, in the interval

$$\bar{x} \pm s = 85 \pm 6 = (79, 91)$$

Weekly sales will fall, virtually all of the time, in the interval

$$\bar{x} \pm 3s = 85 \pm 3(6) = (67, 103)$$

b. Weekly sales will have a value more than 2 standard deviations from the mean $(100 - 95) = 5\%$ of the time.

c. The number 97 is two standard deviations greater than the mean: $97 = 85 + 2(6)$. Since a mound-shaped distribution is symmetrical, demand will exceed 97 copies $(5/2) = 2.5\%$ of the time.

2.52 a.

Class	f_i	m_i	$f_i m_i$	$f_i m_i^2$
0 up to 16	50	8	400	3,200
16 up to 32	160	24	3,840	92,160
32 up to 48	110	40	4,400	176,000
48 up to 64	80	56	4,480	250,880
Total	400		13,120	522,240

$$\bar{x} \cong \frac{\sum_{i=1}^{4} f_i m_i}{400} = \frac{13,120}{400} = 32.8$$

$$s^2 \cong \frac{1}{n-1}\left[\sum_{i=1}^{4} f_i m_i^2 - \frac{\left(\sum_{i=1}^{4} f_i m_i\right)^2}{n}\right]$$

$$= \frac{1}{399}\left[522,240 - \frac{(13,120)^2}{400}\right] = 230.34$$

b. $s \cong \dfrac{\text{Range}}{4} \cong \dfrac{64 - 0}{4} = 16$

$s^2 \cong 16^2 = 256$

The range approximation of s indicates that the value computed for s^2 in part (a) is at least in the ballpark.

SUMMATION NOTATION

This appendix offers an introduction to the use of summation notation. Because summation notation is used extensively throughout statistics, you would be well advised to review this appendix even if you've had previous exposure to summation notation. Our coverage of the topic begins with an introduction to the necessary terminology and notation, follows with some examples, and concludes with four rules that are useful in applying summation notation.

Consider *n* numbers $x_1, x_2, \ldots, x_n$. A concise way of representing their sum is

$$\sum_{i=1}^{n} x_i$$

That is,

$$\sum_{i=1}^{n} x_i = x_1 + x_2 + \cdots + x_n$$

Remarks

1. The symbol $\sum$ is the capital Greek letter sigma, and means "the sum of."
2. The letter *i* is called the *index of summation*. The letter chosen to represent the index of summation is arbitrary.
3. The expression $\sum_{i=1}^{n} x_i$ is read "the sum of the terms x_i, where *i* assumes the values from 1 to *n* inclusive."
4. The numbers 1 and *n* are called the *lower* and the *upper limit of summation*, respectively.

Summation notation is best illustrated by means of examples.

EXAMPLES

1. Suppose that $x_1 = 5$, $x_2 = 6$, $x_3 = 8$, and $x_4 = 10$. Then:

(i) $\displaystyle\sum_{i=1}^{4} x_i = x_1 + x_2 + x_3 + x_4 = 5 + 6 + 8 + 10 = 29$

(ii) $\displaystyle\sum_{i=3}^{4} x_i = x_3 + x_4 = 8 + 10 = 18$

(iii) $\displaystyle\sum_{i=1}^{2} x_i(x_i - 1) = x_1(x_1 - 1) + x_2(x_2 - 1)$

$$= 5(5 - 1) + 6(6 - 1) = 50$$

(iv) $\displaystyle\sum_{i=1}^{3} f(x_i) = f(x_1) + f(x_2) + f(x_3)$

$$= f(5) + f(6) + f(8)$$

2. Suppose that $x_1 = 2$, $x_2 = 3$, $x_3 = 4$, $y_1 = 8$, $y_2 = 9$, and $y_3 = 13$. Then:

(i) $\displaystyle\sum_{i=1}^{3} x_i y_i = x_1 y_1 + x_2 y_2 + x_3 y_3$

$$= 2(8) + 3(9) + 4(13) = 95$$

(ii) $\displaystyle\sum_{i=2}^{3} x_i y_i^2 = x_2 y_2^2 + x_3 y_3^2$

$$= 3(9^2) + 4(13^2) = 919$$

(iii) $\displaystyle\sum_{i=1}^{2} (x_i - y_i) = (x_1 - y_1) + (x_2 - y_2)$

$$= (2 - 8) + (3 - 9) = -12$$

Remark.   It is not necessary that the index of summation be a subscript.

EXAMPLES

1. $\displaystyle\sum_{x=0}^{4} x = 0 + 1 + 2 + 3 + 4 = 10$

2. $\displaystyle\sum_{x=1}^{3} (x^2 - x) = (1^2 - 1) + (2^2 - 2) + (3^2 - 3) = 8$

3. $\displaystyle\sum_{x=1}^{2} 5x = 5(1) + 5(2) = 15$

4. $\displaystyle\sum_{x=0}^{3} f(x) = f(0) + f(1) + f(2) + f(3)$

5. $\displaystyle\sum_{x=1}^{2} f(x, y) = f(1, y) + f(2, y)$

6. $\displaystyle\sum_{y=3}^{5} f(x, y^2) = f(x, 3^2) + f(x, 4^2) + f(x, 5^2)$

Remark.   It is not necessary that the index of summation run through a sequence of successive integers. Instead, it may assume all values belonging to some specified set. In the examples that follow, the notation $\sum_{x \in A}$ is read "the sum of all values x belonging to A."

EXAMPLES

If $A = \{2, 3, 5, 8, 15\}$, then

$$\sum_{x \in A} x = 2 + 3 + 5 + 8 + 15 = 33$$

and

$$\sum_{x \in A} (x^2 - 3) 1 = (2^2 - 3) + (3^2 - 3) + (5^2 - 3) + (8^2 - 3) + (15^2 - 3)$$

$$= 1 + 6 + 22 + 61 + 222 = 312$$

Rules of Summation Notation

1. If c is a constant, then

$$\sum_{i=1}^{n} cx_i = c \sum_{i=1}^{n} x_i$$

2. If c is a constant, then

$$\sum_{i=1}^{n} c = nc$$

3. If a and b are constants, then

$$\sum_{i=1}^{n} (ax_i + by_i) = a \sum_{i=1}^{n} x_i + b \sum_{i=1}^{n} y_i$$

4. If c is a constant, then

$$\sum_{i=1}^{n} (x_i + c) = \sum_{i=1}^{n} x_i + nc$$

Remark.   Notice that

$$\sum_{i=1}^{n} x_i^2 \neq \left(\sum_{i=1}^{n} x_i \right)^2$$

To verify this, observe that

$$\sum_{i=1}^{n} x_i^2 = x_1^2 + x_2^2 + \cdots + x_n^2$$

while

$$\left(\sum_{i=1}^{n} x_i \right)^2 = (x_1 + x_2 + \cdots + x_n)^2$$

■■■■■■■■■■■   *EXERCISES*

1.   Evaluate

$$\sum_{i=1}^{5} (i^2 + 2i)$$

2.   Evaluate

$$\sum_{x=0}^{2} (x^3 + 2x)$$

3.   Using the accompanying set of measurements, evaluate

a. $\sum_{i=1}^{13} x_i$

b. $\sum_{i=1}^{13} (2x_i + 5)$

c. $\sum_{i=1}^{6} (x_i - 5)^2$

i	1	2	3	4	5	6	7	8	9	10	11	12	13
x_i	3	12	10	−6	0	11	2	−9	−5	8	−7	4	−5

C H A P T E R *3*

PROBABILITY

INTRODUCTION

Probability theory is an integral part of all statistics, and in particular is essential to the theory of statistical inference. Statistical inference provides the decision maker—perhaps a businessperson or economist—with a body of methods that aid in decision making under uncertainty. The uncertainty arises because, in real-life situations, we rarely have perfect information regarding various inputs to a decision. Whether our uncertainty relates to the future demand for our product, the future level of interest rates, the possibility of a labor strike, or the proportion of defective widgets in the next production run, probability theory can be used to measure the degree of uncertainty involved. Probability theory allows us to go beyond ignoring uncertainty or considering it in a haphazard fashion, by giving us a foundation for dealing with uncertainty in a consistent, rational manner.

EXPERIMENTS, OUTCOMES, AND EVENTS

RANDOM EXPERIMENT

A logical development of probability begins with consideration of a random experiment, since this process generates the uncertain outcomes to which we will assign probabilities. Random experiments are of interest because they provide the raw data for statistical analysis.

> **Random Experiment**
>
> A random experiment is a process or course of action that results in one of a number of possible outcomes. The outcome that occurs cannot be predicted with certainty.

Following is a list of some random experiments, together with their possible outcomes:

1. Experiment: Flip a coin.
   Outcomes: shows heads, shows tails
2. Experiment: Roll a die.
   Outcomes: 1, 2, 3, 4, 5, 6

3. Experiment: Roll a die.
   Outcomes: even number, odd number
4. Experiment: Observe the unit sales of a product for one day.
   Outcomes: 0, 1, 2, 3, ...
5. Experiment: Solicit a consumer's preference between product *A* and product *B.*
   Outcomes: prefer *A*, prefer *B*, indifferent
6. Experiment: Observe change in IBM share price over one week.
   Outcomes: increase, decrease, no change

An important feature of a random experiment is that *the actual outcome cannot be determined in advance.* That is, the outcome of a random experiment may change if the experiment is repeated, unlike the outcomes of most experiments in a physics or chemistry laboratory. The best we can do is to talk about the probability that a particular outcome will occur. You undoubtedly have some idea of what is meant by the word *probability,* but now let's look more closely at its meaning.

THREE INTERPRETATIONS OF PROBABILITY

Beginning students of this subject are usually disconcerted when they learn that *probability* has no precise definition. Any attempt to define it leads you around a circular series of statements consisting of such synonymous terms as *likelihood, chance,* and *odds.* There are, however, three distinct interpretations of probability that offer three approaches to determining the probability that a particular outcome will occur.

The **classical approach** attempts to deduce the probability of an outcome logically from the symmetric nature of the experiment. If a perfectly balanced coin is flipped, for example, it is logical to expect that the outcome heads and the outcome tails are equally likely. Hence we assert that the probability of observing an occurrence of heads is 1/2. More generally, if an experiment has *n* possible outcomes, each of which is equally likely, the probability of any particular outcome's occurring is 1/*n*. The classical approach can often be used effectively in games of chance. Our development of probability frequently uses examples from this area to illustrate a point, since these examples are easy to relate to. Most practical situations, however, do not lend themselves to the classical, deductive approach. A businessperson will usually use either the relative frequency approach or the subjective approach.

The **relative frequency approach** determines the probability of an outcome in terms of its long-run relative frequency of occurrence. Suppose that a random experiment is repeated *n* times, where *n* is a large number. If *x* represents the number of times a particular outcome occurred in those *n* trials, the proportion *x*/*n* provides an estimate of the probability that that particular outcome will occur. For example, if 600 out of the last 1,000 customers entering our store have made a purchase, the probability that any given customer entering our store will make a purchase is approximately .6. The larger n is, the better will be the estimate of the desired probability, which may be thought of as the limiting value of x/n as n becomes infinitely large. Using the relative frequency approach, then, means determining empirically the probability that a particular outcome will occur.

In many practical situations, the experimental outcomes are not equally likely and there is no history of repetitions of the experiment. This might be the case, for example, if you wished to estimate the probability of striking oil at a new offshore drilling site, or the likelihood of your firm's sales' reaching $1 million this year. In such situations, we resort to the **subjective approach,** under which the probability assigned to an outcome simply reflects the degree to which the statistician believes that the outcome will occur. The probability assigned to a particular outcome thus reflects a personal evaluation of the situation and may be based simply on intuition.

In many cases, however, a businessperson's intuition or subjective evaluation has probably been influenced by outcomes in similar situations, so the relative frequency approach may play a role in the formation of the subjective probabilities. Consider, for example, a producer about to launch a new Broadway musical. The producer's subjective estimate of the probability that the show will return a profit to the investors will be based on several factors, such as the reputation of the musical's principals, the quality of other Broadway shows currently running, and the state of the economy; but the producer will also be mindful of the fact that only about 25% of all Broadway musicals are profitable—a fact based on the relative frequency approach.

SAMPLE SPACE AND EVENTS

Before we begin to consider how to determine the probability that various outcomes will occur, we need to establish some terminology regarding experimental outcomes, in order to permit precise expression of ideas and to help impose more structure on a problem. Much of the necessary terminology is summarized in this subsection.

Recall that a random experiment can result in a number of possible outcomes. To determine, in advance of an experiment, the probabilities that various outcomes will occur, we first have to know what outcomes are possible. The first step in finding the probabilities, then, is to list the possible outcomes. For such a listing to suit our needs, of course, the listed outcomes must be **exhaustive;** that is, each trial of the random experiment must result in some outcome on the list. Furthermore, the listed outcomes must be **mutually exclusive;** that is, no two outcomes on the list can both occur on any one trial of the experiment. Such a listing of the possible outcomes is called a **sample space,** denoted S.

> **Sample Space**
>
> A sample space of a random experiment is a list of all possible outcomes of the experiment. The outcomes listed must be mutually exclusive and exhaustive.

Stated another way, the set of possible outcomes constituting a sample space must be defined in such a way that each trial of the experiment results in exactly one outcome in the sample space. For example, if the experiment is to observe the number of spots turning up when a six-sided die is tossed, a correct sample space for this experiment is $S = \{1, 2, 3, 4, 5, 6\}$, where $\{\ \}$ is read "the set consisting of." One (and only one) of these six listed outcomes will result from a single toss of the die. In contrast, the set {number greater than 1, number less than 6}, which consists of two possible outcomes, is *not* a sample space. Although these two outcomes are exhaustive, they are not mutually exclusive: both outcomes occur if the die shows three spots, for example. Likewise, the set $\{1, 2, 3, 4, 5\}$ is not a sample for this experiment, because the listed outcomes are not exhaustive: no outcome in this set occurs if the die shows six spots.

The individual outcomes in a sample space are called **simple events.** In assigning probabilities, you should *define simple events in such a way that they cannot be broken down, or decomposed, into two or more constituent outcomes.* For example, in the die-tossing experiment, the outcome "an even number is observed" should not be used as a simple event in a sample space, since it can be further decomposed into three outcomes: 2, 4, and 6.

EXAMPLE 3.1

Consider the random experiment consisting of flipping a coin twice. A sample space for this experiment is

$$S = \{HH, HT, TH, TT\}$$

where the first letter of each pair denotes the result of the first flip. This sample space has four simple events. A useful geometrical representation of this sample space, called a **Venn diagram,** is presented in Figure 3.1. In a Venn diagram, the entire sample space S is represented by a rectangle; points inside the rectangle represent the individual outcomes, or simple events, in S. For this reason, the simple events constituting a sample space are sometimes referred to as **sample points.**

FIGURE 3.1
VENN DIAGRAM
FOR COIN
EXAMPLE

Notice that the sample space for an experiment is not unique. An alternative sample space for the coin example is

$$S' = \{2 \text{ heads}, 2 \text{ tails}, 1 \text{ heads and } 1 \text{ tails}\}$$

where each sample space outcome indicates the results of the two flips, with no consideration given to the order in which they occur. There is a danger in using S' to assign probabilities, however: someone looking at this sample space might be tempted to reason that the three outcomes it lists are equally likely to occur, although this would be incorrect. It is therefore advisable, for purposes of assigning probabilities, to define the sample space in terms of outcomes that cannot be further decomposed. Since the outcome "1 heads and 1 tails" in S' can be decomposed into the two outcomes HT and TH, the sample space S is preferable to S'.

The two basic types of sample spaces—discrete and continuous—can be distinguished from each other on the basis of the number of simple events they contain. The distinction is important because the method of assigning probabilities differs radically, depending on which type of sample space is involved. A **discrete** sample space has a finite or countably infinite number of simple events. The sample space in the coin-tossing experiment in Example 3.1 is finite. For the experiment consisting of flipping a coin until the first outcome of heads appears, however, a corresponding sample space is

$$S = \{H,\ TH,\ TTH,\ TTTH, \ldots\}$$

Here, the number of simple events in S is **countably infinite** because, conceivably, the simple events can be counted by using the positive integers 1, 2, 3, 4, ... A **continuous** sample space is not discrete and contains uncountably infinitely many outcomes. If the experiment consists of observing the time required to complete a particular task, the sample space might be

$$S = \{\text{all possible times between 0 and 30 seconds}\}$$

The sample space S is continuous, since uncountably infinitely many values are possible in the interval from 0 to 30. *Throughout this chapter, we will restrict our attention to discrete sample spaces.*

Referring to Example 3.1, suppose that we are interested in the probability of getting at least one outcome of heads—an outcome observed if any one of three simple events (HH, HT, or TH) occurs. An outcome such as this one, which comprises a collection of simple events, is called an **event.**

Event

An event is any collection of simple events.

Events are denoted by capital letters and may be defined either in words or by listing their component simple events, using set notation, as in Example 3.2. The convention when listing the simple events that form a sample space is to use E_i to denote the ith simple event in the list. An event A is said to **occur** if the outcome of the experiment is a simple event that belongs to A. Ultimately, we want to find the **probability that an event A will occur,** which is denoted by $P(A)$.

We next consider combining events to form new ones. In arithmetic, new numbers can be created from existing ones by means of operations such as addition and multiplication. Similarly, new events can be created from events already defined by means of operations called *union, intersection,* and *complementation.*

EXAMPLE 3.2

FIGURE 3.2
VENN DIAGRAM
DEPICTING
EVENTS
A AND C

An investor owns six common stocks. At the end of the month, she will note the number of stocks that have risen in price since the beginning of the year. In preparing to assign probabilities to various events related to the number of stocks that rise in price, the investor forms the sample space

$$S = \{0, 1, 2, 3, 4, 5, 6\}$$

where each number belonging to S represents a possible number of stocks that rise in price.

The investor considers three possible events: "between three and five stocks rise," "at least four stocks rise," and "exactly two stocks rise"; these are labeled A, B, and C, respectively. Using set notation, we have

$$A = \{3, 4, 5\}$$
$$B = \{4, 5, 6\}$$
$$C = \{2\}$$

FIGURE 3.3
VENN DIAGRAM
DEPICTING
$A \cup B$

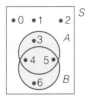

Event A occurs if the number of stocks that rise in price is 3, 4, or 5. This event is represented in a Venn diagram by a closed region containing the simple events that belong to A, as shown in Figure 3.2. Since C is a simple event, it is represented by a closed region containing a single point.

The **union** of any two events A and B, denoted $A \cup B$, is the event consisting of all simple events in A or in B or in both. Thus, the event $A \cup B$ occurs if A occurs, if B occurs, or if both occur. The key word here is *or*. For the events A and B in this example, either A or B occurs if the number of stocks rising in price is 3, 4, 5, or 6. That is,

$$A \cup B = \{3, 4, 5, 6\}$$

The event $A \cup B$, the union of A and B, is depicted by the shaded area in Figure 3.3.

The **intersection** of any two events A and B, denoted $A \cap B$, is the event consisting of all simple events in both A and B. Thus, the event $A \cap B$ occurs only if both event A and event B occur. The key word here is *and*. The event $A \cap B$ is sometimes called the **joint event**. For the events A and B in this example, both A and B occur if the number of stocks rising in price is 4 or 5. That is,

FIGURE 3.4
VENN DIAGRAM
DEPICTING
$A \cap B$

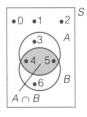

$$A \cap B = \{4, 5\}$$

The event $A \cap B$, the intersection of A and B, is depicted by the shaded area in Figure 3.4.

Two events B and C are said to be **mutually exclusive** if the occurrence of one precludes the occurrence of the other—that is, if $B \cap C$ contains no simple events. The events B and C defined in this example are mutually exclusive because they cannot both occur. If the number of stocks rising in price is 2, it is not 4 or more.

The **complement** of any event A, denoted $\bar{A}$, is the set of all simple events in the sample space S that do not belong to A. Thus, $\bar{A}$ denotes the event "A does not occur." The complement of event A in this example is

$$\bar{A} = \{0, 1, 2, 6\}$$

If the number of stocks that rise is not between 3 and 5, it must be 0, 1, 2, or 6. In Figure 3.2, these are the four simple events represented by the points lying outside the region describing event A.

In the sections that follow, we'll frequently refer to the probability of occurrence of the union, intersection, or complement of events. The notation for these probabilities is as follows:

$$P(A \cup B) = P(A \text{ or } B \text{ or both occur})$$
$$P(A \cap B) = P(A \text{ and } B \text{ both occur})$$
$$P(\bar{A}) = P(A \text{ does not occur})$$

EXERCISES

3.1 Explain what is meant by this statement: "The simple events that constitute a sample space are mutually exclusive and exhaustive."

3.2 Express in your own words what is meant by each of the following terms:

a. Random experiment

b. Sample space

c. Simple event

d. Event

3.3 Specify a sample space S for each of the following random experiments, by listing the simple events in S.

a. The results of three flips of a coin are observed.

b. The time required to complete an assembly is recorded to the nearest minute.

c. The marital status of a loan applicant is solicited.

d. Two six-sided dice are tossed, and the sum of the spots turning up is observed.

e. The number of customers served by a restaurant on a particular day is recorded.

f. The number of positive responses is recorded after 20 shoppers are asked if they are satisfied with parking accessibility.

3.4 A contractor has submitted a bid on each of three separate contracts. Consider the random experiment that consists of observing which of the contracts are won and which are lost.

a. Letting W denote a contract that is won and $\bar{W}$ a contract that is lost, list the simple events in the sample space S.

b. List the simple events in the event "all three contracts are won or all three contracts are lost."

c. Describe in words the event defined by $A = \{W\bar{W}\bar{W}, \bar{W}W\bar{W}, \bar{W}\bar{W}W\}$.

d. Describe in words the event defined by $B = \{WWW, WW\bar{W}, W\bar{W}W, \bar{W}WW\}$.

3.5 A manager must decide which two of four applicants (Anne, Bill, Cynthia, and David) should receive job offers.

a. What is the random experiment?

b. List the simple events in S.

c. List the simple events in the following events:

> L: Cynthia receives an offer.
> M: Bill doesn't receive an offer.
> N: At least one woman receives an offer.

3.6 The number of spots turning up when a six-sided die is tossed is observed. A sample space for this experiment is $S = \{1, 2, 3, 4, 5, 6\}$. Answer each of the following questions, and use a Venn diagram to depict the situation graphically.

a. What is the union of $A = \{2, 3\}$, and $B = \{2, 6\}$?

b. What is the intersection of $A = \{2, 3, 4, 5\}$ and $B = \{3, 5, 6\}$?

c. What is the complement of $A = \{2, 3, 4, 5\}$?

d. Is either $A = \{3\}$ or $B = \{1, 2\}$ a simple event?

e. Are $A = \{3\}$ and $B = \{1, 2\}$ mutually exclusive events? Explain.

3.7 In Example 3.1, we saw that a sample space for the experiment consisting of flipping a coin twice is $S = \{HH, HT, TH, TT\}$. Consider the following events:

$A = \{HT, TH\}$

$B = \{HH, HT, TH\}$

$C = \{TT\}$

a. Describe each of the events A, B, and C in words.

b. List the simple events in $A \cup B$, and use a Venn diagram to depict the union graphically.

c. List the simple events in $A \cap B$, and depict the intersection graphically.

d. List the simple events in $\bar{A}$, and depict the complement graphically.

e. Is A, B, or C a simple event?

f. Is there a pair of mutually exclusive events among A, B, and C? Explain.

3.8 During a recent promotion, a bank offered mortgages with terms of one, two, and three years at a reduced interest rate. Customers could also choose between open and closed mortgages. From the file of approved mortgage applications, the manager selects one application and notes both the term of the mortgage and whether it is open or closed. A sample space for this experiment is $\{O1,$ $O2, O3, C1, C2, C3\}$, where, for example, $O2$ represents an open, two-year mortgage being selected. Consider the following events:

$A = \{O1, O2, O3\}$

$B = \{O2, C2\}$

a. Describe each of the events A and B in words.

b. List the simple events in $A \cup B$, and use a Venn diagram to depict the union graphically.

c. List the simple events in $A \cap B$, and depict the intersection graphically.

d. List the simple events in $\bar{B}$, and depict the complement graphically.

e. Are A and B mutually exclusive events? Explain.

SECTION 3.3   **ASSIGNING PROBABILITIES**

Having established much of the necessary terminology, we now turn to the matter of assigning probabilities to outcomes and events. To each simple event E_i in a sample space, we wish to attach a number $P(E_i)$, called the *probability* of E_i, which represents the likelihood that that particular outcome will occur. Whichever of the three approaches to assigning probabilities (classical, relative frequency, or subjective) is used, the probabilities assigned to simple events must satisfy the two conditions specified in the accompanying box. Keep in mind, too, that the simple events E_i that form a sample space must be mutually exclusive and exhaustive.

Requirements of Probabilities

Given a sample space $S = \{E_1, E_2, \ldots, E_n\}$, the probabilities assigned to the simple events E_i must satisfy **two basic requirements:**

(i) $0 \le P(E_i) \le 1$ for each i

(ii) $\sum\limits_{i=1}^{n} P(E_i) = 1$

Suppose for a moment that probabilities have been assigned to all of the simple events. We still need a method for finding the probability of an event that is not a simple one. Recall that an event A is just a collection of simple events; therefore, its probability can be determined in the following manner.

Probability of an Event

The probability of an event A is equal to the sum of the probabilities assigned to the simple events contained in A.

It follows from the two basic requirements that the probability of an event that is certain to occur is 1, since such an event must contain all of the simple events in the sample space. On the other hand, the probability of an event that cannot possibly occur is 0.

The two basic requirements tell us nothing about how to assign probabilities; they simply state conditions that must be met by probabilities once they have been assigned. In practice, a business manager or economist will usually resort to either the relative frequency approach or the subjective approach in assigning probabilities to events. For example, a promoter choosing a week in which to hold a two-day, outdoor rock concert might consult meteorological records. If a particular week has been rain-free for 35 of the past 50 years, then $35/50 = 0.7$ would be a relative frequency estimate of the probability of that week's being rain-free this year. In many decision-making situations, however, a history of comparable circumstances is not available, and a businessperson must rely on an educated guess (that is, on the subjective approach). Such is the case with a bank manager who must estimate the probability of loan default by a country whose repayment ability has been impaired by declining oil prices.

Once probabilities have been assigned to some of the basic events of interest, the rules of probability (discussed in the next section) can be used to find the probabilities associated with various combinations of events. But first, it is worth discussing briefly how probabilities are assigned to events under the classical approach. Not only will this be helpful in situations that call for the classical approach, it will help clarify basic principles underlying the formulation of a sample space and the assignment of probabilities under any approach.

We now state the basic rule governing the assignment of probabilities under the classical approach.

Probability of an Event

If each simple event in a finite sample space S has the same chance of occurring, the probability that an event A will occur is

$$P(A) = \frac{\text{Number of simple events in } A}{\text{Number of simple events in } S}$$

This rule is simply a special case of the general procedure for finding the probability of an event A: sum the probabilities assigned to the simple events contained in A. For the special case in which the sample space has n simple events, each of which is equally likely to occur, each simple event is assigned the probability $1/n$. The probability of an event A that contains $n(A)$ simple events is therefore obtained by summing $1/n$ a total of $n(A)$ times:

$$P(A) = \sum_{i=1}^{n(A)} \frac{1}{n} = \frac{n(A)}{n} = \frac{\text{Number of simple events in } A}{\text{Number of simple events in } S}$$

To review, the first step in assigning probabilities to events is to list the simple events that form the sample space for the random experiment. Then probabilities are assigned to the simple events, using the classical, relative frequency, or subjective approach. Finally, the probability of an event is determined by summing the probabilities assigned to the simple events that belong to the event of interest.

The following examples illustrate how probabilities are assigned to events under the classical approach. The first step, of course, is to construct the appropriate sample space and to make certain that the simple events are equally likely to occur.

EXAMPLE 3.3

An investor who has $3,000 invested in each of four stocks must sell two to help finance his daughter's education. Since he feels that all four stocks are of comparable quality and have the same likelihood of appreciating in price over the coming year, he simply chooses at random the two stocks to be retained and sells the other two. Suppose that, one year later, two of the original four stocks have increased in value and two have decreased.

a. Find the probability that both of the retained stocks have increased in value.

b. Find the probability that at least one of the retained stocks has increased in value.

Solution.   Let I_1 and I_2 represent the two stocks that increased in value, and let D_1 and D_2 represent the two stocks that decreased in value. Since the random experiment consisted of choosing two stocks from these four, a sample space for the experiment is

$$S = \{I_1I_2, I_1D_1, I_1D_2, I_2D_1, I_2D_2, D_1D_2\}$$

where each simple event represents a possible pair of retained stocks. Each pair of stocks had the same chance of being selected, so the probability that any one of the six pairs of stocks was retained is $1/6$.

a. Let A be the event in which both of the retained stocks increased in value. Then $A = \{I_1I_2\}$ and $P(A) = 1/6$.

b. Let B be the event in which at least one of the retained stocks increased in value. Then the event B consists of all simple events for which either I_1 or I_2 is retained. That is, $B = \{I_1I_2, I_1D_1, I_1D_2, I_2D_1, I_2D_2\}$. Since the probability of an event is the sum of the probabilities of the simple events contained in that event, $P(B) = 5/6$.

EXAMPLE 3.4

A popular game at gambling casinos is roulette. A roulette wheel is divided into 38 equal segments, with the numbers 0 through 36 and 00 (double zero) used to identify the segments. After a player has bet on a number, the wheel is spun. If the wheel stops at the number bet, the player receives \$36 for each \$1 bet, whereas the casino wins the amount bet if the wheel stops at any of the other 37 numbers. A player can also bet that the wheel will stop at an odd number—or, alternatively, at an even number (excluding 0 and 00)—in which case the payoff is \$2 for each \$1 bet if the player wins.

a. What is the probability of winning if the player bets on a single number? On an odd number?

b. Roulette wheels in Europe are often divided into only 37 segments, numbered from 0 to 36. Suppose that a Nevada casino is considering replacing its current (double-zero) roulette wheels with European wheels, in the hope that substantially more gamblers will be attracted to the casino by the improved odds. As input into its decision, the casino wishes to determine its average take (profit) with each type of wheel. Find the average amount that the casino can expect to win for each \$1 bet on a single number, both with the current wheel and with the proposed new wheel.

Solution

a. The sample space consists of 38 numbers—the numbers from 0 to 36 and 00. Since each of the 38 numbers is equally likely to occur, the probability that any one of the numbers will occur is 1/38. The probability of winning if a bet is placed on a single number is therefore 1/38.

Now let A denote the event that an odd number occurs. Since there are 18 simple events in A, the probability of winning when a bet is placed on an odd number is 18/38. Notice that, over the same large number of plays, a player should be indifferent between betting on a single number or on an odd number: although the probability that an odd number will occur is 18 times the probability that a single number will occur, the payoff is only one-eighteenth as much.

b. Although you will be in a better position to handle this part of the example after covering Chapter 4, addressing it now will give you a glimpse of how probabilities can be useful in making business decisions like this one. To find the amount that a roulette player can expect to lose playing the current wheel, suppose that the player bets $1 on a single number 3,800 consecutive times. Since the probability of winning any single bet is 1/38, the relative frequency interpretation of probability suggests that the player can expect to win $(1/38) \cdot (3,800) = 100$ times and lose the remaining 3,700 times. Recall that the payoff is $36 whenever the player wins. Hence, the player's average payoff for each bet placed is

$$\bar{x} = \frac{100(36) + 3,700(0)}{3,800} = \$.947$$

That is, on average, the casino will win $(1 - .947) = \$.053$ on each $1 bet placed on a single number.

With the proposed new wheel, the probability of winning a bet on a single number is 1/37. Reasoning as above, if a player bets $1 on a single number 3,700 times, the player's average payoff for each bet placed is

$$\bar{x} = \frac{100(36) + 3,600(0)}{3,700} = \$.973$$

In this case, on average, the casino wins $(1 - .973) = \$.027$ on each $1 bet placed.

Since, on average, the casino would win only about half as much with the new wheel for each $1 bet, twice as much money would have to be bet on the new roulette wheel before the casino would earn as much as it does currently.

EXAMPLE 3.5

Keep Kool Inc. manufactures window air conditioners in both a deluxe model and a standard model. An auditor engaged in a compliance audit of the firm is validating

TABLE 3.1   CLASSIFICATION OF INVOICES

	Wholesale *W*	Retail $\overline{W}$	Total
Deluxe *D*	36	112	148
Standard $\overline{D}$	㉔	㉘	52
Total	60	⑭⓪	②⓪⓪

the sales account for April. She has collected 200 invoices for the month, some of which were sent to wholesalers and the remainder to retailers. Of the 140 retail invoices, 28 are for the standard model. Only 24 of the wholesale invoices are for the standard model. If the auditor selects one invoice at random, find the following probabilities.

   a. The invoice selected is for the deluxe model.

   b. The invoice selected is a wholesale invoice for the deluxe model.

   c. The invoice selected is either a wholesale invoice or an invoice for the standard model.

Solution.   The sample space *S* here consists of the 200 invoices. Whenever simple events can be classified according to two relevant characteristics—in this case, according to model sold and type of purchaser—it is worthwhile to display the pertinent information in a cross-classification table, such as Table 3.1. The numbers given in this example have been circled in Table 3.1; you should check to confirm that you can fill in the remaining numbers yourself from the given information. The events of interest are as follows:

   W: Wholesale invoice is selected.

   $\overline{W}$:   Retail invoice is selected.

   D: Invoice for deluxe model is selected.

   $\overline{D}$:   Invoice for standard model is selected.

   a. Since each invoice has the same chance of being selected, the probability that any particular invoice will be selected is $1/200$. Since there are 148 invoices for the deluxe model, the event *D* contains 148 simple events. Summing the probabilities of the simple events in *D*, we find that the probability that the one invoice randomly selected was for the deluxe model is

$$P(D) = \frac{148}{200} = .74$$

b. Since there are 36 wholesale invoices for the deluxe model, the event $D \cap W$ contains 36 simple events. Hence, the probability that the invoice selected was a wholesale invoice for the deluxe model is

$$P(D \cap W) = \frac{36}{200} = .18$$

c. The number of invoices that are either wholesale invoices or invoices for the standard model is $36 + 24 + 28 = 88$. Thus, the event $W \cup \bar{D}$ contains 88 simple events. Summing the probabilities of the simple events in $W \cup \bar{D}$, we obtain

$$P(W \cup \bar{D}) = \frac{88}{200} = .44$$

EXERCISES

LEARNING THE TECHNIQUES

3.9 Consider the sample space $S = \{E_1, E_2, E_3, E_4\}$.

a. Find $P(E_1 \cup E_2 \cup E_3 \cup E_4)$.

b. Find $P(E_4)$, if $P(E_1) = P(E_2) = .1$ and $P(E_3) = .5$.

c. Find $P(E_4)$, if $P(E_1) = P(E_2) = P(E_3) = .2$.

3.10 Consider a sample space $S = \{E_1, E_2, E_3, E_4\}$, where $P(E_1) = .25$, $P(E_2) = .40$, $P(E_3) = .15$, and $P(E_4) = .20$. Calculate the following probabilities by summing the probabilities of the appropriate simple events:

a. $P(E_1 \cup E_2)$

b. $P(\bar{E}_2)$

c. $P(\bar{E}_3)$

d. $P(E_3 \cap E_4)$

3.11 The number of spots turning up when a six-sided die is tossed is observed. List the simple events in each of the following events, and find the probability that each event will occur:

S: The number observed is in the sample space.

A: A 6 is observed.

B: The number observed is less than 4.

C: An odd number is observed.

$\vee D$: An even number greater than 2 is observed.

3.12 The result of flipping two fair coins is observed.

a. Define the sample space.

b. Assign probabilities to the simple events.

c. Find the probability of observing one heads and one tails.

d. Find the probability of observing at least one heads.

APPLYING THE TECHNIQUES

MNG **3.13** In Exercise 3.5, we considered a manager who was deciding which two of four applicants (Anne, Bill, Cynthia, and David) should receive job offers. Suppose that the manager, having deemed the applicants equally qualified, chooses at random the two who will receive job offers.

a. Assign probabilities to the simple events in the sample space.

b. Find the probability that Cynthia will receive an offer.

c. Find the probability that one man and one woman will receive an offer.

d. Find the probability that at least one woman will receive an offer.

	Blue-Collar Workers	White-Collar Workers	Managers
For	67	32	11
Against	63	18	9

a. Define a sample space for this experiment.

b. List the simple events belonging to the event F.

c. Find $P(B)$, $P(W)$, $P(M)$, $P(F)$, and $P(\bar{F})$.

d. Find the probability that the employee selected is not a manager.

3.16 Refer to Exercise 3.15. Express each of the following events in words, and find its probability:

a. $B \cup W$

b. $F \cup M$

c. $\bar{F} \cap W$

d. $F \cap \bar{M}$

 3.17 Referring to Exercise 3.8, suppose that 300 mortgage applications are approved and that the number of mortgages of each type were as shown in the following table. The manager selects one mortgage application at random, and the relevant events are defined as follows:

L: The application selected is for a one-year mortgage.
M: The application selected is for a two-year mortgage.
N: The application selected is for a three-year mortgage.
C: The application selected is for a closed mortgage.

	Term of Mortgage (Years)		
	One	Two	Three
Open	32	36	60
Closed	80	48	44

a. Find $P(L)$, $P(M)$, $P(N)$, $P(C)$, and $P(\bar{C})$.

b. Find the probability that the term of the mortgage selected is longer than one year.

Self-Correcting Exercise (See Appendix 3.A for the solution.)

3.14 A store that sells personal computers and related supplies is concerned that it may be overstocking surge suppressors. The store has tabulated the number of surge suppressors sold weekly for each of the last 80 weeks. The results are summarized in the following table:

Number of Suppressors Sold	Number of Weeks
0	36
1	28
2	12
3	2
4	2

The store intends to use the tabulated data as a basis for forecasting what the level of surge-suppressor sales will be in any given week.

a. Define the random experiment of interest to the store.

b. List the simple events in the sample space.

c. Assign probabilities to the simple events.

d. What approach have you used in determining the probabilities in part (c)?

e. Find the probability of selling at least three surge suppressors in any given week.

 3.15 The trustee of a company's pension plan has solicited the employees' feelings toward a proposed revision in the plan. A breakdown of the responses is shown in the accompanying table. Suppose that an employee is selected at random; the relevant events are defined as follows:

B: The employee selected is a blue-collar worker.
W: The employee selected is a white-collar worker.
M: The employee selected is a manager.
F: The employee selected favors the revision.

3.18 Refer to Exercise 3.17. Express each of the following events in words, and find its probability.

a. $L \cup M$

b. $L \cup C$

c. $M \cap \bar{C}$

d. $\bar{N} \cap C$

FIN **3.19** Although the international debt situation no longer captures front-page headlines on a regular basis as it did during the crisis of 1981, the situation continues to pose a serious threat to the banking system. The debt of various high-debt countries, expressed as a percentage of their gross national product (GNP), is shown in the accompanying table. Suppose that one of these countries is selected at random and its debt percentage is observed. Each country has the same chance of being selected.

Country	1984 Debt as Percentage of GNP
Argentina	65%
Bolivia	138
Brazil	53

Country	1984 Debt as Percentage of GNP
Chile	116
Costa Rica	124
Israel	95
Mexico	60
Morocco	94
Turkey	46
Uruguay	67
Venezuela	75

SOURCE: *Finance & Development* (March 1989): 36.

a. Define the random experiment.

b. List the simple events in the sample space.

c. Assign probabilities to the simple events.

d. What approach have you used in determining the probabilities in part (c)?

e. What is the probability that the debt of the country selected is greater than its GNP?

SECTION 3.4 **CONDITIONAL PROBABILITY**

When finding the probability of an event, we can sometimes make use of partial knowledge about the outcome of the experiment. For example, suppose that we are interested in the probability that the share price of IBM increased today. If we hear on the radio that the Dow Jones Industrial Average rose 20 points today (and no individual stock prices are given), that will surely affect the probability that the price of an IBM share has gone up. In light of the new information, we may wish to find the *conditional probability* that the price of IBM increased, given that the DJIA rose 20 points.

For an illustration of the notion of conditional probability, consider once again Example 3.5, involving the audit of Keep Kool Inc. Suppose that we are told that the invoice selected by the auditor is a wholesale invoice (W). We may then determine the probability that this invoice is for the deluxe model (D), making use of our knowledge that it is a wholesale invoice. In other words, we are seeking the **conditional probability** that D will occur, given that W has occurred; this is written

TABLE 3.2   PROBABILITIES FOR INVOICE CLASSIFICATIONS

	Wholesale W	Retail $\overline{W}$	Total
Deluxe D	.18	.56	.74
Standard $\overline{D}$	.12	.14	.26
Total	.30	.70	1.00

$P(D\,|\,W)$. (The vertical stroke | is read "given that," and it is followed by the event that has occurred.) In attempting to find this conditional probability, we first note that knowing that a wholesale invoice was selected restricts our inquiry to the first column of Table 3.1. That is, the new information has reduced the size of the sample space to 60 possible simple events. Of these 60 simple events in the **reduced sample space,** 36 belong to the event D. Hence the desired conditional probability is

$$P(D\,|\,W) = \frac{36}{60} = .6$$

which differs from the (**unconditional**) probability $P(D) = .74$.

We now present a slightly different but equivalent way of calculating $P(D\,|\,W)$. The information displayed in Table 3.1 can be expressed alternatively as probabilities, by dividing the number in each category by the total of 200, as shown in Table 3.2.

The four probabilities in the interior of Table 3.2 are referred to as **joint probabilities,** since they express the likelihood of the occurrence of joint events. For example, .18 is the probability that the joint event $(D \cap W)$ will occur. The four probabilities .30, .70, .74, and .26, which appear at the margins of the table, are called **marginal probabilities.** They are, respectively, the marginal probabilities that W, $\overline{W}$, D, and $\overline{D}$ will occur. Marginal probabilities are simply unconditional probabilities.

Our computation of the conditional probability $P(D\,|\,W)$ as the ratio of two probabilities follows from our previous calculation of $P(D\,|\,W)$:

$$P(D\,|\,W) = \frac{36}{60} = \frac{36/200}{60/200} = \frac{.18}{.30} = \frac{P(D \cap W)}{P(W)}$$

Similarly, we can compute the conditional probability that the invoice selected is to a wholesaler, given that it is for a deluxe model:

$$P(W\,|\,D) = \frac{P(D \cap W)}{P(D)} = \frac{.18}{.74}$$

Having worked through the calculation of a particular conditional probability, we now present the general formula for a conditional probability.

Conditional Probability

Let A and B be two events such that $P(B) > 0$. The conditional probability that A occurs, given that B has occurred, is

$$P(A \mid B) = \frac{P(A \cap B)}{P(B)}$$

In the preceding example, we saw that $P(D) = .74$ and that $P(D \mid W) = .6$, so that $P(D) \neq P(D \mid W)$. In other words, knowing that event W occurred changes the probability that D occurred. Such events D and W are called **dependent** events. On the other hand, if the occurrence of one event does not change the probability of occurrence of the other event, the two events are said to be **independent.**

Independent and Dependent Events

Two events A and B are said to be independent if $P(A \mid B) = P(A)$ or $P(B \mid A) = P(B)$. Otherwise, the events are dependent.

If one equality in the preceding definition holds, so does the other. The concept of independence is illustrated in the following example.

EXAMPLE 3.6

A group of female managers working for an insurance company has lodged a complaint with the personnel department. While the women agree that the company has increased the number of female managers, they assert that women tend to remain in lower-level management positions when promotions are handed out. They have supported their argument by noting that, over the past 3 years, only 8 of the 54 promotions awarded went to women. The personnel department has responded by claiming that these numbers are misleading on two counts: first, there are far fewer female managers than male managers; second, many of the female managers have been hired during the past year, and employees are virtually never promoted during their first year at the managerial level. The personnel department has compiled the data shown in Table 3.3, which classifies those employed as managers for at least one year, according to gender and to promotion record. The department claims that the decision to promote a manager (or not) is independent of the manager's gender. Would you agree?

TABLE 3.3   *CLASSIFICATION OF MANAGERS*

	Promoted	**Not Promoted**	**Total**
Male	46	184	230
Female	8	32	40
Total	54	216	270

Solution.   The events of interest are as follows:

M: A manager is male.

$\bar{M}$:   A manager is female.

A: A manager is promoted.

$\bar{A}$:   A manager is not promoted.

In order to show that the decision about whether or not to promote a manager is independent of the manager's gender, we must verify that

$$P(A \mid M) = P(A)$$

If this equality holds, the probability that a man is promoted is no different from the probability that any manager is promoted. Given no information other than the data in Table 3.3, the probability that a manager is promoted is

$$P(A) = \frac{54}{270} = .20$$

If we now consider only male managers, we restrict our attention to the first row of Table 3.3. Given that a manager is male, the probability that he is promoted is

$$P(A \mid M) = \frac{46}{230} = .20$$

Notice the distinction between this conditional probability and the joint probability that a manager is both male and promoted, which is $P(A \cap M) = 46/270 = .17$. In any case, we have verified that $P(A) = P(A \mid M)$, so the events A and M are independent. Based on the data in Table 3.3, we must agree with the personnel department's contention that there is no discrimination in awarding promotions.

As indicated in the definition of independent events, an alternative way of showing that A and M are independent events is to verify that $P(M \mid A) = P(M)$. The probability that a manager is male is $P(M) = 230/270 = 46/54$, which equals $P(M \mid A)$, the probability that a manager who is promoted is male. Thus, we again conclude that the events A and M are independent.

Before concluding this section, we draw your attention to a common misconception. Students often think that independent events and mutually exclusive events are the same thing. They are not. For example, events A and M in the preceding example are independent events that are not mutually exclusive, since the event $A \cap M$ contains 46 simple events. In fact, it can be shown that *any two independent events A and B that occur with nonzero probabilities cannot be mutually exclusive.* For if A and B were mutually exclusive, we would have $P(A \cap B) = 0$ and $P(A \mid B) = 0$; but since A occurs with nonzero probability, $P(A) \neq P(A \mid B)$, so A and B cannot be independent events.

EXERCISES

LEARNING THE TECHNIQUES

3.20 Consider a sample space $S = \{E_1, E_2, E_3, E_4\}$, where $P(E_1) = .1$, $P(E_2) = .1$, $P(E_3) = .3$, and $P(E_4) = .5$. Define the events:

$A = \{E_1, E_2, E_4\}$

$B = \{E_1, E_4\}$

$C = \{E_1, E_2, E_3\}$

Calculate the following probabilities:

a. $P(A \mid B)$

b. $P(B \mid A)$

c. $P(A \mid C)$

d. $P(C \mid A)$

e. $P(B \mid C)$

f. $P(C \mid B)$

3.21 Consider a sample space $S = \{E_1, E_2, E_3, E_4\}$, where $P(E_1) = .1$, $P(E_2) = .2$, $P(E_3) = .3$, and $P(E_4) = .4$. Define the events:

$A = \{E_1, E_2, E_3\}$

$B = \{E_2, E_3, E_4\}$

$C = \{E_3, E_4\}$.

Calculate the following probabilities:

a. $P(A \mid B)$

b. $P(B \mid A)$

c. $P(A \mid C)$

d. $P(C \mid A)$

e. $P(B \mid C)$

f. $P(C \mid B)$

3.22 Consider a sample space $S = \{E_1, E_2, E_3, E_4\}$, where $P(E_1) = P(E_4) = .3$ and $P(E_2) = P(E_3) = .2$. Define the events:

$A = \{E_1, E_2\}$

$B = \{E_2, E_3\}$

$C = \{E_3, E_4\}$

Which of the following pairs of events are independent? Explain.

a. A and B

b. B and C

c. A and C

3.23 Consider a sample space $S = \{E_1, E_2, E_3, E_4\}$, where $P(E_1) = P(E_4) = .4$ and $P(E_2) = P(E_3) = .1$. Define the events:

$A = \{E_3, E_4\}$

$B = \{E_2, E_3\}$

$C = \{E_1, E_3\}$

Which of the following pairs of events are independent? Explain.

a. A and B

b. B and C

c. A and C

Self-Correcting Exercise (See Appendix 3.A for the solution.)

3.24 An ordinary deck of playing cards has 13 cards of each suit. Suppose that a card is selected at random from the deck.

a. What is the probability that the card selected is an ace?

b. Given that the card selected is a spade, what is the probability that the card is an ace?

c. Are "an ace is selected" and "a spade is selected" independent events?

3.25 Suppose that A and B are two mutually exclusive events. Do A and B represent independent events? Explain.

APPLYING THE TECHNIQUES

3.26 Of a company's employees, 30% are women and 6% are married women. Suppose that an employee is selected at random. If the employee who is selected is a woman, what is the probability that she is married?

FIN 3.27 A firm classifies its customers' accounts according to the balance outstanding and according to whether or not the account is overdue. The accompanying table gives the proportion of accounts falling into various categories. One account is selected at random.

	Overdue	Not Overdue
Under $100	.08	.42
$100–$500	.08	.22
Over $500	.04	.16

a. Given that the account selected is overdue, what is the probability that its balance is under $100?

b. If the balance of the account selected is over $500, what is the probability that it is overdue?

c. If the balance of the account selected is $500 or less, what is the probability that it is overdue?

FIN 3.28 A department store manager wishes to investigate whether the method of payment chosen by customers is related to the size of their purchases. The manager has cross-classified a sample of 250 customer purchases, as shown in the following table. One of these 250 customers is selected at random.

	Method of Payment	
Size of Purchase	Cash	Credit Card
Under $20	51	31
$20 or more	65	103

a. What is the probability that the customer selected paid by credit card?

b. What is the probability that the customer selected made a purchase of under $20?

c. Are the events "Payment by cash" and "Purchase of under $20" mutually exclusive? Explain.

d. Are the events "Payment by cash" and "Purchase of under $20" independent? Explain.

MNG 3.29 A personnel manager has cross-classified the 400 employees of a firm according to their record of absenteeism last year and whether or not they were smokers, as shown in the table. One of these employees is selected at random.

Number of Days Absent	Smoker	Nonsmoker
Less than 10	34	260
10 or more	78	28

a. What is the probability that the employee selected was a nonsmoker?

b. What is the probability that the employee selected was absent for 10 or more days?

c. Are the events "Nonsmoker" and "Absent less than 10 days" mutually exclusive? Explain.

d. Determine if an employee's being absent for 10 or more days last year was independent of whether or not the employee was a smoker.

3.30   Refer to Exercise 3.14. Find the probability that the store sells exactly two surge suppressors in a week, given that it sells at least one that week.

3.31   Refer to Exercise 3.15.

a. Determine whether F and M are independent or dependent events. Explain.

b. Repeat part (a) for events F and B.

3.32   Insurance companies rely heavily on probability theory when computing the premiums to be charged for various life insurance and annuity products. Probabilities are often computed on the basis of life tables like the following one, which tabulates the average number of American males per 100,000 who will die during various age intervals. For example, out of 100,000 male babies born alive, 1,527 will die before their first birthday and 29,721 will live to the age of 80. Answer the following questions based on this life table.

a. What is the probability that a newborn male will reach the age of 50? The age of 70?

b. What is the probability that an American male will reach the age of 70, given that he has just turned 50?

c. What is the probability that an American male will reach the age of 70, given that he has just turned 60?

NUMBER OF DEATHS AT VARIOUS AGES OUT OF 100,000 AMERICAN MALES BORN ALIVE

Age Interval*	Number of Deaths
0–1	1,527
1–10	495
10–20	927
20–30	1,901
30–40	2,105
40–50	4,502
50–60	10,330
60–70	19,954
70–80	28,538
80 and over	29,721
Total	100,000

* Interval contains all ages from lower limit up to (but not including) upper limit.

SOURCE: *Life Tables, Vital Statistics of the United States* (1978), U.S. Department of Health and Human Services.

SECTION 3.5   *RULES OF PROBABILITY*

Once some of the simpler probabilities of experimental outcomes and events have been determined, we may use various rules of probability to compute the probabilities of more complex, related events. Consider, for example, an aerospace company that has submitted bids on two separate federal government defense contracts, A and B. Suppose that the company has estimated $P(A)$ and $P(B)$, the probabilities of winning each of the contracts, as well as $P(A \mid B)$, the probability of winning contract A, given that it wins contract B. Using the rules of probability, the company can then readily calculate various related probabilities—such as $P(\bar{A})$, the probability that it will not win contract A; $P(A \cap B)$, the probability that it will win both contracts; and $P(A \cup B)$, the probability that it will win at least one of the two contracts.

COMPLEMENT RULE

The first rule of probability follows easily from the basic requirement that the sum of the probabilities assigned to the simple events in a sample space must equal 1. Given any event A and its complement $\bar{A}$, each simple event must belong to either A or $\bar{A}$. We therefore must have:

$$P(A) + P(\bar{A}) = 1$$

The complement rule is obtained by subtracting $P(\bar{A})$ from each side of the equality.

Complement Rule

$$P(A) = 1 - P(\bar{A})$$

for any event A.

Despite the simplicity of this rule, it can be very useful. The task of finding the probability that an event will not occur and then subtracting that probability from 1 is often easier than the task of directly computing the probability that it will occur.

EXAMPLE 3.7

Suppose that we intend to flip a coin until heads comes up for the first time; and suppose further that we wish to determine the probability that at least two flips will be required. A possible sample space for this experiment is $S = \{1, 2, 3, 4, \ldots\}$, where each integer indicates a possible number of flips required. If A represents the event that at least two flips are required, then $A = \{2, 3, 4, \ldots\}$. A direct approach to finding $P(A)$ would entail calculating and summing the probabilities $P(2)$, $P(3)$, $P(4), \ldots$. A simpler approach, however, is to recognize that the probability that event A will not occur is the probability that heads will come up on the first flip:

$$P(\bar{A}) = P(1) = 1/2$$

Therefore, the probability that at least two flips will be required before heads comes up for the first time is

$$P(A) = 1 - P(\bar{A}) = 1/2$$

ADDITION RULE

The second rule of probability enables us to find the probability of the union of two events from the probabilities of other events.

Addition Rule

$$P(A \cup B) = P(A) + P(B) - P(A \cap B)$$

where A and B are any two events.

If A and B are mutually exclusive, we have $P(A \cap B) = 0$ and the addition rule simplifies to $P(A \cup B) = P(A) + P(B)$.

FIGURE 3.5
*ENTIRE SHADED
AREA IS A ∪ B*

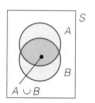

Addition Rule for Mutually Exclusive Events

$$P(A \cup B) = P(A) + P(B)$$

for any two mutually exclusive events A and B.

In general, however, we must subtract the joint probability $P(A \cap B)$, in order to avoid double-counting a simple event that belongs to both A and B. This is apparent from the Venn diagram in Figure 3.5, in which $A \cup B$ is represented by the entire shaded area. When finding the probability $P(A \cup B)$ by summing $P(A)$ and $P(B)$, we must subtract $P(A \cap B)$ to avoid double-counting the probability of the event $A \cap B$, which belongs to both A and B.

EXAMPLE 3.8

Refer to Example 3.5, involving the audit of Keep Kool Inc., and suppose that we wish to find $P(W \cup D)$, the probability that the invoice selected is either a wholesale invoice or an invoice for the deluxe model. For convenience, Tables 3.1 and 3.2 are reproduced in Table 3.4.

We know from Table 3.4(b) that $P(W) = .30$, $P(D) = .74$, and $P(W \cap D) = .18$. Using the addition rule,

$$P(W \cup D) = P(W) + P(D) - P(W \cap D)$$
$$= .30 + .74 - .18$$
$$= .86$$

Thus, the probability that the invoice selected is either a wholesale invoice or an invoice for the deluxe model is .86.

To check the answer by means of the basic counting procedure, let's count simple events, using Table 3.4(a). The number of simple events in W is 60, and the number in D is 148. But the number of points in $W \cup D$ is $60 + 148 - 36$, since 36

TABLE 3.4   CLASSIFICATION OF INVOICES

a. Invoice Frequencies

	Wholesale W	Retail $\overline{W}$	Total
Deluxe: D	36	112	148
Standard: $\overline{D}$	24	28	52
Total	60	140	200

b. Invoice Probabilities

	Wholesale W	Retail $\overline{W}$	Total
D	.18	.56	.74
$\overline{D}$	.12	.14	.26
Total	.30	.70	1.00

simple events are common to both W and D. We therefore have

$$P(W \cup D) = \frac{60}{200} + \frac{148}{200} - \frac{36}{200}$$
$$= .30 + .74 - .18$$
$$= P(W) + P(D) - P(W \cap D)$$

MULTIPLICATION RULE

The third rule of probability, which is used to find the probability of a joint event, is simply a rearrangement of the definition of conditional probability. Since

$$P(A \mid B) = \frac{P(A \cap B)}{P(B)}$$

and

$$P(B \mid A) = \frac{P(A \cap B)}{P(A)}$$

we obtain the following rule for computing the joint probability $P(A \cap B)$.

Multiplication Rule

$$P(A \cap B) = P(A) \cdot P(B \mid A)$$
$$= P(B) \cdot P(A \mid B)$$

for any two events A and B.

Note that the two expressions for finding a joint probability using the multiplication rule are equivalent. The expression that should be used in a particular situation depends on the information that is given.

For the special case in which A and B are independent events, we have $P(B \mid A) = P(B)$, so we can simply write $P(A \cap B) = P(A) \cdot P(B)$.

Multiplication Rule for Independent Events

$$P(A \cap B) = P(A) \cdot P(B)$$

for any two independent events A and B.

EXAMPLE 3.9

A computer software supplier has developed a new record-keeping package for use by hospitals. The company feels that the probability that the new package will show a profit in its first year is .6, unless a competitor introduces a product of comparable quality this year, in which case the probability of a first-year profit drops to .3. The supplier suggests that there is a 50–50 chance that a comparable product will be introduced this year. Define the following events:

A: A competitor introduces a comparable product.

B: The record-keeping package is profitable in its first year.

a. What is the probability that both A and B will occur?

b. What is the probability that either A or B will occur?

c. What is the probability that neither A nor B will occur?

Solution.   Summarizing the given information, we know that

$$P(A) = .5$$
$$P(B) = .6$$
$$P(B \mid A) = .3$$

a. According to the multiplication rule, the probability that a competitor will introduce a comparable product and that the first year will be profitable is

$$P(A \cap B) = P(A) \cdot P(B \mid A)$$
$$= (.5)(.3)$$
$$= .15$$

b. Notice that $P(A \cup B)$ can be determined only after $P(A \cap B)$ has been calculated. The probability that either a competitor will introduce a comparable product or the record-keeping package will be profitable in its first year is

$$P(A \cup B) = P(A) + P(B) - P(A \cap B)$$
$$= .5 + .6 - .15$$
$$= .95$$

c. This part is somewhat more difficult, but it illustrates the effective use of event relations. The easiest way to find $P(\bar{A} \cap \bar{B})$—the probability that neither A nor B will occur—is to recognize that $P(\bar{A} \cap \bar{B}) = P(\overline{A \cup B})$ and to use the complement rule. You should convince yourself that events $(\bar{A} \cap \bar{B})$ and $(\overline{A \cup B})$ are one and the same, with the help of the Venn diagram in Figure 3.6. It follows that the probability that a competitor will not introduce a comparable product and that the first year will not be profitable is

$$P(\bar{A} \cap \bar{B}) = P(\overline{A \cup B})$$
$$= 1 - P(A \cup B)$$
$$= 1 - .95$$
$$= .05$$

FIGURE 3.6

SHADED AREA IS $\bar{A} \cap \bar{B} = \overline{A \cup B}$

![section marker] **EXERCISES**

LEARNING THE TECHNIQUES

3.33 If $P(A) = .6$, $P(B) = .5$, and $P(A \cup B) = .9$, find $P(A \cap B)$ and $P(A \mid B)$.

3.34 If $P(A) = .2$, $P(B) = .4$, and $P(A \cup B) = .5$, find $P(A \cap B)$ and $P(B \mid A)$.

3.35 Given that $P(A) = .3$, $P(B) = .6$, and $P(B \mid A) = .4$, find the following probabilities:

a. $P(A \cap B)$

b. $P(A \cup B)$

c. $P(A \mid B)$

3.36 Given the information in Exercise 3.35, find $P(\bar{A} \cap \bar{B})$. (HINT: Make use of a Venn diagram.)

3.37 Given that $P(A) = .4$, $P(B) = .5$ and $P(B \mid A) = .8$, find the following probabilities:

a. $P(A \cap B)$

b. $P(A \cup B)$

c. $P(A \mid B)$

3.38 Given the information in Exercise 3.37, find $P(\bar{A} \cap \bar{B})$. (HINT: Make use of a Venn diagram.)

3.39 Let A and B be two mutually exclusive events for which $P(A) = .25$ and $P(B) = .6$. Find the following probabilities:

a. $P(A \cap B)$

b. $P(A \cup B)$

c. $P(A \mid B)$

3.40 Let A and B be two independent events for which $P(A) = .25$ and $P(B) = .6$. Find the following probabilities:

a. $P(A \mid B)$

b. $P(B \mid A)$

c. $P(A \cap B)$

d. $P(A \cup B)$

3.41 Let A and B be two mutually exclusive events for which $P(A) = .15$ and $P(B) = .4$. Find the following probabilities:

a. $P(A \cap B)$

b. $P(A \cup B)$

c. $P(B \mid A)$

3.42 Let A and B be two independent events for which $P(A) = .15$ and $P(B) = .4$. Find the following probabilities:

a. $P(A \mid B)$

b. $P(B \mid A)$

c. $P(A \cap B)$

d. $P(A \cup B)$

APPLYING THE TECHNIQUES

MNG **3.43** An aerospace company has submitted bids on two separate federal government defense contracts, A and B. The company feels that it has a 60% chance of winning contract A and a 30% chance of winning contract B. Given that it wins contract B, the company believes it has an 80% chance of winning contract A.

a. What is the probability that the company will win both contracts?

b. What is the probability that the company will win at least one of the two contracts?

c. If the company wins contract B, what is the probability that it will not win contract A?

Self-Correcting Exercise (See Appendix 3.A for the solution.)

MNG **3.44** Suppose that the aerospace company in Exercise 3.43 feels that it has a 50% chance of winning contract A and a 40% chance of winning contract B. Furthermore, it believes that winning contract A is independent of winning contract B.

a. What is the probability that the company will win both contracts?

b. What is the probability that the company will win at least one of the two contracts?

GEN **3.45** A sporting goods store estimates that 20% of the students at a nearby university ski downhill and 15% ski cross-country. Of those who ski downhill, 40% also ski cross-country.

a. What percentage of these students ski both downhill and cross-country?

b. What percentage of the students do not ski at all?

MNG **3.46** A union's executive conducted a survey of its members to determine what the members felt were the important issues to be discussed during upcoming negotiations with management. Results showed that 74% felt that job security was an important issue, while 65% felt that pension benefits were an important issue. Of those who felt that pension benefits were an important issue, 60% also felt that job security was an important issue.

a. What percentage of the members felt that both job security and pension benefits were important?

b. What percentage of the members felt that at least one of these two issues was important?

GEN **3.47** Two six-sided dice are rolled, and the number of spots turning up on each is observed. Determine the probability of observing four spots on at least one of the dice. (HINT: Use the complement rule.)

GEN **3.48** Young Presidents' Organization is an international group whose membership is restricted to those who have become president or chairman and CEO of relatively large companies before the age of 40. Members must leave the organization upon reaching 50. *Canadian Business* (September 1985) reported that three-quarters of the members are 40 years and over, and that 67% are under 45. One member of the organization is chosen at random. Define the events:

A: The member chosen is at least 40 years old.
B: The member chosen is under the age of 45.

Express in words, and compute, the following probabilities:

a. $P(\bar{A})$

b. $P(\bar{B})$

c. $P(A \cup B)$

d. $P(A \cap B)$

e. $P(A \mid B)$

f. $P(B \mid A)$

GEN **3.49** A certain city has one morning newspaper and one evening newspaper. It is estimated that 20% of the city's households subscribe to the morning paper and that 60% subscribe to the evening paper. Of those who subscribe to the morning paper, 80% also subscribe to the evening paper. What proportion of households

a. subscribe to both papers?

b. subscribe to at most one of the papers?

c. subscribe to neither paper?

FIN **3.50** Individuals wishing to pursue a career in investment analysis are often encouraged to obtain the professional designation of Chartered Financial Analyst (CFA). A candidate must pass three exams to obtain this designation and can take only one exam in a given year. The results of the exams held in 1984, reported by the Institute of Chartered Financial Analysts in *The CFA Study Guide* (1985), are summarized in the accompanying table. One candidate is selected at random from among those who took a CFA exam in 1984.

Exam	Number of Candidates Writing	Percentage Who Passed
I	2,075	58%
II	1,147	61%
III	808	81%

a. What is the probability that the selected candidate passed?

b. What is the probability that the selected candidate took Exam I and passed?

c. If the selected candidate passed, what is the probability that the candidate took Exam III?

PROBABILITY TREES

Another way of calculating probabilities is to use a probability tree, in which the various possible events of an experiment are represented by lines or branches of the tree. In the construction of a sample space for an experiment, a probability tree is a useful device to ensure that all simple events have been identified and to assign the associated probabilities. The mechanics of using a probability tree will now be illustrated by reference to the simple coin example encountered earlier.

In Example 3.1, we stated that a sample space for the random experiment consisting of flipping a coin twice is $S = \{HH, HT, TH, TT\}$, where the first letter of each pair denotes the result of the first flip. An alternative representation of S, differing only in the notation used, is

$$S = \{H_1 \cap H_2, H_1 \cap T_2, T_1 \cap H_2, T_1 \cap T_2\}$$

where the events are defined as:

H_1: Heads is observed on the first flip.

H_2: Heads is observed on the second flip.

T_1: Tails is observed on the first flip.

T_2: Tails is observed on the second flip.

A probability tree for this example is shown in Figure 3.7.

Whenever an experiment can be broken down into stages, with a different aspect of the result being observed at each stage, the various possible sequences of observations can be represented in a probability tree. In the coin example, stage 1 observes the outcome of the first flip, and stage 2 observes the outcome of the second flip. The heavy dots in Figure 3.7 are called *nodes,* and the branches emanating from

FIGURE 3.7   PROBABILITY TREE FOR COIN EXAMPLE

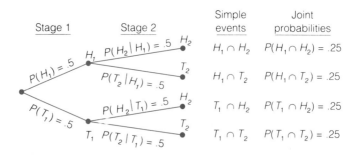

a particular node represent the alternative outcomes that may occur at that point. The probability attached to each branch is the conditional probability that that particular branch outcome will occur, given that the outcomes represented by preceding branches have all occurred. For example, the probability attached to the top branch at stage 2 is $P(H_2 | H_1) = .5$—the probability of obtaining a result of heads on the second flip, given that a result of heads was obtained on the first flip. Since the branches emanating from any particular node represent all possible outcomes that may occur at that point, the sum of the probabilities on those branches must equal 1.

The initial (unlabeled) node is called the *origin*. Any path through the tree from the origin to a terminal node corresponds to one possible simple event, the probability of which is the product of the probabilities attached to the branches forming that path. For example, if we follow along the top two branches of the tree, we observe the simple event $H_1 \cap H_2$, which (according to the multiplication rule) has the probability

$$P(H_1 \cap H_2) = P(H_1) \cdot P(H_2 | H_1) = (.5) \cdot (.5) = .25$$

You may be wondering why we went to all the trouble of using a probability tree to determine that each of the four possible simple events occurs with a probability of 1/4, since this may have been obvious to you from the beginning. The main point of this example was to introduce the mechanics of probability trees; the next two examples illustrate the advantages of using probability trees. In Example 3.10, the probability tree helps sort out the given information and clarify what has to be calculated to reach a solution. The benefits of using a probability tree to identify the possible simple events and their associated probabilities should become even more apparent from Example 3.11. If you are unconvinced, attempt to solve Example 3.11 without the aid of a probability tree.

EXAMPLE 3.10

The proprietor of a men's clothing store has recorded the buying behavior of customers over a long period of time. He has established that the probability that a

FIGURE 3.8   PROBABILITY TREE FOR SHIRTS AND TIES

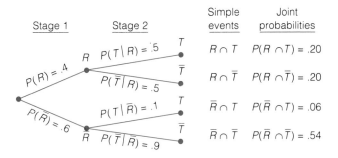

		Simple events	Joint probabilities
		$R \cap T$	$P(R \cap T) = .20$
		$R \cap \bar{T}$	$P(R \cap \bar{T}) = .20$
		$\bar{R} \cap T$	$P(\bar{R} \cap T) = .06$
		$\bar{R} \cap \bar{T}$	$P(\bar{R} \cap \bar{T}) = .54$

customer will buy a shirt is about .4. A customer buys a tie 50% of the time when a shirt is purchased, but only 10% of the time when a shirt is not purchased. Find the probability that a customer will buy the following:

a. A shirt and a tie

b. A tie

c. A shirt or a tie

d. A tie but not a shirt

Solution.   The random experiment consists of observing, for each customer, whether a shirt is purchased and whether a tie is purchased. The two basic events of interest are therefore:

R: A customer buys a shirt.

T: A customer buys a tie.

Summarizing the given information, we have $P(R) = .4$, $P(T|R) = .5$, and $P(T|\bar{R}) = .1$. Before constructing a probability tree, we should search the given probabilities for an unconditional probability. In this example, we are given the unconditional probability that event R will occur, so event R will be considered at the first stage and event T at the second. We can now construct the probability tree for this experiment, as shown in Figure 3.8.

Collecting the simple events at the end of the tree, we find that a sample space for the experiment is

$$S = \{R \cap T, R \cap \bar{T}, \bar{R} \cap T, \bar{R} \cap \bar{T}\}$$

Calculating the required probabilities is now quite simple, amounting to little more than reading off the joint (simple event) probabilities from the tree.

a. The probability that a customer will buy a shirt and a tie is

$$P(R \cap T) = .20$$

b. The probability that a customer will buy a tie is
$$P(T) = P\{R \cap T, \bar{R} \cap T\}$$
$$= P(R \cap T) + P(\bar{R} \cap T)$$
$$= .20 + .06$$
$$= .26$$

c. The probability that a customer will buy a shirt or a tie is
$$P(R \cup T) = P\{R \cap T, R \cap \bar{T}, \bar{R} \cap T\}$$
$$= P(R \cap T) + P(R \cap \bar{T}) + P(\bar{R} \cap T)$$
$$= .20 + .20 + .06$$
$$= .46$$

d. The probability that a customer will buy a tie but not a shirt is
$$P(\bar{R} \cap T) = .06$$

EXAMPLE 3.11

Suppose that you have one nickel, two dimes, and one quarter in a box. If you select two coins from the box without looking, what is the probability of your selecting a dime and a quarter?

Solution.   An organized procedure for solving this problem entails first constructing a relevant sample space, and then assigning probabilities to the simple events. As we have already seen, the sample space associated with a random experiment is not unique. One possibility in this case is

$$S' = \{\text{nickel and dime, nickel and quarter, two dimes, dime and quarter}\}$$

where, for example, "nickel and dime" represents the selection of a nickel and a dime, with no consideration given to the order of selection. With this sample space, however, you might be tempted to assign (incorrectly) a probability of 1/4 to each simple event. How can you be sure that the probabilities you assign are correct?

Using a probability tree is an effective method of simplifying the assignment of probabilities. A probability tree essentially presupposes that there is an order in which the observations of outcomes occur, each stage corresponding to one observation. For this example, the process of observing which two coins are selected can be broken down into two stages, as shown in Figure 3.9. (Rather than resorting to subscripts, as we did in the previous example, we have chosen here to denote each simple event by a pair of letters, where the first letter of each pair indicates the first coin selected.) Once the branches are drawn, assigning the corresponding branch probabilities becomes relatively easy. For example, consider the top branch of the

FIGURE 3.9   *PROBABILITY TREE FOR SELECTING TWO COINS FROM FOUR*

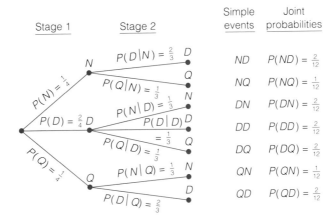

second stage. If the first coin selected is a nickel, two dimes and a quarter remain in the box. Thus $P(D|N) = 2/3$. We next identify the seven simple events corresponding to the seven terminal nodes, and we obtain the sample space

$$S = \{ND, NQ, DN, DD, DQ, QN, QD\}$$

Finally, we obtain the probability of a simple event by taking the product of the probabilities attached to the branches leading to that simple event. This is simply an application of the multiplication rule. For example,

$$P(ND) = P(N) \cdot P(D|N) = (1/4) \cdot (2/3) = 2/12$$

Having constructed the probability tree, we can next determine the probability of selecting a dime and a quarter. Let the event E be the selection of a dime and a quarter; then $E = \{DQ, QD\}$, so

$$P(E) = P(DQ) + P(QD) = 2/12 + 2/12 = 1/3$$

Before leaving this question, notice that we can now go back and easily assign probabilities to the outcomes in the first sample space, S', that was suggested:

P(nickel and dime) $= 4/12$

P(nickel and quarter) $= 2/12$

P(two dimes) $= 2/12$

P(dime and quarter) $= 4/12$

███████████   **EXERCISES**

LEARNING THE TECHNIQUES

3.51 Let $P(A) = .6$, $P(B \mid A) = .1$ and $P(B \mid \bar{A}) = .3$.

a. Sketch a properly labeled probability tree to depict this situation.

b. Use the probability tree to find $P(A \cap \bar{B})$ and $P(\bar{B})$.

3.52 Let $P(\bar{A}) = .7$, $P(\bar{B} \mid A) = .8$, and $P(B \mid \bar{A}) = .4$.

a. Sketch a properly labeled probability tree to depict this situation.

b. Use the probability tree to find $P(A \cap B)$ and $P(\bar{B})$.

3.53 Let $P(A) = .3$, $P(B \mid A) = .4$, and $P(B \mid \bar{A}) = .8$.

a. Sketch a properly labeled probability tree to depict this situation.

b. Use the probability tree to find $P(A \cup B)$ and $P(\bar{A} \cap B)$.

3.54 Let $P(\bar{A}) = .4$, $P(\bar{B} \mid A) = .3$, and $P(B \mid \bar{A}) = .6$.

a. Sketch a properly labeled probability tree to depict this situation.

b. Use the probability tree to find $P(A \cup B)$ and $P(\bar{A} \cap B)$.

3.55 A fair coin is flipped three times. Use a probability tree to find the probability of observing:

a. No heads

b. Exactly one heads

c. Exactly two heads

d. At least one tails

APPLYING THE TECHNIQUES

Self-Correcting Exercise (See Appendix 3.A for the solution.)

POM **3.56** An assembler has been supplied with ten electronic components, of which three are defective. If two components are selected at random,

what is the probability that neither component is defective?

─────────────────────

GEN **3.57** Approximately three out of every four Americans who filed a 1986 tax return received a refund. If three individuals are chosen at random from among those who filed a 1986 tax return, find the probabilities of the following events:

a. All three received a refund.

b. None of the three received a refund.

c. Exactly one received a refund.

RET **3.58** A door-to-door saleswoman sells rug shampoo in three tube sizes: small, large, and giant. The probability of finding a person at home is .6. If the saleswoman does find someone at home, the probabilities are .5 that she will make no sale, .2 that she will sell a small tube, .2 that she will sell a large tube, and .1 that she will sell a giant tube. The probability of selling more than one tube of shampoo at a house is 0.

a. Find the probability that, in one call, she will not sell any shampoo.

b. Find the probability that, in one call, she will sell either a large tube or a giant tube.

GEN **3.59** To determine who pays for coffee, three students each toss a coin and the odd person pays. If all coins show heads or all show tails, the students toss again. What is the probability that a decision will be reached in five or fewer tosses?

MNG **3.60** Of 20,000 small businesses surveyed, "about 82% said they employed women in some capacity." Of the businesses that employed women, 19.5% employed no female supervisors, 50% employed only one female supervisor, and the remainder employed more than one female supervisor (*Globe and Mail,* October 1985).

a. How many of the businesses surveyed employed no women?

b. What proportion of businesses surveyed employed exactly one female supervisor?

c. What proportion of businesses surveyed employed no female supervisors?

d. Given that a firm employed women, what is the probability that it employed at least one female supervisor?

POM **3.61** All printed circuit boards (PCBs) that are manufactured at a certain plant are inspected for flaws. Experience has shown that 50% of the PCBs produced are flawed in some way. Of the flawed PCBs, 60% are repairable, while the remainder are seriously flawed and must be discarded. A newly manufactured PCB is selected before undergoing inspection. What is the probability that it will not have to be discarded?

POM **3.62** In a forest plantation, it is important that trees grow very straight so that they can be used to produce lumber. A forest products firm estimates that 20% of all trees planted will die before maturity. Of the trees that survive, 90% will grow straight enough to be used to produce lumber. If a newly planted tree is selected at random, what is the probability that it will not be used to produce lumber?

POM **3.63** A manufacturer of biodegradable plastic bags has determined that different lighting conditions lead to different lengths of time required for complete degradation to occur. In a lab study, using several different lighting conditions, it was found that 85% of the bags degraded within 10 days of light exposure. Of the bags that had not degraded after 10 days, 20% also had not degraded after 20 days. If a bag is exposed to a lighting condition chosen at random, what is the probability that the bag will degrade within 20 days?

SECTION 3.7   ## BAYES' THEOREM

In Section 3.4, we learned that the conditional probability that a particular event A will occur, given that B has occurred, is

$$P(A \mid B) = \frac{P(A \cap B)}{P(B)}$$

Bayes' theorem, named after the English clergyman and mathematician Thomas Bayes, provides us with an alternative formula for computing this conditional probability. The alternative formula simplifies the computation of $P(A \mid B)$ when $P(A \cap B)$ and $P(B)$ are not given directly.

Beyond its usefulness in simplifying computations, Bayes' theorem is of interest because of its special application in decision analysis (see Chapter 21). Suppose that we are interested in the condition of a machine that produces a particular item. Let A be the event "the machine is in good operating condition"; then $\bar{A}$ represents "the machine is not in good operating condition." We might know from experience that the machine is in good condition 90% of the time. That is, the initial or **prior probabilities** regarding the machine's condition are $P(A) = .9$ and $P(\bar{A}) = .1$. Given the machine's condition, we might also know the probability that a defective item will be produced (event B). Suppose that, when the machine is in good condition, only 1% of the items produced are defective, while 10% are defective when the machine is in poor condition. We therefore have the following conditional probabilities:

$$P(B \mid A) = .01$$
$$P(B \mid \bar{A}) = .10$$

FIGURE 3.10   *PROBABILITY TREE FOR MACHINE PRODUCING ITEMS*

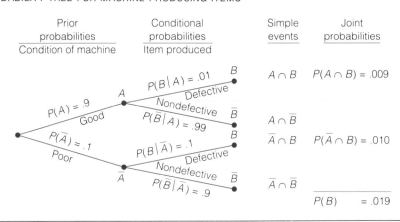

The situation just described can be treated as a two-stage experiment and represented by a probability tree, as in Figure 3.10.

We are primarily concerned with the machine's condition, and we know from historical information that there is a 90% chance of its being in good condition. We can get a better idea of the likelihood that the machine is in good condition right now, however, by obtaining more information. Suppose that, without knowing the condition of the machine, we select an item from the current production run and observe that it is defective. It is then possible to revise the prior probability that the machine is in good condition (event *A*) in light of the new information that event *B* has occurred. That is, we can find the revised or **posterior probability:**

$$P(A \mid B) = \frac{P(A \cap B)}{P(B)}$$

The value of the numerator is obtained easily from the probability tree:

$$P(A \cap B) = P(A) \cdot P(B \mid A)$$
$$= .009$$
$$= (.9)(.01)$$

We next note that event *B* occurs only if one of two simple events, $(A \cap B)$ or $(\bar{A} \cap B)$, occurs. The denominator is therefore

$$P(B) = P(A \cap B) + P(\bar{A} \cap B)$$
$$= .009 + .010$$
$$= .019$$

By using the rules of addition and multiplication, or simply by reading from the probability tree, we obtain

$$P(A \mid B) = \frac{P(A \cap B)}{P(A \cap B) + P(\bar{A} \cap B)}$$

$$= \frac{P(A) \cdot P(B \mid A)}{[P(A) \cdot P(B \mid A)] + [P(\bar{A}) \cdot P(B \mid \bar{A})]}$$

$$= \frac{.009}{.019} = .47$$

In light of the sample information, we have drastically revised downward the probability that the machine is currently in good condition—from .9 to .47. Based on this posterior (after sampling) probability of .47, it is likely to be worth paying a mechanic to check and repair the machine.

The formula just developed, which was used to find the revised or posterior probability of A, given that B has occurred, is the formulation of Bayes' theorem for the case in which the first stage consists of only two events. The two events in our example are A and $\bar{A}$—which alternatively could have been denoted A_1 and A_2, in order to fit the notation of the general formula for Bayes' theorem.

Bayes' theorem can be generalized to the situation in which the first stage consists of n mutually exclusive events $A_1, A_2, \ldots, A_n$. The following statement of Bayes' theorem gives the formula for finding the posterior probabilities $P(A_i \mid B)$, where B is an event observed at the second stage.

Bayes' Theorem

If A_i is one of the n mutually exclusive events $A_1, A_2, \ldots, A_n$ at the first stage, and B is an event at the second stage, then

$$P(A_i \mid B) =$$

$$\frac{P(A_i) \cdot P(B \mid A_i)}{[P(A_1) \cdot P(B \mid A_1)] + [P(A_2) \cdot P(B \mid A_2)] + \cdots + [P(A_n) \cdot P(B \mid A_n)]}$$

Before presenting a second example, we should note that using the probability tree approach is much easier than memorizing Bayes' formula. Once you become familiar with the tree approach that incorporates Bayes' theorem, you may wish to use a tabular format to summarize the given prior and conditional probabilities, identify the probabilities to be computed, and record the computed joint probabilities and posterior probabilities. This type of format will be used in Chapter 21 in our discussion of decision analysis. Table 3.5 displays such a tabular format for the foregoing example. For convenience, the notation has been changed slightly: A_1 instead of A, and A_2 instead of $\bar{A}$. Notice that $P(B)$ is found easily by summing the joint probabilities, and the posterior probabilities are obtained by dividing each of the joint probabilities by $P(B)$.

TABLE 3.5   TABULAR ALTERNATIVE TO FIGURE 3.10

Events	Prior $P(A_i)$	Conditional $P(B \mid A_i)$	Joint $P(A_i \cap B)$	Posterior $P(A_i \mid B)$
A_1	.9	.01	.009	.47
A_2	.1	.10	.010	.53
			$P(B) = .019$	

EXAMPLE 3.12

Each morning, coffee is prepared for the entire office staff by one of three employees, depending on who first arrives at work. Veronica arrives first 20% of the time; Gita and Michael are each the first to arrive on half of the remaining mornings. The probability that the coffee is bitter when it is prepared by Veronica is .1, while the corresponding probabilities when it is prepared by Gita and Michael are .2 and .3, respectively. If you arrive one morning and find the coffee bitter, what is the probability that it was prepared by Veronica? What is the probability that the coffee will not be bitter on a given morning?

Solution.   Let B denote the event "the coffee is bitter." Let V represent the event "the coffee is prepared by Veronica," and let G and M represent the corresponding events when Gita and Michael, respectively, are the preparers. Since $P(V) = .2$, we know that $P(G \cup M) = .8$, so $P(G) = P(M) = .4$. The given prior and conditional probabilities are shown on the probability tree in Figure 3.11. The probability tree allows us to determine quickly the simple events belonging to the event B—namely, $B = \{V \cap B, G \cap B, M \cap B\}$. Hence,

$$P(B) = P(V \cap B) + P(G \cap B) + P(M \cap B)$$
$$= .02 + .08 + .12$$
$$= .22$$

Therefore, the probability that the coffee was prepared by Veronica, given that it is bitter, is

$$P(V \mid B) = \frac{P(V \cap B)}{P(B)} = \frac{.02}{.22} = .09$$

Finally, the probability that the coffee will not be bitter on any given morning is

$$P(\bar{B}) = 1 - P(B) = 1 - .22 = .78$$

FIGURE 3.11   *PROBABILITY TREE FOR COFFEE PREPARATION*

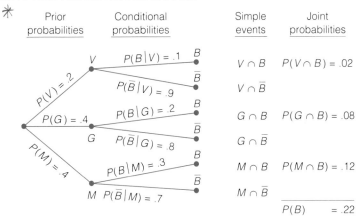

EXERCISES

LEARNING THE TECHNIQUES

3.64 Let $P(A) = .6$, $P(B \mid A) = .2$, and $P(B \mid \bar{A}) = .3$. Use a probability tree to find $P(A \mid B)$ and $P(A \mid \bar{B})$.

3.65 Let $P(A) = .3$, $P(\bar{B} \mid A) = .1$, and $P(B \mid \bar{A}) = .2$. Use a probability tree to find $P(A \mid B)$ and $P(A \mid \bar{B})$.

3.66 Let $P(A) = .2$, $P(B \mid A) = .4$, and $P(\bar{B} \mid \bar{A}) = .3$. Use a probability tree to find $P(A \mid B)$ and $P(A \mid \bar{B})$.

3.67 Let $P(\bar{A}) = .4$, $P(\bar{B} \mid A) = .5$, and $P(\bar{B} \mid \bar{A}) = .6$. Use a probability tree to find $P(\bar{A} \mid B)$ and $P(\bar{A} \mid \bar{B})$.

APPLYING THE TECHNIQUES

Self-Correcting Exercise (See Appendix 3.A for the solution.)

3.68 Due to turnover and absenteeism at an assembly plant, 20% of the items are assembled by inexperienced employees. Management has determined that customers return 12% of the items assembled by inexperienced employees, whereas only 3% of the items assembled by experienced employees are returned. Given that an item has been returned, what is the probability that it was assembled by an inexperienced employee?

MNG **3.69** A consumer goods company recruits several graduating students from universities each year. Concerned about the high cost of training new employees, the company instituted a review of attrition among new recruits. Over 5 years, 30% of new recruits came from the local university, and the balance came from more distant schools. Of the new recruits, 20% of those who were students from the local university resigned within 2 years, while 45% of other students did. Given that a student resigned within 2 years, what is the probability that she was hired from the local university? From a more distant university?

FIN **3.70** The vice-president of a hardware wholesaler has asked the bookkeeper to call all customers five days before their account payments are due, as a means of reducing the number of late payments. As a result of time constraints, however, (only 60% of customers receive such a call from the bookkeeper;) 90% of the customers called pay on time, while only

50% of those not called pay on time. The company has just received a payment on time from a customer. What is the probability that the bookkeeper called this customer?

POM **3.71** A foreman for an injection molding firm admits that, on 10% of his shifts, he forgets to shut off the injection machine on his line. This causes the machine to overheat and increases the chance that a defective molding will be produced during the early morning run from .5% to 5%. If the plant manager randomly selects a molding from the morning run and finds it to be defective, what is the probability that the foreman forgot to shut off the machine the previous night?

3.72 An adhesive technologist concludes from laboratory results that a bond from a new adhesive fails 3% of the time if oil is present on the bonding surface, 12% of the time if the surface is too smooth, and 6% of the time if grit is present on the bonding surface. The bond never fails if the surface is clean. For a particular application by an industrial customer, it is estimated that there is a 5% chance that oil will be on the surface, a 1% chance that the surface will be too smooth, and a .5% chance that grit will be present. This customer has decided to use the new adhesive.

a. What is the probability that the bond will be successful?

b. If the bond is later reported to have failed, what is the probability that grit was present on the bonding surface?

3.73 When a test is conducted to determine whether or not someone is infected with a particular

---

virus, an incorrect test result can occur in two ways: an infected person may test negative, or a noninfected person may test positive. The latter is called a *false positive* test. It has been pointed out that the social consequences of false positive tests for the AIDS virus are particularly serious.* Such a false positive test will unnecessarily "stigmatize and frighten many healthy people," since "most people consider a positive AIDS test to be a sentence to ghastly suffering and death." Meyer and Pauker therefore assert that it is important that a patient who tests positive for the AIDS virus have a high probability of really being infected. In order to focus on the false positive rate of the test, assume throughout this question that we are dealing with a test that properly identifies all persons who really are infected with the AIDS virus.

a. Assume that 5% of a population to be tested for the AIDS virus really is infected and that the test has a false positive rate of .5%. Find the probability that a person who tests positive really is infected.

b. Would your answer to part (a) be higher or lower if more than 5% of the population to be tested were actually infected? Answer the question by referring to the formula for conditional probability without performing any calculations.

c. Assume now that a low-risk population is to be tested. Specifically, assume that .01% of the population to be tested is actually infected with the AIDS virus and that the test has a false positive rate of .005% (which is unusually low). Find the probability that a person who tests positive really is infected.

d. What would your answer to part (c) be if you assumed a false positive rate of .5%?

e. Summarize the implications of your findings in parts (a) through (d).

---

* Klemens Meyer and Stephen Pauker, "Screening for HIV: Can We Afford the False Positive Rate?" *New England Journal of Medicine* (1987): 238–41.

SECTION 3.8 **SUMMARY**

Gamblers, businesspeople, and economists frequently find themselves in decision-making situations involving uncertain events. Probability is the basic tool they use to make rational judgments in such situations. The first step in assigning probabilities to uncertain events is to form a **sample space**—a listing of all of the simple events that can result from a random experiment. A **probability** (number between 0 and 1) is then assigned to each simple event, measuring the likelihood of occurrence of that outcome. The use of a **probability tree** often facilitates both the formation of a sample space and the assignment of probabilities to its simple events. Probabilities may then be computed for more complex events in accordance with rules of probability dealing with the **complement, union,** and **intersection** of events. The notion of **conditional probability** allows us to express the probability that a particular event will occur when some partial knowledge of the experimental outcome is available. In particular, **Bayes' theorem** is used to revise the probability that an event will occur, in light of newly acquired information.

SUPPLEMENTARY EXERCISES

GEN 3.74 The results of three flips of a fair coin are observed. Consider the following events:

- A: At least two heads are observed.
- B: Exactly one tails is observed.
- C: Exactly two tails are observed.

a. Define an appropriate sample space S for this experiment.

b. Assign probabilities to the simple events in S.

c. Find $P(A)$, by summing the probabilities of the simple events in A.

d. Find $P(\bar{B})$.

e. Find $P(B \cap C)$.

f. Find $P(A \cap B)$.

g. Find $P(B \mid A)$.

h. Is there a pair of independent events among A, B, and C?

i. Is there a pair of mutually exclusive events among A, B, and C?

3.75 There are three approaches to determining the probability that an outcome will occur: classical, relative frequency, and subjective. Which is appropriate in determining each of the following probabilities?

a. It will rain tomorrow.

b. A coin toss will result in heads.

c. A Michelin tire will last more than 40,000 miles.

d. When a single card is selected from a well-shuffled deck, it will be a diamond.

e. An automobile will pass quality-control inspection.

f. A firm's sales will grow by at least 10% next year.

3.76 Two six-sided dice are rolled, and the number of spots turning up on each is observed. Find the probability of each of the following:

a. Observing three spots on one die and five spots on the other

b. Observing exactly one die that has two spots showing

c. Observing that the sum of the spots showing is 7

d. Observing that the sum of the spots showing is 8

e. Observing that the sum of the spots showing is an even number

f. Observing that the sum of the spots showing is 8, given that the sum is an even number

3.77 Referring to Exercise 3.76, define the following events:

- A: The sum of the spots showing is 2, 3, or 12.
- B: The sum of the spots showing is an even number.

Are A and B independent events? Explain.

GEN 3.78 Exactly 100 employees of a firm have each purchased one ticket in a lottery, with the draw to be held at the firm's annual party. Of the 80 men who purchased tickets, 25 are single. Only 4 of the women who purchased tickets are single.

a. Find the probability that the lottery winner is married.

b. Find the probability that the lottery winner is a married woman.

c. If the winner is a man, what is the probability that he is married?

MNG **3.79**   A customer service supervisor regularly conducts a survey of customer satisfaction as part of a management control system. The results of his latest survey show that 5% of those surveyed are not satisfied with the service they receive. While only 30% of those surveyed are in arrears, 80% of the dissatisfied customer are in arrears. If the report on one customer surveyed is selected at random, find the probability that this customer is as follows:

a. In arrears and dissatisfied

b. Either in arrears or dissatisfied or both

RET **3.80**   As input into his pricing policy, the owner of an appliance store is interested in the relationship between the price at which an item is sold (regular or sale price) and the customer's decision on whether or not to purchase an extended warranty. The owner has constructed the accompanying table of probabilities, based on a study of 2,000 sales invoices. Suppose that one sales invoice is selected at random, with the relevant events being defined as follows:

- A: Item is purchased at regular price.
- B: Item is purchased at sale price.
- C: Extended warranty is purchased.
- D: Extended warranty is not purchased.

	Extended Warranty	
	Purchased	Not Purchased
Regular price	.21	.57
Sale price	.14	.08

Express each of the following probabilities in words, and find its value:

a. $P(A)$

b. $P(\bar{A})$

c. $P(C)$

d. $P(C \mid A)$

e. $P(C \mid B)$

f. $P(D \mid B)$

g. $P(B \mid D)$

h. $P(C \mid D)$

i. $P(A \cup B)$

j. $P(A \cap D)$

EDUC **3.81**   A *Forbes* survey of students attending leading American MBA schools determined that 96% expect a starting salary in excess of $25,000, while 92% expect a starting salary of under $50,000 (*Forbes,* 3 June 1985). If one of these students is selected at random, what is the probability that the student expects a starting salary of between $25,000 and $50,000?

MNG **3.82**   The director of an insurance company's computing center estimates that the company's computer has a 20% chance of "catching" a computer virus. However, she feels that there is only a 6% chance of the computer's "catching" a virus that will completely disable its operating system. If the company's computer should "catch" a virus, what is the probability that the operating system will be completely disabled?

GEN **3.83**   It is known that 3% of the tickets in a certain scratch-and-win game are winners, in the sense that the purchaser of such a ticket will receive a prize. If three tickets are purchased at random, what is the probability of each of the following?

a. All three tickets are winners.

b. Exactly one of the tickets is a winner.

c. At least one of the tickets is a winner.

FIN **3.84**   A financial analyst estimates that a certain mutual fund has a 60% chance of rising in value by more than 15% over the coming year. She also predicts that the stock market in general, as measured by the S&P 500 Index, has only a 20% chance of rising more than 15%. But if the Index does so, she feels that the mutual fund has a 95% chance of rising by more than 15%.

a. Find the probability that both the S&P 500 Index and the mutual fund will rise in value by more than 15%.

b. Find the probability that either the Index or the mutual fund, or both, will rise by more than 15%.

GEN **3.85** Because the likelihood of an event's occurring is sometimes expressed in terms of betting **odds** rather than probability, it is useful to be able to convert odds into probabilities, and vice versa. If the odds of an event's occurring are a to b, then the probability that the event will occur is $a/(a + b)$. The probability that the event will not occur is therefore $b/(a + b)$. Find the probability that an event A will occur, if the odds that A will occur are as follows:

a. 4 to 1   b. 3 to 2   c. 3 to 5

FIN **3.86** Many authors have developed models, based on financial ratios, that predict whether or not a company will go bankrupt in the next year. In a test of one such model, the model correctly predicted the bankruptcy of 85% of firms that in fact did fail, and it correctly predicted nonbankruptcy for 82% of firms that did not fail.* Suppose that the model maintains the same reliability when applied to a new group of 100 firms, of which 4 fail in the year following the time at which the model makes its predictions.

a. Determine the number of firms for which the model's prediction will prove to be correct.

b. Find the probability that one of these firms will go bankrupt, given that the model has predicted it will do so.

POM **3.87** A gas plant in Texas is equipped with a standby generator that automatically starts up if the main power fails. It is estimated that, on any given day, there is a 1.5% chance that the main power supply will fail. The standby generator is 95% reliable; should it fail, there is also a battery-driven utility power system (UPS) available. The UPS consists of six batteries connected in parallel so that power is supplied by the UPS if any one of the six batteries is properly charged. The UPS can supply sufficient power for n hours, where n is the number of batteries properly charged. For each of the six batteries, there is a probability of .1 that it is not properly charged.

---

* Edward Altman and Mario Lavallee, "Business Failure Classification in Canada," *Journal of Business Administration* 12 (1980): 147–64.

a. Find the probability that all three power sources will fail at the same time.

b. Find the probability that the UPS can supply power for at least 2 hours.

POM **3.88** The foreman in an iron foundry knows that the sand used for molding iron castings is too dry 5% of the time and too wet 2% of the time. He also knows that defective castings occur .5% of the time when the sand has the correct amount of moisture, 5% of the time when the sand is too dry, and 25% of the time when the sand is too wet. Suppose that a casting is selected at random from the batch just produced and is found to be defective. What is the probability that each of the following is true?

a. The sand was too wet.

b. The sand was too dry.

c. The sand had the correct amount of moisture.

MKT **3.89** The size of the price discount offered by an industrial marketing manager varies according to order size. During the last quarter, the manager offered price discounts of 20% to one-half of his customers and 30% to one-quarter of his customers, and no discount to the rest. He estimates that the probability of receiving a reorder this quarter is .90 if the customer received a 20% discount, .92 if the customer received a 30% discount, and .70 if the customer received no discount. If a customer is selected at random and is observed not to have reordered, what is the probability that this customer was offered no discount last quarter?

GEN **3.90** A novelty shop sells coins that come up heads two-thirds of the time. The result of flipping two of these coins is observed.

a. Define a sample space for this experiment.

b. Assign probabilities to the simple events.

c. Find the probability of observing exactly one heads.

GEN **3.91** A modern version of Russian roulette was invented the other day on a small southern Ontario campus by three students (Able, Baker, and Carter):

Line up six identical cars, two of which have had the master brake cylinder secretly removed by participating sweethearts. Each player then randomly selects one car, and one by one (in alphabetical order) they drive at high speed toward the edge of the cliff. At the cliff, they slam on the brakes in time to stop. The first player over the cliff loses, and the game stops.

Before they will agree to play the game, however, they want to understand the odds better, so they have posed the following two questions:

a. What is each player's probability of losing?

b. What is the probability that there will be no loser?

If it were your job to advise them, how would you answer each of these probing questions?

GEN **3.92** Rachel has reached the finals of her tennis club's annual tournament, but she must await the outcome of a match between Linda and Mary Ann before knowing who her opponent will be. Observers feel that Rachel has a 50% chance of winning if she plays Linda and a 75% chance of winning if she plays Mary Ann. They also believe that the probability that Linda will reach the finals is .8. After the final match is played, you are told that Rachel won. What is the probability that she played Linda?

GEN **3.93** Consider a roulette wheel that is divided into 36 equal segments, numbered from 1 to 36. The wheel has stopped at an even number on each of the last 16 spins. On the next spin of the wheel, would you bet on an even number or an odd number? Explain your answer.

GEN **3.94** Bill and Irma are planning to take a two-week vacation in Hawaii, but they can't decide whether to spend one week on each of the islands of Maui and Oahu, two weeks on Maui, or two weeks on Oahu. Agreeing to leave the decision to chance, Bill places two Maui brochures in one envelope, two Oahu brochures in a second envelope, and a brochure from each of the two islands in a third envelope. Irma is to select one envelope, and they will spend two weeks on Maui if it contains two Maui brochures, and so on. After selecting one envelope at random, Irma removes one brochure from the envelope and notes that it is a Maui brochure. What is the probability that the other brochure in the envelope is a Maui brochure? (HINT: Proceed with caution!)

■■■■■■■■ **CASE 3.1*** *GAINS FROM MARKET TIMING*

Many investment managers employ a strategy called *market timing,* according to which they forecast the direction of the overall stock market and adjust their investment holdings accordingly. A study conducted by Sharpe[†] provides insight into how accurate a manager's forecasts must be in order to make a market-timing strategy worthwhile.

Sharpe considers the case of a manager who, at the beginning of each year, either invests all funds in stocks for the entire year (if a good year is forecast) or places all funds in cash equivalents for the entire year (if a bad year is forecast). A good year is defined as one in which the rate of return on stocks (as represented by the Standard and Poor's Composite Index) is higher than the rate of return on cash equivalents (as represented by U.S. Treasury bills). A bad year is one that is not good. The average annual returns for the period from 1934 to 1972 on stocks and on cash equivalents, both for good years and for bad years, are shown in the accompanying table. Two-thirds of the years from 1934 to 1972 were good years.

---

* Some may wish to postpone this case until expected value has been covered, in Chapter 4.

† William F. Sharpe, "Likely Gains from Market Timing," *Financial Analysts' Journal* 31 (1975): 60–69.

a. Suppose that a manager decides to remain fully invested in the stock market at all times rather than employing market timing. What annual rate of return can this manager expect?

b. Suppose that a market timer accurately predicts a good year 80% of the time and accurately predicts a bad year 80% of the time. What is the probability that this manager will predict a good year? What annual rate of return can this manager expect?

c. What is the expected rate of return for a manager who has perfect foresight?

d. Consider a market timer who has no predictive ability whatsoever, but who recognizes that a good year will occur two-thirds of the time. Following Sharpe's description, imagine this manager "throwing a die every year, then predicting a good year if numbers 1 through 4 turn up, and a bad year if number 5 or 6 turns up." What is the probability that this manager will make a correct prediction in any given year? What annual rate of return can this manager expect?

	Average Annual Returns	
	Stocks	Cash Equivalents
Good year	22.99%	2.27%
Bad year	−7.70%	2.68%

SOLUTIONS TO SELF-CORRECTING EXERCISES

3.14 a. The random experiment consists of observing the number of surge suppressors sold in any given week.

b. $S = \{0, 1, 2, 3, 4\}$

c. $P\{0\} = 36/80$, $P\{1\} = 28/80$, $P\{2\} = 12/80$, $P\{3\} = P\{4\} = 2/80$

d. The relative frequency approach was used.

e. $P\{3, 4\} = P\{3\} + P\{4\} = 2/80 + 2/80 = 4/80 = .05$

3.24 Define the events:

A: An ace is selected.
B: A spade is selected.

a. Since 4 of the 52 cards in the deck are aces, $P(A) = \dfrac{4}{52} = \dfrac{1}{13}$.

b. Since there are 13 spades and 1 ace of spades in the deck,

$$P(A \mid B) = \frac{P(A \cap B)}{P(B)} = \frac{1/52}{13/52} = \frac{1}{13}$$

c. Yes, since $P(A) = P(A \mid B)$.

3.44 Define the events:

A: The company wins contract A.
B: The company wins contract B.

Since A and B are independent,

$$P(A \mid B) = P(A) = .5$$

$$P(B \mid A) = P(B) = .4$$

a. $P(A \cap B) = P(A) \cdot P(B \mid A)$
    $= (.5)(.4)$
    $= .2$

b. $P(A \cup B) = P(A) + P(B) - P(A \cap B)$
    $= .5 + .4 - .2$
    $= .7$

3.56 Refer to Figure S3.56. Define the events:

D_1: First component selected is defective.
D_2: Second component selected is defective.

The probability that neither component is defective is 42/90, or .47.

3.68 Refer to Figure S3.68. Define the events:

I: Item was assembled by inexperienced employee.
R: Item was returned.

Then $P(I) = .2$, $P(R \mid I) = .12$, and $P(R \mid \bar{I}) = .03$.

$$P(I \mid R) = \frac{P(I \cap R)}{P(R)} = \frac{.024}{.048} = .5$$

The probability that a returned item was assembled by an inexperienced employee is .5.

Figure S3.56

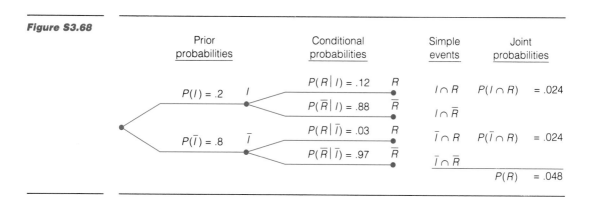

$$P(\overline{D}_1 \cap \overline{D}_2) = P(\overline{D}_1)P(\overline{D}_2 \mid \overline{D}_1)$$
$$= \left(\tfrac{7}{10}\right)\left(\tfrac{6}{9}\right) = \tfrac{42}{90}$$

Figure S3.68

Prior probabilities	Conditional probabilities		Simple events	Joint probabilities	
$P(I) = .2$ I	$P(R \mid I) = .12$	R	$I \cap R$	$P(I \cap R)$	$= .024$
	$P(\overline{R} \mid I) = .88$	$\overline{R}$	$I \cap \overline{R}$		
$P(\overline{I}) = .8$ $\overline{I}$	$P(R \mid \overline{I}) = .03$	R	$\overline{I} \cap R$	$P(\overline{I} \cap R)$	$= .024$
	$P(\overline{R} \mid \overline{I}) = .97$	$\overline{R}$	$\overline{I} \cap \overline{R}$		
				$P(R)$	$= .048$

PROBABILITY DISTRIBUTIONS

INTRODUCTION

This chapter extends our development of probability by first introducing the concept of a random variable, which allows us to summarize the results of an experiment in terms of numerical-valued outcomes. For example, if the experiment consists of selecting five items from a production run and observing how many are defective, the appropriate random variable would be defined as "the number of defective items." This random variable enables us to focus solely on the number of defective items observed, rather than having to concern ourselves with exactly which of the items selected are defective, the nature of the defects, and other such nonessential details.

After introducing random variables, we consider probability distributions, which summarize the probabilities of observing the various numerical observations. Two descriptive measures of a random variable and its probability distribution—expected value and variance—are covered next. The remainder of the chapter looks in detail at four specific, commonly used probability distributions: the binomial, Poisson, normal, and exponential distributions.

RANDOM VARIABLES AND PROBABILITY DISTRIBUTIONS

In most random experiments, we're interested only in a certain aspect of the experimental outcomes. The instrument we use to focus our attention on this particular aspect of an outcome (and to assign a numerical value to the outcome accordingly) is called a **random variable.** Consider once again the experiment described in Example 3.11, involving the selection of two coins from a box containing a nickel, two dimes, and a quarter. Recall that the sample space for this experiment was $S = \{ND, NQ, DN, DD, DQ, QN, QD\}$. Our primary interest in this experiment might be in the total sum of money selected, the number of dimes selected, or whether the quarter was selected. Each of these aspects of the outcome corresponds to a different random variable. Suppose, for example, that we're interested in the total sum of money selected. If X denotes the total sum of money observed, the value that X takes on will vary randomly from one trial of the experiment to the next, and X is called a *random variable*. In fact, X is a function that assigns a numerical value to each simple event in the sample space S, with the possible values of X being 15, 20, 30, and 35, as shown in Figure 4.1.

FIGURE 4.1   *RANDOM VARIABLE X ASSIGNING VALUES TO SIMPLE EVENTS*

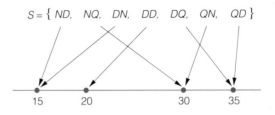

$$S = \{\ ND,\ \ NQ,\ \ DN,\ \ DD,\ \ DQ,\ \ QN,\ \ QD\ \}$$

15   20   30   35

A formal definition of a random variable might therefore read as follows.

Random Variable

A random variable is a function that assigns a numerical value to each simple event in a sample space.

Less formally, we might simply state that a *random variable is a variable whose numerical value is determined by the outcome of a random experiment.* Throughout this chapter, we will stress the distinction between a random variable and the values it can assume, by following the convention of using capital letters such as X and Y to denote random variables, and using lower-case letters such as x and y to denote their values. Although many people feel that this distinction in notation is unnecessary, we believe it is a useful one to maintain while you are becoming familiar with the notion of a random variable. The notational distinction is dropped in subsequent chapters, however, since the interpretation of x is usually clear from the context in which it is used.

A random variable summarizes the results of an experiment in such a way that the numerical-valued outcomes represent the events of interest to us. If our interest in the preceding experiment centers on the number of dimes selected from the box of four coins, we can define a new random variable, Y, to be "the number of dimes selected." The possible values of this random variable Y would be 0, 1, and 2. In practical situations, a random variable may have a similarly small number of possible values, or it may have a very large (or even infinite) number of possible values. The two main types of random variables—discrete and continuous—are distinguished from one another by the number of possible values that they can assume.

Discrete and Continuous Random Variables

A random variable is discrete if it can assume only a countable number of possible values. A random variable that can assume an uncountable number of values is continuous.

A discrete random variable has a finite or countably infinite number of possible values. In most practical situations, a discrete random variable counts the number of times a particular attribute is observed. Examples of discrete random variables include the number of defective items in a production batch, the number of telephone calls received in a given hour, and the number of customers served by a tavern on a given day. If X denotes the number of customers served by a tavern on a particular day, then X can take any one of the values $x = 0, 1, 2, \ldots$.

A continuous random variable has an uncountably infinite number of possible values; that is, it can take on any value in one or more intervals of values. Continuous random variables typically record the value of a measurement such as time, weight, or length. For example, if X represents the time taken by a student to write a 60-minute exam, X can take any one of infinitely many possible values: $0 \leq x \leq 60$.

For the time being, we will restrict our attention to discrete random variables; and having considered the values of a random variable, we now turn to the probabilities with which those values are assumed. Once we know the possible values of a random variable and the probabilities with which those values are assumed, we have the **probability distribution** of the random variable—our main object of interest.

Discrete Probability Distribution

A table, formula, or graph that lists all of the possible values a discrete random variable can assume, together with their associated probabilities, is called a *discrete probability distribution*.

The probability associated with a particular value of a random variable is determined in a manner you can probably anticipate. If x is a value of a random variable X, then the probability that X assumes the value x, denoted either by $P(X = x)$ or by $p(x)$, is the sum of the probabilities associated with the simple events for which X assumes the value x.

Let's apply this rule to the experiment involving the selection of two coins from a box of four coins (Example 3.11). If the random variable X represents the total sum of money selected, X can assume any one of the values 15, 20, 30, or 35. Probabilities can be assigned to the values of X with the help of Table 4.1, which records each simple event, its probability, and the corresponding value of x. (Recall that the simple event probabilities shown in Table 4.1 were calculated in Example 3.11, with the help of a probability tree.) For example, X takes the value 15 if either the simple event ND or the simple event DN occurs, so

$$P(X = 15) = P(ND) + P(DN)$$
$$= 2/12 + 2/12$$
$$= 4/12$$

The distinct values of X and their associated probabilities are summarized in Table 4.2, which gives the probability distribution of X. The probability distribution

TABLE 4.1	VALUES OF X CORRESPONDING TO SIMPLE EVENTS

Simple Event	x	Probability
ND	15	2/12
NQ	30	1/12
DN	15	2/12
DD	20	2/12
DQ	35	2/12
QN	30	1/12
QD	35	2/12

TABLE 4.2	PROBABILITY DISTRIBUTION OF X

x	$p(x)$
15	4/12
20	2/12
30	2/12
35	4/12

of X can be presented in the tabular form shown in Table 4.2, in the graphical form of Figure 4.2, or in terms of the following formula:

$$p(x) = \begin{cases} 2/12 & \text{if } x = 20 \text{ or } 30 \\ 4/12 & \text{if } x = 15 \text{ or } 35 \end{cases}$$

In an example such as this one, where the formula is rather cumbersome, the tabular representation of the probability distribution of X is most convenient. Whichever representation is used, a discrete probability distribution must satisfy two conditions, which follow from the basic requirements for probabilities outlined in Chapter 3.

Requirements of Discrete Probability Distribution

If a random variable X can take values $x_1, x_2, \ldots, x_n$, then

(i) $0 \le p(x_i) \le 1$ for $i = 1, 2, \ldots, n$

(ii) $\sum_{i=1}^{n} p(x_i) = 1$

FIGURE 4.2   GRAPHICAL PRESENTATION OF PROBABILITY DISTRIBUTION

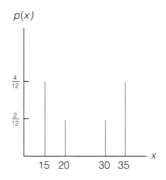

Once a probability distribution has been defined for a random variable X, we may talk about the probability that X takes a value in some range of values. The probability that X takes a value between a and b inclusive, denoted by $P(a \leq X \leq b)$, is obtained by summing the probabilities $p(x)$ for all values of x such that $a \leq x \leq b$. In the preceding example, we would have

$$P(15 \leq X \leq 20) = p(15) + p(20)$$
$$= 4/12 + 2/12$$
$$= 6/12$$

In other words, the probability that the total sum of money selected is either 15 or 20 cents is 6/12, or .5.

EXERCISES

LEARNING THE TECHNIQUES

4.1 Consider a random variable X with the following probability distribution:

x	$p(x)$
-4	.2
0	.3
1	.4
2	.1

Find the following probabilities:

a. $P(X > 0)$ b. $P(X \geq 0)$

c. $P(0 \leq X \leq 1)$ e. $P(X = -2)$

d. $P(X = -4)$ f. $P(X < 2)$

4.2 Consider a random variable X with the following probability distribution:

$p(x) = .1x,$ $x = 1, 2, 3,$ or 4

Express the probability distribution in tabular form, and use it to find the following probabilities:

a. $P(X \geq 1)$ d. $P(X = 4)$

b. $P(X > 1)$ e. $P(X = 3.5)$

c. $P(2 \leq X \leq 3)$

4.3 Determine which of the following are not valid probability distributions, and explain why not.

a.

x	*p(x)*
1	.2
2	.2
3	.3
4	.4

b.

x	*p(x)*
0	−.1
2	.2
4	.3
5	.4

c.

x	*p(x)*
−2	.1
−1	.1
1	.1
2	.7

4.4 Let *X* be the number of spots turning up when a six-sided die is tossed.

a. Express the probability distribution of *X* in tabular form.

b. Express the probability distribution of *X* in graphical form.

4.5 Let *X* be the number of heads that are observed when a fair coin is flipped three times.

a. Express the probability distribution of *X* in tabular form.

b. Express the probability distribution of *X* in graphical form.

APPLYING THE TECHNIQUES

Self-Correcting Exercise (See Appendix 4.A for the solution.)

GEN **4.6** Let *X* represent the number of children under 18 years old in an American family. According to the *Statistical Abstract of the United States: 1985*, the probability distribution of *X* is as follows:

x	0	1	2	3	4	5
p(x)	.50	.21	.19	.07	.02	.01

a. Express the probability distribution of *X* in graphical form.

b. Comment on the symmetry or skewness of the distribution.

c. What is the most likely number of children in a family?

d. What is the probability of a family's having more than two children?

GEN **4.7** Let *X* represent the number of people in an American household. According to the *Statistical Abstract of the United States: 1988*, the probability distribution of *X* is as follows (rounded to two decimal places):

x	1	2	3	4	5	6	7
p(x)	.23	.31	.18	.16	.07	.03	.02

a. Express the probability distribution in graphical form.

b. Comment on the symmetry or skewness of the distribution.

c. What is the most likely number of people in a household?

d. What is the probability of a household's having fewer than four people? More than seven people?

MNG **4.8** Using historical data, the personnel manager of a plant has determined that the probability distribution of *X*, the number of employees absent on any given day, is as follows:

x	0	1	2	3	4	5	6	7
p(x)	.005	.025	.310	.340	.220	.080	.019	.001

a. Express the probability distribution of *X* in graphical form.

b. Comment on the symmetry or skewness of the distribution.

c. Find the probability that $2 \leq X \leq 4$.

d. Find the probability of there being more than one absentee on a given day.

RET **4.9** A mutual fund saleswoman has arranged to call upon three households tomorrow. Based on past experience, she feels that there is a 20% chance of closing a sale on each call, and that the outcome of each call is independent of the others. Let *X* represent the number of sales she closes tomorrow.

a. Find the probability distribution of *X*.

b. Express the probability distribution of *X* graphically.

c. What is the probability that more than one sale will be closed tomorrow?

SECTION 4.3   ## EXPECTED VALUE AND VARIANCE

A probability distribution is the distribution of a population. Consider, for example, the probability distribution shown in Table 4.3, where the random variable X represents the payoff (in dollars) from a proposed investment of $25.

We can conceive of the underlying population in the following way. Imagine a barrel containing infinitely many chips, of which one-half are labeled 20, one-quarter are labeled 40, and one-quarter are labeled 60. If X denotes the label on a chip that is randomly selected from the population of chips, the probability distribution of X is as shown in Table 4.3.

Now, consider the population of labels on all chips. We may wish to find the mean of this population, just as we did with the populations encountered back in Chapter 2, where we defined the *mean of a population* of N values of x to be

$$\mu = \frac{\sum_{i=1}^{N} x_i}{N} = \sum_{i=1}^{N} x_i \cdot 1/N$$

For the infinitely large population of labels, however, we must replace $1/N$ with the probability, or relative frequency, with which x_i occurs. The mean of such a population, called the **mean value** of X, is therefore given by

$$\mu = \sum x \cdot p(x)$$

where the sum is taken over all values of X. This is also referred to as the **expected value** of X, written $E(X)$. Hence, the expected value of the payoff from the $25 investment is

$$E(X) = \mu$$
$$= 20(\tfrac{1}{2}) + 40(\tfrac{1}{4}) + 60(\tfrac{1}{4}) = \$35$$

In general, we have the following definition.

> **Expected Value**
>
> Given a discrete random variable X with values $x_1, x_2, \ldots, x_n$ that occur with probabilities $p(x_i)$, the expected value of X is
>
> $$E(X) = \sum_{i=1}^{n} x_i \cdot p(x_i)$$

TABLE 4.3   *PROBABILITY DISTRIBUTION OF X*

x	$p(x)$
20	1/2
40	1/4
60	1/4

The expected value of a random variable X is the weighted average of the possible values it may assume, where the weights are the probabilities of occurrence of those values. The expected value of X should be interpreted simply as a weighted average of the possible values of X, rather than as a value that X is expected to assume. In fact, as the preceding example illustrates, $E(X)$ may not even be a possible value of X.

An alternative interpretation of the expected value of X employs the long-run relative frequency approach to probability described in Chapter 3. If the investment in the foregoing example were undertaken repeatedly a large number of times, the expected value of X, $35, would be a good approximation to the average payoff resulting from the many investments.

LAWS OF EXPECTED VALUE

Various algebraic identities or laws are available to help simplify the calculation of an expected value. Although the proofs are not difficult, the laws are stated here without proof. The end-of-section Exercises 4.21 and 4.22 provide you with opportunities to verify these laws.

If X and Y are random variables and c is any constant, the following identities hold:

(i) $E(c) = c$

(ii) $E(cX) = cE(X)$

(iii) $E(X + Y) = E(X) + E(Y)$
$E(X - Y) = E(X) - E(Y)$

(iv) $E(XY) = E(X)E(Y)$, if X and Y are independent random variables*

The utility of these laws derives from the fact that, given a function of one or more random variables, the expected value of the terms the function comprises may already be known or may be easier to compute than is the expected value of the function itself. For example, if the random variable X is the number of units of an item that are produced daily, a is the variable cost of production per unit, and b is the daily fixed cost of production, the total daily production cost is $Y = aX + b$. The expected daily production cost is $E(Y) = aE(X) + b$. Calculating $E(X)$ and then using the formula is normally easier than finding $E(Y)$ directly.

---

* Although beginning students of statistics will not normally find occasion to use this law, it is included for completeness. Two random variables X and Y are said to be *independent* if the value assumed by one variable in no way affects the probability of a particular value's being assumed by the other. That is, X and Y are independent if $P(X = x \mid Y = y_0) = P(X = x)$ or, equivalently, if $P(Y = y \mid X = x_0) = P(Y = y)$, for all x_0 and y_0.

VARIANCE

The expected value of a random variable X is a weighted average of the values of X; it therefore provides us with a measure of the central location of the distribution of X. It does not tell us, however, whether the values of X are clustered closely about the expected value or are widely scattered. That is, the mean, or expected value, of a random variable does not by itself adequately describe the random variable. Just as was the case in Chapter 2, we need a measure of dispersion.

Recall that a popular measure of the dispersion of a population of N measurements $x_1, \ldots, x_N$ is the variance, given by

$$\sigma^2 = \frac{\sum_{i=1}^{N}(x_i - \mu)^2}{N} = \sum_{i=1}^{N}(x_i - \mu)^2 \cdot 1/N$$

The variance of a random variable X is defined in a similar manner, with $1/N$ being replaced by $p(x_i)$. We may then describe the variance of a random variable X as the weighted average of the squared deviations of the values of X from their mean μ, with the weight attached to $(x_i - \mu)^2$ being $p(x_i)$—the probability with which that squared deviation occurs. In other words, the variance of X is the expected value of the random variable $(X - \mu)^2$.

Variance

Let X be a discrete random variable with possible values $x_1, x_2, \ldots, x_n$ that occur with probabilities $p(x_i)$, and let $E(X) = \mu$. The variance of X is defined to be

$$\sigma^2 = E[(X - \mu)^2] = \sum_{i=1}^{n}(x_i - \mu)^2 p(x_i)$$

Notice that a variance is always nonnegative, since each item in the summation is nonnegative. Alternative notations for the variance of X are σ_X^2 and $V(X)$, both of which are useful ways to indicate the random variable in question.

To illustrate the computation of variance, consider once again the probability distribution (Table 4.3) for X, the payoff from an investment of \$25. The variance of the payoff is

$$\sigma_X^2 = (20 - 35)^2\left(\frac{1}{2}\right) + (40 - 35)^2\left(\frac{1}{4}\right) + (60 - 35)^2\left(\frac{1}{4}\right)$$
$$= 275 \text{ (dollars)}^2$$

A variance, considered by itself, is somewhat difficult to interpret. The notion of variance is therefore chiefly used to compare the variabilities of different distributions, which may (for example) represent the possible outcomes of alternative courses of action under consideration. One important application arises in finance, where variance is the most popular numerical measure of risk; the underlying assumption is that a larger variance corresponds to a higher level of risk.

Let Y represent the payoff from a second proposed investment of $25. The possible payoffs in this case are $10, $40, and $80, occurring with probabilities 1/2, 1/4, and 1/4, respectively. The expected value of Y can be shown to be $35—the same as the expected value of X—but the variance of Y is 825 (dollars)^2, as you can verify. If the riskiness of the investments is measured by the variance of their payoffs, the second proposed investment is riskier than the first, since $\sigma_Y^2 > \sigma_X^2$. This risk assessment is probably consistent with the intuitive impression you would obtain from a casual comparison of the distributions of X and Y.

The variance of X is defined to be $E[(X - \mu)^2]$. By expanding $(X - \mu)^2$ and applying the laws of expected value, we can identify an alternative formulation of the variance of X:

$$\sigma_X^2 = E(X^2) - \mu^2$$

This **shortcut for computing the variance** is useful because the calculation of $E(X^2)$ is often simpler than the direct computation of σ_X^2, which involves squared deviations. Like that of any other random variable, the expected value of X^2 is obtained by taking the weighted average of its possible values:

$$E(X^2) = \sum_{i=1}^{n} x_i^2 p(x_i)$$

As was the case in Chapter 2 with a set of measurement data, we may wish to express the variability of X in terms of a measure having the same units as does X. Once again, this is accomplished by taking the positive square root of the variance.

Standard Deviation

The standard deviation of a random variable X, denoted σ, is the positive square root of the variance of X.

For instance, the standard deviation of X, the payoff from the first proposed investment, is

$$\sigma_X = \sqrt{275} = \$16.58$$

EXAMPLE 4.1

Now that the new models are available, a car dealership has lowered the prices on last year's models in order to clear its holdover inventory. With prices slashed, a young and aggressive salesman estimates the following probability distribution of

X, the total number of cars that he'll sell next week:

x	0	1	2	3	4
$p(x)$	.05	.15	.35	.25	.20

Determine the expected value and the standard deviation of X.

Solution. The expected value, variance, and standard deviation of X can be calculated directly from their definitions:

$$E(X) = \mu = \sum_{i=1}^{5} x_i p(x_i)$$
$$= 0(.05) + 1(.15) + 2(.35) + 3(.25) + 4(.20)$$
$$= 2.40$$
$$V(X) = \sigma^2 = \sum_{i=1}^{5} (x_i - 2.4)^2 p(x_i)$$
$$= (0 - 2.4)^2(.05) + (1 - 2.4)^2(.15) + (2 - 2.4)^2(.35)$$
$$+ (3 - 2.4)^2(.25) + (4 - 2.4)^2(.20)$$
$$= 1.24$$
$$\sigma = \sqrt{1.24}$$
$$= 1.11$$

The expected number of cars that the salesman will sell next week is 2.4, with a standard deviation of 1.11.

A convenient alternative for computational purposes is to record the probability distribution of X (and subsequent computations) in a table such as Table 4.4. Rather than having a column for $(x - \mu)^2$, we have chosen to use the

---

TABLE 4.4   *COMPUTATIONS FOR $E(X)$ AND $E(X^2)$*

x	$p(x)$	$xp(x)$	x^2	$x^2 p(x)$
0	.05	0	0	0
1	.15	.15	1	.15
2	.35	.70	4	1.40
3	.25	.75	9	2.25
4	.20	.80	16	3.20
Total		$2.40 = E(X)$		$7.00 = E(X^2)$

shortcut formula for variance, which entails finding the expected value of X^2. Therefore, from Table 4.4,

$$E(X) = \mu = 2.4$$
$$V(X) = E(X^2) - \mu^2 = 7 - (2.4)^2 = 1.24$$
$$\sigma = \sqrt{1.24} = 1.11$$

While the mean of 2.4 is a measure of the center of the distribution, the standard deviation 1.11 measures the dispersion of the values about the center. Knowing only these two measures, rather than the entire distribution, we could state (using Chebyshev's theorem from Chapter 2) that at least $(1 - 1/2^2)$ of the values of X lie within two standard deviations of the mean. That is, at least three-quarters of the values of X lie in the interval

$$(\mu - 2\sigma, \mu + 2\sigma) = [2.4 - 2(1.11), 2.4 + 2(1.11)]$$
$$= (.18, 4.62)$$

The foregoing statement is valid for any distribution that has a mean of 2.4 and a standard deviation of 1.11. For this particular example, where we know the entire distribution, we observe that in fact 95% of the values of X lie in the interval (.18, 4.62). In other words, there is a 95% chance that our young salesman will sell at least one car.

LAWS OF VARIANCE

Just as with the calculation of expected value, various laws help simplify the calculation of variance; they are stated here without proof.

If X and Y are random variables and c is a constant, the following identities hold:

(i) $V(c) = 0$

(ii) $V(cX) = c^2 V(X)$

(iii) $V(X + c) = V(X)$

(iv) $V(X + Y) = V(X) + V(Y)$, and
$V(X - Y) = V(X) + V(Y)$, if X and Y are independent

EXAMPLE 4.2

In Example 4.1, the young salesman estimated the probability distribution of X (the total number of cars he would sell next week) to be

x	0	1	2	3	4
$p(x)$	.05	.15	.35	.25	.20

TABLE 4.5	*COMPUTATIONS FOR $E(Y)$ AND $E(Y^2)$*			

y	$p(y)$	$yp(y)$	y^2	$y^2p(y)$
150	.05	7.5	22,500	1,125
350	.15	52.5	122,500	18,375
550	.35	192.5	302,500	105,875
750	.25	187.5	562,500	140,625
950	.20	190.0	902,500	180,500
Total		$630.0 = E(Y)$		$446,500 = E(Y^2)$

Subsequent calculations revealed that $E(X) = 2.4$ and $V(X) = 1.24$. Now suppose that this salesman earns a fixed weekly wage of \$150 plus a \$200 commission for each car sold. His weekly wage is therefore $Y = 200X + 150$. What is his expected wage for next week? What is the variance of Y?

Solution.   The probability distribution of Y and the computations for $E(Y)$ and $E(Y^2)$ are shown in Table 4.5. From it, we know that $E(Y) = 630$ and that $V(Y) = E(Y^2) - \mu^2 = 446,500 - (630)^2 = 49,600$. Rather than performing the mind-numbing calculations in Table 4.5, we could simply use the laws of expected value and variance:

$$
\begin{aligned}
E(Y) &= E(200X + 150) \\
&= 200E(X) + 150 \\
&= 200(2.4) + 150 \\
&= 630 \\
V(Y) &= V(200X + 150) \\
&= (200)^2 V(X) \\
&= (200)^2 (1.24) \\
&= 49,600
\end{aligned}
$$

The young salesman's expected wage for next week is therefore \$630, with a variance of 49,600 (dollars)^2.

EXAMPLE 4.3

Theresa, an avid baseball fan, is planning an excursion from Detroit to Toronto to watch her beloved Tigers play a weekend series against the Blue Jays in August. She has read that the daily high temperatures for August in Toronto have a mean of

27.5°C and a variance of 6.2 (Celsius degrees)^2. Now she wants to find the mean and the variance of the high temperatures in Fahrenheit degrees.

Solution.   Temperature readings in Celsius (C) can be converted into Fahrenheit (F) by means of the linear transformation

$$F = 1.8C + 32$$

In Fahrenheit degrees, the expected high temperature is

$$\begin{aligned} E(F) &= 1.8E(C) + 32 \\ &= (1.8)(27.5) + 32 \\ &= 81.5°F \end{aligned}$$

and the variance is

$$\begin{aligned} V(F) &= (1.8)^2 V(C) \\ &= (3.24)(6.2) \\ &= 20.09 \text{ (Fahrenheit degrees)}^2 \end{aligned}$$

EXERCISES

LEARNING THE TECHNIQUES

4.10   Let X be a random variable with the following probability distribution:

x	1	2	3	4
$p(x)$	.4	.3	.2	.1

a. Find $E(X)$ and $V(X)$.

b. Is $E(X)$ a possible value of X?

4.11   Let X be a random variable with the following probability distribution:

x	−4	0	1	2
$p(x)$	.2	.3	.4	.1

a. Find μ and σ.

b. Is μ a possible value of X?

c. Find $E(X^2)$ and $E(3X^2 + 2)$.

4.12   Let X be a random variable with the following probability distribution:

x	5	10	15	20	25
$p(x)$	.05	.30	.25	.25	.15

a. Find the expected value and variance of X.

b. Find the expected value and variance of $Y = 4X - 3$.

4.13   Let X be a random variable with the following probability distribution:

x	−10	−5	0	5	10
$p(x)$	.10	.20	.20	.20	.30

a. Find the mean and standard deviation of X.

b. Find the mean and standard deviation of $2X$.

c. Find the mean and standard deviation of $2X + 5$.

4.14   Let X be a random variable with the following probability distribution:

x	0	5	10	20
$p(x)$	.2	.3	.3	.2

a. Find the mean and standard deviation of X.

b. Find $E(X^2)$.

c. Find $E(5X^2)$.

APPLYING THE TECHNIQUES

GEN **4.15** Let X represent the number of times a student visits a nearby pizza parlor in a 1-month period. Assume that the following table is the probability distribution of X:

x	$p(x)$
0	.1
1	.3
2	.4
3	.2

a. Find the mean (μ) and the standard deviation (σ) of this distribution.

b. What is the probability that the student visits the pizza parlor at least twice in a month?

c. Find $P(X \geq 1.5)$.

d. Construct a graph of the probability distribution, and locate μ and the interval $\mu \pm \sigma$ on the graph.

Self-Correcting Exercise (See Appendix 4.A for the solution.)

MNG **4.16** The owner of a small firm has just purchased a microcomputer, which she expects will serve her for the next 2 years. The owner has been told that she "must" buy a surge suppressor to provide protection for her new hardware against possible surges or variations in the electrical current. Her son David, a recent university graduate, advises that an inexpensive suppressor could be purchased that would provide protection against one surge only. He notes that the amount of damage without a suppressor would depend on the extent of the surge. David conservatively estimates that, over the next 2 years, there is a 1% chance of incurring $400 damage and a 2% chance of incurring $200 damage. But the probability of incurring $100 damage is .1.

a. How much should the owner be willing to pay for a surge suppressor?

b. Determine the standard deviation of the possible amounts of damage.

FIN **4.17** In Exercise 3.32, it was noted that insurance companies rely heavily on probability theory when computing the premiums to charge for various life insurance and annuity products. Suppose that a 40-year-old male purchases a $100,000 10-year term life policy from an insurance company, meaning that the insurance company must pay out $100,000 if the insured male dies within the next 10 years.

a. Use the accompanying life table to determine the insurance company's expected payout on this policy.

b. What would the expected payout be if the same policy were taken out by a 50-year-old male?

NUMBER OF DEATHS AT VARIOUS AGES OUT OF 100,000 AMERICAN MALES BORN ALIVE

Age Interval*	Number of Deaths
0–1	1,527
1–10	495
10–20	927
20–30	1,901
30–40	2,105
40–50	4,502
50–60	10,330
60–70	19,954
70–80	28,538
80 and over	29,721
Total	100,000

* Interval contains all ages from lower limit up to (but not including) upper limit.

SOURCE: *Life Tables, Vital Statistics of the United States* (1978), U.S. Department of Health and Human Services.

GEN **4.18** Suppose that you have the choice of receiving $500 in cash or receiving a gold coin that has a face value of $100. The actual value of the gold coin depends on its gold content. You are told that the coin has a 40% chance of being worth $400, a 30% chance of being worth $900, and a 30% chance of being worth its face value. If you base your decision on expected value, which should you choose?

MKT **4.19** In order to examine the effectiveness of its four annual advertising promotions, a mail-order company has sent a questionnaire to each of its customers, asking how many of the previous year's promotions prompted orders that otherwise would not have been made. The following table summarizes the data received, where the random variable X is the number of promotions indicated in the customer's responses:

x	$p(x)$
0	.10
1	.25
2	.40
3	.20
4	.05

a. Assuming that the responses received were accurate evaluations of individual effectiveness, and that customer behavior in the coming year will not change, what is the expected number of promotions that each customer will take advantage of next year by ordering goods that otherwise would not be purchased?

b. What is the variance of X?

c. A previous analysis of historical data found that the mean value of orders for promotional goods is $12.50, with the company earning a gross profit of 20% on each order. The fixed cost of conducting the four promotions next year is estimated to be $15,000, with a variable cost of $3.00 per customer for mailing and handling costs. Assuming that the survey results can be used as an accurate predictor of behavior for existing and potential customers, how large a customer base must the company have to cover the cost of the promotions?

4.20 Let X be a random variable with mean μ and standard deviation σ. Consider a new random variable, Z, obtained by subtracting the constant μ from X and dividing the result by the constant σ: $Z = (X - \mu)/\sigma$. The variable Z is called a **standardized random variable.** Use the laws of expected value and variance to show the following:

a. $E(Z) = 0$

b. $V(Z) = 1$

4.21 Let X and Y be two independent random variables with the following probability distributions:

x	$p(x)$		y	$p(y)$
2	.3		0	.2
4	.5		1	.6
6	.2		2	.2

To illustrate the laws of expected value and variance, verify the following equalities by separately evaluating the two sides of each.

a. $E(3X) = 3E(X)$
$V(3X) = 9V(X)$

b. $E(Y + 4) = E(Y) + 4$
$V(Y + 4) = V(Y)$

c. $E(X + Y) = E(X) + E(Y)$
$V(X + Y) = V(X) + V(Y)$

d. $E(X - Y) = E(X) - E(Y)$
$V(X - Y) = V(X) + V(Y)$

4.22 Refer to Exercise 4.21. Since X and Y are independent random variables, the probability $p(xy)$ is given by $P(X = x$ and $Y = y) = p(x)p(y)$.

a. Verify that the probability distribution of the random variable XY is given by

xy	0	2	4	6	8	12
$p(xy)$	.20	.18	.36	.12	.10	.04

b. Verify that $E(XY) = E(X)E(Y)$, by separately evaluating each side of the equality.

SECTION 4.4 ***BINOMIAL DISTRIBUTION***

Having considered the basic properties of probability distributions in general, we now consider in detail the binomial distribution—the first of four important specific probability distributions. The binomial distribution is probably the single most important discrete distribution. An important characteristic of the underlying binomial random experiment is that there are only two possible outcomes. Experiments having such a dichotomy of outcomes are numerous: a coin flip results in heads or tails; an election candidate is favored or not; a product is defective or nondefective; an employee is male or female; and an invoice being audited is correct or incorrect. It is conventional to apply the generic labels **success** and **failure** to the two possible outcomes. Binomial experiments of interest usually involve several repetitions or trials of the basic experiment, and these trials must satisfy the conditions outlined in the definition of a binomial experiment.

Binomial Experiment

A binomial experiment possesses the following properties:

1. The experiment consists of a fixed number n of trials.
2. The result of each trial can be classified into one of two categories: success or failure.
3. The probability p of a success remains constant for each trial.
4. Each trial of the experiment is independent of the other trials.

An example of a binomial experiment is to flip a coin ten times and observe the result of each flip. Which of the two possible outcomes of each trial (flip) is designated a success is arbitrary. We will designate the appearance of heads as a success. Assuming that the coin is fair, the probability of a success is $p = .5$ for each of the ten trials. Clearly, each trial is independent of the others. Our main interest in a binomial experiment such as this is the number of successes (heads) observed in the ten trials. The random variable that records the number of successes (heads) observed in the $n = 10$ trials is called the *binomial random variable*.

Binomial Random Variable

The binomial random variable indicates the number of successes in the n trials of a binomial experiment.

A binomial random variable is therefore a discrete random variable that can take on any one of the values 0, 1, 2, . . . , n. The probability distribution of this random variable, called the **binomial probability distribution,** gives us the probability

FIGURE 4.3   PROBABILITY TREE FOR THREE TRIALS OF A BINOMIAL EXPERIMENT

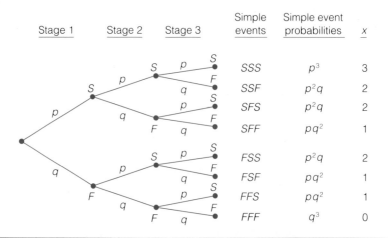

that a success will occur x times in the n trials, for $x = 0, 1, 2, \ldots, n$. Rather than working out binomial probabilities from scratch each time, we would do better to have a general formula for calculating the probabilities associated with any binomial experiment. As a first step toward developing this formula, let's look at another binomial experiment.

Consider a binomial experiment consisting of $n = 3$ trials, with the two possible outcomes of each trial being designated S (success) and F (failure). The binomial random variable X indicates the number of successes in the three trials. Let p denote the probability of a success in any trial, and let q denote the probability of a failure, where $\boldsymbol{q = (1 - p)}$. The possible outcomes of any binomial experiment can be represented by a probability tree, with the stages corresponding to the trials of the experiment. The probability tree for this experiment is shown in Figure 4.3.

Recall from Chapter 3 that the probability attached to a branch of the tree is the conditional probability of that branch outcome's occurring. But because the trials of a binomial experiment are independent, the conditional probability that any branch outcome will occur is the same as the unconditional probability that it will. The simple event probabilities are obtained by applying the multiplication rule for independent events. As an example, the probability that SSF will occur is $p \cdot p \cdot q = p^2 q$.

Once all of the simple event probabilities are found, the binomial probabilities appearing in Table 4.6 can be determined by summing the (simple event) probabilities associated with a given value x. For example, there is only one simple event (FFF) for which $x = 0$, and its probability is q^3. Hence, $p(0) = q^3$. But there are three simple events with exactly $x = 1$ success: SFF, FSF, and FFS. Since each of these simple events occurs with probability $p^2 q$, the probability of exactly one suc-

TABLE 4.6	*BINOMIAL DISTRIBUTION FOR n = 3*

x	$p(x)$
0	q^3
1	$3pq^2$
2	$3p^2q$
3	p^3

cess is $p(1) = 3pq^2$. The probabilities $p(2)$ and $p(3)$ are obtained in a similar manner. The complete probability distribution of X is shown in Table 4.6.

It is impractical to resort to a probability tree each time we wish to find a binomial probability distribution. Instead, we need a general formula for the probability $p(x)$ of obtaining x successes in the n trials, when the probability of a success is p. To this end, notice that we will observe exactly x successes in the n trials whenever we observe a simple event with a total of x S's and $(n - x)$ F's. One such simple event is

$$\underbrace{SS \quad \cdots \quad S}_{x \text{ times}}\underbrace{FF \quad \cdots \quad F}_{(n - x) \text{ times}}$$

Applying the multiplication rule for independent events, we see that the probability that any such simple event will occur is $p^x q^{n-x}$, since p is the probability of a success and $q = (1 - p)$ is the probability of a failure. We must now multiply this probability by the number of simple events having exactly x successes. But the number of simple events with exactly x successes is the same as the number of ways of choosing the x stages at which a success occurs. This number is given by the following counting rule, where the notation $n!$ is read "n factorial." A common alternative to the notation C_x^n used here is $\binom{n}{x}$.

Counting Rule

The number of different ways of choosing x objects from a total of n objects is

$$C_x^n = \frac{n!}{x!(n - x)!}$$

where

$$n! = n(n - 1)(n - 2)\cdots(2)(1)$$

and $0!$ is defined to be 1.

TABLE 4.7	*BINOMIAL COEFFICIENTS* ($n = 3$)

x	C_x^3
0	$C_0^3 = \dfrac{3!}{0!(3-0)!} = \dfrac{3!}{0!3!} = \dfrac{3 \cdot 2 \cdot 1}{(1)(3 \cdot 2 \cdot 1)} = 1$
1	$C_1^3 = \dfrac{3!}{1!(3-1)!} = \dfrac{3!}{1!2!} = \dfrac{3 \cdot 2 \cdot 1}{(1)(2 \cdot 1)} = 3$
2	$C_2^3 = \dfrac{3!}{2!(3-2)!} = \dfrac{3!}{2!1!} = \dfrac{3 \cdot 2 \cdot 1}{(2 \cdot 1)(1)} = 3$
3	$C_3^3 = \dfrac{3!}{3!(3-3)!} = \dfrac{3!}{3!0!} = \dfrac{3 \cdot 2 \cdot 1}{(3 \cdot 2 \cdot 1)(1)} = 1$

Let's use this counting rule to determine the number of simple events that have exactly x successes (for $x = 0$, 1, 2, and 3) in the $n = 3$ trials of the experiment depicted by the probability tree in Figure 4.3. The four values to be calculated (called binomial coefficients, with values recorded in Table 4.7) can be checked against the values that were previously determined by counting the simple events at the end of the probability tree, on page 162. The binomial probabilities $p(x)$ in Table 4.6 are now obtained by multiplying these four (binomial) coefficients by the corresponding probabilities $p^x q^{n-x}$, for $x = 0$, 1, 2, and 3.

We are now in a position to give the general formulation of the binomial probability distribution.

Probability Distribution of a Binomial Experiment

If the random variable X is the number of successes in the n trials of a binomial experiment that has probability p of a success on any given trial, the probability distribution of X is given by

$$P(X = x) = p(x) = C_x^n p^x q^{n-x}$$

$$= \left(\frac{n!}{x!(n-x)!}\right) p^x q^{n-x}, \quad x = 0, 1, \ldots, n$$

Each pair of values (n, p) determines a distinct binomial distribution. Graphical representations of three binomial distributions are shown in Figure 4.4. Each of the $(n + 1)$ possible values of a binomial random variable X has a positive probability of occurring. The fact that some possible values of X do not have a vertical line above them in Figure 4.4 simply means that the probability that those values will occur is too small to be displayed on the graph. A binomial distribution is symmetrical whenever $p = .5$, and it is asymmetrical otherwise.

FIGURE 4.4   *GRAPHS OF THREE BINOMIAL DISTRIBUTIONS*

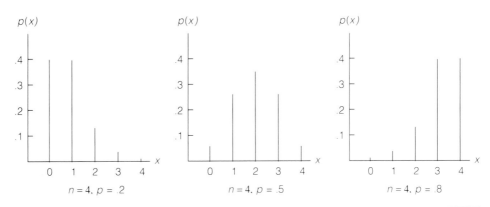

EXAMPLE 4.4

The quality-control department of a manufacturer tested the most recent batch of 1,000 catalytic converters produced and found 50 of them defective. Subsequently, an employee unwittingly mixed the defective converters in with the nondefective ones. If a sample of <u>three</u> converters is randomly selected from the mixed batch, what is the probability distribution of the number of defective converters in the sample?

Solution.   The first thing to do is to make sure that the conditions for a binomial experiment are satisfied. The experiment consists of a fixed number of $n = 3$ trials, with each trial resulting in one of two possible outcomes: a defective converter (success) or a nondefective converter (failure). The probability p of selecting a defective converter does not remain constant for each trial, however, since the probability of selecting a defective converter on a given trial depends on the results of the previous trials. In other words, the trials are not independent. The probability of selecting a defective converter on the first trial is $50/1,000 = .05$. But if a defective converter is selected on the first trial, the probability of selecting a defective converter on the second trial is $49/999 = .049$. In practical situations, this slight violation of the conditions of a binomial experiment is often considered negligible. While p does vary from trial to trial, it remains quite close to .05. The violation would become important, however, if we were sampling from a batch of 100 widgets of which only 5 were defective. In that case, p would change appreciably from trial to trial—especially if one of the defective widgets were selected on an earlier trial—and the binomial model should not be used.

  Returning to the original problem, let's assume that the binomial model adequately describes the situation and that $p = .05$ for each trial. Let X be the binomial random variable indicating the number of defective converters in the sample of three. We may then compute

$$P(X = 0) = p(0) = \frac{3!}{0!3!}(.05)^0(.95)^3 = .8574$$

$$P(X = 1) = p(1) = \frac{3!}{1!2!}(.05)^1(.95)^2 = .1354$$

$$P(X = 2) = p(2) = \frac{3!}{2!1!}(.05)^2(.95)^1 = .0071$$

$$P(X = 3) = p(3) = \frac{3!}{3!0!}(.05)^3(.95)^0 = .0001$$

We thereby obtain the probability distribution of the number of defective converters in the sample of three, as shown in Table 4.8.

USING THE BINOMIAL TABLES

An alternative way of presenting the binomial distribution ($n = 3, p = .05$) in Table 4.8 is depicted in Table 4.9. The difference here is that the probabilities in Table 4.9 are **cumulative probabilities** that represent the sum of binomial probabilities from $x = 0$ to $x = k$. If $k = 1$, for example, we have

$$P(X \leq 1) = \sum_{x=0}^{1} p(x) = p(0) + p(1)$$

$$= .8574 + .1354$$

$$= .9928$$

The advantage of working with such a table of cumulative binomial probabilities is that it enables us to find, more quickly, the probability that X will assume some value within a range of values.

Individual binomial probabilities are obtained from Table 4.9 by subtraction. For example, the probability of exactly two successes is

$$p(2) = P(X \leq 2) - P(X \leq 1)$$

$$= \sum_{x=0}^{2} p(x) - \sum_{x=0}^{1} p(x)$$

$$= .9999 - .9928$$

$$= .0071$$

Calculating binomial probabilities by means of the formula, as illustrated in Example 4.4, is time-consuming and tiresome when n is large. Fortunately, tables identifying these probabilities are available. One such table is Table 1 in Appendix B at the back of this book, which presents cumulative binomial distributions for various values of n and p. (Although the probabilities in the preceding example were computed to four decimal places, the binomial probabilities provided by Table 1 are

TABLE 4.8	BINOMIAL DISTRIBUTION ($n = 3$, $p = .05$)

x	$p(x)$
0	.8574
1	.1354
2	.0071
3	.0001

TABLE 4.9	CUMULATIVE BINOMIAL DISTRIBUTION ($n = 3$, $p = .05$)

k	$\sum\limits_{x=0}^{k} p(x)$
0	.8574
1	.9928
2	.9999
3	1.0000

rounded to three decimal places.) A partial reproduction of this table, for $n = 5$, is shown in Table 4.10. The 15 columns in Table 4.10, corresponding to 15 different values of p, represent 15 distinct binomial distributions. Individual tabulated values are of the form

$$P(X \leq k) = \sum_{x=0}^{k} p(x)$$

To find the probability of at most three successes in $n = 5$ trials of a binomial experiment with $p = .2$, we locate the entry corresponding to $k = 3$ and $p = .2$:

$$P(X \leq 3) = \sum_{x=0}^{3} p(x)$$
$$= p(0) + p(1) + p(2) + p(3)$$
$$= .993$$

Notice that the final probability in each column (distribution) of the table—that is, reading horizontally, the row corresponding to $k = n$—has been omitted. This probability will always be equal to 1, since, for $k = n$

$$P(X \leq k) = P(X \leq n) = 1$$

TABLE 4.10 PARTIAL REPRODUCTION OF TABLE I: BINOMIAL PROBABILITIES FOR $n = 5$*

				p				
k	.01	.05	.10	.20	.25	.30	.40	.50
0	.951	.774	.590	.328	.237	.168	.078	.031
1	.999	.977	.919	.737	.633	.528	.337	.188
2	1.000	.999	.991	.942	.896	.837	.683	.500
3	1.000	1.000	1.000	.993	.984	.969	.913	.812
4	1.000	1.000	1.000	1.000	.999	.998	.990	.969

k	.60	.70	.75	.80	.90	.95	.99	
0	.010	.002	.001	.000	.000	.000	.000	
1	.087	.031	.016	.007	.000	.000	.000	
2	.317	.163	.104	.058	.009	.001	.000	
3	.663	.472	.367	.263	.081	.023	.001	
4	.922	.832	.763	.672	.410	.226	.049	

* Tabulated values are $P(X \leq k) = \sum_{x=0}^{k} p(x)$. (Entries are rounded to three decimal places.)

We have just seen how to use Table 1 in Appendix B to save time in finding binomial probabilities. There is also a time-saving procedure for finding the mean and the variance of a binomial random variable. While these two parameters could be calculated in the usual time-consuming way—using the definitional formulas involving summations—it can be shown that the mean and the variance of a binomial random variable are given by the following pair of formulas.

Mean and Variance of Binomial Random Variables

If X is a binomial random variable, the mean and the variance of X are

$$E(X) = \mu = np$$
$$V(X) = \sigma^2 = npq$$

EXAMPLE 4.5

A shoe store's records show that 30% of customers making a purchase use a credit card to make payment. This morning, 20 customers purchased shoes from the store.

a. Using Table 1 of Appendix B, find the probability that at least 12 of the customers used a credit card.

b. What is the probability that at least 3 customers, but not more than 6, used a credit card?

c. What is the expected number of customers who used a credit card?

d. Find the probability that exactly 14 customers did not use a credit card.

e. Find the probability that at least 9 customers did not use a credit card.

Solution.   If making payment with a credit card is designated as a success, we have a binomial experiment with $n = 20$ and $p = .3$. Let X denote the number of customers who used a credit card.

a. We must first express the probability we seek in the form $P(X \leq k)$, since this is the form in which probabilities are tabulated in Table 1:

$$P(X \geq 12) = P(X = 12) + P(X = 13) + \cdots + P(X = 20)$$
$$= P(X \leq 20) - P(X \leq 11)$$

Because the probabilities in a binomial distribution must sum to 1, $P(X \leq 20) = 1$. From Table 1, $P(X \leq 11) = .995$. Therefore,

$$P(X \geq 12) = 1 - .995 = .005$$

The probability that at least 12 customers used a credit card is .005.

b. Expressing the probability we seek in the form used for the probabilities tabulated in Table 1, we have

$$P(3 \leq X \leq 6) = P(X = 3) + P(X = 4) + P(X = 5) + P(X = 6)$$
$$= P(X \leq 6) - P(X \leq 2)$$
$$= .608 - .035 = .573$$

The probability that between 3 and 6 customers used a credit card is .573.

c. The expected number of customers who used a credit card is

$$E(X) = np = 20(.3) = 6$$

d. Let Y denote the number of customers who did not use a credit card. The probability that a customer did not use a credit card is $(1 - .3) = .7$. This part of the example can be solved in either of two ways:

   (i) You can interchange the designations of success and failure and work with $p = .7$.

   (ii) You can express the required probability in terms of the number of customers who did not use a credit card, and proceed with $p = .3$.

Method (i) is probably easier to use with the tables in the text. In many cases, however, binomial tables with p values above .5 are not available, and method (ii) must be used.

   Using method (i) begins with recognizing that, since the original assignment of the designations *success* and *failure* was arbitrary, we may interchange them. If not using a credit card is designated as a success, then $p = .7$. From Table 1, we find that

$$P(Y = 14) = P(Y \leq 14) - P(Y \leq 13)$$
$$= .584 - .392$$
$$= .192$$

In method (ii) we retain the original designation, according to which using a credit card is a success and $p = .3$. If 14 customers did not use a credit card, the number of customers who did use one is $(20 - 14) = 6$. Hence,

$$P(Y = 14) = P(X = 6)$$
$$= P(X \leq 6) - P(X \leq 5)$$
$$= .608 - .416$$
$$= .192$$

Using either method, we find that the probability that exactly 14 customers did not use a credit card is .192.

e. Again, let Y denote the number of customers who did not use a credit card. If not using a credit card is designated as a success, then $p = .7$. Expressing the required probability in terms of values tabulated in Table 1, we have

$$P(Y \geq 9) = 1 - P(Y \leq 8)$$
$$= 1 - .005$$
$$= .995$$

The probability that at least 9 customers did not use a credit card is .995.

EXERCISES

LEARNING THE TECHNIQUES

4.23 Evaluate the following binomial coefficients:

a. C_2^5

b. C_2^6

c. C_4^6

d. C_0^7

e. C_7^7

4.24 Consider a binomial random variable X with $n = 4$ and $p = .6$.

a. Find the probability distribution of X, and graph it.

b. Find $P(X \leq 2)$.

c. Find the mean and the variance of X.

4.25 Let X be a binomial random variable. Use the formula to compute the following probabilities:

a. $P(X = 2)$, if $n = 8$ and $p = .1$

b. $P(X = 5)$, if $n = 9$ and $p = .5$

c. $P(X = 9)$, if $n = 10$ and $p = .95$

4.26 Use Table 1 in Appendix B to check your answers to Exercise 4.25.

4.27 Let X be a binomial random variable. Use the formula to compute the following probabilities:

a. $P(X = 3)$, if $n = 5$ and $p = .2$

b. $P(X = 2)$, if $n = 6$ and $p = .3$

c. $P(X = 5)$, if $n = 7$ and $p = .75$

4.28 Use Table 1 in Appendix B to check your answers to Exercise 4.27.

4.29 Given a binomial random variable X with $n = 15$ and $p = .3$, find the following probabilities, using Table 1 in Appendix B.

a. $P(X \leq 2)$

b. $P(X \geq 7)$

c. $P(X = 6)$

d. $P(4 \leq X \leq 8)$

e. $P(X \geq 12)$

f. $P(7 < X < 10)$

4.30 Given a binomial random variable X with $n = 25$ and $p = .6$, find the following probabilities, using Table 1 in Appendix B.

a. $P(X \leq 10)$

b. $P(X \geq 12)$

c. $P(X = 15)$

d. $P(18 \leq X \leq 21)$

e. $P(18 < X < 21)$

GEN **4.31** A sign on the gas pumps of a certain chain of gasoline stations encourages customers to have their oil checked, claiming that one out of every four cars should have its oil topped up.

a. Of the next 10 cars entering a station, what is the probability that exactly three of them should have their oil topped up?

b. What is the probability that at least half of the next 10 cars entering a station should have their oil topped up? At least half of the next 20 cars?

APPLYING THE TECHNIQUES

Self-Correcting Exercise (See Appendix 4.A for the solution.)

EDUC **4.32** A multiple-choice quiz has 15 questions. Each question has five possible answers, of which only one is correct.

a. What is the probability that sheer guesswork will yield at least seven correct answers?

b. What is the expected number of correct answers by sheer guesswork?

EDUC **4.33** A student majoring in accounting is trying to decide upon the number of firms to which she

should apply. Given her work experience, grades, and extracurricular activities, she has been told by a placement counselor that she can expect to receive a job offer from 80% of the firms to which she applies. Wanting to save time, the student applies to five firms only. Assuming the counselor's estimate is correct, find the probability that the student receives

a. no offers

b. at most two offers

c. between two and four offers (inclusive)

d. five offers

ACC **4.34** An auditor is preparing for a physical count of inventory as a means of verifying its value. Items counted are reconciled with a list prepared by the storeroom supervisor. Normally 20% of the items counted cannot be reconciled without reviewing invoices. The auditor selects ten items.

a. Find the probability of each of the following:
   (i) Up to four items cannot be reconciled.
   (ii) At least six items cannot be reconciled.
   (iii) Between four and six items (inclusive) cannot be reconciled.

b. If it normally takes 20 minutes to review the invoice for an item that cannot be reconciled and one hour for the balance of the count, how long should the auditor expect the physical count to take?

GEN **4.35** Flight delays at major American airports are an increasing source of exasperation to executives, who may miss important appointments as a result. About 190,000 flights were delayed by more than 15 minutes during the first six months of 1984, with many of the delays lasting hours (*Fortune*, 1 October 1984). During this period, 13% of all arrivals and departures at New York's LaGuardia Airport experienced delays of at least 15 minutes. The corresponding level of delays at Denver's Stapleton Airport was about 5%. Suppose that an executive made three round trips from Denver and New York during this period.

a. Find the probability that the executive experienced at least four delays of 15 minutes or more at Stapleton Airport during arrival or departure.

b. Find the probability that the executive experienced no delays of 15 minutes or more upon arrival at, or departure from, LaGuardia Airport during the three trips.

c. Find the probability that the executive experi-

enced no delays of 15 minutes or more during the three round trips.

d. What assumptions have you made in solving the first three parts of this exercise?

SECTION 4.5   ## *POISSON DISTRIBUTION*

A second important discrete distribution is the Poisson distribution. Whereas a binomial random variable counts the number of successes that occur in a fixed number of trials, a Poisson random variable counts the number of rare events that occur (successes) in a specified time interval or a specified region. Activities to which the Poisson distribution can be successfully applied include counting the number of telephone calls received by a switchboard in a specified time period, counting the number of arrivals at a service location (such as a service station, tollbooth, or grocery checkout counter) in a given time period, and counting the number of bacteria in a specified culture. In order that the Poisson distribution may be appropriately applied to situations such as these, three conditions must be satisfied, as enumerated in the accompanying box. In the following description of a Poisson experiment, *success* refers to the occurrence of the event of interest, and *interval* refers to either an interval of time or an interval of space (such as an area or region).

Poisson Experiment

A Poisson experiment possesses the following properties:

1. The number of successes that occur in any interval is independent of the number of successes that occur in any other interval.

2. The probability that a success will occur in an interval is the same for all intervals of equal size and is proportional to the size of the interval.

3. The probability that two or more successes will occur in an interval approaches zero as the interval becomes smaller.

The Poisson model thus is applicable when the events of interest occur *randomly, independently* of one another, and *rarely,* as specified by the preceding conditions. In particular, condition 3 specifies what is meant by *rarely*. The arrival of individual diners at a restaurant, for example, would not fit the Poisson model because diners usually arrive with companions, violating the independence condition.

Poisson Random Variable

The Poisson random variable indicates the number of successes that occur during a given time interval or in a specified region in a Poisson experiment.

Probability Distribution of Poisson Random Variables

If X is a Poisson random variable, the probability distribution of X is given by

$$P(X = x) = p(x) = \frac{e^{-\mu}\mu^x}{x!}, x = 0, 1, 2, \ldots$$

where μ is the average number of successes occurring in the given time interval or region, and $e = 2.71828\ldots$ is the base of the natural logarithms.

Notice that, since μ (the average number of successes occurring in a specified interval) appears in the formula for the Poisson probability $p(x)$, we must obtain an estimate of μ—usually from historical data—before we can apply the Poisson distribution. Care must be taken to ensure that the intervals specified in the definitions of X and μ are the same size, and that the same units are used for each.

Although the computation of a Poisson probability may be performed by using the formula, it requires us to calculate $e^{-\mu}$. If your calculator will not perform this calculation, you must resort to tabulated values of $e^{-\mu}$, but this becomes impractical when you wish to find the probability that a Poisson random variable will assume any one of a large number of specified values. Fortunately, there is an easier method. To ease the computation of Poisson probabilities, we have included tabulated values of cumulative Poisson probabilities in Table 2 of Appendix B.

There is no limit to the number of values a Poisson random variable can assume. The Poisson random variable is a discrete random variable with infinitely many possible values—unlike the binomial random variable, which has only a finite number. If X is a Poisson random variable for which μ is the average number of successes that occur in a specified interval, the expected value and the variance of X have the same value:

$$E(X) = V(X) = \mu$$

The graphs of three specific Poisson distributions are shown in Figure 4.5.

FIGURE 4.5   GRAPHS OF THREE POISSON DISTRIBUTIONS

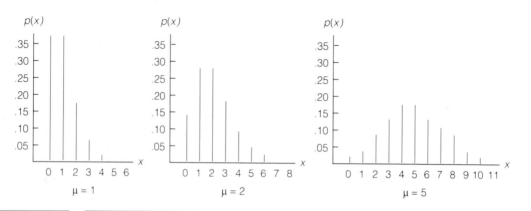

μ = 1   μ = 2   μ = 5

EXAMPLE 4.6

A tollbooth operator has observed that cars arrive randomly at an average rate of 360 cars per hour.

a. Using the formula, calculate the probability that only 2 cars will arrive during a specified 1-minute period.

b. Using Table 2 of Appendix B, find the probability that only 2 cars will arrive during a specified 1-minute period.

c. Using Table 2, find the probability that at least 4 cars will arrive during a specified 1-minute period.

Solution.   Let X denote the number of arrivals during the 1-minute period. Then the mean value of X is $\mu = 360/60 = 6$ cars per minute. Notice that we have defined both X and μ in terms of the same time interval: 1 minute.

a. According to the formula for a Poisson probability, the probability of exactly two arrivals is

$\lambda = u$
$\lambda = 6v$

$$P(X = 2) = \frac{(e^{-6})(6^2)}{2!}$$

$P(x) = \dfrac{e^{-\lambda} \lambda^x}{x!}$ or $\dfrac{e^{-u} u^x}{x!}$

$$= \frac{(.00248)(36)}{2 \cdot 1}$$

$e = 2.718$

$$= .0446$$

The value of e^{-6} was obtained by using a calculator.

b. According to the cumulative Poisson probabilities in Table 2, the probability of exactly two arrivals is

$$P(X = 2) = P(X \le 2) - P(X \le 1)$$
$$= .0620 - .0174$$
$$= .0446$$

c. The probability of at least four arrivals is

$$P(X \ge 4) = 1 - P(X \le 3)$$
$$= 1 - .1512$$
$$= .8488$$

POISSON APPROXIMATION OF THE BINOMIAL

Although binomial and Poisson random variables have distinct distributions, the two distributions are related. If we imagine a Poisson random variable whose interval has been subdivided into n (where n is large) very small subintervals, the probability of a success in any subinterval is approximately $p = \mu/n$, and we have an approximate binomial random variable. Similarly, a binomial distribution for which the number of trials n is large and the probability p of a success is very small can be approximated by a Poisson distribution. This is useful because, for large values of n, binomial probability tables are often unavailable.

The appropriate Poisson distribution to use for the approximation will have $\mu = np$, the mean for the binomial distribution. In order for the approximation to be a good one, p should be very small. It is conventional to suggest that p be sufficiently small to make $np < 5$ when n is large—say, $n > 100$. Hence, at the least, we should have $p < .05$.

EXAMPLE 4.7

A warehouse engages in **acceptance sampling** to determine if it will accept or reject incoming lots of designer sunglasses, some of which invariably are defective. Specifically, the warehouse has a policy of examining a sample of 50 sunglasses from each lot and of accepting the lot only if the sample contains no more than 2 defective pairs. What is the probability of a lot's being accepted if, in fact, 2% of the sunglasses in the lot are defective?

Solution.   We are dealing with a binomial experiment for which $n = 50$ and $p = .02$. The required probability cannot be found by using the binomial tables in this text because n is too large. But since n is reasonably large and the expected number of defective sunglasses in the sample is $np = 50(.02) = 1$, which is less than 5, the required probability can be approximated by using the Poisson distribution with

TABLE 4.11 COMPARISON OF BINOMIAL AND POISSON PROBABILITIES

x	Binomial Probability ($n = 50$, $p = .02$)	Poission Probability ($\mu = np = 1$)
0	.364	.368
1	.372	.368
2	.186	.184
3	.061	.061
4	.014	.015
5	.003	.003
6	.000	.001

$\mu = 1$. From Table 2 of Appendix B, we find that the probability that a sample contains at most 2 defective pairs of sunglasses is .920.

For purposes of illustrating how well the Poisson distribution approximates the binomial distribution in this example, we have reproduced the two distributions in Table 4.11. Probabilities corresponding to values of x greater than 7 are omitted because they consist entirely of zeroes to four decimal places. Summing the first three probabilities in the table, we see that the true (binomial) probability of accepting a lot containing 2% defective sunglasses is .922, while the Poisson approximation to this probability is .920. The Poisson approximation to the binomial distribution in this example is excellent.

EXERCISES

LEARNING THE TECHNIQUES

4.36 Compute the following Poisson probabilities, using the formula.

a. $P(X = 4)$, if $\mu = 1$

b. $P(X \leq 1)$, if $\mu = 1.5$

c. $P(X \geq 2)$, if $\mu = 2$

4.37 Repeat Exercise 4.36 using Table 2 of Appendix B.

4.38 Let X be a Poisson random variable with $\mu = 5$. Use Table 2 to find the following probabilities:

a. $P(X \leq 5)$

b. $P(X = 5)$

c. $P(X \geq 7)$

4.39 Suppose that X is a Poisson random variable whose distribution has a mean of 2.5. Use Table 2 to find the following probabilities:

a. $P(X \leq 3)$

b. $P(X = 6)$

c. $P(X \geq 2)$

d. $P(X > 2)$

4.40 Graph the probability distribution of a Poisson random variable with $\mu = .5$.

4.41 Let X be a binomial random variable with $n = 25$ and $p = .01$.

a. Use Table 1 in Appendix B to find $P(X = 0)$, $P(X = 1)$, and $P(X = 2)$.

b. Approximate the three probabilities in part (a), using the appropriate Poisson distribution. (You will need a calculator.) Compare your approximations with the exact probabilities found in part (a).

4.42 Let X be a binomial random variable with $n = 25$ and $p = .05$.

a. Use Table 1 in Appendix B to find $P(X = 0)$, $P(X = 1)$, and $P(X = 2)$.

b. Approximate the three probabilities in part (a), using the appropriate Poisson distribution. (You will need a calculator.) Compare your approximations with the exact probabilities found in part (a).

APPLYING THE TECHNIQUES

4.43 The number of calls received by a switchboard operator between 9 and 10 A.M. has a Poisson distribution with a mean of 12. Find the probability that the operator received at least 5 calls during the following periods:

a. between 9 and 10 A.M.

b. between 9 and 9:30 A.M.

c. between 9 and 9:15 A.M.

Self-Correcting Exercise (See Appendix 4.A for the solution.)

MKT **4.44** The marketing manager of a company has noted that she usually receives 10 complaint calls from customers during a week (consisting of 5 working days), and that the calls occur at random. Find the probability of her receiving 5 such calls in a single day.

POM **4.45** The numbers of accidents that occur on an assembly line have a Poisson distribution, with an average of 3 accidents per week.

a. Find the probability that a particular week will be accident-free.

b. Find the probability that at least 3 accidents will occur in a week.

c. Find the probability that exactly 5 accidents will occur in a week.

d. If the accidents occurring in different weeks are independent of one another, find the expected number of accidents in a year.

GEN **4.46** During the summer months (June to August inclusive), an average of 5 marriages per month take place in a small city. Assuming that these marriages occur randomly and independently of one another, find the probability that:

a. fewer than 4 marriages will occur in June

b. at least 14 but not more than 18 marriages will occur during the entire 3 months of summer

c. exactly 10 marriages will occur during the 2 months of July and August

4.47 The number of arrivals at a service counter between 1:00 and 3:00 P.M. has a Poisson distribution with a mean of 14.

a. Find the probability that the number of arrivals between 1:00 and 3:00 P.M. is at least 8.

b. Find the probability that the number of arrivals between 1:30 and 2:00 P.M. is at least 8.

c. Find the probability of there being exactly 1 arrival between 2:00 and 3:00 P.M.

FIN **4.48** A snow-removal company bills its customers on a per snowfall basis, rather than at a flat monthly rate. Based on the fee it charges per snowfall, the company will just break even in a month that has exactly 6 snowfalls. Suppose that the average number of snowfalls per month (during the winter) is 8.

a. What is the probability that the company will just break even in a given winter month?

b. What is the probability that the company will make a profit in a given winter month?

GEN **4.49** A biologist knows that about 1% of a certain breed of frogs mutate. Given a random sample of 50 developing frogs, what is the probability that the sample will contain at least 1 mutated frog?

POM **4.50** A paper manufacturer claims that less than 1 in 100 of its reels (two-ton rolls) of paper is flawed. A large customer has just received a shipment of these reels and proceeds to check a random sample of 600 of them for flaws. Of this sample, 14 reels are found to be flawed.

a. What was the probability of finding at least 14 flawed reels in this sample?

b. Based on your answer to part (a), what would you conclude about the manufacturer's claim?

SECTION 4.6   CONTINUOUS PROBABILITY DISTRIBUTIONS

Up to this point, we have focused our attention on discrete distributions — distributions of random variables that have either a finite number of possible values (for example: $x = 0, 1, 2, \ldots, n$) or a countably infinite number of values ($x = 0, 1, 2, \ldots$). In contrast, a continuous random variable has an uncountably infinite number of possible values and can assume any value in the interval between two points a and b ($a < x < b$). Whereas discrete random variables typically involve counting, continuous random variables typically involve measurement attributes such as length, weight, time, and temperature.

One major distinction between a continuous random variable and a discrete one relates to the numerical events of interest. We can list all of the possible values of a discrete random variable, and it is meaningful to consider the probability that a particular individual value will be assumed. On the other hand, we cannot list all of the values of a continuous random variable — since there is always another possible value between any two of its values — so the only meaningful events for a continuous random variable are intervals. The probability that a continuous random variable X will assume any particular value is zero. While this may appear strange at first, it becomes reasonable when you consider that you could not possibly assign a positive probability to each of the (uncountably) infinitely many values of X and still have the probabilities sum to one. This situation is analogous to the fact that, while a line segment has a positive length, no point on the line segment does. For a continuous random variable X, then, it is only meaningful to talk about the probability that the value assumed by X will fall within some interval of values.

We first encountered continuous data in Chapter 2, when we measured the durations of long-distance telephone calls. The relative frequency histogram for telephone-call durations (Figure 2.2) is reproduced in Figure 4.6, with one slight alteration: the heights of the rectangle have been scaled down so that the total area under the histogram is equal to 1. The area under a rectangle now represents the proportion of measurements falling into that class. For example, the area under the first rectangle is 3(3/90) = 3/30, which is the proportion of telephone-call durations falling between two and five minutes. If we had taken a very large sample of measurements, the resulting relative frequency distribution would closely approximate the relative frequency distribution of the entire population of telephone-call durations, and the proportion represented by the area of a rectangle would be a very good approximation of the true probability of obtaining a measurement in the class interval corresponding to that rectangle. Experience has shown that, as the size of

FIGURE 4.6   *RELATIVE FREQUENCY HISTOGRAM*

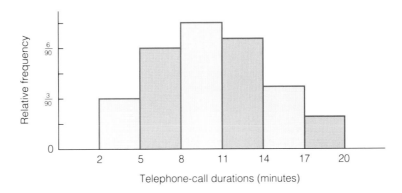

the sample of measurements becomes larger and as the class width is reduced, the outline of the relative frequency distribution tends toward a smooth curve. That is, the shape of the relative frequency polygon (adjusted to have a total area equal to 1) for the entire population of measurements progressively approaches a smooth curve.

When dealing with continuous data, we attempt to find a function $f(x)$, called a *probability density function,* whose graph approximates the relative frequency polygon for the population. A probability density function $f(x)$ must satisfy two conditions:

1. $f(x)$ is nonnegative.
2. The total area under the curve representing $f(x)$ equals 1.

It is important to note that $f(x)$ is not a probability. That is, $f(x) \neq P(X = x)$. As previously mentioned, the probability that X will take any specific value is zero: $P(X = x) = 0$. Given a probability density function $f(x)$, the area under the graph of $f(x)$ between the two values a and b is the probability that X will take a value between a and b.* This area is the shaded area in Figure 4.7.

A continuous random variable X has an expected value and a variance, just as a discrete random variable does. Earlier in this chapter, we saw how to compute the expected value and the variance of any discrete random variable; we also saw that,

---

* Students who have taken calculus will recognize that

$$P(a < X < b) = \int_a^b f(x)\,dx$$

The two conditions to be satisfied by a probability density function $f(x)$ are $f(x) \geq 0$ and

$$\int_{-\infty}^{\infty} f(x)\,dx = 1$$

FIGURE 4.7   *PROBABILITY DENSITY FUNCTION f(x) (SHADED AREA IS P(a < X < b))*

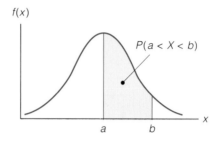

when dealing with a well-known discrete distribution such as the binomial or Poisson, we need not calculate the expected value and the variance from their definitions, since these parameters are well-known. Similarly, most continuous distributions used in practice are well-known ones having expected values and variances that are also well-known and therefore need not be computed.*

UNIFORM DISTRIBUTION

A continuous distribution that possesses appealing descriptive simplicity but unfortunately has limited practical application (except as a theoretical tool) is the *uniform distribution.* The domain of a uniform random variable X consists of all values within some interval $a \leq x \leq b$.

Uniform Distribution

A random variable X, defined over an interval $a \leq x \leq b$, is uniformly distributed if its probability density function is given by

$$f(x) = \frac{1}{b - a}, \qquad a \leq x \leq b$$

---

* For students who are interested and know calculus, the expected value and the variance of a continuous random variable X with probability density function $f(x)$ are given by

$$E(X) = \mu = \int_{-\infty}^{\infty} xf(x)\,dx$$

$$V(X) = \sigma^2 = \int_{-\infty}^{\infty} (x - \mu)^2 f(x)\,dx$$

These expressions are the same as those for the discrete case, except that summation is replaced by integration.

FIGURE 4.8   UNIFORM DISTRIBUTION

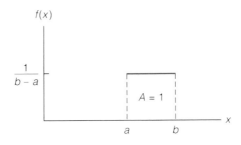

It can be shown that the expected value and the variance of a uniform random variable X are as follows:

$$E(X) = \frac{a + b}{2}$$

$$V(X) = \frac{(b - a)^2}{12}$$

Notice that the expected value of X is simply the midpoint of the domain of X, which should appeal to your intuition, given the symmetrical shape of the probability density function of X. As is evident from Figure 4.8, the values of a uniform random variable X are distributed evenly, or uniformly, across the domain of X. In other words, intervals of equal size within the domain of X are equally likely to contain the value that the variable X will assume.

Notice that the total area A under the uniform density function $f(x)$ equals 1, as is required for any probability density function. The area A of the rectangle under $f(x)$ is the height of the rectangle, $1/(b - a)$, times its base:

$$A = \left(\frac{1}{b - a}\right) \cdot (b - a) = 1$$

The probability that X will take a value within any given interval is found in a similar manner, by multiplying $1/(b - a)$ by the width of the interval in question.

EXAMPLE 4.8

A manufacturer has observed that the time that elapses between the placement of an order with a just-in-time supplier and the delivery of the parts is uniformly distributed between 100 and 180 minutes.

a. Define and graph the density function.

b. What proportion of orders take between 2 and 2.5 hours to be delivered?

FIGURE 4.9   SHADED AREA IS $P(120 \leq X \leq 150)$

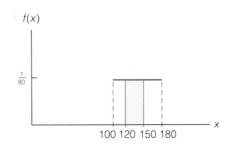

Solution

a. If X denotes the number of minutes that elapse between the placement and delivery of the order, then X can take any value in the interval $100 \leq x \leq 180$. Since the width of the interval is 80, the height of the density function must be $1/80$, in order for the total area under the density function to equal 1. That is, the density function is

$$f(x) = 1/80, \ 100 \leq x \leq 180$$

the graph of which is shown in Figure 4.9.

b. The required probability, which is represented by the shaded area in Figure 4.9, is

$$P(120 \leq x \leq 150) = (\text{Base})(\text{Height}) = (150 - 120)(1/80) = .375$$

EXERCISES

4.51   Consider a random variable X with a probability density function described by

$$f(x) = -.5x + 1, \ 0 \leq x \leq 2$$

a. Graph the density function $f(x)$.

b. Verify that $f(x)$ is a probability density function.

c. Find $P(X \geq 1)$.

d. Find $P(X \leq .5)$.

e. Find $P(X = 1.5)$.

Self-Correcting Exercise (See Appendix 4.A for the solution.)

4.52   Consider a random variable X having the uniform density function $f(x)$, with $a = 20$ and $b = 30$.

a. Define and graph the density function $f(x)$.

b. Verify that $f(x)$ is a probability density function.

c. Find $P(22 \leq X \leq 30)$.

d. Find $P(X = 25)$.

4.53   Consider a random variable X with a probability density function described by

$$f(x) = \begin{cases} .2 + .04x, & -5 \leq x \leq 0 \\ .2 - .04x, & 0 \leq x \leq 5 \end{cases}$$

a. Graph the density function $f(x)$.

b. Verify that $f(x)$ is a probability density function.

c. Find $P(X \geq -2)$.

d. Find $P(X \le 3)$

e. Find $P(3 \le X \le 5)$.

4.54 A hospital receives a pharmaceutical delivery each morning at a time that varies uniformly between 7:00 A.M. and 8:00 A.M.

a. Find the probability that the delivery on a given morning will occur between 7:15 and 7:30.

b. What is the expected time of delivery?

c. Find the probability that the time of delivery will be within one standard deviation of the expected time—that is, within the interval $\mu - \sigma \le x \le \mu + \sigma$.

SECTION 4.7   *NORMAL DISTRIBUTION*

The normal distribution is the most important specific continuous distribution that we will consider in some detail. Other important continuous distributions (most of which we will encounter in later chapters) include the exponential distribution, the Student t distribution, the chi-square distribution, and the F distribution. The graph of the normal distribution is the familiar symmetrical, bell-shaped curve shown in Figure 4.10. One reason for the importance of the normal distribution is that it usefully models or describes the distributions of numerous random variables that arise in practice, such as the heights or weights of a group of people, the total annual sales of a firm, the grades of a class of students, and the measurement errors that arise in the performance of an experiment. In examples such as these, the observed measurements tend to cluster in a symmetrical fashion about the central value, giving rise to a bell-shaped distribution curve.

A second reason for the normal distribution's importance is that this distribution provides a useful approximation to many other distributions, including discrete ones such as the binomial distribution. Finally, as we shall see in Chapter 6, the normal distribution is the cornerstone distribution of statistical inference, representing the distribution of the possible estimates of a population parameter that may arise from different samples. This last point, in fact, is primarily responsible for the importance of the normal distribution.

FIGURE 4.10   SYMMETRICAL, BELL-SHAPED NORMAL DISTRIBUTION

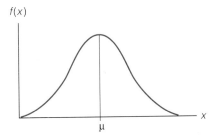

Normal Distribution

A random variable X with mean μ and variance σ^2 is normally distributed if its probability density function is given by

$$f(x) = \left(\frac{1}{\sigma\sqrt{2\pi}}\right)e^{-(1/2)[(x-\mu)/\sigma]^2}, \qquad -\infty < x < \infty$$

where $\pi = 3.14159\ldots$ and $e = 2.71828\ldots$

A random variable that is normally distributed is called a **normal random variable**. A normal random variable can take on any real value from $-\infty$ to $+\infty$, and the normal probability density function $f(x)$ is continuous and has a positive value for all values of x. As is the case with any other probability density function, the value of $f(x)$ here is not the probability that X assumes the value x, but an expression of the height of the curve at the value x. Moreover, the entire area under the curve depicting $f(x)$ must equal 1.

It is apparent from the formula for the probability density function that a normal distribution is completely determined once the parameters μ and σ^2 are specified. That is, a whole family of different normal distributions exists, but one differs from another only in the location of its mean μ and in the variance σ^2 of its values; all normal distributions have the same symmetrical, bell-shaped appearance. Figure 4.11 depicts three normal distributions having the same variance but different means, while Figure 4.12 shows three normal distributions having the same mean but different variances. Notice that the shape of the distribution becomes flatter and more spread out as the variance becomes larger.

FINDING NORMAL PROBABILITIES

Once we determine that a situation can be modeled appropriately by using a normal distribution, we'll want to find various normal probabilities, which are represented by areas under the normal curve. The procedure for finding normal probabilities is illustrated in the following example.

Suppose that the length of time students take in writing a standard entrance examination is known to be normally distributed, with a mean of 60 minutes and a standard deviation of 8 minutes. If we observe the time taken by a particular student, what is the probability that the student's time will be between 60 and 70 minutes?

Given that X denotes the time taken to write the entrance examination, the probability we seek is written $P(60 < X < 70)$.* This probability is given by the area

---

* Recall that the probability that a continuous random variable X will assume any particular value is zero. Hence, $P(60 \le X \le 70) = P(60 < X < 70)$. These two forms for expressing a normal probability will therefore be used interchangeably.

FIGURE 4.11   *NORMAL DISTRIBUTIONS WITH THE SAME VARIANCE BUT DIFFERENT MEANS*

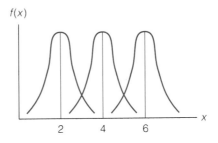

FIGURE 4.12   *NORMAL DISTRIBUTIONS WITH THE SAME MEAN BUT DIFFERENT VARIANCES*

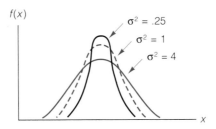

under the normal curve between 60 and 70, depicted by the shaded region in Figure 4.13(a). The actual calculation of such an area (probability) is difficult, however, so we will resort to the tabulated areas provided by Table 3 in Appendix B.*

Since each pair of values for the parameters μ and σ^2 gives rise to a different normal distribution, there are infinitely many possible normal distributions, making it impossible to provide a table of areas for each one. Fortunately, we can make do with just one table.

The particular normal distribution for which Table 3 in Appendix B has been constructed is the normal distribution with $\mu = 0$ and $\sigma = 1$, called the **standard normal distribution.** The corresponding normal random variable, with a mean of 0 and a standard deviation of 1, is called the **standard normal random variable** and is denoted Z. Thus, before using Table 3, we must convert or transform our normal random variable X into the standard normal random variable Z. This is accomplished by applying the following transformation.

---

* For students familiar with calculus, the probability that X takes a value between a and b is given by

$$P(a < X < b) = \int_a^b \left(\frac{1}{\sigma\sqrt{2\pi}}\right) e^{-(1/2)[(x-\mu)/\sigma]^2} \, dx$$

FIGURE 4.13   *SHADED AREA IS $P(60 < X < 70) = P(0 < Z < 1.25)$*

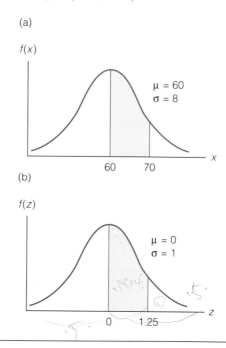

(a)

(b)

Standard Normal Random Variable

$$Z = \frac{X - \mu_x}{\sigma_x}$$

For our example, we obtain:

$$Z = \frac{X - 60}{8}$$

We can easily verify, using the laws of expected value and of variance, that we have created a random variable Z, with a mean of 0 and a standard deviation of 1 (see Exercise 4.20). Moreover, it can be shown that Z is normally distributed. The interpretation of Z is most important. A value of Z equals the distance from the corresponding value of X to μ, measured in standard deviations.

In order to find the desired probability, $P(60 < X < 70)$, we must first determine the interval of z-values corresponding to the interval of x-values of interest: $60 < x < 70$. Using elementary algebra, we know that

$$60 < x < 70$$

holds whenever

$$\frac{60 - 60}{8} < \frac{x - 60}{8} < \frac{70 - 60}{8}$$

or

$$0 < z < 1.25$$

We therefore obtain

$$P(60 < X < 70) = P(0 < Z < 1.25)$$

Thus we can find the required area (probability) by finding the corresponding area under the standard normal curve, which is depicted by the shaded area in Figure 4.13(b). Areas like this one that correspond to probabilities of the form $P(0 < Z < z_0)$ are tabulated in Table 3 in Appendix B. Table 3 is reproduced here as Table 4.12.

In Table 3 (and in Table 4.12), a value of z that is correct to the first decimal place is found in the left-hand column; the second decimal place is located across the top row. We need to find $P(0 < Z < 1.25)$, which is represented by the area over the interval from 0 to 1.25. To find this area corresponding to $z = 1.25$, first locate 1.2 in the left-hand column, and then move across that row until you reach the column with .05 at the top. The area corresponding to $z = 1.25$ is .3944, so that

$$P(60 < X < 70) = P(0 < Z < 1.25)$$
$$= .3944$$

The probability that a particular student will take between 60 and 70 minutes to write the entrance exam is therefore .3944.

We repeat that the z-value corresponding to a given value x_0 has an important interpretation. Since $(x_0 - \mu)$ expresses how far x_0 is from the mean, the corresponding z-value

$$z_0 = \frac{x_0 - \mu}{\sigma}$$

tells us how many standard deviations x_0 is from the mean. Moreover, if z_0 is positive, then x_0 lies to the right of the mean; and conversely, if z_0 is negative, then x_0 lies to the left of the mean. Thus, in the preceding example, the value 70 lies 1.25 standard deviations to the right of the mean value of 60; that is, $70 = 60 + 1.25(8)$.

As we have just seen, we can obtain desired probabilities for any normal distribution from probabilities tabulated for the standard normal distribution. A table of probabilities for just one normal distribution supplies us with all the information we need, because normal distributions differ from one another only in their means and variances. The probability that the variable will assume a value within z_0 standard deviations of the mean remains constant from one normal random variable to the next. In other words, if X is any normal random variable

TABLE 4.12   *REPRODUCTION OF TABLE 3: STANDARD NORMAL CURVE AREAS*

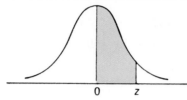

z	.00	.01	.02	.03	.04	.05	.06	.07	.08	.09
0.0	.0000	.0040	.0080	.0120	.0160	.0199	.0239	.0279	.0319	.0359
0.1	.0398	.0438	.0478	.0517	.0557	.0596	.0636	.0675	.0714	.0753
0.2	.0793	.0832	.0871	.0910	.0948	.0987	.1026	.1064	.1103	.1141
0.3	.1179	.1217	.1255	.1293	.1331	.1368	.1406	.1443	.1480	.1517
0.4	.1554	.1591	.1628	.1664	.1700	.1736	.1772	.1808	.1844	.1879
0.5	.1915	.1950	.1985	.2019	.2054	.2088	.2123	.2157	.2190	.2224
0.6	.2257	.2291	.2324	.2357	.2389	.2422	.2454	.2486	.2517	.2549
0.7	.2580	.2611	.2642	.2673	.2704	.2734	.2764	.2794	.2823	.2852
0.8	.2881	.2910	.2939	.2967	.2995	.3023	.3051	.3078	.3106	.3133
0.9	.3159	.3186	.3212	.3238	.3264	.3289	.3315	.3340	.3365	.3389
1.0	.3413	.3438	.3461	.3485	.3508	.3531	.3554	.3577	.3599	.3621
1.1	.3643	.3665	.3686	.3708	.3729	.3749	.3770	.3790	.3810	.3830
1.2	.3849	.3869	.3888	.3907	.3925	.3944	.3962	.3980	.3997	.4015
1.3	.4032	.4049	.4066	.4082	.4099	.4115	.4131	.4147	.4162	.4177
1.4	.4192	.4207	.4222	.4236	.4251	.4265	.4279	.4292	.4306	.4319
1.5	.4332	.4345	.4357	.4370	.4382	.4394	.4406	.4418	.4429	.4441
1.6	.4452	.4463	.4474	.4484	.4495	.4505	.4515	.4525	.4535	.4545
1.7	.4554	.4564	.4573	.4582	.4591	.4599	.4608	.4616	.4625	.4633
1.8	.4641	.4649	.4656	.4664	.4671	.4678	.4686	.4693	.4699	.4706
1.9	.4713	.4719	.4726	.4732	.4738	.4744	.4750	.4756	.4761	.4767
2.0	.4772	.4778	.4783	.4788	.4793	.4798	.4803	.4808	.4812	.4817
2.1	.4821	.4826	.4830	.4834	.4838	.4842	.4846	.4850	.4854	.4857
2.2	.4861	.4864	.4868	.4871	.4875	.4878	.4881	.4884	.4887	.4890
2.3	.4893	.4896	.4898	.4901	.4904	.4906	.4909	.4911	.4913	.4916
2.4	.4918	.4920	.4922	.4925	.4927	.4929	.4931	.4932	.4934	.4936
2.5	.4938	.4940	.4941	.4943	.4945	.4946	.4948	.4949	.4951	.4952
2.6	.4953	.4955	.4956	.4957	.4959	.4960	.4961	.4962	.4963	.4964
2.7	.4965	.4966	.4967	.4968	.4969	.4970	.4971	.4972	.4973	.4974
2.8	.4974	.4975	.4976	.4977	.4977	.4978	.4979	.4979	.4980	.4981
2.9	.4981	.4982	.4982	.4983	.4984	.4984	.4985	.4985	.4986	.4986
3.0	.4987	.4987	.4987	.4988	.4988	.4989	.4989	.4989	.4990	.4990

SOURCE: Abridged from Table 1 of A. Hald, *Statistical Tables and Formulas* (New York: John Wiley & Sons), 1952. Reproduced by permission.

with mean μ and standard deviation σ, then

$$P(\mu - z_0\sigma < X < \mu + z_0\sigma) = P(-z_0 < Z < z_0)$$

We first caught a glimpse of this concept when we took up the Empirical Rule in Chapter 2. According to this rule, about 68% of the values from a mound-shaped distribution (such as the normal distribution) lie within one standard deviation of the mean, about 95% of the values lie within two standard deviations of the mean, and almost 100% of the values lie within three standard deviations.*

Therefore, probabilities of the form $P(-z_0 < Z < z_0)$ have to be tabulated for only one normal distribution, since they are the same for all others. In fact, since a normal distribution is symmetrical, it suffices to tabulate probabilities of the form $P(0 < Z < z_0)$. The probabilities found in Table 3 in Appendix B, then, are of the form $P(0 < Z < z_0)$, for values of z_0 from .00 to 3.09. Given that the total area under the normal curve equals 1, any desired probability may be obtained by adding and subtracting probabilities of this form.

EXAMPLE 4.9

Determine the following probabilities:

    a. $P(Z \geq 1.47)$

    b. $P(-2.25 \leq Z \leq 1.85)$

    c. $P(0.65 \leq Z \leq 1.36)$

Solution.   It is always advisable to begin by sketching a diagram and indicating the area of interest under the normal curve, as shown in Figure 4.14. In part (a), area A_1 corresponds to the required probability, and area A_2 is the area between $z = 0$ and $z = 1.47$. Since the entire area under the normal curve equals 1, and since the

FIGURE 4.14   SHADED AREAS ARE $P(0 < Z < 1.47)$ AND $P(Z \geq 1.47)$ IN EXAMPLE 4.9a

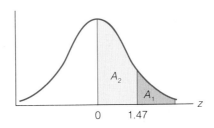

---

* For the special mound-shaped distribution called the *normal distribution*, Table 3 in Appendix B identifies the precise percentages as 68.26, 95.44, and 99.74, respectively.

FIGURE 4.15 *SHADED AREA IS $P(-2.25 \leq Z \leq 1.85)$ IN EXAMPLE 4.9b*

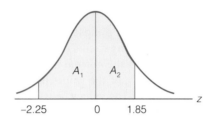

---

curve is symmetrical about $z = 0$, the entire area to the right of $z = 0$ is .5; so

$$A_1 + A_2 = .5$$

Area A_2 is of the form that can be found in Table 3. Locating $z = 1.47$ in Table 3, we find that area A_2 is .4292, so $P(0 < Z < 1.47) = .4292$. The required probability is therefore

$$P(Z \geq 1.47) = A_1$$
$$= .5 - A_2$$
$$= .5 - .4292$$
$$= .0708$$

Whenever the area of interest straddles the mean, as in part (b), we must express it as the sum of the portions to the left and to the right of the mean. The required probability $P(-2.25 \leq Z \leq 1.85)$ corresponds to the sum of the areas A_1 and A_2 in Figure 4.15. That is,

$$P(-2.25 \leq Z \leq 1.85) = A_1 + A_2$$

From Table 3, we find that $A_2 = .4678$. Because the normal distribution is symmetrical, we can write

$$A_1 = P(-2.25 \leq Z \leq 0) = P(0 \leq Z \leq 2.25)$$

Locating $z = 2.25$ in Table 3, we find that $A_1 = .4878$. Therefore, the required probability is

$$P(-2.25 \leq Z \leq 1.85) = A_1 + A_2$$
$$= .4878 + .4678$$
$$= .9556$$

In part (c), $P(.65 \leq Z \leq 1.36)$ corresponds to the shaded area A in Figure 4.16. Since Table 3 only provides areas from 0 up to some positive value of Z, we must express A as the difference between two such areas. If A_1 is the area between $z = 0$ and $z = 1.36$, then $A_1 = .4131$ (from Table 3). Similarly, if A_2 is the area between

FIGURE 4.16   *SHADED AREA IS P(.65 < Z < 1.36) IN EXAMPLE 4.9c*

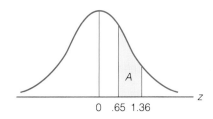

$$z = 0 \text{ and } z = .65, \text{ then } A_2 = .2422. \text{ Therefore,}$$

$$
\begin{aligned}
P(.65 \le Z \le 1.36) &= A \\
&= A_1 - A_2 \\
&= P(0 \le Z \le 1.36) - P(0 \le Z \le .65) \\
&= .4131 - .2422 \\
&= .1709
\end{aligned}
$$

EXAMPLE 4.10

If Z is a standard normal variable, determine the value z_0 for which $P(Z \le z_0) = .6331$.

Solution.   Since the area to the left of $z = 0$ is .5, z_0 must be a positive number, as indicated in Figure 4.17. If A is the area between $z = 0$ and $z = z_0$, then

$$.6331 = .5 + A$$

so

$$A = .6331 - .5 = .1331$$

FIGURE 4.17   *SHADED AREA IS P(0 $\le$ Z $\le$ z$_0$) IN EXAMPLE 4.10*

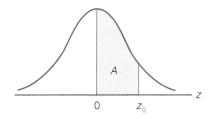

Locating the area .1331 in the body of Table 3, we find that the corresponding value of z_0 is $z_0 = .34$. Therefore,

$$P(z \le .34) = .6331$$

EXAMPLE 4.11

This example introduces some notation that you will use frequently in statistical inference, beginning in Chapter 7. If Z is a standard normal random variable and α is any probability, then $z_{\alpha/2}$ represents that value for which the area under the standard normal curve to the right of $z_{\alpha/2}$ is $\alpha/2$. In other words,

$$P(Z > z_{\alpha/2}) = \alpha/2$$

Thus, because the normal distribution is symmetrical, $-z_{\alpha/2}$ represents that value for which the area under the standard normal curve to the left of $-z_{\alpha/2}$ is $\alpha/2$. Determine $z_{.025}$.

Solution. If A represents the area in Figure 4.18 between $z = 0$ and $z = z_{.025}$, then the desired value $z_{.025}$ is the z-value in Table 3 corresponding to the area A. Since the area under the curve to the right of $z_{.025}$ is .025,

$$A = .5 - .025 = .475$$

From Table 3, the z-value corresponding to the area .475 is

$$Z_{.025} = 1.96$$

so

$$P(Z > 1.96) = .025$$

From symmetry, the area to the left of $z = -1.96$ is also .025. That is,

$$P(Z < -1.96) = .025$$

EXAMPLE 4.12

A venture capital company feels that the rate of return (X) on a proposed investment is approximately normally distributed, with a mean of 30% and a standard deviation of 10%.

    a. Find the probability that the return will exceed 55%.

    b. Find the probability that the return will be less than 22%.

FIGURE 4.18   *LOCATING $z_{.025}$ IN EXAMPLE 4.11*

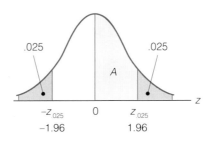

FIGURE 4.19   *CORRESPONDING VALUES OF X AND Z FOR EXAMPLE 4.12*

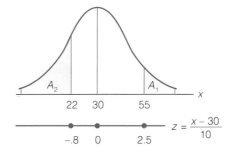

Solution

a. Figure 4.19 shows the required area A_1, together with values of Z corresponding to selected values of X. The value of Z corresponding to $x = 55$ is

$$z = \frac{x - \mu}{\sigma} = \frac{55 - 30}{10} = 2.5$$

Therefore,

$$
\begin{aligned}
P(X > 55) &= A_1 \\
&= P(Z > 2.5) \\
&= .5 - P(0 \le Z \le 2.5) \\
&= .5 - .4938 \\
&= .0062
\end{aligned}
$$

The probability that the return will exceed 55% is .0062.

b. Figure 4.19 shows the required area A_2. By the same logic as was used in part (a),

$$P(X < 22) = A_2$$

$$= P\left(Z < \frac{22 - 30}{10}\right)$$

$$= P(Z < -.8) = P(Z > .8)$$

$$= .5 - P(0 \le Z \le .8)$$

$$= .5 - .2881$$

$$= .2119$$

The probability that the return will be less than 22% is .2119.

NORMAL APPROXIMATION TO THE BINOMIAL

The normal distribution can be used to approximate a number of other probability distributions, including the binomial distribution. The normal approximation to the binomial is useful whenever the number of trials n is so large that the binomial tables cannot be used. Since the normal distribution is symmetrical, it best approximates binomial distributions that are reasonably symmetrical. Therefore, since a binomial distribution is symmetrical when the probability p of a success equals .5, the best approximation is obtained when p is reasonably close to .5. The farther p is from .5, the larger n must be in order for a good approximation to result.

The normal approximation to the binomial distribution works best when only a very small probability exists that the approximating normal random variable will assume a value that falls outside the binomial range ($0 \le X \le n$). Generally, this is satisfied if $np \ge 5$ and $nq \ge 5$; so a conventional rule of thumb is that the normal distribution will provide an adequate approximation of a binomial distribution if $np \ge 5$ and $nq \ge 5$. Recall that the Poisson distribution may be used to approximate binomial probabilities when p is small and n is large.

Given a binomial distribution with n trials and probability p of a success on any trial, the mean of the binomial distribution is $\mu = np$ and the variance is $\sigma^2 = npq$. We therefore choose the normal distribution with $\mu = np$ and $\sigma^2 = npq$ to be the approximating distribution.

To see how the approximation works, consider the binomial distribution with $n = 20$, and $p = .5$, the graph of which is shown in Figure 4.20. Although it is not necessary to use the normal approximation in this case, we have purposely chosen n to be small enough that the binomial tables can be used as a check against the normal approximation. We will approximate the binomial probabilities by using the normal distribution with mean $\mu = (20)(.5) = 10$ and variance $\sigma^2 = 20(.5)(.5) = 5$ (or standard deviation $\sigma = 2.24$). Let X denote the binomial random variable, and let Y denote the normal random variable. The binomial probability $P(X = 10)$, represented by the height of the line above $x = 10$ in Figure 4.20, is equal to the area of the rectangle erected above the interval from 9.5 to 10.5. This area (or probability)

FIGURE 4.20   *NORMAL APPROXIMATION TO BINOMIAL DISTRIBUTION*

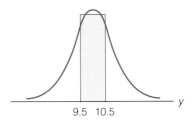

9.5 10.5

is approximated by the area under the normal curve between 9.5 and 10.5. That is,

$$P(X = 10) \cong P(9.5 \leq Y \leq 10.5)$$

The .5 that is added to and subtracted from 10 is called the *continuity correction factor;* it corrects for the fact that we are using a continuous distribution to approximate a discrete distribution. To check the accuracy of this particular approximation, we can use the binomial tables to obtain

$$P(X = 10) = .176$$

From Table 3, the normal approximation is

$$P(9.5 \leq Y \leq 10.5) = P\left(\frac{9.5 - 10}{2.24} \leq Z \leq \frac{10.5 - 10}{2.24}\right)$$

$$= P(-.22 \leq Z \leq .22)$$

$$= 2(.0871)$$

$$= .1742$$

The approximation for any other value of X would proceed in the same manner. In general, the binomial probability $P(X = x_0)$ is approximated by the area under the normal curve between $(x_0 - .5)$ and $(x_0 + .5)$.

Suppose, in the present example, that we wish to approximate the binomial probability $P(5 \leq X \leq 12)$. This probability would be approximated by the area under the normal curve between 4.5 and 12.5. That is,

$$P(5 \leq X \leq 12) \cong P(4.5 \leq Y \leq 12.5)$$

$$= P\left(\frac{4.5 - 10}{2.24} \leq Z \leq \frac{12.5 - 10}{2.24}\right)$$

$$= P(-2.46 \leq Z \leq 1.12)$$

$$= P(0 \leq Z \leq 2.46) + P(0 \leq Z \leq 1.12)$$

$$= .4931 + .3686$$

$$= .8617$$

As a check, the binomial tables yield

$$P(5 \leq X \leq 12) = .862$$

As a final note, we point out that including the continuity correction factor when finding the probability associated with an interval becomes less important as n becomes larger. In subsequent chapters, we will ignore the continuity correction factor when n exceeds 25.

███████   **EXERCISES**

LEARNING THE TECHNIQUES

4.55 Use Table 3 of Appendix B to find the area under the standard normal curve between the following values:

a. $z = 0$ and $z = 2.3$

b. $z = 0$ and $z = 1.68$

c. $z = .24$ and $z = .33$

d. $z = -2.58$ and $z = 0$

e. $z = -2.81$ and $z = -1.35$

f. $z = -1.73$ and $z = .49$

4.56 Use Table 3 to find the following probabilities:

a. $P(Z \geq 1.7)$

b. $P(Z \geq -.95)$

c. $P(Z \leq -1.96)$

d. $P(Z \leq 2.43)$

e. $P(-2.97 \leq Z \leq -1.38)$

f. $P(-1.14 \leq Z \leq 1.55)$

4.57 Use Table 3 to find the value z_0 for which:

a. $P(0 \leq Z \leq z_0) = .41$

b. $P(Z \geq z_0) = .025$

c. $P(Z \geq z_0) = .9$

d. $P(Z \leq z_0) = .95$

e. $P(Z \leq z_0) = .2$

f. $P(-z_0 \leq Z \leq z_0) = .88$

4.58 Determine $z_{\alpha/2}$, and locate its value on a graph of the standard normal distribution, for each of the following values of α:

a. .01

b. .02

c. .10

4.59 Let X be a normal random variable with a mean of 50 and a standard deviation of 8. Find the following probabilities:

a. $P(X \geq 52)$

b. $P(X < 40)$

c. $P(X = 40)$

d. $P(X > 40)$

e. $P(35 < X \leq 64)$

f. $P(32 \leq X \leq 37)$

4.60 If X is a normal random variable with a mean of 50 and a standard deviation of 8, how many standard deviations away from the mean is each of the following values of X?

a. $x = 52$

b. $x = 40$

c. $x = 35$

d. $x = 64$

e. $x = 32$

f. $x = 37$

4.61 Let X be a binomial random variable with $n = 100$ and $p = .6$. Approximate the following probabilities, using the normal distribution:

a. $P(X = 65)$

b. $P(X \leq 70)$

c. $P(X > 50)$

APPLYING THE TECHNIQUES

Self-Correcting Exercise (See Appendix 4.A for the solution.)

POM **4.62** The time required to assemble an electronic component is normally distributed, with a mean of 12 minutes and a standard deviation of 1.5 minutes. Find the probability that a particular assembly takes:

a. more than 14 minutes

b. more than 8 minutes

c. less than 14 minutes

d. less than 10 minutes

e. between 10 and 15 minutes

RET **4.63** The lifetime of a certain brand of tires is approximately normally distributed, with a mean of 45,000 miles and a standard deviation of 2,500 miles. The tires carry a warranty for 40,000 miles.

a. What proportion of the tires will fail before the warranty expires?

b. What proportion of the tires will fail after the warranty expires but before they have lasted for 41,000 miles?

MKT **4.64** A firm's marketing manager believes that total sales for the firm next year can be modeled by using a normal distribution, with a mean of $2.5 million and a standard deviation of $300,000.

a. What is the probability that the firm's sales will exceed $3 million?

b. What is the probability that the firm's sales will fall within $150,000 of the expected level of sales?

c. In order to cover fixed costs, the firm's sales must exceed the break-even level of $1.8 million. What is the probability that sales will exceed the break-even level?

d. Determine the sales level that has only a 9% chance of being exceeded next year.

FIN **4.65** Empirical studies have provided support for the belief that a common stock's annual rate of return is approximately normally distributed. Suppose that you have invested in the stock of a company for which the annual return has an expected value of 16% and a standard deviation of 10%.

a. Find the probability that your one-year return will exceed 30%.

b. Find the probability that your one-year return will be negative.

c. Suppose that this company embarks on a new, high-risk, but potentially highly profitable venture. As a result, the return on the stock now has an expected value of 25% and a standard deviation of 20%. Answer parts (a) and (b) in light of the revised estimates regarding the stock's return.

d. As an investor, would you approve of the company's decision to embark on the new venture?

POM **4.66** A steel fabricator produces pipes with a diameter that is approximately normally distributed, with a mean of 10 cm and a variance of .01 cm^2.

a. Suppose that the tolerance limit for these pipes is .2 cm, so pipes with a diameter falling within the interval $10 \pm .2$ cm are acceptable. What proportion of the pipes produced will be acceptable?

b. Suppose that pipes with too small a diameter can be reworked, but that pipes with too large a diameter must be scrapped. Suppose also that the tolerance has been reduced to .1 cm. What proportion of the pipes must be scrapped?

GEN **4.67** Mensa is an organization whose members possess IQs in the top 2% of the population.

a. If IQs are normally distributed, with a mean of 100 and a standard deviation of 16, what is the minimum IQ necessary for admission?

b. If three individuals are chosen at random from the general population, what is the probability that all three satisfy the minimum requirement for admission to Mensa?

c. If two individuals are chosen at random from the general population, what is the probability that at least one of them exceeds the minimum requirement for admission to Mensa?

EDUC **4.68** Universities throughout the United States and Canada are concerned about the aging of their faculty members, as the average age of professors is at an historic high. A very large number of faculty members will retire within the next decade, making it difficult to find adequate replacements to fill all of the positions that will become available. In 1989, Canadian professors had a median age of 46.4 years, and 36% of them were at least 50 years of age (*Globe and Mail*, 29 March 1989, p. A1). Assume that the ages of these professors are normally distributed.

a. Determine the standard deviation of the ages.

b. Assume that there are currently 40,000 professors at Canadian universities and that the mandatory retirement age is 65. What is the minimum number of professors who will retire during the next decade?

POM **4.69** The maintenance department of a city's electric power company finds that it is cost-efficient to replace all streetlight bulbs at once, rather than to replace the bulbs individually as they burn out. Assume that the lifetime of a bulb is normally distributed, with a mean of 3,000 hours and a standard deviation of 200 hours.

a. If the department wants no more than 1% of the bulbs to burn out before they are replaced, after how many hours should all of the bulbs be replaced?

b. If two bulbs are selected at random from among those that have been replaced, what is the probability that at least one of them has burned out?

MKT **4.70** Companies are interested in the demographics of those who listen to the radio programs they sponsor. A radio station has determined that only 20% of listeners phoning into a morning talk program are male. During a particular week, 200 calls are received by this program.

a. What is the probability that at least 50 of these 200 callers are male?

b. What is the probability that more than half of these 200 callers are female?

c. There is a 30% chance that the number of male callers among the 200 total callers does not exceed what?

FIN **4.71** Due to an increasing number of nonperforming loans, a Texas bank now insists that several stringent conditions be met before a customer is granted a consumer loan. As a result, 60% of all customers applying for a loan are *rejected*. If 40 new loan applications are selected at random, what is the probability that:

a. at least 12 are accepted

b. at least half of them are accepted

c. no more than 16 are accepted

d. the number of applications *rejected* is between 20 and 30, inclusive

POM **4.72** Historical data collected at a paper mill reveal that 40% of sheet breaks are due to water drops, which result from the condensation of steam. Suppose that the causes of the next 50 sheet breaks are monitored and that the sheet breaks are independent of one another.

a. Find the expected value and the standard deviation of the number of sheet breaks that will be caused by water drops.

b. What is the probability that at least 25 of the breaks will be due to water drops?

c. What is the probability that the number of breaks due to water drops will be between 10 and 25, inclusive?

SECTION 4.8   # EXPONENTIAL DISTRIBUTION

Another important continuous distribution, the **exponential distribution,** is closely related to the Poisson distribution, even though the latter distribution is discrete. Recall that a Poisson random variable counts the number of occurrences of an event during a given time interval. In contrast, an exponential random variable, X, can be used to measure the time that elapses before the first occurrence of an event, where occurrences of the event follow a Poisson distribution. Equivalently, an exponential random variable can be used to measure the time that elapses between occurrences of an event. For example, the exponential distribution may be used to model the length of time before the first telephone call is received by a switchboard, or the length of time between arrivals at a service location (such as a service station, tollbooth, or grocery checkout counter). It has been used with considerable success in applications involving waiting times, and it may also be used to model the length of life of various electronic components, such as tubes and transistors.

Exponential Distribution

A random variable X is exponentially distributed if its probability density function is given by

$$f(x) = \lambda e^{-\lambda x}, x \geq 0$$

where $e = 2.71828\ldots$ and λ is the parameter of the distribution ($\lambda > 0$).

It can be shown that the mean and the standard deviation of an exponential probability distribution are equal to one another:

$$\mu = \sigma = 1/\lambda$$

Recall that the normal distribution is a two-parameter distribution: the distribution is completely specified once the values of the two parameters μ and σ are known. In contrast, the exponential distribution is a one-parameter distribution: the distribution is completely specified once the value of the parameter λ is known. If X is an exponential random variable that measures the time that elapses before the first occurrence of an event, where occurrences of the event follow a Poisson distribution, then λ is the average number of occurrences of the event per unit of time.

The graphs of three exponential distributions, corresponding to three different values of λ, are shown in Figure 4.21. Notice that, for any exponential density function $f(x)$, $f(0) = \lambda$ and $f(x)$ approaches zero as x approaches infinity.

Recall that, for a continuous random variable, probabilities are represented by areas under the graph of the probability density function $f(x)$. In the case of an exponential random variable X, it can be shown that the probability that X will take a value greater than a specified nonnegative number a is $e^{-\lambda a}$.*

---

* For students familiar with calculus,

$$P(X \geq a) = \int_a^\infty \lambda e^{-\lambda x}\, dx = -e^{-\lambda x}\Big|_a^\infty = e^{-\lambda a}$$

FIGURE 4.21 GRAPHS OF THREE EXPONENTIAL DISTRIBUTIONS

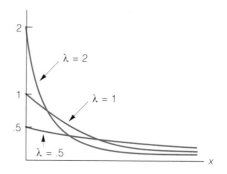

Probability That an Exponential Variable Exceeds the Number a

If X is an exponential random variable,

$$P(X \geq a) = e^{-\lambda a}$$

The value of $e^{-\lambda a}$ can be obtained with the aid of a calculator. Since the total area under the graph of $f(x)$ must equal 1,

$$P(X \leq a) = 1 - e^{-\lambda a}$$

for any nonnegative number t.

The probability that X will take a value between two numbers a and b can now be obtained by subtraction:

$$P(a \leq X \leq b) = P(X \leq b) - P(X \leq a)$$
$$= e^{-\lambda a} - e^{-\lambda b}$$

As an illustration of the relationship between the exponential and Poisson distributions, consider once again the situation described in Example 4.6.

EXAMPLE 4.13

A tollbooth operator has observed that cars arrive randomly and independently at an average rate of 360 cars per hour.

    a. Use the exponential distribution to find the probability that the next car will *not* arrive within half a minute.

    b. Use the Poisson distribution to find the probability required in part (a).

FIGURE 4.22   *SHADED AREA IS $P(X \geq .5)$ IN EXAMPLE 4.13*

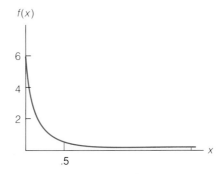

Solution

a. Let X denote the time *in minutes* that will elapse before the next car arrives. It is important that X and λ be defined in terms of the same units. Thus, λ is the average number of cars arriving per minute: $\lambda = 360/60 = 6$. According to the formula for exponential probabilities, the probability that at least half a minute will elapse before the next car arrives is

$$P(X \geq .5) = e^{-6(.5)}$$
$$= e^{-3}$$
$$= .0498$$

This probability is represented by the shaded area shown in Figure 4.22.

b. Let Y be the number of cars that will arrive in the next half minute. Then Y is a Poisson random variable, with $\mu = .5(\lambda) = 3$ cars per half minute. We wish to find the probability that no cars will arrive within the next half minute. Using the formula for a Poisson probability, we find

$$P(Y = 0 \mid \mu = 3) = \frac{(e^{-3})(3^0)}{0!}$$
$$= .0498$$

EXAMPLE 4.14

The lifetime of a transistor is exponentially distributed, with a mean of 1,200 hours. Find the probability that such a transistor will last between 1,000 and 1,500 hours.

Solution.   Let X denote the lifetime (in hours) of a transistor. Since the mean lifetime is 1,000 hours, $\lambda = 1/\mu = 1/1,000 = .001$. The required probability is therefore

$$P(1{,}000 \le X \le 1{,}500) = e^{-.001(1000)} - e^{-.001(1500)}$$
$$= e^{-1} - e^{-1.5}$$
$$= .3679 - .2231$$
$$= .1448$$

EXERCISES

LEARNING THE TECHNIQUES

4.73 Let X be an exponential random variable with $\lambda = 1$. Sketch the graph of the distribution of X by plotting and connecting the points representing $f(x)$ for $x = 0, .5, 1, 1.5$, and 2.

4.74 Let X be an exponential random variable with $\lambda = 3$. Sketch the graph of the distribution of X by plotting and connecting the points representing $f(x)$ for $x = 0, .5, 1, 1.5$, and 2.

4.75 Let X be an exponential random variable with $\lambda = 1.5$. Find the following probabilities:

a. $P(X \ge 1)$

b. $P(X \le 3)$

c. $P(2 \le X \le 4)$

d. $P(X \ge .5)$

4.76 Let X be an exponential random variable with $\lambda = 3$. Find the following probabilities:

a. $P(X \ge 2)$

b. $P(X \le 4)$

c. $P(1 \le X \le 3)$

d. $P(X = 2)$

4.77 Let X be an exponential random variable with $\lambda = 2$.

a. Find the probability that X will take a value within 1.5 standard deviations of its mean.

b. Is your answer to part (a) consistent with the claim made by Chebyshev's theorem? Explain.

4.78 Let X be an exponential random variable with $\lambda = 4$.

a. Find the probability that X will take a value within 1.2 standard deviations of its mean.

b. Is your answer to part (a) consistent with the claim made by Chebyshev's theorem? Explain.

4.79 The expected value of an exponential random variable, X, is $1/\lambda$. Find the probability that X will take value that is less than its expected value.

APPLYING THE TECHNIQUES

Self-Correcting Exercise (See Appendix 4.A for the solution.)

RET **4.80** Suppose that customers arrive at a checkout counter at an average rate of two customers per minute, and that their arrivals follow the Poisson model.

a. Sketch a graph of the (exponential) distribution of the time that will elapse before the next customer arrives, by plotting and joining the points representing $f(t)$ for $t = 0, .5, 1, 1.5$, and 2.

b. Use the appropriate exponential distribution to find the probability that the next customer will arrive within 1 minute; within 2 minutes.

c. Use the exponential distribution to find the probability that the next customer will not arrive within the next 1.5 minutes.

d. Use the appropriate Poisson distribution to answer part (c).

POM **4.81** The length of life of a certain type of electronic tube is exponentially distributed, with a mean of 400 hours.

a. Find the probability that a tube will last more than 1,000 hours.

b. Find the probability that a tube will fail within the first 300 hours.

c. Find the probability that the length of life of a tube will be between 600 and 800 hours.

MNG **4.82** A firm has monitored the duration of long-distance telephone calls placed by its employees, to help it decide which long-distance package to purchase. The duration of calls was found to be exponentially distributed, with a mean of 5 minutes.

a. What proportion of calls last more than 2 minutes?

b. What proportion of calls last more than 5 minutes?

c. What proportion of calls are shorter than 10 minutes?

GEN **4.83** Airplanes arrive at an airport according to the Poisson model, with a mean time between arrivals of 5 minutes.

a. Find the probability that a plane will arrive within the next 5 minutes.

b. Find the probability that no planes will arrive during a given 30-minute period.

c. Find the probability that no more than one plane will arrive during a given 30-minute period.

SECTION 4.9 ## *SUMMARY*

The concept of a random variable permits us to summarize the results of an experiment in terms of numerical-valued events. Specifically, a **random variable** assigns a numerical value to each simple event of an experiment. A random variable is **discrete** if it can assume at most a countably infinite number of values; it is **continuous** if it can take any of infinitely many values within some interval of values. Once the **probability distribution** of a random variable is known, we can determine its **expected value,** its **variance,** and the probability that it will assume various values. These abilities will stand us in good stead when we reach the study of statistical inference, where we will want to determine the probability that any particular sample will be selected from a population over which the random variable is defined.

Two discrete random variables that frequently arise in real-world applications are the **binomial** and the **Poisson.** We described the characteristics of random experiments that give rise to each of these random variables, and we gave the formulas for their probability distributions. The **normal probability distribution** is the most important continuous distribution. Besides approximating the distribution of numerous random variables that arise in practice, the normal distribution is the cornerstone distribution of statistical inference. Finally, we considered the **exponential distribution,** a continuous distribution that is especially useful in application involving waiting lines, or queuing.

SUPPLEMENTARY EXERCISES

4.84 Let X be a random variable with the following probability distribution:

x	0	2	4	6	8
$p(x)$	.10	.20	.25	.30	.15

a. Find the expected value and the standard deviation of X.

b. Find $E(X^2)$.

c. Find $E(4X^2 - 5)$.

d. Find the expected value and the standard deviation of $3X + 7$.

4.85 Two coins are selected from a box containing four coins: a nickel, two dimes, and a quarter. Let X be the number of dimes selected.

a. Express the probability distribution of X in tabular form.

b. Express the probability distribution of X in graphical form.

4.86 A large manufacturer has purchased an insurance policy for $500,000 per year to insure itself against four specific types of losses. The cost associated with each type of loss and its probability are listed in the following table.

Cost	Probability
$100,000	.15
$800,000	.10
$1,500,000	.08
$2,500,000	.04

Of the total cost of the policy, 20% goes to cover administrative expenses.

a. What is the expected *profit* to the insurance company on this policy?

b. What is the standard deviation of the profits to the insurance company?

4.87 Let X, Y, and W be the three random variables with the following probability distributions:

x	$p(x)$	y	$p(y)$	w	$p(w)$
2	1/4	2	1/8	1	1/4
4	1/4	4	3/8	4	1/4
6	1/4	6	3/8	6	1/4
8	1/4	8	1/8	9	1/4

a. Determine the means of X, Y, and W simply by inspection.

b. Verify your answers to part (a) by calculating the means.

c. Without performing any calculations, determine which of the three distributions has the smallest variance and which has the largest. Explain your reasoning. (HINT: Compare X with Y and X with W.)

d. Verify your answer to part (c) by computing the variances.

FIN **4.88** An investor intends to place one-quarter of his funds in a real estate venture and the remaining three-quarters in a portfolio of common stocks. The real estate venture has an expected return of 28% with a standard deviation of 20%, while the stock portfolio has an expected return of 12% with a standard deviation of 6%. Assume that the returns on these two investments are independent.

a. What are the expected value and the standard deviation of the return on the total funds invested? (HINT: Let X be the return on the real estate venture, let Y be the return on the stock portfolio, and express the return on the total funds invested as a function of X and Y.)

b. Using the variance of the possible returns on an investment as a measure of its relative riskiness, rank the real estate venture, the stock portfolio, and the combination of the two, in order of increasing riskiness.

GEN **4.89** Exercise 4.6 gave the probability distribution of the number of children in American families. Use the data in that exercise to find the probability distribution of the number of children in families having at least one child. (This is called a **conditional probability distribution**.)

4.90 Let X be a binomial random variable with $n = 20$ and $p = .4$. Use Table 1 of Appendix B to find the following probabilities:

a. $P(X \le 3)$

b. $P(X = 3)$

c. $P(X \ge 6)$

d. $P(X > 9)$

e. $P(4 < X \le 8)$

f. $P(7 \le X \le 9)$

RET **4.91** The BDW car dealership sells one sports model, the FX500. Of the customers who buy this model, 50% choose fire-engine red as the color, 30% choose snow white, and 20% choose jet black.

a. What is the probability that at least 6 of the next 10 customers who buy an FX500 model will choose red cars?

b. On average, a customer who buys a red FX500 orders options worth $3,000. Customers who buy white FX500 models buy only $2,000 worth of options, and those who buy black FX500 models buy $1,500 worth of options. What is the expected value of the options bought by the next 10 customers who buy an FX500?

4.92 *FIN* Financing acquisitions often takes the form of putting together a leveraged buyout (LBO), in which case a substantial portion of the purchase price is financed by debt. Bankers look at a number of factors when evaluating an LBO proposal. In the United States, an estimated 70% of all LBO proposals are not accepted by bankers (*Canadian Business*, August 1985). If 25 LBO proposals are randomly selected for consideration by a bank, find the probability that:

a. not more than 8 are accepted

b. exactly 8 are accepted

c. more than 8 are accepted

d. at least 5 but fewer than 12 are accepted

4.93 What assumptions did you make in answering Exercise 4.92?

4.94 *POM* ACME Plumbing Supply has just received a shipment of 5,000 stainless steel valves that are designed to be used in chemical plants producing acidic chemicals that corrode regular steel valves. Minutes after receiving the valves, the supplier calls to inform ACME that one of their employees inadvertently included 100 regular steel valves in the shipment. Unfortunately there is no way to distinguish the regular valves from the stainless ones without extensive testing. At about the same time, ACME receives an emergency order for 5 of the stainless steel valves from one of its largest customers.

a. If ACME decides to fill the order for 5 stainless steel valves, what is the probability that one or more will be regular steel valves?

b. If ACME explains its predicament to the customer and ships 6 valves, which the customer is to test prior to use, what is the probability that at least 5 of them will be stainless steel?

4.95 *POM* Suppose that a machine breaks down occasionally as a result of a particular part that wears out, and suppose that these breakdowns occur randomly and independently. The average number of breakdowns per 8-hour day is four, and the distribution of breakdowns is stable within the 8-hour day.

a. Find the probability that no breakdowns will occur during a given day.

b. Find the probability that at most two breakdowns will occur during the first hour of the day.

c. What is the minimum number of spare parts that management should have on hand on a given day if it wishes to be at least 90% sure that the machine will not be idle at any time during the day because of a lack of parts?

4.96 *POM* The MacTell Toy Company produces toy firetrucks. Suppose that records kept on the imperfections per firetruck show that the imperfections observed arise independently of one another and are unpredictable in nature. That is, the distribution of the number of imperfections approximates a Poisson distribution. The records also indicate that the firetrucks are produced with a mean imperfection rate of .5 per truck.

An order for 1,000 toy firetrucks has been received. The cost department must estimate the total cost of repairing the trucks before the work begins. Past experience indicates that the first imperfection on each firetruck costs 20¢ to repair while each subsequent imperfection on a firetruck costs 10¢ to repair. (Thus a truck with three imperfections costs 40¢ to repair.) Find the total expected repair cost involved in supplying the order for 1,000 firetrucks.

4.97 *POM* In 1986, the Bank of Canada made some changes in the design and coloring of its $5 bills. Users of banks' automated teller machines soon discovered that the machines would sometimes make a mistake, due to the coloring, and would issue two $5 bills when only one was called for. The manufacturer of the machines claims that remedying the problem isn't worth the cost, since the chance that a mistake will be made on any one transaction is only 1 in 500. If one of these machines handles 250 transactions on a given day, what is the probability that the machine will make more than two mistakes that day?

RET **4.98** The sales manager for a national women's apparel distributor claims that 20% of the company's orders are for a low-end line of apparel, 70% are for a medium line, and 10% are for a high-end line.

a. If the next 5 orders are independent of one another, what is the probability that at least 3 of them will be for a medium line of apparel?

b. If the next 15 orders are independent of one another, what is the probability that at most 8 of them will be for a low-end line of apparel?

c. Suppose that 30% of orders for a low-end line of apparel include an order for some accessories (such as hats or jewelry), 50% of orders for a medium line include an order for accessories, and 40% of orders for a high-end line include an order for accessories. What is the probability that an order for accessories will be included in the next order for an apparel line?

RET **4.99** A boat broker in Florida receives an average of 26 orders per year for an exotic model of cruiser. Assuming that the demand for this model is uniform throughout the year, what is the probability that the boat broker will receive:

a. exactly 1 order for this model in a given week

b. exactly 2 orders for this model over a given 2-week period

c. exactly 4 orders for this model over a given 4-week period

POM **4.100** A maintenance worker in a large paper-manufacturing plant knows that, on average, the main pulper (which beats solid materials to a pulp) breaks down 6 times per 30-day month. Find the probability that, on a given day, she will have to repair the pulper:

a. Exactly once

b. At least once

c. At least once but not more than twice

POM **4.101** The scheduling manager for a certain hydro power utility company knows that there are an average of 12 emergency calls regarding power failures per month. Assume that a month consists of 30 days.

a. Find the probability that the company will receive at least 12 emergency calls during a specified month.

b. Suppose that the utility company can handle a maximum of 3 emergency calls per day. What is the probability that there will be more emergency calls than the company can handle on a given day?

4.102 Use Table 3 of Appendix B to find the following probabilities:

a. $P(Z > 1.64)$

b. $P(1.23 \leq Z \leq 2.71)$

c. $P(Z < .52)$

d. $P(-.68 < Z \leq 2.42)$

4.103 Use Table 3 of Appendix B to find the following probabilities, where X has a normal distribution with $\mu = 24$ and $\sigma = 4$:

a. $P(X > 30)$

b. $P(25 < X < 27)$

c. $P(X \leq 26)$

d. $P(18 \leq X \leq 23)$

POM **4.104** Suppose that the actual amount of instant coffee that a filling machine puts into 6-ounce cans varies from can to can, and that the actual fill may be considered a random variable having a normal distribution, with a standard deviation of .04 ounces. If only 2 out of every 100 cans contains less than 6 ounces of coffee, what must be the mean fill of these cans?

POM **4.105** A soft-drink bottling plant uses a machine that fills bottles with drink mixture. The contents of the bottles filled are normally distributed, with a mean of 16 ounces and a variance of 4 (ounces)^2.

a. Determine the weight exceeded by only the heaviest 10% of the filled bottles.

b. Determine the probability that the combined weight of two of these bottles is less than 30 ounces. (HINT: If X_1 and X_2 are normally distributed variables, then $Y = X_1 + X_2$ is also normally distributed.)

GEN **4.106** Consumer advocates frequently complain about the large variation in the prices charged by different pharmacies for the same prescription. A survey of pharmacies in Chicago by one such advocate revealed that the prices charged for 100 tablets of Tylenol 3 were normally distributed, with about 90% of the prices ranging between $8.25 and $11.25. The mean price charged was $9.75. What proportion of the pharmacies charged over $10.25 for the prescription?

GEN **4.107** Suppose that men's height is normally distributed, with a mean of 5 feet 9 inches and a standard deviation of 2 inches. Find the minimum ceiling height of an airplane in which at most 2% of the men walking down the aisle will have to duck their heads.

4.108 Suppose that X is a binomial random variable with $n = 100$ and $p = .20$. Use the normal approximation to find the probability that X takes a value between 22 and 25 (inclusive).

FIN **4.109** Venture-capital firms provide financing for small, high-risk enterprises that have the potential to become highly profitable. A successful venture-capital firm notes that it provides financing for only 10% of the proposals it reviews. Of the 200 proposals submitted this year, what is the probability that more than 30 will receive financing?

CASE 4.1   CALCULATING PROBABILITIES ASSOCIATED WITH THE STOCK MARKET

The Value Line Investment Survey is a stock market advisory service that is well known for its fine performance record. Value Line follows 1,700 stocks. Each week it assigns each stock a ranking of from 1 (best) to 5 (worst), indicating the stock's timeliness for purchase. There are always 100 stocks in the (top) Rank 1 group.

Suppose that, at the beginning of a calendar year, a portfolio (called the passive Rank 1 portfolio) consisting of the 100 Rank 1 stocks is formed and is held (unchanged) for one year. At the end of the year, the rate of return on this passive Rank 1 portfolio is compared to the return on the market portfolio, which consists of all 1,700 stocks. Holloway observed that the passive Rank 1 portfolio outperformed the market portfolio in each of the 14 years from 1965 to 1978, with the exception of 1970.* The probability that this would occur by chance is .00085. After noting that the performances of the two portfolios were almost identical in two of the years (1975 and 1976), Holloway stated: "Even if we count these two years as failures, the probability of obtaining the Value Line results by *chance* is only .0286." Subsequently, Gregory took exception to this statement and wrote: "That observation is a misuse of statistics."† He pointed out that, while the probability of .0286 would be correct if applied to an advisory service selected at random, Value Line was selected *because of* its fine performance record. Gregory then noted that "out of a population of, say, 20 investment advisory services, the probability of finding at least one with 3 [or fewer] bad years out of 14 is .44." In other words, it isn't all that surprising to find one advisory service with such a good performance record.

---

* Clark Holloway, "A Note on Testing an Aggressive Investment Strategy Using Value Line Ranks," *Journal of Finance* 36(3) (1981): 711–19.

† N. A. Gregory, "Testing an Aggressive Investment Strategy Using Value Line Ranks: A Comment," *Journal of Finance* 38(1) (1983): 257–70.

Holloway also examined an active portfolio strategy, in which the Rank 1 portfolio was "updated weekly to consist always of the 100 Rank 1 stocks." This strategy "outperformed the market in each of the 14 consecutive years" from 1965 to 1978, neglecting the brokerage commission incurred whenever a stock was bought or sold. Although the probability of achieving this performance by chance is only .000061, analysis of results that included brokerage commissions indicated that performance under this active strategy was not significantly superior to the performance of the passive Rank 1 portfolio.

In another phase of Holloway's study, the 100 Rank 1 stocks were partitioned into 5 subportfolios. Holloway monitored the performance of each of the 5 subportfolios over the 4 years from 1974 to 1977, thereby observing 20 returns. These were compared with the 20 corresponding returns from a passive (buy-and-hold) strategy. The active strategy performed better than the passive strategy in 17 of these 20 cases, when brokerage commissions were not considered, but it was superior in only 12 of these cases when brokerage costs were included. Are either of these two results significantly different from what could be expected to happen simply by chance?

Verify the values of the four different probabilities mentioned in this case.

SOLUTIONS TO SELF-CORRECTING EXERCISES

4.6   a. $p(x)$

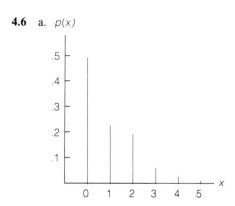

b. The distribution is positively skewed (skewed to the right).

c. The most likely number of children in a family is zero, which occurs with probability .5.

d. $P(X > 2) = P(X \geq 3) = .10$

4.16 Let X represent the amount of damage incurred.

x	$p(x)$	$xp(x)$	x^2	$x^2p(x)$
0	.87	0	0	0
100	.10	10	10,000	1,000
200	.02	4	40,000	800
400	.01	4	160,000	1,600
Total		$18 = E(X)$		$3,400 = E(X^2)$

a. The owner should be willing to pay up to $18, which is the expected amount of damage to be incurred.

b. $V(X) = E(X^2) - \mu^2 = 3400 - (18)^2 = 3,076$
    $\sigma = \sqrt{3,076} = \$55.46$

4.32 Let X be the number of correct answers for $n = 15$ questions, with $p = .2$.

a. $P(X \geq 7) = 1 - P(X \leq 6) = 1 - .982 = .018$

b. The expected number of correct answers is $E(X) = np = 15(.2) = 3$.

4.44   Let X denote the number of calls in a day, with $\mu = 10/5 = 2$. From Table 2,

$$P(X = 5) = P(X \leq 5) - P(X \leq 4)$$
$$= .983 - .947$$
$$= .036.$$

4.52   a. $f(x) = 1/(30 - 20) = .1$ (for $20 \leq x \leq 30$)
  $f(x) = 0$ (elsewhere)

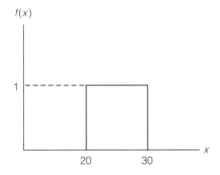

b. $f(x)$ is a probability density function, since:
  (1) $f(x) \geq 0$ for all values of x.
  (2) The total area under the curve representing $f(x)$ is $(10)(.1) = 1$.

c. $P(22 \leq X \leq 30) = (\text{Base})(\text{Height})$
  $= (30 - 22)(.1)$
  $= (8)(.1)$
  $= .8$

d. $P(X = 25) = 0$

4.62   Let X be the time required to assemble a component, where $\mu = 12$ and $\sigma = 1.5$.

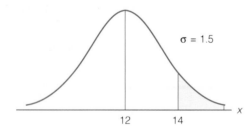

a. $P(X > 14) = P\left(Z > \dfrac{14 - 12}{1.5}\right)$
  $= P(Z > 1.33)$
  $= .5 - P(0 \leq Z \leq 1.33)$
  $= .5 - .4082$
  $= .0918$

b. $P(X > 8) = P\left(Z > \dfrac{8 - 12}{1.5}\right)$
  $= P(Z > -2.67)$
  $= .5 + P(0 \leq Z \leq 2.67)$
  $= .5 + .4962$
  $= .9962$

c. $P(X < 14) = 1 - P(X \geq 14)$
  $= 1 - .0918$ (from part (a))
  $= .9082$

d. $P(X < 10) = P\left(Z < \dfrac{10 - 12}{1.5}\right)$
  $= P(Z < -1.33)$
  $= P(Z > 1.33)$
  $= .0918$ (from part (a))

e. $P(10 \leq X \leq 15) = P\left(\dfrac{10 - 12}{1.5} \leq Z \leq \dfrac{15 - 12}{1.5}\right)$
  $= P(1.33 \leq Z \leq 2)$
  $= P(0 \leq Z \leq 2) - P(0 \leq Z \leq 1.33)$
  $= .4772 - .4080$
  $= .0690$

4.80   Let T be the elapsed time before the next customer arrives. Then the probability density function for T is

$$f(t) = \lambda e^{-\lambda t}   (t \geq 0)$$

where $\lambda = 2$ customers per minute. That is,

$$f(t) = 2e^{-2t}   (t \geq 0)$$

a. $f(0) = 2e^{-2(0)} = 2$
  $f(.5) = 2e^{-2(.5)} = 2e^{-1} = .736$
  $f(1) = 2e^{-2(1)} = 2e^{-2} = .271$
  $f(1.5) = 2e^{-2(1.5)} = 2e^{-3} = .100$
  $f(2) = 2e^{-2(2)} = 2e^{-4} = .037$

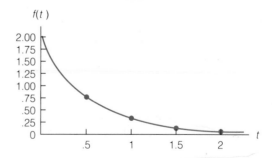

b. $P(T \leq t) = 1 - e^{-2t}$

$$P(T \leq 1) = 1 - e^{-2(1)}$$
$$= 1 - e^{-2}$$
$$= 1 - .135$$
$$= .865$$

$$P(T \leq 2) = 1 - e^{-2(2)}$$
$$= 1 - e^{-4}$$
$$= 1 - .018$$
$$= .982$$

c. $P(T \geq t) = e^{-2t}$

$$P(T \geq 1.5) = e^{-2(1.5)}$$
$$= e^{-3}$$
$$= .050$$

d. Let X be the number of customer arrivals in the next 1.5 minutes. Then X is a Poisson random variable, with $\mu = 1.5\lambda = 1.5(2) = 3$. Using Table 2 in Appendix B, we find that

$$P(X = 0 \,|\, \mu = 3) = .050$$

STATISTICAL INFERENCE

The goal of statistics is to draw inferences about populations on the basis of sample statistics. The 14 chapters in this part of the book present approximately three dozen different techniques directed at satisfying this goal. Chapter 5 introduces statistical inference, explains why so many techniques are required, and develops the system alluded to in the book's title. Chapter 6 presents a central concept of inference, the sampling distribution. Chapters 7 through 10 and 12 through 17 discuss the actual techniques and illustrate them with numerous examples, exercises, and cases. Chapters 11 and 18 are included for review and as contributions to the understanding and execution of the system; these two chapters also contain flowcharts designed to help students identify which technique is to be used to solve a particular problem.

C H A P T E R **5**

STATISTICAL INFERENCE: INTRODUCTION

INTRODUCTION

Much of the remainder of this book deals with problems that attempt to say something about the properties of a population. Because populations are generally quite large, the information we usually have available to work with comes from a relatively small sample taken from the population. The process of drawing conclusions about the properties of a population based on information obtained from a sample is called *statistical inference.*

Examples of statistical inference include the following: estimating the mean annual household income of families in New York; determining whether or not a new advertising compaign has increased the proportion of customers who buy a company's product; estimating the average monthly sales of home computers for next year; and determining whether or not a fuel additive is actually effective in increasing the gas mileage of automobiles. In each case, we are interested in a specific characteristic of the population in question. Most of these characteristics can be determined by using the numerical descriptive measures described in Chapter 2. Recall from Chapter 1 that descriptive measures of a population are called *parameters,* while descriptive measures calculated from a sample are called *statistics.* In many applications of statistical inference, we draw conclusions about a parameter of a population by using sample statistics.

In the course of this textbook, we will present about three dozen different statistical techniques that have proved useful to business managers and economists. You will find that the arithmetic needed for each method is quite simple. The only mathematical skills required are the abilities to add, subtract, multiply, and divide. Even these skills may be less in demand if you use a calculator to do much of the work; and if you use a computer, virtually no mathematics is needed. In fact, because of the availability of inexpensive computers and statistical software, many students will do very few computations by hand. This is certainly true in real-life (defined as anything outside a college or university) applications of statistics.

Thus the real challenge of the subject of statistics relates to your ability to determine which technique is the most appropriate one for answering a given question. Most students who are taking their first course in statistics have some difficulty in recognizing the particular kind of statistical problem involved in practice exercises—and hence the appropriate statistical technique to use. This difficulty intensifies when you are faced with applying statistical techniques to real-life practical problems, where the questions to be addressed may themselves be vague and ill-defined. In this textbook, most of the exercises and examples depict situations in which the data have already been gathered, and your task is to answer a specific question by applying one of the statistical techniques you've studied. In a real-life situation, you will probably have to design the experiment, define the questions, and perform and interpret the statistical computations yourself. The difficulty of determining what to do can be formidable.

Because people encounter such difficulty both during and after studying this subject, we have adopted a systematic approach that is designed to help you identify the statistical problem.

SECTION 5.2 ## DATA SCALES

A number of factors determine which statistical technique should be used, but two of these are especially important: the type of data being measured, and the purpose of the statistical inference. The data generated as a result of an experiment can be classified under four different headings called the **data scales.** Consider the following experiment.

In order to learn more about the plans of tourists, a travel agent has commissioned a survey. The survey questionnaire contains (among others) the following four questions and possible responses:

1. Which continent did you visit on your last vacation?

    Responses: North America
    South America
    Europe
    Asia
    Africa
    Australia
    Antarctica

2. How would you rate the facilities (hotel, restaurants, attractions, and so on)?

    Responses: Excellent
    Good
    Fair
    Poor

3. What was the approximate temperature during your stay?

4. Approximately how many miles is it from your home to the vacation site?

If you examine the possible responses to each question, you will see differences among them. Questions 1 and 2 elicit nonquantitative answers, while questions 3 and 4 ask for quantitative data. But there are other differences, as well. In fact, each of the four questions will produce results that have different data scales.

The set of possible responses to question 1 comprises the seven continents. In order to help record the responses, we could assign numbers to these seven responses; in fact, when such data are stored and processed by a computer, they are often converted into numbers. Data produced in this way are said to have a **nominal scale,** because the numbers only represent the name of the result: they have no real numerical meaning. As a result, any calculations performed on a nominal scale are also meaningless. For example, suppose that we recorded the responses to question 1 as follows:

North America   1
South America   2
Europe   3
Asia   4
Africa   5
Australia   6
Antarctica   7

Suppose further that the first 10 people interviewed answered 1, 1, 3, 4, 1, 1, 2, 3, 1, 3. If we were to calculate the sample mean, we would find that $\bar{x} = 2$. Does this mean that the average person vacationed in South America? Suppose that two more people were interviewed, and they said that they had spent their vacation in Africa. Then $\bar{x} = 2.5$. Does this mean that the average person vacationed halfway between South America and Europe? Obviously, the answer to both questions is no, and the reason why is that descriptive measures such as means and variances are meaningless for nominal data. All we can do when the data scale is nominal is count the number of times each value has occurred, and then calculate the proportion of (in this case) vacationers who visited each of the seven continents.

Since the answers to question 2 are nonquantitative, they, too, appear to be nominal. Notice, however, that the responses to this question are ranked in preferential order, by the quality of the facilities. The first response (Excellent) is the highest rating; the second response (Good) is the second-highest rating; and so on. Any numerical representation of the four answers should maintain the ranked ordering of the responses. Such a numerical system is called an **ordinal scale.** The only constraint upon our choice of numbers for this scale is that they must represent the order of the responses; the actual values to be used are arbitrary. For example, we could record the responses as

Excellent   4
Good   3
Fair   2
Poor   1

But another, equally valid representation of the ratings is

Excellent   9
Good   5
Fair   3
Poor   2

And indeed we could simply reverse our original 4-3-2-1 rating so that Excellent $= 1$ and Poor $= 4$, with no effect on the statistical technique to be used.

The only information provided by an ordinal scale that is not provided by a nominal scale is the ranked order of the responses. We still cannot interpret the difference between values in an ordinal scale, since the actual numbers used are arbitrary. For example, the 4-3-2-1 rating implies that the difference between excellent and good $(4 - 3 = 1)$ is equal to the difference between fair and poor $(2 - 1 = 1)$, whereas the 9-5-3-2 rating implies that the difference between excellent and good $(9 - 5 = 4)$ is four times as large as the difference between fair and poor $(3 - 2 = 1)$. Since both numbering systems are valid (though arbitrary), no inferences can be drawn as to the differences between values of an ordinal scale. Thus, calculations of descriptive measures such as means and variances are again invalid. The only valid statistics that can be calculated from an ordinal scale are descriptive measures based on the ranking process. For example, the appropriate measure of central location of an ordinal scale is the median. You will see in Chapter 14 that any statistical technique properly applied to ordinal data must be based on a ranking process.

Unlike the first two questions, questions 3 and 4 produce answers that are real numbers. Consequently, we do not have to assign an arbitrary number to each response, as we did with the nominal and ordinal scales. Because the numbers are not arbitrary, the intervals between values can be interpreted. Scales that possess these characteristics are called **interval scales.** But although questions 3 and 4 both fit this category, they are not identical in scale. You can see why when you consider that, whereas in question 3 we cannot say (for example) that 80°F is twice as warm as 40°F, we can in question 4 say that 80 miles is twice as far as 40 miles. Therefore, the data scale of question 4 goes beyond that of question 3 and is called a **ratio scale.** All types of statistical calculations are permitted on a ratio scale, and the only limitation on an interval scale is that no calculations of ratios are valid. Thus, means and variances are valid descriptive measures for both interval and ratio scales. In relation to the statistical techniques presented in this text, there are no real differences between interval and ratio scales, so they will be grouped together in future discussions.

The data scales can be ranked according to the valid calculations they permit. The nominal scale has the lowest rank, since no calculations are permitted with it. The ordinal scale comes next, since we may calculate medians and other measures based on rank. Then comes the interval scale, for which all calculations except ratios are valid. And topping the list is the ratio scale, for which every computation is valid. It is important to recognize that we can treat a higher-ranked scale as if it were a lower-ranked one. We have already indicated that we will treat all ratio scales as interval scales in this book (because the two are not distinguishable for purposes of statistical inference). By the same token, we can treat interval scales as ordinal or even nominal, if it suits our purpose.

For example, suppose we wanted to measure the weights of bags of potato chips that are supposed to weigh 8 ounces. (You should recognize at once that the data scale of this measurement is ratio.) Suppose further that our only interest in this experiment is to find the bags that weigh less than 8 ounces, which are considered unacceptable. As a result, for each bag of potato chips, the outcome of the experiment is either *acceptable* or *unacceptable*—classifications that can be handled by a nominal scale. Later in this book, you will find examples and exercises in which it is advantageous to treat higher-ranking scales as lower-ranking ones. (Of course, we cannot reverse the process and treat a lower-ranking scale as a higher-ranking one.)

We conclude our discussion of data scales with the following summary.

Data Scales

Nominal Scale: values assigned completely arbitrarily.
    Valid computations: counts of each value.
    Valid descriptive measure: proportion.

Ordinal Scale: values arbitrarily assigned, but values must represent the ranked order of the responses.
    Valid computations: must be based on a ranking process.
    Valid descriptive measures: median and any other measure based on ranking.

Interval and Ratio Scales: values are real numbers, and differences between values are meaningful.
    Valid computations: all (except ratios on interval scale).
    Valid descriptive measures: all, including means and variances.

SECTION 5.3   ## *PROBLEM OBJECTIVES*

The second key factor in determining the appropriate statistical technique to use is the purpose in doing the work. You will find that every statistical method has some specific objective. We will now identify and describe five such objectives.

1. Description of a Single Population.   Our objective here is to describe some property of a population of interest. The decision about which property to describe is generally dictated by the data scale. For example, suppose that the population of interest consists of all purchasers of home computers. If we are interested in the purchasers' incomes (for which the data scale is ratio), we may calculate the mean or the variance to describe that aspect of the population. But if we are interested in the brand of computer that has been bought (for which the data scale is nominal), all we can do is compute the proportion of the population that purchases each brand.

2. Comparison of Two Populations.   In this case, our goal is to compare a property of one population with a corresponding property of a second population. For example, suppose the populations of interest are male and female purchasers of computers. We could compare the means and variances of their incomes, or we could compare the proportion of each population that purchases a certain brand. Once again, the data scale generally determines what kind of properties we compare.

3. Comparison of Two or More Populations. We may wish to compare the average or the variance of incomes in each of several locations, in order (for example) to decide where to build a new shopping center. Or we may wish to compare the proportions of defective items in a number of production lines, to determine which line is the best. In each case, the problem objective involves comparing two or more populations.

4. Analysis of the Relationship Between Two Variables. There are numerous situations in which we want to know how one variable is related to another. Governments need to know what effect rising interest rates have on the unemployment rate. Companies want to investigate how the size of their advertising budget influences sales volume. In most of the problems we deal with in this introductory text, the two variables to be analyzed possess the same scale; we will not attempt to cover the fairly large body of statistical techniques that have been developed to deal with two variables having different scales.

5. Analysis of the Relationship Among Two or More Variables. Our objective here is usually to forecast one variable (called the **dependent variable**) on the basis of several other variables (called **independent variables**). We will deal with this problem only in situations in which all variables have interval scales.

SECTION 5.4

HOW, WHEN, AND WHY OF STATISTICAL INFERENCE

In Chapters 6 through 17 of this textbook, we will present a number of different statistical techniques, and in the course of developing them we will answer three types of questions pertaining to each—namely, how, when, and why the statistical method is performed.

For the most part, knowing *how* to calculate the relevant statistics involves nothing more than knowing simple arithmetic. If you can add, subtract, multiply, and divide, you will be able to perform most of the computations. Several techniques are so time-consuming that computers are used almost exclusively in solving problems with them. The recent trend is toward using computers on a greater variety of problems, including ones that could easily be done on an inexpensive calculator. If you have ready access to a computer and the appropriate software, you may not need to do the calculations by hand. Nonetheless, in order to understand the logic of the technique, you probably should do several problems of each type by hand or with the aid of a calculator. You will find that we never simply provide a formula in this book without explaining how the technique is used to provide an answer to a problem.

The most difficult issue for students is to determine *when* to apply each technique. We believe that using our systematic approach should alleviate this difficulty. We have observed that graduates of statistics courses hesitate to use statistical techniques because they remain uncertain about the appropriateness of a method. To combat this problem, we detail all of the relevant conditions required to use a method, and we show how to determine whether these conditions are met.

The question of *why* statistical methods are used is somewhat more difficult to answer. This is not because of any shortage of real-life applications of statistics—we can easily produce a long list of such applications as they pertain to the areas of accounting, finance, production, marketing, and organizational behavior—but because statistics plays so integral a role in many managerial decisions that the statistical application is often difficult to show by itself, outside the wider context of the manager's decision problem. Moreover, real-life problems often involve several different techniques, in which case understanding the complete problem requires understanding a number of methods. This circumstance conflicts somewhat with the step-by-step approach necessary in a statistics book.

We propose to deal with the why issue in several ways. In most of the worked examples, we set up the problem in a decision context; and even though some are quite simplistic, they should give you some idea of the motivation for using statistics. Many of the exercises also stress the reason for the application. We acknowledge that these reasons are frequently simplified; but as we progress, the assumptions become much more reasonable, and problems that in practice involve the use of several methods can be addressed. Additionally, in most chapters we provide workable cases that have been adapted from actual studies (as reported in academic journals, conference proceedings, and magazines) and feature real data. To solve these problems, you must repeat the statistical analyses performed by the original author. Most cases in Chapter 18 require the use of several different methods. As such, the cases are as realistic as possible. For about half of the cases, the computer is either recommended or required; the data for these have been stored on a computer disk, which is available from the publisher. A thorough analysis of at least some of the cases in this book will give you greater insight into the how, when, and why of statistical inference.

SECTION 5.5

SUMMARY TABLE

In the next 12 chapters, we will develop approximately 40 statistical techniques, each of which will be identified by problem objective and data scale. Table 5.1 shows the five problem objectives and the three data scales (we have combined the interval and ratio scales). For each combination, one or more techniques are used to answer relevant questions, and Table 5.1 identifies the chapter and section where these methods are described.

Where possible, we will group the statistical techniques according to their common problem objectives. Because of similarities in some of the techniques, however, this order of presentation cannot always be strictly adhered to. Table 5.1 should help you keep track of the actual order of presentation.

TABLE 5.1   *GUIDE TO STATISTICAL TECHNIQUES, SHOWING CHAPTERS AND SECTIONS WHERE EACH TECHNIQUE IS INTRODUCED*

Problem Objective	Nominal Data Scale	Ordinal Data Scale	Interval Data Scale
Description of a single population	Ch. 8 Sec. 13.2	—	Ch. 7
Comparison of two populations	Ch. 10	Sec. 14.2 Sec. 14.3	Ch. 9 Sec. 14.2 Sec. 14.4
Comparison of two or more populations	Sec. 13.3	Sec. 14.5 Sec. 14.6	Ch. 12 Sec. 14.5 Sec. 14.6
Analysis of the relationship between two variables	Sec. 13.3	Sec. 15.10	Ch. 15
Analysis of the relationship among two or more variables	—	—	Ch. 16 Ch. 17

EXERCISES

5.1 Provide two examples each of a nominal scale, an ordinal scale, and an interval scale.

5.2 What factor differentiates a nominal scale from an ordinal scale?

5.3 What factor differentiates an ordinal scale from an interval scale?

5.4 Identify the scale type of the following:

a. numbers on the backs of baseball players' uniforms

b. identification numbers of students enrolled in a university

c. prices of objects in a department store

d. the time it takes for runners to complete the Boston Marathon

e. the ranking of the completion times of runners competing in the Boston Marathon

5.5 For each of the following experiments, identify the variable being measured and indicate whether the data scale is nominal, ordinal, or interval.

a. A survey asks respondents how seriously they take the possibility of another gasoline shortage in the next 5 years. Possible responses are very seriously, somewhat seriously, not too seriously, and not at all seriously.

b. Annual surveys measure trends in the popularity of televised baseball games. Individuals are asked whether or not they regularly watch baseball on television.

c. A government agency randomly selects containers of packaged goods to make certain that the packages weigh what their manufacturers advertise.

d. A breakfast-cereal manufacturer surveys customers to determine which of three new package designs is most popular.

e. A fast-food franchiser wants to know if the position of items on the menu board influences sales. He organizes an experiment in which the sales of an item are counted during one week when the item appears in one position on the board and during a second week when the item appears in another position.

5.6 For each of the following, identify the problem objective.

a. A firm wishes to determine if increasing the advertising budget will result in an increase in sales volume. Analysts determine the monthly advertising expenses and the monthly sales volume for the past 12 months.

b. In the recent recession, a number of workers had to work reduced hours. An economist wants to determine if there are differences among five industries in the average number of hours of work per week.

c. The manager of a large department store has decided that drastic action must be taken to reduce losses caused by shoplifting. Several different, expensive alternatives have been proposed. As each alternative is investigated in depth, it becomes clear that the firm needs an accurate estimate of the percentage of shoppers who engage in shoplifting.

d. In order to design advertising campaigns, a marketing manager needs to know if different segments of the population prefer her company's product to competing products. She decides to perform a survey that will determine if different proportions of people in five age categories purchase the product.

e. The same marketing manager (as in part (d)) also wants to know if the proportion of men pur-

chasing the product is different from the proportion of women.

f. An industrial psychologist is hired by an automobile manufacturer to determine the factors that influence absenteeism. She decides to investigate a number of demographic variables: age, number of years of work experience, number of years of education, and household income.

g. The production manager of a large plant is contemplating changing the process by which a certain product is produced. Since workers in this plant are paid on the basis of their output, it is essential to demonstrate that the rate of assembling a unit will increase under the new system. Ten workers are randomly selected to participate in an experiment in which each worker assembles one unit under the old process and one unit under the new process.

h. The management of a large pension fund is interested in studying the distribution of monthly rates of return on large, well-diversified portfolios of common stock. In particular, the management is interested in finding out whether the mean monthly return exceeds 1%.

i. The electric company in a large city is considering an incentive plan to encourage its customers to pay their bills promptly. The plan is to discount the bills 1% if the customer pays within 5 days rather than within the usual 25 days. An experiment is performed to determine if the incentive plan is effective in reducing the average payment period.

SAMPLING AND SAMPLING DISTRIBUTIONS

SECTION 6.1   *INTRODUCTION*

In Chapter 5, we briefly introduced the concept of statistical inference—the process of inferring information about a population from a sample. Since properties of populations can usually be described by means of parameters, the statistical technique used generally deals with drawing inferences about population parameters from sample statistics.

Working inside the ivy-covered walls of a university or within the covers of a statistics textbook, we may assume that population parameters are known. In real life, however, calculating parameters becomes prohibitive because populations tend to be quite large. As a result, most population parameters are unknown. For example, in order to determine the mean annual income of North American blue-collar workers, we would have to ask each North American blue-collar worker what his or her income is, and then calculate the mean of all the responses. Because this population consists of several million people, the task is both expensive and impractical. If we are willing to accept less than 100% accuracy, we can use statistical inference to obtain an estimate.

Rather than investigating the entire population, we take a sample, determine the annual income of the workers in this group, and calculate the sample mean, $\bar{x}$. While there is very little chance that $\bar{x}$ is identical to the population mean, we would expect $\bar{x}$ to be reasonably close; and sampling distributions allow us to measure how close the value of the sample statistic is likely to be to the value of the population parameter. The sampling distribution plays a critical role in statistics because the measure of proximity it provides is the key to statistical inference. In Section 6.4, we will discuss the sampling distribution of the sample mean; and in later chapters, we will present other sampling distributions, as they are needed. To begin, however, we need to discuss the concepts and techniques of sampling itself.

SECTION 6.2   *SAMPLING*

The chief motive for examining a sample rather than a population is cost. Statistical inference permits us to draw conclusions about a population parameter based on a sample that is quite small in comparison to the size of the population. For example, television executives want to know the proportion of television viewers who watch that network's programs. Since 100 million people may be watching television in the United States on a given evening, determining the proportions that are watching certain programs is impractical and prohibitively expensive. The Nielsen ratings provide approximations of the desired information by observing what a sample of 1,000 television viewers watch. Thus they estimate the population proportion by calculating the sample proportion.

The field of quality control illustrates yet another reason for sampling. In order to ensure that a production process is operating properly, the operations manager needs to know the proportion of defective units that are being produced. If the quality-control technician must destroy the unit in order to determine whether or not it is defective, there is no alternative to sampling: a complete inspection of the population would destroy the entire output of the production process.

We know that the sample proportion of television viewers or of defective items is probably not exactly equal to the population proportion we want it to estimate. Nonetheless, the sample statistic can come quite close to the parameter it is designed to estimate, if the **target population** (the population about which we want to draw inferences) and the **sampled population** (the population from which we've actually taken a sample) are the same. In practice these may not be the same.

For example, the Nielsen ratings are supposed to provide information about the television shows that all Americans are watching. Hence, the target population is the television viewers of the United States. If the sample of 1,000 viewers were drawn exclusively from the state of New York, however, the sampled population would be the television viewers of New York. In this case, the target population and the sampled population are not the same, and no valid inferences about the target population can be drawn. To allow proper estimation of the proportion of all American television viewers watching a specific program, the sample should contain men and women of varying ages, incomes, occupations, and residences in a pattern similar to that of the target population. The importance of sampling from the target population cannot be overestimated, since the consequences of drawing conclusions from improperly selected samples can be costly. One of the most spectacular examples of how not to conduct a survey took place in 1936.

The *Literary Digest* was a popular magazine of the 1920s and 1930s, which had correctly predicted the outcomes of several presidential elections. In 1936, the *Digest* predicted that the Republican candidate, Alfred Landon, would defeat the Democrat incumbent, Franklin D. Roosevelt, by a 3–2 margin. But in that election, Roosevelt defeated Landon in a landslide victory, garnering the support of 62% of the electorate. The source of this blunder was the sampling procedure: the *Digest* sent out 10 million sample ballots to prospective voters, but only 2.3 million ballots were returned, resulting in a self-selected sample.

Self-selected samples are almost always biased, because the individuals who participate in them are more keenly interested in the issue than are the other members of the population. You often see similar surveys conducted today when radio stations ask people to call and give their opinion on an issue of interest. Again, only those who are concerned about the topic and have enough patience to get through to the station will be included in the sample. Hence, the sampled population is composed entirely of people who are interested in the issue, whereas the target population is made up of all the people within the listening radius of the radio station. As a result, the conclusions drawn from such surveys are frequently wrong. Unfortunately, because the true value of the parameter being estimated is never known (unlike the situation in a political survey, where the election provides the true parametric value), these surveys give the impression of providing useful information. In fact, the results of such surveys are likely to be no more accurate than the results of the 1936 *Literary Digest* poll.*

In the next section, we discuss a number of different ways in which we can survey populations. In all cases, we assume that the surveys are properly performed and that the target population and the sampled population are very similar.

EXERCISE

6.1 For each of the following sampling plans, indicate why the target population and the sampled population are not the same.

a. In order to determine the opinions and attitudes of customers who regularly shop at a particular mall, a surveyor stands outside a large department store in the mall and randomly selects people to participate in the survey.

b. A library wishes to estimate the proportion of its books that have been damaged. They decide to select one book per shelf as a sample, by measuring 12 inches from the left edge of each shelf and selecting the book in that location.

c. A political survey visits 200 residences and asks the eligible voters present in the house at the time whom they intend to vote for. The visits take place during the afternoons.

SECTION 6.3   SAMPLING PLANS

Our objective in this section is to introduce several different sampling plans. We begin our presentation with the most basic design.

SIMPLE RANDOM SAMPLING

Simple Random Sample

A simple random sample is a sample in which each member of the population is equally likely to be included.

One way to conduct a simple random sample is to assign a number to each element in the population, write these numbers on individual slips of paper, toss them into a hat, and draw the required number of slips (the sample size, n) from the hat. This is the kind of procedure that occurs in raffles, when all of the ticket stubs go into a large rotating drum from which the winners are selected.

---

* Many statisticians ascribe the *Literary Digest's* statistical debacle to the wrong causes. For a better understanding of what really happened read Maurice C. Bryson "The *Literary Digest* Poll: Making of a Statistical Myth," *American Statistician* 30(4) (November 1976): 184–85.

Sometimes the elements of the population are already numbered. For example, virtually all adults have Social Security numbers; all employees of large corporations have employee numbers; many people have driver's license numbers, medical plan numbers, student numbers, and so on. In such cases, choosing the procedure to use is simply a matter of deciding how to select from among these numbers.

In other cases, a common form of numbering has built-in flaws that make it inappropriate as a source of samples. Not everyone has a phone number, for example, so the telephone book does not list all of the people in a given area. Some people do not have phones, some have unlisted phones, some have more than one; and these differences mean that each element of the population does not have an equal probability of being selected.

Once each element of the chosen population has been assigned a unique number, sample numbers can be selected at random. It is usual to employ a computer-generated random-numbers table, such as Table 14 in Appendix B, for this purpose.

Conceptually the numbers are derived as follows. There are only ten digits: 0 through 9. Working from a rectangular probability distribution, wherein each of these ten numbers has the same probability of being selected, the computer picks a number at random and records it. These individual integers are then formatted to be printed in columns of 5 or 10 integers, with 50 or 100 rows per page.

Using the tables involves picking a row and a column at random, and then reading off the numbers systematically from that point on. For example, we might proceed horizontally to the right or left, or vertically downward or upward. If you are making extensive use of a random-number table, you should replace it every so often. Human nature is such that each of us has a propensity to start in about the same place and to proceed in a similar manner repeatedly. Repeated use of the same table, therefore, can lead to selection of the same string of random numbers.

EXAMPLE 6.1

A department-store audit involves checking a random sample from a population of 30 outstanding credit-account balances. The 30 accounts are listed in the accompanying table.

Account No.	Balance	Account No.	Balance	Account No.	Balance
1	25	6	34	11	918
2	0	7	245	12	801
3	605	8	59	13	227
4	1010	9	67	14	0
5	527	10	403	15	47

(continued)

Account No.	Balance	Account No.	Balance	Account No.	Balance
16	0	21	159	26	291
17	102	22	279	27	16
18	215	23	115	28	0
19	429	24	27	29	402
20	197	25	27	30	17

Use a random-number table to select 5 accounts at random.

Solution.   Going to our random number table, we select row 1, column 8 as our starting point. We shall go down that column, selecting the first two digits as our random numbers. The random numbers are reproduced here for convenience.

Random Numbers			
22	✓	19	✓
17	✓	51	
83		39	
57		59	
27	✓	84	
54		20	✓

Notice that we had to select more than five numbers, since some of them were of no use to us.

The following 5 accounts, therefore, are to be audited:

Random Number (account number)	Balance
22	$279
17	$102
27	$16
19	$429
20	$197

This yields a sample mean of $\bar{x} = \$204.60$, which is quite close to the population mean of $\mu = \$241.47$.

STRATIFIED RANDOM SAMPLING

In making inferences about a population, we attempt to extract as much information as possible from a sample. The basic sampling plan, simple random sampling, often accomplishes this goal at low cost. Other methods, however, can be used to increase the amount of information about the population. One such procedure is stratified random sampling.

Stratified Random Sample

A stratified random sample is obtained by separating the population into mutually exclusive sets or strata and then drawing simple random samples from each stratum.

Examples of criteria for separating a population into strata (and the strata themselves) are as follows:

1. Sex   male
           female

2. Age   under 20
           20–30
           31–40
           41–50
           51–60
           over 60

3. Occupation   professional
                  clerical
                  blue-collar
                  other

Any stratification must be done so that the strata are mutually exclusive. This means that each member of the population must be assigned to exactly one stratum. Once the population has been stratified in this way, we can employ simple random sampling to generate the complete sample.

As you'll see later in this book, we can improve the quality of the statistical inference by reducing the variability associated with the sample. One advantage of this sampling procedure is that, if the strata are relatively homogeneous (similar), the variability within each stratum and the overall variability are reduced. A second advantage is that we can draw inferences about each stratum individually. For example, suppose that we wanted to estimate the average annual individual income of people living in a large city, on the basis of a sample of 1,000. A simple random sample would be generated by randomly selecting a sample of 1,000 individuals. With stratified random sampling, we can improve our estimation by stratifying the population in a number of different ways. We can, for instance, stratify by age; that is, we can separate the population into age categories,

> under 20
> 21–40
> 41–60
> over 60

and draw random samples of 250 from each of the subgroups. The advantage of this approach is that the incomes within each age group are likely to be somewhat similar, and as a result our estimate will be better. Additionally, we can estimate the average income for each age group.

CLUSTER SAMPLING

> **Cluster Sample**
>
> A cluster sample is a simple random sample of groups or clusters of elements.

This sampling plan is particularly useful when it is difficult or costly to develop a complete list of the population members (making it difficult and costly to generate a simple random sample). It is also useful whenever the population elements are widely dispersed geographically. For example, suppose that we wanted to estimate the average annual household income in a large city. If we wish to use simple random sampling, we would need a complete list of households in the city from which to sample. To use stratified random sampling, we would need the list of households, and we would also need to have each household categorized by some other variable (such as age of household head) in order to develop the strata. A less expensive alternative would be to let each block within the city represent a cluster. A sample of clusters could then be randomly selected, and every household within these clusters could be interviewed to determine income. By reducing the distances the surveyor must cover to gather the data, cluster sampling reduces the cost.

SECTION 6.4   ## *SAMPLING DISTRIBUTION OF $\bar{x}$*

An illustration of the importance of the sampling distribution in statistical inference is given in the following problem. The management of a large oil company is trying to assess the effectiveness of its periodic sales campaigns. During the campaign, customers who buy at least 5 gallons of gasoline are given free coupons that can be used to get discounts in local restaurants. Because of the advertising, printing, and other costs involved, management is willing to continue to schedule the campaigns only if it is satisfied that mean daily sales of gasoline during the sales push are at least 18,000 gallons per station. In a random sample of 50 stations during the last campaign, mean daily sales were 18,500 liters. On the basis of the statistical data, should the oil company continue the coupon giveaways?

Before we attempt to answer the question, let's be sure that the issues are clear. The parameter of interest is μ, the mean daily sales during the campaign by all of the stations owned by the company. If management were satisfied that μ exceeds 18,000 gallons, it would approve of the campaign. The only statistic available, however, is the sample mean, $\bar{x}$, of 50 stations. Our initial reaction is that, since $\bar{x}$ (which equals 18,500) exceeds 18,000, μ exceeds 18,000; however, this is not necessarily correct. The conclusion that can be drawn about μ very much depends on how close $\bar{x}$ is expected to be to μ. If management believes that $\bar{x}$ is close to μ, it will be confident that μ is greater than 18,000. Conversely, if $\bar{x}$ can be quite different from μ, μ may actually be less than 18,000. Unfortunately, from the information provided, we cannot determine the expected proximity of $\bar{x}$ and μ. That is the function of the sampling distribution, which is discussed next. When we have completed our discussion of the sampling distribution, we will return to this problem and answer it.

To grasp the idea of a sampling distribution, consider the population created by throwing a fair die infinitely many times, with the random variable x indicating the number of spots showing on any one throw. The probability distribution of the random variable x is

x	$p(x)$
1	1/6
2	1/6
3	1/6
4	1/6
5	1/6
6	1/6

The population is infinitely large, since we can throw the die infinitely many times (or at least imagine doing so). From the definitions of expectation and variance, we can show that the population mean is

$$\mu = E(x)$$
$$= \sum x \cdot p(x)$$
$$= 1(\tfrac{1}{6}) + 2(\tfrac{1}{6}) + \cdots + 6(\tfrac{1}{6})$$
$$= 3.5$$

and that the population variance is

$$\sigma^2 = \text{Var}(x)$$
$$= \sum (x - \mu)^2 \cdot p(x)$$
$$= (1 - 3.5)^2(\tfrac{1}{6}) + (2 - 3.5)^2(\tfrac{1}{6}) + \cdots + (6 - 3.5)^2(\tfrac{1}{6})$$
$$= 2.92$$

Now pretend that μ is unknown and that we wish to estimate its value by using the sample mean $\bar{x}$, calculated from a sample of size $n = 2$. In actual practice, only one sample would be drawn, and hence there would be only one value of $\bar{x}$; but in order to assess how closely $\bar{x}$ estimates the value of μ, we will develop the sampling distribution of $\bar{x}$.

Consider all of the possible different samples of size 2 that could be drawn from the parent population. Figure 6.1 depicts this process. With each of these possible samples, we can associate a value equal to that sample's mean, as shown in Table 6.1. The function making this association is represented by $\bar{x}$, the sample mean. Since the value of the sample mean $\bar{x}$ varies randomly from sample to sample, we can regard $\bar{x}$ as a new random variable created by sampling. Table 6.1 lists all the possible samples and their corresponding values of $\bar{x}$.

There are 36 different possible samples of size 2, and since each sample is equally likely, the probability of any one sample's being selected is 1/36. However, $\bar{x}$ can assume only 11 different possible values: 1.0, 1.5, 2.0, ..., 6.0, with certain values of $\bar{x}$ occurring more frequently than others. The value $\bar{x} = 1.0$ occurs only once, so its probability is $1/36$. The value $\bar{x} = 1.5$ can occur in two ways; hence, $p(1.5) = 2/36$. The probabilities of the other values of $\bar{x}$ are determined similarly, and the sampling distribution of $\bar{x}$ that results is shown in Table 6.2. This same distribution can be approximated by tossing two fair dice many times; the distribution of $\bar{x}$ thus created should be similar to the one shown in Table 6.2.

The most interesting aspect of the sampling distribution of $\bar{x}$ is how dissimilar it is from the distribution of x, as can be seen in Figure 6.2. It is also important to be able to compute the mean and the variance of $\bar{x}$. Using our rules of expectation and variance, we have the mean of $\bar{x}$,

$$
\begin{aligned}
\mu_{\bar{x}} &= E(\bar{x}) \\
&= \sum \bar{x} \cdot p(\bar{x}) \\
&= 1.0(\tfrac{1}{36}) + 1.5(\tfrac{2}{36}) + \cdots + 6.0(\tfrac{1}{36}) \\
&= 3.5
\end{aligned}
$$

and the variance of $\bar{x}$,

$$
\begin{aligned}
\sigma_{\bar{x}}^2 &= \mathrm{Var}(\bar{x}) \\
&= E(\bar{x} - \mu_{\bar{x}})^2 \\
&= \sum (\bar{x} - \mu_{\bar{x}})^2 \cdot p(\bar{x}) \\
&= (1.0 - 3.5)^2(\tfrac{1}{36}) + (1.5 - 3.5)^2(\tfrac{2}{36}) + \cdots + (6.0 - 3.5)^2(\tfrac{1}{36}) \\
&= 1.46
\end{aligned}
$$

It is important to recognize that the distribution of $\bar{x}$ is different from the distribution of x. Figure 6.2 shows that the shapes of the two distributions differ. From our previous calculations, we know that the mean of the sampling distribution of $\bar{x}$ is equal to the mean of the distribution of x; that is, $\mu_{\bar{x}} = \mu$. However, the variance of $\bar{x}$ is not equal to the variance of x; we calculated $\sigma^2 = 2.92$,

---

FIGURE 6.1   *DRAWING SAMPLES OF SIZE 2 FROM A POPULATION*

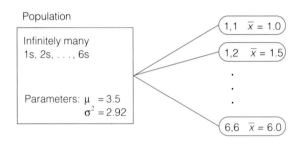

TABLE 6.1   *ALL SAMPLES OF SIZE 2 AND THEIR MEANS*

Sample	$\bar{x}$	Sample	$\bar{x}$
1,1	1.0	4,1	2.5
1,2	1.5	4,2	3.0
1,3	2.0	4,3	3.5
1,4	2.5	4,4	4.0
1,5	3.0	4,5	4.5
1,6	3.5	4,6	5.0
2,1	1.5	5,1	3.0
2,2	2.0	5,2	3.5
2,3	2.5	5,3	4.0
2,4	3.0	5,4	4.5
2,5	3.5	5,5	5.0
2,6	4.0	5,6	5.5
3,1	2.0	6,1	3.5
3,2	2.5	6,2	4.0
3,3	3.0	6,3	4.5
3,4	3.5	6,4	5.0
3,5	4.0	6,5	5.5
3,6	4.5	6,6	6.0

TABLE 6.2 SAMPLING DISTRIBUTION OF $\bar{x}$

$\bar{x}$	$p(\bar{x})$
1.0	1/36
1.5	2/36
2.0	3/36
2.5	4/36
3.0	5/36
3.5	6/36
4.0	5/36
4.5	4/36
5.0	3/36
5.5	2/36
6.0	1/36

FIGURE 6.2 DISTRIBUTIONS OF x AND $\bar{x}$

Distribution of x

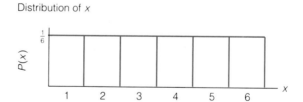

Distribution of $\bar{x}$

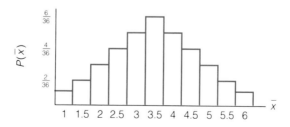

while $\sigma_{\bar{x}}^2 = 1.46$. It is no coincidence that the variance of $\bar{x}$ is exactly half the variance of x, as we shall see shortly.

Don't get lost in the terminology and notation. Remember that μ and σ^2 are the parameters of the population of x. In order to create the sampling distribution of $\bar{x}$, we repeatedly drew samples of size 2 from the population and calculated $\bar{x}$ for each sample. As a result, the values of $\bar{x}$ are not all the same. Thus, we treat $\bar{x}$ as a brand-new random variable, with its own distribution, mean, and variance. The mean is denoted $\mu_{\bar{x}}$, and the variance is denoted $\sigma_{\bar{x}}^2$.

If we now repeat the sampling process with the same population but with other values of n, we produce somewhat different sampling distributions of $\bar{x}$. Figure 6.3 shows the sampling distributions of $\bar{x}$ when $n = 5$, 10, and 25. As n grows larger, the number of possible values of $\bar{x}$ also grows larger; consequently, the histograms depicted in Figure 6.3 have been smoothed (to avoid drawing a large number of rectangles). Observe that, in each case, $\mu_{\bar{x}} = \mu$ and $\sigma_{\bar{x}}^2 = \sigma^2/n$.

The variance of the sampling distribution is less than that of the parent population. That is, $\sigma_{\bar{x}}^2 < \sigma^2$; and given that $\sigma_{\bar{x}}^2 < \sigma^2$, a randomly selected value of $\bar{x}$ (the mean of the number of spots observed in, say, five throws of the die) is likely to be closer to the mean value of 3.5 than is a randomly selected value of x (the number of spots observed in one throw). Indeed, this is what you would expect, since in five throws of the die you are likely to get some large values and some small ones, which will tend to offset one another in the averaging process and produce a sample mean reasonably close to 3.5. As the number of throws of the die increases, the likelihood that the sample mean will be close to 3.5 also increases. Thus we observe in Figure 6.3 that the sampling distribution of $\bar{x}$ becomes narrower (or more concentrated about the mean) as n increases.

Another thing that happens as n gets larger is that the sampling distribution of $\bar{x}$ becomes increasingly bell-shaped. This phenomenon is summarized in the Central Limit Theorem.

FIGURE 6.3   *SAMPLING DISTRIBUTIONS OF $\bar{x}$ WHEN $n = 5$, 10, AND 25*

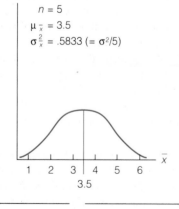
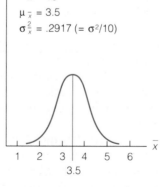
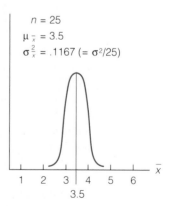

$n = 5$
$\mu_{\bar{x}} = 3.5$
$\sigma_{\bar{x}}^2 = .5833 \ (= \sigma^2/5)$

$n = 10$
$\mu_{\bar{x}} = 3.5$
$\sigma_{\bar{x}}^2 = .2917 \ (= \sigma^2/10)$

$n = 25$
$\mu_{\bar{x}} = 3.5$
$\sigma_{\bar{x}}^2 = .1167 \ (= \sigma^2/25)$

Central Limit Theorem

If relatively large samples of size n are drawn from any population, the sampling distribution of $\bar{x}$ is approximately normal. The approximation is better for larger sample sizes.

In our previous discussion, we established that the mean of $\bar{x}$ is equal to the mean of the original population. That is,

$$\mu_{\bar{x}} = \mu$$

We also showed that the variance of $\bar{x}$ is equal to the population variance divided by the sample size. That is,

$$\sigma_{\bar{x}}^2 = \frac{\sigma^2}{n}$$

We can now summarize what we know about the sampling distribution of the sample mean.

Sampling Distribution of $\bar{x}$

1. $\bar{x}$ is approximately normally distributed
2. $\mu_{\bar{x}} = \mu$
3. $\sigma_{\bar{x}}^2 = \dfrac{\sigma^2}{n}$, or $\sigma_{\bar{x}} = \dfrac{\sigma}{\sqrt{n}}$

The standard deviation of $\bar{x}$ is often called the **standard error** of the mean.

The accuracy of the approximation alluded to in the Central Limit Theorem depends on the probability distribution of the parent population and on the sample size. If the population is normal, then $\bar{x}$ is normally distributed for all values of n. If the population is nonnormal, then $\bar{x}$ is approximately normal only for larger values of n. In Figure 6.3, the distribution of $\bar{x}$ starts looking normal when $n \geq 10$. In many practical situations, a sample size of $n \geq 30$ may be sufficiently large to allow us to use the normal distribution as an approximation for the sampling distribution of $\bar{x}$. We urge you, however, to be cautious about the sample size. If a population is quite nonnormal, the sampling distribution will also be nonnormal—even for moderately large values of n.

Figure 6.4 depicts the sampling distribution of $\bar{x}$ for a variety of populations and sample sizes. Notice that, when x is normal distributed, $\bar{x}$ is also normally distributed for both $n = 5$ and $n = 30$. When x is uniformly distributed, the shape of the sampling distribution of $\bar{x}$ is much closer to the normal shape when $n = 30$ than

FIGURE 6.4   *SAMPLING DISTRIBUTIONS OF x̄ FROM DIFFERENT POPULATIONS*

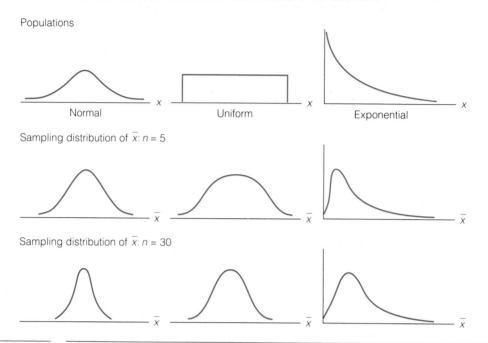

Populations

Sampling distribution of x̄: n = 5

Sampling distribution of x̄: n = 30

when $n = 5$. Obviously, the statement that $\bar{x}$ is approximately normally distributed when x is uniformly distributed and $n = 5$ is quite weak. When $n = 30$, the normal approximation of the sampling distribution of $\bar{x}$ is reasonable. Finally, when x is exponentially distributed, the sampling distribution of $\bar{x}$ for both $n = 5$ and $n = 30$ is clearly nonnormal. In order for the normal approximation of the sampling distribution to be valid, n would have to be larger. In general, when x follows a symmetric distribution, $\bar{x}$ is approximately normal for smaller values of n than it is when x is asymmetric.

EXAMPLE 6.2

The foreman of a bottling plant has observed that the amount of soda pop in each "32-ounce" bottle is actually a normally distributed random variable, with a mean of 32.2 ounces and a standard deviation of 0.3 ounces.

   a. Find the probability that, if a customer buys one bottle, that bottle will contain at least 32 ounces.

   b. Find the probability that, if a customer buys a carton of four bottles, the mean of the four will be at least 32 ounces.

Solution

a. Since the random variable is the amount of fill of one bottle, we want to find

$$P(x > 32)$$

where x is normally distributed, with $\mu = 32.2$ and $\sigma = .3$. Hence

$$P(x > 32) = P\left(\frac{x - \mu}{\sigma} > \frac{32 - 32.2}{.3}\right)$$
$$= P(z > -.67)$$
$$= .7486$$

b. Now we want to find the probability that the mean of four fills exceeds 32 ounces. That is, we want

$$P(\bar{x} > 32)$$

From our previous analysis and from the Central Limit Theorem, we know the following:

1. $\bar{x}$ is normally distributed
2. $\mu_{\bar{x}} = \mu = 32.2$
3. $\sigma_{\bar{x}} = \dfrac{\sigma}{\sqrt{n}} = \dfrac{.3}{\sqrt{4}} = .15$

FIGURE 6.5   *DISTRIBUTION OF x AND SAMPLING DISTRIBUTION OF x̄ IN EXAMPLE 6.2*

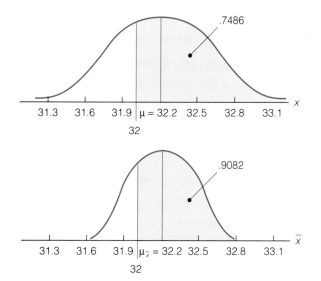

Hence,

$$P(\bar{x} > 32) = P\left(\frac{\bar{x} - \mu_x}{\sigma_{\bar{x}}} > \frac{32 - 32.2}{.15}\right)$$

$$= P(z > -1.33)$$

$$= .9082$$

Figure 6.5 describes the distributions used in this example.

In Example 6.2(b) we began with the assumption that both μ and σ were known. Then, using the sampling distribution, we made a probability statement about $\bar{x}$. This use of the sampling distribution is of no great interest to us, since the values of the parameters μ and σ are generally unknown. We can, however, use the sampling distribution to infer something about the unknown value of μ, on the basis of a sample mean.

EXAMPLE 6.3

The dean of the business school claims that the average weekly income of graduates of his school one year after graduation is $400.

a. If the dean's claim is correct and if weekly incomes are normally distributed with a standard deviation of $60, what is the probability that 36 randomly selected graduates have an average weekly income of less than $375?

b. If a random sample of 36 graduates had an average weekly income of $375, what would you conclude about the validity of the dean's claim?

Solution

a. We want to find

$$P(\bar{x} < 375)$$

Since $\bar{x}$ is normally distributed, with $\mu_{\bar{x}} = 400$ and $\sigma_{\bar{x}} = 60/\sqrt{36} = 10$,

$$P(\bar{x} < 375) = P\left(\frac{\bar{x} - \mu_{\bar{x}}}{\sigma_{\bar{x}}} < \frac{375 - 400}{10}\right)$$

$$= P(z < -2.5)$$

$$= .0062$$

b. The probability of observing a sample mean as low as $375 when the population mean is $400 is extremely small, as Figure 6.6 indicates. Since this event is quite rare and thus quite unlikely, we would have to conclude that the dean's claim is probably unjustified.

Our conclusion in part (b) illustrates one form of statistical inference, called **hypothesis testing.** Another form of inference is **estimation,** which we will

FIGURE 6.6 SAMPLING DISTRIBUTION OF $\bar{x}$ FOR EXAMPLE 6.3

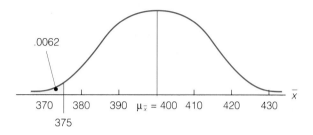

now use to answer part (b) in a different way. We know that about 95% of the values of $\bar{x}$ will fall within two standard errors of μ. Thus, 95% of the values of $\bar{x}$ will fall within \$20 of μ. As a result, we would infer that μ lies somewhere between \$355 and \$395. Since the dean claimed that $\mu = 400$, which does not fall into this interval, we would conclude that the claim is not supported by the statistical result. Both forms of statistical inference will be explained in Chapter 7.

Let's now return to the problem introduced at the beginning of this section and see how the sampling distribution allows us to answer that question. Recall the issue: does a sample of 50 gas stations showing a mean daily sale of 18,500 gallons give management a basis for confidently concluding that the mean sale of all gas stations exceeds 18,000?

Suppose that the population standard deviation of daily sales is known to be 5,000 gallons. From the discussion in this section, we know the following:

1. $\bar{x}$ is approximately normally distributed
2. $\mu_{\bar{x}} = \mu$
3. $\sigma_{\bar{x}} = \dfrac{\sigma}{\sqrt{n}} = \dfrac{5,000}{\sqrt{50}} = 707.11$

If we assume that the mean daily sale of all gas stations during the campaign is only 18,000, then

$$\mu_{\bar{x}} = \mu = 18,000$$

We can then calculate

$$P(\bar{x} > 18,500) = P\left(\frac{\bar{x} - \mu_{\bar{x}}}{\sigma_{\bar{x}}} > \frac{18,500 - 18,000}{707.11}\right)$$
$$= P(z > .71)$$
$$= .2389$$

This means that there is a fairly large probability that $\bar{x}$ can be 18,500 or more when in fact μ is equal to 18,000. As a result, management would not have reason to be very confident that the coupons are effective.

To put this in perspective, suppose that the population standard deviation was 1,500 gallons, instead of 5,000 gallons. Now,

$$\sigma_{\bar{x}} = \frac{\sigma}{\sqrt{n}} = \frac{1,500}{\sqrt{50}} = 212.13$$

and

$$P(\bar{x} > 18,500) = P\left(\frac{\bar{x} - \mu_{\bar{x}}}{\sigma_{\bar{x}}} > \frac{18,500 - 18,000}{212.13}\right)$$
$$= P(z > 2.36)$$
$$= .0091$$

This indicates that we would be quite unlikely to observe a value of $\bar{x}$ as large as 18,500 from a population whose mean is only 18,000. Hence, in this case, management would be justified in concluding that μ is actually larger than 18,000 and that the campaigns are successful.

As you've just seen, the sampling distribution allows us to draw inferences about population parameters. In Chapters 7 through 17 we will use various sampling distributions to test and estimate several different parameters. In each application, the sampling distribution is a critical component of the technique.

SAMPLING FROM A FINITE POPULATION

The definition of the variance of $\bar{x}$, $\sigma_{\bar{x}}^2$, is based on the assumption that the population from which we have sampled is very large (in fact, infinite). In most practical situations, this assumption is quite reasonable, since the purpose of sampling is to avoid the cost of investigating large populations. Nonetheless, situations do arise that are marked by a relatively small population. It turns out that $\bar{x}$ is still approximately normally distributed with $\mu_{\bar{x}} = \mu$. The variance of $\bar{x}$, however, is now defined as

$$\sigma_{\bar{x}}^2 = \left(\frac{\sigma^2}{n}\right)\left(\frac{N - n}{N - 1}\right)$$

where N = population size and $(N - n)/(N - 1)$ is called the **finite population correction factor.** With a little algebra, you can see that the finite population correction factor is approximately equal to $1 - n/N$. Thus, when the sample size is small relative to the population size, the correction factor is close to 1, and $\sigma_{\bar{x}}^2$ is approximately equal to σ^2/n. For example, if $n/N = .05$, then the correction factor is close to .95, and $\sigma_{\bar{x}}^2 \approx .95\sigma^2/n$. As a result, some practitioners use the correction factor only when the population size is small and n/N is relatively large (at least 10%). Since including the correction factor is quite easy, however, we recommend its use whenever the population is finite.

SECTION 6.5   ## *OTHER SAMPLING DISTRIBUTIONS*

For each parameter about which we wish to draw inferences, there will be one best sample statistic to use. In Chapter 7, we discuss how that sample statistic is chosen. Each statistic has its own sampling distribution, which is essential to the process of statistical inference. While the form of these sampling distributions varies, the concept underlying them is the same as that underlying the sampling distribution of $\bar{x}$ we just developed. That is, the sampling distribution is created by repeatedly drawing samples from the parent population, calculating the relevant sample statistic, and producing the distribution.

In later chapters, we will develop the sampling distributions of the sample variance and the sample proportion, as well as other more complex statistics.

SECTION 6.6   ## *SUMMARY*

Because most populations are so large, it is extremely costly and impractical to investigate each member of the population to determine the value of the parameters. As a practical alternative, we **sample** the population and use the sample statistics to draw inferences about the parameters. Care must be taken to ensure that the **target population** is the same as the **sampled population.**

There are several different **sampling plans.** These include **simple random sampling, stratified random sampling,** and **cluster sampling.** The **sampling distribution** represents the probability distribution created by repeated sampling and by calculation of the sample statistics. This allows us to calculate the probability that the statistic falls into a range of values, given that we know the population parameters.

The **Central Limit Theorem** states that the sampling distribution of $\bar{x}$ is approximately normal (for large n), with mean μ and variance σ^2/n. The sampling distribution of $\bar{x}$ and other sampling distributions (developed in later chapters) play a critical role in statistics by providing a probability link between the sample statistics and the population parameters.

■■■■■■■■   ### *EXERCISES*

6.2 A sample of $n = 100$ observations is drawn from a normal population, with $\mu = 1,000$ and $\sigma = 200$. Find

a. $P(\bar{x} > 1,050)$

b. $P(\bar{x} < 960)$

c. $P(\bar{x} > 1,100)$

6.3 Suppose that the sample size in Exercise 6.2 was 16. Find

a. $P(\bar{x} > 1,050)$

b. $P(\bar{x} < 960)$

c. $P(\bar{x} > 1,100)$

6.4 A sample of 50 observations is taken from a normal population, with $\mu = 100$ and $\sigma = 10$. If the population is finite with $N = 250$, find

a. $P(\bar{x} > 103)$

b. $P(98 < \bar{x} < 101)$

6.5 Repeat Exercise 6.4 with $N = 500$.

6.6 Repeat Exercise 6.4 with $N = 1,000$.

6.7   Table 14 in Appendix B is the random-numbers table. The single-digit numbers that appear there are drawn from a discrete uniform distribution. That is,

$$p(x) = \frac{1}{10}, \quad \text{where } x = 0, 1, \ldots, 9$$

a. Using your formula for expected value, find the mean of the probability distribution.

b. Find the variance of this probability distribution.

c. If a sample of $n = 100$ observations is taken from the discrete uniform population, what are the mean and the variance of the sampling distributions of the sample mean?

d. Find the following probabilities:
   (i) $P(4.4 < \bar{x} < 4.55)$
   (ii) $P(\bar{x} > 5.0)$
   (iii) $P(\bar{x} < 4.2)$

6.8   Consider the following experiment, which is similar to the dice-throwing experiment used to illustrate the sampling distribution of $\bar{x}$.

A container holds 6 tokens, each marked with a different number between 1 and 6. The experiment consists of drawing tokens at random without replacement.

a. List all possible samples of size 2 from this population.

b. Compare your results with those listed in Table 6.1. What differences do you notice?

c. Find the sampling distribution of $\bar{x}$.

d. Find the mean and the variance of the sampling distribution of $\bar{x}$. Check that

$$\mu_{\bar{x}} = \mu$$

and

$$\sigma_{\bar{x}}^2 = \left(\frac{\sigma^2}{n}\right)\left(\frac{N-n}{N-1}\right)$$

6.9   Repeat Exercise 6.8, with the container holding tokens numbered 1 to 5.

6.10   Repeat Exercise 6.8, with the container holding tokens numbered 1 to 4.

6.11   Referring to Table 6.1, find the sampling distribution of the sample variance s^2.

6.12   Referring to Table 6.1, find the sampling distribution of the sample proportions of "ones." Compare this with a binomial distribution with $n = 2$ and $p = 1/6$.

We recommend that the following three exercises be performed as a class exercise.

6.13   In order to investigate sampling distributions further, take 100 samples of 50 observations (single digits) from the discrete uniform population (Table 14 in Appendix B).

a. For each sample, calculate the mean (that is, the sample mean, $\bar{x}$).

b. Draw the histogram of $\bar{x}$.

c. From the Central Limit Theorem, find
   (i) $P(4.09 < \bar{x} < 4.91)$
   (ii) $P(3.69 < \bar{x} < 5.31)$

   (HINT: From Exercise 6.7, $\mu = 4.5$ and $\sigma^2 = 8.25$.)

d. Find the proportion of the 100 sample means computed in part (a) that fall between
   (i) 4.09 and 4.91
   (ii) 3.69 and 5.31

e. What do the results of parts (c) and (d) tell you about the sampling distribution of $\bar{x}$?

6.14   For the 100 samples of 50 observations drawn in Exercise 6.13, find the median of each sample.

a. Draw the histogram of the sample median.

b. What are the similarities and differences between the sampling distribution of the sample mean and that of the sample median?

6.15   For the 100 samples of 50 observations drawn in Exercise 6.13, find the variance of each sample.

a. Draw the histogram of the sample variance.

b. What are the similarities and differences between the sampling distribution of the sample mean and that of the sample variance?

6.16   Given a large population whose mean is 1,000 and whose standard deviation is 200, find the probability that a random sample of 400 has a mean that lies between 995 and 1,020.

6.17   An automatic machine in a manufacturing process is operating properly if the lengths of an important subcomponent are normally distributed, with mean $\mu = 117$ cm and standard deviation $\sigma = 2.1$.

a. Find the probability that one randomly selected unit has a length greater than 120 cm.

b. Find the probability that, if three units are randomly selected, all three have lengths exceeding 120 cm.

c. Find the probability that, if three units are randomly selected, their mean length exceeds 120 cm.

d. Explain the differences between parts (a), (b), and (c).

6.18 The manufacturer of cans of salmon that are supposed to have a net weight of 6 ounces tells you that the net weight is actually a random variable with a mean of 6.05 ounces and a standard deviation of .18 ounces. Suppose that you take a random sample of 36 cans.

a. Find the probability that the sample mean will be less than 5.97 ounces.

b. Suppose that your random sample of 36 cans produces a mean of 5.95 ounces. Comment on the statement made by the manufacturer.

6.19 A shipment of 500 cereal boxes is delivered to a supermarket. The manager is told that the weights of the cereal boxes are normally distributed, with a mean of 16.5 ounces and a standard deviation of .5 ounces.

a. Find the probability that a random sample of 200 boxes has a mean weight of between 16.49 and 16.51 ounces.

b. Repeat part (a), assuming that the shipment consists of 1,000 boxes; 2,000 boxes; 10,000 boxes.

c. Comment on the effect that the population size has on the probability.

6.20 The sign on the elevator in a large skyscraper states, "Maximum capacity 2,500 pounds or 16 persons." A professor of statistics wonders what the probability is that 16 people would weigh more than 2,500 pounds. If the weights of the people who use the elevator are normally distributed, with a mean of 150 pounds and a standard deviation of 20 pounds, what is the probability that the professor seeks?

INFERENCE ABOUT THE DESCRIPTION OF A SINGLE POPULATION: INTERVAL SCALE

INTRODUCTION

This chapter introduces the concepts and foundations of estimation and hypothesis testing. Throughout this chapter and in all chapters up to Chapter 18, we employ these techniques for various combinations of data scales and problem objectives. You will find that, by and large, the techniques remain the same but the applications vary. Except in Chapter 14, we will be dealing with what is called *parametric* statistical inference, since our goal is to draw inferences about specific population parameters. (Chapter 14 discusses drawing inferences about populations without specifying parameters.) This chapter illustrates uses of these techniques when the problem objective is to describe a single population and when the data scale is interval. As you know, when the scale is interval, we can calculate both means and variances to describe the population. Hence, in this chapter we'll present the statistical inference of the population mean, μ, and of the population variance, σ^2.

CONCEPTS OF ESTIMATION

There are two general types of statistical inference: estimation and hypothesis testing. In this section we will introduce the general concepts of estimation; the introduction to hypothesis testing will be presented in Section 7.4.

As its name suggests, the objective of *estimation* is to determine the approximate value of a population parameter on the basis of a sample statistic. An **estimator** of a population parameter is a random variable that is a function of the sample data. An **estimate** is the calculation of a specific value of this random variable. Later in this chapter, you will learn that the sample mean $\bar{x}$ is an estimator of the population mean μ, and that s^2 is an estimator of the population variance σ^2; once the sample has been drawn and the statistics calculated, the value of $\bar{x}$ becomes the estimate of μ and the value of s^2 becomes the estimate of σ^2.

POINT AND INTERVAL ESTIMATORS

We can use sample data to estimate a population parameter in two ways. First, we can compute the value of the estimator and consider that value as the estimate of the parameter. Such an estimator is called a **point estimator.**

Point Estimator

A point estimator draws inferences about a population by estimating the value of an unknown parameter, using a single value or point.

In drawing inferences about a population, it is intuitively reasonable to expect that a large sample will produce more accurate results, since it contains more information than a smaller sample does. But point estimators don't have the capacity to reflect the effects of larger sample sizes. The second way of estimating a population parameter is to use an **interval estimator.**

Interval Estimator

An interval estimator draws inferences about a population by estimating the value of an unknown parameter, using an interval that is likely to include the value of the population parameter.

As you will see, the interval estimator is affected by the sample size; and because it possesses this feature, we will deal mostly with interval estimators in this textbook.

Numerous applications of estimation occur in the real world. For example, television network executives want to know the proportion of television viewers who are tuned into their network; a production manager wishes to know the average daily production in his plant; a union negotiator would like to know the average annual income of North American blue-collar workers. In each of these cases, in order to accomplish the objective exactly, the interested party would have to examine each member of the population and then calculate the parameter of interest. For instance, the union negotiator would have to ask every North American blue-collar worker what his or her annual income is, and then calculate the average of these values—a task that is both impractical and prohibitively expensive. An alternative would be to take a random sample from this population, calculate the sample mean, and use that as an estimator of the population mean. The use of the sample mean to estimate the population mean seems logical. The selection of the sample statistic to be used as an estimator, however, depends on the characteristics of that statistic. Naturally, we want to use the statistic with the most desirable qualities for our purposes.

One such desirable quality of an estimator is **unbiasedness.**

Unbiased Estimator

An unbiased estimator of a population parameter is one whose expected value is equal to that parameter.

This means that, if you were to take an infinite number of samples, calculate the value of the estimator in each sample, and then average these values, the average value would equal the parameter. Essentially this amounts to saying that, on average, the sample statistic is equal to the parameter.

As an illustration, $\bar{x}$ is an unbiased estimator of μ, since $E(\bar{x}) = \mu$, which we established in Chapter 6. As a second illustration, recall that in Chapter 2 we defined the sample variance s^2 to be $\Sigma(x_i - \bar{x})^2/(n - 1)$. At the time, it seemed odd that we divided by $(n - 1)$ rather than by n. The reason for choosing $(n - 1)$ was to make $E(s^2) = \sigma^2$, so that the definition of s^2 produces an unbiased estimator of σ^2. Defining s^2 as $\Sigma(x_i - \bar{x})^2/n$ would have resulted in a biased estimator of σ^2—one that produced an average s^2 that was smaller than the true value of σ^2.

Knowing that an estimator is unbiased only assures us that its expected value equals the parameter; it does not tell us how close the estimator is to the parameter. Another desirable quality is for the estimator to be as close to its parameter as possible; and certainly, as the sample size grows larger, the sample statistic should come closer to the population parameter. This quality is called **consistency.**

Consistency

An unbiased estimator is said to be consistent if the difference between the estimator and the parameter grows smaller as the sample size grows larger.

The measure we use to gauge closeness is the variance (or the standard deviation). Thus, $\bar{x}$ is a consistent estimator of μ, since the variance of $\bar{x}$ is σ^2/n. This implies that, as n grows larger, the variance σ^2/n grows smaller. As a consequence, an increasing proportion of the statistics $\bar{x}$ fall close to μ.

In the next eleven chapters, we will present the statistical inference of a number of different population parameters, and in each case we will select a sample statistic that is both unbiased and consistent to serve as the estimator. Because this has already been done for you, once you identify the parameter that you want to estimate, you will also know which statistic is its best estimator.

SECTION 7.3   ## ESTIMATING μ WITH σ^2 KNOWN

Suppose that we have a population whose mean is μ and whose variance is σ^2. The population mean μ is assumed to be unknown, and our task is to estimate its value. As we have just discussed, the technique of estimation involves drawing a random sample of size n and calculating the sample mean $\bar{x}$.

In Chapter 6 we showed that $\bar{x}$ is normally distributed (if x is normally distributed) or approximately normally distributed (if x is nonnormal and n is sufficiently large*). This means that the variable

$$z = \frac{\bar{x} - \mu}{\sigma/\sqrt{n}}$$

follows a standard normal distribution. Figure 7.1 describes this distribution. (Recall from Chapter 4 that $z_{\alpha/2}$ represents the point such that the area to its right under the standard normal curve is equal to $\alpha/2$.)

When a sample is drawn, the value of $\bar{x}$ calculated from the sample is such that $z = (\bar{x} - \mu)/(\sigma/\sqrt{n})$ can be anywhere along the horizontal axis (theoretically, from $-\infty$ to $+\infty$). We know, however, that the probability that z falls between $-z_{\alpha/2}$ and $+z_{\alpha/2}$ is equal to $1 - \alpha$. This can be expressed as

$$1 - \alpha = P\left(-z_{\alpha/2} < \frac{\bar{x} - \mu}{\sigma/\sqrt{n}} < z_{\alpha/2} \right)$$

With some algebraic manipulation, we have

$$1 - \alpha = P\left(-z_{\alpha/2} \frac{\sigma}{\sqrt{n}} < \bar{x} - \mu < z_{\alpha/2} \frac{\sigma}{\sqrt{n}} \right)$$

$$= P\left(\bar{x} - z_{\alpha/2} \frac{\sigma}{\sqrt{n}} < \mu < \bar{x} + z_{\alpha/2} \frac{\sigma}{\sqrt{n}} \right)$$

FIGURE 7.1

SAMPLING DISTRIBUTION OF $z = \dfrac{\bar{x} - \mu}{\sigma/\sqrt{n}}$

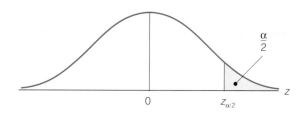

* The value of n required to make the approximation valid depends on the extent of nonnormality in the population.

This says that, with repeated sampling from this population, the proportion of values of $\bar{x}$ for which μ falls between $\bar{x} - z_{\alpha/2}\sigma/\sqrt{n}$ and $\bar{x} + z_{\alpha/2}\sigma/\sqrt{n}$ is equal to $1 - \alpha$. This interval is called the **confidence interval estimator** of μ. A shortcut method of representing this is

$$\bar{x} \pm z_{\alpha/2}\frac{\sigma}{\sqrt{n}}$$

We will also use interval notation:

$$(\bar{x} - z_{\alpha/2}\sigma/\sqrt{n}, \qquad \bar{x} + z_{\alpha/2}\sigma/\sqrt{n})$$

Confidence Interval Estimator of μ

$$\bar{x} \pm z_{\alpha/2}\frac{\sigma}{\sqrt{n}}$$

The probability $1 - \alpha$ is called the *confidence level.*
$\bar{x} - z_{\alpha/2}\sigma/\sqrt{n}$ is called the *lower confidence limit* (LCL).
$\bar{x} + z_{\alpha/2}\sigma/\sqrt{n}$ is called the *upper confidence limit* (UCL).

From the confidence level $1 - \alpha$, we determine α, $\alpha/2$, and finally $z_{\alpha/2}$ from Table 3 in Appendix B. Because the confidence level is equal to the probability that the interval includes the actual value of μ, we generally set $1 - \alpha$ relatively close to 1 (usually between .90 and .99).

In Table 7.1 we list four commonly used confidence levels and their associated values of $z_{\alpha/2}$. Make sure that you know how to use Table 3 to determine these and other values of $z_{\alpha/2}$.

As an illustration, suppose that we want to estimate the mean value of the distribution resulting from the throw of a fair die. Since we know the distribution, we

---

TABLE 7.1 FOUR COMMONLY USED CONFIDENCE LEVELS AND $z_{\alpha/2}$

Confidence Level $1 - \alpha$	α	$\alpha/2$	$z_{\alpha/2}$
.90	.10	.05	1.645
.95	.05	.025	1.96
.98	.02	.01	2.33
.99	.01	.005	2.58

also know that $\mu = 3.5$ and that $\sigma = 1.71$. Pretend now that we only know that $\sigma = 1.71$, that μ is unknown, and that we want to estimate its value. In order to estimate μ, we draw a sample of size $n = 100$ and calculate $\bar{x}$. The confidence interval estimator of μ is

$$\bar{x} \pm z_{\alpha/2} \frac{\sigma}{\sqrt{n}}$$

The 90% confidence interval estimator is

$$\bar{x} \pm z_{\alpha/2} \frac{\sigma}{\sqrt{n}} = \bar{x} \pm 1.645 \frac{1.71}{\sqrt{100}} = \bar{x} \pm .28$$

This notation means that, if we repeatedly draw samples of size 100 from this population, 90% of the values of $\bar{x}$ would be such that μ would lie somewhere between $\bar{x} - .28$ and $\bar{x} + .28$, and 10% of the values of $\bar{x}$ would produce intervals that would not include μ. To illustrate this point, imagine that we draw 40 samples of size 100 observations each. The values of $\bar{x}$ and the resulting confidence interval estimates of μ are shown in Table 7.2. Notice that not all of the intervals include the true value of the parameter. Samples 5, 16, 22, and 34 produce values of $\bar{x}$ that in turn produce confidence intervals that exclude μ. Students often react to this situation by asking, "What went wrong with samples 5, 16, 22, and 34?" The answer is *nothing*. Statistics does not promise 100% certainty. In fact, in this illustration we expected 90% of the intervals to include μ and 10% to exclude μ. Since we produced 40 confidence intervals, we expected that 4.0 (10% of 40) intervals would not contain $\mu = 3.5$.* It is important to understand that, even when the statistician performs experiments properly, a certain proportion (in this example, 10%) of the experiments will produce incorrect estimates by random chance.

We can improve the confidence associated with the interval estimate. If we let the confidence level $1 - \alpha$ equal .95, the confidence interval estimator is

$$\bar{x} \pm z_{\alpha/2} \frac{\sigma}{\sqrt{n}} = \bar{x} \pm 1.96 \frac{1.71}{\sqrt{100}} = \bar{x} \pm .34$$

Because this interval is wider, it is more likely to include the value of μ. If you redo Table 7.2, this time using the 95% confidence interval estimator, only samples 16, 22, and 34 would produce intervals that do not include μ. (Notice that we expected 5% of the intervals to exclude μ and that we actually observed $3/40 = 7.5\%$.) The 99% confidence interval estimate is

$$\bar{x} \pm z_{\alpha/2} \frac{\sigma}{\sqrt{n}} = \bar{x} \pm 2.58 \frac{1.71}{\sqrt{100}} = \bar{x} \pm .44$$

---

* In this illustration exactly 10% of the 40 sample means produced interval estimates that excluded the value of μ, but this will not always be the case. Remember, we expect 10% of the sample means in the long run to result in intervals excluding μ. This group of 40 sample means does not constitute "the long run."

TABLE 7.2   90% CONFIDENCE INTERVAL ESTIMATES OF μ

Sample	$\bar{x}$	LCL = $\bar{x}$ − .28	UCL = $\bar{x}$ + .28	Does Interval Include $\mu = 3.5$?
1	3.55	3.27	3.83	Yes
2	3.61	3.33	3.89	Yes
3	3.47	3.19	3.75	Yes
4	3.48	3.20	3.76	Yes
5	3.80	3.52	4.08	No
6	3.37	3.09	3.65	Yes
7	3.48	3.20	3.76	Yes
8	3.52	3.24	3.80	Yes
9	3.74	3.46	4.02	Yes
10	3.51	3.23	3.79	Yes
11	3.23	2.95	3.51	Yes
12	3.45	3.17	3.73	Yes
13	3.57	3.29	3.85	Yes
14	3.77	3.49	4.05	Yes
15	3.31	3.03	3.59	Yes
16	3.10	2.82	3.38	No
17	3.50	3.22	3.78	Yes
18	3.55	3.27	3.83	Yes
19	3.65	3.37	3.93	Yes
20	3.28	3.00	3.56	Yes
21	3.40	3.12	3.68	Yes
22	3.88	3.60	4.16	No
23	3.76	3.48	4.04	Yes
24	3.40	3.12	3.68	Yes
25	3.34	3.06	3.62	Yes
26	3.65	3.37	3.93	Yes
27	3.45	3.17	3.73	Yes
28	3.47	3.19	3.75	Yes
29	3.58	3.30	3.86	Yes
30	3.36	3.08	3.64	Yes

(continued)

TABLE 7.2   *(continued)*

Sample	$\bar{x}$	LCL = $\bar{x}$ − .28	UCL = $\bar{x}$ + .28	Does Interval Include μ = 3.5?
31	3.71	3.43	3.99	Yes
32	3.51	3.23	3.79	Yes
33	3.42	3.14	3.70	Yes
34	3.11	2.83	3.39	No
35	3.29	3.01	3.57	Yes
36	3.64	3.36	3.92	Yes
37	3.39	3.11	3.67	Yes
38	3.75	3.47	4.03	Yes
39	3.26	2.98	3.54	Yes
40	3.54	3.26	3.82	Yes

Using the sample means listed in Table 7.2, this would result in having all 40 interval estimates include the population mean $\mu = 3.5$. (We expected 1% of the intervals to exclude μ; we observed $0/40 = 0\%$.)

In actual practice, only one sample will be drawn, and thus only one value of $\bar{x}$ will be calculated. The resulting confidence interval estimate will either correctly include the parameter or incorrectly exclude it. Unfortunately, statisticians do not know whether or not in each case they are correct; they only know that, in the long run, they will incorrectly estimate the parameter some of the time. Statisticians accept that as a regrettable fact of life. People who use statistical results should also accept this fact.

EXAMPLE 7.1

The sponsors of television shows targeted at the children's market wanted to know the amount of time children spend watching television, since the types and number of programs and commercials greatly depend on this information. As a result, a survey was conducted to estimate the average number of hours North American children spend watching television per week. From past experience, it is known that the population standard deviation, σ, is 8.0 hours. In a sample of 100 children it was found that $\bar{x} = 27.5$ hours. Find the 95% confidence interval estimate of the average number of hours North American children spend watching television.

Solution.   At this point, there is no uncertainty about which technique to use. You only know one! In order to practice the systematic approach, however, we'll go through the process of identifying the technique.

The problem objective is to describe a single population: the number of hours of television watched per week by North American children. The data scale is interval: the hours spent watching television. Thus the parameter of interest is the population mean μ. Your task is to estimate this parameter.

The confidence interval estimator of μ is

$$\bar{x} \pm z_{\alpha/2} \frac{\sigma}{\sqrt{n}}$$

Since $1 - \alpha = .95$,

$$z_{\alpha/2} = 1.96$$

Hence, the estimate is

$$\bar{x} \pm z_{\alpha/2} \frac{\sigma}{\sqrt{n}} = 27.5 \pm 1.96 \frac{8.0}{\sqrt{100}} = 27.5 \pm 1.57$$

or

$$(25.93, 29.07)$$

Thus, the 95% confidence interval estimate of μ is the interval 25.93 to 29.07 hours per week.

From this estimate, a network executive may decide (for example) that, since the average child watches at least 25.93 hours of television, the number of commercials children see is sufficiently high to satisfy the programs' sponsors. A number of other decisions may follow from that initial one.

Of course, the sample mean ($\bar{x} = 27.5$ hours per week) alone would not provide enough information to the executive. He would also need to know how low the population average is likely to be; and for other decisions, he might need to know how high the population mean is likely to be. A confidence interval estimate gives him that information.

MINITAB COMPUTER OUTPUT FOR EXAMPLE 7.1*

THE ASSUMED SIGMA=8.000

	N	MEAN	STDEV	SE MEAN	95.0 PERCENT C.I.
C1	100	27.50	7.578	0.80	(25.93, 29.07)

This output is a result of inputting all 100 observations into column 1 (C1). The computer calculated the sample standard deviation s (STDEV), the standard error

---

* In Appendix 7.A, we describe the instructions for answering this question.

of the mean $\sigma_{\bar{x}} = \sigma/\sqrt{n}$ (SE MEAN), and of course the 95% confidence interval estimate of μ.

Although the interval estimate is often used to help make decisions, the primary purpose of this technique is to provide some information about the value of the parameter. In other situations, the purpose of the statistical method is to make a decision about the value of a parameter. This is the function of hypothesis testing.

<hr>

EXERCISES

LEARNING THE TECHNIQUES

7.1 In a random sample of 400 observations from a population whose variance is $\sigma^2 = 100$, we calculated $\bar{x} = 75$. Find the 95% confidence interval estimate of the population mean μ.

7.2 Describe what happens to the width of a confidence interval estimate of μ when each of the following occurs.

a. The confidence level increases from 95% to 99%.

b. The sample size decreases.

c. The value of σ increases.

7.3 Suppose that a random sample of five observations is taken from a normal population whose variance is 25. The results are:

8, 15, 12, 6, 7

Find the 99% confidence interval estimate of the population mean.

7.4 A random sample of 400 observations from a population whose standard deviation is 90 produced $\bar{x} = 1500$. Find the 90% confidence interval estimate of μ.

7.5 Given the following information, determine the 95% confidence interval estimate of μ.

$n = 1,000$

$\sigma = 40$

$\bar{x} = 125$

7.6 The following observations were drawn from a normal population whose variance is 100:

12, 8, 22, 15, 30, 6, 39, 48

Determine the 90% confidence interval of the population mean.

7.7 Suppose that the output shown in Figure E7.7 was generated by a computer software package. Briefly describe what each number tells you.

APPLYING THE TECHNIQUES

Self-Correcting Exercise (See Appendix 7.C for the solution.)

FIN **7.8** A bank wishing to determine the average amount of time a customer must wait to be served took a random sample of 100 customers and found that the mean waiting time was 7.2 minutes. Assuming that the population standard deviation is known to be 15 minutes, find the 90% confidence interval estimate of the mean waiting time for all of the bank's customers.

<hr>

FIGURE E7.7

```
        THE ASSUMED SIGMA=150.000

              N      MEAN     STDEV     SE MEAN    95.0 PERCENT C.I.
        C1    250    790.31   163.08    9.48       (771.72, 808.90)
```

TOUR **7.9**   In a survey conducted to determine, among other things, the cost of vacations, 164 individuals were randomly sampled.* Each was asked to assess the total cost of his or her most recent vacation. The average cost was $1,386. Assuming that the standard deviation was $400, estimate with 99% confidence the average cost of all vacation trips.

ECON **7.10**   In an article about disinflation (*Newsweek,* 26 August 1985), various investments were examined. The investments included stocks, bonds, and housing. The annual compound rate of return for each type of investment was calculated for the period June 1980 to June 1985. Suppose that, in order to determine the rate of return for housing, a random sample of 50 residential properties sold

* P. K. Tat and J. R. Thompson, "An Exploratory Study of Brand Loyalty in Selecting Travel Destinations," *Developments in Marketing Science* 6 (1983): 562–65.

during the period 1980 to 1985 was drawn. If the sample mean was 4.3%, estimate with 95% confidence the average rate of return of all houses between 1980 and 1985. (Assume that the standard deviation was 1%.)

MNG **7.11**   A survey of 20 companies indicated that the average annual income of company presidents was $110,000. Assuming that the population standard deviation is $7,000 and that annual incomes are normally distributed, calculate the 90% confidence interval estimate of the average annual income of all company presidents.

EDUC **7.12**   In a random sample of 70 students in a large university, a dean found that the mean weekly time devoted to homework was 14.3 hours. If we assume that homework time is normally distributed, with a standard deviation of 4.0 hours, find the 99% confidence interval estimate of the weekly time spent doing homework for all of the university's students.

SECTION 7.4   ## CONCEPTS OF HYPOTHESIS TESTING

As the previous section indicated, we can use sample data to estimate the value of an unknown parameter. Another way of drawing inferences about a population is called **hypothesis testing.** The objective of this form of statistical inference is to determine whether or not the sample data support some belief or hypothesis about the population. Examples of this type of inference include the following:

1. A company that has a 10% market share launches a new advertising campaign. At the campaign's completion, the company wants to know whether the results of a random sample indicate an increase in market share.

2. A firm that produces fertilizer wants to know whether a new type of fertilizer it has recently produced increases crop yields. The answer is provided by taking a sample of farms and comparing crop yields with the new fertilizer against crop yields with the old fertilizer.

3. A politician is interested in determining whether a new piece of legislation is equally supported by men and women. A random sample of men and women provides her with the information she seeks.

In order to answer these and other similar questions, we must first develop the structure of hypothesis testing.

STRUCTURE OF HYPOTHESIS TESTING

The tests of hypotheses that we present in this chapter (and in all others except Chapter 14) are called **parametric tests,** because they test the value of a population parameter. These tests consist of the following four components:

1. Null hypothesis
2. Alternative hypothesis
3. Test statistic
4. Rejection region

Null Hypothesis.   The null hypothesis, which is denoted H_0 (H-naught), always specifies a single value for the population parameter. For example, if we wished to test to determine whether the mean weight loss of people who have participated in a new weight program is 10 pounds, we would test

$$H_0: \mu = 10$$

Alternative Hypothesis.   This hypothesis, denoted H_A, is the more important one, because it is the hypothesis that answers our question. The alternative hypothesis can assume three possible forms:

1. If a tire company wanted to know whether the average life of its new radial tire exceeds its advertised value of 50,000 miles, the company would specify the alternative hypothesis as
   $$H_A: \mu > 50,000$$
2. If the company wanted to know whether the average life of the tire is less than 50,000 miles, it would test
   $$H_A: \mu < 50,000$$
3. If the company wished to determine whether the average life of the tire differs from that advertised, its alternative hypothesis would be
   $$H_A: \mu \neq 50,000$$

In all three cases the null hypothesis would be

$$H_0: \mu = 50,000$$

The crucial things to remember about the two hypotheses are summarized next.

Null Hypothesis

The null hypothesis H_0 must specify that the parameter is equal to a single value.

Alternative Hypothesis

The alternative hypothesis H_A answers the question by specifying that the parameter is one of the following:

1. Greater than the value shown in the null hypothesis
2. Less than the value shown in the null hypothesis
3. Different from the value shown in the null hypothesis

Test Statistic.   The purpose of the test is to determine whether it is appropriate to reject or not to reject the null hypothesis. (As we will explain later, we use the term *not reject* instead of *accept* because the latter can lead to an erroneous conclusion.)

Test Statistic

The criterion upon which we base our decision is called the *test statistic*.

For parametric tests of hypotheses, the test statistic is the point estimator of the parameter being tested. For example, since the sample mean $\bar{x}$ is the point estimator of the population mean μ, it will be used as the test statistic in tests of hypotheses about μ.

Rejection Region

Rejection Region

The rejection region is a range of values such that, if the test statistic falls into that range, we decide to reject the null hypothesis.

To illustrate, suppose that we wish to test

$$H_0: \mu = 1,000$$

If we find that the sample mean (which is the test statistic) is quite different from 1,000, we say that $\bar{x}$ falls into the rejection region and we reject the null hypothesis. On the other hand, if $\bar{x}$ is close to 1,000, we cannot reject the null hypothesis. The key question answered by the rejection region is, when is the value of the test statistic sufficiently different from the hypothesized value of the parameter to enable us to reject the null hypothesis? The process we use in answering this question depends on the probability of our making a mistake when testing the hypothesis.

Since the conclusion we draw is based on sample data, the chance of our making one of two possible errors will always exist. As indicated in Figure 7.2, the

FIGURE 7.2   RESULTS OF A TEST OF THE NULL HYPOTHESIS

	H_0 is true	H_0 is false
Reject H_0	Type I error $P(\text{Type I error}) = \alpha$	Correct decision
Do not reject H_0	Correct decision	Type II error $P(\text{Type II error}) = \beta$

null hypothesis is either true or false, and we must decide either to reject it or not reject it. Therefore, two correct decisions are possible: rejecting H_0 when it is false, and not rejecting H_0 when it is true. Conversely, two incorrect decisions are possible: rejecting H_0 when it is true (this is called a **Type I error,** and the probability of committing it is α), and not rejecting H_0 when it is false (this is called a **Type II error,** and the probability of committing it is β). The probability α is called the **significance level.**

We would like for both α and β to be as small as possible, but unfortunately there is an inverse relationship between α and β. Thus, for a given sample size, any decrease in α results in an increase in β. (See Section 7.9.) The value of α is selected by the decision maker and is usually between 1% and 10%.

To summarize, the test proceeds as follows:

1. Specify the null hypothesis and the alternative hypothesis.
2. Specify the test statistic.
3. Specify α, and set up the rejection region.
4. Calculate the value of the test statistic.
5. Draw the conclusion: reject or do not reject H_0.

In Section 7.5, we'll demonstrate the technique of hypothesis testing, using the parameter μ.

SECTION 7.5   **TESTING μ WITH σ^2 KNOWN**

Consider the following example.

In the midst of labor–management negotiations, the president of the union claims that her blue-collar workers (whose annual average income is $20,000) are underpaid, since the average annual North American blue-collar income exceeds $20,000. Management claims that the workers are well-paid, since the average annual North American blue-collar income is less than $20,000. An arbitrator believes that the average is really quite close to $20,000. To help resolve the impasse, they decide to test the hypothesis that $\mu = \$20,000$ against the alternative hypothesis that $\mu \neq \$20,000$. The hypotheses are summarized as follows:

$H_0: \mu = 20,000$

$H_A: \mu \neq 20,000$

From other sources, they know (and agree) that the standard deviation of the population of blue-collar incomes is $5,000. The disputants and the arbitrator decide to base their decision on a sample of size 400 drawn from the population of all North American blue-collar workers. In order to conduct the test, they must specify the value of α—the probability of a Type I error. This selection resembles the selection of α in confidence interval estimation. The value of α is usually set at some value between .01 and .10, although we may encounter situations where some other value is selected. Suppose, for our example, we set $\alpha = .05$.

As we discussed in Section 7.4, the test statistic is the best estimator of the parameter. Hence, in this case, our test statistic is $\bar{x}$. If $\bar{x}$ turns out to be a very large number (such as 40,000), or a very small one (such as 5,000), our conclusion is quite clear: reject H_0. On the other hand, if $\bar{x}$ is a number quite close to 20,000 (such as 20,005), we can't reject H_0, since it's entirely possible to observe a sample mean of 20,005 from a population whose mean is 20,000. But if $\bar{x}$ is a number neither far away from nor close to 20,000 (such as 19,000), the decision is less obvious.

It seems reasonable to reject H_0 if the value of $\bar{x}$ is either too small or too large. The key question is, what is "too small" and what is "too large"? That question is answered by reference to the definition of a Type I error. Suppose that we identify the value of $\bar{x}$ that is just small enough to reject H_0 as $\bar{x}_S$, and likewise identify the value of $\bar{x}$ that is just large enough to reject H_0 as $\bar{x}_L$. One element of our hypothesis test—the rejection region—can then be specified: reject H_0 if $\bar{x} < \bar{x}_S$ or if $\bar{x} > \bar{x}_L$. Since a Type I error is defined as rejecting a true hypothesis, it follows that $P(\text{rejecting } H_0 \mid H_0 \text{ is true}) = \alpha$, or

$$P(\bar{x} < \bar{x}_S \text{ or } \bar{x} > \bar{x}_L \mid H_0 \text{ is true}) = \alpha$$

Figure 7.3 depicts the rejection region.

FIGURE 7.3   REJECTION REGION FOR THE TEST OF HYPOTHESIS OF μ

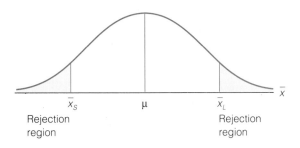

If α is the probability that $\bar{x}$ falls into the rejection region, then $1 - \alpha$ is the probability that it doesn't. Thus,

$$P(\bar{x}_S < \bar{x} < \bar{x}_L \,|\, H_0 \text{ is true}) = 1 - \alpha$$

From Section 6.4 we know that the sampling distribution of $\bar{x}$ is normal (provided that x is normal or that n is sufficiently large), with mean μ and standard deviation $\sigma/\sqrt{n}$. As a result, we can standardize $\bar{x}$ and obtain the following conditional probability:

$$P\left(\frac{\bar{x}_S - \mu}{\sigma/\sqrt{n}} < z < \frac{\bar{x}_L - \mu}{\sigma/\sqrt{n}} \,\middle|\, H_0 \text{ is true}\right) = 1 - \alpha$$

From Chapter 4, we have

$$P(-z_{\alpha/2} < z < +z_{\alpha/2}) = 1 - \alpha$$

Thus,

$$\frac{\bar{x}_S - \mu}{\sigma/\sqrt{n}} = -z_{\alpha/2}$$

and

$$\frac{\bar{x}_L - \mu}{\sigma/\sqrt{n}} = +z_{\alpha/2}$$

In the present example, we know that

$$\sigma = 5,000$$
$$n = 400$$

and

$$z_{\alpha/2} = 1.96 \qquad (\text{since } \alpha = .05)$$

Because we assume that the null hypothesis is true, we let

$$\mu = 20,000$$

which allows us to solve both equations. First, we find

$$\frac{\bar{x}_S - \mu}{\sigma/\sqrt{n}} = -z_{\alpha/2}$$
$$\frac{\bar{x}_S - 20,000}{5,000/\sqrt{400}} = -1.96$$
$$\bar{x}_S = 19,510$$

Similarly, we find

$$\frac{\bar{x}_L - 20,000}{5,000/\sqrt{400}} = 1.96$$
$$\bar{x}_L = 20,490$$

Therefore, our rejection region is

$$\bar{x} < 19,510 \quad \text{or} \quad \bar{x} > 20,490$$

Suppose that we take a random sample of 400 blue-collar annual incomes and find $\bar{x} = 20,500$. Our conclusion would be to reject H_0, and we would then say that there is sufficient evidence to conclude that H_A is true—that is, that $\mu \neq 20,000$. Figure 7.4 graphically represents the rejection region relevant to this discussion.

Notice that the test of hypothesis judges the size of the difference between the hypothesized value of μ and the actual value of the sample mean $\bar{x}$. We decide that any value of $\bar{x}$ between 19,510 and 20,490 represents ordinary random fluctuation. Values of $\bar{x}$ close to 20,000 are considered reasonable and quite possible; after all, even if the null hypothesis is true, it is highly unlikely that, in a sample of 400, $\bar{x}$ will exactly equal 20,000. On the other hand, values of $\bar{x}$ relatively far from 20,000, although theoretically possible, are quite unlikely. This suggests that the assumption that H_0 is true is probably incorrect; and in that case, we reject H_0.

The preceding test used the test statistic $\bar{x}$; as a result, the rejection region had to be set up in terms of $\bar{x}$. An easier method to use specifies that the test statistic be the standardized value of $\bar{x}$. That is, we use the **standardized test statistic,** $z = (\bar{x} - \mu)/(\sigma/\sqrt{n})$, and the rejection region consists of all values of z that are less than $-z_{\alpha/2}$ or greater than $z_{\alpha/2}$. Algebraically, the rejection region is $z < -z_{\alpha/2}$ and $z > z_{\alpha/2}$. This region is usually represented as $|z| > z_{\alpha/2}$.

Standard Testing Format

The standard format for this testing procedure is as follows:

1. Determine H_0 and H_A.
2. Specify the standardized test statistic.
3. Specify α, and set up the rejection region.
4. Calculate the value of the test statistic.
5. Draw your conclusion.

FIGURE 7.4   *REJECTION REGION FOR THE TEST OF HYPOTHESIS OF μ*

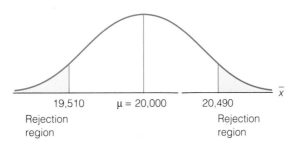

In our example, following the standard testing format, we would have

1. $H_0: \mu = 20,000$
   $H_A: \mu \neq 20,000$

2. Test statistic:

   $$z = \frac{\bar{x} - \mu}{\sigma/\sqrt{n}}$$

3. Rejection region (for $\alpha = .05$): $|z| > 1.96$

4. Value of the test statistic:

   $$z = \frac{\bar{x} - \mu}{\sigma/\sqrt{n}} = \frac{20,500 - 20,000}{5,000/\sqrt{400}} = 2.0$$

5. Conclusion: Since $z = 2.0 > 1.96$, reject H_0 and conclude that there is enough evidence to show that $\mu \neq 20,000$.

Figure 7.5 describes this version of the test.

As you can see, the conclusions we draw from using the test statistic $\bar{x}$ and the standardized test statistic z are identical. Because of its convenience, we will generally use the standardized test statistic for the tests of hypotheses in this textbook. Deferring to popular usage, we will refer to the *standardized test statistic* simply as the *test statistic*.

INTERPRETING THE RESULTS OF THE TEST

In the example just completed, we rejected H_0. Does this prove that H_0 is false? The answer is *no:* because we are dealing only with sample data, we can never prove anything conclusively. We can, however, say that there is sufficient evidence to indicate that H_0 is false and that H_A is true. We would conclude, since $z = 2.0$ (and thus z is in the rejection region), that there is sufficient evidence that $\mu \neq 20,000$.

Suppose that $\bar{x}$ had equaled 20,250 instead of 20,500. We would then have had $z = 1.0$, which is not in the rejection region. Could we conclude on this basis that there is sufficient evidence that $\mu = 20,000$? Again the answer is *no*. To understand

FIGURE 7.5   *REJECTION REGION OBTAINED BY USING THE STANDARDIZED TEST STATISTIC*

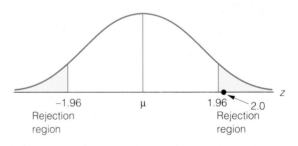

why, imagine for a moment that H_0 specified $\mu = 20{,}001$. In this case, z would still not be in the rejection region and we would conclude that $\mu = 20{,}001$. If we had tested $\mu = 20{,}002$, we would not reject that null hypothesis either. In fact, we would conclude that there is sufficient evidence to support an infinite number of different values of μ. But such a conclusion is absurd, because there is only one value of μ.

Consequently, when z does not fall into the rejection region, we cannot say that there is sufficient evidence to conclude that H_0 is true. What then can we say? When we do not reject H_0, all we can say is that there is not sufficient evidence to indicate that H_0 is not true—or, alternatively, that there is not sufficient evidence to indicate that H_A is true. While it may appear that we've been speaking overly technically and playing semantic games, this is not the case. Your ability to set up tests of hypotheses properly and to interpret their results correctly depends on your understanding of this point.

Ultimately, there are only two possible conclusions of a hypothesis test.

Interpreting the Test Results

If we reject the null hypothesis, we conclude that there is enough evidence to indicate that the alternative hypothesis is true.
If we *do not* reject the null hypothesis, we conclude that there is *not* enough evidence to indicate that the alternative hypothesis is true.

Observe that, in the end, the alternative hypothesis H_A is the more important one. It is H_A that answers the question; not H_0. This point is crucial. Whatever you're trying to show statistically should be represented by the alternative hypothesis (bearing in mind that you have only three possible choices for the alternative hypothesis—greater than, less than, and not equal to).

EXAMPLE 7.2

A manufacturer of a new, cheaper type of light bulb claims that his product is just as well made and just as reliable as the higher-priced competitive light bulbs. The average life of the other light bulbs is known to be 5,000 hours. In order to examine the manufacturer's claim, 50 of his bulbs are left on until they burn out. The average length of life in the sample is 5,100 hours. With $\alpha = .05$, is there sufficient evidence to reject the manufacturer's claim? (Assume that $\sigma = 500$ hours.)

Solution.   The problem objective is to describe a single population, and the data scale is interval; the population is the length of life of light bulbs produced by the manufacturer. Hence, the parameter of interest is μ.

Notice how the question is worded. You are not being asked to determine if there is sufficient evidence to support the claim that $\mu = 5{,}000$. In fact, there can never be enough statistical evidence to show that $\mu = 5{,}000$. All we can conclude is either that there is or that there is not enough evidence to show that $\mu \neq 5{,}000$. The null and alternative hypotheses and the complete test follow.

$H_0: \mu = 5{,}000$

$H_A: \mu \neq 5{,}000$

Test statistic:

$$z = \frac{\bar{x} - \mu}{\sigma/\sqrt{n}}$$

Rejection region:

$|z| > z_{\alpha/2}$

$\quad > z_{.025}$

$\quad > 1.96$

Value of the test statistic:

$$z = \frac{\bar{x} - \mu}{\sigma/\sqrt{n}} = \frac{5{,}100 - 5{,}000}{500/\sqrt{50}} = 1.41$$

Conclusion: Do not reject H_0.

Since z does not fall into the rejection region, we conclude that there is not enough evidence to enable us to reject the manufacturer's claim. Observe that there is some evidence that $\mu \neq 5{,}000$; that is, $\bar{x} = 5{,}100$, but the evidence was not strong enough to push $\bar{x}$ into the rejection region. The interpretation is that it is quite possible to obtain a sample mean of 5,100 from a population whose mean is 5,000 (given that $\sigma = 500$ and $n = 50$). Figure 7.6 shows the results of this test.

FIGURE 7.6   *REJECTION REGION FOR EXAMPLE 7.2*

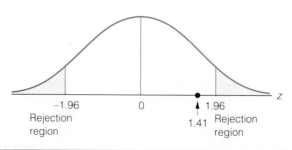

MINITAB COMPUTER OUTPUT FOR EXAMPLE 7.2*

```
TEST OF MU=5000 VS N.E. 5000
THE ASSUMED SIGMA=500.0
      N    MEAN   STDEV   SE MEAN    Z     P VALUE
C1    50   5100   527.3   70.71    1.41    0.1586
```

This printout is quite similar to the one produced for the 95% confidence interval estimate of μ for Example 7.1 in Section 7.3. The decision to reject or not to reject the null hypothesis is not made, since the significance level α is not specified. In Section 7.6, we will discuss the meaning of P VALUE and show how it can be used to make the decision.

ONE-TAIL TEST OF HYPOTHESIS

Suppose that, in Example 7.2, the manufacturer had claimed that his product was better than that of his competitors; that is, suppose that he had claimed that the average life of his product was more than 5,000 hours. If we want to test this claim, our question should be: is there sufficient evidence to show that $\mu > 5,000$? Since whatever we're trying to show statistically is represented by the alternative hypothesis, we have $H_A: \mu > 5,000$. It automatically follows that $H_0: \mu = 5,000$ (since H_0 must specify only a single value for the parameter).[†] Hence, we have

$$H_0: \mu = 5,000$$
$$H_A: \mu > 5,000$$

Test statistic:

$$z = \frac{\bar{x} - \mu}{\sigma/\sqrt{n}}$$

In this situation, we want to reject H_0 in favor of H_A only if the value of the test statistic is too large—that is, if the rejection region is $z > z_\alpha$. Why z_α and not $z_{\alpha/2}$? Because we want the probability of incorrectly rejecting H_0 to be α. Since we reject only when z is too large, the rejection region is $z > z_\alpha$. With $\alpha = .05$, we reject H_0 when $z > 1.645$. (See Figure 7.7.)

Since $z = 1.41$, we conclude that there is not sufficient evidence to establish the truth of the claim.

---

* See Appendix 7.A for the Minitab commands needed in order to answer this question.

[†] Some statisticians prefer to let H_0 represent the opposite of H_A. In this example, they would have $H_0: \mu \leq 5,000$ when $H_A: \mu > 5,000$. The remainder of the statistical technique is the same. That is, we would still use $\mu = 5,000$ in calculating the value of the test statistic. Obviously, we prefer our method where $H_0: \mu = 5,000$, because this forces you to recognize that the question is answered by H_A. It is also less likely to lead to your setting up the hypotheses incorrectly.

FIGURE 7.7 REJECTION REGION FOR A ONE-TAIL TEST

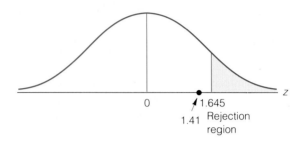

▬▬▬▬▬▬ **EXAMPLE 7.3**

The manager of a department store is thinking about establishing a new billing system for the store's credit customers. After a thorough financial analysis, she determines that the new system will not be cost-effective if the average monthly account is less than $70. A random sample of 200 monthly accounts is drawn, for which the mean monthly account is $66. With $\alpha = .05$, is there sufficient evidence to conclude that the new system will not be cost-effective? Assume that the population standard deviation is $30.

Solution.   The problem objective is to describe a single population, and the data scale is interval (monthly accounts). The parameter of interest is μ. Since we want to know whether there is sufficient evidence to conclude that the mean is less than 70, the alternative hypothesis is

$$H_A: \mu < 70$$

In this example we want to reject the null hypothesis in favor of the alternative only if the value of the test statistic is too small. Hence, we reject if $z < -z_\alpha$.
The complete test is

$$H_0: \mu = 70$$
$$H_A: \mu < 70$$

Test statistic:

$$z = \frac{\bar{x} - \mu}{\sigma/\sqrt{n}}$$

Rejection region:

$$z < -z_\alpha$$
$$< -z_{.05}$$
$$< -1.645$$

FIGURE 7.8 REJECTION REGION FOR EXAMPLE 7.3

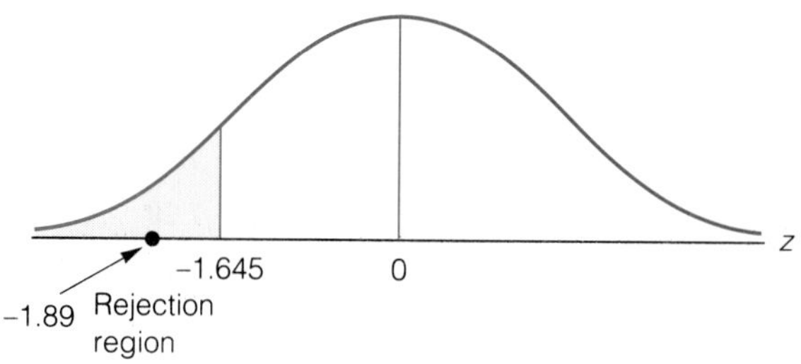

Value of the test statistic:

$$z = \frac{\bar{x} - \mu}{\sigma/\sqrt{n}} = \frac{66 - 70}{30/\sqrt{200}} = -1.89$$

Conclusion: Reject H_0.

There is sufficient evidence from the sample to allow us to conclude that the mean monthly account is less than $70 and that the new system will not be cost-effective. (See Figure 7.8.) Given this statistical result, the manager should argue against proceeding with the new billing system.

MINITAB COMPUTER OUTPUT FOR EXAMPLE 7.3*

```
TEST OF MU=70 VS MU L.T. 70
THE ASSUMED SIGMA=30.0
        N     MEAN     STDEV    SE MEAN      Z       P VALUE
C1    200    66.00     28.62    2.121      -1.89     0.0294
```

EXERCISES

LEARNING THE TECHNIQUES

7.13 Define the following terms:

a. Type I error

b. Type II error

c. significance level

d. rejection region

e. β

7.14 For each of the following tests of hypotheses about μ, determine the rejection region:

a. $H_0: \mu = 1{,}000$
$H_A: \mu \neq 1{,}000$
$\alpha = .05$

b. $H_0: \mu = 50$
$H_A: \mu > 50$
$\alpha = .01$

* See Appendix 7.A for the Minitab computer commands needed to answer this question.

c. $H_0: \mu = 15$
$H_A: \mu < 15$
$\alpha = .10$

7.15 Sketch the sampling distribution and indicate the rejection region for the tests in Exercise 7.14.

7.16 A random sample of 200 observations from a normal population whose variance is 10,000 produced a mean of 150. Test the hypothesis $H_0: \mu = 160$ against the alternative hypothesis $H_A: \mu < 160$. Use $\alpha = .05$.

7.17 A machine that produces ball bearings is set so that the average diameter is .500 inch. In a sample of 100 ball bearings, it was found that $\bar{x} = .51$ inch. Assuming that the standard deviation is .05 inch, can we conclude (with $\alpha = .05$) that the mean diameter is not .500 inch?

7.18 For the following tests of hypotheses, determine the rejection regions in terms of $\bar{x}$.

a. $H_0: \mu = 500$
$H_A: \mu > 500$
$\alpha = .02, \sigma = 25, n = 100$

b. $H_0: \mu = 20$
$H_A: \mu \neq 20$
$\alpha = .07, \sigma = 2, n = 250$

c. $H_0: \mu = 1,000$
$H_A: \mu \neq 1,000$
$\alpha = .04, \sigma = 50, n = 20$

7.19 Given

$$\bar{x} = 22.3, \qquad \sigma = 12, \qquad n = 100$$

test the following hypotheses, with $\alpha = .01$:

$H_0: \mu = 20$

$H_A: \mu \neq 20$

7.20 Test the following hypotheses, with $\alpha = .01$ given that a sample of size $n = 25$ from a normal population whose variance is 100 produced $\bar{x} = 115$:

$H_0: \mu = 110$

$H_A: \mu > 110$

7.21 Given the computer output shown in Figure E7.21, briefly discuss what each number (with the exception of P VALUE) tells you.

7.22 The computer printout of a test of hypothesis is shown in Figure E7.22. Specify the hypotheses that are being tested and the conclusion that you would draw, with $\alpha = .05$.

APPLYING THE TECHNIQUES

EDUC **7.23** A large university claims that the average GMAT score of applicants to its MBA program has increased during the past five years. Five years ago the mean and the standard deviation of GMAT scores of the university's MBA program applicants were 560 and 50, respectively. In a sample of 20

FIGURE E7.21

```
TEST OF MU=700 VS MU L.T. 700
THE ASSUMED SIGMA=60.0
       N     MEAN    STDEV    SE MEAN      Z     P VALUE
C1     40    681.1   63.98     9.48      -1.99    .0233
```

FIGURE E7.22

```
TEST OF MU=0 VS MU G.T. 0
THE ASSUMED SIGMA=1.00
       N     MEAN    STDEV    SE MEAN      Z     P VALUE
C1    100    0.00    0.95      0.10      0.00     0.50
```

recent applicants for the MBA program, the mean GMAT was 575. At the 5% level of significance, can we conclude that the university's claim is true? (Assume that the standard deviation is unchanged.)

Self-Correcting Exercise (See Appendix 7.C for the solution.)

FIN

7.24 A study in the *Academy of Management Journal* reported that the average annual return on investment for American banks was 10.2%, with a standard deviation of .8%.* The article hypothesized that banks that exercised comprehensive planning would outperform the average bank. In a random sample of 26 banks that used comprehensive planning, the mean return on investment was 14.6%. Can we conclude, at the 5% level of significance, that the article's hypothesis is correct? (Assume that the standard deviation of the return on investment for banks that used comprehensive planning is also .8%.)

ECON

7.25 Past experience indicates that the monthly long-distance telephone bill per household in a

---

* D. R. Wood and R. L. LaForge, "The Impact of Comprehensive Planning on Financial Performance," *Academy of Management Journal* 22(3) (1979): 516–26.

particular community is normally distributed, with a mean of $10.12 and a standard deviation of $3.27. After an advertising campaign that encouraged people to make long-distance telephone calls more frequently, a random sample of 57 households revealed that the mean monthly long distance bill was $10.98. Can we conclude at the 10% significance level that the advertising campaign was successful?

SCI

7.26 North Americans' obsession with sweets is blamed by nutritionists for a variety of ills, including cavities, diabetes, hyperactivity, and even violent crime (*Newsweek*, 26 August 1985). These problems, as well as the evergrowing use of sugar substitutes, have negative implications for sugar refiners. In 1975, the average per capita consumption of refined sugar in the United States was 89.2 pounds per year. Suppose that, in order to determine if in 1989 there was a decrease in sugar consumption, the eating patterns of 100 Americans were surveyed. If the sample mean annual consumption of sugar was 87.5 pounds, can we conclude at the 10% significance level that there has been a decrease in annual per capita consumption of sugar in the United States? (Assume that $\sigma = 10$ pounds.)

SECTION 7.6   ## *THE p-VALUE OF A HYPOTHESIS TEST*

It's important for you to realize that the result of a statistical procedure is only one of several factors that are considered by a manager prior to making a decision. In Example 7.3, for instance, the manager concluded that there was enough statistical evidence to show that the proposed billing system would not be cost-effective. However, other issues must be evaluated, too. For example, the new system may improve customer service, and the increased goodwill may offset the possible cost-ineffectiveness. Moreover, we did not prove that the system would be too costly; we merely showed that statistical evidence existed to that effect. What is really needed in this situation is a measure of how much statistical evidence exists, so it can be weighed in relation to other factors. In this section we will present such a measure: the *p*-**value** of a test.

---

p-**Value**

The *p*-value of a test of hypothesis is the smallest value of α that would lead to rejection of the null hypothesis.

To understand this definition, review Example 7.3, where the value of the test statistic was

$$z = -1.89$$

and where, with $\alpha = .05$, the rejection region was

$$z < -1.645$$

In that instance, we rejected H_0. Notice that our test's conclusion very much depended on the choice of the significance level α. Had we chosen (say) $\alpha = .01$, the rejection region would have been

$$z < -2.33$$

and we'd have concluded that we could not reject H_0. Notice, however, that we did not have to decrease α very much to change the decision. Values of $\alpha = .02$ or $.025$ or even $.029$ lead to the same conclusion as $\alpha = .01$, but $\alpha = .03$ produces the rejection region

$$z < -1.88$$

which does result in rejecting H_0. Table 7.3 summarizes the relationship between the different values of α and our test conclusion. As you can see, the smallest value of α that would lead to the rejection of H_0 (that is, the p-value) must lie between $.029$ and $.030$. We can determine this value more accurately and more simply by realizing that the p-value is the probability that $z < -1.89$. From Table 3 in Appendix B, we find

$$p\text{-value} = P(z < -1.89) = .0294$$

Figure 7.9 demonstrates how we determine this value. Notice that the calculation of the p-value depends on, among other things, the alternative hypothesis. For example, suppose that, upon testing the hypotheses

$$H_0: \mu = 300$$
$$H_A: \mu > 300$$

TABLE 7.3   *REJECTION REGION FOR A VARIETY OF VALUES OF α FOR EXAMPLE 7.3*

Value of α	Rejection Region	Decision with $z = -1.89$
.01	$z < -2.33$	Do not reject H_0
.02	$z < -2.05$	Do not reject H_0
.025	$z < -1.96$	Do not reject H_0
.029	$z < -1.90$	Do not reject H_0
.030	$z < -1.88$	Reject H_0
.05	$z < -1.645$	Reject H_0

FIGURE 7.9   CALCULATION OF THE p-VALUE FOR EXAMPLE 7.3

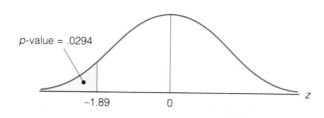

we found $z = 1.50$. Because the rejection region is

$$z > z_\alpha$$

the p-value is the probability that z is greater than 1.50. That is,

$$p\text{-value} = P(z > 1.50) = .0668$$

Figure 7.10 depicts this process.

The p-value of a two-tail test is computed slightly differently. As an illustration, consider Example 7.2, where we tested

$$H_0: \mu = 5,000$$
$$H_A: \mu \neq 5,000$$

and found $z = 1.41$. Since the rejection region in a two-tail test is

$$|z| > z_{\alpha/2}$$

the probability that z is greater than 1.41 must be doubled in order for us to determine the p-value. That is,

$$p\text{-value} = 2P(z > 1.41) = 2(.0793) = .1586$$

Figure 7.11 describes this computation.

FIGURE 7.10   CALCULATION OF THE p-VALUE FOR $H_A: \mu > 300$

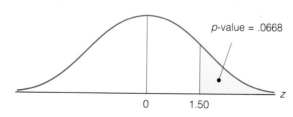

FIGURE 7.11   *CALCULATION OF THE p-VALUE FOR EXAMPLE 7.2*

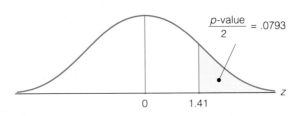

Summary of Calculation of the *p*-Value

Let z_a be the actual value of the test statistic, and let μ_0 be the value of μ specified under the null hypothesis.

If $H_A: \mu > \mu_0$,

p-value $= P(z > z_a)$

If $H_A: \mu < \mu_0$

p-value $= P(z < z_a)$

If $H_A: \mu \neq \mu_0$

p-value $= 2P(z > z_a)$ if $z_a > 0$

$\quad\quad\quad\;\; = 2P(z < z_a)$ if $z_a < 0$

INTERPRETING THE *p*-VALUE

The *p*-value is an important result because it measures the amount of statistical evidence that supports the alternative hypothesis. To understand this interpretation fully, refer again to Example 7.2, where we tested

$H_0: \mu = 5,000$

$H_A: \mu \neq 5,000$

Suppose that the sample mean had been $\bar{x} = 5,200$ and that, as a result, $z = 2.82$. We now find

p-value $= 2P(z > 2.82) = .0048$

Obviously, a larger value of $\bar{x}$ provides more evidence to support H_A. This result is accompanied by a smaller *p*-value. Now suppose that $\bar{x} = 5,050$, which makes $z = .71$ and

p-value $= 2P(z > .71) = .4778$

A value of $\bar{x} = 5,050$ provides very little statistical evidence to indicate that H_A is true. Notice that in this case the *p*-value is large.

Interpreting the *p*-Value

A small *p*-value indicates that there is ample evidence to support the alternative hypothesis.

A large *p*-value indicates that there is little evidence to support the alternative hypothesis.

USING THE *p*-VALUE TO DRAW CONCLUSIONS

In order to draw conclusions about the hypotheses in Section 7.5, we had to use the appropriate table in Appendix B and a predetermined value of α to determine the rejection region in each case and to discover whether or not the test statistic value fell into the rejection region. The *p*-value method is simpler. All we need to do is judge whether the *p*-value is small enough to justify our rejecting the null hypothesis in favor of the alternative. What is considered small enough? The answer to this question is that the manager decides. In Example 7.3 we found the *p*-value to be .0294. If the manager decided that, for this test (taking into account all the other factors), anything less than .01 was small enough to support H_A, then a *p*-value of .0294 would be relatively large and she would conclude that the statistical evidence did not establish that the system was cost-ineffective. However, if she felt that .05 or less was small enough to support H_A, then the *p*-value of .0294 would be relatively small. It follows that she would conclude from the statistical evidence that the system was cost-ineffective.

EXAMPLE 7.4

A major part of waiters' and waitresses' incomes is derived from tips. This income, of course, must be reported on income tax forms. Government tax auditors assume that the average weekly total of tips is $100. A recently hired tax accountant who used to work as a waitress believes that this figure underestimates the true total. As a result she has investigated the weekly tips of a randomly selected group of 150 waiters and waitresses and has found the mean to be $104. Assuming that the population standard deviation is $22, calculate the *p*-value of the test to determine if there is enough evidence to support the tax accountant's assertion.

Solution.   To calculate the *p*-value, we proceed in the usual way to perform a hypothesis test, except that we do not specify a significance level and a rejection region. Because we wish to determine if there is sufficient evidence to show that the average weekly tip total exceeds $100, we set up the null and alternative

FIGURE 7.12   *CALCULATION OF THE p-VALUE FOR EXAMPLE 7.4*

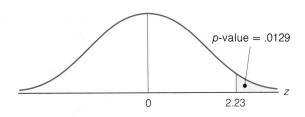

hypotheses as

$$H_0: \mu = 100$$
$$H_A: \mu > 100$$

The test statistic and its value are

$$z = \frac{\bar{x} - \mu}{\sigma/\sqrt{n}} = \frac{104 - 100}{22/\sqrt{150}} = 2.23$$

Since the rejection region is

$$z > z_\alpha$$

the *p*-value is

$$p\text{-value} = P(z > 2.23) = .0129$$

If the accountant judges this value to be small enough, she will conclude that the reported weekly total of tips of $100 underestimates the true total. If not, she will conclude that there is insufficient statistical evidence to support her assertion. Figure 7.12 describes the calculation of the *p*-value for this example.

In subsequent sections of this chapter and in later chapters, we will be dealing with sampling distributions whose tables make calculating the *p*-value quite difficult. Fortunately, most statistical application packages—including the two that are used extensively in this book (Minitab and SAS)—report the *p*-value of the test. Thus, in realistic applications the decision maker only needs to be able to read the *p*-value and judge whether or not it is small enough to justify rejecting H_0. In Section 7.9 we will discuss the calculation of the probability of a Type II error, which will offer you some insight into how to assess *p*-values.

▬▬▬▬▬▬   **EXERCISES**

7.27   For each of the following tests of hypotheses, determine the *p*-value:

a. $H_0: \mu = 200$
    $H_A: \mu > 200$
    $z = 2.63$

b. $H_0: \mu = 500$
    $H_A: \mu \neq 500$
    $z = -2.05$

c. $H_0: \mu = 60$
    $H_A: \mu < 60$
    $z = -3.95$

Self-Correcting Exercise (See Appendix 7.C for the solution.)

7.28   Determine the *p*-value of the test in Exercise 7.16.

7.29   Determine the *p*-value of the test in Exercise 7.24.

7.30   Determine the *p*-value of the test in Exercise 7.25.

7.31   You are told that, in testing of the hypotheses

$H_0: \mu = 1,100$

$H_A: \mu < 1,100$

the *p*-value was computed to be .2365. What does this tell you about the test?

7.32   In testing the hypotheses

$H_0: \mu = 70$

$H_A: \mu > 70$

suppose that you compute

p-value = .0036

What does this value tell you about the test?

SECTION 7.7   *INFERENCE ABOUT μ WITH σ^2 UNKNOWN*

In the preceding sections, the confidence interval estimator and the test statistic were based on knowing that $(\bar{x} - \mu)/(\sigma/\sqrt{n})$ is normally distributed and on having a specific known value for σ^2. This assumption is quite unrealistic because, if the population mean μ is unknown, it is unreasonable to believe that the population variance is known. As a result, $z = (\bar{x} - \mu)/(\sigma/\sqrt{n})$ cannot be the test statistic or the basis of the confidence interval estimator. Because σ^2 is usually unknown, we must substitute the sample standard deviation, s, in place of σ; however, $(\bar{x} - \mu)/(s/\sqrt{n})$ is not normally distributed. In 1908, W. S. Gosset showed that $(\bar{x} - \mu)/(s/\sqrt{n})$ has a particular distribution, called the **Student t distribution,** when the population sampled is normally distributed. The quantity $(\bar{x} - \mu)/(s/\sqrt{n})$ is called the ***t*-statistic.**

STUDENT *t* DISTRIBUTION

Student *t* Distribution

If repeated samples of size n are drawn from a normal population, the sampling distribution of $t = (\bar{x} - \mu)/(s/\sqrt{n})$ is the Student t distribution. This sampling distribution has the following characteristics:

1. It is mound-shaped.

2. It is symmetrical about zero.

3. It is more widely dispersed than the standard normal distribution.

4. Its actual shape depends on the sample size *n*. A convenient way of representing this characteristic is to say that the *t*-statistic has $(n-1)$ degrees of freedom.

Figure 7.13 compares the distribution of *z* with that of a *t*-statistic that has 2 degrees of freedom and with that of another *t*-statistic that has 25 degrees of freedom.

Table 4 in Appendix B specifies values for t_α (where t_α equals the value of *t* such that the area to its right under the *t* curve is equal to α). This table is reproduced in this chapter as Table 7.4. Observe that t_α values are provided for degrees of freedom (d.f.) ranging from 1 through 29 and for ∞. For example, if we want the *t* value with an area .05 to its right with d.f. = 5, we find the column headed by $t_{.05}$ and locate the row with d.f. = 5; the value you should find is $t_{.05} = 2.015$. If d.f. = 10, then $t_{.05} = 1.812$; and if d.f. = 25, then $t_{.05} = 1.708$. As d.f. increases, $t_{.05}$ grows smaller. When d.f. = 29, then $t_{.05} = 1.699$; and if d.f. = ∞, then $t_{.05} = 1.645$, which you should recognize as $z_{.05}$. This is not a coincidence. It can be shown mathematically that, when d.f. is large (theoretically infinite), $t_\alpha = z_\alpha$. You may be wondering why the table does not show t_α for d.f. ≥ 30 (other than ∞). The reason is that t_α with d.f. ≥ 30 is approximately equal to t_α with d.f. = ∞ (that is, z_α). In fact, you can see for yourself that t_α with d.f. = 29 is approximately equal to t_α with d.f. = ∞. We will let $t_{\alpha,\nu}$ represent the value of t_α with *ν* degrees of freedom.

It should be noted that the statistic $(\bar{x} - \mu)/(s/\sqrt{n})$ has the Student *t* distribution only if the sample is drawn from a normal population. Such an application of the *t* distribution is said to be **robust;** this means that the *t* distribution

FIGURE 7.13   *STANDARD NORMAL DISTRIBUTION, t DISTRIBUTION WITH 2 DEGREES OF FREEDOM, AND t DISTRIBUTION WITH 25 DEGREES OF FREEDOM*

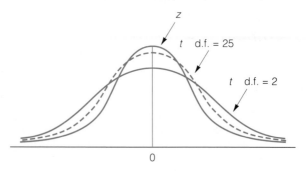

TABLE 7.4   *CRITICAL VALUES OF THE STUDENT t DISTRIBUTION*

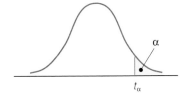

Degrees of Freedom	$t_{.100}$	$t_{.050}$	$t_{.025}$	$t_{.010}$	$t_{.005}$
1	3.078	6.314	12.706	31.821	63.657
2	1.886	2.920	4.303	6.965	9.925
3	1.638	2.353	3.182	4.541	5.841
4	1.533	2.132	2.776	3.747	4.604
5	1.476	2.015	2.571	3.365	4.032
6	1.440	1.943	2.447	3.143	3.707
7	1.415	1.895	2.365	2.998	3.499
8	1.397	1.860	2.306	2.896	3.355
9	1.383	1.833	2.262	2.821	3.250
10	1.372	1.812	2.228	2.764	3.169
11	1.363	1.796	2.201	2.718	3.106
12	1.356	1.782	2.179	2.681	3.055
13	1.350	1.771	2.160	2.650	3.012
14	1.345	1.761	2.145	2.624	2.977
15	1.341	1.753	2.131	2.602	2.947
16	1.337	1.746	2.120	2.583	2.921
17	1.333	1.740	2.110	2.567	2.898
18	1.330	1.734	2.101	2.552	2.878
19	1.328	1.729	2.093	2.539	2.861
20	1.325	1.725	2.086	2.528	2.845
21	1.323	1.721	2.080	2.518	2.831
22	1.321	1.717	2.074	2.508	2.819
23	1.319	1.714	2.069	2.500	2.807
24	1.318	1.711	2.064	2.492	2.797
25	1.316	1.708	2.060	2.485	2.787
26	1.315	1.706	2.056	2.479	2.779
27	1.314	1.703	2.052	2.473	2.771
28	1.313	1.701	2.048	2.467	2.763
29	1.311	1.699	2.045	2.462	2.756
∞	1.282	1.645	1.960	2.326	2.576

SOURCE: From M. Merrington, "Table of Percentage Points of the *t*-Distribution," *Biometrika* 32 (1941): 300. Reproduced by permission of the Biometrika trustees.

also provides an adequate approximate sampling distribution of the *t*-statistic for moderately nonnormal populations. Thus, the statistical inference techniques that follow are valid except when applied to distinctly nonnormal populations.

In actual practice, some statisticians ignore the preceding requirement or blindly assume that the population is normal or only somewhat nonnormal. We urge you not to be one of them. Since we seldom get to know the true value of the parameter in question, our only way of knowing whether the statistical technique is valid is to be certain that the requirements underlying the technique are satisfied. At the very least, you should draw the histogram of any random variable that you are assuming is normal, to ensure that the assumption is not badly violated.

ESTIMATING μ WITH σ^2 UNKNOWN

Using the same algebraic manipulations we employed to produce the confidence interval estimator of μ with σ^2 known, we develop the following estimator.

Confidence Interval Estimator of μ When σ^2 Is Unknown

$$\bar{x} \pm t_{\alpha/2} \frac{s}{\sqrt{n}}$$

We now have two different interval estimators of μ. The basis for deciding which one to use is quite clear.

Two Confidence Interval Estimators of μ

If the population variance is known the confidence interval estimator of μ is

$$\bar{x} \pm z_{\alpha/2} \frac{\sigma}{\sqrt{n}}$$

If the population variance is unknown the confidence interval estimator of μ is

$$\bar{x} \pm t_{\alpha/2} \frac{s}{\sqrt{n}} \qquad \text{d.f.} = n - 1$$

Recall that, when d.f. ≥ 30, $t_{\alpha/2}$ is approximately equal to $z_{\alpha/2}$. If σ^2 is unknown and d.f. ≥ 30, then $t_{\alpha/2}$ can be determined from the standard normal table. You should bear in mind, however, that the interval estimate is still $\bar{x} \pm t_{\alpha/2}s/\sqrt{n}$, with $t_{\alpha/2}$ being approximated by $z_{\alpha/2}$.

EXAMPLE 7.5

The owner of a large fleet of taxis is trying to estimate his costs for next year's operations. One major cost is for fuel purchases. Because of the high cost of gasoline, the owner has recently converted his taxis to operate on propane. He needs to know what the average consumption will be; so he decides to take a random sample of 8 taxis and measure the miles per gallon achieved. The results are as follows:

> 28.1, 33.6, 42.1, 37.5, 27.6, 36.8, 39.0, 29.4

Estimate, with 95% confidence, the mean propane mileage for all taxis in his fleet. (Assume that the distribution of mileage is normal.)

Solution.   The problem objective is to describe a single population (mileage of a fleet of taxis), and the data scale is interval (miles driven per gallon of propane). Since we have no knowledge of the population variance, the confidence interval estimator is $\bar{x} \pm t_{\alpha/2} s / \sqrt{n}$. From the data, we compute

$$\bar{x} = 34.26$$
$$s^2 = 29.61$$
$$s = 5.44$$

Since we want a 95% confidence interval estimate, we know that $1 - \alpha = .95$ and

$$t_{\alpha/2, n-1} = t_{.025, 7}$$
$$= 2.365$$

The 95% confidence interval estimator of μ is

$$\bar{x} \pm t_{\alpha/2} \frac{s}{\sqrt{n}} = 34.26 \pm 2.365 \frac{5.44}{\sqrt{8}} = 34.26 \pm 4.55$$

or

> (29.71, 38.81)

The owner could use this interval estimate to produce an interval estimate of next year's cost of operations.

COMPUTER OUTPUT FOR EXAMPLE 7.5*

Minitab

	N	MEAN	STDEV	SE MEAN	95.0 PERCENT C.I.
C1	8	34.26	5.44	1.92	(29.71, 38.81)

* See Appendixes 7.A and 7.B for the Minitab and SAS commands needed to produce this output.

SAS

```
Analysis Variable : X
N    Minimum        Maximum            Mean         Std Dev
8    27.6000        42.1000         34.2625          5.4410
```

Notice that the confidence interval estimate has not been printed. However, most of the components are here:

$$\bar{x} = 34.26$$
$$s = 5.44$$
$$n = 8$$

All we need to do is find $t_{.025,7}$ from Table 4 in Appendix B and calculate

$$\bar{x} \pm t_{\alpha/2} \frac{s}{\sqrt{n}} = 34.26 \pm t_{.025,7} \frac{5.44}{\sqrt{8}}$$

EXAMPLE 7.6

Suppose that, in Example 7.5, a sample of size 60 had produced $\bar{x} = 33.71$ and $s = 5.51$. Estimate with 95% confidence the mean gas mileage.

Solution. The interval estimator is still

$$\bar{x} \pm t_{\alpha/2} \frac{s}{\sqrt{n}}$$

Since d.f. $= 60 - 1 = 59$, however, $t_{\alpha/2,59}$ is approximately equal to $z_{\alpha/2} = 1.96$. Thus, the 95% confidence interval estimate of μ is

$$\bar{x} \pm t_{\alpha/2} \frac{s}{\sqrt{n}} = 33.71 \pm 1.96 \frac{5.51}{\sqrt{60}} = 33.71 \pm 1.39$$

which simplifies to

$$(32.32, 35.10)$$

TESTING μ WITH σ^2 UNKNOWN

Test Statistic for μ When σ^2 Is Unknown

When the population variance is unknown and the population is normally distributed, the test statistic for testing hypotheses about μ is

$$t = \frac{\bar{x} - \mu}{s/\sqrt{n}}$$

which has a Student t distribution with $n - 1$ degrees of freedom.

As is the case in estimating μ, we have two different test statistics; the choice of which one to use depends on whether or not σ^2 is known.

> **Two Test Statistics for μ**
>
> If σ^2 is known, the test statistic is
>
> $$z = \frac{\bar{x} - \mu}{\sigma/\sqrt{n}}$$
>
> If σ^2 is unknown, the test statistic is
>
> $$t = \frac{\bar{x} - \mu}{s/\sqrt{n}} \qquad \text{d.f.} = n - 1$$

In practice, most applications of statistical inference about μ use the t-statistic, because σ^2 is usually unknown.

EXAMPLE 7.7

A manufacturer of television picture tubes has a production line that produces an average of 100 tubes per day. Because of new government regulations, a new safety device has been installed, which the manufacturer believes will reduce average daily output. A random sample of 15 days' output after the installation of the safety device is shown next.

93, 103, 95, 101, 91, 105, 96, 94, 101, 88, 98, 94, 101, 92, 95

Assuming that the daily output is normally distributed, is there sufficient evidence to conclude that average daily output has decreased following the installation of the safety device? (Use $\alpha = .05$.)

Solution.   The problem objective is to describe the population of television tube production. The scale is interval, since we will be counting the number of picture tubes produced per day. Thus the parameter to be tested is μ. Because σ^2 is unknown, the test statistic is $t = (\bar{x} - \mu)/(s/\sqrt{n})$.

The specifications of H_0 and H_A are based on the same criteria as before. The alternative hypothesis is set up to answer the question. Since we want to know in this problem if there exists sufficient evidence to conclude that μ is less than 100 tubes, we have $H_A: \mu < 100$. The null hypothesis must specify a single value for the parameter. Hence, $H_0: \mu = 100$. The complete test is as follows:

$H_0: \mu = 100$

$H_A: \mu < 100$

Test statistic:

$$t = \frac{\bar{x} - \mu}{s/\sqrt{n}}$$

FIGURE 7.14   REJECTION REGION FOR EXAMPLE 7.7

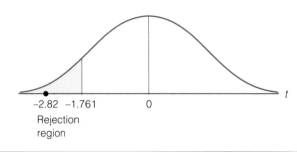

-2.82 -1.761 0

Rejection
region

Rejection region:

$t < -t_{\alpha, n-1}$

$< -t_{.05, 14}$

< -1.761

Value of the test statistic: Since $\bar{x} = 96.47$ and $s = 4.85$,

$$t = \frac{\bar{x} - \mu}{s/\sqrt{n}} = \frac{96.47 - 100}{4.85/\sqrt{15}} = -2.82$$

Conclusion: Reject H_0.

There is enough evidence to show that the average daily output has decreased. Figure 7.14 shows the result of this test. The operations manager should look for ways to restore productivity using the safety device. Perhaps development of another safety device would help.

COMPUTER OUTPUT FOR EXAMPLE 7.7*

Minitab

```
TEST OF MU=100.00 VS MU L.T. 100.00
    N    MEAN    STDEV    SE MEAN      T     P VALUE
C1  15   96.47   4.85     1.25       -2.82   0.0068
```

Given a *p*-value of .0068 and a specified significance level of $\alpha = .05$, we reject the null hypothesis.

* See Appendixes 7.A and 7.B for the Minitab and SAS commands needed to produce this output.

SAS

```
Analysis Variable : Y
  N        Mean              T     Prob > |T|
 15      -3.5333         -2.8197     0.0136
```

SAS automatically tests the hypotheses

$$H_0: \mu = 0$$
$$H_A: \mu \neq 0$$

Thus, to test for

$$H_0: \mu = 100$$
$$H_A: \mu < 100$$

we have to make two adjustments. First, we create a new variable y, which is defined as

$$y = x - 100$$

and test the mean of y. As a result we find $\bar{y} = -3.53$, which implies

$$\bar{x} = \bar{y} + 100 = -3.53 + 100 = 96.47$$

The value of the test statistic $t = -2.82$ is not affected by this transformation. Second, because we want to conduct a one-tail test, we compute the p-value by dividing Prob > |T| by 2. Hence,

$$p\text{-value} = \frac{\text{Prob} > |T|}{2} = \frac{.0136}{2} = .0068$$

EXERCISES

LEARNING THE TECHNIQUES

7.33   In a random sample of 15 observations from a normal population, we found that $\bar{x} = 150$ and $s = 10$. With $\alpha = .01$, test the following hypotheses:

$$H_0: \mu = 160$$
$$H_A: \mu < 160$$

7.34   For Exercise 7.33, estimate μ with 95% confidence.

7.35   For each of the following tests of hypotheses about the mean of a normal population, determine whether or not the null hypothesis should be rejected.

a. $H_0: \mu = 10,000$
      $H_A: \mu > 10,000$
      $n = 10$, $\bar{x} = 11,500$, $s = 3,000$, $\alpha = .05$

b. $H_0: \mu = 75$
      $H_A: \mu > 75$
      $n = 29$, $\bar{x} = 77$, $s = 1$, $\alpha = .01$

c. $H_0: \mu = 200$
      $H_A: \mu < 200$
      $n = 25$, $\bar{x} = 175$, $s = 50$, $\alpha = .10$

7.36   A random sample of 75 observations from a normal population produced the following values:

$$\bar{x} = 56.3, \qquad s^2 = 29.6$$

Test the following hypotheses, with $\alpha = .05$:

$H_0: \mu = 60$

$H_A: \mu < 60$

7.37 For Exercise 7.36, estimate μ with 99% confidence.

7.38 Consider the following data drawn from a normal population:

4, 8, 12, 11, 14, 6, 12, 8, 9, 5

Do they allow us to conclude with $\alpha = .10$ that $\mu > 7$?

7.39 For Exercise 7.38, estimate the population mean with 95% confidence.

7.40 To test the hypotheses

$H_0: \mu = 50,000$

$H_A: \mu < 50,000$

a statistician generated the computer output shown in Figure E7.40. Assuming that the statistician chose $\alpha = .01$, interpret the results and draw a conclusion.

7.41 In testing the hypotheses

$H_0: \mu = 250$

$H_A: \mu > 250$

a statistician used a computer software package to generate the results that follow. If the significance level is set at $\alpha = .05$, what conclusion should we draw?

```
Analysis Variable: Y
 N    Mean      T     Prob > |T|
18   11.30     1.94     0.0717
```

APPLYING THE TECHNIQUES

Self-Correcting Exercise (See Appendix 7.C for the solution.)

SCI **7.42** A diet doctor claims that the average North American is more than 10 pounds overweight. To test his claim, a random sample of 50 North Americans were weighed, and the difference between their actual weight and their ideal weight was calculated. The mean and standard deviation of that difference was 11.5 and 2.2 pounds, respectively. Can we conclude, with $\alpha = .05$, that there is enough evidence to show that the claim is true? What assumption is being made in your test?

SCI **7.43** For Exercise 7.42, find the 99% confidence interval estimate of the average amount by which North Americans are overweight.

MKT **7.44** A courier service advertises that its average delivery time is less than 6 hours for local deliveries. A random sample of the amount of time this courier takes to deliver packages to an address across town produced the following times (rounded to the nearest hour):

7, 3, 4, 6, 10, 5, 6, 4, 3, 8

a. Is this sufficient evidence to support the courier's advertisement, at the 5% level of significance?

b. Find the 99% confidence interval estimate of the mean delivery time.

c. What assumption must be made in order to answer parts (a) and (b)?

GEN **7.45** A highway patrolman believes that the average speed of cars traveling over a certain stretch of highway exceeds the posted limit of 55 mph. A random sample of 10 cars had their speeds measured by radar. The results (in mph) are as follows:

71, 53, 62, 49, 59, 52, 58, 61, 85, 55

a. Do these data provide sufficient evidence to support the highway patrolman's belief, at the 10% level of significance?

b. Estimate with 95% confidence the average speed of cars on this stretch of highway.

c. What assumption did you make in order to answer parts (a) and (b)?

FIGURE E7.40

```
TEST OF MU=50000 VS MU L.T. 50000
       N    MEAN   STDEV   SE MEAN     T    P VALUE
C1    500  49563   3988    178.3    -2.45   0.0071
```

PG **7.46**   A federal agency responsible for enforcing laws concerning weights and measures routinely inspects packages to determine whether the weight of the contents is at least as great as that advertised on the package. A random sample of 25 observations of a product whose container claims that the net weight is 10 ounces yielded the following statistics:

$$\bar{x} = 10.52$$

$$s^2 = 1.43$$

a. Do these data provide sufficient evidence to enable the agency to conclude that the mean net weight exceeds the net weight indicated on the container, at the 10% level of significance?

b. Estimate with 95% confidence the mean weight of the container.

RE **7.47**   A real estate company appraised the market value of 20 homes in a prestigious district of San Francisco. They found that the sample mean and the sample standard deviation were $236,500 and $23,000, respectively.

a. Estimate the mean appraisal value of all the homes in this area, with 90% confidence. (Assume that the appraised values are normally distributed.)

b. Is there sufficient evidence to conclude that the mean appraisal value of all houses is not equal to $250,000? (Use $\alpha = .01$.)

SECTION 7.8   # INFERENCE ABOUT σ^2

In Section 7.7, where we discussed inference about a population mean, our interest lay in the measure of central location of the population. If we are more interested in the measure of variability, however, the parameter of interest is the population variance σ^2. This parameter can be used to describe a number of different situations. For example, quality-control engineers must ensure that products coming off a production line meet specifications. One way of judging the consistency of a production process is to calculate the variance of the size, weight, or volume of the product. Another example comes from the area of finance. Investors use the variance of the returns on a portfolio of investments as a measure of the uncertainty and risk inherent in that portfolio.

We begin the task of drawing inferences about σ^2 by identifying its best estimator. The sample variance s^2 is an unbiased, consistent estimator of σ^2; in this textbook, that means that s^2 is the best estimator of σ^2. In order to proceed with the statistical inference techniques, however, we need to know how s^2 is distributed.

SAMPLING DISTRIBUTION OF s^2

Chi-Square Sampling Distribution

In repeated sampling from a normal population whose variance is σ^2, the variable $(n - 1)s^2/\sigma^2$ is chi-square distributed with $(n - 1)$ degrees of freedom. The variable $(n - 1)s^2/\sigma^2$ is called the *chi-square statistic* and is denoted χ^2 (the Greek letter *chi* squared).

The χ^2 variable can equal any value between 0 and ∞. Figure 7.15 depicts several chi-square distributions that have different degrees of freedom.

FIGURE 7.15   *CHI-SQUARE DISTRIBUTIONS*

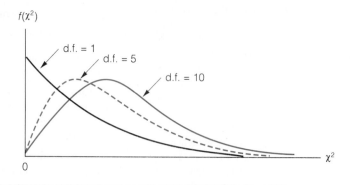

CHI-SQUARE NOTATION

The value of χ^2 such that the area to its right under the chi-square curve is equal to α, is denoted χ^2_α. Because the χ^2 variable assumes only positive values, we need a notation different from the one used for z and t to define the point for which the area to its left is equal to α. We therefore define $\chi^2_{1-\alpha}$ as the point for which the area to its right is $1 - \alpha$ and the area to its left is α. Figure 7.16 describes this notation. Table 5 in Appendix B provides the values of χ^2_α and $\chi^2_{1-\alpha}$ for various values of α and various degrees of freedom. Table 7.5 is a partial reproduction of this table. To illustrate, $\chi^2_{.05} = 18.3070$, with d.f. $= 10$, while $\chi^2_{.95} = 3.94030$, with the same degrees of freedom.

Using the notation just introduced, we can make the following statement:

$$P(\chi^2_{1-\alpha/2} < \chi^2 < \chi^2_{\alpha/2}) = 1 - \alpha$$

FIGURE 7.16 χ^2_α *AND* $\chi^2_{1-\alpha}$

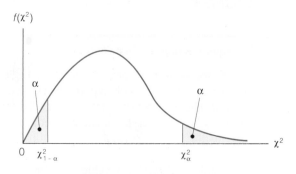

TABLE 7.5 CRITICAL VALUES OF χ^2

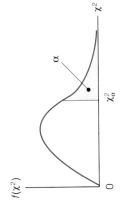

Degrees of Freedom	$\chi^2_{.995}$	$\chi^2_{.990}$	$\chi^2_{.975}$	$\chi^2_{.950}$	$\chi^2_{.050}$	$\chi^2_{.025}$	$\chi^2_{.010}$	$\chi^2_{.005}$
1	.0000393	.0001571	.0009821	.0039321	3.84146	5.02389	6.63490	7.87944
2	.0100251	.0201007	.0506356	.102587	5.99147	7.37776	9.21034	10.5966
3	.0717212	.114832	.215795	.351846	7.81473	9.34840	11.3449	12.8381
4	.206990	.297110	.484419	.710721	9.48773	11.1433	13.2767	14.8602
5	.411740	.554300	.831211	1.145476	11.0705	12.8325	15.0863	16.7496
6	.675727	.872085	1.237347	1.63539	12.5916	14.4494	16.8119	18.5476
7	.989265	1.239043	1.68987	2.16735	14.0671	16.0128	18.4753	20.2777
8	1.344419	1.646482	2.17973	2.73264	15.5073	17.5346	20.0902	21.9550
9	1.734926	2.087912	2.70039	3.32511	16.9190	19.0228	21.6660	23.5893
10	2.15585	2.55821	3.24697	3.94030	18.3070	20.4831	23.2093	25.1882
11	2.60321	3.05347	3.81575	4.57481	19.6751	21.9200	24.7250	26.7569
12	3.07382	3.57056	4.40379	5.22603	21.0261	23.3367	26.2170	28.2995

SOURCE: From C. M. Thompson, "Tables of the Percentage Points of the χ^2-Distribution," *Biometrika* 32 (1941): 188–89. Reproduced by permission of Biometrika trustees.

Substituting $\chi^2 = (n-1)s^2/\sigma^2$, we have

$$P(\chi^2_{1-\alpha/2} < (n-1)s^2/\sigma^2 < \chi^2_{\alpha/2}) = 1 - \alpha$$

Using a little algebraic manipulation, we can isolate σ^2 in the center of the probability statement, which produces the following estimator.

Confidence Interval Estimator of σ^2

$$\text{LCL} = \frac{(n-1)s^2}{\chi^2_{\alpha/2}}$$

and

$$\text{UCL} = \frac{(n-1)s^2}{\chi^2_{1-\alpha/2}}$$

EXAMPLE 7.8

A company manufactures steel shafts for use in engines. One method of judging inconsistencies in the production process is to determine the variance of the lengths of the shafts. A random sample of 10 shafts produced the following measurements of their lengths (in centimeters):

20.5, 19.8, 21.1, 20.2, 18.9, 19.6, 20.7, 20.1, 19.8, 19.0

Find a 90% confidence interval for the population variance σ^2 (assuming that the lengths of the steel shafts are normally distributed).

Solution.   The problem objective is to describe a single population (lengths of steel shafts), and the data scale is interval (the lengths of the shafts, measured in centimeters). The parameter of interest is σ^2 (we wish to describe the inconsistency or variability of the shaft lengths). The interval estimator of σ^2 is:

$$\text{LCL} = \frac{(n-1)s^2}{\chi^2_{\alpha/2}}$$

and

$$\text{UCL} = \frac{(n-1)s^2}{\chi^2_{1-\alpha/2}}$$

From the data, we calculate

$$\sum(x_i - \bar{x})^2 = (n-1)s^2 = 4.44$$

With $1 - \alpha = .90$, we have $\alpha/2 = .05$, $\chi^2_{.05,9} = 16.9190$, and $\chi^2_{.95,9} = 3.32511$. Thus,

$$\text{LCL} = \frac{(n-1)s^2}{\chi^2_{\alpha/2}} = \frac{4.44}{16.9190} = .262$$

and

$$UCL = \frac{(n-1)s^2}{\chi^2_{1-\alpha/2}} = \frac{4.44}{3.32511} = 1.34$$

The 90% confidence interval estimate of σ^2 is (.262, 1.34).

TESTING σ^2

Test Statistic for σ^2

The test statistic used to test hypotheses about σ^2 is

$$\chi^2 = \frac{(n-1)s^2}{\sigma^2}$$

which is chi-square distributed with $(n-1)$ degrees of freedom, provided that the population random variable is normally distributed.

EXAMPLE 7.9

A manufacturer of a bottle-filling machine claims that the standard deviation of the fills from his machine is less than 2 cc. In a random sample of 10 fills, the sample standard deviation was 1.19 cc. Is this sufficient evidence at the 5% level of significance to support the manufacturer's claim? (Assume a normal population.)

Solution.   The problem objective is to describe the population of the fills. The data scale is interval (the size of the fills). We want to measure the inconsistency of the fills, and as a result the parameter of interest is σ^2. Because we want to determine whether we can statistically support the claim that the standard deviation is less than 2 cc, our alternative hypothesis would state that $\sigma^2 < 2^2$. The test is conducted as follows:

$$H_0: \sigma^2 = 4$$
$$H_A: \sigma^2 < 4$$

Test statistic:

$$\chi^2 = \frac{(n-1)s^2}{\sigma^2}$$

Rejection region:

$$\chi^2 < \chi^2_{1-\alpha, n-1}$$
$$< \chi^2_{.95, 9}$$
$$< 3.32511$$

FIGURE 7.17   *REJECTION REGION FOR EXAMPLE 7.9*

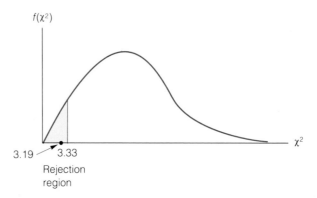

Value of the test statistic:

$$\chi^2 = \frac{(n-1)s^2}{\sigma^2} = \frac{9(1.19)^2}{4} = 3.19$$

Conclusion: Reject H_0.

There is enough evidence to support the manufacturer's claim. Figure 7.17 depicts this test.

████████ **EXERCISES**

LEARNING THE TECHNIQUES

7.48 In a sample of size 15 from a normal population, we find $s^2 = 110$.

a. Estimate σ^2, with 99% confidence.

b. Test with $\alpha = .05$:

   $H_0: \sigma^2 = 100$

   $H_A: \sigma^2 \neq 100$

7.49 Using the data from Exercise 7.45, estimate with 95% confidence the population variance of the speed of cars.

7.50 For each of the following tests of hypotheses about σ^2, find the rejection region in terms of s^2.

a. $H_0: \sigma^2 = 100$
   $H_A: \sigma^2 > 100$
   $\alpha = .05$ $n = 20$

b. $H_0: \sigma^2 = 500$
   $H_A: \sigma^2 < 500$
   $\alpha = .10$ $n = 20$

c. $H_0: \sigma^2 = 20$
   $H_A: \sigma^2 \neq 20$
   $\alpha = .01$ $n = 50$

7.51 Using the data from Exercise 7.44, test with $\alpha = .05$:

   $H_0: \sigma^2 = 10$

   $H_A: \sigma^2 < 10$

7.52 The following observations were drawn from a normal population:

   7, 15, 23, 18, 25, 10, 16, 8

Test the hypotheses, with $\alpha = .10$:

   $H_0: \sigma^2 = 15$

   $H_A: \sigma^2 \neq 15$

7.53 For Exercise 7.52, find a 99% confidence interval estimate of σ^2.

APPLYING THE TECHNIQUES

Self-Correcting Exercise (See Appendix 7.C for the solution.)

MNG **7.54** One important factor in inventory control is the variance of the daily demand for a product. Management believes that demand is normally distributed with the variance equal to 250. In an experiment to test this belief about σ^2, the daily demand was recorded for 25 days. The data have been summarized as follows:

$$\sum x_i = 1,265$$
$$\sum x_i^2 = 76,010$$

Do the data provide sufficient evidence to show that management's belief about the variance is untrue? (Use $\alpha = .01$.)

EDUC **7.55** In a large university, the marks on the final examination of a statistics course are normally distributed. In a random sample of 20 exams, we found that $\bar{x} = 75.2$ and $s^2 = 47.0$. Estimate with 90% confidence the variance of all marks in the final exam of this statistics course.

MNG **7.56** Using the data from Exercise 7.54, determine the 95% confidence interval estimate of σ^2.

GEN **7.57** A consumers' organization is interested in determining the amount of variability in the price of one brand of VCR. A survey of 25 retail outlets produces a mean and a standard deviation of $380 and $20, respectively.

a. Estimate with 99% confidence the variance in price of this brand of VCR.

b. At the 5% level of significance, can we conclude that the variance is less than $500?

c. What assumption did you have to make to answer parts (a) and (b)?

POM **7.58** After an extensive time and motion study at a large plant, the operations manager concluded that the variance of the time for assembly line workers to complete their tasks was critical. Specifically, if the variance exceeds 120 seconds^2, bottlenecks and shortages are inevitable. In a preliminary study of 75 workers, the assembly times were summarized as follows:

$$\sum x_i = 773$$
$$\sum x_i^2 = 22,430$$

a. Can we conclude at the 5% significance level that bottlenecks and shortages are inevitable?

b. Estimate the variance of the assembly times with 99% confidence.

SECTION 7.9 ## *CALCULATING THE PROBABILITY OF A TYPE II ERROR*

In conducting a test of hypothesis, we need to specify only two factors: the significance level α, and the sample size n. The values selected for α and n depend on a number of factors, but perhaps the most important of these is the cost of making a mistake. As you have already seen, it is possible in any hypothesis test to make one of two mistakes. If the cost of making a Type I error is considerably higher than the cost of making a Type II error, a small value of α (perhaps .01 or less) is appropriate. If the cost of making a Type II error is higher, we should set up the test in such a way that β (the probability of a Type II error) is small. To understand this, you must be able to calculate β.

Recall the example at the beginning of this chapter, where the rejection region was $\bar{x} < 19,510$ or $\bar{x} > 20,490$. A Type II error occurs when a false null hypothesis is accepted. Thus,

$$\beta = P(19,510 < \bar{x} < 20,490 \mid H_0 \text{ is false})$$

FIGURE 7.18   CALCULATION OF β

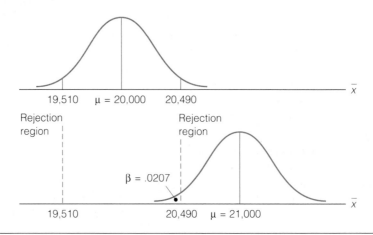

Suppose that we wish to compute β when, in actual fact, $\mu = 21{,}000$. That is,

$$\beta = P(19{,}510 < \bar{x} < 20{,}490 \,|\, \mu = 21{,}000)$$

We can compute this probability by remembering that $\bar{x}$ is approximately normally distributed, with mean μ and standard deviation $\sigma/\sqrt{n}$. We standardize $\bar{x}$ and use Table 3 in Appendix B as follows:

$$\beta = P\left(\frac{19{,}510 - 21{,}000}{5{,}000/\sqrt{400}} < \frac{\bar{x} - \mu}{\sigma/\sqrt{n}} < \frac{20{,}490 - 21{,}000}{5{,}000/\sqrt{400}}\right)$$

$$= P(-5.96 < z < -2.04) = .0207$$

This means that, if μ is actually equal to 21,000, the probability of incorrectly accepting H_0 is .0207. Figure 7.18 graphically represents the calculation of β. Notice that, in order to calculate β, we expressed the rejection region in terms of the unstandardized test statistic. Notice, too, that the value of β depends on our choice of the value of the parameter. In this case, we chose $\mu = 21{,}000$. In a practical setting, we would select a value of interest to us.

EXAMPLE 7.10

The feasibility of constructing a profitable electricity-producing windmill depends on the average velocity of the wind. For a certain type of windmill, the average wind speed would have to exceed 20 mph (miles per hour) in order for that windmill's construction to be feasible. To test whether or not a particular site is appropriate for this windmill, 50 readings of the wind velocity are taken, and the average is calculated. The test is designed to answer the question: is the site feasible? That is, is there sufficient evidence to conclude that the average wind velocity exceeds 20 mph? As a result, we wish to test the following hypotheses:

$$H_0: \mu = 20$$
$$H_A: \mu > 20$$

If, when the test is conducted, a Type I error is committed (rejecting H_0 when it should be accepted), we would conclude mistakenly that the average wind velocity exceeds 20 mph. The consequence of this decision is that the windmill would be built on an inappropriate site. Since this error is quite costly, we set $\alpha = .01$. If a Type II error is committed (accepting H_0 when it's false), we would conclude mistakenly that the wind velocity does not exceed 20 mph. As a result, we would not build the windmill on that site, even though the site is a good one. The cost of this error is not very large, since — if the site under consideration is judged to be inappropriate — the search for a good site would simply continue. But suppose that a site where the wind velocity is greater than or equal to 25 mph is extremely profitable. To judge the effectiveness of this test (to determine if our selection of $\alpha = .01$ and $n = 50$ is appropriate), we compute the probability of committing this error. Our task is to calculate β when $\mu = 25$. (Assume that we know that $\sigma = 12$ mph.)

Solution.   Our first step is to set up the rejection region in terms of $\bar{x}$. Since the rejection region is

$$z > z_\alpha = 2.33$$

we have

$$z = \frac{\bar{x} - \mu}{\sigma/\sqrt{n}} = \frac{\bar{x} - 20}{12/\sqrt{50}} > 2.33$$

Solving the inequality, we express the rejection region as

$$\bar{x} > 23.95$$

The second step is to describe the region where H_0 is accepted as

$$\bar{x} < 23.95$$

Thus,

$$\beta = P(\bar{x} < 23.95 \,|\, \mu = 25) = P\left(\frac{\bar{x} - \mu}{\sigma/\sqrt{n}} < \frac{23.95 - 25}{12/\sqrt{50}}\right)$$
$$= P(z < -.62) = .2676$$

The probability of accepting H_0 when $\mu = 25$ is .2676. (See Figure 7.19.) This means that, when the mean wind velocity is 25 mph, there is a 26.76% probability of erroneously concluding that the site is not profitable. If this probability is considered too large, we can reduce it by either increasing α or increasing n.

For example, if we increase α to .10 and leave $n = 50$, then $\beta = .0475$. With $\alpha = .10$, however, the probability of building on a site that is not profitable is too large. If we let $\alpha = .01$ but increase n to 100, then $\beta = .0336$. Now both α and

---

FIGURE 7.19   *CALCULATION OF β FOR EXAMPLE 7.10*

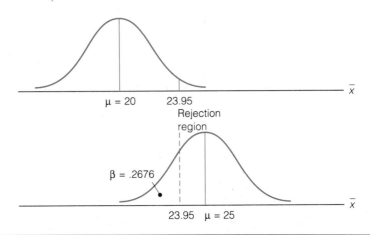

$β$ are quite small, but the cost of sampling has increased. Nonetheless, the cost of sampling is quite small in comparison to the costs of making Type I and Type II errors in this question.

Another way of judging a test is to measure its *power*—the probability of its leading us to reject H_0 when it is false—rather than measuring the probability of a Type II error. Thus the power of the test is equal to $1 - β$. In the present example, the power of the test with $n = 50$ and $α = .01$ is $1 - .2676 = .7324$. When more than one test can be performed in a given situation, we would naturally prefer to use the one that is correct more frequently. If (given the same alternative hypothesis, sample size, and significance level) one test has a higher power than another test, the first test is said to be more powerful.

In this section we have discussed calculating the probability of a Type II error only when testing $μ$ with $σ^2$ known, because only the standard normal table (Table 3 in Appendix B) allows us to perform this computation. In Chapter 8 you will encounter another test statistic that is approximately normally distributed; and in that case, too, you will be able to compute $β$.

EXERCISES

LEARNING THE TECHNIQUE

7.59 For each of the following tests of hypotheses, calculate the probability of a Type II error.

a. $H_0: μ = 200$
  $H_A: μ \neq 200$
  $α = .05, σ = 10, n = 100$

Find $β$, given that $μ = 203$.

b. $H_0: μ = 1,000$
  $H_A: μ > 1,000$
  $α = .01, σ = 50, n = 25$

Find $β$, given that $μ = 1,050$.

c. $H_0: \mu = 50$
$H_A: \mu < 50$
$\alpha = .05, \sigma = 10, n = 40$

Find β, given that $\mu = 48$.

7.60   For the test of hypothesis

$H_0: \mu = 1,000$
$H_A: \mu \neq 1,000$
$\alpha = .05, \sigma = 200, n = 100$

find β when $\mu = 900, 940, 980, 1,020, 1,060, 1,100$.

7.61   For Exercise 7.60, graph μ (on the horizontal axis) versus β (on the vertical axis). If necessary, calculate β for additional values of μ. The resulting graph is called the **operating characteristic (OC) curve.**

7.62   For Exercise 7.60, graph μ versus $1 - \beta$. Recall that $1 - \beta$ is called the *power* of the test; as a consequence, the graph is called the **power curve.**

7.63   Repeat Exercises 7.60 through 7.62, with $n = 25$. What do you notice about these graphs when compared to the graphs drawn in Exercises 7.61 and 7.62?

APPLYING THE TECHNIQUES

Self-Correcting Exercise (See Appendix 7.C for the solution.)

7.64   For Exercise 7.23, determine the probability of concluding that the average GMAT score did not increase, when the population mean score μ actually equals 600.

EDUC **7.65**   A school-board administrator believes that the average number of days absent per year among its students is less than 10 days. From past experience, he knows that the population standard deviation is 3 days. In testing to determine whether his belief is true, he could use either of the following plans:

(i) $n = 100, \alpha = .05$

(ii) $n = 250, \alpha = .01$

Which plan has the lower probability of a Type II error, given that the true population average is 9 days?

SECTION 7.10   **SELECTING THE SAMPLE SIZE TO ESTIMATE μ**

One of the most common questions asked of statisticians is, how large should the sample taken in a survey be? The answer to this question depends on three factors:

1. The parameter to be estimated
2. The desired confidence level of the interval estimator
3. The maximum error of estimation, where **error of estimation** is the absolute difference between the point estimator and the parameter; for example, the point estimator of μ is $\bar{x}$, so in that case

$$\text{Error of estimation} = |\bar{x} - \mu|$$

The maximum error of estimation is also called the **error bound** and is denoted B. Suppose that the parameter of interest in an experiment is the population mean μ. The confidence interval estimator (assuming a normal population, with σ^2 known) is

$$\bar{x} \pm z_{\alpha/2} \frac{\sigma}{\sqrt{n}}$$

If we wish to estimate μ to within a certain specified bound B, we will want the confidence interval estimator to be

$$\bar{x} \pm B$$

As a consequence we have

$$z_{\alpha/2} \frac{\sigma}{\sqrt{n}} = B$$

Solving for *n* we get

Sample Size Necessary to Estimate μ to Within a Bound B

$$n = \left[\frac{z_{\alpha/2}\sigma}{B} \right]^2$$

Suppose that we want to determine the sample size necessary to estimate, with 95% confidence, the average weight gain of rats on a special cereal diet, to within 2 ounces. Thus, $B = 2$; and since $1 - \alpha = .95$, it follows that $z_{\alpha/2} = 1.96$. As a result,

$$n = \left[\frac{1.96\sigma}{2} \right]^2$$

If we assume that σ is known (let's suppose that, from some other source, we know that $\sigma = 15$), we can solve for *n*. That is,

$$n = \left[\frac{(1.96)(15)}{2} \right]^2 = [14.7]^2 = 217$$

In order to solve for *n*, we had to have some value for σ. This value could be approximated from previous experiments or from knowledge about the population. The basic rule of thumb when approximating σ is that we should err on the high side. This will result in a value of *n* that estimates μ at the desired confidence level, and the size of the interval will be at least as good as was specified.

Suppose that, when the previously mentioned experiment was run, *s* was calculated as 30. The confidence interval then would be $\bar{x} \pm 1.96(30)/\sqrt{217}$, which simplifies to $\bar{x} \pm 4$. Hence, the interval is twice as wide as was desired. If *s* is less than 15, the interval would be narrower (and better) than specified. Consistent with this principle, our solution to the equation for *n* is

$$n = (14.7)^2 = 216.09$$

which we round upward to ensure that the confidence interval estimate is at least as good as was specified.

A popular method of approximating σ is to begin by approximating the range of the random variable. In practice, this task is relatively simple. A conservative estimate of σ is the range divided by 4; that is, $\sigma \approx \text{Range}/4$. This method is quite effective (particularly for normal random variables), since 2 standard deviations on either side of the mean create an interval that contains about 95% of the population. You might wonder why we don't divide the range by 6, since 3 standard deviations on either side of the mean is an interval that contains almost 100% of the population. The answer is that approximating σ by Range/4 produces a larger value of σ, which results in a larger value of n, which then estimates μ with an interval at least as good as was specified.

■■■■■■■■■ **EXAMPLE 7.11**

The operations manager of a large production plant would like to estimate the average amount of time a worker takes to assemble a new electronic component. After observing a number of workers assembling similar devices, she noted that the shortest time taken was 10 minutes and that the longest time taken was 22 minutes. How large a sample of workers should she sample if she wishes to estimate the mean assembly time to within 20 seconds? Assume that the confidence level is to be 99%.

Solution.   The parameter to be estimated is μ, the confidence level is .99, and the error bound is 20 seconds. Since Range = 12 minutes, we approximate σ by $12/4 = 3$ minutes = 180 seconds. Hence,

$$B = 20$$
$$z_{\alpha/2} = z_{.005} = 2.58$$
$$\sigma = 180$$

and

$$n = \left[\frac{z_{\alpha/2}\sigma}{B}\right]^2 = \left[\frac{(2.58)(180)}{20}\right]^2 = (23.22)^2 = 540$$

The operations manager should randomly sample 540 workers in order to estimate the mean assembly time to within 20 seconds, with 99% confidence.

■■■■■■■■■ **EXERCISES**

7.66   Find n, given that we wish to estimate μ to within 10 units with 95% confidence, assuming that $\sigma = 100$.

7.67   Determine the sample size necessary to estimate μ to within 10 units with 99% confidence. We know that the range of the population is 200 units.

GEN   **7.68**   A forester would like to estimate the mean tree diameter of a large tract of trees. He would like to estimate μ to within .5 inch with 99% confidence. A quick survey reveals that the smallest tree has a diameter of 2 inches, while the largest tree has a diameter of 27 inches. How large a sample should he take?

POM   **7.69**   A production manager would like to estimate the mean time required for workers to complete a task on an assembly line. How large a sample should she draw to estimate μ to within 5 seconds with 90% confidence? Assume that she knows that σ is 80 seconds.

POM   **7.70**   Repeat Exercise 7.69, changing the confidence level to 99%.

POM   **7.71**   Repeat Exercise 7.69, with $\sigma = 10$ seconds.

SECTION 7.11 ## SUMMARY

There are two types of statistical inference: **estimation** and **hypothesis testing.** Both types of inference can be applied to problems in which the objective is to describe a single population and in which the data scale is interval.

We estimate the **parameters μ and σ^2** by using an **interval estimator** with a specified **confidence level.** There are two different estimators of μ: the **standard normal sampling distribution** (z formula), which is used when σ^2 is known; and the **Student t formula,** which is used when σ^2 is unknown. The estimate of σ^2 is based on the **chi-square sampling distribution.** Student t and chi-square distributions both require that the population from which we're sampling be normally distributed.

The parameters μ and σ^2 are tested by reference to the same sampling distributions. The **alternative hypothesis** is set up to answer the question, while the **null hypothesis** states that the parameter equals a fixed value. The test is conducted by specifying the **significance level α.** The formulas for the estimators and test statistics are summarized in Table 7.6.

This chapter also presented **p-values,** the **calculation of β,** and a method for determining the sample size.

TABLE 7.6   *SUMMARY OF INFERENCES ABOUT μ AND σ^2*

Parameter	Estimator	Test Statistic	Required Conditions
μ	$\bar{x} \pm z_{\alpha/2} \dfrac{\sigma}{\sqrt{n}}$	$z = \dfrac{\bar{x} - \mu}{\sigma/\sqrt{n}}$	σ^2 is known; x is normally distributed, or n is sufficiently large.
	$\bar{x} \pm t_{\alpha/2} \dfrac{s}{\sqrt{n}}$	$t = \dfrac{\bar{x} - \mu}{s/\sqrt{n}}$	σ^2 is unknown; x is normally distributed.
σ^2	$\text{LCL} = \dfrac{(n-1)s^2}{\chi^2_{\alpha/2}}$ $\text{UCL} = \dfrac{(n-1)s^2}{\chi^2_{1-\alpha/2}}$	$\chi^2 = \dfrac{(n-1)s^2}{\sigma^2}$	x is normally distributed.

SUPPLEMENTARY EXERCISES

POM **7.72** The "just-in-time" policy of inventory control (developed by the Japanese) is growing in popularity. For example, General Motors recently announced that it intends to spend $2 billion on its

Oshawa, Ontario, plant so that it will be less than 1 hour from most suppliers. Suppose that an automobile parts supplier claims to deliver parts to any local manufacturer in an average time of 1 hour or less. In an effort to test the claim, a manufacturer recorded the times of 25 deliveries from this supplier. The sample mean and the sample standard deviation were $\bar{x} = 1.1$ hours and $s = .3$ hour.

a. Can we conclude at the 5% level of significance that the supplier's claim is incorrect?

b. Estimate the mean delivery time with 99% confidence.

c. Estimate with 95% confidence the variance of the delivery time.

d. What assumption must you make in order to answer parts (a) through (c)?

EDUC **7.73** In a survey reported in the *Wall Street Journal* (9 February 1987), people selected in a random sample of the high-school class of 1972 were asked how many years it took for them to complete their bachelor's degrees in college. The results (in percentages) are as follows:

Years	Frequency
4	49%
5	27%
6	9%
7	15%

SOURCE: Center for Education Statistics.

If 1,000 graduates were surveyed, estimate with 95% confidence the mean number of years taken to complete the bachelor's degree.

MNG **7.74** For the past few years, the number of customers of a drive-in bank in New York has averaged 20 per hour, with a standard deviation of 3 per hour. This year, another bank 1 mile away opened a drive-in window. The manager believes that this will result in a decrease in the number of customers. A random sample taken over 15 hours

showed that the mean number of customers per hour was 18.7.

a. Can we conclude at the 5% level of significance that the manager's belief is correct?

b. Find the *p*-value of this test.

c. What assumption must we make in order to answer parts (a) and (b)?

RET **7.75** A manufacturer of a brand of designer jeans realizes that many retailers charge less than the suggested retail price of $40. A random sample of 20 retailers reveals that the mean and the standard deviation of the price of the jeans are $32 and $2.50, respectively.

a. Estimate with 90% confidence the mean retail price of the jeans.

b. Estimate with 95% confidence the variance of the retail price of the jeans.

c. What assumption must you make in order to answer parts (a) and (b)?

FIN **7.76** A department store wants to estimate the average account of all its credit-card customers to within $10.00, with 99% confidence. A quick analysis tells us that the smallest account shows $0 while the largest is $500.

a. Determine the sample size.

b. Suppose that a survey is performed, and the sample mean is found to be $150. Find a 99% confidence interval estimate of μ, assuming that the value of σ used in part (a) is correct. (HINT: This question should take you no more than 5 seconds to answer.)

GEN **7.77** An automotive expert claims that the large number of self-serve gasoline stations has resulted in poor automobile maintenance, and that the average tire pressure is at least 4 psi (pounds per square inch) below its manufacturer's specification. As a quick test, ten tires are examined, and in each case the number of psi below specification is recorded. The data are as follows:

7, 9, 2, 0, 5, 6, 3, 5, 8, 9

Do these data allow us to conclude that the expert is correct? (Use $\alpha = .05$.)

MNG **7.78** A fast-food franchiser is considering building a restaurant at a certain location. According to a financial analysis, a site is acceptable only if the number of pedestrians passing the location averages more than 100 per hour. A random sample of 50 hours produced $\bar{x} = 110$ and $s = 12$ pedestrians per hour.

a. Do these data provide sufficient evidence to establish that the site is acceptable? (Use $\alpha = .05$.)

b. What are the consequences of Type I and Type II errors? Which error is the more expensive to make?

c. Considering your answer to part (b), should you select α to be large or small? Explain.

d. Would it be preferable to ask instead whether there is enough evidence to establish that the site is unacceptable? Explain.

TOUR **7.79** People selected in a random sample of business executives were asked how many vacation days they take annually. The results (in percentages), which were reported in the *Wall Street Journal* (6 February 1987), are as follows:

Vacation Days	Frequency
Less than 5 days	9%
At least 5 but less than 10 days	24%
At least 10 but less than 15 days	31%
At least 15 but less than 20 days	23%
At least 20 but less than 25 days	13%

SOURCE: Karn/Ferry International.

If the sample size was 800, estimate with 99% confidence the mean number of days spent on vacation by business executives.

MKT **7.80** An advertisement for a major home-appliance manufacturer claims that its repair personnel are the loneliest in the world, because its appliances require so few service calls. To examine this claim, a random sample of 100 owners of 5-year-old washing machines of this brand was drawn. The mean and the standard deviation of the number of service calls over the 5-year period are 4.3 and 1.8, respectively. Find the 90% confidence interval estimate for the number of service calls for all 5-year-old washing machines of this brand.

MNG **7.81** A large company is considering moving from its present downtown location to one in the suburbs. One factor in this decision is the amount of time its employees spend commuting to work. In a survey, a random sample of 20 employees indicates that the mean and the standard deviation of the time required to get to work are 36.5 and 11.3 minutes, respectively.

a. Estimate with 95% confidence the mean time required to arrive at work.

b. Can we conclude that the average time required to arrive at work exceeds 30 minutes? (Use $\alpha = .01$.)

c. What assumption must you make in order to answer parts (a) and (b)?

GEN **7.82** The owner of a downtown parking lot suspects that the person she hired to run the lot is stealing some money. The receipts as provided by the employee indicate that the average number of cars parked in the lot is 125 per day and that, on average, each car is parked for 3.5 hours. In order to determine whether the employee is stealing, the owner watches the lot for 5 days. On those days the number of cars parked is as follows:

120, 130, 124, 127, 128

For the 629 cars that the owner observed during the 5 days, the mean and the standard deviation of the time spent on the lot were 3.6 and 0.4 hours, respectively.

a. Can the owner conclude at the 5% level of significance that the employee is stealing? (HINT: Since there are two ways to steal, two tests should be performed.)

b. Discuss the consequences of Type I and Type II errors.

c. If you're the owner, do you want a small or large value of α? Explain.

d. If you're the employee, do you want a small or large value of α? Explain.

FIN **7.83** An oil company sends out monthly statements to customers who purchased gasoline and other items using the company's credit card. Up to now, the company did not include a preaddressed envelope for returning payments. The average and the standard deviation of the number of days before payment is received are 10.5 and 3.3, respectively. As an experiment to determine if enclosing preaddressed envelopes speeds up payment, 100 customers selected at random were sent preaddressed envelopes with their bills. The mean number of days to payment was 9.3, and the standard deviation was 2.2.

a. Do the data provide sufficient evidence at the 5% level of significance to establish that enclosing the preaddressed envelopes improves the average speed of payments?

b. Can we conclude from the data that the standard deviation of the speed of payments also decreases when the preaddressed envelopes are enclosed? (Use $\alpha = .01$.)

EDUC **7.84** A large university wants to determine the average income their students earn during the summer. A random sample of 25 second-year business students produced the following statistics (where x is measured in hundreds of dollars):

$$\sum x_i = 826.6$$

$$\sum x_i^2 = 27{,}935.7$$

a. Estimate the mean summer employment income for all second-year business students, with 99% confidence.

b. Does the estimate in part (a) pertain to all business students? To all university students? Explain.

c. What assumption must be made in order to answer part (a)?

POM **7.85** A time study of a large production facility was undertaken to determine the average time required to assemble a widget. A random sample of 15 assemblies produced $\bar{x} = 12.2$ minutes, with a standard deviation of 2.4 minutes.

a. Assuming that the assembly times are normally distributed, estimate the mean assembly time, with 95% confidence.

b. How would your answer to part (a) change if the population standard deviation were known to be 2.0 minutes?

ECON **7.86** Suppose that annual household incomes in a certain city have a standard deviation of $3,000. A random sample of 50 families reveals that the mean annual income is $27,500.

a. Estimate the mean annual family income of all families in this city, with 95% confidence.

b. Without doing the calculations, specify what happens to the width of the interval in each of the following circumstances.
 (i) σ is $5,000, not $3,000.
 (ii) The confidence level is 90%, not 95%.
 (iii) The sample mean is $30,000, not $27,500.

FIN **7.87** In a study to determine the size of loan requests at a suburban bank, the mean in a random sample of 25 requests was $7,500, with a standard deviation of $2,000. Assuming that loan requests are normally distributed, estimate with 95% confidence:

a. The mean loan request

b. The variance of the loan requests

MNG **7.88** Suppose that hourly wages in the chemical industry are normally distributed, with a mean of $7.60 and a standard deviation of $0.60. A large company in this industry took a random sample of 50 of its workers and determined that their average hourly wage was $7.50.

a. Can we conclude at the 10% level of significance that this company's average hourly wage is less than that of the entire industry?

b. Find the probability of making a Type II error, given that the company's average wage is actually $7.45 per hour.

7.89 A sample size of $n = 100$ has been drawn from a population whose variance is 2,250 in order to test:

$$H_0: \mu = 1{,}000$$

$$H_A: \mu \neq 1{,}000$$

It is decided to reject H_0 if $\bar{x} > 1{,}008$ or if $\bar{x} < 992$.

a. Find the probability of a Type I error.

b. Find the probability of a Type II error if $\mu = 1{,}005$.

■■■■■■■■■   **CASE 7.1***   *NATIONAL PATENT DEVELOPMENT CORPORATION*

FIN This case requires the use of a computer. The data are not shown below but are stored on the data disk.

The National Patent Development Corporation (NPD) has recently acquired a new product that can be used to replace the dentist's drill. The product, called Caridex, is a solution that dissolves decayed matter in cavities without requiring drilling.

It is known that 100,000 dentists in the United States treat cavities. A preliminary analysis has revealed that 10% of all dentists would use Caridex in the first year after its introduction. However, Caridex is only effective on certain types of cavities. In a survey of 400 dentists, each was asked to estimate the number of cavities each week he or she would treat with Caridex. The results, which range from 1 to 10, are stored on the data disk.

The dispensing unit costs NPD $200, and it intends to sell the unit at cost price. The solution costs $0.50 per cavity and will be sold to dentists at a price of $2.50 per cavity. Fixed annual costs are expected to be $4 million.

NPD would like an estimate of the profit it can expect in the first year of operation.

■■■■■■■■■   **CASE 7.2†**   *AUTOMATIC TELLER MACHINE*

FIN The automatic teller machine (ATM), first introduced in the 1960s, was a major technological innovation. With it, a customer can make deposits, withdrawals, and other transactions without the aid of a teller. It is estimated that, for each transaction performed by an ATM instead of a teller, the bank saves about $1. In an effort to persuade as many customers as possible to use ATMs, banks install the machines in as many locations as are feasible. Because of installation and maintenance costs, however, the machines should only be placed in locations where the demand warrants it.

In a survey to determine the frequency of use of a proposed ATM, 542 individuals who work in the building where the machine would be installed were asked how frequently they would use it. Their responses appear in the accompanying table. The bank would like to estimate the average annual use of the ATM. (Assume that those who state "less than once per month" would use the machine twice per year.) Given that the potential population of users numbers 10,000, the bank would also like to estimate the annual savings achieved by using the ATM in place of a bank teller.

---

* Based on a report by Ladenburg Thalman—a large, New York–based investment firm. The survey is fictitious.

† Based on D. L. Varble and J. M. Hawes, "Profiling the Users of Automated Teller Machines," *Developments in Marketing Science* 9 (1986): 369–72.

FREQUENCY OF PROPOSED USE OF AN ATM

Frequency of Use	Number of Users
Twice per week	23
Once per week	37
Once per two weeks	18
Once per month	35
Less than once per month	44
Never	385
Total	542

MINITAB INSTRUCTIONS

ESTIMATING μ WITH σ^2 KNOWN

To produce a 95% confidence interval estimate of μ, type

```
ZINTERVAL K1 C1
```

which specifies that $\sigma = $ K1 and that the data are stored in column 1. The command

```
ZINTERVAL .90 25 C1
```

produces the 90% confidence interval estimate of μ when $\sigma = 25$. If the .90 is omitted, a 95% confidence interval estimate will be produced.

Suppose that the 100 observations alluded to in Example 7.1 are stored in column 1. The command

```
ZINTERVAL 8 C1
```

would produce the following output:

```
THE ASSUMED SIGMA=8.000
        N     MEAN    STDEV    SE MEAN    95.0 PERCENT C.I.
C1    100    27.50    7.578     0.80      (25.93,    29.07)
```

Notice that STDEV would equal the sample standard deviation s, which is not necessary for this confidence interval estimate because σ is known. (The value 7.578 was invented to fill the space.) SE MEAN is the standard error of the mean, which is $\sigma_{\bar{x}} = \sigma/\sqrt{n} = .80$.

TESTING μ WITH σ^2 KNOWN

In order to perform a two-tail test of μ, type

```
ZTEST K1 K2 C1
```

where K1 is the value of μ under the null hypothesis, $\sigma = $ K2, and the data are in column 1. For example,

```
ZTEST 100 10 C1
```

tests

$$H_0: \mu = 100$$
$$H_A: \mu \neq 100$$

when $\sigma = 10$. If the data for Example 7.2 were stored in column 1, the command

```
ZTEST 5000 500 C1
```

would produce the following output:

```
TEST OF MU=5000 VS MU N.E. 5000
THE ASSUMED SIGMA=500.0
        N     MEAN    STDEV    SE MEAN     Z     P VALUE
C1     50     5100    527.3    70.71      1.41   0.1586
```

To perform a one-tail test, we employ the subcommand ALTERNATIVE. (Remember that, in order to use a subcommand, you must end the preceding command with a semicolon, and you must end the subcommand with a period.) The subcommand

```
ALTERNATIVE 1
```

performs a one-tail test with

$$H_A: \mu > \text{K1}$$

The subcommand

```
ALTERNATIVE -1
```

employs the alternative hypothesis

$$H_A: \mu < \text{K1}$$

For example,

```
ZTEST 100 10 C1;
ALTERNATIVE -1.
```

tests

$$H_0: \mu = 100$$
$$H_A: \mu < 100$$

when $\sigma = 10$. Thus, to have Minitab do Example 7.3, we would type

```
ZTEST 70 30 C1;
ALTERNATIVE -1.
```

The output would appear as follows:

```
TEST OF MU=70 VS MU L.T. 70
THE ASSUMED SIGMA=30.0
        N     MEAN    STDEV   SE MEAN      Z    P VALUE
C1    200    66.00    28.62    2.121    -1.89    0.0294
```

ESTIMATING μ WITH σ^2 UNKNOWN

The command

```
TINTERVAL .90 C1
```

produces the 90% confidence interval estimate of μ (when σ^2 is unknown) from the data in column 1. Example 7.5 would be done by the computer as follows (since we actually show the data in the example, we'll show how the data are input):

```
SET C1
28.1 33.6 42.1 37.5 27.6 36.8 39.0 29.4
END
TINTERVAL .95 C1
```

The output that would be produced is

```
        N     MEAN    STDEV   SE MEAN   95.0 PERCENT C.I.
C1      8    34.26     5.44      1.92    (29.71,    38.81)
```

TESTING μ WITH σ^2 UNKNOWN

The command

```
TTEST K1 C1
```

performs a two-tail test. The subcommand ALTERNATIVE allows us to perform a one-tail test. For example,

```
TTEST 40 C1;
ALTERNATIVE 1.
```

tests

$$H_0: \mu = 40$$
$$H_A: \mu > 40$$

when σ^2 is unknown. The computer output includes the value of the test statistic t and the *p*-value.

As an illustration, we now show how Example 7.7 is answered:

```
SET C1
93 103 95 101 91 105 96 94 101 88 98 94 101 92 95
END
TTEST 100 C1;
ALTERNATIVE -1.
```

The output is

```
TEST OF MU=100.00 VS MU L.T. 100.00
        N     MEAN    STDEV   SE MEAN      T     P VALUE
C1     15    96.47     4.85     1.25    -2.82    0.0068
```

SAS INSTRUCTIONS

INFERENCE ABOUT μ WITH σ^2 UNKNOWN: TESTING μ

The MEANS procedure is used to test hypotheses about μ when σ^2 is unknown. If we wish, we can specify which statistics are to be provided. For example, if we typed

```
PROC MEANS N MEAN T PRT;
```

the computer would output the sample size n, the sample mean $\bar{x}$, the value of the test statistic

$$t = \frac{\bar{x} - \mu}{s/\sqrt{n}}$$

and the p-value. If no statistics were specified, the computer would print out a variety of statistics, including n, $\bar{x}$, s, and s^2, but not the t-statistic or the p-value.

The PROC MEANS statement is followed by a statement identifying which variables the calculations are to be performed on. The test computed is a two-tail test of

$$H_0: \mu = 0$$
$$H_A: \mu \neq 0$$

In order to test for some value of μ other than zero, we need to create a new variable (say, y), where

$$y = x - \mu$$

and μ is the value we wish to test. Then we test y against zero (which is equivalent to testing x against μ). To illustrate, we solve Example 7.7 as follows:

```
DATA;
INPUT X;
Y=X-100;
```

```
CARDS;
93
103
95
101
91
105
96
94
101
88
98
94
101
92
95
PROC MEANS N MEAN T PRT;
VAR Y;
```

Notice that the new variable is created right after the INPUT X statement and that we subtract the value of μ under the null hypothesis ($H_0: \mu = 100$) from x. The following output would be produced:

```
Analysis Variable: Y
  N       Mean          T       Prob > |T|
  15    -3.5333     -2.8197      0.0136
```

INFERENCE ABOUT μ WITH σ^2 UNKNOWN: ESTIMATING μ

If the MEANS procedure does not specify any statistics, the output will include n, the minimum, the maximum, $\bar{x}$, and s. We could then construct the confidence interval estimate ourselves, with the assistance of the Student t table.

Thus, to estimate μ in Example 7.5, we would proceed as follows:

```
DATA;
INPUT X;
CARDS;
28.1
33.6
42.1
37.5
27.6
36.8
39.0
29.4
```

```
PROC MEANS;
VAR X;
```

The resulting printout would be

```
Analysis Variable: X
N    Minimum    Maximum        Mean    Std Dev
8    27.6000    42.1000     34.2625     5.4410
```

And the confidence interval estimate of μ would be

$$34.26 \pm t_{\alpha/2} \frac{5.44}{\sqrt{8}}$$

■■■■■■■■■ **COMPUTER EXERCISES**

7.90 Given the following observations drawn from a normal population with variance $\sigma^2 = 70$, test to determine whether the mean is greater than 40. (Use $\alpha = .05$.)

36	45	53	60	52
27	40	38	36	62
53	47	48	25	39
78	39	52	43	22

7.91 For Exercise 7.90, estimate the population mean with 99% confidence.

7.92 The following observations were drawn from a normal population whose variance is $\sigma^2 = 15$. Estimate the population mean with 95% confidence.

26	34	24
20	16	29
19	21	18
28	22	30
31	29	17

7.93 In Exercise 7.92, is there enough evidence at the 1% significance level to conclude that the population mean differs from 25?

7.94 The following data were gathered in a sample of 20 observations from a normal population. Do these results allow us to conclude at the 1% significance level that the population mean is less than 75?

89	93	71	88
93	80	98	86
76	88	75	77
79	77	83	91
85	72	84	93

7.95 For Exercise 7.94, estimate the population mean with 90% confidence.

7.96 Given the following 10 observations drawn from a normal population, estimate the population mean with 99% confidence:

7.7, 8.8, 8.3, 9.5, 7.5, 9.3, 8.6, 8.0, 8.1, 9.0

7.97 For Exercise 7.96, test to determine whether the population mean is greater than 9.0. (Use $\alpha = .10$.)

SOLUTIONS TO SELF-CORRECTING EXERCISES

7.8 $\bar{x} \pm z_{\alpha/2}\sigma\sqrt{n} = 7.2 \pm 1.645(15/\sqrt{100})$
$$= 7.2 \pm 2.47$$

The bank estimates that the mean waiting time is between 4.73 and 9.67 minutes.

7.24 $H_0: \mu = 10.2$
   $H_A: \mu > 10.2$

Rejection region: $z > 1.645$

Test statistic: $z = \dfrac{\bar{x} - \mu}{\sigma/\sqrt{n}} = \dfrac{14.6 - 10.2}{0.8/\sqrt{26}} = 28$

Conclusion: Reject H_0.

Yes, there is sufficient evidence to indicate that banks that exercise comprehensive planning outperform the average bank.

7.28 p-value $= P(z < -1.41) = .0793$

7.42 $H_0: \mu = 10$
   $H_A: \mu > 10$

Rejection region: $t > 1.645$

Test statistic: $t = \dfrac{\bar{x} - \mu}{s/\sqrt{n}} = \dfrac{11.5 - 10}{2.2/\sqrt{50}} = 4.82$

Conclusion: Reject H_0.

Yes, we can conclude that the average North American is more than 10 pounds overweight. We must assume that weights are normally distributed.

7.54 $H_0: \sigma^2 = 250$
   $H_A: \sigma^2 \neq 250$

Rejection region: $\chi^2 < 9.88623, \chi^2 > 45.5585$

Test statistic:

$$s^2 = \frac{\sum x_i^2 - (\sum x_i)^2/n}{n-1} = \frac{76{,}010 - (1{,}265)^2/25}{24} = 500$$

$$\chi^2 = \frac{(n-1)s^2}{\sigma^2} = \frac{24(500)}{250} = 48.0$$

Conclusion: Reject H_0.

Yes, there is sufficient evidence to show that the variance differs from 250.

7.64   Rejection region:

$$z > 1.645$$

$$\frac{\bar{x} - \mu}{\sigma/\sqrt{n}} > 1.645$$

$$\frac{\bar{x} - 560}{50/\sqrt{20}} > 1.645$$

$$\bar{x} > 578.39$$

$$\beta = P(\bar{x} < 578.39 \mid \mu = 600)$$

$$= P\left(\frac{\bar{x} - \mu}{\sigma/\sqrt{n}} < \frac{578.39 - 600}{50/\sqrt{20}}\right)$$

$$= P(z < -1.93) = .0268$$

INFERENCE ABOUT THE DESCRIPTION OF A SINGLE POPULATION: NOMINAL SCALE

INTRODUCTION

In Chapter 5 we pointed out that, when the data scale is nominal, the only computation that makes any sense is one to determine the proportion of times each value occurs. If the problem objective is to describe a single population, the parameter of interest is the proportion p of times when certain outcomes occur. In keeping with the concepts and notation of the binomial experiment, we label the outcome of interest to us a *success*. Any other outcomes are labeled *failures*. Our task in this chapter is to develop the techniques of statistical inference about the proportion of successes in a binomial experiment. Three cases where this inference is applied are described for illustrative purposes.

Case 1. The profits of television networks greatly depend on the **proportion** of television viewers who are tuned into each network. In most North American cities, viewers can choose from among the major networks plus an assortment of independent stations. Naturally each network or station would identify anyone tuned into one of its programs as a success, and all others as failures. Labeling of this type gives us a binomial experiment, and television executives are keenly interested in the proportion of successes. The problem objective is to describe the population of television viewers. Since this population is very large, random samples are drawn from it, and statistical techniques are used either to estimate or to test the parameter p. In North America this service is provided by A. C. Nielsen, and the results are known as the *Nielsen ratings*.

Case 2. Items that are manufactured in large production facilities occasionally do not meet specifications or do not function properly. One of the functions of a quality-control engineer is to determine the **fraction** of defective units that are produced. Upon inspection, each unit is labeled *defective* or *nondefective*. You should recognize the nominal scale in this situation. The objective is to describe the population of products being manufactured. In situations where the number of units is quite large or where testing destroys the product, sampling procedures are employed.

Case 3. Most firms periodically introduce new products or services into the marketplace. Before doing so, however, they need to know how well (or poorly) consumers will receive the innovation. That is, they want to know the **market share** of consumers who will purchase their product. Once again, we have a nominal scale in which consumers are either successes (will purchase the product) or failures (will not purchase). The problem objective is to describe the population of consumers.

Sampling procedures are used to estimate or test hypotheses about the population parameter p. This service is often provided by market research consultants. You may be surprised at the large number of such companies listed in the Yellow Pages of your local telephone directory.

In this chapter we will develop methods of estimating and of hypothesis testing for the parameter p. You will find that this development is quite similar to those you've already encountered in Chapter 7. We begin by identifying the best estimator of p, and then we discuss the sampling distribution of the estimator. From this sampling distribution, we branch off into a presentation of the methods of estimation and hypothesis testing. Although it's traditional in textbooks of this kind to present estimation before hypothesis testing (as we did in Chapter 7), we will reverse that order here and in all subsequent chapters. This approach is easier, since the formula that describes the sampling distribution is often the same as the formula for the test statistic. In addition, a number of problem-objective data-scale combinations exist for which the estimation method makes no sense (and of course will not be presented at all).

SECTION 8.2   *SAMPLING DISTRIBUTION OF $\hat{p}$*

The logical statistic used in making inferences about a population proportion is the sample proportion. Thus, given a sample drawn from the population of interest, we will calculate the number of successes divided by the sample size. As we did in Chapter 4, when we discussed the binomial distribution, we label the number of successes x; hence, the sample proportion is x/n. We denote this sample proportion by $\hat{p}$.

Figure 8.1 describes the sampling process. The proportion of successes in the population is p. A random sample of n observations contains x successes. Hence, the proportion of successes in the sample is $\hat{p}$.

Recall (from Chapter 4) that the mean of x is

$$E(x) = np$$

FIGURE 8.1   SAMPLING FROM A POPULATION WITH A NOMINAL SCALE

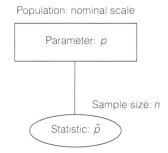

Population: nominal scale

Parameter: p

Sample size: n

Statistic: $\hat{p}$

---

and that the standard deviation of x is

$$\sigma_x = \sqrt{npq}$$

Using the rules of expectation and variance (again, from Chapter 4), we can show without difficulty that

$$E(\hat{p}) = p$$

and that the standard deviation of $\hat{p}$ is

$$\sigma_{\hat{p}} = \sqrt{\frac{pq}{n}}$$

(See Exercise 8.10.) Hence, $\hat{p}$ is an unbiased and consistent estimator of p. Put simply, this means that $\hat{p}$ is the best estimator of p.

Since x is a binomial random variable, its probability distribution is described by the following formula:

$$P(x) = C_x^n p^x q^{n-x}$$

When we divide x by n to create $\hat{p}$, the probability remains unchanged:

$$P(\hat{p}) = C_x^n p^x q^{n-x}$$

That is, $\hat{p}$ is binomially distributed. Unfortunately, the binomial distribution is awkward when used in statistical inference. But in Chapter 4 we demonstrated that the binomial distribution can be approximated by the normal, provided that n is sufficiently large. As a result we have the following definition.

Sampling Distribution of $\hat{p}$

The sample proportion $\hat{p}$ is approximately normally distributed, with mean p and standard deviation $\sqrt{pq/n}$, provided that n is large ($np \geq 5$ and $nq \geq 5$).

Figure 8.2 depicts this distribution.

Since $\hat{p}$ is approximately normal, it follows that the standardized variable

$$z = \frac{\hat{p} - p}{\sqrt{\dfrac{pq}{n}}}$$

is approximately standard normally distributed.* This variable will be the basis for the hypothesis tests and estimation of p. We begin with the hypothesis testing technique.

---

* This requires that $np \geq 5$ and $nq \geq 5$. Some students wrongly assume that, if the sample size is too small, the sampling distribution is Student t. In fact, when n is too small for $np \geq 5$ and $nq \geq 5$, any inference about p must be based on the actual distribution of $\hat{p}$, which is binomially distributed.

FIGURE 8.2	*APPROXIMATE SAMPLING DISTRIBUTION OF $\hat{p}$*

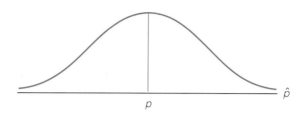

SECTION 8.3   *TESTS OF HYPOTHESES ABOUT p*

The null and alternative hypotheses of tests of p are set up in the same way as are the hypotheses of tests of μ. That is, the alternative hypothesis answers the question, while the null hypothesis indicates that p is equal to some specific value. The test statistic is derived from the sampling distribution of $\hat{p}$.

Test Statistic for p

$$z = \frac{\hat{p} - p}{\sqrt{\dfrac{pq}{n}}}$$

And, as we said in Chapter 7, the rejection region depends on the alternative hypothesis. You will find that calculating the test statistic and determining the rejection region are quite straightforward. Since this is the third parameter (μ and σ^2 were the first two) with which we have dealt, however, the difficulty of correctly identifying the parameter is increasing. Naturally, the examples and the exercises in this chapter all deal with the parameter p. But as you read each problem, make certain that you figure out why that question deals with inference about p. It might be helpful to imagine that you are gathering the data yourself. As you record the responses, ascertain whether those responses are interval, ordinal, or nominal. Recall that nominal data are qualitative and that any numbers assigned to record the values of a nominal scale are arbitrary.

EXAMPLE 8.1

After careful analysis, a company contemplating the introduction of a new product has determined that it will need to capture more than 10% of the market in order to be profitable. In a survey, 100 potential customers were asked whether or not they would purchase this product. If 14 people responded affirmatively, would this be enough evidence for the company to conclude that the product will be profitable? (Use $\alpha = .05$.)

Solution.   The responses to this survey are: "Yes, I would purchase this product" and "No, I would not purchase this product." The scale is nominal, and since we are dealing with a single population (the population of potential customers), the parameter is p. We want to know whether there is sufficient evidence to establish that the product will be profitable, so we have H_A: $p > .10$. The remainder of the test easily follows:

$$H_0: p = .10$$
$$H_A: p > .10$$

Test statistic:

$$z = \frac{\hat{p} - p}{\sqrt{\dfrac{pq}{n}}}$$

Rejection region:

$$z > z_\alpha$$
$$> z_{.05}$$
$$> 1.645$$

Value of the test statistic:

$$z = \frac{\hat{p} - p}{\sqrt{\dfrac{pq}{n}}} = \frac{.14 - .10}{\sqrt{\dfrac{(.10)(.90)}{100}}} = 1.33$$

Conclusion: Do not reject H_0.

Figure 8.3 describes this test of hypothesis.

There are insufficient grounds to conclude that the product will be profitable. Observe that we did find some evidence to support a conclusion that the population proportion is more than 10% (the sample proportion was 14%). But the evidence was not strong enough to allow us to say that the population proportion exceeds

FIGURE 8.3   *REJECTION REGION FOR EXAMPLE 8.1*

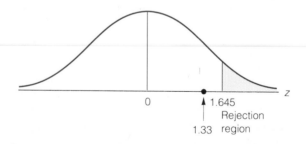

10%. (Remember, the statistical evidence must be strong enough for us to say something with any degree of confidence.)

---

p-VALUE OF THE TEST

In Chapter 7, we pointed out that the *p*-value of a test is the smallest value of α that leads to rejection of the null hypothesis. As a result, a small *p*-value allows the statistician to conclude that there is enough evidence to justify rejecting the null hypothesis in favor of the alternative hypothesis.

The *p*-value of a test of hypothesis about a population proportion is determined in the same way as was shown in Chapter 7. For Example 8.1, we find

$$p\text{-value} = P(z > 1.33) = .0918$$

Thus, if the decision maker chooses a significance level larger than .0918, the *p*-value will be considered small, and H_0 will be rejected. If a significance level less than .0918 is chosen, the *p*-value will be considered large, and the null hypothesis will not be rejected.

PROBABILITY OF A TYPE II ERROR

In Example 8.1, we specified that the probability of a Type I error was .05, meaning that there was a 5% chance we might conclude that the product would be profitable when in fact it would not. If we're interested in determining the probability of our concluding that the product would not be profitable when in fact it would be, we can calculate β, the probability of a Type II error. As in Chapter 7, the process of calculating β is broken into two steps. The first step is to determine the rejection region in terms of the unstandardized test statistic, $\hat{p}$. The rejection region is $z > 1.645$; therefore,

$$z = \frac{\hat{p} - p}{\sqrt{\dfrac{pq}{n}}} = \frac{\hat{p} - .10}{\sqrt{\dfrac{(.10)(.90)}{100}}} > 1.645$$

which holds whenever $\hat{p} > .149$.

The second step is to calculate the probability that $\hat{p}$ will not fall into the rejection region when p is actually greater than 10% (since $H_A: p > .10$). Suppose that we want to know β when p is really .25. That is,

$$\beta = P(\hat{p} < .149 \,|\, p = .25) = P\left(\frac{\hat{p} - p}{\sqrt{\dfrac{pq}{n}}} < \frac{.149 - .25}{\sqrt{\dfrac{(.25)(.75)}{100}}} \right)$$

$$= P(z < -2.33) = .0099$$

In this calculation we assume that $p = .25$, and as a result the standard deviation of $\hat{p}$ changes.

FIGURE 8.4 CALCULATION OF THE PROBABILITY OF A TYPE II ERROR

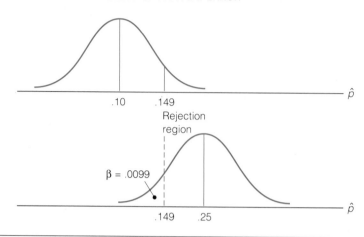

The probability of mistakenly concluding that the product would not be profitable when 25% of the potential customers actually would buy the product is .0099. Figure 8.4 depicts this calculation.

▬▬▬▬▬▬ **EXERCISES**

LEARNING THE TECHNIQUES

8.1 Test each of the following hypotheses:

a. $H_0: p = .45$
$H_A: p \neq .45$
$\alpha = .05, n = 100, \hat{p} = .40$

b. $H_0: p = .7$
$H_A: p > .7$
$\alpha = .01, n = 1,000, \hat{p} = .75$

c. $H_0: p = .25$
$H_A: p < .25$
$\alpha = .10, n = 2,000, \hat{p} = .23$

8.2 If $\hat{p} = .57$ and $n = 100$, can we conclude at the 5% level of significance that the population proportion p is greater than .50?

8.3 In Exercise 8.1, determine the p-value of each test.

8.4 In Exercise 8.1, determine β for the following:

a. true value of $p = .50$

b. true value of $p = .73$

c. true value of $p = .22$

8.5 Repeat Exercise 8.4a, with $n = 500$.

8.6 In a sample of 200, we observe 140 successes. Is this sufficient evidence at the 1% significance level to indicate that the population proportion of successes is at least 65%?

8.7 Find the p-value of the test described in Exercise 8.6.

8.8 For Exercise 8.6, find the probability of erroneously concluding that p does not exceed 65% when in fact p is 68%.

8.9 Test the following hypotheses, with $\alpha = .10$:

$H_0: p = .05$

$H_A: p < .05$

$x = 1, n = 100$

8.10 Using the rules of expectation and variance

that you learned in Chapter 4, show that $E(\hat{p}) = p$ and $\text{Var}(\hat{p}) = \dfrac{pq}{n}$.

APPLYING THE TECHNIQUES

GEN **8.11**   A coin is flipped 100 times. If the number of heads that occur is 60, is this sufficient evidence at the 5% level of significance to conclude that the coin is unfair?

Self-Correcting Exercise (See Appendix 8.A for the solution.)

MKT **8.12**   A tire manufacturer claims that more than 90% of her product will last at least 50,000 miles. In a random sample of 200 tires, 10 tires wore out before reaching 50,000 miles. Do the data support the manufacturer's claim, with $\alpha = .01$?

MKT **8.13**   Find the *p*-value of the test described in Exercise 8.12.

POM **8.14**   In a random sample of 100 units from an assembly line, 22 were defective. Does this provide sufficient evidence at the 10% significance level to allow us to conclude that the defective rate among all units exceeds 10%?

POM **8.15**   For Exercise 8.14, find a 99% confidence interval estimate of the defective rate.

POM **8.16**   Find the *p*-value of the test described in Exercise 8.14.

MKT **8.17**   In a television commercial, the manufacturer of a toothpaste claims that 4 out of 5 dentists recommend its product. In order to test the claim, a consumer-protection group randomly samples 400 dentists and finds that 310 recommended that toothpaste. At the 5% level of significance, test to determine if there is sufficient evidence to refute the manufacturer's claim. (Interpret the claim to say that *at least* 4 out of 5 dentists recommend the product.) What is the *p*-value of the test?

MKT **8.18**   In a test to evaluate the effectiveness of a new drug for combating acne, a drug company found that 120 out of a random sample of 220 acne sufferers improved after being treated with this new preparation. The leading acne treatment has a 50% improvement rate. Can we conclude from the data that this new drug is more effective in treating acne? (Use $\alpha = .01$.)

MKT **8.19**   Find the *p*-value of the test described in Exercise 8.18.

SECTION 8.4   # ESTIMATING p

In Section 8.2, we stated that the best estimator of the population proportion *p* is the sample proportion $\hat{p}$, and that $\hat{p}$ is approximately normal, with mean *p* and standard deviation $\sqrt{pq/n}$.* Applying a little algebra, we now attempt to construct the interval estimator of *p* in the usual manner. The result is

$$\hat{p} \pm z_{\alpha/2}\sqrt{\frac{pq}{n}}$$

This formula is useless, however, since *p* and *q* are unknown. (If they were known, there would be no need to estimate *p*.) As a result, we estimate the standard deviation of $\hat{p}$ with $\sqrt{\hat{p}\hat{q}/n}$, to produce the formula on the following page.

---

* This requires that $np \geq 5$ and $nq \geq 5$. Since these are unknown values, we will use the technique discussed in this section with the proviso that $n\hat{p} \geq 5$ and $n\hat{q} \geq 5$.

Confidence Interval Estimator of p

$$\hat{p} \pm z_{\alpha/2} \sqrt{\frac{\hat{p}\hat{q}}{n}}$$

EXAMPLE 8.2

A factory produces a component that is used in manufacturing computers. Each component is tested prior to shipment to determine whether or not it is defective. In a random sample of 400 units, 60 were found to be defective. Estimate with 99% confidence the true proportion of defective components produced by the factory.

Solution.   The scale is nominal because the values of the variable are *defective* and *nondefective*. The problem objective is to describe a single population (the population of components produced in the factory). Hence, we wish to estimate p. The interval estimator is

$$\hat{p} \pm z_{\alpha/2} \sqrt{\frac{\hat{p}\hat{q}}{n}}$$

Since $\hat{p} = 60/400 = .15$ and $z_{\alpha/2} = 2.58$, the 99% confidence interval estimate of p is

$$\hat{p} \pm z_{\alpha/2} \sqrt{\frac{\hat{p}\hat{q}}{n}} = .15 \pm 2.58 \sqrt{\frac{(.15)(.85)}{400}} = .15 \pm .046$$

which works out to

$$(.104, .196)$$

The operations manager might decide that since the defective rate may be as high as 19.6%, corrective action is required.

SELECTING THE SAMPLE SIZE TO ESTIMATE p

In Chapter 7, when we discussed how to determine the sample size to estimate μ, we pointed out that the value of n depends on three things: the parameter to be estimated, the confidence level, and the desired degree of accuracy. If the parameter to be estimated is p, then $z_{\alpha/2}$ reflects the desired confidence level, and $z_{\alpha/2} \sqrt{\hat{p}\hat{q}/n}$ is equal to the error bound B. To determine the required sample size, we find the following value.

Sample Size Necessary to Estimate p

$$n = \left[\frac{z_{\alpha/2} \sqrt{\hat{p}\hat{q}}}{B} \right]^2$$

Suppose that, working with the data in Example 8.2, we want to estimate the proportion of defective components to within .03, with 95% confidence. This means that, when the sample is taken, we wish the interval estimate to be $\hat{p} \pm .03$. Hence, $B = .03$. Since $1 - \alpha = .95$, we know that $z_{\alpha/2} = 1.96$; therefore,

$$n = \left[\frac{1.96 \sqrt{\hat{p}\hat{q}}}{.03} \right]^2$$

To solve for n we need to know $\hat{p}$ and $\hat{q}$. Unfortunately, these values are unknown, since the sample has not yet been taken. At this point, we can use either of two methods to solve for n.

Method 1.   If we have no knowledge even of the approximate values of $\hat{p}$ and $\hat{q}$, we let $\hat{p} = \hat{q} = .5$. We choose $\hat{p} = .5$ (and thus, $\hat{q} = .5$) because the product $\hat{p}\hat{q}$ equals its maximum value for this value of $\hat{p}$. (Figure 8.5 illustrates this point.) This in turn results in a conservative value of n, and as a result the confidence interval will be no wider than the interval $\hat{p} \pm .03$. If, when the sample is drawn, $\hat{p}$ does not equal .5, the interval estimate will be better (that is, narrower) than planned. Thus,

$$n = \left[\frac{1.96 \sqrt{(.5)(.5)}}{.03} \right]^2 = (32.67)^2 = 1,068$$

If it turns out that $\hat{p} = .5$, the interval estimate is .5 $\pm$ .03. If not, the interval estimate will be narrower. For instance, if it turns out that $\hat{p} = .2$, the estimate is .2 $\pm$ .024,

---

FIGURE 8.5   *GRAPHING $\hat{p}\hat{q}$ VERSUS $\hat{p}$*

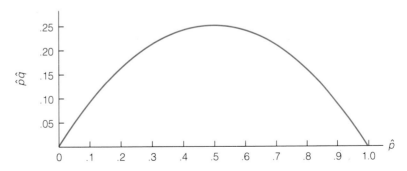

which is better than we had planned. Incidentally, this is the sample size used in opinion polls of the type frequently referred to in newspapers, magazines, and television. These polls usually estimate proportions to within 3%, with 95% confidence. (The media often state the confidence level as "19 times out of 20.")

Method 2. If we have some idea about the value of $\hat{p}$, we can use that quantity to determine n. For example, if we believe that $\hat{p}$ will turn out to be approximately .2, we can solve for n as follows:

$$n = \left[\frac{1.96 \sqrt{(.2)(.8)}}{.03} \right]^2 = (26.13)^2 = 683$$

Notice that this produces a smaller value of n (thus reducing sampling costs) than does method 1. If $\hat{p}$ actually lies between .2 and .8, however, the estimate will not be as good as we wanted, because the interval will be wider than desired.

EXERCISES

LEARNING THE TECHNIQUES

8.20 Given that $\hat{p} = .84$ and $n = 600$, estimate p with 90% confidence.

8.21 In a random sample of 250, we found 75 successes. Estimate the population proportion of successes, with 99% confidence.

8.22 Estimate p with 95% confidence, given

$x = 27$

$n = 110$

8.23 Estimate p with 95% confidence, given that a random sample of 100 produced $\hat{p} = .2$.

8.24 Repeat Exercise 8.23, with $n = 400$.

8.25 Repeat Exercise 8.23, with $n = 10,000$.

8.26 Repeat Exercise 8.23, with $\hat{p} = .5$.

8.27 How large a sample should be taken in order to estimate p to within .01 with 95% confidence? Assume that you have no information about the value of p.

8.28 How large a sample should be taken in order to estimate p to within .01 with 95% confidence if p is believed to be approximately .10?

8.29 Repeat Exercise 8.28, with p believed to be approximately 90%.

APPLYING THE TECHNIQUES

Self-Correcting Exercise (See Appendix 8.A for the solution.)

POM **8.30** In a random sample of 1,000 picture tubes produced in a large plant, 80 were defective. Estimate with 95% confidence the true proportion of defective picture tubes produced at this plant.

PG **8.31** In a survey of 250 voters prior to an election, 40% indicated that they would vote for the incumbent candidate. Estimate with 90% confidence the population proportion of voters who support the incumbent.

MKT **8.32** Women selected in a random sample were asked what factor was the most important to them in deciding where to shop. The results, which appeared in the Wall Street Journal (5 February 1987) are reproduced in the accompanying table. If the sample size was 1,200, estimate with 95%

Factor	Percentage
Price and value	44%
Quality and selection of merchandise	34
Service	11
Shopping environment	11

Source: Newspaper Advertising Bureau Inc.

confidence the proportion of women who identified price and value as the most important factor.

EDUC **8.33** In a survey, 1,039 adults were asked "How much respect and confidence do you have in the public school system?" The results, which were reported in the *Toronto Star* (26 September 1988), are shown in the accompanying table. Estimate with 90% confidence the proportion of all adults who answered "A great deal" or "Quite a lot."

Responses	Percentage
A great deal	12%
Quite a lot	30
Some	35
Very little	13
No opinion	10

SECTION 8.5   ## SUMMARY

We have just completed a discussion of the techniques of statistical inference when the problem objective is to describe a single population and when the data scale is nominal. The parameter tested and estimated was the population proportion p. The estimate and tests are based on the best estimator of p, which is the **sample proportion** $\hat{p}$. Because $\hat{p}$ is approximately normally distributed, the formulas used to estimate and test p both involve the standard normal random variable z. These techniques are summarized in Table 8.1.

This chapter also presented a method for determining the sample size required to estimate p.

TABLE 8.1   *SUMMARY OF INFERENCE ABOUT p*

Parameter	Estimator	Test Statistic	Required Condition
p	$\hat{p} \pm z_{\alpha/2}\sqrt{\dfrac{\hat{p}\hat{q}}{n}}$	$z = \dfrac{\hat{p} - p}{\sqrt{\dfrac{pq}{n}}}$	$n\hat{p}$ and $n\hat{q} \geq 5$ (for estimation) np and $nq \geq 5$ for test statistic)

SUPPLEMENTARY EXERCISES

8.34 In a poll of 1,500 Americans, 30% stated that in 10 years' time the world will be a better place to live in than it is today (*Toronto Star,* 4 April 1985). Estimate with 99% confidence the proportion of all Americans who believe that the world will be a better place to live in 10 years from now than it is today.

PG **8.35** The television networks often compete on the evening of the day of an election to be the first to identify correctly the winner of the election. One of the techniques often used is the random sampling of voters as they exit the polling booth. Suppose that, in a two-candidate race, 55% of a random sample of 500 voters indicate that they voted Republican.

a. Can we conclude at the 5% level of significance that the Republican candidate will win?

b. What is the *p*-value of this test?

c. Assuming that networks wish to avoid making a mistake and later having to withdraw their conclusion, what value of α seems appropriate?

PG **8.36** As a result of a recent Federal Trade Commission ruling, doctors are allowed to advertise. In a survey designed to examine this issue, 91 doctors were asked whether or not they believed that doctors should be allowed to advertise.* A total of 23 physicians supported advertising by doctors. Estimate with 90% confidence the proportion of all doctors who support advertising.

PG **8.37** For Exercise 8.35, with $n = 500$ and $\alpha = .05$, what is the probability of concluding that not enough evidence exists to determine that the Republican has won when in actual fact the proportion of all voters who voted for that candidate is 60%?

MKT **8.38** Officials of Via Rail (the Canadian version of Amtrak) claim that less than 10% of all its trains are late. If a random sample of 70 trains shows that only 60 of them are on schedule, can we conclude that the claim is false? (Use $\alpha = .10$.)

MKT **8.39** The management of a firm is contemplating modifying one of its products. Before making a decision, management representatives wish to conduct a market survey that will enable them to estimate the proportion of potential customers who would buy the new product. They wish to estimate this proportion to within 3%, with 99% confidence. How large a sample should be drawn if the following circumstances are true?

a. Management has no idea about the value of *p*.

b. It is known that the proportion will be less than 20%.

c. It is known that the proportion will be somewhere between 40 and 70%.

POM **8.40** A manufacturer of computer chips claims that more than 90% of his product conforms to specifications. In a random sample of 1,000 chips drawn from a large production run, 75 were defective. Do the data provide sufficient evidence at the 1% level of significance to enable us to conclude that the manufacturer's claim is true? What is the *p*-value of the test?

GEN **8.41** Suppose that we want to test the following hypotheses:

$H_0: p = .4$

$H_A: p \neq .4$

$n = 500, \alpha = .01$

Find β if the true value of *p* is .45.

MKT **8.42** In a large city, 22% of the households had the afternoon newspaper delivered to their doors. After the newspaper conducted an aggressive marketing campaign to increase that figure, a random sample of 200 households was taken. Of the sample group, 61 households now have the paper delivered.

a. Can we conclude at the 5% significance level that the campaign was a success?

b. Find the *p*-value of the test.

PG **8.43** In the 1988 presidential election campaign, George Bush and Michael Dukakis participated in a television debate on September 25, 1988. In an ABC-TV poll, 639 registered voters were surveyed and asked who won the debate. The results, as reported in the *Toronto Star* (26 September 1988), were as follows:

George Bush	36%
Michael Dukakis	44%
Tie	20%

a. Estimate with 95% confidence the proportion of all registered voters who thought that George Bush won.

b. Estimate with 95% confidence the proportion of all registered voters who thought that Michael Dukakis won.

---

* G. Riecker and G. Yavas, "Do Medical Professionals Favor Advertising?" *Developments in Marketing Science* 7 (1984): 239–43.

PG **8.44** In response to the same debate discussed in Exercise 8.43, people interviewed in a *Newsweek* poll of 337 registered voters had answered as follows: 42% said Michael Dukakis won, and 41% said George Bush won. Do these results contradict the results of the ABC-TV poll?

PG **8.45** Last year in an election, a politician received 58% of the ballots cast. Several months later, a survey of 700 people revealed that 54% now supported her. Is this sufficient evidence to conclude that her popularity has decreased? (Let $\alpha = .05$.) What is the *p*-value of this test?

MKT **8.46** A rock promoter is in the process of deciding whether or not to book a new band for a rock concert. He knows that this band appeals almost exclusively to teenagers. According to the latest census, there are 400,000 teenagers in the area. The promoter decides to do a survey to try to estimate the proportion of teenagers who will attend the concert. How large a sample should he take in order to estimate the proportion to within .02 with 99% confidence?

MKT **8.47** In Exercise 8.46 suppose that the promoter decides to draw a sample of size 600 (because of financial considerations). Of these 600, 75 respondents indicate that they would attend the concert.

a. Estimate the population proportion, with 99% confidence.

b. The promoter needs to sell at least 40,000 tickets to break even. At the 5% significance level, do the data provide sufficient evidence to justify concluding that the concert will at least break even?

c. What is the *p*-value of the test in part *b*?

TOUR **8.48** In an examination of consumer loyalty in the travel business, 24 out of a total of 72 first-time visitors to a tourist attraction stated that they would not return.* Estimate with 95% confidence the proportion of all first-time visitors who would not return to the same destination.

GEN **8.49** (Extremely difficult exercise.) Suppose that we want to test the following hypotheses:

$H_0: p = .7$

$H_A: p > .7$

$\alpha = .05$

Find the value of *n* such that $\beta = .05$ when $p = .75$.

---

* P. K. Tat and J. R. Thompson, "An Exploratory Study of Brand Loyalty in Setting Travel Destinations," *Developments in Marketing Science* 6 (1983): 562–65.

■■■■■■■■ **CASE 8.1   MIAMI HERALD SURVEY**

PG Political surveys play such an important role in election campaigns that it's hard to imagine an election devoid of extensive polling. Besides selecting people to fill various political offices, voters also decide issues such as gun control and tax limitation. The November 4, 1986 ballot in the state of Florida contained questions about proposed casinos and lotteries, as well as choices for senator and governor. A survey of 959 registered voters, reported by the *Miami Herald* (30 October 1986), produced the following results:

Casinos

Q: If the election were held today, would you vote for or against the amendment to allow casino gambling in counties that want it?

For	35%
Against	60%
Don't Know	5%

U.S. Senate Race

Q: Suppose the election for U.S. Senate were held today. Would you vote for Paula Hawkins, the Republican, or Bob Graham, the Democrat?

Graham	47%
Hawkins	41%
Undecided	7%
Refused	5%

Governor's Race

Q: Suppose the election for governor were held today. Would you vote for Bob Martinez, the Republican, or Steve Pajcic, the Democrat?

Martinez	43%
Pajcic	40%
Undecided	14%
Refused	3%

Lottery

Q: If the election were held today, would you vote for or against a state-run lottery to help public education?

For	58%
Against	34%
Don't Know	8%

What conclusions can you draw from these data?

CASE 8.2* FACULTY ATTITUDES ABOUT STUDENT EVALUATIONS

EDUC | Student evaluations of professors and instructors in colleges and universities are a common practice. These evaluations provide feedback so that professors can improve their classroom performance; they are also used as factors in considering salary increases, promotions, and tenure. Most students favor the evaluations because they hold potential for improving the overall quality of university and college instruction. Faculty members do not universally support the evaluations, however, for a variety of reasons.

In a study designed to determine the attitudes of faculty members about student evaluations, 250 professors at a large university were randomly selected and asked whether or not they agreed with a number of statements concerning evaluations. One of the purposes of the research was to test the idea that the majority of faculty members would agree with each of the following views:

1. Student evaluations serve a useful purpose.

2. High evaluations are related to high grades.

* Adapted from M. A. Stutts, "Faculty Perceptions of Student Evaluations," *Developments in Marketing Science* 8 (1985): 157–62.

3. High evaluations are related to the "entertaining personality."

4. Too much emphasis is placed on evaluations by superiors.

5. Evaluations from freshmen and sophomores are lower than those from juniors and seniors.

6. Evaluations from large classes are lower than those from small classes.

7. Evaluations from quantitatively oriented courses are lower than those from qualitatively oriented courses.

8. Evaluations from required courses are lower than those from elective courses.

The number of respondents who agreed with each of the eight statements is shown in the accompanying table. Is there sufficient statistical evidence to support the idea that the eight views are shared by a majority of faculty members?

Statement	Respondents Agreeing
1	173
2	136
3	195
4	137
5	125
6	164
7	114
8	168

SOLUTIONS TO SELF-CORRECTING EXERCISES

8.12 $H_0: p = .90$
$H_A: p > .90$

Rejection region: $z > 2.33$

Test statistic: $z = \dfrac{\hat{p} - p}{\sqrt{pq/n}} = \dfrac{.95 - .90}{\sqrt{(.90)(.10)/200}} = 2.36$

Conclusion: Reject H_0.

Yes, there is enough evidence to support the claim that more than 90% of the tires will last at least 50,000 miles.

8.30 $\hat{p} \pm z_{\alpha/2}\sqrt{\hat{p}\hat{q}/n}$

$= .08 \pm 1.96\sqrt{(.08)(.92)/1,000} = .08 \pm .017$

The proportion of defective picture tubes is estimated to be between 6.3% and 9.7%.

INFERENCE ABOUT THE COMPARISON OF TWO POPULATIONS: INTERVAL SCALE

INTRODUCTION

The mechanism of the hypothesis testing and estimation techniques should be quite routine by this point; and if you now understand how the techniques work, you should have no difficulty understanding the remaining chapters devoted to statistical inference. In this chapter, we present statistical methods that deal with the problem objective of comparing two populations when the data scale is interval. As you know, calculations of parameters and statistics such as the mean and the variance are valid when the scale is interval. As a result, we can compare the means and the variances of the two populations. Four examples of such situations are described in the following cases.

Case 1. Operations managers of production facilities are always looking for ways of improving productivity in their plants. This can be accomplished by rearranging sequences of operations, acquiring new technology, or improving the training of workers. When one or more such changes are made, their effect on the operation of the entire plant is of interest. The manager can measure the effect by comparing productivity after the innovation with productivity before the innovation. In this case, the data scale is interval (we often measure productivity in terms of the number of units produced), and the problem objective is to compare two populations (the productivity before and after the change). The descriptive measurement to be used is the mean, and hence the parameter of interest is $\mu_1 - \mu_2$.

Case 2. Firms that use subcomponents manufactured by other companies in producing their own finished products are often concerned about the quality, reliability, and price of the subcomponents. If two competing suppliers of a component are available, the firm's manager may wish to compare the reliability of the two products. For example, a car manufacturer currently equips its product with a certain brand of tire. If a similarly priced brand of tire becomes available, the decision about which brand to use should be based on which tire, on average, lasts longer. In this situation, the data scale is interval (tire life is usually measured by the number of miles until wear-out), and the problem objective is to compare the two populations of tires. The parameter to be estimated or tested is $\mu_1 - \mu_2$.

Case 3. Portfolio managers are concerned with the returns that are realized on their clients' investment portfolios and with the risks that are undertaken to achieve those returns. Since the returns on investment portfolios are uncertain, portfolio returns can be treated as random variables. As was previously mentioned, the variance of returns is often used as a measure of the riskiness of a portfolio. In comparing the performance of two portfolios, a manager may compare their average annual returns, in which case the parameter is $\mu_1 - \mu_2$. To compare their riskiness as measured by the variance of the returns, the manager might estimate the parameter σ_1^2/σ_2^2 (for statistical purposes, dealing with the **ratio** of the two variances instead of with the differences, because of the nature of the sampling distribution).

Case 4. Machines that perform certain operations must function consistently. Too often, those that don't function consistently produce products unsatisfactorily. For example, a bottling plant has machines that automatically fill bottles and/or cans with soda pop. In comparing two different machines, the manager will examine them to ensure that, on average, they both produce the required fill. Equally important, however, is the variability of the fills: too little fill, and the customer (not to mention several government agencies) will be unhappy; too much fill, and soda pop ends up on the bottling-plant floor. In order to compare the quality of the two machines, the manager needs to know their relative variances. In such a case, the parameter is σ_1^2/σ_2^2.

SECTION 9.2

INFERENCE ABOUT $\mu_1 - \mu_2$ WHEN σ_1^2 AND σ_2^2 ARE KNOWN

In Chapter 6, we showed that $\bar{x}$ is the best estimator of μ and that $\bar{x}$ is approximately normally distributed. By a similar analysis, we can show that $\bar{x}_1 - \bar{x}_2$ is the best estimator of $\mu_1 - \mu_2$, where $\bar{x}_1$ is the mean of a sample of size n_1 from a large population whose mean and variance are μ_1 and σ_1^2, respectively, and where $\bar{x}_2$ is the mean of a sample of size n_2 from another large population with mean and variance μ_2 and σ_2^2, respectively. Figure 9.1 depicts the sampling process.

The sampling distribution of $\bar{x}_1 - \bar{x}_2$ is derived from an extension of the Central Limit Theorem and from the basic rules of expectation and variance. The Central Limit Theorem (see Chapter 6) states that $\bar{x}$ is normally distributed when x is normally distributed or when n is sufficiently large. It can be shown that $\bar{x}_1 - \bar{x}_2$,

FIGURE 9.1   INDEPENDENT SAMPLES FROM TWO POPULATIONS

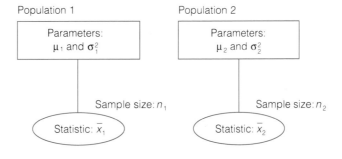

FIGURE 9.2   *SAMPLING DISTRIBUTION OF $\bar{x}_1 - \bar{x}_2$*

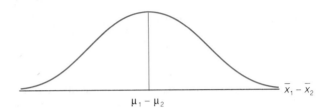

$\mu_1 - \mu_2$

$\bar{x}_1 - \bar{x}_2$

too, is normally distributed (or approximately normally distributed) when x_1 and x_2 are normal or when n_1 and n_2 are large enough.* By the rules of expectation and variance, we can establish that

$$E(\bar{x}_1 - \bar{x}_2) = \mu_1 - \mu_2$$

and

$$\text{Var}(\bar{x}_1 - \bar{x}_2) = \frac{\sigma_1^2}{n_1} + \frac{\sigma_2^2}{n_2}$$

or equivalently

$$\sigma_{\bar{x}_1 - \bar{x}_2} = \sqrt{\frac{\sigma_1^2}{n_1} + \frac{\sigma_2^2}{n_2}}$$

The sampling distribution of $\bar{x}_1 - \bar{x}_2$ is depicted in Figure 9.2.

We assume that the samples are independent. This means that the selection of sample members drawn from one population is not affected by the selection of sample members drawn from the other population. The issue of dependent samples will be discussed in greater detail in Section 9.4. Until then, all the examples and exercises will deal with independent samples. We also assume that the two population variances are known—although this assumption is quite unrealistic. The more realistic case is dealt with in Section 9.3, where we assume that σ_1^2 and σ_2^2 are unknown.

TESTING $\mu_1 - \mu_2$

The test statistic used in testing $\mu_1 - \mu_2$ is the standardized value of $\bar{x}_1 - \bar{x}_2$.

---

* As we pointed out in Chapter 6, the sample size that is considered "large enough" depends on the extent of nonnormality of x_1 and x_2.

Test Statistic for $\mu_1 - \mu_2$ When σ_1^2 and σ_2^2 Are Known

$$z = \frac{(\bar{x}_1 - \bar{x}_2) - (\mu_1 - \mu_2)}{\sqrt{\dfrac{\sigma_1^2}{n_1} + \dfrac{\sigma_2^2}{n_2}}}$$

This test statistic is standard normally distributed (on the condition that x_1 and x_2 are normally distributed or that n_1 and n_2 are sufficiently large). The process of determining the null and alternative hypotheses and the rejection region is identical to the process described in the last two chapters.

EXAMPLE 9.1

The selection of a new store location depends on many factors, one of which is the level of household income in areas around the proposed site. Suppose that a large department-store chain is trying to decide whether to build a new store in Kitchener or in the nearby city of Waterloo. Building costs are lower in Waterloo, and the company decides it will build there unless the average household income is higher in Kitchener than in Waterloo. In a survey of 100 residences in each of the cities, the mean annual household income was $29,980 in Kitchener and $28,650 in Waterloo. From other sources, it is known that the population standard deviations of annual household incomes are $4,740 in Kitchener and $5,365 in Waterloo. At the 5% significance level, can it be concluded that the mean household income in Kitchener exceeds that of Waterloo? Assume that incomes are normally distributed.

Solution. The data scale is interval (annual household incomes), and the problem objective is to compare two populations. Hence, the parameter of interest is $\mu_1 - \mu_2$. The question requires that we determine if there is enough evidence to indicate that the mean income in Kitchener (labeled μ_1) exceeds the mean income in Waterloo (μ_2). Thus, the alternative hypothesis is $H_A: (\mu_1 - \mu_2) > 0$.

$$H_0: (\mu_1 - \mu_2) = 0$$
$$H_A: (\mu_1 - \mu_2) > 0$$

Test statistic:

$$z = \frac{(\bar{x}_1 - \bar{x}_2) - (\mu_1 - \mu_2)}{\sqrt{\dfrac{\sigma_1^2}{n_1} + \dfrac{\sigma_2^2}{n_2}}}$$

Rejection region:

$$z > z_\alpha$$
$$> z_{.05}$$
$$> 1.645$$

FIGURE 9.3   *REJECTION REGION FOR EXAMPLE 9.1*

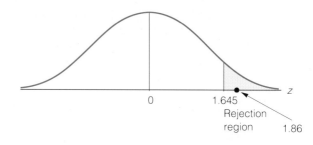

Value of the test statistic:

$$z = \frac{(\bar{x}_1 - \bar{x}_2) - (\mu_1 - \mu_2)}{\sqrt{\dfrac{\sigma_1^2}{n_1} + \dfrac{\sigma_2^2}{n_2}}} = \frac{(29,980 - 28,650) - 0}{\sqrt{\dfrac{4,740^2}{100} + \dfrac{5,365^2}{100}}} = 1.86$$

Conclusion: Reject H_0.

There is enough evidence to allow us to conclude that the mean annual household income in Kitchener exceeds that in Waterloo. And based on this statistical conclusion, the new store should be built in Kitchener. This test is depicted in Figure 9.3.

ESTIMATING $\mu_1 - \mu_2$

From the sampling distribution of $\bar{x}_1 - \bar{x}_2$, we develop the interval estimate of $\mu_1 - \mu_2$.

> **Confidence Interval Estimator of $\mu_1 - \mu_2$ When σ_1^2 and σ_2^2 Are Known**
>
> $$(\bar{x}_1 - \bar{x}_2) \pm z_{\alpha/2} \sqrt{\frac{\sigma_1^2}{n_1} + \frac{\sigma_2^2}{n_2}}$$

Keep in mind that this estimator is valid as long as the populations are normal or the sample sizes are large enough.

EXAMPLE 9.2

Periodically, coupons that can be used to purchase products at discount prices appear in newspapers. A supermarket chain has two different types of coupon for its own brand of bread. Coupon 1 offers 2 loaves for the price of 1, and coupon 2 offers a

25¢ discount on the purchase of each loaf. In order to determine the relative selling power of the two plans, the supermarket chain performs the following experiment. The coupons appear in four consecutive weeks (coupon 1 in weeks 1 and 2, and coupon 2 in weeks 3 and 4) in the local newspaper. The company wants to estimate the average daily sales under each coupon plan. The average number of loaves sold per day during the first 14 days (supermarkets are open 7 days per week) was 151. The average number per day during the second 14 days was 142. Assuming that the population standard deviation was 15 loaves per week, estimate with 99% confidence the difference in mean daily sales under the two coupon plans. The number of loaves sold per day is normally distributed.

Solution.   The data scale is interval (number of loaves per day), and the problem objective is to compare sales under the two coupon plans. The parameter to be estimated is $\mu_1 - \mu_2$. Because σ_1 and σ_2 are known (they are both equal to 15) and because x_1 and x_2 are normally distributed, the interval estimator is

$$(\bar{x}_1 - \bar{x}_2) \pm z_{\alpha/2} \sqrt{\frac{\sigma_1^2}{n_1} + \frac{\sigma_2^2}{n_2}}$$

With $1 - \alpha = .99$, we know that $z_{\alpha/2} = z_{.005} = 2.58$. The 99% confidence interval estimate of $\mu_1 - \mu_2$ is

$$(\bar{x}_1 - \bar{x}_2) \pm z_{\alpha/2} \sqrt{\frac{\sigma_1^2}{n_1} + \frac{\sigma_2^2}{n_2}} = (151 - 142) \pm 2.58 \sqrt{\frac{15^2}{14} + \frac{15^2}{14}} = 9 \pm 14.6$$

which simplifies to

$$(-5.6, 23.6)$$

The 99% confidence interval estimate of the difference between average daily sales is the interval -5.6 to 23.6 loaves.

SELECTING THE SAMPLE SIZES TO ESTIMATE $\mu_1 - \mu_2$

The method used to determine the sample sizes required to estimate $\mu_1 - \mu_2$ is a simple extension of the method used to determine the sample size to estimate μ (Chapter 7). Since the confidence interval estimator is

$$(\bar{x}_1 - \bar{x}_2) \pm z_{\alpha/2} \sqrt{\frac{\sigma_1^2}{n_1} + \frac{\sigma_2^2}{n_2}}$$

the error bound is set equal to

$$B = z_{\alpha/2} \sqrt{\frac{\sigma_1^2}{n_1} + \frac{\sigma_2^2}{n_2}}$$

In order to solve for n_1 and n_2, we specify the confidence level $1 - \alpha$, and we approximate the values of σ_1^2 and σ_2^2. Finally, we let $n_1 = n_2$, and solve the equation below.

Sample Sizes Necessary to Estimate $\mu_1 - \mu_2$

$$n_1 = n_2 = \left[\frac{z_{\alpha/2}\sqrt{\sigma_1^2 + \sigma_2^2}}{B} \right]^2$$

EXAMPLE 9.3

An advertising consultant for a major brewer wants to compare the annual beer consumption of men and women. She decides to estimate the difference in mean annual consumption to within 10 liters, with 99% confidence. How large should the sample sizes be, if we assume that the range of consumption is 400 liters for males and 200 liters for females?

Solution.   The error bound is 10 and the confidence level is .99. Hence, $B = 10$ and $z_{\alpha/2} = 2.58$. We approximate σ_1 and σ_2 by using the formulas

$$\sigma_1 \cong \frac{\text{Range}}{4} = \frac{400}{4} = 100 \qquad \text{(for males)}$$

and

$$\sigma_2 \cong \frac{\text{Range}}{4} = \frac{200}{4} = 50 \qquad \text{(for females)}$$

Thus,

$$n_1 = n_2 = \left[\frac{2.58\sqrt{100^2 + 50^2}}{10} \right]^2 = 833$$

In order to estimate $\mu_1 - \mu_2$ to within 10 liters with 99% confidence, we should take samples of 833 men and 833 women.

EXERCISES

LEARNING THE TECHNIQUES

9.1   You are given the following information:

$n_1 = 50$ \qquad $n_2 = 100$

$\bar{x}_1 = 52.3$ \qquad $\bar{x}_2 = 49.0$

$\sigma_1 = 6.1$ \qquad $\sigma_2 = 7.9$

a. Test

$H_0: (\mu_1 - \mu_2) = 0$

$H_A: (\mu_1 - \mu_2) \neq 0$

$\alpha = .05$

b. What is the *p*-value of this test?

c. Estimate $\mu_1 - \mu_2$, with 99% confidence.

9.2   Assume that, from samples drawn from two

normal populations, we have:

$n_1 = 15$ $\qquad n_2 = 10$

$\bar{x}_1 = 150$ $\qquad \bar{x}_2 = 135$

$\sigma_1 = 10$ $\qquad \sigma_2 = 15$

a. Is there sufficient evidence to allow us to conclude that μ_1 is greater than μ_2? (Use $\alpha = .05$.)

b. What is the p-value of this test?

c. Estimate $\mu_1 - \mu_2$, with 98% confidence.

9.3 Test the following hypotheses:

$H_0: (\mu_1 - \mu_2) = 0$

$H_A: (\mu_1 - \mu_2) > 0$

given

$n_1 = 40$ $\qquad n_2 = 70$

$\bar{x}_1 = 27.3$ $\qquad \bar{x}_2 = 24.6$

$\sigma_1 = 7.2$ $\qquad \sigma_2 = 6.9$

$\alpha = .05$

9.4 Find the p-value for the test in Exercise 9.3.

9.5 For Exercise 9.3, estimate $\mu_1 - \mu_2$ with 95% confidence.

9.6 Samples of 50 observations from each of two normal populations were drawn. The sample means were

$\bar{x}_1 = 28.3$ $\qquad \bar{x}_2 = 31.5$

If $\sigma_1 = 6.4$ and $\sigma_2 = 5.8$, can we conclude with $\alpha = .01$ that μ_1 is less than μ_2?

9.7 What is the p-value of the test in Exercise 9.6?

9.8 For Exercise 9.6, estimate the difference between population means, with 95% confidence.

9.9 What size samples should be drawn from two normal populations in order to estimate $\mu_1 - \mu_2$ to within 5 with 99% confidence. Assume that $\sigma_1 = 40$ and $\sigma_2 = 50$.

9.10 Given that $\sigma_1 = \sigma_2 = 100$, find the values of n_1 and n_2 necessary to estimate $\mu_1 - \mu_2$ to within 2 with 90% confidence.

9.11 Repeat Exercise 9.10, changing the confidence level to 99%.

APPLYING THE TECHNIQUES

Self-Correcting Exercise (See Appendix 9.C for the solution.)

GEN **9.12** A sporting-goods manufacturer has just produced a new type of baseball, which he claims will have the same playing characteristics as the standard type but can be produced much more cheaply. In a test, 20 baseballs of the currently used type and 15 of the new type are placed in an automatic ball-hitting machine and the distance the machine hits each is recorded. The average distance for the baseball now used is 352 feet, while the average for the new ball is 375 feet. Assuming that $\sigma_1 = 20$ feet and $\sigma_2 = 25$ feet, test at the 5% level of significance to determine if there is sufficient evidence to show that the average distances of the two types of baseball differ. What is the p-value of the test? (You may assume that the distances are normally distributed.)

FIN **9.13** In order to compare the wages paid to workers in two large industries, random samples of 50 hourly wage earners are drawn from each. The averages are $\bar{x}_1 = \$7.50$ and $\bar{x}_2 = \$7.90$. Assuming that $\sigma_1 = 2.00$ and $\sigma_2 = 1.80$, estimate with 95% confidence the difference in average wages between the two industries.

FIN **9.14** Does your answer in Exercise 9.13 provide sufficient evidence for us to conclude that the average hourly wage in industry 2 is greater than the average in industry 1? (Use $\alpha = .01$.)

MNG **9.15** The management of a chain of department stores wants to know if there is a difference in the average annual income of potential customers at two possible sites for a new store. In one location, a random sample of 100 households had a mean annual income of \$27,000. In the other location, the mean annual income of 75 households was \$29,000. Assuming that $\sigma_1 = \sigma_2 = 5,000$, estimate with 99% confidence the difference between average annual incomes in the two locations.

MNG **9.16** For Exercise 9.15, how large should the sample sizes be in order to estimate the difference between average incomes in the two areas to within \$1,000 with 99% confidence?

SCI **9.17** One of the least-known environmental threats to our health is lead, which appears in both soil and air after originating in leaded gasoline. Its effect on small children is especially worrisome: lead seems to have an adverse impact on the intelligence of children who are regularly exposed to it. To examine this phenomenon, researchers randomly selected 100 nine-year-old children from an inner-city neighborhood where the lead con- tent in the air is more than three times the danger limit. Their IQs were measured, and the mean was $\bar{x}_1 = 97.3$. The researchers also selected 100 nine-year-old children from another inner-city neighborhood where the lead content is low. Their mean IQ was $\bar{x}_2 = 102.3$. If we assume that $\sigma_1 = \sigma_2 = 15$, can we conclude at the 5% significance level that high lead content in the atmosphere has a harmful effect on children's IQ level?

SECTION 9.3   # INFERENCE ABOUT $\mu_1 - \mu_2$ WHEN σ_1^2 AND σ_2^2 ARE UNKNOWN

In the previous section, our inferences about $\mu_1 - \mu_2$ assumed that the population variances σ_1^2 and σ_2^2 were known. Unfortunately, it is quite unusual for μ_1 and μ_2 to be unknown while σ_1^2 and σ_2^2 are known. In this section, we address the more realistic problem of making inferences about $\mu_1 - \mu_2$ when σ_1^2 and σ_2^2 are unknown.

The proper way to handle this problem depends on several factors, one of which is the size of the samples. If the sample sizes are large enough (that is, if $n_1 > 30$ and $n_2 > 30$), we can simply substitute the sample variances for the un- known population variances in the formula for the test statistic given in Section 9.2.

Test Statistic for $\mu_1 - \mu_2$ When σ_1^2 and σ_2^2 Are Unknown and $n_1 > 30$ and $n_2 > 30$

$$z = \frac{(\bar{x}_1 - \bar{x}_2) - (\mu_1 - \mu_2)}{\sqrt{\dfrac{s_1^2}{n_1} + \dfrac{s_2^2}{n_2}}}$$

The rationale for this formula is based on our experience in Chapter 7, where, when $n > 30$, the test statistic

$$t = \frac{\bar{x} - \mu}{s/\sqrt{n}}$$

was approximately normally distributed. Based on this experience, it would seem that, if the sample size is small, the test statistic should be

$$t = \frac{(\bar{x}_1 - \bar{x}_2) - (\mu_1 - \mu_2)}{\sqrt{\dfrac{s_1^2}{n_1} + \dfrac{s_2^2}{n_2}}}$$

Unfortunately, the actual distribution of this test statistic is not clear.* As a result, when σ_1^2 and σ_2^2 are unknown and either of the sample sizes is too small (that is, when $n_1 \leq 30$ or $n_2 \leq 30$), the test statistic is as follows.

Test Statistic for $\mu_1 - \mu_2$ When σ_1^2 and σ_2^2 Are Unknown and $n_1 \leq 30$ or $n_2 \leq 30$

$$t = \frac{(\bar{x}_1 - \bar{x}_2) - (\mu_1 - \mu_2)}{\sqrt{s_p^2 \left(\dfrac{1}{n_1} + \dfrac{1}{n_2}\right)}}$$

where

$$s_p^2 = \frac{(n_1 - 1)s_1^2 + (n_2 - 1)s_2^2}{n_1 + n_2 - 2}$$

The test statistic is Student t distributed, with $n_1 + n_2 - 2$ degrees of freedom, provided that the following three conditions are satisfied:

1. The two population random variables (x_1 and x_2) are normally distributed.
2. The two population variances are equal; that is, $\sigma_1^2 = \sigma_2^2$.
3. The two samples are independent.

The quantity s_p^2 is called the *pooled variance estimate* of the common variance. It is the weighted average of the two sample variances. Condition 2 makes this calculation feasible, since, if $\sigma_1^2 = \sigma_2^2$ (where both values are unknown), we need only one estimate of the common value of σ_1^2 and σ_2^2. It makes sense for us to use the pooled variance estimate because, in combining both samples, we produce a better estimate. Later in this chapter we will present a statistical technique to test if this required condition is satisfied.

If condition 1 is not valid, the effect on the distribution of the test statistic may not be drastic. If the populations are only slightly nonnormal, the distribution may still be approximately Student t if the sample sizes are somewhat larger. Thus, larger values of n_1 and n_2 can offset the effects of nonnormality.

---

* Some statisticians and computer application packages treat this statistic as an approximate Student t distributed random variable with degrees of freedom equal to

$$\frac{(s_1^2/n_1 + s_2^2/n_2)^2}{\dfrac{(s_1^2/n_1)^2}{n_1 - 1} + \dfrac{(s_2^2/n_2)^2}{n_2 - 1}}$$

We take the conservative view that, since the distribution of this test statistic is uncertain, we should use it only when the sample sizes are sufficiently large. Since (in that case) the degrees of freedom will be large enough to make the Student t distribution approximately equal to the standard normal, we will label this statistic z and use it to test $\mu_1 - \mu_2$ only when $n_1 > 30$ and $n_2 > 30$ (and σ_1^2 and σ_2^2 are unknown).

Deviations from condition 3 require the use of another test statistic, which is discussed in Section 9.4.

The confidence interval estimation of $\mu_1 - \mu_2$ is produced in the same way here as in Chapters 7 and 8. The formulas of the test statistic and the confidence interval estimators of $\mu_1 - \mu_2$ are summarized next.

Inference About $\mu_1 - \mu_2$

1. If σ_1^2 and σ_2^2 are known:

   Test statistic:
   $$z = \frac{(\bar{x}_1 - \bar{x}_2) - (\mu_1 - \mu_2)}{\sqrt{\dfrac{\sigma_1^2}{n_1} + \dfrac{\sigma_2^2}{n_2}}}$$

   Estimator:
   $$(\bar{x}_1 - \bar{x}_2) \pm z_{\alpha/2} \sqrt{\frac{\sigma_1^2}{n_1} + \frac{\sigma_2^2}{n_2}}$$

   Required conditions:

   x_1 and x_2 are normally distributed, or n_1 and n_2 are sufficiently large. Samples are independent.

2. If σ_1^2 and σ_2^2 are unknown, and $n_1 > 30$ and $n_2 > 30$:

   Test statistic:
   $$z = \frac{(\bar{x}_1 - \bar{x}_2) - (\mu_1 - \mu_2)}{\sqrt{\dfrac{s_1^2}{n_1} + \dfrac{s_2^2}{n_2}}}$$

   Estimator:
   $$(\bar{x}_1 - \bar{x}_2) \pm z_{\alpha/2} \sqrt{\frac{s_1^2}{n_1} + \frac{s_2^2}{n_2}}$$

   Required conditions:

   x_1 and x_2 are normally distributed, or n_1 and n_2 are sufficiently large. Samples are independent.

3. If σ_1^2 and σ_2^2 are unknown, and $n_1 \leq 30$ or $n_2 \leq 30$:

   Test statistic:
   $$t = \frac{(\bar{x}_1 - \bar{x}_2) - (\mu_1 - \mu_2)}{\sqrt{s_p^2 \left(\dfrac{1}{n_1} + \dfrac{1}{n_2} \right)}}$$

Estimator:

$$(\bar{x}_1 - \bar{x}_2) \pm t_{\alpha/2} \sqrt{s_p^2 \left(\frac{1}{n_1} + \frac{1}{n_2} \right)}$$

Required conditions:

x_1 and x_2 are normally distributed.

$\sigma_1^2 = \sigma_2^2$.

Samples are independent.

EXAMPLE 9.4

The manager of a large production facility believes that worker productivity is a function of, among other things, the *design* of the job, which refers to the sequence of worker movements. Two designs are being considered for the production of a new product. In an experiment, six workers using design A had a mean assembly time of 7.60 minutes, with a standard deviation of 2.36 minutes, for this product. (The six observations were 8.2, 5.3, 6.5, 5.1, 9.7, and 10.8.) Eight workers using design B had a mean assembly time of 9.20 minutes, with a standard deviation of 1.35 minutes. (The eight observations were 9.5, 8.3, 7.5, 10.9, 11.3, 9.3, 8.8, and 8.0.) Can we conclude at the 5% significance level that the average assembly times differ for the two designs? Assume that the times are normally distributed.

Solution.   The data scale is interval (assembly times), and the problem objective is to compare two populations (assembly times for designs A and B). Since we wish to compare average assembly times, the parameter of interest is $\mu_1 - \mu_2$. We are asked to determine if there is sufficient evidence to justify concluding that $\mu_1 \neq \mu_2$, so the alternative hypothesis is $H_A: (\mu_1 - \mu_2) \neq 0$. Since σ_1^2 and σ_2^2 are not known (but since s_1^2 and s_2^2 are close to each other, we can assume that $\sigma_1^2 = \sigma_2^2$) and since the sample sizes are small, the test statistic is the t-statistic. The complete test follows:

$$H_0: (\mu_1 - \mu_2) = 0$$
$$H_A: (\mu_1 - \mu_2) \neq 0$$

Test statistic:

$$t = \frac{(\bar{x}_1 - \bar{x}_2) - (\mu_1 - \mu_2)}{\sqrt{s_p^2 \left(\frac{1}{n_1} + \frac{1}{n_2} \right)}}$$

Rejection region:

$$|t| > t_{\alpha/2, n_1 + n_2 - 2}$$
$$> t_{.025, 12}$$
$$> 2.179$$

FIGURE 9.4   *REJECTION REGION FOR EXAMPLE 9.4*

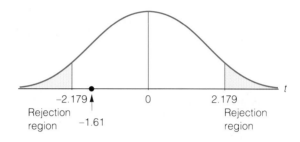

Value of the test statistic: Since

$$s_p^2 = \frac{5(2.36)^2 + 7(1.35)^2}{12} = 3.38$$

it follows that

$$t = \frac{(\bar{x}_1 - \bar{x}_2) - (\mu_1 - \mu_2)}{\sqrt{s_p^2\left(\dfrac{1}{n_1} + \dfrac{1}{n_2}\right)}} = \frac{(7.60 - 9.20) - 0}{\sqrt{3.38\left(\dfrac{1}{6} + \dfrac{1}{8}\right)}} = -1.61$$

Conclusion: Do not reject H_0.

There is not sufficient evidence to allow us to conclude that a difference in mean assembly times exists between designs A and B. The test is depicted in Figure 9.4.

COMPUTER OUTPUT FOR EXAMPLE 9.4*

Minitab

```
TWOSAMPLE T FOR C1 VS C2
       N    MEAN    ST DEV    SE MEAN
C1     6    7.60    2.36      0.96
C2     8    9.20    1.35      0.48
95 PCT CI FOR MU C1-MU C2: (-3.76, 0.56)
TTEST MU C1=MU C2 (VS NE): T=-1.61 P=0.13 DF=12.0
```

Minitab presents the 95% confidence interval estimate of $\mu_1 - \mu_2$, as well as the value of the test statistic (T = −1.61) and its p-value (P = 0.13).

---

* See Appendixes 9.A and 9.B for the Minitab and SAS commands needed to produce these printouts.

SAS

Variable: X

SAMPLE	N	Mean	Std Dev	Std Error
1	6	7.6000	2.3562	0.9619
2	8	9.2000	1.3469	0.4762

Variances	T	DF	Prob > |T|
Unequal	-1.4906	7.4	0.1774
Equal	-1.6134	12.0	0.1326

The output includes the sample sizes, means, standard deviations, and standard errors. There are also two test statistic values, two degrees of freedom, and two *p*-values. The first value of $t (t = -1.4906)$ is the calculated value of the test statistic

$$z = \frac{(\bar{x}_1 - \bar{x}_2) - (\mu_1 - \mu_2)}{\sqrt{\dfrac{s_1^2}{n_1} + \dfrac{s_2^2}{n_2}}}$$

which we use only when $n_1 > 30$ and $n_2 > 30$. The formula for the degrees of freedom (d.f. = 7.4) is shown in the footnote on page 343. The second value of $t (t = -1.6134)$ is the value of the test statistic

$$t = \frac{(\bar{x}_1 - \bar{x}_2) - (\mu_1 - \mu_2)}{\sqrt{s_p^2 \left(\dfrac{1}{n_1} + \dfrac{1}{n_2} \right)}}$$

which requires that $\sigma_1^2 = \sigma_2^2$. This explains the appearance of the words Unequal and Equal in the printout preceding the value of the *t*-statistics.

In this example, $n_1 \leq 30$ and $n_2 \leq 30$, and we assume that $\sigma_1^2 = \sigma_2^2$. Hence, we use the second test statistic, $t = -1.6134$, with d.f. = 12, as our test statistic. The *p*-value (Prob > |T| = .1326) is based on a two-tail test. If a one-tail test is being performed, Prob > |T| must be adjusted.

EXAMPLE 9.5

If in Example 9.4 we wish only to estimate $\mu_1 - \mu_2$ (with 99% confidence), rather than to test it, we use the confidence interval estimator

$$(\bar{x}_1 - \bar{x}_2) \pm t_{\alpha/2} \sqrt{s_p^2 \left(\frac{1}{n_1} + \frac{1}{n_2} \right)}$$

Since $t_{\alpha/2, n_1 + n_2 - 2} = t_{.005, 12} = 3.055$, the estimate is

$$(\bar{x}_1 - \bar{x}_2) \pm t_{\alpha/2} \sqrt{s_p^2 \left(\frac{1}{n_1} + \frac{1}{n_2} \right)} = (7.6 - 9.2) \pm 3.055 \sqrt{3.38 \left(\frac{1}{6} + \frac{1}{8} \right)}$$

$$= -1.6 \pm 3.03$$

or

$$(-4.63, 1.43)$$

Thus, the difference between the mean assembly times is estimated to fall between -4.63 and 1.43 minutes.

EXAMPLE 9.6

A senior at a prestigious eastern university is trying to decide whether to enter a one-year teacher's college and become a high-school teacher or go to graduate school, obtain an M.A. and Ph.D., and become a university professor. After careful consideration, he concludes that the decision should be made on the basis of the average annual income of the two groups ten years after getting the bachelor's degree. In particular he will become a university professor unless there is enough evidence to conclude that high-school teachers earn more money. The senior takes a sample of 50 university professors and 50 high-school teachers, all of whom graduated with their bachelor's degrees ten years ago. The results are shown in the accompanying table.

MEAN AND VARIANCE OF ANNUAL INCOMES (in $1,000s)

High-School Teachers	University Professors
$\bar{x}_1 = 43.7$	$\bar{x}_2 = 41.5$
$s_1^2 = 11.8$	$s_2^2 = 46.3$

---

a. At the 5% significance level, should he become a university professor or a high-school teacher?

b. What is the p-value of this test?

c. Estimate with 95% confidence the difference between the mean annual incomes of professors and teachers.

Solution. The problem objective is to compare two populations, and the data scale is interval. The parameter of interest is therefore $\mu_1 - \mu_2$. The population variances σ_1^2 and σ_2^2 are unknown, but since n_1 and n_2 are greater than 30 ($n_1 = 50$ and $n_2 = 50$), the test statistic is

$$z = \frac{(\bar{x}_1 - \bar{x}_2) - (\mu_1 - \mu_2)}{\sqrt{\dfrac{s_1^2}{n_1} + \dfrac{s_2^2}{n_2}}}$$

a. Since the senior will become a university professor unless there is sufficient evidence that high-school teachers earn more on the average than professors, he wishes to determine whether or not μ_1 is greater than μ_2. Hence, the alternative hypothesis is

$$H_A : (\mu_1 - \mu_2) > 0$$

The complete test is

$$H_0 : (\mu_1 - \mu_2) = 0$$
$$H_A : (\mu_1 - \mu_2) > 0$$

Test statistic:

$$z = \frac{(\bar{x}_1 - \bar{x}_2) - (\mu_1 - \mu_2)}{\sqrt{\dfrac{s_1^2}{n_1} + \dfrac{s_2^2}{n_2}}}$$

Rejection region:

$$z > z_\alpha$$
$$> z_{.05}$$
$$> 1.645$$

Value of the test statistic:

$$z = \frac{(\bar{x}_1 - \bar{x}_2) - (\mu_1 - \mu_2)}{\sqrt{\dfrac{s_1^2}{n_1} + \dfrac{s_2^2}{n_2}}} = \frac{(43.7 - 41.5) - 0}{\sqrt{\dfrac{11.8}{50} + \dfrac{46.3}{50}}} = 2.04$$

Conclusion: Reject H_0.

There is sufficient evidence to allow us to conclude that $\mu_1 > \mu_2$. Thus, the senior will enter teacher's college next fall. Figure 9.5 describes this test.

b. p-value $= p(z > 2.04) = .0207$

c. The confidence interval estimator of $\mu_1 - \mu_2$ is

$$(\bar{x}_1 - \bar{x}_2) \pm z_{\alpha/2} \sqrt{\dfrac{s_1^2}{n_1} + \dfrac{s_2^2}{n_2}}$$

FIGURE 9.5   REJECTION REGION FOR EXAMPLE 9.6

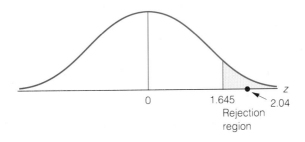

which, since $z_{\alpha/2} = 1.96$, is equal to

$$(\bar{x}_1 - \bar{x}_2) \pm z_{\alpha/2}\sqrt{\frac{s_1^2}{n_1} + \frac{s_2^2}{n_2}} = (43.7 - 41.5) \pm 1.96\sqrt{\frac{11.8}{50} + \frac{46.3}{50}}$$

$$= 2.2 \pm 2.11$$

or

(.09, 4.31)

It is estimated that high-school teachers annually earn, on average, between $90 and $4,310 more than university professors ten years after their bachelor's degrees.

COMPUTER OUTPUT FOR EXAMPLE 9.6*

Minitab

```
TWOSAMPLE T FOR C1 VS C2
        N     MEAN    ST DEV    SE MEAN
C1      50    43.7    3.44      0.486
C2      50    41.5    6.80      0.962
95 PCT CI FOR MU C1-MU C2 (0.09, 4.31)
TTEST MU C1=MU C2 (VS GT): T=2.04 P=.022 DF=72.5
```

The value of the test statistic is $z = 2.04$. The *p*-value (.022) is different from that calculated (.0207) in part *b* because Minitab's *p*-value is based on the *t* distribution.

SAS

```
Variable: X
SAMPLE    N     Mean       Std Dev    Std Error
-------------------------------------------------
    1     50    43.7000    3.4415     0.4867
    2     50    41.5000    6.8016     0.9619


Variances       T       DF      Prob > |T|
-------------------------------------------------
Unequal     2.0409    72.5      0.0448
Equal       2.0409    98.0      0.0440
```

In this example we use the Unequal test statistic value, which we label $z = 2.0409$. The two-tail *p*-value is .0448, which we divide by 2 to produce the one-tail *p*-value ($.0448/2 = .0224$).

---

* Appendixes 9.A and 9.B provide the Minitab and SAS instructions to produce these outputs.

VIOLATIONS OF THE REQUIRED CONDITIONS

We've already pointed out that, to ensure the validity of a statistical technique, the statistician must be certain that the technique is appropriate and that all requirements for its use are satisfied. For example, all the methods in this section require that the populations from which we've sampled are normally distributed. In the inference about $\mu_1 - \mu_2$, with σ_1^2 and σ_2^2 unknown and $n_1 \leq 30$ or $n_2 \leq 30$, we can only use the pooled variance estimator when $\sigma_1^2 = \sigma_2^2$. It is important for you to realize that, if a requirement is not satisfied, the technique should not be used, because its results may be invalid. Some students believe that the techniques should be used even when the required conditions are unsatisfied, since we do not have any alternative. This is quite untrue. When the data are not normally distributed—a required condition for the use of the z- or t-statistics—we can use another technique. To draw inferences about $\mu_1 - \mu_2$ from nonnormal populations, we use the nonparametric technique—the Wilcoxon rank sum test for independent samples (described in Section 14.2).

■■■■ *EXERCISES*

LEARNING THE TECHNIQUES

9.18 Test the following hypotheses:

a. $H_0: (\mu_1 - \mu_2) = 0$
$H_A: (\mu_1 - \mu_2) > 0$
$n_1 = 10$ $n_2 = 8$
$\bar{x}_1 = 200$ $\bar{x}_2 = 185$
$s_1 = 20$ $s_2 = 15$

$\alpha = .05$ (Assume that x_1 and x_2 are normally distributed.)

b. $H_0: (\mu_1 - \mu_2) = 0$
$H_A: (\mu_1 - \mu_2) \neq 0$
$n_1 = 50$ $n_2 = 70$
$\bar{x}_1 = 25$ $\bar{x}_2 = 20$
$s_1 = 2$ $s_2 = 3$

$\alpha = .01$ (Assume that x_1 and x_2 are normally distributed.)

9.19 For each of the problems in Exercise 9.18, estimate $\mu_1 - \mu_2$, with 95% confidence.

9.20 Suppose that samples of size $n_1 = 20$ and $n_2 = 15$ are drawn from two normal populations. The sample statistics are as follows:

$\bar{x}_1 = 110$ $\bar{x}_2 = 125$
$s_1^2 = 225$ $s_2^2 = 150$

a. Can we conclude at the 5% level of significance that μ_1 is less than μ_2?

b. Estimate $\mu_1 - \mu_2$, with 99% confidence.

9.21 Samples of $n_1 = 60$ and $n_2 = 80$ were drawn from two normal populations. The following statistics were produced:

$\bar{x}_1 = 70.6$ $\bar{x}_2 = 68.3$
$s_1 = 14.9$ $s_2 = 12.3$

Do these results allow us to conclude that μ_1 is greater than μ_2? (Use $\alpha = .05$.)

9.22 For Exercise 9.21, estimate $\mu_1 - \mu_2$, with 99% confidence.

9.23 The following two samples were drawn from two normal populations:

Sample 1: $n_1 = 20$ $\bar{x}_1 = 2.5$ $s_1 = 9.8$
Sample 2: $n_2 = 25$ $\bar{x}_2 = -1.6$ $s_2 = 7.8$

Do these data provide sufficient evidence at the 5% significance level to allow us to conclude that μ_1 is not equal to μ_2?

FIGURE E9.26

```
TWOSAMPLE T FOR C1 VS C2
        N    MEAN    STDEV    SE MEAN
C1     40    126.3   21.4     3.38
C2     70    132.4   25.3     3.02
95 PCT CI FOR MU C1-MU C2: (-14.99, 2.79)
TTEST MU C1=MU C2 (VS LT): T=-1.34 P=.0917 DF=92.7
```

FIGURE E9.27

```
TWOSAMPLE T FOR C1 VS C2
        N    MEAN    STDEV    SE MEAN
C1     12    29.3    5.8      1.67
C2      9    34.9    6.9      2.30
95 PCT CI FOR MU C1-MU C2: (-11.40, 0.20)
TTEST MU C1=MU C2 (VS NE): T=-2.02 P=.0578 DF=19
```

9.24 For Exercise 9.23, estimate $\mu_1 - \mu_2$, with 90% confidence.

9.25 What assumption(s) did you make in order to answer Exercises 9.23 and 9.24?

9.26 Given the output shown in Figure E9.26, briefly describe what each number tells you.

9.27 The computer printout of a hypothesis test is shown in Figure E9.27. Specify the hypotheses being tested and the conclusion you would draw at the 1% significance level.

9.28 To test the hypotheses

$H_0: (\mu_1 - \mu_2) = 0$

$H_A: (\mu_1 - \mu_2) < 0$

we generated the computer output shown in Figure E9.28. Interpret the results and—assuming that we want the significance level to be .01—draw a conclusion. What other assumption(s) must you make in answering this question?

9.29 Given the computer output shown in Figure E9.29 for testing the hypotheses

$H_0: (\mu_1 - \mu_2) = 0$

$H_A: (\mu_1 - \mu_2) > 0$

what conclusion would you draw, with $\alpha = .10$? What assumption(s) did you make in answering the question?

FIGURE E9.28

```
Variable: X
SAMPLE     N     Mean     Std Dev     Std Error
-------------------------------------------------
    1     10     126.3     17.23        5.45
    2     16     149.3     23.61        5.90
Variances       T       DF      Prob > |T|
-------------------------------------------------
Unequal       -2.86     23.3      0.0086
Equal         -2.66     24.0      0.0138
```

FIGURE E9.29

```
Variable: X
SAMPLE    N     Mean    Std Dev    Std Error
------------------------------------------------
  1      32     77.1      6.03       1.07
  2      58     75.2      4.21       0.55
Variances     T      DF      Prob > |T|
------------------------------------------------
Unequal      1.58    48.0     0.1206
Equal        1.74    88.0     0.0848
```

9.30   For Exercise 9.28, find the 99% confidence interval estimate of $\mu_1 - \mu_2$.

9.31   For Exercise 9.29, find the 90% confidence interval estimate of $\mu_1 - \mu_2$.

APPLYING THE TECHNIQUES

Self-Correcting Exercise (See Appendix 9.C for the solution.)

MKT   **9.32**   A baby-food producer claims that her product is superior to that of her leading competitor, in that babies gain weight faster with her product. As an experiment, ten healthy newborn infants are randomly selected. For 2 months, five of the babies are fed the producer's product and the other five are fed the competitor's product. Each baby's weight gain (in ounces) is recorded in the accompanying table.

WEIGHT GAIN (ounces)

Producer's Product	Competitor's Product
30	32
36	24
28	30
37	29
40	27

a. Can we conclude that the average weight gain for babies fed on the producer's baby food is greater than the average weight gain for babies fed on the competitor's baby food? (Use $\alpha = .05$.)

b. Estimate the difference in average weight gain between the two groups of babies. (Use a confidence level of 90%.)

c. What assumption(s) must you make in order to answer parts (a) and (b)?

POM   **9.33**   Kool Kat, a manufacturer of automobile air conditioners, is considering switching its supplier of condensers. Supplier A, the current producer of condensers for Kool Kat, prices its product 5% higher than supplier B does. Since Kool Kat wants to maintain its reputation for quality, however, Kool Kat wants to be sure that supplier B's condensers last at least as long as those of supplier A. The management of Kool Kat has decided to retain supplier A if there is sufficient statistical evidence that supplier A's condensers last longer on the average than supplier B's condensers. In an experiment, ten mid-sized cars were equipped with air conditioners using type A condensers while another ten mid-sized cars were equipped with type B condensers. The number of miles driven by each car before the condenser broke down was recorded, and the relevant statistics are listed in the accompanying table.

Type A Condensers	Type B Condensers
$\bar{x}_1 = 75{,}000$	$\bar{x}_2 = 70{,}000$
$s_1 = 6{,}000$	$s_2 = 5{,}000$

Assuming that the distance traveled is normally distributed, should Kool Kat retain Supplier A? (Use $\alpha = .05$.)

POM   **9.34**   Estimate $\mu_1 - \mu_2$ with 95% confidence, using the data in Exercise 9.33.

EDUC **9.35** Do students at four-year universities work harder than those at two-year junior colleges? To help answer this question, 47 randomly selected university students and 36 college students were asked how many hours per week they spent doing homework. The means and variances for both groups are shown next. Do these results allow us to answer our opening question affirmatively? (Use $\alpha = .10$.)

University Students	College Students
$\bar{x}_1 = 18.6$	$\bar{x}_2 = 14.7$
$s_1^2 = 22.4$	$s_2^2 = 20.9$

EDUC **9.36** What is the p-value of the test in Exercise 9.35?

SECTION 9.4 ## INFERENCE ABOUT $\mu_1 - \mu_2$: MATCHED PAIRS EXPERIMENT

In the two previous sections, we dealt with statistical techniques for computing the difference between two population means when the samples were independent. Now consider the following experiment, in which the samples are not independent.

The president of a pharmaceutical company that has recently developed a new nonprescription sleeping pill wants to test its effectiveness. Her assistant recruits five individuals selected at random to participate in a preliminary experiment. The experiment is performed over two nights. On one night the subject takes the sleeping pill, and on the other he or she takes a placebo (a pill that looks like a sleeping pill but contains no medication). The order in which the pills are taken by each individual is random. The hours of sleep in each case are shown in the following table.

	Number of Hours of Sleep	
Subject	Sleeping Pill	Placebo
1	7.3	6.8
2	8.5	7.9
3	6.4	6.0
4	9.0	8.4
5	6.9	6.5

To determine whether or not sufficient evidence exists to allow us to conclude that the sleeping pill is effective, we test

$$H_0: (\mu_1 - \mu_2) = 0$$
$$H_A: (\mu_1 - \mu_2) > 0$$

where μ_1 is the average amount of sleep with the sleeping pill, and μ_2 is the average amount of sleep with the placebo. If we use the test statistic described in Section 9.3, we have

$$t = \frac{(\bar{x}_1 - \bar{x}_2) - (\mu_1 - \mu_2)}{\sqrt{s_p^2 \left(\dfrac{1}{n_1} + \dfrac{1}{n_2}\right)}} = \frac{(7.62 - 7.12) - 0}{\sqrt{1.097 \left(\dfrac{1}{5} + \dfrac{1}{5}\right)}} = .75$$

and the rejection region is

$$t > t_{\alpha, n_1 + n_2 - 2}$$

If we select $\alpha = .05$, we reject H_0 when

$$t > t_{.05, 8}$$
$$> 1.860$$

Since t does not fall into the rejection region, we cannot conclude that the sleeping pill is effective. If you examine the individual times of sleep, however, you will see that for all five subjects the amount of sleep with the sleeping pill was between .4 and .6 hours more than the amount of sleep with the placebo. This suggests that, contrary to the test conclusion, there is evidence that the sleeping pill is effective.

This apparent contradiction is the result of the large variation in the amounts of sleep among the five subjects. The variation is so large that it hides the actual differences in amounts of sleep with the sleeping pill and with the placebo. The way in which the experiment was conducted, however, enables us to remedy this problem. This experiment is called a **matched pairs experiment,** because each subject's amount of sleep was measured twice—once with the sleeping pill, and once with the placebo. As a result, there is a natural pairing between the two samples. This means that the samples are *not independent;* once we selected the five subjects to take the sleeping pill, the experiment dictated that we measure the amount of sleep of the *same five subjects* with the placebo.

If we had measured the amount of sleep of five individuals with the sleeping pill and the amount of sleep of *another five* individuals with the placebo, the samples would have been independent. The correct test statistic in that case would be the one encountered in Section 9.3. However, because our example was conducted as a matched pairs experiment, we can produce a better test that resolves the apparent contradiction.

TESTING THE PAIRED DIFFERENCES

In order to eliminate the effect of the variations in the subjects' sleeping times, we test the **mean difference** for each subject, as opposed to the difference between means. This is done by calculating the difference D between the amounts of sleep with the sleeping pill and with the placebo for each of the five subjects, as shown in the table on the next page.

	Number of Hours of Sleep		
Subject	Sleeping Pill	Placebo	Difference
1	7.3	6.8	.5
2	8.5	7.9	.6
3	6.4	6.0	.4
4	9.0	8.4	.6
5	6.9	6.5	.4

The result of this computation is to eliminate the effect of differences in the subjects' sleeping times. We now test the mean difference, denoted μ_D, which is equivalent to the difference between means; that is, $\mu_D = \mu_1 - \mu_2$. As you are about to see, eliminating the effects of differences between subjects enables us to produce a better test.

Since the parameter now is μ_D, the test statistic is as follows.

Test Statistic for Testing the Matched Pairs' Mean Difference

$$t = \frac{\bar{x}_D - \mu_D}{s_D/\sqrt{n_D}} \qquad \text{d.f.} = n_D - 1$$

where $\bar{x}_D$ and s_D are the sample mean and the sample standard deviation, respectively, of the n_D differences.

As we've explained before, use of the Student t distribution requires the condition of normality; and in this application, we require that the differences be normally distributed. Our test is

$H_0: \mu_D = 0$

$H_A: \mu_D > 0$

Test statistic:

$$t = \frac{\bar{x}_D - \mu_D}{s_D/\sqrt{n_D}}$$

Rejection region:

$t > t_{\alpha, n_D - 1}$

$> t_{.05, 4}$

> 2.132

Value of the test statistic:

$$t = \frac{\bar{x}_D - \mu_D}{s_D/\sqrt{n_D}} = \frac{.5 - 0}{.1/\sqrt{5}} = 11.18$$

(You should check that $\bar{x}_D = .5$ and $s_D = .1$.)

Conclusion: Reject H_0.

There is sufficient evidence to allow us to conclude that the sleeping pill is effective in increasing the user's amount of sleep.

Observe that the large difference in the two test statistics was not caused by a difference in their numerators (both of which were equal to .5), but by a difference in their denominators. The test statistic for μ_D is much larger, because the variance of the differences is $s_D^2 = .01$, while the variance used in the test statistic for $\mu_1 - \mu_2$ is $s_p^2 = 1.097$. The quantity s_D^2 is substantially smaller because we removed the variation caused by differences in sleeping time among the subjects.

EXAMPLE 9.7

A nationally known manufacturer of replacement shock absorbers claims that its product lasts longer than does the type of shock absorber that the car manufacturer installs. To test this claim, 8 cars each had one new original and one new replacement shock absorber installed on the rear end and were driven until the shock absorbers were no longer effective. In each case, the number of miles until this happened was recorded, and the results are shown in the accompanying table.

	Number of Miles (1,000s)	
Car	Original Shock Absorber	Replacement Shock Absorber
1	42.6	43.8
2	37.2	41.3
3	50.0	49.7
4	43.9	45.7
5	53.6	52.5
6	32.5	36.8
7	46.5	47.0
8	39.3	40.7

Is there sufficient evidence at the 5% significance level to support the manufacturer's claim?

Solution.   The data scale is interval (number of miles driven), and the problem objective is to compare two populations (miles driven with the original and with the replacement shock absorbers). The observations are paired, because each car was equipped with both kinds of shock absorbers. Hence, the parameter of interest is μ_D. We arbitrarily define D as the number of miles driven on the original shock minus the number of miles driven on the replacement shock. Since the manufacturer claims that his shock absorbers are better, we want to know if the data provide sufficient evidence to justify our concluding that $\mu_D < 0$. The values of D are as follows:

Car	D
1	-1.2
2	-4.1
3	0.3
4	-1.8
5	1.1
6	-4.3
7	-0.5
8	-1.4

From the data, we calculate

$$\bar{x}_D = -1.49$$

and

$$s_D = 1.92$$

Hence,

$$H_0: \mu_D = 0$$
$$H_A: \mu_D < 0$$

Test statistic:

$$t = \frac{\bar{x}_D - \mu_D}{s_D/\sqrt{n_D}}$$

Rejection region:

$$t < -t_{\alpha, n_D - 1}$$
$$< -t_{.05, 7}$$
$$< -1.895$$

FIGURE 9.6   *REJECTION REGION FOR EXAMPLE 9.7*

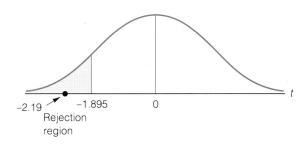

Value of the test statistic:

$$t = \frac{\bar{x}_D - \mu_D}{s_D/\sqrt{n_D}} = \frac{-1.49 - 0}{1.92/\sqrt{8}} = -2.19$$

Conclusion: Reject H_0.

Hence, there is sufficient evidence to allow us to conclude that the replacement shocks last longer than the original shocks. This test is described in Figure 9.6.

COMPUTER OUTPUT FOR EXAMPLE 9.7*

Minitab

```
TEST OF MU=0.00 VS MU L.T. 0.00
        N    MEAN    STDEV    SE MEAN      T    P VALUE
C3      8   -1.487   1.919    0.679    -2.19    0.032
```

To conduct this test, we calculated the paired differences and stored them in column 3. We then conducted a *t*-test (as in Chapter 7).

SAS

```
Analysis Variable: D
N      Mean            T     Prob > |T|
8    -1.4875      -2.1919     0.0645
```

SAS produces the two-tail *p*-value. The *p*-value for this test is

$$p\text{-value} = \frac{\text{Prob} > |\text{T}|}{2} = \frac{.0645}{2} = .0325$$

---

* The Minitab and SAS commands that were used to create these printouts are shown in Appendixes 9.A and 9.B, respectively.

ESTIMATING THE MEAN DIFFERENCE

We estimate the difference between means by estimating the mean difference μ_D, when the data are produced by a matched pairs experiment.

> **Confidence Interval Estimator of μ_D**
>
> $$\bar{x}_D \pm t_{\alpha/2} \frac{s_D}{\sqrt{n_D}} \qquad \text{d.f.} = n_D - 1$$

If in Example 9.7 we want to estimate the mean difference μ_D with 95% confidence, we get

$$\bar{x}_D \pm t_{\alpha/2} \frac{s_D}{\sqrt{n_D}} = -1.49 \pm 2.365 \frac{1.92}{\sqrt{8}} = -1.49 \pm 1.61$$

which simplifies to

$$(-3.10, 0.12)$$

The 95% confidence interval estimate of the mean difference is the interval -3.10 to 0.12.

RECOGNIZING THE MATCHED PAIRS EXPERIMENT

Many students of statistics experience some degree of difficulty in determining whether a particular experiment is independent or matched pairs. We suggest that students try asking and answering the following question: Does some natural relationship exist between *each pair* of observations? That is, is there a logical reason why we would compare the first observation of sample 1 with the first observation of sample 2, the second observation of sample 1 with the second observation of sample 2, and so on? If not, the samples are independent.

▬▬▬▬▬▬ *EXAMPLE 9.8*

In an effort to determine whether or not a new type of fertilizer is more effective than the type currently in use, researchers subdivided a 20-acre farm into twenty 1-acre plots. Ten plots were randomly selected and treated with the new fertilizer, and the remaining ten plots were treated with the current fertilizer. Wheat was planted on the farm, and at the end of the season the number of bushels reaped was measured. The resulting figures are shown in the accompanying table.

Is this a matched pairs experiment?

Number of Bushels Produced	
Current Fertilizer	New Fertilizer
30	35
20	27
14	36
36	33
29	16
22	35
18	28
31	13
30	26
25	18

Solution. You might be tempted to answer *yes,* arguing that—since all of the plots of land come from one farm—a relationship exists between the ten plots treated with the current fertilizer and the ten plots treated with the new fertilizer. But this is wrong, because it fails to recognize that there was no natural relationship between each pair of observations. For example, is it reasonable to compare the crop yield of 30 bushels obtained from the first plot treated with the current fertilizer to the crop yield of 35 bushels obtained from the first plot treated with the new fertilizer? The answer is a definite *no.* Since no pairwise relationship exists, we identify the experimental design as consisting of independent samples. The parameter to be tested is $\mu_1 - \mu_2$, and the test statistic is

$$t = \frac{(\bar{x}_1 - \bar{x}_2) - (\mu_1 - \mu_2)}{\sqrt{s_p^2\left(\dfrac{1}{n_1} + \dfrac{1}{n_2}\right)}}$$

EXAMPLE 9.9

Suppose that the experiment described in Example 9.8 has been redesigned in the following way. Ten 2-acre plots of land scattered throughout the county are randomly selected. Each plot is divided into two subplots, one of which is treated with the current fertilizer, and the other of which is treated with the new fertilizer. Wheat is planted, and the crop yields are measured and recorded. The resulting figures are shown in the table on the next page.

Is this a matched pairs experiment?

	Number of Bushels Produced	
Plot	Current Fertilizer	New Fertilizer
1	25	28
2	19	25
3	32	30
4	23	21
5	28	33
6	21	25
7	14	20
8	31	28
9	26	26
10	20	19

Solution.   Yes. In this experiment, it is logical to compare pairs of observations, since each pair of observations comes from the same plot of land and since there is only one pair of observations per plot. The parameter to be tested is μ_D, and the test statistic is

$$t = \frac{\bar{x}_D - \mu_D}{s_D/\sqrt{n_D}}$$

Recognizing a Matched Pairs Experiment

The key to recognizing a matched pairs experiment is to watch for a natural pairing between one observation in the first sample and one observation in the second sample. If a natural pairing exists, the experiment involves matched pairs.

VIOLATION OF THE REQUIRED CONDITION

The t-test and estimator of μ_D require that the differences are normally distributed. When the differences are not normally distributed this method should not be used. Instead we will employ a nonparametric technique: the Wilcoxon signed rank sum test for matched pairs (see Section 14.4).

EXERCISES

LEARNING THE TECHNIQUES

9.37   Given the following data generated from a matched pairs experiment, test at the 1% level of significance to determine if there is enough evidence to conclude that the mean of population I exceeds the mean of population II. Assume that the random variables are normally distributed.

Observation	I	II
1	20	17
2	23	16
3	15	9
4	18	19
5	19	15

9.38   Estimate the difference in means, with 95% confidence, using the data from Exercise 9.37.

9.39   Test the following hypotheses:

a. $H_0: \mu_D = 0$
   $H_A: \mu_D \neq 0$
   $\bar{x}_D = 2, s_D = 4, n_D = 15, \alpha = .05$

b. $H_0: \mu_D = 0$
   $H_A: \mu_D < 0$
   $\bar{x}_D = -8, s_D = 20, n_D = 50, \alpha = .01$

9.40   For each of the problems in Exercise 9.39, estimate μ_D with 95% confidence.

9.41   With $\alpha = .01$, test the hypotheses

$H_0: \mu_D = 0$

$H_A: \mu_D \neq 0$

given the following data generated from a matched pairs experiment:

Observation	Sample 1	Sample 2
1	25	32
2	11	14
3	17	16
4	7	14
5	29	36
6	21	22

9.42   Estimate μ_D with 90% confidence in Exercise 9.41.

9.43   In order to test the hypotheses

$H_0: \mu_D = 0$

$H_A: \mu_D > 0$

we produced the computer output shown in Figure E9.43. Interpret each of the numbers, and state what they tell you.

9.44   Specify the hypotheses that are being tested, and interpret the numbers listed in the computer printout shown in Figure E9.44.

FIGURE E9.43

```
TEST OF MU=0.00 VS MU G.T. 0.00
        N    MEAN    STDEV    SE MEAN    T      P VALUE
C3     70    8.63    48.36    5.78      1.49    .0704
```

FIGURE E9.44

```
TEST OF MU=0.00 VS MU N.E. 0.00
        N    MEAN     STDEV    SE MEAN    T       P VALUE
C3     20   -12.05    23.34    5.22      -2.31    .0322
```

9.45   To test the following hypotheses

$H_0: \mu_D = 0$

$H_A: \mu_D > 0$

we generated the following computer output. Interpret the results, and draw a conclusion. (Use $\alpha = .05$.)

```
Analysis Variable: D
 N    Mean      T      Prob > |T|
22   63.571    1.88      0.0740
```

9.46   Given the accompanying computer output, test the following hypotheses at the 10% significance level:

$H_0: \mu_D = 0$

$H_A: \mu_D < 0$

```
Analysis Variable: D
 N    Mean       T      Prob > |T|
18  -0.73615  -1.52      0.1468
```

9.47   The computer printout of the hypothesis test

$H_0: \mu_D = 0$

$H_A: \mu_D \neq 0$

is shown next. What conclusion would you draw with $\alpha = .01$?

```
Analysis Variable: D
 N    Mean      T      Prob > |T|
60   12.702   2.53      0.0140
```

9.48   For Exercise 9.43, Estimate μ_D with 95% confidence.

9.49   For Exercise 9.44, Estimate μ_D with 90% confidence.

APPLYING THE TECHNIQUES

Self-Correcting Exercise (See Appendix 9.C for the solution.)

GEN **9.50**   In a test to compare the speeds of two types of equal-sized computers, eight large programs written in FORTRAN were run on both computers. Then the amount of CPU time in minutes was measured and recorded. The CPU times are normally distributed.

Program	CPU Time (minutes)	
	Computer 1	Computer 2
1	28	32
2	52	47
3	103	110
4	15	12
5	72	75
6	49	55
7	62	72
8	26	30

Can we conclude that the average CPU time for computer 1 is less than the average CPU time for computer 2? (Use $\alpha = .10$.)

GEN **9.51**   For Exercise 9.50, estimate the mean difference in CPU time between computers 1 and 2, with 99% confidence.

SCI **9.52**   In their quest to understand the relative effects of environment and heredity on intelligence, social scientists recognize the desirability of studying sets of identical twins who have been raised apart since birth. If intelligence is primarily determined by heredity, the twins' IQs should be more or less equal. On the other hand, if environment is a major factor in intelligence, the twins' IQs should differ — in some cases, considerably. In a preliminary study, ten sets of twins separated at birth had their IQs tested. The results are shown in the following table. (The twin with the higher IQ is shown first.) What can we conclude about the roles of heredity and environment in determining intelligence? (Test with $\alpha = .05$.)

Twin Set	Intelligence Quotient	
	Higher	Lower
1	107	102
2	95	92
3	114	106

Twin Set	Intelligence Quotient	
	Higher	Lower
4	121	120
5	99	98
6	104	100
7	89	86
8	93	90
9	101	100
10	103	98

Years of Experience	Commissions ($1,000s)
12	49
1	14
7	44

The next step in the experiment involved finding eight salesmen who had the same number of years of experience as the eight saleswomen. The years of experience and last year's commissions for these salesmen are shown in the following table.

SCI **9.53** For Exercise 9.52, estimate the mean difference in IQ between twins, with 95% confidence.

RET **9.54** Until recently most car salespeople have been men. However, in the past decade, numerous automobile dealers have hired women as salespeople in the hope that they will succeed in selling more cars to women customers. A researcher decided to test the proposition that female salespeople are actually superior to their male counterparts. She took a random sample of eight saleswomen and determined the commission that each earned in the last year. Her original plan was simply to take a random sample of eight salesmen and compare their commissions with those of the saleswomen. However, she felt that, since years of sales experience would be a factor, she should also determine the numbers of years of sales experience for each of the eight women. The years of experience and last year's commissions are shown in the following table.

YEARS OF EXPERIENCE AND LAST YEAR'S COMMISSION FOR EIGHT SALESWOMEN

Years of Experience	Commissions ($1,000s)
5	35
3	27
2	24
4	22
10	55

YEARS OF EXPERIENCE AND LAST YEAR'S COMMISSION FOR EIGHT SALESMEN

Years of Experience	Commissions ($1,000s)
5	29
3	28
2	19
4	20
10	51
12	52
1	12
7	31

Can we conclude at the 5% significance level that female salespeople do better than male salespeople?

RET **9.55** How do you know that the experiment described in Exercise 9.54 is a matched pairs experiment?

9.56 In a study to determine whether gender affects salary offers for graduating BBA students, ten pairs of students were selected. Each pair consisted of a male student and a female student who had almost identical grade-point averages, courses taken, ages, and previous work experience. The highest salary offered to each student upon graduation is shown in the following table. Assume that these salaries follow a normal distribution.

	Annual Salary Offer ($1,000s)	
Student Pair	**Female Student**	**Male Student**
1	22	25
2	17	18
3	21	27
4	19	17
5	26	29
6	23	25
7	21	19
8	31	27
9	25	36
10	18	23

a. Is there sufficient evidence to allow us to conclude that the average salary offer differs between males and females? (Use $\alpha = .01$.)

b. Estimate the average difference in salary offers, with 90% confidence.

c. How should the experiment be redesigned in order to have independent samples? Which design is superior? Explain.

SECTION 9.5   ## INFERENCE ABOUT σ_1^2/σ_2^2

In the preceding three sections of this chapter, we dealt with statistical inference concerning $\mu_1 - \mu_2$. The problem objective in each case was to compare two populations, the data scale was interval, and our interest was in comparing measures of central location. This section will discuss the statistical techniques to use when the problem objective and the data scale are the same as those in the previous sections, but when our interest is in comparing measures of variability. Here, we will compare the ratio of two population variances, σ_1^2/σ_2^2.

In Chapter 7, we used the sample variance s^2 to draw inferences about the population variance σ^2. In this section, we use the ratio of two independent sample variances, s_1^2/s_2^2, to draw inferences about σ_1^2/σ_2^2.

If samples of sizes n_1 and n_2 are drawn from two normal populations, with variances σ_1^2 and σ_2^2, the random variable

$$F = \frac{s_1^2/\sigma_1^2}{s_2^2/\sigma_2^2}$$

created by repeated sampling follows a distribution known as the **F distribution.** The shape of the F distribution is similar to that of the chi-square distribution. The exact shape of the F distribution, however, is determined by two sets of degrees of freedom: $v_1 = n_1 - 1$, which is the number of degrees of freedom associated with the numerator; and $v_2 = n_2 - 1$, which is the number of degrees of freedom associated with the denominator. Figure 9.7 illustrates the F distribution.

Table 6 in Appendix B provides values of F_{α, v_1, v_2}, where F_{α, v_1, v_2} is the value of F with v_1 and v_2 degrees of freedom such that the probability that this value will be exceeded is α. That is,

$$P(F > F_{\alpha, v_1, v_2}) = \alpha$$

FIGURE 9.7   *F DISTRIBUTION*

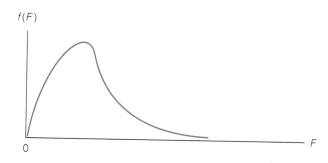

Part of Table 6 is reproduced here as Table 9.1. Notice that, with 5 numerator degrees of freedom and 7 denominator degrees of freedom, we get from the table

$$F_{.05,5,7} = 3.97$$

TABLE 9.1   *CRITICAL VALUES OF THE F DISTRIBUTION, $\alpha = .05$*

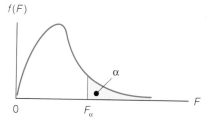

v_1	Numerator Degrees of Freedom								
v_2	1	2	3	4	5	6	7	8	9
1	161.4	199.5	215.7	224.6	230.2	234.0	236.8	238.9	240.5
2	18.51	19.00	19.16	19.25	19.30	19.33	19.35	19.37	19.38
3	10.13	9.55	9.28	9.12	9.01	8.94	8.89	8.85	8.81
4	7.71	6.94	6.59	6.39	6.26	6.16	6.09	6.04	6.00
5	6.61	5.79	5.41	5.19	5.05	4.95	4.88	4.82	4.77
6	5.99	5.14	4.76	4.53	4.39	4.28	4.21	4.15	4.10
7	5.59	4.74	4.35	4.12	3.97	3.87	3.79	3.73	3.68
8	5.32	4.46	4.07	3.84	3.69	3.58	3.50	3.44	3.39
9	5.12	4.26	3.86	3.63	3.48	3.37	3.29	3.23	3.18
10	4.96	4.10	3.71	3.48	3.33	3.22	3.14	3.07	3.02

(Denominator Degrees of Freedom)

SOURCE: From M. Merrington and C. M. Thompson, "Tables of Percentage Points of the Inverted Beta(F)-Distribution," *Biometrika* 33 (1943): 73–88. Reproduced by permission of the Biometrika Trustees.

which means that

$$P(F > 3.97) = .05$$

In our notation, the order of the degrees of freedom is important. For example, observe that

$$F_{.05,7,5} = 4.88$$

This represents the point with 7 numerator degrees of freedom and 5 denominator degrees of freedom such that the area to its right is .05.

Table 6 provides values of F_α for $\alpha = .01, .025, .05,$ and .10; however, the table does not show values of F such that the area to the left of that value is equal to α. We denote such a value by $F_{1-\alpha}$. That is,

$$P(F < F_{1-\alpha}) = \alpha$$

Figure 9.8 illustrates this notation. The values of $F_{1-\alpha}$ are not given, because they are not necessary. It can be shown that

$$F_{1-\alpha,v_1,v_2} = \frac{1}{F_{\alpha,v_2,v_1}}$$

For example,

$$F_{.95,8,5} = \frac{1}{F_{.05,5,8}} = \frac{1}{3.69} = .271$$

Thus, for any F_α value shown in Table 6, we can calculate $F_{1-\alpha}$.

FIGURE 9.8 F_α AND $F_{1-\alpha}$

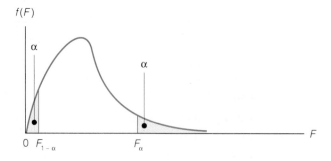

TESTING σ_1^2/σ_2^2

In comparing two population variances, we will almost always test the null hypothesis specifying that the population variances are equal. That is,

$$H_0: \sigma_1^2/\sigma_2^2 = 1$$

As was the case in all other tests, we can formulate any of three possible alternative hypotheses.

1. $H_A: \sigma_1^2/\sigma_2^2 \neq 1$, where the rejection region is $F > F_{\alpha/2}$ or $F < F_{1-\alpha/2}$.
2. $H_A: \sigma_1^2/\sigma_2^2 > 1$, where the rejection region is $F > F_{\alpha}$.
3. $H_A: \sigma_1^2/\sigma_2^2 < 1$, where the rejection region is $F < F_{1-\alpha}$.

Because we will always be testing $\sigma_1^2/\sigma_2^2 = 1$, the test statistic is

---

Test Statistic for σ_1^2/σ_2^2

$$F = \frac{s_1^2}{s_2^2} \qquad \text{d.f.} \quad \begin{array}{l} v_1 = n_1 - 1 \\ v_2 = n_2 - 1 \end{array}$$

EXAMPLE 9.10

In Example 9.4, we assumed that the two unknown population variances were equal. We now want to determine whether there is sufficient evidence to allow us to conclude that the test was invalid because $\sigma_1^2 \neq \sigma_2^2$. (Use $\alpha = .10$.) Assume that the random variables (assembly times) are normally distributed.

Solution

$$H_0: \sigma_1^2/\sigma_2^2 = 1$$
$$H_A: \sigma_1^2/\sigma_2^2 \neq 1$$

Test statistic:

$$F = \frac{s_1^2}{s_2^2}$$

Rejection region:

$$F > F_{\alpha/2, v_1, v_2} \quad \text{or} \quad F < F_{1-\alpha/2, v_1, v_2}$$

$$> F_{.05, 5, 7} \qquad\qquad < F_{.95, 5, 7} = \frac{1}{F_{.05, 7, 5}} = \frac{1}{4.88} = .205$$

$$> 3.97$$

FIGURE 9.9   REJECTION REGION FOR EXAMPLE 9.10

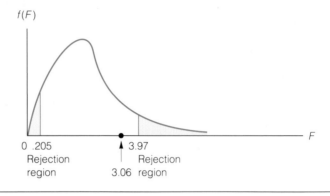

Value of the test statistic:

$$F = \frac{s_1^2}{s_2^2} = \frac{2.36^2}{1.35^2} = 3.06$$

Conclusion: Do not reject H_0.

There is not enough evidence to conclude that the t-test conducted in Example 9.4 is invalid. Figure 9.9 describes this test.

ESTIMATING σ_1^2/σ_2^2

From the notation developed in the preceding subsection, we can state that

$$P(F_{1-\alpha/2} < F < F_{\alpha/2}) = 1 - \alpha$$

Substituting

$$F = \frac{s_1^2/\sigma_1^2}{s_2^2/\sigma_2^2}$$

into that equation, we get

$$P\left(F_{1-\alpha/2} < \frac{s_1^2/\sigma_1^2}{s_2^2/\sigma_2^2} < F_{\alpha/2}\right) = 1 - \alpha$$

By using some mathematical manipulations, we can isolate σ_1^2/σ_2^2 in the center of the probability statement. Incorporating the formula

$$F_{1-\alpha/2, v_1, v_2} = \frac{1}{F_{\alpha/2, v_2, v_1}}$$

we get the following interval estimator.

Confidence Interval Estimator of σ_1^2/σ_2^2

$$\text{LCL} = \left(\frac{s_1^2}{s_2^2}\right)\frac{1}{F_{\alpha/2, v_1, v_2}}$$

$$\text{UCL} = \left(\frac{s_1^2}{s_2^2}\right)F_{\alpha/2, v_2, v_1}$$

EXAMPLE 9.11

The variability of fills in a bottling plant is almost as important as the average, since a large variance would result in some bottles' being quite underfilled and in others' being overfilled. In a test of two automatic bottle-filling machines, random samples from the two machines were drawn; 25 observations (measured in ounces) from machine 1 had a variance of $s_1^2 = 1.63$, and 16 observations from machine 2 produced $s_2^2 = 1.23$. Estimate with 90% confidence the ratio of the two population variances.

Solution.   The data scale is interval (the amount of fill), and the problem objective is to compare two populations (the fills of the two machines). Because we are interested in the variability of fills, the parameter to be estimated is σ_1^2/σ_2^2. Since $1 - \alpha = .90$, we know that $\alpha/2 = .05$; therefore,

$$F_{.05, 24, 15} = 2.29$$

and

$$F_{.05, 15, 24} = 2.11$$

Thus,

$$\text{LCL} = \left(\frac{s_1^2}{s_2^2}\right)\frac{1}{F_{\alpha/2, v_1, v_2}} = \left(\frac{1.63}{1.23}\right)\frac{1}{F_{.05, 24, 15}} = \left(\frac{1.63}{1.23}\right)\frac{1}{2.29} = .58$$

and

$$\text{UCL} = \left(\frac{s_1^2}{s_2^2}\right)F_{\alpha/2, v_2, v_1} = \left(\frac{1.63}{1.23}\right)F_{.05, 15, 24} = \left(\frac{1.63}{1.23}\right)2.11 = 2.80$$

We estimate that σ_1^2/σ_2^2 falls between .58 and 2.80. Notice that the interval is not symmetrical about the point estimate.

EXERCISES

LEARNING THE TECHNIQUES

9.57   Test the following hypotheses:

a. $H_0: \sigma_1^2/\sigma_2^2 = 1$
   $H_A: \sigma_1^2/\sigma_2^2 \neq 1$
   $n_1 = 10$ $n_2 = 16$
   $s_1^2 = 250$ $s_2^2 = 200$
   $\alpha = .05$

b. $H_0: \sigma_1^2/\sigma_2^2 = 1$
   $H_A: \sigma_1^2/\sigma_2^2 > 1$
   $n_1 = 8$ $n_2 = 11$
   $s_1^2 = 16.0$ $s_2^2 = 5.0$
   $\alpha = .05$

9.58   For each of the problems in Exercise 9.57, estimate σ_1^2/σ_2^2 with 95% confidence.

9.59   Given

$n_1 = 16$ $n_2 = 25$
$s_1^2 = 43.6$ $s_2^2 = 101.8$

test (with $\alpha = .05$) to determine whether there is enough evidence to justify concluding that σ_2^2 exceeds σ_1^2.

9.60   For Exercise 9.59, estimate σ_1^2/σ_2^2 with 90% confidence.

9.61   Given the following observations from two normal populations, test to determine whether the population variances differ. (Use $\alpha = .05$.)

Sample 1:   27   19   33   18   15   25
Sample 2:   37   27   20   43   18

9.62   For Exercise 9.61, estimate σ_1^2/σ_2^2 with 98% confidence.

9.63   Test the following hypotheses (with $\alpha = .05$)

$H_0: \sigma_1^2/\sigma_2^2 = 1$

$H_A: \sigma_1^2/\sigma_2^2 > 1$

given the following summations determined from samples taken from normal populations.

Sample 1	Sample 2
$n_1 = 21$	$n_2 = 27$
$\sum x_i = 263$	$\sum x_i = 358$
$\sum x_i^2 = 13{,}406$	$\sum x_i^2 = 12{,}317$

APPLYING THE TECHNIQUES

Self-Correcting Exercise (See Appendix 9.C for the solution.)

FIN **9.64**   The risk of an investment is often measured by the variance of the return on investment. In a comparison of the risk associated with two investments, monthly returns on two $1,000 investments were recorded, as listed in the accompanying table.

RETURNS ON $1,000 INVESTMENT ($)

| Investment 1 | 12 6 25 -5 18 6 -3 10 9 15 |
| Investment 2 | 18 0 -15 32 25 -20 37 -15 |

a. Do these data provide sufficient evidence to indicate that investment 2 is riskier than investment 1? (Use $\alpha = .05$.)

b. What assumption(s) must you make in order to answer part (a)?

c. Estimate σ_1^2/σ_2^2 with 98% confidence.

POM **9.65** An important statistical measurement in service facilities (such as restaurants, banks, and car washes) is the variability in service times. As an experiment, two tellers at a bank were observed, and the service times of ten customers served by each of the tellers were recorded (in seconds). The sample standard deviations of the service times were 32 seconds for teller 1 and 45 seconds for teller 2. Can we conclude at a 10% significance level that the tellers' variabilities in service times differ? (The service times are normally distributed.)

POM **9.66** For Exercise 9.65, estimate σ_1^2/σ_2^2 with 95% confidence.

ECON **9.67** Social scientists are interested in measuring the variability in incomes among different countries, since great variability often signifies social inequities. In random samples of 25 individuals randomly selected from each of two countries, the following summations were computed:

Country 1	Country 2
$\sum x_i = 676$	$\sum x_i = 803$
$\sum x_i^2 = 20{,}693$	$\sum x_i^2 = 29{,}379$

Can we conclude at the 5% significance level that the variability in incomes in country 1 is less than that in country 2?

ECON **9.68** Estimate the ratio of the two population variances in Exercise 9.67, with 98% confidence.

GEN **9.69** In Exercise 9.32, the statistical inference depended on the assumption that $\sigma_1^2 = \sigma_2^2$. Is there sufficient evidence to indicate that this assumption is incorrect? (Use $\alpha = .05$.)

SECTION 9.6   **SUMMARY**

There are several methods of drawing inferences about two populations when the data scale is interval. We can test and estimate $\mu_1 - \mu_2$ with three different formulas. When the two population variances are known or when the two sample sizes are each larger than 30 and the samples are independent, the **z-statistic** is used. When the two population variances are unknown but equal and two independent samples are drawn, the **t-statistic** allows us to draw inferences. If the normally distributed data are generated from a **matched pairs experiment,** we estimate and test the mean difference μ_D, which is equivalent to $\mu_1 - \mu_2$. The **F sampling distribution** is used to draw inferences about the ratio of two population variances σ_1^2/σ_2^2, where it is assumed that the samples are independent of one another and that the populations are normally distributed. These various techniques are summarized in Table 9.2.

TABLE 9.2   *SUMMARY OF INFERENCE ABOUT $\mu_1 - \mu_2$ AND σ_1^2/σ_2^2*

Parameter	Estimator	Test Statistic	Required Conditions
$\mu_1 - \mu_2$	$(\bar{x}_1 - \bar{x}_2) \pm z_{\alpha/2}\sqrt{\dfrac{\sigma_1^2}{n_1} + \dfrac{\sigma_2^2}{n_2}}$	$z = \dfrac{(\bar{x}_1 - \bar{x}_2) - (\mu_1 - \mu_2)}{\sqrt{\dfrac{\sigma_1^2}{n_1} + \dfrac{\sigma_2^2}{n_2}}}$	σ_1^2 and σ_2^2 are known. x_1 and x_2 are normally distributed, or n_1 and n_2 are large enough. Samples are independent.

(continued)

TABLE 9.2   SUMMARY OF INFERENCE ABOUT $\mu_1 - \mu_2$ AND σ_1^2/σ_2^2 (continued)

Parameter	Estimator	Test Statistic	Required Conditions
$\mu_1 - \mu_2$	$(\bar{x}_1 - \bar{x}_2) \pm z_{\alpha/2}\sqrt{\dfrac{s_1^2}{n_1} + \dfrac{s_2^2}{n_2}}$	$z = \dfrac{(\bar{x}_1 - \bar{x}_2) - (\mu_1 - \mu_2)}{\sqrt{\dfrac{s_1^2}{n_1} + \dfrac{s_2^2}{n_2}}}$	x_1 and x_2 are normally distributed, or n_1 and n_2 are large enough. Samples are independent. $n_1 > 30$ and $n_2 > 30$.
$\mu_1 - \mu_2$	$(\bar{x}_1 - \bar{x}_2) \pm t_{\alpha/2}\sqrt{s_p^2\left(\dfrac{1}{n_1} + \dfrac{1}{n_2}\right)}$	$t = \dfrac{(\bar{x}_1 - \bar{x}_2) - (\mu_1 - \mu_2)}{\sqrt{s_p^2\left(\dfrac{1}{n_1} + \dfrac{1}{n_2}\right)}}$	x_1 and x_2 are normally distributed. $\sigma_1^2 = \sigma_2^2$. Samples are independent.
μ_D	$\bar{x}_D \pm t_{\alpha/2}\dfrac{s_D}{\sqrt{n_D}}$	$t = \dfrac{\bar{x}_D - \mu_D}{s_D/\sqrt{n_D}}$	D is normally distributed. Samples are matched pairs.
σ_1^2/σ_2^2	$\text{LCL} = \left(\dfrac{s_1^2}{s_2^2}\right)\dfrac{1}{F_{\alpha/2, v_1, v_2}}$ $\text{UCL} = \left(\dfrac{s_1^2}{s_2^2}\right)F_{\alpha/2, v_2, v_1}$	$F = \dfrac{s_1^2}{s_2^2}$	x_1 and x_2 are normally distributed. Samples are independent.

SUPPLEMENTARY EXERCISES

POM **9.70** A chicken farmer who supplies an international fast-food chain is experimenting with ways to make chickens grow faster. His latest scheme is to remove the feathers of young chickens so that the energy normally used to grow feathers will be used instead to make their bodies grow faster. In order to test his scheme, the farmer takes 20 young chickens and removes the feathers from 10 of them. He then treats them exactly alike for two months, at which point he measures their weight and calculates the percentage weight gain. The statistics are as follows:

"Defeathered" Chickens	"Feathered" Chickens
$n_1 = 10$	$n_2 = 10$
$\bar{x}_1 = 112.5$	$\bar{x}_2 = 102.0$
$s_1^2 = 98.6$	$s_2^2 = 79.5$

a. Can we conclude from these statistics that the scheme is effective? (Use $\alpha = .05$.)

b. What assumption(s) must you make in order to answer part (a)?

c. Explain the consequences of a Type I error and of a Type II error. Which is more damaging? Which value of α would you select: $\alpha = .01$, or $\alpha = .10$?

d. Is the requirement of equal population variances unsatisfied? (Test with $\alpha = .05$.)

e. Estimate the difference in mean percentage weight gain, with 99% confidence.

SCI **9.71** In a preliminary study to determine the effectiveness of a new cavity-fighting toothpaste, 16 ten-year-old children were randomly selected. Of these, 8 were told to use the new product, while the other 8 continued to use one of the leading brands.

The experiment began with all of the children visiting a dentist and having any cavities filled. After a year, the children visited their dentist again, and the number of new cavities was counted. It is assumed that the number of new cavities is a normally distributed variable. The results are as follows:

NUMBER OF NEW CAVITIES

New Toothpaste	Leading Brand of Toothpaste
0	2
3	4
2	3
4	3
1	2
0	4
2	4
1	3

a. Can we conclude at the 5% significance level that the new toothpaste is effective in reducing cavities?

b. What assumption must you make in order to answer part (a)? Test that assumption with $\alpha = .05$.

9.72 Suppose that the experiment described in Exercise 9.71 were redone in the following way: 8 ten-year-old children are told to use the leading brand for one year, and then to use the new toothpaste for one year (with any cavities that occur in the first year to be filled before the start of the second year). The numbers of cavities occurring in each year of the experiment are as follows:

	Number of New Cavities	
Child	New Toothpaste	Leading Brand of Toothpaste
1	2	3
2	1	0

	Number of New Cavities	
Child	New Toothpaste	Leading Brand of Toothpaste
3	2	2
4	3	3
5	0	2
6	0	3
7	2	3
8	1	4

Can we conclude at the 5% significance level that the new toothpaste is effective in reducing cavities?

9.73 Discuss the advantages and disadvantages of the two experimental designs described in Exercises 9.71 and 9.72.

9.74 A restaurant located in an office building decides to adopt a new strategy for attracting customers to the restaurant. Every week it advertises in the city newspaper. In the 10 weeks immediately prior to the advertising campaign, the average weekly gross was $10,500, with a standard deviation of $750. In the 8 weeks after the campaign began, the average weekly gross was $12,000, with a standard deviation of $1,000.

a. Assuming that the weekly grosses are normally distributed, can we conclude, with $\alpha = .10$, that the advertising campaign was successful?

b. Assume that the net profit is 20% of the gross. If the ads cost $100 per week, can we conclude at the 10% significance level that the ads are worthwhile?

9.75 The owners of two downtown restaurants (whose customers are mostly office workers on coffee breaks) each claim to serve more coffee than the other. They decide to test their claims by counting the number of cups of coffee sold for one working week. The data are presented below. (After some analysis, it is determined that the number of cups of coffee is normally distributed.)

	Number of Cups of Coffee Sold	
Weekday	Restaurant 1	Restaurant 2
Monday	670	640
Tuesday	420	440
Wednesday	515	500
Thursday	690	650
Friday	825	800

a. Can we conclude that there is a difference between the average coffee sales of the two restaurants? (Use $\alpha = .10$.)

b. Estimate the average difference in coffee sales, with 95% confidence.

GEN **9.76** Three years ago, a 100-acre site was planted with 250,000 white spruce seedlings. Half the site was scarified (soil turned up) and the seedlings spot-fertilized; the other half was not fertilized. In order to assess the effect of fertilization, a forester would like to estimate the difference in the average weight of foliage between the fertilized and unfertilized trees. If she believes that the standard deviation of the foliage weight is approximately .90 grams, how many fertilized and unfertilized trees should she sample in order to estimate the difference in average weight to within .1 gram, with 95% confidence?

GEN **9.77** Suppose that, in Exercise 9.76, the mean and the variance of the foliage weight (in grams) of the samples taken are as shown in the accompanying table.

Fertilized Trees	**Unfertilized Trees**
$\bar{x}_1 = 5.98$	$\bar{x}_2 = 4.79$
$s_1^2 = .61$	$s_2^2 = .77$

Estimate the difference in average foliage weight between the fertilized trees and the unfertilized trees, with 95% confidence.

GEN **9.78** Because of the cost of the fertilizer referred to in Exercise 9.76, using fertilizer is considered to be cost-effective only if there is sufficient evidence

(with $\alpha = .01$) that the average foliage weight of the fertilized trees exceeds the average foliage weight of the unfertilized trees by at least 1 gram. Using the sample data, can we conclude that the fertilizer is cost-effective?

MNG **9.79** In an effort to reduce absenteeism, an electronics company initiated a program under which employees could participate in a monthly lottery, provided that they had perfect attendance and punctuality during the month.* A $10 cash prize was awarded to the winner of each monthly lottery. Approximately 80 employees participated in the program. In order to assess the impact of the program, comparisons were made between sick-leave expenditures for the first year before and the first year after the system was instituted. The results are shown in the accompanying table. Estimate the difference, with 90% confidence, between the average monthly costs before and those after the program. The costs are normally distributed.

Months	**Prior Monthly Costs ($)**	**Post Monthly Costs ($)**
September	553	935
October	755	562
November	1,088	315
December	563	576
January	1,209	737
February	1,075	585
March	1,136	746
April	1,394	775
May	826	596
June	814	767
July	755	469
August	690	670

* J. A. Wallin and R. D. Johnson, "The Use of Positive Reinforcement to Reduce Costs Associated with Employee Absenteeism," *Proceedings of the Twenty-Eighth Annual Winter Meeting of the Industrial Relations Research Association* (1975), pp. 41–46.

9.80 Megaflop Inc. is a large company employing several thousand employees. The company is located in the downtown core of a large city. Because of heavy traffic conditions, Megaflop's employees have complained for several years about the length of time it takes them to commute to work. Megaflop is considering a move to a more remote area where traffic moves more quickly. Because of the relatively high cost of the move, the company will proceed with it only if the average commuting time can be reduced by at least 15 minutes. As an experiment, ten employees were asked to measure the average amount of time it takes them to drive to the present location of Megaflop and the amount of time it takes them to drive to the new location. The times (in minutes) are shown in the accompanying table.

Employee	Time to Drive to Present Location (minutes)	Time to Drive to New Location (minutes)
1	63	40
2	72	59
3	55	35
4	42	29
5	81	60
6	58	33
7	67	41
8	52	27
9	39	21
10	32	32

At a significance level of 5%, should Megaflop make the move? (Assume that the times are normally distributed.)

CASE 9.1*   STUDENT SURROGATES IN MARKET RESEARCH

Researchers in both the business world and the academic world often treat college students as representative of the adult population. This practice reduces sampling costs enormously, but its effectiveness is open to question. An experiment was performed to determine the suitability of using student surrogates in research.

The study used three groups of people:

1. The first consisted of 59 adults (18 years of age or older) chosen so that they represented by age and occupation the adult population of a midwestern state.
2. The second consisted of 42 students enrolled in an introductory marketing course at a public university. Many of the students were registered in a business program, but few were marketing majors.
3. The third consisted of 33 students enrolled in an advanced marketing course, almost all of whom were marketing majors.

* Adapted from R. Kesavan, D. G. Anderson, and O. Mascarenhas, "Students as Surrogates in Advertising Research," *Developments in Marketing Science* 7 (1984): 438–41.

TABLE A   COMPARISON OF RESPONSES OF INTRODUCTORY MARKETING STUDENTS, ADVANCED
                   MARKETING STUDENTS, AND ADULTS: BELIEVABILITY OF AD

Advertisement	Introductory Marketing Students		Advanced Marketing Students		Adults	
	$\bar{x}$	s	$\bar{x}$	s	$\bar{x}$	s
1	6.7	2.5	6.6	3.1	6.9	2.7
2	7.3	2.6	7.2	2.3	6.1	3.0
3	5.9	2.7	6.6	2.8	7.0	2.9

TABLE B   COMPARISON OF RESPONSES OF INTRODUCTORY MARKETING STUDENTS, ADVANCED
                   MARKETING STUDENTS, AND ADULTS: INTEREST IN AD

Advertisement	Introductory Marketing Students		Advanced Marketing Students		Adults	
	$\bar{x}$	s	$\bar{x}$	s	$\bar{x}$	s
1	4.5	3.2	4.3	2.8	5.9	2.4
2	6.0	2.7	6.1	2.5	4.5	2.9
3	4.0	2.6	4.3	2.8	5.8	3.1

The experiment consisted of showing each group a sequence of three 30-second television advertisements dealing with financial institutions. Each respondent was asked to assess each commercial on the basis of believability and interest. The responses were recorded on a 10-point graphic rating scale, where a higher rating represented greater believability or interest. The responses were treated as interval data, and the sample means and standard deviations were calculated. These are shown in Tables A and B.

What conclusions can you draw regarding the suitability of using students as surrogates in marketing research?

CASE 9.2*   BONANZA INTERNATIONAL

We recommend the use of a computer for this case. The data listed below are also stored on the data disk.

Bonanza International is one of the top 15 fast-food franchisers in the United States. Like McDonald's, Burger King, and most others, Bonanza uses a menu

---

* Adapted from M. G. Sobol and T. E. Barry, "Item Positioning for Profits: Menu Boards at Bonanza International," *Interfaces* (February 1980): 55–60.

board to inform customers about its products. One of Bonanza's bright young executives believes that not all positions on the board are equal; that is, the position of the menu item on the board influences sales. If this hypothesis is true, Bonanza would be well-advised to place its high-profit items in the positions that produce the highest sales.

After watching the eye movements of several people, the executive determined that customers first look at the upper right-hand corner, then cross the top row toward the left-hand side, then move down to the lower left-hand corner, and finally scan across the bottom toward the right. (See Figure 9.10.)

This analysis suggests that items listed in the upper right-hand corner may achieve higher sales than items listed in the lower left-hand corner. In order to test this hypothesis, ten stores with similar characteristics were selected as test restaurants, and two moderately popular items were selected as test menu items. During weeks 1 and 3 (of a four-week study), item *A* was placed in the upper right-hand corner and item *B* was placed in the lower left-hand corner. During weeks 2 and 4, the positions were reversed. The number of sales of each item was recorded, and the results are summarized in Tables A and B.

On the basis of the data, what can you conclude regarding the executive's belief?

FIGURE 9.10   *DIRECTION OF EYE MOVEMENT ACROSS MENU BOARD*

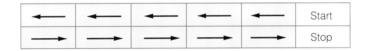

TABLE A   *SALES OF ITEM **A***

Store	Sales with Item *A* in Upper Right-hand Corner	Sales with Item *A* in Lower Left-hand Corner
1	642	485
2	912	681
3	221	138
4	312	237
5	295	258
6	775	725
7	511	553
8	726	524
9	476	384
10	570	529

| TABLE B | SALES OF ITEM *B* |

Store	Sales with Item *B* in Upper Right-hand Corner	Sales with Item *B* in Lower Left-hand Corner
1	372	351
2	334	312
3	160	136
4	285	305
5	271	189
6	464	430
7	327	310
8	642	557
9	213	215
10	493	446

CASE 9.3*   SEXUAL CONTENT ADVERTISEMENTS

This case requires the use of a computer. The data are not shown below but are stored on the data disk.

MKT   A successful television advertisement must attract and hold the attention of the viewer. Numerous techniques are used for this purpose, but one of the most popular is to use ads with sexual content. A potential negative consequence of this approach is that some viewers may be offended. In an investigation of the effect of advertisements with sexual content, two groups of university students were selected: class *A* (*n* = 53) was shown ten ads with sexual content, and class *B* (*n* = 60) was shown ten similar ads without sexual content. Immediately after viewing each ad, the two groups were asked to rate it (on a scale from 1 to 5, where 1 is high and 5 is low) on its power to attract attention and to hold attention. For each student, the ratings for all ten ads were totaled.

Two days after viewing the advertisements, each student was asked to name the specific brands mentioned in the ads. The totals (out of 10) for each student were computed. What conclusions can you draw from these data?

The data are stored on the data disk using the following format.

* Adapted from L. T. Patterson and J. K. Ross, "A Study of Sex in Advertising," *Developments in Marketing Science* 7 (1984): 244–48.

TABLE A   CLASS A

Student	Attract Attention Ratings	Hold Attention Ratings	Correct Responses
1	11	20	10
2	15	32	8
3	18	34	9
⋮	⋮	⋮	⋮
53	8	37	5

TABLE B   CLASS B

Student	Attract Attention Ratings	Hold Attention Ratings	Correct Responses
1	32	32	7
2	14	27	6
3	17	13	4
⋮	⋮	⋮	⋮
60	26	32	5

CASE 9.4*   ACCOUNTING COURSE EXEMPTIONS

ACC One of the problems encountered in teaching accounting in a business program is the issue of what to do with students who have taken one or more accounting courses in high school. Should these students be exempted from the university accounting course, or can it be assumed that the high-school course does not cover

---

* Adapted from E. Morash, G. Walsh, and N. M. Young, "Accounting for Performance: An Analysis of the Relationship Between Success in Introductory Accounting in University and Prior Study of Accounting in High School," *Proceedings of the 14th Annual Atlantic Schools of Business Conference* (1984), pp. 13–44.

sufficient material and that students with high-school accounting are not likely to outperform students without high-school accounting?

In order to examine this issue, the students enrolled in the third year of the Bachelor of Commerce program at St. Mary's University were sampled. In the third year of this program, two introductory accounting half-credits are required: ACC 241 and ACC 242. Of the 638 students enrolled in ACC 241 in the fall semesters of 1982 and 1983, 374 were selected because of the similarities in their high-school backgrounds (excluding high-school accounting). Student files were examined for all 374 students, of whom 275 continued on to ACC 242 in the winter quarters of 1983 and 1984. Table A summarizes the high-school accounting background of these students. Assume that the 99 students who took ACC 241 but not ACC 242 failed ACC 241. The average grades for each group of students are shown in Table B. What conclusions can you draw on the basis of these data? What exemption policy would you recommend?

TABLE A   *HIGH-SCHOOL ACCOUNTING BACKGROUNDS OF STUDENTS IN THE SAMPLE*

Number of Years of High-School Accounting	Number of Students in ACC 241	Number of Students in ACC 242
0	296	210
1	24	15
2	54	50
All students	374	275

TABLE B   *AVERAGE GRADES OF STUDENTS IN THE SAMPLE*

Number of Years of High-School Accounting	Grades in ACC 241		Grades in ACC 242	
	Mean	Standard Deviation	Mean	Standard Deviation
0	2.0281	1.4189	2.2081	1.2721
1	2.0238	1.5611	1.9583	1.1172
2	2.7778	1.1313	2.1591	1.1653
All students	2.1528	1.4089	2.1867	1.2426

████████ *CASE 9.5**   *STUDENT PERFORMANCE AND CLASS SIZE*

This case requires the use of a computer. The data are not shown below but are stored on the data disk.

EDUC   The rapid increase in enrollment in North American business schools has led to larger classes. What effect does class size have on student performance? In an experiment to answer this question, two sections—one large and one small—in a marketing class were offered during each of three semesters. The numbers of students in the large sections were 121, 156, and 179. The numbers of students in the small sections were 40, 27, and 27. In all classes, the same material was covered, identical tests and grading policies were used, and the same instructor taught all sections.

The grades (A = 4, B = 3, C = 2, D = 1, and F = 0) and the number of absences for each student were recorded. What conclusions can you draw? These data are stored on the data disk in the following way.

TABLE A   LARGE CLASSES

Student	Grade	Number of Absences
1	3	3
2	3	2
3	4	1
⋮	⋮	⋮
456	1	7

TABLE B   SMALL CLASSES

Student	Grade	Number of Absences
1	2	3
2	2	0
3	2	4
⋮	⋮	⋮
94	2	2

* Adapted from C. E. Vincent and S. E. Lamb, "The Effect of Class Size on Quality of Instruction—Large Class Size Versus Small," *Developments in Marketing Science* 6 (1983): 246–47.

MINITAB
INSTRUCTIONS

INFERENCE ABOUT $\mu_1 - \mu_2$ WITH σ_1^2 AND σ_2^2 UNKNOWN: INDEPENDENT SAMPLES

Two different sets of commands can be used to make inferences about $\mu_1 - \mu_2$. If the observations of sample 1 are stored in one column and the observations of sample 2 are stored in a second column, the data are said to be *unstacked*. The following example illustrates the input of unstacked data:

```
READ C1 C2
10      15
12      13
17      14
20      16
END
```

If all of the observations of both samples are stored in one column, and the second column simply keeps track of which sample the data were drawn from, the data are said to be *stacked*. For example, the preceding data could be input as follows:

```
READ C1 C2
10     1
12     1
17     1
20     1
15     2
13     2
14     2
16     2
END
```

In certain situations, it may be necessary or desirable to change the format of the data. The STACK command converts unstacked data into stacked data. For instance, if the data base appears as

```
C1    C2
10    15
12    13
17    14
20    16
```

the command

```
STACK (C1) ON (C2) PUT IN (C3)
```

creates a third column consisting of

```
C3
10
12
17
20
15
13
14
16
```

The subcommand SUBSCRIPTS is used to create the index or subscript of the variables. The commands

```
STACK (C1) ON (C2) PUT IN (C3);
SUBSCRIPTS INTO C4.
```

would create the following columns:

```
C3    C4
10    1
12    1
17    1
20    1
15    2
13    2
14    2
16    2
```

The UNSTACK command can be used to convert stacked data into unstacked data. For example, suppose that we have data in the following form:

```
C1    C2
22    1
18    2
```

```
37    1
91    3
83    3
65    1
35    2
```

The command and subcommand

```
UNSTACK (C1) INTO (C3) (C4) (C5);
SUBSCRIPTS C2.
```

would convert the data into

```
C3    C4    C5
22    18    91
37    35    83
65
```

The appropriate technique to use in making inferences about $\mu_1 - \mu_2$ depends on the sample size and on whether or not σ_1^2 equals σ_2^2. If $n_1 > 30$ and $n_2 > 30$, the appropriate test statistic is

$$z = \frac{(\bar{x}_1 - \bar{x}_2) - (\mu_1 - \mu_2)}{\sqrt{\dfrac{s_1^2}{n_1} + \dfrac{s_2^2}{n_2}}}$$

If the data are unstacked, we perform a test of $\mu_1 - \mu_2$ by using the command

```
TWOSAMPLE T C1 C2
```

where the observations of sample 1 are stored in column 1, and the observations of sample 2 are stored in column 2. The command tests the hypotheses

$$H_0 : (\mu_1 - \mu_2) = 0$$
$$H_A : (\mu_1 - \mu_2) \neq 0$$

The subcommand ALTERNATIVE is used for a one-tail test. That is,

```
ALTERNATIVE 1
```

tests

$$H_A : (\mu_1 - \mu_2) > 0$$

whereas

```
ALTERNATIVE -1
```

tests

$$H_A : (\mu_1 - \mu_2) < 0$$

If the data are stacked, we use the command

```
TWOT C1 C2
```

where the observations of both samples are stored in column 1, and column 2 indicates the sample each observation is from. The output includes the value of the test statistic, the *p*-value, and the 95% confidence interval estimate of $\mu_1 - \mu_2$. If you examine this output, you will see that the test statistic is referred to as *t* and that the degrees of freedom are provided even though we perform a *z*-test. This discrepancy is explained in the footnote on page 343. We suggest that you simply read the *t*-statistic value, label it *z*, and draw your conclusion about the test from this value. To answer Example 9.6, we would proceed as follows (assuming that the data are unstacked):

```
TWOSAMPLE T C1 C2;
ALTERNATIVE 1.
```

The output would be

```
TWOSAMPLE T FOR C1 VS C2
        N     MEAN    ST DEV    SE MEAN
C1     50     43.7     3.44      0.486
C2     50     41.5     6.80      0.962

95 PCT CI FOR MU C1-MU C2 (0.09, 4.31)
TTEST MU C1=MU C2 (VS GT): T=2.04 P=.022 DF=72.5
```

The commands

```
TWOT C1 C2;
ALTERNATIVE 1.
```

would produce exactly the same output if the data were stacked.

If the two population variances are equal and $n_1 \le 30$ or $n_2 \le 30$, we use the test statistic

$$t = \frac{(\bar{x}_1 - \bar{x}_2) - (\mu_1 - \mu_2)}{\sqrt{s_p^2\left(\dfrac{1}{n_1} + \dfrac{1}{n_2}\right)}}$$

The subcommand POOLED instructs the computer to use this statistic. With unstacked data, we would test $\mu_1 - \mu_2$ as follows:

```
TWOSAMPLE T C1 C2;
POOLED.
```

With stacked data, we would type

```
TWOT C1 C2;
POOLED.
```

We'll illustrate these commands by doing Example 9.4 in two different ways: with unstacked data, and with stacked data. With unstacked data, the commands are

```
SET C1
8.2 5.3 6.5 5.1 9.7 10.8
END
```

```
SET C2
9.5 8.3 7.5 10.9 11.3 9.3 8.8 8.0
END
TWOSAMPLE T C1 C2;
POOLED.
```

With stacked data, the commands are

```
READ C1 C2
  8.2  1
  5.3  1
  6.5  1
  5.1  1
  9.7  1
 10.8  1
  9.5  2
  8.3  2
  7.5  2
 10.9  2
 11.3  2
  9.3  2
  8.8  2
  8.0  2
END
TWOT C1 C2;
POOLED.
```

The output in either case is

```
TWOSAMPLE T FOR C1 VS C2
       N    MEAN    STDEV    SE MEAN
C1     6    7.60    2.36      0.96
C2     8    9.20    1.35      0.48
95 PCT CI FOR MU C1-MU C2: (-3.76, 0.56)
TTEST MU C1=MU C2 (VS NE): T=-1.61 P=0.13 DF=12.0
```

INFERENCE ABOUT $\mu_1 - \mu_2$: MATCHED PAIRS EXPERIMENT

If the paired observations are stored in columns 1 and 2, the command

```
LET C3=C1-C2
```

calculates the differences and stores them in column 3. The command

```
TTEST 0 C3
```

performs a two-tail test of μ_D, where the null hypothesis is

$$H_0: \mu_D = 0$$

The **ALTERNATIVE** subcommand performs a one-tail test. The command

```
TINTERVAL.90 C3
```

computes the 90% confidence interval estimate of μ_D. Example 9.7 is answered as follows:

```
READ C1 C2
42.6   43.8
37.2   41.3
50.0   49.7
43.9   45.7
53.6   52.5
32.5   36.8
46.5   47.0
39.3   40.7
END
LET C3=C1-C2
TTEST 0 C3;
ALTERNATIVE -1.
```

The computer will then respond in the following way:

```
TEST OF MU=0.00 VS MU L.T. 0.00
      N    MEAN    STDEV   SE MEAN     T     P VALUE
C3    8   -1.487   1.919    0.679    -2.19    0.032
```

SAS INSTRUCTIONS

INFERENCE ABOUT $\mu_1 - \mu_2$ WITH σ_1^2 AND σ_2^2 UNKNOWN: INDEPENDENT SAMPLES

TESTING $\mu_1 - \mu_2$

Two different test statistics are used in making inferences about $\mu_1 - \mu_2$, with σ_1^2 and σ_2^2 unknown, when the samples are independent. If $n_1 > 30$ and $n_2 > 30$, the test statistic is

$$z = \frac{(\bar{x}_1 - \bar{x}_2) - (\mu_1 - \mu_2)}{\sqrt{\dfrac{s_1^2}{n_1} + \dfrac{s_2^2}{n_2}}}$$

When either $n_1 \leq 30$ or $n_2 \leq 30$, and $\sigma_1^2 = \sigma_2^2$, we use the test statistic

$$t = \frac{(\bar{x}_1 - \bar{x}_2) - (\mu_1 - \mu_2)}{\sqrt{s_p^2 \left(\dfrac{1}{n_1} + \dfrac{1}{n_2} \right)}}$$

The TTEST procedure performs both tests and lets you choose the one you want to use. Before you can use this procedure, however, the data must be input in the following way. Two variables are input: the first represents the values of both samples, and the second indicates which sample the observation is from. This procedure performs a two-tail test of $\mu_1 - \mu_2$, with the following hypotheses:

$$H_0 : (\mu_1 - \mu_2) = 0$$
$$H_A : (\mu_1 - \mu_2) \neq 0$$

To illustrate, the procedure solves Example 9.4 as follows:

```
DATA;
INPUT X SAMPLE;
```

```
CARDS;
 8.2  1
 5.3  1
 6.5  1
 5.1  1
 9.7  1
10.8  1
 9.5  2
 8.3  2
 7.5  2
10.9  2
11.3  2
 9.3  2
 8.8  2
 8.0  2
PROC TTEST;
CLASS SAMPLE;
VAR X;
```

Notice that the PROC TTEST is followed by the statement CLASS SAMPLE, which identifies the sample that the observation is from. The test is to be performed on the variable x.

The output appears as follows:

```
Variable: X
```

SAMPLE	N	Mean	Std Dev	Std Error
1	6	7.6000	2.3562	0.9619
2	8	9.2000	1.3469	0.4762

Variances	T	DF	Prob > |T|
Unequal	-1.4906	7.4	0.1774
Equal	-1.6134	12.0	0.1326

We can solve Example 9.6 in a similar manner, except that (since $n_1 > 30$, and $n_2 > 30$) we must use the first value of t shown in the output. The output for Example 9.6 appears as follows (assuming that all 100 observations have been input):

```
Variable: X
```

SAMPLE	N	Mean	Std Dev	Std Error
1	50	43.7000	3.4415	0.4867
2	50	41.5000	6.8016	0.9619

Variances	T	DF	Prob > |T|
Unequal	2.0409	72.5	0.0448
Equal	2.0409	98.0	0.0440

ESTIMATING $\mu_1 - \mu_2$

Since the values of $\bar{x}_1, \bar{x}_2, s_1,$ and s_2 are output as part of the test of $\mu_1 - \mu_2$, we can easily construct the confidence interval estimate of $\mu_1 - \mu_2$. When $n_1 \leq 30$ or $n_2 \leq 30$, and $\sigma_1^2 = \sigma_2^2$, we first have to compute s_p^2. The interval estimate is

$$(\bar{x}_1 - \bar{x}_2) \pm t_{\alpha/2} \sqrt{s_p^2 \left(\frac{1}{n_1} + \frac{1}{n_2} \right)}$$

When $n_1 > 30$ and $n_2 > 30$, we estimate $\mu_1 - \mu_2$ with

$$(\bar{x}_1 - \bar{x}_2) \pm z_{\alpha/2} \sqrt{\frac{s_1^2}{n_1} + \frac{s_2^2}{n_2}}$$

INFERENCE ABOUT $\mu_1 - \mu_2$: MATCHED PAIRS EXPERIMENT

TESTING μ_D

In order to test μ_D, we calculate each of the paired differences with the statement

```
D=X1-X2
```

We then perform a *t*-test on those differences, using the MEANS procedure. To illustrate, we will solve Example 9.7. Notice that input variables X1 and X2 are in separate columns, unlike their layout when we tested $\mu_1 - \mu_2$ from independent samples. The commands for solving Example 9.7 are as follows:

```
DATA;
INPUT X1 X2;
D=X1-X2;
CARDS;
42.6   43.8
37.2   41.3
50.0   49.7
43.9   45.7
53.6   52.5
32.5   36.8
46.5   47.0
39.3   40.7
PROC MEANS N MEAN T PRT;
VAR D;
```

The computer then prints out the following statistics:

```
Analysis Variable: D
N       Mean            T      Prob>|T|
8      -1.4875      -2.1919      0.0645
```

ESTIMATING μ_D

If we type the statements

```
PROC MEANS;
VAR D;
```

instead of (or after) the last two statements in Example 9.7, the output includes $\bar{x}_D$ and $s_D/\sqrt{n_D}$, from which we could produce the confidence interval estimate of μ_D.

COMPUTER EXERCISES

9.81 Convert the following unstacked data into stacked data:

x_1	x_2
29	42
23	36
36	39
41	30
40	33
38	45
34	35
28	38
39	46
	31
	32
	40
	33

9.82 Convert the following stacked data into unstacked data:

x_1	x_2
13	1
6	1
5	1
7	1
7	1
9	2
7	2
8	2
12	2
9	2
13	2
15	2
17	2

9.83 The following data were generated from samples of size $n_1 = 9$ and $n_2 = 13$ drawn from two normal populations. Test at the 5% significance level to determine if μ_1 is greater than μ_2.

x_1	x_2
11.3	11.0
17.5	10.9
10.6	10.3
12.3	11.5
11.5	16.3
	10.8
	11.9

9.84 Convert the data in Exercise 9.83 into stacked data, and repeat the test.

9.85 An experiment was conducted in which samples of size $n_1 = 8$ and $n_2 = 11$ were drawn from two normal populations. Do the resulting data (shown next) allow us to conclude at the 10% significance level that μ_1 differs from μ_2?

x (observations from both samples)	Sample
136	1
128	1
115	1
129	1
153	1
141	1
166	1
125	1
152	2
162	2
154	2

(continued)

x (observations from both samples)	Sample
148	2
163	2
171	2
160	2
175	2
166	2
141	2
132	2

9.86 The following observations were drawn from two normal populations. Test with $\alpha = .01$ to determine if μ_2 is greater than μ_1.

x (observations from both samples)	Sample
3.6	1
2.5	1
2.1	1
0.9	1
2.8	1
2.5	1
3.6	2
3.8	2
2.7	2
3.1	2
3.4	2
3.9	2
2.9	2
3.9	2

9.87 The following observations were drawn from a matched pairs experiment. Do these data allow us to conclude that the mean of population 1 is greater than the mean of population 2? (Use $\alpha = .01$.)

Matched Pair	x_1	x_2	Matched Pair	x_1	x_2
1	17	20	11	16	15
2	25	24	12	14	18
3	18	14	13	23	22
4	16	18	14	29	21
5	23	21	15	17	17
6	25	24	16	21	20
7	12	15	17	16	15
8	17	13	18	20	18
9	19	19	19	18	19
10	15	13	20	23	18

9.88 Given the following observations generated from a matched pairs experiment, can we conclude at the 5% significance level that the mean of population 2 is greater than the mean of population 1?

Matched Pair	x_1	x_2	Matched Pair	x_1	x_2
1	6	8	9	9	7
2	5	9	10	3	6
3	5	4	11	1	4
4	7	11	12	5	6
5	4	6	13	7	4
6	5	5	14	9	11
7	9	8	15	3	7
8	11	14			

9.89 The following data were generated from a matched pairs experiment. Do these results allow us to conclude at the 10% significance level that the two population means differ?

Matched Pair	x_1	x_2	Matched Pair	x_1	x_2
1	21.6	19.5	6	17.5	17.7
2	27.3	26.5	7	30.6	25.7
3	23.6	25.3	8	29.3	25.4
4	32.0	29.8	9	18.6	15.6
5	26.5	26.3	10	29.3	28.8

SOLUTIONS TO SELF-CORRECTING EXERCISES

9.12 $H_0: (\mu_1 - \mu_2) = 0$
$H_A: (\mu_1 - \mu_2) \neq 0$

Rejection region: $|z| > 1.96$

Test statistic:

$$z = \frac{(\bar{x}_1 - \bar{x}_2) - (\mu_1 - \mu_2)}{\sqrt{\dfrac{\sigma_1^2}{n_1} + \dfrac{\sigma_2^2}{n_2}}} = \frac{(352 - 375) - 0}{\sqrt{\dfrac{400}{20} + \dfrac{625}{15}}}$$

$= -2.93$

Conclusion: Reject H_0.

There is enough evidence to allow us to conclude that the average distances traveled by the two types of baseball differ.

p-value $= 2P(z < -2.93) = 2(.0017) = .0034$

9.32 a. $H_0: (\mu_1 - \mu_2) = 0$
$H_A: (\mu_1 - \mu_2) > 0$

Rejection region: $t > 1.860$

Test statistic:

$$t = \frac{(\bar{x}_1 - \bar{x}_2) - (\mu_1 - \mu_2)}{\sqrt{s_p^2\left(\dfrac{1}{n_1} + \dfrac{1}{n_2}\right)}} = \frac{(34.2 - 28.4) - 0}{\sqrt{17.25\left(\dfrac{1}{5} + \dfrac{1}{5}\right)}}$$

$= 2.21$

Conclusion: Reject H_0.

At the 5% significance level, there is enough evidence to show that the average weight gain for babies fed on the producer's baby food exceeds that for babies fed on the competitor's product.

b. $(\bar{x}_1 - \bar{x}_2) \pm t_{\alpha/2}\sqrt{s_p^2\left(\dfrac{1}{n_1} + \dfrac{1}{n_2}\right)}$

$= (34.2 - 28.4) \pm 1.860\sqrt{17.25\left(\dfrac{1}{5} + \dfrac{1}{5}\right)}$

$= 5.8 \pm 4.89$

c. You must assume that weight gains are normally distributed.

9.50 Let $D = x_1 - x_2$

$H_0: \mu_D = 0$

$H_A: \mu_D < 0$

Rejection region: $t < -1.415$

Test statistic: $t = \dfrac{\bar{x}_D - \mu_D}{s_D/\sqrt{n_D}} = \dfrac{-3.25 - 0}{5.01/\sqrt{8}} = -1.83$

Conclusion: Reject H_0.

Yes, there is enough evidence to allow us to conclude that the average CPU time for computer 1 is less than that for computer 2.

9.64 a. $H_0: \sigma_1^2/\sigma_2^2 = 1$
$H_A: \sigma_1^2/\sigma_2^2 < 1$

Rejection region: $F < .304$

Test statistic: $F = \dfrac{s_1^2}{s_2^2} = \dfrac{82.23}{530.21} = .155$

Conclusion: Reject H_0.

There is sufficient evidence to allow us to conclude that investment 2 is riskier than investment 1.

b. You must assume that the returns are normally distributed.

c. $\text{LCL} = \left(\dfrac{s_1^2}{s_2^2}\right)\dfrac{1}{F_{\alpha/2, v_1, v_2}} = \left(\dfrac{82.23}{530.21}\right)\dfrac{1}{6.72} = .023$

$\text{UCL} = \left(\dfrac{s_1^2}{s_2^2}\right)F_{\alpha/2, v_2, v_1} = \left(\dfrac{82.23}{530.21}\right)5.61 = .870$

INFERENCE ABOUT THE COMPARISON OF TWO POPULATIONS: NOMINAL SCALE

INTRODUCTION

In this chapter we present statistical inference techniques that are used when the problem objective is to compare two populations and the data scale is nominal. Unlike the previous chapter, where we dealt with two parameters and three different formulas for drawing inferences about $\mu_1 - \mu_2$, this chapter will be quite short and simple. The material's simplicity should not, however, be interpreted as a sign of its impracticality. The techniques presented here can be extremely useful in a wide range of applications, of which the following cases are illustrative.

Case 1. Market managers and advertisers are eager to know which segments of the population are buying their products. If they can determine these groups, they can target their advertising messages and tailor their products to these customers. For example, if advertisers determine that the decision to purchase a particular household product is made more frequently by men than by women, the interests and concerns of men will be the focus of most commercial messages. The advertising media also depend on whether the product is of greater interest to men or to women. The most common way of measuring this factor is to find the **difference in the proportions** of men and women buying the product. In these situations, the parameter to be tested or estimated is $p_1 - p_2$.

Case 2. Production supervisors and quality-control engineers are responsible for measuring, controlling, and minimizing the number of defective units that are produced. Frequently more than one method or machine can be used to perform the manufacturing function. The decision as to which one of two machines to acquire and use often depends on which machine produces a smaller proportion of defective units—or in other words on the parameter $p_1 - p_2$, the **difference in the proportions** of defective units from each machine.

Case 3. Politicians are constantly concerned about how the voting public perceives their actions and behavior. Of particular interest are the extent to which constituents approve of a politician's behavior, and the ways in which that approval changes over time. As a result, they frequently poll the public to determine the **proportion** of voters who support them, and whether that support has changed since the previous survey. The parameter of interest to them is $p_1 - p_2$, where p_1 is the proportion of support at present, and p_2 is the proportion of support in the previous poll.

In the next section, we will present the techniques of hypothesis testing and estimation for the parameter $p_1 - p_2$. The pattern adopted in Chapters 7, 8, and 9 will be repeated here. We identify the best estimator and its sampling distribution, and from this we derive the two inference methods. The process of estimation and hypothesis testing is the same as before, as are the determination of the null and alternative hypotheses and the type of conclusions drawn. In fact, everything will be so familiar that we hope we won't bore you needlessly.

SECTION 10.2 **INFERENCE ABOUT $p_1 - p_2$**

In order to draw inferences about $p_1 - p_2$, we take a sample of size n_1 from population 1 and a sample of size n_2 from population 2. For each sample, we calculate the sample proportion of successes and then obtain $\hat{p}_1 = x_1/n_1$ (where x_1 is the number of successes in sample 1) and $\hat{p}_2 = x_2/n_2$ (where x_2 is the number of successes in sample 2). It can be shown that the statistic $\hat{p}_1 - \hat{p}_2$ is an unbiased and consistent estimator of $p_1 - p_2$. Figure 10.1 describes the sampling process.

SAMPLING DISTRIBUTION OF $p_1 - p_2$

In repeated samples of size n_1 from population 1 and of size n_2 from population 2, we calculate $\hat{p}_1 - \hat{p}_2$. Using the same logic we used in Chapter 8 to develop the sampling distribution of $\hat{p}$, we can demonstrate that $(\hat{p}_1 - \hat{p}_2)$ is approximately normally distributed (provided that the sample sizes are sufficiently large—that is, provided that $n_1 p_1$ and $n_1 q_1 \geq 5$, and $n_2 p_2$ and $n_2 q_2 \geq 5$), with mean $p_1 - p_2$ and standard deviation

$$\sqrt{\frac{p_1 q_1}{n_1} + \frac{p_2 q_2}{n_2}}$$

Thus, the variable

$$z = \frac{(\hat{p}_1 - \hat{p}_2) - (p_1 - p_2)}{\sqrt{\frac{p_1 q_1}{n_1} + \frac{p_2 q_2}{n_2}}}$$

is approximately standard normally distributed, provided that the sample sizes are sufficiently large. Since p_1 and p_2 are unknown, we express the sample size

---

FIGURE 10.1 SAMPLING FROM TWO POPULATIONS WHOSE DATA SCALE IS NOMINAL

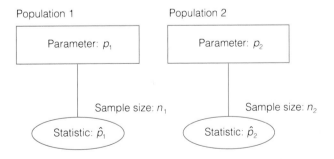

requirement as $n_1\hat{p}_1$, $n_1\hat{q}_1$, $n_2\hat{p}_2$, and $n_2\hat{q}_2 \geq 5$. This variable is the source of the statistical inference that follows.

TESTING $p_1 - p_2$

We would like to use the z-formula just described as our test statistic; however, the standard deviation of $\hat{p}_1 - \hat{p}_2$ is

$$\sqrt{\frac{p_1 q_1}{n_1} + \frac{p_2 q_2}{n_2}}$$

which is unknown, since both p_1 and p_2 are unknown. As a result, the standard deviation of $\hat{p}_1 - \hat{p}_2$ must be estimated from the sample data. There are two different estimators of this quantity, and the determination of which one to use depends on the null hypothesis. If the null hypothesis states that $p_1 - p_2 = 0$, the hypothesized equality of the two population proportions allows us to pool the data from the two samples. Thus the estimated standard deviation of $\hat{p}_1 - \hat{p}_2$ is

$$\sqrt{\hat{p}\hat{q}\left(\frac{1}{n_1} + \frac{1}{n_2}\right)}$$

where $\hat{p}$ is the **pooled proportion estimate,** defined as

$$\hat{p} = \frac{x_1 + x_2}{n_1 + n_2}$$

and where

$$\hat{q} = 1 - \hat{p}$$

The principle used in estimating the standard deviation of $\hat{p}_1 - \hat{p}_2$ is analogous to that applied in Section 9.3 to produce the pooled variance estimate s_p^2, which is used to test $\mu_1 - \mu_2$ with σ_1^2 and σ_2^2 unknown but equal. That principle roughly states that, where possible, pooling data from two samples produces a better estimator of the standard deviation. Here, this is made possible by hypothesizing (under H_0) that $p_1 = p_2$. (In Section 9.3, we used the pooled variance estimate because we assumed that $\sigma_1^2 = \sigma_2^2$.) We will call this application *Case 1.*

Test Statistic for $p_1 - p_2$: Case 1

If the null hypothesis specifies

$$H_0: (p_1 - p_2) = 0$$

the test statistic is

$$z = \frac{(\hat{p}_1 - \hat{p}_2) - (p_1 - p_2)}{\sqrt{\hat{p}\hat{q}\left(\dfrac{1}{n_1} + \dfrac{1}{n_2}\right)}}$$

The second case applies when, under the null hypothesis, we state that $p_1 - p_2 = D$, where D is some value *other than zero*. Under such circumstances, we cannot pool the sample data to estimate the standard deviation of $\hat{p}_1 - \hat{p}_2$. The appropriate test statistic is described next, as *Case 2*.

Test Statistic for $p_1 - p_2$: Case 2

If the null hypothesis specifies

$$H_0: (p_1 - p_2) = D \qquad (D \neq 0)$$

the test statistic is

$$z = \frac{(\hat{p}_1 - \hat{p}_2) - (p_1 - p_2)}{\sqrt{\dfrac{\hat{p}_1 \hat{q}_1}{n_1} + \dfrac{\hat{p}_2 \hat{q}_2}{n_2}}}$$

Notice that this test statistic is determined by simply substituting the sample statistics $\hat{p}_1$, $\hat{q}_1$, $\hat{p}_2$, and $\hat{q}_2$ in the standardized version of the sampling distribution.

You will find that, in most practical applications (including the exercises and cases in this text), Case 1 applies—since, in most problems, we wish to know if the two population proportions differ $(H_A: (p_1 - p_2) \neq 0)$ or if one proportion exceeds the other $(H_A: (p_1 - p_2) > 0$ or $H_A: (p_1 - p_2) < 0)$. In some problems, however, the objective is to determine if one proportion exceeds the other by a specific nonzero quantity. In such situations, Case 2 applies.

EXAMPLE 10.1

An insurance company is thinking about offering discounts on its life insurance policies to nonsmokers. As part of its analysis, it randomly selects 200 men who are 50 years old and asks them if they smoke at least one pack of cigarettes per day, and if they have ever suffered from heart disease. The results indicate that 20 out of 80 smokers and 15 out of 120 nonsmokers suffer from heart disease. Can we conclude at the 5% level of significance that smokers have a higher incidence of heart disease than nonsmokers?

Solution.   The problem objective is to compare two populations (50-year-old men who smoke is one population, and 50-year-old men who don't smoke is the other). The data scale is nominal, since the responses are "suffer from heart disease" and "don't suffer from heart disease." The parameter of interest is therefore $p_1 - p_2$, where p_1 is the proportion of smokers who suffer from heart disease, and p_2 is the proportion of nonsmokers who suffer from heart disease. Since we want to know if p_1 is greater than p_2, the alternative hypothesis is $H_A: (p_1 - p_2) > 0$. As a result, the null hypothesis states that $p_1 - p_2 = 0$. This example is described in Case 1, where the test statistic is

$$z = \frac{(\hat{p}_1 - \hat{p}_2) - (p_1 - p_2)}{\sqrt{\hat{p}\hat{q}\left(\dfrac{1}{n_1} + \dfrac{1}{n_2}\right)}}$$

The complete test is as follows:

$H_0 : (p_1 - p_2) = 0$

$H_A : (p_1 - p_2) > 0$

Test statistic:

$$z = \frac{(\hat{p}_1 - \hat{p}_2) - (p_1 - p_2)}{\sqrt{\hat{p}\hat{q}\left(\dfrac{1}{n_1} + \dfrac{1}{n_2}\right)}}$$

Rejection region:

$z > z_\alpha$

$> z_{.05}$

> 1.645

Value of the test statistic:

$$\hat{p}_1 = \frac{20}{80} = .25$$

$$\hat{p}_2 = \frac{15}{120} = .125$$

$$\hat{p} = \frac{20 + 15}{80 + 120} = \frac{35}{200} = .175$$

$$z = \frac{(\hat{p}_1 - \hat{p}_2) - (p_1 - p_2)}{\sqrt{\hat{p}\hat{q}\left(\dfrac{1}{n_1} + \dfrac{1}{n_2}\right)}} = \frac{(.25 - .125) - 0}{\sqrt{(.175)(.825)\left(\dfrac{1}{80} + \dfrac{1}{120}\right)}} = 2.28$$

Conclusion: Reject H_0.

There is sufficient evidence to show that the proportion of smokers who suffer from heart disease is greater than the proportion of nonsmokers who do. Figure 10.2 describes this test.

EXAMPLE 10.2

The process that is used to produce a complex component used in medical instruments typically results in defective rates in the 40% range. Recently two

FIGURE 10.2   REJECTION REGION FOR EXAMPLE 10.1

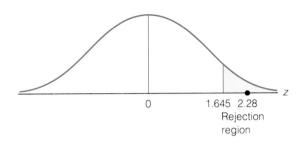

0   1.645 2.28
Rejection
region

innovations have been developed. Innovation 1 appears to be more promising but is considerably more expensive to purchase and operate than innovation 2. After a careful analysis of the costs, management decides that it will adopt innovation 1 only if the proportion of defective components it produces is at least 8% smaller than that produced by innovation 2. In a random sample of 300 units produced by innovation 1, 33 are found to be defective. In a sample of 300 components produced by innovation 2, 84 are found to be defective. At the 1% significance level, can we conclude that there is sufficient evidence to justify adopting innovation 1?

Solution.   The problem objective is to compare two populations (components produced by the two innovations), and the data scale is nominal (the value of the variable is either "defective" or "nondefective"). It follows that the parameter of interest is $p_1 - p_2$. Because we wish to know if there is sufficient statistical evidence to conclude that p_1 is at least .08 less than p_2, the alternative hypothesis is

$$H_A : (p_1 - p_2) < -.08$$

which means that the test statistic is described in Case 2. The complete test is as follows:

$$H_0 : (p_1 - p_2) = -.08$$
$$H_A : (p_1 - p_2) < -.08$$

Test statistic:

$$z = \frac{(\hat{p}_1 - \hat{p}_2) - (p_1 - p_2)}{\sqrt{\dfrac{\hat{p}_1 \hat{q}_1}{n_1} + \dfrac{\hat{p}_2 \hat{q}_2}{n_2}}}$$

Rejection region:

$$z < -z_\alpha$$
$$< -z_{.01}$$
$$< -2.33$$

FIGURE 10.3   *REJECTION REGION FOR EXAMPLE 10.2*

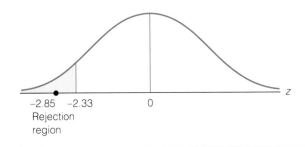

Value of the test statistic:

$$\hat{p}_1 = \frac{33}{300} = .11$$

$$\hat{p}_2 = \frac{84}{300} = .28$$

$$z = \frac{(\hat{p}_1 - \hat{p}_2) - (p_1 - p_2)}{\sqrt{\dfrac{\hat{p}_1 \hat{q}_1}{n_1} + \dfrac{\hat{p}_2 \hat{q}_2}{n_2}}} = \frac{(.11 - .28) - (-.08)}{\sqrt{\dfrac{(.11)(.89)}{300} + \dfrac{(.28)(.72)}{300}}} = -2.85$$

Conclusion: Reject H_0.

There is sufficient evidence to conclude that the proportion of defective components produced by innovation 1 is at least 8% smaller than the proportion of defective components produced by innovation 2. Therefore, the firm should adopt innovation 1. Figure 10.3 describes this test.

ESTIMATING $p_1 - p_2$

The interval estimator of $p_1 - p_2$ can very easily be developed from the sampling distribution of $\hat{p}_1 - \hat{p}_2$.

> **Confidence Interval Estimator of $p_1 - p_2$**
>
> $$(\hat{p}_1 - \hat{p}_2) \pm z_{\alpha/2} \sqrt{\frac{\hat{p}_1 \hat{q}_1}{n_1} + \frac{\hat{p}_2 \hat{q}_2}{n_2}}$$

This formula is valid when $n_1 \hat{p}_1$, $n_1 \hat{q}_1$, $n_2 \hat{p}_2$, and $n_2 \hat{q}_2$ exceed 5. Notice that the standard deviation of $\hat{p}_1 - \hat{p}_2$ is estimated using $\hat{p}_1$, $\hat{q}_1$, $\hat{p}_2$, and $\hat{q}_2$. In this application, we cannot use the pooled proportion estimate because we cannot assume that $p_1 = p_2$.

EXAMPLE 10.3

In 1979, a survey of 1,654 Canadians found that 37% believed that the "energy crisis" (the shortage of gasoline that first appeared in 1973) was a hoax.* In 1984, of 1,814 Canadians, 42% believed that the energy crisis was a hoax. In order to determine the real size of the change, estimate with 90% confidence the difference between the 1979 and 1984 proportions.

Solution.   The scale is nominal (the possible responses are "believe" or "don't believe"), and the problem objective is to compare two populations (the populations in 1979 and in 1984). The parameter to be estimated is $p_1 - p_2$, and its interval estimator is:

$$(\hat{p}_1 - \hat{p}_2) \pm z_{\alpha/2} \sqrt{\frac{\hat{p}_1 \hat{q}_1}{n_1} + \frac{\hat{p}_2 \hat{q}_2}{n_2}}$$

Since $1 - \alpha = .90$, we know that $z_{\alpha/2} = z_{.05} = 1.645$. The 90% confidence interval estimator of $p_1 - p_2$ is

$$(\hat{p}_1 - \hat{p}_2) \pm z_{\alpha/2} \sqrt{\frac{\hat{p}_1 \hat{q}_1}{n_1} + \frac{\hat{p}_2 \hat{q}_2}{n_2}} = (.37 - .42) \pm 1.645 \sqrt{\frac{(.37)(.63)}{1,654} + \frac{(.42)(.58)}{1,814}}$$

$$= -.05 \pm .027$$

or

$$(-.077, -.023)$$

The difference in the 1979 and 1984 proportions lies between $-.077$ and $-.023$; that is, the proportion of Canadians who believed that the energy crisis was a hoax in 1984 is between 2.3 and 7.7 percentage points greater than the 1979 proportion. The increased cynicism was of concern to the government.

SELECTING THE SAMPLE SIZES TO ESTIMATE $p_1 - p_2$

The sample size required to estimate $p_1 - p_2$ is calculated in essentially the same way as was the sample size needed to estimate p. First, we specify the confidence level and the error bound B. Second, we set $\hat{p}_1$ and $\hat{p}_2$ equal to .5 or to some specific values that we believe $\hat{p}_1$ and $\hat{p}_2$ are likely to assume. Finally, we solve for the sample sizes by letting $n_1 = n_2$.

---

* "A Survey of the Canadian Public's Attitudes Towards the Energy Situation," *Consumer and Corporate Affairs, Canada.*

Sample Sizes Necessary to Estimate $p_1 - p_2$

$$n_1 = n_2 = \left[\frac{z_{\alpha/2} \sqrt{\hat{p}_1 \hat{q}_1 + \hat{p}_2 \hat{q}_2}}{B} \right]^2$$

EXAMPLE 10.4

A market surveyor wants to estimate the difference in the proportion of male and female automobile owners who have their cars' oil changed by a national chain of no-wait service centers. The surveyor wishes to estimate the difference in proportions to within .04, with 90% confidence. If she believes that the proportion of men who regularly use the service center is no more than 20% and that the proportion of women who regularly use it is no more than 30%, how large should the samples be?

Solution.   Because we want to estimate $p_1 - p_2$ to within .04, with 90% confidence,

$$B = .04$$

and

$$z_{\alpha/2} = 1.645$$

Since p_1 is believed to be no more than 20% and p_2 no more than 30%, we use $\hat{p}_1 = .20$ and $\hat{p}_2 = .30$. Thus,

$$n_1 = n_2 = \left[\frac{z_{\alpha/2} \sqrt{\hat{p}_1 \hat{q}_1 + \hat{p}_2 \hat{q}_2}}{B} \right]^2 = \left[\frac{1.645 \sqrt{(.2)(.8) + (.3)(.7)}}{.04} \right]^2$$

$$= (25.02)^2 = 626$$

In order for the surveyor to estimate $p_1 - p_2$ to within .04 with 90% confidence, the sample sizes should be $n_1 = 626$ and $n_2 = 626$.

EXAMPLE 10.5

Repeat Example 10.4, but this time assume that the market surveyor has no idea about what the values of $\hat{p}_1$ and $\hat{p}_2$ are.

Solution.   Since the surveyor has no idea about what the values of $\hat{p}_1$ and $\hat{p}_2$ are, she should use the values that produce the largest sample sizes—namely, $\hat{p}_1 = .5$ and $\hat{p}_2 = .5$. The result is

$$n_1 = n_2 = \left[\frac{z_{\alpha/2} \sqrt{\hat{p}_1 \hat{q}_1 + \hat{p}_2 \hat{q}_2}}{B} \right]^2 = \left[\frac{1.645 \sqrt{(.5)(.5) + (.5)(.5)}}{.04} \right]^2$$

$$= (29.08)^2 = 846$$

The surveyor must draw samples of 846 men and 846 women in order to estimate the difference in proportions to within .04 with 90% confidence. Because she has to use $\hat{p}_1 = .5$ and $\hat{p}_2 = .5$ in her preliminary calculation, she must increase each sample size by 220 (when compared to the sample sizes computed in Example 10.4).

SECTION 10.3   ## *SUMMARY*

When the problem objective is to compare two populations and when the data scale is nominal, the parameter of interest is the difference between two binomial proportions, $p_1 - p_2$. In this short chapter, we presented the estimation and hypothesis testing techniques for this parameter. The formulas are summarized in Table 10.1.

TABLE 10.1   SUMMARY OF INFERENCE ABOUT $p_1 - p_2$

Parameter	Estimator	Test Statistic	Required Condition
$p_1 - p_2$	$(\hat{p}_1 - \hat{p}_2) \pm z_{\alpha/2} \sqrt{\dfrac{\hat{p}_1\hat{q}_1}{n_1} + \dfrac{\hat{p}_2\hat{q}_2}{n_2}}$	Case 1: $H_0: (p_1 - p_2) = 0$ $z = \dfrac{(\hat{p}_1 - \hat{p}_2) - (p_1 - p_2)}{\sqrt{\hat{p}\hat{q}\left(\dfrac{1}{n_1} + \dfrac{1}{n_2}\right)}}$ Case 2: $H_0: (p_1 - p_2) = D(\neq 0)$ $z = \dfrac{(\hat{p}_1 - \hat{p}_2) - (p_1 - p_2)}{\sqrt{\dfrac{\hat{p}_1\hat{q}_1}{n_1} + \dfrac{\hat{p}_2\hat{q}_2}{n_2}}}$	$n_1\hat{p}_1$ and $n_1\hat{q}_1 \geq 5$ $n_2\hat{p}_2$ and $n_2\hat{q}_2 \geq 5$

EXERCISES

LEARNING THE TECHNIQUES

10.1   Test the following hypotheses:

a. $H_0: (p_1 - p_2) = 0$
    $H_A: (p_1 - p_2) \neq 0$
    $n_1 = 100 \quad n_2 = 150 \quad \alpha = .01$
    $x_1 = 50 \quad x_2 = 90$

b. $H_0: (p_1 - p_2) = .05$
    $H_A: (p_1 - p_2) > .05$
    $n_1 = 500 \quad n_2 = 400 \quad \alpha = .05$
    $x_1 = 200 \quad x_2 = 100$

10.2   Calculate the *p*-value of each test in Exercise 10.1.

10.3   Determine the 95% confidence interval estimate of $p_1 - p_2$ for the following:

$n_1 = 93$ $n_2 = 121$

$x_1 = 16$ $x_2 = 29$

10.4   Test the following hypotheses:

$H_0: (p_1 - p_2) = 0$

$H_A: (p_1 - p_2) < 0$

$n_1 = 250$ $n_2 = 400$ $\alpha = .01$

$\hat{p}_1 = .17$ $\hat{p}_2 = .24$

10.5   Calculate the *p*-value of the test in Exercise 10.4.

10.6   Given $n_1 = 40$, $\hat{p}_1 = .25$, $n_2 = 50$, and $\hat{p}_2 = .32$, test to determine if there is enough evidence at the 5% significance level to show that $p_2 > p_1$.

10.7   A random sample of $n_1 = 1,000$ from population 1 produced $x_1 = 500$, and a random sample of $n_2 = 1,500$ produced $x_2 = 500$. Can we conclude with $\alpha = .10$ that p_1 exceeds p_2 by at least .10?

10.8   Estimate $p_1 - p_2$ with 90% confidence, given the following:

$n_1 = 500$ $n_2 = 500$

$\hat{p}_1 = .46$ $\hat{p}_2 = .51$

10.9   Test the following hypotheses:

$H_0: (p_1 - p_2) = .25$

$H_A: (p_1 - p_2) < .25$

$n_1 = 200$ $n_2 = 500$ $\alpha = .01$

$x_1 = 60$ $x_2 = 50$

10.10   Find the *p*-value of the test in Exercise 10.9.

10.11   A random sample of $n_1 = 200$ from population 1 produced $x_1 = 50$, and a random sample of $n_2 = 100$ from population 2 yielded $x_2 = 35$.

a. Can we conclude with $\alpha = .10$ that $p_1 \neq p_2$?

b. What is the *p*-value of this test?

c. Estimate $p_1 - p_2$, with 95% confidence.

10.12   Given the following data, can we conclude with $\alpha = .01$ that $p_1 < p_2$?

$n_1 = 1,000$ $n_2 = 500$

$x_1 = 200$ $x_2 = 150$

10.13   Find the sample sizes necessary to estimate $p_1 - p_2$ to within .05 with 95% confidence if we have no idea about the value of p_1 and p_2.

10.14   Find the sample sizes necessary to estimate $p_1 - p_2$ to within .05 with 95% confidence if we believe that p_1 is approximately .1 and p_2 is approximately .4.

10.15   Suppose that the samples with n_1 and n_2 determined in Exercise 10.13 were taken and it was found that $\hat{p}_1 = .1$ and $\hat{p}_2 = .4$. Estimate $p_1 - p_2$ with 95% confidence.

10.16   Suppose that the samples with n_1 and n_2 determined in Exercise 10.14 were taken and it was found that $\hat{p}_1 = .6$ and $\hat{p}_2 = .5$. Estimate $p_1 - p_2$ with 95% confidence.

10.17   Discuss why the intervals computed in Exercises 10.15 and 10.16 are not the size specified in Exercises 10.13 and 10.14, respectively.

APPLYING THE TECHNIQUES

Self-Correcting Exercise (See Appendix 10.A for the solution.)

PG **10.18**   In a public opinion survey, 60 out of a sample of 100 high-income voters and 40 out of 75 low-income voters supported a decrease in sales tax.

a. Can we conclude at the 5% level of significance that the proportion of voters favoring a sales tax decrease differs between high- and low-income voters?

b. What is the *p*-value of this test?

c. Estimate the difference in proportions, with 99% confidence.

POM **10.19**   In a random sample of 500 television sets from a large production line, there were 80 defective sets. In a random sample of 200 television sets from a second production line, there were 10 defective sets. Do these data provide sufficient evidence that the proportion of defective sets from the first line exceeds the proportion of defective sets from the second line by at least 3%? (Use $\alpha = .05$.)

SCI **10.20**   A pharmaceutical company has produced a

flu vaccine. In a test of its effectiveness, 1,000 people were randomly selected; of these, 500 were injected with the vaccine, and the other 500 went untreated. The number of people in each group who contracted the flu during the next three months is summarized in the accompanying table.

Condition	Number of People	
	Treated with Vaccine	Untreated
Developed the flu	80	120
Did not develop the flu	420	380

a. Do these data provide sufficient evidence that the vaccine is effective in preventing the flu? (Use $\alpha = .05$.)

b. What is the *p*-value of this test?

c. Discuss the consequences of Type I and Type II errors. From the perspective of the pharmaceutical company, should you choose a large or a small value of α?

POM **10.21** A survey (reported in the 6 May 1985 *Toronto Star*) to study the usefulness of computers used a sample of 330 managers, professionals, and executives. This group included 132 computer users, 102 people who did not use computers, and 96 who said they would use them relatively soon. Asked if computers boost personal productivity, 50% of the nonusers and "intenders" said no, as did 25% of the users. Can we conclude from the data, at the 1% level of significance, that users and nonusers differ in their opinion of the usefulness of computers?

PG **10.22** Surveys have been widely used by politicians in North America as a way of monitoring the opinions of the electorate. Six months ago, a survey was undertaken to determine the proportion of voters who supported a national leader. Of a sample of 1,100, 56% indicated that they would vote for this politician. This month, another survey of 800 voters indicated that 53% now support that leader. At the 5% level of significance, can we infer that the national leader's popularity has decreased in the last six months?

PG **10.23** Using the data from Exercise 10.22, estimate with 95% confidence the decrease in the proportion of supporters between six months ago and now.

PG **10.24** In light of your answers to Exercises 10.22 and 10.23, how would you report the survey results if you were a newspaper reporter?

EDUC **10.25** Over the past 30 years, the public has grown increasingly critical of the educational system. In a series of surveys between 1948 and 1982, people were asked: "Do you think children today are being better educated or worse educated than you were?" The results are shown in the accompanying table.

Assessment of Educational System				
Year	Better	Worse	Same	Can't Say
1948	74%	12%	10%	4%
1971	63	20	12	5
1976	49	33	13	5
1981	47	38	9	6
1982	52	31	12	6

Assuming that the 1981 and 1982 surveys were each based on 1,049 interviews, can we conclude that there is a significant difference in the proportion of those who responded "Better" between 1981 and 1982? (Use $\alpha = .10$, and omit those who responded "Can't Say.")

SCI **10.26** In a study that was widely publicized, doctors discovered that aspirin seems to help prevent heart attacks. The research project, which was scheduled to last for five years, employed 22,000 American physicians. Half took an aspirin tablet three times per week while the other half took a placebo on the same schedule. After three years, researchers determined that 104 of those who took aspirin and 189 of those who took the placebo had had heart attacks.

a. At the .005 level of significance, do these results indicate that aspirin is effective in reducing the incidence of heart attacks?

b. A not-so-widely-publicized British study attempted to replicate the American research plan; however, it used only 5,000 men (2,500 took aspirin and 2,500 took the placebo). Suppose that the respective proportions of men who suffered heart attacks were exactly the same as in the American study. Do such results allow us to draw the same conclusion, with $\alpha = .005$? If the appropriate conclusion is not the same in the British study as in the U.S. study, explain why not.

GEN **10.27** Have North Americans grown to distrust television and newspaper journalists? A survey was conducted to compare what Americans think of the press in 1988 versus what they said they thought in 1985. The results are shown in the accompanying table.

	Percent in Agreement	
Proposed Opinion	**1985**	**1988**
1. Press reports are "often inaccurate"	34%	48%
2. Press "tends to favor one side" when reporting on political and social issues	53%	59%
3. Press "often invades people's privacy"	73%	78%
4. Rate TV news "very favorably"	25%	18%
5. Rate daily newspaper "very favorably"	25%	21%

SOURCE: *Times Mirror* survey. Results reported in *Newsweek* (21 March 1988).

Can we conclude at the 5% significance level that Americans are more distrustful of television and newspaper reporting in 1988 than they were in 1985? (Assume that the number of respondents in each survey was 400.)

GEN **10.28** In October 1979, February 1981, and November 1981, 1,020 people were asked,* "Do you favor or oppose capital punishment . . .

a. For the killing of a prison guard or an on-duty policeman?

_____

* *The Gallup Report,* 13 February 1982.

b. For the killing of any innocent person?

c. For murders committed by terrorists?"

The results are shown in the accompanying table.

Category	Favor	Oppose	Don't Know
Prison Guard/ Policeman:			
November 1981	730	210	80
February 1981	745	204	71
October 1979	714	224	82
Any Innocent Person:			
November 1981	704	235	81
February 1981	683	255	82
October 1979	690	240	90
Terrorists:			
November 1981	755	194	71
February 1981	755	184	81
October 1979	720	200	100

For each of the three categories (a, b, and c), can we conclude at the 5% significance level that the proportion of those who favor capital punishment has changed between October 1979 and November 1981? (Omit those who responded "Don't Know.")

SCI **10.29** The National Center for Health Statistics keeps track of a number of important statistical trends. Suppose that the center wants to survey women to determine the difference between the proportion of women between 20 and 24 and the proportion of women between 45 and 64 who smoke. How large a sample should be taken in order to estimate the difference to within .05, with 95% confidence?

SCI **10.30** Suppose that, in Exercise 10.29, 36.1% of women between 20 and 24 and 30.5% of women between 45 and 64 smoke at least one pack of cigarettes per day. Can we conclude at the 10% significance level that the younger age group contains a higher percentage of smokers than the older age group does?

PG **10.31** Company policies that force people who are 65 years old to retire are coming under attack from various sources. In a poll reported in the *Toronto Star* (20 January 1986), 1,025 people were interviewed and asked "Do you think that mandatory retirement at age 65 is or is not a good idea?" The survey was performed in January 1985 and repeated in December 1985. The results are given in the following table:

Survey Date	Good Idea	Not a Good Idea	Don't Know
January 1985	492	492	41
December 1985	513	482	30

Referring only to those who expressed an opinion (that is, to those who did not respond "Don't Know"), can we conclude at the 5% significance level that support for mandatory retirement increased during 1985?

PG **10.32** In the December 1985 survey referred to in Exercise 10.31, the age categories of the interviewees were also recorded. Suppose that the responses by age were as shown in the accompanying table.

Age Category	Good Idea	Not a Good Idea	Don't Know
18 to 29 years	168	187	11
30 to 49 years	233	210	13
50 years & over	112	85	6

a. Is there sufficient evidence, with $\alpha = .05$, to conclude that those who are at least 50 years old more strongly support mandatory retirement than do those who are 30 to 49 years old? (Include only those who express an opinion for or against.)

b. Estimate with 99% confidence the difference in the proportion of support between the people aged 18–29 years and the people aged 30–49 years.

EDUC **10.33** Have career expectations changed in the last five years? That was the question addressed by a survey whose results were reported in *Newsweek* (27 January 1986). In the survey, 1,000 university freshmen were asked in 1980 and another 1,000 freshmen were asked in 1985 about their career

expectations. The results appear in the accompanying table.

a. Can we conclude at the 5% significance level that there has been an increase in the proportion of students who expect to become business executives?

b. Can we conclude at the 5% significance level that there has been a decrease in the proportion of students who expect to become computer programmers or analysts?

Career	1980	1985
Accounting	58	63
Business executive	101	127
Computer programmer/analyst	53	44
Engineer	107	100
Lawyer/Judge	41	39
Military career	9	11
Physician	35	38
Teacher	38	38
Other/Undecided	558	540
Total	1,000	1,000

GEN **10.34** In a Gallup poll (reported in the 4 April 1985 *Toronto Star*) conducted in 16 nations, respondents were asked "Do you think for people like yourself, the world in 10 years' time will be a better place to live than it is now, a worse place, or just about the same as it is today?" The results are shown in the accompanying table.

a. Considering only the respondents who expressed one of the three defined opinions, is there statistical evidence at the 5% significance level that Americans are more optimistic than Canadians? (An optimistic respondent is one who responded "Better.")

b. Can we conclude that Americans are more optimistic than Brazilians? (Use $\alpha = .05$.)

c. Estimate with 99% confidence the difference in the proportion of respondents who answered "Worse," between Australia and Great Britain. (Exclude those who answered "Can't say.")

RESPONSES TO GALLUP POLL, BY NATION

Nation	Better	Worse	About Same	Can't Say	Approximate Sample Size
North America:					
Canada	19%	35%	41%	4%	(1,000)
United States	30	30	35	5	(1,500)
South America:					
Argentina					
(Buenos Aires only)	44	27	21	8	(700)
Brazil	27	48	17	8	(2,700)
Uruguay	54	23	15	9	(800)
Europe:					
Belgium	15	31	37	17	(1,000)
Germany	4	31	46	19	(1,000)
Great Britain	18	45	31	6	(1,000)
Greece	46	29	15	10	(1,000)
Netherlands	15	26	53	6	(1,000)
Portugal	16	37	9	38	(2,000)
Switzerland	23	33	40	4	(4,000)
Turkey	26	38	12	24	(1,000)
Other:					
Australia	14	41	38	7	(1,000)
Japan	12	53	18	17	(1,400)
South Africa					
(white population only)	13	52	28	7	(1,000)

CASE 10.1   DEGREE OF OPTIMISM SURVEY

GEN An important factor in predicting consumer demand is the degree of optimism felt by consumers. In general, if most people are optimistic about the economy, their jobs, and the political climate, they are more likely to buy a wide range of luxury items.

A large multinational company commissions a series of annual surveys in the countries in which it operates. These surveys, conducted in December of each year, ask 500 people in each country, "Do you think that this year will be better or worse than the previous year?" The results of this survey (reported in the 31 December 1986 *Toronto Star*) are shown in the accompanying table. What conclusions can be drawn about each country regarding the degree of consumer optimism about the coming year in comparison to what it was for the previous year?

PERCENTAGE SAYING COMING YEAR WILL BE "BETTER," BY COUNTRY

Country	1987	1986
United States	53%	64%
Canada	46	53
United Kingdom	40	37
West Germany	29	27
France	26	26
Sweden	46	43
Austria	18	17
Japan	18	18

CASE 10.2*   SPECIALTY ADVERTISING RECALL

Advertisers are extremely interested not only in having consumers hear about their products but also in having consumers remember the product and its name. It is generally believed that, if an advertisement is seen only once, the amount of recall diminishes over time. In an experiment to study the amount of recall in specialty advertising, 355 people were randomly selected. Each received by mail three specialty items with imprinted advertising: a ball-point pen with the name *American Airlines* printed on it, a key ring with the letters *TIW* on it, and a note pad with the name *General Electric* imprinted on the cover. One week later, 164 of these people were asked if they remember the products received and if they could also recall the products' sponsors. One month after the products were received, the remaining 191 people were asked the same questions. The numbers of those who could recall the products and the sponsors' names are shown in the tables on page 416.

Do these data indicate that the level of recall about these specialty items decreases over time?

---

* Adapted from A. Raj, C. R. Stoner, and R. A. Schreiber, "Advertising Specialties: A Note on Recall," *Developments in Marketing Science* 8 (1985): 308–11.

TABLE A *PRODUCT RECALL*

Product	Number Who Recalled Product	
	1 Week	1 Month
Ball-point pen	140	159
Key ring	141	125
Note pad	149	150

TABLE B *SPONSOR'S NAME RECALL*

Sponsor's Name	Number Who Recalled Sponsor's Name	
	1 Week	1 Month
American Airlines	74	63
TIW	45	36
General Electric	74	58

SOLUTION TO SELF-CORRECTING EXERCISE

10.18   a. $H_0: (p_1 - p_2) = 0$
$H_A: (p_1 - p_2) \neq 0$

Rejection region: $|z| > 1.96$

Test statistic:

$$z = \frac{(\hat{p}_1 - \hat{p}_2) - (p_1 - p_2)}{\sqrt{\hat{p}\hat{q}\left(\dfrac{1}{n_1} + \dfrac{1}{n_2}\right)}}$$

$$= \frac{(.6 - .53) - 0}{\sqrt{(.571)(.429)\left(\dfrac{1}{100} + \dfrac{1}{75}\right)}} = .93$$

Conclusion: Do not reject H_0.

At the 5% significance level, we cannot conclude that the two proportions differ.

b. p-value $= 2P(z > .93) = 2(.1762) = .3524$

c. $(\hat{p}_1 - \hat{p}_2) \pm z_{\alpha/2} \sqrt{\dfrac{\hat{p}_1 \hat{q}_1}{n_1} + \dfrac{\hat{p}_2 \hat{q}_2}{n_2}}$

$= (.6 - .53) \pm 2.58 \sqrt{\dfrac{(.6)(.4)}{100} + \dfrac{(.53)(.47)}{75}}$

$= .07 \pm .195$

The difference between the two proportions is estimated to lie between $-.125$ and $.265$.

C H A P T E R   **11**

STATISTICAL INFERENCE: A REVIEW OF CHAPTERS 7 THROUGH 10

INTRODUCTION

In the preceding four chapters, we have introduced the methods of hypothesis testing and estimation and have applied them to two different problem objectives and two data scales. This entire chapter is devoted to a review of the material in Chapters 7 through 10. In the following section, we summarize our systematic way of identifying which technique from among the dozen or so that have been covered thus far should be used to answer a particular question. The exercises at the end of this chapter are drawn from the types that you have already seen in the preceding four chapters. Since they are not identified by chapter, however, these exercises should provide good practice in recognizing techniques.

GUIDE TO IDENTIFYING THE CORRECT TECHNIQUE: CHAPTERS 7–10

As you have already seen, the two most important determinants of the appropriate technique to use are the problem objective and the data scale. In some situations, once these have been identified, the method automatically follows. In other cases, however, several additional factors must be determined before you can proceed. For example, when the problem objective is to describe a single population and the data scale is interval, two other significant factors must be investigated: the type of descriptive measurement (location or variability), and whether or not σ^2 is known (if the measurement is location). All of the relevant factors for different problem objectives and data scales are summarized in the following outline list.

I. Problem Objective: Description of a Single Population
    A. Data scale: interval
        1. Type of descriptive measurement: location
           a. σ^2 known

Parameter: μ

Test statistic:

$$z = \frac{\bar{x} - \mu}{\sigma/\sqrt{n}}$$

Interval estimator:

$$\bar{x} \pm z_{\alpha/2}\sigma/\sqrt{n}$$

Required condition: x is normally distributed, or n is large enough.

b. σ^2 unknown

Parameter: μ

Test statistic:

$$t = \frac{\bar{x} - \mu}{s/\sqrt{n}} \qquad \text{d.f.} = n - 1$$

Interval estimator:

$$\bar{x} \pm t_{\alpha/2}s/\sqrt{n}$$

Required condition: x is normally distributed.

2. Type of descriptive measurement: variability

Parameter: σ^2

Test statistic:

$$\chi^2 = \frac{(n - 1)s^2}{\sigma^2} \qquad \text{d.f.} = n - 1$$

Interval estimator:

$$\text{LCL} = \frac{(n - 1)s^2}{\chi^2_{\alpha/2}}$$

$$\text{UCL} = \frac{(n - 1)s^2}{\chi^2_{1 - \alpha/2}}$$

Required condition: x is normally distributed.

B. Data scale: nominal

Parameter: p

Test statistic:

$$z = \frac{\hat{p} - p}{\sqrt{\dfrac{pq}{n}}}$$

Interval estimator:

$$\hat{p} \pm z_{\alpha/2} \sqrt{\frac{\hat{p}\hat{q}}{n}}$$

Required conditions: $np \geq 5$ and $nq \geq 5$ (for test statistic).
$n\hat{p} \geq 5$ and $n\hat{q} \geq 5$ (for estimation).

II. Problem Objective: Comparison of Two Populations
  A. Data scale: interval
    1. Type of descriptive measurement: location
      a. Independent samples
        (i) σ_1^2 and σ_2^2 known

Parameter: $\mu_1 - \mu_2$

Test statistic:

$$z = \frac{(\bar{x}_1 - \bar{x}_2) - (\mu_1 - \mu_2)}{\sqrt{\sigma_1^2/n_1 + \sigma_2^2/n_2}}$$

Interval estimator:

$$(\bar{x}_1 - \bar{x}_2) \pm z_{\alpha/2} \sqrt{\sigma_1^2/n_1 + \sigma_2^2/n_2}$$

Required condition: x_1 and x_2 are normally distributed, or n_1 and n_2 are large enough.

(ii) σ_1^2 and σ_2^2 unknown; $n_1 > 30$ and $n_2 > 30$

Parameter: $\mu_1 - \mu_2$

Test statistic:

$$z = \frac{(\bar{x}_1 - \bar{x}_2) - (\mu_1 - \mu_2)}{\sqrt{s_1^2/n_1 + s_2^2/n_2}}$$

Interval estimator:

$$(\bar{x}_1 - \bar{x}_2) \pm z_{\alpha/2} \sqrt{s_1^2/n_1 + s_2^2/n_2}$$

Required condition: x_1 and x_2 are normally distributed, or n_1 and n_2 are large enough.

(iii) σ_1^2 and σ_2^2 unknown; $n_1 \leq 30$ or $n_2 \leq 30$

Parameter: $\mu_1 - \mu_2$

Test statistic:

$$t = \frac{(\bar{x}_1 - \bar{x}_2) - (\mu_1 - \mu_2)}{\sqrt{s_p^2(1/n_1 + 1/n_2)}} \qquad \text{d.f.} = n_1 + n_2 - 2$$

Interval estimator:

$$(\bar{x}_1 - \bar{x}_2) \pm t_{\alpha/2} \sqrt{s_p^2(1/n_1 + 1/n_2)}$$

Required conditions: x_1 and x_2 are normally distributed; $\sigma_1^2 = \sigma_2^2$.

b. Matched pairs samples

Parameter: $\mu_D = \mu_1 - \mu_2$

Test statistic:

$$t = \frac{\bar{x}_D - \mu_D}{s_D/\sqrt{n_D}} \qquad \text{d.f.} = n_D - 1$$

Interval estimator:

$$\bar{x}_D \pm t_{\alpha/2} s_D/\sqrt{n_D}$$

Required condition: D is normally distributed.

2. Type of descriptive measurement: variability

Parameter: σ_1^2/σ_2^2

Test statistic:

$$F = \frac{s_1^2}{s_2^2} \qquad \text{d.f.} \quad \begin{aligned} v_1 &= n_1 - 1 \\ v_2 &= n_2 - 1 \end{aligned}$$

Interval estimator:

$$\text{LCL} = \left(\frac{s_1^2}{s_2^2}\right) \frac{1}{F_{\alpha/2, v_1, v_2}}$$

$$\text{UCL} = \left(\frac{s_1^2}{s_2^2}\right) F_{\alpha/2, v_2, v_1}$$

Required conditions: x_1 and x_2 are normally distributed; samples are independent.

B. Data scale: nominal

Parameter: $p_1 - p_2$

Test statistic:

Case 1: $H_0: (p_1 - p_2) = 0$

$$z = \frac{(\hat{p}_1 - \hat{p}_2) - (p_1 - p_2)}{\sqrt{\hat{p}\hat{q}\left(\dfrac{1}{n_1} + \dfrac{1}{n_2}\right)}}$$

Case 2: $H_0: (p_1 - p_2) = D \qquad (D \neq 0)$

$$z = \frac{(\hat{p}_1 - \hat{p}_2) - (p_1 - p_2)}{\sqrt{\dfrac{\hat{p}_1\hat{q}_1}{n_1} + \dfrac{\hat{p}_2\hat{q}_2}{n_2}}}$$

Interval estimator:

$$(\hat{p}_1 - \hat{p}_2) \pm z_{\alpha/2}\sqrt{\frac{\hat{p}_1\hat{q}_1}{n_1} + \frac{\hat{p}_2\hat{q}_2}{n_2}}$$

Required conditions: $n_1\hat{p}_1$, $n_1\hat{q}_1$, $n_2\hat{p}_2$, and $n_2\hat{q}_2 \geq 5$.

FIGURE 11.1   *FLOWCHART OF THE SYSTEMATIC APPROACH*

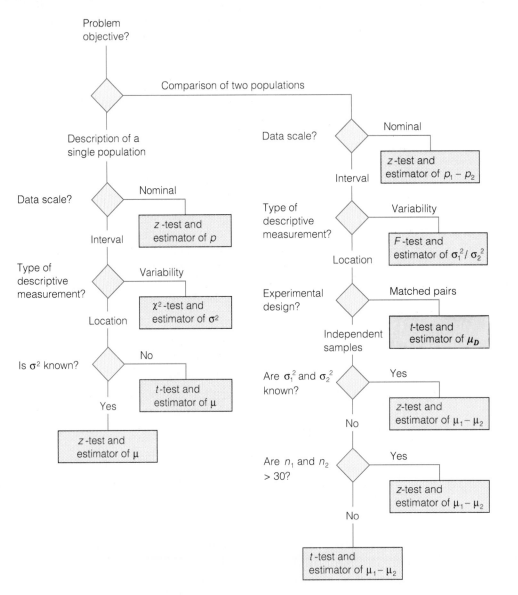

By referring to the guide, you will be able to identify the formulas of the test statistics, interval estimators, and conditions required for each technique. To help you decide which technique to use, a flowchart of the decision process is provided in Figure 11.1. Notice that the process begins with recognizing the problem objective and the data scale. Thus far, we've only discussed two problem objectives, and the interval and nominal data scales. A complete guide and flowchart for all statistical inference techniques covered in this book will be presented in Chapter 18.

As you can see, in some cases the problem objective and the data scale alone determine the technique to be used, while in other cases several more factors must be determined.

■■■■■■■ **EXAMPLE 11.1**

The executives of a company that manufactures an adhesive that is used to attach heat-shield tiles to the space shuttle are concerned about the performance of their product. They find that the drying time is excessive and that the fraction of tiles requiring reattachment is too large. As a result, they're looking for an improved product. The research and development laboratory has produced a new adhesive that the company hopes is superior to the old one. To test the new adhesive, 25 tiles are attached using the old adhesive, and another 25 are attached using the new adhesive. The number of hours of drying time required and an expert's judgment as to whether or not the tile has been properly attached are recorded in Table 11.1. Because of the cost of changing adhesives, the executives are willing to switch only if the new adhesive can be shown to be superior to the old one.

a. At the 5% significance level, can we conclude that the new adhesive has a superior drying time?

b. At the 5% significance level, can we conclude that the new adhesive is superior in fraction of proper attachments?

c. Estimate with 99% confidence the average drying time of the new adhesive.

d. Estimate with 99% confidence the fraction of proper attachments achieved by the new adhesive.

e. What assumptions must you make in order to answer part (a)?

f. If we assume that the drying times are normally distributed, test at the 5% significance level to determine if the other assumption made in part (a) is invalid.

Solution. The various parts of this example require a number of different statistical techniques. We'll proceed through the flowchart, in order to identify each of the needed techniques.

In part (a), the problem objective is to compare two populations, and the data scale is interval (the drying times of the two adhesives). The descriptive measure to be compared is location (we're interested in the relative positions of the two populations). The samples are independent, the population variances are unknown, and $n_1 \leq 30$ and $n_2 \leq 30$. As a result of all of these factors, we identify the t-test of $\mu_1 - \mu_2$ as the appropriate test.

Since we want to know if we can conclude that the mean drying time of the new adhesive (labeled μ_2) is less than the mean drying time of the old adhesive

TABLE 11.1   RECORDED DATA FOR EXAMPLE 11.1

	Old Adhesive			New Adhesive	
Tile	Drying Time (hours)	Properly Attached (Y or N)	Tile	Drying Time (hours)	Properly Attached (Y or N)
1	7.1	Y	1	8.3	Y
2	6.3	Y	2	8.5	Y
3	9.2	N	3	7.3	Y
4	8.6	Y	4	6.5	Y
5	5.5	N	5	7.0	Y
6	7.3	N	6	6.4	Y
7	6.6	Y	7	6.3	N
8	8.0	N	8	7.7	Y
9	7.7	Y	9	5.2	Y
10	8.9	N	10	7.6	N
11	9.1	Y	11	6.1	Y
12	8.6	N	12	5.7	Y
13	5.7	Y	13	6.3	Y
14	4.9	Y	14	7.0	N
15	6.0	N	15	8.8	Y
16	6.8	Y	16	6.9	Y
17	6.7	N	17	6.5	Y
18	7.5	Y	18	5.8	N
19	8.3	Y	19	4.3	Y
20	8.0	N	20	4.9	Y
21	6.1	Y	21	6.6	N
22	9.1	Y	22	6.8	Y
23	5.8	N	23	7.0	Y
24	6.0	Y	24	6.5	Y
25	7.3	N	25	6.0	Y

(labeled μ_1), the alternative hypothesis is

$$H_A: (\mu_1 - \mu_2) > 0$$

In order to perform the t-test, we need the following statistics:

$$\bar{x}_1 = 7.24$$
$$\bar{x}_2 = 6.64$$
$$s_1^2 = 1.62$$
$$s_2^2 = 1.13$$
$$s_p^2 = 1.375$$

The complete test is as follows:

$$H_0: (\mu_1 - \mu_2) = 0$$
$$H_A: (\mu_1 - \mu_2) > 0$$

Test statistic:

$$t = \frac{(\bar{x}_1 - \bar{x}_2) - (\mu_1 - \mu_2)}{\sqrt{s_p^2 \left(\frac{1}{n_1} + \frac{1}{n_2}\right)}}$$

Rejection region:

$$t > t_{\alpha, n_1 + n_2 - 2}$$
$$> t_{.05, 48}$$
$$> 1.645$$

Value of the test statistic:

$$t = \frac{(\bar{x}_1 - \bar{x}_2) - (\mu_1 - \mu_2)}{\sqrt{s_p^2 \left(\frac{1}{n_1} + \frac{1}{n_2}\right)}} = \frac{(7.24 - 6.64) - 0}{\sqrt{1.375 \left(\frac{1}{25} + \frac{1}{25}\right)}} = 1.81$$

Conclusion: Reject H_0.

There is sufficient evidence to conclude that the new adhesive has a superior drying time.

In part (b), we have the same problem objective: to compare two populations. Here, however, the data scale is nominal, because the responses to the question are either *yes* (the tile is properly attached) or *no* (the tile is not properly attached). The correct technique is therefore the z-test of $p_1 - p_2$. To conduct this test, we need to know the proportions of tiles that are not properly attached. (Alternatively, we could perform this test by determining the proportions of properly attached tiles.) By counting, we find

$$\hat{p}_1 = .44$$
$$\hat{p}_2 = .20$$

Since we want to know if the proportion of tiles improperly attached with the new adhesive is smaller than the corresponding proportion for the old adhesive, the alternative hypothesis is

$$H_A: (p_1 - p_2) > 0$$

The complete test is as follows:

$$H_0: (p_1 - p_2) = 0$$
$$H_A: (p_1 - p_2) > 0$$

Test statistic:

$$z = \frac{(\hat{p}_1 - \hat{p}_2) - (p_1 - p_2)}{\sqrt{\hat{p}\hat{q}\left(\frac{1}{n_1} + \frac{1}{n_2}\right)}}$$

Rejection region:

$$z > z_\alpha$$
$$> z_{.05}$$
$$> 1.645$$

Value of the test statistic:

$$z = \frac{(\hat{p}_1 - \hat{p}_2) - (p_1 - p_2)}{\sqrt{\hat{p}\hat{q}\left(\frac{1}{n_1} + \frac{1}{n_2}\right)}} = \frac{(.44 - .20) - 0}{\sqrt{(.32)(.68)\left(\frac{1}{25} + \frac{1}{25}\right)}} = 1.82$$

Conclusion: Reject H_0.

There is enough evidence to conclude that the new adhesive is superior to the old adhesive in the fraction of proper attachments it achieves.

In part (c), the problem is to describe a single population, and the data scale is interval. Hence we wish to estimate μ; and since σ^2 is unknown, the estimator is

$$\bar{x} \pm t_{\alpha/2}\frac{s}{\sqrt{n}} = 6.64 \pm 2.797\frac{1.06}{\sqrt{25}} = 6.64 \pm .59$$

The average drying time of the new adhesive is between 6.05 and 7.23 hours.

In part (d), the problem objective is to describe a single population, and the data scale is nominal. The interval estimator of p is

$$\hat{p} \pm z_{\alpha/2}\sqrt{\frac{\hat{p}\hat{q}}{n}} = .80 \pm 2.58\sqrt{\frac{(.80)(.20)}{25}} = .80 \pm .21$$

We estimate that the true proportion of properly attached tiles achieved by using the new adhesive lies between 59% and 100% (since p cannot exceed 100%).

In answer to part (e), in order to conduct the t-test of $\mu_1 - \mu_2$, we must assume that the drying times are normally distributed and that $\sigma_1^2 = \sigma_2^2$.

In part (f), the assumption we wish to test is $\sigma_1^2 = \sigma_2^2$. Our complete test is as follows:

$H_0: \sigma_1^2/\sigma_2^2 = 1$

$H_A: \sigma_1^2/\sigma_2^2 \neq 1$

Test statistic:

$$F = \frac{s_1^2}{s_2^2}$$

Rejection region:

$F > F_{\alpha/2, n_1 - 1, n_2 - 1}$ or $F < F_{1 - \alpha/2, n_1 - 1, n_2 - 1}$

$\quad > F_{.025, 24, 24}$ $\quad < \dfrac{1}{F_{.025, 24, 24}} = \dfrac{1}{2.27} = .441$

$\quad > 2.27$

Value of the test statistic:

$$F = \frac{s_1^2}{s_2^2} = \frac{1.62}{1.13} = 1.43$$

Conclusion: Do not reject H_0.

There is not enough evidence to allow us to conclude that the assumption in part (a) is invalid.

COMPUTER OUTPUT FOR EXAMPLE 11.1*

Minitab

Columns 1 and 3 are used to store the adhesive drying times, and columns 2 and 4 are used to store the code representing whether the tile has been properly attached (Yes = 1 and No = 0).

Here is the Minitab output for part (a):

```
TWOSAMPLE T FOR C1 VS C3
       N     MEAN    STDEV    SE MEAN
C1    25     7.24    1.27     0.25
C3    25     6.64    1.06     0.21
95 PCT CI FOR MU C1-MU C3: (-0.06, 1.27)
TTEST MU C1=MU C3 (VS GT): T=1.82 P=0.037 DF=48.0
```

---

* See Appendixes 11.A and 11.B for the Minitab and SAS commands used to answer this question.

Here is the Minitab output for part (b):

```
ROWS C2
        COUNT
0        11
1        14
ALL      25


ROWS C4
        COUNT
0         5
1        20
ALL      25
```

From this output we learn that

$$\hat{p}_1 = \frac{11}{25} = .44$$

and

$$\hat{p}_2 = \frac{5}{25} = .20$$

We can then compute the value of the z-test statistic.

    Here is the output for part (c):

```
      N     MEAN    STDEV    SE MEAN    99.0 PERCENT C.I.
C3    25    6.640   1.062    0.212       (6.046, 7.234)
```

The output for parts (a) through (c) provides the statistics needed to answer parts (d) and (f) of the question.

SAS

Here is the SAS output for part (a):

```
Variable: TIME
ADHESIVE     N      Mean     Std Dev     Std Error
NEW         25     6.6400    1.0618       0.2123
OLD         25     7.2440    1.2731       0.2546


Variances             T      DF     Prob > |T|
Unequal           -1.8217   46.5     0.0749
Equal             -1.8217   48.0     0.0747
```

Because SAS identified the new adhesive as sample 1 and the old adhesive as sample 2, the test statistic is $t = -1.82$ (equal variances). We compute the p-value as $.0747/2 = .0374$.

Here is the SAS output for part (b):

```
    TABLE OF ATTACHED BY ADHESIVE
   ATTACHED           ADHESIVE
   Frequency │
   Percent   │
   Row Pct   │
   Col Pct   │ NEW   │ OLD   │  Total
   ----------+-------+-------+
   NO        │     5 │    11 │      16
             │ 10.00 │ 22.00 │   32.00
             │ 31.25 │ 68.75 │
             │ 20.00 │ 44.00 │
   ----------+-------+-------+
   YES       │    20 │    14 │      34
             │ 40.00 │ 28.00 │   68.00
             │ 58.82 │ 41.18 │
             │ 80.00 │ 56.00 │
   ----------+-------+-------+
   Total          25      25       50
               50.00   50.00   100.00
```

From this output we have

$$\hat{p}_1 = \frac{11}{25} = .44$$

and

$$\hat{p}_2 = \frac{5}{25} = .20$$

Using the output from parts (a) and (b), we can answer parts (c), (d), and (f) of the question.

EXERCISES

11.1 RE A real estate company employs agents on a commission basis. It claims that, during their first year, agents will earn a mean commission of at least $25,000. It also claims that, because of its unique training program, there is very little variability among individual agents' annual commissions. In fact, it claims that the standard deviation will not exceed $5,000. In an examination of these claims, a random sample of 20 first-year employees is selected, and their commissions are recorded. The sample mean and the standard deviation are $27,500 and $3,800, respectively.

a. Test the claim about the mean commission. (Use $\alpha = .05$.)

b. Test the claim about the standard deviation. (Use $\alpha = .01$.)

11.2 POM The production manager of a large plant is contemplating changing the process by which a certain product is produced. Since workers in this plant are paid on the basis of their output, it is necessary for the manager to demonstrate that the rate of assembling a unit will be increased under the new system. Ten workers are randomly selected to participate in an experiment in which each worker assembles one unit under the old process and one unit under the new process. The assembly times, which are normally distributed, are shown in the accompanying table.

	Assembly Time (minutes)	
Worker	Old Process	New Process
1	20	20
2	27	25
3	19	18
4	23	20
5	17	15
6	22	24
7	18	18
8	25	22
9	29	26
10	18	16

a. Can we conclude that the average time required to assemble the unit is greater with the old process than with the new process? Use $\alpha = .01$.

b. Estimate the difference in mean assembly time between the two processes, with 95% confidence.

SCI **11.3** Random samples of two brands of whole milk are checked for their fat content as follows: 33 half-gallon containers of each brand are selected, and the fat content is measured (in grams). The resulting data are shown in the accompanying table.

Brand *A*			Brand *B*		
30	26	36	24	33	17
26	33	35	27	20	21
31	20	32	22	18	18
27	28	27	31	26	25
37	27	29	30	25	27

Brand *A*			Brand *B*		
28	31	33	25	20	24
31	35	27	22	22	24
29	30	30	26	24	20
25	26	36	29	33	18
27	29	30	22	25	20
25	31	27	30	26	27

$\sum x_i = 974$	$\sum x_i = 801$
$\sum x_i^2 = 29{,}200$	$\sum x_i^2 = 20{,}037$

a. Estimate with 95% confidence the difference in mean fat content between Brand *A* and Brand *B*.

b. Any container that contains 30 grams or more of fat is considered unacceptable. Is there enough evidence to conclude that Brand *A* has a higher fraction of unacceptable containers than Brand *B*? (Use $\alpha = .01$.)

c. What is the *p*-value of the test in part (b)?

d. The owner of Brand *B* claims that no more than 10% of his containers are unacceptable. Is there sufficient evidence at the 5% significance level to refute this claim?

e. Estimate with 90% confidence the fraction of unacceptable Brand *A* containers.

f. Can we conclude at the 5% significance level that the variability in fat content of Brand *A* is different from that of Brand *B*?

RET **11.4** A random sample consisting of 20 McDonald's outlets revealed a mean of 20.5 employees, with a standard deviation of 4.3. A random sample of 25 Wendy's outlets had a mean of 16.7, with a standard deviation of 6.9. Do these results provide sufficient evidence at the 5% significance level that Wendy's and McDonald's employ an unequal average number of employees nationwide?

PG **11.5** The use of seat belts in automobiles is now mandatory in more than half of the states in the United States and in most of the provinces in Canada. In order to investigate whether these laws reduce auto fatalities, researchers recorded the number of fatalities for several months before and for the same months after mandatory seat-belt laws were passed in New York, Illinois, and Michigan; the results appear in the accompanying table. For each state, can we conclude with $\alpha = .01$ that mandatory seat-belt laws are effective in reducing fatalities? (The data are based on a 3 February 1986 article in *Newsweek*, citing data from the National Highway Traffic Safety Administration, Highway Users Federation, and state figures.) The monthly fatalities are normally distributed.

MONTHLY FATALITIES

New York

Before Law		After Law	
Month	Fatalities	Month	Fatalities
Jan 1984	980	Jan 1985	802
Feb 1984	916	Feb 1985	753
March 1984	849	March 1985	702
April 1984	793	April 1985	652
May 1984	829	May 1985	683
June 1984	1,012	June 1985	843
July 1984	1,027	July 1985	827
Aug 1984	1,133	Aug 1985	983
Sept 1984	1,101	Sept 1985	910

Illinois

Before Law		After Law	
Month	Fatalities	Month	Fatalities
July 1984	763	July 1985	695
Aug 1984	767	Aug 1985	598
Sept 1984	539	Sept 1985	501
Oct 1984	473	Oct 1985	422
Nov 1984	428	Nov 1985	356
Dec 1984	504	Dec 1985	440

Michigan

Before Law		After Law	
Month	Fatalities	Month	Fatalities
July 1984	556	July 1985	493
Aug 1984	528	Aug 1985	456
Sept 1984	560	Sept 1985	502
Oct 1984	584	Oct 1985	519
Nov 1984	503	Nov 1985	451
Dec 1984	611	Dec 1985	549

MNG **11.6** Laurier Trucking Company is trying to decide whether to purchase its tires from Alpha Tire Co. or Beta Tire Co. Laurier currently buys its tires from Alpha and will continue to do so unless the Beta tires can be shown to last more than 5,000 km longer (on average) than the Alpha tires. Recently Laurier conducted an experiment by running 10 Alpha tires and 14 Beta tires until they wore out. The number of miles each traveled before wearing out was recorded, and the data were summarized with the following statistics:

Alpha	Beta
$\bar{x}_1 = 46,384$	$\bar{x}_2 = 52,050$
$s_1^2 = 985,000$	$s_2^2 = 856,000$

Is there sufficient evidence to allow us to conclude that Laurier should buy from Beta? (Use $\alpha = .05$.) The miles traveled by either type of tire before wearing out are normally distributed.

RE **11.7** It's important for a politician to know if different groups within her constituency support her to a greater or lesser extent than others. If she finds support lagging in one group, she can take action to remedy the problem. Suppose that the politician discovers in a survey that 187 out of 417 men interviewed approve of her performance, while 225 out of 632 women approve of it. Can the politician conclude at the 1% significance level that men and women do not support her equally?

GEN **11.8** Suppose that we want to test a null hypothesis that the mean of a population is 145 against an alternative hypothesis that the mean is less than 145. A sample of 100 measurements drawn from the population (whose standard deviation is 20) yields a mean of 140. If the probability of a Type I error is chosen to be .05, calculate the probability of a Type II error, assuming that the true population mean equals 142.

MNG **11.9** The managers of a large department store have decided that drastic action must be taken to reduce losses caused by shoplifting. Several different, expensive alternatives have been proposed. As each alternative is investigated in depth, it becomes clear that the firm needs an accurate estimate of the percentage of shoppers who engage in shoplifting. An examination of secondary sources reveals estimates of shoppers who shoplifted an item in the past week that range from .1% to 9%. In view of the serious nature of the countermeasures proposed, the firm wants an estimate of the percentage of shoppers who actually shoplift an item during their visit to the store. The incidence of shoplifting will be determined by having specially trained store detectives discreetly follow a random sample of shoppers throughout their store visit—an expensive process. If the firm's management wants to be 99% confident that its estimate will not differ from the actual figure by more than 2%, how large should the sample be?

GEN **11.10** When an analyst was considering using the *t*-test to test the difference between two means, two samples of size 10 yielded variances of 28.5 and 9.5, respectively. Do the data indicate that the *t*-test is inappropriate, on the basis of the requirement of equality of population variances? (Use $\alpha = .05$.)

FIN **11.11** The electric company in a large city is considering an incentive plan to encourage its customers to pay their bills promptly. The plan is to discount the bills 1% if the customer pays within 5 days, as opposed to the usual 25 days. As an experiment, 20 customers are offered the discount on their September bill. The mean and the variance of the number of days before payment is received from this group are 6.3 and 9.1, respectively. A random sample of 20 customers who were not offered the discount took an average of 23.1 days (with a variance of 26.3) to pay their bills. (Assume that the time elapsed before payment is normally distributed.)

a. Estimate with 99% confidence the difference between the mean payment periods for the two groups.

b. Calculate the 95% confidence interval estimate of the average number of days before payment for the group of customers who were not offered the discount for paying early.

c. Estimate with 90% confidence the ratio of the two population variances.

FIN **11.12** The management of a large pension fund is interested in studying the distribution of monthly rates of return on large, well-diversified portfolios of common stock. In particular, management is interested in finding out whether the mean exceeds .5%. Intensive data gathering yielded 90 monthly returns on various large and well-diversified portfolios. These returns are expressed as gross returns per $1,000 invested. The data have been classified into intervals, with the frequency distribution shown in the accompanying table.

FREQUENCY DISTRIBUTION OF GROSS RETURNS

Range*	Frequency
$960–970	4
$970–980	4
$980–990	10
$990–1,000	13
$1,000–1,010	16
$1,010–1,020	15
$1,020–1,030	13
$1,030–1,040	8
$1,040–1,050	5
$1,050–1,060	2

* Each closed interval includes the lower limit but excludes the upper limit.

Is there sufficient evidence to allow us to conclude that the mean monthly return exceeds .5%? (Use $\alpha = .05$.)

TABLE E11.13

						Number of Accidents (by location)							
Year	A	B	C	D	E	F	G	H	I	J	K	L	
Before lights	8	12	5	4	6	3	4	3	2	6	6	9	
After lights	5	3	2	1	4	2	2	4	3	5	4	3	

11.13 A study is conducted to investigate how effectively street lighting placed at various locations reduces automobile accidents in a certain town. Table E11.13 shows the number of nighttime accidents at 12 locations (*A* through *L*) one year before and one year after the installation of lighting. Do these data provide sufficient evidence to indicate that lighting reduces nighttime automobile accidents? (It is known that the number of accidents is normally distributed. Use $\alpha = .05$.)

11.14 North American Oil is considering sites for new gas stations. An estimate of the mean traffic flow (average number of passing cars per day) at each site is to be determined by taking traffic counts for a random sample of days. The mean for each site is to be estimated to within 5 cars per day, with 90% confidence. Experience at existing sites indicates that the standard deviation of the number of cars passing in a day can be as low as 70 or as high as 100. What sample size should be used?

11.15 Amcar Motor Company has test-driven a random sample of 35 new Amcars. Gasoline mileage figures for the sample cars (in miles per gallon) are given in the accompanying table. Construct a 95% confidence interval for the proportion of cars that get more than 20 miles per gallon.

GASOLINE MILEAGE (mpg)

15.4	18.3	19.1	20.4	21.0	21.8	19.3
16.3	18.7	19.4	20.5	21.3	21.8	20.8
16.7	18.7	19.4	20.6	21.4	22.5	22.0
17.2	19.0	19.8	20.9	21.5	23.2	20.1
18.1	19.0	20.4	21.0	21.6	25.0	17.8

11.16 A firm that makes insecticide wants the percentage of impurities in its product not to exceed an average of 3%. A random sample of 30 1-gallon cans yields the following percentages of impurities:

3	3	1	1	.5	2	2	4	5	4	5	3	1	3	1
4	2	2	4	2	5	3	1	1	1	.75	1.5	3	3	2

On the basis of these data, can we conclude that the true average is less than 3%? (Let $\alpha = .05$.)

11.17 In order to determine the effect of advertising in the Yellow Pages, Bell Telephone took a sample of ten retail stores that did not advertise in the Yellow Pages in 1988 and recorded their annual sales (which are normally distributed). Each of the ten stores took out a Yellow Pages ad in 1989, and the annual sales for that year were recorded, as well. Both sets of figures are shown in the accompanying table.

Retail Store	1988 Annual Sales ($1,000s)	1989 Annual Sales ($1,000s)
1	52	57
2	116	125
3	105	100
4	75	85
5	48	68
6	99	110
7	77	77
8	125	150
9	110	130
10	66	88

a. Estimate the difference in average sales between 1988 and 1989, with 99% confidence.

b. Estimate the average percentage increase in sales between 1988 and 1989, with 99% confidence.

POM **11.18**   The Barbarian Ball Company of Baden produces ball bearings. The contract that Barbarian has requires that it produce ball bearings whose diameters are 1,010 microns each, with a tolerance of ± 2.5 microns. That is, each diameter must fall between 1,007.5 and 1,012.5 microns. Any bearings whose diameters are outside this interval are considered to be defective. Barbarian owns two machines that produce ball bearings; in order to compare them, an engineer draws a sample of 25 ball bearings from each machine and measures each ball bearing's diameter. The samples are as follows (measured in microns):

Machine 1:

1,007	1,011	1,012	1,010	1,011
1,009	1,007	1,006	1,010	1,011
1,012	1,008	1,009	1,013	1,015
1,009	1,010	1,009	1,011	1,012
1,006	1,010	1,009	1,010	1,011

$$\sum x_i = 25,248$$
$$\sum x_i^2 = 25,498,570$$

Machine 2:

1,011	1,010	1,011	1,009	1,008
1,008	1,010	1,009	1,009	1,013
1,010	1,011	1,015	1,010	1,008
1,009	1,010	1,008	1,010	1,011
1,007	1,010	1,009	1,011	1,018

$$\sum x_i = 25,255$$
$$\sum x_i^2 = 25,512,733$$

a. Do these data provide sufficient evidence at the 1% significance level to allow us to conclude that the average diameters of ball bearings produced by the two machines differ?

b. Can we conclude (with $\alpha = .05$) that machine 2 has a lower defective rate than machine 1?

c. Estimate the fraction of defective ball bearings produced on machine 1, with 98% confidence.

d. Test to determine if the requirement of equal variances made in part (a) is not satisfied. (Use $\alpha = .05$.)

MKT **11.19**   In an attempt to increase business, a major credit-card company is thinking of offering a 1% discount on all monthly accounts that exceed $1,000. Currently, average monthly billings are $273. As an experiment, 100 cardholders were offered the discount. In the following month, the mean and the standard deviation of the billings were $285 and $53, respectively. Do these statistics provide sufficient evidence at the 5% significance level to indicate that the discount plan will increase business?

EDUC **11.20**   The administration at a large state university has proposed to the faculty a new policy for promotion. It is believed that the proportion favoring the proposal among untenured faculty is different from the proportion favoring the proposal among tenured faculty. In a sample of 64 faculty without tenure, it is found that only 20 favor the proposal; while in a sample of 36 tenured faculty, 18 favor the proposal. Can we conclude at the 10% level of significance that there is a difference in opinion between tenured and untenured faculty?

PG **11.21**   Suppose that a politician has engaged a team of public opinion surveyors to determine the percentage of constituents who favor his stand on a current issue. The survey company will conduct a random survey of public opinion at a cost of 35 cents per interview. How much will it cost the politician if he insists that the error of estimation be less than 5% for 95% of the time, and if:

a. He has no idea about the percentage of constituents who favor his stand.

b. He knows that the percentage in favor of his stand lies somewhere between 10 and 30%.

c. He knows that the percentage in favor of his stand lies somewhere between 25 and 60%.

MKT **11.22**   A cereal manufacturer has recently redesigned its product's container. In a random sample of 1,000 households prior to the switch, the manufacturer found that 220 purchased its brand of cereal. After the switch, a survey of 1,000 households determined that 250 bought that brand. Estimate with 99% confidence the difference in the cereal's market share before and after the design change.

POM **11.23** In Yankee Stadium, the labor costs of changing light bulbs are quite high. If all of the light bulbs tend to last about the same length of time, they can all be replaced periodically, saving labor costs. An industrial statistician has calculated that it will pay to replace all of the bulbs at fixed time intervals if the standard deviation is less than 100 hours. In an experiment, a sample of 50 bulbs lasted an average of 5,750 hours with a variance of 8,000. Can we conclude at the 1% level of significance that all of the bulbs should be replaced periodically?

POM **11.24** In an attempt to reduce the number of man-hours lost as a result of industrial accidents, a large company installed new safety equipment. In a test of the effectiveness of the equipment, a random sample of five departments was examined. The numbers of man-hours lost in the month before installation of the safety equipment and in the month after installation were recorded. The data, which are normally distributed, are reproduced in the following table.

Month	Hours Lost (by department)				
	1	2	3	4	5
Before safety equipment	17	25	42	16	19
After safety equipment	15	20	30	17	14

Estimate with 99% confidence the difference between the average man-hours lost before and after the safety equipment's installation.

EDUC **11.25** Many college and university professors have been accused of grade inflation over the past several years. This means that they assign higher grades now than they did in the past, even though students' work is of the same caliber. If grade inflation has occurred, the mean grade-point average of today's students should exceed the mean of 10 years ago. To test the grade inflation theory at one university, a business professor randomly selects 75 business majors who are graduating with the present class and 50 who graduated 10 years ago. The results are shown in the following table.

Present	10 Years Ago
$\bar{x}_1 = 3.04$	$\bar{x}_2 = 2.82$
$s_1 = .38$	$s_2 = .43$
$n_1 = 75$	$n_2 = 50$

Test to see whether or not the data support the hypothesis of grade inflation in the business school of this university. (Use $\alpha = .05$.)

GEN **11.26** Suppose that we have just conducted a paired difference experiment (with 36 pairs of observations), and we wish to test

$$H_0: \mu_D = 0$$
$$H_A: \mu_D < 0$$

with $\alpha = .05$. From a previous analysis, we know that the standard deviation of the paired difference is 6.0. Find β, if μ_D really equals -1.

PG **11.27** The chief of police wishes to estimate the mean number of accidents per weekend at a busy intersection. In a sample of 50 randomly selected weekends, the police found 2 weekends with two accidents, 18 weekends with one accident, and the remainder with no accidents. Estimate with 96.4% confidence the true mean number of accidents per weekend at this intersection.

GEN **11.28** The federal government is interested in determining whether the variability of men's salaries differs from the variability of women's salaries. Suppose that random samples of 15 women and 22 men are drawn from the population of first-level managers in the private sector. The resulting information is summarized in the following table.

Women	Men
$\bar{x}_1 = \$18,400$	$\bar{x}_2 = \$19,700$
$s_1 = \$2,300$	$s_2 = \$3,100$
$n_1 = 15$	$n_2 = 22$

Test this question at the 10% level of significance.

FIN **11.29** Suppose that you want to estimate the mean percentage of gain in per-share value for growth-type mutual funds over a specific two-year period. Ten mutual funds are randomly selected from the population of all commonly listed funds. The percentage-gain figures are as follows:

12 −3 7 6 −2 4 8 18 9 3

Find a 90% confidence interval for the mean percentage of gain for the population of funds. (Assume that the gains are normally distributed.)

MKT **11.30** Last year a local television station determined that 70% of the people who watch news at 11:00 P.M. watch its station. The station's management believes that the current audience share may have changed. In an attempt to determine whether or not the audience share has in fact changed, the station questions a random sample of 80 local viewers and finds that 60 watch its news show. Does the sample evidence support the management's belief that its audience share has changed? (Test at the $\alpha = .10$ level of significance.)

GEN **11.31** (Extremely difficult exercise) Suppose that you are testing

$H_0: \mu = 100$

$H_A: \mu > 100$

With $\sigma = 20$ and $\alpha = .05$, find the sample size that produces $\beta = .10$, when $\mu = 105$.

PG **11.32** A national market-survey company has just received a contract to survey voters in order to estimate the proportion of the population that favors gun control, abortion on demand, and continued UN membership. After careful analysis, the survey manager determines that the proportion favoring gun control lies between 70% and 90%, the proportion favoring abortion on demand lies between 10% and 35%, and the proportion favoring continued UN membership is at least 80%. If the purpose of the survey is to estimate each proportion to within 3%, with 90% confidence, how large a sample should be taken? (Remember, all questionnaires will contain all three questions.)

SCI **11.33** An entomologist wants to determine the extent of a spruce budworm infestation. This is done by counting the number of budworm larvae on a representative sampling of 18-inch branch tips. If the entomologist believes that the variance of the number of larvae per branch tip is 400, determine how many branch tips should be sampled to estimate the mean number of budworm larvae per branch tip to within 2, with 95% confidence.

SCI **11.34** Suppose that in Exercise 11.33 the mean and the variance of the sample taken were $\bar{x} = 41.0$ and $s^2 = 352.0$.

a. Estimate with 95% confidence the mean number of spruce budworm larvae per branch tip.

b. If the policy of the Forestry Service is to spray the spruce trees when sufficient evidence exists (with $\alpha = .01$) to indicate that the average number of larvae per branch tip exceeds 38.0, should the trees be sprayed?

■■■■■■ CASE 11.1* DEMOGRAPHIC PROFILE OF THE AUTOMATIC TELLER MACHINE USER

MKT Case 7.2 discussed an article that presented the results of a survey designed to determine the frequency of use of an automatic teller machine (ATM). Another

---

* Adapted from D. L. Varble and J. M. Hawes, "Profiling the Users of Automated Teller Machines," *Developments in Marketing Science* 9 (1986): 369–72.

purpose of the survey was to draw a demographic profile of individuals who use these banking machines. This profile would help the bank persuade more customers to use the ATM instead of a teller. (The bank would save approximately one dollar for each such transaction.)

An ATM is about to be installed in a large office tower. As a random sample, 530 people who work in this building were asked whether or not they own an ATM card, and they have also been asked several questions to identify various demographic characteristics. These results appear in Tables A through E. What are the demographic characteristics that distinguish those who possess an ATM card from those who do not?

TABLE A   FREQUENCY OF POSSESSION OF AN ATM CARD AND GENDER

	Possession of an ATM Card	
Gender	Yes	No
Female	102	302
Male	48	78

TABLE B   FREQUENCY OF POSSESSION OF AN ATM CARD AND INCOME

	Possession of an ATM Card	
	Yes	No
Income	$\bar{x} = 15,190$	$\bar{x} = 13,580$
	$s = 5,398$	$s = 5,636$

TABLE C   FREQUENCY OF POSSESSION OF AN ATM CARD AND FAMILY EMPLOYMENT PATTERN

	Possession of an ATM Card	
Family Employment Pattern	Yes	No
Both spouses work	70	202
Only one spouse works	80	178

TABLE D   FREQUENCY OF POSSESSION OF AN ATM CARD AND YEARS OF EDUCATION

	Possession of an ATM Card	
	Yes	No
Years of Education	$\bar{x} = 17.07$	$\bar{x} = 14.83$
	$s = 2.82$	$s = 2.88$

TABLE E   FREQUENCY OF POSSESSION OF AN ATM CARD AND AGE

	Possession of an ATM Card	
	Yes	No
Age	$\bar{x} = 39.40$	$\bar{x} = 38.67$
	$s = 11.95$	$s = 11.69$

CASE 11.2*   *EFFECT OF THE DEATH OF KEY EXECUTIVES*
ON STOCK MARKET RETURNS

We recommend the use of a computer for this case. The data listed below are also stored on the data disk.

FIN   How does the death of a key executive affect a company? This question was addressed by two researchers. In particular they wanted to know how the stock market would react to the deaths of the chief executive officer and/or chairman of the board of companies whose stock trades over the counter. A sample of 21 companies whose CEO or chairman died during a 17-year period from 1966 to 1982 was selected. For each company the weekly stock returns were recorded for 55 weeks prior to the executives' deaths and for 5 weeks after. A market model (see Case 15.1) was used to determine expected returns, and the difference between the actual and expected returns was calculated. These are called *abnormal returns*. The abnormal returns for each company for the periods 3 weeks prior to the deaths and 5 weeks after are shown in the accompanying table.

Under stable conditions the average abnormal return should equal zero, and we should observe an equal number of positive and negative abnormal returns. The researchers believed that in the weeks before the deaths ($t = -3, -2, -1$) the abnormal returns would indicate stable conditions. However, after the deaths

* Adapted from D. L. Warnell and W. N. Davidson, III, "The Death of Key Executives in Small Firms: Effects on Investor Wealth," *Journal of Small Business Management* 27(2) (April 1989): 10–16.

($t = 0$, 1, 2, 3, 4, 5) they would exhibit the effects of bad news—the abnormal returns would be negative. What conclusions can you draw from the data?

ABNORMAL RETURNS (IN %) FOR WEEKS $t = -3, -2, \ldots, 5$

Company	$t = -3$	-2	-1	0	1	2	3	4	5
1	-2.73	-6.03	6.67	2.50	-11.63	5.59	-4.53	-2.09	-2.65
2	-1.01	-3.30	-0.69	7.97	-4.37	1.63	-0.98	4.14	2.31
3	-2.53	6.89	-2.03	-7.17	-1.01	-1.51	-4.97	-1.48	0.27
4	-3.87	-2.53	-2.60	-0.45	-0.32	6.91	-2.19	3.12	-1.62
5	7.22	-1.21	2.19	-0.02	-1.52	-2.36	-5.16	-8.31	1.45
6	9.88	6.51	-1.17	-5.04	-1.26	0.03	3.05	-4.10	4.01
7	2.20	-6.26	9.93	-5.32	-4.14	-4.45	-5.97	11.54	3.67
8	-1.72	3.40	-2.68	-0.59	-0.11	-4.93	2.12	-1.59	1.89
9	3.68	-6.36	10.41	-0.22	5.71	-3.63	-1.01	0.65	-4.54
10	-5.90	2.58	-1.34	-1.90	-0.83	8.51	-1.80	0.73	-1.75
11	0.15	6.09	-0.16	-0.73	-3.10	-3.31	6.05	-3.89	-0.27
12	-1.19	-0.87	-0.26	-2.48	3.42	4.54	4.33	-0.44	3.66
13	-2.06	4.32	1.67	-0.62	-0.66	0.08	3.57	6.79	1.91
14	1.60	1.22	-4.04	-1.33	-0.85	0.66	-4.72	-2.49	0.84
15	6.82	5.94	6.46	3.08	-0.68	-2.71	9.19	0.14	0.98
16	2.40	-1.39	2.94	-3.19	-10.91	8.11	3.99	4.27	-0.68
17	3.51	-3.49	7.32	-5.53	-2.13	-0.49	0.55	1.49	-3.80
18	-5.03	0.32	-2.49	-7.46	-0.66	0.14	1.35	1.44	-2.35
19	-6.02	1.68	-1.26	-7.51	1.19	-2.67	-0.67	-0.13	-1.85
20	-0.54	0.68	-0.17	-5.33	-2.38	-7.56	1.10	1.21	0.26
21	-8.65	1.22	7.06	-0.75	1.77	-1.96	5.99	-1.64	-2.32

CASE 11.3*   HOST SELLING AND ANNOUNCER COMMERCIALS

MKT A study was undertaken to compare the effects of host selling commercials and announcer commercials on children. Announcer commercials are straightforward

---

* Adapted from J. H. Miller, "An Empirical Evaluation of the Host Selling Commercial and the Announcer Commercial When Used on Children," *Developments in Marketing Science* 8 (1985): 276–78.

commercials in which the announcer describes to viewers why they should buy a particular product. Host selling commercials feature a children's show personality or television character who extols the virtues of the product. In 1975, the National Association of Broadcasters prohibited using show characters to advertise products during the same program in which they appear. This was overturned in 1982, however, by a judge's decree.

The objective of the study was to determine whether the two types of advertisements have different effects on children viewing them. The experiment utilized two groups of children, ranging in age from 6 to 10. One group of 121 children watched a program in which two host selling commercials appeared. (The commercials tried to sell Canary Crunch, a breakfast cereal.) A second group of 121 children watched the same program, but this group was exposed to two announcer commercials for the same product. Immediately after the show the children were given a questionnaire that tested their memory concerning the commercials they had watched. Each child was marked (on a scale of 10) on his or her ability to remember details of the commercial. In addition, each child was offered a free box of cereal. The children were shown four different boxes of cereal—Froot Loops, Boo Berries, Kangaroo Hops, and Canary Crunch (the advertised cereal)—and asked to pick the one they wanted.

The summarized results of the experiment are shown in Tables A and B. What conclusions can be drawn from these data?

TABLE A   CHILDREN'S RECALL (10-POINT SCALE)

	Type of Commercial	
	Host	Announcer
Scores	$\bar{x} = 7.81$	$\bar{x} = 7.28$
	$s^2 = 2.87$	$s^2 = 1.94$

TABLE B   CHILDREN'S CHOICE OF BREAKFAST CEREAL

Cereal	Type of Commercial	
	Host	Announcer
Froot Loops	28	35
Boo Berries	15	11
Kangaroo Hops	34	38
Canary Crunch	44	37

■■■■■■■■■   **CASE 11.4***   *TEXACO'S SEASONAL PROMOTIONS*

We recommend the use of a computer for this case. The data listed below are also stored on the data disk.

MKT   Texaco Canada is the fourth largest retailer of gasoline in Canada, with a market share of 12%. An important part of Texaco's marketing strategy is a sales promotion in which customers receive free gifts with purchases of at least 25 liters. It is company policy to make a profit on the promotion, and it is anticipated that additional profits will result after the promotion because customers will continue to buy Texaco gasoline even when there are no free gifts.

The country is divided into 11 divisions, and decisions regarding promotions are made by executives in charge of each division. The executives of one division that has 200 stations are considering a Christmas promotional campaign (October 15 to December 31) in which customers who buy at least 25 liters of gasoline will receive a free package of Christmas wrapping paper. The cost per package is $0.27. Currently, the mean retail price is 41.9 cents per liter. The costs, including delivery, are 29.2 cents per liter. An integral part of the campaign is additional advertising, which is estimated to cost $40,000. From previous promotional campaigns, it is known that 100 stations will participate in this Christmas campaign.

Before launching the campaign, Texaco wants to be quite confident that the program will at least break even. The decision is usually based on sales experience with previous, similar promotions. In the previous year, a similar promotional campaign was undertaken. Each of the 32 stations that participated kept track of the monthly gasoline volume before, during, and after the campaign, as well as of the number of free gifts given away during the month that the campaign lasted. These data are shown in the accompanying table.

Based on these data, can the executives of this division confidently conclude that the campaign will at least break even? What are the prospects for additional profits after the campaign?

PROMOTIONAL CAMPAIGN DATA

Station	Monthly Vol. Before Campaign (1,000 liters)	Monthly Vol. During Campaign (1,000 liters)	Monthly Vol. After Campaign (1,000 liters)	Monthly Free Gifts
1	205	220	207	4,903
2	182	191	180	4,275
3	237	263	246	5,862

(*continued*)

---

* The authors are grateful to Texaco Canada for providing assistance in writing this case.

PROMOTIONAL CAMPAIGN DATA (continued)

Station	Monthly Vol. Before Campaign (1,000 liters)	Monthly Vol. During Campaign (1,000 liters)	Monthly Vol. After Campaign (1,000 liters)	Monthly Free Gifts
4	236	241	242	5,269
5	198	217	202	4,818
6	242	271	232	6,183
7	151	159	155	3,475
8	253	271	248	5,962
9	156	153	159	3,571
10	163	175	159	3,725
11	211	228	210	5,100
12	225	242	231	5,306
13	192	205	191	4,455
14	175	187	172	4,243
15	252	262	261	5,739
16	181	200	170	4,291
17	217	230	214	5,008
18	188	195	190	4,362
19	170	179	170	3,877
20	363	393	359	9,512
21	169	180	174	4,125
22	293	320	292	7,837
23	171	169	172	3,448
24	210	230	209	5,653
25	193	210	192	4,348
26	312	342	316	8,985
27	225	253	222	5,492
28	183	183	183	3,961
29	288	321	294	6,873
30	171	185	171	3,888
31	209	235	207	4,675
32	235	266	252	5,911

■■■■■ *CASE 11.5**   *ALTERING REPORTED INCOMES*

ACC   It is often in the interest of companies to report incomes in a favorable light. A recent study investigated the possibility that firms make minor alterations in their reported figures to make the results look better. Psychologists have noted that humans have a tendency to simplify numbers by rounding up or down. Thus, changing one or two digits in a number may make an important difference. There are often rewards for managers who meet goals as opposed to those who just fall short. Managers in such situations may take steps to give the appearance that goals are being met. Consequently income figures such as $295,086 may be rounded to $300,000 because the latter figure appears to be so much better than the former. It is possible to detect this phenomenon by observing the second digit. If small changes are being made, there will be a greater number of zeros and a smaller number of nines than expected in the second digit.

It would appear logical that the proportion of times any digit will occur in a given place in a number would be 1/9 for the first digit (which cannot be zero) and 1/10 for all other digits. However, this is not the case. By a complex mathematical formula, the expected frequencies of the first and second digits were computed, as shown in Table A.[†]

TABLE A   *EXPECTED FREQUENCIES OF FIRST AND SECOND DIGITS*

	Expected Frequencies	
Digit	First Digit	Second Digit
0	—	.120
1	.301	.114
2	.176	.109
3	.125	.104
4	.097	.100
5	.079	.097
6	.067	.093
7	.058	.090
8	.051	.088
9	.046	.085
Total	1	1

---

* C. A. P. N. Carslaw, "Anomalies in Income Numbers: Evidence of Goal-Oriented Behavior," *Accounting Review* 63(2) (April 1988): 321–27.

† See W. Feller, *An Introduction to Probability Theory,* Vol. 2 (New York: John Wiley & Sons, 1966) pp. 62–63.

TABLE B

ACTUAL FREQUENCIES OF FIRST AND SECOND DIGITS IN REPORTED
ORDINARY AND NET INCOME

	First Digits		**Second Digits**	
Digit	Ordinary Income	Net Income	Ordinary Income	Net Income
0	—	—	133	129
1	262	235	95	89
2	119	123	78	87
3	110	119	86	82
4	82	82	72	68
5	55	56	70	74
6	53	60	76	71
7	45	42	76	72
8	43	46	68	77
9	36	42	51	56
Total	805	805	805	805

A random sample of financial statements from 220 firms during the years 1981 to 1985 was selected. Statements acknowledging losses were excluded, resulting in a usable sample of 805 statements. The number of occurrences of each first and second digit for ordinary and net income is shown in Table B. The data and expected frequencies of the first digits are shown to ensure that the formulas that produced the expected frequencies in Table A are reasonable.

What conclusions can you draw from these data?

CASE 11.6* UNDERPRICING IN INITIAL PUBLIC OFFERINGS

FIN | When a company offers its common shares to the public for the first time, the process is referred to as the company's initial public offering (IPO). The company retains an investment banker to establish the price at which the shares will be sold initially (at $t = 0$). If the price is set too high, there will be insufficient demand to sell all of the shares. On the other hand, if the shares are underpriced, the company will receive less money for its shares than the maximum possible.

Studies concerning IPOs in the U.S. indicate that, on average, "IPOs tend to be underpriced by 11 to 18%." Studies concerning IPOs in Canada, using pre-1970

---

* Adapted from Vijay M. Jog and Allan L. Riding, "Underpricing in Canadian IPOs," *Financial Analysts' Journal* (Nov.–Dec. 1987): 48–55.

data, "reported an average degree of underpricing in excess of 40%." The evidence of excessive underpricing has caused the Canadian government to consider direct intervention in the capital markets to reduce this underpricing, and thereby encourage entrepreneurs to raise capital through public offerings.

Jog and Riding have suggested that, before the government decides to intervene, it should consider the results of their underpricing study that used more recent data. Jog and Riding took a sample of 100 Canadian IPOs issued between 1971 and 1983. For each IPO they computed (for three-time intervals) the values of the following underpricing measure:

U_{jt} = the percentage of underpricing of the jth IPO measured from $t = 0$ to day t of public trading (for $t = 1, 35$)

The value U_{jt} is essentially the percentage price appreciation of the jth IPO, measured from $t = 0$ to day t of public trading. Thus, underpricing is indicated by positive values of U_{jt}.

The average values of the underpricing measure across all stocks in the sample, for each of the three time intervals, are shown in the table. For example, on average, the IPOs appreciated by 9.33% during their first day of public trading.

The government would be interested in knowing if there is evidence of (a positive percentage of) underpricing; and also if this percentage exceeds 5%, in which case the degree of underpricing would be sufficiently high to allow traders to profit from it even after paying brokerage commissions. What conclusions might the government draw from this study?

UNDERPRICING OF IPOS

Underpricing Measure	Mean	Std. Dev.
U_1	9.33	25.91
U_3	9.24	26.86
U_5	9.38	27.15

CASE 11.7*   COMPREHENSIVE PLANNING FOR BANKS

We recommend the use of a computer for this case. The data listed below are also stored on the data disk.

FIN   Wood and Laforge examined a number of banks to test their belief that "large U.S. banks that had more comprehensive planning would financially outperform

---

* Adapted from D. R. Wood., Jr., and R. L. Laforge. "The Impact of Comprehensive Planning on Financial Performance," *Academy of Management Journal* 22(3) (1979): 516–26.

those that had less comprehensive planning." A total of 61 banks were involved. Of this total, 26 had comprehensive formal plans, 6 had partial formal plans, and 9 had no formal planning system. The remaining 20 banks represented a random sample of all banks.

TABLE A COMPREHENSIVE FORMAL PLANNERS

Bank	Percent Increase in Net Income	Percent Return on Investment
1	11.02	12.02
2	7.34	12.33
3	9.81	12.56
4	11.53	13.10
5	10.75	13.41
6	14.10	13.66
7	13.28	12.48
8	12.56	12.80
9	7.27	12.45
10	16.53	13.58
11	13.56	11.55
12	0.70	11.96
13	14.22	13.59
14	13.06	13.20
15	12.70	12.96
16	9.51	12.04
17	9.00	13.65
18	14.29	12.79
19	6.56	13.07
20	16.93	12.41
21	14.32	13.68
22	14.17	12.41
23	9.15	13.08
24	12.27	12.94
25	17.46	12.21
26	18.01	12.35

The financial performance over a five-year period (1972–1976) was analyzed with respect to two different performance measures: growth in net income, and return on owner's investment. The results appear in the accompanying tables. What conclusions can you draw from these data?

TABLE B   PARTIAL FORMAL PLANNERS

Bank	Percent Increase in Net Income	Percent Return on Investment
1	7.67	13.29
2	12.22	14.83
3	21.56	13.48
4	9.42	12.55
5	10.56	12.67
6	− 1.59	14.75

TABLE C   NO FORMAL PLANNING

Bank	Percent Increase in Net Income	Percent Return on Investment
1	3.50	10.80
2	15.72	11.75
3	7.62	10.21
4	− 11.88	9.20
5	− 0.60	7.87
6	12.94	10.79
7	5.21	10.11
8	− 17.60	10.67
9	3.95	9.33

TABLE D   RANDOM SAMPLE OF ALL BANKS

Bank	Percent Increase in Net Income	Percent Return on Investment
1	7.65	10.60
2	5.07	10.19
3	1.82	11.41
4	9.37	9.46
5	2.11	10.20
6	9.62	11.29
7	7.07	9.95
8	7.57	10.99
9	5.64	10.08
10	10.28	10.47
11	2.79	8.35
12	1.62	10.49
13	6.31	9.95
14	−2.98	11.16
15	8.49	9.77
16	3.80	11.30
17	−0.95	10.04
18	13.98	9.84
19	−2.16	9.57
20	1.62	9.53

CASE 11.8*   GENERIC PRODUCTS

This case requires the use of a computer. The data are not shown below but are stored on the data disk.

MKT   The growth in sales of generic grocery products has been quite impressive in recent years. Their share of the total grocery bill is now in excess of 5%. In an effort by a supermarket to improve sales, a random sample of 150 grocery shoppers was taken, and the surveyor attempted to determine if she could identify the

* Adapted from N. Hanna, B. Ahuja, and D. Kumar, "The Generic User/Nonuser and the Process of Adoption," *Developments in Marketing Science* 6 (1983): 68–71.

demographic characteristics of users of generic grocery products. Individuals were asked whether they were users of generic grocery products as well as their age, sex, marital status, occupation, income, and education. What conclusions can be drawn from the survey results?

The data are stored on the data disk using the following format.

TABLE A   *USERS OF GENERIC PRODUCTS*

Respondent	Age	Sex (female = 1, male = 0)	Marital Status (single = 1, other = 0)	Occupation (white-collar = 1, other = 0)	Income	Years of Education
1	22	1	0	1	6,000	10
2	20	0	0	0	7,500	10
3	19	1	0	1	9,000	10
⋮	⋮	⋮	⋮	⋮	⋮	⋮
120	50	1	0	1	42,500	17

TABLE B   *NONUSERS OF GENERIC PRODUCTS*

Respondent	Age	Sex	Martial Status	Occupation	Income	Education
1	23	1	1	1	5,000	10
2	20	1	0	1	7,500	10
3	19	0	0	1	10,000	11
⋮	⋮	⋮	⋮	⋮	⋮	⋮
30	47	0	1	0	30,000	16

MINITAB INSTRUCTIONS

In this appendix we use the Minitab statistical application package to answer Example 11.1. We begin by typing in the data. Columns 1 and 3 are the values of the drying times of the old and new adhesives, respectively. Columns 2 and 4 represent the nominal scale specifying whether the tile has been properly attached. We arbitrarily let Yes = 1 and No = 0. The commands we enter for this part of Example 11.1 are as follows:

```
READ C1-C4
7.1    1   8.3   1
6.3    1   8.5   1
9.2    0   7.3   1
8.6    1   6.5   1
5.5    0   7.0   1
7.3    0   6.4   1
6.6    1   6.3   0
8.0    0   7.7   1
7.7    1   5.2   1
8.9    0   7.6   0
9.1    1   6.1   1
8.6    0   5.7   1
5.7    1   6.3   1
4.9    1   7.0   0
6.0    0   8.8   1
6.8    1   6.9   1
6.7    0   6.5   1
7.5    1   5.8   0
8.3    1   4.3   1
8.0    0   4.9   1
```

```
6.1    1   6.6   0
9.1    1   6.8   1
5.8    0   7.0   1
6.0    1   6.5   1
7.3    0   6.0   1
END
```

For part (a) of the example, to test

$$H_0: (\mu_1 - \mu_2) = 0$$
$$H_A: (\mu_1 - \mu_2) > 0$$

we type the commands

```
TWOSAMPLE T C1 C3;
POOLED;
ALTERNATIVE 1.
```

The output is

```
TWOSAMPLE T FOR C1 VS C3
        N    MEAN    ST DEV    SE MEAN
C1     25    7.24     1.27      0.25
C3     25    6.64     1.06      0.21
95 PCT CI FOR MU C1-MU C3: (-0.06, 1.27)
TTEST MU C1=MU C3 (VS GT): T=1.82 P=0.037 D=48.0
```

In order to answer part (b), we test

$$H_0: (p_1 - p_2) = 0$$
$$H_A: (p_1 - p_2) > 0$$

Although there is no direct test for these hypotheses, we can use Minitab to count the number of times each value of the variables occurs. This involves using the TABLE command for columns 2 and 4. That is, the command

```
TABLE C2
```

causes the computer to print

```
ROWS C2
        COUNT
0        11
1        14
ALL      25
```

The command

```
TABLE C4
```

prints

```
ROWS C4
        COUNT
0        5
1       20
ALL     25
```

Once the values of $\hat{p}_1$ and $\hat{p}_2$ are computed, the z-test of $p_1 - p_2$ can be completed manually (or with a calculator).

For part (c), the command

```
TINTERVAL .99 C3
```

outputs

```
        N    MEAN    ST DEV   SE MEAN   99.0 PERCENT C.I.
C3     25    6.640   1.062    0.212     (6.046, 7.234)
```

For part (d) we use the calculation of $\hat{p}_2 = .20$ to produce the confidence interval estimate of p_2.

In part (f), we wish to test

$$H_0: \sigma_1^2/\sigma_2^2 = 1$$
$$H_A: \sigma_1^2/\sigma_2^2 \neq 1$$

for which we need the test statistic

$$F = \frac{s_1^2}{s_2^2}$$

In part (a), we found that $s_1 = 1.27$ and $s_2 = 1.06$, and these values permit us to compute the value of the test statistic.

SAS INSTRUCTIONS

In this appendix, we use the SAS statistical application package to answer Example 11.1. We begin by inputting the data. The variable TIME represents the drying times for both adhesives; ATTACHED is the nominally scaled variable indicating whether or not the tile has been properly attached; and ADHESIVE is the variable identifying the adhesive as either old or new. We do not convert the latter two variables into numerical values. We type them in as Yes or No for the ATTACHED variable, and as Old or New for the ADHESIVE variable. We identify these variables as nonnumerical by putting a $ sign after the variable names in the INPUT statement.

The data input for Example 11.1 is as follows:

```
DATA;
INPUT TIME ATTACHED $ ADHESIVE $;
CARDS;
7.1    YES        OLD
6.3    YES        OLD
9.2    NO         OLD
8.6    YES        OLD
5.5    NO         OLD
7.3    NO         OLD
6.6    YES        OLD
8.0    NO         OLD
7.7    YES        OLD
8.9    NO         OLD
9.1    YES        OLD
8.6    NO         OLD
5.7    YES        OLD
4.9    YES        OLD
6.0    NO         OLD
6.8    YES        OLD
```

(continued)

6.7	NO	OLD
7.5	YES	OLD
8.3	YES	OLD
8.0	NO	OLD
6.1	YES	OLD
9.1	YES	OLD
5.8	NO	OLD
6.0	YES	OLD
7.3	NO	OLD
8.3	YES	NEW
8.5	YES	NEW
7.3	YES	NEW
6.5	YES	NEW
7.0	YES	NEW
6.4	YES	NEW
6.3	NO	NEW
7.7	YES	NEW
5.2	YES	NEW
7.6	NO	NEW
6.1	YES	NEW
5.7	YES	NEW
6.3	YES	NEW
7.0	NO	NEW
8.8	YES	NEW
6.9	YES	NEW
6.5	YES	NEW
5.8	NO	NEW
4.3	YES	NEW
4.9	YES	NEW
6.6	NO	NEW
6.8	YES	NEW
7.0	YES	NEW
6.5	YES	NEW
6.0	YES	NEW

For part (a) of Example 11.1, to test $\mu_1 - \mu_2$, we type (after all the data have been input) the following commands:

```
PROC TTEST;
CLASS ADHESIVE;
VAR TIME;
```

The output is

```
Variable: TIME
ADHESIVE      N      Mean     Std Dev    Std Error
-----------------------------------------------------
NEW          25    6.6400     1.0618      0.2123
OLD          25    7.2440     1.2731      0.2546


Variances        T        DF      Prob > |T|
-----------------------------------------------------
Unequal      -1.8217     46.5      0.0749
Equal        -1.8217     48.0      0.0747
```

In order to answer part (b), we test

$$H_0: (p_1 - p_2) = 0$$
$$H_A: (p_1 - p_2) > 0$$

Although there is no direct test for these hypotheses, we can use SAS to count the number of times each value of the ATTACHED variable occurs. This involves using the FREQ procedure. That is, the statements

```
PROC FREQ;
TABLES ATTACHED*ADHESIVE;
```

cause the computer to print the following:

```
TABLE OF ATTACHED BY ADHESIVE
ATTACHED         ADHESIVE
Frequency |        |        |
Percent   |        |        |
Row Pct   |        |        |
Col Pct   | NEW    | OLD    |   Total
----------+--------+--------+
NO        |    5   |   11   |    16
          | 10.00  | 22.00  |  32.00
          | 31.25  | 68.75  |
          | 20.00  | 44.00  |
----------+--------+--------+
YES       |   20   |   14   |    34
          | 40.00  | 28.00  |  68.00
          | 58.82  | 41.18  |
          | 80.00  | 56.00  |
----------+--------+--------+
Total         25       25        50
            50.00    50.00    100.00
```

This provides the answer to part (b).

From part (a), we find $\bar{x}_2 = 6.6400$ and $s_2 = 1.0618$, which we use to produce the confidence interval estimate of μ_2 required in part (c).

For part (d), recall that, in the solution to part (b), we found $\hat{p}_2 = .20$. We use this value to construct the interval estimate of p_2.

In part (f), we wish to test

$$H_0: \sigma_1^2/\sigma_2^2 = 1$$
$$H_A: \sigma_1^2/\sigma_2^2 \neq 1$$

for which we need the test statistic

$$F = \frac{s_1^2}{s_2^2}$$

In part (a), we found that $s_1 = 1.2731$ and $s_2 = 1.0618$, and these values permit us to compute the value of the test statistic.

ANALYSIS OF VARIANCE

INTRODUCTION

The techniques presented in this chapter allow us to compare two or more populations in terms of their population means when the data scale is interval. We will not present the technique for population variances: ironically, the statistical technique employed here analyzes the sample variance in order to test and estimate the means, and for this reason the method is called the **analysis of variance.** Examples of applications of the analysis of variance include the following:

Case 1. A supermarket chain-store executive needs to determine whether or not the sales of a new product are affected by the aisle in which the product is stored. If there are eight aisles in the store, the experiment would consist of locating the product in a different aisle in each of eight weeks and recording the weekly sales. The test would assess whether or not the mean weekly sales differ.

Case 2. A farm-products manufacturer wants to determine if the yield of a crop is different when the soil is treated with various fertilizers. Similar plots of land are planted with the same type of seed but are fertilized differently. At the end of the growing season, the mean yields from the sample plots can be compared. Historically, this type of experiment was one of the first to use the analysis of variance, and the terminology of the original experiment is still used. No matter what the experiment, the test is designed to determine if there are significant differences among the **treatment means.**

COMPLETELY RANDOMIZED DESIGN

As was the case in Chapter 9, the experimental design is a determinant in identifying the appropriate statistical technique. We begin our presentation by describing the proper method to use when the samples are independently drawn. Such an experiment is said to have a **completely randomized design.** Figure 12.1 depicts this experimental design.

Each population has mean μ_j and variance σ_j^2, where both parameters are unknown. From each population, we draw independent random samples; thus the selection of one sample does not affect the selection of any other sample. For each sample we can compute the mean, $\bar{x}_j$, and the variance, s_j^2.

EXAMPLE 12.1

An apple juice manufacturer has developed a new product—a liquid concentrate that, when mixed with water, produces 1 liter of apple juice. After careful analysis

FIGURE 12.1   SAMPLING SCHEME FOR COMPLETELY RANDOMIZED DESIGN

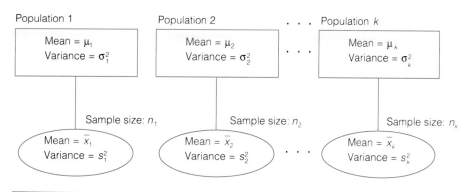

she has decided to market the product in one of three ways: emphasizing convenience, emphasizing quality, or emphasizing price. In order to help make a decision she conducts an experiment. In three different small cities, she launches the product with advertising stressing convenience in one city, quality in the second city, and price in the third city. The number of packages sold weekly is recorded for the eight weeks following the beginning of the campaign; these data are shown in the accompanying table. Can we conclude at the 5% significance level that there are differences in the weekly sales of the product among the three cities?

WEEKLY SALES (100s of units)

City 1 (convenience)	City 2 (quality)	City 3 (price)
15	10	13
17	12	18
22	15	19
20	17	16
18	12	17
16	13	16
14	15	15
19	16	18

You should confirm that the data scale is interval (weekly sales) and that the problem objective is to compare three populations (the three types of advertising).

Following the same pattern that we used to conduct tests in Chapters 7 through 10, we now proceed to conduct this test. We begin with the null and alternative hypotheses. The null hypothesis states that there are no differences among the population means. Hence,

$$H_0: \mu_1 = \mu_2 = \mu_3$$

The alternative hypothesis, as usual, answers the question being addressed. Since we'd like to know if there is evidence of a difference among the population means, the alternative hypothesis states

H_A: At least two means differ.

The next step is to determine the test statistic, which is somewhat more involved than the test statistics we have developed previously. The testing process will be facilitated by the following notation.

Notation

$x_{ij} = i$th observation of the jth sample

$n_j =$ Number of observations in the sample taken from the jth population

$$\bar{x}_j = \text{Mean of the } j\text{th sample} = \frac{\sum_{i=1}^{n_j} x_{ij}}{n_j}$$

$$\bar{\bar{x}} = \text{Grand mean of all the values of } x_{ij} = \frac{\sum_{j=1}^{k} \sum_{i=1}^{n_j} x_{ij}}{n}$$

where $n = n_1 + n_2 + \cdots + n_k$ and k is the number of populations to be compared. Table 12.1 provides another view of the notation. Notice that we allow the sample sizes to be different.

TABLE 12.1   *NOTATION FOR THE COMPLETELY RANDOMIZED DESIGN OF THE ANALYSIS OF VARIANCE*

Independent Samples from k Populations (Treatments)

	Treatment			
	1	2	$\cdots$	k
	x_{11}	x_{12}	$\cdots$	x_{1k}
	x_{21}	x_{22}	$\cdots$	x_{2k}
	$\vdots$	$\vdots$		$\vdots$
	$x_{n_1 1}$	$x_{n_2 2}$		$x_{n_k k}$
For each treatment (column):				
Sample sizes	n_1	n_2		n_k
Sample means	$\bar{x}_1$	$\bar{x}_2$		$\bar{x}_k$

Test Statistic.   The test statistic is computed in accordance with the following rationale. If the null hypothesis were true, the population means would all be equal to each other. We would then expect that the sample means would be close to one another. If the alternative hypothesis were true, however, some of the sample means would exhibit relatively large differences. The calculation that measures the proximity of the sample means to each other is called the **between-treatments variability**, denoted SST (sum of squares for treatments), where

$$\text{SST} = \sum_{j=1}^{k} n_j(\bar{x}_j - \bar{\bar{x}})^2$$

As you can deduce from this formula, if the sample means are close to each other, all sample means are close to the grand mean and consequently SST is small. In fact, SST achieves its smallest possible value (0) when all of the sample means are equal. That is, if

$$\bar{x}_1 = \bar{x}_2 = \cdots = \bar{x}_k$$

then

$$\text{SST} = 0$$

It follows that a small value of SST supports the null hypothesis.

To illustrate, consider Example 12.1. We compute the sample means and the grand mean as

$$\bar{x}_1 = \frac{(15 + 17 + \cdots + 19)}{8} = \frac{141}{8} = 17.625$$

$$\bar{x}_2 = \frac{(10 + 12 + \cdots + 16)}{8} = \frac{110}{8} = 13.75$$

$$\bar{x}_3 = \frac{(13 + 18 + \cdots + 18)}{8} = \frac{132}{8} = 16.5$$

$$\bar{\bar{x}} = \frac{(15 + 17 + \cdots + 18)}{24} = \frac{383}{24} = 15.9583$$

Then

$$\begin{aligned}
\text{SST} &= \sum_{j=1}^{3} n_j(\bar{x}_j - \bar{\bar{x}})^2 \\
&= 8(17.625 - 15.9583)^2 + 8(13.75 - 15.9583)^2 + 8(16.5 - 15.9583)^2 \\
&= 63.59
\end{aligned}$$

If large differences exist among the sample means, at least some sample means differ considerably from the grand mean, producing a large value of SST. It is then reasonable to reject the null hypothesis in favor of the alternative. The key question to be answered in this test (as in all of the tests that we've encountered thus far) is how large must SST be in order for us to be justified in rejecting the null hypothesis? In our example, SST = 63.59. Is this value large enough to indicate that the population means differ? To answer this question, we compare SST to the variability within the treatments. The **within-treatments variability** offers a measure of the degree of variability we can expect from the random variable we're measuring.

To understand this concept, examine Tables 12.2 and 12.3. Table 12.2 describes an example in which, because the variability within each sample is quite small, SST is relatively large. Table 12.3 depicts a case in which, because the variability within the samples is large, the same value of SST could by comparison be considered small. The term that measures the amount of variability within the samples is the sum of squares for error, denoted SSE, where

$$\text{SSE} = \sum_{j=1}^{k} \sum_{i=1}^{n_j} (x_{ij} - \bar{x}_j)^2$$

When SSE is partially expanded, we get

$$\text{SSE} = \sum_{i=1}^{n_1} (x_{i1} - \bar{x}_1)^2 + \sum_{i=1}^{n_2} (x_{i2} - \bar{x}_2)^2 + \cdots + \sum_{i=1}^{n_k} (x_{ik} - \bar{x}_k)^2$$

If you examine each of the k components of SSE, you'll see that each is a measure of the variability of that sample. If we divide each component by $n_j - 1$, the results of our computation are the sample variances of each sample. We can express this by rewriting SSE as

$$\text{SSE} = (n_1 - 1)s_1^2 + (n_2 - 1)s_2^2 + \cdots + (n_k - 1)s_k^2$$

where s_j^2 is the sample variance of sample j. SSE is thus the combined or pooled variability of all k samples. This is an extension of a calculation we made in Section 9.3, where we determined the pooled estimate of the common population variance (denoted s_p^2). In that case, it was a required condition that the population variances were equal. That same condition is now necessary in order for us to use SSE. That is, we require that

$$\sigma_1^2 = \sigma_2^2 = \cdots = \sigma_k^2$$

Returning to the example, we compute the following:

$$\begin{aligned}
\text{SSE} &= \sum_{j=1}^{3} \sum_{i=1}^{8} (x_{ij} - \bar{x}_j)^2 \\
&= \sum_{i=1}^{8} (x_{i1} - \bar{x}_1)^2 + \sum_{i=1}^{8} (x_{i2} - \bar{x}_2)^2 + \sum_{i=1}^{8} (x_{i3} - \bar{x}_3)^2 \\
&= (15 - 17.625)^2 + (17 - 17.625)^2 + \cdots + (19 - 17.625)^2 \\
&\quad + (10 - 13.75)^2 + (12 - 13.75)^2 + \cdots + (16 - 13.75)^2 \\
&\quad + (13 - 16.5)^2 + (18 - 16.5)^2 + \cdots + (18 - 16.5)^2 \\
&= 49.875 + 39.5 + 26.0 \\
&= 115.375
\end{aligned}$$

Both SST and SSE are measures of variability of the variable x_{ij}. In Section 9.5 we showed that, if two such independent measures of variability are divided by their

TABLE 12.2   *RELATIVELY LARGE VARIABILITY BETWEEN SAMPLES*

Treatment		
1	2	3
10	15	20
10	16	20
11	14	20
10	16	20
9	14	20
$\bar{x}_1 = 10$	$\bar{x}_2 = 15$	$\bar{x}_3 = 20$

TABLE 12.3   *RELATIVELY SMALL VARIABILITY BETWEEN SAMPLES*

Treatment		
1	2	3
1	19	5
12	31	33
20	4	20
10	9	12
7	12	30
$\bar{x}_1 = 10$	$\bar{x}_2 = 15$	$\bar{x}_3 = 20$

respective degrees of freedom, the ratio is *F*-distributed, provided that the population random variable is normally distributed. The degree of freedom of SST is the number of populations being tested minus one. That is,

$$v_1 = k - 1$$

The degree of freedom of SSE is the total sample size minus the number of populations. Thus,

$$v_2 = n - k$$

The sums of squares divided by their degrees of freedom are called **mean squares.** The mean square for treatments is

$$\text{MST} = \frac{\text{SST}}{k - 1}$$

The mean square for error is

$$\text{MSE} = \frac{\text{SSE}}{n-k}$$

The ratio

$$F = \frac{\text{MST}}{\text{MSE}}$$

is F-distributed, with $k-1$ and $n-k$ degrees of freedom.

Using our previous calculations in this example, we find

$$\text{MST} = \frac{\text{SST}}{k-1} = \frac{63.59}{3-1} = 31.80$$

$$\text{MSE} = \frac{\text{SSE}}{n-k} = \frac{115.375}{24-3} = 5.49$$

The value of the test statistic is

$$F = \frac{\text{MST}}{\text{MSE}} = \frac{31.80}{5.49} = 5.79$$

Rejection Region. The purpose of calculating the F-statistic is to determine whether or not the value of SST is large enough to allow us to reject the null hypothesis. As you can see from the formula of the test statistic, if SST is large, then F is also large. It follows that we reject H_0 only if F is large enough. Specifically, we reject H_0 only if

$$F > F_{\alpha, k-1, n-k}$$

Figure 12.2 exhibits the F-distribution and the rejection region.

FIGURE 12.2   F-DISTRIBUTION AND REJECTION REGION FOR THE ANALYSIS OF VARIANCE

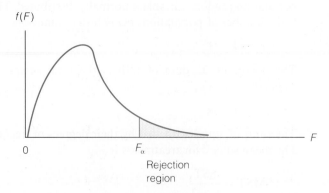

FIGURE 12.3   REJECTION REGION FOR EXAMPLE 12.1

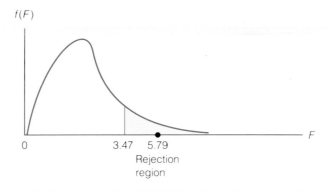

The rejection region for the present example is

$$F > F_{\alpha, k-1, n-k}$$
$$> F_{.05, 2, 21}$$
$$> 3.47$$

Figure 12.3 depicts this rejection region and the value of the test statistic. Since the value of the test statistic $F = 5.79$ falls into the rejection region, we reject the null hypothesis and conclude that there are differences in the weekly sales of the product among the three cities. If we assume that the three cities are similar in all respects, we may infer that there are differences in effectiveness among the three marketing approaches. The company should perform more analyses in the hope of determining which approach is likely to be the most successful.

The results of the analysis of variance test are usually reported in an analysis of variance (ANOVA) table. Table 12.4 shows the general organization of the

TABLE 12.4   GENERAL ORGANIZATION OF THE ANOVA TABLE

Source of Variability	Degrees of Freedom	Sum of Squares	Mean Squares	F-Ratio
Treatments	$k - 1$	SST	$\text{MST} = \text{SST}/(k-1)$	$F = \dfrac{\text{MST}}{\text{MSE}}$
Error	$n - k$	SSE	$\text{MSE} = \text{SSE}/(n-k)$	
Total	$n - 1$	SS(Total)		

TABLE 12.5   ANOVA TABLE FOR EXAMPLE 12.1

Source of Variability	Degrees of Freedom	Sum of Squares	Mean Squares	F-Ratio
Treatments	2	63.59	31.80	5.79
Error	21	115.375	5.49	
Total	23	178.96		

ANOVA table, while Table 12.5 shows the specific ANOVA table for the data in the present example. The terminology used in the ANOVA table (and for that matter in the test itself) is based on the **partitioning of the sum of squares.** Such partitioning is derived from the following equation (whose validity can be demonstrated by using the rules of summation):

$$\sum_{j=1}^{k} \sum_{i=1}^{n_j} (x_{ij} - \bar{\bar{x}})^2 = \sum_{j=1}^{k} n_j(\bar{x}_j - \bar{\bar{x}})^2 + \sum_{j=1}^{k} \sum_{i=1}^{n_j} (x_{ij} - \bar{x}_j)^2$$

The term on the left represents the total variability of all the data. This expression is denoted SS(Total). If we divide SST(Total) by the total sample size minus one (that is, by $n - 1$), we would compute the sample variance. The first term to the right of the equal sign is SST, and the second term is SSE. As you can see, the total variability SS(Total) is partitioned into two sources of variability. The sum of squares for treatments (SST) is the variability attributed to the differences between the treatment means, while the sum of squares for error (SSE) measures the amount of variability within the samples. The preceding equation can be restated as

$$SS(Total) = SST + SSE$$

The test is then based on comparing the relative sizes of SST and SSE (after taking into consideration the degrees of freedom). The partitioning of the sum of squares is depicted in Figure 12.4.

If you have carefully followed the method we used to calculate the test statistic, you are aware that these computations are simple but quite time-consuming. In Appendix 12.A we provide the details of shortcut methods that are available. These methods are derived in the same way as the shortcut approach to determining the sample variance discussed in Chapter 2. Unfortunately the computations are still very lengthy for relatively small problems. In a realistic application of the analysis of variance, the amount of data is typically too large even for shortcut methods, leaving us no alternative except to use the computer. Consequently, instead of discussing how to calculate the necessary statistics, we will focus our attention on how to interpret the computer output. This discussion, of course, is above and beyond our usual guidance on how to recognize when to use the analysis of variance.

FIGURE 12.4   PARTITIONING SS(Total)

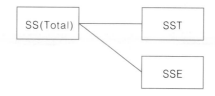

COMPUTER OUTPUT FOR EXAMPLE 12.1*

Minitab

```
ANALYSIS OF VARIANCE
SOURCE     DF      SS       MS      F
FACTOR      2    63.58    31.79    5.79
ERROR      21   115.37     5.49
TOTAL      23   178.96
```

```
                                INDIVIDUAL 95 PCT CI'S FOR MEAN
                                      BASED ON POOLED STDEV

LEVEL    N     MEAN    STDEV    --------|-------|-------|--------
 C1      8    17.625   2.669                      (-----x-----)
 C2      8    13.750   2.375    (-----x-----)
 C3      8    16.500   1.927              (-----x-----)
                                --------|-------|-------|--------
                                   14.0    16.0    18.0
```

POOLED STDEV=2.344

The first half of the printout presents the ANOVA table. The second half shows the sample sizes n_j, the sample means $\bar{x}_j$, and the sample standard deviations s_j. It also shows 95% confidence intervals for μ_j, using the pooled standard deviation. We will discuss these estimates later in this section.

SAS

```
Dependent Variable: X

                            Sum of        Mean
Source            DF       Squares      Square    F Value    Pr > F
Model              2       63.5833      31.7916      5.79     0.0100
Error             21      115.3750       5.4940
Corrected Total   23      178.9583
```

---

* Appendixes 12.B and 12.C provide Minitab and SAS instructions that produced these outputs.

The SAS output includes the complete ANOVA table, as well as the *p*-value of the test, which is represented as Pr > *F*.

Before doing another example, let's summarize what we know.

Analysis of Variance: Completely Randomized Design

Test statistic:

$$F = \frac{MST}{MSE} \qquad \text{d.f.} \quad \begin{aligned} v_1 &= k - 1 \\ v_2 &= n - k \end{aligned}$$

Rejection region:

$$F > F_{\alpha, k-1, n-k}$$

Required conditions:

1. Population random variables $x_1, x_2, \ldots, x_k$ are normally distributed.
2. Population variances are equal. That is, $\sigma_1^2 = \sigma_2^2 = \cdots = \sigma_k^2$.
3. Samples are independent.

Partitioning the sum of squares:

$$SS(Total) = SST + SSE$$

Mean squares:

$$MST = \frac{SST}{k - 1}$$

$$MSE = \frac{SSE}{n - k}$$

EXAMPLE 12.2

A department-store chain is considering building a new store at one of four different sites. One of the important factors in the decision is the average annual household income of the residents of the four areas. Suppose that, in a preliminary study, various residents in each area are asked what their annual household incomes are. The results of this survey are shown in the accompanying table. Is there sufficient evidence to conclude that differences exist in average annual household incomes among the four communities? (Use $\alpha = .01$.)

ANNUAL HOUSEHOLD INCOMES ($1,000s)

Area 1	Area 2	Area 3	Area 4
25	32	27	18
27	35	32	23
31	30	48	29
17	46	25	26
29	32	20	42
30	22	12	
	19	18	
	51		
	27		

Solution. The problem objective is to compare the four communities, and the data scale is interval (annual household income). The samples were drawn independently of one another. If we assume that the incomes are normally distributed and that $\sigma_1^2 = \sigma_2^2 = \sigma_3^2 = \sigma_4^2$, the appropriate test is the completely randomized design of the analysis of variance:

The complete test is shown next.

$H_0: \mu_1 = \mu_2 = \mu_3 = \mu_4$

H_A: At least two means differ.

Test statistic:

$$F = \frac{\text{MST}}{\text{MSE}}$$

Rejection region:

$F > F_{\alpha, k-1, n-k}$

$> F_{.01, 3, 23}$

> 4.76

Value of the test statistic: From the computer output that follows, we have $F = .82$.

Conclusion: Do not reject H_0.

There is not enough evidence to allow us to conclude that average annual household incomes differ among the four communities. The department-store chain's management would be advised to ignore household income as a factor in its decision about the new store location. Figure 12.5 depicts this test.

FIGURE 12.5   REJECTION REGION FOR EXAMPLE 12.2

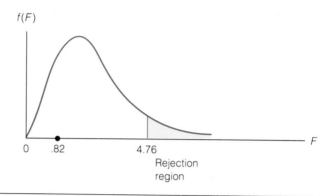

COMPUTER OUTPUT FOR EXAMPLE 12.2

Minitab

ANALYSIS OF VARIANCE

SOURCE	DF	SS	MS	F
FACTOR	3	227.6	75.9	0.82
ERROR	23	2134.7	92.8	
TOTAL	26	2362.3		

INDIVIDUAL 95 PCT CI'S FOR MEAN
BASED ON POOLED STDEV

LEVEL	N	MEAN	STDEV	
C1	6	26.500	5.128	(--------- x --------)
C2	9	32.667	10.368	(---------- x ----------)
C3	7	26.000	11.676	(-------- x --------)
C4	5	27.600	9.017	(---------- x -----------)

```
          -------|-------|-------|--------
                24.0    30.0    36.0
```

POOLED STDEV=9.634

SAS

Dependent Variable: X

Source	DF	Sum of Squares	Mean Square	F Value	Pr > F
Model	3	227.5962	75.8654	0.82	0.4975
Error	23	2134.7000	92.8130		
Corrected Total	26	2362.2962			

CONFIDENCE INTERVAL ESTIMATES OF TREATMENT MEANS

Although the primary function of the analysis of variance is to test for differences in treatment means, the results can also be used to estimate single population means and the difference between two means. In Chapter 7, we developed the confidence interval estimate of the population mean μ, when σ^2 is unknown. That formula is

$$\bar{x} \pm t_{\alpha/2, n-1} \frac{s}{\sqrt{n}}$$

where s is the estimator of the unknown population standard deviation σ.

We can use this formula to estimate each of the k population means that we dealt with in the analysis of variance. For example, we can determine $\bar{x}_1$ and s_1 and use these statistics to estimate μ_1 in Example 12.1. Turning back to Example 12.1, we find

$$\bar{x}_1 = 17.625$$

and

$$s_1 = 2.67$$

The 95% confidence interval estimate of μ_1 is

$$\bar{x}_1 \pm t_{\alpha/2, n_1 - 1} \frac{s_1}{\sqrt{n_1}} = 17.625 \pm 2.365 \frac{(2.67)}{\sqrt{8}}$$

$$= 17.625 \pm 2.23$$

It is possible to improve this estimate by using the calculations in the analysis of variance. Because we assumed that there was a common but unknown population variance, we calculated the common or pooled variability of the data, denoted SSE. When SSE is divided by its degrees of freedom, the result (MSE) is an estimator of the population variance. Since it is based on a larger sample size, however, the confidence interval estimator of μ_1 based on MSE is likely to be a better estimator than the one based only on the data in the sample drawn from population 1. The confidence interval estimator of μ_1 based on all of the data is

$$\bar{x}_1 \pm t_{\alpha/2, n-k} \sqrt{\frac{\text{MSE}}{n_1}}$$

Hence, the 95% confidence interval estimate of μ_1 is

$$17.625 \pm 2.080 \sqrt{\frac{5.49}{8}} = 17.625 \pm 1.72$$

Notice that the interval that incorporates MSE is narrower (and thus better) than the one based on s_1.

Confidence Interval Estimator of μ_j

$$\bar{x}_j \pm t_{\alpha/2,n-k}\sqrt{\frac{\text{MSE}}{n_j}}$$

We can also use all of the data to estimate the difference between two population means.

Confidence Interval Estimator of $\mu_j - \mu_m$

$$(\bar{x}_j - \bar{x}_m) \pm t_{\alpha/2,n-k}\sqrt{\text{MSE}\left(\frac{1}{n_j}+\frac{1}{n_m}\right)}$$

For example, the 95% confidence interval estimate of $\mu_1 - \mu_2$ from Example 12.1 is

$$(\bar{x}_1 - \bar{x}_2) \pm t_{.025,21}\sqrt{\text{MSE}\left(\frac{1}{n_1}+\frac{1}{n_2}\right)}$$

$$= (17.625 - 13.75) \pm 2.080\sqrt{5.49\left(\frac{1}{8}+\frac{1}{8}\right)}$$

$$= 3.875 \pm 2.44$$

Thus, the 95% confidence interval estimate of $\mu_1 - \mu_2$ is (1.435, 6.315).

All we need in order to produce the confidence interval estimates are the sample means and the mean square for error MSE. Both Minitab and SAS print MSE as part of the ANOVA table. In addition, Minitab provides the sample means (as well as the sample standard deviations) and graphically shows the 95% confidence interval estimates of the treatment means, using what Minitab calls the *pooled standard deviation*, which is $\sqrt{\text{MSE}}$. Fortunately, this leaves very little computation for us to do.

VIOLATIONS OF REQUIRED CONDITIONS

The analysis of variance test described in this section is only valid if the random variables $x_1, x_2, \ldots, x_k$ are normally distributed. If this condition is unsatisfied, the F-test is invalid. In that case, we must employ a different test: the nonparametric Kruskal–Wallis test for the completely randomized design. This test is described in Section 14.5.

■■■■■■   **EXERCISES**

LEARNING THE TECHNIQUES

12.1   What are the required conditions for performing the F-test of the analysis of variance?

12.2   Describe in ordinary English what SST measures.

12.3   Describe in ordinary English what SSE measures.

12.4   Provide an example with $k = 4$ where SST $= 0$.

12.5   Provide an example with $k = 4$ where SSE $= 0$.

12.6   Use of the analysis of variance in handling a particular problem has resulted in the following ANOVA table.

Source	d.f.	SS	MS	F
Treatment	2	457.1241	228.5621	52.74
Error	17	117.0165	4.3339	

Complete the test at a significance level of 5%.

12.7   Complete the following ANOVA table, and test with $\alpha = .01$.

Source	d.f.	SS	MS	F
Treatment	2	1.0214		
Error	12	1.2159		

12.8   Given the following information, complete the ANOVA table and conduct the F-test with $\alpha = .05$.

SS(Total) $= 1052.0$
SST $= 581.6$
SSE $= 470.4$
$k = 3$
$n_1 = n_2 = n_3 = 10$

12.9   Given the following information, complete the test for analysis of variance at a significance level of 1%.

SST(Total) $= 468.86$
SST $= 254.57$
$k = 4$
$n_1 = n_2 = n_3 = n_4 = 7$

12.10   Given the following information, perform an analysis of variance test with $\alpha = .05$.

Variable	Treatment 1	2	3
n	26	31	18
$\sum x_i$	537	718	454
$\sum x_i^2$	13,470	19,256	13,007

12.11   The completely randomized design of an analysis of variance experiment produced the statistics that follow. Produce the ANOVA table.

Variable	Treatment 1	2	3	4
n	16	16	16	16
$\bar{x}$	158.6	149.2	151.3	157.6
s^2	95.3	102.1	96.8	99.1

12.12   The following statistics were generated by sampling from four normal populations. Do these statistics provide enough evidence at the 5% significance level to allow us to conclude that differences exist among the four population means?

Variable	Treatment 1	2	3	4
n	11	11	11	11
$\sum x_i$	653	712	507	698
$\sum x_i^2$	40,975	48,210	25,493	46,431

12.13 Using the following statistics, test with $\alpha = .01$ to determine whether differences exist among the population means.

$$n_1 = 49 \qquad n_2 = 45 \qquad n_3 = 29$$

$$\bar{x}_1 = 8.36 \qquad \bar{x}_2 = 7.91 \qquad \bar{x}_3 = 9.02$$

$$s_1 = 2.98 \qquad s_2 = 3.15 \qquad s_3 = 3.62$$

12.14 Suppose that you are given the following treatment means and sample sizes:

$$\bar{x}_1 = -2.150 \qquad n_1 = 5$$

$$\bar{x}_2 = 5.147 \qquad n_2 = 7$$

$$\bar{x}_3 = 6.021 \qquad n_3 = 6$$

With MSE = 44.8101, compute 95% confidence intervals for μ_1, μ_2, and μ_3.

12.15 For Exercise 12.8, suppose that we've calculated the following sample means:

$$\bar{x}_1 = 17.6 \qquad \bar{x}_2 = 8.8 \qquad \bar{x}_3 = 18.6$$

Compute the 99% confidence interval estimates of

a. μ_1 c. $\mu_1 - \mu_2$

b. μ_2 d. $\mu_1 - \mu_3$

12.16 For Exercise 12.9, suppose that the following sample means were computed:

$$\bar{x}_1 = 3.21 \qquad \bar{x}_2 = 5.78 \qquad \bar{x}_3 = 4.19 \qquad \bar{x}_4 = 6.01$$

$$n_1 = 5 \qquad n_2 = 8 \qquad n_3 = 7 \qquad n_4 = 4$$

Find the 90% confidence interval estimates of

a. μ_1 c. $\mu_1 - \mu_2$

b. μ_3 d. $\mu_2 - \mu_3$

12.17 Suppose that you are given the following statistics:

$$\bar{x}_1 = 3.21 \qquad \bar{x}_2 = 5.78 \qquad \bar{x}_3 = 4.19 \qquad \bar{x}_4 = 6.01$$

$$n_1 = 5 \qquad n_2 = 8 \qquad n_3 = 7 \qquad n_4 = 4$$

With MSE = 34.12, compute 95% confidence interval estimates of

a. μ_1 c. $\mu_2 - \mu_3$

b. μ_4 d. $\mu_2 - \mu_4$

12.18 The observations that follow were drawn from three normally distributed populations whose variances are equal.

Treatment		
1	2	3
7	15	8
9	11	15
16	12	21
3	4	18
	8	19
	6	

The following statistics were produced:

SST = 168.9   SSE = 274.9

Compute 90% confidence interval estimates of

a. μ_1

b. $\mu_1 - \mu_3$

12.19 For Exercise 12.18, using the formulas shown in Chapters 7 and 9, find 90% confidence interval estimates of

a. μ_1

b. $\mu_1 - \mu_3$

12.20 Compare the results of Exercises 12.18 and 12.19.

12.21 The observations that follow were taken from four normally distributed populations whose variances are equal.

Treatment			
1	2	3	4
27	48	31	25
43	41	35	29
31	36	46	18
37	41	28	20
26	32	36	
	33	40	
		24	

FIGURE E12.21

```
ANALYSIS OF VARIANCE
SOURCE    DF      SS       MS      F
FACTOR     3    593.2    197.7   4.51
ERROR     18    789.7     43.9
TOTAL     21   1383.0


                      INDIVIDUAL 95 PCT CI'S FOR MEAN
                         BASED ON POOLED STDEV

LEVEL    N     MEAN    STDEV   -------|-------|-------|-------
C1       5   32.800    7.155                (----x----)
C2       6   38.500    6.025                     (----x----)
C3       7   34.286    7.410               (----x----)
C4       4   23.000    4.967    (----x----)
                                -------|-------|-------|-------
POOLED STDEV=6.624              24.0    32.0    40.0
```

The Minitab command analysis of variance (AOVONEWAY) was used to produce the output shown in Figure E12.21. Compute 95% confidence interval estimates of

a. μ_2 c. $\mu_1 - \mu_3$

b. μ_3 d. $\mu_2 - \mu_4$

12.22 For Exercise 12.21, using the formulas shown in Chapters 7 and 9, find 95% confidence interval estimates of

a. μ_2 c. $\mu_1 - \mu_3$

b. μ_3 d. $\mu_2 - \mu_4$

12.23 Compare the results of Exercises 12.21 and 12.22.

Use the shortcut formulas shown in Appendix 12.A to answer the questions in Exercises 12.24–12.27.

12.24 Perform an analysis of variance to determine whether there is enough evidence at the 5% significance level to allow us to conclude that differences exist among the following treatment means.

Treatment			
1	2	3	4
12	10	10	9
15	12	8	6
13	11	12	8
18	14	15	7
20	10	13	9

12.25 Do the data that follow provide enough evidence at the 10% significance level to allow us to conclude that the treatment means differ?

Treatment				
1	2	3	4	5
16	8	6	17	14
21	12	9	19	9
19	15	9	14	11
18	13	8	18	12
23		5	20	16
		3		17

12.26 Perform an analysis of variance to determine whether there are differences among the treatment means for the following data, with $\alpha = .05$.

Treatment		
1	2	3
15	12	16
18	21	18
17	14	18
20	30	17
	28	15
		16

12.27 Undertake the appropriate test for analysis of variance needed to examine the following data for possible differences at a significance level of 1%.

Treatment			
1	2	3	4
62	45	61	48
61	49	55	27
67	51	59	31
71	47	68	37
73	48	62	39

APPLYING THE TECHNIQUES

Self-Correcting Exercise (See Appendix 12.D for the solution.)

MKT **12.28** The management of a computer company that has previously specialized in the home computer market wishes to expand into business applications. In order to determine which areas of business are most likely to purchase their computers and software, a preliminary survey was performed. A total of 150 middle managers were randomly selected, 50 of whom were in the banking industry, 50 from resource-based companies, and the remaining 50 from retail companies. Each was asked how many hours per week he or she spent working at a computer at work. The computer company's management decided that, if there is no evidence of differences among the industries, the company's marketing strategy will be to attempt to sell to all industries. If there are differences, however, it will tailor marketing and advertising toward the industry that uses the computer most. Based on the following statistics, what would you recommend? (Use $\alpha = .05$.)

$SS(Total) = 1,621.88$

$SST = 73.18$

EDUC **12.29** An engineering student who is about to graduate decided to survey various firms in Silicon Valley to see which offered the best chance for early promotion and career advancement. In approaching 15 different high-tech firms, the student asked (among other things) how much time must elapse after the initial hiring before a really good technician can receive a promotion. Suspecting that there might be differences depending on whether it was a small new firm, a medium-size firm, or a large international firm, the student grouped the data by size of firms, as follows.

NUMBER OF WEEKS UNTIL FIRST PROMOTION

Small Firms	Medium Firms	Large Firms
26	30	42
30	34	43
38	32	48
32	30	45
36	25	
24		
$\bar{x}_1 = 31.0$	$\bar{x}_2 = 30.2$	$\bar{x}_3 = 44.5$
$s_1 = 5.477$	$s_2 = 3.347$	$s_3 = 2.646$

Do these data provide sufficient evidence at the 1% significance level to indicate differences among the three sizes of firms?

EDUC **12.30** For Exercise 12.29, estimate with 90% confidence

a. the mean promotion time for large firms

b. the differences in mean promotion times between large and small firms

FIN **12.31** In attempting to compare the returns on four different types of stocks trading on the New York Stock Exchange, an investor selected a random sample from each category and computed the rates of return. To conduct an analysis of variance test, he computed the following statistics:

$$SS(Total) = 3272.5$$
$$SST = 438.1$$
$$SSE = 2,834.4$$

$\bar{x}_1 = 11.04 \qquad n_1 = 14$
$\bar{x}_2 = 14.51 \qquad n_2 = 20$
$\bar{x}_3 = 7.12 \qquad n_3 = 12$
$\bar{x}_4 = 12.88 \qquad n_4 = 18$

a. Do these data provide sufficient evidence to allow the investor to conclude that the rates of return differ among the four stock types? (Use $\alpha = .05$.)

b. Suppose that the investor decides to invest in type 3 stocks. Determine a 99% confidence interval estimate of the mean percentage return for this type of stock.

c. After further consideration, the investor decides that type 2 stocks are less risky than type 3 stocks. He would therefore like to know the difference between their mean returns. Determine a 90% confidence interval estimate of the difference between the mean returns of type 2 and type 3 stocks.

ACC **12.32** The Internal Revenue Service (IRS) is always looking for ways to improve the wording and format of their tax return forms. Three new formats have been developed recently. To determine which, if any, are superior to the current form, 20 individuals were asked to participate in an experiment. Each of the three new forms and the old form were filled out by 5 different people. The amount of time taken by each person to complete the task is recorded in the accompanying table. At the 10% significance level, can we conclude that differences in the completion times exist among the four forms?

COMPLETION TIMES (HOURS)

	New Forms			Current Form
	A	B	C	D
	9.2	12.6	7.5	6.3
	8.6	10.9	9.3	9.8
	10.3	11.8	8.8	10.1
	11.4	10.8	7.8	8.5
	8.5	10.1	9.1	7.1
Sample means	9.60	11.24	8.50	8.36
Sample variances	1.525	.9428	.6448	2.739

ACC **12.33** Another way of determining the effectiveness of tax returns is to count the number of errors made by the taxpayer in filling out his or her return. An IRS tax auditor examined each of the 20 returns described in Exercise 12.32 and computed the number of errors. These data are shown next. At the 10% significance level, can we conclude that there are differences in the number of errors among the four forms?

NUMBER OF ERRORS

	New Forms			Current Form
	A	B	C	D
	3	1	6	4
	5	3	8	1
	6	2	3	0
	2	4	3	6
	1	1	2	2
$\sum x_i$	17	11	22	13
$\sum x_i^2$	75	31	122	57

12.34   For Exercise 12.32, estimate with 99% confidence

a. the mean completion time for the current form

b. the difference in mean completion time between Form C and the current form

12.35   In an experiment to measure the amount of tar contained in five brands of "low-tar" cigarettes, random samples of 200 cigarettes from each brand were "smoked" by a tar-content machine. From these data, the following incomplete ANOVA table was prepared. Complete the table to determine if, at the 1% significance level, we can conclude that differences exist among the five brands of cigarettes.

ANOVA TABLE

Source	d.f.	Sum of Squares	Mean Squares	F Ratio
Factor		.00109		
Error		.1088		

SECTION 12.3   ## *RANDOMIZED BLOCK DESIGN*

In Section 9.4, we encountered the matched pairs experiment, which allowed us to draw inferences about $\mu_1 - \mu_2$ when the samples were not independent. This type of experimental design reduces the variability within the samples, making it easier to detect differences between the two population means. When the problem objective is to compare more than two populations, the experimental design that decreases the variability within samples is called the **randomized block design.** The term **block** refers to a matched group of observations from each of the populations.

In the completely randomized design, we partitioned the total variability into the between-treatments and the within-treatments variability. That is,

SS(Total) = SST + SSE

This allowed us to express the sum of squares for error as

SSE = SS(Total) − SST

In the randomized block design, we partition the total variability into three sources of variability.

SS(Total) = SST + SSB + SSE

where SSB, the **sum of squares for blocks** measures the variability among the blocks. As a result we can express the sum of squares for error as

SSE = SS(Total) − SST − SSB

This equation reveals the advantage of the randomized block design. By removing the effect of differences among the blocks, we reduce SSE.

Just as was the case in the matched pairs experiment described in Section 9.4, this design of the experiment results in a statistical test that more easily identifies true differences among the population means. Figure 12.6 describes the partitioning of the total sum of squares for the randomized block design.

FIGURE 12.6   *PARTITIONING SS(Total) IN THE RANDOMIZED BLOCK DESIGN*

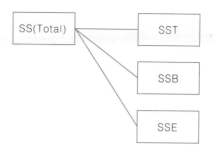

EXAMPLE 12.3

A dean of a business school wanted to determine whether or not there were differences in annual salaries two years after graduation among those who majored in accounting, marketing, and finance. As a preliminary experiment, he surveyed six graduates from each of the three subject areas and asked how much they earned annually. The results are shown in the accompanying table. Do these data provide sufficient evidence to allow the dean to conclude that there are differences among the majors' incomes? (Use $\alpha = .05$.)

ANNUAL INCOME ($1,000s), BY MAJOR

Accounting	Marketing	Finance
27	23	48
22	36	35
33	27	46
25	44	36
38	39	28
29	32	29

Solution.   The problem objective is to compare three populations, and the data scale is interval (annual income). Since the samples are independent, the appropriate statistical technique is the completely randomized design of the analysis of variance. The following hypotheses were tested:

$H_0: \mu_1 = \mu_2 = \mu_3$

$H_A:$ At least two means differ.

TABLE 12.6   *ANOVA TABLE FOR EXAMPLE 12.3*

Source of Variability	Degrees of Freedom	Sum of Squares	Mean Squares	*F*-Ratio
Treatments	2	193.0	96.5	1.77
Error	15	819.5	54.63	
Total	17	1,012.5		

From the data, the ANOVA table shown as Table 12.6 was produced. Since $F_{.05,2,15} = 3.68$, we conclude that there is insufficient evidence to indicate a difference among the three majors' incomes.

The conclusion was puzzling to the dean because, when he calculated the sample means, he had observed the following statistics:

Accounting majors: $\bar{x}_1 = 29.0$

Marketing majors: $\bar{x}_2 = 33.5$

Finance majors: $\bar{x}_3 = 37.0$

In desperation, he sought the advice of a statistics professor. After examining how the experiment was done, she pointed out that many other factors are involved in a graduate's salary, one of which is average grade. As a result, the variability within the samples is potentially so large that real differences among the three majors might be hidden. The experimental results support her comment. Notice that the sum of squares for treatments is 193.0 while the sum of squares for error is 819.5. From the raw data, considerable differences in annual incomes within each of the majors are evident.

At the recommendation of the statistics professor, the experiment was redone. This time the graduates were matched according to their grade average on graduation. From the files, the dean selected one student from each major, each of whom had an A^+ average. He then selected five other matched groups or blocks, whose averages were A, B^+, B, C^+, and C. When these eighteen graduates were asked their annual income two years after graduation, the data shown in the following table were produced.

ANNUAL INCOME ($1,000s), BY MAJOR

Average	Accounting	Marketing	Finance
A^+	41	45	51
A	36	38	45
B^+	27	33	31

Average	Accounting	Marketing	Finance
B	32	29	35
C$^+$	26	31	32
C	23	25	27

EXAMPLE 12.4

Is there sufficient evidence at the 5% significance level to indicate that differences exist among the three majors?

Solution. The problem objective and the data scale are the same as they were in Example 12.3. Consequently, we test the same hypotheses. That is,

$H_0: \mu_1 = \mu_2 = \mu_3$

H_A: At least two means differ.

However, the experiment was performed differently. The samples in this experiment are not independent: they were matched or blocked according to average grade. This experimental design is called the *randomized block design*. The experiment was designed in this way to eliminate the variability in annual income attributable to differences in average grades. This is accomplished by computing SSB in addition to SST and SSE.

The total variability is measured by

$$SS(Total) = \sum_{j=1}^{k} \sum_{i=1}^{b} (x_{ij} - \bar{\bar{x}})^2$$

Notice that in the randomized block design the number of observations of each treatment is b. As a result, b is used instead of n_j in the formulas for the sums of squares. The between-treatments variability is

$$SST = \sum_{j=1}^{k} b(\bar{x}(t)_j - \bar{\bar{x}})^2$$

where $\bar{x}(t)_j$ is the mean of the observations in the jth treatment. The between-blocks variability is

$$SSB = \sum_{i=1}^{b} k(\bar{x}(b)_i - \bar{\bar{x}})^2$$

where $\bar{x}(b)_i$ is the mean of the observations in the ith block. Finally, the sum of squares for error is

$$SSE = SS(Total) - SST - SSB$$

From the data, we find the following.

Grand Mean:

$$\bar{\bar{x}} = 33.722$$

Total Variability:

$$\text{SS(Total)} = \sum_{j=1}^{k} \sum_{i=1}^{b} (x_{ij} - \bar{\bar{x}})^2$$
$$= (41 - 33.722)^2 + (36 - 33.722)^2 + \cdots + (27 - 33.722)^2 = 1015.61$$

Treatment Means:

$$\bar{x}(t)_1 = 30.833$$
$$\bar{x}(t)_2 = 33.5$$
$$\bar{x}(t)_3 = 36.833$$

Between-Treatments Variability:

$$\text{SST} = \sum_{j=1}^{k} b(\bar{x}(t)_j - \bar{\bar{x}})^2$$
$$= 6(30.833 - 33.722)^2 + 6(33.5 - 33.722)^2 + 6(36.833 - 33.722)^2$$
$$= 108.44$$

Block Means:

$$\bar{x}(b)_1 = 45.667$$
$$\bar{x}(b)_2 = 39.667$$
$$\bar{x}(b)_3 = 30.833$$
$$\bar{x}(b)_4 = 32.0$$
$$\bar{x}(b)_5 = 29.667$$
$$\bar{x}(b)_6 = 25.0$$

Between-Blocks Variability:

$$\text{SSB} = \sum_{i=1}^{b} k(\bar{x}(b)_i - \bar{\bar{x}})^2$$
$$= 3(45.667 - 33.722)^2 + 3(39.667 - 33.722)^2 + \cdots + 3(25.0 - 33.722)^2$$
$$= 854.94$$

Sum of Squares for Error:

$$\text{SSE} = \text{SS(Total)} - \text{SST} - \text{SSB} = 1015.61 - 108.44 - 854.94 = 52.23$$

Compare these results with those obtained in Example 12.3; both sets of results are shown in Table 12.7. As you can see, the total variability is about the same for both experiments. The sum of squares for treatments in the randomized block design is somewhat smaller in Example 12.4. Notice, however, the large difference between the two values of SSE: in Example 12.3 SSE = 819.5, whereas in Example 12.4

TABLE 12.7   *SUMS OF SQUARES FOR EXAMPLES 12.3 AND 12.4*

Sum of Squares	Example 12.3 Completely Randomized Design	Example 12.4 Randomized Block Design
SST	193.0	108.44
SSB	—	854.94
SSE	819.5	52.23
SS(Total)	1,012.5	1,015.61

SSE = 52.23. Most of the difference is explained by SSB. The sum of squares for error has been dramatically reduced by removing the variability caused by the differences among the blocks. If you examine the block means, you will see that (as might be expected) the graduates' average grades influence what they earn. By ignoring this factor in Example 12.3, the dean could not establish that the majors' incomes are different. Next we will show that removing the effect of the differences among the grades produces an *F*-test that allows the dean to conclude that differences among the majors' incomes do indeed exist.

The test statistic for the randomized block design is

$$F = \frac{MST}{MSE}$$

where

$$MST = \frac{SST}{k-1}$$

and

$$MSE = \frac{SSE}{n-k-b+1}$$

Notice that the denominator of MSE is different from that given in Section 12.2. The test statistic is *F*-distributed (provided that the random variable is normally distributed) with degrees of freedom

$$v_1 = k - 1$$
$$v_2 = n - k - b + 1$$

The rejection region is

$$F > F_{\alpha, k-1, n-k-b+1}$$

For Example 12.4, we find

$$MST = \frac{SST}{k-1} = \frac{108.44}{3-1} = 54.22$$

$$\text{MSE} = \frac{\text{SSE}}{n - k - b + 1} = \frac{52.23}{18 - 3 - 6 + 1} = 5.22$$

$$F = \frac{\text{MST}}{\text{MSE}} = \frac{54.22}{5.22} = 10.39$$

Since the rejection region is

$$F > F_{\alpha, k-1, n-k-b+1}$$
$$> F_{.05, 2, 10}$$
$$> 4.10$$

the dean should reject H_0 and conclude that there is sufficient evidence to indicate that differences exist among the majors' incomes. (See Figure 12.7.)

Here, as in Section 12.2, we report our statistical findings in an ANOVA table. The general form of the ANOVA table for the randomized block design is shown in Table 12.8. The calculations from the present example are shown in Table 12.9.

FIGURE 12.7   *REJECTION REGION FOR TEST OF TREATMENT MEANS IN EXAMPLE 12.4*

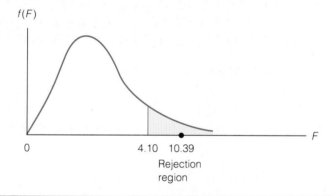

TABLE 12.8   *GENERAL ANOVA TABLE FOR RANDOMIZED BLOCK DESIGN*

Source of Variability	Degrees of Freedom	Sum of Squares	Mean Squares	F-Ratio
Treatments	$k - 1$	SST	$\text{MST} = \text{SST}/(k-1)$	$F = \text{MST}/\text{MSE}$
Blocks	$b - 1$	SSB	$\text{MSB} = \text{SSB}/(b-1)$	$F = \text{MSB}/\text{MSE}$
Error	$n - k - b + 1$	SSE	$\text{MSE} = \text{SSE}/(n-k-b+1)$	
Total	$n - 1$	SS(Total)		

TABLE 12.9   *ANOVA TABLE FOR EXAMPLE 12.4*

Source of Variability	Degrees of Freedom	Sum of Squares	Mean Squares	F-Ratio
Treatments	2	108.44	54.22	10.39
Blocks	5	854.94	170.99	32.76
Error	10	52.23	5.22	
Total	17	1,015.61		

Notice that there are two *F*-ratios in the ANOVA tables. The first,

$$F = \frac{MST}{MSE}$$

satisfies our problem objective of determining whether or not there are differences among treatment means. The second *F*-ratio,

$$F = \frac{MSB}{MSE}$$

provides a useful by-product: it enables us to test for differences among block means. The degrees of freedom associated with this *F*-ratio are

$$v_1 = b - 1$$
$$v_2 = n - k - b + 1$$

Thus, the rejection region for the test of differences among block means is

$$F > F_{\alpha, b-1, n-k-b+1}$$

In the present example, we compute

$$MSB = \frac{SSB}{b-1} = \frac{854.94}{6-1} = 170.99$$

$$F = \frac{MSB}{MSE} = \frac{170.99}{5.22} = 32.76$$

The rejection region (assuming $\alpha = .05$) is

$$F > F_{\alpha, b-1, n-k-b+1}$$
$$> F_{.05, 5, 10}$$
$$> 3.33$$

Therefore, there is enough evidence to allow the dean to conclude that the block means differ. This is no surprise, since the experiment was designed to remove the variability due to block differences.

Obviously the calculations required to perform the randomized block design of the analysis of variance are no easier (they are actually more time-consuming) than those for the completely randomized design. Consequently we will generally depend on the computer to do the arithmetic. For those who wish to do the calculations by hand, Appendix 12.A presents the shortcut methods.

COMPUTER OUTPUT FOR EXAMPLE 12.4*

Minitab

SOURCE	DF	SS	MS
C2	2	108.44	54.22
C3	5	854.94	170.99
ERROR	10	52.22	5.22
TOTAL	17	1015.61	

Column 2 contains the variable identifying the treatment, and column 3 identifies the block. The *F*-ratios must be computed by hand.

SAS

Dependent Variable: X

Source	DF	Anova SS	Mean Square	F Value	Pr > F
T	2	108.4444	54.2222	10.38	0.0036
B	5	854.9444	170.9888	32.74	0.0001

The actual output contains a number of additional statistics that are not shown here because we did not discuss them in this book.

A summary of the randomized block design of the analysis of variance is shown next.

Analysis of Variance: Randomized Block Design

Test statistics:

For Treatments

$$F = \frac{\text{MST}}{\text{MSE}} \quad \begin{aligned} \text{d.f. } v_1 &= k - 1 \\ v_2 &= n - k - b + 1 \end{aligned}$$

For Blocks

$$F = \frac{\text{MSB}}{\text{MSE}} \quad \begin{aligned} \text{d.f. } v_1 &= b - 1 \\ v_2 &= n - k - b + 1 \end{aligned}$$

Rejection region:

$$F > F_{\alpha, k-1, n-k-b+1}$$

$$F > F_{\alpha, b-1, n-k-b+1}$$

---

* Appendixes 12.B and 12.C describe the Minitab and SAS commands that produced these printouts.

Required conditions:

1. Population random variables $x_1, x_2, \ldots, x_k$ are normally distributed.
2. Population variances are equal. That is, $\sigma_1^2 = \sigma_2^2 = \cdots = \sigma_k^2$.
3. Samples are blocked.

Partitioning the sum of squares:

SS(Total) = SST + SSB + SSE

Mean squares:

$$\text{MST} = \frac{\text{SST}}{k-1}$$

$$\text{MSB} = \frac{\text{SSB}}{b-1}$$

$$\text{MSE} = \frac{\text{SSE}}{n-k-b+1}$$

EXAMPLE 12.5

The advertising revenues commanded by a radio station depend on the number of listeners it has. The manager of a station that plays mostly hard rock music wants to learn more about its listeners—mostly teenagers and young adults. In particular he wants to know if the amount of time they spend listening to radio music varies by day of the week. If the manager discovers that the mean time per day is about the same, he will schedule the most popular music evenly throughout the week. Otherwise, the top hits will be played mostly on the days that attract the greatest audience. An opinion survey company is hired, and it randomly selects 200 teenagers and asks them each to record the amount of time they spend listening to music on the radio for each day of one week in October. Some of the data are listed in the accompanying table. At the 5% significance level, what can the manager conclude from these results?

Time Spent Listening to Radio Music (minutes)

Teenager	Sunday	Monday	Tuesday	Wednesday	Thursday	Friday	Saturday
1	65	40	32	48	60	75	110
2	90	85	75	90	78	120	100
3	30	30	20	25	30	60	70
$\vdots$	$\vdots$	$\vdots$	$\vdots$	$\vdots$	$\vdots$	$\vdots$	$\vdots$
200	80	95	90	80	80	120	120

Solution.   The problem objective is to compare seven populations, and the data scale is interval (time spent listening to radio music each day). Because the survey company recorded the times for each day for each teenager, we identify the experiment as randomized block design. The treatments are the days of the week, and the blocks are the 200 teenagers. The complete test is as follows:

$H_0: \mu_1 = \mu_2 = \cdots = \mu_7$

H_A : At least two means differ.

Test statistic:

$$F = \frac{\text{MST}}{\text{MSE}}$$

Rejection region:

$F > F_{\alpha, k-1, n-k-b+1}$

$> F_{.05, 6, 1194}$

$> 2.10 \quad \text{(approximately)}$

Value of the test statistic: From the computer output that follows, we find $F = 8.01$.

Conclusion: Reject H_0.

There is enough evidence to allow the manager to conclude that the mean time teenagers spend listening to music on the radio is not the same for each day of the week. The next step is to determine which days have the greatest audience and to program the music accordingly. Figure 12.8 depicts this test.

FIGURE 12.8   *REJECTION REGION FOR TEST OF TREATMENT MEANS IN EXAMPLE 12.5*

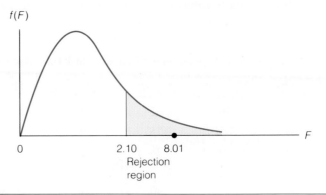

COMPUTER OUTPUT FOR EXAMPLE 12.5

Minitab

Source	DF	SS	MS
C2	6	18632	3105.3
C3	199	103415	519.67
ERROR	1194	462799	387.60
TOTAL	1399	584846	

As in Example 12.4, column 2 identifies the treatment and column 3 identifies the block. The value of the test statistic is

$$F = \frac{3105.3}{387.6} = 8.01$$

SAS

Dependent Variable: X

Source	DF	Anova SS	Mean Square	F Value	Pr > F
T	6	18632.3162	3105.3860	8.0118	0.0000
B	199	103415.0184	519.6746	1.3407	0.0023

Notice that the results indicate that differences among the teenagers also exist. The value of the F-statistic is

$$F = 1.3407$$

and its rejection region is

$$F > F_{\alpha, b-1, n-k-b+1}$$
$$> F_{.05, 199, 1194}$$
$$> 1.22 \text{ (approximately)}$$

CONFIDENCE INTERVALS

The confidence interval estimators developed in Section 12.2 for the completely randomized design are also applicable to the randomized block design. The formulas for the four estimators are given next.

Estimating Treatment Means

$$\bar{x}(t)_j \pm t_{\alpha/2, n-k-b+1} \sqrt{\frac{\text{MSE}}{b}}$$

Estimating Block Means

$$\bar{x}(b)_i \pm t_{\alpha/2, n-k-b+1} \sqrt{\frac{\text{MSE}}{k}}$$

Estimating the Difference Between Treatment Means

$$(\bar{x}(t)_j - \bar{x}(t)_m) \pm t_{\alpha/2, n-k-b+1} \sqrt{\text{MSE}\left(\frac{1}{b} + \frac{1}{b}\right)}$$

Estimating the Difference Between Block Means

$$(\bar{x}(b)_i - \bar{x}(b)_r) \pm t_{\alpha/2, n-k-b+1} \sqrt{\text{MSE}\left(\frac{1}{k} + \frac{1}{k}\right)}$$

VIOLATION OF REQUIRED CONDITIONS

Like the test for the completely randomized design of the analysis of variance, the test for the randomized block design requires that the data be drawn from normal populations. If this is not the case, the test that we use instead is a nonparametric technique: the Friedman test for the randomized block design. This test is described in Section 14.6.

EXERCISES

LEARNING THE TECHNIQUES

12.36 Provide an example with $k = 3$ and $b = 4$ in which SST $= 0$ and SSB and SSE are not equal to 0.

12.37 Provide an example with $k = 3$ and $b = 4$ in which SSB $= 0$ and SST and SSE are not equal to 0.

12.38 Is it possible to have a randomized block design of the analysis of variance in which SSE $= 0$ and SSB is not equal to 0? Explain.

12.39 Complete the following ANOVA table.

Source	d.f.	SS	MS	F
Treatments	5	500		
Blocks	20	1,000		
Error	100	2,000		

12.40 Complete the following ANOVA table, and test for equal treatment means with a significance level of 5%.

Source	d.f.	SS	MS	F
Treatments	8	150		
Blocks		250		
Error	120	1,640		

12.41 Given the following statistics, produce the ANOVA table and test for differences among treatment means with $\alpha = .01$.

SS(Total) = 1,563.7

SST = 501.1

SSB = 336.4

$k = 4, b = 10$

12.42 The following sums of squares were computed from a randomized block design of the analysis of variance with 5 treatments and 12 blocks:

SS(Total) = 79.3

SST = 11.6

SSB = 9.0

Determine whether there is enough evidence at the 10% significance level to allow us to conclude that the treatment means differ.

12.43 For Exercise 12.42, test with $\alpha = .10$ to determine if the block means differ.

12.44 The observations shown in the accompanying table were drawn from a randomized block design.

	Treatment		
Block	1	2	3
1	17	28	26
2	24	25	31
3	16	20	24
4	21	21	22

The following statistics were computed:

SST = 80.17

SSB = 76.92

SSE = 49.83

Compute 95% confidence interval estimates of:

a. treatment mean 2

b. the difference between treatment means 2 and 3

c. block mean 3

d. the difference between block means 1 and 4.

12.45 The observations shown in the accompanying table were drawn from four normal populations with equal variances.

	Treatment			
Block	1	2	3	4
1	9	7	6	8
2	8	12	9	12
3	6	10	7	12

The following statistics were produced:

SS(Total) = 55.67

SST = 23.00

SSB = 15.17

SSE = 17.50

Do these results allow us to conclude at the 5% significance level that the treatment means differ?

12.46 For Exercise 12.45, can we conclude at the 5% significance level that the block means differ?

12.47 For Exercise 12.45, estimate with 95% confidence:

a. treatment mean 4

b. the difference between treatment means 1 and 2

c. block mean 1

d. the difference between block means 1 and 3

Use the shortcut formulas shown in Appendix 12.A to answer the questions asked in Exercises 12.48– 12.51.

12.48 Given the following data generated from a randomized block experiment, test at the 5% level of significance to determine whether the treatment means differ.

	Treatment		
Block	1	2	3
1	25	31	26
2	30	38	28
3	32	40	29
4	26	32	24
5	20	29	21

12.49 The following observations were drawn from four normal populations with equal variances. The experimental design is randomized block.

a. Test with $\alpha = .01$ to determine whether the treatment means differ.

b. Test with $\alpha = .01$ to determine whether the block means differ.

	Treatment			
Block	1	2	3	4
1	93	102	90	105
2	99	105	84	83
3	86	88	82	99
4	101	102	98	89

12.50 The following data were generated from a randomized block experiment. Do these results allow us to conclude at the 1% significance level that the treatment means differ?

	Treatment		
Block	1	2	3
1	3.1	4.2	3.8
2	6.2	6.1	6.5
3	4.5	4.8	5.0
4	4.4	4.5	5.0
5	2.8	2.8	3.1

12.51 Do the following data (drawn from four normal populations with equal variances) allow us to conclude at the 10% significance level that the population means differ?

	Treatment			
Block	1	2	3	4
1	51	55	56	52
2	58	60	61	55
3	55	52	58	59

APPLYING THE TECHNIQUES

Self-Correcting Exercise (See Appendix 12.D for the solution.)

GEN **12.52** In recent years, lack of confidence in the Postal Service has led many companies to send all of their correspondence by private courier. A large company is in the process of selecting one of three possible couriers to act as their sole delivery method. To help in making the decision, an experiment was performed whereby letters were sent using each of the three couriers at ten different times of the day to a delivery point across town. The number of hours required for delivery was recorded in each case and summarized as follows:

SS(Total) = 150.97

SST = 5.98

SSB = 122.49

Can we conclude at the 1% significance level that there are differences in delivery times among the three couriers?

ACC **12.53** Exercise 12.32 described an experiment that involved comparing the completion times associated with four different income tax forms. Suppose that the experiment is redone in the following way. Five people are asked to fill out all four forms. The times are recorded in the accompanying table, together with the sums of squares. At the 10% significance level, can we conclude that differences in the completion times exist among the four forms?

COMPLETION TIMES (hours)

	New Forms			**Current Form**
Person	**A**	**B**	**C**	**D**
1	8.3	10.9	8.0	8.1
2	11.5	13.6	11.6	10.8
3	7.4	9.3	10.1	9.1
4	8.8	9.5	8.7	8.8
5	10.5	13.1	9.8	9.5

SS(Total) = 52.422

SST = 13.690

SSB = 29.962

ACC **12.54** For Exercise 12.53, estimate with 95% confidence

a. the mean completion time for form C

b. the difference in mean completion times between forms C and D

c. the mean completion time for the first person

EDUC **12.55** A recruiter for a computer company would like to determine whether there are differences in sales ability among business, arts, and science graduates. She takes a random sample of six business graduates who have been working for the company for the past 2 years. Each is then matched with an arts graduate and a science graduate with similar educational and working experience. The commission each earned in the last year is shown in the accompanying table. Is there sufficient evidence at the 5% significance level to allow the recruiter to conclude that there are differences in sales ability among the holders of the three types of degrees?

	Commission Income ($1,000s)		
Group	**Business**	**Arts**	**Science**
1	17	22	19
2	25	26	28
3	31	28	25
4	21	18	18
5	33	25	26
6	25	23	26

Types-of-degree sum of squares	11.11
Group sum of squares	253.11
Total sum of squares	337.11

EDUC **12.56** For Exercise 12.55, estimate with 90% confidence

a. the mean income of business graduates

b. the mean income of group 1

c. the difference in mean incomes between business and arts graduates

d. the difference in mean incomes between groups 2 and 3

SCI **12.57** Many North Americans suffer from high levels of cholesterol, which can lead to heart attacks. For those with very high levels (over 280), doctors prescribe drugs to reduce cholesterol levels. A pharmaceutical company has recently developed three such drugs. To determine if any differences exist in their benefits, an experiment was organized. The company selected 25 groups of 3 men, each of whom had levels in excess of 280. In each group the men were matched according to age and weight. The drugs were administered over a 2-month period, and the reduction in cholesterol was recorded. The data were summarized as follows:

Drug sum of squares	41.6
Group sum of squares	722.9
Total sum of squares	1,283.6

Do these results allow the company to conclude at the 5% significance level that differences exist among the three new drugs?

12.58 Four judges were asked to test the sensory quality of four different frozen orange juices. After the complex scoring system was explained to them, the judges assigned the points shown in the accompanying table.

a. Do these data provide enough evidence at the 10% significance level to indicate that there are differences in sensory quality among the orange-juice brands?

b. What do these results indicate about the consistency of the four judges' opinions?

	Brand			
Judge	1	2	3	4
1	81	79	55	36
2	63	69	65	45
3	57	59	58	62
4	77	69	73	58

Brand sum of squares	963.25
Judge sum of squares	245.25
Total sum of squares	2,171.75

SECTION 12.4   # MULTIPLE COMPARISON METHODS

When the null hypothesis is rejected in the analysis of variance, which treatment means are responsible for the difference among treatment means? For example, if an experiment is undertaken to determine whether or not different locations within a store produce different mean sales, the manager would be keenly interested in determining which locations result in higher sales and which locations result in lower sales. Similarly, a stockbroker would like to know which one of several mutual funds outperforms the others. And a television executive would like to know which television commercials hold the viewers' attention and which ones are ignored.

There are several ways to deal with this problem. For instance, we could perform a series of t-tests on all possible combinations of pairs of treatment means to determine which are significantly different. If we have $k = 4$ treatments, we could test each of

$$\mu_1 - \mu_2 \quad \mu_1 - \mu_3 \quad \mu_1 - \mu_4 \quad \mu_2 - \mu_3 \quad \mu_2 - \mu_4 \quad \mu_3 - \mu_4$$

In general, given k treatments, there will be C_2^k (which is the combinatorial formula—first seen in the binomial formula, where $C_2^k = k(k-1)/2$) hypotheses to test. The problem with performing numerous tests is that, for each test, there exists the probability α of making a Type I error. Thus, if we perform 100 tests with $\alpha = .05$, we can expect to reject five null hypotheses that in fact are correct; that means we will conclude that some of the treatment means differ when they really don't.

One way to avoid this problem is to perform each test at a significance level of α/C_2^k. This method, referred to as the **least significant difference (LSD) method,** ensures that the overall significance level does not exceed α; however, the overall power of this test is low, making the probability of a Type II error relatively high.

A more powerful test is **Tukey's multiple comparison method.** This technique determines a critical number such that, if any pair of sample means has a difference greater than this critical number, we conclude that the pair's two corresponding population means are different. This test can be employed only when the following conditions are satisfied.

Tukey's Multiple Comparison Method: Conditions

1. The design of the experiment is completely randomized. (In other words, the samples are independent.)

2. The sizes of the samples selected from each population are equal. We'll denote that sample size as n_g.

3. The conditions necessary to perform the F-test of the analysis of variance are satisfied; that is, the populations from which we sampled are normally distributed, with common variance.

The test is based on the standardized range, which is

$$q = \frac{\bar{x}_{max} - \bar{x}_{min}}{s/\sqrt{n}}$$

where $\bar{x}_{max}$ and $\bar{x}_{min}$ are the largest and smallest sample means, respectively. If we assume that there are no differences among all of the population means, we can find a critical number ω (Greek letter *omega*) such that $\bar{x}_{max} - \bar{x}_{min} < \omega$. If the difference in any pair of sample means exceeds ω, we would take this as sufficient evidence that the pair's two corresponding population means differ. We define the number ω as follows.

Critical Number ω

$$\omega = q_\alpha(k, v) \sqrt{\frac{MSE}{n_g}}$$

where

k = number of samples

v = number of degrees of freedom associated with MSE ($v = n - k$)

n_g = number of observations in each of the k samples

α = significance level

$q_\alpha(k, v)$ = critical value of the Studentized range

Table 7 in Appendix B (reproduced here as Table 12.10) provides values of $q_\alpha(k, v)$ for a variety of values of k and v and for $\alpha = .05$ and .01. Suppose that $k = 3$, $v = 15$, and $\alpha = .05$. From the table, we find $q_{.05}(3, 15) = 3.67$.

a. $\alpha = .05$

v										k									
	2	3	4	5	6	7	8	9	10	11	12	13	14	15	16	17	18	19	20
1	18.0	27.0	32.8	37.1	40.4	43.1	45.4	47.4	49.1	50.6	52.0	53.2	54.3	55.4	56.3	57.2	58.0	58.8	59.6
2	6.08	8.33	9.80	10.9	11.7	12.4	13.0	13.5	14.0	14.4	14.7	15.1	15.4	15.7	15.9	16.1	16.4	16.6	16.8
3	4.50	5.91	6.82	7.50	8.04	8.48	8.85	9.18	9.46	9.72	9.95	10.2	10.3	10.5	10.7	10.8	11.0	11.1	11.2
4	3.93	5.04	5.76	6.29	6.71	7.05	7.35	7.60	7.83	8.03	8.21	8.37	8.52	8.66	8.79	8.91	9.03	9.13	9.23
5	3.64	4.60	5.22	5.67	6.03	6.33	6.58	6.80	6.99	7.17	7.32	7.47	7.60	7.72	7.83	7.93	8.03	8.12	8.21
6	3.46	4.34	4.90	5.30	5.63	5.90	6.12	6.32	6.49	6.65	6.79	6.92	7.03	7.14	7.24	7.34	7.43	7.51	7.59
7	3.34	4.16	4.68	5.06	5.36	5.61	5.82	6.00	6.16	6.30	6.43	6.55	6.66	6.76	6.85	6.94	7.02	7.10	7.17
8	3.26	4.04	4.53	4.89	5.17	5.40	5.60	5.77	5.92	6.05	6.18	6.29	6.39	6.48	6.57	6.65	6.73	6.80	6.87
9	3.20	3.95	4.41	4.76	5.02	5.24	5.43	5.59	5.74	5.87	5.98	6.09	6.19	6.28	6.36	6.44	6.51	6.58	6.64
10	3.15	3.88	4.33	4.65	4.91	5.12	5.30	5.46	5.60	5.72	5.83	5.93	6.03	6.11	6.19	6.27	6.34	6.40	6.47
11	3.11	3.82	4.26	4.57	4.82	5.03	5.20	5.35	5.49	5.61	5.71	5.81	5.90	5.98	6.06	6.13	6.20	6.27	6.33
12	3.08	3.77	4.20	4.51	4.75	4.95	5.12	5.27	5.39	5.51	5.61	5.71	5.80	5.88	5.95	6.02	6.09	6.15	6.21
13	3.06	3.73	4.15	4.45	4.69	4.88	5.05	5.19	5.32	5.43	5.53	5.63	5.71	5.79	5.86	5.93	5.99	6.05	6.11
14	3.03	3.70	4.11	4.41	4.64	4.83	4.99	5.13	5.25	5.36	5.46	5.55	5.64	5.71	5.79	5.85	5.91	5.97	6.03
15	3.01	3.67	4.08	4.37	4.59	4.78	4.94	5.08	5.20	5.31	5.40	5.49	5.57	5.65	5.72	5.78	5.85	5.90	5.96
16	3.00	3.65	4.05	4.33	4.56	4.74	4.90	5.03	5.15	5.26	5.35	5.44	5.52	5.59	5.66	5.73	5.79	5.84	5.90
17	2.98	3.63	4.02	4.30	4.52	4.70	4.86	4.99	5.11	5.21	5.31	5.39	5.47	5.54	5.61	5.67	5.73	5.79	5.84
18	2.97	3.61	4.00	4.28	4.49	4.67	4.82	4.96	5.07	5.17	5.27	5.35	5.43	5.50	5.57	5.63	5.69	5.74	5.79
19	2.96	3.59	3.98	4.25	4.47	4.65	4.79	4.92	5.04	5.14	5.23	5.31	5.39	5.46	5.53	5.59	5.65	5.70	5.75
20	2.95	3.58	3.96	4.23	4.45	4.62	4.77	4.90	5.01	5.11	5.20	5.28	5.36	5.43	5.49	5.55	5.61	5.66	5.71
24	2.92	3.53	3.90	4.17	4.37	4.54	4.68	4.81	4.92	5.01	5.10	5.18	5.25	5.32	5.38	5.44	5.49	5.55	5.59
30	2.89	3.49	3.85	4.10	4.30	4.46	4.60	4.72	4.82	4.92	5.00	5.08	5.15	5.21	5.27	5.33	5.38	5.43	5.47
40	2.86	3.44	3.79	4.04	4.23	4.39	4.52	4.63	4.73	4.82	4.90	4.98	5.04	5.11	5.16	5.22	5.27	5.31	5.36
60	2.83	3.40	3.74	3.98	4.16	4.31	4.44	4.55	4.65	4.73	4.81	4.88	4.94	5.00	5.06	5.11	5.15	5.20	5.24
120	2.80	3.36	3.68	3.92	4.10	4.24	4.36	4.47	4.56	4.64	4.71	4.78	4.84	4.90	4.95	5.00	5.04	5.09	5.13
∞	2.77	3.31	3.63	3.86	4.03	4.17	4.29	4.39	4.47	4.55	4.62	4.68	4.74	4.80	4.85	4.89	4.93	4.97	5.01

b. $\alpha = .01$

									k										
v	2	3	4	5	6	7	8	9	10	11	12	13	14	15	16	17	18	19	20
1	90.0	135	164	186	202	216	227	237	246	253	260	266	272	277	282	286	290	294	298
2	14.0	19.0	22.3	24.7	26.6	28.2	29.5	30.7	31.7	32.6	33.4	34.1	34.8	35.4	36.0	36.5	37.0	37.5	37.9
3	8.26	10.6	12.2	13.3	14.2	15.0	15.6	16.2	16.7	17.1	17.5	17.9	18.2	18.5	18.8	19.1	19.3	19.5	19.8
4	6.51	8.12	9.17	9.96	10.6	11.1	11.5	11.9	12.3	12.6	12.8	13.1	13.3	13.5	13.7	13.9	14.1	14.2	14.4
5	5.70	6.97	7.80	8.42	8.91	9.32	9.67	9.97	10.2	10.5	10.7	10.9	11.1	11.2	11.4	11.6	11.7	11.8	11.9
6	5.24	6.33	7.03	7.56	7.97	8.32	8.61	8.87	9.10	9.30	9.49	9.65	9.81	9.95	10.1	10.2	10.3	10.4	10.5
7	4.95	5.92	6.54	7.01	7.37	7.68	7.94	8.17	8.37	8.55	8.71	8.86	9.00	9.12	9.24	9.35	9.46	9.55	9.65
8	4.74	5.63	6.20	6.63	6.96	7.24	7.47	7.68	7.87	8.03	8.18	8.31	8.44	8.55	8.66	8.76	8.85	8.94	9.03
9	4.60	5.43	5.96	6.35	6.66	6.91	7.13	7.32	7.49	7.65	7.78	7.91	8.03	8.13	8.23	8.32	8.41	8.49	8.57
10	4.48	5.27	5.77	6.14	6.43	6.67	6.87	7.05	7.21	7.36	7.48	7.60	7.71	7.81	7.91	7.99	8.07	8.15	8.22
11	4.39	5.14	5.62	5.97	6.25	6.48	6.67	6.84	6.99	7.13	7.25	7.36	7.46	7.56	7.65	7.73	7.81	7.88	7.95
12	4.32	5.04	5.50	5.84	6.10	6.32	6.51	6.67	6.81	6.94	7.06	7.17	7.26	7.36	7.44	7.52	7.59	7.66	7.73
13	4.26	4.96	5.40	5.73	5.98	6.19	6.37	6.53	6.67	6.79	6.90	7.01	7.10	7.19	7.27	7.34	7.42	7.48	7.55
14	4.21	4.89	5.32	5.63	5.88	6.08	6.26	6.41	6.54	6.66	6.77	6.87	6.96	7.05	7.12	7.20	7.27	7.33	7.39
15	4.17	4.83	5.25	5.56	5.80	5.99	6.16	6.31	6.44	6.55	6.66	6.76	6.84	6.93	7.00	7.07	7.14	7.20	7.26
16	4.13	4.78	5.19	5.49	5.72	5.92	6.08	6.22	6.35	6.46	6.56	6.66	6.74	6.82	6.90	6.97	7.03	7.09	7.15
17	4.10	4.74	5.14	5.43	5.66	5.85	6.01	6.15	6.27	6.38	6.48	6.57	6.66	6.73	6.80	6.87	6.94	7.00	7.05
18	4.07	4.70	5.09	5.38	5.60	5.79	5.94	6.08	6.20	6.31	6.41	6.50	6.58	6.65	6.72	6.79	6.85	6.91	6.96
19	4.05	4.67	5.05	5.33	5.55	5.73	5.89	6.02	6.14	6.25	6.34	6.43	6.51	6.58	6.65	6.72	6.78	6.84	6.89
20	4.02	4.64	5.02	5.29	5.51	5.69	5.84	5.97	6.09	6.19	6.29	6.37	6.45	6.52	6.59	6.65	6.71	6.76	6.82
24	3.96	4.54	4.91	5.17	5.37	5.54	5.69	5.81	5.92	6.02	6.11	6.19	6.26	6.33	6.39	6.45	6.51	6.56	6.61
30	3.89	4.45	4.80	5.05	5.24	5.40	5.54	5.65	5.76	5.85	5.93	6.01	6.08	6.14	6.20	6.26	6.31	6.36	6.41
40	3.82	4.37	4.70	4.93	5.11	5.27	5.39	5.50	5.60	5.69	5.77	5.84	5.90	5.96	6.02	6.07	6.12	6.17	6.21
60	3.76	4.28	4.60	4.82	4.99	5.13	5.25	5.36	5.45	5.53	5.60	5.67	5.73	5.79	5.84	5.89	5.93	5.98	6.02
120	3.70	4.20	4.50	4.71	4.87	5.01	5.12	5.21	5.30	5.38	5.44	5.51	5.56	5.61	5.66	5.71	5.75	5.79	5.83
∞	3.64	4.12	4.40	4.60	4.76	4.88	4.99	5.08	5.16	5.23	5.29	5.35	5.40	5.45	5.49	5.54	5.57	5.61	5.65

SOURCE: E. S. Pearson and H. O. Hartley, *Biometrika Tables for Statisticians*, Vol. 1, pp. 176–77. Reproduced by permission of the Biometrika Trustees.

Because the procedure we will be using actually tests several hypotheses at the same time, we will dispense with our usual method of listing the hypotheses, the test statistic, the rejection region, the value of the test statistic, and the conclusion. In place of all that, we will summarize the procedure.

Tukey's Multiple Comparison Method

1. Perform the analysis of variance to ascertain that there are differences among the population means.

2. From the relevant ANOVA table, determine MSE and its degrees of freedom.

3. From Table 7 of Appendix B (Table 12.10), determine $q_\alpha(k, v)$ and calculate
$$\omega = q_\alpha(k, v)\sqrt{\text{MSE}/n_g}\,.$$

4. List the sample means in ascending order, and determine which pairs differ by at least ω. If any such pairs exist, conclude that sufficient evidence exists to indicate that their corresponding population means differ.

EXAMPLE 12.6

Automobile manufacturers have become more concerned with quality because of overseas competition. One aspect of quality is the cost of repairing damage caused by accidents. A manufacturer is considering several new types of bumpers. In order to test how well they react to low-speed collisions, seven bumpers of each of four different types were installed on mid-sized cars, which were then driven into a wall at 5 miles per hour. The cost of repairing the damage in each case was assessed, and the relevant data are shown in the accompanying table.

COST ($) OF REPAIRING LOW-SPEED COLLISION DAMAGE

	Bumper Type		
1	2	3	4
315	285	269	255
288	292	277	287
293	263	273	265
306	249	252	279
299	275	263	241
310	266	251	312
282	252	272	310

a. At the 5% level of significance, can we conclude that there are differences in the degree of damage incurred among the four types of bumpers?

b. If there are differences, which bumpers can be judged to be different, with $\alpha = .05$?

Solution.   In part (a), the problem objective is to compare four populations, and the data scale is interval (dollar cost of damages). Since the samples are independently drawn, the appropriate technique is the completely randomized design of the analysis of variance. The ANOVA table for these data appears as Table 12.11.

$H_0: \mu_1 = \mu_2 = \mu_3 = \mu_4$

H_A: At least two means differ.

Test statistic:

$$F = \frac{\text{MST}}{\text{MSE}}$$

Rejection region:

$F > F_{\alpha, k-1, n-k}$

$> F_{.05, 3, 24}$

> 3.01

Value of the test statistic: $F = 5.20$

Conclusion: Reject H_0.

There is sufficient evidence to indicate that significant differences exist in the degree of damage incurred among the four types of bumpers.

In part (b), since we wish to determine which types of bumpers are different, we employ Tukey's multiple comparison method. We find the sample means to be

$\bar{x}_1 = 299.0$

$\bar{x}_2 = 268.9$

$\bar{x}_3 = 265.3$

$\bar{x}_4 = 278.4$

TABLE 12.11   ANOVA TABLE FOR EXAMPLE 12.6

Source of Variability	Degrees of Freedom	Sum of Squares	Mean Squares	F-Ratio
Treatments	3	4,804.7	1,601.6	5.20
Error	24	7,396.0	308.2	
Total	27	12,200.7		

The critical value is

$$\omega = q_\alpha(k, v) \sqrt{\frac{\text{MSE}}{n_g}}$$

with

$\alpha = .05$

$k = 4$

$v = 24$

From Table 7 in Appendix B (or Table 12.10), we find

$q_{.05}(4, 24) = 3.90$

Since $\text{MSE} = 308.2$ and $n_g = 7$, we find

$$\omega = 3.90 \sqrt{\frac{308.2}{7}} = 25.9$$

If we put the values of the sample means in ascending order, we have

$\bar{x}_3$	$\bar{x}_2$	$\bar{x}_4$	$\bar{x}_1$
265.3	268.9	278.4	299.0

As you can see,

$\bar{x}_1 - \bar{x}_3 = 33.7$

and

$\bar{x}_1 - \bar{x}_2 = 30.1$

both of which exceed $\omega = 25.9$. No other differences exceed ω. As a result, we conclude that sufficient evidence exists to indicate that μ_2 and μ_3 significantly differ from μ_1. There is not enough evidence, however, to allow us to conclude that differences exist among μ_2, μ_3, and μ_4 and between μ_1 and μ_4.

The automobile manufacturer should be advised not to use bumper 1; the choice from among bumpers 2, 3, and 4 should be made on the basis of some other criterion, such as cost.

SAS COMPUTER OUTPUT FOR EXAMPLE 12.6*

Dependent Variable: X

Source	DF	Sum of Squares	Mean Square	F Value	Pr > F
Model	3	4804.6785	1601.5595	5.20	0.0066
Error	24	7396.0000	308.1667		
Corrected Total	27	12200.6785			

---

* Appendix 12.C describes the SAS commands that produced this output.

```
Tukey's Studentized Range (HSD) Test for variable: X

NOTE: This test controls the type I experimentwise error rate, but
      generally has a higher type II error rate than REGWQ.

               Alpha=0.05 df=24 MSE=308.1667
            Critical Value of Studentized Range=3.901
               Minimum Significant Difference=25.885


Means with the same letter are not significantly different.

Tukey Grouping        Mean     N    T
              A      299.000    7    1
              A
        B     A      278.429    7    4
        B
        B             268.857    7    2
        B
        B             265.286    7    3
```

The first part of the output is the ANOVA table. In the next part we see that the critical value of the studentized range is

$$q_\alpha(k, v) = q_{.05}(4, 24) = 3.901$$

and that

$$\omega = q_\alpha(k, v)\sqrt{\frac{MSE}{n_g}} = (3.901)\sqrt{\frac{308.1667}{7}} = 25.885$$

Finally the treatment means are grouped. Means 1 and 4 (Group A) do not significantly differ and Means 2, 3, and 4 (Group B) are not significantly different. As a result we conclude that μ_1 differs from μ_2 and μ_3.

EXERCISES

LEARNING THE TECHNIQUES

12.59 Use Tukey's multiple comparison method to determine which means differ in the following problems.

a. $k = 5$ $n_g = 5$ MSE $= 125$ $\alpha = .01$

$\bar{x}_1 = 227$

$\bar{x}_2 = 205$

$\bar{x}_3 = 219$

$\bar{x}_4 = 248$

$\bar{x}_5 = 202$

b. $k = 3$ $n_g = 11$ MSE $= 63$ $\alpha = .05$

$\bar{x}_1 = 28$

$\bar{x}_2 = 25$

$\bar{x}_3 = 36$

c. $k = 4$ $n_g = 16$ MSE $= 172$ $\alpha = .01$

$\bar{x}_1 = 655$

$\bar{x}_2 = 674$

$\bar{x}_3 = 653$

$\bar{x}_4 = 677$

12.60   In an attempt to compare three populations, independent random samples consisting of five observations per sample were drawn. Some of the statistical results are as follows:

$$SSE = 350$$
$$\bar{x}_1 = 82$$
$$\bar{x}_2 = 73$$
$$\bar{x}_3 = 85$$

Using Tukey's multiple comparison method, determine which means differ at the 5% significance level.

12.61   Use Tukey's multiple comparison method to determine which means differ in Exercise 12.11. (Use $\alpha = .05$.)

12.62   The following data were drawn from four normally distributed populations whose variances are equal.

a. Is there sufficient evidence at the 1% significance level to conclude that differences exist among the treatment means?

b. Use Tukey's multiple comparison method to determine which treatment means differ. (Use $\alpha = .01$.)

	Treatment		
1	2	3	4
18	25	29	25
16	33	38	20
17	28	24	14
22	41	29	29
10	21	41	12
$\bar{x}$ 16.6	29.6	32.2	20.0

$SST = 839.6$ $SSE = 719.2$

12.63   Use Tukey's multiple comparison method to determine which means differ in Exercise 12.12. (Use $\alpha = .05$.)

APPLYING THE TECHNIQUES

Self-Correcting Exercise (See Appendix 12.D for the solution.)

 12.64   With Tukey's multiple comparison method to help you, determine which means differ in Exercise 12.32. (Use $\alpha = .05$.)

POM **12.65**   A manufacturer of outdoor brass lamps and mailboxes has received numerous complaints about premature corrosion. The manufacturer has identified the cause of the problem as being the low-quality lacquer that is used to coat the brass. He decides to replace his current supplier of lacquer with one of five possible alternatives. In order to judge which is the best, he uses each of the five lacquers to coat a set of 6 brass mailboxes and puts all 30 mailboxes outside. He records, for each, the number of days before the first sign of corrosion is observed. The results are listed in the accompanying table.

a. Is there sufficient evidence at the 5% significance level to allow the manufacturer to conclude that differences exist among the five lacquers?

b. Use Tukey's multiple comparison method to determine which lacquers are relatively effective and which are relatively ineffective. (Use $\alpha = .05$.)

NUMBER OF DAYS BEFORE CORROSION IS OBSERVED

	Lacquer			
1	2	3	4	5
73	110	68	89	99
56	108	75	93	121
61	92	99	90	110
83	95	81	81	117
92	93	77	79	112
73	112	79	88	115
$\bar{x}$ 73.00	101.67	79.83	86.67	112.33

$SST = 6,215.46$ $SSE = 2,300.83$

EDUC **12.66** A common complaint about university professors is that they don't work very much and that the higher their rank the less work they do. To examine this claim a statistics student determined the number of hours of work per week for a random sample of university instructors of different ranks. The data appear in the accompanying table.

HOURS OF WORK

Lecturer	Assistant Professor	Associate Professor	Full Professor
31	45	41	43
38	53	39	46
37	38	44	38
41	52	48	37

	Lecturer	Assistant Professor	Associate Professor	Full Professor
	36	55	47	41
	32	44	52	34
	37	36	48	37
$\bar{x}$	36.00	46.143	45.571	39.429
s	3.464	7.471	4.504	4.117

a. Can the student conclude at the 1% significance level that the hours of work differ among the four ranks of instructor?

b. Use Tukey's multiple comparison method to determine which ranks differ in terms of hours of work. (Use $\alpha = .01$.)

SECTION 12.5 **SUMMARY**

The technique for analysis of variance allows us to test for differences among populations when the data scale is interval. Two experimental designs were discussed: the **completely randomized design** produces data from independent samples; and the **randomized block design** assumes that measurements were taken over similar experimental units. The test statistic is F-distributed, which requires that the populations from which we've sampled are normally distributed. We can use the calculations to estimate single population means, as well as to estimate the difference between means. **Tukey's multiple comparison method** allows us to determine if there are differences between members of any pair of population means in the completely randomized design.

▓▓▓▓▓▓▓▓ **SUPPLEMENTARY EXERCISES**

GEN **12.67** Police cars, ambulances, and other emergency vehicles are required to carry road flares. One of the most important features of flares is their burning time. As a preliminary study to help decide which of four brands of flares to use, a police laboratory measured the burning times of five flares of each brand. The results, recorded to the nearest minute, are shown in the accompanying table. Is there sufficient evidence at the 5% significance level to indicate that differences exist among the four brands?

BURNING TIME (minutes)

	Brands		
1	2	3	4
16	15	14	18
19	20	19	22
22	18	16	19

(continued)

	Brands			
	1	2	3	4
	21	16	12	23
	23	14	15	20
$\bar{x}$	20.2	16.6	15.2	20.4
s	2.775	2.408	2.588	2.074

GEN **12.68** For Exercise 12.67, estimate with 90% confidence

a. the mean burning time for brand 4

b. the difference in mean burning times between brands 3 and 4

GEN **12.69** For Exercise 12.67, use Tukey's multiple comparison method to determine which means differ, at the 5% significance level.

MKT **12.70** Detergent manufacturers frequently make claims about the effectiveness of their products. A consumer-protection service decides to test five brands of detergent, each of whose manufacturer claims that its product produces the "whitest whites" in all water temperatures. The "whiteness" scores shown in the accompanying table were produced by laser equipment for white sheets washed in each of the detergents at three different water temperatures. Sum of squares information is also provided.

a. Can we conclude at the 1% significance level that there are differences in effectiveness among the five detergents?

b. Do these data indicate at the 1% significance level that water temperature affects the detergents' effectiveness?

c. What assumption(s) must be made to answer parts (a) and (b)?

	Brand of Detergent				
Water Temperature	1	2	3	4	5
Cool	76	82	75	63	83
Lukewarm	79	83	80	69	87
Hot	80	87	78	71	91

Brand of detergent sum of squares	658.93
Water temperature sum of squares	81.73
Total sum of squares	760.93

MKT **12.71** In marketing children's products, it's extremely important to produce television commercials that hold the attention of the children who view them. A psychologist hired by a marketing research firm wants to determine whether differences in attention span exist among advertisements for different types of products. Fifteen children under 10 years of age are asked to watch one 60-second commercial for one of three types of products, and their attention spans are measured in seconds. The results are shown next. Do these data provide enough evidence to conclude that there are differences in attention span among the three products advertised? (Use $\alpha = .05$.)

CHILDREN'S ATTENTION SPANS (seconds)

Type of Product Advertised		
Toys/Games	Food/Candy	Children's Clothing
42	55	30
45	58	35
48	52	42
40	60	32
50	57	38

SST = 1,105.20

SSE = 196.40

MKT **12.72** Use Tukey's multiple comparison method in Exercise 12.71 to determine which means differ. (Use $\alpha = .05$.)

MKT **12.73** Upon reconsidering the experiment in Exercise 12.71, the psychologist decides that the age of the child may influence the attention span. Consequently, the experiment is redone in the following way. Three 10-year-olds, three 8-year-olds, three 6-year-olds, and three 4-year-olds are randomly assigned to watch one of the commercials, and their attention spans are measured. Do the results that follow indicate, at the 5% significance level, that there are differences in the ability of the products advertised to hold children's attention?

CHILDREN'S ATTENTION SPANS (seconds)

	Type of Product Advertised		
Age	Toys/Games	Food/Candy	Children's Clothing
10	52	60	35
8	48	58	36
6	49	54	32
4	43	52	33

Type of product sum of squares	992.00
Age sum of squares	68.67
Total sum of squares	1,084.00

EDUC **12.74** Henry Blank is trying to choose a university to attend in order to get his MBA. Since money is the only thing that matters to him, he has decided to judge schools on the basis of the average annual salary their graduates receive one year after graduation. If there are differences, Henry will attend the university with the highest average income. If there is no evidence of a difference, he will select the U. of A., because he likes the school song. A random sample of the annual salaries of graduates of each of the four universities that have accepted him is shown in the accompanying table. What should Henry do? (Use $\alpha = .05$.)

ANNUAL SALARY ($1,000s)

U. of A.	U. of B.	U. of C.	U. of D.
24	41	27	19
18	38	26	22
19	29	29	33
28	24	33	40
22	28	22	27
33	18	25	26

U. of A.	U. of B.	U. of C.	U. of D.
27	22	31	19
21		27	33
43			32
			21
			20

SS(Total) = 1,535.89

SST = 28.56

PG **12.75** The possible imposition of a residential property tax has been a sensitive political issue in a large city that consists of 5 boroughs. Currently, property tax is based on an assessment system that dates back to 1950. This system has produced numerous inequities whereby newer homes tend to be assessed at higher values than older homes. A new system has been proposed that is based on the market value of the house. Opponents of the plan argue that residents of some boroughs would have to pay considerably more on the average, while residents of other boroughs would pay less. As part of a study examining this issue, several homes in each borough were assessed under both plans. The percentage increase or decrease in each case is recorded in the accompanying table. Can we conclude at the 5% significance level that there are differences in the effect the new assessment system would have on the 5 boroughs?

PERCENTAGE CHANGE IN ASSESSMENT

		Borough		
1	2	3	4	5
7	22	7	−2	7
16	18	10	12	10
5	10	12	18	15
17	14	11	14	11
8	9	18	0	14
14	16	21	20	12
12	18	14	16	18

(continued)

Borough				
1	2	3	4	5
−1	11	10	12	7
3	7	11	15	0
	12	15	11	9
	15	17	19	8
	16			−3

SS(Total) = 1,838.76

SST = 244.38

GEN **12.76** The editor of the student newspaper was in the process of making some major changes in the newspaper's layout. He was also contemplating changing the typeface of the print used. To help him make a decision, he set up an experiment in which six individuals were asked to read four newspaper pages, with each page printed in a different typeface. If the reading speed differed, then the typeface that was read fastest would be used. However, if there was not enough evidence to allow the editor to conclude that such differences existed, the current typeface would be continued. Based on the results shown in Table E12.76, what should the editor do? (Test with $\alpha = .05$.)

GEN **12.77** For Exercise 12.76, estimate with 90% confidence

a. the mean reading time for typeface 1

b. the difference in mean reading time between typefaces 2 and 3

FIN **12.78** For many years automobile insurance companies have charged young men higher premiums, reflecting this group's relatively poor driving record. An executive in the insurance industry believes that different premiums should be charged according to age for all drivers, because drivers in some age groups drive considerably more than others. To examine this issue, 50 young (25–40), 50 middle-age (40–55), and 50 older (over 55) drivers were questioned concerning the number of miles they drove in the previous 12 months. The results are summarized in the following table. Do these data allow us to conclude at the 1% significance level that there are differences in miles driven among the three age groups?

MILES DRIVEN (1,000s), BY AGE

	Age of Driver		
	Young	Middle-age	Older
$\sum x_i$	830.3	855.4	548.8
$\sum x_i^2$	14,263.7	15,049.4	6,599.1

TABLE E12.76

Respondent	Reading Time (seconds)			
	Typeface 1	Typeface 2	Typeface 3	Typeface 4
1	98	102	92	99
2	105	107	99	106
3	84	91	90	88
4	112	110	112	115
5	110	106	108	108
6	88	93	90	93

Reading time sum of squares	40.50
Respondent sum of squares	1,823.50
Total sum of squares	1,982.50

12.79 For Exercise 12.78, estimate with 95% confidence

a. the mean miles driven by young drivers

b. the difference in mean miles driven between young and older drivers

12.80 The research and development department of a sporting goods manufacturer has been experimenting with several new designs of skateblades. The designs are aimed at increasing skating speeds. In order to test their developments, the researchers recruited the services of eight professional hockey players. Each was asked to try all four new types of skates, as well as the ones they currently used. Each player's skating speed was measured on a regulation hockey rink. These data are shown in the accompanying table. Sums of squares are also provided. At the 10% significance level, is there enough evidence to allow the researchers to conclude that differences exist among the five types of blade?

SKATING SPEEDS (MILES PER HOUR)

| Player | \multicolumn{5}{c}{Type of Blade} |
	1	2	3	4	5
Geoff Courtnall	29.3	29.1	29.2	29.3	29.0
Wayne Gretzky	28.2	28.5	28.5	28.3	28.2
Guy LaFleur	26.3	26.5	26.6	26.8	26.2
Rod Langway	25.6	25.5	25.6	25.9	25.6
Mario Lemieux	28.2	28.4	28.3	28.3	28.4
Mark Messier	28.4	27.8	27.9	27.8	28.0
Joey Mullen	27.1	27.0	26.9	27.0	26.5
Steve Yzerman	28.4	28.5	28.5	28.6	28.4

Blade sum of squares	.1960
Player sum of squares	50.1670
Total sum of squares	51.1710

12.81 An economist wants to determine if differences exist among the salaries of university professors in different departments. In a prelimi-

nary study, she took a random sample of six professors from each of the departments of business, history, and psychology. These data are shown in the following table. Can she conclude at the 5% significance level that differences exist among the salaries in the three departments?

SALARIES ($1,000s)

	Business	History	Psychology
	48	28	37
	56	48	43
	33	62	28
	41	45	48
	60	39	51
	52	43	40
$\bar{x}$	48.333	44.167	41.167
s	9.973	11.161	8.232

SS(Total) = 1,614.4   SST = 155.4

12.82 For Exercise 12.81, estimate with 95% confidence

a. the mean salary of business professors

b. the difference in mean salary between business and psychology professors

12.83 In a recent report, a group of scientists claimed that Americans are consuming an excessive amount of selenium in their diets. The National Science Foundation has stated that the safe upper limit is 200 micrograms per day. In order to determine the extent of the problem, researchers drew samples of people from each of five widely separated cities and measured their daily consumption of selenium. The researchers decided that, if there were no differences among the cities, there must be numerous sources of selenium in the diet. On the other hand, if differences exist, the sources may be quite localized. From the data in Table E12.83, what conclusions can be drawn? (Use $\alpha = .05$.)

TABLE E12.83 DAILY SELENIUM INTAKE (MICROGRAMS)

	New York	Minneapolis	San Diego	Dallas	Atlanta
	227	181	175	221	183
	183	163	166	183	225
	219	175	188	195	228
	248	189	195	188	203
	163	193	175	203	195
	175	188	171	201	198
$\bar{x}$	202.50	181.50	178.33	198.50	205.33
s	33.58	11.10	10.95	13.38	17.69

SS(Total) = 13,033

SST = 3,718

SSE = 9,315

MNG **12.84** Some restaurants appear to prefer to hire older waiters and waitresses, while others seem to prefer younger ones. To help establish hiring policies for a large restaurant chain, a management consultant wanted to determine whether restaurant customers generally prefer younger or older waiters and waitresses. She decided that a reasonable measure of a customer's satisfaction is the size of the tip that the customer leaves. The consultant took a random sample of 7 young (20–30), 7 middle-age (40–50), and 7 older (55–65) waiters and waitresses and measured the percentage of the total bill left as a tip during one evening. The resulting data appear in the accompanying table. Can the consultant conclude at the 10% significance level that there are differences in the tips left to the three age groups?

PERCENTAGE TIPS

Young	Middle-Age	Older
14.5	13.3	9.8
10.9	16.5	10.6
11.6	12.4	8.5

	Young	Middle-Age	Older
	9.8	10.9	10.6
	11.9	11.6	11.1
	12.6	13.5	9.8
	11.1	12.8	9.2
$\bar{x}$	11.771	13.000	9.943
s	1.487	1.796	0.902

SS(Total) = 70.64   SST = 33.13   SSE = 37.51

POM **12.85** Billions of dollars are lost each year because of industrial accidents. As a consequence, companies regularly invest in safety-training programs. A large company has recently developed two new programs designed to teach its workers to work safely. In order to determine the new programs' effectiveness in comparison to the currently used program, three groups of 50 new workers were assembled. Each group underwent a different safety-training program. The workers then were assigned identical tasks. The numbers of monthly man-hours lost as a result of industrial accidents were recorded for the next 12 months. These results are shown in the accompanying table.

a. What conclusions can be drawn about the relative effectiveness of the three programs? (Use $\alpha = .05$.)

b. What do these data tell you about the effect of the training programs shortly after their completion versus 8–12 months after?

MAN-HOURS LOST, BY MONTH

Month	Safety-Training Program		
	1	2	3
April	11	10	6
May	15	10	12
June	8	11	10
July	14	8	11
August	18	15	16
September	23	14	12

Month	Safety-Training Program		
	1	2	3
October	27	20	18
November	26	16	18
December	32	24	22
January	28	28	30
February	35	26	28
March	32	28	26

Program sum of squares	196.72
Month sum of squares	2,002.22
Total sum of squares	2,347.56

CASE 12.1*   EFFECTS OF FINANCIAL PLANNING ON SMALL BUSINESSES

This case requires the use of a computer. The data are not shown below but are stored on the data disk.

FIN   In the United States, approximately $\frac{1}{2}$ million small businesses fail annually. Many researchers have investigated small businesses to determine the factors that distinguish those that succeed from those that fail. One set of researchers suggested that a potential factor is the degree of planning. They identified three different levels of planning:

1. Structural Strategic Planning—This involves producing a formalized written description of long-term plans with a 3- to 15-year horizon.

2. Structural Operational Planning—This type of planning deals with short-term issues such as action plans for the current fiscal year.

3. Unstructured Planning—This covers arrangements where there is no formal or informal planning.

A random sample of 73 firms participated in the study. The mean age of the firms was 9.2 years, mean annual revenues were $4.25 million, and mean net income was $300,000. On average, 71 people were employed. These statistics suggest that the

---

* Adapted from J. S. Bracker, B. W. Keats, and J. N. Pearson, "Planning and Financial Performance Among Small Firms in a Growth Industry," *Strategic Management Journal* 9 (1988): 591–603.

73 participating companies are fairly representative of the population to be investigated.

The companies were analyzed over a 5-year period (1979 to 1984), and the following four measures of performance were used:

1. Growth in revenue—average sales growth in percent over the 5 years
2. Net income growth—growth in percent average net income (before taxes) over the 5 years
3. Present value growth—average book value growth in percent over the 5 years
4. CEO cash compensation growth—percent average growth in the cash payments to chief executive officers over the 5 years

The results are stored on the data disk in the following way. What conclusions and recommendations can be derived from these data?

TABLE A   *PERFORMANCE MEASUREMENTS FOR COMPANIES WITH STRUCTURAL STRATEGIC PLANNING*

Company	Revenue Growth	Income Growth	Present Value Growth	Compensation Growth
1	126	53	75	84
2	46	57	60	85
3	29	70	85	32
⋮	⋮	⋮	⋮	⋮
11	100	57	106	121

TABLE B   *PERFORMANCE MEASUREMENTS FOR COMPANIES WITH STRUCTURAL OPERATIONAL PLANNING*

Company	Revenue Growth	Income Growth	Present Value Growth	Compensation Growth
1	−23	0	27	55
2	55	48	69	4
3	34	39	18	31
⋮	⋮	⋮	⋮	⋮
27	46	15	84	34

TABLE C   *PERFORMANCE MEASUREMENTS FOR COMPANIES WITH UNSTRUCTURED PLANNING*

Company	Revenue Growth	Income Growth	Present Value Growth	Compensation Growth
1	25	35	−43	26
2	20	−9	9	57
3	87	4	22	22
⋮	⋮	⋮	⋮	⋮
35	31	17	26	−19

CASE 12.2*   *DIVERSIFICATION STRATEGY FOR MULTINATIONAL COMPANIES*

This case requires the use of a computer. The data are not shown below but are stored on the data disk.

FIN

One of the many goals of management researchers is to identify factors that differentiate between success and failure and among different levels of success in businesses. In this way it may be possible to help more businesses become successful. Among multinational enterprises (MNEs), two factors to be examined are the degree of product diversification and the degree of internationalization. *Product diversification* refers to efforts by companies to increase the range and variety of the products they produce. The more unrelated the products are, the greater is the degree of diversification created. *Internationalization* is a term for expressing geographic diversification. Companies that sell their products to many countries are said to employ a high degree of internationalization.

Three management researchers set out to examine these issues. In particular they wanted to test two hypotheses:

1. MNEs employing strategies that result in more product diversification outperform those with less product diversification.

2. MNEs employing strategies that result in more internationalization outperform those with less internationalization.

Company performance was measured in two ways:

1. Profit-to-sales is the ratio of profit to total sales, expressed as a percentage.

2. Profit-to-assets is the ratio of profit to total assets, expressed as a percentage.

---

* Adapted from J. M. Geringer, P. W. Beamish, and R. C. da Costa, "Diversification Strategy and Internationalization: Implications for MNE Performance," *Strategic Management Journal* 10 (1989): 109–19.

A random sample of 189 companies was selected. For each company, the profit-to-sales and profit-to-assets were measured. In addition, each company was judged to have a low (1), medium (2), or high (3) level of diversification. The degree of internationalization was measured on a 5-point scale where 1 = Lowest level and 5 = Highest level. The resulting data are stored on the data disk using the following format. What do these results tell you about the researchers' hypotheses?

PERFORMANCE MEASURES

Company	Profit-to-Sales	Profit-to-Assets	Diversification	Internationalization
1	2.79	3.21	1	3
2	6.39	6.94	1	4
3	5.53	1.04	1	2
⋮	⋮	⋮	⋮	⋮
189	6.20	4.66	3	2

████████████   **CASE 12.3***   *OLYMPIC FIGURE-SKATING JUDGMENTS*

PG Most North Americans believe that politics plays an important role in almost all aspects of the Olympic Games. This politicization is often seen in the way that judges assign scores in judgmental competitions, where scores are suspected of being influenced by the nationality of the judges and the competitors. In an attempt to determine the validity of these beliefs, two researchers examined the results of four figure-skating competitions from the 1980 Winter Olympics in Lake Placid, New York. The competitions were men's, women's, and pairs' figure skating, and ice dancing.

Each event involves several subevents that are evaluated by nine judges. For each subevent, the judges provide scores from 1 to 6. The subevent scores are then combined to produce a single event score. The scores are ordinally scaled, but they were treated as interval for purposes of the statistical analysis. An analysis of variance was performed on each of the four events. We can identify two sources of variation: the contestants, and the judges. The experiment is a randomized block design. The accompanying tables present some of the relevant calculations. What conclusions can be drawn from the results?

---

* Based on an article by Ian Fenwick and Songit Chatterjee, "Perception, Preference, and Patriotism: An Exploratory Analysis of the 1980 Winter Olympics," *American Statistician* 35(3) (1981): 170–73.

TABLE A   MEN'S FIGURE SKATING

Number of competitors = 16
Number of judges = 9
SS(Total) = 402.35
SST(Competitors) = 273.38
SSB(Judges) = 2.48

TABLE B   WOMEN'S FIGURE SKATING

Number of competitors = 22
Number of judges = 9
SS(Total) = 518.86
SST = 364.50
SSB = .81

TABLE C   PAIRS' FIGURE SKATING

Number of competitors = 11
Number of judges = 9
SS(Total) = 42.30
SST = 40.22
SSB = .23

TABLE D   ICE DANCING

Number of competitors = 12
Number of judges = 9
SS(Total) = 66.74
SST = 60.10
SSB = 1.65

SHORTCUT COMPUTATIONS

SHORTCUT COMPUTATIONS FOR THE COMPLETELY RANDOMIZED DESIGN

To find SS(Total), we use

$$\text{SS(Total)} = \sum\sum(x_{ij} - \bar{\bar{x}})^2 = \sum\sum x_{ij}^2 - \text{CM}$$

where

$$\text{CM} = \frac{(\sum\sum x_{ij})^2}{n}$$

To find SST, we use

$$\text{SST} = \sum\left(\frac{T_j^2}{n_j}\right) - \text{CM}$$

where

$$T_j = \text{Total of the } j\text{th sample}$$

And to find SSE, we use

$$\text{SSE} = \text{SS(Total)} - \text{SST}$$

As an illustration of these shortcut computations, we will calculate the value of the test statistic for Example 12.1. From the data, we find

$$\sum\sum x_{ij} = 383$$
$$\sum\sum x_{ij}^2 = 6,291$$
$$T_1 = 141, T_2 = 110, T_3 = 132$$
$$n_1 = 8, n_2 = 8, n_3 = 8, n = 24$$

$$CM = \frac{\left(\sum\sum x_{ij}\right)^2}{n} = \frac{(383)^2}{24} = 6{,}112.04$$

$$SS(\text{Total}) = \sum\sum x_{ij}^2 - CM = 6{,}291 - 6{,}112.04 = 178.96$$

$$SST = \frac{T_1^2}{n_1} + \frac{T_2^2}{n_2} + \frac{T_3^2}{n_3} - CM$$

$$= \frac{(141)^2}{8} + \frac{(110)^2}{8} + \frac{(132)^2}{8} - 6{,}112.04 = 63.59$$

$$SSE = SS(\text{Total}) - SST = 178.96 - 63.59 = 115.37$$

The mean squares can now be computed:

$$MST = \frac{SST}{k-1} = \frac{63.59}{3-1} = 31.795$$

$$MSE = \frac{SSE}{n-k} = \frac{115.37}{24-3} = 5.49$$

Therefore, the value of the test statistic is

$$F = \frac{MST}{MSE} = \frac{31.795}{5.49} = 5.79$$

SHORTCUT COMPUTATIONS FOR THE RANDOMIZED BLOCK DESIGN

The shortcut formulas for SS(Total), SST, and SSB are as follows:

$$SS(\text{Total}) = \sum\sum x_{ij}^2 - CM$$

$$SST = \frac{\sum T_j^2}{b} - CM$$

$$SSB = \frac{\sum B_i^2}{k} - CM$$

where

$B_i = $ total of the ith block

And the formula for SSE is

$$SSE = SS(\text{Total}) - SST - SSB$$

To illustrate, in Example 12.4, we find the value of the test statistics

$$\sum\sum x_{ij} = 607$$

$$\sum\sum x_{ij}^2 = 21{,}485$$

$$T_1 = 185,\ T_2 = 201,\ T_3 = 221$$

$$B_1 = 137,\ B_2 = 119,\ B_3 = 91,\ B_4 = 96,\ B_5 = 89,\ B_6 = 75$$

From these, we calculate

$$CM = \frac{(\sum\sum x_{ij})^2}{n} = \frac{(607)^2}{18} = 20{,}469.39$$

$$SS(Total) = \sum\sum x_{ij}^2 - CM = 21{,}485 - 20{,}469.39 = 1{,}015.61$$

$$SST = \frac{\sum T_j^2}{b} - CM = \frac{(185)^2 + (201)^2 + (221)^2}{6} - 20{,}469.39 = 108.44$$

$$SSB = \frac{\sum B_i^2}{k} - CM$$

$$= \frac{(137)^2 + (119)^2 + (91)^2 + (96)^2 + (89)^2 + (75)^2}{3} - 20{,}469.39$$

$$= 854.94$$

$$SSE = SS(Total) - SST - SSB = 1{,}015.61 - 108.44 - 854.94 = 52.23$$

The mean squares are

$$MST = \frac{SST}{k-1} = \frac{108.44}{3-1} = 54.22$$

$$MSB = \frac{SSB}{b-1} = \frac{854.94}{6-1} = 170.99$$

$$MSE = \frac{SSE}{n-k-b+1} = \frac{52.23}{18-3-6+1} = 5.22$$

The *F*-ratios are calculated differently for treatments and for blocks. For treatments, the computation is

$$F = \frac{MST}{MSE} = \frac{54.22}{5.22} = 10.39$$

For blocks, the computation is

$$F = \frac{MSB}{MSE} = \frac{170.99}{5.22} = 32.76$$

MINITAB INSTRUCTIONS

COMPLETELY RANDOMIZED DESIGN

As was the case with the inference concerning $\mu_1 - \mu_2$, the data can be stored in either stacked or unstacked form.

UNSTACKED DATA

If, in a question involving the analysis of variance, there are three treatments, and if the observations of treatment 1 are stored in column 1, the observations of treatment 2 are stored in column 2, and the observations of treatment 3 are stored in column 3, then the command

```
AOVONEWAY C1-C3
```

performs the analysis of variance. The output includes the ANOVA table, the means and standard deviations of each treatment, and a graphical depiction of a 95% confidence interval estimate of each treatment mean. For instance, the following series of keyboard entries will perform the analysis of variance for Example 12.1:

```
SET C1
15   17   22   20   18   16   14   19
END
SET C2
10   12   15   17   12   13   15   16
END
SET C3
13   18   19   16   17   16   15   18
END
AOVONEWAY C1-C3
```

The output is

```
ANALYSIS OF VARIANCE
SOURCE    DF      SS       MS       F
FACTOR     2    63.58    31.79    5.79
ERROR     21   115.37     5.49
TOTAL     23   178.96
                              INDIVIDUAL 95 PCT CI'S FOR MEAN
                                   BASED ON POOLED STDEV

LEVEL     N     MEAN    STDEV   --------|-------|-------|--------
C1        8   17.625    2.669                  (-----x-----)
C2        8   13.750    2.375    (-----x-----)
C3        8   16.500    1.927           (-----x-----)
                                --------|-------|-------|--------
POOLED STDEV=2.344                  14.0    16.0    18.0
```

STACKED DATA

If the data are stacked, the command

```
ONEWAY C1 C2
```

(where the observations of all treatments are in column 1, and the values in column 2 show the treatment number of each observation) triggers the computations. The output is essentially the same as that produced by the AOVONEWAY command for unstacked data.

RANDOMIZED BLOCK DESIGN

To perform the analysis of variance when the data have been taken from the randomized block design, type

```
TWOWAY C1 C2 C3
```

where the first column stores all of the observations (stacked data), the second column specifies which treatment each observation is from, and the third column identifies which block each observation is from. For example, the data from Example 12.4 would be input and analyzed as follows:

```
READ C1-C3
41       1    1
36       1    2
27       1    3
32       1    4
26       1    5
23       1    6
45       2    1
```

```
38          2    2
33          2    3
29          2    4
31          2    5
25          2    6
51          3    1
45          3    2
31          3    3
35          3    4
32          3    5
27          3    6
END
TWOWAY  C1  C2  C3
```

The computer would then show the following output:

```
SOURCE      DF        SS         MS
C2          2       108.44      54.22
C3          5       854.94     170.99
ERROR      10        52.22       5.22
TOTAL      17      1015.61
```

SAS INSTRUCTIONS

COMPLETELY RANDOMIZED DESIGN

In order to perform the completely randomized design of the analysis of variance, we must input the data as described here. The observations of all treatments are input as one variable (say, x), and another variable (say, t) identifies the treatment each observation is from. (This is identical to the manner in which the data were input in the test of $\mu_1 - \mu_2$, with independent samples.) The ANOVA procedure is then used. The procedure statement must be followed by a statement identifying the treatment variable (which is t) and the model. The model states that the variable x depends on the treatment t.

Thus, for Example 12.1, the following information and commands are input from the keyboard:

```
DATA;
INPUT X T;
CARDS;
15    1
17    1
22    1
20    1
18    1
16    1
14    1
19    1
10    2
12    2
15    2
17    2
12    2
13    2
15    2
16    2
```

```
13    3
18    3
19    3
16    3
17    3
16    3
15    3
18    3
PROC ANOVA;
CLASS T;
MODEL X=T;
```

The computer will then print the following output:

```
Dependent Variable: X
                             Sum of      Mean
Source              DF      Squares     Square    F Value    Pr > F
Model                2      63.5833    31.7916       5.79    0.0100
Error               21     115.3750     5.4940
Corrected Total     23     178.9583
```

RANDOMIZED BLOCK DESIGN

The randomized block design of the analysis of variance is performed in the same way as the completely randomized design, except that we must include the blocks. Three variables must be input: variable x is the value of each observation, variable t identifies the treatment, and variable b identifies the block. After the ANOVA procedure statement is entered, we need to identify the variables representing the treatments and blocks, which we do with the statement

```
CLASS T B
```

We also need the MODEL statement, which tells the computer that the variable x depends on both blocks and treatments. This is done with the statement

```
MODEL X=T B
```

Thus, for Example 12.4, the following information and commands are input from the keyboard:

```
DATA;
INPUT X T B;
CARDS;
41    1    1
36    1    2
27    1    3
32    1    4
26    1    5
```

```
23   1   6
45   2   1
38   2   2
33   2   3
29   2   4
31   2   5
25   2   6
51   3   1
45   3   2
31   3   3
35   3   4
32   3   5
27   3   6
PROC ANOVA;
CLASS T B;
MODEL X=T B;
```

The output for this program includes a number of statistics that we have not discussed. An explanation of these is available in the SAS manual. The output is

```
Dependent Variable: X
Source    DF    Anova SS    Mean Square    F Value    Pr > F
T          2    108.4444       54.2222       10.38     0.0036
B          5    854.9444      170.9888       32.74     0.0001
```

TUKEY'S MULTIPLE COMPARISON METHOD

By adding the command

```
MEANS T/TUKEY
```

on the line after the model specification (MODEL X = T), the computer will print the means and standard deviations of each sample as well as perform Tukey's multiple comparison test. The variable after MEANS is the variable used to identify the treatments. Thus the command MEANS T tells the computer to produce the means and standard deviation for each treatment. The instruction TUKEY is an option of the MEANS procedure. To solve Example 12.6, we proceed as follows:

```
DATA;
INPUT X T;
CARDS;
315  1
288  1
 .   .
 .   .
 .   .
310  4
```

```
PROC ANOVA;
CLASS T;
MODEL X=T;
MEANS T/TUKEY;
```

![bar] **COMPUTER EXERCISES**

12.86 For the data in the following table, perform an analysis of variance to determine if differences exist among the treatment means, with $\alpha = .10$.

Treatment			
1	2	3	4
6	19	8	12
12	23	9	20
25	27	15	13
18	18	14	
21		13	
		8	

12.87 Do the data that follow allow us to conclude that there are differences among the treatment means? (Use $\alpha = .05$.)

Treatment		
1	2	3
125	110	127
141	153	120
112	145	132
162	140	108

12.88 The following data were generated by a completely randomized experiment. Variable X represents all of the observations, and variable T represents the sample that each observation is from. Conduct an analysis of variance test to determine at the 5% significance level whether the treatment means differ.

X	T
7	1
14	1
16	1
19	2
11	2
15	2
18	2
21	2
16	3
15	3
19	3
22	3
25	4
29	4
20	4

12.89 Do the following data drawn from a randomized block experiment provide sufficient evidence at the 10% significance level to allow us to conclude that the treatment means differ?

	Treatment		
Block	1	2	3
1	55	48	47
2	63	59	56
3	52	53	50
4	69	61	65
5	60	59	61 .

12.90   The data that follow were generated by a randomized block experiment. Variable X represents all of the observations, variable T identifies the treatment, and variable B the block. Test with $\alpha = .01$ to determine whether the treatment means differ.

X	T	B
4.6	1	1
3.1	1	2
3.8	1	3
4.9	1	4
4.7	2	1
3.3	2	2
3.7	2	3
4.9	2	4
4.4	3	1
3.3	3	2
3.6	3	3
4.8	3	4
4.8	4	1
3.1	4	2
3.6	4	3
4.8	4	4

SOLUTIONS TO SELF-CORRECTING EXERCISES

12.28 $H_0: \mu_1 = \mu_2 = \mu_3$
   H_A: At least two means differ.

Rejection region: $F > 3.07$ (approximately)

Value of the test statistic:

Source	DF	SS	MS	F
Treatments	2	73.18	36.59	3.47
Error	147	1548.7	10.54	

Conclusion: Reject H_0.

There is enough evidence to allow us to conclude that differences in computer use exist among the three industries surveyed. We recommend that the company marketing strategy be focused on the industry that uses the computer most.

12.52 $H_0: \mu_1 = \mu_2 = \mu_3$
   H_A: At least two means differ.

Rejection region: $F > 6.01$

Value of the test statistic:

Source	DF	SS	MS	F
Treatments	2	5.98	2.99	2.39
Blocks	9	122.49	13.61	10.89
Error	18	22.50	1.25	

Conclusion: Do not reject H_0.

There is not enough evidence to allow us to conclude that there are differences in delivery times among the three couriers.

12.64   MSE $= 1.46$ $n_g = 5$ $v = n - k = 16$

$$\omega = q_\alpha(k, v)\sqrt{\frac{\text{MSE}}{n_g}} = q_{.05}(4, 16)\sqrt{\frac{1.46}{5}}$$

$$= (4.05)(.540) = 2.19$$

$\bar{x}_4 = 8.36$ $\bar{x}_3 = 8.50$ $\bar{x}_1 = 9.60$ $\bar{x}_2 = 11.24$

There is sufficient evidence to conclude that μ_2 differs from μ_3 and μ_4.

CHI-SQUARE TESTS

INTRODUCTION

The chi-square distribution was introduced in Chapter 7 as a way to test hypotheses concerning the population variance σ^2. The objective there was to describe a single population for which the data scale was interval. This chapter makes use of the chi-square distribution to conduct two statistical tests involving data having a nominal scale. (Recall that nominal data are categorical in nature.) The first of these statistical tests is a **goodness-of-fit test** applied to data generated by a multinomial experiment—which is a generalization of a binomial experiment. The second test uses data arranged in a table (called a **contingency table**) to determine whether or not two classifications of a population of nominal data are statistically independent; this test can also be interpreted as a comparison of two or more populations of nominal data. Finally, the goodness-of-fit test is applied to a sample of data to determine whether or not it is reasonable to assume that the sample was drawn from a normal population. The Lilliefors test, an alternative to this test for normality, will be presented in Chapter 14.

The chi-square distribution is one of the most widely used statistical distributions for conducting tests of hypotheses in practical situations. Following are two examples of situations in which the statistical tests mentioned above could be applied.

Case 1. Firms periodically estimate the proportion (or market share) of consumers who prefer their product, as well as the market shares of competitors. These market shares may change over time as a result of advertising campaigns or the introduction of new and improved products. To determine if the actual current market shares are in accord with its beliefs, a firm might sample several consumers and compute, for each of k competing companies, the proportion of consumers sampled who prefer that company's product. Such an experiment, in which each consumer is classified as preferring one of the k companies, is called a **multinomial experiment.** If only two companies were considered ($k = 2$), we would be dealing with the familiar binomial experiment. After computing the proportion of consumers preferring each of the k companies, a goodness-of-fit test could be conducted to determine whether or not the sample proportions (or market shares) differ significantly from those hypothesized by the firm. The problem objective is to describe the population of consumers, and the data scale is nominal.

Case 2. For advertising and other purposes, it is important for a company to understand which segments of the market prefer which of its products. For example, it would be helpful for an automotive manufacturer to know if there is a relationship between the buyer preferences for its various models and the sex of the consumer. After conducting a survey to solicit consumers' preferences, the firm could classify each respondent according to two nominal variables: model preferred, and sex. A test could then be conducted to determine whether or not consumers' preferences are independent of their sex. Rather than interpreting this test as a test of the independence of two nominal variables defined over a single population, we could view male and female consumers as representing two different populations. Then we could interpret the test as testing for differences in preferences between these two populations.

CHI-SQUARE TEST OF A MULTINOMIAL EXPERIMENT

This section presents another test concerned with describing a single population that has a nominal data scale. The first such test was presented in Chapter 8, where we discussed inferences concerning the population proportion p. In that case, the data for the statistical tests were provided by a binomial experiment. Recall that the result of each trial of a binomial experiment is measured on a nominal scale, using dichotomous categories such as *defective* and *nondefective,* or *favor* and *disfavor.* In some important experiments (called *multinomial experiments*), however, the result of each trial is measured on a nominal scale involving more than two categories. For example, apparel produced by a machine might be classified as having a tear, improper stitching, or no defects. Or a consumer might prefer product $A, B, C,$ or D. **A multinomial experiment** is a generalized version of a binomial experiment that allows for more than two possible outcomes on each trial of the experiment—as is evident from the following description, which parallels that of a binomial experiment.

Multinomial Experiment

A multinomial experiment is one possessing the following properties:

1. The experiment consists of a fixed number n of trials.
2. The outcome of each trial can be classified into exactly one of k categories, called **cells.**
3. The probability p_i that the outcome of a trial will fall into cell i remains constant for each trial, for $i = 1, 2, \ldots, k$. Moreover, $p_1 + p_2 + \cdots + p_k = 1$.
4. Each trial of the experiment is independent of the other trials.

Just as we count the number of successes and failures in the n trials of a binomial experiment, we count the number of outcomes falling into each of the k cells in a multinomial experiment. We thereby obtain a set of observed frequencies

$(o_1, o_2, \ldots, o_k)$, where o_i is the **observed frequency** of outcomes falling into cell i, for $i = 1, 2, \ldots, k$. Since an outcome must fall into some cell,

$$o_1 + o_2 + \cdots + o_k = n$$

These observed frequencies may then be used to test hypotheses about the values of the probabilities p_i ($i = 1, 2, \ldots, k$).

As an illustration, consider Willy Winn, the bookie, who is searching for ways to improve the profitability of his business. He regularly establishes odds and accepts bets on races at the local racetrack, which runs six horses in each race. Willy believes that some post positions may be more favorable than others, so that horses starting in these post positions win more frequently than horses starting in other positions. If this hunch is correct, he can use the information to advantage in setting his odds.

The population in question is the population of winning post positions for all races at this track. Although the data scale may appear at first glance to be interval, it is in fact nominal. The numbers from one to six simply give unique names to each of the post positions. The relevant parameters are the probabilities $p_1, p_2, \ldots, p_6$ that post positions 1 to 6 are the winning positions. To test Willy's belief, we will have the null hypothesis specify that each of the post positions is equally likely to win. That means that each of the probabilities $p_1, p_2, \ldots, p_6$ equals $1/6$. Thus,

$$H_0: p_1 = 1/6, p_2 = 1/6, p_3 = 1/6, p_4 = 1/6, p_5 = 1/6, p_6 = 1/6$$

Because we want to know if at least one post position wins more frequently than the others, the alternative hypothesis is

H_A: At least one p_i is not equal to the specified value.

To test these hypotheses, Willy has obtained the results of a random sample of 300 races and counted the number of times each post position was the winning position. These observed frequencies o_i are recorded in Table 13.1. We proceed, as usual, by *assuming that the null hypothesis is true*. In that case, we would expect each of the post positions to win one-sixth of the time; and since $n = 300$, our expectation under H_0 would be that each position won $300(1/6) = 50$ times. In general, the **expected frequency** for each post position is given by

$$e_i = np_i$$

This expression is based on the formula for the expected value of a binomial random variable:

$$E(X) = np$$

TEST STATISTIC

Table 13.1 summarizes the observed frequencies (o_i) and the expected frequencies (e_i). If the null hypothesis is true, the observed and expected frequencies should be

TABLE 13.1 COMPUTATION OF χ^2 FOR 300 HORSE RACES

Post Position i	Observed Frequency o_i	Expected Frequency e_i	$(o_i - e_i)^2$	$\dfrac{(o_i - e_i)^2}{e_i}$
1	44	50	36	.72
2	65	50	225	4.50
3	42	50	64	1.28
4	60	50	100	2.00
5	46	50	16	.32
6	43	50	49	.98
Total	300	300		$\chi^2 = 9.80$

similar. (Because we're dealing with random variables, they wouldn't be required—or expected—to be identical.) If there are large differences between the observed and expected frequencies, however, this would cast doubt on the null hypothesis, and we would reject H_0 in favor of H_A. The test statistic for judging this is

$$\chi^2 = \sum_{i=1}^{k} \frac{(o_i - e_i)^2}{e_i}$$

If the null hypothesis is true, this test statistic will have an approximate chi-square distribution, with $k - 1$ degrees of freedom, where k is the number of cells. This number of degrees of freedom corresponds to the number of independent cell frequencies. Thus, once we know the observed frequencies for $k - 1$ cells, the observed frequency for the one remaining cell is automatically determined, since the frequencies must sum to n.

Notice that, if the observed frequencies are similar to the expected frequencies, the value of χ^2 will be small. Conversely, if there are large differences between observed and expected frequencies, χ^2 will be large. Hence, we reject H_0 in favor of H_A if χ^2 is sufficiently large. The rejection region is therefore located in the right tail of the chi-square distribution and is determined by the level of significance chosen. If $\alpha = .05$, then the rejection region is given by

$$\chi^2 > \chi^2_{\alpha, k-1}$$
$$> \chi^2_{.05, 5}$$
$$> 11.0705$$

as depicted in Figure 13.1.

FIGURE 13.1 REJECTION REGION FOR COMPARING POST POSITIONS

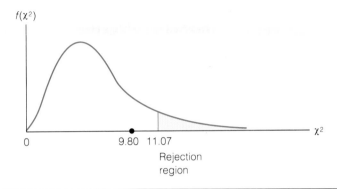

From Table 13.1, we find that the value of the test statistic, using Willy's data, is

$$\chi^2 = \frac{(44 - 50)^2}{50} + \frac{(65 - 50)^2}{50} + \cdots + \frac{(43 - 50)^2}{50} = 9.80$$

Since the computed value of 9.80 does not exceed the critical value of 11.0705, insufficient evidence exists to allow us to conclude that some post positions are more favorable than others, at the 5% level of significance. There is sufficient evidence for us to reach this conclusion at the 10% level, however, since $\chi^2_{.10,5} = 9.23635$.

While it is common to test for no differences in the cell probabilities p_1, $p_2, \ldots, p_k$ (as we did in the foregoing example), we are not restricted to this formulation. Based on prior expectations, we may hypothesize a different value for each p_i, as long as they sum to 1. The following example illustrates such a test, in which the null hypothesis asserts values for the cell probabilities that differ from one another.

EXAMPLE 13.1

Two companies, A and B, have recently conducted aggressive advertising campaigns in order to maintain and possibly increase their respective shares of the market for a particular product. These two companies enjoy a dominant position in the market. Before the advertising campaigns began, the market share for company A was $p_1 = .45$, while company B had a market share of $p_2 = .40$. Other competitors accounted for the remaining market share of $p_3 = .15$. To determine whether these market shares changed after the advertising campaigns, a marketing analyst solicited the preferences of a random sample of 200 consumers of this product. Of the 200 consumers, 100 indicated a preference for company A's product, 85 preferred company B's product, and the remainder preferred one or another of the products

TABLE 13.2 COMPUTATION OF χ^2 FOR 200 CONSUMERS

Company	Observed Frequency o_i	Expected Frequency e_i	$(o_i - e_i)^2$	$\dfrac{(o_i - e_i)^2}{e_i}$
A	100	90	100	1.11
B	85	80	25	.31
Others	15	30	225	7.50
Total	200	200		$8.92 = \chi^2$

distributed by the competitors. Table 13.2 reproduces the relevant data. Conduct a test to determine, at the 5% level of significance, whether the market shares have changed from the levels they were at before the advertising campaigns occurred.

Solution. There is only one population (the population of preferences of all consumers), and the data scale is nomina!. The parameters of interest are the proportions of consumers preferring the product marketed by A, by B, and by the other competitors. Since we wish to determine whether or not the proportions have changed from their previous levels, the alternative hypothesis states that at least one proportion has changed. We therefore have

$H_0: p_1 = .45, p_2 = .40, p_3 = .15$

$H_A:$ At least one p_i is not equal to its specified value.

Test statistic:

$$\chi^2 = \sum_{i=1}^{k} \frac{(o_i - e_i)^2}{e_i} \qquad \text{d.f.} = k - 1$$

Rejection region:

$$\chi^2 > \chi^2_{\alpha, k-1}$$
$$> \chi^2_{.05, 2}$$
$$> 5.99147$$

Value of the test statistic: Assuming that H_0 is correct, we can expect the number of consumers who prefer A to be $(200)(.45) = 90$. The other two expected frequencies are as shown in Table 13.2, so

$$\chi^2 = \frac{(100 - 90)^2}{90} + \frac{(85 - 80)^2}{80} + \frac{(15 - 30)^2}{30} = 8.92$$

Conclusion: Reject H_0.

There is sufficient evidence at the 5% level of significance to allow us to conclude that the market shares have changed from the levels they were at before the advertising campaigns occurred.

RULE OF FIVE

The test statistic used to compare the relative sizes of observed and expected frequencies is

$$\chi^2 = \sum_{i=1}^{k} \frac{(o_i - e_i)^2}{e_i}$$

We previously stated that this test statistic has an approximate chi-square distribution. The distribution of this test statistic is actually discrete, but it can be conveniently approximated by using a continuous chi-square distribution when the sample size n is large, just as we approximated the discrete binomial distribution by using the normal distribution. This approximation may be poor, however, if the expected cell frequencies are small. For the (discrete) distribution of the test statistic χ^2 to be adequately approximated by the (continuous) chi-square distribution, the conventional (and conservative) rule is to **require that the expected frequency for each cell be at least 5.**[*] Where necessary, cells should be combined in order to satisfy this condition. The choice of cells to be combined should be made in such a way that meaningful categories result from the combination.

Consider the following modification of Example 13.1. Suppose that three companies (A, B, and C) have recently conducted aggressive advertising campaigns; the market shares prior to the campaigns were $p_1 = .45$ for company A, $p_2 = .40$ for company B, $p_3 = .13$ for company C, and $p_4 = .02$ for other competitors. In a test to see if the market shares changed after the advertising campaigns, the null hypothesis would now be

$$H_0: p_1 = .45, \, p_2 = .40, \, p_3 = .13, \, p_4 = .02$$

If the preferences of a sample of 200 consumers were solicited, the expected frequencies would be

$$e_1 = 90$$
$$e_2 = 80$$
$$e_3 = 26 \,\Big\}$$
$$e_4 = 4 \,\Big\} \; 30$$

---

[*] To be on the safe side, this rule of thumb is somewhat conservative. A discussion of alternatives to the rule of five can be found in W. J. Conover, *Practical Nonparametric Statistics* (New York: John Wiley, 1971), p. 152 and in S. Siegel, *Nonparametric Statistics for the Behavioral Sciences* (New York: McGraw-Hill, 1956), p. 178.

Since the expected cell frequency e_4 is less than 5, the rule of five requires that it be combined with one of the other expected frequencies (say, e_3) to obtain a combined cell frequency of (in this case) 30. Although e_4 could have been combined with e_1 or e_2, we have chosen to combine it with e_3 so that we still have a separate category representing each of the two dominant companies (A and B). After this combination is made, the null hypothesis reads

$$H_0: p_1 = .45, p_2 = .40, p_3 = .15$$

where p_3 now represents the market share of all competitors of companies A and B. The appropriate number of degrees of freedom for the chi-square test statistic would be $k - 1 = 3 - 1 = 2$, where k is the number of cells remaining after some have been combined to satisfy the rule of five.

EXERCISES

LEARNING THE TECHNIQUES

13.1 Describe the properties of a multinomial experiment. How do they compare with the properties of a binomial experiment?

13.2 Describe an example of a multinomial experiment. Formulate a pair of hypotheses that could be tested by using the data from this experiment.

13.3 Determine the rejection region for a test of hypothesis based on the results of a multinomial experiment with:

a. $k = 5$ and $\alpha = .05$

b. $k = 8$ and $\alpha = .01$

c. $k = 10$ and $\alpha = .10$

13.4 Consider a multinomial experiment involving $n = 300$ trials and $k = 5$ cells. The observed frequencies resulting from the experiment are shown in the accompanying table, and the null hypothesis to be tested is

$$H_0: p_1 = .1, p_2 = .2, p_3 = .3, p_4 = .2, p_5 = .2$$

Cell	1	2	3	4	5
Frequency	24	65	86	70	55

a. State the alternative hypothesis.

b. Test the hypotheses, using $\alpha = .01$.

13.5 Consider a multinomial experiment involving $n = 150$ trials and $k = 4$ cells. The observed frequencies resulting from the experiment are shown in the accompanying table, and the null hypothesis to be tested is

$$H_0: p_1 = .3, p_2 = .3, p_3 = .2, p_4 = .2$$

Cell	1	2	3	4
Frequency	38	50	38	24

a. State the alternative hypothesis.

b. Test the hypotheses, using $\alpha = .05$.

13.6 For Exercise 13.5, retest the hypotheses, assuming that the experiment involved twice as many trials ($n = 300$) and that the observed frequencies were twice as high as before, as shown in the accompanying table. (Use $\alpha = .05$.)

Cell	1	2	3	4
Frequency	76	100	76	48

13.7 Explain what is meant by the *rule of five*.

APPLYING THE TECHNIQUES

Self-Correcting Exercise (See Appendix 13.C for the solution.)

GEN **13.8** To determine if a single die is balanced, or fair, the die was rolled 600 times. The observed frequencies with which each of the six sides of the die turned up are recorded in the following table. Is there sufficient evidence to conclude, at the 5% level of significance, that the die is not fair?

Face	Observed Frequency
1	114
2	92
3	84
4	101
5	107
6	102

GEN **13.9** For Exercise 13.8, suppose that the die were rolled 1,200 times and that the observed frequencies were twice as high as before, as recorded in the accompanying table. Is there now sufficient evidence to conclude, at the 5% level of significance, that the die is not fair?

Face	Observed Frequency
1	228
2	184
3	168
4	202
5	214
6	204

EDUC **13.10** Grades assigned by an economics instructor have historically followed a symmetrical distribution: 5% A's, 25% B's, 40% C's, 25% D's, and 5% F's. This year, a sample of grades revealed 11 A's, 32 B's, 62 C's, 29 D's, and 16 F's. Can you conclude, at the 1% level of significance, that this year's grades are distributed differently than grades were in the past?

MNG **13.11** A firm has been accused of engaging in prejudicial hiring practices. According to the most recent census, the percentages of whites, blacks, and Hispanics in the community where the firm is located are 70%, 12%, and 18%, respectively. A random sample of 200 employees of the firm revealed that 165 were white, 14 were black, and 21 were Hispanic. What would you conclude, at the 5% level of significance?

FIN **13.12** Financial managers are interested in the speed with which customers who make purchases on credit pay their bills. In addition to calculating the average number of days that unpaid bills (called *accounts receivable*) remain outstanding, they often prepare an aging schedule. An aging schedule classifies outstanding accounts receivable according to the time that has elapsed since billing and records the proportion of accounts receivable belonging to each classification. A large firm has estimated its current aging schedule on the basis of a sample of 250 of its accounts receivable. With the economy moving into a recession, the firm wishes to determine whether the distribution of its current aging schedule differs from what it was one year ago. Using the data in the accompanying table, conduct an appropriate test at the 5% level of significance.

Number of Days Outstanding	Proportion of Accounts Receivable	
	Year Ago	Current
0–29	.72	.64
30–59	.15	.14
60–89	.10	.18
Over 90	.03	.04

SECTION 13.3   *CONTINGENCY TABLES*

This section deals with a test that addresses the relationship between two variables for which the data scale is nominal. Defining two nominal variables over a population amounts to classifying the items in the population according to two different criteria. Specifically, the test discussed here investigates whether a dependence relationship exists between two variables or whether the variables are statistically independent.

To see how the **test for statistical independence** is conducted, consider the following example. A certain cola company sells four types of cola throughout North America. To help determine if the same marketing approach used in the United States can be used in Canada and Mexico, one of the firm's marketing analysts wishes to ascertain if there is an association between the type of cola preferred and the nationality of the consumer. She first classifies the population of cola drinkers according to the type of cola preferred: regular (A); both caffeine- and sugar-free (B); caffeine-free only (C); and sugar-free only (D). Her second classification consists of the three nationalities: American (N_1); Canadian (N_2); and Mexican (N_3). The marketing analyst then interviews a random sample of 250 cola drinkers from the three countries, classifies each according to the two criteria, and records the observed frequency of drinkers falling into each of the 12 possible cells, as shown in Table 13.3. A rectangular table such as this, in which items from a population are classified according to two characteristics, is called a **contingency table.**

Since the marketing analyst wishes to determine whether there is an association between cola preference and nationality, the hypotheses to be tested are:

H_0: The two classifications are independent.

H_A: The two classifications are dependent.

The appropriate test statistic is the same chi-square test statistic used for the multinomial experiment. Here, however, the null hypothesis doesn't specify values for the cell probabilities, which are needed if we are to calculate the expected cell

TABLE 13.3   CONTINGENCY TABLE CLASSIFYING COLA DRINKERS

| Nationality | Cola Preference | | | | |
	A	B	C	D	Total
N_1	72	8	12	23	115
N_2	26	10	16	33	85
N_3	7	10	14	19	50
Total	105	28	42	75	250

frequencies. As a result, we must estimate the cell probabilities—and hence the expected frequencies—from the sample data.

Let A represent the event that a cola drinker prefers type A cola. Events B, C, and D are defined similarly. Let N_i denote the event that a drinker belongs to nationality N_i, for $i = 1, 2$, and 3.

As before, the expected cell frequencies will be obtained by multiplying the sample size n by the cell probabilities. But before we can do that, we must estimate the cell probabilities. This is achieved by estimating the marginal column probabilities (the proportions of drinkers preferring each type of cola) and the marginal row probabilities (the proportions of drinkers belonging to each nationality).

The marginal column probabilities are estimated by dividing the column sums by the total sample size.

$$P(A) \cong \frac{105}{250} \qquad P(B) \cong \frac{28}{250} \qquad P(C) \cong \frac{42}{250} \qquad P(D) \cong \frac{75}{250}$$

The notation $\cong$ indicates that these probabilities are only approximations (because they are determined on the basis of sample data).

In a similar manner, the marginal row probabilities are estimated by dividing the row sums by the total sample size:

$$P(N_1) \cong \frac{115}{250} \qquad P(N_2) \cong \frac{85}{250} \qquad P(N_3) \cong \frac{50}{250}$$

Having estimated the marginal column and row probabilities, we can proceed to estimate the cell probabilities. Recall from Chapter 3 that, if events E_1 and E_2 are independent, $P(E_1 \cap E_2) = P(E_1) \cdot P(E_2)$. Thus, assuming the null hypothesis to be true, we may apply this multiplication rule for independent events to obtain the joint probability that a drinker falls into the first cell:

$$P(A \cap N_1) = P(A) \cdot P(N_1) \cong \left(\frac{105}{250}\right)\left(\frac{115}{250}\right)$$

By multiplying this joint probability by the sample size, we obtain the expected number of drinkers who fall into the first cell:

$$e_{11} = n \cdot P(A \cap N_1) = 250\left(\frac{105}{250}\right)\left(\frac{115}{250}\right) = \frac{(105)(115)}{250}$$

Observe that e_{11} was calculated by multiplying the total of row 1 by the total of column 1 and dividing by n. The other expected frequencies are estimated in a similar manner, using the following general formula for the expected frequency of the cell in row i and column j:

$$e_{ij} = \frac{(\text{Row } i \text{ total}) \cdot (\text{Column } j \text{ total})}{\text{Sample size}}$$

TABLE 13.4   CONTINGENCY TABLE CLASSIFYING COLA DRINKERS

Nationality	Cola Preference				Total
	A	B	C	D	
N_1	72(48.30)	8(12.88)	12(19.32)	23(34.50)	115
N_2	26(35.70)	10(9.52)	16(14.28)	33(25.50)	85
N_3	7(21.00)	10(5.60)	14(8.40)	19(15.00)	50
Total	105	28	42	75	250

The expected cell frequencies for the cola-drinkers example are shown in parentheses in Table 13.4. Since the row and column sums of the expected frequencies must be the same as the corresponding sums for the observed frequencies, a quick means of checking the accuracy of the expected frequency calculations is available. As in the case of multinomial experiments, the expected frequencies here should satisfy the *rule of five* (discussed in the previous section).

Having determined the observed and expected cell frequencies, we use the same chi-square test statistic as we did for the multinomial experiment to assess whether or not the differences between them are sufficiently great to allow us to reject the null hypothesis. For convenience of notation, we will continue to use single subscripts to denote observed and expected frequencies in the test statistic. From the calculations in Table 13.5, we obtain

$$\chi^2 = \sum_{i=1}^{12} \frac{(o_i - e_i)^2}{e_i}$$
$$= \frac{(72 - 48.30)^2}{48.30} + \frac{(26 - 35.70)^2}{35.70} + \cdots + \frac{(19 - 15.00)^2}{15.00}$$
$$= 42.75$$

We must now locate the critical value, and hence the rejection region. To locate the critical value, we have to know the appropriate number of degrees of freedom for the chi-square distribution of the test statistic. The number of degrees of freedom for a contingency table with r rows and c columns is

$$\text{d.f.} = (r - 1)(c - 1)$$

We will briefly indicate why this is so. In general, the number of degrees of freedom for a chi-square distribution is $(k - 1 - m)$, where k is the number of cells and m is the number of independent population parameters that must be estimated from the sample data before the expected frequencies can be determined. No parameters were estimated in the test involving a multinomial experiment, so m was equal to zero and the number of degrees of freedom was $k - 1$. For a contingency table with r rows

TABLE 13.5   *COMPUTATION OF χ^2 FOR COLA DRINKERS*

Cell i	Observed Frequency o_i	Expected Frequency e_i	$(o_i - e_i)^2$	$\dfrac{(o_i - e_i)^2}{e_i}$
1	72	48.30	561.69	11.63
2	26	35.70	94.09	2.64
3	7	21.00	196.00	9.33
4	8	12.88	23.81	1.85
5	10	9.52	.23	.02
6	10	5.60	19.36	3.46
7	12	19.32	53.58	2.77
8	16	14.28	2.96	.21
9	14	8.40	31.36	3.73
10	23	34.50	132.25	3.83
11	33	25.50	56.25	2.21
12	19	15.00	16.00	1.07
Total	250	250.00		$42.75 = \chi^2$

and c columns, however, there are $k = rc$ cells, and the sample data are used to estimate $r - 1$ row probabilities and $c - 1$ column probabilities. Once these are estimated, the one remaining row probability and the one remaining column probability are automatically determined, since both the row probabilities and the column probabilities must sum to 1. Therefore, the number of degrees of freedom for a contingency table with r rows and c columns is

$$\text{d.f.} = rc - 1 - [(r - 1) + (c - 1)] = (r - 1)(c - 1)$$

If you didn't understand our perfectly clear analysis of how the degrees of freedom are determined, don't worry. The important thing for you to know is that *the number of degrees of freedom for the chi-square test of a contingency table is* $(r - 1)(c - 1)$.

The chi-square distribution for the test statistic in the cola-drinkers example, therefore, has $(3 - 1)(4 - 1) = 6$ degrees of freedom. If we take $\alpha = .01$, then the critical value is $\chi^2_{.01, 6} = 16.8119$. Since the computed value of our test statistic is 42.75, we reject the null hypothesis that the two classifications are independent. Based on the sample data, we conclude at the 1% level of significance that there is a relationship between the preferences of cola drinkers and their nationality.

COMPARISON OF TWO OR MORE POPULATIONS

When analyzing the data in a contingency table, we are interested in determining whether or not two nominal variables, or classifications, are statistically independent. But the results of a chi-square test for independence can also be interpreted in terms of a different problem objective: the comparison of two or more populations of nominal data. In such a comparison, each of the categories belonging to one of the two classifications is considered to be a population. In the cola-drinkers example, for instance, we could think of the three nationalities as representing three distinct populations of cola drinkers; then we could test for differences among these three populations with respect to cola preference.

The null hypothesis stated that nationality and cola preference were independent. If that were the case, we could state that

$$P(A \mid N_1) = P(A)$$
$$P(A \mid N_2) = P(A)$$
$$P(A \mid N_3) = P(A)$$

or, equivalently,

$$P(A \mid N_1) = P(A \mid N_2) = P(A \mid N_3)$$

This would mean that the preference for cola A is the same for all three populations (American, Canadian, and Mexican). We could make similar statements of independence for colas B, C, and D:

$$P(B \mid N_1) = P(B \mid N_2) = P(B \mid N_3)$$
$$P(C \mid N_1) = P(C \mid N_2) = P(C \mid N_3)$$
$$P(D \mid N_1) = P(D \mid N_2) = P(D \mid N_3)$$

The alternative hypothesis in the cola-drinkers example asserted that the two variables were dependent. If this were true, the statement of independence would not hold for one of the colas—say, cola A. That is, at least one of $P(A \mid N_1)$, $P(A \mid N_2)$, and $P(A \mid N_3)$ would not be equal to $P(A)$. Hence, there would be differences in the preferences for cola A among the three populations.

From the preceding discussion above, it should be clear that testing for differences between two or more nominally scaled populations is equivalent to testing for dependence between two nominal variables. The only differences are in the interpretation and in the problem objective.

EXAMPLE 13.2

The foreman at a shirt manufacturer, which operates three shifts daily, wishes to determine if there are differences in the quality of workmanship among the three shifts. After an inspection of the 600 shirts produced on a particular day, the foreman compiled the data in Table 13.6, showing the number of "seconds" (shirts with flaws) produced by each shift. Do these data indicate that there are differences in the quality of workmanship among the three shifts? (Use $\alpha = .10$.)

TABLE 13.6   CONTINGENCY TABLE CLASSIFYING SHIRTS

| | Shift | | | |
Shirt Condition	1	2	3	Total
Flawed	10(12.5)	9(10)	11(7.5)	30
No flaws	240(237.5)	191(190)	139(142.5)	570
Total	250	200	150	600

Solution.   We can view the 600 shirts as representing a sample from a single population, classified both according to the shift that produced them and according to their condition. The data have a nominal scale. We may then conduct a chi-square test to determine whether or not these two classifications are statistically independent. Alternatively, we may view the data as consisting of three populations: the populations of shirts produced on each of the three shifts. In this regard, notice that, if the two classifications are independent, the shift producing the shirt and the shirt's condition are unrelated—meaning that there are no differences in workmanship among the shifts. The alternative hypothesis states that the shift and the shirt condition are related, and hence that there are differences in workmanship among the shifts.

H_0: The two classifications are independent.

H_A: The two classifications are dependent.

Test statistic:

$$\chi^2 = \sum_{i=1}^{6} \frac{(o_i - e_i)^2}{e_i} \text{ with d.f.} = (1)(2) = 2$$

Rejection region:

$$\chi^2 > \chi^2_{.10, 2}$$
$$> 4.60517$$

Value of the test statistic: The expected cell frequencies, which are estimated in the same way as in the preceding cola-drinkers example, are shown in parentheses in Table 13.6.

$$\chi^2 = \frac{(10 - 12.5)^2}{12.5} + \frac{(240 - 237.5)^2}{237.5} + \cdots + \frac{(139 - 142.5)^2}{142.5} = 2.36$$

Conclusion: Do not reject H_0.

We cannot reject the hypothesis that the two classifications are independent: there is insufficient evidence to allow us to conclude, at the 10% level, that differences in workmanship exist among the three shifts.

COMPUTER OUTPUT FOR EXAMPLE 13.2*

Minitab

```
Expected counts are printed below observed counts

            C1        C2        C3     Total
    1       10         9        11       30
          12.5      10.0       7.5
    2      240       191       139      570
         237.5     190.0     142.5
Total     250       200       150      600
ChiSq=0.50+0.10+1.63+
      0.03+0.01+0.09=2.36
df=2
```

The output includes observed and expected values, the test statistic, and the degrees of freedom.

SAS

```
TABLE OF CONDITION BY SHIFT

CONDITION    SHIFT

Frequency |
Percent   |
Row Pct   |
Col Pct   |     1 |     2 |     3 | Total
----------+-------+-------+-------+
        1 |    10 |     9 |    11 |    30
          |  1.67 |  1.50 |  1.83 |  5.00
          | 33.33 | 30.00 | 36.67 |
          |  4.00 |  4.50 |  7.33 |
----------+-------+-------+-------+
        2 |   240 |   191 |   139 |   570
          | 40.00 | 31.83 | 23.17 | 95.00
          | 42.11 | 33.51 | 24.39 |
          | 96.00 | 95.50 | 92.67 |
----------+-------+-------+-------+
Total         250     200     150     600
            41.67   33.33   25.00  100.00


STATISTICS FOR TABLE OF CONDITION BY SHIFT
Statistic    DF    Value     Prob
---------------------------------------
Chi-Square    2    2.356     0.309

Sample Size=600
```

---

* Appendixes 13.A and 13.B describe the Minitab and SAS commands that produced these outputs.

We've omitted some of the output showing statistical techniques not covered in this book. For each cell in the table, SAS lists the observed value, the percentage frequency, row percentage, and column percentage. It also presents the chi-square statistic and its *p*-value (Prob = 0.309).

EXERCISES

LEARNING THE TECHNIQUES

13.13 Consider a chi-square test of statistical independence.

a. What is the problem objective?

b. What is the data scale?

c. What is meant by *statistical independence*?

13.14 A test of statistical independence is to be conducted, using the data in a contingency table with *r* rows and *c* columns. Determine the rejection region if:

a. $r = 3$, $c = 3$, and $\alpha = .01$

b. $r = 4$, $c = 6$, and $\alpha = .05$

13.15 A test of statistical independence is to be conducted, using the data in a contingency table with *r* rows and *c* columns. Determine the rejection region if:

a. $r = 4$, $c = 4$, and $\alpha = .025$

b. $r = 3$, $c = 5$, and $\alpha = .10$

13.16 Conduct a test to determine whether the two classifications *L* and *M* are independent, using the data in the accompanying contingency table and $\alpha = .01$.

L	*M*	
	M_1	M_2
L_1	29	67
L_2	56	38

13.17 Conduct a test to determine whether the two classifications *R* and *C* are independent, using the data in the accompanying contingency table and $\alpha = .10$.

R	*C*		
	C_1	C_2	C_3
R_1	40	32	48
R_2	30	48	52

APPLYING THE TECHNIQUES

Self-Correcting Exercise (See Appendix 13.C for the solution.)

MNG **13.18** The trustee of a company's pension plan has solicited the opinions of a sample of the company's employees toward a proposed revision of the plan. A breakdown of the responses is shown in the accompanying table. Is there evidence that the responses differ among the three groups of employees? (Test at the 5% level of significance.)

Responses	Blue-Collar Workers	White-Collar Workers	Managers
For	67	32	11
Against	63	18	9

MKT **13.19** To determine if commercials viewed during happy television programs are more effective than those viewed during sad television programs, a study was conducted in which a random sample of students viewed an upbeat segment from *Real People* with commercials, while another random sample of students viewed a very sad segment from *Sixty Minutes* with commercials. The students were then asked what they were thinking about during the final commercial. From their responses, they were categorized as thinking primarily about the commercial, thinking primarily about the program, or thinking about both. The results are summarized in the table. Do commercials viewed during happy television programs appear to be more effective than those viewed during sad television programs? (Test using $\alpha = .01$.)

Program Viewed	What Viewers Were Thinking About		
	Commercial	Program	Both
Real People	50	15	8
Sixty Minutes	11	42	25

SOURCE: Adapted from Marvin E. Goldberg and Gerald J. Gorn, "Happy and Sad TV Programs: How They Affect Reactions to Commercials," *Journal of Consumer Research* 14 (1987): 387–403.

MKT **13.20** In a study comparing characteristics of television commercials in the United States, Mexico, and Australia, characters from a random sample of commercials in the three countries were cross-classified, as shown in Table E13.20. For each of the three countries, conduct a test to determine whether men and women are portrayed in significantly different settings in commercials. (Test using $\alpha = .01$.)

MKT **13.21** The study referred to in Exercise 13.20 also cross-classified characters in commercials according to age and gender, as shown in Table E13.21. For each of the three countries, conduct a test to determine whether women are significantly more likely than men to be portrayed in commercials as being young. (Test using $\alpha = .005$.)

MKT **13.22** A market survey was conducted for the purpose of forming a demographic profile of individuals who would like to own a compact disk player. This profile will help to establish the target market for compact disk players, which in turn will be used in developing an advertising strategy. The

TABLE E13.20		United States		Mexico		Australia	
	Setting	Women	Men	Women	Men	Women	Men
	Home	57	30	31	21	15	8
	Store	15	9	19	14	3	7
	Occupational	6	20	1	3	0	2
	Outdoors	19	10	14	19	3	7
	Other	72	63	55	45	31	25

SOURCE: Adapted from Mary C. Gilly, "Sex Roles in Advertising: A Comparison of Television Advertisements in Australia, Mexico, and the United States," *Journal of Marketing* 52 (1988): 75–85.

TABLE E13.21		United States		Mexico		Australia	
	Age	Women	Men	Women	Men	Women	Men
	Under 35	68	26	85	21	37	15
	35–50	86	82	28	74	13	32
	Over 50	15	24	7	7	2	2

SOURCE: Adapted from Mary C. Gilly, "Sex Roles in Advertising: A Comparison of Television Advertisements in Australia, Mexico, and the United States," *Journal of Marketing* 52 (1988): 75–85.

portion of data collected that relate to the consumers' gender is summarized in the table. Is there sufficient evidence to conclude that the desire to own a compact disk player is related to the consumer's gender? (Test using $\alpha = .05$.)

Response	Men	Women
Want player	32	20
Don't want player	118	130

GEN **13.23** The Equal Credit Opportunity Act forbids lenders in the United States from soliciting the marital status of women who are applying for personal loans. Many women feel that this act should be extended to include business loans. They cite instances in which women have received business loans only after the lender determined that they were married to men who had good credit ratings (*Business Week*, 27 May 1985). Suppose that a women's group has collected data on the business loan applications of 600 women, and that the results are as summarized in the accompanying table. Is there evidence of bias on the part of lenders regarding marital status? (Use $\alpha = .05$.)

Marital Status	Loan Granted	Loan Denied
Single	253	119
Married	181	47

GEN **13.24** An antismoking group recently had a large advertisement published in local newspapers throughout Florida. Several statistical facts and medical details were included, in the hope that it would have a meaningful impact on smokers. The antismoking group is concerned, however, that smokers may have read less of the advertisement than did nonsmokers. This concern is based on the belief that a reader tends to spend more time reading articles that agree with the reader's predisposition. The antismoking group has conducted a survey asking those who saw the advertisement if they had read the headline only, some detail, or most of the advertisement. Do the data in the table

indicate that the antismoking group has reason to be concerned? (Use $\alpha = .05$.)

Type of Reader	Headline Only	Some Detail	Most of the Advertisement
Smoker	42	28	16
Nonsmoker	44	57	41

FIN **13.25** An investor who can correctly forecast the direction and size of changes in foreign currency exchange rates is able to reap huge profits in the international currency markets. A knowledgeable reader of the *Wall Street Journal* (in particular, of the currency futures market quotations) can determine the direction of change in various exchange rates that is predicted by all investors, viewed collectively. These predictions, together with the subsequent actual directions of change, are summarized in the accompanying table for a sample of 216 observations.

a. Test the hypothesis that a relationship exists between the predicted and actual directions of change, at the 5% level of significance.

b. To what extent would you make use of these predictions in formulating your forecasts of future exchange rate changes?

EXCHANGE RATE CHANGES

Predicted Change	Actual Change	
	Positive	Negative
Positive	65	64
Negative	39	48

Source: Lee R. Thomas, III, "A Winning Strategy for Currency Futures Speculation," *Journal of Portfolio Management* 11 (1985): 65–69.

POM **13.26** There are three distinct types of hardware wholesalers: independents (independently owned), wholesaler voluntaries (groups of independents acting together), and retailer cooperatives (retailer-owned). In a random sample of 137 retailers, the retailers were categorized according to the type of wholesaler they primarily used and according to their store location, as shown in the accompanying table. Is there sufficient evidence to conclude that the type of wholesaler primarily used by a retailer is related to the retailer's location? (Test using $\alpha = .05$.)

Store Location	Retailer Cooperatives	Wholesaler Voluntaries	Independents
Multiple locations	14	10	5
Free-standing	29	26	13
Other (mall, strip)	20	14	6

SOURCE: Adapted from F. Robert Dwyer and Sejo Oh, "A Transaction Cost Perspective on Vertical Contractual Structure and Interchannel Competitive Strategies," *Journal of Marketing* 52 (1988): 21–34.

SECTION 13.4 *CHI-SQUARE TEST FOR NORMALITY*

The goodness-of-fit test for a multinomial population was introduced in Section 13.2. The chi-square test described therein can be used to test the hypothesis that a population has a particular probability distribution. Because use of the normal distribution is so prevalent—particularly in the assumptions adopted for many statistical techniques—it would be useful to be able to test whether or not a sample of data has been drawn from a normal population. This section describes one such test.

The chi-square goodness-of-fit test for a normal distribution proceeds in essentially the same way as the chi-square test for a multinomial population. But the multinomial test presented in Section 13.2 dealt with a single population having a nominal data scale, whereas a normal distribution has an interval scale. Therefore, we must begin by subdividing the range of the normal distribution into a set of intervals, or categories, in order to obtain a nominal scale.

Consider, for example, a battery manufacturer that wishes to determine if the lifetimes of its batteries are normally distributed. Such information would be helpful in establishing the guarantee that should be offered. The lifetimes of a sample of 200 batteries are measured, and the resulting data are grouped into a frequency distribution, as shown in Table 13.7. The mean and the standard deviation of the sample of lifetimes are calculated to be $\bar{x} = 164$ and $s = 10$.

Notice that, by grouping the lifetimes into categories, we have obtained a nominal scale. Moreover, once we find the probability that an observation will fall into each of these categories, we have a multinomial experiment and can proceed as before. That is, the chi-square test statistic can be used to compare the observed frequencies of lifetimes falling into the various categories with the expected frequencies that are calculated under the assumption that the data are normally distributed. We therefore have

H_0: The data are normally distributed.

H_A: The data are not normally distributed.

TABLE 13.7   *FREQUENCY DISTRIBUTION OF BATTERY LIFETIMES*

Lifetime in Hours	Number of Batteries
140 up to 150	15
150 up to 160	54
160 up to 170	78
170 up to 180	42
180 up to 190	11
Total	200

Test statistic:

$$\chi^2 = \sum_{i=1}^{k} \frac{(o_i - e_i)^2}{e_i} \qquad \text{d.f.} = k - 3$$

Recall from the previous section that the number of degrees of freedom for a chi-square distribution is $k - 1 - m$, where k is the number of categories and m is the number of population parameters that must be estimated from the sample data. Since we are estimating μ and σ from the sample data, $m = 2$ and d.f. $= k - 3$. The number of categories in the frequency distribution is 5. To accommodate all possible values in the hypothesized normal population, however, the first and last categories should be redefined as open-ended categories (less than 150 and 180 or more, respectively). We therefore have $k = 5$ categories and $k - 3 = 2$ degrees of freedom. Hence, if we conduct the test at the 10% level of significance, we have

Rejection region:

$$\chi^2 > \chi^2_{\alpha, k-3}$$
$$> \chi^2_{.10, 2}$$
$$> 4.60517$$

VALUE OF THE TEST STATISTIC

Before computing the value of the test statistic, we must first determine the expected frequency for each category. In a sample of 200 observations, the expected frequency for any category is simply 200 times the probability that an observation will fall into that category. Assuming that the null hypothesis is correct, this probability can be found by using the standard normal table. The hypothesized normal distribution is shown in Figure 13.2, together with the probabilities that a lifetime x will fall into the various categories. For example, the z-value corresponding to $x = 160$ is $z = (160 - 164)/10 = -.4$; and for $x = 170$, $z = (170 - 164)/10 = .6$. Thus, the

FIGURE 13.2   HYPOTHESIZED NORMAL DISTRIBUTION OF BATTERY LIFETIMES

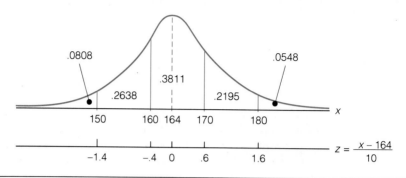

probability that a lifetime falls between 160 and 170 hours is

$$P(160 \le x \le 170) = P(-.4 \le z \le .6) = .3811$$

The expected frequency for this category is therefore $(200)(.3811) = 76.22$. Similarly, the expected number of lifetimes falling below 150 hours is $(200)(.0808) = 16.16$. The remaining expected frequencies—each calculated in a similar manner—are recorded in Table 13.8, which also contains the computation of the chi-square test statistic. Since the computed value of $\chi^2 = .236$ does not exceed the critical value of 4.60517, we cannot reject the hypothesis that the lifetimes of the manufacturer's batteries are normally distributed.

We conclude this section by making three points. First, if the value of either the mean or the standard deviation of the population is hypothesized, rather than estimated from the sample data, the number of degrees of freedom for the chi-square

TABLE 13.8   COMPUTATION OF χ^2 FOR 200 LIFETIMES

Lifetime (in hours)	Observed Frequency o_i	Expected Frequency e_i	$(o_i - e_i)^2$	$\dfrac{(o_i - e_i)^2}{e_i}$
Less than 150	15	16.16	1.35	.083
150 up to 160	54	52.76	1.54	.029
160 up to 170	78	76.22	3.17	.042
170 up to 180	42	43.90	3.61	.082
180 or more	11	10.96	.00	.000
Total	200	200.00		$.236 = \chi^2$

test statistic must be adjusted accordingly. The number of degrees of freedom is $(k - 2)$ if only one of the parameters is estimated, and it is $(k - 1)$ if neither parameter is estimated. Second, when applied to small samples of data, the chi-square test usually fails to reject the hypothesis of normality when the data have a symmetrical distribution with a single mode—even though the distribution may be nonnormal. It is therefore advisable to work with sample sizes greater than 100 whenever possible. An alternative test (called the **Lilliefors test**) of the null hypothesis of normality, with unspecified mean and standard deviation, is presented in Chapter 14. Although it is somewhat more powerful than the chi-square test, the Lilliefors test requires that you work with the individual sample observations. If you only have access to grouped data—as might be the case if the data have been obtained from a secondary source—you must resort to the chi-square test for normality. The final point is that the procedure described in this section can also be used to test the fit of other distributions, such as the binomial and Poisson distributions. We have singled out the normal distribution for attention because of its importance.

EXERCISES

LEARNING THE TECHNIQUES

13.27 Determine the rejection regions for tests of normality having the following null hypotheses (assuming that there are seven categories and that $\alpha = .05$).

a. The data are normally distributed.

b. The data are normally distributed, with a mean of 25.

c. The data are normally distributed, with a mean of 25 and a standard deviation of 8.

13.28 Test the hypothesis that the following sample of data is drawn from a normal population. The sample mean and the standard deviation are 34 and 12, respectively. (Use $\alpha = .01$.)

Class	Frequency
10 up to 20	15
20 up to 30	24
30 up to 40	30
40 up to 50	18
50 up to 60	13

13.29 Test the hypothesis that the following sample of data is drawn from a normal population. (Use $\alpha = .10$.)

Class	Frequency
-20 up to -10	8
-10 up to 0	21
0 up to 10	43
10 up to 20	48
20 up to 30	25
30 up to 40	15

APPLYING THE TECHNIQUES

Self-Correcting Exercise (See Appendix 13.C for the solution.)

13.30 A common measure of a firm's liquidity is its **current ratio,** defined as its current assets divided by its current liabilities. A relatively high current ratio provides some evidence that a firm can meet its short-term financial obligations. The current ratios for a sample of 200 firms are recorded in the

accompanying table. Is there evidence at the 10%
level of significance that this sample was drawn
from a normal population?

Current Ratio	Frequency
.0 up to 1.0	20
1.0 up to 1.5	33
1.5 up to 2.0	47
2.0 up to 2.5	40
2.5 up to 3.0	31
3.0 up to 4.0	29

EDUC **13.31** The instructors for an introductory accounting course attempt to construct the final
examination so that the grades are normally distributed, with a mean of 65. From the sample of
grades appearing in the accompanying frequency
distribution table, can you conclude that they have
achieved their objective? (Use $\alpha = .05$.)

Grade	Frequency
30 up to 40	4
40 up to 50	17
50 up to 60	29
60 up to 70	49

Grade	Frequency
70 up to 80	33
80 up to 90	18

EDUC **13.32** Universities throughout the United States
and Canada are concerned about the aging of their
faculty members, since the average age of professors is at a historic high. A very large number of
professors will retire within the next decade, making it difficult to find adequate replacements to
fill all of the positions that will become available.
Suppose that the ages of a sample of professors are
as recorded in the accompanying table. Is there
evidence at the 5% level of significance that professors' ages are normally distributed?

Age Group	Frequency
25 up to 30	18
30 up to 35	84
35 up to 40	138
40 up to 45	192
45 up to 50	212
50 up to 55	163
55 up to 60	120
60 up to 65	73

SECTION 13.5 SUMMARY

This chapter describes two statistical tests that are based on samples taken from a
single population of nominal data. The first is a **goodness-of-fit test,** used to
determine the validity of a hypothesis concerning the **multinomial distribution** of a
single population of nominal data. The second test uses data arranged in a
contingency table to determine whether or not two classifications of a population of
nominal data are statistically independent. Both tests are based on the same test
statistic, which has an approximate chi-square distribution. In order for this
approximation to be adequate, the sample must be sufficiently large so that no
expected cell frequency is less than 5. The test for statistical independence can also be
interpreted as the comparison of two or more populations of nominal data. The
goodness-of-fit test can be used to determine whether a sample has been drawn from
a normal population.

SUPPLEMENTARY EXERCISES

13.33 Consider a multinomial experiment involving $n = 200$ trials and $k = 4$ cells. The observed frequencies resulting from the experiment are shown in the accompanying table, and the null hypothesis to be tested is

$$H_0: p_1 = .4, p_2 = .3, p_3 = .2, p_4 = .1$$

Cell	1	2	3	4
Frequency	96	54	28	22

a. State the alternative hypothesis.

b. Test the hypotheses, using $\alpha = .05$.

GEN **13.34** An organization dedicated to ensuring fairness in television game shows is investigating *Wheel of Fortune*. In this show, three contestants are required to solve puzzles by selecting letters. Each contestant gets to select the first letter and continues selecting until he or she chooses a letter that is not in the phrase, place, or name. The order of contestants is random. However, contestant 1 starts game 1, contestant 2 starts game 2, and so on. The contestant who wins the most money is declared the winner, and he or she is given an opportunity to win a grand prize. Usually, more than three games are played per show, and as a result it appears that contestant 1 has an advantage: contestant 1 will start two games while contestant 3 will start only one game. To see if this is the case, a random sample of 30 shows was taken, and the starting position of the winning contestant was recorded. These are shown in the following table.

Starting Position	Number of Winners
1	14
2	10
3	6

Do the tabulated results allow us to conclude that the game is unfair? (Use $\alpha = .05$.)

MNG **13.35** Econetics Research Corporation, a well-known Montreal-based consulting firm, desires to test how it can influence the proportion of questionnaires returned from surveys. Believing that the inclusion of an inducement to respond may be important, it sends out 1,000 questionnaires: 200 promise to send respondents a summary of the survey results, 300 indicate that 10 respondents (selected by lottery) will be awarded gifts, and 500 are accompanied by no inducements. Of these, 80 questionnaires promising a summary, 100 questionnaires offering gifts, and 120 questionnaires offering no inducements are returned. What can you conclude, at the 1% level of significance?

MNG **13.36** It has been estimated that employee absenteeism costs North American companies more than $100 billion per year. As a first step in addressing the rising cost of absenteeism, the personnel department of a large corporation recorded the weekdays during which individuals in a sample of 362 absentees were away over the past several months. Do these data suggest that absenteeism is higher on some days of the week than on others? (Use $\alpha = .05$.)

Day of the Week	Mon	Tues	Wed	Thurs	Fri
Number Absent	87	62	71	68	74

MNG **13.37** Suppose that the personnel department in Exercise 13.36 continued its investigation by categorizing absentees according to the shift on which they worked, as shown in the accompanying table. Is there evidence of a relationship between the days on which employees were absent and the shift on which the employees worked? (Use $\alpha = .10$.)

Shift	Mon	Tues	Wed	Thurs	Fri
Day	52	28	37	31	33
Evening	35	34	34	37	41

| MKT | **13.38** A manufacturer of automobile batteries wishes to determine whether there are any differences among three different media (TV, radio, magazine) in terms of the audience's recall of an ad. The results of an advertising study are shown in Table E13.38. Conduct the appropriate test (with $\alpha = .10$), and interpret the results for the manufacturer. |

	Credit Card Held (1984)		
Sex	VISA Only	MC Only	Both Cards
Male	128	66	137
Female	295	165	287

SOURCE: Adapted from Douglass K. Hawes, "Profiling VISA and MasterCard Holders: An Overview of Changes–1973 to 1984, and Some Thoughts for Future Research," *Journal of the Academy of Marketing Science* 15 (1987): 62–69.

| MKT | **13.39** The use of bank cards as a source of consumer credit has become increasingly prevalent over the last 10 to 15 years. A recent study has attempted to profile holders of VISA (Bank Americard) and MasterCard. From the data shown in the accompanying table, would you conclude that there is a relationship between gender and the bank card that is held? (Test using $\alpha = .05$.) |

| MKT | **13.40** The author of the study mentioned in Exercise 13.39 also investigated credit-card users' payment habits. From the data given in Ta- |

TABLE E13.38

	Medium			
Recall Ability	Magazine	TV	Radio	Totals
Number of people remembering ad	25	10	5	40
Number of people not remembering ad	75	60	25	160
Total	100	70	30	200

TABLE E13.40

	Credit Card Held (1984)		
Amount Paid Monthly	VISA Only	MC Only	Both Cards
In full	204	99	148
Minimum amount due	55	37	81
More than minimum but not in full	148	85	174

SOURCE: Adapted from Douglass K. Hawes, "Profiling VISA and MasterCard Holders: An Overview of Changes–1973 to 1984, and Some Thoughts for Future Research," *Journal of the Academy Marketing Science* 15 (1987): 62–69.

ble E13.40, would you conclude that there is a relationship between the bank card that is held and the amount that is paid monthly? (Test using $\alpha = .05$.)

SCI **13.41** A relationship has long been suspected between smoking and susceptibility to having a stroke. Strong statistical evidence on this issue has been lacking, however, since a convincing study would involve monitoring a large number of individuals over a long period of time. The *Toronto Star* (March 1987) reported that one such study has now been conducted, involving over 2,000 residents outside of Boston who were studied over a 26-year period. Because of the large number of individuals observed, researchers were able to maintain reasonable sample sizes even after segmenting the observed group to control for factors other than smoking that might influence the individual susceptibility to a stroke, such as gender and blood-pressure level. Suppose that the results for men with low blood-pressure levels were as shown in the accompanying table. What would you conclude at the 5% level of significance?

Individual	Stroke	No Stroke
Smoker	37	183
Nonsmoker	21	274

SCI **13.42** Acute otitis media, an infection of the middle ear, is a very common childhood illness. Although it is normally treated with amoxicillin, emerging resistance to this antibiotic has prompted the search for an alternative. Your friend David has just read about a study that tested the efficacy of one such alternative: trimethoprim-sulfamethoxazole. In this study, 203 "patients were randomly assigned to receive either amoxicillin or trimethoprim-sulfamethoxazole by means of a computer-generated table of random numbers." The data are summarized in the accompanying table. Being a specialist, David's interest in the study centered on the reported gastrointestinal side effects of the two drugs. But his inquisitive nature induced him to seek your help in understanding the chi-square test that was conducted on the tabulated data.

a. Reconstruct the test to determine if there are differences, at the 10% level of significance, in the outcomes for children treated with amoxicillin and for children treated with trimethoprim-sulfamethoxazole.

b. The chi-square test was reported to have a *p*-value of .42. For David's benefit, explain what this means.

Outcome	Treatment	
	Amoxicillin	Trimethoprim-Sulfamethoxazole
Cure	60	65
Improvement	31	22
Treatment failure	12	13

SOURCE: William Feldman, Joanne Momy, and Corinne Dulberg, "Trimethoprim-sulfamethoxazole v. Amoxicillin in the Treatment of Acute Otitis Media," *Canadian Medical Association Journal* 139 (1988): 961–64.

MKT **13.43** Research into the meaning of object ownership and consumption may improve our understanding of demand and consumer behavior. Two researchers (Wallendorf and Arnould) have conducted a study involving 298 individuals that, among other things, investigated "differences between Southwest American men and women in their selection of favorite objects." From the researchers' data, shown in the following table, would you conclude that men and women exhibit differences in the type of object that is their favorite? (Test using $\alpha = .01$.)

TYPE OF FAVORITE OBJECT BY SOUTHWEST AMERICAN GENDER GROUPS

Type of Favorite Object	Female	Male
Functional (chair, clock)	24	48
Entertainment (stereo, TV)	28	36
Personal items	27	15
Art piece	11	18

(continued)

Type of Favorite Object	Female	Male
Photograph	18	6
Plants	8	16
Handicraft	18	7
Antique	14	4

SOURCE: Adapted from Melanie Wallendorf and Eric J. Arnould, "My Favorite Things: A Cross-Cultural Inquiry into Object Attachment, Possessiveness, and Social Linkage," *Journal of Consumer Research* 14 (1988): 531–47.

Type of Favorite Object	Age Group			
	18–24	25–35	36–44	45+
Photograph/ plants	9	18	5	10
Handicraft/ antiques	6	15	14	6

SOURCE: Adapted from Melanie Wallendorf and Eric J. Arnould, "My Favorite Things: A Cross-Cultural Inquiry into Object Attachment, Possessiveness, and Social Linkage," *Journal of Consumer Research* 14 (1988): 531–47.

MKT **13.44** The researchers mentioned in Exercise 13.43 also investigated the relationship between age and favorite object. On the basis of their data, which are shown in the accompanying table, what would you conclude at the 1% level of significance? (Some object categories have been combined to satisfy the rule of five.)

TYPE OF FAVORITE OBJECT BY
SOUTHWEST AMERICAN AGE GROUPS

Type of Favorite Object	Age Group			
	18–24	25–35	36–44	45+
Functional	14	29	13	10
Entertainment	9	32	11	9
Personal items/ art	7	20	19	21

MNG **13.45** A management behavior analyst has been studying the relationship between male/female reporting structures in the workplace and the level of employees' job satisfaction. The results of a recent survey are shown in Table E13.45. Using $\alpha = .10$, conduct a test to determine whether the level of job satisfaction depends on the boss/ employee gender relationship.

MNG **13.46** A discount video shop sells televisions, video cassette recorders, and video cameras. The store's manager wishes to determine if there is a relationship between the method of payment and the item purchased. The relevant data on last month's purchases are shown in the accompanying table. Using $\alpha = .10$, test to see if the data in the table suggest such a relationship.

TABLE E13.45

Level of Satisfaction	Boss/Employee				
	Female/Male	Female/Female	Male/Male	Male/Female	Total
Satisfied	20	25	50	75	170
Neutral	40	50	50	40	180
Dissatisfied	30	45	10	15	100
Total	90	120	110	130	450

Payment Method	VCR	TV	Camera
Cash	11	4	7
Credit card	52	19	12
Installment	27	32	11

MKT **13.47** Suppose that the marketing analyst for the cola company referred to in Section 13.3 believes that the cola preferences of Americans and Canadians are quite similar and wishes to determine only if there are differences in cola preferences between this combined group and Mexicans. She obtains the accompanying table of data by collapsing the first two rows of Table 13.3. Using $\alpha = .025$, test for a difference in cola preferences.

Nationality	Cola Preference				
	A	B	C	D	Total
American/Canadian	98	18	28	56	200
Mexican	7	10	14	19	50
Total	105	28	42	75	250

13.48 Use a chi-square test to answer part (a) of Exercise 10.20.

POM **13.49** A bottling plant's quality-control engineer has taken a sample of 125 fills from one of the bottle-filling machines, which is set to produce an average fill of 10 ounces. Given the data in the following table and using $\alpha = .10$, test the hypothesis that the fills are normally distributed with a mean of 10 ounces.

Fill	Frequency
9.6 up to 9.7	4
9.7 up to 9.8	10
9.8 up to 9.9	15
9.9 up to 10.0	32
10.0 up to 10.1	43
10.1 up to 10.2	15
10.2 up to 10.3	6

FIN **13.50** The proportion of a company's earnings that is paid out to its shareholders in the form of dividends is called the company's **dividend payout ratio.** A frequency distribution of the dividend payout ratios (expressed as percentages) for a sample of 125 companies is shown in the accompanying table. Ten of these companies paid no dividend.

a. Construct a histogram for these data.

b. Using $\alpha = .10$, test the hypothesis that dividend payout ratios are normally distributed.

c. Repeat part (b), considering only companies that paid a dividend.

Dividend Payout Ratio (%)	Frequency
0 up to 10	13
10 up to 20	7
20 up to 30	10
30 up to 40	23
40 up to 50	28
50 up to 60	21
60 up to 70	14
70 up to 80	5
80 up to 90	3
90 up to 100	1

FIN **13.51** The management of a large pension fund is interested in studying the distribution of monthly rates of return on large, well-diversified portfolios of common stock. Intensive gathering of data has yielded 90 monthly returns on various large portfolios. These returns are summarized in the following frequency distribution. Is there sufficient evidence to allow management to conclude that the monthly rates of return are not normally distributed? (Use $\alpha = .05$.)

Return (%)	Frequency
−4 up to −3	4
−3 up to −2	4
−2 up to −1	10
−1 up to 0	13
0 up to 1	16
1 up to 2	15
2 up to 3	13
3 up to 4	8
4 up to 5	5
5 up to 6	2

Exercises 13.52 and 13.53 are based on the following political analysis.

In 1988 (prior to the presidential elections), *Newsweek* started a new feature that attempted to determine what differences existed among several different groups of prospective voters. These groups were defined on the basis of a number of characteristics including (but not limited to) the person's age, income, and degree of religious commitment, and the political party of which each person was a registered member. After extensive polling, ten different groups were identified, and the proportion of those surveyed who belong to each group was determined. The characteristics of each group and their proportions are listed in Table E13.52.

TABLE E13.52	Group	Characteristics	Proportion
	Republicans		
	Enterprisers	Affluent, educated, pro-business, and anti-government; worry about deficit.	10%
	Moralists	Middle-aged, middle-income, anti-abortion, pro-school prayer, and military.	13%
	Independents		
	Upbeats	Young, optimistic, strongly patriotic, and pro-government; worry about deficit.	10%
	Disaffecteds	Middle-aged, alienated, pessimistic, anti-government, anti-business, and pro-military.	10%
	Followers	Young; little faith in America or interest in politics; worry about unemployment.	6%
	Seculars	Middle-aged, educated, nonreligious, and nonmilitant; pro-personal freedoms.	7%
	Democrats		
	'60s Democrats	Upper middle-class; identify with '60s peace, civil rights, and environmental movements.	9%
	New Dealers	Older, middle-income, protectionist, pro-unions, and pro-government.	14%
	Partisan poor	Militantly Democratic; pro–social spending and anti–tax hikes.	12%
	Passive poor	Older; strong faith in America's institutions; pro–social spending and anti-communist.	9%

PG **13.52** During the 1988 primary campaign, two ministers (Pat Robertson and Jesse Jackson) were seeking their parties' nomination. In a survey conducted by the Gallup Organization on January 8–17, 1988, and reported in *Newsweek* (22 February 1988), 2,110 Americans were asked "Is it a good thing if a minister is a presidential candidate?" The following table summarizes the answers to this question.

RESPONSE TO MINISTER AS PRESIDENTIAL CANDIDATE*

Group	Good Thing	Bad Thing	Makes No Difference	No Opinion
Enterprisers	11%	38%	46%	5%
Moralists	17	45	34	4
Upbeats	16	39	40	5
Disaffecteds	12	46	41	1
Followers	14	32	42	12
Seculars	6	54	36	4
'60s Democrats	9	30	58	3
New Dealers	20	39	38	3
Partisan poor	23	26	44	7
Passive poor	19	46	34	1

* Recall that the chi-square test statistic is computed from (observed and expected) frequencies, not from proportions.

a. Can we conclude, at the 5% significance level, that differences in opinion about the desirability of having a minister as a presidential candidate exist among the ten groups?

b. Can we conclude, at the 5% significance level, that differences exist among Republicans, Independents, and Democrats?

c. Can we conclude, at the 5% significance level, that differences exist among the four groups of Independents?

PG **13.53** In the period 1980–1988, the United States went from being the #1 creditor nation inter-

nationally to being the #1 debtor nation. The key reason for this transformation was the country's enormous trade deficit. As a result, one of the issues in the 1988 campaign was a proposal to increase taxes on imported goods. In a survey conducted by the Gallup Organization (January 8–17, 1988) and reported in *Newsweek* (7 March 1988), 2,110 Americans were asked "Are you more likely, or less likely, to vote for a candidate who favors increasing import taxes?" The table below shows the percentage of each group who responded "more likely."

PERCENT RESPONDING "MORE LIKELY"*

Group	Percent
Enterprisers	48
Moralists	75
Upbeats	81
Disaffecteds	82
Followers	56
Seculars	50
'60s Democrats	65
New Dealers	84
Partisan poor	80
Passive poor	70

* Recall that the chi-square statistic is computed from (observed and expected) frequencies, not from proportions.

a. Do these results allow us to conclude, at the 5% significance level, that differences in the perception of a candidate who favors increasing import taxes exist among the ten groups?

b. Do these results allow us to conclude that differences exist among Republicans, Independents, and Democrats? (Use $\alpha = .05$.)

c. Do these results allow us to conclude that differences exist among the four groups of Democrats? (Use $\alpha = .05$.)

■■■■■■■■ *CASE 13.1** WOMEN IN TELEVISION COMMERCIALS

MKT Television advertisers have frequently been criticized for using stereotyped portrayals of women in television commercials. Caballero and Solomon have suggested the following summary of a profile of the female stereotype:

> She is young and beautiful, usually found in the home—especially the bathroom or kitchen. She is relatively helpless and requires a male authority to solve her problems and give her advice. She often appears in an essentially decorative role or solely as a sex object, and her primary function in life is to nurture and care for the male.

In a study investigating whether the portrayal of women in television commercials has been changing in recent years, Caballero and Solomon analyzed 2,095 commercials appearing on the three major U.S. networks in 1977 and 1,872 commercials appearing in 1980. To help put the study in perspective, the authors pointed out that the proportion of women in the population who fall into the higher age categories is on the rise, as is women's participation in the workforce and society's acceptance of "the changing roles of women." Furthermore, women were the targeted consumers for over 75% of commercials both in 1977 and 1980.

When comparing 1977 commercials to 1980 commercials, one might therefore expect to observe the following:

A shift in the distribution of ages of the main female characters portrayed

Changes in the characterization of women portrayed (for example, a trend toward career roles)

Differences in the setting used (for example, fewer scenes set in the home)

A significant increase in the proportion of commercials that used women as announcers (or voice-overs)

Are these expectations supported by the study results that appear in the accompanying tables?

TABLE A FEMALE MODELS' AGES

Age	1977	1980
Young (under 36)	861	893
Middle (36 to 55)	451	399
Older (56 and over)	55	82
Total	1,367	1,374

---

* Marjorie Caballero and Paul J. Solomon, "A Longitudinal View of Women's Role Portrayal in Television Advertising," *Journal of the Academy of Marketing Science* 12 (1984): 93–108.

TABLE B   *CHARACTERIZATION OF FEMALE MODELS*

Role	1977	1980
Family	699	699
Career	192	137
Fashion	151	82
Sex	110	151
Neutral	219	302
Total	1,371	1,371

TABLE C   *SETTINGS OF ADVERTISEMENTS*

Setting	1977	1980
House	509	467
Outdoors	358	288
Business	248	138
Combination	124	192
Undeterminable	138	288
Total	1,377	1,373

TABLE D   *ANNOUNCER'S SEX*

Sex	1977	1980
Female	118	95
Male	1,358	1,268
Total	1,476	1,363

██████████ *CASE 13.2**   *AUDITOR SWITCHING IN FAILING COMPANIES*

ACC The phenomenon of auditor switching has broad implications for the auditing profession, and the Securities and Exchange Commission has expressed its concern over this issue (see, for example, SEC ASR No. 165 [1974]). There may be a variety

---

* Adapted from K. B. Schwartz and K. Menon, "Auditor Switches by Failing Firms," *Accounting Review* (April 1985): 248–61.

of reasons behind any switch in auditor. In a study designed to examine the issue, the following factors were hypothesized to influence auditor switching:

The financial health of the company

The desire for a more prestigious auditor when the company is failing

Receipt of a qualified opinion from the current auditor in a failing company

A change in company management in a failing company

The experiment consisted of examining a random sample of 132 companies that went bankrupt in the period from 1974 to 1982 and another 132 similar, but financially healthy, companies. Each company was asked if it had switched CPA firms, and (if so) whether the switch involved a Big Eight CPA firm, whether their audit statements were qualified, and whether the firm changed management. The results are laid out in the accompanying tables.

Comment on the factors that influence an auditor switch.

TABLE A   ASSOCIATION BETWEEN FINANCIAL DISTRESS AND AUDITOR SWITCHES

Action Taken	Bankrupt	Nonbankrupt
Switched CPA firms	35	13
Did not switch CPA firms	97	119

TABLE B   DIRECTION OF AUDITOR SWITCHES BY FAILING COMPANIES

Action Taken	Switched to Big Eight CPA Firm	Switched to Non–Big Eight CPA Firm
Switched from Big Eight CPA firm	11	10
Switched from non–Big Eight CPA firm	12	2

TABLE C   ASSOCIATION BETWEEN AUDIT QUALIFICATION AND AUDITOR SWITCHES FOR FAILING COMPANIES

Action Taken	Qualified	Not Qualified
Switched CPA firms	14	17
Did not switch CPA firms	63	34

TABLE D   *ASSOCIATION BETWEEN MANAGEMENT CHANGES AND AUDITOR SWITCHES FOR FAILING COMPANIES*

Action Taken	Changed Management	Did Not Change Management
Switched CPA firms	13	18
Did not switch CPA firms	34	63

▮▮▮▮ CASE 13.3   LOTTO 6/49

GEN Lotto 6/49 is a lottery that operates as follows. Players select six different numbers between 1 and 49 for each $1.00 ticket. Several times each month, the corporation that runs the lottery selects seven numbers at random between 1 and 49. Winners are determined by how many numbers on their tickets agree with the drawn numbers. In selecting their numbers, players often look at past patterns as a way to help predict future drawings. A regular feature that appears in the newspaper identifies the number of times each number has occurred in the previous year. The data recorded in the accompanying table appears in the January 21 edition of the *Toronto Star*.

What would you recommend to anyone who believes that past patterns of the lottery numbers are useful in predicting future drawings?

DRAWING FREQUENCY OF LOTTO NUMBERS

Lotto Number	Number of Times Drawn in the Last Year	Lotto Number	Number of Times Drawn in the Last Year
1	12	7	13
2	9	8	9
3	10	9	16
4	13	10	7
5	8	11	11
6	12	12	9

(continued)

Lotto Number	Number of Times Drawn in the Last Year	Lotto Number	Number of Times Drawn in the Last Year
13	7	32	14
14	8	33	13
15	5	34	9
16	6	35	10
17	6	36	10
18	13	37	3
19	16	38	10
20	12	39	11
21	15	40	10
22	8	41	11
23	9	42	7
24	12	43	10
25	7	44	10
26	11	45	16
27	13	46	13
28	2	47	12
29	8	48	6
30	14	49	8
31	13		

■■■■■■■■   **CASE 13.4*   *MARKETING APPEALS TO BLACK CONSUMERS***

This case requires the use of a computer. The data are not shown below but are stored on the data disk.

MKT   In the last decade, a number of special marketing efforts have been directed at black consumers. Many companies have noted the increase in sales to this group. A number of projects have been undertaken to examine similarities and dissimilarities

---

* Adapted from A. C. Samil, E. F. Tozler, and D. V. Harps, "Social Class Differences in the Apparel Purchase Behavior of Single, Professional Black Women," *Journal of the Academy of Marketing Science* 6(1, 2) (1978): 25–38.

between black and white consumers. In one study, the relationship between social class and clothing-purchase behavior among black women was examined. The authors of this study wanted to determine whether the method of payment differs among social classes.

A sample of 141 single black women was used in the experiment. On the basis of several questions, each was classified as belonging to the upper middle, lower middle, or upper lower socioeconomic class. In order to explore the respondents' purchasing patterns, the following questions were asked:

1. Do you carry credit cards?
2. Do you use revolving accounts?
3. To what extent do you use bank credit?
4. Do you use regular charge accounts?
5. How often do you use layaway plans?
6. What is the maximum charge limit on your account?

The responses to these questions and the classifications of the respondents' socioeconomic classes are stored on the data disk, using the format below.

Can we conclude that the method of payment varies significantly among social classes?

PURCHASING PATTERNS OF SINGLE BLACK WOMEN

Respondent	Socioeconomic Class	Carry Credit Cards	Revolving Account	Bank Credit Cards	Regular Charge	Use of Layaway	Maximum Charge
1	1	1	0	1	0	1	2
2	1	0	1	1	0	0	2
3	1	0	1	1	1	0	2
⋮	⋮	⋮	⋮	⋮	⋮	⋮	⋮
141	3	0	0	0	0	0	0

The coded responses are interpreted as follows:

Socioeconomic class: 1 = Upper middle

2 = Lower middle

3 = Upper lower

Question	Coded Response
1–4	0 = No
	1 = Yes
5	0 = Almost never
	1 = Sometimes
	2 = Often
6	0 = Don't have charge accounts
	1 = Up to $400
	2 = $400–no limit

■■■■■■■■ **CASE 13.5***   *STOCK RETURN DISTRIBUTIONS*

FIN   When investors purchase common stock, the rate of return that they realize over the forthcoming period (which could be taken as a day, a week, a month, or a year) is a continuous random variable. The investors might, for example, enjoy a 20% return (a gain) or suffer a -10% return (a loss). Since the beginning of the century, numerous students of the stock market have hypothesized that distributions of stock returns are approximately normal.

In two well-known studies of stock price behavior, Eugene Fama observed both the daily returns and the monthly returns for the 30 stocks in the Dow Jones Industrial Average (DJIA) over a 5-year period. Fama's results are summarized in Tables A and B, which show the average percentages of returns (over the 30 stocks) that fell into various intervals. For example, 46.7% of the daily returns were within .5 standard deviations of the mean daily return.

Fisher and Lorie later observed the returns over a 1-year period on approximately 32,000 portfolios. Each portfolio consisted of 8 stocks, randomly selected from those listed on the New York Stock Exchange. (The authors noted that the total number of portfolios consisting of 8 stocks that could be selected from 1,000 stocks is about 2.4×10^{19}!) Various percentiles of the distribution of returns

---

* Adapted from the following sources:

Eugene F. Fama, "Behavior of Stock Market Prices," *Journal of Business* 38 (1965): 34–105.

Eugene F. Fama, *Foundations of Finance* (New York: Basic Books, 1976), pp. 28–29.

Lawrence Fisher and James H. Lorie, "Some Studies of Variability of Returns on Investments in Common Stocks," *Journal of Business* 43 (1970): 99–117.

Seha M. Tinic and Richard R. West, *Investing in Securities: An Efficient Markets Approach* (Cambridge, Mass.: Addison-Wesley, 1979), pp. 488–89.

TABLE A   AVERAGE RELATIVE FREQUENCY OF 1,200 DAILY RETURNS OF DJIA COMMON STOCKS

Intervals in Terms of Standardized z-Values	Percentage of Observed Daily Returns
Less than -2.0	2.1%
-2.0 to -1.5	3.1%
-1.5 to -1.0	7.4%
-1.0 to $-.5$	14.4%
$-.5$ to $.5$	46.7%
$.5$ to 1.0	13.6%
1.0 to 1.5	6.4%
1.5 to 2.0	3.2%
Greater than 2.0	3.1%

TABLE B   AVERAGE RELATIVE FREQUENCY OF 200 MONTHLY RETURNS OF DJIA COMMON STOCKS

Intervals in Terms of Standardized z-Values	Percentage of Observed Monthly Returns
Less than -2.0	1.6%
-2.0 to -1.5	3.7%
-1.5 to -1.0	9.3%
-1.0 to $-.5$	15.9%
$-.5$ to $.5$	40.1%
$.5$ to 1.0	14.7%
1.0 to 1.5	8.0%
1.5 to 2.0	3.9%
Greater than 2.0	2.8%

observed on these portfolios are shown in Table C, together with the mean and the standard deviation of the observed returns.

What would you conclude about the normality of stock returns? Answer the question both from a visual inspection of the relevant histograms and after conducting the appropriate statistical tests.

TABLE C DISTRIBUTION OF 32,000 OBSERVED RETURNS ON PORTFOLIOS OF EIGHT STOCKS

Percentile	Return
5th	8.1%
10th	11.7%
20th	16.3%
30th	20.0%
40th	23.2%
50th	26.4%
60th	29.9%
70th	33.8%
80th	38.9%
90th	46.7%
95th	54.3%
Mean	28.2%
Standard deviation	14.4%

MINITAB INSTRUCTIONS

CHI-SQUARE TEST OF A CONTINGENCY TABLE

The command

```
CHISQUARE C1-C3
```

causes Minitab to calculate the chi-square statistic for a contingency table whose columns are stored in columns 1 to 3. To illustrate, we solve Example 13.2 as follows:

```
READ C1-C3
10      9     11
240    191    139
END
CHISQUARE C1-C3
```

The output is

```
Expected counts are printed below observed counts

             C1       C2       C3    Total
     1       10        9       11       30
           12.5     10.0      7.5
     2      240      191      139      570
          237.5    190.0    142.5
Total      250      200      150      600
ChiSq=0.50+0.10+1.63+
      0.03+0.01+0.09=2.36
df=2
```

The CHISQUARE command can be used whenever the contingency table has been determined; if the contingency table has not been determined, another command must be employed. If the first column lists the values of the first nominally scaled variable and the second column lists the values of the second nominally scaled variable, the command

```
CONTINGENCY TABLE C1 C2
```

will elicit output of the observed and expected values and of the test statistic. If we had the raw data in Example 13.2 (where variable Shift = 1, 2, or 3 and variable Condition = 1 [Flawed] or 2 [No flaws]) we would proceed as follows:

```
READ  C1  C2
2      3
2      1
1      1
.      .  } 600 observations
.      .
.      .
2      2
END
CONTINGENCY TABLE C1 C2
```

The output is almost identical to that produced by the CHISQUARE command above.

SAS INSTRUCTIONS

CHI-SQUARE TEST OF A CONTINGENCY TABLE

In this application, we assume that the contingency table has not been constructed. That is, we assume that we have a list of the nominal values for variables 1 and 2, from which the contingency table will be created. In Appendix 2.B we showed that the statements

```
PROC FREQ;
TABLES X1*X2;
```

would output the cross-classification table. If we now include the option CHISQ, the chi-square statistic (among other things) will be printed. For instance, if we had the raw data in Example 13.2 (where variable Shift = 1, 2, or 3 and variable Condition = 1 [Flawed] or 2 [No Flaws]), we would proceed as follows:

```
DATA;
INPUT CONDITION SHIFT;
CARDS;
2    3 ⎫
2    1 ⎪
1    1 ⎪
.    . ⎬ 600 observations
.    . ⎪
.    . ⎪
2    2 ⎭
PROC FREQ;
TABLES CONDITION*SHIFT/CHISQ;
```

The output is

```
TABLE OF CONDITION BY SHIFT

CONDITION   SHIFT

Frequency
Percent
Row Pct
Col Pct          1      2      3    Total
          ---------------------------
       1     10      9     11       30
             1.67   1.50   1.83     5.00
            33.33  30.00  36.67
             4.00   4.50   7.33
          ---------------------------
       2    240    191    139      570
            40.00  31.83  23.17    95.00
            42.11  33.51  24.39
            96.00  95.50  92.67
          ---------------------------
   Total    250    200    150      600
            41.67  33.33  25.00   100.00
```

```
STATISTICS FOR TABLE OF CONDITION BY SHIFT
Statistic    DF   Value   Prob
---------------------------------
Chi-Square    2   2.356   0.309

Sample Size=600
```

SOLUTIONS TO SELF-CORRECTING EXERCISES

13.8 Let p_i be the probability that side i will turn up on any one roll ($i = 1, 2, \ldots, 6$).

$H_0: p_1 = p_2 = p_3 = p_4 = p_5 = p_6 = 1/6$

H_A: At least one p_i is not equal to its specified value.

Rejection region:

$\chi^2 > \chi^2_{.05,5}$

> 11.0705

Test statistic:

$$\chi^2 = \sum_{i=1}^{6} \frac{(o_i - e_i)^2}{e_i}$$

$$= \frac{(114 - 100)^2}{100} + \frac{(92 - 100)^2}{100} + \frac{(84 - 100)^2}{100}$$

$$+ \frac{(101 - 100)^2}{100} + \frac{(107 - 100)^2}{100}$$

$$+ \frac{(102 - 100)^2}{100} = 5.70$$

Conclusion: Do not reject H_0.

There is not sufficient evidence to allow us to conclude that the die is not fair.

13.18 H_0: The two classifications are independent.

H_A: The two classifications are dependent.

Rejection region:

$\chi^2 > \chi^2_{.05,2}$

> 5.99147

Test statistic:

$$\chi^2 = \frac{(67 - 71.5)^2}{71.5} + \frac{(63 - 58.5)^2}{58.5} + \frac{(32 - 27.5)^2}{27.5}$$

$$+ \frac{(18 - 22.5)^2}{22.5} + \frac{(11 - 11)^2}{11} + \frac{(9 - 9)^2}{9}$$

$$= 2.27$$

Conclusion: Do not reject H_0.

There is not sufficient evidence to allow us to conclude that the responses differ among the three groups of employees.

13.30 H_0: The current ratios are normally distributed.

H_A: The current ratios are not normally distributed.

Rejection region:

$\chi^2 > \chi^2_{.10,3}$

> 6.25139

Test statistic: Approximating $\bar{x}$ and s for the grouped data, we obtain $\bar{x} \cong 2.05$ and $s \cong .87$.

Therefore,

$$\chi^2 = \frac{(20 - 22.62)^2}{22.62} + \frac{(33 - 30.24)^2}{30.24}$$

$$+ \frac{(47 - 42.36)^2}{42.36} + \frac{(40 - 44.48)^2}{44.48}$$

$$= \frac{(31 - 32.72)^2}{32.72} + \frac{(29 - 27.58)^2}{27.58} = 1.68$$

Conclusion: Do not reject H_0.

We cannot reject the hypothesis that current ratios are normally distributed.

NONPARAMETRIC STATISTICS

575

INTRODUCTION

Up to this point, all of the statistical techniques we have dealt with have addressed problems involving either nominal or interval data scales. In this chapter, we present a body of statistical techniques designed to deal with *ordinal data*. As was noted in Chapter 5, when data are not interval-scaled, the calculation of means and variances is invalid. As a result, the methods in this chapter do not enable us to test the value of means or variances; instead, we will test characteristics of populations without referring to specific parameters. (For this reason, these techniques are called **nonparametric techniques.**) Rather than testing the difference between two population means, for example, we will test to determine whether or not the two population locations are different.

Although the nonparametric methods presented here are designed to test ordinal data, they have another area of application, as well. In Chapters 7, 9, and 12, we encountered problems in which the data scale was interval and the sampling distribution was either Student t or F. One of the required conditions for using these methods is that the population being sampled must be normally distributed. These situations are as follows:

Test of μ, with σ^2 unknown

Test of $\mu_1 - \mu_2$, with σ_1^2 and σ_2^2 unknown and with independent samples

Test of μ_D

Test of $\mu_1, \mu_2, \ldots, \mu_k$ (analysis of variance)

If the data are not normally distributed, the results of these techniques are invalid. However, the nonparametric methods described in this chapter can be used instead.

In the next section, we present the nonparametric technique for comparing two populations when the samples are independent. The parametric counterpart of this test is the test of $\mu_1 - \mu_2$ when σ_1^2 and σ_2^2 are unknown but equal and when the samples are independent. In Sections 14.3 and 14.4, we discuss the same problem objective when the samples are matched pairs. In Sections 14.5 and 14.6, the problem objective is to compare two or more populations. The parametric counterparts are the two models of the analysis of variance: the completely randomized design, and the randomized block design.

A large number of nonparametric techniques are available for our use. In this book, we only present a small group of such methods—omitting, for example, tests that deal with descriptions of a single population (the parametric counterpart of which is the test of μ with σ^2 unknown) and other tests that deal with comparisons of two populations.

SECTION 14.2 *WILCOXON RANK SUM TEST FOR INDEPENDENT SAMPLES*

The test we develop in this section deals with problems in which the following conditions are satisfied:

1. The problem objective is to compare two populations.
2. The data scale is either ordinal or interval (where the conditions necessary to perform the parametric test are unsatisfied).
3. The samples are independent.

Because the data may be ordinal, we do not test the difference between two means. (When the scale is ordinal, calculating means and variances is pointless, since they have no real meaning.) Rather, we test to determine whether the *locations* of the two populations are different. We conclude that two population locations differ if all or most of the values of one population exceed those of the other.

Figure 14.1 depicts a situation in which the two population locations differ, while Figure 14.2 shows two populations whose locations are about the same. Notice that, since we don't know (or care) anything about the shape of the distribution, we represent them as completely nonnormal. For this reason, nonparametric techniques are often (perhaps more accurately) called **distribution-free statistics.**

As we've done in all previous tests, we begin by specifying the hypotheses. The null hypothesis states that the two population locations are the same; the alternative hypothesis can take any one of three different forms:

1. If we want to know whether sufficient evidence exists to show a difference between the two populations, the alternative hypothesis is

   H_A: The location of population A is different from the location of population B.

FIGURE 14.1   *POPULATION LOCATIONS DIFFER*

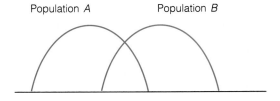

Population *A*   Population *B*

FIGURE 14.2   *POPULATION LOCATIONS ARE THE SAME*

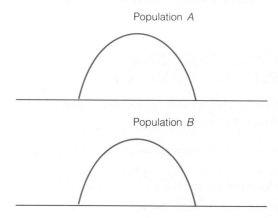

Population *A*

Population *B*

2. If we want to know whether we can conclude that population *A* is larger in general than population *B*, the alternative hypothesis is

   H_A: The location of population *A* is to the right of the location of population *B*.

3. If we want to know whether we can conclude that population *A* is smaller in general than population *B*, the alternative hypothesis is

   H_A: The location of population *A* is to the left of the location of population *B*.

The process of testing these hypotheses is basically the same as that of testing hypotheses in all the earlier chapters. The next steps in the procedure are to determine the appropriate test statistic and to determine the rejection region, based on its sampling distribution. Because the data may be ordinal, the test statistic used in this section is based on a ranking process. You will find that these calculations are simpler and less time-consuming than any of the techniques previously encountered.

TEST STATISTIC

We illustrate the calculation of the test statistic with an example.

EXAMPLE 14.1

Suppose that we wish to determine whether the following observations drawn from two populations allow us to conclude, with $\alpha = .05$, that the location of population *A* is to the right of the location of population *B*.

A	B
18	20
28	21
23	14
29	18
32	14

Solution.   We wish to test the hypotheses

H_0: The two population locations are the same.

H_A: The location of population A is to the right of the location of population B.

Calculation of the Test Statistic.   The first step is to rank all 10 observations, where rank 1 is assigned to the smallest observation and rank 10 is assigned to the largest.

A	Rank	B	Rank
18	3.5	20	5
28	8	21	6
23	7	14	1.5
29	9	18	3.5
32	10	14	1.5
	$T_A = 37.5$		$T_B = 17.5$

Observe that the value 14 appears twice and occupies ranks 1 and 2. Where ties exist, we average the ranks; thus, both observations of 14 are assigned the rank of 1.5. The next larger observation is 18; and since there are two of these, they are both assigned ranks of 3.5—the average of ranks 3 and 4. The process continues until all of the observations have been ranked. Because there are 10 observations, the largest one is ranked 10.

The second step is to calculate the sum of ranks of each sample. The rank sum of sample A, denoted T_A, is 37.5. The rank sum of sample B, denoted T_B, is 17.5. (You should confirm that $T_A + T_B$ equals the sum of the integers 1 through 10, which is 55.) In applications of this test, we will arbitrarily select as the test statistic the rank sum of the sample with fewer observations. For convenience, we will label that sample A and the other sample B. In this example, since both sample sizes are 5, we do not have to change labels. The test statistic is denoted T. Hence $T = T_A$.

FIGURE 14.3   *LOCATION OF POPULATION A TO THE RIGHT OF THE LOCATION OF POPULATION B*

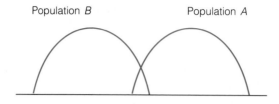

TABLE 14.1   *CRITICAL VALUES OF THE WILCOXON RANK SUM TEST FOR INDEPENDENT SAMPLES*

a. $\alpha = .025$ One-Tail; $\alpha = .05$ Two-Tail

n_2 \ n_1	3 T_L	3 T_U	4 T_L	4 T_U	5 T_L	5 T_U	6 T_L	6 T_U	7 T_L	7 T_U	8 T_L	8 T_U	9 T_L	9 T_U	10 T_L	10 T_U
3	5	16														
4	6	18	11	25												
5	6	21	12	28	18	37										
6	7	23	12	32	19	41	26	52								
7	7	26	13	35	20	45	28	56	37	68						
8	8	28	14	38	21	49	29	61	39	73	49	87				
9	8	31	15	41	22	53	31	65	41	78	51	93	63	108		
10	9	33	16	44	24	56	32	70	43	83	54	98	66	114	79	131

b. $\alpha = .05$ One-Tail; $\alpha = .10$ Two-Tail

n_2 \ n_1	3 T_L	3 T_U	4 T_L	4 T_U	5 T_L	5 T_U	6 T_L	6 T_U	7 T_L	7 T_U	8 T_L	8 T_U	9 T_L	9 T_U	10 T_L	10 T_U
3	6	15														
4	7	17	12	24												
5	7	20	13	27	19	36										
6	8	22	14	30	20	40	28	50								
7	9	24	15	33	22	43	30	54	39	66						
8	9	27	16	36	24	46	32	58	41	71	52	84				
9	10	29	17	39	25	50	33	63	43	76	54	90	66	105		
10	11	31	18	42	26	54	35	67	46	80	57	95	69	111	83	127

SOURCE: F. Wilcoxon and R. A. Wilcox, "Some Rapid Approximate Statistical Procedures" (1964), pp. 20–23. Reproduced with permission of the American Cyanamid Company.

Rejection Region.   A *large* value of T indicates that most of the larger observations are in sample A and that most of the smaller ones are in sample B. This would imply that the location of population A is to the *right* of the location of population B, as shown in Figure 14.3. Therefore, in order for us to conclude statistically that this is the case, T must be large enough. The definition of "large enough" comes from the sampling distribution of T, the critical values of which appear in Table 8 in Appendix B and are repeated in Table 14.1.

Table 14.1 provides values of T_L and T_U for various combinations of sample sizes. The values of T_L and T_U in part (a) of the table are such that

$$P(T \le T_L) = P(T \ge T_U) = .025$$

The value of T_L and T_U in part (b) of the table are such that

$$P(T \le T_L) = P(T \ge T_U) = .05$$

Part (a) is used either in a two-tail test with $\alpha = .05$ or in a one-tail test with $\alpha = 0.25$. Part (b) is used either in a two-tail test with $\alpha = .10$ or in a one-tail test with $\alpha = .05$. Since no other values are provided, we are restricted to those values of α. Notice that, since n_1 must be less than or equal to n_2, we do not show values of T_L and T_U when $n_1 > n_2$.

In our example, the null hypothesis is rejected in favor of the alternative hypothesis if T is too large. This means that the rejection region is

$$T \ge T_U$$

where

$$P(T \ge T_U) = \alpha$$

Since $n_1 = 5$, $n_2 = 5$, and $\alpha = .05$ in the present example, we find from Table 14.1(*b*) (or from Table 8 in Appendix B) that

$$T_U = 36$$

It follows that we should reject H_0 if $T \ge 36$. Therefore, since $T = 37.5$, we reject H_0 and conclude that there is enough evidence to show that the location of population A is to the right of the location of population B.

Figure 14.4 (on page 582) depicts the sampling distribution of T and the rejection region for this test.* The unusual shape of this distribution is due to the fact that T is a discrete random variable (whereas the test statistics used previously have all been continuous random variables).

---

* The actual shape of the sampling distributions of T depends on n_1 and n_2. For values of n_1 and $n_2 > 4$, it is extremely time-consuming to draw the exact distribution. Consequently, Figure 14.4 and other figures depicting discrete sampling distributions in this section and in Section 14.4 are not drawn completely accurately.

FIGURE 14.4   SAMPLING DISTRIBUTION AND REJECTION REGION FOR EXAMPLE 14.1

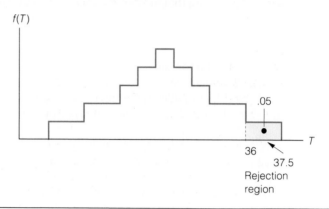

REJECTION REGIONS FOR OTHER ALTERNATIVE HYPOTHESES

As was the case throughout Chapters 7 through 10, the alternative hypothesis dictates how the rejection region is determined. Thus, if we wish to determine whether the location of population A is to the left of the location of population B, the rejection region is

$$T \leq T_L$$

where T_L is defined as

$$P(T \leq T_L) = \alpha$$

For example, if $n_1 = 7$ and $n_2 = 9$ with $\alpha = .025$, the one-tail (left-tail) rejection region determined from Table 14.1(a) is

$$T \leq 41$$

as shown in Figure 14.5.

If we wish to determine whether the two population locations differ, the rejection region is

$$T \leq T_L \quad \text{or} \quad T \geq T_U$$

where T_L and T_U are such that

$$P(T \leq T_L) = P(T \geq T_U) = \alpha/2$$

For example, suppose that we want to test for a difference in locations in samples of $n_1 = 4$ and $n_2 = 8$, at the 10% significance level. The rejection region from Table 14.1(b) is

$$T \leq 16 \quad \text{or} \quad T \geq 36.$$

Figure 14.6 describes this rejection region.

FIGURE 14.5 *REJECTION REGION FOR LEFT-TAIL HYPOTHESIS TEST WITH $n_1 = 7$ AND $n_2 = 9$, WITH $\alpha = .025$*

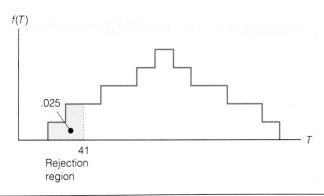

FIGURE 14.6 *REJECTION REGION FOR TWO-TAIL HYPOTHESIS TEST WITH $n_1 = 4$ AND $n_2 = 8$, WITH $\alpha = .10$*

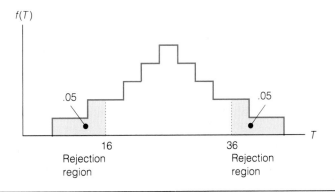

REQUIRED CONDITIONS

The Wilcoxon rank sum test (like all of the tests discussed in Sections 14.3 through 14.6) actually tests to determine whether the population distributions are identical. This means that it not only tests for identical locations but for identical spreads (dispersions) and shapes as well. Unfortunately this means that the rejection of the null hypothesis may not necessarily signify that there is a difference in population locations. The rejection of H_0 may be due instead to a difference in distribution shapes and/or spreads. To avoid this problem, we will require that the two probability distributions be identical except with respect to location, which then becomes the sole focus of the test. This requirement is made for all tests described in Sections 14.2 through 14.6.

Let's review what we have learned thus far about the Wilcoxon rank sum test.

Summary of Wilcoxon Rank Sum Test

Factors to Identify

Problem objective: comparison of two populations

Data scale: ordinal or interval

Experimental design: independent samples

Calculation of the Test Statistic

Step 1: Rank all observations, where 1 is the smallest observation and n is the largest observation. Average the ranks of tied observations. Note that $n = n_1 + n_2$, where n_1 and n_2 are the sample sizes drawn from populations A and B, respectively. The label A is arbitrarily assigned to the population with the smaller sample size.

Step 2: Calculate the rank sums of the two samples T_A and T_B. As a check on your computations, confirm that

$$T_A + T_B = n(n + 1)/2.$$

The test statistic is $T = T_A$.

Rejection Region

Case 1. Alternative hypothesis:

H_A: The location of population A is different from the location of population B.

Rejection region: $T \leq T_L$ or $T \geq T_U$

Case 2. Alternative hypothesis:

H_A: The location of population A is to the right of the location of population B.

Rejection region: $T \geq T_U$

Case 3. Alternative hypothesis:

H_A: The location of population A is to the left of the location of population B.

Rejection region: $T \leq T_L$

Required Condition

The two population distributions are identical in shape and spread.

The next two examples demonstrate how and (more importantly) where to use the Wilcoxon rank sum test for independent samples.

EXAMPLE 14.2

A pharmaceutical company is planning to introduce a new painkiller. In an experiment to determine its effectiveness, 20 people were randomly selected, of whom 10 were given the new painkiller and the other 10 were given aspirin. All 20 were told to use the drug when headaches or other minor pains occurred and to rate the effectiveness of the product on a 7-point scale. (On this scale, 1 represents least effective, and 7 represents most effective.) The results were as follows:

RATINGS

Aspirin	New Painkiller
4	6
3	4
4	5
2	7
2	3
3	6
2	4
3	3
4	5
5	4

Do these data provide sufficient evidence, at the 5% significance level, to allow us to conclude that the new painkiller is perceived as more effective?

Solution.   The data scale is ordinal (the scale rates the level of effectiveness), and the problem objective is to compare two populations (ratings of the new painkiller and of aspirin). Because 10 individuals used the new painkiller and 10 different individuals used aspirin, the samples are independent. Recognizing these three factors allows us to identify the appropriate technique as the Wilcoxon rank sum test for independent samples.

The sample sizes are the same ($n_1 = n_2 = 10$), so we arbitrarily label the aspirin ratings A and the new painkiller ratings B. Because we want to know whether the new painkiller generally has higher ratings (and thus whether aspirin has lower ratings), the alternative hypothesis is

H_A: The location of population A is to the left of the location of population B.

The complete test follows.

H_0: The two population locations are the same.

H_A: The location of population A is to the left of the location of population B.

Rejection region: With $n_1 = 10$ and $n_2 = 10$, we need to find T_L such that

$P(T \leq T_L) = .05$

From Table 8 in Appendix B (or from Table 14.1), we find $T_L = 83$. Thus, the rejection region is

$T \leq 83$

Value of the test statistic:

Population *A* (Aspirin)		Population *B* (New Painkiller)	
Rating	Rank	Rating	Rank
4	11.5	6	18.5
3	6	4	11.5
4	11.5	5	16
2	2	7	20
2	2	3	6
3	6	6	18.5
2	2	4	11.5
3	6	3	6
4	11.5	5	16
5	16	4	11.5
	$T_A = 74.5$		$T_B = 135.5$

$T = T_A = 74.5$

Conclusion: Reject H_0.

There is enough evidence to show that the new painkiller is perceived as more effective than aspirin. The company should consider using this experiment and others like it as the basis for their advertising.

COMPUTER OUTPUT FOR EXAMPLE 14.2*

Minitab

```
C1   N=10   MEDIAN=3.0000
C2   N=10   MEDIAN=4.5000
```

---

* See Appendixes 12.A and 12.B for the Minitab and SAS commands that produced these printouts.

```
POINT ESTIMATE FOR ETA1-ETA2 IS -0.9999
95.5 PCT C.I. FOR ETA1-ETA2 IS (-2.99, 0.00)
W=74.5
TEST OF ETA1=ETA2 VS. ETA1 N.E. ETA2 IS SIGNIFICANT AT 0.0233
```

Minitab preforms the Mann–Whitney test rather than the Wilcoxon test. However, the two tests are equivalent and quite similar. The only difference between them is that the Mann–Whitney test calculates

$$U_A = n_1 n_2 + \frac{n_1(n_1 + 1)}{2} - T_A$$

and

$$U_B = n_1 n_2 + \frac{n_2(n_2 + 1)}{2} - T_B$$

The conclusion is based on judging whether either U_A or U_B (depending on the alternative hypothesis) is too small. In the preceding printout, ETA represents the population median. The results include a point estimate and a confidence interval estimate of the difference between the two medians. It also includes the value of the test statistic $W(= 74.5)$, which is the value of the Wilcoxon rank sum test statistic. That is,

$$T = W = 74.5$$

In addition to the value of the test statistic, we also have the two-tail p-value (.0233). Since we're performing a one-tail test, the p-value is $.0233/2 = .0117$.

SAS

```
            Wilcoxon Scores (Rank Sums) for Variable X
                 Classified by Variable SAMPLE


            Sum of    Expected    Std Dev     Mean
SAMPLE   N   Scores   Under H0    Under H0    Score
1        10  74.5000    105.0     12.9065    7.4500
2        10  135.5000   105.0     12.9065    13.5500
            Average Scores were used for Ties
Wilcoxon 2-Sample Test (Normal Approximation)
(with Continuity Correction of .5)

S=74.5000    Z=-2.3244    Prob > |Z|=0.0201

Kruskal-Wallis Test (Chi-Square Approximation)
CHISQ=5.5844    DF=1    Prob > CHISQ=0.0181
```

Some of the actual output from the SAS program test has been omitted. The output shown includes the rank sums for each sample. Much of the other output is useful for situations in which the sample sizes are large. We will discuss this circumstance when we present the large sample-size version of the Wilcoxon test later in this section.

The Kruskal–Wallis test is described in Section 14.5. The value of the test statistic is

$$S = 74.5$$

As was pointed out in the introduction to this chapter, the Wilcoxon rank sum test is used to compare two populations when the data scale is either ordinal or interval. Example 14.2 illustrated the use of the Wilcoxon rank sum test when the scale was ordinal. In the next example, we demonstrate its use when the scale is interval.

EXAMPLE 14.3

The manager of a large production facility believes that worker productivity is a function of (among other things) the design of the job—that is, to the sequence of worker movements involved in it. Two designs are being considered for the production of a new product. In an experiment, the assembly times taken by 6 workers using design *A* and 8 workers using design *B* were recorded and are shown in the following table. Can we conclude at the 5% significance level that the assembly times differ for the two designs? Assume that the times are not normally distributed.

ASSEMBLY TIMES (MINUTES)

Design *A*	Design *B*
8.2	9.5
5.3	8.3
6.5	7.5
5.1	10.9
9.7	11.3
10.8	9.3
	8.8
	8.0

Solution. The problem objective is to compare two populations (assembly times for designs *A* and *B*). The data scale is interval, but the condition required to test $\mu_1 - \mu_2$ is not satisfied. (That is, the assembly times are not normally distributed.) Notice that, aside from this point, this example is the same as Example 9.4. Since the samples are independent, the appropriate technique is the Wilcoxon rank sum test for independent samples. Because we wish to know whether adequate evidence of a difference between the assembly times exists, the alternative hypothesis is

H_A: The location of population A is different from the location of population B.

The complete test follows.

H_0: The two population locations are the same.

H_A: The location of population A is different from the location of population B.

Rejection region:

$T \leq T_L$ or $T \geq T_U$

≤ 29 ≥ 61

Value of the test statistic:

Design A		Design B	
Time	Rank	Time	Rank
8.2	6	9.5	10
5.3	2	8.3	7
6.5	3	7.5	4
5.1	1	10.9	13
9.7	11	11.3	14
10.8	12	9.3	9
		8.8	8
		8.0	5
	$T_A = 35$		$T_B = 70$

$T = T_A = 35$

Conclusion: Do not reject H_0.

There is not enough evidence to allow us to conclude that a difference in assembly times exists between designs A and B. You may recall that a similar conclusion was drawn when the data were assumed to be normally distributed and we used the t-test of $\mu_1 - \mu_2$.

LARGE SAMPLE SIZES

You may have noticed that the values of n_1 and n_2 in Table 8 of Appendix B (Table 14.1) are less than or equal to 10. If n_1, n_2, or both exceed 10, the sampling distribution of T is approximately normal, with mean $E(T)$ and standard deviation σ_T calculated, respectively, as

$$E(T) = \frac{n_1(n_1 + n_2 + 1)}{2}$$

and

$$\sigma_T = \sqrt{\frac{n_1 n_2(n_1 + n_2 + 1)}{12}}$$

When either of the sample sizes is large, the test statistic is

$$z = \frac{T - E(T)}{\sigma_T}$$

which is standard normally distributed. The rejection region is one of the following:

$|z| > z_{\alpha/2}$ (two-tail test)

$z > z_\alpha$ (one-tail test)

$z < -z_\alpha$ (one-tail test)

In most practical applications of the Wilcoxon rank sum test when the sample sizes are large, statisticians turn to the computer to produce some or all of the needed statistics. As you've already seen from the computer output for Example 14.2, both of the statistical software systems discussed in this book provide you with enough statistical output to allow you to complete the test. Minitab gives you the value of the test statistic, as well as its two-tail p-value. SAS presents values for T, $E(T)$, and σ_T as well as the value of z and its two-tail p-value. The value for σ_T is computed using a correction for tied values, and z is calculated with a correction factor for continuity. We recommend that you ignore SAS's values for σ_T and z and calculate these values by hand using the outputted values of T and $E(T)$ (which are not "corrected"). To illustrate the differences, in Example 14.2 we compute

$$\sigma_T = \sqrt{\frac{n_1 n_2(n_1 + n_2 + 1)}{12}} = \sqrt{\frac{(10)(10)(21)}{12}} = 13.2288$$

compared to SAS's value of $\sigma_T = 12.9065$. We calculate the test statistic as

$$z = \frac{T - E(T)}{\sigma_T} = \frac{74.5 - 105}{13.2288} = -2.3056$$

SAS found z to be -2.3244.

EXAMPLE 14.4

Because of the high cost of hiring and training new employees, employers would like to ensure that they retain highly qualified workers. To help develop a hiring program, the personnel manager of a large company wanted to compare business and nonbusiness university graduates in terms of the number of years they worked for the company before quitting to accept a position elsewhere. The manager selected a random sample of 100 business and 80 nonbusiness graduates who had quit during the preceding 5 years. The amount of time that elapsed between the day they were hired and the day they quit was determined. When the results were analyzed, it was determined that the times were not normally distributed. Subsequently, in preparation for application of a nonparametric technique, all the times were ranked and the rank sums were computed. These results are shown in the following table. At the 5% level of significance, is the personnel manager justified in concluding that a difference in the duration of employment exists between business and nonbusiness graduates?

Business Graduates	**Nonbusiness Graduates**
Sample size = 100	Sample size = 80
Rank sum = 8,398	Rank sum = 7,892

Solution.   The problem objective is to compare two populations whose data scales are interval. The samples are independent. However, the data are not normally distributed, precluding the use of the t-test of $\mu_1 - \mu_2$. Thus the appropriate technique is the Wilcoxon rank sum test. Since the sample sizes are large (greater than 10), we will use the test statistic

$$z = \frac{T - E(T)}{\sigma_T}$$

Because the sample of nonbusiness graduates is smaller than that of the business graduates, we label the nonbusiness sample A and the business sample B. The test proceeds as follows.

H_0: The two population locations are the same.

H_A: The location of population A is different from the location of population B.

Test statistic:

$$z = \frac{T - E(T)}{\sigma_T}$$

Rejection region:

$$|z| > z_{\alpha/2}$$
$$> z_{.025}$$
$$> 1.96$$

Value of the test statistic:

$$T = T_A = 7{,}892$$

$$E(T) = \frac{n_1(n_1 + n_2 + 1)}{2} = \frac{80(181)}{2} = 7{,}240$$

$$\sigma_T = \sqrt{\frac{n_1 n_2 (n_1 + n_2 + 1)}{12}} = \sqrt{\frac{(80)(100)(181)}{12}} = 347.4$$

$$z = \frac{T - E(T)}{\sigma_T} = \frac{7{,}892 - 7{,}240}{347.4} = 1.88$$

Conclusion: Do not reject H_0.

There is not enough evidence at the 5% significance level to establish that a difference in duration of employment exists between business and nonbusiness graduates.

EXERCISES

LEARNING THE TECHNIQUES

14.1 Specify the test statistic and the rejection region for each of the following Wilcoxon rank sum tests for independent samples.

a. H_0: The two population locations are the same.
   H_A: The location of population A is to the right of the location of population B.

   $n_A = 8$ $n_B = 9$ $\alpha = .05$

b. H_0: The two population locations are the same.
   H_A: The location of population A is to the left of the location of population B.

   $n_A = 4$ $n_B = 6$ $\alpha = .025$

c. H_0: The two population locations are the same.
   H_A: The location of population A is different from the location of population B.

   $n_A = 20$ $n_B = 25$ $\alpha = .01$

14.2 Use the Wilcoxon rank sum test for independent samples to determine whether the location of population A is to the left of the location of population B. (Use $\alpha = .05$.)

A	B
75	90
60	70
75	100
65	80
80	80

14.3 Perform the Wilcoxon rank sum test to determine whether the location of population A is different from the location of population B. (Use $\alpha = .05$.)

A	B
5	7
12	10
11	15
10	12

(continued)

A	B
9	16
	20

14.4 Use the Wilcoxon rank sum test for independent samples to determine whether the location of population A is to the right of the location of population B. (Use $\alpha = .05$.)

A	B
27	29
38	24
26	23
33	28
39	26
41	22
	20
	25

14.5 Perform the Wilcoxon rank sum test with $\alpha = .05$ to determine whether the two population locations differ, given the following information.

Sample	Sample Size	Rank Sum
1	9	90
2	6	30

14.6 Using the Wilcoxon rank sum test, with $\alpha = .05$, test to determine whether there is enough evidence to indicate that the location of population A differs from that of population B, given the following information.

Sample	Sample Size	Rank Sum
1	30	1,162
2	40	1,323

14.7 Given the results that follow, conduct the Wilcoxon rank sum test to determine whether the location of population 1 is to the left of the location of population 2. (Use $\alpha = .025$.)

Sample	Sample Size	Rank Sum
1	50	2,120
2	40	1,975

APPLYING THE TECHNIQUES

Self-Correcting Exercise (See Appendix 14.6 for the solution.)

POM **14.8** In recent years insurance companies offering medical coverage have given discounts to companies that are committed to improving the health of their employees. To help determine whether this policy is reasonable, the general manager of one large insurance company organized a study. He took a random sample of 10 workers who regularly participate in their company's lunchtime exercise program and 10 workers who do not. Over a two-year period he observed the total dollar amount of medical expenses for each individual. Do the resulting data allow the manager to conclude at the 5% significance level that companies that provide exercise programs should be given discounts? (Assume that the data are not normally distributed.)

MEDICAL CLAIMS ($)

Employees Who Exercise	Employees Who Do Not Exercise
$403	$229
38	99
0	385
55	526
121	415
354	367
183	504

(continued)

Employees Who Exercise	Employees Who Do Not Exercise
106	298
95	601
210	422

1985	1988
15	
21	
25	
18	

14.9 To producers of household products, the question of who does the housework is important because of the way advertising campaigns are designed. One of many issues that affect advertising campaigns is the extent to which women are doing less housework and men are doing more. Suppose that, in a 1988 study, 10 women were asked how many hours of work around the home they perform weekly, and that these results are to be compared with the results of a similar 1985 survey that included 14 women. If we know that the data are not normally distributed, can we conclude at the 5% significance level that women are doing less housework in 1988 than in 1985?

Weekly Hours of Housework

1985	1988
23	17
18	21
27	16
14	20
17	14
26	13
19	18
22	10
28	12
18	15

14.10 Repeat Exercise 9.32(a), but assume that the weight gains are not normally distributed.

14.11 Repeat Exercise 9.71(a), but assume that the number of new cavities is not normally distributed.

14.12 Certain drugs differ in their side effects, depending on the gender of the patient. In a study to determine whether men or women suffer more serious side effects when taking a powerful penicillin substitute, eight men and eight women were given the drug. Each was asked to evaluate the level of stomach upset that occurred, on a 7-point scale where 1 = No effect and 7 = Very badly upset. The results were as shown in the following table. Can we conclude at the 10% significance level that men and women experience different levels of stomach upset from the drug?

Men	Women
6	2
3	2
5	4
4	7
1	3
3	3
5	2
6	1

SECTION 14.3 **SIGN TEST**

In the preceding section, we discussed the nonparametric technique for comparing two populations whose data scales are either ordinal or interval, and whose samples are independent. In this section, the problem objective and the data scales remain as they were in Section 14.2, but now we will be working with data that were generated from a matched pairs experiment. We have dealt with this type of experiment twice before: in Section 9.4, we dealt with the mean of the paired differences represented by the parameter μ_D; and in Section 12.3, we discussed the analysis of variance of the randomized block design. In both cases, the samples were blocked (or paired), and the interval data were normally distributed. In this section, we again assume that the samples are blocked (or paired), but here the data scale may be ordinal or interval. That is, we present the technique for testing hypotheses of problems that have the following characteristics:

1. The problem objective is to compare two populations.
2. The data scale is either ordinal or interval (where the condition necessary for performing the parametric test is unsatisfied).
3. The samples are matched pairs.

The requirement for parametric testing alluded to in characteristic 2 is that the differences must be normally distributed.

The null and alternative hypotheses that we encounter in this section are identical to the ones we dealt with in Section 14.2. The technique to be employed is called the **sign test.**

The sign test is quite simple. For each matched pair, we calculate the difference between the observation in sample A and the related observation in sample B. We then count the number of positive differences and negative differences. If the null hypothesis is true, we expect the number of positive differences to be approximately equal to the number of negative differences. Expressed another way, we expect the number of positive differences and the number of negative differences each to be approximately half the total sample size. If either number is too large or too small, we reject H_0. By now you know that the determination of what is too large or too small comes from the sampling distribution of the test statistic. We will arbitrarily decide that the test statistic is the number of positive differences, which we denote x. The test statistic x is a binomial random variable, and under the null hypothesis the binomial proportion is $p = .50$. Thus, the sign test is none other than the z-test of p first developed in Chapter 8.

Recall from Chapter 4 that x is binomially distributed and that, for sufficiently large n ($np \geq 5$ and $nq \geq 5$), x is approximately normally distributed with mean $\mu = np$ and standard deviation $\sigma = \sqrt{npq}$. Thus the standardized test statistic is

$$z = \frac{x - np}{\sqrt{npq}}$$

Since the null hypothesis is

H_0: The two population locations are the same.

which is equivalent to testing H_0: $p = .5$, the test statistic becomes

$$z = \frac{x - np}{\sqrt{npq}} = \frac{x - .5n}{\sqrt{n(.5)(.5)}} = \frac{x - .5n}{.5\sqrt{n}}$$

It is common practice in this type of test to eliminate the matched pairs of observations when the differences equal zero. Consequently, n equals the number of nonzero differences in the sample.

We summarize the sign test next.

Summary of the Sign Test

Factors to Identify

Problem objective: comparison of two populations

Data scale: ordinal or interval

Experimental design: matched pairs

Calculation of the Test Statistic

Step 1: Calculate the difference for each matched pair; $D = A - B$.

Step 2: Eliminate all differences that equal zero ($D = 0$), and adjust n so that it represents the number of nonzero differences.

Step 3: x is the number of positive differences and

$$z = \frac{x - .5n}{.5\sqrt{n}}$$

which is normally distributed, provided that n is sufficiently large ($np \geq 5$ and $nq \geq 5$). This condition is satisfied for $p = q = .5$ when $n \geq 10$.

Alternative Hypotheses and the Rejection Region

Case 1. Alternative hypothesis:

H_A: The location of population A is different from the location of population B. (This is equivalent to H_A: $p \neq .5$.)

Rejection region: $|z| > z_{\alpha/2}$

Case 2. Alternative hypothesis:

H_A: The location of population A is to the right of the location of population B (H_A: $p > .5$).

Rejection region: $z > z_\alpha$

Case 3. Alternative hypothesis:

H_A: The location of population A is to the left of the location of population B (H_A: $p < .5$).

Rejection region: $z < -z_\alpha$

Required Conditions

The two population distributions are identical in shape and spread.

EXAMPLE 14.5

In an experiment to determine which of two cars is perceived to have the more comfortable ride, 30 people rode (separately) in the back seat of an expensive European model and also in the back seat of a North American model. Each of the 30 people were asked to rate the ride on a 9-point scale, where 1 = very uncomfortable and 9 = very comfortable. The ratings are shown in the following table. Do these data provide sufficient evidence at the 5% significance level to allow us to conclude that the North American car is perceived by riders as more comfortable than the European car?

Respondent	European Car Rating	North American Car Rating	Respondent	European Car Rating	North American Car Rating
1	6	7	16	4	5
2	9	5	17	2	3
3	4	5	18	7	8
4	7	7	19	4	6
5	8	9	20	4	7
6	5	7	21	6	8
7	4	6	22	9	7
8	5	4	23	3	4
9	8	9	24	7	8
10	3	6	25	7	4
11	4	8	26	5	2
12	9	9	27	4	1
13	5	6	28	6	8
14	7	4	29	5	9
15	7	6	30	2	4

Solution.   The problem objective is to compare two populations. The data scale is ordinal, and the data were drawn from a matched pairs experiment.

The sign test is employed, with the following results.

H_0: The two population locations are the same ($p = .50$).

H_A: The location of population A (European car rating) is to the left of the location of population B (North American car rating) ($p < .50$).

Test statistic:

$$z = \frac{x - .5n}{.5\sqrt{n}}$$

Rejection region:

$z < -z_\alpha$

$< -z_{.05}$

< -1.645

Value of the test statistic:

Number of positive differences $x = 8$

Number of zero differences $= 2$ (thus $n = 28$)

$$z = \frac{x - .5n}{.5\sqrt{n}} = \frac{8 - .5(28)}{.5\sqrt{28}} = -2.27$$

Conclusion: Reject H_0.

There is sufficient evidence to allow us to conclude that the North American car is perceived as providing a more comfortable ride than the European car.

MINITAB COMPUTER OUTPUT FOR EXAMPLE 14.5*

```
SIGN TEST OF MEDIAN=0 VERSUS L.T. 0

         N    BELOW    EQUAL    ABOVE    P-VALUE    MEDIAN
C3      30     20        2        8      0.0178    -1.000
```

Minitab tests the median of the differences. The printout reveals that there are 20 negative differences (BELOW), 2 zero differences (EQUAL), and 8 positive differences (ABOVE). The p-value is calculated by using the binomial (and not the approximate normal) distribution, with $n = 28$.

---

* Appendix 14.A describes how to produce the Minitab output shown here.

■■■■■■■■   ***EXERCISES***

LEARNING THE TECHNIQUES

14.13   If in a matched pairs experiment we find 30 negative, 5 zero, and 15 positive differences, perform the sign test to determine whether the two population locations differ. (Use $\alpha = .10$.)

14.14   Given the following results from a matched pairs experiment, use the sign test to determine whether the location of population A is to the right of the location of population B. (Use $\alpha = .01$.)

Total sample size	150
Pairs where $A > B$	88
$A < B$	54
$A = B$	8

14.15   A matched pairs experiment produced the following results (where $D = A - B$).

Positive values of D	235
Negative values of D	306
Cases where $D = 0$	21

Use the sign test to determine whether there is enough evidence at the 5% significance level to allow us to conclude that the location of population A is to the left of the location of population B.

APPLYING THE TECHNIQUES

Self-Correcting Exercise (See Appendix 14.C for the solution.)

MKT   **14.16**   At the height of the energy shortage during the 1970s, governments were actively seeking ways to persuade consumers to reduce their energy consumption. Among other efforts undertaken, several advertising campaigns were launched. To provide input on how to design effective advertising messages, a poll was taken in which people were asked how concerned they were about shortages of gasoline and electricity. There were four possible responses to both questions:

> 1 = Not concerned at all
> 2 = Not too concerned
> 3 = Somewhat concerned
> 4 = Very concerned

A poll of 40 individuals produced the results shown in Table E14.16. At the 10% significance level, do these data provide enough evidence to allow us to conclude that concern about a gasoline shortage exceeded concern about an electricity shortage?

MKT   **14.17**   Does the brand name of an ice cream affect consumers' perceptions of it? This question was pondered by the marketing manager of a major dairy. She decided to ask 28 randomly selected people to taste the same flavor of ice cream in two different dishes (Table E14.17). The dishes contained exactly the same ice cream, but they were labeled differently. One was given a name that suggested that its maker was European and sophisticated; the other was given a name that implied that the product was domestic and inexpensive. The tasters were asked to rate each ice cream on a 10-point scale, where 1 = Poor and 10 = Excellent. Do the results that follow allow the manager to conclude, at a significance level of 5%, that the "European" brand was preferred?

EDUC   **14.18**   Admissions officers at universities and colleges face the problem of comparing grades achieved at different high schools. As a step toward developing a more informed interpretation of such grades, an admissions officer at a large state university conducts the following experiment. The records of 100 students from the same local high school who just completed their first year at the university were selected. Each of these students was paired (according to their average grade in the last year of high school) with a student from another local high school who also just completed the first year at the university. For each matched pair, the average marks in the first year of university study were recorded. The results are summarized as follows:

Matched pair with identical averages	2
Matched pair in which student from high school 1 has higher average	67
Matched pair in which student from high school 2 has higher average	31

Do these results allow us to conclude at the 5% significance level that, in comparing two students with the same high-school average (one from high school 1 and the other from high school 2), preference in admissions should be given to the student from high school 1?

Respondent	Concern About Shortage		Respondent	Concern About Shortage	
	Electricity	Gasoline		Electricity	Gasoline
1	3	4	21	3	4
2	2	4	22	3	4
3	2	3	23	3	3
4	2	2	24	2	4
5	3	4	25	1	4
6	1	3	26	3	2
7	1	4	27	4	2
8	4	2	28	4	2
9	4	1	29	2	4
10	2	3	30	2	3
11	3	2	31	4	2
12	3	4	32	4	2
13	3	4	33	1	4
14	4	3	34	2	3
15	2	3	35	3	4
16	1	3	36	3	4
17	2	3	37	4	4
18	2	4	38	3	4
19	3	2	39	4	2
20	1	4	40	4	3

Taster	Ice Cream Labels		Taster	Ice Cream Labels	
	European	Inexpensive		European	Inexpensive
1	10	8	15	9	8
2	8	6	16	5	5
3	7	8	17	8	5
4	9	8	18	7	4
5	8	9	19	6	4
6	7	4	20	8	10
7	10	9	21	5	7
8	7	6	22	6	8
9	6	6	23	10	7
10	8	9	24	8	9
11	6	5	25	9	6
12	8	10	26	7	6
13	9	6	27	6	5
14	10	8	28	6	3

WILCOXON SIGNED RANK SUM TEST FOR THE MATCHED PAIRS EXPERIMENT

The sign test presented in the preceding section can be used to test for differences between population locations when the data scale is ordinal or interval. However, when the scale is interval, the sign test has a major deficiency. The test is based on the number of positive and negative differences, but it ignores the magnitude of these differences. When the scale is ordinal, this feature is appropriate since calculating differences between the values of an ordinal variable is meaningless. However, ignoring differences between the values of an interval scale can result in the loss of potentially useful information. Consequently, when the data scale is interval, we will use the *Wilcoxon signed rank sum test for the matched pairs experiment* instead of the sign test. The sign test will be used only when the data scale is ordinal (and the problem objective is to compare two populations with data drawn from a matched pairs experiment).

The Wilcoxon signed rank sum test for the matched pairs experiment is used under the following circumstances:

1. The problem objective is to compare two populations.
2. The data scale is interval and the data are not normally distributed.
3. The samples are matched pairs.

The Wilcoxon signed rank sum test is the nonparametric counterpart of the *t*-test of the mean paired difference μ_D (Section 9.4).

Because the data are interval-scaled, we may refer to the Wilcoxon ranked sum test as a test of μ_D. However, to be consistent with the other nonparametric techniques and to avoid confusion, we will express the hypotheses to be tested in the same way as in Sections 14.2 and 14.3.

EXAMPLE 14.6

Traffic congestion on roads and highways costs industry billions of dollars annually as workers struggle to get to and from work. Several suggestions have been made about how to improve the situation, one of which involves allowing workers to change their schedules to avoid rush-hour traffic. In a preliminary experiment to investigate such a program, the general manager of a large company wanted to compare the average times it took workers to arrive at work in the morning and to return home in the evening. A random sample of seven workers was selected. For each, the time taken to get to work from home and the time taken to return home were measured on the same day. These observations are shown in the following table. An analysis of the data established that the times are not normally distributed. Perform the Wilcoxon signed rank sum test for the matched pairs experiment, with $\alpha = .05$, to determine whether there is a difference in the average times taken to arrive at work and to return home.

Worker	Time to Arrive at Work (minutes)	Time to Return Home (minutes)
1	42	43
2	28	32
3	32	37
4	29	29
5	18	30
6	32	24
7	36	40

Solution.   The Wilcoxon signed rank sum test is the appropriate test to use because we wish to compare two populations with interval data drawn from a matched pairs experiment. Because of nonnormality, the t-test of μ_D is not appropriate.

Even though we wish to test for a difference between means (or more precisely, even though we wish to test the mean difference), we will express the hypotheses as follows:

H_0: The two population locations are the same.

H_A: The location of population A is different from the location of population B.

Calculating the Test Statistic.   We begin by computing the paired differences $D = A - B$, where A represents the times taken to get to work and B represents the times taken to return home. All differences where $D = 0$ are eliminated (as in the sign test). Next we rank the absolute values of D, where $1 =$ Smallest value of $|D|$ and $n =$ Largest value of $|D|$ (where $n =$ Number of nonzero differences). All ties are resolved (as in Section 14.2) by assigning the average of the tied ranks. The sum of the ranks of the positive differences (denoted T^+) and the sum of the ranks of the negative differences (denoted T^-) are then calculated. These calculations are shown in the following table.

Worker	A	B	D = A − B	|D|	Ranks
1	42	43	−1	1	1
2	28	32	−4	4	2.5
3	32	37	−5	5	4
4	29	29	0	—	

(continued)

Worker	A	B	D = A − B	|D|	Ranks	
5	18	30	− 12	12	6	
6	32	24	8	8		5
7	36	40	− 4	4	2.5	
					$T^- = 16$	$T^+ = 5$

Observe that we ignore the results for worker 4, since the time difference there equals zero. We resolve the tie for ranks 2 and 3 ($|D| = 4$) by assigning the rank of 2.5. There are five negative differences, whose rank sum is $T^- = 16$, and there is one positive difference, whose rank sum is $T^+ = 5$. As a check on our calculations, we note that $T^+ + T^-$ equals the sum of the integers from 1 to 6, which is 21.

As was the case with the Wilcoxon rank sum test for independent samples in Section 14.2, we must select one of T^+ and T^- to be the test statistic. This selection, however, depends on the alternative hypothesis and the rejection region.

Rejection Region.   The null hypothesis asserts that the two population locations are the same. If this were true, we would expect T^+ to be approximately equal to T^-. Since we are trying to determine whether enough evidence exists to enable us to conclude that they are different, we should reject H_0 if there is a large difference between T^+ and T^-. In other words, we would reject H_0 if either T^- (the larger of the two rank sums) is too large or T^+ (the smaller of the two rank sums) is too small. To determine which of the two rank sums to use as the test statistic (which we denote T), we need to know the sampling distribution of the test statistic. Refer now to Table 9 in Appendix B (which is reproduced as Table 14.2).

Table 9 provides values of T_L such that the probability that T is less than or equal to T_L is .005, .01, .025, or .05. This means that only the critical values of the left side of the sampling distribution are provided (the critical values of the right side are unnecessary).

In our example, we reject H_0 if either T^- is too large or T^+ is too small. Because we only know the critical values of the left side of the distribution, we can only determine whether the test statistic is too small. As a result, the test statistic T equals T^+. With $\alpha = .05$ and $n = 6$, the rejection region is

$$T \le T_L$$

where $(P(T \le T_L) = \alpha/2 = .025$. Hence, $T_L = 1$. Since $T = T^+ = 5$, we don't reject the null hypothesis. Figure 14.7 depicts the results of this test. (Like the test statistic in the Wilcoxon rank sum test for independent samples, this test statistic is discrete; consequently, the graph in Figure 14.7 appears terraced, rather than describing a smooth curve.) We conclude that there is insufficient evidence to indicate a difference in the times taken to reach work from home and the times taken to arrive at home from work.

TABLE 14.2 CRITICAL VALUES OF T_L IN THE WILCOXON SIGNED RANK SUM TEST FOR THE MATCHED PAIRS EXPERIMENT

n	$P(T \le T_L) = .05$	.025	.01	.005	n	$P(T \le T_L) = .05$	.025	.01	.005
	T_L	T_L	T_L	T_L		T_L	T_L	T_L	T_L
5	1	—	—	—	28	130	117	102	92
6	2	1	—	—	29	141	127	111	100
7	4	2	0	—	30	152	137	120	109
8	6	4	2	0	31	163	148	130	118
9	8	6	3	2	32	175	159	141	128
10	11	8	5	3	33	188	171	151	138
11	14	11	7	5	34	201	183	162	149
12	17	14	10	7	35	214	195	174	160
13	21	17	13	10	36	228	208	186	171
14	26	21	16	13	37	242	222	198	183
15	30	25	20	16	38	256	235	211	195
16	36	30	24	19	39	271	250	224	208
17	41	35	28	23	40	287	264	238	221
18	47	40	33	28	41	303	279	252	234
19	54	46	38	32	42	319	295	267	248
20	60	52	43	37	43	336	311	281	262
21	68	59	49	43	44	353	327	297	277
22	75	66	56	49	45	371	344	313	292
23	83	73	62	55	46	389	361	329	307
24	92	81	69	61	47	408	379	345	323
25	101	90	77	68	48	427	397	362	339
26	110	98	85	76	49	446	415	380	356
27	120	107	93	84	50	466	434	398	373

SOURCE: F. Wilcoxon and R. A. Wilcox, "Some Rapid Approximate Statistical Procedures" (1964), p. 28. Reproduced with permission of the American Cyanamid Company.

Test Statistic and Rejection Regions for Other Alternative Hypotheses. Had we tested to see whether the time taken to arrive at work were longer, that result would have been indicated only if the ranks of the positive differences (since $D = A - B$) were large. That is, we would have rejected H_0 only if T^+ were large and T^- were small. In this situation, the test statistic would be $T = T^-$, and the rejection region

FIGURE 14.7   *SAMPLING DISTRIBUTION AND REJECTION REGION FOR EXAMPLE 14.6*

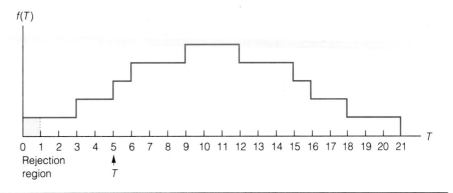

would be

$$T \le T_L$$

where

$$P(T \le T_L) = \alpha$$

If we had wanted to test to determine whether the time taken to return home were longer, the test statistic would have been T^+ and the rejection region would have been

$$T \le T_L$$

where

$$P(T \le T_L) = \alpha$$

The Wilcoxon signed rank sum test for the matched pairs experiment is summarized next.

Summary of Wilcoxon Signed Rank Sum Test for Matched Pairs

Factors to Identify

Problem objective: comparison of two populations

Data scale: interval

Experimental design: matched pairs

Calculation of the Test Statistic

Step 1:   Calculate the difference $D = A - B$ for each pair of observations. Eliminate all values of $D = 0$.

Step 2:   Rank the absolute values of D, where $1 =$ Smallest value of $|D|$ and $n =$ Largest value of $|D|$. The effective sample size n is the number of nonzero differences.

Step 3:   Calculate the rank sum of the positive differences T^+ and the rank sum of the negative differences T^-. As a check, confirm that $T^- + T^+ = n(n + 1)/2$.

Test Statistic and the Rejection Region

Case 1.   Alternative hypothesis:

H_A: The location of population A is different from the location of population B.

Test statistic: $T =$ smaller of T^+ and T^-

Rejection region: $T \leq T_L$ (where $P(T \leq T_L) = \alpha/2$)

Case 2.   Alternative hypothesis:

H_A: The location of population A is to the right of the location of population B.

Test statistic: $T = T^-$

Rejection region: $T \leq T_L$ (where $P(T \leq T_L) = \alpha$)

Case 3.   Alternative hypothesis:

H_A: The location of population A is to the left of the location of population B.

Test statistic: $T = T^+$

Rejection region: $T \leq T_L$ (where $P(T \leq T_L) = \alpha$)

Required Condition

The two population distributions are identical in shape and spread.

EXAMPLE 14.7

A nationally known manufacturer of replacement shock absorbers claims that its product lasts longer than the type of shock absorbers that the car manufacturer installs. In an experiment to test the company's claim, eight cars equipped with one original and one replacement shock absorber installed on the rear end were driven until the shock absorbers were no longer effective. The number of miles each was driven before this happened was recorded, as shown in the accompanying table.

NUMBER OF MILES (1,000s)

Car	Original Shock Absorber	Replacement Shock Absorber
1	42.6	43.8
2	37.2	41.3
3	50.0	49.7
4	43.9	45.7
5	53.6	52.5
6	32.5	36.8
7	46.5	47.0
8	39.3	40.7

Is there sufficient evidence at the 5% significance level to support the manufacturer's claim? (Assume that the number of miles is *not* normally distributed. Notice that this is identical to Example 9.7, except that here we assume nonnormality.)

Solution.   The problem objective is to compare two populations (the miles driven on the two types of shock absorbers). The data scale is interval, but the condition required to perform the parametric test is unsatisfied. The experiment is matched pairs (because the same eight cars are used to measure the miles driven until the shock absorbers wear out). Hence, the appropriate test is the Wilcoxon signed rank sum test for the matched pairs experiment. Because we want to know if we can conclude that the replacement shock is better (lasts longer) than the original one, the alternative hypothesis is:

H_A: The location of population A (original shock) is to the left of the location of population B (replacement shock).

The complete test is as follows:

H_0: The two population locations are the same.

H_A: The location of population A is to the left of the location of population B.

Test statistic: $T = T^+$

Rejection region: With $n = 8$ and $\alpha = .05$, we want to find T_L such that

$P(T \leq T_L) = .05$

From Table 9 of Appendix B (or from Table 14.2), we find $T_L = 6$. The rejection region is therefore

$T \le 6$

Value of the test statistic:

Car	A	B	D = A − B	|D|	Ranks	
1	42.6	43.8	− 1.2	1.2	4	
2	37.2	41.3	− 4.1	4.1	7	
3	50.0	49.7	.3	.3		1
4	43.9	45.7	− 1.8	1.8	6	
5	53.6	52.5	1.1	1.1		3
6	32.5	36.8	− 4.3	4.3	8	
7	46.5	47.0	− .5	.5	2	
8	39.3	40.7	− 1.4	1.4	5	
					$T^- = 32$	$T^+ = 4$

Hence, $T = T^+ = 4$.

Conclusion: Reject H_0.

There is sufficient evidence to enable us to conclude that the replacement shock absorber lasts longer than the original shock absorber.

___

COMPUTER OUTPUT FOR EXAMPLE 14.7*

Minitab

```
TEST OF MEDIAN=0 VERSUS MEDIAN L.T.  0
            N FOR    WILCOXON                ESTIMATED
         N   TEST    STATISTIC   P-VALUE      MEDIAN
C3       8    8        4.0        0.029       -1.450
```

The output includes the original sample size, the number of nonzero differences (N FOR TEST), the value of T^+ (WILCOXON STATISTIC), the p-value, and the estimated median. If you require T^-, this value can be calculated from T^+, since $T^+ + T^- = n(n + 1)/2$. Caution should be exercised in interpreting the p-value, since the outputted statistic will always be T^+, even though in some cases you may need T^-.

___

* Appendixes 14.A and 14.B describe the Minitab and SAS commands needed to answer this question.

SAS

In Chapter 2 we discussed the univariate procedure where we pointed out that the output includes a number of statistics other than the mean, variance, and standard deviation. One of these statistics is what SAS refers to as the signed rank statistic, which is

$$S = T^+ - \frac{n(n + 1)}{4}$$

The quantity $\frac{n(n + 1)}{4}$ is the mean of the Wilcoxon signed rank sum test statistic (which is described in the next subsection). The relevant part of the output is

```
Sgn Rank    -14    Prob > |S|    0.0547
```

Since $n = 8$, $\frac{n(n + 1)}{4} = 18$. Thus, since

$$S = T^+ - 18 = -14$$

we find

$$T^+ = 4$$

The two-tail *p*-value (Prob > |S|) is .0547. If the test that we apply requires T^-, we can compute that value from T^+. If the test is one-tailed, the *p*-value will have to be adjusted.

LARGE SAMPLE SIZES

When the sample size *n* is large ($n > 50$), the test statistic *T* is approximately normally distributed, with mean $E(T)$ and standard deviation σ_T calculated as

$$E(T) = \frac{n(n + 1)}{4}$$

and

$$\sigma_T = \sqrt{\frac{n(n + 1)(2n + 1)}{24}}$$

We can then use the standardized test statistic, which is

$$z = \frac{T - E(T)}{\sigma_T}$$

where *T* is determined just as it is when $n \leq 50$. The rejection region is either

$$z < -z_{\alpha/2} \qquad \text{(two-tail test)}$$

or

$$z < -z_{\alpha} \qquad \text{(one-tail test)}$$

████████████ *EXAMPLE 14.8*

Advertising is critical in the residential real estate industry. Agents are always seeking ways to increase sales through improved advertising methods. A particular agent believes that he can increase the number of inquiries (and thus the probability of making a sale) by describing the house for sale without indicating its asking price. To support his belief he conducted an experiment in which 100 different houses for sale are advertised in two ways—with and without the asking price. The number of inquiries associated with each ad was recorded. Since the data were not normally distributed (the agent took a statistics course and as a consequence he knows things like this), the agent prepared to perform the appropriate nonparametric technique. He calculated the differences in the number of inquiries between the two ads for each house, with the following results:

D = Number of inquiries associated with ads not showing the price
    minus number of inquiries associated with ads showing the price

Number of ties = 10

$T^+ = 2,667$

$T^- = 1,428$

Do these results allow the agent to conclude that the ads without the price are more effective in generating interest in a house? (Use $\alpha = .01$.)

Solution.   The problem objective is to compare two populations, and the data scale is interval. Since the data are not normally distributed and the experimental design is matched pairs, we use the Wilcoxon signed rank sum test for matched pairs.

Suppose that we denote A and B as follows:

A = Population of inquiries from ads without the price

B = Population of inquiries from ads with the price

Because we wish to show that the ads without the price are more effective, our alternative hypothesis is

H_A: The location of population A is to the right of the location of
    population B.

The details of the test are as follows:

H_0: The two population locations are the same.

H_A: The location of population A is to the right of the location of
    population B.

Test statistic:

$$z = \frac{T - E(T)}{\sigma_T}$$

where $T = T^-$.

Rejection region:

$$z < -z_\alpha$$
$$< -z_{.01}$$
$$< -2.33$$

Value of the test statistic:

$$T = T^- = 1,428$$

$$E(T) = \frac{n(n + 1)}{4} = \frac{90(91)}{4} = 2,047.5$$

$$\sigma_T = \sqrt{\frac{n(n + 1)(2n + 1)}{24}} = \sqrt{\frac{(90)(91)(181)}{24}} = 248.5$$

$$z = \frac{T - E(T)}{\sigma_T} = \frac{1,428 - 2,047.5}{248.5} = -2.49$$

Conclusion: Reject H_0.

There is enough evidence to allow the agent to conclude that the ads without prices elicit more interest than the ads with prices.

EXERCISES

LEARNING THE TECHNIQUES

14.19 Perform the Wilcoxon signed rank sum test for matched pairs on the following problem, to determine whether the location of population A differs from the location of population B. (Use $\alpha = .10$.)

Pair	A	B
1	9	5
2	12	10
3	13	11
4	8	9
5	7	3
6	10	10

14.20 Specify the test statistic and the rejection region for each of the following Wilcoxon signed rank sum tests for matched pairs.

a. H_0: The two population locations are the same.
H_A: The location of population A is to the left of the location of population B.

$n = 8$ $\alpha = .05$

b. H_0: The two population locations are the same.
H_A: The location of population A is different from the location of population B.

$n = 20$ $\alpha = .01$

c. H_0: The two population locations are the same.
H_A: The location of population A is to the right of the location of population B.

$n = 10$ $\alpha = .05$

14.21 Use the Wilcoxon signed rank sum test for matched pairs to determine whether the location of population A is to the right of population B. (Use $\alpha = 05$.)

Pair	A	B
1	108	103
2	125	114
3	119	121
4	96	94
5	163	149
6	75	76
7	98	94
8	81	80

14.22 Given the results that follow, use the Wilcoxon signed rank sum test for matched pairs to determine whether the location of population A is to the left of the location of population B. (Use $\alpha = .10$.)

$$n = 88 \qquad T^+ = 1,764 \qquad T^- = 2,152$$

14.23 Given the following data drawn from two nonnormal populations and generated from a matched pairs experiment, is there sufficient evidence at the 5% significance level to allow us to conclude that the location of population A is to the left of the location of population B?

Pair	A	B
1	3.2	3.5
2	6.5	6.6
3	7.1	7.0
4	4.8	5.3
5	11.9	13.8
6	10.5	12.9
7	7.4	7.7

14.24 In a matched pairs experiment, $n = 60$ pairs of observations were drawn from two nonnormal populations. Do the following results allow us to conclude at the 1% significance level that the location of population A is to the right of the location of population B?

$$T^+ = 1,016 \qquad T^- = 814$$

14.25 Use the Wilcoxon signed rank sum test to determine whether the results that follow allow us to conclude at the 5% significance level that the two population locations differ.

$$n = 143 \qquad T^+ = 5,011 \qquad T^- = 5,285$$

APPLYING THE TECHNIQUES

Self-Correcting Exercise (See Appendix 14.C for the solution.)

MKT **14.26** Some movie studios believe that, by adding sexually explicit scenes to the home-video version of movies, they can increase the movie's appeal and profitability (*Wall Street Journal,* 14 October 1988). A studio executive decided to test this belief. She organized a study that involved eight movies that were rated PG-13. Versions of each movie were created by adding scenes that changed the rating to R. The two versions of the movies were then made available to rental shops. For each of the eight pairs of movies, the total number of rentals in one major city during a 1-week period was recorded, and the results are reproduced in the accompanying table. Do these data provide enough evidence at the 5% significance level to support the belief? (Assume that weekly rentals are not normally distributed.)

Movie	Number of Rentals	
	PG-13	R
1	326	358
2	413	425
3	258	244
4	127	125
5	379	502
6	205	221
7	428	433
8	307	315

MKT **14.27** Suppose that the housework study referred to in Exercise 14.9 was repeated with some changes. In the revised experiment, 12 women were asked in 1985 and again in 1988 how many hours of housework they perform weekly. The results are shown in the following table. If we assume that the hours of housework are not normally distributed, can we conclude at the 5% significance level that women as a group are doing less housework in 1988 than in 1985?

	Hours of Housework	
Woman	1985	1988
1	22	20
2	18	15
3	27	28
4	16	14
5	23	18
6	21	19
7	15	10
8	20	21
9	19	16
10	25	20
11	18	14
12	17	13

GEN **14.28** Repeat Exercise 9.50 for the case where the times are not normally distributed. (Use $\alpha = .05$.)

EDUC **14.29** Repeat Exercise 9.56 (a) for the case where the salary offers are not normally distributed.

MNG **14.30** A large sporting-goods store located in Florida is planning a renovation that will result in an increase in the floor space for one department. The manager of the store has narrowed her choice about which department to increase to two possi-

bilities: the tennis-equipment department or the swimming-accessories department. The manager would like to enlarge the tennis-equipment department because she believes that this department improves the overall image of the store. She decides, however, that, if the swimming-accessories department can be shown to have higher gross sales, she will choose that department. She has collected the monthly gross sales data for the past year for each department; these appear in the accompanying table.

Month	Tennis Equipment	Swimming Accessories
January	$6,573	$4,950
February	$4,570	$5,921
March	$7,818	$8,920
April	$10,650	$12,514
May	$12,492	$14,650
June	$14,862	$15,202
July	$16,253	$17,319
August	$14,198	$12,444
September	$10,608	$8,309
October	$7,215	$8,460
November	$6,751	$8,653
December	$5,915	$6,793

After some analysis, the manager concludes that the gross sales are not normally distributed. At the 5% significance level, which department should be enlarged?

SECTION 14.5   **KRUSKAL–WALLIS TEST FOR THE COMPLETELY RANDOMIZED DESIGN**

The technique described in this section is a relatively simple extension of two techniques we have already covered. In Sections 12.2 and 12.3, we considered one of these—the analysis of variance, which enables us to compare two or more populations whose data scale is interval. We discussed two models: the completely randomized design, which uses independent samples; and the randomized block design, in which the observations are blocked. In this section, we discuss the equivalent of the completely randomized design of the analysis of variance; the only difference between Section 12.2 and this section is that the data scale is now assumed to be ordinal. The data scale may actually be interval, but we'll treat it as ordinal anyway, because the assumption necessary to perform the analysis of variance is unsatisfied. As was mentioned in Section 12.2, the test statistic of the analysis of variance was F-distributed, which required that the population from which we sampled be normally distributed.

The other technique that is extended by the test now being discussed is the Wilcoxon rank sum test for independent samples, presented in Section 14.2. You will find that the kinds of calculations performed in that section are, by and large, repeated here.

The **Kruskal–Wallis test for the completely randomized design** is applied to problems that have the following characteristics:

1. The problem objective is to compare two or more populations.

2. The data scale is either ordinal or interval. If the scale is interval, the Kruskal–Wallis test is applied when the variable is *not* normally distributed.

3. The samples are independent.

The null hypothesis for this test is similar to that encountered in the analysis of variance. Because the data may be ordinal, however, we test population locations instead of population means. In all applications of this nonparametric technique, the null and alternative hypotheses are

H_0: The locations of all k populations are the same.

H_A: At least two population locations differ.

Here, k represents the number of populations to be compared.

EXAMPLE 14.9

A manufacturer of high-quality calculators is trying to decide which one of three types of battery to include with each calculator sold. The two key determinants of the decision are the cost and the length of life of the battery. In order to assess the latter factor, 5 calculators were equipped with type 1 batteries, another 5 calculators were equipped with type 2 batteries, and yet another 5 calculators were equipped with type 3 batteries. The 15 calculators were then run until the batteries wore out. The times until battery wear-out were recorded and are shown in the table below.

HOURS UNTIL BATTERY WEAR-OUT

Type 1	Type 2	Type 3
15.5	20.5	13.3
17.2	18.3	18.9

(continued)

Type 1	Type 2	Type 3
13.3	21.2	19.5
20.6	15.7	15.2
19.2	16.3	13.8

At the 5% level of significance, is there a difference in the length of life of the three batteries? Assume that the wear-out times are not normally distributed.

Solution.   The problem objective is to compare three populations, the data scale is interval, and the condition necessary to perform the analysis of variance is not satisfied. Because the samples are independent, the appropriate technique is the Kruskal–Wallis test for the completely randomized design. The null and alternative hypotheses automatically follow. That is,

H_0: The locations of all three populations are the same.

H_A: At least two population locations differ.

The test statistic is calculated in a way that closely resembles the way in which the test statistic of the Wilcoxon rank sum test for independent samples is calculated.

The first step is to rank all of the observations. As before, 1 = Smallest observation and n = Largest observation, where $n = n_1 + n_2 + n_3$. We average the ranks of any tied observations. This task is described in the following table.

Type 1 (rank)	Type 2 (rank)	Type 3 (rank)
15.5 (5)	20.5 (13)	13.3 (1.5)
17.2 (8)	18.3 (9)	18.9 (10)
13.3 (1.5)	21.2 (15)	19.5 (12)
20.6 (14)	15.7 (6)	15.2 (4)
19.2 (11)	16.3 (7)	13.8 (3)
$T_1 = 39.5$	$T_2 = 50$	$T_3 = 30.5$

If the null hypothesis is true, the ranks should be evenly distributed among the three groups. The degree to which this is true is judged by calculating the rank sums of the three samples (labeled T_1, T_2, and T_3). In our example, $T_1 = 39.5$, $T_2 = 50$, and $T_3 = 30.5$.

The next step is to calculate the test statistic, denoted H, where

$$H = \left[\frac{12}{n(n+1)} \sum_{j=1}^{k} \frac{T_j^2}{n_j} \right] - 3(n+1)$$

Although it is difficult to see this from the formula, if the rank sums T_1, T_2, and T_3 are similar, then H is small. As a result, a small value of H supports the null hypothesis. Conversely, if considerable differences exist between any two of the rank sums, then H is large. In this example, we have

$$H = \left[\frac{12}{15(16)} \left(\frac{39.5^2}{5} + \frac{50^2}{5} + \frac{30.5^2}{5} \right) \right] - 3(16)$$
$$= 1.91$$

The key question addressed by this test is whether H is large enough to allow us to reject the null hypothesis. The question is answered by examining the sampling distribution of H, which is approximately chi-square with $k - 1$ degrees of freedom, provided that all sample sizes are greater than or equal to 5. (That is, $n_j \geq 5$ for $j = 1, 2, \ldots, k$.) Hence, the rejection region is

$$H > \chi^2_{\alpha, k-1}$$

In our example, we reject H_0 if

$$H > \chi^2_{.05, 2}$$
$$> 5.99147$$

Therefore, since H does not exceed χ^2_α, we do not reject H_0. There is insufficient evidence to allow us to conclude that the battery lives differ. Presumably, the calculator manufacturer would equip its product with the lowest-cost battery, given that there are evidently no significant differences in longevity among the three types.

COMPUTER OUTPUT FOR EXAMPLE 14.9*

Minitab

LEVEL	NOBS	MEDIAN	AVE RANK	Z VALUE
1	5	17.20	7.9	-0.06
2	5	18.30	10.00	1.22
3	5	15.20	6.1	-1.16
OVERALL	15		8.0	

H=1.905
H (ADJ FOR TIES)=1.908

The value of the test statistic is identified by H = 1.905. The rest of the output can be ignored.

---

* See Appendix 14.A for the Minitab commands and Appendix 14.B for the SAS commands that produced these printouts.

SAS

Wilcoxon Scores (Rank Sums) for Variable X
Classified by Variable SAMPLE

SAMPLE	N	Sum of Scores	Expected Under H0	Std Dev Under H0	Mean Score
1	5	39.5000	40.0	8.1576	7.9000
2	5	50.0000	40.0	8.1576	10.0000
3	5	30.5000	40.0	8.1576	6.1000

Average Scores were used for Ties

Kruskal-Wallis Test (Chi-Square Approximation)
CHISQ=1.9084   DF=2   Prob > CHISQ=0.3851

The output includes T_1, T_2, T_3, the test statistic (CHISQ = 1.9084), and the *p*-value (Prob > CHISQ = 0.3851).

We now summarize the Kruskal–Wallis test for the completely randomized design.

Summary of Kruskal–Wallis Test

Factors to Identify

Problem objective: comparison of two or more populations

Data scale: ordinal or interval

Experimental design: independent samples

Calculation of the Test Statistic

Step 1:   Rank all of the observations, where 1 = Smallest observation and n = Largest observation. Average the ranks of the tied observations.

Step 2:   Calculate the rank sums of the samples. As a check, you should confirm that

$$\sum T_j = \frac{n(n + 1)}{2}$$

Step 3:   Calculate the test statistic:

$$H = \left[\frac{12}{n(n + 1)} \sum_{j=1}^{k} \frac{T_j^2}{n_j}\right] - 3(n + 1)$$

Rejection Region

$$H > \chi_{\alpha, k - 1}^2$$

Required Conditions

The k population distributions are identical in shape and spread, $n_j \geq 5$ for $j = 1, 2, \ldots, k$.

▬▬▬▬▬▬▬ **EXERCISES**

LEARNING THE TECHNIQUES

14.31 Using the Kruskal–Wallis test, determine if there is enough evidence to enable us to conclude that at least two population locations differ. (Use $\alpha = .05$.)

Population		
1	2	3
25	19	27
15	21	25
20	23	22
22	22	29
23	28	28

14.32 Test to determine whether there is sufficient evidence to indicate that at least two population locations differ for the following Kruskal–Wallis test:

$n_1 = 7 \qquad n_2 = 10 \qquad n_3 = 8 \qquad n_4 = 12$

$T_1 = 133 \qquad T_2 = 190 \qquad T_3 = 152 \qquad T_4 = 228$

$\alpha = .10$

14.33 Given the following data drawn independently from four nonnormal populations, can we conclude at the 10% significance level that at least two population locations differ?

Population			
1	2	3	4
14.5	15.3	18.3	18.8
17.3	14.6	19.5	19.3
19.8	16.8	16.6	16.5
17.4	12.1	23.3	17.0
11.9	11.6	18.8	23.5
	11.4	17.1	

14.34 In random samples of 10 from each of five nonnormal populations, the following results were generated. Can we conclude at the 5% significance level that the locations of at least two populations differ?

$T_1 = 241 \qquad T_2 = 281 \qquad T_3 = 262$

$T_4 = 233 \qquad T_5 = 258$

14.35 Use the Kruskal–Wallis test to determine whether there is enough evidence, with $\alpha = .05$, to allow us to conclude that at least two population locations differ.

$n_1 = 23 \qquad n_2 = 41 \qquad n_3 = 31$

$T_1 = 1,201 \qquad T_2 = 1,852 \qquad T_3 = 1,507$

APPLYING THE TECHNIQUES

Self-Correcting Exercise (See Appendix 14.C for the solution.)

GEN **14.36** A consumer testing service is comparing the effectiveness of four different brands of drain cleaners. The experiment consists of using each product on six different clogged sinks and measuring the amount of time until the drain becomes unclogged. The resulting times, measured in minutes, are shown in the accompanying table. If a statistical analysis has shown that the times are not normally distributed, can the service conclude with $\alpha = .10$ that differences exist among the speeds at which the four brands perform?

TIMES TO UNCLOG

Brand			
1	2	3	4
17	12	19	12
25	23	29	10
19	19	31	11
12	26	26	6
14	18	29	8
16	25	33	13

EDUC **14.37**   Repeat Exercise 12.29, but this time assume that the data are not normally distributed.

EDUC **14.38**   In an effort to determine whether differences exist among three methods of teaching statistics, a professor of business taught his course differently in each of three large sections. In the first section, he taught the traditional way; in the second, he taught by the case method; and in the third, he incorporated a canned computer package extensively. At the end of the semester, each student was asked to evaluate the course on a 7-point scale, where 1 = Poor and 7 = Excellent. From each section, the professor chose five evaluations at random. These are listed in the accompanying table.

Section 1 (traditional)	Section 2 (case method)	Section 3 (computer method)
6	4	6
4	5	7
5	5	6
4	3	7
5	3	5

At the 5% level of significance, is there evidence that differences in student satisfaction exist with respect to at least two of the three teaching methods?

GEN **14.39**   A recent development in the manufacturing of golf balls is to increase the number of dimples, which manufacturers believe increases the distance they travel when hit. Three new designs were compared with the existing design by having a machine hit each of the balls seven times and measuring the yardage traveled. The existing design has about 350 dimples, and the three experimental designs have about 370, 390, and 410 dimples, respectively. The number of yards traveled by each is shown in the accompanying table.

350 Dimples	370 Dimples	390 Dimples	410 Dimples
255	248	265	267
233	247	253	258
248	249	259	272
261	253	275	265
253	261	260	266
244	252	255	258
271	244	258	268

After analyzing the data, researchers concluded that the distances are not normally distributed. Can we conclude at the 1% significance level that there are differences in length of flight among the golf balls?

ACC **14.40**   Repeat Exercise 12.32, but this time assume that the completion times are not normally distributed.

SECTION 14.6   # FRIEDMAN TEST FOR THE RANDOMIZED BLOCK DESIGN

The second model for the analysis of variance is the randomized block design. This model is used whenever data are generated from relatively similar blocks and represents an extension of the matched pairs experiment such that, when more than two populations are to be compared, the experimental units are called blocks. The technique described in Section 12.3 requires that the data scale be interval and that the populations from which we sample be normally distributed. If the normality requirement is unsatisfied or if the scale is ordinal, the **Friedman test for the randomized block design** must be used. This test is applied to problems that have the following characteristics:

1. The problem objective is to compare two or more populations.
2. The data scale is either ordinal or interval. If the scale is interval, the Friedman test is applied when the variable is *not* normally distributed.
3. The data are generated from a randomized block design.

━━━━━━━━━━ *EXAMPLE 14.10*

Suppose that, for economic reasons, a large company wants each of its secretaries to use the same make of typewriter. After a preliminary study, the company has reduced its choice to four kinds of typewriter. Over a period of 4 days, six secretaries randomly selected by the company are asked to use each of the typewriters for 1 day each and then to evaluate them on the basis of speed, convenience, ease of handling, and noise level. The typewriters were rated on a 7-point scale, where 1 = Poor and 7 = Excellent. The ratings assigned are shown in the accompanying table.

	Typewriter			
Secretary	1	2	3	4
1	3	7	7	4
2	4	2	5	5
3	2	3	4	3
4	4	6	5	4
5	5	4	7	5
6	4	5	6	4

Can we conclude at the 5% level of significance that the secretaries' ratings indicate that differences exist among the typewriters?

Solution.   The problem objective is to compare four populations (the evaluations of the four kinds of typewriter), and the data scale is ordinal. The experiment was performed as the randomized block design (the typewriters are the treatments, and the secretaries are the blocks). The appropriate statistical technique to use is therefore the Friedman test for the randomized block design.

The null hypothesis states that all treatments (typewriters) are the same. The alternative hypothesis asserts that at least two kinds of typewriter differ. In keeping with the terminology introduced in this chapter, the null and alternative hypotheses are

H_0: The locations of all four populations are the same.

H_A: At least two population locations differ.

To calculate the test statistic, we first rank each observation within each block. That is, for each secretary (block), we rank the four ratings that each produced, as shown in the following table.

	Typewriter			
Secretary	i(Rank)	2(Rank)	3(Rank)	4(Rank)
1	3(1)	7(3.5)	7(3.5)	4(2)
2	4(2)	2(1)	5(3.5)	5(3.5)
3	2(1)	3(2.5)	4(4)	3(2.5)
4	4(1.5)	6(4)	5(3)	4(1.5)
5	5(2.5)	4(1)	7(4)	5(2.5)
6	4(1.5)	5(3)	6(4)	4(1.5)
	$T_1 = 9.5$	$T_2 = 15$	$T_3 = 22$	$T_4 = 13.5$

Since there are four kinds of typewriter, the ranks are 1, 2, 3, and 4. Once again, we average the ranks of any tied observations. Next, we calculate the rank sums for each typewriter. That is,

$$T_1 = 9.5 \qquad T_2 = 15 \qquad T_3 = 22 \qquad T_4 = 13.5$$

Then we calculate the test statistic, which is

$$F_r = \left[\frac{12}{b(k)(k + 1)} \sum_{j=1}^{k} T_j^2 \right] - 3b(k + 1)$$

where k = Number of treatments and b = Number of blocks. In this case, $k = 4$ typewriters, and $b = 6$ secretaries. As a result,

$$F_r = \left[\frac{12}{(6)(4)(5)} (9.5^2 + 15^2 + 22^2 + 13.5^2) \right] - 3(6)(5) = 8.15$$

Finally, we set up the rejection region. If the rank sums are similar, then F_r is small. Obviously a small value of F_r supports the null hypothesis. When F_r is large, we reject H_0. The sampling distribution of F_r is approximately chi-square distributed, with $k - 1$ degrees of freedom, provided that k or b is greater than or equal to 5. Thus the rejection region is

$$F_r > \chi^2_{\alpha, k-1}$$

In this example, we reject H_0 if

$$F_r > \chi^2_{.05, 3}$$
$$> 7.81473$$

As a result, we reject H_0 and conclude that at least two of the typewriters' evaluations differ. Management's next step should be to try to identify the best typewriter from among the four types sampled.

We review the Friedman test in summarized form next.

Summary of Friedman Test

Factors to Identify

Problem objective: comparison of two or more populations

Data scale: ordinal or interval

Experimental design: randomized block

Calculation of the Test Statistic

Step 1: Within each block, rank all of the observations from 1 to k. Average the ranks of tied observations.

Step 2: Calculate the rank sum of each treatment. As a check, confirm that

$$\sum T_j = bk(k + 1)/2$$

Step 3: Calculate the test statistic:

$$F_r = \left[\frac{12}{(b)(k)(k + 1)} \sum T_j^2 \right] - 3b(k + 1)$$

Rejection Region

$$F_r > \chi^2_{\alpha, k-1}$$

Required Conditions

The k population distributions are identical in shape and spread, k or $b \geq 5$.

EXERCISES

LEARNING THE TECHNIQUES

14.41 Apply the Friedman test to the accompanying table of data to determine whether we can conclude that at least two population locations differ. (Use $\alpha = .05$.)

	Treatment			
Block	1	2	3	4
1	10	12	15	9
2	8	10	11	6

	Treatment			
Block	1	2	3	4
3	13	14	16	11
4	9	9	12	13
5	7	8	14	10

14.42 Based on the following calculations of the Friedman test, can we conclude that at least two treatment locations differ? (Use $\alpha = .01$.)

$k = 5$ $T_1 = 14$
$b = 6$ $T_2 = 22$
  $T_3 = 18$
  $T_4 = 12$
  $T_5 = 24$

14.43   Given the following data drawn from three nonnormal populations and generated by a blocked experiment, can we conclude at the 10% significance level that differences exist among the population locations?

	Treatment		
Block	1	2	3
1	17.1	16.3	18.3
2	23.2	22.5	25.1
3	16.5	13.9	17.2
4	18.1	19.0	18.7
5	28.7	25.6	27.9
6	14.7	14.6	15.3

14.44   Use the following results to complete the Friedman test, with $\alpha = .05$.

$k = 6$ $T_1 = 48$
$b = 15$ $T_2 = 73$
  $T_3 = 41$
  $T_4 = 52$
  $T_5 = 40$
  $T_6 = 61$

14.45   The data that follow were drawn from four nonnormal populations by means of a randomized block experiment. Do these data provide sufficient evidence at the 10% significance level to allow us to conclude that at least two population locations differ?

	Treatment			
Block	1	2	3	4
1	6.2	6.5	4.4	7.2
2	7.3	7.2	6.2	8.3

	Treatment			
Block	1	2	3	4
3	5.1	5.0	4.1	5.2
4	9.3	10.1	8.1	10.2
5	8.6	9.3	6.9	9.0
6	7.5	7.4	7.3	8.9
7	8.8	7.9	7.1	7.4

APPLYING THE TECHNIQUES

Self-Correcting Exercise (See Appendix 14.C for the solution.)

GEN   **14.46**   The manager of a personnel company is in the process of examining her company's advertising programs. Currently, the company advertises for a wide variety of positions including computer programmers, secretaries, and receptionists in each of the three local newspapers. The manager has decided that only one newspaper will be used if it can be determined that there are differences in the number of inquiries generated among the newspapers. The following experiment was performed. For 1 week (6 days) six different jobs were advertised in each of the three newspapers. The number of inquiries were counted, and the results appear in the accompanying table. Assuming that the data are not normally distributed, can we conclude at the 5% significance level that differences exist among the newspapers' abilities to attract potential employees?

NUMBER OF INQUIRIES

	Newspaper		
Job Advertised	1	2	3
Receptionist	14	17	12
Systems analyst	8	9	6
Junior secretary	25	20	23
Computer programmer	12	15	10
Legal secretary	7	10	5
Office manager	5	9	4

EDUC **14.47** Repeat Exercise 12.55, but this time assume that commission income is not normally distributed.

MKT **14.48** The Crazy-Cola company has used the same secret recipe for its product since its introduction 200 years ago. In response to a decreasing market share, however, the owner of Crazy-Cola, Charles Upchuck, is contemplating changing the recipe. He has two alternative concoctions. In a preliminary study, he had 10 people taste the original recipe and the two new concoctions. He asked each to evaluate the taste of the product on a 5-point scale, where 1 = Abominable and 5 = Wonderful. The results are shown in the accompanying table.

Respondent	Original Recipe	Concoction 1	Concoction 2
1	2	1	3
2	4	3	5
3	5	3	5
4	3	2	4
5	1	1	3
6	3	2	2
7	5	4	3
8	4	4	3
9	2	3	3
10	1	2	3

Chuck decides that, unless significant differences exist among evaluations of the products, he will not make any changes in Crazy-Cola. At the 5% significance level, can we conclude that there are differences in the ratings of the three recipes?

GEN **14.49** A school that has recently been built has four intersections surrounding it. The town council must decide whether to maintain the current stop signs or to switch to traffic lights at the intersections. The total traffic in the area is not sufficient to warrant four traffic lights. The council decides that it will keep the stop signs at all of the intersections unless sufficient evidence exists that there are differences in traffic flow among the intersections. If there are differences, the two busiest intersections will get traffic lights. During one 8-hour period, the number of cars per intersection was counted. The numbers per hour are shown in the accompanying table.

Hour	Intersections			
	1	2	3	4
8–9	60	63	55	44
9–10	43	41	47	43
10–11	25	28	31	29
11–12	32	31	25	35
12–1	58	53	61	65
1–2	41	49	45	44
2–3	22	19	20	25
3–4	37	45	40	42

Assuming that the number of cars is not normally distributed, can we conclude at the 5% significance level that traffic lights should be installed at the two busiest intersections?

SECTION 14.7 ## *CAUTIONARY NOTE ABOUT NONPARAMETRIC STATISTICS*

If you've actually performed the calculations in this chapter, you have undoubtedly noticed that the amount of work required for a nonparametric technique is far less than for its parametric counterpart. Compare the computations necessary to do the analysis of variance, for example, with those involved in the Kruskal–Wallis or Friedman test, and you may wonder why it is necessary to have parametric tests at all. Even if the data are interval-scaled, why not always use the computationally simple nonparametric test? The answer lies in the probability of a Type II error. If the data in a given question are interval and the conditions necessary to perform the parametric test are satisfied, the probability of a Type II error is smaller (and the power is larger) for a parametric test than for a nonparametric test. Hence, when the conditions are satisfied, the parametric test is said to be more powerful. The reason for this is quite simple: by ranking interval data, we lose information—information about the actual value of the observations. Whenever we are restricted to using less information than the full amount available, our decision (in general) becomes less authoritative. Since the probability of a Type I error is fixed at some value of α, the poorer decision is reflected by a smaller power. Consequently, when a parametric technique can be used (because interval data are involved and the relevant required conditions have been met), it should be—so as to reduce the probability of incorrectly accepting the null hypothesis. Think of use of the parametric method as involving a tradeoff: more calculations, but less likelihood of error.

SECTION 14.8
KOLMOGOROV–SMIRNOV TEST AND LILLIEFORS TEST FOR NORMALITY

The assumption of normality is extremely important in applications of statistical inference. We've already seen in Chapters 7, 9, and 12 and we'll see again in Chapters 15, 16, and 17 that the assumption that the population random variable is normally distributed must be satisfied (at least reasonably well) in order for a number of statistical techniques to be valid.

In Chapter 13, we studied the chi-square test, which can be used to test any distribution (including, of course, the normal distribution). In this section, we discuss two nonparametric techniques that can be used to test distributions. The first is called the **Kolmogorov–Smirnov** (shortened to **K–S,** for those who can't spell or pronounce the two Russian mathematicians' names) **test,** and the second is called the **Lilliefors test.** The Kolmogorov–Smirnov test, like the chi-square test, can be used to test for any distribution. The Lilliefors test, however, is specifically designed to test normality.

The advantage of the K–S test over the chi-square test is that it is generally more powerful, does not require a minimum expected frequency (such as the rule of five), and (like other nonparametric methods) is easier to compute.

KOLMOGOROV–SMIRNOV TEST

The Kolmogorov–Smirnov test is conducted by comparing the hypothesized and sample cumulative distribution functions. A cumulative distribution function is defined as

$$F(x) = P(X \le x)$$

We encountered this function in Chapter 4 when we discussed the tables of the cumulative binomial and Poisson distributions (Tables 1 and 2 in Appendix B). In both cases, the tables provide values for

$$P(X \leq k) = \sum_{x=0}^{k} p(x)$$

The sample cumulative distribution function, $S(x)$, is defined as the proportion of sample values that are less than or equal to x. To illustrate how $S(x)$ is computed, suppose that we have the following 10 observations:

110, 89, 102, 80, 93, 121, 108, 97, 105, 103

We begin by placing the values of x in ascending order, as follows:

80, 89, 93, 97, 102, 103, 105, 108, 110, 121

Since $x = 80$ is the smallest of the 10 values, the proportion of values of x that are less than or equal to 80 is

$$S(80) = \frac{1}{10} = .1$$

Similarly, two of the 10 values are less than or equal to 89 (namely, 80 and 89). As a result,

$$S(89) = \frac{2}{10} = .2$$

The remaining values of $S(x)$, each determined in a like manner, are as follows:

x	$S(x)$
80	.1
89	.2
93	.3
97	.4
102	.5
103	.6
105	.7
108	.8
110	.9
121	1.0

Suppose that we wish to test the hypothesis that the data in question were drawn from a normal distribution, with mean $\mu = 100$ and standard deviation

$\sigma = 10$. Our hypotheses for this test are

H_0: Data were drawn from a normal distribution, with $\mu = 100$ and $\sigma = 10$.

H_A: Data were not drawn from a normal distribution, with $\mu = 100$ and $\sigma = 10$.

As we've done in all of our hypothesis tests, we begin by assuming that the null hypothesis is true. This assumption allows us to calculate the hypothesized cumulative distribution function $F(x)$ for each sample value of x. For example, we can find $F(80)$ as follows

$$F(80) = P(x \le 80)$$

$$= P\left(\frac{x - \mu}{\sigma} \le \frac{80 - 100}{10}\right)$$

$$= P(z \le -2)$$

$$= .0228$$

Notice that we standardized x by subtracting 100 and dividing by 10 because we hypothesized that $\mu = 100$ and $\sigma = 10$. The accompanying table lists all of the values of x and $F(x)$.

x	$F(x) = P(X \le x)$		
80	$P(X \le 80)$	$= P(z \le -2)$	$= .0228$
89	$P(X \le 89)$	$= P(z \le -1.1)$	$= .1357$
93	$P(X \le 93)$	$= P(z \le -.7)$	$= .2420$
97	$P(X \le 97)$	$= P(z \le -.3)$	$= .3821$
102	$P(X \le 102)$	$= P(z \le .2)$	$= .5793$
103	$P(X \le 103)$	$= P(z \le .3)$	$= .6179$
105	$P(X \le 105)$	$= P(z \le .5)$	$= .6915$
108	$P(X \le 108)$	$= P(z \le .8)$	$= .7881$
110	$P(X \le 110)$	$= P(z \le 1.0)$	$= .8413$
121	$P(X \le 121)$	$= P(z \le 2.1)$	$= .9821$

If the null hypothesis is true, then $F(x)$ and $S(x)$ should be similar for all values of x. If the null hypothesis is false, however, large differences will exist between $F(x)$ and $S(x)$ for at least some values of x. We define the test statistic D as the largest absolute difference between $F(x)$ and $S(x)$. That is,

$$D = \max|F(x) - S(x)|$$

To calculate D, we first calculate the absolute difference between $F(x)$ and $S(x)$ for each value of x, as shown in the accompanying table.

x	$F(x)$	$S(x)$	$|F(x) - S(x)|$
80	.0228	.1	.0772
89	.1357	.2	.0643
93	.2420	.3	.0580
97	.3821	.4	.0179
102	.5793	.5	$.0793 = D = \max|F(x) - S(x)|$
103	.6179	.6	.0179
105	.6915	.7	.0085
108	.7881	.8	.0119
110	.8413	.9	.0587
121	.9821	1.0	.0179

Clearly, the maximum absolute difference is $D = .0793$.

If D were large, we would conclude that there are large differences between $F(x)$ and $S(x)$, and we would reject the null hypothesis. To judge whether D is large enough to justify rejecting the null hypothesis, we compare D with the critical values of D in the Kolmogorov–Smirnov test shown in Table 10 in Appendix B (reproduced here as Table 14.3). Notice that critical values are provided for $\alpha = .01$, .02, .05, .10, and .20 and for $n = 1, 2, \ldots, 40$. If $n > 40$, a simple formula provides the critical value. If, in our example, we set $\alpha = .05$, then the critical value (with $n = 10$) is .409. If $D > .409$, we reject H_0. Since $D = .0793$, however, we conclude that there is not enough evidence to allow us to reject the null hypothesis. Thus, there is insufficient evidence to indicate that the data are not normally distributed, with $\mu = 100$ and $\sigma = 10$.

LILLIEFORS TEST

In most applications where we wish to test for normality, the population mean and the population variance are unknown. In order to perform the Kolmogorov–Smirnov test, however, we must assume that those parameters are known. The Lilliefors test, which is quite similar to the Kolmogorov–Smirnov test, overcomes this problem. The major difference between the two is that, with the Lilliefors test, the sample mean $\bar{x}$ and the sample standard deviation s are used (instead of μ and σ) to calculate $F(x)$. The sample cumulative function $S(x)$ and the test statistic D are both computed as in the Kolmogorov–Smirnov test. In the Lilliefors test, we compare the computed value of D with the corresponding critical value of D provided by Table 11 in Appendix B (reproduced here as Table 14.4, page 631).

TABLE 14.3   *CRITICAL VALUES OF THE KOLMOGOROV–SMIRNOV TEST*

Sample Size	Significance Level α				
	.20	.10	.05	.02	.01
1	.900	.950	.975	.990	.995
2	.684	.776	.842	.900	.929
3	.565	.636	.708	.785	.829
4	.493	.565	.624	.689	.734
5	.447	.509	.563	.627	.669
6	.410	.468	.519	.577	.617
7	.381	.436	.483	.538	.576
8	.358	.410	.454	.507	.542
9	.339	.387	.430	.480	.513
10	.323	.369	.409	.457	.489
11	.308	.352	.391	.437	.468
12	.296	.338	.375	.419	.449
13	.285	.325	.361	.404	.432
14	.275	.314	.349	.390	.418
15	.266	.304	.338	.377	.404
16	.258	.295	.327	.366	.392
17	.250	.286	.318	.355	.381
18	.244	.279	.309	.346	.371
19	.237	.271	.301	.337	.361
20	.232	.265	.294	.329	.352
21	.226	.259	.287	.321	.344
22	.221	.253	.281	.314	.337
23	.216	.247	.275	.307	.330
24	.212	.242	.269	.301	.323
25	.208	.238	.264	.295	.317
26	.204	.233	.259	.290	.311
27	.200	.229	.254	.284	.305
28	.197	.225	.250	.279	.300
29	.193	.221	.246	.275	.295

(continued)

TABLE 14.3 CRITICAL VALUES OF THE KOLMOGOROV–SMIRNOV TEST (continued)

Sample Size	Significance Level α				
	.20	.10	.05	.02	.01
30	.190	.218	.242	.270	.290
31	.187	.214	.238	.266	.285
32	.184	.211	.234	.262	.281
33	.182	.208	.231	.258	.277
34	.179	.205	.227	.254	.273
35	.177	.202	.224	.251	.269
36	.174	.199	.221	.247	.265
37	.172	.196	.218	.244	.262
38	.170	.194	.215	.241	.258
39	.168	.191	.213	.238	.255
40	.165	.189	.210	.235	.252
Over 40	$\dfrac{1.07}{\sqrt{n}}$	$\dfrac{1.22}{\sqrt{n}}$	$\dfrac{1.36}{\sqrt{n}}$	$\dfrac{1.52}{\sqrt{n}}$	$\dfrac{1.63}{\sqrt{n}}$

SOURCE: L. H. Miller, "Tables of Percentage Points of the Kolmogorov Statistic," *Journal of the American Statistical Association,* 51 (1956): 111–21. Adapted by W. J. Conover, *Practical Nonparametric Statistics* (New York: John Wiley, 1971), p. 397. Reprinted by permission of John Wiley & Sons, Inc., and the American Statistical Association.

EXAMPLE 14.11

In Example 7.7, a random sample of 15 days' production was taken to test a hypothesis about mean daily production. Because σ^2 was unknown, a *t*-test was performed. The daily production was assumed to be normally distributed. Use the Lilliefors test to examine that assumption, with $\alpha = .01$.

Solution. The sample data were as follows:

93, 103, 95, 101, 91, 105, 96, 94, 101, 88, 98, 94, 101, 92, 95

As in the Kolmogorov–Smirnov test, we place the values of x in ascending order and calculate $S(x)$. The resulting values are shown next.

TABLE 14.4   *CRITICAL VALUES OF THE LILLIEFORS TEST*

Sample Size n	Significance Level α				
	.20	.15	.10	.05	.01
4	.300	.319	.352	.381	.417
5	.285	.299	.315	.337	.405
6	.265	.277	.294	.319	.364
7	.247	.258	.276	.300	.348
8	.233	.244	.261	.285	.331
9	.223	.233	.249	.271	.311
10	.215	.224	.239	.258	.294
11	.206	.217	.230	.249	.284
12	.199	.212	.223	.242	.275
13	.190	.202	.214	.234	.268
14	.183	.194	.207	.227	.261
15	.177	.187	.201	.220	.257
16	.173	.182	.195	.213	.250
17	.169	.177	.189	.206	.245
18	.166	.173	.184	.200	.239
19	.163	.169	.179	.195	.235
20	.160	.166	.174	.190	.231
25	.142	.147	.158	.173	.200
30	.131	.136	.144	.161	.187
Over 30	$\dfrac{.736}{\sqrt{n}}$	$\dfrac{.768}{\sqrt{n}}$	$\dfrac{.805}{\sqrt{n}}$	$\dfrac{.886}{\sqrt{n}}$	$\dfrac{1.031}{\sqrt{n}}$

SOURCE: H. W. Lilliefors, "On the Kolmogorov–Smirnov Test for Normality with Mean and Variance Unknown," *Journal of the American Statistical Association,* 62 (1967): 399–402. Adapted by W. J. Conover, *Practical Nonparametric Statistics* (New York: John Wiley, 1971), p. 398.

x	S(x)
88	1/15 = .067
91	2/15 = .133
92	3/15 = .200
93	4/15 = .267
94	6/15 = .400
95	8/15 = .533
96	9/15 = .600
98	10/15 = .667
101	13/15 = .867
103	14/15 = .933
105	15/15 = 1.000

From the data, we compute $\bar{x} = 96.47$ and $s = 4.85$. Using these statistics to estimate μ and σ, respectively, we calculate the cumulative distribution function, $F(x)$, as shown in the accompanying table.

x	F(x)
88	$P(x \leq 88) = P\left(\dfrac{x - \mu}{\sigma} \leq \dfrac{88 - 96.47}{4.85}\right) = P(z \leq -1.75) = .0401$
91	$P(x \leq 91) = P\left(\dfrac{x - \mu}{\sigma} \leq \dfrac{91 - 96.47}{4.85}\right) = P(z \leq -1.13) = .1292$
92	$P(x \leq 92) = P\left(\dfrac{x - \mu}{\sigma} \leq \dfrac{92 - 96.47}{4.85}\right) = P(z \leq -.92) = .1788$
93	$P(x \leq 93) = P\left(\dfrac{x - \mu}{\sigma} \leq \dfrac{93 - 96.47}{4.85}\right) = P(z \leq -.72) = .2358$
94	$P(x \leq 94) = P\left(\dfrac{x - \mu}{\sigma} \leq \dfrac{94 - 96.47}{4.85}\right) = P(z \leq -.51) = .3050$
95	$P(x \leq 95) = P\left(\dfrac{x - \mu}{\sigma} \leq \dfrac{95 - 96.47}{4.85}\right) = P(z \leq -.30) = .3821$
96	$P(x \leq 96) = P\left(\dfrac{x - \mu}{\sigma} \leq \dfrac{96 - 96.47}{4.85}\right) = P(z \leq -.10) = .4602$

(continued)

x	$F(x)$
98	$P(x \le 98) = P\left(\dfrac{x - \mu}{\sigma} \le \dfrac{98 - 96.47}{4.85}\right) = P(z \le .32) \quad = .6255$
101	$P(x \le 101) = P\left(\dfrac{x - \mu}{\sigma} \le \dfrac{101 - 96.47}{4.85}\right) = P(z \le .93) \quad = .8238$
103	$P(x \le 103) = P\left(\dfrac{x - \mu}{\sigma} \le \dfrac{103 - 96.47}{4.85}\right) = P(z \le 1.35) = .9115$
105	$P(x \le 105) = P\left(\dfrac{x - \mu}{\sigma} \le \dfrac{105 - 96.47}{4.85}\right) = P(z \le 1.76) = .9608$

For each value of x, we find the absolute difference $|F(x) - S(x)|$ and the largest absolute difference D. These calculations produce the results given in the following table.

x	$F(x)$	$S(x)$	$|F(x) - S(x)|$
88	.0401	.067	.0269
91	.1292	.133	.0038
92	.1788	.200	.0212
93	.2358	.267	.0312
94	.3050	.400	.0950
95	.3821	.533	$.1509 = D = \max|F(x) - S(x)|$
96	.4602	.600	.1398
98	.6255	.667	.0415
101	.8238	.867	.0432
103	.9115	.933	.0215
105	.9608	1.000	.0392

From Table 11 in Appendix B (or from Table 14.4), we find the critical value (with $\alpha = .01$ and $n = 15$). That value is .257. Since $D = .1509$ is less than .257, we conclude that there is insufficient evidence to establish that the data are not normally distributed. The t-test applied in Example 7.7 is therefore judged to be valid.

▬▬▬▬▬▬   **EXERCISES**

LEARNING THE TECHNIQUES

14.50 For each of the following Kolmogorov–Smirnov tests, determine whether or not the test statistic falls in the rejection region.

a. $n = 20$ $\alpha = .05$ $D = .303$

b. $n = 12$ $\alpha = .10$ $D = .315$

c. $n = 100$ $\alpha = .05$ $D = .166$

14.51 For each of the following Lilliefors tests, determine whether or not the test statistic falls in the rejection region.

a. $n = 8$ $\alpha = .01$ $D = .285$

b. $n = 16$ $\alpha = .10$ $D = .203$

c. $n = 50$ $\alpha = .05$ $D = .139$

14.52 Use the Kolmogorov–Smirnov test, with $\alpha = .05$, to determine whether the following data are normally distributed, with $\mu = 10$ and $\sigma = 2$:

7, 10, 9, 15, 12, 6, 14, 7, 14, 7, 6, 11, 10, 7

14.53 Use the Lilliefors test, with $\alpha = .01$, to determine whether the following data are normally distributed:

25, 27, 29, 27, 25, 24, 26, 22, 29, 22, 28, 23

APPLYING THE TECHNIQUES

POM **14.54** An inspector for a government agency charged with ascertaining that product labels indicating net weight are correct has weighed 12 packages of hamburger meat whose labels say that the packages weigh exactly 1 pound. The inspector would like to test to see whether there is evidence that the average is less than the amount stated, but the applicable test requires that the data are normally distributed. Perform the appropriate test, at the 1% significance level, to check this required condition. The weights of the 12 packages (in pounds) are as follows:

1.02, .97, 1.02, 1.03, .96, .98,
1.03, 1.02, .97, .98, .96, .99

GEN **14.55** A management scientist wants to estimate the variance of lead-time demand for an inexpensive line of compact disk players. She has found the demand for the product during the past eight lead times. Determine, with $\alpha = .05$, whether the condition necessary to draw inferences about σ^2 is satisfied. The past eight values for compact disk demand during lead time are as follows:

125, 170, 136, 141, 163, 158, 159, 162

SECTION 14.9   SUMMARY

Nonparametric statistical tests are applied to problems in which the data scale is either ordinal or interval and in which the conditions required to perform the parametric tests are not satisfied. The **Wilcoxon rank sum test for independent samples,** the **sign test,** and the **Wilcoxon signed rank sum test for the matched pairs experiment** are all used to compare two populations. The **Kruskal–Wallis test** allows us to compare two or more populations when the data are gathered from independent samples. The **Friedman test** also compares two or more populations, but it deals with data generated from the randomized block design. These tests and their parametric counterparts are summarized in Table 14.5. Because of the importance of the normal distribution in many parametric tests, two tests of normality—the **Kolmogorov–Smirnov test** and the **Lilliefors test**—were discussed in detail.

TABLE 14.5   SUMMARY OF NONPARAMETRIC TESTS

Nonparametric Test	Problem Objective	Data Scale	Parametric Counterpart
Wilcoxon rank sum test for independent samples	Comparison of two populations	Ordinal or interval	t-test of $\mu_1 - \mu_2$
Sign test	Comparison of two populations	Ordinal	—
Wilcoxon signed rank sum test for the matched pairs experiment	Comparison of two populations	Interval	t-test of μ_D
Kruskal–Wallis test for the completely randomized design	Comparison of two or more populations	Ordinal or interval	F-test in the analysis of variance
Friedman test for the randomized block design	Comparison of two or more populations	Ordinal or interval	F-test in the analysis of variance

▆▆▆▆▆▆▆   SUPPLEMENTARY EXERCISES

RET **14.56** Do collectors and noncollectors of super-market trading stamps differ in their perceptions of the importance of trading stamps in their patronage of a particular supermarket? This question was addressed by Boone, Johnson, and Ferry.* Suppose that 10 collectors and 10 noncollectors were asked to rate the importance (on a 5-point scale, where 5 = Most important and 1 = Least important) of trading stamps in their choice of a supermarket. The results are shown in the accompanying table.

Collectors	Noncollectors
1	3
2	1
5	2
1	1
3	1

* "Trading Stamps: Their Role in Today's Marketplace," *Journal of Marketing Science* 6 (1978): 71–76.

Collectors	Noncollectors
4	2
3	4
4	3
2	2
2	1

Can we conclude at the 5% level of significance that collectors perceive trading stamps as being more important than do noncollectors?

EDUC **14.57** In a study to determine which of two teaching methods is perceived to be better, two sections of an introductory marketing course were taught in two ways.† At the course's completion, each student rated the course on a boring/stimulating spectrum. In this process,

† R. W. Cook, "An Investigation of the Relationship Between Student Attitudes and Student Achievement," *Journal of the Academy of Marketing Science* 7 (1979): 71–79.

1 = Boring and 7 = Stimulating. Suppose that section 1 had 8 students, while section 2 had 10 students; the results are shown in the accompanying table.

RATINGS OF BORING/STIMULATING

Section 1	Section 2
3	5
5	3
6	4
4	3
5	4
6	6
4	2
7	2
	3
	4

Can we conclude at the 5% significance level that the ratings of the two teaching methods differ?

GEN **14.58** A rancher is trying to find which of four cattle feeds increases the weight of heifers the fastest. The four feeds are approximately equally priced. As an experiment, the rancher selects 20 heifers similar in age and weight, divides them into four groups of five heifers each, and feeds each group exclusively on feed A, B, C, or D. After several months the weight gains are measured, as reported in the accompanying table.

WEIGHT GAIN (KILOGRAMS)

Feed A	Feed B	Feed C	Feed D
100	106	88	98
105	92	95	93
112	98	106	95
98	99	99	101
102	103	98	107

If the weight gains are not normally distributed, can the rancher conclude that the weight gains from the four feeds differ from one another? (Use $\alpha = .05$.)

MNG **14.59** The solution of Exercise 9.80 required the assumption that paired differences were normally distributed. Test the assumption with $\alpha = .05$. If you conclude that there is sufficient evidence to indicate that the differences are not normally distributed, repeat Exercise 9.80, using the appropriate method.

GEN **14.60** Consumer protection groups often test products for quality, effectiveness, and safety. In a study designed to determine which paint is the best one to use under varying conditions, white paints from each of four manufacturers were used to cover a section of six walls, where the walls were originally painted black, blue, red, green, orange, and yellow. The hiding power (the ability of the paint to cover the wall without leaving any of the original color visible underneath) of each of the four white paints was evaluated by a trained technician on a 7-point scale, where 1 = Poor and 7 = Excellent. The results are shown in the accompanying table.

	Paint			
Wall Color	1	2	3	4
Black	4	3	4	2
Blue	4	5	6	2
Red	5	5	6	2
Green	6	5	6	4
Orange	6	5	7	5
Yellow	6	7	7	6

At the 5% significance level, can we conclude that there are differences in the hiding power of the four paints?

GEN **14.61** Suppose that the consumer protection group in Exercise 14.60 performed a more intensive study to determine which of the two least expensive paints is superior. Walls of 40 different colors were covered by paints 1 and 2, and a technician determined which paint hid the color underneath better. The results are as follows:

Number of wall colors where hiding power is the same	0
Number of wall colors where paint 1 is superior	13
Number of wall colors where paint 2 is superior	27

The consumer protection group would like to recommend the least expensive product (paint 1) to its members, but it won't if paint 2 can be shown to be statistically superior. Using $\alpha = .10$, what should they do?

14.62 The reaction of Europeans to U.S. and Soviet nuclear weapons–limitations plans are of great interest to both sides. Of particular interest is whether there are differences among attitudes in Great Britain, France, and West Germany. Surveys were conducted in all three countries, with the results appearing in the 7 October 1985 edition of *Newsweek*. One question asked was "How confident are you that the United States would defend Western Europe, even at the risk of nuclear attack on its own territory?" The responses of 100 people in each country are summarized in Table E14.62. In anticipation of applying a nonparametric technique, researchers ranked the data (the "Don't know" responses were omitted) and computed the rank sums. Can we conclude at the 5% significance level that there are differences in attitudes among our European allies?

14.63 Another question in the survey referred to in Exercise 14.62 asked "What is the likelihood that U.S.–Soviet hostility will escalate into a third world war?" This question was posed in 1983 and again in 1985. The results are shown in Table E14.63. For each country, the responses in 1983 and 1985 were ranked (the "Don't know" responses were omitted), and the rank sums calculated. Is there sufficient evidence at the 5% significance level that, in each of the three countries, the perceived likelihood of a third world war decreased between 1983 and 1985?

TABLE E14.62

Response	Britain	France	West Germany
Very confident (4)	16	9	9
Somewhat confident (3)	26	37	33
Not too confident (2)	33	34	34
Not at all confident (1)	24	15	18
(Don't know)	1	5	6
Rank sums	13,973	14,191	13,452

TABLE E14.63

	Britain		France		West Germany	
Response	1983	1985	1983	1985	1983	1985
Very likely (4)	20	10	7	5	10	4
Somewhat likely (3)	31	24	33	21	24	22
Not too likely (2)	27	36	37	48	38	48
Not at all likely (1)	17	28	17	23	28	23
(Don't know)	5	2	6	3	0	3
Rank sums	10,256	8,465	9,750.5	8,585.5	10,076	9,427

MNG **14.64** A computer retailer who (until several months ago) did not advertise on television decided to experiment by advertising on a local station once a week. His mean weekly gross prior to advertising was $21,500. His weekly gross for the 10 weeks since he began advertising is listed at the end of this exercise. He would like to determine whether his mean weekly gross sales have increased. Perform the Lilliefors test, with $\alpha = .01$, to determine whether the condition of normality necessary to do the *t*-test is satisfied.

22,800	25,200	19,300	21,600	23,800
20,400	22,100	20,900	23,400	25,600

RET **14.65** The owners of two downtown restaurants whose customers are mostly office workers on coffee breaks each claim to serve more coffee than the other. They decide to test their claim by counting the number of cups of coffee sold for one working week. The data are presented in the accompanying table.

	Number of Cups of Coffee Sold	
Weekday	Restaurant 1	Restaurant 2
Monday	650	640
Tuesday	420	440
Wednesday	515	500
Thursday	690	650
Friday	825	800

Can we conclude that there really is a difference between the coffee sales of the two restaurants? (Use $\alpha = .10$, and assume that the number of cups of coffee sold is not normally distributed.)

MNG **14.66** In attempting to decide which of three brands of desk calculators to purchase for a government department, the government purchasing office buys several calculators of each make and asks one operator to solve a given set of arithmetic questions of varying complexity on each machine within a 1-hour time constraint. Each set of questions is then "scored" by another operator for accuracy. The percentage correct is shown in the accompanying table.

Desk Calculator		
1	2	3
85%	93%	97%
79	83	92
87	77	89
62	85	91
87	69	90

Is there sufficient evidence to indicate differences among the desk calculators? (Use $\alpha = .01$, and assume that the accuracy scores are not normally distributed.)

POM **14.67** The researchers at a large carpet manufacturer have been experimenting with a new dyeing process in hopes of reducing the streakiness that has occurred frequently with the current process. As an experiment, eight carpets are dyed using the new process, and another eight are dyed using the existing method. Each carpet is rated on a 10-point scale of streakiness, where 1 is very bad and 10 is very good. The results are shown in the accompanying table.

New Process	Current Process
7	6
6	7
8	5
6	3
6	5
5	5
6	7
7	6

Can we conclude at the 5% significance level that the new process is superior to the old?

POM **14.68** Some of the researchers described in Exercise 14.67 felt that the color of the dye might be a factor. The experiment was rerun, using the new and current processes to dye carpets 100 different colors. For each color, a judgment was made as to which process resulted in more streakiness. These judgments are summarized as follows.

Number of carpet colors with identical streakiness	8
Number of carpet colors for which the new process resulted in more streakiness	32
Number of carpet colors for which the current process resulted in more streakiness	60

Can we conclude at the 5% significance level that the new process is superior?

SCI **14.69** In recent years, consumers have become more safety-conscious, particularly about children's products. A manufacturer of children's pajamas is looking for material that is as non-flammable as possible. In an experiment to compare a new fabric with the kind now being used, 10 pieces of each kind were exposed to an open flame, and the number of seconds until the fabric burst into flames was recorded. The results are shown in the accompanying table. Since the new material is so much more expensive than the current material, the manufacturer will switch only if the new material can be shown to be better. On the basis of these data, what should the manufacturer do? (Assume that the times are not normally distributed, and use $\alpha = .05$.)

IGNITING TIME (seconds)

New Fabric	Old Fabric
28	31
33	35
39	29
36	37
38	36
32	28
39	38
37	36
35	30
37	39

PG **14.70** The American public's support for the space program is important for that program's continuation and for the financial health of the aerospace industry. In a poll conducted by the Gallup Organization and reported in *Newsweek* (10 February 1984), a random sample of Americans were asked "Should the amount of money being spent on the U.S. space program be increased, kept at current levels, decreased, or ended altogether?" The survey was conducted again in January 1986. The results for respondents who expressed an opinion are shown in the accompanying table. The data were ranked, and the rank sums are also shown in the table.

Preferred Funding Level	February 1984	January 1986
Increased (4)	22	27
Same (3)	49	53
Decreased (2)	24	15
Ended (1)	5	5
Rank sums	9,544	10,556

Can we conclude at the 10% significance level that the level of support has increased between 1984 and 1986?

SCI **14.71** The captain of a firefighter training course conducts a test to determine which of five squads of trainees is the fastest at extinguishing a given fire situation. Each squad is presented with four different types of fire, and the times each take to extinguish the fires are as shown in the accompanying table.

EXTINGUISHING TIME (seconds)

	Squad				
Type of Fire	1	2	3	4	5
1	45	51	54	41	50
2	48	39	50	38	40
3	37	38	43	36	33
4	34	44	39	39	34

If the captain believes that the times are not normally distributed, can he conclude at the 10% significance level that there are differences among the five squads?

POM **14.72** A locksmith is in the process of selecting a new key-cutting machine. If there are no differences in key-cutting speed between the two machines under consideration, she will simply purchase the cheaper machine. The times required to cut each of the 10 most common types of keys are shown in the following table. The locksmith has analyzed the times and has determined that they are not normally distributed. At the 5% significance level, what should she do?

CUTTING TIME (seconds)

Key Type	Machine A	B
1	20	18
2	29	29
3	16	18
4	19	23
5	31	38
6	44	48
7	29	34
8	14	15
9	12	16
10	35	36

RET **14.73** The owner of a chain of hamburger outlets wishes to reduce the number of different types of hamburger offered from four to three. Wanting to drop the least popular type of hamburger, the owner monitors the number of burgers sold at each of eight outlets over a certain test period. These data are shown in the accompanying table. Assuming that the number of hamburgers sold is not normally distributed, can the owner conclude at the 10% significance level that there are differences in sales among the four types of hamburger?

Outlet	Hamburger Type 1	2	3	4
1	488	562	412	492
2	512	542	476	565
3	600	597	458	712
4	740	628	563	883
5	726	812	612	941
6	782	776	676	812
7	694	621	655	861
8	606	538	675	723

POM **14.74** The printing department of a publishing company wants to determine whether there are differences in durability among four types of book bindings. Five books are selected with each type of binding and are placed in a machine that continually opens and closes them. Shown in the accompanying table are the number of book openings before the pages separated from the binding. Assuming that the data are not normally distributed, can we conclude with $\alpha = .05$ that there are differences in durability among the four types of binding?

NUMBER OF OPENINGS

Binding 1	2	3	4
2694	2645	3271	2608
2890	2966	3056	2852
2766	2688	2985	2733
2855	2901	3061	2549
3023	2863	3100	2621

MKT **14.75** The marketing manager of a large ski resort wants to advertise that his ski resort has the shortest lift lines of any resort in the area. To avoid the possibility of a false advertising liability suit, he collects data on the average wait in line at his resort and at each of two competing resorts on each of 15 days. These results are shown next. Assuming that waiting times are not normally distributed, can he conclude that there are differences in waiting times among the three resorts? (Use $\alpha = .05$.)

Average Wait (minutes)

Day	Home Resort	Competitor 1	Competitor 2
1	7	4	7
2	4	9	11
3	10	9	12
4	8	9	10
5	8	11	14
6	11	6	15
7	4	8	7
8	11	7	16
9	8	6	10
10	3	9	5
11	2	5	8

Average Wait (minutes)

Day	Home Resort	Competitor 1	Competitor 2
12	2	4	5
13	6	9	8
14	7	9	6
15	8	7	6

MKT **14.76** An advertising firm wants to determine the relative effectiveness of two recently produced commercials for a car dealership. An important attribute of such commercials is their believability. In order to judge this aspect of the commercials, 45 people were randomly selected. Each watched both commercials and then rated them on a 7-point scale where $1 = $ Not believable and $7 = $ Very believable. The ratings are shown in Table E14.76. Do these data provide sufficient evidence at the 5% significance level to indicate that there are differences in believability between the two commercials?

TABLE E14.76

Respondent	Commercial A	Commercial B	Respondent	Commercial A	Commercial B	Respondent	Commercial A	Commercial B
1	2	5	16	4	2	31	6	3
2	6	3	17	6	2	32	7	5
3	5	5	18	3	1	33	4	4
4	7	5	19	3	2	34	5	4
5	3	2	20	6	4	35	5	3
6	7	6	21	4	3	36	6	4
7	7	7	22	5	5	37	7	7
8	6	4	23	7	4	38	7	6
9	4	5	24	4	1	39	6	4
10	3	1	25	1	5	40	3	4
11	3	4	26	4	4	41	2	5
12	5	5	27	4	3	42	4	2
13	6	4	28	2	1	43	5	3
14	2	4	29	1	2	44	1	3
15	1	5	30	3	2	45	2	1

GEN **14.77** The manager of a dry-cleaning chain wants to determine whether there are differences among three outlets in terms of the number of comebacks (garments returned for recleaning) they experience. She was able to collect the following data, which show the number of comebacks per 1,000 garments cleaned. Assuming that the number of comebacks is not normally distributed, can the manager conclude, with $\alpha = .10$, that differences exist among the three outlets?

	Outlet		
Month	1	2	3
June	36	37	48
July	48	52	56
Aug.	21	28	40
Sept.	11	21	23
Oct.	24	24	19
Nov.	29	48	27
Dec.	39	21	44

SCI **14.78** Large potential profits for pharmaceutical companies exist in the area of hair-growth drugs. The head chemist for a large pharmaceutical company is conducting experiments to determine which of two new drugs is more effective in growing hair among balding men. One experiment was conducted as follows. A total of 30 pairs of men—each pair of which were matched according to their degree of baldness—were selected. One man used drug *A*, and the other used drug *B*. After 10 weeks, the men's new hair growth was examined, and for each pair one of the following three determinations was made:

1. There was no difference in hair growth between the two men (N)

2. The man who used drug *A* had greater hair growth (A).

3. The man who used drug *B* had greater hair growth (B).

The results are shown in the following table. At the 5% significance level, do these data provide sufficient evidence that drug *B* is more effective?

Pair	Outcome	Pair	Outcome	Pair	Outcome
1	B	11	A	21	B
2	B	12	B	22	B
3	N	13	B	23	A
4	A	14	B	24	B
5	A	15	B	25	B
6	B	16	A	26	B
7	B	17	B	27	N
8	B	18	A	28	A
9	N	19	B	29	B
10	A	20	B	30	B

SCI **14.79** Suppose that a precise measuring device for new hair growth has been developed and is used in the experiment described in Exercise 14.78. The percentages of new hair growth for the 30 pairs of men involved in the experiment are shown in the accompanying table. Do these data allow the chemist to conclude, with $\alpha = .05$, that drug *B* is more effective? (Note that the chemist has determined that the percentages are not normally distributed.)

PERCENTAGE OF NEW HAIR GROWTH

	Drug			**Drug**			**Drug**	
Pair	*A*	*B*	**Pair**	*A*	*B*	**Pair**	*A*	*B*
1	3.5	7.1	11	2.0	1.8	21	4.0	6.7
2	2.4	6.6	12	5.6	6.9	22	3.5	6.8
3	4.2	4.2	13	4.3	6.8	23	3.1	3.0
4	1.1	1.0	14	7.1	7.9	24	6.0	9.0
5	2.9	2.7	15	3.8	6.2	25	5.3	8.4
6	2.8	4.1	16	3.6	3.5	26	2.6	4.1
7	5.6	8.3	17	4.2	7.3	27	4.8	4.8
8	4.8	8.8	18	2.8	2.7	28	2.2	1.8
9	0.8	0.8	19	6.1	9.5	29	4.2	5.6
10	3.6	3.4	20	3.7	6.2	30	0.8	2.2

■■■■■■■ **CASE 14.1*   *CAPITALIZATION RATIOS IN THE UNITED STATES***
AND JAPAN

We recommend the use of a computer for this case. The data listed below are also stored on the data disk.

FIN

Firms raise funds to finance their operations by issuing debt to lenders and by issuing equity to shareholders. If the amount of debt employed by a firm is high relative to its amount of equity, the firm is said to have a high degree of financial leverage. One measure of a firm's leverage is its *capitalization ratio*–the ratio of the value of a firm's equity to the total value of its equity plus debt. The smaller a firm's capitalization ratio is, the more highly levered the firm is. The size of the capitalization ratio, however, depends on whether its computation is based on the (accounting) book value of equity or the market value of equity.

In a study comparing the leverage of American and Japanese firms, Michel and Shaked computed the capitalization ratios for a sample of American firms and for a sample of Japanese firms, using both book values and market values of equity. As expected, they observed that the shapes of the distributions of capitalization ratios differed between American and Japanese firms. For example, the distribution of book value–based capitalization ratios was reasonably symmetrical for American firms, while the corresponding distribution for Japanese firms exhibited considerable negative skewness. Michel and Shaked were primarily interested in

TABLE A   *BOOK VALUE–BASED CAPITALIZATION RATIOS*

Industry	U.S.A.	Japan
1	.582	.484
2	.597	.435
3	.485	.435
4	.476	.393
5	.435	.353
6	.483	.288
7	.428	.288
8	.392	.182
9	.433	.174
10	.400	.140

* Adapted from Allen Michel and Israel Shaked, "Japanese Leverage: Myth or Reality?" *Financial Analysts Journal* 41 (1985): 61–67.

TABLE B *MARKET VALUE–BASED CAPITALIZATION RATIOS*

Industry	U.S.A.	Japan
1	.734	.654
2	.625	.662
3	.452	.662
4	.499	.546
5	.414	.495
6	.458	.390
7	.372	.390
8	.388	.262
9	.438	.252
10	.275	.226

testing "the commonly held belief among Japanese businessmen, Japanese government officials, and the investment community worldwide that Japanese firms on average are more highly levered than their American counterparts."

From each of 10 industries, Michel and Shaked selected a sample of 13 American firms and 13 Japanese firms. The average book value–based capitalization ratios that were computed for each of the 10 industries, for 1981, are shown in Table A. Table B presents similar information, using market value–based capitalization ratios. What would you conclude from a comparison of these ratios?

CASE 14.2*   *SURVEY OF DEMOCRATS IN 1988*
PRESIDENTIAL CAMPAIGN

This case requires the use of a computer. The data are not shown below but are stored on the data disk.

PG   During the 1988 presidential campaign, the Gallup Organization surveyed a random sample of 200 registered Democrats in January, another 200 in February, and yet another 200 in March. All 600 Democrats were asked to "rate the chances of the Democrats winning the presidential race in your state." The responses and their numerical codes were Excellent (4), Good (3), Fair (2), and Poor (1).

The data from the March, February, and January surveys are stored on the data disk in the format below. What conclusions can be drawn from these results?

---

* SOURCE: *Newsweek* (28 March 1988).

SURVEY RESULTS (THE "DON'T KNOW" RESPONSES HAVE BEEN OMITTED)

March 1988 ($n = 200$)	February 1988 ($n = 196$)	January 1988 ($n = 194$)
2	1	2
2	2	3
3	3	3
⋮	⋮	⋮
3	4	2

■ **CASE 14.3   *TRAVELING BUSINESSMEN AND BUSINESSWOMEN***

This case requires the use of a computer. The data listed below are also stored on the data disk.

> **GEN**   The increasing number of traveling businesswomen represents a large potential clientele for the hotel industry. Many hotel chains have made changes designed to attract more women (*Wall Street Journal*, 14 October 1988). To help direct these changes, a hotel chain commissioned a study to determine whether there are major differences between male and female business travelers. A total of 100 male and 100 female executives were questioned on a variety of topics, one of which was the number of trips they had taken in the previous 12 months.

The results are listed in Tables A and B. What conclusions can we draw regarding any differences between male and female executives' business trips?

TABLE A   *NUMBER OF TRIPS OF 100 BUSINESSMEN*

1	0	1	0	6	3	0	2	0	5	4	4	3	0	0
4	2	3	3	4	1	0	2	2	0	5	2	1	2	5
4	1	2	0	4	1	5	4	6	5	0	1	1	3	6
1	1	2	3	3	4	4	5	4	0	3	0	5	3	0
1	0	0	0	6	1	3	1	2	4	0	3	2	1	2
3	3	1	4	5	1	1	1	2	0	3	6	6	2	1
3	1	0	2	0	0	0	3	0	4					

TABLE B		*NUMBER OF TRIPS OF 100 BUSINESSWOMEN*												

0	3	0	0	3	3	0	3	2	2	3	1	4	0	0
2	3	0	0	4	3	3	0	4	0	2	2	0	4	2
0	2	1	2	4	2	1	2	3	1	1	0	3	0	0
1	2	0	0	1	0	1	4	1	1	2	2	0	0	3
0	0	2	4	2	4	3	0	1	0	3	1	3	3	1
2	1	1	1	4	4	3	1	2	1	4	2	1	3	2
1	1	4	1	2	1	4	0	3	4					

▬▬▬▬▬ CASE 14.4* CUSTOMERS' PERCEPTIONS OF SALESWOMEN

This case requires the use of a computer. The data are not shown below but are stored on the data disk.

[RET]   The number of women entering the workforce each year has been growing. Various studies have compared the performance of men and women in different settings. In 1983, Lundstrom and Ashworth examined how saleswomen in the automobile sales industry were perceived by male and female shoppers. If saleswomen are perceived differently by male and female shoppers, there may be significant advantages to assigning salespeople to customers according to these perceptions.

Suppose that, in this study, responses were obtained from 103 male and 80 female shoppers. Each was asked to evaluate automobile saleswomen on a 7-point scale, with respect to the following dimensions:

Calm/Excitable   (1 = Excitable; 7 = Calm)
Competent/Incompetent   (1 = Incompetent; 7 = Competent)
Intelligent/Unintelligent (1 = Unintelligent; 7 = Intelligent)
Honest/Dishonest   (1 = Dishonest; 7 = Honest)

The results of the survey are stored on the data disk using the following format. What conclusion can we draw about the relative perception of saleswomen by male and female shoppers?

---

* Adapted from W. J. Lundstrom and D. N. Ashworth, "Customers' Perceptions of the Sales Woman: A Study of Personality Task and Evaluative Attributes by Respondent Location and Gender," *Journal of the Academy of Marketing Science* 11(1, 2) (1983): 114–22.

TABLE A   MALE SHOPPERS' PERCEPTIONS

Shopper	Evaluations			
	Calmness	Competence	Intelligence	Honesty
1	3	4	5	5
2	4	5	5	6
3	4	4	5	6
⋮	⋮	⋮	⋮	⋮
103	4	5	6	7

TABLE B   FEMALE SHOPPERS' PERCEPTIONS

Shopper	Evaluations			
	Calmness	Competence	Intelligence	Honesty
1	5	5	7	7
2	2	5	6	5
3	4	5	6	7
⋮	⋮	⋮	⋮	⋮
80	6	7	6	5

MINITAB INSTRUCTIONS

The Minitab system allows us to perform the Wilcoxon rank sum test for independent samples, the sign test, the Wilcoxon signed rank sum for matched pairs, and the Kruskal–Wallis test.

WILCOXON RANK SUM TEST FOR INDEPENDENT SAMPLES

Minitab performs the Mann–Whitney test, rather than the Wilcoxon test. Nonetheless, the command

```
MANN WHITNEY C1 C2
```

will calculate a value of W, which is the rank sum of the sample stored in column 1. If we input the smaller sample size in column 1, then W will equal T_A, the value of the test statistic for the Wilcoxon test. The output includes the p-value of a two-tail test. To perform Example 14.2, we proceed in the following way.

```
SET C1
4   3   4   2   2   3   2   3   4   5
END
SET C2
6   4   5   7   3   6   4   3   5   4
END
MANN WHITNEY C1 C2
```

The resulting output is

```
C1   N=10   MEDIAN=3.0000
C2   N=10   MEDIAN=4.5000
POINT ESTIMATE FOR ETA1-ETA2 IS -0.9999
```

```
95.5 PCT C.I. FOR ETA1-ETA2 IS (-2.99, 0.00)
W=74.5
TEST OF ETA1=ETA2 VS ETA1 N.E. ETA2 IS SIGNIFICANT AT 0.0233
```

SIGN TEST

We begin to perform the sign test by computing the paired differences, using

```
LET C3=C1-C2
```

The required statistics are then produced by

```
STEST   0   C3
```

which actually tests the median to determine whether it is different from zero. As in earlier chapters, a one-tail test can be performed with the ALTERNATIVE subcommand. Example 14.5 is solved by inputting

```
SET C1
6   9   4   7   8   5   4   5   8   3   4   9   5   7   7
4   2   7   4   4   6   9   3   7   7   5   4   6   5   2
END
SET C2
7   5   5   7   9   7   6   4   9   6   8   9   6   4   6
5   3   8   6   7   8   7   4   8   4   2   1   8   9   4
END
LET C3=C1-C2
STEST   0   C3;
ALTERNATIVE -1.
```

This causes Minitab to print

```
SIGN TEST OF MEDIAN=0 VERSUS L.T.  0
        N    BELOW    EQUAL    ABOVE    P-VALUE    MEDIAN
C3     30     20        2        8      0.0178    -1.000
```

WILCOXON SIGNED RANK SUM TEST FOR MATCHED PAIRS

To apply the Wilcoxon signed rank sum test, we proceed as we did in the sign test. We first create the paired differences, using

```
LET C3=C1-C2
```

The statistic T^+ is then generated by the command

```
WTEST C3
```

The WTEST command actually tests the median to determine whether or not it's equal to zero. When C3 represents paired differences, however, the WTEST command performs the Wilcoxon signed rank sum test.

A one-tail test can be performed by using the ALTERNATIVE subcommand. To illustrate, we perform Example 14.7, as follows:

```
READ C1 C2
42.6 43.8
37.2 41.3
50.0 49.7
43.9 45.7
53.6 52.5
32.5 36.8
46.5 47.0
39.3 40.7
END
LET C3=C1-C2
WTEST C3;
ALTERNATIVE -1.
```

The resulting output is

```
TEST OF MEDIAN=0 VERSUS MEDIAN L.T. 0
           N FOR     WILCOXON                   ESTIMATED
      N    TEST      STATISTIC    P-VALUE        MEDIAN
C3    8    8            4.0        0.029          -1.450
```

KRUSKAL–WALLIS TEST

The command

```
KRUSKAL WALLIS C1 C2
```

calculates the *H*-statistic from stacked data. The observations are stored in column 1, and the sample number from which each observation was drawn is stored in column 2. The information and command input for Example 14.9 is as follows:

```
READ C1 C2
15.5 1
17.2 1
13.3 1
20.6 1
19.2 1
20.5 2
18.3 2
21.2 2
15.7 2
16.3 2
```

```
13.3  3
18.9  3
19.5  3
15.2  3
13.8  3
END
KRUSKAL WALLIS C1 C2
```

The resulting output is

```
LEVEL     NOBS    MEDIAN    AVE. RANK    Z VALUE
  1         5      17.20       7.9        -0.06
  2         5      18.30      10.00        1.22
  3         5      15.20       6.1        -1.16
OVERALL    15                  8.0

H=1.905
H(ADJ FOR TIES)=1.908
```

SAS INSTRUCTIONS

WILCOXON RANK SUM TEST FOR INDEPENDENT SAMPLES AND THE KRUSKAL–WALLIS TEST

The procedure NPAR1WAY WILCOXON (that's a numeral one between NPAR and WAY) provides the nonparametric technique for independent samples. When only two populations are being compared, this technique performs the Wilcoxon rank sum test for independent samples. When more than two populations are involved, it performs the Kruskal–Wallis test. Two variables are input: the first represents the observations of all the samples; and the second identifies the sample that each observation came from. In Example 14.2, the following entries are made from the keyboard:

```
DATA;
INPUT    X    SAMPLE;
CARDS;
4        1
3        1
4        1
2        1
2        1
3        1
2        1
3        1
4        1
5        1
6        2
4        2
5        2
7        2
3        2
6        2
4        2
3        2
```

```
5       2
4       2
PROC NPAR1WAY WILCOXON;
CLASS SAMPLE;
VAR X;
```

The resulting output is

```
            Wilcoxon Scores (Rank Sums) for Variable X
                   Classified by Variable SAMPLE


                    Sum of    Expected    Std Dev     Mean
SAMPLE     N        Scores    Under HO    Under HO    Score
1          10      74.5000     105.0      12.9065    7.4500
2          10     135.5000     105.0      12.9065   13.5500
                Average Scores were used for Ties
Wilcoxon 2-Sample Test (Normal Approximation)
(with Continuity Correction of .5)


S=74.5000    Z=-2.3244    Prob > |Z|=0.0201


Kruskal-Wallis Test (Chi-Square Approximation)
CHISQ=5.5844    DF=1    Prob > CHISQ=0.0181
```

We solve for Example 14.9 as follows:

```
DATA;
INPUT X SAMPLE;
CARDS;
15.5   1
17.2   1
13.3   1
20.6   1
19.2   1
20.5   2
18.3   2
21.2   2
15.7   2
16.3   2
13.3   3
18.9   3
19.5   3
15.2   3
13.8   3
PROC NPAR1WAY WILCOXON;
CLASS SAMPLE;
VAR X;
```

The resulting output is

```
            Wilcoxon Scores (Rank Sums) for Variable X
                  Classified by Variable SAMPLE


               Sum of    Expected    Std Dev      Mean
SAMPLE    N    Scores    Under HO    Under HO     Score
1         5   39.5000      40.0       8.1576     7.9000
2         5   50.0000      40.0       8.1576    10.0000
3         5   30.5000      40.0       8.1576     6.1000
            Average Scores were used for Ties


Kruskal-Wallis Test (Chi-Square Approximation)
CHISQ=1.9084    DF=2    Prob > CHISQ=0.3851
```

WILCOXON SIGNED RANK SUM TEST FOR MATCHED PAIRS

The UNIVARIATE procedure described in Chapter 2 performs this test (as well as computing a variety of other statistics). As is the case with the *t*-test of μ_D (Chapter 9), we input the data and then calculate the paired differences. The UNIVARIATE procedure is applied to the differences. Example 14.7 is solved in the following way.

```
DATA;
INPUT X1 X2;
D=X1-X2;
CARDS;
42.6   43.8
37.2   41.3
50.0   49.7
43.9   45.7
53.6   52.5
32.5   36.8
46.5   47.0
39.3   40.7
PROC UNIVARIATE;
VAR D;
```

Part of the output is shown below.

```
Variable=D          Moments


N                  8
Mean         -1.4875    Sum           -11.9
Std Dev     1.919403    Variance    3.684107
Sgn Rank         -14    Prob >|S|     0.0547
```

COMPUTER EXERCISES

14.80 Use the Wilcoxon rank sum test for independent samples (with $\alpha = .05$) to determine whether the following data indicate that the population locations differ.

A	B
17	31
21	16
11	20
19	25
23	28
	18

14.81 The following independent samples were drawn from two nonnormal populations. Can we conclude at the 5% significance level that the location of population *A* is to the right of the location of population *B*?

A	B
103	84
81	79
99	89
115	71
86	68
88	75
101	98
116	
99	

14.82 The data that follow represent observations of an ordinal-scaled variable drawn from two populations by a matched pairs experiment. At the 5% significance level, can we conclude that the location of population *B* is to the right of the location of population *A*?

Pair	A	B	Pair	A	B	Pair	A	B
1	3	5	10	8	12	19	4	6
2	8	11	11	9	12	20	8	9
3	12	10	12	8	6	21	4	3
4	8	9	13	11	12	22	7	8
5	6	8	14	10	8	23	7	3
6	6	8	15	6	9	24	6	8
7	9	11	16	9	11	25	9	8
8	5	4	17	6	12	26	10	12
9	4	8	18	5	10	27	2	10

14.83 What conclusion would you draw in Exercise 14.82 if you were told that the data are interval-scaled but nonnormally distributed?

14.84 Given the following interval-scaled observations drawn from two nonnormal populations by means of a matched pairs experiment, test at the 1% significance level to determine whether the two population locations differ.

Pair	A	B
1	20.3	16.4
2	25.7	21.8
3	19.6	20.1
4	18.4	18.3
5	22.8	20.9
6	16.3	16.5
7	14.9	13.1
8	21.8	19.3
9	23.0	22.8
10	18.0	17.9

14.85 Use the Kruskal–Wallis test, with $\alpha = .10$, to determine whether differences in locations exist among the following four populations.

1	2	3	4
6.3	7.1	6.4	5.5
7.9	8.9	6.2	6.9
4.4	8.8	4.9	6.3
8.6	11.2	7.1	4.9
9.3	9.3	6.9	4.6
5.2		6.4	

14.86 The following observations were drawn from three nonnormal populations. Can we conclude at the 5% significance level that at least two population locations differ?

1	2	3
56	58	73
41	71	61
59	63	74
73	51	69
46	60	78

SOLUTIONS TO SELF-CORRECTING EXERCISES

14.8 H_0: The two population locations are the same.

H_A: The location of population A is to the left of the location of population B.

Rejection region: $T \leq 83$

A: Exercise	Ranks	B: No Exercise	Ranks
403	15	229	10
38	2	99	5
0	1	385	14
55	3	526	19
121	7	415	16
354	12	367	13
183	8	504	18
106	6	298	11
95	4	601	20
210	9	422	17
	$T_A = \quad 67$		$T_B = \quad 143$

Test statistic: $T = 67$

Conclusion: Reject H_0.

Companies that provide exercise programs should be given discounts.

14.16 H_0: The two population locations are the same.

H_A: The location of population A is to the left of the location of population B.

Rejection region: $z < -1.28$

Test statistic: $x = 12 \qquad n = 37$

$$z = \frac{x - .5n}{.5\sqrt{n}} = \frac{12 - 18.5}{3.04} = -2.14$$

Conclusion: Reject H_0.

There is enough evidence to allow us to conclude that concern about a gasoline shortage exceeds concern about an electricity shortage.

14.26 H_0: The two population locations are the same.

H_A: The location of population A is to the left of the location of population B.

Rejection region: $T \leq 6$

A: PG-13	B: R	$D = A - B$	$\lvert D \rvert$	Ranks	
326	358	-32	32	7	
413	425	-12	12	4	
258	244	14	14		5
127	125	2	2		1
379	502	-123	123	8	
205	221	-16	16	6	
428	433	-5	5	2	
307	315	-8	8	3	
				$T^- = 30$	$T^+ = 6$

Conclusion: Reject H_0.

The data provide enough evidence to support the belief that sexually explicit scenes increase movies' appeal.

14.36 H_0: The locations of all four populations are the same.

H_A: At least two population locations differ.

Rejection region: $H > 6.25139$

1	Ranks	2	Ranks	3	Ranks	4	Ranks
17	11	12	6	19	14	12	6
25	17.5	23	16	29	21.5	10	3
19	14	19	14	31	23	11	4
12	6	26	19.5	26	19.5	6	1
14	9	18	12	29	21.5	8	2
16	10	25	17.5	33	24	13	8
	$T_1 = 67.5$		$T_2 = 85$		$T_3 = 123.5$		$T_4 = 24$

$$H = \left[\frac{12}{24(25)} \left(\frac{67.5^2}{6} + \frac{85^2}{6} + \frac{123.5^2}{6} + \frac{24^2}{6} \right) \right]$$
$$- 3(25) = 17.03$$

Conclusion: Reject H_0.

There are differences in speed of performance among the brands.

14.46 H_0: The locations of all three populations are the same.

H_A: At least two population locations differ.

Rejection region: $F_r > 5.99147$

1	Ranks	2	Ranks	3	Ranks
14	2	17	3	12	1
8	2	9	3	6	1
25	3	20	1	23	2
12	2	15	3	10	1
7	2	10	3	5	1
5	2	9	3	4	1
	$T_1 = 13$		$T_2 = 16$		$T_3 = 7$

$$F_r = \left[\frac{12}{(6)(3)(4)}(13^2 + 16^2 + 7^2) \right] - 3(6)(4) = 7.0$$

Conclusion: Reject H_0.

Differences in ability to attract potential employees exist among the newspapers.

SIMPLE LINEAR REGRESSION AND CORRELATION

INTRODUCTION

This chapter is the first in a series of three in which the problem objective is to analyze the relationship among interval-scaled variables. The statistical technique that is developed is called *regression analysis.*

One of the reasons for the importance of regression, particularly in business and economics applications, is that it can be used to forecast variables. As you can easily appreciate, almost all companies and governmental institutions frequently forecast variables such as product demand, interest rates, inflation rates, prices of raw materials, and labor costs. While several different forecasting techniques can be used, regression analysis is one of the most popular (some other techniques are discussed in Chapter 19).

The technique involves developing a mathematical equation that analyzes the relationship between the variable to be forecast and variables that the statistician believes are related to the forecast variable. The variable to be forecast is called the **dependent variable** and is denoted y, while the related variables are called **independent variables** and are denoted $x_1, x_2, \ldots, x_k$ (where k is the number of independent variables). The first step is to identify the independent variables to be used in the analysis. The following examples illustrate this process.

Case 1. The product manager in charge of a particular brand of children's breakfast cereal would like to predict the demand for it during the next year. In order to use regression analysis, he and his staff list the following variables as likely to affect sales:

> Price of the product
>
> Number of children 5 to 12 years of age (the target market)
>
> Price of the competitor's products
>
> Effectiveness of advertising (as measured by advertising exposure)
>
> Annual sales this year
>
> Annual sales in previous years

Case 2. A gold speculator is considering making a major purchase of gold bullion. He would like to forecast the price of gold 2 years from now (his planning horizon), using the regression technique. In preparation, he produces the following list of independent variables:

> Interest rates
>
> Inflation rate

Price of oil

Demand for gold jewelry

Demand for industrial and commercial gold

Dow Jones Industrial Average

Case 3. A real estate agent wants to more accurately predict the selling price of houses. She believes that the following variables affect the price of a house.

Size of the house

Number of bedrooms

Frontage of the lot

Condition

Location

In each of the preceding examples, the primary motive for using regression is forecasting. Nonetheless, analyzing the relationships among variables can also be quite helpful in managerial decision making. For instance, in the first application, the product manager may wish to know how price is related to product demand so that a decision about a prospective change in pricing can be made.

Another application comes from the field of finance. The capital asset pricing model analyzes the relationship between the returns of a particular stock and the behavior of a stock index (such as Standard and Poor's 500). Its function is not to predict the stock's price, but to assess the risk of that stock versus the risk of the stock market in general.

Regardless of why the regression analysis is performed, the next step in the technique is to develop a mathematical equation or model that accurately describes the nature of the relationship that exists between the dependent variable and the independent variables. This stage—which is only a small part of the total project—is described in the next section. In the ensuing sections of this chapter (and in Chapters 16 and 17), we will spend considerable time assessing and testing how well the model fits actual data. Only when we're satisfied that the model is relatively good will we use it to estimate and forecast.

SECTION 15.2 **MODEL**

The job of developing a mathematical equation can be quite complex, since we need to have some idea about the nature of the relationship between each of the independent variables and the dependent variable. For example, the gold speculator mentioned in case 2 needs to know how interest rates affect the price of gold. If he proposes a linear relationship, that may imply that, as interest rates rise (or fall), the price of gold will rise or fall. A quadratic relationship may suggest that the price of gold will increase over a certain range of interest rates but will decrease over a different range. Perhaps certain combinations of values of interest rates and other independent variables influence the price in one way, while other combinations change it in other ways. The number of different mathematical models that could be proposed is virtually infinite.

You may have encountered various models in previous courses. For instance, the following represent relationships in the natural sciences.

$E = mc^2$, where E = Energy, m = Mass, and c = Speed of light

$F = ma$, where F = Force, m = Mass, and a = Acceleration

$S = at^2/2$, where S = Distance, t = Time, and a = Gravitational acceleration

In other business courses you may have seen

Profit = Revenue − Costs

Total cost = Fixed cost + (Variable cost × Number of units produced)

All of the above are examples of **deterministic** models, so named because—except for small measurement errors—such an equation allows us to determine the value of the dependent variable (on the left side of the equation) from the value of the independent variables. In many practical applications of interest to us, deterministic models are unrealistic. For example, is it reasonable to believe that we can determine the selling price of a house solely on the basis of its size? Unquestionably the size of a house affects its price, but many other variables (some of which may not be measurable) also influence price. What must be included in most practical models is a method to represent the randomness that is part of a real-life process. Such a model is called **probabilistic**. To create a probabilistic model, we start with a deterministic model that approximates the relationship we wish to model. We then add a random term that measures the error of the deterministic component. For example, suppose that, in case 3 described earlier, the real estate agent knows that the cost of building a new house is about $40 per square foot and that most lots sell for about $10,000. The approximate selling price would be

$$y = 10{,}000 + 40x$$

where y = Selling price and x = Size of the house in square feet. A house of 2,000 square feet would therefore be estimated to sell for

$$y = 10{,}000 + 40(2{,}000) = \$90{,}000$$

We know, however, that the selling price is not likely to be exactly $90,000. Prices may actually range from $70,000 to $200,000. In other words, the deterministic model is not really suitable. To represent this situation properly, we should use the probabilistic model

$$y = 10{,}000 + 40x + \varepsilon$$

where ε (the Greek letter epsilon) represents the random term—the difference between the actual selling price and the estimated price based on the size of the house. The random term thus accounts for all of the variables—measurable and unmeasurable—that are not part of the model.

In the three chapters devoted to regression analysis (Chapters 15, 16, and 17), we will only present probabilistic models. Additionally, to simplify the presentation, all models will be linear. In this chapter, we restrict the number of independent variables to one. The model to be used in this chapter is called the *first-order linear model*—sometimes called the *simple linear regression model.*

First-Order Linear Model

$$y = \beta_0 + \beta_1 x + \varepsilon$$

where

y = Dependent variable

x = Independent variable

β_0 = y-intercept

β_1 = Slope of the line (defined as the ratio Rise/Run)

ε = Random error term

Figure 15.1 depicts the deterministic component of the model.

The problem objective addressed by the model is to analyze the relationship between two variables, x and y, both of which must have interval scales. To define the relationship between x and y, we need to know the value of the coefficients of the linear model β_0 and β_1. However, these coefficients are population parameters, which are almost always unknown. In the next section, we will discuss how they are estimated.

FIGURE 15.1   *FIRST-ORDER LINEAR MODEL: DETERMINISTIC COMPONENT*

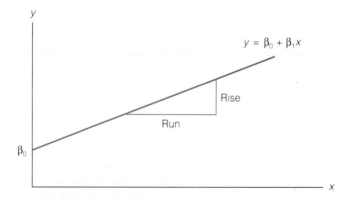

15.1   Graph each of the following straight lines. Identify the intercept and the slope on the graph.

a. $y = 2 + 3x$

b. $y = 5 - 2x$

c. $y = -2 + 4x$

d. $y = x$

e. $y = 4$

15.2   For each of the following data sets, plot the points on a graph to determine whether the first-order linear model is reasonable.

a. x   2   3   5   7   9
   y   6   9   4   7   8

b. x   1   3   5   4   7
   y   5   7   10   9   16

c. x   7   9   2   3   6
   y   4   1   6   10   5

15.3   Graph the following observations of x and y.

x   1   2   3   4   5   6
y   4   6   7   7   9   11

Draw a straight line through the data. What are the intercept and the slope of the line you drew?

SECTION 15.3   *LEAST SQUARES METHOD*

We estimate the parameters β_0 and β_1 in a way similar to the methods used to estimate all the other parameters discussed in this book. We draw a random sample from the populations of interest and calculate the sample statistics that we need. Because β_0 and β_1 represent the coefficients of a straight line, their estimators are based on drawing a straight line through the sample data. To see how this is done, consider the following example.

■■■■■■■■   **EXAMPLE 15.1**

Given the following six observations of variables x and y, determine the straight line that fits these data.

x	y
2	50
4	38
8	26
10	25
13	7
16	2

Solution.   As a first step we graph the data, as shown in Figure 15.2. This graph is called a **scatter diagram** or a **scattergram**. The scattergram usually reveals whether

FIGURE 15.2   *SCATTERGRAM FOR EXAMPLE 15.1*

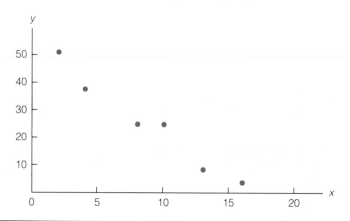

or not a straight line model fits the data reasonably well. Evidently, in this case a linear model is justified. However, notice that the points do not align themselves perfectly in a straight line. Our task is to draw a straight line that provides the *best possible fit.*

We can define what we mean by *best* in various ways. For example, we can draw the line that minimizes the sum of the differences between the line and the points. Because some of the differences will be positive (points above the line) and others will be negative (points below the line), however, a canceling effect may produce a straight line that does not fit the data at all. To eliminate the positive and negative differences, we will draw the line that minimizes the sum of the squared differences. That is, we wish to minimize

$$\sum_{i=1}^{n} (y_i - \hat{y}_i)^2$$

where y_i represents the observed value of y and $\hat{y}_i$ represents the value of y calculated from the line. That is,

$$\hat{y}_i = \hat{\beta}_0 + \hat{\beta}_1 x_i$$

The technique that produces this line is called the **least squares method**. The line itself is called the **least squares line**, the **fitted line**, or the **regression line**. The hats on the coefficients remind us that they are estimators of the parameters β_0 and β_1.

By using calculus, we can produce formulas for $\hat{\beta}_0$ and $\hat{\beta}_1$. Although we know that you're keenly interested in the details of the calculus operation, we will not provide them, since we promised to keep the mathematics to a minimum. Instead, we offer the following formulas derived by calculus.

Calculation of $\hat{\beta}_0$ and $\hat{\beta}_1$

$$\hat{\beta}_1 = \frac{SS_{xy}}{SS_x}$$

where

$$SS_{xy} = \sum(x_i - \bar{x})(y_i - \bar{y}) = \sum x_i y_i - \frac{(\sum x_i)(\sum y_i)}{n}$$

and

$$SS_x = \sum(x_i - \bar{x})^2 = \sum x_i^2 - \frac{(\sum x_i)^2}{n}$$

$$\hat{\beta}_0 = \bar{y} - \hat{\beta}_1 \bar{x}$$

where

$$\bar{y} = \frac{\sum y_i}{n}$$

and

$$\bar{x} = \frac{\sum x_i}{n}$$

It can be shown that the sample statistics $\hat{\beta}_0$ and $\hat{\beta}_1$ are unbiased estimators of the population parameters β_0 and β_1. That is,

$$E(\hat{\beta}_0) = \beta_0$$

and

$$E(\hat{\beta}_1) = \beta_1$$

Notice that there are two formulas each for SS_{xy} and SS_x. The second formula in each pair is the shortcut version. You should realize, however, that SS_x is nothing more than the numerator when the sample variance of x is computed. The shortcut procedure for computing the sample variance of x was described in Chapter 2.

Applying these formulas to Example 15.1, we can compute

$$\sum x = 53$$
$$\sum x^2 = 609$$
$$\sum y = 148$$
$$\sum xy = 833$$

From these summations, we find

$$SS_{xy} = \sum x_i y_i - \frac{(\sum x_i)(\sum y_i)}{n} = 833 - \frac{(53)(148)}{6} = -474.333$$

$$SS_x = \sum x_i^2 - \frac{(\sum x_i)^2}{n} = 609 - \frac{(53)^2}{6} = 140.833$$

$$\bar{y} = \frac{\sum y_i}{n} = \frac{148}{6} = 24.667$$

$$\bar{x} = \frac{\sum x_i}{n} = \frac{53}{6} = 8.833$$

Finally, we calculate

$$\hat{\beta} = \frac{SS_{xy}}{SS_x} = \frac{-474.333}{140.833} = -3.368$$

and

$$\hat{\beta}_0 = \bar{y} - \hat{\beta}_1 \bar{x} = 24.667 - (-3.368)(8.833) = 54.417$$

Thus, the least squares line is

$$\hat{y} = 54.417 - 3.368x$$

Figure 15.3 describes the regression line. As you can see, the line fits the data quite well. We can measure how well by computing the value of the minimized sum of squared differences. The differences between the points and the line are called **residuals,** denoted e_i. That is,

$$e_i = y_i - \hat{y}_i$$

FIGURE 15.3   LEAST SQUARES LINE FOR EXAMPLE 15.1

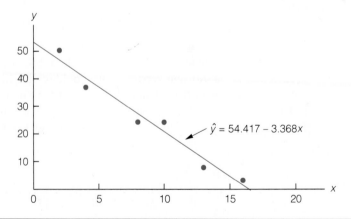

The residuals are the observed values of the error variable. Consequently, the minimized sum of squared differences is called the **sum of squares for error** denoted **SSE**.

Sum of Squares for Error

$$\text{SSE} = \sum(y_i - \hat{y}_i)^2$$

The calculation of SSE for Example 15.1 is shown in Figure 15.4. Notice that we compute $\hat{y}_i$ by substituting x_i into the regression line. The residuals are the differences between the values of y_i from the sample and $\hat{y}_i$ from the line. The following table lists specific values of the variables for Example 15.1.

i	x_i	y_i	$\hat{y}_i = 54.417 - 3.368x$	Residual $y_i - \hat{y}_i$	Residual Squared $(y_i - \hat{y}_i)^2$
1	2	50	47.681	2.319	5.378
2	4	38	40.945	-2.945	8.673
3	8	26	27.473	-1.476	2.179
4	10	25	20.737	4.263	18.173
5	13	7	10.633	-3.633	13.199
6	16	2	.529	1.471	2.164
					$\sum(y_i - \hat{y}_i)^2 = 49.765$

FIGURE 15.4   MEASURING THE RESIDUALS IN EXAMPLE 15.1

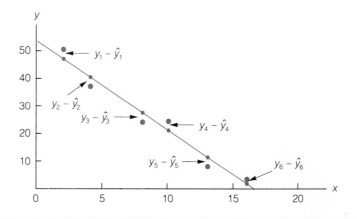

Thus,

SSE = 49.765

No other straight line will produce a sum of squared errors as small as 49.765. In that sense, the regression line fits the data best.

Let's now apply the technique to a more practical problem.

EXAMPLE 15.2

A real estate agent would like to predict the selling price of single-family homes. After careful consideration, he concludes that the variable likely to be most closely related to selling price is the size of the house. As an experiment, he takes a random sample of 15 recently sold houses and records the selling price (in $1,000s) and the size (in 100 ft^2) of each. These are shown in the accompanying table. Find the sample regression line for these data.

House Size (100 ft^2) x	Selling Price ($1,000s) y
20.0	89.5
14.8	79.9
20.5	83.1
12.5	56.9
18.0	66.6
14.3	82.5
27.5	126.3
16.5	79.3
24.3	119.9
20.2	87.6
22.0	112.6
19.0	120.8
12.3	78.5
14.0	74.3
16.7	74.8

Solution.   Both variables are interval scaled. Since we want to predict the selling price, this variable is labeled y and house size is labeled x. The scattergram in Fig-

FIGURE 15.5   *SCATTERGRAM FOR EXAMPLE 15.2*

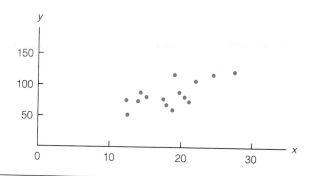

ure 15.5 seems to indicate that a linear model is suitable. The various required summations are shown in the following table. We have also calculated $\sum y_i^2$, which is not necessary now but will be useful later.

x	y	x^2	y^2	xy
20.0	89.5	400.00	8,010.25	1,790.00
14.8	79.9	219.04	6,384.01	1,182.52
20.5	83.1	420.25	6,905.61	1,703.55
12.5	56.9	156.25	3,237.61	711.25
18.0	66.6	324.00	4,435.56	1,198.80
14.3	82.5	204.49	6,806.25	1,179.75
27.5	126.3	756.25	15,951.69	3,473.25
16.5	79.3	272.25	6,288.49	1,308.45
24.3	119.9	590.49	14,376.01	2,913.57
20.2	87.6	408.04	7,673.76	1,769.52
22.0	112.6	484.00	12,678.76	2,477.20
19.0	120.8	361.00	14,592.64	2,295.20
12.3	78.5	151.29	6,162.25	965.55
14.0	74.3	196.00	5,520.49	1,040.20
16.7	74.8	278.89	5,595.04	1,249.16
$\sum x_i = 272.6$	$\sum y_i = 1{,}332.6$	$\sum x_i^2 = 5{,}222.24$	$\sum y_i^2 = 124{,}618.42$	$\sum x_i y_i = 25{,}257.97$

From these summations, we produce

$$SS_{xy} = \sum x_i y_i - \frac{(\sum x_i)(\sum y_i)}{n} = 25,257.97 - \frac{(272.6)(1,332.6)}{15} = 1,040.18$$

$$SS_x = \sum x_i^2 - \frac{(\sum x_i)^2}{n} = 5,222.24 - \frac{(272.6)^2}{15} = 268.19$$

$$\bar{y} = \frac{\sum y_i}{n} = \frac{1,332.6}{15} = 88.84$$

$$\bar{x} = \frac{\sum x_i}{n} = \frac{272.6}{15} = 18.17$$

It then follows that

$$\hat{\beta}_1 = \frac{SS_{xy}}{SS_x} = \frac{1,040.18}{268.19} = 3.88$$

and

$$\hat{\beta}_0 = \bar{y} - \hat{\beta}_1 \bar{x} = 88.84 - 3.88(18.17) = 18.34$$

The sample regression line is

$$\hat{y} = 18.34 + 3.88x$$

Figure 15.6 graphs the points and the regression line.

Interpreting the Coefficients. The coefficient $\hat{\beta}_1$ is equal to 3.88 (in $1,000s), which means that, for each additional 100 square feet, the price of the house increases by an average of $3,880. If we change the units, $\hat{\beta}_1$ tells us that each additional square foot increases the price by $38.80.

The intercept is $\hat{\beta}_0 = 18.34$. Technically the intercept is the point at which the regression line and the y-axis intersect. This means that, when $x = 0$ (no house),

---

FIGURE 15.6   *GRAPH OF EXAMPLE 15.2*

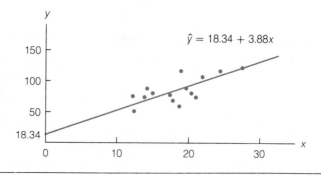

$\hat{y} = 18.34$ (in $1,000s). We might be tempted to interpret this to mean that the lot the house is built on is worth \$18,340, on average; however, it is often misleading to interpret $\hat{\beta}_0$ in this way. Since our sample did not include the sale of any empty lots, we really have no basis for concluding that the lots are worth \$18,340. As a general rule, we cannot interpret the value of y for a value of x that is far outside the observed range of the values of x. In this example, the range of x was

$$12.3 \le x \le 27.5$$

Since $x = 0$ is not in the range, we cannot safely interpret the value of y when $x = 0$.

COMPUTER OUTPUT FOR EXAMPLE 15.2*

As you will see shortly, several different statistics are typically computed as part of regression analysis. Most statistical software systems calculate and print all of these at once. We will show these complete printouts here, and as we proceed through this chapter we will ask you to refer back to them so that we can discuss how each system presents the different components of regression analysis. As usual, what follows is the output from Minitab and SAS.

Minitab

```
The regression equation is

C1=18.4+3.88C2

Predictor      Coef      Stdev      t-ratio
Constant      18.35      14.81        1.24
C2           3.8786     0.7936        4.89

s=13.00    R-sq=64.8%    R-sq(adj)=62.0%

Analysis of Variance

SOURCE        DF       SS         MS
Regression     1     4034.4     4034.4
Error         13     2195.8      168.9
Total         14     6230.2
```

Minitab presents the sample regression line at the top of the printout. Column 1 (C1) stores the values of y, and column 2 (C2) stores the values of x. Thus we have

```
C1=18.4+3.88C2
```

---

* See Appendixes 15.A and 15.B for the Minitab and SAS commands that perform the regression analysis.

SAS

```
Dependent Variable: Y
```

Analysis of Variance

Source	DF	Sum of Squares	Mean Square	F Value	Prob > F
Model	1	4034.4144	4034.4144	23.885	0.0003
Error	13	2195.8215	168.9093		
C Total	14	6230.2360			

Root MSE	12.9965	R-square	0.6476
Dep Mean	88.8400	Adj R-sq	0.6204
C.V.	14.6291		

Parameter Estimates

Variable	DF	Parameter Estimate	Standard Error	T for H0: Parameter=0	Prob > |T|
INTERCEP	1	18.3538	14.8077	1.239	0.2371
X	1	3.8785	0.7936	4.887	0.0003

The values of $\hat{\beta}_0$ and $\hat{\beta}_1$ are shown at the bottom of the printout:

Variable	Parameter Estimate
INTERCEP	18.3538
X	3.8785

EXERCISES

LEARNING THE TECHNIQUES

15.4 Given the following six points, find the least squares regression line.

x	−5	−2	0	3	4	7
y	15	9	7	6	4	1

15.5 Find the least squares regression for the following data.

x	15	6	27	19	14	24	20
y	10	3	21	13	10	11	8

15.6 A set of 10 observations to be analyzed by a regression model yields the following summations:

$$\sum x = 31 \qquad \sum y = 37 \qquad \sum xy = 75$$
$$\sum x^2 = 102 \qquad \sum y^2 = 445$$

Find the least squares regression line.

15.7 A set of 25 observations of two variables x and y produced the following summations:

$$\sum x = 62.5 \qquad \sum y = 129.0 \qquad \sum xy = 114.1$$
$$\sum x^2 = 317.8 \qquad \sum y^2 = 936.4$$

Find the least squares regression line.

APPLYING THE TECHNIQUES

Self-Correcting Exercise (See Appendix 15.C for the solution.)

RET **15.8**   The accompanying table exhibits the annual profit per dollar of sales y (measured in cents) for eight grocery stores and the number of employees per store x.

x	3	6	4	5	2	5	4	1
y	22	30	20	25	18	26	22	19

a. Find the least squares regression line to help predict profit per sales dollar on the basis of the number of employees.

b. Plot the points, and graph the regression line.

c. Does it appear that a straight line model is reasonable?

d. Make an economic interpretation of the slope.

ACC **15.9**   A custom-jobber of specialty fiberglass-bodied cars wished to estimate overhead expenses (labeled y and measured in $1,000s) as a function of the number of cars (x) it produced monthly. A random sample of 12 months was recorded, and the following statistics were calculated:

$$\sum x = 157 \qquad \sum y = 57 \qquad \sum xy = 987$$
$$\sum x^2 = 4,102 \qquad \sum y^2 = 413$$

a. Find the least squares regression line.

b. What does the value of $\hat{\beta}_1$ tell you?

MNG **15.10**   Twelve secretaries were asked to take a special 3-day intensive course to improve their typing skills. They were given a particular two-page letter and asked to type it flawlessly at the beginning and again at the end of the course. The data shown in Table E15.10 were recorded.

a. Find the equation of the regression line.

b. As a check of your calculations in part (a), plot the 12 points and graph the line.

c. Does it appear that the typists' experience is linearly related to their typing improvement?

TABLE E15.10

Typist	Number of Years of Experience x	Improvement (words per minute) y
A	2	9
B	6	11
C	3	8
D	8	12
E	10	14
F	5	9
G	10	14
H	11	13
I	12	14
J	9	10
K	8	9
L	10	10
	$\sum x = 94$	$\sum y = 133$ $\sum xy = 1,102$
	$\sum x^2 = 848$	$\sum y^2 = 1,529$

EDUC **15.11** Students in a small class were polled by a surveyor attempting to establish a relationship between hours of study in the week immediately preceding a major midterm exam and the marks received on the exam. The surveyor gathered the data listed in the accompanying table.

Hours of Study (x)	Exam Score (y)
25	93
12	57
18	55
26	90
19	82
20	95
23	95
15	80
22	85
8	61

$\sum x = 188$ $\sum y = 793$ $\sum xy = 15,540$

$\sum x^2 = 3,832$ $\sum y^2 = 65,143$

a. Find the equation of the regression line to help predict the exam score on the basis of study hours.

b. As a check of your calculations in part (a), plot the 10 points and graph the line.

c. Interpret the meaning of the coefficients.

d. Is the sign of the slope logical? If the slope had the opposite sign, what would that tell you?

MKT **15.12** Advertising is often touted as the key to success. In seeking to determine just how influential advertising is, the management of a recently set-up retail chain has collected data over the previous 15 weeks on sales revenue and advertising expenditures, with the results shown in the following table.

Advertising Expenditures ($1,000s) x	Sales ($1,000s) y
3	50
5	250
7.	700
6	450
6.5	600
8	1,000
3.5	75
4	150
4.5	200
6.5	550
7	750
7.5	800
7.5	900
8.5	1,100
7	600

$\sum x = 91.5$ $\sum y = 8,175$ $\sum xy = 57,787.5$

$\sum x^2 = 598.75$ $\sum y^2 = 6,070,625$

a. Find the coefficients of the regression line, using the least squares method.

b. Make an economic interpretation of the slope.

c. If the sign of the slope were negative, what would that say about the advertising?

d. What does the value of the intercept tell you?

SECTION 15.4   **ERROR VARIABLE: REQUIRED CONDITIONS**

In the previous section, we developed the least squares method of estimating the coefficients of the probabilistic model. A critical part of this model is the error variable ε. In the next three sections, we present methods of assessing how well the straight line fits the data. In order for the methods to be valid, however, four requirements involving the probability distribution of the error variable must be satisfied.

Required Conditions for ε

1. The probability distribution of ε is normal.
2. The mean of the distribution of ε is zero; that is, $E(\varepsilon) = 0$.
3. The variance of ε is σ_ε^2, which is a constant no matter what the value of x is.
4. The errors associated with any two values of y are independent. As a result, the value of the error variable at one point does not affect the value of the error variable at another point.

Requirements 1, 2, and 3 can be interpreted in another way: for each value of x, y is a normally distributed random variable whose mean is

$$E(y) = \beta_0 + \beta_1 x$$

and whose variance is σ_ε^2. Notice that the mean of y depends on x. To reflect this, the expected value is sometimes expressed as

$$E(y \mid x) = \beta_0 + \beta_1 x$$

The variance however, is not influenced by x, since it is a constant over all values of x. Figure 15.7 depicts this interpretation.

In many real-life applications of regression analysis, these requirements are satisfied reasonably well. In Chapter 16, we will discuss how departures from the requirements are recognized and dealt with.

FIGURE 15.7   *THE DISTRIBUTION OF THE ERROR VARIABLE*

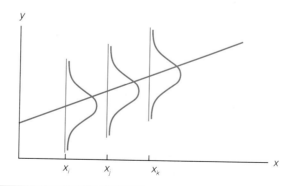

SECTION 15.5 ## *ASSESSING THE MODEL: ESTIMATING σ_ε^2*

As we discussed in Section 15.3, the least squares method produces the best straight line (where *best* is defined as minimizing the sum of squared errors). This does not mean that a linear relationship exists between x and y. In reality, there may be no relationship or perhaps a nonlinear (for example, quadratic) relationship between x and y. If so, the use of a linear model for analysis or forecasting will produce poor results. Hence, it is important for us to assess how well the linear model fits the data. If the fit is poor, we would do better to discard the model and seek another one.

Three different methods can be used to evaluate the model. In this section, we will discuss assessing the model by analyzing the error variable ε.

Since ε equals the deviation between the actual data points and the regression line, large positive or negative values indicate large deviations. Such a result implies that the straight line does not fit the data well. The presence of large positive or negative deviations reflects considerable variability (since the mean of the deviations is assumed to equal zero), and as a result the variance of ε, σ_ε^2, is large. Figure 15.8 depicts an example in which a straight line is a poor model for the relationship between the two variables. Figure 15.9 depicts the resulting distribution of ε. Contrast these figures with Figures 5.10 and 15.11, where the linear model is entirely appropriate and the error term and its variance are small.

We have established that we can assess the model by determining σ_ε^2, but σ_ε^2 is a population parameter whose value (unfortunately) is unknown. Still, σ_ε^2 can be estimated from the data in the random sample. Recall from Section 15.3 that the minimum sum of squared errors was labeled SSE. The sample statistic

$$s_\varepsilon^2 = \frac{\text{SSE}}{n-2}$$

is an unbiased estimator of σ_ε^2. The square root of s_ε^2 is called the standard error of estimate.

Standard Error of Estimate

$$s_\varepsilon = \sqrt{\frac{\text{SSE}}{n-2}}$$

In order to compute s_ε^2, we need to calculate SSE. Recall that we determined SSE in Example 15.1 by calculating $\hat{y}_i$ from the regression line, taking the difference between the observed y_i and $\hat{y}_i$, squaring the differences, and summing the squares. When the sample size is relatively large, this process can be extremely time-consuming. You've probably noticed that, every time we've commented about the amount of time required to do a calculation in this textbook, a shortcut technique has followed. We won't disappoint you. Once again, we dispense with the mathematical derivation and simply present the method that we use to find SSE.

FIGURE 15.8   STRAIGHT LINE AS A POOR MODEL

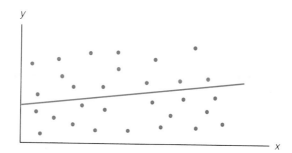

FIGURE 15.9   LARGE ERROR VARIANCE

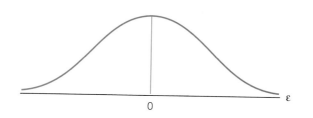

FIGURE 15.10   STRAIGHT LINE AS A GOOD MODEL

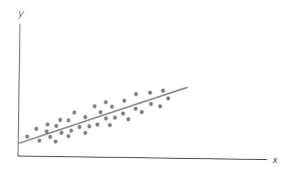

FIGURE 15.11   SMALL ERROR VARIANCE

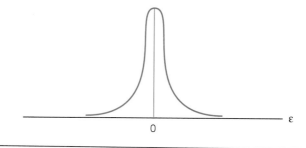

SHORTCUT METHOD FOR SSE

The sum of squared errors is defined as

$$SSE = \sum [y_i - (\hat{\beta}_0 + \hat{\beta}_1 x_i)]^2$$

When we substitute the formulas for $\hat{\beta}_0$ and $\hat{\beta}_1$, we produce the shortcut formula.

Shortcut Calculation of SSE

$$SSE = SS_y - \frac{SS_{xy}^2}{SS_x}$$

where

$$SS_y = \sum (y_i - \bar{y})^2$$

---

which has its own shortcut method.

You should recognize SS_y as the numerator in the calculation of the sample variance of y. Using the shortcut procedure described in Chapter 2, we get

$$SS_y = \sum y_i^2 - \frac{(\sum y_i)^2}{n}$$

In anticipation of this equation, we computed $\sum y_i^2$ in the table accompanying Example 15.2.

EXAMPLE 15.3

From the data developed in Example 15.2, determine the estimate of σ_ε^2 and the standard error of estimate.

Solution. We begin by calculating SS_y. In the course of Example 15.2, we found

$$\sum y_i^2 = 124{,}618.42$$

and

$$\sum y_i = 1{,}332.6$$

From these, we find

$$SS_y = \sum y_i^2 - \frac{(\sum y_i)^2}{n} = 124{,}618.42 - \frac{(1{,}332.6)^2}{15} = 6{,}230.24$$

While calculating $\hat{\beta}_1$ in Example 15.2, we found

$$SS_{xy} = 1{,}040.18$$

and

$$SS_x = 268.19$$

Thus, we have

$$SSE = SS_y - \frac{SS_{xy}^2}{SS_x} = 6{,}230.24 - \frac{(1{,}040.18)^2}{268.19} = 2{,}195.88$$

Finally,

$$s_\varepsilon^2 = \frac{SSE}{n-2} = \frac{2{,}195.88}{15-2} = 168.91$$

The estimate of σ_ε^2 is $s_\varepsilon^2 = 168.91$. The standard error of estimate is

$$s_\varepsilon = \sqrt{168.91} = 13.00$$

Interpreting the Value of s_ε.   The smallest value that s_ε can assume is zero, which occurs when $SSE = 0$; that is, when all the points fall on the regression line. Therefore, if s_ε is close to zero, the fit is excellent and the linear model is likely to be a useful and effective analytical and forecasting tool. If s_ε is large, the model is a poor one, and the statistician should either improve it or discard it.

We judge the value of s_ε by comparing it to the values of the dependent variable y or (more particularly) to the sample mean $\bar{y}$. In this case, because $s_\varepsilon = 13.00$ and $\bar{y} = 88.84$, we would say that s_ε is not very small. Since there is no predefined upper limit on s_ε, however, it is difficult to assess the model definitively in this way (except when s_ε is close to zero). In general, the standard error of estimate cannot be used as an absolute measure of the model's utility.

Nonetheless, s_ε is useful in comparing models. If the statistician has several models to choose from, the one with the smallest value of s_ε should generally be the one used. As you'll see in subsequent sections of this chapter, s_ε is also an important statistic in the other techniques associated with regression analysis. It will be used in Section 15.6 to test the model, and it will be used later in the chapter to estimate and predict the value of y.

COMPUTER OUTPUT FOR EXAMPLE 15.3

Refer to page 673 to examine the Minitab and SAS computer outputs for Example 15.2.

Minitab

Minitab denotes the standard error of estimate s and prints

```
s=13.00
```

SAS

For reasons that we'll explain later, the standard error of estimate is reported by SAS as

Root MSE   12.9965

▬▬▬▬▬▬ **EXERCISES**

LEARNING THE TECHNIQUES

15.13 A set of 15 observations to be analyzed by regression analysis yields the following summations:

$$\sum x = 75 \qquad \sum y = 525 \qquad \sum xy = 3{,}145$$
$$\sum x^2 = 455 \qquad \sum y^2 = 25{,}146$$

Compute the standard error of estimate (s_ε).

15.14 For Exercise 15.4, calculate the sum of squared errors (SSE) by computing each value of $\hat{y}$, subtracting y, squaring the differences and summing the squared differences. Check your computation by calculating SSE using the shortcut method.

15.15 For Exercise 15.5, calculate SSE by computing each value of $\hat{y}$, subtracting y, squaring the differences, and summing the squared differences. Compute SSE by the shortcut method, and compare the results.

15.16 In a study of the relationship between two variables x and y, the following summations were computed:

$$\sum x = 105 \qquad \sum y = 4{,}414 \qquad \sum xy = 37{,}525$$
$$\sum x^2 = 956 \qquad \sum y^2 = 1{,}818{,}421 \qquad n = 15$$

Compute SSE, s_ε^2, and s_ε.

15.17 Calculate SSE and s_ε for Exercise 15.6.

15.18 Provide an example of five observations of x and y for which $s_\varepsilon = 0$.

15.19 Calculate SSE and s_ε for Exercise 15.7.

APPLYING THE TECHNIQUES

Self-Correcting Exercise (See Appendix 15.C for the solution.)

RET **15.20** For Exercise 15.8, find the standard error

of estimate. What does this value tell you about the linear regression model?

───────

ECON **15.21** An economist wanted to investigate the relationship between office rents and vacancy rates. She took a random sample of the monthly office rents per square foot and the percentage of vacant office space in 10 different cities. The results are shown in the following table.

City	Vacancy Rate x	Monthly Rent y
1	3	5.00
2	11	2.50
3	6	4.75
4	5	4.50
5	9	3.00
6	2	4.50
7	5	4.00
8	7	3.00
9	10	3.25
10	8	2.75

$$\sum x = 66 \qquad \sum y = 37.25 \qquad \sum xy = 225.0$$
$$\sum x^2 = 514 \qquad \sum y^2 = 146.44$$

a. Compute the least squares regression line.

b. Calculate the standard error of estimate. How well does the linear model fit the data?

───────

MNG **15.22** Calculate the standard error of estimate in Exercise 15.10, in order to determine how well the model fits the data.

TABLE E15.23

Years on Assembly Line x	Number of Units Manufactured Daily y
15.1	110
7.0	105
18.6	115
23.7	127
11.5	98
16.4	103
6.3	87
15.4	108
19.9	112
$\sum x = 133.9$	$\sum y = 965$ $\sum xy = 14,801.2$
$\sum x^2 = 2,258.73$	$\sum y^2 = 104,469$

MNG **15.23** A new profit-sharing plan was introduced at an automobile parts manufacturing plant last year. Both management and union representatives were interested in determining how a worker's years of experience influence his or her productivity gains. Before the profit-sharing plan was introduced, the average output of a particular auto part was 104 units per day; previous time-and-motion studies had indicated that this was a realistic goal. After the plan had been in effect for a while, the data shown in Table E15.23 were collected:

a. Find the least squares regression line.

b. Calculate the standard error of estimate.

c. What does the value of s_ε tell you about the relationship between x and y?

MKT **15.24** Calculate the standard error of estimate for Exercise 15.12. What does this value tell you about the relationship between sales and advertising expenditures?

SECTION 15.6   **ASSESSING THE MODEL: DRAWING INFERENCES ABOUT β_1**

A second method of assessing the model involves determining whether a linear relationship actually exists between x and y. Suppose that in Example 15.2 we had examined the relationship between the selling price and the house size for all houses in the region. We could then determine the population regression line

$$E(y) = \beta_0 + \beta_1 x$$

Notice that, since we are dealing in this case with the entire population, we refer to the population parameters β_0 and β_1 (no hats).

FIGURE 15.12   *POPULATION REGRESSION LINE: NO LINEAR RELATIONSHIP*

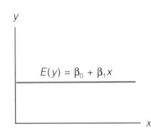

Suppose that, when the regression line is drawn, it produces the graph shown in Figure 15.12. The line is horizontal, which means that the value of y is unaffected by the value of x. A horizontal straight line has a slope of zero; hence, $\beta_1 = 0$ means that no linear relationship exists and that the linear model is inappropriate.

In general, however, β_1 is unknown, because it's a population parameter (and as we've pointed out countless times, population parameters are usually unknown). Here, again, we can use the sample slope, $\hat{\beta}_1$, to make inferences about the population slope, β_1. Most often we test β_1, but we can also produce a confidence interval estimate.

TESTING β_1

The process of testing hypotheses about β_1 is identical to the process of testing any other parameter. We begin with the hypotheses. As usual we can test any one of three alternative hypotheses:

1. If we want to test the slope, in order to determine whether some linear relationship exists between x and y, we test
   $H_A\colon \beta_1 \neq 0$
2. If we want to test for a positive linear relationship, we test
   $H_A\colon \beta_1 > 0$
3. A negative linear relationship is tested with
   $H_A\colon \beta_1 < 0$

In all cases, the null hypothesis specifies that no linear relationship exists. That is,

$H_0\colon \beta_1 = 0$

The test statistic is as follows.

Test Statistic for β_1

$$t = \frac{\hat{\beta}_1 - \beta_1}{s_{\hat{\beta}_1}}$$

where $s_{\hat{\beta}_1}$ is the standard deviation of $\hat{\beta}_1$ (also called the standard error of $\hat{\beta}_1$) and is equal to

$$s_{\hat{\beta}_1} = \frac{s_\varepsilon}{\sqrt{SS_x}}$$

Assuming that the error variable ε is normally distributed, the test statistic follows a Student t distribution with $n - 2$ degrees of freedom.

EXAMPLE 15.4

Can we conclude at the 1% level of significance that the size of a house is linearly related to its selling price in Example 15.2?

Solution.   We wish to test the following hypotheses:

$H_0: \beta_1 = 0$

$H_A: \beta_1 \neq 0$

Test statistic:

$$t = \frac{\hat{\beta}_1 - \beta_1}{s_{\hat{\beta}_1}}$$

Rejection region:

$|t| > t_{\alpha/2, n-2}$

$\quad > t_{.005, 13}$

$\quad > 3.012$

Value of the test statistic: From previous work, we have

$\hat{\beta}_1 = 3.88$

$$s_{\hat{\beta}_1} = \frac{s_\varepsilon}{\sqrt{SS_x}} = \frac{13.00}{\sqrt{268.19}} = .794$$

Therefore,

$$t = \frac{\hat{\beta}_1 - \beta_1}{s_{\hat{\beta}_1}} = \frac{3.88 - 0}{.794} = 4.89$$

Conclusion: Reject H_0.

FIGURE 15.13   *QUADRATIC RELATIONSHIP*

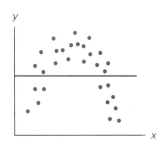

There is sufficient evidence to indicate that house size linearly affects selling price.

In effect, we are saying that there is a linear relationship and that the slope of the line is significantly different from zero. Notice that, if we had not been able to reject the null hypothesis, our conclusion would have been that there was insufficient evidence to show that the slope is *not* equal to zero, and consequently that there may be no linear relationship between *x* and *y*.

We must caution you about how the results of the test of β_1 should be reported. The technique tests to determine whether there is evidence that *x* and *y* are *linearly* related. If we do not reject the null hypothesis, we are saying that there is not enough evidence to indicate that a linear relationship exists. It may be, however, that a nonlinear relationship exists; for example, a quadratic relationship is depicted in Figure 15.13. In such a case, a straight line would be a very poor model, and consequently the slope would be approximately equal to zero.

COMPUTER OUTPUT FOR EXAMPLE 15.4

Both statistical software systems allow the statistician to test β_0 and β_1. However, as we've pointed out before, interpreting the value of the *y*-intercept can lead to erroneous conclusions. As a result, we will not test β_0. The outputs from Minitab and SAS include the standard deviation of $\hat{\beta}_1(s_{\hat{\beta}_1})$ and the *t*-statistic. The latter package provides the *p*-value of this test. To see where in the printout these values appear, again refer to the computer output for Example 15.2 on page 673.

Minitab

The relevant part of the printout is

```
Predictor    Coef      Stdev     t-ratio
Constant     18.35     14.81     1.24
C2            3.8786    0.7936    4.89
```

The standard deviation (Stdev) of $\hat{\beta}_1$ is .7936, and the value of the test statistic

$$t = \frac{\hat{\beta}_1 - \beta_1}{s_{\hat{\beta}_1}}$$

is 4.89.

SAS

The tests of the coefficients appear as follows:

Parameter Estimates

Variable	DF	Parameter Estimate	Standard Error	T for HO: Parameter=0	Prob > |T|
INTERCEP	1	18.3538	14.8077	1.239	0.2371
X	1	3.8785	0.7936	4.887	0.0003

For the test of β_1, the standard deviation of $\hat{\beta}_1$ is Standard Error (.7936), the value of the test statistic is T for HO: Parameter $= 0$ (4.887), and the two-tail p-value is Prob $> |T|$ (.0003).

ESTIMATING β_1

In addition to (or instead of) carrying out the hypothesis-testing procedure, we can form a confidence interval estimate of the true slope parameter.

Confidence Interval Estimator of β_1

$$\hat{\beta}_1 \pm t_{\alpha/2} s_{\hat{\beta}_1}$$

The 99% confidence interval estimate of β_1 for Example 15.2 is

$$3.88 \pm 3.012(.794) = 3.88 \pm 2.39$$

or

$$(1.49, 6.27)$$

Thus the 99% confidence interval estimate of the slope is the interval from 1.49 to 6.27.

EXERCISES

LEARNING THE TECHNIQUES

15.25 Test each of the following hypotheses:

a. $H_0: \beta_1 = 0$
$H_A: \beta_1 \neq 0$
$\hat{\beta}_1 = 1.87$ $s_{\hat{\beta}_1} = .63$ $n = 25$ $\alpha = .05$

b. $H_0: \beta_1 = 0$
$H_A: \beta_1 < 0$
$\hat{\beta}_1 = -26.32$ $s_{\hat{\beta}_1} = 14.51$ $n = 100$
$\alpha = .01$

c. $H_0: \beta_1 = 0$
   $H_A: \beta_1 > 0$
   $\hat{\beta}_1 = .056$ $s_{\hat{\beta}_1} = .021$ $n = 10$
   $\alpha = .05$

15.26 Estimate with 95% confidence the slope of the regression line, given the following data:

$$\sum x = 55 \qquad \sum y = 325 \qquad \sum xy = 929$$
$$\sum x^2 = 175 \qquad \sum y^2 = 6{,}051 \qquad n = 20$$

15.27 Test with $\alpha = .01$ to determine whether there is evidence of a linear relationship for the following data:

x	7	12	0	-2	5
y	9	6	12	15	10

15.28 Twelve observations of x and y produced the following summations:

$$\sum x = 65 \qquad \sum y = 515 \qquad \sum xy = 3{,}085$$
$$\sum x^2 = 445 \qquad \sum y^2 = 24{,}815$$

a. Is there sufficient evidence at the 1% significance level to determine whether a positive linear relationship exists between x and y?

b. Determine the 99% confidence interval estimate of the population slope.

15.29 For Exercise 15.5, test with $\alpha = .10$ to determine whether there is enough evidence to allow us to conclude that a linear relationship exists between x and y.

APPLYING THE TECHNIQUES

Self-Correcting Exercise (See Appendix 15.C for the solution.)

EDUC **15.30** Frank Jones is a student in the class referred to in Exercise 15.11. He doesn't believe that more hours of study result in a higher exam score. Using the data in Exercise 15.11, produce a test with $\alpha = .05$ to convince Frank that he's wrong.

ECON **15.31** In an attempt to get a better idea of some of the determinants of medical expenditures by families, a social worker collected data on family size and average monthly medical bills, with the results shown in the following table.

Family Size x	Monthly Medical Expenses (in dollars) y
2	20
2	28
4	52
5	50
7	78
3	35
8	102
10	88
5	51
2	22
3	29
5	49
2	25
$\sum x = 58$	$\sum y = 629$ $\sum xy = 3{,}582$
$\sum x^2 = 338$	$\sum y^2 = 38{,}797$

Do these data present sufficient evidence (with $\alpha = .05$) that larger families have larger monthly medical expenses?

MKT **15.32** The owner of the company alluded to in Exercise 15.12 does not believe that his advertising is effective in increasing sales. Perform an appropriate test, with $\alpha = .01$, to examine the problem.

SCI **15.33** Physicians have been recommending more exercise for their patients, particularly those who are overweight. One benefit of regular exercise appears to be a reduction in cholesterol, a substance associated with heart disease. In order to study the relationship more carefully, a physician took a random sample of 8 patients who do not exercise. He measured their cholesterol levels. He then started them on regular exercise programs. After 4 months he asked each patient how many minutes per week (on the average) he or she exercised, and he also measured their cholesterol levels. The results are shown in the accompanying table. Can the physician conclude at the 5%

significance level that more exercise leads to greater cholesterol reduction?

Patient	Weekly Exercise (minutes)	Cholesterol Level Before	Cholesterol Level After
1	75	240	180
2	80	210	195
3	105	230	200
4	40	220	200
5	20	235	230
6	150	205	180
7	60	190	180
8	90	200	185

MKT **15.34** Corporate sponsors of television commercials want people who see their commercials at least to remember the brand name of the product. A marketing manager of a major computer manufacturer believes that, all other things being equal, the more frequently the name of the product is mentioned in a television commercial, the greater

will be the percentage of people who remember the name. To examine this potentially important phenomenon, she prepares five commercials that are essentially identical except in the number of times they mention the name of the computer company. Each commercial is shown to five different groups of 100 people. (At the same time, each group is also shown various other products' commercials.) Three days later they are asked to name the computer that was advertised. The number of correct responses was recorded. All the results are shown in the following table. Do these data support the marketing manager's belief? (Use $\alpha = .10$.)

Number of Times Product Mentioned	Number of People Identifying Product Name
2	40
3	45
5	41
7	48
8	55

SECTION 15.7

ASSESSING THE MODEL: MEASURING THE STRENGTH OF THE LINEAR RELATIONSHIP

The test of β_1 discussed in the previous section only addresses the question of whether there is enough evidence to allow us to conclude that a linear relationship does exist. In many cases, however, it is also useful to measure the strength of the linear relationship. This is particularly important when we wish to compare different models to see which one fits the data better. In this section, we will present two such measures: the coefficient of correlation, and the coefficient of determination.

COEFFICIENT OF CORRELATION

The coefficient of correlation, denoted ρ (the Greek letter *rho*), measures the similarity of the changes in the values of x and y. Its range is

$$-1 \leq \rho \leq +1$$

If (in general) y increases when x increases, ρ is positive. If y generally decreases when x increases, ρ is negative. If y is unaffected by x, then $\rho = 0$. The absolute value of ρ measures how closely changes in x mirror changes in y. When $|\rho| = 1$, for example, a change in the value of x is reflected by a perfectly predictable change in the value of y, and every point falls on the regression line. When $\rho = 0$, the values of x and y are not correlated. This is equivalent to saying that there is no linear relationship between x and y. Figure 15.14 depicts examples of different values of ρ. When $\rho = +1$, the slope is positive and all data points fall exactly on the line; when $\rho = -1$, the slope is negative but again all data points fall exactly on the line; when $\rho = 0$, the line is horizontal and no linear relationship exists between the two variables. Other values of ρ must be interpreted with reference to these three

FIGURE 15.14   GRAPHICAL PRESENTATIONS OF FIVE VALUES OF CORRELATION COEFFICIENT (ρ)

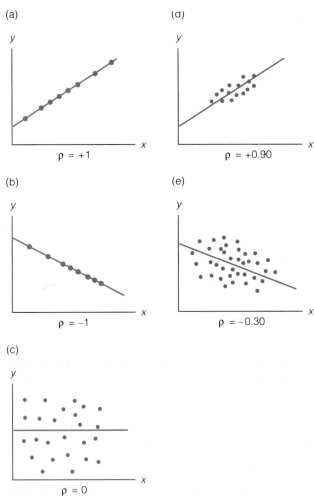

values. For example, $\rho = +.90$ tells us that there is a strong (but not perfect) positive linear relationship; similarly, $\rho = -.30$ indicates a weak negative relationship.

Since ρ is a population parameter, we estimate its value from the data. The sample coefficient of correlation, denoted r, is defined as follows.

Sample Coefficient of Correlation

$$r = \frac{SS_{xy}}{\sqrt{SS_x \cdot SS_y}}$$

Each component has previously been calculated, so r can quickly be determined. In Example 15.2, we found that

$$SS_{xy} = 1{,}040.18$$
$$SS_x = 268.19$$
$$SS_y = 6{,}230.24$$

Hence,

$$r = \frac{SS_{xy}}{\sqrt{SS_x \cdot SS_y}} = \frac{1{,}040.18}{\sqrt{(268.19)(6{,}230.24)}} = .805$$

This value of r tells us two things. First, because r is positive, the slope of the sample regression line is also positive. This is not new information to us, since we already calculated $\hat{\beta}_1$ and found it to be positive. If you examine the formulas of r and $\hat{\beta}_1$, you'll find that their numerators are the same and that their denominators are positive (since they're sums of squares).

$$r = \frac{SS_{xy}}{\sqrt{SS_x \cdot SS_y}}$$
$$\hat{\beta}_1 = \frac{SS_{xy}}{SS_x}$$

Thus, r and $\hat{\beta}_1$ will always have the same sign; and when r equals zero, $\hat{\beta}_1$ will also equal zero. Second, since .805 is close to 1, the fit is fairly good. Unfortunately, when interpreting the value of r, we can only use vague terms such as *close* and *fairly good*. Except when $r = +1$, -1, or 0, we cannot interpret r (or ρ) precisely. This shortcoming will be remedied when we get to the coefficient of determination.

TESTING THE COEFFICIENT OF CORRELATION

If $\rho = 0$, the values of x and y are uncorrelated and the linear model is not appropriate. We can test to determine if x and y are correlated by testing the following hypotheses:

$$H_0: \rho = 0$$
$$H_A: \rho \neq 0$$

Test Statistic for ρ

$$t = \frac{r - \rho}{s_r}$$

where

$$s_r = \sqrt{\frac{1 - r^2}{n - 2}}$$

The test statistic is Student t distributed, with $n - 2$ degrees of freedom (if the error variable is normally distributed). The complete test for Example 15.2 is as follows.

$$H_0: \rho = 0$$
$$H_A: \rho \neq 0$$

Test statistic:

$$t = \frac{r - \rho}{s_r}$$

Rejection region:

$$|t| > t_{\alpha/2, n-2}$$
$$> t_{.005, 13} \text{ (assuming that } \alpha = .01)$$
$$> 3.012$$

Value of the test statistic: Since $r = .805$,

$$s_r = \sqrt{\frac{1 - r^2}{n - 2}} = .165$$
$$t = \frac{.805 - 0}{.165} = 4.89$$

Conclusion: Reject H_0.

There is sufficient evidence to enable us to conclude that x and y are correlated, and as a result that a linear relationship exists between them.

These results are identical to those obtained when we tested the slope, β_1. In fact, the values of the test statistic, the rejection region, and (of course) the conclusion are all the same. This is not a coincidence. Since in both cases we're testing to determine whether a linear association exists, the results must agree. We presented this test to establish that you can test ρ directly, rather than testing β_1. In practice, you need perform only one of the tests.

COEFFICIENT OF DETERMINATION

The coefficient of determination, denoted r^2, is defined to be the coefficient of correlation squared.

Coefficient of Determination

$$r^2 = \frac{SS_{xy}^2}{SS_x SS_y}$$

With a little algebra, we can show that

$$r^2 = \frac{SS_y - SSE}{SS_y}$$

The significance of this formula is evident by analogy to an argument we made in Chapter 12, where the technique for analysis of variance was based on the partitioning of the total sum of squares into two sources of variability. Here, the discussion begins by observing that the deviation between y_i and $\bar{y}$ can be decomposed into two parts. That is,

$$(y_i - \bar{y}) = (y_i - \hat{y}_i) + (\hat{y}_i - \bar{y})$$

This relationship is represented graphically in Figure 15.15.

Now we ask, why are the values of y different from one another? In Example 15.2, we observe that the house prices vary, and we'd like to explain this variation. From Figure 15.15, we see that part of the difference between y_i and $\bar{y}$ is the difference between $\hat{y}_i$ and $\bar{y}$, which is accounted for by the difference between x_i and $\bar{x}$. That is, some of the price variation is *explained* by the size variation. The other part of the difference between y_i and $\bar{y}$, however, is accounted for by the difference

---

FIGURE 15.15   *ANALYSIS OF THE DEVIATION*

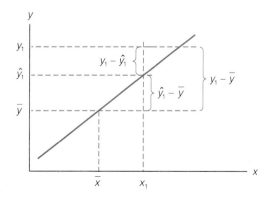

between y_i and $\hat{y}_i$. This difference is the error term, which to some degree reflects variables not otherwise represented in the model. (These variables likely included factors such as the number of bedrooms, the number of bathrooms, the lot size, and whether or not the basement (if any) is finished.) As a result, we say that this part of the difference is *unexplained* by the size variability.

If we now square the left side of the preceding equation, sum over all the points, and perform some algebra, we produce

$$\sum(y_i - \bar{y})^2 = \sum(y_i - \hat{y}_i)^2 + \sum(\hat{y}_i - \bar{y})^2$$

You should recognize the quantity on the left side of this equation as SS_y and the first quantity on the right side as SSE. The last term is denoted SSR (sum of squares of regression). That is,

$$SS_y = SSE + SSR$$

where

$$SS_y = \sum(y_i - \bar{y})^2$$
$$SSE = \sum(y_i - \hat{y}_i)^2$$

and

$$SSR = \sum(\hat{y}_i - \bar{y})^2$$

As we did in the analysis of variance in Chapter 12, we partition the variability of y here into two parts: SSE, which measures the amount of variability of y that remains unexplained; and SSR, which measures the amount of variability of y that is explained by the variability of the independent variable x.

Returning to our formula for r^2, we see that

$$r^2 = \frac{SS_y - SSE}{SS_y}$$

or

$$r^2 = \frac{SSR}{SS_y}$$

since

$$SSR = SS_y - SSE$$

It follows that r^2 measures the proportion of the variability of y that is explained by the variability of x. In Example 15.2, we find that

$$r^2 = \frac{SS_y - SSE}{SS_y} = \frac{6,230.24 - 2,195.88}{6,230.24} = .648$$

(Alternatively, we could simply have squared $r = .805$ to compute r^2.) This value of r^2 tells us that 64.8% of the price variability is explained by the size variability. The remaining 35.2% of the price variability remains unexplained.

COMPUTER OUTPUT SHOWING r^2 AND THE SUMS OF SQUARES

The two computer systems produce the coefficient of determination labeled R-sq by Minitab and R-square by SAS. They also print a second related value called the adjusted coefficient of determination. We will discuss this coefficient in Chapter 16. The remaining part of the output relates to our discussion of the interpretation of the value of r^2, where its meaning is derived from the partitioning of the total variability. The values of SSR and SSE are shown in an analysis of variance table similar to the tables encountered in Chapter 12. The general format of this table is shown next. The *F*-test performed in the ANOVA table will be explained in Chapter 16.

GENERAL FORM OF THE ANOVA TABLE

Source	d.f.	Sum of Squares	Mean Square	F-ratio
Regression	1	SSR	MSR = SSR/1	F = MSR/MSE
Error	$n - 2$	SSE	MSE = SSE/$(n - 2)$	
Total	$n - 1$	SS_y		

Turn to page 673 to examine the computer output for Example 15.2.

Minitab

The values of r^2, adjusted r^2, and the sums of squares used to compute r^2 are presented as follows.

```
            R-sq=64.8%      R-sq (adj)=62.0%

Analysis of Variance

SOURCE         DF      SS       MS
Regression      1    4034.4    4034.4
Error          13    2195.8     168.9
Total          14    6230.2
```

SAS

The analysis of variance table and the coefficient of determination and related values are outputted by SAS as follows.

```
                   Analysis of Variance

                 Sum of       Mean
Source     DF    Squares      Square     F Value    Prob > F
Model       1   4034.4144   4034.4144    23.885     0.0003
Error      13   2195.8215    168.9093
C Total    14   6230.2360
```

```
Root MSE      12.9965    R-square    0.6476
Dep Mean      88.8400    Adj R-sq    0.6204
C.V.          14.6291
```

The mean square for error is

$$MSE = \frac{SSE}{n-2} = \frac{2,195.8215}{15-2} = 168.9093$$

which is s_ε^2. The square root of MSE is $s_\varepsilon = \sqrt{168.9093} = 12.9965$. For this reason, SAS refers to the standard error of estimate s_ε as Root MSE.

The Dep Mean, which is the value of $\bar{y}$, is shown to help you judge whether or not s_ε is large. The remaining value in the output is C.V., the coefficient of variation, defined as

$$C.V. = \left(\frac{s_\varepsilon}{\bar{y}}\right) \times 100 = \left(\frac{12.9965}{88.84}\right) \times 100 = 14.6291$$

This definition differs slightly from the one presented in Chapter 2, where the numerator was the standard deviation of y.

■■■■■■■■■■ **EXERCISES**

LEARNING THE TECHNIQUES

15.35 A set of data consisting of 12 observations yields the following results:

$$\sum x = 35 \qquad \sum y = 84 \qquad \sum xy = 185$$
$$\sum x^2 = 190 \qquad \sum y^2 = 719$$

a. Calculate the coefficient of correlation.

b. Calculate the coefficient of determination.

15.36 Given the following observations, determine the coefficient of correlation:

x	0	5	-1	0	3	2	4
y	3	10	2	4	6	5	7

15.37 Compute the coefficients of correlation and determination for Exercise 15.4.

15.38 Test each of the following sets of hypotheses:

a. $H_0: \rho = 0$
$\quad H_A: \rho > 0$
$\quad r = .30 \qquad n = 20 \qquad \alpha = .05$

b. $H_0: \rho = 0$
$\quad H_A: \rho < 0$
$\quad r = -.28 \qquad n = 10 \qquad \alpha = .01$

c. $H_0: \rho = 0$
$\quad H_A: \rho \neq 0$
$\quad r = .48 \qquad n = 18 \qquad \alpha = .05$

15.39 Given the following sums of squares, find the proportion of total variation explained by the regression model.

$$SSR = 650 \qquad SSE = 350 \qquad SS_y = 1,000$$

15.40 Invent some values of x and y (about five pairs) that have a correlation of:

a. $+1$

b. -1

c. 0

15.41 Explain what the sign of the correlation coefficient means, and state how you would interpret the magnitude of r.

APPLYING THE TECHNIQUES

Self-Correcting Exercise (See Appendix 15.C for the solution.)

| EDUC | **15.42** Calculate the coefficients of correlation and determination for Exercise 15.11. What do these values tell you?

| MNG | **15.43** A supermarket chain performed a survey to help determine desirable locations for new stores. The management of the chain wanted to know whether there was a linear relationship between weekly take-home pay and weekly food expenditures. A random sample of eight households produced the data shown in the accompanying table.

Family	Weekly Take-Home Pay (x)	Weekly Food Expenditures (y)
1	300	160
2	200	110
3	270	150
4	180	90
5	250	130
6	360	200
7	225	120
8	340	180

a. Find the least squares regression line.

b. Compute the standard error of estimate.

c. Do these data provide sufficient evidence (with $\alpha = .01$) to allow us to conclude that there is a linear relationship between x and y?

d. Calculate the coefficients of correlation and determination.

e. What does the value of r^2 tell you about the strength of the linear relationship?

| GEN | **15.44** A computer-manufacturing plant offers one year of free service with the sale of each computer. As part of an internal cost-control program, checks are being made to ascertain the time needed for a customer service call and the number of tape drives that customers ask to have adjusted. The results of this study (shown in the accompanying table) should allow for better time use and for cost reduction.

No. of Tape Drives x	Minutes on Service Call y
5	310
3	240
7	380
2	120
1	90
9	510
8	450
6	320
5	410
3	390

a. Determine the least squares regression line.

b. Interpret the coefficients.

c. Calculate SSE and the standard error of estimate.

d. Can we conclude that a positive linear relationship exists between x and y? (Use $\alpha = .05$.)

e. Compute the coefficient of determination, and comment on what it says about the strength of the linear relationship.

| FIN | **15.45** In order to determine a realistic price for a new product that a company wishes to market, the company's research department selected 10 sites thought to have essentially identical sales potential and offered the product in each at a different price. The resulting sales are recorded in the accompanying table.

Location	Price x	Sales ($1,000s) y
1	15.00	15
2	15.50	14

(continued)

Location	Price x	Sales ($1,000s) y
3	16.00	16
4	16.50	9
5	17.00	12
6	17.50	10
7	18.00	8
8	18.50	9
9	19.00	6
10	19.50	5

a. Find the equation of the regression line.

b. Is there sufficient evidence at the 10% significance level to allow us to conclude that a negative linear relationship exists between price and sales?

c. Calculate the coefficients of correlation and determination.

 15.46 Calculate the coefficient of determination for Exercise 15.31. What does this value tell you about the strength of the linear relationship?

SECTION 15.8   **USING THE REGRESSION EQUATION**

As we pointed out in Section 15.1, the regression model can be used for forecasting and analytical purposes. By analyzing the regression equation in Example 15.2, for instance, we learned that, for each additional square foot, the selling price of the house increases (on average) by $38.80. This information may be useful to real estate agents, property-tax assessors, banks (in determining mortgage limits), and insurance agents (in calculating replacement costs).

We can also use the regression model to predict and estimate values of y. Again referring to Example 15.2, suppose that a real estate agent wanted to predict the selling price of a house that occupies 2,000 square feet. Using the regression equation, with $x = 20$ (recall that the unit of measurement of x is hundreds of square feet), we get

$$\hat{y} = 18.34 + 3.88x = 18.34 + 3.88(20) = 95.94$$

Thus, he would predict that the house will sell for $95,940. (The unit of measurement of y is thousands of dollars.)

By itself, however, this value does not provide any information about how closely it will match the true selling price of a 2,000-square-foot house. To discover that information, we must use a confidence interval. In fact, we can use one of two intervals: the prediction interval (for a particular value of y), or the confidence interval estimate (for the expected value of y).

**PREDICTING THE PARTICULAR VALUE OF y
FOR A GIVEN x**

The first confidence interval we will discuss is used whenever we want to predict one particular value of the dependent variable, given a specific value of the independent variable. This confidence interval, often called the **prediction interval,** is calculated as follows.

Prediction Interval

$$\hat{y} \pm t_{\alpha/2, n-2} s_{\varepsilon} \sqrt{1 + \frac{1}{n} + \frac{(x_g - \bar{x})^2}{SS_x}}$$

where x_g is the given value of x and

$$\hat{y} = \hat{\beta}_0 + \hat{\beta}_1 x_g$$

EXAMPLE 15.5

Predict with 95% confidence the selling price of a house that occupies 2,000 square feet.

Solution.   From previous calculations we have

$$\hat{y} = 18.34 + 3.88x_g = 18.34 + 3.88(20) = 95.94$$
$$s_{\varepsilon} = 13.00$$
$$SS_x = 268.19$$
$$\bar{x} = 18.17$$
$$t_{.025, 13} = 2.160$$

The 95% prediction interval is

$$\hat{y} \pm t_{\alpha/2, n-2} s_{\varepsilon} \sqrt{1 + \frac{1}{n} + \frac{(x_g - \bar{x})^2}{SS_x}}$$

$$= 95.94 \pm (2.160)(13.00) \sqrt{1 + \frac{1}{15} + \frac{(20 - 18.17)^2}{268.19}}$$

$$= 95.94 \pm 29.17$$

or

$$(66.77, 125.11)$$

We predict that the selling price will fall between $66,770 and $125,110.

If you think that this interval is awfully wide, you're right. Even though there is sufficient evidence of a linear relationship, and even though we have determined that the coefficient of determination is .648, the size of the interval apparently makes the value of the model dubious. Bear in mind, however, that this sample is quite small — likely much smaller than the sample that would be used in a real application. More importantly, restricting the number of independent variables to one precluded us from producing a better model and hence a better prediction.

ESTIMATING THE EXPECTED VALUE OF *y* FOR A GIVEN *x*

The conditions described in Section 15.4 imply that, for a given value of x, there is a population of values of y whose mean is

$$E(y) = \beta_0 + \beta_1 x$$

To estimate this value, we would use the following interval (known informally as the *confidence interval*).

> **Confidence Interval Estimator of the Expected Value of *y***
>
> $$\hat{y} \pm t_{\alpha/2, n-2} s_\varepsilon \sqrt{\frac{1}{n} + \frac{(x_g - \bar{x})^2}{SS_x}}$$

Unlike the formula for the prediction interval described previously, this formula does not include the 1 under the square-root sign. As a result, the interval it produces is narrower than that of the prediction interval. This is reasonable, given that predicting a single value is more difficult than estimating the average of a population of values.

EXAMPLE 15.6

In a certain part of the city, a developer built several thousand houses whose floor plans and exteriors differ, but whose sizes are all 2,000 square feet. To date they've been rented, but the builder now wishes to sell them and wants to know approximately how much money in total he can expect from the sale of the houses. Help him by producing a 95% confidence interval estimate of the mean selling price of the houses.

Solution.   Since we now want to estimate the expected value of a large population of selling prices, we use the following formula:

$$\hat{y} \pm t_{\alpha/2, n-2} s_\varepsilon \sqrt{\frac{1}{n} + \frac{(x_g - \bar{x})^2}{SS_x}}$$

Substituting the values previously calculated, we have

$$\hat{y} \pm t_{\alpha/2, n-2} s_\varepsilon \sqrt{\frac{1}{n} + \frac{(x_g - \bar{x})^2}{SS_x}} = 95.94 \pm (2.160)(13.00)\sqrt{\frac{1}{15} + \frac{(20 - 18.17)^2}{268.19}}$$

$$= 95.94 \pm 7.90$$

or

(88.04, 103.84)

Thus, the mean selling price is estimated to lie between \$88,040 and \$103,840.

FIGURE 15.16   CONFIDENCE INTERVALS AND PREDICTION INTERVALS FOR y

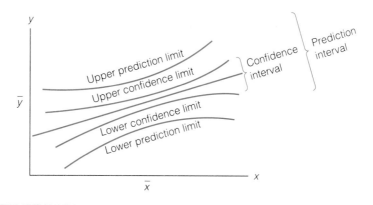

From the interval calculated in Example 15.5, we predict that the price of each house will be between $66,770 and $125,110; now we estimate, in addition, that the mean price of all houses will be between $88,040 and $103,840. Again, since predicting a single value is relatively difficult, the prediction interval for one house is wider than the confidence interval estimate of the expected value of all the houses.

If the two intervals were calculated for various values of x, Figure 15.16 would be produced. Notice that both intervals are represented by curved lines. This is due to the fact that, the farther the given value of x lies from $\bar{x}$, the greater the estimation error becomes. This factor is measured by the quantity

$$\frac{(x_g - \bar{x})^2}{SS_x}$$

which appears in both the prediction interval formula and the confidence interval formula.

COMPUTER OUTPUT FOR EXAMPLES 15.5 AND 15.6*

Minitab

```
  Fit    Stdev. Fit      95% C.I.           95% P.I.
 95.92      3.66      (88.03, 103.82)    (66.75, 125.10)
```

The output includes the calculated value of y, Fit (95.92), the standard deviation of y

---

* See Appendixes 15.A and 15.B for the Minitab and SAS commands that produced these printouts.

(3.66), which is

$$s_\varepsilon \sqrt{\frac{1}{n} + \frac{(x_g - \bar{x})^2}{SS_x}}$$

and the 95% confidence interval estimate of the expected value of y (88.03, 103.82) and the 95% prediction interval (66.75, 125.10).

SAS

Obs	Dep Var Y	Predict Value	Std Err Predict
1	89.5000	95.9	3.655
2	79.9000	75.7564	4.293
3	83.1000	97.9	3.830
4	56.9000	66.8357	5.615
5	66.6000	88.1677	3.359
6	82.5000	73.8171	4.551
7	126.3	125.0	8.127
8	79.3000	82.3499	3.609
9	119.9	112.6	5.908
10	87.6000	96.7	3.721
11	112.6	103.7	4.526
12	120.8	92.0463	3.419
13	78.5000	66.0600	5.743
14	74.3000	72.6535	4.715
15	74.8000	83.1256	3.554
16		95.9	3.655

Lower95% Mean	Upper95% Mean	Lower95% Predict	Upper95% Predict
88.0278	103.8	66.7581	125.1
66.4825	85.0302	46.1872	105.3
89.5896	106.1	68.5930	127.1
54.7044	78.9669	36.2498	97.4
80.9121	95.4	59.1681	117.2
63.9857	83.6484	44.0684	103.6
107.5	142.6	91.8993	158.1
74.5534	90.1464	53.2103	111.5
99.8	125.4	81.7607	143.4
88.6613	104.7	67.4950	125.9
93.9044	113.5	73.9510	133.4
84.6595	99.4	63.0136	121.1
53.6521	78.4678	35.3633	96.8
62.4677	82.8393	42.7858	102.5
75.4486	90.8026	54.0177	112.2
88.0278	103.8	66.7581	125.1

For each value of x, SAS prints the observed value of y, the value of $\hat{y}$, a quantity called the standard error of the prediction, which is

$$s_\varepsilon \sqrt{\frac{1}{n} + \frac{(x_g - \bar{x})^2}{SS_x}}$$

plus the confidence interval estimates and the prediction intervals. As we explain in Appendix 15.B, the intervals we want appear in the 16th row. Thus the 95% confidence interval estimate of the expected value of y when $x = 20$ is

(88.0278, 103.8)

The 95% prediction interval of the particular value of y when $x = 20$ is

(66.7581, 125.1)

EXERCISES

LEARNING THE TECHNIQUES

15.47 On the basis of eight observations of x and y, the following summations were computed:

$$\sum x = 40 \qquad \sum y = 100 \qquad \sum xy = 600$$
$$\sum x^2 = 250 \qquad \sum y^2 = 2{,}000$$

a. Determine a 95% confidence interval for the expected value of y when $x = 6$.

b. Determine a 95% prediction interval for the value of y when $x = 3$.

15.48 Consider the following statistics based on 25 observations.

$$\hat{\beta}_0 = 6.5 \qquad \hat{\beta}_1 = -2.0 \qquad s_\varepsilon = 5.0$$
$$SS_x = 100 \qquad \bar{x} = 25.0$$

a. Find the 90% prediction interval for the value of y when $x = 22.0$.

b. Find the 99% confidence interval estimate of the expected value of y when $x = 27.0$.

15.49 For Exercise 15.5, find the 95% prediction interval for the value of y when $x = 12.0$.

15.50 What happens to the prediction interval and the confidence interval when SSE $= 0$?

15.51 Suppose that you are given the following six observations:

| x | 3 | 6 | 5 | 4 | 3 | 8 |
| y | 10 | 8 | 6 | 9 | 9 | 4 |

a. Determine a 99% confidence interval for the expected value of y when $x = 8$.

b. Determine a 99% prediction interval for the value of y when $x = 3$.

APPLYING THE TECHNIQUES

Self-Correcting Exercise (See Appendix 15.C for the solution.)

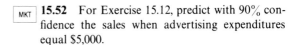

MKT **15.52** For Exercise 15.12, predict with 90% confidence the sales when advertising expenditures equal $5,000.

ECON **15.53** The E-Z Sleepwear Company decided to examine whether personal disposable income nationwide was a decisive factor in predicting overall company sales. Data collected over the past 15 years yielded the information shown in Table E15.53.

a. Find the equation of the regression line.

b. Use the equation you found in part (a) to produce a 90% prediction interval of company sales when disposable income is $500 billion.

c. What assumptions are being made about the data?

TABLE E15.53

Year	Disposable Income ($billions) x	Company Sales ($millions) y
1970	137	202
1971	154	212
1972	175	221
1973	196	233
1974	209	245
1975	224	259
1976	245	273
1977	270	285
1978	291	294
1979	310	303
1980	341	313
1981	375	323
1982	402	335
1983	441	350
1984	487	368

$\sum x = 4{,}257$ $\sum y = 4{,}216$ $\sum xy = 1{,}273{,}299$

$\sum x^2 = 1{,}369{,}249$ $\sum y^2 = 1{,}222{,}430$

EDUC **15.54** Use your regression equation to predict with 95% confidence the exam score of a student who studied for 21 hours in Exercise 15.11.

EDUC **15.55** Find the 95% confidence interval estimate of the mean exam score of all students who have studied for 21 hours in Exercise 15.11.

15.56 Briefly explain the difference between your answers to Exercises 15.54 and 15.55.

FIN **15.57** The different interest rates charged by some financial institutions may reflect how stringent their standards are for their loan appraisals; that is, the lower the rate, the higher the standards (and hence, the lower the default rate). The following data were collected from a sample of 9 financial companies that were selected at random:

Interest Rate (%) x	Default Rate (per 1,000 loans) y
7.0	38
6.6	40
6.0	35
8.5	46
8.0	48
7.5	39
6.5	36
7.0	37
8.0	44

$\sum x = 65.1$ $\sum y = 363$ $\sum xy = 2{,}652.5$

$\sum x^2 = 476.31$ $\sum y^2 = 14{,}811$

a. Find the least squares regression line.

b. Do these data provide sufficient evidence to indicate that there is a positive linear relationship between the interest rate and the default rate? (Use $\alpha = .10$.)

c. Calculate the coefficients of correlation and determination.

d. Find a 95% prediction interval for the default rate when the interest rate is 8%.

ECON **15.58**   Estimate with 95% confidence the mean monthly medical expenses of a family of four people in Exercise 15.31.

ECON **15.59**   A family of eight people is trying to produce a budget. Help them by determining a 90% prediction interval for their monthly medical expenses (Exercise 15.31).

SECTION 15.9   **COMPLETE EXAMPLE**

EXAMPLE 15.7

Car dealers across North America use the "Red Book" to help them determine the value of used cars that their customers trade in when purchasing new cars. The book, which is published monthly, lists average trade-in values for all basic models of North American, Japanese, and European cars. These averages are determined on the basis of the amounts paid at recent used-car auctions. The book indicates alternative values of each car model according to its condition and optional features, but it does not inform dealers as to how the odometer reading affects the trade-in value. In an experiment to determine whether the odometer reading should be included in the Red Book, an interested student of statistics and used cars randomly selects ten 3-year-old cars of the same make, condition, and optional features. The trade-in value and mileage for each are shown in the accompanying table.

Car	Odometer Reading (1,000 miles) x	Trade-In Value ($100s) y
1	59	37
2	92	31
3	61	43
4	72	39
5	52	41
6	67	39
7	88	35
8	62	40
9	95	29
10	83	33

a. Find the sample regression line for determining how the odometer reading affects the trade-in value of the car.

b. What does the regression line tell us about the relationship between the two variables?

c. Find the standard error of estimate.

d. Can we conclude at the 5% significance level that, for all cars of the type described in this experiment, higher mileage results in a lower trade-in value?

e. Measure the strength of the linear relationship by calculating the coefficients of correlation and determination.

f. Predict with 95% confidence the trade-in value of a car that has been driven 60,000 miles.

g. A large national courier company has a policy of selling its cars once the odometer reaches 75,000 miles. The company is about to sell a large number of 3-year-old cars, each equipped with the same optional features and in the same condition as the ten cars described in the original experiment. The company president would like to know the cars' mean trade-in price. Determine the 95% confidence interval estimate of the expected value of all the cars that have been driven 75,000 miles.

Solution, Part (a).   The problem objective is to analyze the relationship between two variables whose data scale is interval. Because we want to determine how the odometer reading influences trade-in value, we identify the latter as the dependent variable, y, and the former as the independent variable, x.

From the data, we compute the following summations:

$$\sum x_i = 731$$
$$\sum x_i^2 = 55{,}545$$
$$\sum y_i = 367$$
$$\sum y_i^2 = 13{,}657$$
$$\sum x_i y_i = 26{,}265$$

We then find the sum of squares:

$$SS_x = \sum x_i^2 - \frac{(\sum x_i)^2}{n} = 55{,}545 - \frac{(731)^2}{10} = 2{,}108.9$$

$$SS_y = \sum y_i^2 - \frac{(\sum y_i)^2}{n} = 13{,}657 - \frac{(367)^2}{10} = 188.1$$

$$SS_{xy} = \sum x_i y_i - \frac{(\sum x_i)(\sum y_i)}{n} = 26{,}265 - \frac{(731)(367)}{10} = -562.7$$

Finally, we calculate the coefficients:

$$\hat{\beta}_1 = \frac{SS_{xy}}{SS_x} = \frac{-562.7}{2{,}108.9} = -.267$$

$$\hat{\beta}_0 = \bar{y} - \hat{\beta}_1\bar{x} = \frac{367}{10} - (-.267)\frac{731}{10} = 56.203$$

The sample regression line is

$$\hat{y} = 56.203 - .267x$$

Solution, Part (b).   The intercept is the value of y when $x = 0$. Obviously, no 3-year-old cars have no mileage on the odometer. We cannot realistically interpret the value of $\hat{\beta}_0$.

The slope ($\beta_1 = -.267$) tells us that, for each additional 1,000 miles driven, the car's value decreases by an average of .267 (in \$100s) or \$26.70. By altering the units, we find that each additional mile results in an average reduction of 2.67 cents in trade-in value.

Solution, Part (c).   We want to calculate

$$s_\varepsilon = \sqrt{\frac{SSE}{n-2}}$$

Using our shortcut method, we find

$$SSE = SS_y - \frac{SS_{xy}^2}{SS_x} = 188.1 - \frac{(-562.7)^2}{2,108.9} = 37.96$$

Hence,

$$s_\varepsilon = \sqrt{\frac{37.96}{10-2}} = 2.18$$

Therefore, the standard error of estimate is 2.18.

Solution, Part (d).   This question is answered by testing the population slope, β_1. Since we want to know whether there is sufficient evidence to indicate a *negative* linear relationship, the alternative hypothesis is $H_A: \beta_1 < 0$. The complete test is as follows:

$$H_0: \beta_1 = 0$$
$$H_A: \beta_1 < 0$$

Test statistic:

$$t = \frac{\hat{\beta}_1 - \beta_1}{s_{\hat{\beta}_1}}$$

Rejection region:

$$t < -t_{\alpha, n-2}$$
$$< -t_{.05, 8}$$
$$< -1.860$$

Value of the test statistic: From the calculations in parts (a) and (c), we have

$$\hat{\beta}_1 = -.267$$

$$s_\varepsilon = 2.18$$

$$SS_x = 2,108.9$$

$$s_{\hat{\beta}_1} = \frac{s_\varepsilon}{\sqrt{SS_x}} = .047$$

Hence,

$$t = \frac{\hat{\beta}_1 - \beta_1}{s_{\hat{\beta}_1}} = \frac{-.267 - 0}{.047} = -5.68$$

Conclusion: Reject H_0.

There is sufficient evidence to conclude that higher mileage results in a lower trade-in value.

Solution, Part (e).   The coefficient of correlation is

$$r = \frac{SS_{xy}}{\sqrt{SS_x \cdot SS_y}} = \frac{-562.7}{\sqrt{(2,108.9)(188.1)}} = -.893$$

The coefficient of determination is

$$r^2 = (-.893)^2 = .798$$

The value of the coefficient of determination tells us that 79.8% of the variability in trade-in values is explained by the variability in odometer readings. The remaining 20.2% is unexplained. This indicates a strong linear relationship.

Solution, Part (f).   Since we want to predict the value of only one car, the prediction interval is

$$\hat{y} \pm t_{\alpha/2, n-2} s_\varepsilon \sqrt{1 + \frac{1}{n} + \frac{(x_g - \bar{x})^2}{SS_x}}$$

where

$$\hat{y} = 56.203 - .267 x_g = 56.203 - .267(60) = 40.19$$

and

$$s_\varepsilon = 2.18$$

$$x_g = 60$$

$$\bar{x} = 73.1$$

$$SS_x = 2,108.9$$

$$t_{\alpha/2, n-2} = t_{.025, 8} = 2.306$$

The 95% prediction interval is

$$\hat{y} \pm t_{\alpha/2, n-2} S_\varepsilon \sqrt{1 + \frac{1}{n} + \frac{(x_g - \bar{x})^2}{SS_x}}$$

$$= 40.19 \pm 2.306(2.18) \sqrt{1 + \frac{1}{10} + \frac{(60 - 73.1)^2}{2,108.9}}$$

$$= 40.19 \pm 5.46$$

which simplifies to

$$(34.73, 45.65)$$

We therefore predict that the trade-in value of the car will be between $3,473 and $4,565.

Solution, Part (g).   Since we now want to estimate the mean value of a large number of cars, the confidence interval estimator is

$$\hat{y} \pm t_{\alpha/2, n-2} S_\varepsilon \sqrt{\frac{1}{n} + \frac{(x_g - \bar{x})^2}{SS_x}}$$

where

$$\hat{y} = 56.203 - .267(75) = 36.19$$

and

$$t_{.025, 8} = 2.306$$

The 95% confidence interval estimate of the expected value is

$$\hat{y} \pm t_{\alpha/2, n-2} S_\varepsilon \sqrt{\frac{1}{n} + \frac{(x_g - \bar{x})^2}{SS_x}}$$

$$= 36.19 \pm 2.306(2.18) \sqrt{\frac{1}{10} + \frac{(75 - 73.1)^2}{2,108.9}}$$

$$= 36.19 \pm 1.60$$

which simplifies to

$$(34.59, 37.79)$$

We therefore predict that the mean price of the cars will be between $3,459 and $3,779.

COMPUTER OUTPUT FOR EXAMPLE 15.7

Minitab

```
The regression equation is

C1=56.2-0.267C2
```

```
Predictor    Coef        Stdev       t-ratio
Constant     56.205      3.535       15.90
C2           -0.26682    0.04743     -5.63

s=2.178    R-sq=79.8%    R-sq (adj)=77.3%

Analysis of Variance

SOURCE        DF      SS        MS
Regression    1     150.14    150.14
Error         8      37.96      4.74
Total         9     188.10
```

Separate subcommands are used to answer parts (f) and (g). For part (f), the output is

```
 Fit      Stdev. Fit       95% C.I.           95% P.I.
40.195      0.928     (38.056, 42.335)   (34.734, 45.657)
```

The 95% prediction interval (95% P.I.) is

```
(34.734, 45.657)
```

For part (g), the output is

```
 Fit      Stdev. Fit       95% C.I.           95% P.I.
36.193      0.695     (34.591, 37.795)   (30.919, 41.467)
```

The 95% confidence interval estimate (95% C.I.) of the mean trade-in value of all such cars with 75,000 miles is

```
(34.591, 37.795)
```

SAS

```
Dependent Variable: Y


                              Analysis of Variance


                    Sum of        Mean
Source       DF     Squares       Square     F Value    Prob > F
Model        1     150.1405     150.1405     31.642     0.0005
Error        8      37.9595       4.7449
C Total      9     188.1000


Root MSE      2.1782     R-square    0.7982
Dep Mean     36.7000     Adj R-sq    0.7730
C.V.          5.9353
```

Parameter Estimates

Variable	DF	Parameter Estimate	Standard Error	T for H0: Parameter=0	Prob > |T|
INTERCEP	1	56.2046	3.5351	15.899	0.0001
X	1	-0.2668	0.0474	-5.625	0.0005

SECTION 15.10 *SPEARMAN RANK CORRELATION*

In the previous eight sections of this chapter, we have dealt only with interval-scaled variables and have assumed that all conditions for the validity of the hypothesis tests and confidence interval estimates have been met (see Section 15.4). In many situations, however, one or both variables may be ordinal-scaled; or if both are interval-scaled, some of the required conditions may not be satisfied. In such cases, we cannot employ the regression technique to analyze the relationship between the two variables. We can, however, calculate and test the correlation coefficient—provided that we make two fundamental changes.

The first change relates to calculating the **Spearman rank correlation coefficient,** which utilizes the ranks of the data rather than the original data themselves. Recall, from Chapters 5 and 14, that the only legitimate calculations involving ordinal data are those based on a ranking process. The sample Spearman rank correlation is denoted r_s (the population coefficient is denoted ρ_s) and it is defined as follows.

Spearman Rank Correlation Coefficient

$$r_s = \frac{SS_{xy}}{\sqrt{SS_x \cdot SS_y}}$$

where x and y are the ranks of the data.

The second change involves the hypothesis test. There is a specific test for the parameter ρ_s, where the test statistic is r_s and the critical values of the rejection region are determined from Table 12 in Appendix B. Table 12 provides values of r_0 such that

$$P(r_s > r_0) = \alpha$$

for values of n ranging from 1 to 30 and for several values of α.

EXAMPLE 15.8

In a recent publication, a consumer group rated all self-propelled lawnmowers sold coast-to-coast, on factors including evenness of cut, convenience, and safety. The overall quality of each of the eight brands of lawnmower was rated on a 10-point scale, where 10 = Excellent and 1 = Poor. The lawnmowers' suggested retail prices were also recorded and (together with the ratings) are shown in the accompanying table. The publication would like to know if higher prices mean higher quality.

Lawnmower Brand	Quality Rating	Price
A	8	$540
B	9	$570
C	3	$430
D	3	$495
E	6	$620
F	4	$510
G	6	$580
H	4	$475

Solution.*   The problem objective is to analyze the relationship between price and quality. Price has an interval scale, but the quality rating is ordinal. We begin by assuming that both variables are ordinal-scaled, and we rank each variable from 1 to 8, where 1 is the smallest value and 8 is the largest. This is shown in the following table.

Lawnmower Brand	Quality Rating	Rank (x)	Price	Rank (y)
A	8	7	$540	5
B	9	8	$570	6
C	3	1.5	$430	1
D	3	1.5	$495	3
E	6	5.5	$620	8
F	4	3.5	$510	4
G	6	5.5	$580	7
H	4	3.5	$475	2

We've arbitrarily labeled the quality ranks x and the price ranks y. (The results would be the same if we reversed the labels.) Notice that the ranks were averaged

---

* See Appendix 15.A for the Minitab commands that compute the Spearman rank correlation coefficient for this example.

when ties occurred (just as in Chapter 14). To calculate the Spearman rank correlation coefficient, we find the relevant summations of the ranks:

$$\sum x_i = 36$$
$$\sum x_i^2 = 202.5$$
$$\sum y_i = 36$$
$$\sum y_i^2 = 204$$
$$\sum x_i y_i = 192.5$$

From these, we compute

$$SS_{xy} = \sum x_i y_i - \frac{(\sum x_i)(\sum y_i)}{n} = 192.5 - \frac{(36)(36)}{8} = 30.5$$

$$SS_x = \sum x_i^2 - \frac{(\sum x_i)^2}{n} = 202.5 - \frac{(36)^2}{8} = 40.5$$

$$SS_y = \sum y_i^2 - \frac{(\sum y_i)^2}{n} = 204 - \frac{(36)^2}{8} = 42$$

Finally,

$$r_s = \frac{SS_{xy}}{\sqrt{SS_x \cdot SS_y}} = \frac{30.5}{\sqrt{(40.5)(42)}} = .740$$

This tells us that, since r_s is positive, higher prices are associated with higher-quality lawnmowers. In order to determine if this result is statistically significant, however, we test the population Spearman rank correlation coefficient. Since we want to know whether higher prices are related to higher quality, we test

$$H_0: \rho_s = 0$$
$$H_A: \rho_s > 0$$

The test statistic is r_s, and the critical value of the rejection region is found in Table 12 of Appendix B. Assuming that $\alpha = .05$, and given $n = 8$, we find r_0 such that

$$P(r_s > r_0) = .05$$

Thus $r_0 = .643$. The rejection region is

$$r_s > .643$$

Since $r_s = .740$, we reject the null hypothesis and conclude that there is sufficient evidence to indicate that $\rho_s > 0$. Hence, there is enough evidence to allow us to conclude that, in general, higher prices indicate higher quality.

Incidentally, had we wanted to perform a one-tail test with

$$H_A: \rho_s < 0$$

the rejection region would have been

$$r_s < -.643$$

A two-tail test with

$$H_A: \rho_s \neq 0$$

would have had the following rejection region (with $\alpha = .05$):

$$r_s > .738 \quad \text{or} \quad r_s < -.738$$

SHORTCUT CALCULATION FOR r_s

A shortcut method can be used to calculate r_s, provided that there are not too many ties in the rankings of the original data. If there are no tied observations, the following formula produces the same value of r_s as the other formula.

> **Shortcut Calculation of r_s**
>
> $$r_s = 1 - \frac{6 \sum d_i^2}{n(n^2 - 1)}$$
>
> where $d_i = x_i - y_i$.

If some ties are present, the shortcut formula provides an approximation of the actual value of r_s. In Example 15.8, there were three pairs of tied observations. To use the shortcut method, we first find the values shown in the following table.

Quality Rank x_i	Price Rank y_i	Difference $d_i = x_i - y_i$	d_i^2
7	5	2	4
8	6	2	4
1.5	1	.5	.25
1.5	3	-1.5	2.25
5.5	8	-2.5	6.25
3.5	4	-.5	.25
5.5	7	-1.5	2.25
3.5	2	1.5	2.25
			$\sum d_i^2 = 21.5$

From these it follows that

$$r_s \cong 1 - \frac{6 \sum d_i^2}{n(n^2 - 1)}$$

$$\cong 1 - \frac{6(21.5)}{8(64 - 1)}$$

$$\cong .744$$

which is very close to the actual value of .740.

LARGE SAMPLE SIZE

When $n > 30$, then (under the null hypothesis $H_0: \rho_s = 0$) r_s is approximately normally distributed, with mean

$$E(r_s) = 0$$

and standard deviation

$$\sigma_{r_s} = \frac{1}{\sqrt{n - 1}}$$

Thus, the standardized test statistic is as follows.

Standardized Test Statistic for ρ_s when $n > 30$

$$z = \frac{r_s - 0}{\dfrac{1}{\sqrt{n - 1}}} = r_s \sqrt{n - 1}$$

EXAMPLE 15.9

In the last decade society in general and the judicial system in particular have altered their opinion of the seriousness of drunken driving. In most jurisdictions a blood-alcohol level in excess of .08 in an automobile driver is a felony. However, because of a number of factors, it is difficult to provide guidelines on when it is safe for someone who has consumed alcohol to drive his or her car. In an experiment to examine the relationship between blood-alcohol level and the weight of the drinker, 36 men of varying weights were given 3 beers to drink, and 1 hour later their blood-alcohol level was measured. Because the statistician in charge of the experiment concluded that a regression analysis was invalid (because he determined that the error term was nonnormal) the data for each variable were ranked. The ranks (where 1 = Lowest and 36 = Highest) are shown in the accompanying table. Can we conclude at the 5% significance level that the blood-alcohol level in heavier men is in general less than that in lighter men? (In this table, the ranks for weight were placed in order.)

Ranks		Ranks		Ranks	
Weight	Blood-Alcohol Level	Weight	Blood-Alcohol Level	Weight	Blood-Alcohol Level
1	34	13	26	25	18
2	28	14	30	26	11
3	31	15	17	27	16
4	36	16	19	28	9
5	29	17	24	29	13
6	27	18	15	30	6
7	33	19	14	31	4
8	35	20	22	32	7
9	25	21	12	33	5
10	20	22	21	34	3
11	32	23	10	35	1
12	23	24	8	36	2

Solution. The problem objective is to analyze the relationship between two interval-scaled variables. The identification of these two factors would ordinarily lead us to use regression analysis and to test β_1 in order to answer the question. However, because the error variable is not normally distributed, the appropriate technique is the test of the Spearman rank correlation coefficient. The test proceeds as follows.

$H_0: \rho_s = 0$

$H_A: \rho_s < 0$

Test statistic:

$z = r_s \sqrt{n - 1}$

Rejection region:

$z < -z_\alpha$

$\quad < -z_{.05}$

$\quad < -1.645$

Value of the test statistic: From the data we compute

$\sum d_i^2 = 14{,}944$

Thus,

$$r_s = 1 - \frac{6 \sum d_i^2}{n(n^2 - 1)} = 1 - \frac{6(14{,}944)}{36(36^2 - 1)} = -.923$$

$$z = r_s \sqrt{n - 1} = -.923 \sqrt{36 - 1} = -5.46$$

Conclusion: Reject H_0.

There is enough evidence to allow us to conclude that the blood-alcohol level of heavier men is in general less than that of lighter men. It follows that lighter men should be particularly careful about drinking and driving.

EXERCISES

LEARNING THE TECHNIQUES

15.60 Calculate the Spearman rank correlation coefficient for the following data.

x	115	220	86	99	50	110
y	1.0	1.3	.6	.8	.5	.7

15.61 Suppose that 10 pairs of observations of ordinal-scaled variables produced the following rankings. Calculate the Spearman rank correlation coefficient.

Observation	x	y
1	1	2
2	3	3
3	4	5
4	7	6
5	6	8
6	5	4
7	8	9
8	2	1
9	10	7
10	9	10

15.62 Test the following hypotheses:

a. $H_0: \rho_s = 0$
   $H_A: \rho_s > 0$
   $r_s = .482$ $n = 20$ $\alpha = .01$

b. $H_0: \rho_s = 0$
   $H_A: \rho_s \neq 0$
   $r_s = .413$ $n = 25$ $\alpha = .05$

c. $H_0: \rho_s = 0$
   $H_A: \rho_s < 0$
   $r_s = -.588$ $n = 10$ $\alpha = .05$

15.63 For the following data, compute the Spearman rank correlation coefficient.

x	−15	−6	10	5	0	−22	3
y	10	25	32	36	29	13	28

15.64 Test the following hypotheses:

$H_0: \rho_s = 0$
$H_A: \rho_s > 0$
$r_s = .205$ $n = 100$ $\alpha = .01$

15.65 Suppose that, in a sample of 60 sets of observations of x and y, we found $r_s = -.28$. Does this statistic allow us to conclude at the 5% significance level that, as x increases, y decreases?

APPLYING THE TECHNIQUES

Self-Correcting Exercise (See Appendix 15.C for the solution.)

GEN **15.66** Assume that the conditions for the test performed in Exercise 15.44 are not met. Do the data allow us to conclude (with $\alpha = .05$) that, the larger the number of tape drives, the greater the service time?

GEN **15.67** The general manager of an engineering firm wanted to know if a draftsman's experience influenced the quality of his work. She selects nine draftsmen at random and records their years of work experience and their quality rating (as assessed by their supervisors). These data are exhibited in the accompanying table. (The quality rating is on a 7-point scale, where 7 = Excellent and 1 = Poor.)

Do these data provide sufficient evidence at the 5% significance level to indicate that quality increases with amount of experience?

Draftsman	Years of Experience	Quality Rating
1	1	3
2	3	5
3	1	4
4	2	3
5	4	6
6	3	4
7	5	6
8	4	5
9	5	6

POM **15.68** The production manager of a firm wishes to examine the relationship between aptitude test scores given prior to hiring production-line workers and performance ratings the employees receive 3 months after starting. The results of this study would allow the firm to decide how much weight to give to these aptitude tests relative to

other work-history information obtained, including references. A random sample of 10 production workers yielded the results shown in the following table.

Worker	Aptitude Test Score	Performance Rating
1	3	5
2	5	4
3	3	4
4	2	3
5	3	2
6	1	4
7	4	2
8	1	2
9	4	5
10	5	5

(Both the aptitude test score and the performance rating are on 5-point scales, where 5 = Very good and 1 = Poor.) Do these data provide sufficient evidence at the 1% significance level to allow the manager to conclude that higher aptitude test scores are predictive of higher performance ratings?

FIN **15.69** If we assume that the error variable in Exercise 15.45 is not normally distributed, can we conclude at the 5% significance level that as the price increases, sales decrease?

SECTION 15.11   **SUMMARY**

Simple linear regression and **correlation** are techniques for analyzing the relationship between two interval-scaled variables. Regression analysis assumes that the two variables are linearly related. The **least squares method** produces estimates of the **intercept** and the **slope** of the regression line. Considerable effort must be expended in attempting to assess how well the linear model fits the data. We calculate the **standard error of estimate,** which is the standard deviation of the error variable. We test the population slope to determine whether there is evidence of a linear relationship. The strength of the linear association is measured by the coefficients of **correlation** and **determination.** When we're satisfied that the model provides a good fit, we can use it to **predict the particular value** and to **estimate the expected value** of the dependent variable. The **Spearman rank correlation** analyzes the relationship between two variables, at least one of which is ordinal-scaled.

Many formulas were presented in this chapter; we summarize them in Table 15.1.

TABLE 15.1   SUMMARY OF FORMULAS

$$SS_x = \sum x_i^2 - \frac{(\sum x_i)^2}{n}$$

$$SS_y = \sum y_i^2 - \frac{(\sum y_i)^2}{n}$$

$$SS_{xy} = \sum x_i y_i - \frac{(\sum x_i)(\sum y_i)}{n}$$

$$\hat{\beta}_1 = \frac{SS_{xy}}{SS_x}$$

$$\hat{\beta}_0 = \bar{y} - \hat{\beta}_1 \bar{x}$$

$$SSE = SS_y - \frac{SS_{xy}^2}{SS_x}$$

$$s_\varepsilon = \sqrt{\frac{SSE}{n-2}}$$

$$s_{\hat{\beta}_1} = \frac{s_\varepsilon}{\sqrt{SS_x}}$$

$$t = \frac{\hat{\beta}_1 - \beta_1}{s_{\hat{\beta}_1}}$$

$$r = \frac{SS_{xy}}{\sqrt{SS_x \cdot SS_y}}$$

$$r^2 = \frac{SS_y - SSE}{SS_y} = \frac{SSR}{SS_y}$$

$$r_s = \frac{SS_{xy}}{\sqrt{SS_x \cdot SS_y}} \qquad \text{(where } x \text{ and } y \text{ are the ranks of the data)}$$

$$\cong 1 - \frac{6 \sum d_i^2}{n(n^2 - 1)} \qquad \text{(where } d_i = x_i - y_i\text{)}$$

$$\hat{y} \pm t_{\alpha/2} s_\varepsilon \sqrt{1 + \frac{1}{n} + \frac{(x_g - \bar{x})^2}{SS_x}}$$

$$\hat{y} \pm t_{\alpha/2} s_\varepsilon \sqrt{\frac{1}{n} + \frac{(x_g - \bar{x})^2}{SS_x}}$$

SUPPLEMENTARY EXERCISES

MKT **15.70** The store manager of Colonial Furniture Inc. has been reviewing quarterly advertising expenditures. TV spot ads in particular caught her eye, because they were the major expenditure item. In order to maximize cost-effectiveness, she would like to get a better idea of the relationship between the TV spot advertising she sponsors and the number of people (adults) who visit her store because of them. To this end, she has compiled the data contained in the accompanying table.

Number of TV Ads x	Number of People y
7	42
5	32
1	10
8	40
10	61
2	8
6	35
7	39
8	48
9	51
5	30
7	45
8	41
2	7
6	37
5	33

$\sum x = 96$ $\sum y = 559$ $\sum xy = 3,930$
$\sum x^2 = 676$ $\sum y^2 = 23,037$

a. Find the estimated regression line that expresses the number of people coming to the store as a function of the number of TV ads run.

b. Is there enough evidence to allow the manager to conclude that there is a linear relationship between the two variables? (Use $\alpha = .10$.)

c. What proportion of the variability in the number of people coming into the store is explained by the variability in the number of TV ads?

d. Find a 99% prediction interval for the number of people entering the store if the store manager intends to sponsor five TV ads this quarter.

ECON **15.71** In recent years, fishermen on both the east and west coasts have suffered financial hardship because of shortened fishing seasons, reduced catches, and lower market prices. Moreover, fishermen have complained about price fluctuations and have called for a system of minimum prices. One suggestion made was that the size of the catch had an immediate impact on prices, and that this relationship should be clarified before potential solutions were discussed.

In an investigation of this issue, the following data were collected for analysis. A random 12-week period was selected during which to study the price of fish versus the average daily catch.

Average Daily Catch (100 pounds) x	Price per Pound ($) y
357	1.95
621	1.05
485	2.15
927	.55
520	1.70
645	1.40
515	1.60
395	1.00
485	1.75
615	1.15
695	1.10
710	1.05

$\sum x = 6,970$ $\sum y = 16.45$ $\sum xy = 8,972.8$
$\sum x^2 = 4,315,894$ $\sum y^2 = 24.94$

a. Determine the sample regression line that shows the price per pound as a function of average daily catch.

b. Calculate the standard error of estimate. What does this value tell you about the relationship between the two variables?

c. Do these data provide sufficient evidence at the 5% significance level to allow you to conclude that large catches result in lower prices?

d. Calculate the coefficient of determination. What does this value tell you about the relationship between the two variables?

e. Find a 90% confidence interval estimate for the expected value of the price per pound if the daily catch is 75,000 pounds.

ECON **15.72** Assume that some of the conditions required to perform the regression analysis in Exercise 15.71 are not being met. Do the data provide sufficient evidence at the 5% significance level to indicate that large catches result in lower prices?

MNG **15.73** The head office of a medium-sized New England life insurance company believed that regional managers should have weekly meetings with their salesmen, not only to keep them abreast of current market trends but also to provide them with important facts and figures that would help them in their sales. Furthermore, the company felt that these meetings should be used for pep talks. One of the points management felt strongly about was the high value of new contact initiation and follow-up phone calls. To dramatize the importance of phone calls on prospective clients and (ultimately) on sales, the company undertook the following small study.

Twenty randomly selected life insurance salesmen were surveyed to determine the number of weekly sales calls they made and the number of policy sales they concluded. The data shown in the accompanying table were collected.

Weekly Calls x	Weekly Sales y
66	20
43	15

Weekly Calls x	Weekly Sales y
57	18
32	12
18	2
59	21
61	18
32	8
48	14
39	12
58	17
54	16
48	13
37	9
29	9
21	5
43	12
62	18
51	17
44	14
$\sum x = 902$	$\sum y = 270$ $\sum xy = 13{,}432$
$\sum x^2 = 44{,}318$	$\sum y^2 = 4{,}120$

a. Find the least squares regression line that expresses the number of sales as a function of the number of calls.

b. What do the coefficients tell you?

c. Is there enough evidence (with $\alpha = .05$) to indicate that, the larger the number of calls, the larger the number of sales?

d. What proportion of the variability in the number of sales can be attributed to the variability in the number of calls?

e. Find a 90% confidence interval estimate of the mean number of sales if many salesmen make 50 calls each.

f. Predict with 99% confidence the number of sales concluded by a salesman who makes 30 calls.

POM **15.74** In order to control maintenance costs more effectively, the production manager at a factory divided the machines on the floor into five age classes and for each class selected three machines at random for which to investigate maintenance cost records over the preceding 3 months. The data compiled appear in the accompanying table.

Age (months)	Monthly Costs ($)		
6	51.27	24.30	48.00
12	102.50	140.70	125.00
18	227.00	185.90	200.20
24	285.50	265.30	205.10
30	352.75	333.80	359.90

a. Do these data provide sufficient evidence at the 10% significance level to indicate that older machines incur higher monthly maintenance costs?

b. Estimate with 95% confidence the mean monthly maintenance cost of all machines that are 2 years old.

c. Predict with 99% confidence next month's maintenance cost of a machine that is 12 months old.

TOUR **15.75** The Miami Beach Hotel Association has expressed concern about increased pollution in the area and the deterioration of some beaches. As part of their overall study of the problem, they wish to determine the relationship between beach attendance and mean daily temperature. The following data were obtained for a random sample of weekends last summer in the local area.

Mean Daily Temperature	Number of People on Beach
72°F	270
68	170
85	430
80	400

Mean Daily Temperature	Number of People on Beach
78	420
89	380
78	400
80	440
82	480

a. Find the slope and intercept of the least squares regression line for these data.

b. Plot the data and draw the regression line.

c. Test the hypothesis (with $\alpha = .10$) of a linear relationship, and compare this to your graphical evidence.

d. Predict with 99% confidence the number of people on the beach when the mean daily temperature is 88°.

e. Calculate the coefficients of correlation and determination. What do these values tell you about the relationship between the two variables?

GEN **15.76** Baseball fans are intensely interested in statistics about their favorite sport. Of particular interest is any statistic that might help them predict a team's winning percentage. A major newspaper (*Toronto Star,* 17 June 1986) published the data shown in Table E15.76.

a. Can you conclude from these results that a team's batting average is linearly related to its winning percentage? (Use $\alpha = .10$.)

b. Predict with 90% confidence the winning percentage of a team whose batting average is .275.

GEN **15.77** An agriculture student at Texas A&M has pulled some data from his father's farm records relating crop yield to amount of fertilizer used, mean seasonal rainfall, mean number of hours of sunshine, and mean daily temperature. As a first approximation, he wishes to regress crop yield on amount of fertilizer used, based on the data provided in Table E15.77.

TABLE E15.76   AMERICAN LEAGUE TEAMS

Team	Team Batting Average x	Team Winning Percentage y
Baltimore	.266	.574
Boston	.269	.661
California	.256	.508
Chicago	.246	.410
Cleveland	.271	.500
Detroit	.259	.467
Kansas City	.250	.508
Milwaukee	.271	.525
Minnesota	.274	.403
New York	.268	.587
Oakland	.252	.422
Seattle	.246	.391
Texas	.263	.548
Toronto	.270	.500
	$\sum x = 3.661$	$\sum y = 7.004$ $\sum xy = 1.8365$
	$\sum x^2 = .9586$	$\sum y^2 = 3.5826$

TABLE E15.77

Fertilizer (pounds/acre) x	Crop Yield (tons/acre) y	Fertilizer (pounds/acre) x	Crop Yield (tons/acre) y
220	36	240	39
450	72	280	45
250	48	370	62
320	51	400	71
500	80	410	79
250	40	450	75
330	55	$\sum x = 4,900$	$\sum y = 825$ $\sum xy = 307,190$
430	72	$\sum x^2 = 1,825,600$	$\sum y^2 = 51,891$

a. Find the least squares regression line for these data.

b. Test to determine whether there is a linear relationship between the two variables. (Use $\alpha = .05$.)

c. Compute the coefficient of determination, and interpret its value.

d. Forecast the crop yield, with 99% confidence, based on using 500 pounds of fertilizer. How does this compare to the actual yield when 500 pounds were used?

EDUC **15.78** In response to both students' and parents' complaints about the high cost of school materials, the local school board has attempted to keep track of students' cost of supplies. It has selected three students at random from each of the four grades (9–12) in high school, with the results shown in the following table.

Grade	Annual Cost ($) Student		
	1	2	3
9	$215	$200	$210
10	210	205	220
11	210	220	235
12	225	225	215

a. Find the equation of the regression line.

b. Do these data provide enough evidence to indicate that students in higher grades incur higher costs? (Use $\alpha = .10$.)

c. Predict with 95% confidence the annual cost of sending a child to grade 11.

d. Estimate with 98% confidence the mean annual cost of sending children to grade 9.

RE **15.79** A homebuilders' association lobbying for various home subsidy programs argued that, during periods of high interest rates, the number

of building permits issued decreased drastically, which in turn reduced the availability of new housing. The following raw data (grouped monthly) were presented as part of their argument.

Interest Rates (%) x	Building Permits y
18.00	427
10.75	1,189
15.25	825
12.45	904
15.56	800
14.25	880
13.95	950
16.85	628
11.45	1,027
16.95	610
17.50	582
17.00	600

$\sum x = 179.96$ $\sum y = 9,422$ $\sum xy$
$\sum x^2 = 2,764.48$ $\sum y^2 = 7,930,728$ $= 135,609.75$

a. Find the equation of the regression line.

b. What is the exact meaning of the slope coefficient?

c. Test to see whether there is evidence of a linear relationship. (Use $\alpha = .05$.)

d. Calculate the coefficient of determination, and comment about its meaning.

e. Predict with 90% confidence the number of building permits that will be issued if the interest rate is 16%.

RE **15.80** Repeat Exercise 15.79(c), assuming that the error variable is nonnormal.

■ CASE 15.1*   *MARKET MODEL OF STOCK RETURNS*

We recommend the use of a computer for this case. The data listed below are also stored on the data disk.

A well-known model in finance, called the *market model,* assumes that the monthly rate of return on a stock (R) is linearly related to the monthly rate of return on the overall stock market (R_m). The mathematical description of the model is

$$R = \beta_0 + \beta_1 R_m + \varepsilon$$

where the error term ε is assumed to satisfy the requirements of the linear regression model. For practical purposes, R_m is taken to be the monthly rate of return on some major stock market index, such as the New York Stock Exchange Composite Index.

The coefficient β_1, called the stock's *beta coefficient,* measures how sensitive the stock's rate of return is to changes in the level of the overall market. For example, if $\beta_1 > 1$ ($\beta_1 < 1$), the stock's rate of return is more (less) sensitive to changes in the level of the overall market than is the average stock. The monthly rates of return to Host International Inc. stock and to the overall market (as approximated by the NYSE Composite Index) over a 5-year period are shown in the accompanying table.

a. Is Host International more sensitive than average to overall stock market movements?

b. Estimate next month's expected rate of return to Host International stock, given that the corresponding expected rate of return to the overall market is 0 percent.

c. What proportion of the variability of R is explained by overall stock market movements?

MONTHLY PERCENTAGE STOCK RETURNS TO HOST INTERNATIONAL AND TO THE MARKET OVERALL, JANUARY 1975–DECEMBER 1979

Month	Host International	Market	Month	Host International	Market
January 1975	26.7	13.5	May 1975	−6.0	5.5
February 1975	7.0	6.1	June 1975	−4.2	5.2
March 1975	15.9	2.9	July 1975	4.0	−6.4
April 1975	18.6	4.7	August 1975	−5.2	−2.0

(continued)

---

* Adapted from James H. Lorie, Peter Dodd, and Mary Hamilton Kimpton, *The Stock Market: Theories and Evidence,* 2d Ed. (Homewood, Ill.: Richard D. Irwin, 1985). Original source: Center for Research in Securities Prices.

Month	Host International	Market	Month	Host International	Market
September 1975	−1.7	−3.6	November 1977	11.0	4.2
October 1975	28.2	6.1	December 1977	−1.0	.5
November 1975	17.6	3.1	January 1978	−2.7	−5.7
December 1975	1.6	−1.0	February 1978	10.4	−1.2
January 1976	17.6	12.5	March 1978	10.2	3.2
February 1976	−13.4	.1	April 1978	15.6	8.3
March 1976	−12.1	3.0	May 1978	5.4	1.9
April 1976	−6.2	−1.1	June 1978	1.2	−1.3
May 1976	−12.1	3.0	July 1978	22.3	5.7
June 1976	−2.5	4.7	August 1978	3.1	3.8
July 1976	−9.3	−.7	September 1978	−13.6	−.6
August 1976	.0	.0	October 1978	−28.8	−10.2
September 1976	−1.5	2.6	November 1978	19.0	3.1
October 1976	−5.3	−2.1	December 1978	−2.1	1.6
November 1976	9.7	.5	January 1979	−7.8	4.7
December 1976	18.7	5.8	February 1979	−10.1	−2.9
January 1977	−10.7	−4.0	March 1979	11.4	6.2
February 1977	−8.4	−1.6	April 1979	−5.5	.7
March 1977	6.3	−1.1	May 1979	−6.6	−1.5
April 1977	1.2	.4	June 1979	19.6	4.5
May 1977	2.5	−1.2	July 1979	3.7	1.5
June 1977	14.3	5.3	August 1979	7.9	6.3
July 1977	−4.2	−1.5	September 1979	−3.2	.0
August 1977	2.2	−1.4	October 1979	−10.4	−6.9
September 1977	3.1	.1	November 1979	−12.4	6.0
October 1977	6.4	−3.9	December 1979	−4.2	2.3

CASE 15.2*   *RUN LENGTH AND PERCENTAGE WASTE IN A PAPER MILL*

We recommend the use of a computer for this case. The data listed below are also stored on the data disk.

* We are grateful to Frank Belchamber for suggesting this case to us, as well as for providing the actual data.

POM

A major Canadian commercial printer has sought to control the amount of waste associated with particular printing runs. As part of this effort, the firm's general manager has asked that printing-press crews be given a table of percentage waste targets or standards. It was recognized that the firm gets less waste (expressed as a percentage of good impressions produced) on long runs, so the table was broken down by various lengths of runs.

The available data, gathered during one particular period of time, relate to one type of paper stock only (coated paper) and are shown in the accompanying table. The data apply to a single press and are collected automatically by a computer that is connected to sensors on the press. The system is complete and tamperproof.

On investigation, some of the data were deemed unsuitable for use. Some short runs occurred at very low waste, for example, but were not independent runs and therefore benefited unduly from being tacked onto longer runs (for instance, because plate changes were made with no other adjustments required, in order to create different regional advertisements in a national publication). There were also some "disasters"—not typical of the press—that should not be included in the study. Both of these types of "unsuitable" data are indicated by asterisks in the table, and the analyst may choose to omit them.

Analyze the data, and (casting yourself in the role of an industrial engineer) prepare a well-founded recommendation to management. (Your recommendations can be either positive—to continue using the table and/or to improve on it—or negative—to discontinue using the table.) Comment on the current practice of disciplining press operators for runs having in excess of 5% waste.

RUN LENGTH AND PERCENTAGE WASTE FOR A SINGLE PRINTING PRESS

Run Length (no. of impressions)	Waste (%)	Run Length (no. of impressions)	Waste (%)
51,372	22.8	33,752	4.9*
68,434	3.5*	67,192	5.4*
207,583	8.5	114,812	14.9
64,568	15.1	103,148	1.8*
90,167	9.9	92,230	29.3*
183,574	8.8	303,848	8.9
48,724	15.3	16,380	2.9*
121,752	8.7	90,939	6.9*
371,545	10.6	130,350	5.1*
138,076	13.1	214,162	19.2*
37,872	1.2*	124,245	5.9*
122,136	13.3	125,260	10.8
138,738	11.3	53,444	11.7

(continued)

Run Length (no. of impressions)	Waste (%)	Run Length (no. of impressions)	Waste (%)
134,730	9.5	64,447	6.3*
135,372	14.1	109,119	.7*
32,501	2.7*	832,635	5.8
402,383	8.3	99,322	17.4
72,707	12.9	124,423	10.9
90,293	23.8*	177,868	11.7
124,890	7.2	321,562	6.4

* Runs identified as anomalous that should (perhaps) be omitted.

CASE 15.3*   DO TALLER MBAs EARN MORE THAN SHORTER ONES?

We recommend the use of a computer for this case. The data listed below are also stored on the data disk.

GEN   One general belief held by observers of the business world is that taller men earn more than shorter men. In a University of Pittsburgh study, MBA graduates were polled and asked their monthly incomes and their heights. Suppose that 30 of the observations are as listed in the accompanying table. What can we conclude about the relationship between height and income?

HEIGHTS AND INCOMES OF MBA GRADUATES

MBA Graduate	Height (inches)	Monthly Income
1	70	$2,990
2	67	2,870
3	69	2,950
4	70	3,140
5	65	2,790
6	73	3,230
7	64	2,880
8	70	3,140
9	69	3,000

(continued)

* Adapted from an article that appeared in the *Wall Street Journal*, 30 December 1986.

MBA Graduate	Height (inches)	Monthly Income
10	73	3,170
11	68	2,910
12	66	2,840
13	71	3,180
14	68	3,020
15	73	3,220
16	73	3,370
17	70	3,180
18	71	3,340
19	69	2,970
20	73	3,240
21	75	3,150
22	68	2,860
23	69	2,930
24	76	3,210
25	71	3,180
26	66	2,670
27	69	3,050
28	65	2,750
29	67	2,960
30	70	3,050

CASE 15.4*   CONSUMER REPORTS' QUALITY RATING AND PRICE

We recommend the use of a computer for this case. The data listed below are also stored on the data disk.

GEN   Consumers often wonder if paying more for one particular brand over another gives them a better-quality product. Among the most useful sources of information for comparing brand names of specific products are the various consumers' associations.

In a recent issue of *Consumer Reports,* 18 top-of-the-line stereo large-screen TV sets (mostly 25-inchers, and the rest 26- and 27-inchers) were compared; the

---

* Adapted from *Consumer Reports* (January 1986): 12–20.

results are shown in the accompanying table. Notice that the various brands are ranked in order of estimated overall quality—that is, by the overall ratings score. The ratings table in the article also states that differences of less than 7 points in the overall ratings score—and differences of less than 10 points in the tone quality/accuracy score—were judged not very significant. Furthermore, the article concluded that all of the sets tested had acceptable picture quality—the factor that was used as the chief criterion in rating the TVs.

On the basis of the available data, can you conclude that "you get what you pay for"?

RATINGS OF TOP-OF-THE-LINE LARGE-SCREEN TV SETS

Brand and Model	Overall Ratings Score	Tone Quality/ Accuracy Score	Manufacturer's Suggested List Price	Price Consumers Union Paid
Wards Cat. No. 17737	90	86	$850	$750
Philco R5883WAK	90	83	$750	$610
Magnavox RF4950AK	88	87	$899	$725
RCA GLR2538P	86	83	$800	$650
Sony KV-2680R	84	87	$1,250	$825
Panasonic CTG-2587R	82	81	$1,099	$845
JVC AV-2590	81	77	$1,100	$750
Quasar TV9950YP	81	56	$975	$650
Fisher PC-340W	80	75	$850	$610
Mitsubishi CK-2587R	80	81	$1,100	$995
Toshiba CZ2685	80	78	$1,490	$850
GE 26CP6869	79	78	$899	$757
Zenith SB2527P	77	88	$960	$685
Zenith SB2729N	73	77	$1,080	$823
Sanyo AVM260	72	74	$800	$660
Sears Cat. No. 4870	68	79	$780	$780
Curtis Mather M2658RL	67	65	$1,250	$1,250
Hitachi CT-2559	65	72	$1,080	$740

CASE 15.5   BASEBALL TEAM SALARIES AND WINNING PERCENTAGES

We recommend the use of a computer for this case. The data listed below are also stored on the data disk.

GEN

A well-worn cliché states that money can't buy happiness. However, this may not be true if you are the owner of a major league baseball team. With the goal of winning pennants and World Series, some owners have participated in bidding wars for the services of expensive free agents and have offered lucrative contracts to keep star players. In 1988, the National League's divisional playoff participants (New York Mets and Los Angeles Dodgers) had the highest player payrolls in their respective divisions. The following table lists all major league baseball teams, their divisional rank, their winning percentage, and their average salary paid per player during the 1988 season. Upon analysis of these data, can you conclude that money can buy successful teams and thus, to some degree, happiness?

WINNING PERCENTAGES AND AVERAGE SALARIES OF MAJOR LEAGUE BASEBALL TEAMS IN 1988

American League

Division	Team	Rank in Division	Winning Percentage	Average Salary
East	Boston Red Sox	1	.549	610,172
	Detroit Tigers	2	.543	612,326
	Toronto Blue Jays	3	.537	484,427
	Milwaukee Brewers	3	.537	385,335
	New York Yankees	5	.528	718,670
	Cleveland Indians	6	.482	305,841
	Baltimore Orioles	7	.335	424,568
West	Oakland Athletics	1	.642	424,581
	Minnesota Twins	2	.562	446,598
	Kansas City Royals	3	.522	522,555
	California Angels	4	.463	417,278
	Chicago White Sox	5	.441	226,392
	Texas Rangers	6	.435	241,389
	Seattle Mariners	7	.422	242,880

(continued)

National League

Division	Team	Rank in Division	Winning Percentage	Average Salary
East	New York Mets	1	.617	605,895
	Pittsburgh Pirates	2	.531	307,088
	Montreal Expos	3	.500	343,047
	Chicago Cubs	4	.475	472,008
	St. Louis Cardinals	5	.469	522,296
	Philadelphia Phillies	6	.404	501,954
West	Los Angeles Dodgers	1	.584	573,441
	Cincinnati Reds	2	.540	304,647
	San Diego Padres	3	.516	409,930
	San Francisco Giants	4	.512	403,567
	Houston Astros	5	.506	545,595
	Atlanta Braves	6	.338	384,641

SOURCE: Creative Statistics Company.

MINITAB
INSTRUCTIONS

The command

REGRESS C1 1 C2

computes the least squares line

$$\hat{y} = \hat{\beta}_0 + \hat{\beta}_1 x$$

where the observed values of y and x are stored in columns 1 and 2, respectively. The term 1 refers to the use of only one independent variable—in this case, the variable stored in column 2. The REGRESS command may be preceded by the command

BRIEF K

where K can equal 1, 2, or 3. Increasing the value of K causes the computer to print out more statistical results. Generally, K = 1 will produce enough statistics for most applications. If the BRIEF command is not given, Minitab will assume that the command BRIEF 1 was given. For Example 15.2, the following data are input:

```
READ C1 C2
  89.5    20.0
  79.9    14.8
  83.1    20.5
  56.9    12.5
  66.6    18.0
  82.5    14.3
 126.3    27.5
  79.3    16.5
 119.9    24.3
  87.6    20.2
 112.6    22.0
```

```
120.8     19.0
 78.5     12.3
 74.3     14.0
 74.8     16.7
END
REGRESS C1 1 C2
```

(Notice that we regress y on x. Hence, we stored the values of y in column 1 and the values of x in column 2.)

The following output is printed:

```
The regression equation is

C1=18.4+3.88C2

Predictor    Coef      Stdev     t-ratio
Constant     18.35     14.81     1.24
C2           3.8786    0.7936    4.89


s=13.00    R-sq=64.8%    R-sq(adj)=62.0%

Analysis of Variance

SOURCE          DF      SS        MS
Regression      1       4034.4    4034.4
Error           13      2195.8    168.9
Total           14      6230.2
```

The subcommand **PREDICT** is used to produce the 95% confidence interval estimate of the expected value of y for a given x, and the 95% prediction interval of y for a given x. To answer the questions in Examples 15.5 and 15.6, we type the command and subcommand

```
REGRESS C1 1 C2;
PREDICT 20.
```

Here we specified the given value of x in the **PREDICT** subcommand. The computer will print out

```
  Fit     Stdev. Fit      95% C.I.          95% P.I.
95.92        3.66      (88.03, 103.82)   (66.75, 125.10)
```

To produce a scattergram, we type

```
PLOT C1 C2
```

If this command is used for Example 15.2, Minitab outputs the following.

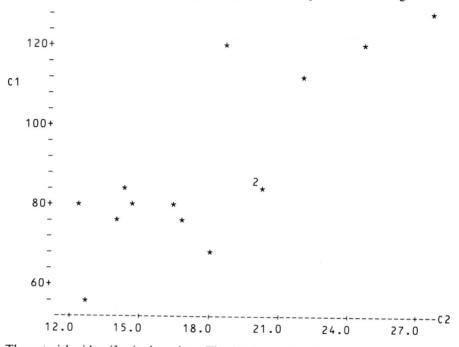

The asterisks identify single points. The 2 tells us that there are 2 points in that location.

SPEARMAN RANK CORRELATION COEFFICIENT

Minitab does not compute the Spearman rank correlation coefficient directly. However, the following sequence of commands will accomplish the task. The command

```
RANK C1 C2
```

ranks each observation in column 1 and places the ranks in column 2 (averaging the ranks of tied observations). If we rank both variables, we can use the CORRELATION command to compute the coefficient of correlation of the ranks. To illustrate, we answer the question in Exercise 15.8 as follows:

```
SET C1
8    9    3    3    6    4    6    4
END
SET C2
540    570    430    495    620    510    580    475
END
RANK C1 C3
```

```
RANK C2 C4
CORRELATION C3 C4
```

The output is

```
Correlation of C3 and C4=0.740
```

SAS INSTRUCTIONS

The REG procedure is used to perform both simple and multiple regressions. The procedure statement is followed by the MODEL statement, which specifies the dependent variable and the independent variable(s). In Example 15.2, the following commands and data are input:

```
DATA;
INPUT Y X;
CARDS;
 89.5    20.0
 79.9    14.8
 83.1    20.5
 56.9    12.5
 66.6    18.0
 82.5    14.3
126.3    27.5
 79.3    16.5
119.9    24.3
 87.6    20.2
112.6    22.0
120.8    19.0
 78.5    12.3
 74.3    14.0
 74.8    16.7
PROC REG;
MODEL Y=X;
```

The following output is printed.

```
Dependent Variable: Y
```

Analysis of Variance

Source	DF	Sum of Squares	Mean Square	F Value	Prob > F
Model	1	4034.4144	4034.4144	23.885	0.0003
Error	13	2195.8215	168.9093		
C Total	14	6230.2360			

Root MSE	12.9965	R-square	0.6476	
Dep Mean	88.8400	Adj R-sq	0.6204	
C.V.	14.6291			

Parameter Estimates

Variable	DF	Parameter Estimate	Standard Error	T for H0: Parameter=0	Prob > |T|
INTERCEP	1	18.3538	14.8077	1.239	0.2371
X	1	3.8785	0.7936	4.887	0.0003

We can use the CLI and CLM options to produce the 95% prediction intervals of the particular value of y and the 95% confidence interval estimates of the expected value of y. However, these predictions and estimates can only be based on the observed values of the independent variable x. Fortunately, SAS can be "fooled" into providing the prediction and estimate for some other values of x. To do so, we add an extra observation consisting of the given value of $x(x_g)$ and a period for y. SAS reads the period as a missing observation and ignores it when computing the least squares line. However, it does produce the prediction interval and the interval estimate for that value of x when the CLI and CLM options are asked for. To answer Examples 15.5 and 15.6, we add a 16th observation ($y = .$ and $x = 20$).

    20.0

and we change the MODEL statement to

```
MODEL Y=X/CLI CLM;
```

which produces the following output (in addition to that shown above).

Obs	Dep Var Y	Predict Value	Std Err Predict
1	89.5000	95.9	3.655
2	79.9000	75.7564	4.293
3	83.1000	97.9	3.830
4	56.9000	66.8357	5.615

Obs	Dep Var Y	Predict Value	Std Err Predict
5	66.6000	88.1677	3.359
6	82.5000	73.8171	4.551
7	126.3	125.0	8.127
8	79.3000	82.3499	3.609
9	119.9	112.6	5.908
10	87.6000	96.7	3.721
11	112.6	103.7	4.526
12	120.8	92.0463	3.419
13	78.5000	66.0600	5.743
14	74.3000	72.6535	4.715
15	74.8000	83.1256	3.554
16		95.9	3.655

Lower95% Mean	Upper95% Mean	Lower95% Predict	Upper95% Predict
88.0278	103.8	66.7581	125.1
66.4825	85.0302	46.1872	105.3
89.5896	106.1	68.5930	127.1
54.7044	78.9669	36.2498	97.4
80.9121	95.4	59.1681	117.2
63.9857	83.6484	44.0684	103.6
107.5	142.6	91.8993	158.1
74.5534	90.1464	53.2103	111.5
99.8	125.4	81.7607	143.4
88.6613	104.7	67.4950	125.9
93.9044	113.5	73.9510	133.4
84.6595	99.4	63.0136	121.1
53.6521	78.4678	35.3633	96.8
62.4677	82.8393	42.7858	102.5
75.4486	90.8026	54.0177	112.2
88.0278	103.8	66.7581	125.1

SAS will draw the scattergram if we type

```
PLOT Y*X;
```

after the MODEL statement. If we did that in Example 15.2, the scattergram below would be drawn.

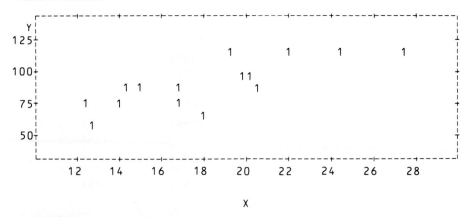

The 1s represent the observed points.

COMPUTER EXERCISES

15.81   Suppose that you are given the following set of data.

a. Determine the least squares line.

b. Test to determine whether there is evidence of a linear relationship with $\alpha = .10$.

c. Determine the coefficients of correlation and determination.

x	6	3	8	9	14	11	5	6
y	35	21	49	68	100	82	38	39

15.82   Refer to Exercise 15.81.

a. Estimate with 95% confidence the expected value of y when $x = 10$.

b. Predict with 95% confidence the value of y when $x = 10$.

15.83   The following 10 pairs of observations were drawn in order to allow you to analyze the relationship between the two variables.

a. Determine the least squares regression line.

b. Do these data provide sufficient evidence at the 5% significance level to establish that a negative linear relationship exists between x and y?

c. Interpret the coefficient of determination.

x	21	14	33	42	28	16	29	34	38	51
y	18	20	11	6	15	25	11	10	9	4

15.84   Refer to Exercise 15.83.

a. Predict with 95% confidence the value of y when $x = 30$.

b. Estimate with 95% confidence the mean value of y when $x = 30$.

SOLUTIONS TO SELF-CORRECTING EXERCISES

15.8 a. $SS_{xy} = 724 - \dfrac{(30)(182)}{8} = 41.5$

$SS_x = 132 - \dfrac{(30)^2}{8} = 19.5$

$\hat{\beta}_1 = \dfrac{41.5}{19.5} = 2.13$

$\hat{\beta}_0 = 22.75 - (2.13)(3.75) = 14.77$

The regression line is

$\hat{y} = 14.77 + 2.13x$

d. For each additional employee, the average profit per dollar of sales increases by 2.13 cents.

15.20 $\sum y = 182, \sum y^2 = 4{,}254$

$SS_y = 4{,}254 - \dfrac{(182)^2}{8} = 113.5$

$SSE = 113.5 - \dfrac{(41.5)^2}{19.5} = 25.18$

$s_\varepsilon^2 = \dfrac{25.18}{8-2} = 4.20$

The standard error of estimate is

$s_\varepsilon = 2.05$

15.30 $SS_y = 65{,}143 - \dfrac{(793)^2}{10} = 2{,}258.1$

$SSE = 2{,}258.1 - \dfrac{(631.6)^2}{297.6} = 917.65$

$s_\varepsilon = \sqrt{\dfrac{917.65}{8}} = 10.71$

$s_{\hat{\beta}_1} = \dfrac{10.71}{\sqrt{297.6}} = .62$

$H_0: \beta_1 = 0$

$H_A: \beta_1 > 0$

Rejection region:

$t > 1.860$

Test statistic:

$t = \dfrac{2.12 - 0}{.62} = 3.418$

Conclusion: Reject H_0.

There is sufficient evidence to indicate that more hours of study result in higher exam scores.

15.42 $r = \dfrac{631.6}{\sqrt{(297.6)(2{,}258.1)}} = .770$

$r^2 = (.770)^2 = .593$

15.52 $SS_y = 6{,}070{,}625 - \dfrac{(8{,}175)^2}{15} = 1{,}615{,}250$

$SSE = 1{,}615{,}250 - \dfrac{(7{,}920)^2}{40.6} = 70{,}264.8$

$$s_\varepsilon = \sqrt{\frac{70,264.8}{15-2}} = 73.52$$

$$\hat{y} = -644.95 + 195.07(5) = 330.4$$

$$\hat{y} \pm t_{\alpha/2} s_\varepsilon \sqrt{1 + \frac{1}{n} + \frac{(x_g - \bar{x})^2}{SS_x}}$$

$$= 330.4 \pm (1.771)(73.52)$$

$$\times \sqrt{1 + \frac{1}{15} + \frac{(5-6.1)^2}{40.6}} = 330.4 \pm 136.3$$

When advertising expenditures equal $5,000, we predict that sales will be between $194,100 and $466,700.

15.66

Tape Drives	Rank (x)	Service Call	Rank (y)
5	5.5	310	4
3	3.5	240	3
7	8	380	6
2	2	120	2
1	1	90	1
9	10	510	10
8	9	450	9
6	7	320	5
5	5.5	410	8
3	3.5	390	7
	$\sum x = 55$		$\sum y = 55$
	$\sum x^2 = 384$		$\sum y^2 = 385$

$\sum xy = 370$

$$SS_{xy} = 370 - \frac{(55)(55)}{10} = 67.5$$

$$SS_x = 384 - \frac{(55)^2}{10} = 81.5$$

$$SS_y = 385 - \frac{(55)^2}{10} = 82.5$$

$$r_s = \frac{67.5}{\sqrt{(81.5)(82.5)}} = .823$$

$H_0: \rho_s = 0$

$H_A: \rho_s > 0$

Rejection region:

$r_s > .564$

Test statistic:

$r_s = .823$

Conclusion: Reject H_0.

There is enough evidence to conclude that the larger the number of tape drives is, the greater the service time will be.

CHAPTER 16

MULTIPLE REGRESSION

INTRODUCTION

In this chapter we extend the statistical technique introduced in Chapter 15. In that chapter we employed the simple linear regression model to analyze how one variable (the dependent variable y) is affected by another variable (the independent variable x). We acknowledged, however, that by restricting the number of independent variables to one, we reduce the potential usefulness of the model.

In this chapter we remove the restriction and allow for any number of independent variables. In so doing, we expect to improve our ability to predict the value of the dependent variable and estimate its expected value.

The improved performance of the multiple regression model, however, is not cost-free. Because additional variables are included, calculating the required statistics becomes quite lengthy. Fortunately, the availability of computer software packages designed for this purpose enables us to avoid having to perform these calculations ourselves. As a result, our focus in this chapter is on recognizing and interpreting various computer systems' output.

MODEL AND REQUIRED CONDITIONS

We now assume that k independent variables are potentially related to the dependent variable. Thus, the model is represented by the following equation:

$$y = \beta_0 + \beta_1 x_1 + \beta_2 x_2 + \cdots + \beta_k x_k + \varepsilon$$

where y is the dependent variable, $x_1, x_2, \ldots, x_k$ are the independent variables, $\beta_0, \beta_1, \ldots, \beta_k$ are the coefficients, and ε is the error variable. The independent variables may actually be functions of other variables. For example, we may define some of the independent variables as follows:

$$x_2 = x_1^2$$
$$x_3 = x_1 \cdot x_2$$
$$x_5 = \log(x_4)$$

In Chapter 17, we will discuss how and under what circumstances such functions can be used in regression analysis. In this chapter, for the most part, we keep the models relatively uncomplicated.

The error variable is retained because—even though we have included additional independent variables—deviations between values in the model and the

FIGURE 16.1   *RESPONSE SURFACE PRODUCED BY MULTIPLE REGRESSION, WITH $k = 2$*

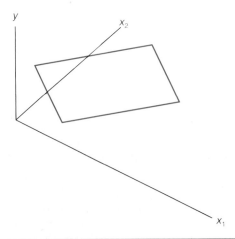

actual values of y will still occur. Incidentally, when there is more than one independent variable in the regression analysis, we refer to the graphical depiction of the equation as a **response surface** rather than as a straight line. Figure 16.1 depicts such a surface when $k = 2$. Of course, whenever $k > 2$ we can only imagine the curve; we cannot draw it.

An important part of regression analysis comprises several statistical techniques that evaluate how well the model fits the data. These techniques require the accompanying conditions, which we first discussed in Chapter 15.

Required Conditions of Regression Analysis

1. The error variable ε is normally distributed.
2. The mean value of the error variable is zero; that is, $E(\varepsilon) = 0$.
3. The variance of the error variable is
   $$\text{Var}(\varepsilon) = \sigma_\varepsilon^2$$
   which is a fixed but unknown value.
4. The values of the error variable are independent of one another.

In Section 16.6 we will discuss how to recognize when the requirements are unsatisfied, what the consequences of departing from these requirements are, and how to deal with the situation. Nonetheless, we will assume that these conditions are satisfied in all of the examples and exercises in this book.

Our initial goal is to determine the values of the coefficients $\beta_0, \beta_1, \ldots, \beta_k$. Since these are population parameters, we estimate their values from a random sample by using the least squares method. That is, we calculate the estimates of the coefficients $\beta_0, \beta_1, \ldots, \beta_k$ by minimizing.

$$SSE = \sum(y_i - \hat{y}_i)^2$$

Unlike the computations encountered in applying simple regression, however, the calculations involved in applying multiple regression are so time-consuming that—except for those with masochistic tendencies—no one ever does the analysis by hand (even with the aid of a calculator). Instead, all of the analyses are performed by statistical applications packages.

Consistent with the way we've presented computer output thus far, we will show the printouts for Minitab and SAS for the examples and exercises in this chapter. In Appendixes 16.A and 16.B, we provide instructions for using both packages.

EXERCISES

16.1 In Chapter 15, the simplifying assumption was made that one explanatory variable could adequately explain the dependent variable of interest. For the following examples, suggest two or three additional independent variables that could be added to the simple regression model.

Dependent Variable	Independent Variable
House price	Size of house
Car price	Odometer reading
Crop yield	Amount of fertilizer used
Team winning percentage	Team batting average
Weekly food expenditure	Weekly net income

16.2 Underlying the multiple regression model are certain assumptions, one of which relates to *linearity*.

a. Discuss at least one way you might be able to check for linearity *before* you run your regression.

b. Discuss at least one way you might be able to check for linearity *after* you have run your regression.

c. What other required conditions for the use of the model should be tested for?

16.3 a. Go to your library and collect an actual set of data that you would like to run as a multiple regression.

b. Discuss the model you would like to test.

c. Discuss the relationship between the variables you thought of using and the actual empirical counterpart of each variable you found.

SECTION 16.3 **INTERPRETING AND TESTING THE COEFFICIENTS**

▬▬▬▬▬▬ **EXAMPLE 16.1**

In Example 15.2, we described the problem of a real estate agent who wanted to predict the selling price of single-family homes. In order to use the simple regression model, he gathered the prices and sizes of 15 recently sold houses. In the analysis that followed, we found that the standard error of estimate was

$$s_\varepsilon = 13.00$$

and the coefficient of determination was

$$r^2 = .648$$

The coefficient of determination indicates that 64.8% of the variation in selling price is explained by the variation in house size. The remaining 35.2% is unexplained. To reduce the proportion of unexplained variation (and so increase r^2 and decrease s_ε), the agent decides to include two additional independent variables: the age of the house, and the lot size (in 1,000s ft^2). All of these data are exhibited in Table 16.1.

The model being proposed is

$$y = \beta_0 + \beta_1 x_1 + \beta_2 x_2 + \beta_3 x_3 + \varepsilon$$

Estimate the coefficients and interpret the results.

Solution. From either one of the two computer printouts that we will present shortly, we find the following estimates of the coefficients

$$\hat{\beta}_0 = -16.06$$
$$\hat{\beta}_1 = 4.146$$
$$\hat{\beta}_2 = -0.236$$
$$\hat{\beta}_3 = 4.831$$

Thus, the sample regression line is

$$\hat{y} = -16.06 + 4.146x_1 - 0.236x_2 + 4.831x_3$$

The intercept $\hat{\beta}_0 = -16.06$ represents the value of $\hat{y}$ when $x_1 = x_2 = x_3 = 0$. As we observed in Chapter 15, it is often misleading to try to interpret the value of the intercept, particularly when the range of values of the independent variables does not include zero.

The relationship between x_1 and y is measured by $\hat{\beta}_1 = 4.146$. This indicates that, in this model, for each additional 100 square feet, the price of the house increases (on average) by \$4,146 (assuming that the other independent variables are fixed).

The coefficient $\hat{\beta}_2 = -.236$ specifies that, for each additional year in the age of

TABLE 16.1   *DATA FOR EXAMPLE 16.1*

House	Selling Price ($1,000s) y	House Size (100s ft^2) x_1	Age (years) x_2	Lot Size (1,000s ft^2) x_3
1	89.5	20.0	5	4.1
2	79.9	14.8	10	6.8
3	83.1	20.5	8	6.3
4	56.9	12.5	7	5.1
5	66.6	18.0	8	4.2
6	82.5	14.3	12	8.6
7	126.3	27.5	1	4.9
8	79.3	16.5	10	6.2
9	119.9	24.3	2	7.5
10	87.6	20.2	8	5.1
11	112.6	22.0	7	6.3
12	120.8	19.0	11	12.9
13	78.5	12.3	16	9.6
14	74.3	14.0	12	5.7
15	74.8	16.7	13	4.8

the house, the price decreases by an average of $236 (as long as the values of the other independent variables do not change).

Finally the coefficient $\hat{\beta}_3 = 4.831$ means that, for each additional 1,000 square feet of lot size, the price increases by an average of $4,831 (assuming that x_1 and x_2 remain the same).

COMPUTER OUTPUT FOR EXAMPLE 16.1*

Minitab

```
The regression equation is

C1=-16.1+4.15C2-0.236C3+4.83C4
```

---

* Appendixes 16.A and 16.B provide details about how Minitab and SAS, respectively, perform the multiple regression analysis for this example.

```
Predictor      Coef       Stdev     t-ratio
Constant     -16.06      19.07      -0.84
      C2       4.1462     0.7512     5.52
      C3      -0.2361     0.8812    -0.27
      C4       4.8309     0.9011     5.36


s=6.894   R-sq=91.6%   R-sq (adj)=89.3%

Analysis of Variance

SOURCE          DF      SS        MS
Regression       3    5707.4    1902.5
Error           11     522.8      47.5
Total           14    6230.2
```

The values of y were stored in column 1, while columns 2, 3, and 4 contained independent variables x_1, x_2, and x_3, respectively.

SAS

```
Dependent Variable: Y


                               Analysis of Variance


                 Sum of     Mean
Source     DF    Squares    Square     F Value    Prob > F
Model       3    5707.44    1902.48    40.029     0.0000
Error      11     522.80      47.53
C Total    14    6230.24


Root MSE     6.894    R-square    0.916
Dep Mean    88.840    Adj R-sq    0.893
C.V.         7.760


                               Parameter Estimates


                 Parameter   Standard   T for H0:
Variable    DF   Estimate    Error      Parameter=0    Prob > |T|
INTERCEP     1    -16.058    19.071     -0.842         0.418
X1           1      4.146     0.751      5.520         0.000
X2           1     -0.236     0.881     -0.268         0.794
X3           1      4.831     0.901      5.361         0.000
```

TESTING THE COEFFICIENTS

In Chapter 15, we tested to determine whether there was sufficient evidence of a linear relationship between y and x. The null and alternative hypotheses were

$$H_0: \beta_1 = 0$$
$$H_A: \beta_1 \neq 0$$

The test statistic was

$$t = \frac{\hat{\beta}_1 - \beta_1}{s_{\hat{\beta}_1}}$$

which is Student t distributed with $n - 2$ degrees of freedom.

In multiple regression, we have more than one independent variable; and for each such variable, we can test to determine if there is evidence of a linear relationship between it and y.

Testing the Coefficients

$$H_0: \beta_i = 0$$
$$H_A: \beta_i \neq 0$$

(for $i = 1, 2, \ldots, k$), and the test statistic is

$$t = \frac{\hat{\beta}_i - \beta_i}{s_{\hat{\beta}_i}}$$

which is Student t distributed with d.f. $= n - k - 1$.

Care should be taken in interpreting the results of these tests. We may find that in one model there is enough statistical evidence to show that a particular independent variable is linearly related to y, while in another model not enough evidence exists to establish a linear relationship. As a result, whenever we do not reject H_0, we will state that there is not enough evidence to show that the independent variable and y are linearly related *in this model*. This issue will be examined further when we discuss collinearity in Section 16.6.

EXAMPLE 16.2

Using the data developed in Example 16.1, test at the 5% level of significance to determine whether we can conclude that there is evidence of a linear relationship between x_1 and y, x_2 and y, and x_3 and y.

Solution.   The tests that follow are performed just as all preceding tests in this book have been. We set up the null and alternative hypotheses, define the rejection region, and identify the value of the test statistic. The only difference is that here the value of the test statistic comes from the computer printout. For each independent variable, we test

$$H_0: \beta_i = 0$$
$$H_A: \beta_i \neq 0$$

($i = 1, 2, 3$). The rejection region is

$$|t| > t_{\alpha/2, n-k-1}$$
$$> t_{.025, 11}$$
$$> 2.201$$

From the computer output for Example 16.1, we find the value of the test statistics for each coefficient (other than β_0).

Test of β_1

Value of the test statistic: $t = 5.520$

Conclusion: Reject H_0.

There is enough evidence to allow us to conclude that there is a linear relationship between house price and house size. We can come to the same conclusion by observing (from SAS) that the p-value is .000.

Test of β_2

Value of the test statistic: $t = -.268$ (p-value $= .794$)

Conclusion: Do not reject H_0.

There is not enough evidence to allow us to conclude that there is a linear relationship between age and price (in this model).

Test of β_3

Value of the test statistic: $t = 5.361$ (p-value $= .000$)

Conclusion: Reject H_0.

There is enough evidence to allow us to conclude that lot size and price are linearly related.

Thus we have discovered that the size of the house and the lot size are linearly related to the price, while the age of the house is not necessarily linearly related to the price. If the real estate agent has confidence in the reliability of these results, he will not make the age of the house a factor in recommending a price to either the buyer or the seller of the property.

A couple of warnings must attend this conclusion. First, if one or more of the required conditions are violated, the results may be invalid. This possibility will be investigated in Section 16.6. Second, because the age of the houses in the random sample fell between 1 and 16 years, the conclusions we drew apply only to houses in that age range. It is likely that a much older home's selling price would be influenced by its age. Remember, we can only draw valid conclusions about the model for values within the range of the observed values of the independent variables.

EXERCISES

LEARNING THE TECHNIQUES

16.4 Can we conclude with $\alpha = .01$ from the following output that

a. x_1 and y are positively correlated?

b. x_2 and y are negatively correlated?

	Coefficients	Standard Error
Constant	125.6	52.0
x_1	12.3	3.9
x_2	−6.1	1.6

$k = 2$ $n = 30$

16.5 Do the results below allow us to conclude that there are linear relationships between each of x_1, x_2, and x_3 and y? (Use $\alpha = .05$.)

	Coefficients	Standard Error
Constant	−30.0	10.0
x_1	−7.5	4.2
x_2	18.0	10.1
x_3	−0.5	0.2

$k = 3$ $n = 100$

16.6 Suppose that, in an effort to estimate the equation,

$$y = \beta_0 + \beta_1 x_1 + \beta_2 x_2 + \varepsilon$$

18 observations produced the following estimates and standard deviations:

$\hat{\beta}_0 = 5.5$ $s_{\hat{\beta}_0} = 2.0$

$\hat{\beta}_1 = 2.4$ $s_{\hat{\beta}_1} = .8$

$\hat{\beta}_2 = 6.0$ $s_{\hat{\beta}_2} = 3.6$

Test the following hypotheses, with $\alpha = .01$:

a. $H_0: \beta_1 = 0$
   $H_A: \beta_1 \neq 0$

b. $H_0: \beta_2 = 0$
   $H_A: \beta_2 \neq 0$

16.7 From 25 observations of the variables y, x_1, x_2, and x_3, output on coefficients and standard errors of coefficients was produced in an attempt to estimate the model

$$y = \beta_0 + \beta_1 x_1 + \beta_2 x_2 + \beta_3 x_3 + \varepsilon$$

Here are the output data:

$\hat{\beta}_0 = $ 51.2 $s_{\hat{\beta}_0} = 10.6$

$\hat{\beta}_1 = $ 48.6 $s_{\hat{\beta}_1} = 12.8$

$\hat{\beta}_2 = $ 19.3 $s_{\hat{\beta}_2} = 14.3$

$\hat{\beta}_3 = -22.5$ $s_{\hat{\beta}_3} = $ 5.6

Test the following hypotheses, with $\alpha = .05$:

a. $H_0: \beta_1 = 0$
   $H_A: \beta_1 \neq 0$

b. $H_0: \beta_2 = 0$
   $H_A: \beta_2 > 0$

c. $H_0: \beta_3 = 0$
   $H_A: \beta_3 < 0$

16.8 In estimating the regression model

$$y = \beta_0 + \beta_1 x_1 + \beta_2 x_2 + \beta_3 x_3 + \beta_4 x_4 + \varepsilon$$

with 50 observations, a statistician observed the following partial Minitab output:

```
The regression equation is

Y=110.5+32.8X1-56.3X2+85.0X3-27.6X4

Predictor    Coef    Stdev    t-ratio
Constant    110.5    52.1      2.12
   X1        32.8    12.6      2.60
```

Predictor	Coef	Stdev	t-ratio
X2	-56.3	48.5	-1.16
X3	85.0	69.1	1.23
X4	-27.6	5.6	-4.93

a. Do these data allow us to conclude at the 5% significance level that a linear relationship exists between x_1 and y?

b. Can we conclude (with $\alpha = .01$) that there is a negative linear relationship between x_2 and y?

c. Can we conclude at the 10% significance level that there is a positive linear relationship between x_3 and y?

16.9 To estimate the multiple regression model

$$y = \beta_0 + \beta_1 x_1 + \beta_2 x_2 + \varepsilon$$

a researcher took 200 observations. The partial SAS output shown in Figure E16.9 was created.

a. Can we conclude (with $\alpha = .05$) that there is a positive linear relationship between x_1 and y?

b. Can we conclude (with $\alpha = .05$) that there is a negative linear relationship between x_2 and y?

APPLYING THE TECHNIQUES

Self-Correcting Exercise (See Appendix 16.C for the solution.)

RE **16.10** The owner of a drywall-manufacturing plant wants to predict the monthly demand for drywall (in 100s of 4 × 8 sheets) as a function of the number of building permits issued in the county, the 5-year-term mortgage rates, and overall economic activity as measured by per capita GNP (in $1,000s). Taking monthly data over the last three years, he used the SAS statistical applications package to produce the results shown in Figure E16.10:

a. Interpret the coefficients, $\hat{\beta}_1$, $\hat{\beta}_2$, and $\hat{\beta}_3$.

b. Test to determine whether there is a linear relationship between each of the independent variables and the dependent variable. (Use $\alpha = .05$.)

FIGURE E16.9

Parameter Estimates

Variable	DF	Parameter Estimate	Standard Error	T for H0: Parameter=0	Prob > |T|
INTERCEP	1	75.0	45.5	1.65	0.099
X1	1	6.5	2.1	3.10	0.002
X2	1	-10.4	8.8	-1.18	0.238

FIGURE E16.10

Parameter Estimates

Variable	DF	Parameter Estimate	Standard Error	T for H0: Parameter=0	Prob > |T|
INTERCEP	1	5.127	1.325	3.869	.0004
PERMITS	1	0.062	0.030	2.067	.0444
RATES	1	-1.212	0.659	-1.839	.0722
GNP	1	0.022	0.005	4.400	.0000

ECON **16.11** A meat packer was interested in getting a better understanding of the variables that influence the price of beef in the state. After some thought, he produced the following list of four variables that he believes affect the price of beef (in hundredweights, on the hoof). These are

Average beef consumption
Price of chicken
Price of pork
Price of lamb

Using data from the last 120 months and a computer package, he produced the statistics shown in Figure E16.11:

a. Are the signs of $\hat{\beta}_1, \hat{\beta}_2, \hat{\beta}_3$, and $\hat{\beta}_4$ in the expected direction? Explain.

b. Which of the four independent variables are linearly related to the dependent variable? (Test with $\alpha = .05$.)

FIGURE E16.11

Variable	Coefficient $\hat{\beta}_i$	Standard Error $s_{\hat{\beta}_i}$	t-statistic
BEEF	1.259	.397	3.174
CHICKEN	1.214	.601	2.020
PORK	2.386	2.708	.881
LAMB	1.366	.544	2.513
CONSTANT	5.260	7.982	.659

RE **16.12** A developer who specializes in summer cottage properties is considering purchasing a large tract of land adjoining a lake, approximately 60 miles from a large urban area. The current owner of the tract has already subdivided the land into separate building lots and has prepared the lots by removing some of the trees. The developer wants to forecast the value of each lot. From previous experience, she knows that the most important factors affecting the price of a lot (in $1,000s) are lot size (in square feet), number of mature trees remaining, and distance to the lake (in feet). From a nearby area, she gathers relevant data about 60 recently sold lots. Using Minitab computer software, she produces the output shown in Figure E16.12.

a. What do the values of $\hat{\beta}_0, \hat{\beta}_1, \hat{\beta}_2$, and $\hat{\beta}_3$ tell you?

b. Is there sufficient evidence to indicate that price and size are linearly related? (Use $\alpha = .05$.)

c. Do these data provide enough evidence to enable the developer to conclude, at the 1% significance level, that price and distance from the lake are negatively linearly related?

FIGURE E16.12

The regression equation is

PRICE=8.242+.102SIZE+1.348TREES-2.137DISTANCE

Predictor	Coef	Stdev	t-ratio
Constant	8.242	3.257	2.531
SIZE	.102	.048	2.125
TREES	1.348	.513	2.628
DISTANCE	-2.137	.676	-3.161

ECON **16.13** Some economists believe that a number of companies suffer from having too many white-collar workers and not enough blue-collar workers. To examine this issue, a statistician took a random sample of 25 companies. For each she measured the annual profit (in $millions) and counted the number of white-collar and blue-collar workers (in 100s). A multiple regression model run of SAS produced the *partial* output shown in Figure E16.13.

a. What do the values of $\hat{\beta}_0$, $\hat{\beta}_1$, and $\hat{\beta}_2$ tell you?

b. Do these results allow the statistician to conclude that numbers of white-collar and blue-collar workers are linearly related to profit. Use $\alpha = .05$.

MKT **16.14** Why do some door-to-door salespeople perform better than others? To investigate the factors that lead to successful selling, the general manager of a cosmetics company that sells its products door-to-door took a random sample of 50 salespeople in 50 different districts. For each he determined the dollar sales last month (the dependent variable), the number of homes visited by the salesperson, and the density of the district (the number of residents per square mile). The partial computer output of the multiple regression model appears in Figure E16.14. Can the general manager conclude at the 5% significance level that the number of homes visited and the district density are both linearly related to monthly sales?

FIGURE E16.13

Parameter Estimates

Variable	DF	Parameter Estimate	Standard Error	T for H0: Parameter=0	Prob > |T|
INTERCEP	1	-2.83	1.11	-2.55	0.0182
WHITE	1	1.67	1.24	1.35	0.1908
BLUE	1	0.96	0.66	1.45	0.1612

FIGURE E16.14

Variable	Coefficient $\hat{\beta}_i$	Standard Error $s_{\hat{\beta}_i}$	t-statistic
VISITS	0.36	0.14	2.57
DENSITY	0.15	0.06	2.50
CONSTANT	3.62	1.23	2.94

SECTION 16.4 **ASSESSING THE MODEL**

In almost all applications of regression analysis, it is important (for at least two reasons) that we assess or judge the usefulness of the model. First, we frequently have more than one model available that we could use; thus, we need a measure that allows us to compare competing models. Second, we need to know whether the model selected is likely to be useful in forecasting and analyzing relationships. In this section, we discuss three methods of assessing the model: the standard error of estimate (s_ε), the coefficient of determination (r^2), and the analysis of variance F-test.

STANDARD ERROR OF ESTIMATE

Recall that σ_ε is the standard deviation of the error variable ε and that, since σ_ε is a population parameter, it is necessary to estimate its value by using s_ε. In multiple regression, the standard error of estimate is defined as follows.

> **Standard Error of Estimate**
>
> $$s_\varepsilon = \sqrt{\frac{\text{SSE}}{n - k - 1}}$$

As we discussed in Chapter 15, each of our software packages reports the standard error of estimate s_ε in a different way. Minitab outputs s_ε as

```
s=6.894
```

and SAS outputs this value as

```
Root MSE  6.894
```

In the simple regression model in Chapter 15 (Example 15.2), we found $s_\varepsilon = 13.00$. Obviously, including the two additional variables x_2 and x_3 has improved the model.

COEFFICIENT OF DETERMINATION

The coefficient of determination is defined by the following formula.

> **Coefficient of Determination**
>
> $$r^2 = \frac{\text{SS}_y - \text{SSE}}{\text{SS}_y}$$

As the value for the coefficient of determination in the present case, Minitab outputs

```
R-sq=91.6%
```

and SAS outputs

```
R-square  0.916
```

This means that 91.6% of the variation in house prices is explained by the three independent variables, while 8.4% remains unexplained. The simple regression model produced $r^2 = 64.8\%$.

Notice that the computer output includes a second r^2 statistic, called the **coefficient of determination adjusted for degrees of freedom,** which has been adjusted to take into account the sample size and the number of independent variables. The rationale for this statistic is that, if the number of independent variables k is large relative to the sample size n, the unadjusted r^2 value may be unrealistically high. To avoid creating a false impression, the adjusted r^2 is often calculated. Its formula is as follows.

Coefficient of Determination Adjusted for Degrees of Freedom

$$\text{Adjusted } r^2 = 1 - \frac{\text{SSE}/(n - k - 1)}{\text{SS}_y/(n - 1)}$$

If n is considerably larger than k, the actual and adjusted r^2 values will be similar. But if SSE is quite different from zero and k is large compared to n, the actual and adjusted values of r^2 will differ substantially. If such differences exist, the analyst should be alerted to a potential problem in interpreting the coefficient of determination. In our example,

$$\text{Adjusted } r^2 = 89.3\%$$

indicating that, no matter how we measure the coefficient of determination, the model's fit is very good.

TESTING THE UTILITY OF THE MODEL

In Section 16.3, we tested the individual coefficients to determine whether sufficient evidence existed to allow us to conclude that there was a linear relationship between each independent variable and the dependent variable. As we saw in Chapter 15, if there is only one independent variable, the t-test of β_1 also tests whether the model is reasonable. When there is more than one independent variable, however, we need another technique for testing the overall utility of the model. This technique is called the **analysis of variance.**

When we discussed the coefficient of determination in Chapter 15, we noted that the variability of the dependent variable (measured by SS_y) can be decomposed into two parts: the explained variability (measured by SSR), and the unexplained variability (measured by SSE). That is,

$$\text{SS}_y = \text{SSR} + \text{SSE}$$

Furthermore, we established that, if SSR is large relative to SSE, the coefficient of determination r^2 is high—signifying a good model. On the other hand, if SSE is large, most of the variation of y remains unexplained, which indicates that the model provides a poor fit and consequently has little utility.

The hypotheses to be tested are

$$H_0: \beta_1 = \beta_2 = \cdots = \beta_k = 0$$

H_A: At least one β_i is not equal to zero

If the null hypothesis is true, none of the independent variables $x_1, x_2, \ldots x_k$ is linearly related to y, and therefore the model is useless. If at least one β_i is not equal to zero, the model does have some utility.

The test statistic is basically the same one we encountered in Chapter 12, where we tested for the equivalence of k population means. In order to judge whether SSR is large enough relative to SSE to allow us to conclude that at least one $\beta_i \neq 0$, we compute the ratio of the two mean squares. (Recall that the **mean square** is the sum of squares divided by the degrees of freedom; recall, too, that the ratio of the mean squares is F-distributed, as long as the underlying population is normal—a required condition of this application.) The calculation of the test statistic is summarized in an analysis of variance table, which in general appears as follows.

ANALYSIS OF VARIANCE

Source of Variation	Degrees of Freedom	Sum of Squares	Mean Squares	F-ratio
Regression	k	SSR	$MSR = SSR/k$	$F = MSR/MSE$
Residual	$n - k - 1$	SSE	$MSE = SSE/(n - k - 1)$	
Total	$n - 1$	SS_y		

Again, using Minitab or SAS, we get the following analysis of variance table for Example 16.1.

ANALYSIS OF VARIANCE

Source of Variation	Degrees of Freedom	Sum of Squares	Mean Squares	F-ratio
Regression	3	5,707.4	1,902.5	40.053
Residual	11	522.8	47.5	
Total	14	6,230.2		

A large value of F indicates that most of the variation of y is explained by the regression equation and that the model is useful. A small value of F indicates that most of the variation of y remains unexplained. The rejection region allows us to determine whether F is large enough to justify our rejecting H_0. For our test, the rejection region is

$$F > F_{\alpha, k, n-k-1}$$

In Example 16.1, the rejection region is

$$F > F_{\alpha, k, n-k-1}$$
$$> F_{.05, 3, 11}$$
$$> 3.59$$

Since the computed value of F is 40.053, we reject H_0. We conclude that at least one β_i is not equal to zero and that the model can be useful.

t-TESTS AND THE ANALYSIS OF VARIANCE

The t-tests of the individual coefficients allow us to determine whether $\beta_i \neq 0$ (for $i = 1, 2, \ldots, k$), which tells us whether a linear relationship exists between x_i and y. There is a t-test for each independent variable. Consequently, we typically perform the t-test k times.

The F-test in the analysis of variance essentially combines these k tests into a single test. That is, we test all of the β_i at one time to determine if at least one of them is not equal to zero. The question naturally arises: why do we need the F-test, if it's nothing more than a combination of the previously performed t-tests? The answer is that, in many cases, the F-test is more reliable. There are two possible reasons for this.

First, when numerous tests are performed, a certain percentage of true null hypotheses will be rejected. (This issue was previously discussed in Section 12.4.) For example, if $k = 100$ and 100 t-tests with $\alpha = .05$ are performed, then—even if all population coefficients β_i are zero—an average of five hypotheses (100 times .05) will be rejected. It is almost certain that at least one valid null hypothesis will be rejected. As a result, you will conclude erroneously that, since at least one β_i is not equal to zero, the model has some value. The F-test on the other hand is performed only once. Since the probability that a Type I error will occur in a single trial is equal to α, the chance of erroneously concluding that the model is useful is less with the F-test than with multiple t-tests.

Second, through a commonly occurring problem called **collinearity** (or **multicollinearity**), the standard deviations of the coefficients may be overestimated, resulting in t-statistics that are smaller than they should be. (The problem of collinearity is discussed in Section 16.6.) Thus, we may conclude that some β_i equals zero when it really doesn't. The problem of collinearity does not affect the F-test.

F-TEST, r^2, AND s_ε

Although each of the assessment measurements offers a different perspective, they agree in their assessment of how well the model fits the data. This is because they are all based on the sum of squares for error, SSE. The standard error of estimate is

$$s_\varepsilon = \sqrt{\frac{SSE}{n - k - 1}}$$

and the coefficient of determination is

$$r^2 = 1 - \frac{SSE}{SS_y}$$

When the curve hits every single point,

$$SSE = 0$$

Hence,

$$s_\varepsilon = 0$$
$$r^2 = 1$$

If the model provides a poor fit, we know that SSE is large (its maximum value is SS_y), s_ε is large, and (since SSE is close to SS_y) r^2 is close to zero.

The F-statistic also depends on SSE. That is,

$$F = \frac{(SS_y - SSE)/k}{SSE/(n - k - 1)}$$

When SSE = 0,

$$F = \frac{SS_y/k}{0/(n - k - 1)}$$

which is infinitely large. When SSE is large, SSE is close to SS_y and F is quite small.

The relationship among s_ε, r^2, and F is summarized in the accompanying table.

SSE	s_ε	r^2	F	Assessment of Model
0	0	1	∞	Perfect
Small	Small	Close to 1	Large	Good
Large	Large	Close to 0	Small	Poor
SS_y	$\sqrt{\dfrac{SS_y}{n - k - 1}}$ *	0	0	Useless

* When n is large and k is small, this quantity is approximately equal to the standard deviation of y.

LEARNING THE TECHNIQUES

16.15   Suppose that, in an attempt to estimate the model,

$$y = \beta_0 + \beta_1 x_1 + \beta_2 x_2 + \beta_3 x_3 + \beta_4 x_4 + \varepsilon$$

a researcher obtained 28 observations, which produced the following analysis of variance table.

ANALYSIS OF VARIANCE

Source	DF	SS	MS
Regression	4	126.30	31.58
Error	23	269.10	11.70
Total	27	395.40	

Test (with $\alpha = .01$) the following hypotheses:

$H_0: \beta_1 = \beta_2 = \beta_3 = \beta_4 = 0$

$H_A:$ At least one $\beta_i \neq 0$

16.16   In analyzing a multiple regression model, with $n = 70$ and $k = 8$, a statistician found

$SS_y = 1,526.3$ $SSE = 1,162.2$

Determine the following:

a. s_ε

b. r^2

c. F

16.17   A random sample of 34 observations of five variables produced the following summations:

$SSR = 2,512.6$ $SSE = 4,509.2$

Do these data provide sufficient evidence to indicate that the model is useful? (Test the appropriate hypothesis with $\alpha = .10$.)

16.18   In calculations undertaken to estimate the model

$$y = \beta_0 + \beta_1 x_1 + \beta_2 x_2 + \varepsilon$$

50 observations of the variables y, x_1, and x_2 produced the following summations:

$SS_y = 321.2$ $SSE = 259.0$

a. Find SSR.

b. Calculate the standard error of estimate.

c. Calculate the coefficient of determination.

d. Calculate the coefficient of determination adjusted for degrees of freedom.

e. Test the overall utility of the model, with $\alpha = .01$.

16.19   A random sample of 100 observations was taken to estimate the regression model

$$y = \beta_0 + \beta_1 x_1 + \beta_2 x_2 + \varepsilon$$

Minitab was employed to produce the output shown in the accompanying table. Because of a printer malfunction, however, some values from the analysis of variance table are missing; at present, these are replaced by the letters (a) through (f). Fill in the missing values.

ANALYSIS OF VARIANCE

Source	DF	SS	MS
Regression	(a)	573.6	(e)
Error	(b)	(d)	(f)
Total	(c)	925.9	

APPLYING THE TECHNIQUES

Self-Correcting Exercise (See Appendix 16.C for the solution.)

MKT **16.20**   A Florida hardware cooperative wanted to study advertising effectiveness by relating total dollar volume of sales of individual stores to dollar expenditures on localized direct mailings, local newspaper ads, and local TV spot ads. The results of the analysis are shown in the computer printout of Figure E16.20.

a. What does the value of the coefficient of determination tell you?

b. Test the overall utility of the model, with $\alpha = .01$.

FIGURE E16.20

```
The regression equation is

Y=-2.572+3.422X1+5.216X2+7.314X3

Predictor     Coef     Stdev     t-ratio
Constant     -2.572    2.543     -1.011
X1            3.422    1.744      1.962
X2            5.216    2.542      2.052
X3            7.314    3.448      2.121

s=9.319    R-sq=12.7%    R-sq(adj)=9.8%

Analysis of Variance

SOURCE        DF       SS        MS
Regression     3    1115.25    371.75
Error         88    7641.89     86.84
Total         91    8757.14
```

MKT **16.21** For Exercise 16.20, find SSR, SSE, and SS_y. From these values (and from their degrees of freedom), calculate r^2 and s_ε. Confirm that these values are the same as those shown in the computer output.

GEN **16.22** In an effort to explain to customers why their electricity bills have been so high lately and how, specifically, they could save money by reducing thermostat settings on both space heaters and water heaters, an electric utility company has collected total kilowatt consumption figures for last year's winter months, as well as average thermostat settings on space heaters and water heaters. These data are shown in the accompanying table.

Consumption (KWH/100)	Thermostat Settings (°F)	
y	Space Heater x_1	Water Heater x_2
20	70°	125°
24	72	130
16	68	120

Consumption (KWH/100)	Thermostat Settings (°F)	
y	Space Heater x_1	Water Heater x_2
28	74	135
32	75	140
19	68	120
24	71	130
29	72	135
35	75	140

The SAS-generated computer output is as shown in Figure E16.22.

a. What does the value of s_ε tell you about the fit of the model?

b. What proportion of the variability in consumption is not explained by the model?

c. Is there sufficient evidence, with $\alpha = .05$, to allow you to conclude that consumption is affected by both space-heater and water-heater use?

FIGURE E16.22

Dependent Variable: Y

Analysis of Variance

Source	DF	Sum of Squares	Mean Square	F Value	Prob > F
Model	2	304.41587	152.20793	69.503	0.0001
Error	6	13.13969	2.18995		
C Total	8	317.55556			

Root MSE	1.47985	R-square	0.9586	
Dep Mean	25.22222	Adj R-sq	0.9448	
C.V.	5.86724			

Parameter Estimates

Variable	DF	Parameter Estimate	Standard Error	T for H0: Parameter=0	Prob > |T|
INTERCEP	1	-68.88470	26.07207	-2.642	0.0384
X1	1	-0.39467	0.90855	-0.434	0.6792
X2	1	0.93747	0.31841	2.944	0.0258

EDUC **16.23** The administrator of a school board in a large southern state was analyzing the average mathematics score in the schools in his district. He noticed that there were enormous differences in scores among schools. In an attempt to determine some of the factors that influenced student perfor-

mance on mathematics tests, he took a random sample of 30 high schools across the state and determined the mean mathematics score (y), the percentage of mathematics teachers who have at least one university degree in mathematics (x_1), the mean age of the mathematics teachers (x_2), and

FIGURE E16.23

Analysis of Variance

Source	DF	Sum of Squares	Mean Square	F Value
Model	2	141.4	70.70	1.10
Error	27	1732.2	64.16	
C Total	29	1873.6		

Root MSE	8.010	R-square	.0755
Dep Mean	62.348		

the mean annual salary of teachers (x_3). Part of the SAS computer output appears in Figure E16.23.

a. What proportion of the variability in mathematics scores is not explained by the model?

b. What is the value of the standard error of estimate? What does it tell you about the model's fit?

c. Can we conclude at the 10% significance level that the model is useful in predicting mean mathematics scores?

16.24 The Christmas break (December 10–January 5) is a critical period for the tourist industry of Miami Beach. If a relatively small number of people visit during this time period, the hotels, restaurants, and other tourist attractions will suffer financial losses. A marketing analyst hired by the chamber of commerce to promote more tourism wants to analyze the factors that influence people to come to Miami Beach during Christmas break. She believes that the crucial factors affecting hotel vacancy rates are tied to weather conditions in the previous year. As a result, she proposes the model

$$y = \beta_0 + \beta_1 x_1 + \beta_2 x_2 + \varepsilon$$

where

y = Vacancy rate during Christmas break in year i

x_1 = Mean daily high temperature (in degrees Fahrenheit) during Christmas break in year $i - 1$

x_2 = Number of rainy days during Christmas break in year $i - 1$

The results for the past 15 years are as follows:

Year	y	x_1	x_2
1988	6	75	1
1987	12	68	4
1986	11	67	3
1985	8	73	2

Year	y	x_1	x_2
1984	13	65	3
1983	9	71	4
1982	6	73	1
1981	8	74	1
1980	4	76	2
1979	10	73	3
1978	8	69	3
1977	9	71	4
1976	8	66	2
1975	12	64	4
1974	2	73	5

The complete Minitab output is shown next.

```
The regression equation is
C1=53.4-0.627C2-0.267C3

Predictor     Coef      Stdev    t-ratio
Constant     53.38      12.60       4.24
C2          -0.6272    0.1693      -3.71
C3          -0.2672    0.5080      -0.53

s=2.195   R-sq=55.4%   R-sq(adj)=47.9%

Analysis of Variance

SOURCE        DF        SS        MS
Regression     2     71.766    35.883
Error         12     57.834     4.820
Total         14    129.600
```

a. At the 5% significance level can we conclude that the model is useful?

b. At the 5% significance level can we conclude that y and x_2 are linearly related?

SECTION 16.5   ## USING THE REGRESSION EQUATION

As was the case with simple linear regression (Chapter 15), the multiple regression equation can be used in two ways: we can produce the prediction interval for a particular value of y, and we can produce the confidence interval estimate of the expected value of y. Like the other computations associated with multiple regression, however, the formulas for the prediction interval and the confidence interval estimate are usually too complicated for us to calculate by hand. Instead, we call on the computer to produce the results we want.

Suppose that in Example 16.1 we wanted to produce a 95% confidence interval estimate of the expected value of y and a 95% prediction interval of y when the ground area of the house is 2,000 square feet ($x_1 = 20$), the house is 10 years old ($x_2 = 10$), and the lot size is 10,000 square feet ($x_3 = 10$). Minitab would produce the following output:

```
 Fit       Stdev. Fit        95% C.I.             95% P.I.
112.81       3.58       (104.94, 120.69)    (95.71, 129.91)
```

SAS would print

```
          Dep Var    Predict    Std Err
Obs          Y        Value     Predict
 16                    112.8      3.579

Lower 95%    Upper 95%    Lower 95%    Upper 95%
  Mean         Mean       Predict      Predict
  104.9        120.7        95.7        129.9
```

As you can see, the 95% confidence interval estimate of the expected value of y is (104.94, 120.69), and the 95% prediction interval (P.I.) of y is (95.71, 129.91).

SECTION 16.6   ## VIOLATION OF REQUIRED CONDITIONS AND OTHER PROBLEMS

In order for the statistical tests described in this chapter to be valid, a number of conditions must be satisfied. These were listed in Section 16.2 and are repeated here for your convenience.

Required Conditions of Regression Analysis

1 The error variable ε is normally distributed.

2. $E(\varepsilon) = 0$

3. σ_ε^2 is fixed.

4. The values of ε are independent.

FIGURE 16.2   HISTOGRAM OF RESIDUALS IN EXAMPLE 16.1

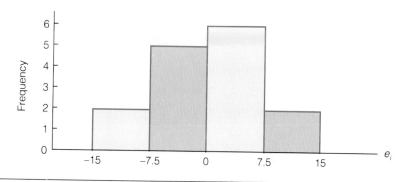

Most departures from these requirements can be diagnosed by examining the **residuals** (denoted e_i)—the differences between the observed values of y and the values of y determined from the regression equation. That is,

$$e_i = y_i - \hat{y}_i$$

Most computer packages allow you to print out the values of the residuals and then apply various graphical and statistical techniques to this variable. In our discussion of the subject, we assume that you have access to such a system.

NONNORMALITY

We can use several methods to determine whether the error variable is nonnormal. First, we can employ an inferential technique such as the Lilliefors test (discussed in Section 14.8) or the chi-square goodness-of-fit test (Section 13.4). Second, we can draw a histogram and judge whether or not the distribution appears to be bell-shaped. Figure 16.2 depicts the histogram of the residuals in Example 16.1. Notice that the residuals form a histogram that suggests the error variable is approximately normally distributed. It should be noted that the tests applied in regression analysis are robust, which means that only when the error variable is quite nonnormal are the test results called into question.

When and if we decide that the error variable is sufficiently nonnormal to cause problems, the most effective remedial procedure is to transform the dependent variable. We will discuss this procedure later in this section.

HETEROSCEDASTICITY

When the requirement that the variance of $\varepsilon(\sigma_\varepsilon^2)$ is a fixed value is violated, the condition is called **heteroscedasticity.** (You can impress friends and relatives by using this term. If you can't pronounce it, try **homoscedasticity,** which refers to the

FIGURE 16.3   *PLOT OF RESIDUALS DEPICTING HETEROSCEDASTICITY*

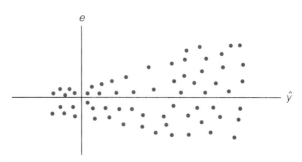

FIGURE 16.4   *PLOT OF RESIDUALS DEPICTING HOMOSCEDASTICITY*

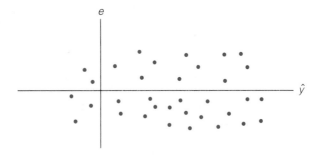

condition where the requirement is satisfied.) One method of diagnosing hetero-scedasticity is to plot the residuals against the predicted values of $y(\hat{y})$. We then look for a change in the spread or dispersion of the plotted points. Figure 16.3 describes such a situation.

Notice that, in this illustration, σ_ε^2 appears to be small when $\hat{y}$ is small and large when $\hat{y}$ is large. Of course, many other patterns could be used to depict this problem.

Figure 16.4 illustrates a case in which σ_ε^2 is constant. As a result, there is no apparent change in the variability of the residuals. Like the problem of nonnormality, heteroscedasticity is dealt with by transforming y.

AUTOCORRELATION

Condition 4 states that the values of the error variable are independent. In most applications, this condition is valid. But when the data are gathered sequentially over a period of time (the process is referred to as a **time series**), the residuals often are correlated. For example, suppose that, in an analysis of the relationship between annual gross profits and a number of independent variables, we observe the gross profits for the years 1960 to 1986. The observed values of y are denoted $y_1, y_2, \ldots, y_{27}$, where y_1 is the gross profit for 1960, y_2 is the gross profit for 1961, and so on. If we label the residuals $e_1, e_2, \ldots, e_{27}$, then—if the independence requirement is satisfied—there should be no relationship among the errors.

We can often detect problematic relationships by graphing e against the time periods. If a pattern emerges, it is likely that the requirement is violated. Figures 16.5 and 16.6 exhibit patterns indicating autocorrelation, while Figure 16.7 exhibits no pattern and thus likely represents independent errors.

The **Durbin–Watson** test allows the statistician to determine whether there is evidence of **first-order autocorrelation**—a condition in which a relationship exists between residuals e_i and e_{i-1}, where i is the time period. The Durbin–Watson statistic is defined as

$$d = \frac{\sum_{i=2}^{n}(e_i - e_{i-1})^2}{\sum_{i=1}^{n} e_i^2}$$

Most computer packages automatically produce this statistic. In general, unless the observations are drawn from a time series, however, the Durbin–Watson statistic should be ignored; it provides a meaningful test of autocorrelation only for a time series.

FIGURE 16.5   *PLOT OF RESIDUALS VERSUS TIME INDICATING AUTOCORRELATION*

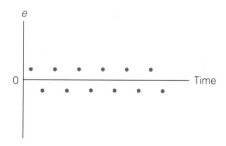

FIGURE 16.6   *PLOT OF RESIDUALS VERSUS TIME INDICATING AUTOCORRELATION*

FIGURE 16.7   *PLOT OF RESIDUALS VERSUS TIME INDICATING INDEPENDENCE*

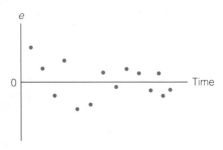

The null hypothesis of the Durbin–Watson test is always

H_0: There is no first-order autocorrelation

The alternative hypothesis can take on any one of three different forms. In most cases, we simply want to determine whether evidence exists that the required condition of no first-order autocorrelation is violated. Thus, the alternative hypothesis is usually

H_A: There is first-order autocorrelation

Table 13 in Appendix B provides critical values for the test statistic for a variety of values of n between 15 and 100 and for values of $k = 1, 2, 3, 4,$ and 5. Table 13(a) exhibits values of d_L and d_U such that $P(d < d_L) = P(d > d_U) = .05$. Table 13(b) gives values of d_L and d_U such that $P(d < d_L) = P(d > d_U) = .01$.

The rejection region for the two-tail test is $d < d_L$ or $d > d_U$. As an example, if $n = 20$, $k = 3$, and $\alpha = .10$, the rejection region is $d < 1.00$ or $d > 1.68$.

If the statistician wishes to test for positive first-order autocorrelation, the rejection region is $d < d_L$, where d_L is such that $P(d < d_L) = \alpha$. (Positive first-order autocorrelation produces a small value of d.) For example, if $n = 25$, $k = 2$, and $\alpha = .05$, the rejection region is $d < 1.21$.

The rejection region for the test of negative first-order autocorrelation is $d > d_U$, where d_U is such that $P(d > d_U) = \alpha$. (Negative first-order autocorrelation produces a large value of d.) When $n = 28$, $k = 4$, and $\alpha = .05$, for example, the rejection region is $d > 1.75$.

When the requirement that the errors are independent is unsatisfied, the appropriate response is to use the autoregressive model described in Chapter 19.

COLLINEARITY

Collinearity is a condition that exists when the independent variables are correlated with one another. The adverse effect of collinearity is that the standard deviations of the coefficients may be overestimated. As a result, when the coefficients are tested, the t-statistic is smaller than it should be, and some independent variables appear not to be linearly related to y when in fact they are.

EXAMPLE 16.3

The executives of a company that manufactures backyard satellite antennae want to predict sales by geographic sales district. They believe that the two most important variables in predicting sales are the number of households and the number of owner-occupied households in each district. To develop and test a model, they randomly selected nine districts; for each district, the number of antennae sold in the previous month, the number of households, and the number of owner-occupied households were recorded. The data are shown in the accompanying table. Analyze the relationships among the variables.

District	Monthly Sales y	Number of Households (in 10,000s) x_1	Number of Owner-Occupied Households (in 10,000s) x_2
1	50	14	11
2	73	28	18
3	32	10	5
4	121	30	20
5	156	48	30
6	98	30	21
7	62	20	15
8	51	16	11
9	80	25	17

Solution.   The proposed model is

$$y = \beta_0 + \beta_1 x_1 + \beta_2 x_2 + \varepsilon$$

When the data were run on a computer system, the following results were observed.

RELATIONSHIPS AMONG x_1, x_2, AND y

$\hat{y} = -2.380 + 2.402 x_1 + 1.444 x_2$

Predictor	Coefficient	Standard Error	t-statistic
Constant	-2.380	10.910	$-.22$
x_1	2.402	2.221	1.08
x_2	1.444	3.525	.41

$s_\varepsilon = 12.10$
$r^2 = 92.8\%$

ANALYSIS OF VARIANCE

Source	DF	SS	MS	F
Regression	2	11,318.9	5,659.5	38.63
Residual	6	879.1	146.5	
Total	8	12,198.0		

The critical value (with $\alpha = .05$) of the t-tests is

$$t_{.025,6} = 2.447$$

Since the t-statistics for β_1 and β_2 are both less than this critical value, we would conclude that neither x_1 nor x_2 is linearly related to y. Notice, however, that the coefficient of determination is 92.8% while the value of F is 38.63. The critical value of the F-test is

$$F_{.05,2,6} = 5.14$$

which indicates that at least one of β_1 and β_2 is significantly different from zero; as a result, we must conclude that at least one of x_1 and x_2 is linearly related to y. How is it possible that the results of the two t-tests are so different from the results of the F-test? The answer is that collinearity has destroyed the t-tests.

To help you understand this, we've produced more statistical results. First, we calculated the coefficient of correlation between x_1 and x_2; we found that $r = .985$, which indicates that x_1 and x_2 are highly correlated. This was quite predictable, since—in most cities in the country—there is a close relationship between the number of households and the number of owner-occupied households.

Then we examined two simple linear regression models: one in which x_1 is the independent variable; and another in which x_2 is the independent variable. The results are shown in the accompanying tables. First consider the variables x_1 and y.

RELATIONSHIP BETWEEN x_1 AND y

$$\hat{y} = -.657 + 3.298x_1$$

Predictor Value	Coefficient	Standard Error	t-statistic
Constant	−.657	9.451	−.07
x_1	3.298	.353	9.35

$$s_\varepsilon = 11.36$$
$$r^2 = 92.6\%$$

ANALYSIS OF VARIANCE

Source	DF	SS	MS	F
Regression	1	11,294	11,294	87.48
Residual	7	904	129.1	
Total	8	12,198		

The critical value of the t-test of β_1 is

$$t_{.025,7} = 2.365$$

while the critical value of the F-test is

$$F_{.05,1,7} = 5.59$$

All of the statistics concur. There is clearly a strong linear relationship between x_1 and y.

Now consider the variables x_2 and y.

RELATIONSHIP BETWEEN x_2 AND y

$\hat{y} = -5.18 + 5.200x_2$

Predictor	Coefficient	Standard Error	t-statistic
Constant	-5.18	10.73	$-.48$
x_2	5.200	.6033	8.62

$s_\varepsilon = 12.25$
$r^2 = 91.4\%$

ANALYSIS OF VARIANCE

Source	DF	SS	MS	F
Regression	1	11,148	11,148	74.32
Residual	7	1,050	150	
Total	8	12,198		

Once again, there is clearly a strong linear relationship between x_2 and y.

We have established with this analysis that both x_1 and x_2 are linearly related to y. Yet when we tested β_1 and β_2 in the multiple regression model, we found that both *t*-statistics were small. This led us to the erroneous conclusion that both x_1 and x_2 were not linearly related to y. The contradiction was caused by *collinearity*—the correlation of two independent variables. Notice, however, that the *F*-test in the multiple regression model did indicate that at least one of x_1 and x_2 was linearly associated with y. Thus, only the *t*-tests are adversely affected by collinearity; the *F*-test is unaffected.

This discussion raises two important questions for the statistician. First, how do we recognize the problem when it occurs, and second, how do we avoid or correct it?

Collinearity exists in virtually all multiple regression problems. In fact, finding or even creating two uncorrelated variables is a difficult task. The problem only becomes serious, however, when two or more independent variables are highly correlated. Unfortunately, we do not have a critical value that indicates when the correlation between two independent variables is large enough to cause problems. To complicate the issue, collinearity also occurs when a combination of several independent variables is correlated with another independent variable or with a combination of other independent variables. Determining when the collinearity problem has reached the serious stage may be extremely difficult if you are dealing with a large number of independent variables.

Minimizing the effect of collinearity is often easier than recognizing it. The statistician must try to include independent variables that are truly independent of one another. For example, in the real estate problem (Example 16.1) the independent variables house size and lot size are likely to be correlated. (People tend to build large houses on large lots, and small lots cannot contain large houses.) Other variables that might be used to predict the selling price of a house but are correlated include house size and number of bedrooms, house size and age, and number of bedrooms and number of bathrooms. Rather than including all such variables in the model, the statistician may choose to include only house size, plus several other variables that measure other aspects of a house's value.

Another alternative is to use a stepwise regression package, which most of the statistical applications systems have. Stepwise regression, discussed in Section 16.8, brings independent variables into the equation one at a time. Only if an independent variable improves the fit is it included. If two variables are strongly correlated, the inclusion of one of them in the model makes the second one unnecessary. Because the stepwise technique excludes the redundant variables, it minimizes collinearity.

TRANSFORMATIONS

When either of required conditions 1 and 3 is violated (ε is nonnormal or σ_ε^2 is not constant) we can transform the dependent variable in order to alleviate the problem. There are several points to note about this procedure. First, the actual form of the transformation depends on which condition is unsatisfied and on the specific nature of the violation of the requirement. Since there are many different ways to violate the required conditions of the statistical techniques, the list of transformations given here is unavoidably incomplete. Second, these transformations can also be useful in improving the model. That is, if the linear model appears to be quite poor, we often can increase r^2 (and decrease s_ε) by transforming y. Third, many computer software systems allow us to make transformations quite easily. You may wish to experiment to see the effects these transformations have on your statistical results.

Common Transformations

1. *Log Transformation*: $y' = \log y$ (provided $y > 0$). The log transformation is used when (a) the variance of the error variable σ_ε^2 increases as y increases (heteroscedasticity); and (b) the distribution of the error variable is positively skewed (nonnormality).

2. *Square Transformation*: $y' = y^2$. Use this transformation when (a) σ_ε^2 is proportional to the expected value of y; and (b) the distribution of ε is negatively skewed.

3. *Square-Root Transformation*: $y' = \sqrt{y}$ (provided that $y > 0$). The square-root transformation is helpful when σ_ε^2 is proportional to the expected value of y.

4. *Reciprocal Transformation*: $y' = 1/y$. When σ_ε^2 appears to significantly increase when y increases beyond some critical value, the reciprocal transformation is recommended.

EXERCISES

LEARNING THE TECHNIQUES

16.25 Given the following information, perform the Durbin–Watson test to determine whether first-order autocorrelation exists.

$n = 25 \qquad k = 5 \qquad \alpha = .10 \qquad d = 1.96$

16.26 Test each of the following hypotheses:

a. H_0: There is no first-order autocorrelation
H_A: There is positive first-order autocorrelation
$n = 50 \qquad k = 2 \qquad \alpha = .05 \qquad d = 1.38$

b. H_0: There is no first-order autocorrelation
H_A: There is first-order autocorrelation
$n = 90 \qquad k = 5 \qquad \alpha = .02 \qquad d = 1.60$

c. H_0: There is no first-order autocorrelation

H_A: There is negative first-order autocorrelation
$n = 33 \qquad k = 4 \qquad \alpha = .01 \qquad d = 1.63$

16.27 In a multiple regression application, where the observations are made over a period of time, 22 observations were taken to estimate the model $y = \beta_0 + \beta_1 x_1 + \beta_2 x_2 + \beta_3 x_3 + \varepsilon$. The Durbin–Watson statistic is 1.51. Can we conclude at the 2% significance level that there is first-order autocorrelation?

16.28 Each of the following pairs of columnar values represents an actual value of y and a predicted value of y (based on a regression model). Graph the predicted values of y versus the residuals. In each case, determine from the graph whether the requirement that σ_ε^2 is constant is satisfied.

a.

y	$\hat{y}$
155	143
112	108
163	180
130	133
143	146
182	193
160	140
104	101
125	126
161	176
189	200
102	97
142	145
149	151
180	158

b.

y	$\hat{y}$
10	7
22	21
29	29
15	13
24	25
13	16
17	19
23	22
11	14
27	27
19	17
26	27
20	22
14	11

c.

y	$\hat{y}$
46	48
40	43
53	54
60	63
56	54
62	65
44	46
49	47
52	49
59	56
45	41
55	53
47	44
61	57
42	45
57	62
50	51

16.29 Each of the following sets of data represents the actual and predicted values of a time series. Graph the residuals versus the time periods

to determine whether the requirement that the values of ε are independent of one another is satisfied.

a.

Time Period	y	$\hat{y}$
1	60	58
2	71	68
3	53	57
4	59	60
5	75	71
6	50	48
7	52	55
8	65	68
9	72	67
10	54	53
11	61	65
12	66	68

b.

Time Period	y	$\hat{y}$
1	325	303
2	265	257
3	350	326
4	375	361
5	290	272
6	280	304
7	360	371
8	250	270
9	300	309
10	330	352

APPLYING THE TECHNIQUES

Exercises 16.30 through 16.34 refer to Exercise 15.53. The least squares regression line is

$$\hat{y} = 145.786 + 0.4777x$$

The values of $\hat{y}_i$ and e_i were computed, with the following results:

Predicted Value $\hat{y}_i$	Residual e_i
211.09	−9.09
219.19	−7.19
229.20	−8.20
239.21	−6.21
245.41	−.41
252.56	6.44
262.57	10.43
274.49	10.51
284.50	9.50
293.56	9.44
308.33	4.67
324.54	−1.54
337.41	−2.41
356.00	−6.00
377.93	−9.93

16.30 Draw a histogram of the residuals to determine whether the error variable is normally distributed.

16.31 Plot the residuals versus the predicted value of y to see whether the requirement that σ_ε^2 is fixed is satisfied.

16.32 Plot the residuals versus time to examine the required condition that the errors be independent.

16.33 Suppose that the Durbin–Watson statistic was computed as $d = 0.23$. What does this tell you about the possibility of first-order autocorrelation?

16.34 How are your answers to the questions in Exercise 15.53 affected by what you've learned from Exercises 16.30–16.33?

Exercises 16.35 through 16.40 refer to Exercise 16.22, where the least squares regression line is

$$\hat{y} = -68.88 - 0.3947x_1 + 0.9375x_2$$

The values of $\hat{y}_i$ and e_i were calculated and are shown below.

Predicted Value $\hat{y}_i$	Residual e_i
20.672	−.672
24.570	−.570
16.774	−.774
28.468	−.468
32.761	−.761
16.774	2.226
24.965	−.965
29.257	−.257
32.761	2.239

16.35 Plot y versus x_1 and y versus x_2 to see whether each of the independent variables is apparently linearly related to the dependent variable.

16.36 The correlation matrix showing the correlations between y and x_1, y and x_2, and x_1 and x_2 is shown next.

a. Does it appear that collinearity is a problem?

b. What are the likely consequences of collinearity?

	y	x_1
x_1	.948	
x_2	.978	.977

16.37 The Durbin–Watson statistic is $d = 1.98$. What does this tell you about the independence of the error variable?

16.38 Draw a histogram of the residuals. What does this tell you about the distribution of the error variable?

16.39 Plot e_i versus $\hat{y}_i$. Does it appear that σ_ε^2 is fixed?

16.40 How are your answers to the questions in Exercise 16.22 affected by what you've learned from Exercises 16.35–16.39?

Exercises 16.41 through 16.47 refer to Exercise 16.24. The least squares regression line is

$$\hat{y} = 53.38 - 0.6272x_1 - 0.2673x_2$$

The values of $\hat{y}_i$ and e_i are as follows:

Predicted Value $\hat{y}_i$	Residual e_i
6.0795	−.0795
9.6682	2.3318
10.5626	.4374
7.0667	.9333
11.8169	1.1831
7.7867	1.2133
7.3339	−1.3339
6.7067	1.2933
5.1852	−1.1852
6.7996	3.2004
9.3082	−1.3082
7.7867	1.2133
11.4569	−3.4569
12.1769	−.1769
6.2652	−4.2652

16.41 Plot y versus x_1 and y versus x_2 to see whether there is an obvious linear relationship between each of the independent variables and y.

16.42 The correlation matrix for all three variables is

	y	x_1
x_1	−.737	
x_2	.208	−.408

Does it appear that collinearity is a problem? What are the consequences of collinearity?

16.43 Draw a histogram of the residuals. Does it appear that the error variable is normally distributed?

16.44 Plot the residuals versus the predicted values. Does it appear that σ_ε^2 is fixed?

16.45 Plot the residuals versus time. Does it appear that the errors are independent?

16.46 The Durbin–Watson statistic is $d = 2.15$. What does this tell you about the possible existence of first-order autocorrelation?

16.47 How do your answers to Exercises 16.41–16.46 affect your answers to Exercise 16.24?

SECTION 16.7 **WORKED EXAMPLE**

EXAMPLE 16.4

Jack Miles has just been hired as general manager of an American League baseball team. In recent years, the team has not fared very well—a state of affairs that Jack intends to change. Unlike his peers, Jack has a degree in business administration. Since one of his favorite courses was statistics (obviously, this is fiction), he decides to apply the multiple regression technique to analyzing baseball statistics. As a first step, he gathers data on each of the 14 American League teams. The variables to be recorded are as follows:

y = Team's winning percentage at this point in the season (July)

x_1 = Team's batting average

x_2 = Average number of home runs hit per game for each team

x_3 = Team's earned run average

x_4 = Average number of errors per game made by each team

The data for these variables are shown in the accompanying table.

Team	y	x_1	x_2	x_3	x_4
Baltimore	.532	.263	1.00	3.99	.89
Boston	.620	.276	.73	3.82	.99
California	.533	.262	1.02	4.30	.51
Chicago	.462	.251	.74	4.22	.73
Cleveland	.544	.273	.98	4.35	.94
Detroit	.511	.260	1.15	4.18	.65
Kansas City	.462	.250	.75	3.87	.84
Milwaukee	.473	.260	.62	3.84	.82
Minnesota	.419	.264	1.38	5.09	.82
New York	.564	.277	1.19	4.25	.88
Oakland	.400	.253	.96	4.46	.79
Seattle	.442	.256	1.05	4.80	.98
Texas	.505	.263	1.06	4.12	.72
Toronto	.537	.279	1.12	4.53	.73

SOURCE: *Toronto Star*, 22 July 1986.

The regression model that Jack proposes is

$$y = \beta_0 + \beta_1 x_1 + \beta_2 x_2 + \beta_3 x_3 + \beta_4 x_4 + \varepsilon$$

When Jack inputs the data into a computer and runs the Minitab package, he obtains the following output:

```
The regression equation is

Y=-0.370+4.827X1+0.0232X2-0.0947X3-0.0241X4

Predictor      Coef      Stdev     t-ratio
Constant      -0.370     0.286     -1.294
X1             4.827     0.981      4.920
X2             0.0232    0.0671     0.346
X3            -0.0947    0.0352    -2.690
X4            -0.0241    0.0655    -0.368

s=0.0282   R-sq=85.0%   R-sq(adj)=78.3%
```

```
Analysis of Variance

SOURCE         DF    SS         MS
Regression      4    0.0405     0.0101
Error           9    0.00715    0.000794
Total          13    0.0476
```

To provide further analysis, the actual (y_i) and predicted ($\hat{y}_i$) values of y and the residuals ($e_i = y_i - \hat{y}_i$) were output, as shown in the accompanying table.

ROW	VALUE OF Y	PREDICTED VALUE OF Y	RESIDUAL
1	.532	.52375	.00825
2	.620	.59391	.02609
3	.533	.49920	.03380
4	.462	.44186	.02014
5	.544	.53625	.00775
6	.511	.50055	.01045
7	.462	.46776	-.00576
8	.473	.51633	-.04333
9	.419	.43492	-.01592
10	.564	.57136	-.00736
11	.400	.43245	-.03245
12	.442	.41217	.02983
13	.505	.51687	-.01187
14	.537	.55643	-.01943

a. What are the values of the standard error of estimate and the coefficient of determination? What do they tell you about how well the model fits the data?

b. Which independent variables are linearly related to the dependent variable? (Test using $\alpha = .05$.)

c. Interpret the coefficients. Are the signs of the coefficients reasonable?

d. Test the overall utility of the model, with $\alpha = .01$.

e. Does it appear that the requirement of a constant σ_ε^2 is violated? Explain.

f. Which variables appear to be the most important in predicting winning percentage? What should this suggest to Jack with regard to future trades?

g. Pretend that Jack is the general manager of your favorite team. What do these results indicate about how well your team has performed compared to how well they were predicted (by the model) to perform?

Solution

a. The standard error of estimate is

$$s_\varepsilon = .0282$$

In relation to the values of y, s_ε is a small value, which indicates a good fit. This judgment is supported by the coefficient of determination, which is

$$r^2 = 85.0\%$$

This value tells us that 85% of the variation in winning percentages is explained by the variation in the independent variables; only 15% is unexplained.

b. We begin by testing the following set of hypotheses for $i = 1, 2, 3, 4$:

$H_0: \beta_i = 0$

$H_A: \beta_i \neq 0$

The rejection region is

$t| > t_{\alpha/2, n-k-1}$

$\quad > t_{.025, 9}$

$\quad > 2.262$

Since the t-statistics for x_1 and x_3 (4.920 and -2.690, respectively) fall into the rejection region, we conclude that the team batting average and the team earned run average are linearly related to winning percentage. The average number of home runs and the average number of errors are not linearly related to winning percentage (in this model).

c. As usual, $\hat{\beta}_0$ cannot be interpreted. If you attempted to do so, you would find that a team that can't hit at all but gives up no earned runs and makes no errors (great defense, but no offense) should have a winning percentage of $-.370$.

The value $\hat{\beta}_1 = 4.827$ means that, for each .001 increase in batting average, the winning percentage should increase by .004827.

Since $\hat{\beta}_2 = .0232$, each .01 increase in the average number of home runs increases y by .000232. To put this number in perspective, the difference in winning percentage between a team averaging .70 home runs per game and another averaging 1.20 home runs per game is expected to be .0116.

Since $\hat{\beta}_3 = -.0947$, each earned run allowed per 9-inning game results in a .0947 decrease in the average winning percentage.

With $\hat{\beta}_4 = -.0241$, we would expect each additional .01 in the average number of errors per game to result in a decrease of .000241 in the average winning percentage.

All of the signs of the coefficients are reasonable and expected. Larger values for the offensive statistics are related to better teams, while larger values of the defensive statistics are related to poorer teams.

d. The overall utility of the model is tested by the analysis of variance. That is, we perform the following complete test:

$H_0: \beta_1 = \beta_2 = \beta_3 = \beta_4 = 0$

H_A: At least one β_i is not equal to zero.

Rejection region:

$F > F_{\alpha, k, n-k-1}$

$\quad > F_{.01, 4, 9}$

$\quad > 6.42$

FIGURE 16.8   *GRAPH OF THE PREDICTED VALUES OF y VERSUS THE RESIDUALS IN EXAMPLE 16.4*

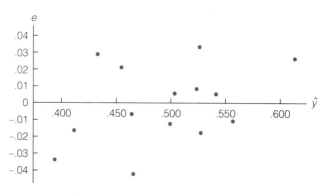

Value of the test statistic:

$$F = \frac{\text{MSR}}{\text{MSE}} = \frac{.0101}{.000794} = 12.72$$

Conclusion: Reject H_0.

There is evidence that the model is useful in predicting a team's winning percentage.

e. Figure 16.8 depicts the graph of the predicted values of y versus the residuals. There appears to be no violation of the requirement that σ_ε^2 is constant.

f. The variable with the largest absolute t-statistic is the variable that is most strongly linearly related to y. Hence the team's batting average, x_1, followed by the team's earned run average, x_3, are the two most important variables.

Using this model (other models may produce different results), Jack would be encouraged to try to trade good pitchers for players who can hit for high averages. Evidently, home-run hitters who have low batting averages are not particularly desirable.

g. The favorite teams of the authors of this textbook are the New York Yankees and the Toronto Blue Jays. For the Yankees, the predicted winning percentage is .57136, while the actual value is .564. (The residual is −.00736.) The Blue Jays' predicted winning percentage is .55643, and their actual winning percentage is .537. (The residual is −.01943.) Both teams have performed more poorly than predicted. The teams' general managers should seek reasons for these results. Possibilities include poor coaching, bad strategy by the teams' managers, players' "choking" in important situations, meddling by top executives, and unrealistic expectations (and subsequent disillusioned harassment) by fans and media.

SECTION 16.8 **STEPWISE REGRESSION**

In preparing to use a multiple regression model, most statisticians assemble a relatively long list of potential independent variables. The task of determining which ones belong in the model can be challenging. We could, of course, include all potential variables and use the t-test of β_i to determine which of them are linearly related to the dependent variable. Problems such as collinearity, however, may make the t-tests misleading. A technique that can be used to help overcome these problems is **stepwise regression.**

In stepwise regression, one independent variable at a time is included in the equation. At step 1, the variable most strongly related to the dependent variable is included in the model. At step 2, the next most strongly related variable from among the remaining variables is included. This continues until only variables that are not linearly related to y (given the other variables already in the model) remain out of the equation. Although the actual calculations of this technique vary from one computer package to the next, most work as follows.

The statistician inputs the values of y and of the k potential independent variables. The computer then produces the statistics for k simple regression applications. That is, for each independent variable, the model

$$y = \beta_0 + \beta_1 x_i + \varepsilon$$

is estimated. Included in the ouput is the t-statistic for the test of β_1. The independent variable with the largest absolute t-statistic is the variable most strongly related to y. This variable is recoded (if necessary) and labeled x_1, and it becomes the first variable included in the model.

The second step is to examine the remaining $k - 1$ independent variables to determine which one of them, when combined with x_1, provides the best two-variable model of the form

$$y = \beta_0 + \beta_1 x_1 + \beta_2 x_i + \varepsilon$$

This is accomplished by calculating the t-statistic for β_2 for all $k - 1$ remaining independent variables and selecting the largest absolute value of the t-statistics. This variable is labeled x_2.

Because x_1 and x_2 are probably correlated to some degree, the inclusion of x_2 changes the value of β_1 and its t-statistic. Some programs then recheck x_1 to ensure that it remains sufficiently strongly related to y to remain in the model. If it does not, the computer searches for the best replacement (based on the largest absolute t-statistic).

The process continues with a search for the third independent variable. The remaining $k - 2$ independent variables are examined to determine which one produces the best fit for the model

$$y = \beta_0 + \beta_1 x_1 + \beta_2 x_2 + \beta_3 x_i + \varepsilon$$

When x_3 is selected, the process resumes as before until no remaining independent variable has a β coefficient that is significantly different from zero (for some specified value of α).

TABLE 16.2 *STEPWISE REGRESSION FOR EXAMPLE 16.1*

Stepwise Procedure for Dependent Variable Y

Step 1   Variable X1 Entered   R-square=0.6475

	DF	Sum of Squares	Mean Square	F	Prob > F
Regression	1	4034.4144	4034.4144	23.89	0.0003
Error	13	2195.8215	168.9093		
Total	14	6230.2360			

Variable	Parameter Estimate	Standard Error	Sum of Squares	T	Prob > |T|
INTERCEP	18.3538	14.8077	259.4943	1.24	0.2371
X1	3.8785	0.7936	4034.4144	4.89	0.0003

Step 2   Variable X3 Entered   R-square=0.9155

	DF	Sum of Squares	Mean Square	F	Prob > F
Regression	2	5704.0273	2852.0136	65.04	0.0001
Error	12	526.2086	43.8507		
Total	14	6230.2360			

Variable	Parameter Estimate	Standard Error	Sum of Squares	T	Prob > |T|
INTERCEP	-20.3721	9.8139	188.9589	-2.08	0.0601
X1	4.3117	0.4104	4840.0010	10.51	0.0001
X3	4.7177	0.7645	1669.6129	6.17	0.0001

All variables in the model are significant at the 0.1500 level.

No other variable met the 0.1500 significance level for entry into the model

Summary of Stepwise Procedure for Dependent Variable Y

Step	Variable Entered Removed	Number In	Partial R**2	Model R**2		T	Prob > |T|
1	X1	1	0.6475	0.6475	5	4.89	0.0003
2	X3	2	0.2680	0.9155	18	6.17	0.0001

This process is illustrated in Table 16.2, which shows the SAS output for the stepwise regression involved in Example 16.1.*

In the first step, as you can see from Table 16.2, house size is judged to be the variable most strongly related to price. The resulting equation, with one indepen-

---

* The output has been slightly modified to make it easier to interpret.

dent variable, is

$$\hat{y} = 18.3538 + 3.8785x_1$$

where x_1 is house size. Other important statistics are

$$r^2 = .6475$$

$$s_\varepsilon = \sqrt{168.9093} = 12.9965$$
$$F\text{-statistic} = 23.89$$

At step 2, the variable for lot size is included in the equation, which becomes

$$\hat{y} = -20.3721 + 4.3117x_1 + 4.7177x_2$$

Notice that r^2 has increased and s_ε has decreased from step 1. That is, at step 2,

$$r^2 = .9155$$

$$s_\varepsilon = \sqrt{43.8507} = 6.6220$$

The new value of F has increased to 65.04. The p-value (Prob $> F$) has decreased from .0003 to .0001.

The variable for age was not included, since its t-statistic is too low for it to enter the model.

The advantage of the stepwise regression technique over ordinary regression is that stepwise regression includes only variables that are significantly linearly related to the dependent variable. It also tends to reduce the problem of collinearity because, if there are two highly correlated independent variables, including one usually eliminates the second. It should be noted that a certain degree of collinearity does remain.

WARNING ABOUT STEPWISE REGRESSION

Like most statistical techniques, stepwise regression can be (and unfortunately, often is) misused. Statisticians developing a regression model are often tempted to produce a long list of potential independent variables and then let the stepwise regression eliminate all or most of the ineffective ones. However, you should resist this temptation. If you input a long list of independent variables, many t-tests will be performed, and a certain number of Type I errors will likely be made. As a result, you will include in the model at least some variables that are not linearly related to the dependent variable.

To avoid this pitfall, the careful statistician uses his or her judgment and experience to screen the independent variables in advance, discarding most of the ones that are not likely to be included in the model anyway. In other words, the statistician should take the initiative to remove these variables, rather than trying to get the stepwise regression technique to do it. We strongly recommend that you regard the regression technique as a method of testing a postulated model rather than as a search technique for putting together a good model. This is not to suggest that stepwise regression should not be used. Rather, we believe that stepwise regression should be used in conjunction with the statistician's judgment. Then it can serve as an effective means of improving the model selection.

COMMENT ABOUT STATISTICAL SOFTWARE SYSTEMS OUTPUT

There are many statistical software systems available to the statistician for applying the multiple regression method and many other techniques. Unfortunately, the method, instructions, and output of each program vary. Throughout this book, we've shown the output from two of the most popular systems and provided instructions for them in the chapter appendixes. Of course, if you intend to use some other computer system, you will need to acquire specific details on its use. As a matter of fact, because of inevitable changes in Minitab and SAS and the introduction of newly developed versions, you will probably need to be aware of changes in the form of the printouts produced by these programs. We refer you to your own computer center for particular instructions.

In most applications of multiple regression, your task is to read and interpret computer output. In this section, we facilitate your job by briefly discussing variations in the terminology and notation employed by representative programs. The large number of such programs and the tendency of their inventors to make changes incline us to provide guidelines on the output that are not overly specific.

STANDARD ERROR OF ESTIMATE

The standard error of estimate appears in numerous forms, including the following:

```
THE ST. DEV. OF Y ABOUT REGRESSION LINE
S
STD. ERROR OF EST.
Root MSE
STD. DEV.
STANDARD ERROR
```

COEFFICIENT OF DETERMINATION

Most computer programs output the coefficient of determination as R-SQUARE. Some systems also include the adjusted coefficient as ADJUSTED R SQUARE. R-sq(adj), or R-SQUARED, ADJUSTED FOR D.F. Some packages also print the coefficient of correlation, as MULTIPLE R.

COEFFICIENTS, STANDARD DEVIATIONS, AND *t*-TESTS

The $\hat{\beta}_i$ coefficients and their associated test statistics appear in a variety of forms. Most packages print out a table in which the headings appear in one of the following sets of ways:

Predictor	Coef	Stdev	t-ratio
VARIABLE	PARAMETER ESTIMATE	STANDARD ERROR	T FOR H0: PARAMETER=0
VARIABLE	COEFFICIENT	STD ERROR	T-VALUE
VARIABLE	B	STD ERROR B	F

The first column of the table typically provides the independent variable's name. The value of $\hat{\beta}_0$ is referred to as either CONSTANT or INTERCEPT.

The standard deviation of the estimators, a statistic represented in this textbook as $s_{\hat{\beta}_i}$, usually appears in the output as one of the following:

```
Stdev
Standard Error
ST DEV. OF COEF.
STD. ERROR OF ESTIMATE
STD. ERROR B
STD. ERROR
```

You may have observed that the terms **standard error** and **standard error of estimate** can represent both s_ε and $s_{\hat{\beta}_i}$. The location of these statistics in the printout, however, will make it obvious (we hope) which value is being referred to.

The test statistic required to test the hypotheses concerning β_i is also included in the table. Some programs produce the t-statistic, which (as you've seen in this chapter) is defined as

$$t = \frac{\hat{\beta}_i - \beta_i}{s_{\hat{\beta}_i}}$$

where, under the null hypothesis, $\beta_i = 0$. Many packages, however, produce the F-statistic for this purpose. Both the t-test and the F-test of the coefficient β_i produce the same results, because of the relationship between a t-statistic and an F-statistic. That relationship is described by the equation

$$t^2_{n-k-1} = F_{1, n-k-1}$$

In other words, if you square a t-statistic (with d.f. $= n - k - 1$), the result is equal to the F-statistic (with d.f. $v_1 = 1$ and $v_2 = n - k - 1$). Thus, we can test the hypotheses

$$H_0 : \beta_i = 0$$
$$H_A : \beta_i \neq 0$$

in either of two ways: we can use the test statistic

$$t = \frac{\hat{\beta}_i}{s_{\hat{\beta}_i}}$$

where the rejection region is

$$|t| > t_{\alpha/2, n-k-1}$$

or we can use the test statistic

$$F = \left[\frac{\hat{\beta}_i}{s_{\hat{\beta}_i}}\right]^2$$

where the rejection region is

$$F > F_{\alpha, 1, n-k-1}$$

Notice that, although this is a two-tail test when we use the *t*-statistic, the rejection region is one-tailed when we use the *F*-statistic. This is because, when the *t*-statistic is squared, any values of *t* less than $-t_{\alpha/2}$ become positive values of $F(=t^2)$. As a result, we cannot perform a one-tail test of β_i ($H_A: \beta_i > 0$ or $H_A: \beta_i < 0$) with the *F*-test. To do so, we must use the *t*-statistic (even if we have to calculate it ourselves by taking the ratio of $\hat{\beta}_i$ over $s_{\hat{\beta}_i}$—both of which are provided by the output).

The interpretation of the test is sometimes facilitated by calculating the *p*-values, which are often reported in one of the following ways:

```
Prob > |T|
SIG  T
PR > |T|
```

It should be noted that, when the *p*-values are printed, they refer to a two-tail test.

ANALYSIS OF VARIANCE

The format of the analysis of variance tables also varies. The structures of some of these are as follows:

```
Analysis of Variance
SOURCE          DF              SS              MS
Regression
Error
Total
```

	DF	Sum of Squares	Mean Square	F Value	Prob > F
Source					
Model					
Error					
C Total					

Analysis of Variance

```
ANALYSIS OF VARIANCE
                DF    SUM OF SQUARES    MEAN SQUARE    F RATIO
REGRESSION
RESIDUAL
```

Several printouts do not include the F-statistic (in which case you must compute it yourself); others print the F-value as well as the corresponding p-value (represented by Prob > F, P > F, or SIGNIF F).

OTHER OUTPUT

Various other statistics are available. For example, we can obtain the Durbin–Watson statistic, the list of errors (residuals) and confidence interval estimates of the expected value of y, and prediction intervals of y for given values of the independent variables. Details about instructions and the format of the output can be found in manuals available from the creators of the packages and at your computer centers.

▮▮▮▮▮ *EXERCISES*

16.48 Assume that the computer application package you are using produces the F-statistic for testing the β_i coefficients. Test each of the following hypotheses:

a. $H_0: \beta_1 = 0$
   $H_A: \beta_1 \neq 0$
   $\alpha = .01$ $n = 25$ $k = 3$ $F = 9.01$

b. $H_0: \beta_2 = 0$
   $H_A: \beta_2 \neq 0$
   $\alpha = .05$ $n = 20$ $k = 2$ $F = 4.93$

16.49 For each of the following hypotheses, set up the rejection region in terms of the F-statistic:

a. $H_0: \beta_1 = 0$
   $H_A: \beta_1 \neq 0$
   $\alpha = .05$ $n = 27$ $k = 3$

b. $H_0: \beta_1 = 0$
   $H_A: \beta_1 \neq 0$
   $\alpha = .10$ $n = 15$ $k = 1$

SECTION 16.10   *SUMMARY*

In this chapter we discussed the **multiple regression technique.** With this technique, because of the difficulty of performing the calculations by hand, we must use the computer extensively in estimating and testing the parameters. The computer output also includes the **standard error of estimate,** the **coefficient of determination,** and the **analysis of variance** (which allows us to test the utility of the model).

The required conditions, first presented in Chapter 15, were again enumerated; we also discussed how to recognize and test for situations where the requirements are violated. As a possible remedy for the problem of **collinearity,** we presented the technique of stepwise regression. Finally, we discussed various types of output that you may see, depending on the computer package available to you.

SUPPLEMENTARY EXERCISES

GEN **16.50**   An auctioneer of semi-antique and antique Persian rugs kept records of his weekly auctions in order to determine the relationships among price, age of carpet or rug, number of people attending the auction, and number of times the winning bidder had previously attended his auctions. He felt that, with this information, he could plan his auctions better, serve his steady customers better, and make a higher profit overall for himself. The results shown in the accompanying table were obtained.

Price	Age	Audience Size	Previous Attendance
y	x_1	x_2	x_3
1,080	80	40	1
2,540	150	80	12
1,490	85	55	3
960	55	45	0
2,100	140	70	8
1,820	95	65	5
2,230	140	80	7
1,490	80	60	9
1,620	90	65	10
1,260	60	55	8
1,880	90	70	7
2,080	100	100	5
2,150	120	85	3
1,940	95	80	0
1,860	90	80	6
2,240	135	90	8
2,950	175	120	10
2,370	150	115	10
1,240	55	55	3
1,620	70	75	5
2,120	120	100	0
1,090	50	50	8

Price	Age	Audience Size	Previous Attendance
y	x_1	x_2	x_3
1,850	65	65	9
2,220	125	95	7
1,420	60	45	8
2,140	115	95	5

The SAS statistical application package was used to estimate the model, $y = \beta_0 + \beta_1 x_1 + \beta_2 x_2 + \beta_3 x_3 + \varepsilon$. The resulting output is given in Figure E16.50.

a. Do the signs of the coefficients conform to what you expected?

b. Do the results allow us to conclude at the 5% significance level that price is linearly related to each of age, audience size, and previous attendance?

c. What proportion of the variation in y is explained by the independent variables?

d. Test the utility of the overall regression model, with $\alpha = .05$.

e. What price would you forecast for a 100-year-old rug, given an audience size of 120 that had on average attended three of the auctioneer's auctions before?

Exercises 16.51 through 16.55 refer to Exercise 16.50, where the predicted values and the residuals were determined to be as follows:

Predicted Values $\hat{y}_i$	Residuals e_i
1,254.48	− 174.48
2,368.73	171.27
1,478.72	11.28
1,103.58	− 143.58
2,123.88	− 23.88
1,688.95	131.05

Predicted Values $\hat{y}_i$	Residuals e_i
2,208.38	21.62
1,596.58	−106.58
1,738.60	−118.60
1,380.77	−120.77
1,737.57	142.43
2,082.19	−2.19
2,042.45	107.55
1,755.12	184.88
1,822.08	37.92
2,290.60	−50.60
2,925.85	24.15

Predicted Values $\hat{y}_i$	Residuals e_i
2,690.45	−320.45
1,257.32	−17.32
1,606.26	13.74
2,143.24	−23.24
1,256.06	−166.06
1,536.79	313.21
2,250.40	−30.40
1,278.96	141.04
2,141.98	−1.98

FIGURE E16.50

```
Dependent Variable: Y

                              Analysis of Variance

                        Sum of              Mean
        Source    DF    Squares             Square        F VALUE    Prob > F
        Model      3    5530974.5959    1843658.1986      88.256      0.0001
        Error     22     459579.25024     20889.96592
        C Total   25    5990553.8462


        Root MSE      144.53362    R-square    0.9233
        Dep Mean     1836.92308    Adj R-sq    0.9128
        C.V.            7.86825


                              Parameter Estimates

                      Parameter    Standard     T for H0:
        Variable  DF  Estimate     Error        Parameter=0    Prob > |T|
        INTERCEP   1  239.53258    108.87614      2.200         0.0386
        X1         1    7.37991      1.45947      5.057         0.0001
        X2         1   10.18120      2.27321      4.479         0.0002
        X3         1   17.30921      9.04095      1.915         0.0686
```

16.51   The correlation matrix is

	y	x_1	x_2
x_1	0.920		
x_2	0.890	0.803	
x_3	0.382	0.326	0.206

What (if anything) do the correlations tell you about your original answers in Exercise 16.50?

16.52   Check to determine whether the error variable is normally distributed.

16.53   Check to determine whether σ_ε^2 is fixed.

16.54   Check whether the errors are independent.

16.55   How do your answers in Exercises 16.52–16.54 affect your answers in Exercise 16.50?

ACC **16.56**   An electronic parts manufacturing firm can cost out a particular job easily in terms of direct labor and direct materials costs. Allocating in-direct costs, however, is somewhat more difficult. In an effort to come to grips with this problem, the firm's controller instructed one of the accountants to regress total manufacturing overhead costs on the number of direct labor hours used (x_1) and on the quantity of direct materials used (x_2), with the results shown in Figure E16.56. (This output was produced by the SAS software package.)

a. Write out the estimated regression equation.

b. Is there sufficient evidence (with $\alpha = .05$) to indicate that total costs and direct labor are linearly related?

c. Is there sufficient evidence (with $\alpha = .05$) to indicate that total costs and direct materials are linearly related?

d. Test the overall usefulness of the regression model, with $\alpha = .05$.

e. Interpret the coefficient of determination.

f. What can you say about the magnitude of the standard error of estimate?

FIGURE E16.56

```
Dependent Variable: Y


                                            Analysis of Variance


                        Sum of       Mean
        Source    DF    Squares      Square     F Value    Prob > F
        Model      2    1249.3114    624.6557    8.49       .0059
        Error     11     809.3301     73.5755
        C Total   13    2058.6415


        Root MSE      8.5776     R-square    .6069
        Dep Mean     23.6511     Adj R-sq    .5354
        C.V.         36.2672


                                            Parameter Estimates


                        Parameter     Standard     T for H0:
        Variable    DF    Estimate      Error     Parameter=0    Prob > |T|
        INTERCEP     1    12432.1171    6346.4787    1.9589        .0760
        X1           1       11.6432       2.7879    4.1763        .0016
        X2           1        6.1135       1.5699    3.8942        .0026
```

ECON **16.57** In order to examine the cause of large price fluctuations in the lettuce market over the last year, a study was undertaken on the possible effects of volume of harvest and amount of sunshine on lettuce prices. In regressing the price of crates containing 24 iceberg lettuce heads each on monthly harvest figures in California and mean monthly sunshine in the same growing regions, an agricultural analyst ended up with the results produced by the Minitab applications package that are shown in Figure E16.57A. Somewhat discouraged and confused by the results, the analyst decided to rerun the equation, this time omitting the sunshine variable x_2. This led to the results shown in Figure E16.57B, again produced by the Minitab applications package. Compare the results of the two regressions, and discuss why such a change might have taken place.

FIGURE E16.57A

```
The regression equation is

C1=57.3-15.3C2+3.12C3

Predictor       Coef       Stdev      t-ratio
Constant       57.247     25.874       2.213
C2            -15.277      9.223      -1.656
C3              3.125      3.174       0.985

s=2.663    R-sq=43.6%    R-sq(adj)=38.3%

Analysis of Variance

SOURCE        DF       SS        MS
Regression     2     115.27     57.63
Error         21     148.94      7.09
Total         23     264.21
```

FIGURE E16.57B

```
The regression equation is
C1=183-29.2C2

Predictor       Coef       Stdev      t-ratio
Constant      183.418     44.228       4.147
C2            -29.217      8.787      -3.325

s=2.746    R-sq=37.2%    R-sq(adj)=34.3%

Analysis of Variance

SOURCE        DF       SS        MS
Regression     1      98.27     98.27
Error         22     165.94      7.54
Total         23     264.21
```

16.58 The president of a national real estate company wanted to know why certain branches of the company outperformed others. He felt that the key factors in determining total annual sales (in $millions) were the advertising budget (in $1,000s) x_1 and the number of sales agents x_2. To analyze the situation, he took a sample of 15 offices and ran the data through the Minitab software system. The data are shown next. The output is shown in Figure E16.58.

Office	Annual Sales ($millions) y	Advertising ($1,000s) x_1	Number of Agents x_2
1	32	249	15
2	47	292	18
3	18	183	14
4	25	201	16
5	49	310	21
6	41	248	20

Office	Annual Sales ($millions) y	Advertising ($1,000s) x_1	Number of Agents x_2
7	52	246	18
8	38	241	14
9	36	288	13
10	29	191	15
11	43	248	21
12	28	210	18
13	24	256	20
14	36	275	16
15	41	241	19

a. Interpret the coefficients.

b. Test to determine whether there is a linear relationship between each independent variable and the dependent variable, with $\alpha = .05$.

FIGURE E16.58

```
The regression equation is

Y=-19.5+0.158X1+0.962X2

Predictor       Coef       Stdev     t-ratio
Constant       -19.47      15.84      -1.23
X1             0.15838     0.05613     2.82
X2             0.9625      0.7781      1.24

s=7.362    R-sq=52.4%    R-sq(adj)=44.5%

Analysis of Variance

SOURCE         DF      SS        MS
Regression      2     716.58    358.29
Error          12     650.35     54.20
Total          14    1366.93
```

Exercises 16.59 through 16.63 refer to Exercise 16.58. In Exercise 16.58, the predicted values and the residuals are as follows.

Office	Predicted Value $\hat{y}_i$	Residuals e_i
1	34.41	−2.41
2	44.10	2.90
3	22.99	−4.99
4	27.77	−2.77
5	49.84	−0.84
6	39.06	1.94
7	36.82	15.18
8	32.18	5.82
9	38.66	−2.66
10	25.22	3.78
11	40.02	2.98
12	31.12	−3.12
13	40.33	−16.33
14	39.49	−3.49
15	36.99	4.01

16.59   The correlation matrix is

	y	x_1
x_1	0.681	
x_2	0.457	0.329

Is collinearity a problem?

16.60   Does it appear that the error variable is normal?

16.61   Does it appear that σ_ε^2 is fixed?

16.62   Does it appear that the errors are independent?

16.63   Do any of your answers in Exercises 16.59–16.62 cause you to doubt your answers in Exercise 16.58?

16.64   Suppose that in Exercise 16.58, a third independent variable was included—the average number of years of experience in the real estate business x_3 for each office. These data are as follows.

Office	Average Years of Experience x_3
1	12
2	15
3	8
4	12
5	16
6	14
7	13
8	10
9	12
10	8
11	17
12	9
13	11
14	10
15	13

The Minitab computer output is shown in Figure E16.64 on page 796.

a. What differences do you observe between this output and the output in Exercise 16.58? How do you account for any differences?

b. The correlation matrix is

	y	x_1	x_2
x_1	0.681		
x_2	0.457	0.329	
x_3	0.743	0.647	0.679

FIGURE E16.64

```
The regression equation is

Y=-8.2+0.0905X1-0.071X2+1.93X3

Predictor       Coef        Stdev      t-ratio
Constant       -8.17        16.21       -0.50
X1              0.09054      0.06601      1.37
X2             -0.0714       0.9500      -0.08
X3              1.927        1.145        1.68

s=6.857    R-sq=62.2%    R-sq(adj)=51.8%

Analysis of Variance
SOURCE          DF      SS         MS
Regression       3    849.78     283.26
Error           11    517.16      47.01
Total           14   1366.93
```

Does this help explain some of the differences? Why or why not?

16.65 The capital asset pricing model is an extremely important tool for financial analysts. The model, which allows analysts to assess the risk associated with portfolios of stocks, is based on constructing a regression line for which the dependent variable is the return of a particular stock and the independent variables are various stock-market indices. A business student decided to develop her own model using the following variables:

y = Price of a stock

x_1 = TSE (Toronto Stock Exchange) Composite Price-Earnings Ratio

x_2 = TSE300 Index

The accompanying data from 21 months in 1977 and 1978 were gathered.

Month	Stock Price ($)	TSE Composite Price/Earnings Ratio	TSE300 Index
1977-J	8 7/8	8.80	996.6
F	9	8.85	1,008.9
M	8 3/4	8.96	1,022.1
A	8 5/8	8.48	994.8
M	8 1/2	8.19	981.2
J	9 3/8	8.62	1,031.2
J	9 5/8	8.70	1,033.5
A	9 3/8	8.31	1,003.3
S	9 1/8	8.20	1,000.1
O	8 7/8	7.93	970.5
N	9 3/8	7.90	1,017.5
D	9 3/4	8.24	1,059.6

(continued)

FIGURE E16.65

```
Dependent Variable: PRICE

                                  Analysis of Variance

                       Sum of      Mean
        Source   DF   Squares    Square    F Value    Prob > F
        Model     2   16.32357   8.16178   147.889    0.0001
        Error    18    0.99340   0.05519
        C Total  20   17.31696

        Root MSE    0.23492   R-square   0.9426
        Dep Mean    9.71429   Adj R-sq   0.9363
        C.V.        2.41832

                                  Parameter Estimates

                       Parameter   Standard    T for H0:
        Variable   DF   Estimate      Error    Parameter=0   Prob > |T|
        INTERCEP    1    2.62501    1.08985        2.409      0.0269
        PE          1   -0.57296    0.14007       -4.090      0.0007
        TSE300      1    0.01121    0.00066       16.905      0.0001
```

Month	Stock Price ($)	TSE Composite Price/Earnings Ratio	TSE300 Index
1978-J	9 1/4	7.64	998.4
F	9 5/8	7.65	1,005.7
M	10	8.09	1,063.3
A	10 1/8	8.06	1,081.5
M	10 7/8	8.25	1,128.8
J	10 7/8	8.23	1,126.2
J	11 1/8	8.58	1,193.8
A	11 3/8	8.66	1,232.2
S	11 1/2	9.12	1,284.7

SOURCE: Bank of Canada Review.

The data were input, and the SAS system was used to produce the printout shown in Figure E16.65.

a. Test for the overall usefulness of the model, at $\alpha = .05$.

b. Test each of the coefficients for significance, at $\alpha = .05$.

Exercises 16.66 through 16.70 refer to Exercise 16.65, where the predicted values and the residuals are as follows.

Predicted Values $\hat{y}_i$	Residuals e_i
8.7622	.1128
8.8715	.1285
8.9566	−.2066
8.9254	−.3004

(continued)

Predicted Values $\hat{y}_i$	Residuals e_i
8.9390	$-.4390$
9.2535	.1215
9.2334	.3916
9.1181	.2569
9.1452	$-.0202$
8.9679	$-.0929$
9.5123	$-.1373$
9.7898	$-.0398$
9.4470	$-.1970$
9.5232	.1018
9.9172	.0828
10.1386	$-.0136$
10.5603	.3147
10.5426	.3324
11.1003	.0247
11.4853	$-.1103$
11.8106	$-.3106$

16.66   Does it appear that the error variable is normally distributed?

16.67   Does it appear that σ_e^2 is fixed?

16.68   Does it appear that the errors are independent?

16.69   The Durbin–Watson statistic is $d = 1.03$. What conclusion can you draw from this statistic?

16.70   The correlation matrix is

	y	x_1
x_1	0.179	
x_2	0.943	0.412

Is collinearity a problem?

FIN **16.71**   Stock-market analysts are keenly interested in determining what factors influence the price of a stock. After some examination, a statistician hypothesized that a stock price would be affected by its quarterly dividends x_1, its price/ earnings ratio x_2, and the interest rate of treasury bills x_3. The values of the relevant variables were observed for a period of 40 quarters. When the data were run on the SAS computer system, the output shown in Figure E16.71 was created.

a. Test the overall utility of the model, with $\alpha = .05$.

b. Is the stock price explained by quarterly dividends? (Test with $\alpha = .05$.)

c. Is the stock price negatively related to the price/earnings ratio? (Test with $\alpha = .05$.)

MNG **16.72**   The sales manager of a large retail chain has been given the task of determining why certain stores have been performing more poorly than expected. She believes that part of the problem is that some stores appear to be the victims of an inefficient distribution system. Other possible factors include the size of the population in the surrounding area and the amount of advertising used. She decides to take a sample of 50 stores, and for each she determines the following variables:

y = Total sales last year (in \$1,000s)

x_1 = Population (in 1,000,000s)

x_2 = Advertising expenditures (in \$1,000s)

x_3 = Distribution-efficiency index, ranging from 1 = Poor distribution to 10 = Excellent distribution; this is an ordinal scale, but x_3 will be treated as an interval-scaled variable.

The data were run on the Minitab software package, with the results shown in Figure E16.72.

a. Can we conclude at the 5% significance level that this model is useful in analyzing annual sales?

b. Do these data provide sufficient evidence at the 5% significance level to enable us to conclude that the distribution-efficiency index is a factor in determining total annual sales?

c. Does the amount of advertising influence sales? (Test with $\alpha = .05$.)

MNG **16.73**   In preparing for upcoming union–management talks about pensions, benefits, and other nonsalary items, a labor union wishes to determine the relationships among hourly wages,

Dependent Variable: Y

Analysis of Variance

Source	DF	Sum of Squares	Mean Square	F Value	Prob > F
Model	3	516.9036	172.3012	34.4341	0.0000
Error	36	180.1368	5.0038		
C Total	39	697.0404			

Root MSE	2.2369	R-square	0.7416
Dep Mean	25.0962	Adj R-sq	0.7200
C.V.	8.9133		

Parameter Estimates

Variable	DF	Parameter Estimate	Standard Error	T for H0: Parameter=0	Prob > |T|
INTERCEP	1	17.3925	5.5254	3.1477	0.0032
X1	1	41.2991	7.5016	5.5054	0.0000
X2	1	-0.4158	0.5228	-0.7953	0.4316
X3	1	0.5709	0.4083	1.3982	0.1706

The regression equation is

$$C1 = 13.6 + 34.1C2 + 0.126C3 - 0.993C4$$

Predictor	Coef	Stdev	t-ratio
Constant	13.623	6.720	2.027
C2	34.079	4.114	8.284
C3	0.126	0.106	1.184
C4	-0.993	0.655	-1.516

s=6.905   R-sq=58.1%   R-sq (adj)=55.4%

Analysis of Variance

SOURCE	DF	SS	MS
Regression	3	3046.165	1015.388
Error	46	2193.298	47.680
Total	49	5239.463	

FIGURE E16.73

```
The regression equation is

C1=6.76+0.317C2+0.439C3

Predictor    Coef     Stdev     t-ratio
Constant     6.759    1.162     5.817
C2           0.317    0.141     2.248
C3           0.439    0.0824    5.328

s=0.621    R-sq=87.2%    R-sq (adj)=84.9%

Analysis of Variance

SOURCE        DF      SS        MS
Regression     2    28.919    14.459
Error         11     4.239     0.385
Total         13    33.158
```

years of schooling, and years of experience on the job. Selecting a random sample of workers on a production line, the union recorded the accompanying data.

Hourly Wages y	Years of Schooling x_1	Years of Experience x_2
10.00	8	3
11.00	8	4
12.50	9	5
14.00	12	8
10.50	10	2
13.25	11	4
15.20	10	10
12.10	9	6
11.75	8	5
10.85	8	4
12.35	10	7

Hourly Wages y	Years of Schooling x_1	Years of Experience x_2
14.55	12	10
13.80	10	9
13.60	12	8

Then, using the Minitab statistical application package, the union generated the output shown in Figure E16.73.

a. Is there sufficient evidence to allow you to conclude that the linear model as a whole is significant? (Test at $\alpha = .10$.)

b. What do the values of $\hat{\beta}_1$ and $\hat{\beta}_2$ tell you?

Exercises 16.74 through 16.77 refer to Exercise 16.73.

16.74 The histogram of the residuals appears next. Does it appear that the error variable is normal?

Histogram of C4   N=14

```
Midpoint    Count
 -0.500       5      *****
  0.000       5      *****
  0.500       2      **
  1.000       2      **
```

16.75 Applying the Lilliefors test (Chapter 14) to the residuals, we find the value of the test statistic to be $D = .2499$. Can we conclude with $\alpha = .05$ that the normality requirement is unsatisfied?

16.76 The plot of the residuals versus $\hat{y}$ is shown in Figure E16.76.

a. What does it tell you about σ_ε^2?

b. What does it tell you about the independence of the error variable?

16.77 The correlation coefficient of x_1 and x_2 is 0.601. Is collinearity a problem in this case?

 16.78 Economists have stated that the willingness of individuals to hold cash in safety deposit boxes or non-interest-bearing checking accounts is a function of an individual's income x_1, and of the prevailing interest rate x_2. A bank executive has decided to test this theory. He has selected a random sample of individuals at different times during the past 2 years and has gathered from them the relevant data. With the assistance of the Minitab system, he produces the output given in Figure E16.78.

a. Do these data provide sufficient evidence to support the theory? (Test with $\alpha = .01$.)

b. Would you conclude that the prevailing interest rates are very important to an individual's willingness to hold cash? (Test with $\alpha = .01$.)

FIGURE E16.76

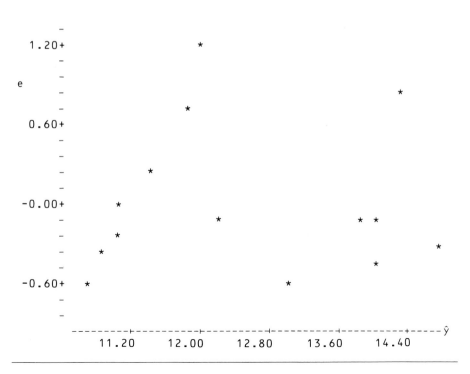

FIGURE E16.78

```
The regression equation is

C1=15.7+1.63C2+2.11C3

Predictor     Coef      Stdev     t-ratio
Constant      15.721    10.256    1.533
C2            1.634     0.431     3.791
C3            2.112     1.742     1.212

s=16.555    R-sq=73.0%    R-sq(adj)=72.1%

Analysis of Variance

SOURCE        DF        SS        MS
Regression    2         42320.1   21160.0
Error         57        15621.3   274.1
Total         59        57941.4
```

CASE 16.1*   **RISK ASSESSMENT FROM FINANCIAL REPORTS**

This case requires the use of a computer. The data listed below are also stored on the data disk.

FIN

    Investors are interested in assessing the riskiness of a company's common stock, as well as its expected rate of return. It is therefore desirable to potential investors that a company's financial reports provide information to help them assess the company's risk.

    Farrelly, Ferris, and Reichenstein conducted an investigation into the relationship between seven accounting-determined measures of risk and the average risk assessment of financial analysts. The seven accounting-determined measures of risk (all of which could be computed from a company's financial reports) and their definitions are as follows:

    Dividend payout = (Cash dividends)/(Earnings)

    Current ratio = (Current assets)/(Current liabilities)

    Asset size = Log (Total assets)[†]

---

* Gail E. Farrelly, Kenneth R. Ferris, and William R. Reichenstein, "Perceived Risk, Market Risk and Accounting-Determined Risk Measures," *Accounting Review* 60 (1985): 278–88.

[†] In this definition, Log is the natural logarithm.

Asset growth = Average growth rate in asset size for the years 1977–1981

Leverage = (Total senior debt)/(Total assets)

Variability in earnings = Standard deviation of the price–earnings ratio for the years 1977–1981

Covariability in earnings = Strength of the relationship between a firm's price–earnings ratio and the average price–earnings ratio of the market overall

These seven measures were computed for 25 well-known stocks, based on data from the companies' annual reports from 1977 to 1981. The results are summarized in the accompanying table.

The names of the 25 stocks were then sent to a random sample of 500 financial analysts, who "were requested to assess the risk of each of the 25 companies on a scale of 1 (low) to 9 (high), assuming that the stock was to be added to a diversified portfolio." The mean rating assigned by the 209 financial analysts who responded is recorded for each of the 25 stocks. This measure of the financial analysts' risk perception was taken to be a reasonable surrogate for the (market) risk of each stock.

Based on the data given in the accompanying table, what would you conclude concerning the usefulness of the information provided by financial reports for the purpose of assessing a company's risk?

SUMMARY DATA FOR SELECT STUDY VARIABLES

Name of Stock	Dividend Payout	Current Ratio	Asset Size	Asset Growth	Leverage	Variability Earnings	Covariability Earnings	Mean Risk Assessment
American Telephone	.63	.70	11.83	.093	.165	1.09	.62	1.89
Procter & Gamble	.47	1.76	8.85	.106	.318	2.79	.46	2.36
IBM	.61	1.41	10.30	.103	.338	1.95	.21	2.39
General Electric	.43	1.24	9.95	.111	.468	1.29	.97	2.69
Exxon	.47	1.34	11.33	.165	.277	2.25	.56	2.70
Commonwealth Edison	.88	.72	9.32	.128	.620	1.76	.21	3.20
Dow Jones & Co.	.40	.78	6.28	.177	.477	2.96	.67	3.57
McDonald's	.15	.50	7.97	.150	.413	2.32	.62	3.87
Sears Roebuck	.66	1.24	10.24	.177	.573	1.42	.67	3.91
Du Pont	.60	2.05	10.08	.244	.508	1.64	.67	4.11
Safeway	.59	1.08	8.21	.093	.691	2.01	.55	4.28
Citicorp	.36	1.47	11.69	.124	.467	1.52	.87	4.30
Dr. Pepper	.54	2.17	5.11	.121	.215	2.26	.31	4.32

(continued)

Name of Stock	Dividend Payout	Current Ratio	Asset Size	Asset Growth	Leverage	Variability Earnings	Covariability Earnings	Mean Risk Assessment
General Motors	2.24	1.09	10.57	.093	.422	2.79	.32	4.59
Xerox	.42	1.74	8.95	.102	.397	1.04	.21	4.69
American Broadcasting	.31	2.63	7.37	.127	.370	.47	.16	4.86
Holiday Inns	.20	.87	7.43	.155	.536	1.34	.36	5.13
Tandy	.00	3.48	6.84	.168	.225	3.27	.31	5.54
Litton Ind.	.17	1.53	8.21	.117	.552	2.52	1.00	5.66
RCA	.58	1.18	8.97	.143	.855	2.79	.51	5.67
Georgia Pacific	.80	1.48	8.53	.134	.450	3.13	.67	5.88
Emery Air Freight	.83	1.78	5.62	.135	.697	2.28	.46	5.92
E. F. Hutton	.18	1.47	8.64	.181	.467	1.80	.82	6.37
U.S. Homes	1.30	1.47	6.63	.136	.467	20.18	.10	7.23
International Harvester	8.58	1.48	8.58	.081	.704	2.79	.51	8.78

CASE 16.2*   BUSINESS FAILURES AND KEY
ECONOMIC INDICATORS

This case requires the use of a computer. The data listed below are also stored on the data disk.

ECON   Many people have attempted to get an overall picture of business failures and bankruptcies—both by studying the incidence of business failure on a national or industry-wide scale and by analyzing individual firms one by one—with varying degrees of success. In the latter instance, promising results have been achieved by using various accounting and financial ratios to predict bankruptcies.

In looking at the overall picture, some analysts have been tempted by dramatic swings in the number of business failures from year to year to try to relate them to overall economic conditions. The annual percentage change in certain key economic indicators is reproduced in the accompanying table.

Undertake the analysis necessary to enable you to discuss changes in the number of business failures.

---

* This case is based on ideas from various studies. At the level of the firm, considerable work has been done by Altman. See, for example, E. I. Altman, "Financial Ratios, Discriminant Analysis and the Prediction of Corporate Bankruptcy," *Journal of Finance* (September 1968): 589–609.

ANNUAL PERCENTAGE CHANGES IN BUSINESS FAILURES AND IN KEY ECONOMIC INDICATORS IN CANADA*

	1968	1969	1970	1971	1972	1973	1974	1975	1976	1977	1978	1979	1980
Business failures	.3	−5.1	24.3	4.0	1.2	−4.8	−4.9	5.1	−4.9	40.0	40.4	2.7	15.8
Real domestic product	3.5	5.5	6.2	2.2	5.9	5.6	7.8	4.7	.7	5.3	2.8	3.5	3.2
Wages and salaries	10.9	8.7	12.1	8.4	9.9	11.3	15.8	19.4	16.4	15.4	10.0	8.8	11.0
Unemployment rate	3.8	4.5	4.4	5.7	6.2	6.2	5.5	5.3	6.9	7.1	8.1	8.4	7.5
Retail sales	6.8	6.0	6.9	2.3	8.9	11.3	12.6	16.9	14.5	10.8	8.4	11.7	11.9
Housing starts	22.0	20.0	6.9	−9.5	22.6	7.0	7.4	−17.3	4.2	−7.3	−10.1	−7.3	−13.4
C.P.I.	3.6	4.0	4.6	3.3	2.9	4.8	7.6	10.8	10.8	7.5	8.0	9.0	8.8

* "Canadian Business Failure Record, Various Years," compiled by the Business Education Division, Dun and Bradstreet.

■■■■■■■ **CASE 16.3[†]** **TESTING POPULAR BELIEFS ABOUT GOVERNMENT LOTTERIES**

> [PG] Lotteries have become important sources of revenue for governments. Many people have criticized lotteries, however—often referring to them as a tax on the poor or a tax on the uneducated. In an examination of this issue, a random sample of 100 people were asked how much they spend on lottery tickets and were interviewed about various sociodemographic variables. The purpose of this work was to test the following beliefs:
>
> 1. Relatively poor people spend a greater proportion of their income on lotteries than do relatively rich people.
> 2. Older people buy more lottery tickets than do younger people.
> 3. People who have children spend more on lotteries than do those without children.
> 4. Relatively uneducated people spend more on lotteries than do relatively educated people.
>
> As part of the study, the following model was proposed:
>
> $$y = \beta_0 + \beta_1 x_1 + \beta_2 x_2 + \beta_3 x_3 + \beta_4 x_4 + \varepsilon$$
>
> In this model
>
> $y =$ Amount spent on lottery tickets as a percentage of total household income

---

[†] This case is based on several different studies. The results are simulated.

x_1 = Number of years of education

x_2 = Age

x_3 = Number of children

x_4 = Personal income

The data were run on a statistical applications package, with the results shown in the accompanying table.

COMPUTER-GENERATED DATA RESULTS

Variable	Coefficients	t-Statistic
Constant	−7.35	−4.58
x_1	−.46	−2.83
x_2	.55	2.61
x_3	.09	.71
x_4	−5.81	−6.05
$r^2 =$ .41		
$F = 89.0$		

Comment on the validity of the enumerated beliefs, in light of the statistical results.

MINITAB
INSTRUCTIONS

The command

```
REGRESS C1 2 C2 C3
```

will produce the regression equation

$$\hat{y} = \hat{\beta}_0 + \hat{\beta}_1 x_1 + \hat{\beta}_2 x_2$$

where y, x_1, and x_2 are stored in columns 1, 2, and 3, respectively. The 2 in the command specifies the number of independent variables in the equation. The output includes the coefficients, t-statistics, s_ε, r^2, and the analysis of variance.

The subcommand

```
PREDICT X1, X2
```

will produce the 95% confidence intervals and prediction intervals of y, when the given values of the independent variables are X1 and X2.

In Example 16.1, the following data are input:

```
READ C1-C4
  89.5  20.0     5    4.1
  79.9  14.8    10    6.8
  83.1  20.5     8    6.3
  56.9  12.5     7    5.1
  66.6  18.0     8    4.2
  82.5  14.3    12    8.6
 126.3  27.5     1    4.9
  79.3  16.5    10    6.2
 119.9  24.3     2    7.5
  87.6  20.2     8    5.1
 112.6  22.0     7    6.3
```

```
120.8   19.0    11    12.9
 78.5   12.3    16     9.6
 74.3   14.0    12     5.7
 74.8   16.7    13     4.8
END
REGRESS C1 3 C2-C4
```

And the following output is produced:

```
The regression equation is

C1=-16.1+4.15C2-0.236C3+4.83C4

Predictor     Coef        Stdev      t-ratio
Constant     -16.06       19.07       -0.84
C2             4.1462      0.7512       5.52
C3            -0.2361      0.8812      -0.27
C4             4.8309      0.9011       5.36

s=6.894    R-sq=91.6%    R-sq(adj)=89.3%

Analysis of Variance

SOURCE        DF       SS         MS
Regression     3     5707.4     1902.5
Error         11      522.8       47.5
Total         14     6230.2
```

We can use the subcommand **PREDICT** to produce the 95% confidence interval estimate of the expected value of y and the 95% prediction interval of y. Thus, the commands

```
REGRESS C1 3 C2-C4;
PREDICT 20 10 10.
```

will elicit the following statistical data:

```
 Fit     Stdev. Fit      95% C.I.           95% P.I.
112.81      3.58     (104.94, 120.69)   (95.71,129.91)
```

DIAGNOSING VIOLATIONS OF THE REQUIRED CONDITIONS AND OTHER PROBLEMS

COLLINEARITY

Some forms of collinearity may be identified by computing the correlations among the independent variables. The command

```
CORRELATION C1, C2, C3
```

will cause the computer to print the correlation matrix showing the correlations between C1 and C2, C1 and C3, and C2 and C3. After inputting the data in Example 16.1, the command (not a subcommand)

```
CORRELATION C1-C4
```

produces the output

```
         C1        C2        C3
C2     0.805
C3    -0.521    -0.809
C4     0.372    -0.171    0.410
```

From this matrix we learn, for example, that the correlation between x_1 and x_2 (C2 and C3) is $-.809$, a value large enough to make us suspect that collinearity is a problem in this example.

AUTOCORRELATION

First-order autocorrelation can be detected by the subcommand

```
DW
```

which produces the Durbin–Watson statistic. Thus, in Example 16.1 the commands

```
REGRESS C1 3 C2-C4;
DW.
```

will output all of the regression statistics plus the Durbin–Watson statistic:

```
Durbin-Watson statistic=2.05
```

ANALYZING THE RESIDUALS

If we type the command

```
BRIEF 3
```

prior to typing the REGRESS command, the output will include (among other things) the predicted values $\hat{y}_i$ and the residuals e_i. To perform various statistical techniques on the residuals, we would proceed as follows:

```
BRIEF 3
REGRESS C1 3 C2-C4;
RESIDUAL C5.
```

(Note that BRIEF 3 is a command, not a subcommand.)
The RESIDUAL C5 subcommand will tell the computer to store the residuals in column 5. If we follow this up by typing

```
LET C6=C1-C5
```

Minitab will store the predicted values $\hat{y}_i$ in column 6. To graph the residuals versus the predicted values, we would command

```
PLOT C5 C6
```

We can examine the graph to see if σ_ε^2 appears to be fixed. We can also look for any signs that the errors are not independent. As an illustration, we made the following commands and subcommands after inputting the data in Example 16.1:

```
BRIEF 3
REGRESS C1 3 C2-C4;
RESIDUAL C5.
```

In response, Minitab produced the following output (in addition to the regression statistics already shown):

Obs.	C2	C1	Fit	Stdev. Fit	Residual	St. Resid
1	20.0	89.50	85.49	2.86	4.01	0.64
2	14.8	79.90	75.79	2.50	4.11	0.64
3	20.5	83.10	97.48	2.24	-14.38	-2.21R
4	12.5	56.90	58.75	5.51	-1.85	-0.45
5	18.0	66.60	76.97	2.60	-10.37	-1.63
6	14.3	82.50	81.95	2.79	0.55	0.09
7	27.5	126.30	121.40	4.37	4.90	0.92
8	16.5	79.30	79.94	1.97	-0.64	-0.10
9	24.3	119.90	120.45	4.18	-0.55	-0.10
10	20.2	87.60	90.44	2.55	-2.84	-0.44
11	22.0	112.60	103.94	2.60	8.66	1.36
12	19.0	120.80	122.44	5.44	-1.64	-0.39
13	12.3	78.50	77.54	3.96	0.96	0.17
14	14.0	74.30	66.69	2.78	7.61	1.21
15	16.7	74.80	73.30	4.37	1.50	0.28

```
R denotes an obs. with a large st. resid.
```

The predicted values $\hat{y}_i$ are listed under Fit. The values of e_i are listed under Residual. If we then type

```
LET C6=C1-C5
PRINT C5 C6
```

Minitab outputs the values of e_i and $\hat{y}_i$ shown next.

ROW	C5	C6
1	4.0080	85.49
2	4.1052	75.79
3	-14.3848	97.48
4	-1.8543	58.75
5	-10.3745	76.97

6	0.5549	81.95
7	4.9025	121.40
8	-0.6448	79.94
9	-0.5539	120.45
10	-2.8439	90.44
11	8.6598	103.94
12	-1.6411	122.44
13	0.9607	77.54
14	7.6083	66.69
15	1.4975	73.30

The command

```
PLOT C5 C6
```

will then cause Minitab to produce the following graph.

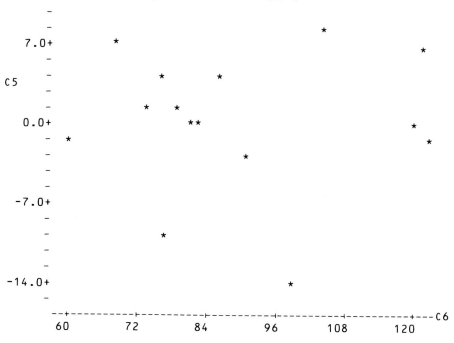

SAS INSTRUCTIONS

The SAS applications package performs multiple regression in the same way as it does simple regression. Thus, we handle Example 16.1 by entering the following statements:

```
DATA;
INPUT Y X1 X2 X3;
CARDS;
  89.5   20.0    5    4.1
  79.9   14.8   10    6.8
  83.1   20.5    8    6.3
  56.9   12.5    7    5.1
  66.6   18.0    8    4.2
  82.5   14.3   12    8.6
 126.3   27.5    1    4.9
  79.3   16.5   10    6.2
 119.9   24.3    2    7.5
  87.6   20.2    8    5.1
 112.6   22.0    7    6.3
 120.8   19.0   11   12.9
  78.5   12.3   16    9.6
  74.3   14.0   12    5.7
  74.8   16.7   13    4.8
PROC REG;
MODEL Y=X1 X2 X3;
```

The resulting output is as follows:

Dependent Variable: Y

Analysis of Variance

Source	DF	Sum of Squares	Mean Square	F Value	Prob > F
Model	3	5707.44	1902.48	40.029	0.0000
Error	11	522.80	47.53		
C Total	14	6230.24			

Root MSE	6.894	R-square	0.916	
Dep Mean	88.840	Adj R-SQ	0.893	
C.V.	7.760			

Parameter Estimates

Variable	DF	Parameter Estimate	Standard Error	T for H0: Parameter=0	Prob > |T|
INTERCEP	1	-16.058	19.071	-0.842	0.418
X1	1	4.146	0.751	5.520	0.000
X2	1	-0.236	0.881	-0.268	0.794
X3	1	4.831	0.901	5.361	0.000

If the CLI and CLM options are activated in the MODEL statement as follows

MODEL Y=X1 X2 X3/CLI CLM;

and we add a 16th observation ($y = .$, $x_1 = 20$, $x_2 = 10$, and $x_3 = 10$)

    20.0   10   10.0

we produce the following output:

Obs	Dep Var Y	Predict Value	Std Err Predict
1	89.5000	85.4920	2.860
2	79.9000	75.7948	2.495
3	83.1000	97.5	2.244
4	56.9000	58.7543	5.511
5	66.6000	76.9745	2.603
6	82.5000	81.9451	2.788
7	126.3	121.4	4.366
8	79.3000	79.9448	1.975
9	119.9	120.5	4.185
10	87.6000	90.4439	2.552
11	112.6	103.9	2.601
12	120.8	122.4	5.436

13	78.5000	77.5393	3.960
14	74.3000	66.6917	2.777
15	74.8000	73.3025	4.365
16		112.8	3.579

Lower95% Mean	Upper95% Mean	Lower95% Predict	Upper95% Predict
79.1969	91.7871	69.0644	101.9
70.3033	81.2862	59.6580	91.9315
92.5468	102.4	81.5279	113.4
46.6252	70.8834	39.3287	78.1799
71.2449	82.7040	60.7551	93.1938
75.8084	88.0817	65.5775	98.3
111.8	131.0	103.4	139.4
75.5981	84.2914	64.1608	95.7
111.2	129.7	102.7	138.2
84.8270	96.1	74.2640	106.6
98.2	109.7	87.7225	120.2
110.5	134.4	103.1	141.8
68.8230	86.2555	60.0404	95.0
60.5793	72.8041	50.3332	83.0502
63.6949	82.9101	55.3430	91.2620
104.9	120.7	95.7	129.9

Thus we can produce the 95% confidence interval estimates of the expected value of y and the 95% prediction intervals of the particular value of y for any set of independent variables.

DIAGNOSING VIOLATIONS OF THE REQUIRED CONDITIONS AND OTHER PROBLEMS

COLLINEARITY

We may be able to identify some forms of collinearity by examining the correlation among the independent variables. We produce the correlation matrix by adding the CORR option to the regression procedure. Thus, typing

```
PROC REG CORR
```

(in addition to PROC REG) will produce the same regression output as described above plus the correlation matrix. The correlation matrix for Example 16.1 is

Correlation

CORR	X1	X2	X3	Y
X1	1.0000	-0.8093	-0.1710	0.8047
X2	-0.8093	1.0000	0.4097	-0.5209
X3	-0.1710	0.4097	1.0000	0.3724
Y	0.8047	-0.5209	0.3724	1.0000

As you can see, the correlation between x_1 and x_2 is $-.8093$, a value large enough to indicate that collinearity may be a problem.

AUTOCORRELATION

First-order autocorrelation can be detected by adding

```
DW
```

to the model statement. Thus, if we type the following in Example 16.1,

```
MODEL Y=X1 X2 X3/DW;
```

SAS will output

```
Durbin-Watson D                2.052
(For Number of Obs.)              15
1st Order Autocorrelation     -0.043
```

The Durbin–Watson statistic is 2.052 with $n = 15$. The coefficient of correlation is $-.043$.

ANALYZING THE RESIDUALS

To compute the residuals and plot them against $\hat{y}$, we input the following instructions (after the PROC REG statement):

```
MODEL Y=X1 X2 X3/R;
PLOT R.*P.;
```

The option R calculates the predicted values of y, the residuals, and several other statistics that we have omitted from our presentation. The command

```
PLOT R.*P.;
```

instructs SAS to plot the residuals (R.) against the predicted values of y (P.). The output for Example 16.1 is

Obs	Dep Var Y	Predict Value	Std Err Predict	Residual	Std Err Residual	Student Residual
1	89.5000	85.4920	2.860	4.0080	6.273	0.639
2	79.9000	75.7948	2.495	4.1052	6.427	0.639

(*continued*)

Obs	Dep Var Y	Predict Value	Std Err Predict	Residual	Std Err Residual	Student Residual
3	83.1000	97.5	2.244	-14.3848	6.519	-2.207
4	56.9000	58.7543	5.511	-1.8543	4.142	-0.448
5	66.6000	76.9745	2.603	-10.3745	6.384	-1.625
6	82.5000	81.9451	2.788	0.5549	6.305	0.088
7	126.3	121.4	4.366	4.9025	5.335	0.919
8	79.3000	79.9448	1.975	-0.6448	6.605	-0.098
9	119.9	120.5	4.185	-0.5539	5.478	-0.101
10	87.6000	90.4439	2.552	-2.8439	6.404	-0.444
11	112.6	103.9	2.601	8.6598	6.385	1.356
12	120.8	122.4	5.436	-1.6411	4.240	-0.387
13	78.5000	77.5393	3.960	0.9607	5.643	0.170
14	74.3000	66.6917	2.777	7.6083	6.310	1.206
15	74.8000	73.3025	4.365	1.4975	5.336	0.281

Sum of Residuals   4.973799E-14
Sum of Squared Residuals   522.7975
Predicted Resid SS (Press)   768.5089

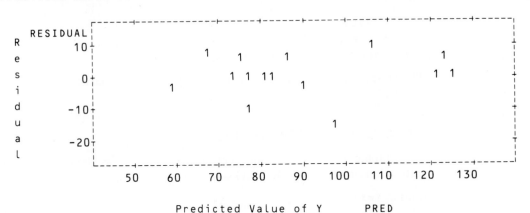

Predicted Value of Y   PRED

████████████   **COMPUTER EXERCISES**

16.79 Given the following observations of variables y, x_1, x_2, and x_3, conduct a multiple regression analysis.

y	x_1	x_2	x_3
506	10	6	55
811	18	10	32
816	20	11	34
752	16	9	48
610	15	5	58
903	21	12	29
685	11	7	52
830	18	10	36
650	14	8	60
793	15	6	49
961	19	8	24
692	18	10	63
752	12	7	45
488	10	7	61
848	17	8	38
611	15	9	59
709	14	10	41
919	22	10	26
827	20	9	39
526	9	6	65

a. What is the regression equation?

b. What are the results of the t-tests?

c. What does the standard error of estimate tell you about the model?

d. What does the coefficient of determination tell you about the model?

e. What is the result of the F-test of the analysis of variance?

Exercises 16.80 through 16.84 refer to Exercise 16.79.

16.80 Is collinearity a problem?

16.81 Does it appear that the error is normally distributed?

16.82 If the data had been recorded as a time series, would there be evidence of first-order autocorrelation?

16.83 Does it appear that σ_ε^2 is fixed?

16.84 Does it appear that the errors are independent?

16.85 The following 12 observations were drawn to estimate the model

$$y = \beta_0 + \beta_1 x_1 + \beta_2 x_2 + \varepsilon$$

y	x_1	x_2
38	2	1
39	4	2
44	5	3
47	9	5
52	9	4
56	11	6
59	13	7
66	14	7
71	18	9
78	23	12
79	28	15
83	30	16

a. Determine the regression equation.

b. Test (with $\alpha = .10$) to determine whether each of the independent variables is linearly related to the dependent variable.

c. Test (with $\alpha = .10$) the overall utility of the model.

d. What proportion of the variability of y is explained by the model?

Exercises 16.86 through 16.89 refer to Exercise 16.85.

16.86 Is it likely that collinearity adversely affects the t-tests in Exercise 16.85(b)?

16.87 Is it likely that the requirement of normality is violated?

16.88 Does it appear that the homoscedasticity requirement is violated?

16.89 Does it appear that the requirement that the errors be independent is violated?

16.90 The following observations were drawn over 16 consecutive time periods to analyze the relationship between y and x_1 and x_2.

Time	y	x_1	x_2
1	100	7	28
2	104	11	27
3	106	13	29
4	109	15	31
5	115	16	26
6	118	18	24
7	123	20	20
8	131	23	18
9	136	25	22
10	139	28	20
11	150	33	19
12	151	34	17
13	153	39	14
14	158	41	12
15	159	42	14
16	164	44	13

a. Identify the regression equation.

b. Is there sufficient evidence at the 5% significance level to establish a positive linear relationship between x_1 and y?

c. Is there sufficient evidence at the 5% significance level to indicate that there is a negative linear relationship between x_2 and y?

d. Do the data provide enough evidence at the 1% significance level to establish that the regression model is useful?

e. What proportion of the variation in y is unexplained by the model?

Exercises 16.91 through 16.95 refer to Exercise 16.90.

16.91 Is collinearity a likely problem? If so, what effect does it have on your answers in Exercise 16.90?

16.92 What does the Durbin–Watson statistic tell you about the possibility of first-order autocorrelation?

16.93 Does it appear that the model suffers from heteroscedasticity?

16.94 Does it appear that the error variable is nonnormal?

16.95 How are your answers in Exercise 16.90 affected by your responses to Exercises 16.92–16.94?

SOLUTIONS TO SELF-CORRECTING EXERCISES

16.10 a. $\hat{\beta}_1 = .062$: For each additional building permit issued, the drywall demand increases by .062 hundred sheets (on the average).

$\hat{\beta}_2 = -1.212$: For each 1-point increase in the mortgage rate, drywall demand decreases by 1.212 hundred sheets (on the average).

$\hat{\beta}_3 = .022$: For each $1,000 increase in per capita GNP, drywall demand increases by .022 hundred sheets (on the average).

b. Rejection region: $|t| > 1.96$

   (i) Test of β_1: $t = 2.067$
      Reject H_0.

  (ii) Test of β_2: $t = -1.839$
      Do not reject H_0.

 (iii) Test of β_3: $t = 4.400$
      Reject H_0.

There is evidence of a linear relationship between the number of building permits and GNP, and drywall demand.

16.20 a. $r^2 = 12.7\%$. Thus, 12.7% of the variation in sales volume is explained by the variation in the independent variables.

b. H_0: $\beta_1 = \beta_2 = \beta_3 = 0$
   H_A: At least one β_i is not equal to zero

Rejection region: $F > 4.13$ (approximately)

Test statistic:

$$F = \frac{371.75}{86.84} = 4.28$$

Conclusion: Reject H_0.

There is sufficient evidence to indicate that the model is useful.

C H A P T E R **17**

MULTIPLE REGRESSION MODELS

INTRODUCTION

In this chapter, we discuss regression analysis models that are somewhat more complex than the model presented in Chapter 16. In Chapter 16, we discussed how to read and interpret the computer output for the basic regression model represented by the equation

$$y = \beta_0 + \beta_1 x_1 + \cdots + \beta_k x_k + \varepsilon$$

We pointed out that the independent variables could be functions of other variables, and in this chapter we will consider such possibilities. Before we do so, however, we must discuss the proper way to deal with regression analysis.

HUNTING, FISHING, AND OTHER PURSUITS

Regression analysis can be a very powerful tool, but for this reason it may be dangerous in the hands of those who are not cautious. In this chapter we make the technique more powerful by increasing the number of possible models. At the same time, however, we will be increasing the chances of making a common but serious mistake. This mistake involves what is often called a hunting or fishing expedition. The expedition is organized in the erroneous belief that the ideal model to use in forecasting is the one with the largest coefficient of determination or the smallest standard error of estimate. Unquestionably, these are desirable characteristics, but they are not the only ones. It is equally important for the statistician to select a model that is valid.

For example, suppose that an economist wants to forecast monthly housing starts, using the current interest rate. It is quite reasonable to believe that there is a negative linear relationship between the two variables. Obviously, high interest rates produce high mortgage rates, making it difficult for people to purchase homes. But suppose that, when graphed, a randomly selected sample of months produces the points shown in Figure 17.1.

The relationship appears to be nonlinear. By trying a number of different mathematical expressions, even an amateur statistician can produce a model that fits extremely well (Figure 17.2). This model clearly fits the data much better than does the linear model depicted in Figure 17.3. Despite this, it is extremely likely that the linear model will produce more accurate predictions than the nonlinear model will, because the true relationship is far more likely to resemble that described by the linear model than that described by any nonlinear one.

FIGURE 17.1   HOUSING STARTS VERSUS INTEREST RATES

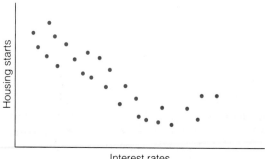

FIGURE 17.2   NONLINEAR MODEL DESCRIBING HOUSING STARTS VERSUS INTEREST RATES

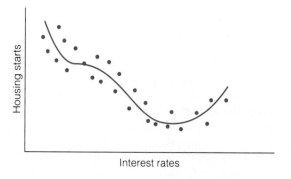

FIGURE 17.3   LINEAR MODEL DESCRIBING HOUSING STARTS VERSUS INTEREST RATES

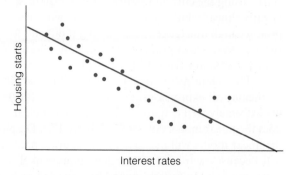

The major function of regression analysis is to test several possible models — all of which should be based on sound economic, scientific, or other foundations. Consequently, the statistician should have reason to believe in every model that will be tested; when this approach is followed, the regression tests simply serve to determine which one of these models is the best.

The alternative is to launch a hunting expedition, wherein the statistician first accumulates a long list of possible independent variables and mathematical expressions, and then hunts for the model with the smallest s_ε (or largest r^2). Thousands of combinations of independent variables may be involved, but since the computer and not the statistician is doing the calculations, the job is relatively easy. The only problem is that the end result is a model that fits past data extremely well but produces poor forecasts.

Now that we've warned you about the pitfalls, let's proceed to discuss various multiple regression models.

SECTION 17.3   ## POLYNOMIAL MODELS WITH ONE INDEPENDENT VARIABLE

If the dependent variable seems to depend on only one variable, the statistician may use the polynomial model.

Polynomial Model

$$y = \beta_0 + \beta_1 x + \beta_2 x^2 + \cdots + \beta_k x^k + \varepsilon$$

In this model, k is the **order** of the equation. For reasons we discuss later, we rarely propose a model whose order is greater than three. However, it is worthwhile to devote individual attention to situations where $k = 1, 2,$ or 3.

FIRST-ORDER MODEL

When $k = 1$, we have the simple linear regression model

$$y = \beta_0 + \beta_1 x + \varepsilon$$

Obviously, this model should be selected when the statistician believes that there is a straight-line relationship over the range of the values of x.

SECOND-ORDER MODEL

With $k = 2$, the polynomial model is

$$y = \beta_0 + \beta_1 x + \beta_2 x^2 + \varepsilon$$

The basic shape of this equation is a parabola, as shown in Figures 17.4 and 17.5.

FIGURE 17.4   SECOND-ORDER MODEL WITH $\beta_2 < 0$

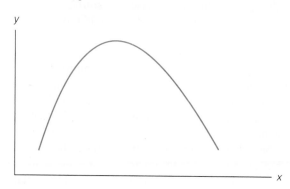

FIGURE 17.5   SECOND-ORDER MODEL WITH $\beta_2 > 0$

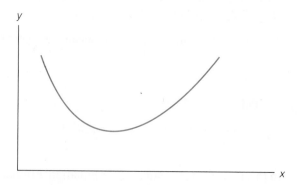

The coefficient β_0 represents the intercept where the response surface strikes the y-axis. The signs of β_1 and β_2 control the position of the parabola relative to the y-axis. If $\beta_1 = 0$, for example, the parabola is symmetric and centered around $y = 0$. If β_1 and β_2 have the same sign, the parabola shifts to the left. If β_1 and β_2 have oppposite signs, the parabola shifts to the right. The coefficient, β_2, describes the curvature. If $\beta_2 = 0$, there is no curvature. If $\beta_2 < 0$, the equation is *concave* (as in Figure 17.4). If $\beta_2 > 0$, the equation is *convex* (as in Figure 17.5). The greater the absolute value of β_2 the greater the rate of curvature, as can be seen in Figure 17.6.

THIRD-ORDER MODEL

By setting $k = 3$, we produce the third-order model

$$y = \beta_0 + \beta_1 x + \beta_2 x^2 + \beta_3 x^3 + \varepsilon$$

Figures 17.7 and 17.8 depict this equation, whose curvature can change twice.

FIGURE 17.6   SECOND-ORDER MODEL WITH VARIOUS VALUES OF β_2

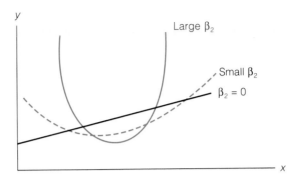

FIGURE 17.7   THIRD-ORDER MODEL WITH $\beta_3 < 0$

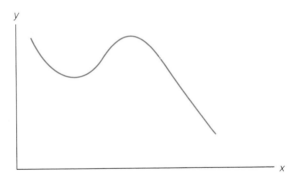

FIGURE 17.8   THIRD-ORDER MODEL WITH $\beta_3 > 0$

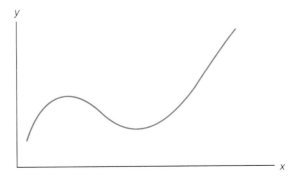

As you can see, when $\beta_3 < 0$ over the range of x, y is decreasing; and when $\beta_3 > 0$, y is increasing. The other coefficients determine the position of the curvature changes and the point at which the curve intersects the y-axis.

The number of real-life applications of this model is quite small. Statisticians rarely encounter situations involving more than one curvature reversal. Therefore, we will not discuss any higher-order models.

EXERCISES

LEARNING THE TECHNIQUES

17.1   Draw a rough sketch of each of the following equations:

a. $y = 6 + 3x$

b. $y = 6 + 3x + 2x^2$

c. $y = 6 + 3x - 2x^2$

d. $y = 6 - 3x + 2x^2$

e. $y = 6 - 3x - 2x^2$

17.2   What equation describes a second-order model with one independent variable?

17.3   For each of the following graphs, identify the sign of β_1 and the sign of β_2.

(a)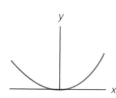

(b)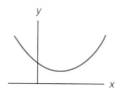

(c)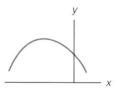

APPLYING THE TECHNIQUES

GEN **17.4**   The general manager of a supermarket chain believes that there is a relationship between weekly sales and the amount of space allotted to most products. If true, this would have great significance, since the more profitable items could be given more space. The manager realizes that sales would increase with increases in space only up to a certain point. Beyond that point, sales would likely flatten and perhaps eventually decrease (since customers often are dismayed by very large exhibits). Which multiple regression model would you suggest?

GEN **17.5**   Suppose that the manager referred to in Exercise 17.4 observed 25 stores in the chain. The number of square feet allotted to a particular brand of laundry detergent and the number of boxes of it sold in the previous week were recorded. When used as input for the SAS system, the data produced the results shown in the block of computer output given in Figure E17.5.

a. Can we conclude at the 5% significance level that the second-order model, with allotted space as the independent variable, provides a reasonable model for predicting sales?

b. Is there sufficient evidence at the 1% significance level to allow us to conclude that, beyond a certain point, additional space results in a decrease in sales?

POM **17.6**   A person starting a new job always takes a certain amount of time to adjust fully. In repetitive task situations, such as on a production line, significant productivity gains can occur within the first few days. Assume that data have been collected on the number of units produced per day (y) and the number of days on the job (x) for 55 workers. In fitting a regression model to these data, the analyst believed that a second-order model of the type $y = \beta_0 + \beta_1 x + \beta_2 x^2 + \varepsilon$ was likely to give the best results. The Minitab system was used to produce the computer ouput shown in Figure E17.6.

FIGURE E17.5

```
Dependent Variable: Y
                                    Analysis of Variance
                        Sum of      Mean
        Source    DF    Squares     Square      F Value    Prob > F
        Model      2    12063.57    6031.785    247.426    0.0000
        Error     22      536.32      24.378
        C Total   24    12599.89


        Root MSE      4.9374    R-square    0.9574
        Dep Mean    126.3851    Adj R-sq    0.9536
        C.V.          3.9066


                                    Parameter Estimates
                        Parameter   Standard    T for H0:
        Variable  DF    Estimate    Error       Parameter=0    Prob > |T|
        INTERCEP   1      5.135     1.131         4.540        0.0002
        SPACE      1     30.246     4.225         7.159        0.0000
        SPACE-SQ   1     -2.031     0.398        -5.103        0.0000
```

FIGURE E17.6

```
        The regression equation is

        Y=30.8+3.06X+.102XSQ

        Predictor    Coef      Stdev     t-ratio
        Constant    30.775     1.516     20.30
        X            3.056     1.344      2.27
        XSQ          0.102     0.026      3.90


        S=4.890    R-sq=54.1%    R-sq(adj)=52.3%

        Analysis of Variance

        SOURCE        DF    SS        MS
        Regression     2    1465.7    732.8
        Error         52    1243.3     23.9
        Total         54    2709.0
```

a. Test for the overall usefulness of the model, using $\alpha = .05$.

b. Is the x^2 term related to y? (Test with $\alpha = .05$.)

ECON **17.7** The relationship between quantity demanded and price charged for any particular good or service is called a *demand curve*; generally, such a curve slopes downward from left to right. Demand curves, however, need not be straight lines. To examine the demand curve for her company's product, a marketing executive took a random sample of the number of units demanded and the price per unit in 50 cities across the country.

Because she was not certain that the relationship would be linear, she proposed the second-order model,

$$y = \beta_0 + \beta_1 x + \beta_2 x^2 + \varepsilon$$

The SAS software package generated the output found in Figure E17.7.

a. Test the overall utility of the model, with $\alpha = .05$.

b. Can the x^2 term be omitted without significantly reducing the usefulness of the model? (Test with $\alpha = .05$.)

FIGURE E17.7

Dependent Variable: Y

Analysis of Variance

Source	DF	Sum of Squares	Mean Square	F Value	Prob > F
Model	2	20064.3	10032.15	45.5758	0.0000
Error	47	10345.8	220.12		
C Total	49				

Root MSE	14.8364	R-square	0.6598	
Dep Mean	95.6322	Adj R-sq	0.6453	
C.V.	15.5140			

Parameter Estimates

Variable	DF	Parameter Estimate	Standard Error	T for H0: Parameter=0	Prob > |T|
INTERCEP	1	989.8811	24.1043	41.0666	0.0000
X	1	-6.5132	0.8961	-7.2683	0.0000
XSQ	1	3.7101	2.8457	1.3038	0.1986

SECTION 17.4 **POLYNOMIAL MODELS WITH TWO INDEPENDENT VARIABLES**

If we believe that only two independent variables influence y, we can use a polynomial model with two independent variables. The general form of this model is rather cumbersome, so we will not show it. Instead, we will discuss several specific examples.

FIRST-ORDER MODEL

The first-order model is represented by

$$y = \beta_0 + \beta_1 x_1 + \beta_2 x_2 + \varepsilon$$

This model should be used wherever the statistician believes that, on average, y is linearly related to each of x_1 and x_2 and that the independent variables do not interact. This means that the effect of one independent variable on y is independent of the value of the second independent variable. For example, suppose that the sample regression line of the first-order model is

$$\hat{y} = 5 + 3x_1 + 4x_2$$

If we examine the relationship between y and x_1 for several values of x_2 (say, $x_2 = 1$, 2, and 3) we produce the following table of equations.

x_2	$\hat{y} = 5 + 3x_1 + 4x_2$
1	$\hat{y} = 9 + 3x_1$
2	$\hat{y} = 13 + 3x_1$
3	$\hat{y} = 17 + 3x_1$

The only difference in the three equations is in the intercept. (See Figure 17.9.) The coefficient of x_1 remains the same, which means that the effect of x_1 on y remains the same no matter what the value of x_2 is. (We could also have shown that the effect of x_2 on y remains the same no matter what the value of x_1.) As you see from Figure 17.9, the first-order model with no interaction produces parallel straight lines.

A statistician who does not believe that the effect of one independent variable on y is uninfluenced by the other independent variable can use the next model.

FIGURE 17.9   *FIRST-ORDER MODEL WITH TWO INDEPENDENT VARIABLES: NO INTERACTION*

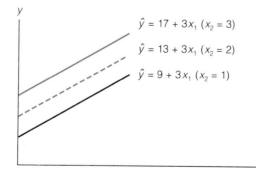

$\hat{y} = 17 + 3x_1 \; (x_2 = 3)$

$\hat{y} = 13 + 3x_1 \; (x_2 = 2)$

$\hat{y} = 9 + 3x_1 \; (x_2 = 1)$

FIRST-ORDER MODEL WITH INTERACTION

Interaction means that the effect of x_1 on y is influenced by the value of x_2. (It also means that the effect of x_2 on y is influenced by x_1.)

First-Order Model with Interaction

$$y = \beta_0 + \beta_1 x_1 + \beta_2 x_2 + \beta_3 x_1 x_2 + \varepsilon$$

Suppose that the sample regression line is

$$\hat{y} = 5 + 3x_1 + 4x_2 - 2x_1 x_2$$

If we examine the relationship between y and x_1 for $x_2 = 1, 2,$ and 3, we produce the following table of equations.

x_2	$\hat{y} = 5 + 3x_1 + 4x_2 - 2x_1 x_2$
1	$\hat{y} = 9 + x_1$
2	$\hat{y} = 13 - x_1$
3	$\hat{y} = 17 - 3x_1$

As you can see, not only is the intercept different, but the coefficient of x_1 also varies. Obviously, the effect of x_1 on y is influenced by the value of x_2. Figure 17.10 depicts these equations. The straight lines they produce are clearly not parallel.

FIGURE 17.10   *FIRST-ORDER MODEL WITH INTERACTION*

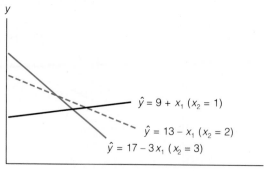

SECOND-ORDER MODEL WITH INTERACTION

A statistician who believes that a quadratic relationship exists between y and each of x_1 and x_2 and that the independent variables interact in their effect on y can use the following model.

> **Second-Order Model with Interaction**
>
> $$y = \beta_0 + \beta_1 x_1 + \beta_2 x_2 + \beta_3 x_1^2 + \beta_4 x_2^2 + \beta_5 x_1 x_2 + \varepsilon$$

Figures 17.11 and 17.12, respectively, depict this model without and with the interaction term.

FIGURE 17.11   *SECOND-ORDER MODEL WITHOUT INTERACTION ($\beta_5 = 0$)*

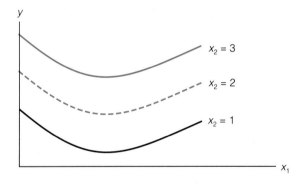

FIGURE 17.12   *SECOND-ORDER MODEL WITH INTERACTION*

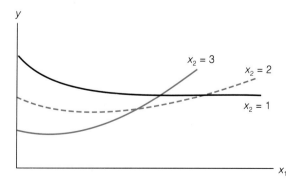

Now that we've examined several different models, how do we know which model to use? The answer is that we must propose a model based on our knowledge of the variables involved and then test the model by means of the various statistical procedures associated with regression analysis.

EXAMPLE 17.1

In trying to find new locations for their restaurants, hamburger emporiums like McDonald's and Wendy's usually consider a number of factors. Suppose that a statistician working for a hamburger restaurant chain wants to construct a regression model that will help her make recommendations about new locations. She knows that this type of restaurant has as its primary market middle-income adults and their children (particularly children between the ages of 5 and 12). Which model should the statistician propose?

Solution.   Since the statistician would like to find locations that generate high gross sales, she'll let the dependent variable y be annual gross sales. The independent variables will be mean annual household income, x_1, and mean age of children, x_2, in the area surrounding the restaurant.

The relationship between y and x_1 and x_2 is probably quadratic. That is, relatively poor households and relatively affluent ones are not likely to eat at this chain's restaurants, since the restaurants attract mostly middle-income customers. Figure 17.13 depicts the proposed relationship.

A similar relationship can be hypothesized between y and x_2. Areas where the mean age of children is either quite low or quite high are likely to yield relatively low gross sales, whereas areas where the mean age of children lies in the middle of the range 5 to 12 are likely to do very well.

The question of whether or not to include the interaction effect is more difficult to answer. It is probably best to include the interaction term and then perform a t-test on β_5 (the coefficient of $x_1 x_2$) to determine whether the interaction effect

FIGURE 17.13   *RELATIONSHIP BETWEEN ANNUAL GROSS SALES AND MEAN ANNUAL HOUSEHOLD INCOME*

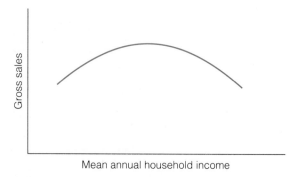

really exists. Thus, the model to be tested is

$$y = \beta_0 + \beta_1 x_1 + \beta_2 x_2 + \beta_3 x_1^2 + \beta_4 x_2^2 + \beta_5 x_1 x_2 + \varepsilon$$

where y is the gross annual sales, x_1 is the mean income of the residents in the area, and x_2 is the mean age of children in the area.

EXAMPLE 17.2

To determine whether the second-order model with interaction is appropriate, the statistician selects 25 areas at random. Each area consists of approximately 5,000 households, as well as one of her employer's restaurants and exactly one competitor's restaurant. The statistician then records the previous year's annual gross sales, the mean annual household income, and the mean age of children (the latter two figures are available from the latest census); these data are listed in the accompanying table. The SAS computer output for the second-order model with interaction is also shown.

What conclusions can you draw from these results? In particular, does the inclusion of the interaction term appear to be appropriate?

Area	Annual Gross Sales ($1,000s) y	Mean Annual Household Income ($1,000s) x_1	Mean Age of Children x_2
1	1,128	23.5	10.5
2	1,005	17.6	7.2
3	1,212	26.3	7.6
4	893	16.5	5.9
5	1,073	22.3	6.6
6	1,179	26.1	6.3
7	1,109	24.3	12.1
8	1,019	20.9	14.9
9	1,228	27.1	8.9
10	812	15.6	3.4
11	1,193	25.7	10.5
12	983	30.5	6.0
13	1,281	26.5	8.6
14	1,156	25.7	11.6
15	1,032	21.8	13.7

(continued)

Area	Annual Gross Sales ($1,000s) y	Mean Annual Household Income ($1,000s) x_1	Mean Age of Children x_2
16	856	33.6	5.8
17	978	17.9	10.3
18	1,017	18.3	5.3
19	1,091	30.1	6.3
20	1,048	29.8	5.3
21	1,192	28.5	10.4
22	1,256	27.5	8.7
23	1,215	26.8	9.5
24	1,233	24.3	8.3
25	950	17.8	6.1

```
Dependent Variable: Y
                                    Analysis of Variance
                   Sum of      Mean
Source      DF    Squares     Square    F Value    Prob > F
Model        5    366129     73225.8    34.8098     0.0000
Error       19     39968      2103.6
C Total     24    406097


Root MSE    45.8603    R-square    0.9022
Dep Mean  1085.56     Adj R-sq    0.8757
C.V.         4.2246

                                    Parameter Estimates
                   Parameter    Standard     T for H0:
Variable    DF     Estimate      Error     Parameter=0    Prob > |T|
INTERCEP     1    -1244.937     297.609       -4.183        0.0006
X1           1      178.091      36.371        4.896        0.0002
X2           1       42.005      37.293        1.126        0.2742
X1SQ         1       -3.740       0.820       -4.561        0.0002
X2SQ         1       -4.129       1.396       -2.958        0.0080
X1X2         1        1.311       0.739        1.774        0.0920
```

Solution.   The value of r^2 (90.22%) and the standard error of estimate (45.8603) both indicate that this model fits the data quite well. In the analysis of variance test of the overall utility of the model, we find $F = 34.8098$. Since this is greater than $F_{.01,5,19}(4.17)$, we conclude that the model is useful in predicting gross annual sales.

We can determine whether there is an interaction effect by testing β_5. That is, we test

$$H_0: \beta_5 = 0$$
$$H_A: \beta_5 \neq 0$$

If we wish to test with $\alpha = .05$, the rejection region is

$$|t| > t_{\alpha/2, n-k-1}$$
$$> t_{.025, 19}$$
$$> 2.093$$

Since the t-value is 1.774, we conclude that there is not enough (although there is some) evidence to show that $\beta_5 \neq 0$. Hence, the inclusion of the interaction term does not significantly enhance the model.

EXERCISES

LEARNING THE TECHNIQUES

17.8   Graph y versus x_1 for $x_2 = 1, 2,$ and 3, for the following equations:

a. $y = 1 + 2x_1 + 4x_2$

b. $y = 1 + 2x_1 + 4x_2 - x_1 x_2$

17.9   Graph y versus x_1 for $x_2 = 2, 4,$ and 5, for the following equations:

a. $y = 0.5 + 1x_1 - 0.7x_2 - 1.2x_1^2 + 1.5x_2^2$

b. $y = 0.5 + 1x_1 - 0.7x_2 - 1.2x_1^2$
    $\quad + 1.5x_2^2 + 2x_1 x_2$

17.10   Examine the following graphs of y versus x_1 for a variety of values of x_2. Determine whether or not the interaction term exists.

(a)

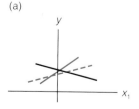

(b)

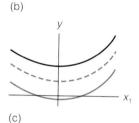

(c)

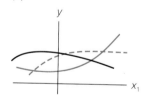

APPLYING THE TECHNIQUES

EDUC   **17.11**   The assistant dean of the school of business at a large university wanted to find a better way of deciding which students should be accepted into the MBA program. Currently, the records of the applicants are examined by the admissions committee, which looks at the undergraduate GPA and the score on the Graduate Management Aptitude Test (GMAT). In order to provide a more systematic method, the assistant dean took a random sample of 50 students who entered the program 2 years ago. She recorded each student's undergraduate GPA, GMAT score, and MBA GPA. The School of Business requires students to maintain a minimum GPA of 2.00 in the MBA program in order to graduate. Thus, any student whose MBA GPA was less than 2.00 did not graduate. The assistant dean believed that a first-order model with interaction would be the best model. When the data were run on the SAS package, the computer output in Figure E17.11 was obtained.

a. Can you conclude that the first-order model with interaction provides information to predict the MBA GPA? (Use $\alpha = .05$.)

b. Test to determine whether the interaction term is related to the dependent variable. (Use $\alpha = .01$.)

c. Provide a point estimate for the MBA GPA of a student whose undergraduate GPA was 3.2 and whose GMAT was 625.

17.12 The manager of the food concession at a major league baseball stadium wanted to be able to predict the attendance of a game 24 hours in advance, in order to prepare the correct amount of food to be sold. He believed that the two most important factors were the home team's and visiting team's winning percentages. He proposed a first-order model with interaction. In order to test his belief, he found the attendance figures y, the home team's winning percentage x_1, and the visiting team's winning percentage x_2, for 40 randomly selected games. The accompanying output of the Minitab computer system shown in Figure E17.12 was obtained.

a. Do these results indicate that the first-order model with interaction is useful in predicting attendance? (Use $\alpha = .01$.)

FIGURE E17.11

```
Dependent Variable: Y
                                     Analysis of Variance
                      Sum of     Mean
    Source    DF     Squares    Square    F Value    Prob > F
    Model      3      3.522     1.174      6.106      0.0014
    Error     46      8.843     0.192
    C Total   49     12.365

    Root MSE      0.4385     R-square    0.2848
    Dep Mean      2.9882     Adj R-sq    0.2393
    C.V.         14.6744

                                    Parameter Estimates
                      Parameter    Standard    T for H0:
    Variable    DF    Estimate      Error     Parameter=0    Prob > |T|
    INTERCEP     1      0.434       0.132        3.288         0.0020
    GPA          1      0.586       0.273        2.147         0.0370
    GMAT         1     -0.00057     0.00031     -1.839         0.0724
    GPA*GMAT     1      0.00062     0.00086      0.721         0.4746
```

FIGURE E17.12

```
The regression equation is

Y=25603+19816X1+8554X2+1506X1X2

Predictor      Coef       Stdev      t-ratio
Constant       25603.5    1928.5     13.27
X1             19816.2    4667.3      4.25
X2              8554.0    3961.6      2.16
X1X2            1506.1    1019.9      1.48

s=51.27    R-sq=54.1%    R-sq(adj)=50.3%

Analysis of Variance

SOURCE         DF        SS          MS
Regression      3     111704.4     37234.8
Error          36      94625.1      2628.5
Total          39     206329.5
```

b. Is there sufficient evidence to indicate that the interaction term is helpful? (Use $\alpha = .05$.)

TOUR **17.13** The manager of a large hotel on the Riviera in southern France wanted to forecast the monthly vacancy rate (as a percentage) during the peak season. After considering a long list of potential variables, she identified two variables that she believed were most closely related to the vacancy rate: the average daily temperature x_1, and the value of the currency in American dollars x_2. A second-order model with interaction was tested. The results of the SAS computer program with 50 observations produced the output shown in Figure E17.13 on page 838.

a. Do these data allow us to conclude that this model is useful? (Test with $\alpha = .01$.)

b. Test to determine whether there is a linear relationship between x_1 and y. What about between x_1^2 and y? (Use $\alpha = .05$.)

c. Test (with $\alpha = .05$) to determine whether the interaction term can be eliminated from the model.

GEN **17.14** The coach and the general manager of a team in the National Hockey League are trying to decide what kinds of players to draft. To help them in making a decision, they need to know which variables are most closely related to the goals differential. This is the difference between the number of goals their team scores and the number of goals scored by their team's opponents. (A positive differential means that their team wins, and a negative differential is a loss.) After some consideration they decide that there are two important variables; the percentage of faceoffs won x_1, and the penalty-minutes differential x_2. The latter variable is the difference between the number of penalty minutes assessed against their team and the number of penalty minutes assessed against their team's op-

Dependent Variable: Y

Analysis of Variance

Source	DF	Sum of Squares	Mean Square	F Value	Prob > F
Model	5	121.62	24.324	18.983	0.0000
Error	44	56.38	1.281		
C Total	49	178.00			

Root MSE	1.132	R-square	0.6833
Dep Mean	3.669	Adj R-sq	0.6474
C.V.	30.853		

Parameter Estimates

Variable	DF	Parameter Estimate	Standard Error	T for H0: Parameter=0	Prob > |T|
INTERCEP	1	8.637	1.536	5.623	0.0000
X1	1	-0.0158	0.0024	-6.583	0.0000
X2	1	-0.00009	0.00003	-3.000	0.0044
X1SQ	1	0.286	0.0765	3.739	0.0006
X2SQ	1	-0.00021	0.00016	-1.313	0.1960
X1X2	1	0.0038	0.0045	0.844	0.4032

The regression equation is

Y=.0638+.0063X1-.0021X2-.0015X1X2

Predictor	Coef	Stdev	t-ratio
Constant	.0638	.0416	1.534
X1	.0063	.0031	2.032
X2	-.0021	.0034	-0.618
X1X2	-.0015	.0005	-3.00

s=1.355   R-sq=13.3%   R-sq(adj)=10.6%

Analysis of Variance

SOURCE	DF	SS	MS
Regression	3	27.090	9.030
Residual	96	176.461	1.838
Total	99	203.551	

ponents. A first-order model with interaction is believed to be appropriate.

A random sample of 100 games played recently was drawn. The results obtained by using Minitab are exhibited in the output shown in Figure 17.14.

a. Do these data provide sufficient evidence at the 1% significance level to indicate that the first-order model with interaction is useful in predicting the goals differential?

b. Test each of the coefficients with $\alpha = .05$. What are your conclusions?

POM **17.15** The production manager of a chemical plant wants to determine the roles that temperature and pressure play in the yield of a particular chemical produced at the plant. From past experience she believes that, when pressure is held constant, lower and higher temperatures tend to reduce the yield. When temperature is held constant, higher and lower pressures tend to increase the yield. She does not have any idea about how the yield is affected for various combinations of pressure and temperature.

a. What model should the production manager propose?

b. What signs should she expect for each of the coefficients?

POM **17.16** Suppose that, in Exercise 17.15, the production manager observed 100 different batches of the chemical in which the pressure and the temperature were allowed to vary, in order to test a second-order model with interaction. The accompanying Minitab computer output given in Figure E17.16 was observed.

a. Is the second-order model with interaction appropriate? (Test with $\alpha = .01$.)

b. Interpret each of the t-tests. (Use $\alpha = .05$.)

c. What does the coefficient of determination tell you?

FIGURE E17.16

The regression equation is

$$Y = 57.62 + .091X1 - .130X2 + .00031X1X1 + .00052X2X2 - .00069X1X2$$

Predictor	Coef	Stdev	t-ratio
Constant	57.62	5.735	10.05
X1	.091	.039	2.33
X2	-.130	.056	-2.32
X1X1	.00031	.00024	1.29
X2X2	.00052	.00049	1.06
X1X2	-.00069	.00013	-5.31

s=13.32   R-sq=39.6%   R-sq(adj)=36.4%

Analysis of Variance

SOURCE	DF	SS	MS
Regression	5	10936.3	2187.26
Error	94	16669.1	177.33
Total	99	27605.4	

SECTION 17.5   ## NOMINALLY SCALED INDEPENDENT VARIABLES

When we introduced regression analysis, we pointed out that the data scale of all variables must be interval. But in many real-life cases, one or more independent variables are nominal-scaled. For example, suppose that the real estate agent in Example 16.1 believed that the energy source used to heat the house is a factor in determining its selling price. Most homes in North America are heated by one of three energies: heating oil, natural gas, or electricity. This variable is obviously nominal-scaled. Nonetheless, it is possible to transform it so that it can be used in the regression model. This is accomplished by using dummy variables.

A **dummy variable** is a variable that can assume either of only two values (usually 0 and 1), where one value represents the existence of a certain condition and the other value indicates that the condition does not hold. Suppose that in Example 16.1 we wish to forecast selling price, using as independent variables house size and type of heating energy. Because energy source has a nominal scale (as before, we label selling price y and house size x_1), we create the following two dummy variables to represent this variable:

$x_2 = 1$ (if house is heated by heating oil)

$\quad = 0$ (if not)

and

$x_3 = 1$ (if house is heated by natural gas)

$\quad = 0$ (if not)

Notice first that, since both x_2 and x_3 can assume only two values (0 and 1), there is only one interval; thus, it is consistent and constant. Therefore, x_2 and x_3 are interval-scaled variables. Second, we need only two dummy variables to represent the three energy sources. A house that is heated by heating oil is represented by $x_2 = 1$ and $x_3 = 0$. A house heated by natural gas specifies $x_2 = 0$ and $x_3 = 1$. Since a house heated by electricity is not heated by heating oil nor by natural gas, we represent such a house by $x_2 = 0$ and $x_3 = 0$. It should be apparent that we cannot have $x_2 = 1$ and $x_3 = 1$, if we assume that a house can have only one primary heating system.

In general, to represent a nominal variable that has m possible values, we must create $m - 1$ dummy variables.

INTERPRETING AND TESTING THE COEFFICIENTS OF THE DUMMY VARIABLES

Suppose that we recorded the energy source for each of the 15 houses in the sample in Example 16.1. If we then created dummy variables x_2 and x_3, the data shown in Table 17.1 would be produced. When these data were input into the Minitab system, the accompanying computer output was obtained.

TABLE 17.1   *REAL ESTATE EXAMPLE WITH DUMMY VARIABLES*

House	Price, y	Size, x_1	Heating	x_2	x_3
1	89.5	20.0	electricity	0	0
2	79.9	14.8	electricity	0	0
3	83.1	20.5	heating oil	1	0
4	56.9	12.5	heating oil	1	0
5	66.6	18.0	heating oil	1	0
6	82.5	14.3	natural gas	0	1
7	126.3	27.5	electricity	0	0
8	79.3	16.5	electricity	0	0
9	119.9	24.3	natural gas	0	1
10	87.6	20.2	heating oil	1	0
11	112.6	22.0	natural gas	0	1
12	120.8	19.0	natural gas	0	1
13	78.5	12.3	natural gas	0	1
14	74.3	14.0	electricity	0	0
15	74.8	16.7	heating oil	1	0

```
The regression equation is

Y=21.406+3.688X1-12.446X2+13.664X3

Predictor     Coef      Stdev     t-ratio
Constant      21.406    8.251      2.59
X1             3.688    0.4138     8.91
X2           -12.446    4.283     -2.91
X3            13.664    4.265      3.20

s=6.742   R-sq=92.0%   R-sq(adj)=89.8%

Analysis of Variance

SOURCE        DF      SS        MS
Regression     3    5730.2    1910.1
Error         11     500.0      45.5
Total         14    6230.2
```

The intercept $(\hat{\beta}_0)$ and the coefficient of x_1 $(\hat{\beta}_1)$ are interpreted in the usual manner. When $x_1 = x_2 = x_3 = 0$, the dependent variable y equals 21.406. For each additional 100 square feet, the price of the house increases by an average of \$3,688. Now examine the remaining two coefficients:

$$\hat{\beta}_2 = -12.446$$
$$\hat{\beta}_3 = 13.664$$

These tell us that, on average, a house heated by heating oil sells for \$12,446 less than one heated by electricity and that a house heated by natural gas sells for an average of \$13,664 more than one heated by electricity. The reason that both comparisons are made with the electrically heated house is that such a house is represented by $x_2 = x_3 = 0$. Thus, for an electrically heated house, the equation is

$$\hat{y} = \hat{\beta}_0 + \hat{\beta}_1 x_1 + \hat{\beta}_2(0) + \hat{\beta}_3(0)$$

which is

$$\hat{y} = \hat{\beta}_0 + \hat{\beta}_1 x_1$$

or

$$\hat{y} = 21.406 + 3.688 x_1$$

For a house heated by oil $(x_2 = 1, x_3 = 0)$, the regression equation is

$$\hat{y} = \hat{\beta}_0 + \hat{\beta}_1 x_1 + \hat{\beta}_2(1) + \hat{\beta}_3(0)$$

which is

$$\hat{y} = \hat{\beta}_0 + \hat{\beta}_2 + \hat{\beta}_1 x_1$$

or

$$\hat{y} = 21.406 - 12.446 + 3.688 x_1$$

or

$$\hat{y} = 8.960 + 3.688 x_1$$

Finally, for a house heated by natural gas $(x_2 = 0, x_3 = 1)$, the equation is

$$\hat{y} = \hat{\beta}_0 + \hat{\beta}_1 x_1 + \hat{\beta}_2(0) + \hat{\beta}_3(1)$$

which simplifies to

$$\hat{y} = \hat{\beta}_0 + \hat{\beta}_3 + \hat{\beta}_1 x_1$$

which is

$$\hat{y} = 21.406 + 13.664 + 3.688 x_1$$

or

$$\hat{y} = 35.070 + 3.688 x_1$$

FIGURE 17.14   GRAPH OF $\hat{y}$ VERSUS x_1 FOR (x_2, x_3) = (0, 0), (1, 0), AND (0, 1)

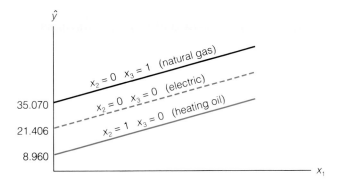

Figure 17.14 depicts the graph of $\hat{y}$ versus x_1 for the three different heating systems. Notice that the three lines are parallel (with slope = $\hat{\beta}_1$ = 3.688), while the intercepts differ.

We can also perform the usual t-tests of β_2 and β_3; however, since the variables x_2 and x_3 represent different groups (the three different heating systems), these t-tests allow us to draw conclusions about the differences between the groups. For example, if the real estate agent wanted to know whether there is enough evidence (with $\alpha = .05$) to justify concluding that the average price of a house heated by oil is different from the average price of an electrically heated house, he would perform the following test.

$H_0: \beta_2 = 0$

$H_A: \beta_2 \neq 0$

Test statistic:

$$t = \frac{\hat{\beta}_2 - \beta_2}{s_{\hat{\beta}_2}}$$

Rejection region:

$|t| > t_{\alpha/2, n-k-1}$

$\quad > t_{.025, 11}$

$\quad > 2.201$

Value of the test statistic: $t = -2.91$

Conclusion: Reject H_0.

There is sufficient evidence to indicate that a difference exists between the average price of houses heated by oil and the average price of houses heated by electricity.

If you are uncertain as to why we chose to test β_2 in this situation, examine Figure 17.14. It shows that, for any size house (any value of x_1), the average difference in prices between oil-heated and electrically heated houses is the value of $\hat{\beta}_2 = -12.446$. The *t*-test of β_2 allows us to decide whether the value of the statistic $\hat{\beta}_2$ indicates that the population parameter β_2 is not equal to zero (and thus that a price difference exists between the two types of houses).

We can also perform a one-tail test. For example, if the real estate agent wanted to know whether there was sufficient evidence (with $\alpha = .05$) to indicate that, on average, a house heated by natural gas sells for more than an electrically heated house, he would perform the following test.

$H_0: \beta_3 = 0$

$H_A: \beta_3 > 0$

Test statistic:

$$t = \frac{\hat{\beta}_3 - \beta_3}{s_{\hat{\beta}_3}}$$

Rejection region:

$t > t_{\alpha/2, n-k-1}$

$\quad > t_{.05, 11}$

$\quad > 1.796$

Value of the test statistic: $t = 3.20$

Conclusion: Reject H_0.

We conclude that sufficient evidence exists to show that gas-heated houses sell for more, on average, than do electrically heated houses.

EXERCISES

LEARNING THE TECHNIQUES

17.17 Create and identify dummy variables to represent the following nominally scaled variables:

a. Religious affiliation (Catholic, Protestant, and others)

b. Working shift (8:00 A.M.–4:00 P.M., 4:00 P.M.–12:00 midnight, and 12:00 midnight–8:00 A.M.)

c. Supervisor (Jack Jones, Mary Brown, George Fosse, and Elaine Smith)

17.18 In a study of computer applications, a survey asked which microcomputer a number of companies used. The following dummy variables were created:

$x_1 = 1$ (if IBM)

$\quad = 0$ (if not)

$x_2 = 1$ (if Apple)

$\quad = 0$ (if not)

What computer is being referred to by each of the following pairs of values?

a. $x_1 = 0$ $\quad x_2 = 1$

b. $x_1 = 1$ $\quad x_2 = 0$

c. $x_1 = 0$ $\quad x_2 = 0$

APPLYING THE TECHNIQUES

EDUC **17.19** Suppose that in Exercise 17.11 the assistant dean believed that the type of undergraduate degree also influenced the student's GPA as a graduate student. The most common undergraduate degrees of students attending the graduate school of business are B.B.A. (Business Administration), B.Eng., B.Sc., and B.A. Because the type of degree has a nominal scale, the following three dummy variables were created:

$x_3 = 1$ (if degree is B.B.A.)

$\quad = 0$ (if not)

$x_4 = 1$ (if degree is B.Eng.)

$\quad = 0$ (if not)

$x_5 = 1$ (if degree is B.Sc.)

$\quad = 0$ (if not)

The model to be estimated is

$y = \beta_0 + \beta_1 x_1 + \beta_2 x_2 + \beta_3 x_3 + \beta_4 x_4 + \beta_5 x_5 + \varepsilon$

where

$x_1 =$ Undergraduate GPA

$x_2 =$ GMAT score

The SAS computer output shown in Figure E17.19 was observed.

a. Test to determine (with $\alpha = .05$) whether each of the independent variables is linearly related to y.

b. Can we conclude at the 5% significance level that, on average, the B.B.A. graduate performs better than the B.A. graduate?

c. Provide a point estimate for the graduate school GPA of a B.Eng. whose undergraduate GPA was 3.0 and whose GMAT score was 700.

d. Repeat part (c) for a B.A. student.

RE **17.20** The real estate agent of Example 16.1 has become so fascinated by the multiple regression technique that he decides to improve the model by

FIGURE E17.19

Dependent Variable: Y

Analysis of Variance

Source	DF	Sum of Squares	Mean Square	F Value	Prob > F
Model	5	6.644	1.333	10.248	0.0000
Error	44	5.721	0.130		
C Total	49	12.365			

Root MSE	0.3607	R-square	0.5372	
Dep Mean	2.9882	Adj R-sq	0.4849	
C.V.	12.0708			

Parameter Estimates

Variable	DF	Parameter Estimate	Standard Error	T for H0: Parameter=0	Prob > |T|
INTERCEP	1	0.336	0.245	1.371	0.1774
X1	1	0.672	0.199	3.377	0.0016
X2	1	0.00035	0.00042	0.833	0.4094
X3	1	0.572	0.255	2.243	0.0300
X4	1	0.745	0.376	1.981	0.0538
X5	1	0.256	0.120	2.133	0.0386

including the following variables in the equation:

y = Value of house (in \$1,000s)

x_1 = Square feet of living space (in 100s ft^2)

x_2 = Age of house (in years)

x_3 = Lot size (in 1,000s ft^2)

x_4 = Number of bedrooms

x_5 = Number of bathrooms

x_6 = Finished basement; dummy variable

x_6 = 1 (if yes)

  = 0 (if no)

x_7 = Ravine view; dummy variable

x_7 = 1 (if yes)

  = 0 (if no)

x_8 = Attached garage; dummy variable

x_8 = 1 (if yes)

  = 0 (if no)

x_9 = House condition; dummy variable

x_9 = 1 (if good)

  = 0 (if not)

x_{10} = Swimming pool; dummy variable

x_{10} = 1 (if yes)

  = 0 (if no)

FIGURE E17.20

Dependent Variable: Y

Analysis of Variance

SOURCE	DF	Sum of Squares	Mean Square	F Value	Prob > F
Model	10	2752.149	275.215	9.328	0.0000
Error	79	2330.882	29.505		
C Total	89	5083.031			

Root MSE	5.4319	R-square	0.5414
Dep Mean	93.1677	Adj R-sq	0.4834
C.V.	5.8302		

Parameter Estimates

Variable	DF	Parameter Estimate	Standard Error	T for H0: Parameter=0	Prob > |T|
INTERCEP	1	-13.2175	15.6492	-0.845	0.4006
X1	1	2.9857	1.0049	2.971	0.0040
X2	1	-0.8753	0.6606	-1.325	0.1890
X3	1	3.1249	1.0368	3.014	0.0034
X4	1	1.2715	0.2415	5.264	0.0000
X5	1	0.9875	0.2806	3.519	0.0008
X6	1	11.5102	11.5914	0.993	0.3236
X7	1	0.5908	0.2982	1.981	0.0510
X8	1	0.2146	1.7731	0.121	0.9040
X9	1	5.3490	1.2521	4.272	0.0000
X10	1	-0.6126	0.2263	-2.747	0.0074

The SAS computer output using a sample of $n = 90$ is shown in Figure E17.20.

a. Test the overall utility of the model, with $\alpha = .05$.

b. Test to determine each of the following (with $\alpha = .05$):

(i) Does a finished basement increase the selling price?

(ii) It is generally believed that a swimming pool decreases the house price. Do these data support this belief?

(iii) Does an attached garage increase the price?

c. Interpret the value of $\hat{\beta}_9$ and comment on the

desirability of keeping the house in good condition.

17.21 The manager of an amusement park would like to be able to predict daily attendance, in order to develop more accurate plans about how much food to order and how many ride operators to hire. After some consideration, he decides that the following three factors are critical:

Day of the week (weekday or weekend)
Predicted weather (rain or no rain)
Whether or not special events are planned

He then took a random sample of 16 days, the data for which are shown in Table E17.21.

TABLE E17.21

y Attendance (1,000s)	x_1 Weekend Dummy (0 = weekday) (1 = weekend)	x_2 Predicted Weather Dummy (0 = rain) (1 = no rain)	x_3 Special Events Dummy (0 = no special event) (1 = special event)
25	0	0	1
37	0	1	0
40	1	1	0
22	0	0	0
45	1	1	1
21	0	0	0
29	0	0	0
34	0	1	0
39	0	1	1
44	1	1	0
48	1	1	1
37	0	1	0
49	1	1	1
28	0	0	0
39	0	1	0
44	1	1	0

Minitab was then used to produce the accompanying output.

The regression equation is

Y=24.4+6.95X1+12.2X2+2.84X3

Predictor	Coef	Stdev	t-ratio
Constant	24.432	1.290	18.94
X1	6.948	1.759	3.95
X2	12.200	1.768	6.90
X3	2.839	1.588	1.79

s=2.796   R-sq=92.3%   R-sq(adj)=90.4%

Analysis of Variance

SOURCE	DF	SS	MS
Regression	3	1121.62	373.87
Error	12	93.82	7.82
Total	15	1215.44	

a. Can we conclude at the 1% significance level that weather is a factor in determining attendance?

b. Do these results provide sufficient evidence that weekend attendance is, on average, larger than weekday attendance? (Use $\alpha = .05$.)

SECTION 17.6 ## TESTING PARTS OF THE MODEL

In any application of regression analysis, we would like to choose the best possible model. As we've previously discussed, accomplishing this involves selecting a logical and meaningful model that fits the data well. Frequently, in order to improve the model's fit, we add additional variables or (in the case of polynomial models) we increase the order. For example, we know that a second-order model will fit the data at least as well as a first-order model will. However, adding additional variables to provide only a small improvement in the fit is not advisable. Besides increasing the likelihood of problems associated with collinearity, additional variables are costly to gather, store, and process on the computer. In general, we would like to keep the model simple, unless there is a good reason for including additional variables.

We've already seen a method by which we can determine whether a particular variable should be included in the model or not. We've also discussed some of the disadvantages of performing numerous t-tests to test for significant coefficients.

The technique presented in this section allows us to test several coefficients together in a single test. This method will allow us to determine whether the full model

$$y = \beta_0 + \beta_1 x_1 + \cdots + \beta_{k_1} x_{k_1} + \beta_{k_1+1} x_{k_1+1} + \cdots + \beta_{k_2} x_{k_2} + \varepsilon$$

is significantly better than the shortened model

$$y = \beta_0 + \beta_1 x_1 + \cdots + \beta_{k_1} x_{k_1} + \varepsilon$$

HYPOTHESES

The technique works by testing the following hypotheses.

Hypotheses for Testing Parts of the Model

H_0: $\beta_{k_1+1} = \beta_{k_1+2} = \cdots = \beta_{k_2} = 0$

H_A: At least one of $\beta_{k_1+1}, \beta_{k_1+2}, \ldots, \beta_{k_2}$ is not equal to zero.

If the full model offers no improvement over the shortened model, the variables $x_{k_1+1}, x_{k_1+2}, \ldots, x_{k_2}$ are not linearly related to y (given that $x_1, x_2, \ldots, x_{k_1}$ are also in the model). This is indicated whenever the coefficients of these variables are all zero. If, however, the full model is superior to the shortened model, at least one of the variables $x_{k_1+1}, x_{k_1+2}, \ldots, x_{k_2}$ is linearly related to y, and thus at least one of the coefficients is not zero.

TEST STATISTIC

The first step in calculating the test statistic is to compute (or more precisely, to let the computer output) the sum of squares for error for each model. We'll denote the sum of squares for error of the shortened model SSE_1 and the sum of squares for error of the full model SSE_2.

The sum of squares for error is a measure of how well the model fits the data: a small value of SSE indicates a good fit. The next step is to compare SSE_1 and SSE_2. If the full model were significantly better than the shortened model, we would find that SSE_2 was considerably smaller than SSE_1. If the full model were not really superior, however, we would find that SSE_2 was only somewhat smaller (it cannot be larger) than SSE_1.

The test statistic for assessing the size of the difference between SSE_1 and SSE_2 is as follows.

Test Statistic

$$F = \frac{(SSE_1 - SSE_2)/(k_2 - k_1)}{SSE_2/(n - k_2 - 1)}$$

which is F-distributed, with $v_1 = k_2 - k_1$ and $v_2 = n - k_2 - 1$ degrees of freedom.

Notice that v_1 is the number of coefficients being tested and that $n - k_2 - 1$ is the number of degrees of freedom associated with the full model.

We remind you that the statistic is F-distributed if ε is normally distributed and the other requirements listed in Chapter 16 are satisfied.

REJECTION REGION

If the full model's fit is not significantly better than the shortened model's fit, then $SSE_1 - SSE_2$ will be approximately equal to zero, and the value of the F-statistic will be small. Thus, a small value of F indicates that the null hypothesis should not be rejected.

  If the full model's fit is better, SSE_2 will be much smaller than SSE_1. As a result, $SSE_1 - SSE_2$ will be large, and hence F will be large. Therefore a large value of F signals us to reject the null hypothesis. As usual, providing guidance as to whether F is large or small is the function of the appropriate statistical table—in this case, the F table (Table 6 in Appendix B). The rejection region for this test is

$$F > F_{\alpha, k_2 - k_1, n - k_2 - 1}$$

EXAMPLE 17.3

In Example 17.2, we proposed a second-order model with interaction. In order to determine whether the terms x_1^2, x_2^2, and $x_1 x_2$ are useful, we now estimate a first-order model with no interaction. This model's equation is

$$y = \beta_0 + \beta_1 x_1 + \beta_2 x_2 + \varepsilon$$

where

$x_1 =$ Mean household income

$x_2 =$ Mean age of children

The accompanying computer output is produced when the data from Example 17.2 are run.

```
Dependent Variable: Y
```

				Analysis of Variance	
		Sum of	Mean		
Source	DF	Squares	Square	F Value	Prob > F
Model	2	132072	66036	5.302	0.0132
Error	22	274025	12455		
C Total	24	406097			

Root MSE	11.602	R-square	0.3252
Dep Mean	1085.56	Adj R-sq	0.2639
C.V.	10.2806		

			Parameter Estimates		
		Parameter	Standard	T for H0:	
Variable	DF	Estimate	Error	Parameter=0	Prob > |T|
INTERCEP	1	667.83	132.30	5.05	0.0000
X1	1	11.43	4.677	2.44	0.0232
X2	1	16.82	8.000	2.10	0.0474

Is there sufficient evidence at the 5% level of significance to enable us to conclude that the second-order model with interaction is superior to the first-order model with no interaction?

Solution.   The full model is

$$y = \beta_0 + \beta_1 x_1 + \beta_2 x_2 + \beta_3 x_1^2 + \beta_4 x_2^2 + \beta_5 x_1 x_2 + \varepsilon$$

The sum of squares for error is

$$SSE_2 = 39{,}968$$

The shortened model produced a sum of squares for error of

$$SSE_1 = 274{,}025$$

The complete test is as follows:

$H_0: \beta_3 = \beta_4 = \beta_5 = 0$
$H_A:$ At least one of β_3, β_4, and β_5 is not equal to zero.

Test statistic:

$$F = \frac{(SSE_1 - SSE_2)/(k_2 - k_1)}{SSE_2/(n - k_2 - 1)}$$

Rejection region:

$$F > F_{\alpha, k_2 - k_1, n - k_2 - 1}$$
$$> F_{.05, (5 - 2), (25 - 5 - 1)}$$
$$> F_{.05, 3, 19}$$
$$> 3.13$$

Value of the test statistic:

$$F = \frac{(274{,}025 - 39{,}968)/3}{39{,}968/19}$$
$$= \frac{78{,}019}{2{,}103.6}$$
$$= 37.09$$

Conclusion: Reject H_0.

There is sufficient evidence to allow us to conclude that the second-order model with interaction is superior to the first-order model with no interaction.

▬▬▬▬▬▬▬ **EXERCISES**

17.22   Test each of the following hypotheses:

a. $H_0: \beta_3 = \beta_4 = \beta_5 = 0$
    H_A: At least one of β_3, β_4, and β_5 is not equal to zero.
    $k_1 = 2$ $k_2 = 5$ $n = 100$ $\alpha = .05$
    $SSE_1 = 6,806.2$ $SSE_2 = 6,111.5$

b. $H_0: \beta_4 = \beta_5 = \beta_6 = \beta_7 = 0$
    H_A: At least one of $\beta_4, \beta_5, \beta_6,$ and β_7 is not equal to zero.
    $k_1 = 3$ $k_2 = 7$ $n = 45$ $\alpha = .01$
    $SSE_1 = 1,562.7$ $SSE_2 = 928.5$

c. $H_0: \beta_3 = \beta_4 = 0$
    H_A: At least one of β_3 and β_4 is not equal to zero.

$k_1 = 2$ $k_2 = 4$ $n = 25$ $\alpha = .05$
$SSE_1 = 128.0$ $SSE_2 = 101.3$

17.23   The sum of squares for error of the second-order model

$$y = \beta_0 + \beta_1 x_1 + \beta_2 x_2 + \beta_3 x_1^2 + \beta_4 x_2^2$$
$$+ \beta_5 x_1 x_2 + \varepsilon$$

is $SSE_2 = 528.3$. The sum of squares for error of the first-order model

$$y = \beta_0 + \beta_1 x_1 + \beta_2 x_2 + \varepsilon$$

is $SSE_1 = 706.9$. Test at the 1% significance level to determine whether the full model is better than the shortened model. (Assume that $n = 50$.)

SECTION 17.7   ## SUMMARY

This chapter completes our discussion of the regression technique, which began in Chapter 15. Here we presented several additional models for predicting the value of one variable on the basis of other variables. We dealt with **polynomial models** with one and two independent variables, and we also discussed how **dummy variables** allow us to use nominal-scaled independent variables. Since this is the last chapter that involves statistical inference, we couldn't resist the opportunity to introduce one more test of hypothesis—a test that allows us to test for portions of the regression model. This is particularly useful in testing the models introduced in this chapter, but it is also helpful in assessing any regression model.

▬▬▬▬▬▬▬ **SUPPLEMENTARY EXERCISES**

POM   **17.24**   Utilization of machinery, number of hours worked, and length of production runs are all considered important factors affecting per unit variable costs. A statistical analyst has been given the task of estimating the relationship between variable cost and daily plant output. After collecting data on per unit variable cost y (measured in dollars) and daily plant output of grapplegramits x (measured in individual units), she plotted the data and concluded that the model $y = \beta_0 + \beta_1 x + \beta_2 x^2 + \varepsilon$ might be appropriate. The computer yielded the results (SAS output) shown in Figure E17.24.

a. Write out the regression equation.

b. Are both β_1 and β_2 statistically significant? (Test with $\alpha = .05$.)

ACC   **17.25**   In allocating overhead, accountants sometimes regress it against direct labor hours used. direct materials used, or a combination of both. A recent accounting graduate decided not only that he would regress overhead y (measured in dollars) on labor used x_1 (measured in hours) and on direct materials used x_2 (measured in units), he also felt that there might be some interaction between the two independent variables. He therefore specified the model $y = \beta_0 + \beta_1 x_1 + \beta_2 x_2 + \beta_3 x_1 x_2 + \varepsilon$, with the results (Minitab output) shown in Figure E17.25.

FIGURE E17.24

```
Dependent Variable: Y
                                Analysis of Variance
                     Sum of     Mean
         Source   DF  Squares   Square   F Value   Prob > F
         Model    2   46.904    23.452   79.945    0.0000
         Error    57  16.721    0.293
         C Total  59  63.625


         Root MSE    0.5413   R-square   0.7372
         Dep Mean    1.3628   Adj R-sq   0.7283
         C.V.        39.7197


                                Parameter Estimates
                        Parameter   Standard   T for H0:
         Variable   DF  Estimate    Error      Parameter=0   Prob > |T|
         INTERCEP   1   -3.5521     2.5740     -1.3800       0.1730
         X          1    0.0211     0.0091      2.3187       0.0240
         XSQ        1   -0.000131   0.000058   -2.2586       0.0278
```

FIGURE E17.25

```
The regression equation is

Y=-180.91+51.516X1+29.093X2-0.032X1X2

Predictor     Coef      Stdev     t-ratio
Constant     -180.91    14.359    -12.599
X1            51.516    18.021      2.859
X2            29.093     9.632      3.020
X1X2          -0.032     0.014     -2.286

s=2.993   R-sq=63.7%   R-sq (adj)=62.4%

Analysis of Variance

SOURCE       DF     SS         MS
Regression   3      1352.765   450.92
Error        86      770.334     8.96
Total        89     2123.099
```

a. Is the interaction variable significant? (Test with $\alpha = .05$.)

b. Is this model useful in analyzing overhead? (Test with $\alpha = .01$.)

GEN **17.26** The number of car accidents on a particular stretch of highway seems to be related to the number of vehicles that travel over it, plus the speed at which they are traveling. A city alderman has decided to ask the county sheriff to provide him with statistics covering the last few years, with the intention of examining these data statistically so that he can (if possible) introduce new speed laws that will reduce traffic accidents. Using the number of accidents (y) as the dependent variable, he obtains estimates of the number of cars passing along that stretch of road x_1 and their average speeds x_2 (in miles per hour). He decides that the two independent variables probably have an effect on each other, and therefore he asks his assistant to run the model $y = \beta_0 + \beta_1 x_1 + \beta_2 x_2 + \beta_3 x_1 x_2 + \varepsilon$. The results are obtained (SAS output) per Figure E17.26.

a. Test the utility of the entire model, at $\alpha = .01$.

b. Can we eliminate the interaction term without significantly reducing the usefulness of the model? (Test with $\alpha = .01$.)

GEN **17.27** After completing the analysis in Exercise 17.26, the research assistant decides to respecify the model as

$$y = \beta_0 + \beta_1 x_1 + \beta_2 x_2 + \beta_3 x_1 x_2 + \beta_4 x_1^2 + \beta_5 x_2^2 + \varepsilon$$

to see how the results compare. The results are produced (SAS output) as shown in Figure E17.27.

a. Which of the explanatory variables is significant? (Test with $\alpha = .01$.)

b. Is the overall model, as specified, significant? (Test with $\alpha = .05$.)

GEN **17.28** Do the results shown in the two previous exercises allow us to conclude that the model proposed in Exercise 17.27 is superior to the model proposed in Exercise 17.26? (Test using $\alpha = .10$.)

FIGURE E17.26

Dependent Variable: Y

Analysis of Variance

Source	DF	Sum of Squares	Mean Square	F Value	Prob>F
Model	3	3954.71244	1318.23751	287.19771	0.0000
Error	346	1588.14133	4.59000		
C Total	349	5542.85377			

Root MSE	2.14243	R-square	0.71348
Dep Mean	10.86139	Adj R-sq	0.71000
C.V.	19.72519		

Parameter Estimates

Variable	DF	Parameter Estimate	Standard Error	T for H0: Parameter=0	Prob>|T|
INTERCEP	1	8.75138	20.13446	0.435	0.6628
X1	1	0.022864	0.011545	1.980	0.0484
X2	1	0.073136	0.023971	3.051	0.0024
X1X2	1	0.00071335	0.00015112	4.720	0.0000

FIGURE E17.27

Dependent Variable: Y

Analysis of Variance

Source	DF	Sum of Squares	Mean Square	F Value	Prob > F
Model	5	4215.30845	843.06168	218.45843	0.0000
Error	344	1327.54532	3.85914		
C Total	349	5542.85377			

Root MSE	1.96447	R-square	0.76049
Dep Mean	10.86139	Adj R-sq	0.75701
C.V.	18.08673		

Parameter Estimates

Variable	DF	Parameter Estimate	Standard Error	T for HO: Parameter=0	Prob > |T|
INTERCEP	1	-23.65059	40.08471	-0.590	0.5556
X1	1	0.03656	0.014862	2.460	0.0144
X2	1	0.57361	0.27983	2.050	0.0412
X1X2	1	-0.00088077	0.00059463	-1.481	0.1398
X1SQ	1	0.000049231	0.000014612	3.369	0.0008
X2SQ	1	0.0012482	0.00065018	1.920	0.0556

[SCI] **17.29** Growth of some bacteria and viruses often appears to follow a mathematical exponential pattern. One bright high-school student ran repeated experiments on a particular strain of bacteria that she grew in a special supersolution of her own composition in a petri dish. After collecting the data and entering them in the computer, she asked for a graph. Somewhat uncertain about what kind of regression model she should specify, she decided to start with $y = \beta_0 + \beta_1 x + \beta_2 x^2 + \beta_3 x^3 + \varepsilon$, where y is the actual bacteria count and x is the number of hours that have passed; the Minitab output shown in Figure E17.29 on page 856 resulted.

a. Test each of her coefficients, at $\alpha = .05$. Which are statistically significant?

b. What would the respecified model look like?

[ACC] **17.30** An accountant wishes to estimate total assembly costs as a function of the number of standard models produced plus the number of deluxe models produced. Using the total cost y (measured in dollars) as the dependent variable, he collected data on the number of units of the standard model x_1 and the number of units of the deluxe model x_2; then he ran the regression $y = \beta_0 + \beta_1 x_1^2 + \beta_2 x_2^2 + \varepsilon$ as an experimental first step. He obtained the Minitab printout given in Figure E17.30 on page 856.

a. Is the x_2^2 variable significant, at $\alpha = .05$?

b. What would you expect the impact on the overall model to be if the accountant dropped x_2^2?

[GEN] **17.31** In studying the expenditures on new computer hardware y (measured in $millions), a survey of 300 firms revealed that the primary determinants were the price of the computer x_1 (measured in $millions), the age of the existing stock of computers x_2 (measured in years), the company's yearly earnings x_3 (measured in $millions), and the firm's

FIGURE E17.29

```
The regression equation is

Y=-8.10+12.7X-0.905XSQ+2.14XCUBE

Predictor       Coef      Stdev     t-ratio
Constant      -8.101     55.780     -0.145
X             12.683     40.390      0.314
XSQ           -0.905      7.735     -0.117
XCUBE          2.136      0.432      4.944

s=41.845   R-sq=99.8%   R-sq(adj)=99.8%

Analysis of Variance

SOURCE        DF        SS         MS
Regression     3     12331818    4110606
Error         13       22760       1751
Total         16     12354578
```

FIGURE E17.30

```
The regression equation is

Y=3789+0.0105X1SQ+0.00248X2SQ

Predictor       Coef        Stdev     t-ratio
Constant        3789        1219       3.108
X1SQ           0.0105      0.0043      2.442
X2SQ          0.00248      0.0095      0.253

s=23.413   R-sq=55.7%   R-sq(adj)=54.9%

Analysis of Variance

SOURCE        DF        SS          MS
Regression     2     75794.47    37897.24
Error        110     60295.99      548.15
Total        112    136090.46
```

FIGURE E17.31

```
Dependent Variable: Y
                                 Analysis of Variance
                       Sum of      Mean
        Source    DF   Squares     Square    F-Value    Prob > F
        Model      8   8.1104      1.0138    322.95     0.0000
        Error    291   0.9135      0.00314
        C Total  299   9.0239


        Root MSE    0.0560    R-square    0.8988
        Dep Mean    0.8541    Adj R-sq    0.8960
        C.V.        6.5566


                             Parameter Estimates
                          Parameter     Standard     T for H0:
        Variable    DF    Estimate      Error        Parameter=0    Prob > |T|
        INTERCEP     1    0.0719        0.5789       0.12           0.9046
        X1           1    0.4157        0.2535       1.64           0.1020
        X2           1    0.1428        0.0583       2.45           0.0148
        X3           1    0.001169      0.000579     2.02           0.0442
        X4           1    0.07221       0.01675      4.31           0.0000
        X1X2         1    0.1757        0.090567     1.94           0.0534
        X2X3         1   -0.01247       0.02188     -0.57           0.5692
        X3X4         1    0.0001858     0.0000474    3.92           0.0002
        X1X4         1   -0.002541      0.006198    -0.41           0.6820
```

perceived growth potential x_4 (measured—as the average year-over-year growth over the last five years—in percent).

Since each variable was considered potentially important, and since various interactions were equally feasible, the computer industry analyst decided to specify the model as

$$y = \beta_0 + \beta_1 x_1 + \beta_2 x_2 + \beta_3 x_3 + \beta_4 x_4$$
$$+ \beta_5 (x_1 \cdot x_2) + \beta_6 (x_2 \cdot x_3) + \beta_7 (x_3 \cdot x_4)$$
$$+ \beta_8 (x_1 \cdot x_4) + \varepsilon$$

With the SAS statistical applications package, the output shown in Figure E17.31 was produced.

a. Which of the variables is statistically significant, at $\alpha = .05$?

b. Respecify the model, as appropriate, and discuss what you would do next.

c. How important is the firm's growth potential to its future expenditure on computers?

GEN **17.32** A baseball fan has been collecting data from a newspaper on the various American League teams. She wishes to explain each team's winning percentage y as a function of its batting average x_1 and its earned run average x_2, plus a dummy variable for whether or not the team fired its manager within the last 12 months ($x_3 = 1$ if it did and $= 0$ if it did not). Using Minitab, she obtained the results shown in the computer printout of Figure E17.32 on page 858.

a. Interpret $\hat{\beta}_1$.

b. Are the signs of the coefficients expected? Explain.

c. Do these data provide sufficient evidence that a team that fired its manager within the last 12

FIGURE E17.32

The regression equation is

Y=0.4017+2.1562X1-0.1843X2-0.2145X3

Predictor	Coef	Stdev	t-ratio
Constant	0.4017	0.4099	0.9800
X1	2.1562	1.0674	2.0201
X2	-0.1843	0.0589	-3.1290
X3	-0.2145	0.0844	-2.5415

s=0.0362   R-sq=83.9%   R-sq (adj)=79.2%

Analysis of Variance

SOURCE	DF	SS	MS
Regression	3	0.0681	0.0227
Error	10	0.0131	0.0013
Total	13	0.0812	

FIGURE E17.33

The regression equation is

Y=27.053+.926X1+3.273X2+.0786X3+.0824X4+.405X5

Predictor	Coef	Stdev	T-ratio
Constant	27.0531	3.2611	82.96
X1	0.9262	0.1140	8.12
X2	3.2734	2.8622	1.14
X3	0.07859	0.0592	1.33
X4	0.08237	0.0216	3.81
X5	0.4048	0.1018	3.98

S=9.375   R-sq=15.5%   R-sq (adj)=11.1%

Analysis of Variance

SOURCE	DF	SS	MS
Regression	5	1521.2	304.24
Error	94	8261.3	87.89
Total	99	9782.5	

months wins less frequently than a team that did not fire its manager? (Test with $\alpha = .05$.)

EDUC **17.33** Pay equity for men and women has been an ongoing source of conflict for a number of years in North America. Suppose that a statistician is investigating the factors that affect salary differences between male and female university professors. He believes that the following list of variables have some impact on a professor's income.

Number of years since first degree x_1

Highest degree $x_2 = 1$ if highest degree is a Ph.D.

$= 0$ if highest degree is not a Ph.D.

Average score on teaching evaluations x_3

Number of papers in refereed journals x_4

Sex $x_5 = 1$ if professor is male

$= 0$ if professor is female

Annual income y is measured in \$1,000s.

A random sample of 100 university professors was taken, and the Minitab results given in Figure E17.33 were produced.

a. Can the statistician conclude, with $\alpha = .05$, that the model is useful in analyzing salaries?

b. What do the coefficients and their t-values tell you?

c. Can the statistician conclude, with $\alpha = .05$, that there is sex discrimination?

CASE 17.1* *DETERMINANTS OF SUCCESS IN UNIVERSITY ACCOUNTING COURSES*

ACC In the past decade, business school enrollment has increased significantly. This has resulted in a large number of students taking bookkeeping and accounting courses. There has also been increased interest in accounting in high school. One issue of concern to accounting professors is to what extent high-school accounting courses affect performance in university accounting courses. This issue is part of the more general question of what factors determine the degree of success in university accounting courses. This problem was addressed in a study reported in the *Accounting Review* (January 1988). A multiple regression model was proposed to investigate the variables that affect performance in a first-year accounting course. The model is

$$y = \beta_0 + \beta_1 x_1 + \beta_2 x_2 + \beta_3 x_3 + \beta_4 x_4 + \beta_5 x_5 + \beta_6 x_6 + \beta_7 x_7 + \varepsilon$$

where

y = Total mark earned in four examinations

x_1 = Sum of the math and verbal scores from the Scholastic Aptitude Test (SAT), divided by 10

x_2 = Sum of high school English and math grades, where A = 9 and D = 0

x_3 = Last cumulative grade point, where A = 6 and F = 2

x_4 = Number of quizzes taken (this is supposed to measure motivation and effort)

---

* Adapted from R. K. Eskew and R. H. Faley, "Some Determinants of Student Performance in the First College-Level Financial Accounting Course," *Accounting Review* 63(1) (1988): 137–47.

$x_5 = 1$, if the student has had high-school bookkeeping or accounting
$= 0$, otherwise

$x_6 = $ Number of semester hours of completed university-level statistics and mathematics (this is supposed to measure related experience)

$x_7 = $ Number of semester hours of completed university-level courses

A total of 352 students who successfully completed the accounting course were included in the study. The Minitab system was used to estimate the model and produce the correlation matrix. These results are shown in the accompanying computer output.

Discuss what factors are the most important determinants of success in university accounting courses.

```
The regression equation is

Y=5.78+1.88X1+4.18X2+8.00X3+4.08X4+21.32X5+1.08X6+.06X7


Predictor     Coef      Stdev     t-ratio
Constant      5.78      1.23      4.70
X1            1.88      0.200     9.37
X2            4.18      0.822     5.08
X3            8.00      2.98      2.68
X4            4.08      0.591     6.90
X5            21.32     5.46      3.91
X6            1.08      0.431     2.50
X7            0.06      0.117     0.54


Correlation Matrix
```

	x_2	x_3	x_4	x_5	x_6	x_7	y
x_1	.453	.271	.015	-.128	.402	.059	.580
x_2		.322	.151	.012	.272	.053	.517
x_3			.145	-.043	.150	.252	.348
x_4				.117	.016	-.114	.334
x_5					-.071	-.173	.110
x_6						.410	.360
x_7							.078

STATISTICAL INFERENCE: CONCLUSION

INTRODUCTION

You have now studied about 40 statistical techniques in Chapters 7 through 17. If you are like most students, you probably understand estimation and hypothesis testing and are capable of doing the actual calculations of any of the methods. You may feel, however, that the system of identifying which technique to use is still somewhat vague. In this chapter we will complete the systematic approach we began in Chapter 5 and continued in Chapter 11, adding the techniques covered in Chapters 12 through 17 to the methods summarized in Section 11.2. In order to maintain the headings and subheadings of that section, we will continue to identify the sequence of data scales as interval, nominal, and ordinal. This is not the logical sequence, but it does make Chapter 18 compatible with Chapter 11.

In Section 18.2, we present the complete systematic approach, which we hope will make the determination of which technique to use much easier. We begin by stating the problem objective, followed by the data scale. Once these are determined, various specific factors that depend on the particular combinations of problem objective and data scale can be identified. In some cases, as many as five additional factors are involved; other cases involve no additional factors. For each method, we also present the conditions necessary for executing the technique. Use this guide in the exercises and cases shown at the end of the chapter. In many of these, the data are real; consequently, by doing them you will be getting first-hand experience in the use of statistical inference.

In Section 18.3, we address a number of issues that can improve your effectiveness in understanding and applying statistical methods in practical settings.

OUTLINE OF THE COMPLETE SYSTEM

I. Problem Objective: Description of a Single Population

    A. Data scale: interval

        1. Type of descriptive measurement: location
          a. σ^2 known

Parameter: μ

Test statistic:

$$z = \frac{\bar{x} - \mu}{\sigma/\sqrt{n}}$$

Interval estimator: $\bar{x} \pm z_{\alpha/2}\sigma/\sqrt{n}$

Required condition: x is normally distributed, or n is large enough.

b. σ^2 unknown

Parameter: μ

Test statistic:

$$t = \frac{\bar{x} - \mu}{s/\sqrt{n}} \qquad \text{d.f.} = n - 1$$

Interval estimator: $\bar{x} \pm t_{\alpha/2}s/\sqrt{n}$

Required condition: x is normally distributed.

2. Type of descriptive measurement: variability

Parameter: σ^2

Test statistic:

$$\chi^2 = \frac{(n-1)s^2}{\sigma^2} \qquad \text{d.f.} = n - 1$$

Interval estimator:

$$LCL = \frac{(n-1)s^2}{\chi^2_{\alpha/2}}$$

$$UCL = \frac{(n-1)s^2}{\chi^2_{1-\alpha/2}}$$

Required condition: x is normally distributed.

B. Data Scale: nominal

1. Binomial experiment

Parameter: p

Test statistic:

$$z = \frac{\hat{p} - p}{\sqrt{\dfrac{pq}{n}}}$$

Interval estimator:

$$\hat{p} \pm z_{\alpha/2} \sqrt{\frac{\hat{p}\hat{q}}{n}}$$

Required conditions: $np \geq 5$ and $nq \geq 5$ (for test statistic)
$n\hat{p} \geq 5$ and $n\hat{q} \geq 5$ (for estimation)

2. Multinomial experiment

Parameters: $p_1, p_2, \ldots, p_k$

Test statistic:

$$\chi^2 = \sum_{i=1}^{k} \frac{(o_i - e_i)^2}{e_i} \qquad \text{d.f.} = k - 1$$

Required condition: $e_i \geq 5$

C. Data scale: ordinal—not covered in this book

II. Problem Objective: Comparison of Two Populations

A. Data scale: interval

1. Type of descriptive measurement: location
    a. Independent samples

(i) σ_1^2 and σ_2^2 known

Parameter: $\mu_1 - \mu_2$

Test statistic:

$$z = \frac{(\bar{x}_1 - \bar{x}_2) - (\mu_1 - \mu_2)}{\sqrt{\sigma_1^2/n_1 + \sigma_2^2/n_2}}$$

Interval estimator:

$$(\bar{x}_1 - \bar{x}_2) \pm z_{\alpha/2}\sqrt{\sigma_1^2/n_1 + \sigma_2^2/n_2}$$

Required condition: x_1 and x_2 are normally distributed, or n_1 and n_2 are large enough.

If x_1 and x_2 are nonnormal, apply Wilcoxon rank sum test for independent samples.

(ii) σ_1^2 and σ_2^2 unknown: $n_1 > 30$ and $n_2 > 30$

Parameter: $\mu_1 - \mu_2$

Test statistic:

$$z = \frac{(\bar{x}_1 - \bar{x}_2) - (\mu_1 - \mu_2)}{\sqrt{s_1^2/n_1 + s_2^2/n_2}}$$

Interval estimator:

$$(\bar{x}_1 - \bar{x}_2) \pm z_{\alpha/2}\sqrt{s_1^2/n_1 + s_2^2/n_2}$$

Required condition: x_1 and x_2 are normally distributed, or n_1 and n_2 are large enough.

If x_1 and x_2 are nonnormal, apply Wilcoxon rank sum test for independent samples.

(iii) σ_1^2 and σ_2^2 unknown: $n_1 \leq 30$ or $n_2 \leq 30$

Parameter: $\mu_1 - \mu_2$

Test statistic:

$$t = \frac{(\bar{x}_1 - \bar{x}_2) - (\mu_1 - \mu_2)}{\sqrt{s_p^2(1/n_1 + 1/n_2)}} \qquad \text{d.f.} = n_1 + n_2 - 2$$

Interval estimator:

$$(\bar{x}_1 - \bar{x}_2) \pm t_{\alpha/2}\sqrt{s_p^2(1/n_1 + 1/n_2)}$$

Required conditions: x_1 and x_2 are normally distributed; $\sigma_1^2 = \sigma_2^2$.

If x_1 and x_2 are nonnormal, apply Wilcoxon rank sum test for independent samples.

b. Matched pairs samples

Parameter: $\mu_D = \mu_1 - \mu_2$

Test statistic:

$$t = \frac{\bar{x}_D - \mu_D}{s_D/\sqrt{n_D}} \qquad \text{d.f.} = n_D - 1$$

Interval estimator:

$$\bar{x}_D \pm t_{\alpha/2}s_D/\sqrt{n_D}$$

Required condition: D is normally distributed.

If D is nonnormal, apply Wilcoxon signed rank sum test for matched pairs.

Nonparametric technique: Wilcoxon signed rank sum test for matched pairs.

Test statistic: $T = T^-$ or T^+

Required conditions: $n \geq 5$; population distributions are identical in shape and spread.

2. Type of descriptive measurement: variability

Parameter: σ_1^2/σ_2^2

Test statistic:

$$F = \frac{s_1^2}{s_2^2} \qquad \text{d.f.} \quad \begin{aligned} v_1 &= n_1 - 1 \\ v_2 &= n_2 - 1 \end{aligned}$$

Interval estimator:

$$\text{LCL} = \left(\frac{s_1^2}{s_2^2}\right)\frac{1}{F_{\alpha/2,v_1,v_2}}$$

$$\text{UCL} = \left(\frac{s_1^2}{s_2^2}\right)F_{\alpha/2,v_2,v_1}$$

Required conditions: x_1 and x_2 are normally distributed; samples are independent.

B. Data scale: nominal

Parameter: $p_1 - p_2$

Test statistic:

Case 1: $H_0: (p_1 - p_2) = 0$

$$z = \frac{(\hat{p}_1 - \hat{p}_2) - (p_1 - p_2)}{\sqrt{\hat{p}\hat{q}(1/n_1 + 1/n_2)}}$$

Case 2: $H_0: (p_1 - p_2) = D \qquad (D \neq 0)$

$$z = \frac{(\hat{p}_1 - \hat{p}_2) - (p_1 - p_2)}{\sqrt{\dfrac{\hat{p}_1\hat{q}_1}{n_1} + \dfrac{\hat{p}_2\hat{q}_2}{n_2}}}$$

Interval estimator:

$$(\hat{p}_1 - \hat{p}_2) \pm z_{\alpha/2}\sqrt{\frac{\hat{p}_1\hat{q}_1}{n_1} + \frac{\hat{p}_2\hat{q}_2}{n_2}}$$

Required conditions: $n_1\hat{p}_1$, $n_1\hat{q}_1$, $n_2\hat{p}_2$, and $n_2\hat{q}_2 \geq 5$.

C. Data scale: ordinal

   1. Independent samples

Nonparametric technique: Wilcoxon rank sum test for independent samples

Test statistic: $T = T_A$

Required conditions: $n_1 \geq 3$ and $n_2 \geq 3$; population distributions are identical in shape and spread.

   2. Matched pairs samples

Nonparametric technique: sign test

Test statistic: $z = \dfrac{x - .5n}{.5\sqrt{n}}$

Required conditions: $n \geq 10$; population distributions are identical in shape and spread.

III. Problem Objective: Comparison of Two or More Populations

   A. Data scale: interval

      1. Completely randomized design (independent samples)

Parameters: $\mu_1, \mu_2, \ldots, \mu_k$

Test statistic:

$$F = \frac{\text{MST}}{\text{MSE}} \qquad \text{d.f.} \quad \begin{aligned} v_1 &= k - 1 \\ v_2 &= n - k \end{aligned}$$

Required conditions: $x_1, x_2, \ldots, x_k$ are normally distributed; $\sigma_1^2 = \sigma_2^2 = \cdots = \sigma_k^2$.

If $x_1, x_2, \ldots, x_k$ are nonnormal, apply Kruskal–Wallis test.

2. Randomized block design (matched samples)

Parameters: $\mu_1, \mu_2, \ldots, \mu_k$

Test statistic:

$$F = \frac{\text{MST}}{\text{MSE}} \qquad \text{d.f.} \quad \begin{array}{l} v_1 = k - 1 \\ v_2 = n - k - b + 1 \end{array}$$

Required conditions: $x_1, x_2, \ldots, x_k$ are normally distributed; $\sigma_1^2 = \sigma_2^2 = \cdots = \sigma_k^2$.

If $x_1, x_2, \ldots, x_k$ are nonnormal, apply Friedman test.

B. Data scale: nominal

Statistical technique: contingency table

Test statistic:

$$\chi^2 = \sum \frac{(o_i - e_i)^2}{e_i} \qquad \text{d.f.} = (r - 1)(c - 1)$$

Required condition: $e_i \geq 5$.

C. Data scale: ordinal

1. Completely randomized design (independent samples)

Nonparametric technique: Kruskal–Wallis test

Test statistic:

$$H = \left[\frac{12}{n(n + 1)} \sum \left(\frac{T_j^2}{n_j} \right) \right] - 3(n + 1)$$

Chi-square distributed, d.f. $= k - 1$

Required conditions: $n_j \geq 5$; population distributions are identical in shape and spread.

2. Randomized block design (matched samples)

Nonparametric technique: Friedman test

Test statistic:

$$F_r = \left[\frac{12}{bk(k+1)} \sum T_j^2 \right] - 3b(k+1)$$

Chi-square distributed, d.f. $= k - 1$

Required conditions: b or $k \geq 5$; population distributions are identical in shape and spread.

IV. Problem Objective: Analysis of the Relationship Between Two Variables

  A. Data scale: interval

Parameters: β_0, β_1, ρ (simple linear regression and correlation)

Test statistic:

$$t = \frac{\hat{\beta}_0 - \beta_0}{s_{\hat{\beta}_0}} \qquad \text{d.f.} = n - 2$$

$$t = \frac{\hat{\beta}_1 - \beta_1}{s_{\hat{\beta}_1}} \qquad \text{d.f.} = n - 2$$

$$t = \frac{r - \rho}{s_r} \qquad \text{d.f.} = n - 2$$

Confidence intervals:

$$\hat{\beta}_0 \pm t_{\alpha/2} s_{\hat{\beta}_0}$$

$$\hat{\beta}_1 \pm t_{\alpha/2} s_{\hat{\beta}_1}$$

$$\hat{y} \pm t_{\alpha/2} s_\varepsilon \sqrt{\frac{1}{n} + \frac{(x_g - \bar{x})^2}{SS_x}}$$

$$\hat{y} \pm t_{\alpha/2} s_\varepsilon \sqrt{1 + \frac{1}{n} + \frac{(x_g - \bar{x})^2}{SS_x}}$$

Required conditions: ε is normally distributed with mean zero and variance $= \sigma_\varepsilon^2$; ε terms are independent.

B. Data scale: nominal

Statistical technique: contingency table

Test statistic:

$$\chi^2 = \sum \frac{(o_i - e_i)^2}{e_i} \qquad \text{d.f.} = (r-1)(c-1)$$

Required condition: $e_i \geq 5$.

C. Data scale: ordinal

Nonparametric technique: Spearman rank correlation

Test statistic: r_s

V. Problem Objective: Analysis of the Relationship Among Two or More Variables

A. Data scale: interval

Parameters: $\beta_0, \beta_1, \ldots, \beta_k$ (multiple regression)

Test statistic:

$$t = \frac{\hat{\beta}_i - \beta_i}{s_{\hat{\beta}_i}} \qquad \text{d.f.} = n - k - 1$$

$$F = \frac{\text{MSR}}{\text{MSE}} \qquad \begin{array}{l} \text{d.f.} \quad v_1 = k \\ \phantom{\text{d.f.}} \quad v_2 = n - k - 1 \end{array}$$

Confidence intervals:

$$\hat{\beta}_i \pm t_{\alpha/2} s_{\hat{\beta}_i}$$

Required conditions: ε is normally distributed with mean zero and variance $= \sigma_\varepsilon^2$; ε terms are independent.

B. Data scale: nominal—not covered in this book

C. Data scale: ordinal—not covered in this book

In order to help you choose the appropriate method, a flowchart of the complete system is presented in Figure 18.1. The techniques are summarized in Table 18.1.

FIGURE 18.1   FLOWCHART OF THE SYSTEMATIC APPROACH

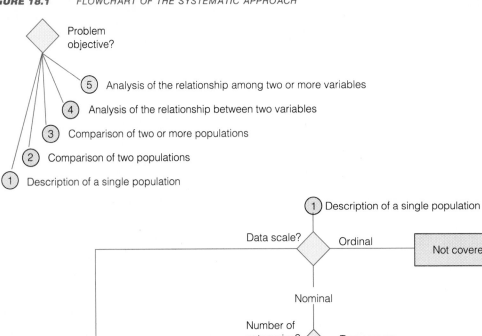

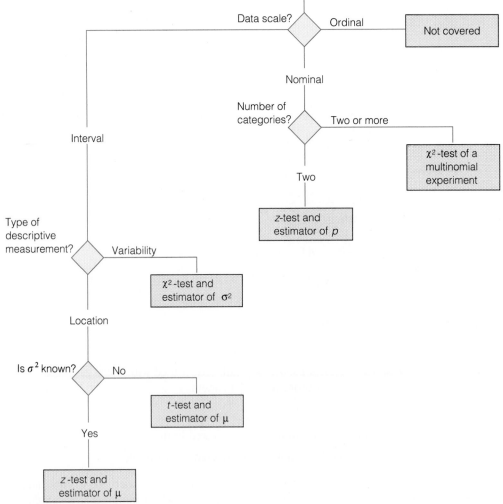

FIGURE 18.1   *(continued)*

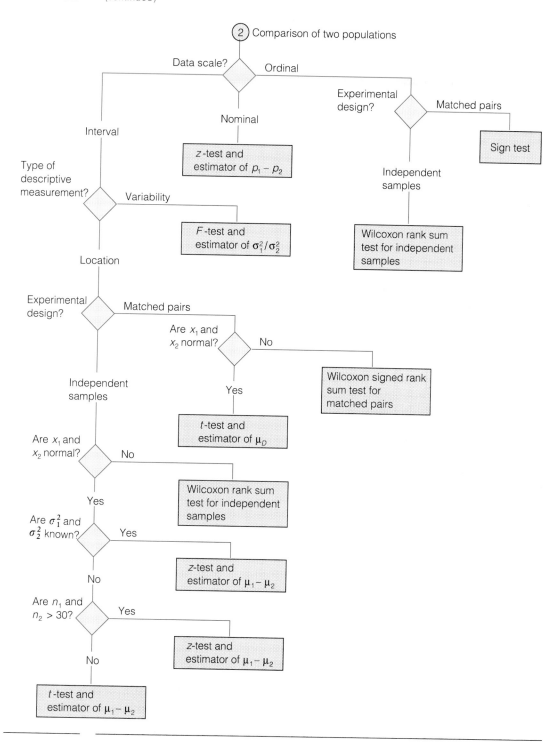

FIGURE 18.1 (continued)

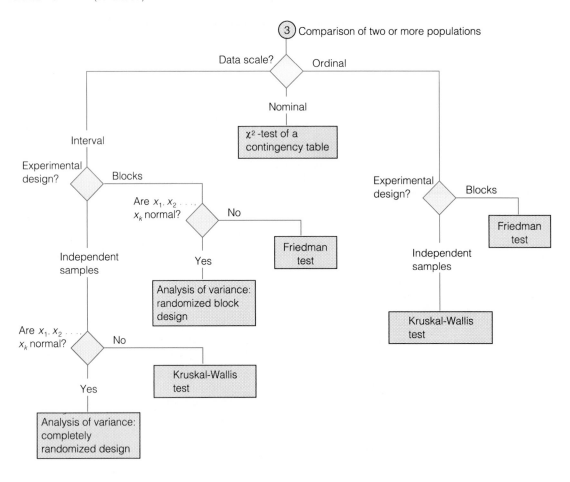

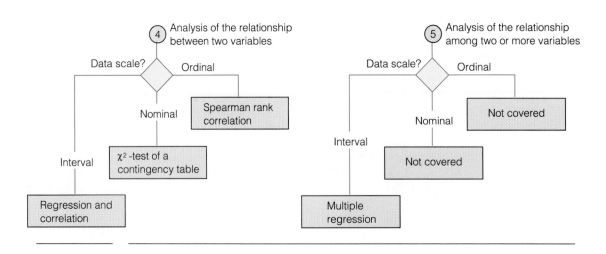

TABLE 18.1   GUIDE TO THE STATISTICAL TECHNIQUES

Scale	Problem Objective				
	Description of a Single Population	Comparisons of Two Populations	Comparisons of Two or More Populations	Analysis of the Relationship Between Two Variables	Analysis of the Relationship Among Two or More Variables
Nominal	z-test and estimator of p χ^2-test of the multinomial experiment	z-test and estimator of $p_1 - p_2$	χ^2-test of a contingency table	χ^2-test of a contingency table	Not covered
Ordinal	Not covered	Wilcoxon rank sum test for independent samples Sign test	Kruskal–Wallis test Friedman test	Spearman rank correlation	Not covered
Interval	z-test and estimator of μ t-test and estimator of μ χ^2-test and estimator of σ^2	z-test and estimator of $\mu_1 - \mu_2$ t-test and estimator of $\mu_1 - \mu_2$ Wilcoxon rank sum test for independent samples t-test and estimator of μ_D Wilcoxon signed rank sum test for matched pairs F-test and estimator of σ_1^2/σ_2^2	ANOVA—completely randomized design Kruskal–Wallis test ANOVA—randomized block design Friedman test	Simple linear regression and correlation	Multiple regression

Many university instructors continually seek better ways to teach their courses. That is, they try to find the teaching style that will result in a more positive attitude toward both the professor and the course, which in turn will result in greater student achievement. In an experiment to determine better teaching methods, two sections of an introductory marketing course were taught in two distinctly different ways. Section 1 was taught primarily with lectures: a minimum of discussion was allowed, several unannounced quizzes were given, and there was no "bell-curving" of grades. Section 2 used a combination of lectures and discussions, no quizzes were given, and the students were graded on the curve.

At the completion of the course, each student rated the fairness of the professor and the relevance of the course on 5-point scales. The ratings were 5 = Fair and 1 = Unfair and 5 = Very relevant and 1 = Irrelevant, respectively. All students also were assigned marks, on a 100-point scale. The results are summarized in the two accompanying tables. The actual data (not shown) were stored in computer memory, and Minitab was used to calculate the required statistics.

DISTRIBUTION OF RATINGS

Type of Rating	Frequency	
Fairness Rating	Section 1	Section 2
1	8	4
2	18	9
3	23	22
4	16	19
5	7	10
Sample size	$n_1 = 72$	$n_2 = 64$
Relevance Rating	Section 1	Section 2
1	4	2
2	19	11
3	25	20
4	20	23
5	4	8
Sample size	$n_1 = 72$	$n_2 = 64$

---

* Adapted from Robert W. Cook, "An Investigation of the Relationship Between Student Attitudes and Student Achievement," *Journal of the Academy of Marketing Science* 7(1, 2) (1979): 71–79.

DISTRIBUTION OF FINAL MARKS

	Frequency	
Class Mark	Section 1	Section 2
0–9.9	0	0
10–19.9	0	0
20–29.9	0	0
30–39.9	0	0
40–49.9	1	3
50–59.9	6	10
60–69.9	14	9
70–79.9	33	28
80–89.9	14	11
90–100	4	3

a. Can we conclude that there is a difference in the fairness ratings received by the professors in the two sections?

b. Can we conclude that there is a difference in the relevance ratings received by the course in the two sections?

c. Can we conclude that there is a difference in the marks received by students in the two sections?

The significance level will be set at $\alpha = .05$.

Solution, Part (a).   The first question we encounter on the flowchart asks us to identify the problem objective. Here the objective is to compare two populations. The data scale is ordinal. Following that, the flowchart asks whether the samples are independent or matched pairs. Since we have two separate sections with differing sample sizes, the samples clearly are independent. The appropriate statistical method is the Wilcoxon rank sum test for independent samples. Because we want to know whether the two populations differ, the alternative hypothesis is

H_A: The location of population A is different from the location of population B.

Recall from Section 14.2 that the test statistic is the rank sum of sample A, where A is the smaller sample (that is, Section 2). The complete test is as follows.

H_0: The two population locations are the same.

H_A: The location of population A is different from the location of population B.

Test statistic: Since the sample sizes are large, the test statistic is

$$z = \frac{T - E(T)}{\sigma_T}$$

Rejection region:

$|z| > z_{\alpha/2}$

$> z_{.025}$

> 1.96

Value of the test statistic: From the Minitab output that follows, we have

$T = W = 4{,}842$

The test statistic is

$$z = \frac{T - E(T)}{\sigma_T}$$

where

$$E(T) = \frac{n_1(n_1 + n_2 + 1)}{2} = \frac{64(64 + 72 + 1)}{2} = 4{,}384$$

and

$$\sigma_T = \sqrt{\frac{n_1 n_2(n_1 + n_2 + 1)}{12}} = \sqrt{\frac{(64)(72)(137)}{12}} = 229$$

Hence,

$$z = \frac{4{,}842 - 4{,}384}{229} = 2.0$$

Conclusion: Reject H_0.

There is sufficient evidence to allow us to conclude that a difference exists in the fairness ratings assigned in the two sections.

Minitab Computer Output

```
C1    N=64    MEDIAN=3.0000
C2    N=72    MEDIAN=3.0000


POINT ESTIMATE FOR ETA1-ETA2 IS    -0.0001
95.0 PCT C.I. FOR ETA1-ETA2 IS (-0.00, 1.00)
W=4842.0
TEST OF ETA1=ETA2 VS. ETA1 N.E. ETA2 IS SIGNIFICANT AT 0.0461
```

Notice that we stored the ratings for Section 2 in column 1 because Section 2 is labeled Population A (smaller sample size).

Solution, Part (b).   The problem objective is to compare two populations, the data scale is ordinal, and the samples are independent. We complete the test as follows (without showing the calculations).

H_0: The two population locations are the same

H_A: The location of population A is different from the location of population B

Test statistic:

$$z = \frac{T - E(T)}{\sigma_T}$$

Rejection region: $|z| > 1.96$

Value of the test statistic: From the printout that follows, we find

$$T = W = 4,836.5$$

Thus,

$$z = \frac{4,836.5 - 4,384}{229} = 1.98$$

Conclusion: Reject H_0.

There is sufficient evidence to allow us to conclude that a difference exists in the relevance ratings assigned in the two sections.

Minitab Computer Output

```
C1    N=64    MEDIAN=3.0000
C2    N=72    MEDIAN=3.0000

POINT ESTIMATE FOR ETA1-ETA2 IS -0.0001
95.0 PCT C.I. FOR ETA1-ETA2 IS (-0.00, 1.00)
W=4836.5
TEST OF ETA1=ETA2 VS. ETA1 N.E. ETA2 IS SIGNIFICANT AT 0.0488
```

Solution, Part (c).   The problem objective is the same as it was for parts (a) and (b): to compare two populations. The data scale, however, is not the same. To answer part (c), we use the assigned marks out of 100; hence, the scale is interval. The flowchart then asks us to identify the type of descriptive measurement involved. We identify that as the location. Next we recognize that the samples are independent, that the marks appear to be normally distributed, that σ_1^2 and σ_2^2 are unknown, and that n_1 and $n_2 > 30$. Hence, we apply the z-test of $\mu_1 - \mu_2$.

H_0: $(\mu_1 - \mu_2) = 0$

H_A: $(\mu_1 - \mu_2) \neq 0$

Test statistic:

$$z = \frac{(\bar{x}_1 - \bar{x}_2) - (\mu_1 - \mu_2)}{\sqrt{\dfrac{s_1^2}{n_1} + \dfrac{s_2^2}{n_2}}}$$

Rejection region: $|z| > 1.96$

Value of the test statistic: From the computer output that follows, we have

$z = 1.42$

Conclusion: Do not reject H_0.

There is not enough evidence to allow us to conclude that the marks received by the two sections differ.

Minitab Computer Output

```
       N    MEAN    STDEV    SE MEAN
C1    72    73.7    10.4      1.2
C2    64    70.9    12.2      1.5

95 PCT CI FOR MU C1-MU C2:  (-1.1, 6.7)
TTEST MU C1=MU C2 (VS NE):  T=1.42  P=0.16  DF=124.7
```

Our overall conclusion is that, although the students do not perceive the fairness of the professor and the relevance of the course equally, there appears to be no significant difference in their performance.

EXAMPLE 18.2

A university researcher hypothesized that dieters who paid for their diets would lose more weight than those who paid nothing (*Science International*, Global Television Network, 8 November 1985). Suppose that, in an experiment to test this belief, 30 dieters are randomly selected. Of these, 10 are asked to pay $100 for a comprehensive diet, another 10 are asked to pay $50 for the same diet, and the remaining 10 are given the same diet for no charge. The total weight loss after 16 weeks of dieting was recorded for each individual and is shown in the accompanying table.

TOTAL WEIGHT LOSS (POUNDS)

Amount Paid		
$0	$50	$100
16	3	20
3	2	23
1	17	21
18	19	17
7	28	16
0	27	19
7	10	11
15	3	29
0	14	23
2	19	33

a. Does sufficient evidence exist to allow us to conclude that there are differences in weight loss among the three groups of dieters?

b. Another researcher pointed out that the amount of weight lost is a function of other variables besides the amount paid for the diet. As part of the experiment, the age, sex, initial weight, and ideal weight were also recorded. These data, together with the amount paid and the weight loss achieved, are shown in the accompanying table. What conclusions can be drawn now?

WEIGHT LOSS CONSIDERED WITH OTHER SIGNIFICANT VARIABLES

Dieter	Amount Paid	Age	Sex	Initial Weight	Ideal Weight	Weight Loss
1	100	25	F	180	120	20
2	0	19	F	166	125	16
3	50	29	F	140	110	3
4	100	40	F	176	120	23
5	100	29	M	265	180	21
6	0	58	F	163	130	3

(continued)

Dieter	Amount Paid	Age	Sex	Initial Weight	Ideal Weight	Weight Loss
7	50	33	F	151	125	2
8	0	51	F	149	115	1
9	50	33	M	220	160	17
10	50	37	F	207	135	19
11	100	42	F	182	120	17
12	0	42	M	200	160	18
13	0	32	F	153	120	7
14	0	36	F	133	115	0
15	50	25	F	213	130	28
16	0	53	F	146	115	7
17	0	27	F	173	130	15
18	100	39	F	198	120	16
19	50	29	M	246	150	27
20	100	29	F	186	120	19
21	100	33	F	163	125	11
22	100	39	M	258	160	29
23	0	41	F	149	135	0
24	50	43	F	148	110	10
25	50	38	F	153	125	3
26	100	48	M	259	150	23
27	0	22	F	142	120	2
28	50	49	F	168	125	14
29	100	39	M	360	170	33
30	50	50	F	195	135	19

Solution, Part (a).   The objective of analyzing the data in the first table is to determine whether differences exist among the three groups. Hence the problem objective is to compare three populations. Since the populations are the weight losses, the data scale is interval. The experiment was performed by selecting ten separate individuals for each group; therefore, the samples are independent. The prescribed technique is the completely randomized design of the analysis of variance. We will assume that the data are normally distributed, and we'll use $\alpha = .05$. The SAS statistical package is used to produce the required statistical results.

$H_0: \mu_1 = \mu_2 = \mu_3$

H_A: At least two means differ.

Test statistic:

$$F = \frac{\text{MST}}{\text{MSE}}$$

Rejection region:

$F > F_{\alpha, k-1, n-k}$

$\quad > F_{.05, 2, 27}$

$\quad > 3.35$

Value of the test statistic: From the SAS output that follows, we have the following ANOVA table.

Source	d. f.	Sum of Squares	Mean Squares	F Ratio
Treatment	2	1,022.6	511.3	8.48
Error	27	1,628.1	60.3	
Total	29	2,650.7		

Conclusion: Reject H_0.

There is sufficient evidence to suggest that differences exist among the three groups. Since $\bar{x}_1 = 6.9$, $\bar{x}_2 = 14.2$, and $\bar{x}_3 = 21.2$, it is reasonable to conclude that, on average, those who pay more for their diets lose more weight.

SAS COMPUTER OUTPUT

```
Dependent Variable: Y
                             Sum of      Mean
Source              DF      Squares     Square    F Value    Pr > F
Model                2    1022.6000   511.3000       8.48    0.0014
Error               27    1628.1000    60.3000
Corrected Total     29    2650.7000
```

Solution Part (b).   The data provided in the second table allow for the possibility that other factors besides the cost of the diet may be related to weight loss. The question is how the variables—amount paid, age, sex, initial weight, and ideal weight—affect weight loss. The technique to be used is multiple regression. The following regression equation was estimated:

$$y = \beta_0 + \beta_1 x_1 + \beta_2 x_2 + \beta_3 x_3 + \beta_4 x_4 + \beta_5 x_5 + \varepsilon$$

In this equation,

y = Weight loss

x_1 = Amount paid for the diet

x_2 = Age

x_3 = Dummy variables representing sex, where

x_3 = 0 (if dieter is male)

x_3 = 1 (if dieter is female)

x_4 = Initial weight

x_5 = Ideal weight

Generally, in analyzing a multiple regression equation, we perform various tests. In this application, however, we're interested only in the effect of the amount paid on the weight loss. As a result, we test β_1, the coefficient of variable x_1 (the amount paid). We want to know whether there is enough evidence to allow us to conclude that, the greater the amount paid, the greater the weight loss; therefore, the alternative hypothesis is

$$H_A: \beta_1 > 0$$

The complete test (with $\alpha = .05$) is as follows.

$$H_0: \beta_1 = 0$$
$$H_A: \beta_1 > 0$$

Test statistic:

$$t = \frac{\hat{\beta}_1 - \beta_1}{s_{\hat{\beta}_1}}$$

Rejection region:

$$t > t_{\alpha, n-k-1}$$
$$> t_{.05, 24}$$
$$> 1.711$$

Value of the test statistic: From the SAS output that follows, we find $t = 1.292$

Conclusion: Do not reject H_0.

There is not enough evidence to allow us to conclude that, in the presence of the other variables, a positive linear relationship between y and x_1 exists. Thus, we cannot conclude that the amount paid is positively related to weight loss.

It should be noted that the conclusion we've drawn may depend on the model chosen. We determined that there was not enough evidence to allow us to conclude that a positive *linear* relationship exists; however, a positive nonlinear relationship may exist. Additionally, if a serious problem of collinearity is present, the test we performed may have been influenced by that collinearity.

SAS Computer Output

Dependent Variable: Y

Analysis of Variance

Source	DF	Sum of Squares	Mean Square	F Value	Prob > F
Model	5	2010.0687	402.0137	15.061	0.0001
Error	24	640.6312	26.6929		
C Total	29	2650.7000			

Root MSE	5.1665	R-square	0.7583
Dep Mean	14.1000	Adj R-sq	0.7080
C.V.	36.6420		

Parameter Estimates

Variable	DF	Parameter Estimate	Standard Error	T for H0: Parameter=0	Prob > |T|
INTERCEP	1	-1.8735	15.5785	-0.120	0.9053
X1	1	0.0390	0.0302	1.292	0.2088
X2	1	-0.1309	0.0996	-1.315	0.2009
X3	1	-0.1411	5.2069	-0.027	0.9786
X4	1	0.1760	0.0444	3.955	0.0006
X5	1	-0.1077	0.1401	-0.768	0.4497

SECTION 18.3   ## *PRACTICAL CONSIDERATIONS*

Before you proceed to the exercises and cases, you should consider some practical issues that often arise in applying statistical techniques. Some of these issues have been alluded to earlier in this book, while others have not been discussed for lack of a suitable setting. Since this is the last chapter in the statistical inference part of the textbook, we now present a hodgepodge of these practical problems.

MEANING OF STATISTICAL SIGNIFICANCE

The term **statistically significant** is used repeatedly in all statistics books. We urge you to be careful about its meaning. A statistically significant test result is one in which sufficient evidence existed to enable the person performing the test to reject the null hypothesis. But even if a statistically significant test result is obtained, it may not mean a great deal in practice. The following example illustrates this point.

EXAMPLE 18.3

In a large national survey designed to determine whether more men than women prefer the taste of a new soft drink, 5,000 men and 5,000 women are asked to try the product. Suppose that 1,100 men and 1,000 women state that they prefer the new drink. Is there sufficient evidence to allow us to conclude that more men than women prefer this drink? (Use $\alpha = .05$.)

Solution. The test would be conducted as follows.

$$H_0: (p_1 - p_2) = 0$$
$$H_A: (p_1 - p_2) > 0$$

where

$p_1 =$ Proportion of men who prefer the product

$p_2 =$ Proportion of women who prefer the product

Test statistic:

$$z = \frac{(\hat{p}_1 - \hat{p}_2) - (p_1 - p_2)}{\sqrt{\hat{p}\hat{q}\left(\dfrac{1}{n_1} + \dfrac{1}{n_2}\right)}}$$

Rejection region:

$$z > z_\alpha$$
$$> z_{.05}$$
$$> 1.645$$

Value of the test statistic:

$$z = \frac{(.22 - .20) - 0}{\sqrt{(.21)(.79)\left(\dfrac{1}{5,000} + \dfrac{1}{5,000}\right)}}$$
$$= 2.46$$

Conclusion: Reject H_0.

There is sufficient evidence to indicate that $p_1 > p_2$. But even so, the difference is not particularly meaningful. A 2% difference in population proportions (remember, though, that we found only a 2% difference in sample proportions) is not likely to have any serious consequences. The soft-drink company is not going to change its advertising media, for instance, because of this result.

Bear in mind that the term *statistically significant* does not imply practical significance. Practical significance depends on both the statistical result and the general context of the problem.

NORMALITY REQUIREMENT

Many of the statistical techniques presented in this book require that the populations from which we have sampled be normally distributed. These techniques include the t-test and estimate of μ and $\mu_1 - \mu_2$, the chi-square test and estimate of σ^2, the F-test and estimate of σ_1^2/σ_2^2, the analysis of variance, and regression. Most practitioners (including many authors of textbooks on statistics) ignore this requirement and apply the statistical technique without checking to see if the data are nonnormal.

A number of statistical methods—including the chi-square test discussed in Chapter 13 and the Kolmogorov—Smirnov and Lilliefors tests presented in Chapter 14—test for normality. We think it prudent at the very least to draw a histogram of the data to determine whether the populations appear to be quite nonnormal. This step is particularly important for techniques that are not robust. In Chapter 7, we pointed out that the t-test is generally valid even when the population is somewhat nonnormal, but the chi-square test for variance is poor when the population is nonnormal. Hence, when testing σ^2, you must examine the population more carefully.

TREATING AN ORDINAL SCALE AS AN INTERVAL SCALE

Practical research often investigates individuals' attitudes toward various issues. For example, a marketing analyst may be interested in respondents' assessments of the quality of a product. The analyst may determine these assessments by measuring the degree to which respondents agree or disagree with a number of statements. The responses might be as follows:

Very strongly disagree	1
Strongly disagree	2
Disagree	3
Neutral	4
Agree	5
Strongly agree	6
Very strongly agree	7

This scale is an ordinal scale. In a very large proportion of applications of statistical techniques where the scale is ordinal, however, the practitioner treats the scale as if it were an interval scale.

In preparing the cases presented at the end of this chapter, we often encountered ordinal scales in the journals that we quote. Unfortunately, all too often the method used by the author of the journal article was one that theoretically should be applied only to *interval* data. Technically, then, the author was wrong to apply that method. Recall, however, the key determinant of an interval scale: if the intervals between values of the variable are meaningful, the scale is judged to be interval. The practitioner who treats ordinal scales like interval scales would undoubtedly argue that the intervals between the values of variables such as the one just described are meaningful enough to be treated as interval scales. This is not unreasonable in many applications—particularly since the result of the technically incorrect parametric test is often similar to the result of the technically correct nonparametric test. (To confirm this, you may wish to apply a *t*-test for $\mu_1 - \mu_2$ in a situation where we applied the Wilcoxon rank sum test to ordinal data and then compare results.) Nonetheless, we continue to advocate that, when the data are ordinal, a nonparametric technique should be applied. If you wish to treat an ordinal scale as an interval scale, you must satisfy yourself that the intervals between values are meaningful.

TRANSFORMING DATA SCALES

When the problem objective is to analyze the relationship between two variables, both variables are assumed to have the same scale. If that is not the case, the higher-ranking scale must be reduced to a lower rank. For example, if one variable is interval and the other is nominal, the interval scale should be grouped and treated as a nominal scale. The appropriate technique to use would then be the chi-square contingency table.

You may be tempted to reduce the variables to a nominal scale in every case, thus simplifying the statistical techniques. The disadvantage of doing so is that, by grouping data, you lose information and thus weaken the conclusion of the statistical inference. In general, you should not transform scales unless you have to.

SECTION 18.4   *SUMMARY*

At this point we think (and hope) you're ready to tackle real-life statistical problems. Some of the exercises and all of the cases deal with real problems or real data. By using the guide presented in this chapter, you should be able to produce accurate solutions within a reasonable amount of time. Have fun!

▰▰▰▰▰▰   *EXERCISES*

MKT **18.1**   Sales of a product can depend on its placement in a store. Cigarette manufacturers often offer cost discounts to retailers who display their products more prominently than competing brands. In order to examine this phenomenon more carefully, a cigarette manufacturer (with the help of a national chain of restaurants) planned the following

experiment. In five restaurants, the manufacturer's brand is displayed behind the cashier's counter with all the other brands. (This was called position 1.) In another five restaurants, the brand was placed separately but close to the other brands (position 2). In a third group of five restaurants, the cigarettes were placed in a special display next to the cash register. The daily sales for one complete week were recorded, and the results appear in the accompanying table.

NUMBER OF CARTONS SOLD

	Position		
Weekday	1	2	3
Sunday	22	25	30
Monday	16	19	20
Tuesday	13	12	12
Wednesday	10	9	8
Thursday	15	12	14
Friday	23	20	22
Saturday	31	28	30

a. Is there sufficient evidence to allow you to conclude that sales of this brand of cigarette differ depending on placement? (Use $\alpha = .05$.)

b. What assumption must you make in order to answer part (a)?

c. Redo the test, assuming that the requirement in part (b) is not satisfied.

d. Comment on the policy of offering discounts to the retailer for displaying the product more prominently.

MKT **18.2** One of the ways advertisers measure the value of television commercials is through telephone surveys shortly after the commercial is aired.

Respondents are asked if they watched a certain television station at a given time period, during which the commercial appeared. People who answer affirmatively are then asked if they can recall the name of the product in the commercial. Suppose that an advertiser wishes to compare the recall proportions of two commercials. The first commercial is relatively inexpensive. A survey of 500 television viewers found that 138 could recall the product name. A second commercial shown a week later features a well-known rock star and (as a result) is quite expensive to produce. The advertiser decides that the second commercial is viable only if its recall proportion is at least 15% higher than the recall proportion of the first commercial. If a survey of 800 viewers finds that 389 people recall the product from the second commercial, can we conclude at the 5% significance level that the second commercial is viable?

GEN **18.3** A large textile firm has been accused by the federal government of discrimination in hiring. In compliance with a court order, the firm produces the results of the last 1,000 job applications; these results are summarized in Table E18.3.

a. On the basis of these data, can we conclude at the 5% significance level that the firm is guilty of discriminatory hiring practices?

b. If yes, can we conclude that the discrimination is on the basis of race, sex, or both?

GEN **18.4** The widespread use of salt on Canadian roads during the winter and acid precipitation throughout the year combine to cause rust on cars. Car manufacturers and other companies offer rustproofing services to help purchasers preserve the

TABLE E18.3

	Caucasian		Black		Hispanic	
	Males	Females	Males	Females	Males	Females
Number Hired	193	75	47	15	14	9
Number Rejected	199	111	114	51	96	76
Number of Applications	392	186	161	66	110	85

value of their cars. A consumer protection agency decides to determine whether there are any differences between the rust protection provided by automobile manufacturers and that provided by two competing types of rust-proofing. As an experiment, 21 identical new cars are selected. Of these, 7 are rust-proofed by the manufacturer. Another 7 are rust-proofed by a method that applies a liquid to critical areas of the car. The liquid hardens, forming a (supposedly) lifetime bond with the metal. The last 7 are treated with oil and are retreated every 12 months. The cars are then driven under similar conditions in a Canadian city. The number of months until the first rust appears is recorded. These data appear in the accompanying table.

a. If we assume that the time until rusting is normally distributed, is there sufficient evidence to conclude that at least one rust-proofing method is different from the others? (Use $\alpha = .05$.)

b. Repeat part (a), with the assumption that the time until rusting is not normally distributed.

NUMBER OF MONTHS UNTIL RUST

Rust-Proofing Method		
Manufacturer	Permanent Bond	Oil Treatment
33	42	47
38	36	39
27	25	43
35	38	42
29	32	46
39	29	47
32	37	38

PG **18.5** In response to the energy crisis of 1973, the U.S. government instituted the 55 mph speed limit on all highways. If states failed to enforce this limit, they risked losing millions of dollars in highway funds (*Newsweek,* 15 July 1985). Suppose that states were judged to be in violation of the law if at least 50% of all motorists exceeded the posted

speed limit or if the average speed exceeded 55 mph. In order to determine whether a state was properly enforcing the law, 500 cars, selected at random, were clocked on radar; the car speeds were as summarized in the accompanying table.

Car Speeds	Frequency
Less than 43	0
43 up to but not including 47	17
47 up to but not including 51	63
51 up to but not including 55	154
55 up to but not including 59	182
59 up to but not including 63	47
63 up to but not including 67	24
67 up to but not including 71	13
More than 71	0

Can we conclude at the 5% significance level that this state was violating the law?

MKT **18.6** In the door-to-door selling of vacuum cleaners, various factors influence sales. The Birk Vacuum Cleaner Company considers its sales pitch and overall package to be extremely important. As a result, it often thinks of new ways to sell its product. Because the company's management dreams up so many new sales pitches each year, there is a two-stage testing process. In stage 1, a new plan is tested with a relatively small sample. If there is sufficient evidence that the plan increases sales, a second, considerably larger test is undertaken. The statistical test is performed so that there is only a 1% chance of concluding that the new pitch is successful in increasing sales when it actually does not increase sales. In a stage-1 test to determine if the inclusion of a "free" 10-year service contract increases sales, 10 sales representatives were selected at random from the company's list of several thousand. The monthly sales of these representatives were recorded for 1 month prior to use of the new sales pitch and for 1 month after its introduction. The results are shown in the accompanying table.

Sales Representative	Sales Before New Sales Pitch	Sales After New Sales Pitch
1	15	20
2	27	29
3	22	24
4	19	22
5	28	27
6	11	15
7	32	31
8	25	25
9	15	19
10	17	21

a. If the sales are normally distributed, should the company proceed to stage 2?

b. If the sales are not normally distributed, should the company proceed to stage 2?

MKT **18.7** In the spring of 1985, the Coca-Cola Company changed the recipe of its product, first introduced in 1886. As might be expected, this change is being carefully monitored by market surveys. Prior to the recipe change, the A. C. Nielsen Company of Canada surveyed soft-drink consumers and found the following percentages:

Coca-Cola   20.6%
Pepsi-Cola   18.1%

In April/May 1985 (after the recipe change), another survey produced the following results:

Coca-Cola   21.4%
Pepsi-Cola   17.5%

(All of the statistics were reported in the *Toronto Star*, 10 July 1985.) Assuming that both surveys were based on samples of 1,000 consumers, can we conclude at the 5% significance level that the popularity of Coca-Cola has increased?

EDUC **18.8** A small but important part of a university library's budget is the amount collected in fines on overdue books. Last year the library collected $25,652.75 in fine payments; however, the head librarian suspects that some employees are not bothering to collect the fines on overdue books. In an effort to learn more about the situation, she asked a sample of 400 students (out of a total student population of 50,000) how many books they returned late to the library in the previous 12 months. They were also asked how many days overdue the books were. The results indicated that the total number of days overdue ranged from 0 (either no books borrowed or all books returned on time) to 58 days (one student borrowed 10 books, returned 6 on time, but kept the remaining 4 books a total of 58 days too long). The average per student was 4.1 days, with a standard deviation of 2.8 days.

a. Estimate with 95% confidence the average number of days overdue for all 50,000 students at the university.

b. If the fine is 25 cents per day, estimate the amount that should be collected annually. Should the librarian conclude that not all the fines were collected?

GEN **18.9** Companies that send us bills naturally seek prompt action and are always seeking methods to induce us to pay quickly. Advertisers and marketing managers who often perform mail surveys are interested in eliciting responses from the people selected to be sampled. An experiment was performed to determine if the enclosure of a mild threat would increase the response rate.* A sample of 600 residents of Cincinnati was randomly selected, and each person selected received a questionnaire. Half of the residents were sent questionnaires that included a casual covering letter requesting action. The other half were sent a questionnaire that included a covering letter implying that, if the questionnaire was not returned by a certain date, the respondent would be called on the telephone and asked to answer the questionnaire. A total of 105 people (out of 300) responded to the threat, while 90 people (out of 300) responded to the casual covering letter. Do these data allow us to conclude that there is a different response rate between the two approaches? (Use $\alpha = .05$.)

MNG **18.10** The image of the U.S. Postal Service has suffered in recent years. One reason may be the perception that postal workers are rude in their

---

* C. J. Dommeyer, "How Does a Threat in the Initial Cover Letter Affect Mail Survey Response?" *Developments in Marketing Science* 6 (1983): 578.

dealings with the public. In an effort to improve its image, the Postal Service is contemplating the introduction of public relations seminars for all of its inside workers. Because of the substantial costs involved, it decided to institute the seminars only if there is at least a 25% reduction in the number of written complaints received by the postmasters about personnel who took the seminars. As a trial the employees of 10 large postal centers attended the seminar. The monthly average number of complaints per center (for all centers) was 640 before the trial. The number of written complaints one month after the trial for the 10 sample centers are shown in the accompanying table.

Postal Center	Number of Written Complaints
1	525
2	386
3	128
4	615
5	319
6	256
7	428
8	388
9	456
10	299

Can we conclude at the 5% significance level that the seminars should be instituted?

MNG **18.11**   Some psychologists believe that there are at least three different personality types: type A is the aggressive workaholic; type B is the relaxed under-achiever; type C displays various characteristics of types A and B. The personnel manager of a large insurance company believes that, among life insurance salespersons, there are equal numbers of all three personality types and that their degree of satisfaction and sales ability are not influenced by personality type. In a survey of 30 randomly selected salespersons, he determined the type of personality, measured their job satisfaction on a 7-point scale (where 1 = Very dissatisfied, and

7 = Very satisfied), and determined the total value of life insurance each sold during the previous year. The results are provided in Table E18.11.

a. Test all three of the personnel manager's beliefs at the 5% level of significance. That is, test to determine whether there is enough evidence to justify concluding that:
   (i) The proportions of each personality type are different.
   (ii) The job satisfaction measures for each personality type are different.
   (iii) The life insurance sales for each personality type are different.

b. State all of the assumptions you made in order to answer each subsection of part (a).

c. How would you perform the test(s) if the assumptions you made turned out not to be satisfied?

EDUC **18.12**   Because of the large number of appli-cations to its graduate school of business, the university admissions officer wants to determine the factors that influence success or failure in the MBA program. The two factors under investiga-tion are the score on the entrance exam (which can range from 200 to 800) and the undergraduate degree. A random sample of 600 students was selected, and from their records the following data were determined: the entrance score result, the undergraduate degree, and whether the student graduated from the MBA program or not. These results are summarized in the two following tables. On the basis of these results, what can you conclude about the value of entrance exam score and type of undergraduate degree as factors in determin-ing success or failure in the MBA program? (Use $\alpha = .01$.)

ENTRANCE EXAM SCORES AND SUCCESS IN THE PROGRAM

	Mean	Standard Deviation
Graduated	579.2	98.2
Did not graduate	537.6	80.9

TABLE E18.11

Salesperson	Personality Type	Job Satisfaction	Total Amount of Life Insurance Sold ($100,000s)
1	B	4	7.5
2	C	5	10.7
3	A	2	9.3
4	B	5	2.3
5	B	5	5.3
6	B	4	2.4
7	C	5	8.1
8	B	4	7.0
9	C	6	18.7
10	B	3	5.6
11	A	3	8.4
12	C	6	6.2
13	B	4	7.2
14	C	5	17.6
15	A	3	9.3
16	C	5	8.1
17	B	2	9.2
18	C	4	4.4
19	A	4	9.8
20	B	3	2.9
21	C	5	13.6
22	B	2	10.4
23	B	3	2.6
24	B	3	2.8
25	C	6	16.1
26	A	1	15.3
27	A	2	14.7
28	C	6	8.1
29	B	4	6.1
30	B	5	6.3

UNDERGRADUATE DEGREE AND SUCCESS
IN THE PROGRAM

	B.A.	B.Sc.	B.Eng.	B.B.A.
Graduated	211	151	68	81
Did not graduate	49	28	8	4

Student	Second Exam Result	First Exam Result
11	928	899
12	1,103	965
13	1,182	1,157
14	1,079	1,025
15	1,165	1,092

EDUC **18.13** The Scholastic Aptitude Test (SAT), which is organized by the Educational Testing Service (ETS), is important to high-school students seeking admission to colleges and universities throughout the United States. There are now a number of companies that offer courses to prepare students for the SAT. The Stanley H. Kaplan Educational Center claims that its students gain an average of 110–150 points by taking its course (*Newsweek,* 12 August 1985). ETS, however, insists that preparatory courses can improve a score by only 30–40 points. (The minimum and maximum scores of the SAT are 400 and 1,600, respectively.) Suppose that a random sample of 15 students wrote the exam, then took the Kaplan preparatory course, and then wrote the exam again. The results are shown in the accompanying table. Do these data provide sufficient evidence at the 5% significance level to refute both the ETS claim and Kaplan's claim?

Student	Second Exam Result	First Exam Result
1	1,289	1,152
2	962	875
3	1,125	1,058
4	1,031	929
5	1,172	1,123
6	829	752
7	1,132	1,058
8	1,522	1,478
9	873	699
10	1,377	1,320

RET **18.14** It is generally believed that salespeople who are paid on a commission basis outperform salespeople who are paid a fixed salary. Some management consultants argue, however, that in certain industries the fixed-salary salesperson may sell more because the consumer will feel less sales pressure and will respond to the salesperson less as an antagonist. In an experiment to study this, a random sample of 15 salespeople from a retail clothing store was selected. Of these, 9 salespeople were paid a fixed salary, and the remaining 6 were paid a commission on each sale. The total dollar amount of one month's sales for each was recorded, and the results are shown in the accompanying table.

a. Can we conclude that the commission salesperson outperforms the fixed-salary salesperson? (Use $\alpha = .05$ and assume that the sales figures are normally distributed.)

b. Estimate the difference in average monthly sales between the two types of salespeople, with 95% confidence.

c. Redo part (a), assuming that the sales are not normally distributed.

MONTHLY SALES ($1,000s)

Fixed Salary	Commission
40.1	37.3
29.6	43.8
33.7	49.6
37.2	25.3
36.0	51.0

(continued)

TABLE E18.15

	Bachelors Degrees			Masters Degrees	Total
	Business	Science	Arts/Music		
Employed	298	11	416	131	856
Unemployed	9	2	37	9	57
Total	307	13	453	140	913

Fixed Salary	Commission
43.5	46.1
39.8	
38.6	
36.3	

EDUC **18.15** Every summer the most recent graduates of Wilfrid Laurier University are surveyed to determine their employment status. The 1989 survey is shown in Table E18.15.

a. Can we conclude at the 5% significance level that the unemployment rate differs among holders of the four types of degrees?

b. Can we conclude at the 5% significance level that the unemployment rate for business graduates is lower than that for the graduates of all the other groups combined?

GEN **18.16** Numerous studies have dealt with various job search methods. A 1975 survey focused attention on the problems of job searching in a rural setting.* In this project, 367 heads of households indicated that they had been job-seekers in the previous 12 months. The purpose of the study was to examine the effectiveness of different methods of job seeking. The methods considered are as follows:

    Direct application to employer (DE)
    Friends and relatives (FR)
    State employment service (ES)
    Other

* B. Rungeling and L. H. Smith, "Job Search in Rural Labor Markets," *Proceedings of the Twenty-eighth Annual Winter Meeting of the Industrial Relations Research Association*, pp. 120–28.

To eliminate other factors from the comparison, the following multiple regression equation was estimated:

$$Job = \beta_0 + \beta_1 DE + \beta_2 FR + \beta_3 ES$$
$$+ \beta_4 SEX + \beta_5 ANGLO + \beta_6 BLACK$$
$$+ \beta_7 ED + \beta_8 AGE + \beta_9 TRAIN$$
$$+ \beta_{10} HEALTH + \varepsilon$$

where

JOB = 1 (if job-seeker obtained a job)
    = 0 (if not)

DE = 1 (if job-seeker used DE most)
    = 0 (if not)

FR = 1 (if job-seeker used FR most)
    = 0 (if not)

ES = 1 (if job-seeker used ES most)
    = 0 (if not)

SEX = 1 (if male)
    = 0 (if female)

ANGLO = 1 (if job-seeker is Anglo)
    = 0 (if not)

BLACK = 1 (if job-seeker is Black)
    = 0 (if not)

(The other racial category is Hispanic.)

ED = education of job-seeker (in years)

AGE = age of job-seeker (in years)

TRAIN = 1 (if job-seeker participated in training program)
    = 0 (if not)

HEALTH = 1 (if job-seeker had a health problem)

= 0 (if not)

The results produced by a computer package are summarized in the accompanying table.

Independent Variable	$\hat{\beta}_i$	t-value
Constant	.81	
DE	.12	2.69
FR	.10	1.90
ES	.07	.73
SEX	.19	4.14
ANGLO	−.07	−1.46
BLACK	−.12	−2.53
ED	−.001	−.21
AGE	−.002	−1.54
TRAIN	−.07	−1.50
HEALTH	−.15	−3.42
r^2	.16	
F	6.99	
n	367	

a. Interpret the meaning of each of the $\hat{\beta}_i$ coefficients.

b. Which job search technique was the most effective? Explain.

SCI **18.17** An insurance company that offers dental plans to large companies is seriously reconsidering its premium structure. Currently, the premium paid by each individual is the same throughout the country. The insurance company's executives believe that the incidence of cavities varies among the different parts of the country. If that is the case, the premiums should also vary according to locale. As part of a preliminary study, the company chooses the records of ten 8-year-old children who are covered by the dental plan in each of four different parts of the country. The number of cavities each child had filled during the previous year was recorded and is shown in the accompanying table.

CAVITIES IN CHILDREN GROUPED GEOGRAPHICALLY

East	Central	Midwest	West
0	5	0	3
2	1	1	2
3	3	2	2
6	1	2	0
4	4	1	4
3	4	1	3
2	1	0	2
3	1	1	2
1	2	3	1
2	0	1	3

a. Assuming that the number of cavities is normally distributed, do these data provide sufficient evidence at the 5% level of significance to indicate that there are differences among geographical locations in the number of cavities in children from each?

b. Repeat part (a), assuming that the number of cavities is *not* normally distributed.

MNG **18.18** The executives of a large supermarket chain are considering introducing new electronic machines for checkout counters. These machines read the code of a product and automatically add the price on the cash register. Because the machines are still not perfected, they may occasionally miss an item, forcing the cashier to punch in the price manually. For this reason, the executives are uncertain about adopting the new technology. They decide to try the machines in one store and adopt them for all stores in the chain if it can be shown that checkouts are faster with the machines than without.

As an experiment, the new device is installed at one of the counters, and the service times for 100 customers are recorded at the counter with the new device. Concurrently the service times of 100 customers are recorded at one of the conventional counters. The means and standard deviations (in seconds) are as follows.

Conventional Counter	New Counter
$\bar{x}_1 = 127.2$	$\bar{x}_2 = 121.8$
$s_1 = 22.1$	$s_2 = 19.3$

Is there sufficient evidence at the 5% significance level to establish that the new device should be installed in all stores?

SCI **18.19** It is generally known that second-hand smoke can be detrimental to one's health. As a result, an insurance company that sells life insurance at group rates to large companies is considering offering discounts to companies that have no-smoking policies. In order to help make the decision, the records of two companies are examined. Company 1 has had a no-smoking policy for the past five years, while company 2 does not have such a policy. A total of 1,000 men between the ages of 50 and 60 are randomly selected from each company. The number who suffer from lung disease, heart disease, heart and lung disease, and neither heart nor lung disease are recorded. These data are shown in the accompanying table.

	Company 1	Company 2
Lung disease	9	17
Heart disease	18	33
Both diseases	4	6
Neither disease	969	944
Total	1,000	1,000

Do the data provide sufficient evidence to indicate that the no-smoking policy reduces the incidence of heart and lung disease? (Use $\alpha = .01$.)

GEN **18.20** In November 1981, 1,020 people were asked whether they favored or opposed capital punishment for the killing of any innocent person.* The results were categorized according to sex, age, and education. The results are shown in the accompanying table.

---

* *The Gallup Report*, 13 February 1982.

	Favor	Oppose	Don't Know
National	704	235	81
*Sex**			
Men	355	115	30
Women	348	125	47
*Age**			
Young	288	135	27
Middle-age	255	85	30
Senior	146	34	20
*Education**			
Elementary	76	13	11
Secondary	432	132	36
University	160	131	29

* The totals for each of these categories were estimated. The percentages are as reported by Gallup.

Ignoring those who responded "Don't Know," can we reach the following conclusions at the 5% significance level?

a. There are differences between men and women with respect to support of capital punishment.

b. There are differences among the age categories with respect to support of capital punishment.

c. There are differences among the educational categories with respect to support of capital punishment.

ECON **18.21** In a recent Gallup Poll (*Toronto Star*, 14 October 1985), people were asked whether they were satisfied or dissatisfied with their family's income. The responses, categorized by age, appear in the accompanying table.

Age	Satisfied	Dissatisfied
Young	162	91
Middle-age	355	159
Senior	183	53

Is there sufficient evidence at the 1% level of significance to enable us to conclude that differences in satisfaction level exist among the three age groups?

GEN **18.22** In a recent letter to *National Geographic* (169[2], February 1986), a reader accused the publication of bias in its published letters. He pointed out that of the 773 letters published between September 1981 and May 1985, 642 came from the United States, 51 from Canada, 11 from England, and 69 from the rest of the world. The Society responded by noting that 82% of its members live in the United States, 7.3% in Canada, 1.8% in England, and 8.9% in the rest of the world. At the 5% level of significance, can we conclude that the number of letters published from each country does not reflect the fraction of members from each country?

■■■■■■■■ **CASE 18.1*** *COMPARING MBAs AND UNDERGRADUATE ACCOUNTING MAJORS*

ACC In recent years many accounting firms have hired MBAs instead of BAs in accounting. It is generally believed that MBAs are more mature and ambitious, have broader business knowledge and problem-solving skills, and possess superior communication and leadership abilities. On the other hand, MBAs usually have less knowledge of accounting and typically demand higher salaries. They also sometimes have unrealistic expectations with regard to promotions and a reluctance to perform routine, uninteresting tasks.

A research project was organized to examine this issue. The study traced the performance of 56 BAs and 54 MBAs who were hired as entry-level accountants in 1973. Over the next 9 years, the performance of these 110 individuals was measured in terms of advancement, turnover, and salary.

Advancement was measured in three different ways:

1. The number of years it took to advance to four possible staff levels (semi-senior, senior, supervisor, and manager)

2. Advancement compared to the office mean, expressed as the ratio

$$\frac{\text{Time to attain a staff level position}}{\text{Office mean time to attain a staff level position}}$$

3. The percentage of individuals who have attained each of the four staff levels

Table A presents the summaries of the advancement performance measures. Turnover was measured in two ways:

1. The amount of time with the company that originally hired the individual

2. The percentage of individuals still with the same company at the end of the 9-year study

Table B summarizes these results.
Table C presents salary data for the years 1973–1981.
Based on these results, what conclusions can you draw?

---

* Based on A. Wright, "The Comparative Performance of MBAs vs. Undergraduate Accounting Majors in Public Accounting," *Accounting Review* 63(1) (1988): 123–36.

TABLE A   *ADVANCEMENT WITHIN THE FIRM*

	BAs		MBAs	
	Mean	Standard Deviation	Mean	Standard Deviation
Years to achieve staff level				
	($n = 51$)		($n = 45$)	
Semi-senior	1.06	.28	.97	.27
	($n = 36$)		($n = 40$)	
Senior	2.29	.58	2.17	.72
	($n = 19$)		($n = 21$)	
Supervisor	3.89	.70	3.48	.58
	($n = 12$)		($n = 14$)	
Manager	5.67	.81	5.54	.72
*Advancement as compared to firm norm**				
To semi-senior	.93	.24	.90	.28
To senior	1.03	.35	.93	.32
To supervisor	1.14	.29	.97	.20
To manager	.96	.13	.96	.15
Percent of hires achieving staff levels[†]				
Semi-senior	91%		83%	
Senior	64		74	
Supervisor	34		39	
Manager	21		26	

* Mean values represents a ratio of actual time/firm average time. Thus, values over 1.0 indicate that greater time than the firm norm was necessary to reach a certain position.

[†] Percentages relate to the original number of individuals hired in each group.

TABLE B   *STAFF TURNOVER*

	BAs ($n = 56$)		MBAs ($n = 54$)	
	Mean	Standard Deviation	Mean	Standard Deviation
Years with the firm	3.56	2.29	3.76	2.54
Percent of hires still with the firm in 1981	16%		22%	

TABLE C BASE PAY DATA

	BAs			MBAs		
Year	*n*	Mean	Standard Deviation	*n*	Mean	Standard Deviation
1973	56	$11,100	$1,194	54	$12,753	$1,016
1974	46	11,886	1,096	51	13,367	1,259
1975	45	13,650	1,402	46	15,241	1,580
1976	40	15,608	1,725	39	17,174	1,892
1977	29	17,300	2,069	25	19,910	1,966
1978	18	20,283	2,082	17	22,839	2,354
1979	16	23,369	2,871	13	26,762	2,481
1980	11	29,141	2,866	13	31,354	3,098
1981	9	33,556	2,465	12	36,183	2,690

CASE 18.2* *PROFILING THE RETAIL BUSINESS SUCCESS*

We recommend the use of a computer in this case. The data listed below are also stored on the data disk.

[RET]   Students of business administration have often wondered what factors determine the success or failure of a business. A group of retail grocers was selected to help determine whether personal characteristics (age, years of experience, and years of education) and attitudes about the importance of five retailing variables (price, customer service, advertising, store location, and personnel quality) influenced the success of their businesses.

The importance of each of the five retailing variables was measured on a 7-point scale, when 1 = Very important and 7 = Unimportant. The degree of success, measured by percent gross profit margin, was categorized as either high (above 20%) or low (below 20%). These data are shown in the accompanying table. What conclusions can we draw?

---

* Adapted from L. L. Judd, "Owner/Manager's Age and Retailing Experience: Do They Influence Business Strategies and Success?" *Developments in Marketing Science* 6 (1983): 12–16.

GROCERS' PERSONAL CHARACTERISTICS AND ATTITUDES TOWARD RETAILING VARIABLES

Grocer	Gross Profit-Margin Category	Age	Years of Experience	Years of Education	Price	Customer Service	Advertising	Store Location	Personnel Quality
1	L	43	15	11	3	4	6	2	4
2	L	52	12	12	4	5	5	1	6
3	L	30	7	8	4	5	6	2	6
4	L	33	6	11	5	6	6	2	7
5	L	24	2	12	2	4	3	2	5
6	L	41	14	12	1	4	6	1	5
7	L	23	3	10	3	4	6	1	2
8	L	26	5	12	3	5	5	1	5
9	L	60	15	8	5	4	5	2	4
10	L	33	10	12	4	6	3	3	5
11	H	47	16	12	6	3	6	4	5
12	H	23	2	11	6	3	6	3	5
13	H	29	8	11	5	2	7	2	4
14	H	49	25	12	4	1	6	2	4
15	H	28	7	16	3	2	5	1	5
16	H	35	12	12	5	3	4	1	4
17	H	50	22	17	7	4	6	1	3
18	H	27	6	12	5	3	6	2	3
19	H	52	32	11	4	2	5	3	2
20	H	37	10	12	3	2	7	3	2
21	H	20	1	16	3	3	4	2	2
22	H	37	8	12	1	4	3	1	3
23	H	46	23	11	2	3	6	2	1
24	H	21	1	10	4	3	4	1	3
25	H	42	21	11	4	2	3	2	2
26	H	28	7	16	5	2	6	3	5
27	H	33	5	12	4	1	6	4	5
28	H	41	9	12	3	1	5	3	2

━━━━━ **CASE 18.3*** *THE CUSTOMER AND THE SALESMAN*

RET In many retail purchases, the customers' decisions depend to a large extent on the customer–salesman interaction. In a project to examine the effect of customer characteristics on the sales approach employed by salesmen, the salesmen of 19 automobile dealers were studied. Male and female researchers posing as potential customers visited the dealerships a number of times. The researchers visited the dealership under four different conditions:

> Male or female shopper
>
> Casual or formal dress
>
> Morning or evening visit
>
> Shopping for a compact or subcompact car

The following five variables of the sales routine were observed:

1. Salesman introduced himself.
2. Salesman inquired about name and address of shopper.
3. Salesman inquired about type of car desired.
4. Salesman gave his card.
5. Salesman gave brochure.

The frequencies of each combination of condition and sales routine are shown in the accompanying table.

Specify the circumstances under which the sales routines varied.

EFFECT OF CUSTOMER CHARACTERISTICS ON SALES ROUTINE

	Sex		Dress		Time		Size	
	Male	Female	Casual	Formal	Morning	Evening	Compact	Subcompact
Salesman Introduced Himself								
Yes	49	31	41	39	36	44	41	39
No	51	69	59	61	64	56	59	61
Salesman Inquired Name and Address								
Yes	42	23	31	34	21	44	35	30
No	58	77	69	66	79	56	65	70

(continued)

---

* Adapted from M. Etgar, A. K. Jain, and M. K. Agarwal, "Salesmen–Customer Interaction: An Experimental Approach," *Journal of the Academy of Marketing Science* 6(1, 2)(1978): 1–11.

	Sex		Dress		Time		Size	
	Male	Female	Casual	Formal	Morning	Evening	Compact	Subcompact
Salesman Inquired								
Type of Car								
Yes	93	83	90	86	86	90	84	92
No	7	17	10	14	14	10	16	8
Salesman Gave Card								
Yes	62	41	51	52	45	58	57	46
No	38	59	49	48	55	42	43	54
Salesman Gave Brochure								
Yes	48	28	38	38	31	45	38	38
No	52	72	62	62	69	55	62	62

CASE 18.4*   PAST PERFORMANCES OF BOND MANAGERS

We recommend the use of a computer in this case. The data listed below are also stored on the data disk.

FIN   Bond-market investors, like stock-market investors, often choose their investment managers on the basis of the managers' past performance. Kritzman has reported on a statistical analysis performed by the Bell System on its bond managers. The purpose of the analysis was to determine the extent to which a manager's past performance was a good predictor of future performance.

The study involved 32 Bell System bond managers, for each of whom 10 years of data were available. Each manager was assigned a percentile ranking for both the 1972–1976 period and the 1977–1981 period, based on the performance of that manager's bond portfolio relative to the performance of the competition's portfolios. These percentile rankings are shown in the accompanying table.

On the basis of the data presented, what would you conclude about the consistency in performance of the Bell System bond managers?

BOND MANAGER PERCENTILE RANKINGS

Manager	1972–1976	1977–1981	Manager	1972–1976	1977–1981
1	18	75	3	22	41
2	91	59	4	72	97

(continued)

* Adapted from Mark Kritzman, "Can Bond Managers Perform Consistently?" *Journal of Portfolio Management* 9 (1983): 54–56.

Manager	1972–1976	1977–1981	Manager	1972–1976	1977–1981
5	63	9	19	38	13
6	16	3	20	47	6
7	34	34	21	81	63
8	25	56	22	31	50
9	28	69	23	53	19
10	44	44	24	84	99
11	78	28	25	3	22
12	59	94	26	41	38
13	67	16	27	75	66
14	56	88	28	94	81
15	6	47	29	66	31
16	69	84	30	9	72
17	99	25	31	50	78
18	13	91	32	88	53

**CASE 18.5*   DO BANKS DISCRIMINATE AGAINST
WOMEN BUSINESS OWNERS? I**

FIN More and more women are becoming owners of small businesses. However, questions concerning how they are treated by banks and other financial institutions have been raised by women's groups. Banks are particularly important to small businesses, since studies show that bank financing represents about one-quarter of total debt and that for medium businesses the proportion rises to approximately one-half. If women's requests for loans are rejected more frequently than are men's requests or if women must pay higher interest charges than men do, women have cause for complaint. Banks may then be subject to criminal as well as civil suits. To examine this issue, a research project was launched.

The researchers surveyed a total of 3,217 business owners, of which 153 were women. The percentage of women in the sample, 4.8%, compares favorably with other sources that indicate that women own about 5% of established small businesses.

The survey asked several questions to determine the nature of the business, its size, and its age. Additionally, the owners were asked about their experience in

---

* Adapted from A. L. Riding and C. S. Swift, "Giving Credit Where It's Due: Women Business Owners and Canadian Financial Institutions," Carleton University Working Paper Series WPS 89-07, 1989.

dealing with banks. The questions asked in the survey are as follows:

1. Did you ever apply for a loan or a line of credit?
2. If so, was it approved?
3. If it was approved, what interest rate did you get? (How much above the prime rate was your rate?)
   a. For loans?
   b. For lines of credit?
4. Did you require a co-signature by your spouse? (This question was only asked if the owner was married.)

The responses to these questions are summarized in Tables A through C. What do these data disclose about possible gender bias by the banks?

TABLE A   *APPLICATIONS AND APPROVALS OF LOANS AND LINES OF CREDIT*

	Applied for Loan or Line of Credit	**Loan or Line of Credit Not Approved**	**Proportion Requiring Co-signature of Spouse**
Women	123	15	39/83
Men	2,208	210	557/1,804

TABLE B   *INTEREST RATES OF LOANS*

	Number of Owners with Loans	**Interest Rates (points above prime)**	
		Mean	Standard Deviation
Women	65	1.48%	.60%
Men	1,499	1.28	.61

TABLE C   *INTEREST RATES OF LINES OF CREDIT*

	Number of Owners with Lines of Credit	**Interest Rates (points above prime)**	
		Mean	Standard Deviation
Women	84	1.61%	.73%
Men	1,808	1.23	.62

████████████ **CASE 18.6   *DO BANKS DISCRIMINATE AGAINST WOMEN***
                              BUSINESS OWNERS? II

FIN To help explain the apparent discrimination against women documented in Case 18.5, researchers performed further analyses. In the original study, the following pieces of information were gathered for each company:

1. Annual gross sales
2. Age of the firm
3. Form of business: proprietorship, partnership, or corporation

The relationship among these three variables, gender, and loan rates are shown in Tables A through D. What do these results tell you about the alleged discrimination against women by banks?

TABLE A   CORRELATIONS BETWEEN INTEREST RATES AND GROSS SALES AND FIRM AGE

	Gross Sales	**Age of Firm**
Loan interest rate (points above prime) ($n = 1564$)	$-.25$	$-.17$
Line of credit interest rate (points above prime) ($n = 1892$)	$-.29$	$-.16$

TABLE B   ANNUAL GROSS SALES AND FIRM AGE

	Annual Gross Sales ($1,000)		**Age of Firm**	
	Mean	Standard Deviation	Mean	Standard Deviation
Women ($n = 153$)	559	241	9.0	4.48
Men ($n = 3,064$)	1,170	695	12.6	5.32

TABLE C

INTEREST RATES AND FORM OF BUSINESS

	Interest Rates (points above prime)								
	Proprietorships			Partnerships			Corporations		
	n	$\bar{x}$	s	n	$\bar{x}$	s	n	$\bar{x}$	s
Loans	209	1.41	0.65	161	1.10	0.56	1194	1.29	0.59
Lines of credit	258	1.40	0.62	206	1.13	0.63	1428	1.24	0.64

TABLE D

NUMBER OF WOMEN AND MEN WHOSE BUSINESSES ARE PROPRIETORSHIPS, PARTNERSHIPS, OR CORPORATIONS

	Proprietorships	Partnerships	Corporations
Women	47	14	92
Men	521	245	2,298

CASE 18.7*   TAX TREATMENT OF DIVIDENDS

FIN

A controversial issue in finance is whether or not changes in the personal tax rate applied to dividends affect the prices of stocks that pay dividends. One school of thought maintains that an increase in the tax rate will cause stock prices to fall, whereas a decrease in the tax rate will cause prices to rise. The opposing school of thought argues that no stock price change will result from a dividend tax change, because investors are able to shelter dividend income from any such tax.

Chan, Pirie, and Wright have conducted a study to determine what effect changes in the Canadian tax treatment of dividends have had on stock prices. In 1977, the Canadian government announced a reduction in the taxes to be paid on dividends; in 1986, it announced an increase in the taxes on dividends. Because these announcements were made in the evening, after the stock markets were closed, any resulting stock price changes should be observable on the following day.

For the years of 1977 and 1986, the researchers took a sample of common stocks and a sample of preferred stocks from both the Toronto Stock Exchange (TSE) and the New York Stock Exchange (NYSE). Thus, four samples of TSE stocks and four samples of NYSE stocks were selected. The percentage changes in

---

* Adapted from B. Chan, W. Pirie and R. E. Wright, "Changes in Tax Treatment of Dividends in Canada: Some Empirical Evidence of Their Effects on Capital Asset Prices," *Conference Proceedings of the Sixteenth Annual Atlantic Schools of Business Conference* (October 1986).

the prices of these stocks on the day following the tax change announcements were then calculated. The frequencies of the price changes are summarized in Table A. "Under the assumption of the existence of a tax effect, a difference in frequency of negative, zero, and positive price movements between the TSE stocks and NYSE would be expected." This assumes that "under normal circumstances the TSE and NYSE price movements are strongly correlated."

In the second part of the experiment, the stocks in each of the four TSE samples were paired with stocks from the NYSE according to dividend yield (where dividend yield = dividend paid/stock price). The percentage price change in each NYSE stock on the day after an announcement was then subtracted from the percentage price change in the corresponding TSE stock. The means and standard deviations of these differences, together with frequency distribution of the differences, are given in Table B.

Finally, the absolute values of the nonzero differences in percentage price changes (TSE-NYSE) were ranked (from smallest to largest). The sums of the ranks of the positive differences (T^+) and of the negative differences (T^-) are given in Table C.

What conclusions can be drawn concerning the effect of changes in the tax treatment of dividends on stock prices?

TABLE A   *FREQUENCIES OF PRICE CHANGES*

	1977 Common		1977 Preferred	
	TSE	NYSE	TSE	NYSE
Positive	15	76	24	72
Zero	10	25	7	52
Negative	7	27	12	52

	1986 Common		1986 Preferred	
	TSE	NYSE	TSE	NYSE
Positive	25	108	12	184
Zero	15	20	17	51
Negative	39	33	100	77

TABLE B   *DIFFERENCES IN PERCENTAGE PRICE CHANGES (TSE-NYSE)*

1977 Common

Mean difference = 0.0023	s.d. = 0.0280
Interval	Observed Frequency
Less than −.0258	2
−.0258 to .0023	18
.0023 to .0303	8
Greater than .0303	4

1977 Preferred

Mean difference = 0.0055	s.d. = 0.0230
Interval	Observed Frequency
Less than −.0175	5
−.0175 to .0055	19
.0055 to .0.286	14
Greater than .0286	5

1986 Common

Mean difference = 0.0244	s.d. = 0.0429
Interval	Observed Frequency
Less than −.0673	13
−.0673 to −.0244	19
−.0244 to .0186	42
Greater than .0186	5

1986 Preferred

Mean difference = −0.0242	s.d. = 0.0267
Interval	Observed Frequency
Less than −.0509	14
−.0509 to −.0242	47
−.0242 to .0025	54
Greater than .0025	14

TABLE C   *SUMS OF RANKS OF DIFFERENCES IN PERCENTAGE PRICE CHANGES (TSE-NYSE)*

	1977		1986	
	Common	Preferred	Common	Preferred
Number of nonzero differences	26	42	75	128
T^+	194	581	543	584.5
T^-	157	322	2,307	7,671.5

CASE 18.8*   CONTINUING EDUCATION TRENDS

EDUC | North American educational institutions are turning their attention increasingly to the market for adult (or continuing) education, in order to bolster declining enrollments. Cooke and Maronick have reported on the results of a survey conducted by an American community college that was designed to provide information on the profile of people interested in continuing education.

A mail survey was conducted by the college, with questionnaires sent to a random sample of households in a suburban community consisting primarily of single-family homes, with few apartments. The questionnaires were addressed, by name, to the heads of the households. A total of 2,354 usable questionnaires were returned.

Table A provides demographic data for the 2,354 survey respondents and for the entire population residing in the survey area. Table B summarizes the interest in continuing education for each of a number of demographic groups.

a. Does the sample appear to be representative of the population? Attempt to explain any deviation that you find.

b. Draw a profile of the individuals most interested in continuing education.

---

* Adapted from Ernest F. Cooke and Thomas J. Maronick, "Identifying the Customer for Continuing Education," *Developments in Marketing Science* 2 (1979): 261–64.

TABLE A   COMPARISON OF SURVEY AND POPULATION DATA

	Survey*	Actual
Sex		
Male	58.8%	45.8%
Female	41.2	54.2
Age (18 and over)		
18 up to 24	6.8	17.7
24 up to 44	45.8	37.1
44 up to 66	47.4	45.2
Age (25 and over)		
25 up to 44	49.2	45.1
45 up to 66	50.8	54.9
Education		
H.S. or less	32.2	74.7
Some college +	67.8	25.3

* n = 2,354 respondents

TABLE B   INTEREST IN CONTINUING EDUCATION, BY GROUP

	Interest	No Interest
Previous Education (n = 2,156)		
H.S. or less	530	157
Some college	1,246	223
Sex (n = 2,204)		
Male	1,044	252
Female	754	154
Employment Status (n = 2,099)		
Employed (full-time)	1,215	232
Not employed (full-time)	513	139
Age Group (n = 2,240)		
18 up to 24	132	23
24 up to 44	900	141
44 up to 66	797	247

████████████ **CASE 18.9*** *ATTITUDES AND BEHAVIORS IN*
ENERGY CONSERVATION

This case requires the use of a computer. The data are not shown below but are
stored on the data disk.

PG   Since 1973, North Americans have experienced both shortages and surpluses
of gasoline and other petroleum products. It is becoming apparent that the periods
of shortages will increase as the world exhausts its supply of crude oil. In an effort
to postpone that event, governments have been trying to persuade consumers to
reduce their consumption of energy. Both the Canadian and United States governments have launched advertising campaigns for this purpose.

In 1983, Epsilon Management Consultants was given a contract to advise the
government. The specific objectives were:

1. To measure current attitudes toward the energy situation, and to evaluate
   whether attitudes are changing over time

2. To measure the extent to which the public is reducing energy consumption,
   and to determine whether energy-conserving behaviors are increasing

3. To design an advertising strategy that appeals to energy consumers to use less
   gasoline, heating oil, natural gas, and electricity

In March of 1983 and 1984, 1,800 respondents were surveyed in 9 major cities
(200 per city). Results of these surveys were based on telephone interviews, where the
numbers were selected at random. Only the male or female head of the household
was interviewed (the gender of the person to be interviewed was specified on each
questionnaire).

The questionnaires dealt with attitudes and behaviors toward the energy
situation, as well as with several demographic characteristics. A partial set of
questions and specified responses is given in the materials that follow. (The actual
questionnaire used was considerably longer.)

1. I would like you to think about the following issues and tell me how seriously
   you feel each one is affecting us today. Would you say it is very seriously
   affecting us, somewhat seriously, not too seriously, or not at all seriously?

   (a) Energy shortage
   (b) Cost of energy

Very seriously	1
Somewhat seriously	2
Not too seriously	3
Not at all seriously	4

---

* This case is based on the authors' consulting project. The data were gathered by professional marketing firms, and the research was sponsored by the federal government.

2. What about the cost of energy? By about what percentage do you think the cost of gasoline has increased in the last 12 months? (Estimate the percentage to the nearest 5%.)

3. Since the start of the energy situation a few years ago, some people have changed some of the things they do. I will now read to you a list of things people have or have not done to conserve energy. Please tell me "yes" or "no" for each statement as it applies to you.

   (a) Turning down thermostat.
   (b) Turning off lights more often.
   (c) Driving less.
   (d) Using public transportation more.

   Yes   1
   No   2

4. If your home has a thermostat,

   (a) What is its setting during the day?
   (b) What is its setting at night?

5. I am going to read some statements about the energy situation. I would like to know, for each, whether you agree or disagree. Do you agree or disagree?

   (a) The "energy crisis" was a hoax.
   (b) I resent utilities and governments asking me to save more energy.
   (c) The oil companies have profited unfairly from the energy situation.

   Agree   1
   Disagree   2

6. What is your age?

7. Male = 1
   Female = 2

8. How many years of formal education have you completed?

9. What was your household income in the last year (to the nearest $5,000)?

A total of 1,800 respondents were actually surveyed. The data for this case, however, represent the results from 60 respondents in a major city on the United States/Canada border in 1983 and another 60 respondents in 1984. (The "Don't Know" responses have been eliminated.) The results are stored on the data disk using the format below.

Questions for You to Answer

a. To what extent has concern over the energy situation changed between 1983 and 1984?

b. Is the concern over the energy shortage more or less serious than the concern over the cost of energy in 1984?

c. Questions 5a–c were designed to measure respondents' hostility about the energy situation. Can we conclude that hostility has increased or decreased between 1983 and 1984?

d. Based on national data, the percentage increase in the price of gasoline in 1983 was 12.6%. In 1984, the price of gasoline decreased by .2%. Can we conclude that the mean overestimate of the gasoline price increase in 1984 was larger than the mean overestimate in 1983?

e. Do the answers of the respondents in the two surveys indicate that more people are engaging in energy-conserving behaviors in 1983 than in 1984?

f. Is the average thermostat setting higher in 1984 than in 1983?

g. Is it possible to construct a demographic profile (age, sex, education, and income) of those in 1984 who use public transportation more? That is, can we conclude that those who use public transportation more are demographically different from those who don't?

h. Does it appear that respondents who, in 1984, are reducing their energy consumption have higher estimates of the gasoline cost increase than do those who are not reducing their energy consumption?

QUESTIONNAIRE RESPONSES

Year	Respondent	1a	1b	2	3a	3b	3c	3d	4a	4b	5a	5b	5c	6	7	8	9
83	1	2	2	30	1	1	1	2	60	60	1	1	2	37	2	15	40
83	2	1	3	10	1	2	2	1	60	60	1	2	2	25	2	5	20
83	3	1	3	10	1	2	1	2	65	65	1	2	2	61	2	16	40
⋮	⋮	⋮	⋮	⋮	⋮	⋮	⋮	⋮	⋮	⋮	⋮	⋮	⋮	⋮	⋮	⋮	⋮
84	60	1	3	40	1	1	1	1	70	70	1	2	2	60	1	11	20

■■■■■■■■ **CASE 18.10*** *IDENTIFYING DIFFERENCES IN ATTITUDES BETWEEN MALE AND FEMALE ACCOUNTANTS*

This case requires the use of a computer. The data are not shown below but are stored on the data disk.

[ACC]   More women are working today than ever before, and more are going into traditionally male-dominated professions. This is particularly true of the account-

---

* The authors are grateful to Dr. Morton Nelson who supplied the data, which were drawn from a longer survey conducted by M. Nelson, P. Andiappan, and R. Schwartz. Some of the results of this work have been published in "Salaries and Attitudes of CGAs," *CGA Magazine* 19(11) (1985): 29–33, and "CMAs: Gender and Equality," *CMA Magazine* 59(6) (1984): 14–20.

ing profession: the number of women enrolled in and graduating from university accounting programs has increased significantly in the past 5 years. Because it is important for potential employers and future students to know whether female accountants face particular problems, a survey was undertaken. The purpose of the survey was to determine whether male and female accountants differ in education, income, and type of employment. The researchers also wanted to know whether there are gender-based differences in the perception of problems and in the degree of satisfaction with work conditions. Part of the purpose of the study was to examine the validity of the following beliefs:

1. Female accountants' incomes are less than male accountants' incomes.
2. Male accountants are older than female accountants.
3. Female accountants are more educated than male accountants.
4. Female accountants are more likely to be single than are male accountants.
5. Male and female accountants work for different types of organizations.
6. Male and female accountants differ in their assessments of problems in their present positions.
7. Male accountants are more likely to think that their career advancement has been commensurate with their abilities and experience.
8. Female accountants are less satisfied with their salaries, employee benefits, and recognition by supervisor.

The survey involved 159 randomly selected accountants who responded to the accompanying questionnaire. What conclusions can you draw?

1. What is your age?
2. You are:
   1. Male
   2. Female
3. What is your marital status?
   1. Single
   2. Married
   3. Divorced
   4. Separated
   5. Widowed
4. Please indicate your highest level of education:
   1. High school graduate
   2. Community college graduate
   3. Some university (no degree completed)
   4. University degree (bachelor's)
   5. Master's degree

5. Please indicate your annual income from your primary occupation:

    1. Below $18,000
    2. $18,000–21,999
    3. $22,000–25,999
    4. $26,000–29,999
    5. $30,000–33,999
    6. $34,000–37,999
    7. $38,000–41,999
    8. $42,000–45,999
    9. $46,000–49,999
    10. $50,000–53,999
    11. Over $54,000

6. Are you currently employed:

    1. Full-time
    2. Part-time
    3. Unemployed

7. Please indicate the type of organization for which you work in your primary occupation:

    1. Private industry
    2. Public practice
    3. Government
    4. Education
    5. Self-employed
    6. Other

8. Please indicate the extent (using one of the following responses) to which each of the issues below is a problem in your present position.

    1. Very much so
    2. To a large extent
    3. To some extent
    4. To a small extent
    5. Not at all
        a. Inadequate leisure time
        b. Lack of opportunities for advancements
        c. Too much overtime required
        d. Inequitable pay relative to your colleagues

9. Do you think that advancement in your career has been commensurate with your abilities and experience?

    1. Very much so
    2. To a large extent
    3. To some extent
    4. To a small extent
    5. Not at all

10. The following questions relate to your perception of satisfaction or dissatisfaction with the conditions of your work. Based on your experience, please indicate which of the following responses apply to the conditions below:

    1. To a large extent satisfied
    2. Somewhat satisfied
    3. Neutral
    4. Somewhat dissatisfied
    5. To a large extent dissatisfied

       a. Salary
       b. Employee benefits
       c. Recognition of your work by your supervisor

The results are stored on the data disk using the following format.

RESPONSES TO SURVEY QUESTIONS

1	2	3	4	5	6	7	8a	8b	8c	8d	9	10a	10b	10c
38	2	2	4	9	3	5	4	5	5	5	3	3	3	2
32	1	3	4	11	1	2	2	4	5	5	2	4	3	3
23	2	1	4	4	1	1	3	5	3	5	2	2	3	1
⋮	⋮	⋮	⋮	⋮	⋮	⋮	⋮	⋮	⋮	⋮	⋮	⋮	⋮	⋮
34	1	2	4	9	1	1	3	3	5	5	3	4	5	1

APPLICATIONS

Part One of this book dealt with the foundation for statistical inference, which was developed in Part Two. In this part of the book we discuss several techniques that in some ways are different from the methods presented earlier. The development of the techniques of statistical inference followed a pattern first seen in Chapter 7. In the parametric methods we started by identifying a parameter of interest, that parameter's best estimator, and the estimator's sampling distribution. The sampling distribution was then used to develop the confidence interval estimator and test statistic. Although in the nonparametric statistics chapter (Chapter 14) we did not deal with a specific parameter and its estimator, the sampling distribution of the test statistic was at the center of the technique. In the three chapters of Part Three, that pattern is not followed. Chapter 19 discusses forecasting time series, which shares the goals of Chapters 15, 16, and 17, but the technique and circumstances are different. In Chapter 20 we present index numbers, which are used to measure how variables change over time. Index numbers are used primarily as descriptive measurements with little or no inference. Finally, the concepts and processes of decision theory are presented in Chapter 21.

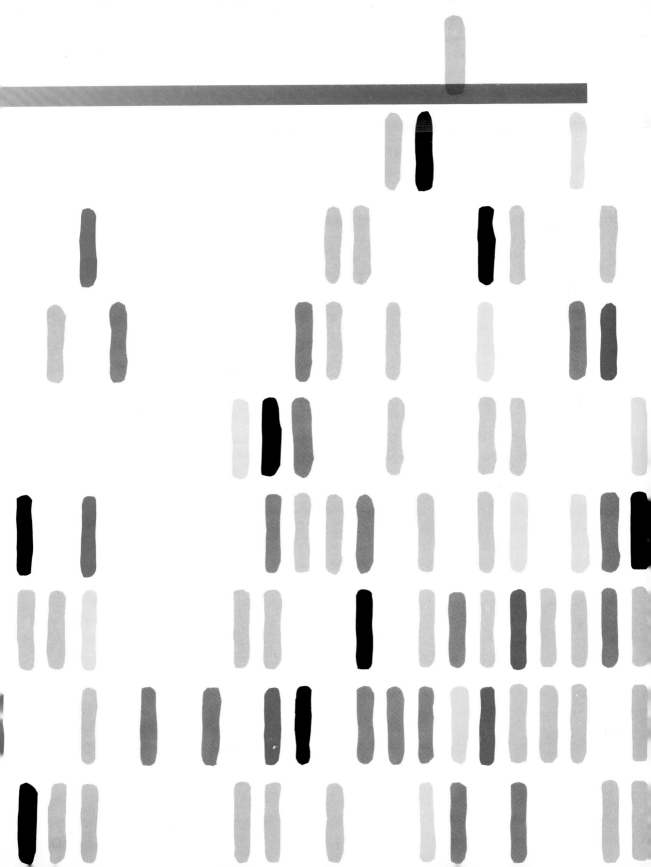

TIME SERIES ANALYSIS AND FORECASTING

INTRODUCTION

Any variable that is measured over time in sequential order is called a **time series**. Our objective in this chapter is to analyze time series to detect patterns that will enable us to forecast the future value of the time series. There is almost an unlimited number of such applications in management and economics. For example:

1. Governments want to know future values of interest rates, unemployment rates, and percentage increases in the cost of living.
2. Housing industry economists must forecast mortgage interest rates, demand for housing, and the cost of building materials.
3. Many companies attempt to predict the demand for their product and their share of the market.
4. Universities and colleges often try to forecast the number of students who will be applying to be accepted at post-secondary-school institutions.

There are many different forecasting techniques. Some are based on developing a model that attempts to analyze the relationship between a dependent variable and one or more independent variables. We presented some of these methods in the chapters on regression analysis (Chapters 15 through 17). The forecasting methods to be discussed in this chapter are all based on time series analysis. The first step is to analyze the components of a time series, which we discuss in the next section. In Sections 19.3 through 19.6, we deal with methods for detecting and measuring which components exist. Once we uncover this information, we can develop forecasting tools. We will only scratch the surface of this topic. Our objective is to expose you to the concepts of forecasting and to introduce some of the simpler techniques. The level of this textbook precludes us from investigating the more complicated methods.

COMPONENTS OF A TIME SERIES

A time series may consist of four different components.

Components of a Time Series

1. Long-term trend (T)
2. Cyclical effect (C)
3. Seasonal effect (S)
4. Random variation (R)

FIGURE 19.1   *POPULATION OF THE UNITED STATES: 1948–1988*

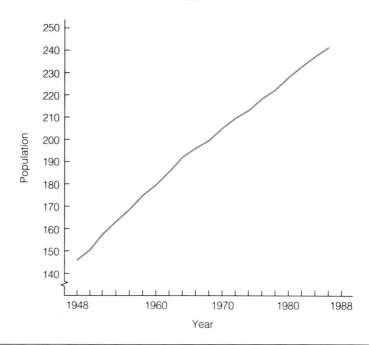

Source: *Statistical Abstract of the United States.*

FIGURE 19.2   *U.S. BEER CONSUMPTION PER PERSON OVER 20*

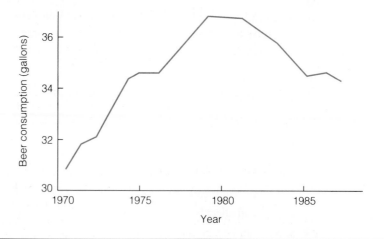

Source: *Standard and Poor's Industry Surveys.*

FIGURE 19.3    *CYCLICAL VARIATION IN A TIME SERIES*

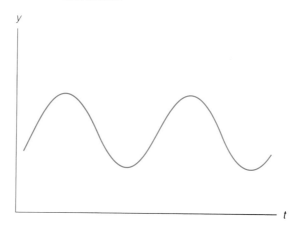

A **trend** (also known as a *secular trend*) is a long-term, relatively smooth pattern or direction that the series exhibits. Its duration is more than 1 year. For example, the population of the United States during the past 40 years has exhibited a trend of relatively steady growth from 147 million in 1948 to 246 million in 1988. (See Figure 19.1.)

The trend of a time series is not always linear. For example, Figure 19.2 describes U.S. beer consumption per person (over 20) from 1970 to 1987. As you can see, such consumption grew between 1970 and 1980, then leveled off, and for the last 5 years decreased. In Section 19.4 we will discuss a model that fits this type of time series quite well.

A **cycle** is a wavelike pattern about a long-term trend that is generally apparent over a number of years. By definition, it has a duration of more than 1 year. Examples of cycles include the well-known business cycles that record periods of economic recession and inflation, long-term product-demand cycles, and cycles in the monetary and financial sectors.

Figure 19.3 displays a series of regular cycles. Unfortunately, in practice, cycles are seldom regular and often appear together with other components. The percentage change in U.S. domestic imports between 1970 and 1986 is depicted in Figure 19.4. There appear to be three irregular cycles and a long-term decrease in this time series.

Seasonal variations are like cycles, but they occur over short repetitive calender periods and, by definition, have durations of less than 1 year. The term *seasonal variation* may refer to the four traditional seasons or to systematic patterns that occur during the period of 1 week or even over the course of 1 day. Stock-market prices, for example, often show highs and lows at particular times during the day.

FIGURE 19.4   *PERCENTAGE CHANGE IN U.S. DOMESTIC IMPORTS*

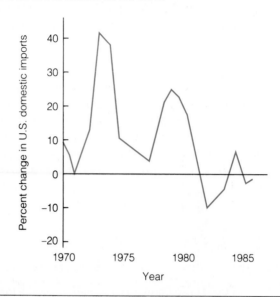

SOURCE: *Statistical Abstract of the United States.*

FIGURE 19.5   *TRAFFIC VOLUME IN BILLIONS OF MILES*

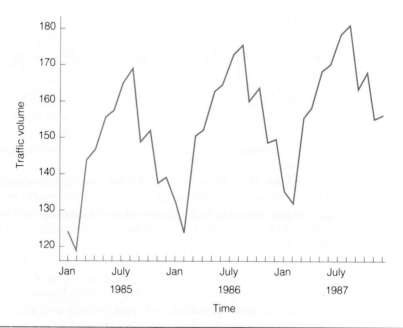

SOURCE: *Standard and Poor's Industry Surveys.*

An illustration of seasonal variation is provided in Figure 19.5, which graphs monthly U.S. traffic volume (in billions of miles). It is obvious from the graph that Americans drive more during the summer months than during the winter.

Random variation comprises the irregular changes in a time series that are not caused by any other component. It tends to hide the existence of the other, more predictable components. Because it exists in almost all time series, one of the functions of this chapter is to present ways to remove the random variation, thereby allowing us to describe and measure the other components and, ultimately, to make accurate forecasts. If you examine Figures 19.1, 19.2, 19.4, and 19.5 you will detect some degree of random variation; because of it, even if we knew precisely about the other components we would not be able to predict the time series with 100% confidence. If you've learned anything from the previous 18 chapters in this book, you will recognize that this is not something new. Statisticians must always live with this fact.

TIME SERIES MODELS

The time series model is generally expressed either as an **additive** model, where the value of the time series at time t is specified as

$$y_t = T_t + C_t + S_t + R_t$$

or as a **multiplicative** model, where the value of the time series at time t is specified as

$$y_t = T_t \cdot C_t \cdot S_t \cdot R_t$$

Both models may be equally acceptable. However, it is frequently easier to understand the techniques associated with time series analysis if we refer to the multiplicative model.

In the next four sections, we will present ways of determining which components are present in the time series.

SECTION 19.3   ## SMOOTHING TECHNIQUES

If we can determine which components actually exist in a time series, we can develop a better forecast. Unfortunately, the existence of the random variation component often hides the other components. One of the simplest ways of removing the random fluctuation is to smooth the time series. In this section we will describe two methods of doing this: *moving averages* and *exponential smoothing*.

MOVING AVERAGES

A *moving average* for a time period is the simple arithmetic average of the values in that time period and those close to it. For example, to compute the three-period moving average for any time period, we would sum the value of the time series in that time period, the value in the previous time period, and the value in the following time period and divide by 3. We calculate the three-period moving average for all time periods except the first and the last. To compute the five-period moving average, we average the value in that time period, the values in the two previous time periods, and the values in the two following time periods. We can choose any number of periods with which to calculate the moving averages.

EXAMPLE 19.1*

As part of an effort to forecast future gasoline sales, an operator of five independent gas stations recorded the quarterly gasoline sales (in 1,000s of gallons) for the past 4 years. These are shown in the accompanying table. Calculate the 3-quarter and 5-quarter moving averages. Then graph the quarterly sales and the moving averages.

QUARTERLY REGIONAL GASOLINE SALES

Time Period	Year	Quarter	Gasoline Sales (1,000s of gallons)
1	1	1	39
2		2	37
3		3	61
4		4	58
5	2	1	18
6		2	56
7		3	82
8		4	27
9	3	1	41
10		2	69
11		3	49
12		4	66
13	4	1	54
14		2	42
15		3	90
16		4	66

---

* In Appendix 19.A we describe the Minitab commands that produce the moving averages for this example.

Solution.   To compute the 3-quarter moving averages, we group the gasoline sales in periods 1, 2, and 3, and then we average them. Thus, the first moving average is

$$\frac{39 + 37 + 61}{3} = \frac{137}{3} = 45.7$$

The second moving average is calculated by dropping the first period's sales (39), adding the fourth period's sales (58), and then computing the new average. Thus, the second moving average is

$$\frac{37 + 61 + 58}{3} = \frac{156}{3} = 52.0$$

The process continues as shown in the following table. Similar calculations are used to produce the 5-quarter moving averages (also shown in the table).

Time Period	Gasoline Sales	3-Quarter Moving Average	5-Quarter Moving Average
1	39	—	—
2	37	45.7	—
3	61	52.0	42.6
4	58	45.7	46.0
5	18	44.0	55.0
6	56	52.0	48.2
7	82	55.0	44.8
8	27	50.0	55.0
9	41	45.7	53.6
10	69	53.0	50.4
11	49	61.3	55.8
12	66	56.3	56.0
13	54	54.0	60.2
14	42	62.0	63.6
15	90	66.0	—
16	66	—	—

Notice that we place the moving averages in the center of the group of values that are being averaged. It is for this reason that we prefer to use an odd number of periods in the moving averages. Later in this section we will discuss how to deal with an even number of periods.

To see how the moving averages remove some of the random variation, examine Figures 19.6 and 19.7. Figure 19.6 depicts the quarterly gasoline sales. It is difficult to discern any of the time series components because of the large amount of random variation. Now consider the 3-quarter moving average in Figure 19.7. You should be able to detect the seasonal pattern that exhibits peaks in the third quarter

FIGURE 19.6   *QUARTERLY GASOLINE SALES*

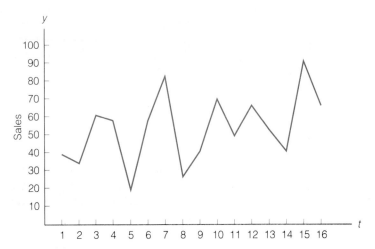

FIGURE 19.7   *QUARTERLY GASOLINE SALES AND THE 3-QUARTER AND 5-QUARTER MOVING AVERAGES*

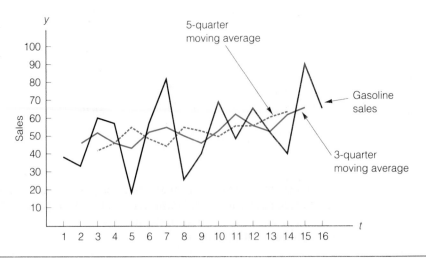

of each year (periods 3, 7, 11, and 15) and valleys in the first quarter of the year (periods 5, 9, and 13). There is also a small but discernible long-term trend of increasing sales.

Notice also in Figure 19.7 that the 5-quarter moving average produces more smoothing than the 3-quarter moving average. In general, the longer the time period over which we average, the smoother the series becomes. Unfortunately, in this case we've smoothed too much, since the seasonal pattern is no longer apparent in the 5-quarter moving average. All that we can see is the long-term trend. It is important to realize that our objective is to smooth the time series sufficiently to remove the random variation and to reveal the other components (trend, cycle, and/or season) present. With too little smoothing, the random variation disguises the real pattern. With too much smoothing, however, some or all of the other effects may be eliminated along with the random variation.

CENTERED MOVING AVERAGE

If we decide to use an even number of periods to calculate the moving averages, we have a problem about where to place the moving averages in a graph. For example, suppose that we calculate the four-period moving average of the following data.

Period	Time Series
1	15
2	27
3	20
4	14
5	25
6	11

The first moving average is

$$\frac{15 + 27 + 20 + 14}{4} = \frac{76}{4} = 19.0$$

However, since this value represents time periods 1, 2, 3, and 4, we must place this value between periods 2 and 3. The next moving average is

$$\frac{27 + 20 + 14 + 25}{4} = \frac{86}{4} = 21.5$$

and it must be placed between periods 3 and 4. The moving average that falls between periods 4 and 5 is

$$\frac{20 + 14 + 25 + 11}{4} = \frac{70}{4} = 17.5$$

Having the moving averages fall between the time periods causes various problems, including the difficulty of graphing. Centering the moving averages corrects the problem. This is performed by computing the two-period moving average of the moving averages. Thus, the centered moving average for period 3 is

$$\frac{19.0 + 21.5}{2} = 20.25$$

The centered moving average for period 4 is

$$\frac{21.5 + 17.5}{2} = 19.5$$

The following table summarizes our results.

Period	Time Series	Four-Period Moving Average	Four-Period Centered Moving Average
1	15		—
2	27	—	—
		19.0	
3	20		20.25
		21.5	
4	14		19.50
		17.5	
5	25		—
		—	
6	11		—

Because of the extra computation involved in centering a moving average, we prefer to use an odd number of periods. However, in some situations we're required to use an even number of periods. Such cases are discussed in Section 19.6.

EXPONENTIAL SMOOTHING

Two drawbacks are associated with the moving average method of smoothing time series. First, we do not have moving averages for the first and last sets of time periods. If the time series has few observations, the missing values can represent an important loss of information. Second, the moving average "forgets" most of the previous time series values. For example in the 5-month moving average described in Example 19.1, the average for month 4 reflects months 2, 3, 4, 5, and 6 but is not affected by month 1. Similarly the moving average for month 5 forgets months 1 and 2. Both of these problems are addressed by **exponential smoothing.**

The exponentially smoothed time series is defined as follows.

Exponentially Smoothed Time Series

$$S_t = wy_t + (1 - w)S_{t-1} \qquad \text{for } t \geq 2$$

where

$S_t = $ Exponentially smoothed time series at time t

$y_t = $ Time series at time t

$S_{t-1} = $ Exponentially smoothed time series at time $t - 1$

$w = $ Smoothing constant, where $0 \leq w \leq 1$

We begin by setting

$$S_1 = y_1$$

Then

$$S_2 = wy_2 + (1 - w)S_1$$
$$= wy_2 + (1 - w)y_1$$
$$S_3 = wy_3 + (1 - w)S_2$$
$$= wy_3 + (1 - w)[wy_2 + (1 - w)y_1]$$
$$= wy_3 + w(1 - w)y_2 + (1 - w)^2 y_1$$

and so on. In general we have

$$S_t = wy_t + w(1 - w)y_{t-1} + w(1 - w)^2 y_{t-2} + \cdots + (1 - w)^{t-1}y_1$$

This formula states that the smoothed time series in period t depends on all of the previous observations of the time series.

The smoothing constant w is chosen on the basis of how much smoothing is required. A small value of w produces a great deal of smoothing. A large value of w results in very little smoothing. Figure 19.8 depicts a time series and two exponentially smoothed series with $w = .1$ and $w = .5$.

EXAMPLE 19.2

Apply the exponential smoothing technique with $w = .2$ and $w = .7$ to the data in Example 19.1, and graph the results.

Solution.   The exponentially smoothed values are calculated from the formula

$$S_t = wy_t + (1 - w)S_{t-1}$$

FIGURE 19.8   *ORIGINAL TIME SERIES AND TWO EXPONENTIALLY SMOOTHED SERIES*

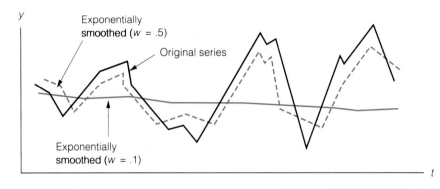

The results with $w = .2$ and $w = .7$ are shown in the following table.

Time Period	Gasoline Sales	Exponentially Smoothed Sales (with $w = .2$)	Exponentially Smoothed Sales (with $w = .7$)
1	39	39	39
2	37	38.6	37.6
3	61	43.1	54.0
4	58	46.1	56.8
5	18	40.5	29.6
6	56	43.6	48.1
7	82	51.2	71.8
8	27	46.4	40.4
9	41	45.3	40.8
10	69	50.1	60.6
11	49	49.8	52.5
12	66	53.1	61.9
13	54	53.3	56.4
14	42	51.0	46.3
15	90	58.8	76.9
16	66	60.2	69.3

Figure 19.9 depicts the graph of the original time series and the exponentially smoothed series. As you can see, $w = .7$ results in very little smoothing, while $w = .2$

FIGURE 19.9   QUARTERLY GASOLINE SALES AND EXPONENTIALLY SMOOTHED SALES
WITH w = .2 AND w = .7

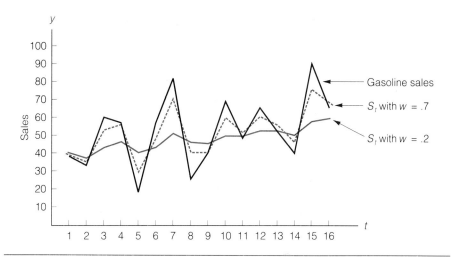

results in perhaps too much smoothing. In both smoothed time series it is difficult to discern the seasonal pattern that we detected by using moving averages. A different value of w (perhaps $w = .5$) would likely produce more satisfactory results.

Moving averages and exponential smoothing are relatively crude methods of removing the random variation in order to discover the existence of other components. In the next three sections, we will attempt to measure the components more precisely.

EXERCISES

LEARNING THE TECHNIQUES

19.1 For the following time series, compute the three-period moving averages.

Period t	y	Period t	y
1	48	7	43
2	41	8	52
3	37	9	60
4	32	10	48
5	36	11	41
6	31	12	30

19.2 For Exercise 19.1, compute the five-period moving averages.

19.3 For Exercises 19.1 and 19.2, graph the time series and the two moving averages.

19.4 Compute the four-period centered moving averages for the following time series.

Period t	y
1	44
2	42
3	49

(continued)

Period *t*	*y*
4	56
5	66
6	62
7	63
8	49

19.5 Apply exponential smoothing with $w = .1$ to help detect the components of the following time series.

Period *t*	*y*
1	12
2	18
3	16
4	24
5	17
6	16
7	25
8	21
9	23
10	14

19.6 Repeat Exercise 19.5, with $w = .8$.

19.7 For Exercises 19.5 and 19.6, draw the time series and the two sets of exponentially smoothed values. Does there appear to be a trend component in the time series?

APPLYING THE TECHNIQUES

Self-Correcting Exercise (See Appendix 19.B for the solution.)

RET **19.8** The following daily sales figures have been recorded in a medium-sized merchandising firm.

	Week 1	Week 2	Week 3	Week 4
Monday	43	51	40	64
Tuesday	45	41	57	58
Wednesday	22	37	30	33
Thursday	25	22	33	38
Friday	31	25	37	25

a. Plot the series on a graph.

b. Use a 3-day moving average, and superimpose it on the same graph.

c. Does there appear to be a seasonal (weekly) pattern?

RET **19.9** For Exercise 19.8, compute the 5-day moving averages, and superimpose these on the same graph. Does this help you answer part (c)?

RET **19.10** The quarterly sales of a department store chain were recorded for the past 4 years. These figures are shown in the accompanying table.

a. Graph the time series.

b. Calculate the 4-quarter centered moving averages, and superimpose those on the time series graph.

c. What can you conclude from your time series smoothing?

Year	Quarter	Sales ($millions)
1986	1	18
	2	33
	3	25
	4	41
1987	1	22
	2	20
	3	36
	4	33
1988	1	27
	2	38
	3	44
	4	52
1989	1	31
	2	26
	3	29
	4	45

RET **19.11** Repeat Exercise 19.10, using exponential smoothing with $w = .4$.

SECTION 19.4   *TREND ANALYSIS*

In the previous section we described how smoothing a time series can give us a clearer picture of which components are present. In order to forecast, however, we often need more precise measurements about trend, cyclical effects, and seasonal effects. In this section we will discuss methods that allow us to describe trend. In subsequent sections we will consider how to measure the cyclical and seasonal effects.

As we pointed out before, a trend can be linear or nonlinear and, indeed, can take on a whole host of other functional forms—some of which we will discuss. The easiest way of isolating the long-term trend is by regression analysis, where the independent variable is time. If we believe that the long-term trend is essentially linear, we will use the following model.

Linear Model for Long-Term Trend

$$y = \beta_1 + \beta_1 t + \varepsilon$$

where t is the time period.

Although various nonlinear models are available, we will only consider the following two.

As described in Chapter 17, if we think that the time series is nonlinear with one change in slope, the polynomial model may be best.

Polynomial Model for Long-Term Trend

$$y = \beta_0 + \beta_1 t + \beta_2 t^2 + \varepsilon$$

Figure 19.10 depicts one form of the polynomial model. This may apply, for example, to a new product that has experienced a rapid early growth rate followed by the inevitable leveling off.

The logarithmic or exponential model described next (and in Figure 19.11) can be used to depict time series that show growth with no sign of leveling off.

Logarithmic Model for Long-Term Trend

$$y = \beta_0(\beta_1)^t \varepsilon$$

which can be converted to the following form to allow us to use regression analysis:

$$\log y = \log \beta_0 + (\log \beta_1)t + \log \varepsilon$$

Expressed more simply, this equation becomes

$$y' = \beta'_0 + \beta'_1 t + \varepsilon'$$

FIGURE 19.10   *POLYNOMIAL MODEL*

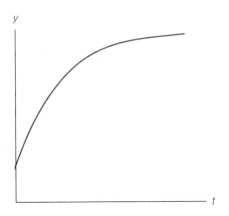

FIGURE 19.11   *LOGARITHMIC MODEL*

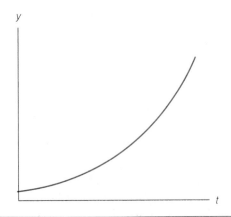

You may use the common logarithm (base 10) or the natural logarithm (base *e*). In our analyses, we use the natural logarithm. Examples 9.3, 9.4, and 9.5 illustrate how and when the models are used.

EXAMPLE 19.3

Annual sales (in millions of dollars) for a pharmaceutical company have been recorded for the past 10 years. These data are shown in the accompanying table. The management of the company believes that the trend over this period is basically linear. Use regression analysis to measure the trend.

Year	Sales ($millions)
1980	18.0
1981	19.4
1982	18.0
1983	19.9
1984	19.3
1985	21.1
1986	23.5
1987	23.2
1988	20.4
1989	24.4

Solution.   It is easier (though not necessary) to change the times from years 1980 to 1989 to time periods 1 through 10. When that was done, the SAS software package was used to estimate the model.

SAS COMPUTER OUTPUT FOR EXAMPLE 19.3

Dependent Variable: SALES

Analysis of Variance

Source	DF	Sum of Squares	Mean Square	F Value	Prob > F
Model	1	32.27345	32.27345	17.657	0.0030
Error	8	14.62255	1.82782		
C Total	9	46.89600			

Root MSE	1.35197	R-square	0.6882	
Dep Mean	20.72000	Adj R-sq	0.6492	
C.V.	6.52494			

Parameter Estimates

Variable	DF	Parameter Estimate	Standard Error	T for H0: Parameter=0	Prob > |T|
INTERCEP	1	17.28000	0.92357	18.710	0.0001
TIME	1	0.62545	0.14884	4.202	0.0030

The fit of the line is relatively good with $r^2 = 68.8\%$. It is important to realize that, because of the possible presence of cyclical and seasonal effects and because of random variation, we do not usually expect a very good fit. Remember, we're only measuring the trend in this analysis and not any other components.

FIGURE 19.12   *TIME SERIES AND TREND LINE FOR EXAMPLE 19.3*

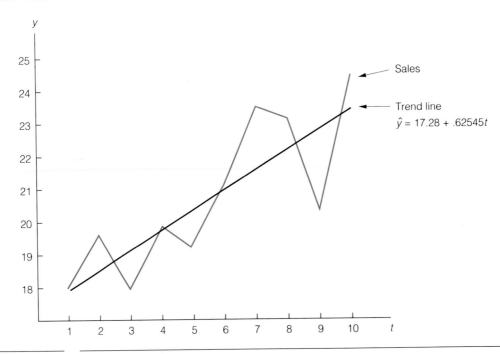

The time series is shown graphically in Figure 19.12. The regression trend line that we just estimated is superimposed on the graph, showing a clear upward trend to the right.

One of the purposes of isolating the trend, as we suggested before, is to use it for forecasting. For example, we could use it for forecasting 1 year in advance—through 1990 ($t = 11$). From our trend equation, we get

$$y = 17.28 + .62545t = 17.28 + .62545(11) = 24.15995$$

This value, however, represents the forecast based only on trend. If we believe that a cyclical pattern also exists, we should incorporate that into the forecast as well.

EXAMPLE 19.4

Americans are among the world's greatest consumers of beef. In the last decade, however, because of health concerns, many Americans have either decreased their consumption of beef or eliminated beef from their diets. The effect has been serious for farmers and processors of meat products. To help analyze the problem, the civilian per capita consumption of beef in the United States has been recorded for the period 1960–1982. These data are shown in the accompanying table. To help forecast future consumption of beef, apply regression analysis to determine the trend. A graph of the data suggests that a polynomial model might be best.

Year	t	Annual Civilian per Capita Consumption of Beef (pounds) y_t
1960	1	85.0
1961	2	87.8
1962	3	88.8
1963	4	94.3
1964	5	99.8
1965	6	99.5
1966	7	104.0
1967	8	106.2
1968	9	109.7
1969	10	110.8
1970	11	113.5
1971	12	113.0
1972	13	116.1
1973	14	109.6
1974	15	116.8
1975	16	118.8
1976	17	127.6
1977	18	123.9
1978	19	117.9
1979	20	105.5
1980	21	103.4
1981	22	104.3
1982	23	104.4

SOURCE: *Statistical Abstract of the United States.*

Solution.   The model

$$y = \beta_0 + \beta_1 t + \beta_2 t^2 + \varepsilon$$

was estimated, using the SAS statistical system, with the following results.

SAS COMPUTER OUTPUT

```
Dependent Variable: CONSUME
                           Analysis of Variance
                     Sum of           Mean
   Source     DF     Squares         Square      F Value     Prob > F
   Model       2   2322.34815     1161.17408      54.848      0.0001
   Error      20    423.41793       21.17090
   C Total    22   2745.76609


   Root MSE        4.60118     R-square    0.8458
   Dep Mean      106.98696     Adj R-sq    0.8304
   C.V.            4.30070


                              Parameter Estimates
                     Parameter    Standard     T for H0:
   Variable    DF    Estimate        Error    Parameter=0     Prob > |T|
   INTERCEP     1    75.92914      3.14802         24.120      0.0001
   TIME         1     5.48025      0.60431          9.068      0.0001
   TIME2        1    -0.18460      0.02444         -7.551      0.0001
```

FIGURE 19.13   *TIME SERIES AND POLYNOMIAL TREND FOR EXAMPLE 19.4*

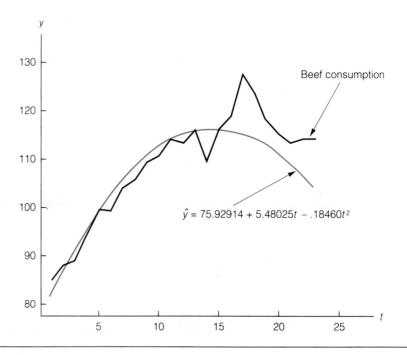

All of the statistics (r^2, F, t-values) indicate that the polynomial model fits the data quite well. Thus, the trend is measured by

$$\hat{y} = 75.92914 + 5.48025t - .18460t^2$$

To forecast the per capita beef consumption for 1983, we use the regression equation with $t = 24$. Thus,

$$\hat{y} = 75.92914 + 5.48025(24) - .18460(24^2) = 101.1$$

The actual 1983 per capita beef consumption turned out to be 106.4. Figure 19.13 describes the time series and the trend line for this example.

EXAMPLE 19.5

The AIDS epidemic in the United States is of great concern to the entire society. Among its many consequences are the effects it has and will have on the life and health insurance industry. If possible, insurance statisticians would like to forecast the number of AIDS cases. To assist in this project, the number of estimated cases in the United States during the period 1981–1989 was recorded. These data are listed in the accompanying table. Because of the rapid growth in estimated cases over this period of time, a logarithmic model is suggested. Use regression analysis to find the logarithmic trend line.

Year	Time Period t	Number of Estimated AIDS Cases y_t (rounded to the nearest 1,000)
1981	1	1
1982	2	6
1983	3	10
1984	4	14
1985	5	25
1986	6	48
1987	7	63
1988	8	108
1989	9	161

SOURCE: *Standard and Poor's Industry Surveys.* (The data are interpreted from a graph.)

Solution.   The proposed model is

$$y = \beta_0 \beta_1^t \varepsilon$$

which can also be represented as

$$\log y = \log \beta_0 + (\log \beta_1)t + \log \varepsilon$$

or

$$y' + \beta'_0 + \beta'_1 t + \varepsilon'$$

To estimate the coefficients, we calculate log y for each year, as shown in the following table.

t	y	$y' = \log y$
1	1	0
2	6	1.792
3	10	2.303
4	14	2.639
5	25	3.219
6	48	3.871
7	63	4.143
8	108	4.682
9	161	5.081

From the computer output that follows, we find the coefficients of the trend line.

$$\hat{\beta}'_0 = .255$$
$$\hat{\beta}'_1 = .561$$

Thus, one form of the model is

$$\hat{y}' = .255 + .561t$$

Since

$$\beta'_0 = \log \hat{\beta}_0$$

and

$$\hat{\beta}'_1 = \log \hat{\beta}_1$$

it follows that

$$\hat{\beta}_0 = e^{\beta'_0} = (2.718)^{.255} = 1.29$$

and

$$\hat{\beta}_1 = e^{\beta'_1} = (2.718)^{.561} = 1.75$$

The trend line expressed in the model's original form is

$$\hat{y} = (1.29)(1.75)^t$$

The values of r^2 and the t-statistics indicate that the logarithmic model fits well. Figure 19.14 confirms this assessment. The forecasted figure for 1990 ($t = 10$) is

$$\hat{y} = 1.29(1.75)^{10} = 347.5$$

MINITAB COMPUTER OUTPUT

```
The regression equation is

Y=0.255+0.561TIME

Predictor      Coef       Stdev      t-ratio
Constant      0.2553     0.2916        0.88
TIME          0.56517    0.05182      10.91

s=0.4014    R-sq=94.4%    R-sq(adj)=93.6%

Analysis of Variance

SOURCE          DF        SS         MS
Regression       1     19.165     19.165
Error            7      1.128      0.161
Total            8     20.293
```

FIGURE 19.14   TIME SERIES AND LOGARITHMIC TREND FOR EXAMPLE 19.5

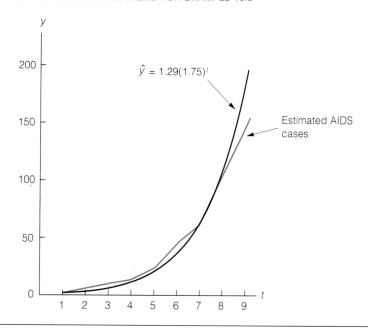

EXERCISES

LEARNING THE TECHNIQUES

19.12   Plot the following time series. Which of the three models (linear, polynomial, or logarithmic) would fit best?

Time Period t	y
1	.5
2	.6
3	1.3
4	2.7
5	4.1
6	6.9
7	10.8
8	19.2

19.13   Plot the following time series to determine which of the three trend models appears to fit best.

Time Period t	y
1	55
2	57
3	53
4	49
5	47
6	39
7	41
8	33
9	28
10	20

19.14   For Exercise 19.12, use the regression technique to calculate the linear trend line.

19.15   For Exercise 19.12, use the regression technique to calculate the logarithmic trend line.

19.16   Calculate the coefficient of determination

in both Exercises 19.14 and 19.15. Do these results confirm your answer to Exercise 19.12?

APPLYING THE TECHNIQUES

19.17   Enrollment in institutions of higher education has grown phenomenally in the postwar years. Forecasting this enrollment pattern, however, has been difficult. As a preliminary step, various attempts have been made to improve our understanding of the historical trend. One particular example consists of historical data on postsecondary enrollment in one midwestern state over the past 11 years. These data are shown in the accompanying table.

Year	t	FTE Enrollment (1,000s)
1975	1	185
1976	2	188
1977	3	192
1978	4	198
1979	5	210
1980	6	225
1981	7	240
1982	8	252
1983	9	260
1984	10	266
1985	11	270

a. Plot the time series.

b. Which of the three trend models appears to fit best? Explain.

Self-Correcting Exercise (See Appendix 19.B for the solution.)

EDUC   **19.18**   In Exercise 19.17, the linear trend line was found to be

$$\hat{y} = 167 + 9.81t \qquad (t = 1, 2, \ldots, 11)$$

a. Plot this line on the graph.

b. Forecast the FTE enrollment for 1986 and 1987.

Year	t	Exports ($millions)
1971	11	43,549
1972	12	49,199
1973	13	70,823
1974	14	97,908
1975	15	107,589
1976	16	115,150
1977	17	121,150
1978	18	143,681
1979	19	181,860
1980	20	220,630

Source: U.S. Department of Commerce, Bureau of Economic Analysis, Business Statistics. Biennial supplement to the *Survey of Current Business* (1984).

EDUC **19.19**   In Exercise 19.17, the logarithmic trend line was estimated, with the following result:

$$\hat{y} = (172)(1.045)^t \qquad (t = 1, 2, \ldots, 11)$$

a. Plot this line on the graph.

b. Forecast the FTE enrollment for 1986 and 1987.

EDUC **19.20**   In Exercise 19.17, the polynomial trend line is

$$\hat{y} = 170 + 8.45t + 0.113t^2 \qquad (t = 1, 2, \ldots, 11)$$

a. Plot this line on the graph.

b. Forecast the FTE enrollment for 1986 and 1987.

EDUC **19.21**   From the time series plot in Exercise 19.17 and from the graphs of the three trend lines, judge which model fits best.

ECON **19.22**   Exports are an important component of the exchange rate and, domestically, are an important indicator of employment and profitability in certain industries. The value of merchandise exports, in particular, seems to have increased dramatically over the past 20 years, as the accompanying table suggests.

Year	t	Exports ($millions)
1961	1	20,188
1962	2	20,973
1963	3	22,472
1964	4	25,690
1965	5	26,691
1966	6	29,379
1967	7	30,934
1968	8	34,063
1969	9	37,332
1970	10	42,659

a. Plot the time series.

b. Which trend model is likely to fit best? Explain.

ECON **19.23**   In Exercise 19.22, the linear trend line is

$$\hat{y} = -22,393 + 8,999t \qquad (t = 1, 2, \ldots, 20)$$

Plot this line on the graph.

ECON **19.24**   In Exercise 19.22, the logarithmic trend line is

$$\hat{y} = (14,005)(1.137)^t \qquad (t = 1, 2, \ldots, 20)$$

Plot this line on the graph.

ECON **19.25**   Refer to Exercise 19.22. The polynomial trend line is

$$\hat{y} = 36,858 - 7160t + 769.5t^2 \qquad (t = 1, 2, \ldots, 20)$$

Plot this line on the graph.

ECON **19.26**   Which of the three trend models in Exercises 19.23 through 19.25 appears to provide the best fit? Use that model to forecast exports for 1981.

MEASURING THE CYCLICAL EFFECT

The fundamental difference between cyclical and seasonal variations is in the length of the time period under consideration. In addition, however, seasonal effects are felt to be predictable, whereas cyclical effects (except in the case of certain well-known economic and business cycles) are often viewed as being unpredictable—varying in both duration and amplitude, and not necessarily even being repetitive. Nevertheless, cycles need to be isolated, and the procedure we will use to identify cyclical variation is the **percentage of trend.**

The percentage of trend is calculated in the following way:

1. Determine the trend line (usually by regression).
2. For each time period, compute the trend value $\hat{y}$.
3. The percentage of trend is $[(y/\hat{y}) \cdot 100]$.

Consider the following example.

▬▬▬▬▬ **EXAMPLE 19.6**

The annual demand for energy in the United States is affected by various factors, including price, availability, and the state of the economy. To help analyze the changes that have taken place and to develop a prediction, the annual total consumption for the United States (measured in quadrillions of Btu) was recorded for the period 1970–1986. These data are shown in the accompanying table. Assuming a linear trend, calculate the percentage of trend for each year.

Year	Time Period t	Annual Energy Consumption y_t
1970	1	66.4
1971	2	69.7
1972	3	72.2
1973	4	74.3
1974	5	72.5
1975	6	70.6
1976	7	74.4
1977	8	76.3
1978	9	78.1
1979	10	78.9
1980	11	76.0
1981	12	74.0
1982	13	70.8

Year	Time Period t	Annual Energy Consumption y_t
1983	14	70.5
1984	15	74.1
1985	16	74.0
1986	17	73.9

Source: *Statistical Abstract of the United States.*

Solution. Minitab* was used to produce the trend line and the percentage of trend. From the output, we observe that the trend line is

$$\hat{y} = 71.313 + .2248t$$

For each value of t ($t = 1, 2, \ldots , 17$), the predicted values $\hat{y}$ and the percentage of trend were determined as follows.

Year	Time Period t	Energy Consumption y	Trend $\hat{y}$	Percentage of Trend $(y/\hat{y}) \cdot 100$
1970	1	66.4	71.5378	92.819
1971	2	69.7	71.7626	97.127
1972	3	72.2	71.9874	100.296
1973	4	74.3	72.2122	102.892
1974	5	72.5	72.4370	100.088
1975	6	70.6	72.6618	97.164
1976	7	74.4	72.8866	102.078
1977	8	76.3	73.1114	104.363
1978	9	78.1	73.3362	106.497
1979	10	78.9	73.5610	107.259
1980	11	76.0	73.7858	103.002
1981	12	74.0	74.0106	99.897
1982	13	70.8	74.2354	95.374
1983	14	70.5	74.4602	94.683
1984	15	74.1	74.6850	99.218
1985	16	74.0	74.9098	98.787
1986	17	73.9	75.1346	98.358

* See Appendix 19.A for the Minitab commands used to produce the accompanying table.

FIGURE 19.15   *TIME SERIES AND TREND LINE FOR EXAMPLE 19.6*

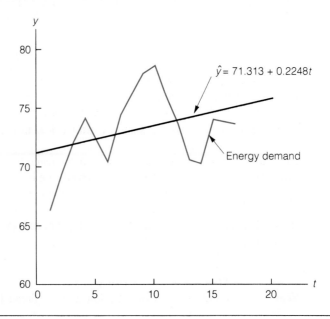

FIGURE 19.16   *PERCENTAGE OF TREND FOR EXAMPLE 19.6*

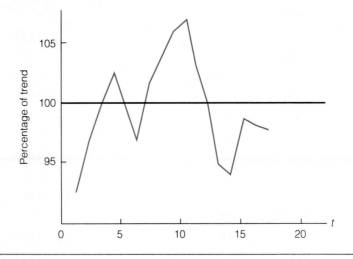

Figure 19.15 describes the time series and the trend line. The percentage of trend represents the amount by which the actual energy consumption lies above or below the line. Figure 19.16 is another way of depicting these values. The trend line now appears as the 100% line.

The problem we face when trying to interpret Figure 19.16 is that of distinguishing between random variation and a cyclical pattern. If there appears to be a random collection of percentage of trend values above and below the 100% line, we could conclude that its cause is random and not cyclical. However, if we see alternating groups of percentage of trend values above and below the 100% line and the patterns are regular, we would confidently identify the cyclical effect. In Figure 19.16 there appears to be a cyclical pattern, although it is not very regular. This highlights the major problem of forecasting time series that possess a cyclical component: the cyclical effect is often quite clearly present but too irregular to forecast with any degree of accuracy. Forecasting methods for this type of problem are available, but they are too advanced for our use. We will be satisfied with simply identifying and measuring the cyclical component of time series.

EXERCISES

LEARNING THE TECHNIQUES

19.27 Consider the time series shown in the following table.

t	y
1	30
2	27
3	24
4	21
5	23
6	27
7	33
8	38
9	41
10	38
11	43
12	36
13	29
14	24
15	20

The linear trend line is

$$\hat{y} = 27.8 + .311t \quad (t = 1, 2, \ldots, 15)$$

a. Calculate the percentage of trend for each time period.

b. Plot the percentage of trend.

19.28 The time series shown in the following table was recorded.

t	y
1	6
2	11
3	21
4	17
5	27
6	23
7	20
8	22
9	18
10	17
11	12
12	15

The linear trend line is

$\hat{y} = 15.9 + .234t$ $(t = 1, 2, \ldots, 12)$

a. Plot the time series.

b. Plot the trend line.

c. Calculate the percentage of trend.

d. Plot the percentage of trend.

b. The trend line is

$\hat{y} = 8.30 + .397t$ $(t = 1, 2, \ldots, 19)$

Graph this line.

c. Compute the percentage of trend.

APPLYING THE TECHNIQUES

RET **19.29**   As a preliminary step in forecasting future values, a large mail-order retail outlet has recorded the sales figures shown in the accompanying table.

Year	t	Sales ($millions)
1970	1	6.7
1971	2	7.4
1972	3	8.5
1973	4	11.2
1974	5	12.5
1975	6	10.7
1976	7	11.9
1977	8	11.4
1978	9	9.8
1979	10	11.5
1980	11	14.2
1981	12	18.1
1982	13	16.0
1983	14	11.2
1984	15	14.8
1985	16	15.2
1986	17	14.1
1987	18	12.2
1988	19	15.7

a. Plot the time series.

Self-Correcting Exercise (See Appendix 19.B for the solution.)

FIN **19.30**   One interesting phenomenon of the past several decades is the extent to which certain classes of assets have kept up with inflation while certain others have not. In terms of nominal interest rates, domestic corporate bond yields in the United States have assumed the values shown in the accompanying table over the years between 1961 and 1980.

Year	t	Domestic Corporate Bond Yields (annual averages; Moody's Aaa rating)
1961	1	4.35
1962	2	4.33
1963	3	4.26
1964	4	4.40
1965	5	4.49
1966	6	5.13
1967	7	5.51
1968	8	6.18
1969	9	7.03
1970	10	8.04
1971	11	7.39
1972	12	7.21
1973	13	7.44
1974	14	8.57
1975	15	8.83
1976	16	8.43
1977	17	8.02

Year	t	Domestic Corporate Bond Yields (annual averages; Moody's Aaa rating)
1978	18	8.73
1979	19	9.63
1980	20	11.94

SOURCE: U.S. Department of Commerce, Bureau of Economic Analysis, Business Statistics. Biennial supplement to the *Survey of Current Business* (1984).

The linear trend line was computed as

$$\hat{y} = 3.42 + .340t \qquad (t = 1, 2, \ldots, 20)$$

a. Plot the time series, and graph the trend line.

b. Calculate the percentage of trend.

c. Plot the percentage of trend. Does there appear to be a cyclical effect?

SECTION 19.6   ## MEASURING THE SEASONAL EFFECT

Seasonal variation may occur within a year or within an even shorter time interval, such as a month, week, or day. In order to measure the seasonal effect, we shall construct **seasonal indices**, which attempt to measure the degree to which the seasons differ from one another. One requirement for this method is that we have a time series sufficiently long to allow us to observe several occurrences of each season. For example, if our seasons are the quarters of a year, we need to observe the time series over a number of years. If the seasons are the days of the week, our time series should be observed for a number of weeks.

The seasonal indices are computed in the following way.

1. Remove the effect of seasonal and random variations by calculating the moving averages. Set the number of periods equal to the number of types of season. For example, we compute 12-month moving averages if the months of the year represent the seasons. A 5-day moving average is used if the seasons are the working days of the week. If the number of periods in the moving average is even, we compute the centered moving averages. The effect of the moving averages is seen in the multiplicative model of time series:

$$y_t = T_t \cdot C_t \cdot S_t \cdot R_t$$

The moving averages remove S_t and R_t, leaving

$$MA_t = T_t \cdot C_t$$

2. Compute the ratio of the time series over the moving average. Thus, we have

$$\frac{y_t}{MA_t} = \frac{T_t \cdot C_t \cdot S_t \cdot R_t}{T_t \cdot C_t} = S_t \cdot R_t$$

The result is a measure of seasonal and random variation.

3. For each type of season, calculate the average of the ratios in Step 2. This procedure removes most (although we can seldom remove all) of the random variation. This average is a measure of the seasonal differences.

4. The seasonal indices are the average ratios from Step 3 adjusted to ensure that the average seasonal index is 1.

The tourist industry is subject to enormous seasonal variation. A hotel in Bermuda has recorded its occupancy rate for each quarter during the past 5 years. These data are shown in the accompanying table. Calculate the seasonal indices for each quarter, to measure the amount of seasonal variation.

Year	Quarter	Hotel Occupancy
1985	1	.561
	2	.702
	3	.800
	4	.568
1986	1	.575
	2	.738
	3	.868
	4	.605
1987	1	.594
	2	.738
	3	.729
	4	.600
1988	1	.622
	2	.708
	3	.806
	4	.632
1989	1	.665
	2	.835
	3	.873
	4	.670

Solution.   Since there are 4 quarters (seasons) per year, we will calculate a 4-quarter centered moving average to remove the seasonal and random effects.

To calculate the 4-quarter centered moving averages, we first determine the 4-quarter moving averages and second compute the two-period moving averages of these values. So, for example, the moving average that falls between quarters 2 and 3 is

$$\frac{.561 + .702 + .800 + .568}{4} = \frac{2.631}{4} = .658$$

---

* In Appendix 19.A we describe the Minitab commands that produce the seasonal indices.

The moving average that falls between quarters 3 and 4 is

$$\frac{.702 + .800 + .568 + .575}{4} = \frac{2.645}{4} = .661$$

Thus the third quarter centered moving average is

$$\frac{.658 + .661}{2} = \frac{1.319}{2} = .660$$

The next step is to find the ratio of the occupancy rates divided by the centered moving averages.

The outcomes of the first two operations are shown in the accompanying table.

Year	Quarter	Occupancy y_t	Centered MA	Ratio y/MA
1985	1	.561	—	—
	2	.702	—	—
	3	.800	.660	1.213
	4	.568	.666	.853
1986	1	.575	.679	.847
	2	.738	.692	1.067
	3	.868	.699	1.242
	4	.605	.701	.863
1987	1	.594	.684	.869
	2	.738	.666	1.108
	3	.729	.669	1.090
	4	.600	.669	.898
1988	1	.622	.675	.922
	2	.708	.688	1.029
	3	.806	.697	1.156
	4	.632	.719	.879
1989	1	.665	.743	.895
	2	.835	.756	1.105
	3	.873	—	—
	4	.670	—	—

If we now group the ratios by quarter, we can see the similarities within each type of quarter and the differences between the different types of quarter. For example, the ratios for quarter 1 are .847, .869, .922, and .895, whereas for quarter 3 they are 1.213, 1.242, 1.090, and 1.156. By averaging these values, we remove most of the random variation. The last step is to adjust the averages by dividing each average by the total 4.008 and multiplying by 4.000. The seasonal indices are these adjusted averages. The following table summarizes Steps 3 and 4.

Year	Quarter				Total
	1	2	3	4	
1985	—	—	1.213	.853	
1986	.847	1.067	1.242	.863	
1987	.869	1.108	1.090	.898	
1988	.922	1.029	1.156	.879	
1989	.895	1.105	—	—	
Average	.883	1.077	1.175	.873	4.008
Seasonal index	.881	1.075	1.173	.871	4.000

The seasonal indices tell us that, on average, the occupancy rates in the first and fourth quarters are below the annual average, and the occupancy rates in the second and third quarters are above the annual average. That is, we expect the occupancy rate in the first quarter to be 11.9% below the annual rate. The second and third quarter's rates are expected to be 7.5% and 17.3%, respectively, above the annual rate. The fourth quarter's rate is 12.9% below the annual rate. Figure 19.17 depicts the time series and the moving averages.

One of the drawbacks of this method is the large number of calculations necessary to do even a relatively small problem. However, if the time series contains no discernible cyclical component we can use regression analysis instead of moving averages in Step 1. When the time series has no cyclical effect, we can represent the model as

$$y_t = T_t \cdot S_t \cdot R_t$$

Since the regression line ($\hat{y} = \beta_0 + \beta_1 t$) represents trend, it follows that

$$\frac{y_t}{\hat{y}_t} = S_t \cdot R_t$$

We can then average these values to remove the random variation as we did using moving averages. And with several additional commands, we can induce Minitab to calculate the ratios for each time period. Since the time series in our example seems to contain no cyclical pattern, we would expect the indices based on moving averages to be quite similar to the indices determined from regression analysis. Using Minitab, we obtained the following information. The trend line is

$$\hat{y} = .639 + .00525t$$

FIGURE 19.17   TIME SERIES AND MOVING AVERAGES FOR EXAMPLE 19.7

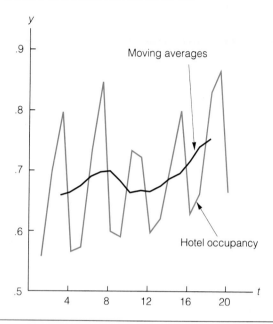

The value of r^2 is 9.3%, which is very low. However, bear in mind that large deviations between the line and the points are inevitable when either seasonal or cyclical components exist. The values of y, $\hat{y}$, and $y/\hat{y}$ are listed in the accompanying table.

Year	Quarter	y	$\hat{y}$	$y/\hat{y}$
1985	1	.561	.644614	.87029
	2	.702	.649860	1.08023
	3	.800	.655106	1.22118
	4	.568	.660352	.86015
1986	1	.575	.665598	.86839
	2	.738	.670844	1.10011
	3	.868	.676089	1.28385
	4	.605	.681335	.88796
1987	1	.594	.686581	.86516
	2	.738	.691827	1.06674
	3	.729	.697073	1.04580
	4	.600	.702319	.85431

(*continued*)

Year	Quarter	y	$\hat{y}$	$y/\hat{y}$
1988	1	.622	.707565	.87907
	2	.708	.712811	.99325
	3	.806	.718056	1.12247
	4	.632	.723302	.87377
1989	1	.665	.728548	.91277
	2	.835	.733794	1.13792
	3	.873	.739040	1.18126
	4	.670	.744286	.90019

The seasonal indices are computed as shown in the following table. (No adjustment was necessary in this case, since the average ratio = 1.000).

	Quarter				
Year	1	2	3	4	Total
1985	.87029	1.08023	1.22118	.86015	
1986	.86389	1.10011	1.28385	.88796	
1987	.86516	1.06674	1.04580	.85431	
1988	.87907	.99325	1.12247	.87377	
1989	.91277	1.13792	1.18126	.90019	
Average	.87824	1.07565	1.17091	.87528	4.000
Seasonal index	.87824	1.07565	1.17091	.87528	4.000

As you can see, the two sets of seasonal indices are almost identical. Although we applied the two methods to the same data, the actual Step 1 technique in a practical application would depend on whether or not we had identified a cyclical pattern in the time series.

At this point the seasonal indices only measure the extent to which the seasons vary from one another. In Section 19.9, however, we will show how the seasonal indices can play a critical role in forecasting.

▬▬▬▬ **EXERCISES**

LEARNING THE TECHNIQUES

19.31 For the following time series, compute the 5-day moving averages to remove the seasonal and random variation.

Day	Week			
	1	2	3	4
Monday	12	11	14	17
Tuesday	18	17	16	21
Wednesday	16	19	16	20
Thursday	25	24	28	24
Friday	31	27	25	32

19.32 For Exercise 19.31, calculate the seasonal (daily) indices.

19.33 Given the following time series, compute the seasonal (quarterly) indices, using a 4-quarter centered moving average.

Quarter	Year				
	1	2	3	4	5
1	50	41	43	36	30
2	44	38	39	32	25
3	46	37	39	30	24
4	39	30	35	25	22

19.34 In Exercise 19.31, the regression trend line is

$$\hat{y} = 16.8 + .366t \quad (t = 1, 2, \ldots, 20)$$

Calculate the seasonal indices, based on the regression trend line.

19.35 In Exercise 19.33, the regression trend line is

$$\hat{y} = 47.7 - 1.19t \quad (t = 1, 2, \ldots, 20)$$

Calculate the seasonal indices, based on this trend line.

APPLYING THE TECHNIQUES

Self-Correcting Exercise (See Appendix 19.B for the solution.)

GEN **19.36** The quarterly earnings of a large soft-drink company have been recorded for the past 4 years. These data are shown in the accompanying table. Using an appropriate moving average, measure the quarterly variation by computing the seasonal (quarterly) indices.

EARNINGS ($MILLIONS)

Quarter	Year			
	1986	1987	1988	1989
1	52	57	60	66
2	67	75	77	82
3	85	90	94	98
4	54	61	63	67

GEN **19.37** In Exercise 19.36, the linear trend line calculated by regression analysis is

$$\hat{y} = 61.7 + 1.18t \quad (t = 1, 2, \ldots, 16)$$

Calculate the seasonal indices, using this trend line.

GEN **19.38** Cable TV subscriptions over the past few years have been growing dramatically, although sometimes somewhat erratically. In one southwestern state, the data shown in the accompanying table were observed.

Year	Quarter	Cable Subscribers (thousands)
1985	1	184
	2	173
	3	160
	4	189
1986	1	191
	2	185

(continued)

Year	Quarter	Cable Subscribers (thousands)
	3	184
	4	200
1987	1	205
	2	192
	3	200
	4	229
1988	1	236
	2	219
	3	211
	4	272
1989	1	280
	2	261
	3	275
	4	322

a. Plot the time series.

b. Calculate the 4-quarter centered moving averages.

c. Plot the moving averages.

GEN **19.39**   Compute the seasonal (quarterly) indices, using the time series and moving averages in Exercise 19.38.

GEN **19.40**   In Exercise 19.38, the linear trend line (from regression analysis) is

$$\hat{y} = 150 + 6.53t \qquad (t = 1, 2, \ldots, 20)$$

Calculate the seasonal indices, using this trend line.

GEN **19.41**   The owner of a pizzeria wants to forecast the number of pizzas she will sell each day. She records the number sold daily during the past 4 weeks. These data are shown in the accompanying table. Calculate the seasonal (daily) indices, using a 7-day moving average.

NUMBER OF PIZZAS SOLD

Day	Week 1	2	3	4
Sunday	240	221	235	219
Monday	85	80	86	91
Tuesday	93	75	74	102
Wednesday	106	121	100	89
Thursday	125	110	117	105
Friday	188	202	205	192
Saturday	314	386	402	377

FIN **19.42**   A manufacturer of ski equipment is in the process of reviewing his accounts receivable. He has noticed that there appears to be a seasonal pattern. Accounts receivable increase in the winter months and decrease during the summer. The quarterly accounts receivable for the past 4 years are shown in the accompanying table. To measure the seasonal variation, compute the seasonal (quarterly) indices based on the regression trend line, which was calculated as

$$\hat{y} = 90.4 + 2.02t \qquad (t = 1, 2, \ldots, 16)$$

ACCOUNTS RECEIVABLE ($MILLIONS)

Quarter	Year 1986	1987	1988	1989
1	106	115	114	121
2	92	100	105	111
3	65	73	79	82
4	121	135	140	163

SECTION 19.7   *INTRODUCTION TO FORECASTING*

As we've noted before, many different forecasting methods are available. One of the factors we consider in making our choice is the type of component that makes up the time series we're attempting to forecast. Even then, however, we have a variety of techniques to choose from. One way of deciding which method to use is to select the technique that results in the greatest forecast accuracy. The two most commonly used measures of forecast accuracy are the **mean absolute deviation (MAD)** and the **sum of squares for forecast error (SSE).** These are defined as follows:

Mean Absolute Deviation

$$\text{MAD} = \frac{\sum_{t=1}^{n} |y_t - F_t|}{n}$$

where

y_t = Actual value of the time series at time t

F_t = Forecast value at time t

n = Number of time periods

Sum of Squares for Forecast Error

$$\text{SSE} = \sum_{t=1}^{n} (y_t - F_t)^2$$

MAD averages the absolute differences between the actual values and the forecast values; in contrast, SSE squares these differences. Which measure to use in judging forecast accuracy depends on the circumstances. If avoiding large errors is extremely important, SSE should be used, since it penalizes large deviations more heavily than does MAD. Otherwise, use MAD.

It is probably best to use some of the observations of the time series to develop several competing forecasting models and then forecast for the remaining time periods. Afterward we can compute either MAD or SSE for the latter period. For example, if we have 5 years of monthly observations, we can use the first 4 years to develop the forecasting techniques and then use them to forecast the fifth year. Since we know the actual values in the fifth year, we can choose the technique that results in the most accurate forecasts.

EXAMPLE 19.8

Annual data from 1960 to 1985 were used to develop three different forecasting models. Each was used to forecast the time series for 1986, 1987, 1988, and 1989. The forecasted and actual values for these years are shown in the accompanying table. Use MAD and SSE to determine which model performed best.

		Forecast Value Using Model		
Year	Actual Value of y	1	2	3
1986	129	136	118	130
1987	142	148	141	146
1988	156	150	158	170
1989	183	175	163	180

Solution.   For Model 1, we have

$$MAD = \frac{|129 - 136| + |142 - 148| + |156 - 150| + |183 - 175|}{4}$$

$$= \frac{7 + 6 + 6 + 8}{4} = \frac{27}{4} = 6.75$$

$$SSE = (129 - 136)^2 + (142 - 148)^2 + (156 - 150)^2 + (183 - 175)^2$$
$$= 49 + 36 + 36 + 64 = 185$$

For Model 2, we compute

$$MAD = \frac{|129 - 118| + |142 - 141| + |156 - 158| + |183 - 163|}{4}$$

$$= \frac{11 + 1 + 2 + 20}{4} = \frac{34}{4} = 8.5$$

$$SSE = (129 - 118)^2 + (142 - 141)^2 + (156 - 158)^2 + (183 - 163)^2$$
$$= 121 + 1 + 4 + 400 = 526$$

The measures of forecast accuracy for Model 3 are

$$MAD = \frac{|129 - 130| + |142 - 146| + |156 - 170| + |183 - 180|}{4}$$

$$= \frac{1 + 4 + 14 + 3}{4} = \frac{22}{4} = 5.5$$

$$SSE = (129 - 130)^2 + (142 - 146)^2 + (156 - 170)^2 + (183 - 180)^2$$
$$= 1 + 16 + 196 + 9 = 222$$

Model 2 is inferior to both Models 1 and 3, no matter how forecast accuracy is measured. Using MAD, Model 3 is best; but using SSE, Model 1 is the most accurate. The choice between Model 1 or Model 3 should be made on the basis of whether we prefer a model that consistently produces moderately accurate forecasts (Model 1) or one whose forecasts come quite close to most actual values but miss badly in a small number of time periods (Model 3).

19.43   The actual values and forecast values of a time series are shown in the following table. Calculate MAD and SSE.

Forecast Value F_t	Actual Value y_t
173	166
186	179
192	195
211	214
223	220

Self-Correcting Exercise (See Appendix 19.B for the solution.)

19.44   Two forecasting models were used to predict the future values of a time series. These are shown next, together with the actual values. For each model, compute MAD to determine which was more accurate.

Forecast Value F_t		Actual Value y_t
Model 1	Model 2	
7.5	6.3	6.0
6.3	6.7	6.6
5.4	7.1	7.3
8.2	7.5	9.4

19.45   Repeat Exercise 19.44, using SSE to measure forecast accuracy.

19.46   Calculate MAD and SSE for the forecasts that follow.

Forecast Value F_t	Actual Value y_t
6.3	5.7
7.2	6.0
8.6	7.0
7.1	7.5
6.0	7.0

19.47   Three forecasting techniques were used to predict the values of a time series. These are given in Table E19.47 below. For each, compute MAD and SSE to determine which was most accurate.

TABLE E19.47	Forecast Value F_t			
	Technique 1	Technique 2	Technique 3	Actual Value y_t
	21	22	17	19
	27	24	20	24
	29	26	25	28
	31	28	31	32
	35	30	39	38

SECTION 19.8 ## *TIME SERIES FORECASTING WITH EXPONENTIAL SMOOTHING*

In Section 19.3 we presented smoothing techniques whose function is to reduce random fluctuation, enabling us to identify the time series components. One of these methods, exponential smoothing, can also be used to forecast. Recall the exponential smoothing formula

$$S_t = wy_t + (1 - w)S_{t-1}$$

where the choice of the smoothing constant w determines the degree of smoothing. A value of w close to 1 results in very little smoothing, whereas a value of w close to 0 results in a great deal of smoothing.

When a time series exhibits a gradual trend and no evidence of cyclical effects or seasonal effects, exponential smoothing can be a useful way of forecasting. Suppose that t represents the current time period and we've computed the smoothed value S_t. This value is then the forecast value at time $t + 1$. That is,

$$F_{t+1} = S_t$$

If we wish, we can forecast 2 or 3 or any number of time periods into the future.

$$F_{t+2} = S_t$$
$$F_{t+3} = S_t$$

As long as we're dealing with a time series that possesses no cyclical or seasonal effect, we can produce reasonably accurate forecasts once we've eliminated the random variation.

EXAMPLE 19.9

An important measure of a nation's manufacturing activity is earnings as a percentage of value added, which is derived by dividing total nominal earnings of employees by the nominal value added. This shows labor's share of income generated in the manufacturing sector. The accompanying table lists Canada's earnings as a percentage of value added from 1970 to 1984. Use exponential smoothing to forecast for 1985.

Year	Earnings as a Percentage of Value Added
1970	53.1
1971	52.4
1972	51.7
1973	49.5
1974	46.7

Year	Earnings as a Percentage of Value Added
1975	49.5
1976	51.2
1977	50.4
1978	48.8
1979	46.8
1980	47.4
1981	47.3
1982	51.4
1983	48.7
1984	48.7

SOURCE: *World Tables* (1987).

Solution.   A plot of the time series (see Figure 19.18) reveals no long-term trend or distinct cyclical pattern. As a consequence, exponential smoothing is an appropriate

FIGURE 19.18   *TIME SERIES, EXPONENTIAL SMOOTHING, AND FORECAST FOR EXAMPLE 19.9*

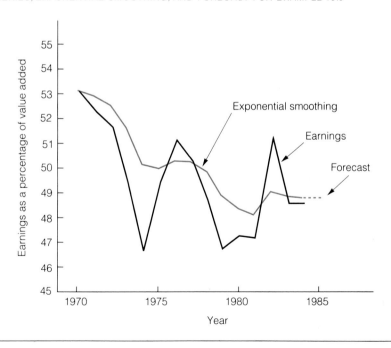

forecasting method. We choose $w = .3$. The results are shown in the table that follows.

Year	Earnings as a Percentage of Value Added y_t	$S_t = wy_t + (1 - w) S_{t-1}$: $w = .3$
1970	53.1	53.1
1971	52.4	52.89
1972	51.7	52.53
1973	49.5	51.62
1974	46.7	50.15
1975	49.5	50.00
1976	51.2	50.33
1977	50.4	50.35
1978	48.8	49.88
1979	46.8	48.96
1980	47.4	48.49
1981	47.3	48.13
1982	51.4	49.11
1983	48.7	48.99
1984	48.7	48.90

The 1985 forecast is

$$F_{1985} = S_{1984} = 48.90$$

The actual 1985 earnings as a percentage of value added is 49.0.

LEARNING THE TECHNIQUES

19.48 Use exponential smoothing, with $w = .6$, to forecast the next value of the time series that follows.

t	y
1	23
2	18
3	26
4	27
5	24
6	22

19.49 Use the exponential smoothing technique, with $w = .3$, to forecast the value of the following time series at time $t = 8$.

t	y
1	12
2	20
3	16
4	19
5	15
6	11
7	14

19.50 Use the following time series for the years 1980–1985 to develop forecasts for 1986–1989, with:

a. $w = .3$

b. $w = .6$

c. $w = .7$

Year	y
1980	110
1981	103
1982	111
1983	117
1984	126
1985	115

19.51 For the data in Exercise 19.50, compare each of the three sets of forecasts with the actual values for 1986–1989 given in the accompanying table. Compute MAD for each model.

Year	y
1986	121
1987	120
1988	115
1989	127

19.52 Continue using the forecasting model that you determined was best in Exercise 19.51 to forecast the time series value for 1990.

APPLYING THE TECHNIQUES

SCI **19.53** The increased awareness among consumers of the effects of cigarettes is expected to have an adverse impact on the tobacco industry. To help analyze the problem, a tobacco industry executive wants to forecast future production of cigarettes. The production amounts for the past 10 years are shown in the table that follows. Because of the relatively small changes that have taken place, it was decided to use exponential smoothing. Forecast the 1987 cigarette production, using a smoothing constant of $w = .5$.

Year	Cigarette Production (billions)
1977	673
1978	688
1979	707
1980	702
1981	744
1982	711
1983	688
1084	657
1985	665
1986	652

SOURCE: *Statistical Abstract of the United States.*

Self-Correcting Exercise (See Appendix 19.B for the solution.)

ECON **19.54** The following table lists U.S. earnings as a percentage of value added (see Example 19.9). Use exponential smoothing, with $w = .7$, to forecast earnings for 1985.

Year	Earnings as a Percentage of Value Added
1975	43.1
1976	41.7

(continued)

Year	Earnings as a Percentage of Value Added
1977	41.4
1978	41.3
1979	39.9
1980	40.9
1981	40.8
1982	41.4
1983	40.1
1984	40.0

Source: *World Tables* (1987).

19.55   Plywood is used in a number of industries, including housing and furniture. Annual U.S. production of plywood for the years 1971–1980 is listed in the accompanying table. Using exponen-

tial smoothing with $w = .7$, predict U.S. production for 1981.

Year	U.S. Plywood Production (1000s of cubic meters)
1971	16,184
1972	17,746
1973	18,054
1974	15,172
1975	14,579
1976	16,726
1977	17,981
1978	17,056
1979	18,200
1980	16,000

Source: *Yearbook of Industrial Statistics.*

SECTION 19.9
TIME SERIES FORECASTING WITH REGRESSION

Regression analysis has been applied to various different problems. It was used in Chapter 15 to analyze what the relationship is between two variables, and it was used in Chapters 16 and 17 to analyze how a dependent variable is influenced by a group of independent variables. In those chapters, regression analysis was used to predict the value of the dependent variable. In this section we again wish to use regression techniques, but now the independent variable or variables will be measures of time. The simplest application would be to a time series in which the only component (in addition to random variation, which is always present) is trend. In that case, the model

$$y = \beta_0 + \beta_1 t + \varepsilon$$

would likely provide excellent forecasts. However, we can take this basic model and augment it so that it can be used in other situations.

FORECASTING TIME SERIES WITH TREND AND SEASONALITY

There are two ways to use regression analysis to forecast time series whose components are trend and seasonal effect. The first involves using the seasonal indices developed in Section 19.6. The second involves using dummy variables, which were introduced in Section 17.5.

FORECASTING WITH SEASONAL INDICES

The seasonal indices measure the season-to-season variation. If we combine these indices with a forecast of the trend, we produce the following formula.

Forecast of Trend and Seasonality

$$F_t = [\hat{\beta}_0 + \hat{\beta}_1 t]\text{SI}_t$$

where

F_t = Forecast for period t

SI_t = Seasonal index for period t

The process that we use to forecast with seasonal indices is as follows.

1. Use simple linear regression to find the trend line
   $$\hat{y} = \hat{\beta}_0 + \hat{\beta}_1 t$$
2. Use the trend line to calculate the seasonal indices.
3. For the future time period t, find the trend value
   $$\hat{y} = \hat{\beta}_0 + \hat{\beta}_1 t$$
4. Multiply the trend value $\hat{y}$ by the seasonal index for the season to forecast:
   $$F_t = \hat{y} \cdot \text{SI}_t$$

EXAMPLE 19.10

Recall that in Example 19.7 we computed the seasonal (quarterly) indices for the hotel occupancy. Use these indices to forecast each quarter's occupancy in 1990.

Solution. The trend line that was calculated from the quarterly data for 1985–1989 is

$$\hat{y} = .639 + .00525t$$

For $t = 21, 22, 23,$ and 24 we find the following values.

Year	Quarter	t	$\hat{y} = .639 + .00525t$
1990	1	21	.749
	2	22	.755
	3	23	.760
	4	24	.765

We now multiply the trend values by the seasonal indices (computed from the trend line rather than from moving averages). Thus, the seasonalized forecasts are as follows.

Year	Quarter	Seasonal Index	$\hat{y}$	Forecast
1990	1	.87824	.749	.658
	2	1.07565	.755	.812
	3	1.17091	.760	.890
	4	.87528	.765	.670

EXAMPLE 19.11

At the end of 1985, a major builder of residential houses in the northeastern United States wanted to predict the number of housing units to be started in 1986. This information would be extremely useful in determining a variety of variables including housing demand, availability of labor, and the prices of building materials. To assist in developing an accurate forecasting model, the number of housing starts for the previous 60 months (1981–1985) were determined. These numbers (in 1,000s of units) are shown in the accompanying table. Forecast the housing starts for the 12 months of 1986.

HOUSING STARTS IN THE NORTHEAST UNITED STATES (1,000s)

					Month							
Year	Jan.	Feb.	Mar.	Apr.	May	June	July	Aug.	Sept.	Oct.	Nov.	Dec.
1981	5.5	2.8	8.5	10.2	12.0	11.2	16.0	11.6	12.0	12.0	7.6	7.8
1982	2.6	3.3	7.3	8.7	11.9	10.0	11.3	12.9	15.9	11.0	14.0	7.8
1983	5.5	7.4	13.1	13.7	17.2	17.8	17.5	21.5	14.6	16.2	13.8	9.3
1984	7.2	8.8	11.1	17.1	18.7	22.8	19.9	21.1	19.5	22.2	21.6	14.2
1985	9.5	7.4	16.3	25.6	24.7	27.0	22.7	25.3	24.1	32.3	19.9	17.0

SOURCE: *Standard and Poor's Industry Surveys.*

Solution. The data display a very clear seasonal pattern. This is as might be expected, since much construction activity ceases during the winter months. Operating under the assumption that there is little cyclical variation, we chose to determine the seasonal indices for 1981–1985 by using linear regression. Minitab was used to produce the following results.

The linear trend line is

$$\hat{y} = 6.15 + 0.267t$$

The ratios $y/\hat{y}$ for each month were computed and are reproduced in the accompanying table.

Year	Month	t	Housing Units Started $y(1,000s)$	Trend Line $\hat{y} = 6.15 + 0.267t$	Ratio $y/\hat{y}$
1981	Jan.	1	5.5	6.417	.857
	Feb.	2	2.8	6.684	.419
	Mar.	3	8.5	6.951	1.223
	Apr.	4	10.2	7.218	1.413
	May	5	12.0	7.484	1.603
	June	6	11.2	7.751	1.445
	July	7	16.0	8.018	1.995
	Aug.	8	11.6	8.285	1.400
	Sept.	9	12.0	8.552	1.403
	Oct.	10	12.0	8.819	1.361
	Nov.	11	7.6	9.086	.836
	Dec.	12	7.8	9.353	.834
1982	Jan.	13	2.6	9.620	.270
	Feb.	14	3.3	9.887	.334
	Mar.	15	7.3	10.154	.719
	Apr.	16	8.7	10.421	.835
	May	17	11.9	10.688	1.113
	June	18	10.0	10.955	.913
	July	19	11.3	11.222	1.007
	Aug.	20	12.9	11.489	1.123
	Sept.	21	15.9	11.756	1.353
	Oct.	22	11.0	12.023	.915
	Nov.	23	14.0	12.290	1.139
	Dec.	24	7.8	12.556	.621

(continued)

Year	Month	t	Housing Units Started $y(1{,}000s)$	Trend Line $\hat{y} = 6.15 + 0.267t$	Ratio $y/\hat{y}$
1983	Jan.	25	5.5	12.823	.429
	Feb.	26	7.4	13.090	.565
	Mar.	27	13.1	13.357	.981
	Apr.	28	13.7	13.624	1.006
	May	29	17.2	13.891	1.238
	June	30	17.8	14.158	1.257
	July	31	17.5	14.425	1.213
	Aug.	32	21.5	14.692	1.463
	Sept.	33	14.6	14.959	.976
	Oct.	34	16.2	15.226	1.064
	Nov.	35	13.8	15.493	.891
	Dec.	36	9.3	15.760	.590
1984	Jan.	37	7.2	16.027	.449
	Feb.	38	8.8	16.294	.540
	Mar.	39	11.1	16.561	.670
	Apr.	40	17.1	16.828	1.016
	May	41	18.7	17.095	1.094
	June	42	22.8	17.362	1.313
	July	43	19.9	17.629	1.129
	Aug.	44	21.1	17.895	1.179
	Sept.	45	19.5	18.162	1.074
	Oct.	46	22.2	18.429	1.205
	Nov.	47	21.6	18.696	1.155
	Dec.	48	14.2	18.963	.749
1985	Jan.	49	9.5	19.230	.494
	Feb.	50	7.4	19.497	.380
	Mar.	51	16.3	19.760	.825
	Apr.	52	25.6	20.031	1.278
	May	53	24.7	20.298	1.217
	June	54	27.0	20.565	1.313
	July	55	22.7	20.832	1.090
	Aug.	56	25.3	21.099	1.199
	Sept.	57	24.1	21.366	1.128
	Oct.	58	32.3	21.633	1.493
	Nov.	59	19.9	21.900	.909
	Dec.	60	17.0	22.167	.767

The ratios for each month were grouped and averaged, and these averages were then adjusted as follows.

	Monthly Ratios					
Year	Jan.	Feb.	Mar.	Apr.	May	June
1981	.857	.419	1.223	1.413	1.603	1.445
1982	.270	.334	.719	.835	1.113	.913
1983	.429	.565	.981	1.006	1.238	1.257
1984	.449	.540	.670	1.016	1.094	1.313
1985	.494	.380	.825	1.278	1.217	1.313
Average	.500	.448	.884	1.110	1.253	1.248
Seasonal index	.496	.444	.877	1.101	1.243	1.238

	Monthly Ratios					
Year	July	Aug.	Sept.	Oct.	Nov.	Dec.
1981	1.995	1.400	1.403	1.361	.836	.834
1982	1.007	1.123	1.353	.915	1.139	.621
1983	1.213	1.463	.976	1.064	.891	.590
1984	1.129	1.179	1.074	1.205	1.155	.749
1985	1.090	1.199	1.128	1.493	.909	.767
Average	1.287	1.273	1.187	1.207	.986	.712
Seasonal index	1.277	1.263	1.177	1.198	.978	.707

The seasonal indices confirm our observation that there are more starts in the summer and far fewer in the winter.

The 1986 forecasts are made by computing the trend line value for each month in 1986 and multiplying these values by the monthly seasonal indices. The resulting values are shown in the accompanying table on p. 972.

FORECASTS

Year	Month	Time Period t	Trend Value $\hat{y} = 6.15 + .267t$	Seasonal Index	Forecast $F_t = \hat{y}_t \cdot SI_t$
1986	Jan.	61	22.437	.496	11.1
	Feb.	62	22.704	.444	10.1
	Mar.	63	22.971	.877	20.1
	Apr.	64	23.238	1.101	25.6
	May	65	23.505	1.243	29.2
	June	66	23.772	1.238	29.4
	July	67	24.039	1.277	30.7
	Aug.	68	24.306	1.263	30.7
	Sept.	69	24.573	1.177	28.9
	Oct.	70	24.840	1.198	29.8
	Nov.	71	25.107	.978	24.6
	Dec.	72	25.374	.707	17.9

Figure 19.19 depicts the time series, the trend line, and the forecasted values.

When we examine the actual data for 1986 monthly housing starts, we see that the forecasts were quite accurate. The following table offers a comparison of the two.

Year	Month	Forecast F_t	Actual Housing Starts y_t
1986	Jan.	11.1	14.1
	Feb.	10.1	12.3
	Mar.	20.1	20.6
	Apr.	25.6	29.3
	May	29.2	27.5
	June	29.4	30.4
	July	30.7	28.1
	Aug.	30.7	34.0
	Sept.	28.9	29.1
	Oct.	29.8	27.2
	Nov.	24.6	21.7
	Dec.	17.9	19.1

FIGURE 19.19   *TIME SERIES, TREND, AND FORECASTS FOR EXAMPLE 19.11*

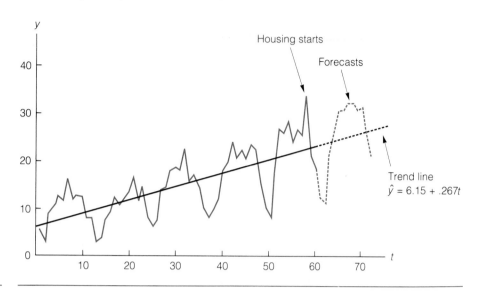

FORECASTING SEASONAL TIME SERIES WITH DUMMY VARIABLES

As an alternative to calculating and using seasonal indices to measure the seasonal variations, we can use dummy variables. For example, if the seasons are the quarters of a year, the multiple regression model

$$y = \beta_0 + \beta_1 t + \beta_2 Q_1 + \beta_3 Q_2 + \beta_4 Q_3 + \varepsilon$$

can be used, where

$$t = \text{Time period}$$
$$Q_1 = 1 \text{ if quarter 1}$$
$$= 0 \text{ if not}$$
$$Q_2 = 1 \text{ if quarter 2}$$
$$= 0 \text{ if not}$$
$$Q_3 = 1 \text{ if quarter 3}$$
$$= 0 \text{ if not}$$

Thus, for each time period, variables Q_1, Q_2, and Q_3 would be used to represent the quarter. The coefficients β_0, β_1, β_2, β_3, and β_4 would be estimated in the usual way, and the regression equation would be used to predict future values.

▬▬▬▬▬▬▬ **EXAMPLE 19.12**

Use dummy variables and regression analysis to forecast hotel occupancy in 1990, using the data in Example 19.7.

Solution.   Because the seasons are the quarters of the year, we begin by creating dummy variables Q_1, Q_2, and Q_3, as described earlier. Thus,

$$Q_1 = 1, Q_2 = 0, Q_3 = 0$$

represents an observation in quarter 1;

$$Q_1 = 0, Q_2 = 1, Q_3 = 0$$

identifies the second quarter measurement;

$$Q_1 = 0, Q_2 = 0, Q_3 = 1$$

represents the third quarter, and

$$Q_1 = 0, Q_2 = 0, Q_3 = 0$$

represents the fourth quarter.
   The model to be estimated is

$$y = \beta_0 + \beta_1 t + \beta_2 Q_1 + \beta_3 Q_2 + \beta_4 Q_3 + \varepsilon$$

The data in the accompanying table were input, and the SAS output that follows was produced.

y	t	Q_1	Q_2	Q_3
.561	1	1	0	0
.702	2	0	1	0
.800	3	0	0	1
.568	4	0	0	0
.575	5	1	0	0
.738	6	0	1	0
.868	7	0	0	1
.605	8	0	0	0
.594	9	1	0	0
.738	10	0	1	0
.729	11	0	0	1
.600	12	0	0	0
.622	13	1	0	0

y	t	Q_1	Q_2	Q_3
.708	14	0	1	0
.806	15	0	0	1
.632	16	0	0	0
.665	17	1	0	0
.835	18	0	1	0
.873	19	0	0	1
.670	20	0	0	0

SAS COMPUTER PRINTOUT

Dependent Variable: Y

Analysis of Variance

Source	DF	Sum of Squares	Mean Square	F Value	Prob > F
Model	4	0.17453	0.04363	30.122	0.0001
Error	15	0.02173	0.00145		
C Total	19	0.19626			

Root MSE	0.03806	R-square	0.8893
Dep Mean	0.69445	Adj R-sq	0.8598
C.V.	5.48053		

Parameter Estimates

Variable	DF	Parameter Estimate	Standard Error	T for H0: Parameter=0	Prob > |T|
INTERCEP	1	0.5545	0.0248	22.350	0.0001
T	1	0.00504	0.0015	3.348	0.0044
Q1	1	0.00351	0.0244	0.143	0.8879
Q2	1	0.1392	0.0242	5.741	0.0001
Q3	1	0.2052	0.0241	8.510	0.0001

$F = 30.122$ (p-value $= .0001$) and $r^2 = .8893$ indicate that the model's fit to the data is very good. The t-value for Q_1 ($t = .143$, p-value $= .8879$) tells us that there is no significant difference in occupancy rates between quarters 1 and 4. The t-values for Q_2 and Q_3 (5.741 and 8.510, respectively) provide enough evidence to allow us to conclude that the occupancy rates in quarters 2 and 3 differ from that in quarter 4.

The model's fit appears to be reasonable, so we can use it to forecast the 1990 quarterly occupancy rates, as shown in the accompanying table.

					Forecast
Quarter	*t*	Q_1	Q_2	Q_3	$\hat{y} = .5545 + .00504t + .00351Q_1 + .1392Q_2 + .2052Q_3$
1	21	1	0	0	.664
2	22	0	1	0	.805
3	23	0	0	1	.876
4	24	0	0	0	.675

These forecasts are quite similar to those produced by using seasonal indices.

AUTOREGRESSIVE MODEL

Recall that one of the requirements for the use of regression analysis is that the errors be independent of one another. In Chapter 16 we developed a test for first-order autocorrelation, called the Durbin–Watson test. While the existence of strong autocorrelation tends to destroy the validity of regression analysis, it is also an opportunity to produce accurate forecasts. If we believe that there is a correlation between consecutive residuals, then the model

$$y_t = \beta_0 + \beta_1 y_{t-1} + \varepsilon_t$$

can be helpful in forecasting future values of *y*. The model specifies that consecutive values of the time series are correlated (which follows from the conclusion that the residuals are correlated). We estimate β_0 and β_1 by least squares and then use the equation to forecast.

EXAMPLE 19.13

The consumer price index (CPI) is used as a general measure of inflation. It is an important measure because it often influences governments to take some corrective action when the rate of inflation is high. The table that follows lists the percentage annual increase in the CPI since 1951. In an attempt to forecast this value on the basis of time alone, we estimated the model

$$y = \beta_0 + \beta_1 t + \varepsilon$$

We found that $r^2 = 29.8\%$ (indicating a poor model), but more importantly we found the Durbin–Watson statistic to be

$$d = .56$$

indicating a strong autocorrelation. Because of this condition, an autoregressive model appears to be a desirable technique. Estimate the autoregressive model, and forecast the increase in the CPI.

ANNUAL PERCENTAGE INCREASE IN THE CPI

Year	% Increase in CPI	Year	% Increase in CPI
1951	7.9	1970	5.9
1952	2.2	1971	4.3
1953	.8	1972	3.3
1954	.5	1973	6.2
1955	−.4	1974	11.0
1956	1.5	1975	9.1
1957	3.6	1976	5.8
1958	2.7	1977	6.5
1959	.8	1978	7.7
1960	1.6	1979	11.3
1961	1.0	1980	13.5
1962	1.1	1981	10.4
1963	1.2	1982	6.1
1964	1.3	1983	3.2
1965	1.7	1984	4.3
1966	2.9	1985	3.6
1967	2.9	1986	1.9
1968	4.2		
1969	5.4		

SOURCE: *Statistical Abstract of the United States.*

Solution.   The model to be estimated is

$$y_t = \beta_0 + \beta_1 y_{t-1} + \varepsilon$$

where y_t = Increase in the CPI in year t and y_{t-1} = Increase in the CPI in year $t-1$. The Minitab output shown next was produced. Thus, to forecast the percentage change in the CPI, we use

$$\hat{y}_t = .730 + .797 y_{t-1}$$

The forecast for 1987 is

$$\hat{y}_{1987} = .730 + .797 y_{1986} = .730 + .797(1.9) = 2.2$$

The autoregressive model predicts that in 1987 the consumer price index should increase by 2.2%.

MINITAB COMPUTER OUTPUT FOR EXAMPLE 19.13

The values of y_t were stored in column 1 and the previous year's values y_{t-1} were stored in column 2.

```
The regression equation is

C1=0.730+0.797C2

Predictor    Coef     Stdev    t-ratio
Constant    0.7303   0.5782     1.26
C2          0.7965   0.1029     7.74

s=2.102    R-sq=64.5%    R-sq(adj)=63.4%

Analysis of Variance

SOURCE        DF      SS       MS
Regression     1    264.66   264.66
Error         33    145.84     4.42
Total         34    410.50
```

███████████ **EXERCISES**

LEARNING THE TECHNIQUES

19.56 The following trend line and seasonal indices were computed from 10 years of quarterly observations:

$\hat{y} = 150 + 3t \qquad (t = 1, 2, \ldots, 40)$

Quarter	SI
1	.7
2	1.2
3	1.5
4	.6

Forecast the next 4 values.

19.57 Regression analysis with $t = 1$ to 96 was used to develop the following forecast equation:

$\hat{y} = 220 + 6.5t + 1.3Q_1 - 1.6Q_2 - 1.3Q_3$

where

$Q_i = 1$ if quarter i \qquad $(i = 1, 2, 3)$

$\quad = 0$ otherwise

Forecast the next 4 values.

19.58 Use the following autoregressive model to forecast the value of the time series if the last observed value is 65:

$\hat{y}_t = 625 - 1.3y_{t-1}$

19.59 A time series has exhibited seasonal variation and a logarithmic trend. The trend line is as follows:

$\hat{y} = (21.5)(1.05)^t \qquad (t = 1, 2, \ldots, 48)$

The seasonal (quarterly) indices are shown in the

accompanying table.

Quarter	SI
1	1.25
2	1.05
3	0.80
4	0.90

Forecast the next 4 quarters.

19.60   Daily observations for 52 weeks (5 days per week) have produced the following regression model:

$$\hat{y} = 1,500 + 250t - 20D_1 + 10D_2 + 20D_3 + 50D_4$$

$$(t = 1, 2, \ldots, 260)$$

where

$D_1 = 1$ if Monday

$\quad = 0$ otherwise

$D_2 = 1$ if Tuesday

$\quad = 0$ otherwise

$D_3 = 1$ if Wednesday

$\quad = 0$ otherwise

$D_4 = 1$ if Thursday

$\quad = 0$ otherwise

Forecast the next week.

19.61   The following autoregressive model was developed:

$$\hat{y}_t = 155 + 21y_{t-1}$$

Forecast the time series if the last observation is 11.

19.62   For Exercise 19.34, forecast the time series for Monday through Friday of week 5.

APPLYING THE TECHNIQUES

GEN | **19.63**   For Exercises 19.38 and 19.40, forecast the number of cable subscribers over the next 8 quarters.

Self-Correcting Exercise (See Appendix 19.B for the solution.)

GEN | **19.64**   The following regression model was produced from the observations in Exercise 19.38:

$$\hat{y} = 164 + 6.51t - 3.66Q_1 - 23.4Q_2 - 29.9Q_3$$

$$(t = 1, 2, \ldots, 20)$$

where

$Q_i = 1$ if quarter $i \quad (i = 1, 2, 3)$

$\quad = 0$ otherwise

Use this model to forecast the number of cable subscribers over the next 4 quarters.

GEN | **19.65**   The following autoregressive model was produced from the time series in Exercise 19.38:

$$\hat{y}_t = 0.2 + 1.03y_{t-1}$$

Forecast the number of cable subscribers in the first quarter of 1990.

ECON | **19.66**   Retail sales in durable goods are an important indicator of overall economic activity. They in turn are affected by people's perception of the economy and especially by prevailing interest rates and financing availability. Sales are said to exhibit considerable seasonal variability. Consider the data in Table E19.66 on page 980.

TABLE E19.66   *TOTAL RETAIL SALES—DURABLE GOODS STORES, UNADJUSTED FOR SEASONAL VARIATION ($MILLIONS)*

	Jan	Feb	Mar	Apr	May	June
1976	14,464	15,025	18,010	18,966	19,014	20,008
1977	16,012	16,928	21,069	21,469	21,942	22,784
1978	17,027	18,043	22,950	23,384	25,349	25,964
1979	21,357	21,380	26,401	25,919	27,479	26,854
1980	22,684	22,971	24,263	23,750	24,383	24,869

	July	Aug	Sept	Oct	Nov	Dec
1976	19,346	18,505	17,640	18,301	18,163	20,343
1977	21,396	21,993	20,342	21,636	20,864	22,201
1978	24,238	25,210	22,820	24,913	24,678	25,821
1979	25,629	27,897	24,956	26,588	25,238	26.655
1980	26,135	25,361	24,582	26,690	25,114	28,171

SOURCE: U.S. Department of Commerce, Bureau of Economic Analysis, *Business Statistics.* Biennial supplement to the *Survey of Current Business* (1984).

The linear trend line was calculated and found to be

$$\hat{y} = 17{,}596 + 162t \qquad (t = 1, 2, \ldots, 60)$$

a. Using the trend line, compute the seasonal (monthly) indices.

b. Forecast the monthly total retail sales for 1981.

19.67   A daily newspaper wanted to forecast 2-day revenues from its classified ads section. The revenues (in $1,000s) were recorded for the past 104 weeks. From these data, the regression equation was computed. Forecast the 2-day revenues for the next week. (Note that the newspaper appears 6 days per week.)

$$\hat{y} = 2{,}550 + 0.5t - 205D_1 - 60D_2$$

$$(t = 1, 2, \ldots, 312)$$

where

$D_1 = 1$ if Monday or Tuesday

$\quad = 0$ otherwise

$D_2 = 1$ if Wednesday or Thursday

$\quad = 0$ otherwise

19.68   In Exercise 19.41, the linear trend line for the time series is

$$\hat{y} = 145 + 1.66t \qquad (t = 1, 2, \ldots, 28)$$

Use this trend line and the seasonal indices calculated in Exercise 19.41 to forecast the number of pizzas that will be sold daily for the next week.

19.69   For Exercises 19.36 and 19.37, forecast the earnings during the 4 quarters of 1990.

SECTION 19.10   *SUMMARY*

In this chapter, we discussed the classical **time series** and its decomposition into **long-term trend** and **cyclical, seasonal,** and **random variation. Moving averages** and **exponential smoothing** were used to remove some of the random fluctuation, enabling us to identify the time series' other components. The long-term trend was measured more scientifically by one of three regression models—linear, polynomial, or logarithmic. The cyclical and seasonal effects are more clearly detected through calculation of **percentage of trend** and **seasonal indices**.

When the components of a time series are identified, we can select one of many available methods to forecast the time series. When there is no or very little trend and cyclical and seasonal variation, exponential smoothing is recommended. When trend and seasonality are present, we can use regression analysis with seasonal indices or dummy variables to make predictions. We can also use the **autoregressive model**.

SUPPLEMENTARY EXERCISES

SCI **19.70** The cost of health care in the United States has been increasing rapidly. The accompanying table lists annual per capital national health expenditures for 1970–1986.

a. Plot the time series.

b. Based on the linear trend line

$\hat{y} = 80.1 + 96.4t \qquad (t = 1, 2, \ldots, 17)$

compute the percentage of trend.

Year	t	Per Capita National Health Expenditures
1984	15	1,597
1985	16	1,710
1986	17	1,837

SOURCE: *Statistical Abstract of the United States.*

Year	t	Per Capita National Health Expenditures
1970	1	349
1971	2	384
1972	3	428
1973	4	467
1974	5	521
1975	6	590
1976	7	665
1977	8	743
1978	9	822
1979	10	921
1980	11	1,054
1981	12	1,207
1982	13	1,348
1983	14	1,473

ECON **19.71** The number of hospital beds is a function of various factors including medical costs, population age, and economic conditions. The number of beds available in the United States between 1975 and 1985 is recorded in the accompanying table. Use exponential smoothing with $w = .4$ to forecast the number of hospital beds available in 1986.

Year	Number of Hospital Beds (1,000s)
1975	1,466
1976	1,434
1977	1,407
1978	1,381
1979	1,372
1980	1,365
1981	1,362
1982	1,360

(continued)

Year	Number of Hospital Beds (1,000s)
1983	1,350
1984	1,339
1985	1,309

SOURCE: *Statistical Abstract of the United States.*

19.72   An important measure of a country's economic health is the difference between the value of its exports and the value of its imports. This quantity is sometimes called the *resource balance.* Canada's resource balance for the past 10 years is shown next. (Use exponential smoothing (with $w = .4$) to forecast the 1987 figure.

Year	Resource Balance ($billions)
1977	6.17
1978	11.09
1979	7.18
1980	5.65
1981	2.51
1982	13.43
1983	13.28
1984	16.58
1985	15.64
1986	13.84

SOURCE: *World Tables* (1987).

Exercises 19.73 through 19.82 are based on the following problem.

The revenues of a chain of ice cream stores are listed for each quarter during the past 5 years in the table at the top of the next column.

19.73   Plot the time series.

19.74   Discuss why exponential smoothing is not recommended as a forecasting method in this case.

REVENUES ($MILLIONS)

	Year				
Quarter	1984	1985	1986	1987	1988
1	16	14	17	18	21
2	25	27	31	29	30
3	31	32	40	45	52
4	24	23	27	24	32

19.75   Calculate the 4-quarter centered moving averages, and plot these values.

19.76   Use the moving averages computed in Exercise 19.75 to calculate the seasonal (quarterly) indices.

19.77   Regression analysis produced the trend line

$\hat{y} = 20.2 + .732t$ $(t = 1, 2, \ldots, 20)$

Using this trend line, compute the seasonal indices.

19.78   Using the trend line and seasonal indices calculated in Exercise 19.77, forecast revenues for the 4 quarters of 1989.

19.79   The following multiple regression model was produced:

$\hat{y} = 18.6 + 0.613t - 6.96Q_1 + 3.62Q_2 + 14.6Q_3$

$(t = 1, 2, \ldots, 20)$

where

$Q_i = 1$ if quarter i, $(i = 1, 2, 3)$

$= 0$ otherwise

Use this model to forecast revenues for the 4 quarters of 1989.

19.80   The Durbin–Watson statistic for the regression line in Exercise 19.77 is $d = 2.08$. What does this tell you about the likelihood that an autoregressive model will produce accurate forecasts?

19.81   Suppose that the actual 1989 revenues are as shown in the following table.

Quarter	1989 Revenues ($millions)
1	25
2	35
3	58
4	37

Calculate MAD for the forecasts in Exercises 19.78 and 19.79.

19.82 Repeat Exercise 19.81, using SSE instead of MAD.

Exercises 19.83 through 19.89 are based on the following problem.

ECON The monthly unemployment rate in Canada typically displays a great deal of seasonal variation, partly because of the country's climate. This factor plays an important role when governments attempt to forecast unemployment. The monthly unemployment rates for 1984–1987 are listed in the accompanying table.

Month	Year 1984	1985	1986	1987
Jan.	12.7	12.6	10.1	10.8
Feb.	12.2	11.9	10.1	10.4
Mar.	12.1	12.3	9.8	10.4
Apr.	12.0	11.3	9.5	9.4
May	11.2	9.7	9.0	7.7
June	10.4	9.3	8.5	7.5
July	9.8	9.0	8.0	7.2
Aug.	9.9	8.5	7.5	7.6
Sept.	10.6	8.7	7.8	7.6
Oct.	10.0	8.9	8.0	7.0
Nov.	10.2	9.7	8.2	7.3
Dec.	10.9	9.2	9.0	7.7

19.83 Plot the time series, to confirm the assertion about seasonal variation.

19.84 The linear trend line (computed by regression analysis) is

$$\hat{y} = 11.7 - .0885t \quad (t = 1, 2, \ldots, 48)$$

Compute the seasonal (monthly) indices.

19.85 Using the trend line and seasonal indices calculated in Exercise 19.84, forecast the monthly unemployment rates for 1988.

19.86 The following multiple regression model was developed from the unemployment rate data:

$$\hat{y} = 11.5 - .076t + 1.51M_1 + 1.19M_2 + 1.26M_3$$
$$+ 0.74M_4 - .33M_5 - .73M_6 - 1.08M_7$$
$$- 1.13M_8 - .75M_9 - .88M_{10} - .43M_{11}$$
$$(t = 1, 2, \ldots, 48)$$

where

$M_i = 1$ if month i, where $i = 1, 2, \ldots, 11$

$\quad$ (1 = January, 11 = November)

$\quad = 0$ otherwise

Use this model to forecast the 1988 monthly unemployment rates.

19.87 The regression line referred to in Exercise 19.84 produced a Durbin–Watson statistic of $d = .47$ indicating strong first-order autocorrelation. The autoregressive model was estimated as

$$\hat{y}_t = 1.08 + .876y_{t-1}$$

Use this model to forecast the 1988 monthly unemployment rates. (Use forecasted values of y_{t-1} for $t \geq 50$.)

19.88 The actual 1988 unemployment rates were as follows.

Month	Unemployment Rates
Jan.	8.4
Feb.	7.6
Mar.	8.7
Apr.	7.7
May	7.2

(continued)

Month	Unemployment Rates
June	6.7
July	6.6
Aug.	6.2
Sept.	7.0
Oct.	7.4
Nov.	7.5
Dec.	7.7

For each set of forecasts in Exercises 19.85–19.87, calculate the mean absolute deviation to determine which model worked best for 1988.

19.89 Repeat Exercise 19.88, using SSE instead of MAD.

MINITAB INSTRUCTIONS

TIME SERIES PLOTTING

To plot the time series stored in column 1, type

`TSPLOT C1`

For example, the time series plot for Example 19.1 appears as follows.

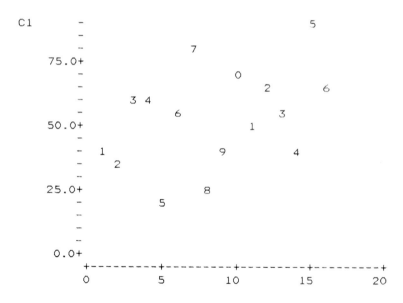

The points are shown in order, where 1 represents the first time series value, 2 represents the second, and so on.

MOVING AVERAGES

Minitab does not calculate moving averages directly. However, by using several commands we can induce Minitab to compute the moving averages using any number of periods. To illustrate, we'll re-do Example 19.1. We begin by inputting the time series in column 1.

```
SET C1
39 37 61 58 18 56 82 27 41 69 49 66 54 42 90 66
END
```

To calculate the 3-quarter moving averages, we copy column 1 into columns 2 and 3.

```
LET C2=C1
LET C3=C1
```

Next, we delete the first observation in column 2 and the first two observations in column 3.

```
DELETE 1 C2
DELETE 1:2 C3
```

If you now print the 3 columns (PRINT C1–C3), you'll observe

39	37	61
37	61	58
61	58	18
58	18	56
18	56	82
56	82	27
82	27	41
27	41	69
41	69	49
69	49	66
49	66	54
66	54	42
54	42	90
42	90	66
90	66	
66		

As you can see, the first row contains observations 1, 2, and 3 of the time series. The mean of these values is the first moving average. The mean of the second row is the second moving average, and so on. The command

```
RMEAN C1-C3 C4
```

calculates the mean for each row in columns 1 to 3 and stores these means in column 4.

```
PRINT C4
```

produces the following output.

```
45.6667    52.0000    45.6667    44.0000    52.0000    55.0000    50.0000
45.6667    53.0000    61.3333    56.3333    54.0000    62.0000    66.0000
78.0000    66.0000
```

Care should be taken when interpreting these values. The first value (45.6667) is the moving average for period 2. (Remember, there is no moving average for period 1.) The second value (52.000) is the moving average for period 3. The last two values (78.000 and 66.000) have no meaning and should be ignored.

You can present the moving averages in a more useful form by deleting the last two values in column 4 and inserting an asterisk (which represents missing data) in the first row.

```
DELETE 15:16 C4
INSERT 0 1 C4
*
END
PRINT C1 C4
```

The output is

```
ROW    C1    C4
 1     39    *
 2     37    45.6667
 3     61    52.0000
 4     58    45.6667
 5     18    44.0000
 6     56    52.0000
 7     82    55.0000
 8     27    50.0000
 9     41    45.6667
10     69    53.0000
11     49    61.3333
12     66    56.3333
13     54    54.0000
14     42    62.0000
15     90    66.0000
16     66
```

To produce the 5-quarter moving average in Example 19.1, we would type the following commands (after inputting the time series in column 1).

```
LET C2=C1
LET C3=C1
```

```
LET C4=C1
LET C5=C1
DELETE 1 C2
DELETE 1:2 C3
DELETE 1:3 C4
DELETE 1:4 C5
RMEAN C1-C5 C6
PRINT C6
```

The output is

```
42.6    46.0    55.0    48.2    44.8    55.0    53.6    50.4    55.8    56.0    60.2
63.6    63.0    66.0    78.0    66.0
```

The first value (42.6) is the moving average for period 3. The last four values (63.0, 66.0, 78.0, and 66.0) should be ignored. Again, we can make the results more presentable in the following way.

```
DELETE 13:16 C4
INSERT 0 1 C4
*
*
END
```

To calculate the centered moving averages we employ our procedure twice. To illustrate, consider the time series from page 929.

Period	Time Series
1	15
2	27
3	20
4	14
5	25
6	11

To compute the 4-period centered moving average, we type the following commands.

```
SET C1
15 27 20 14 25 11
END
LET C2=C1
LET C3=C1
```

```
LET C4=C1
DELETE 1 C2
DELETE 1:2 C3
DELETE 1:3 C4
RMEAN C1-C4 C5
LET C6=C5
DELETE 1 C6
RMEAN C5-C6 C7
PRINT C7
```

The output is

```
20.2500    19.5000    17.0833    17.3333    14.5000    11.0000
```

The centered moving averages for periods 3 and 4 are 20.25 and 19.5, respectively. Ignore the remaining four values.

MEASURING THE CYCLICAL EFFECT

To measure the cyclical effect, we begin by finding the trend line using regression analysis. The LET command is used to calculate the trend values, as well as the percentage of trend. The results for Example 19.6 are produced as follows.

```
READ C1 C2
 1    66.4
 2    69.7
 3    72.2
 4    74.3
 5    72.5
 6    70.6
 7    74.4
 8    76.3
 9    78.1
10    78.9
11    76.0
12    74.0
13    70.8
14    70.5
15    74.1
16    74.0
17    73.9
END
REGRESS C2 1 C1
```

The regression results are

```
C2=71.313+0.2248C1
```

The trend values are computed by

```
LET C3=71.313+0.2248*C1
```

The percentage of trend values are determined by

```
LET C4=(C2/C3)*100
```

PRINT C1-C4 outputs the following:

1	66.4	71.5378	92.819
2	69.7	71.7626	97.127
3	72.2	71.9874	100.296
4	74.3	72.2122	102.892
5	72.5	72.4370	100.088
6	70.6	72.6618	97.164
7	74.4	72.8866	102.078
8	76.3	73.1114	104.363
9	78.1	73.3362	106.497
10	78.9	73.5610	107.259
11	76.0	73.7858	103.002
12	74.0	74.0106	99.987
13	70.8	74.2354	95.374
14	70.5	74.4602	94.683
15	74.1	74.6850	99.218
16	74.0	74.9098	98.787
17	73.9	75.1346	98.358

We can then plot the results to duplicate Figure 19.16.

CALCULATING THE SEASONAL INDICES

Minitab can be used to compute the seasonal indices based on the regression trend line. The REGRESS command, of course, creates the trend line. The LET command calculates the ratios ($y/\hat{y}$). We then use the DESCRIBE command (with the BY subcommand) to produce the unadjusted indices. We illustrate with Example 19.7.

```
SET C1
1 2 3 4 5 6 7 8 9 10 11 12 13 14 15 16 17 18 19 20
END
SET C2
1 2 3 4 1 2 3 4 1 2 3 4 1 2 3 4 1 2 3 4
END
SET C3
.561 .702 .800 .568 .575 .738 .868 .605 .594 .738
.729 .600 .622 .708 .806 .632 .665 .835 .873 .670
```

Notice that column 1 stores t (1, 2, ..., 20), column 2 identifies the quarter, and column 3 stores the time series.

```
REGRESS C3 1 C1
```

computes the regression line

```
C3=.639+.00525C1
LET C4=.639+.00525*C1
LET C5=C3/C4
```

These two commands calculate $\hat{y}$ (C4) and the ratio $y/\hat{y}$ (C5). We can then calculate the average for each quarter by

```
DESCRIBE C5;
BY C2.
```

This instructs Minitab to calculate the mean (plus other statistics) of C5 for each value in C2. These means can then be adjusted so that their total $= 4.000$. The relevant part of the output is shown next.

	C2	N	MEAN
C5	1	5	0.87866
	2	5	1.0762
	3	5	1.1715
	4	5	0.87568

■■■■■■   **COMPUTER EXERCISES**

19.90   Plot the following time series.

t	y
1	0.5
2	0.9
3	1.6
4	3.0
5	5.6
6	10.9
7	18.0
8	32.4
9	70.6
10	125.4

19.91   Plot the following time series.

t	y
1	3.3
2	7.4
3	9.9
4	13.2
5	13.3
6	15.6
7	16.3
8	17.1
9	17.3
10	19.8
11	22.0
12	27.3
13	30.5
14	34.5
15	34.7

19.92   The following daily sales were recorded.

	Week				
	1	2	3	4	5
Monday	25	41	52	26	33
Tuesday	41	28	75	48	52
Wednesday	38	67	26	50	60
Thursday	52	65	82	74	95
Friday	73	42	80	93	88

a. Compute the 3-day moving averages.

b. Compute the 5-day moving averages.

19.93   The following quarterly observations were recorded.

	Year					
Quarter	1	2	3	4	5	6
1	75	88	62	59	45	49
2	92	63	51	53	57	36
3	63	71	83	18	49	30
4	27	50	42	27	28	15

Compute the 4-quarter centered moving averages.

19.94   Fit a logarithmic trend line to the time series in Exercise 19.90.

19.95   Calculate the percentage of trend, assuming a linear trend in Exercise 19.91.

19.96   Given the following quarterly observations, compute the seasonal indices using linear regression.

Time Period	Quarter	y
1	1	20
2	2	15
3	3	12
4	4	27
5	1	18
6	2	13
7	3	11
8	4	24
9	1	14
10	2	12
11	3	9
12	4	20
13	1	13
14	2	11
15	3	7
16	4	15

SOLUTIONS TO SELF-CORRECTING EXERCISES

19.8

Time Period	Sales	3-Day Moving Average
1	43	—
2	45	$(43+45+22)/3 = 36.7$
3	22	$(45+22+25)/3 = 30.7$
4	25	$(22+25+31)/3 = 26.0$
5	31	$(25+31+51)/3 = 35.7$
6	51	$(31+51+41)/3 = 41.0$
7	41	$(51+41+37)/3 = 43.0$
8	37	$(41+37+22)/3 = 33.3$
9	22	$(37+22+25)/3 = 28.0$
10	25	$(22+25+40)/3 = 29.0$
11	40	$(25+40+57)/3 = 40.7$
12	57	$(40+57+30)/3 = 42.3$
13	30	$(57+30+33)/3 = 40.0$
14	33	$(30+33+37)/3 = 33.3$
15	37	$(33+37+64)/3 = 44.7$
16	64	$(37+64+58)/3 = 53.0$
17	58	$(64+58+33)/3 = 51.7$
18	33	$(58+33+38)/3 = 43.0$
19	38	$(33+38+25)/3 = 32.0$
20	25	—

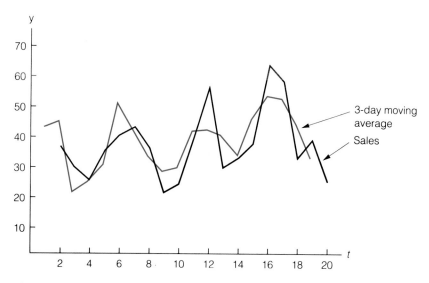

The seasonal pattern is quite distinct.

19.18

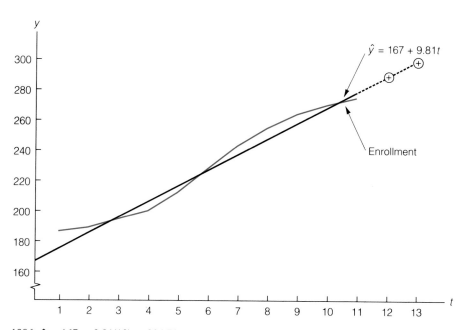

1986: $\hat{y} = 167 + 9.81(12) = 284.72$

1987: $\hat{y} = 167 + 9.81(13) = 294.53$

19.30

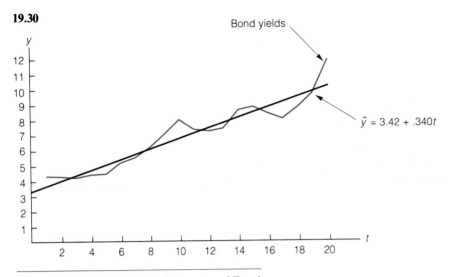

Time Period	Yields	Trend	Percentage of Trend
t	*y*	*ŷ*	*(y/ŷ) · 100*
1	4.35	3.76	115.7
2	4.33	4.10	105.6
3	4.26	4.44	95.9
4	4.40	4.78	92.1
5	4.49	5.12	87.7
6	5.13	5.46	94.0
7	5.51	5.80	95.0
8	6.18	6.14	100.7
9	7.03	6.48	108.5
10	8.04	6.82	117.9
11	7.39	7.16	103.2
12	7.21	7.50	96.1
13	7.44	7.84	94.9
14	8.57	8.18	104.8
15	8.83	8.52	103.6
16	8.43	8.86	95.1
17	8.02	9.20	87.2
18	8.73	9.54	91.5
19	9.63	9.88	97.5
20	11.94	10.22	116.8

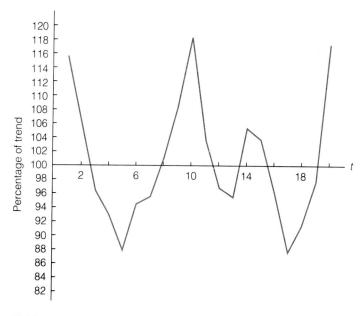

19.36

Period t	Earnings y	4-Quarter Moving Average	4-Quarter Centered Moving Average	Ratio y/MA
1	52		—	—
2	67	—	—	—
		64.50		
3	85		65.125	1.305
		65.75		
4	54		66.750	.809
		67.75		
5	57		68.375	.834
		69.00		
6	75		69.875	1.073
		70.75		
7	90		71.125	1.265
		71.50		
8	61		71.750	.850
		72.00		
9	60		72.500	.828
		73.00		
10	77		73.250	1.051
		73.50		
11	94		74.250	1.266
		75.00		
12	63		75.625	.833
		76.25		
13	66		76.750	.860
		77.25		
14	82		77.750	1.055
		78.25		
15	98		—	—
16	67	—		

| | Quarter | | | | |
Year	1	2	3	4	Total
1986	—	—	1.305	.809	
1987	.834	1.073	1.265	.850	
1988	.828	1.051	1.266	.833	
1989	.860	1.055			
Average	.841	1.060	1.279	.831	4.011
Seasonal index	.839	1.057	1.275	.829	4.000

19.44

Model 1: MAD

$$= \frac{|6.0 - 7.5| + |6.6 - 6.3| + |7.3 - 5.4| + |9.4 - 8.2|}{4}$$

$$= \frac{1.5 + .3 + 1.9 + 1.2}{4} = \frac{4.9}{4} = 1.225$$

Model 2: MAD

$$= \frac{|6.0 - 6.3| + |6.6 - 6.7| + |7.3 - 7.1| + |9.4 - 7.5|}{4}$$

$$= \frac{.3 + .1 + .2 + 1.9}{4} = \frac{2.5}{4} = .625$$

Model 2 is more accurate.

19.54

Year	Earnings as a Percentage of Value Added y_t	$S_t = wy_t + (1 - w)S_{t-1}$ with $w = .7$
1975	43.1	$S_{1975} = 43.1$
1976	41.7	$S_{1976} = .7(41.7) + .3(43.1) = 42.1$
1977	41.4	$S_{1977} = .7(41.4) + .3(42.1) = 41.6$
1978	41.3	$S_{1978} = .7(41.3) + .3(41.6) = 41.4$
1979	39.9	$S_{1979} = .7(39.9) + .3(41.4) = 40.4$
1980	40.9	$S_{1980} = .7(40.9) + .3(40.4) = 40.7$
1981	40.8	$S_{1981} = .7(40.8) + .3(40.7) = 40.8$
1982	41.4	$S_{1982} = .7(41.4) + .3(40.8) = 41.2$
1983	40.1	$S_{1983} = .7(40.1) + .3(41.2) = 40.4$
1984	40.0	$S_{1984} = .7(40.0) + .3(40.4) = 40.1$

The 1985 forecast is $F_{1985} = S_{1984} = 40.1$.

19.64

Year	Quarter	t	Q_1	Q_2	Q_3	Forecast $\hat{y} = 164 + 6.51t - 3.66Q_1 - 23.4Q_2 - 29.9Q_3$
1990	1	21	1	0	0	297.05
	2	22	0	1	0	283.82
	3	23	0	0	1	283.83
	4	24	0	0	0	320.24

INDEX NUMBERS

INTRODUCTION

In Chapter 19 we presented a variety of techniques for analyzing and forecasting time series. This chapter is devoted to the simpler task of developing descriptive measurements of the changes in a time series. These measurements are called **index numbers.** As is the case with the descriptive statistics introduced in Chapter 2 and used throughout this book, index numbers allow the statistician to summarize a large body of data with a single number.

For example, shoppers who observe the price of goods and services change frequently have difficulty assessing what is happening to overall prices. They might know that the price of T-bone steaks has increased, that baby-sitters charge more, and that rental and housing prices seem to have increased; but at the same time, desk calculators and personal computers have gotten cheaper, airline deregulation has lowered the price of many flights, and the cost of certain types of food staples does not seem to have increased significantly. By looking at the Consumer Price Index, they can get an immediate general idea as to what has happened to overall prices.

The **Consumer Price Index (CPI)** measures what has happened to the prices of hundreds of consumer goods and services. In 1967, the CPI was set to equal 100. By 1978, it had risen to 195.4, telling us that prices had generally almost doubled over the preceding 11 years; and by 1982, the CPI reading of almost 300 told us that prices had tripled over the 15-year period.

Another popular index is the Dow Jones Industrial Average, which measures the average daily closing prices of 30 large corporations listed on the New York Stock Exchange. As such, it is perceived by many people (and especially by the media that report it on a daily and sometimes hourly basis) as being a good indicator not only of the current status of the stock market but of the economic well-being of the country as a whole.

In general, the use of indices has become so popular that they have entered our everyday language. Jimmy Carter, for example, invented a "misery index"—defined as the sum of the inflation rate and the unemployment rate—during his 1976 Presidential campaign against Gerald Ford. His use of the index against President Ford later backfired, however, when it rose to some 20% in 1980 and was used by Ronald Reagan to attack his administrations track record.

Although we can develop an index to measure changes in any time series, in practice most indices measure changes in prices. Our notation will reflect this fact.

SECTION 20.2   *SIMPLE AND AGGREGATE INDEX NUMBERS*

We start with the most basic type of index number.

> **Simple Index**
>
> A simple index is a ratio of the price of a commodity at time *t* divided by its value in some base period. We can express the ratio as a percentage by multiplying it by 100. That is,
>
> $$I_1 = \left(\frac{P_1}{P_0}\right) 100$$
>
> where
>
> I_1 = Index in the current period
> P_1 = Price in the current period
> P_0 = Price in the base period

■■■■■   EXAMPLE 20.1

Construct the index of average hourly earnings of private nonagricultural workers for 1981–1986, using the data in the accompanying table. Use 1980 as the base year.

Year	Average Hourly Earnings of Private Nonagricultural Workers
1980	$6.66
1981	$7.25
1982	$7.68
1983	$8.02
1984	$8.32
1985	$8.57
1986	$8.76

SOURCE: U.S. Department of Labor, Bureau of Labor Statistics, *Monthly Labor Reviews.*

Solution.   For each year, we compute

$$I_1 = \left(\frac{P_1}{P_0}\right) 100$$

The results are as follows.

Year	Index Number of Earnings
1980	100
1981	108.9
1982	115.3
1983	120.4
1984	124.9
1985	128.7
1986	131.5

These numbers can be used, for example, by a labor union to compare its members' wage increases since 1980 with those of the average worker. Example 20.2 illustrates this type of comparison.

EXAMPLE 20.2

Suppose that the members of a union were paid the average hourly wages listed in the accompanying table. Compute the index of earnings for 1981–1986 (using 1980 as the base year) for this union, and compare it with those computed in Example 20.1.

Year	Average Hourly Earnings for a Labor Union
1980	$5.50
1981	$6.11
1982	$6.62
1983	$6.71
1984	$6.77
1985	$6.85
1986	$7.05

Solution.   The index of earnings for this union is as follows.

Year	Index Number of Earnings
1980	100
1981	111.1
1982	120.4
1983	122.0
1984	123.1
1985	124.5
1986	128.2

In comparsion to the wages represented by the index numbers in Example 20.1, this union's wages grew faster than the average between 1980 and 1981, 1982, and 1983, but grew more slowly in the periods 1980–1984, 1980–1985, and 1980–1986.

Figures 20.1 and 20.2 describe the actual wages and the indices. As you can see, it is difficult to compare relative increases in wages using Figure 20.1, but graphing the indices in Figure 20.2 provides a great deal more information.

The simple index number measures the price changes of only one item. Very frequently, though, we would like to measure price changes for a group of commodities. Our next index number performs this function.

Simple Aggregate Index

A simple aggregate index is the ratio of the sum of the prices of several commodities in the current period over the sum in the base period, multiplied by 100.

$$I_1 = \left[\frac{\sum_{i=1}^{n} P_{1i}}{\sum_{i=1}^{n} P_{0i}} \right] \cdot 100$$

where

P_{1i} = Price of item i in the current period

P_{0i} = Price of item i in the base period

FIGURE 20.1   *HOURLY WAGES IN EXAMPLES 20.1 AND 20.2*

FIGURE 20.2   *INDICES IN EXAMPLES 20.1 AND 20.2*

EXAMPLE 20.3

Construct a simple aggregate index of the prices for the meat, chicken, and fish items shown in the following table, using July 1988 as the base period.

Item	Meat, Chicken, and Fish Prices per Pound	
	July 1988	July 1989
Beef	$5.50	$5.92
Veal	$7.48	$8.06
Pork	$4.80	$5.05
Chicken	$3.62	$3.45
Fish	$5.13	$6.25

Solution

$$I_1 = \left[\frac{\sum_{i=1}^{5} P_{1i}}{\sum_{i=1}^{5} P_{0i}} \right] \cdot 100$$

$$= \left[\frac{5.92 + 8.06 + 5.05 + 3.45 + 6.25}{5.50 + 7.48 + 4.80 + 3.62 + 5.13} \right] \cdot 100 = 108.3$$

Thus, the 1-year increase in the total prices is 8.3%.

The figure identified in Example 20.3 cannot be interpreted as the price increase in this part of our diets, however, since each food item may not be equally represented. For example, if the average person's diet consisted mostly of chicken, the average costs may actually have decreased. Thus, the simple aggregate index must be modified if we do not consume equal quantities of each item. In the **weighted aggregate index,** each item is weighted by its relative importance.

Weighted Aggregate Index

$$I_1 = \left[\frac{\sum_{i=1}^{n} P_{1i}Q_{1i}}{\sum_{i=1}^{n} P_{0i}Q_{0i}} \right] \cdot 100$$

where

Q_{1i} = Weight assigned to item i in the current period
Q_{0i} = Weight assigned to item i in the base period

Notice that

$$\sum_{i=1}^{n} Q_{1i} = 1 \quad \text{and} \quad \sum_{i=1}^{n} Q_{0i} = 1$$

EXAMPLE 20.4

In July 1988, a family's weekly diet consists of 6 pounds of fish, 2 pounds of beef, and 2 pounds of veal. One year later, because of the cost increases in these products, the family's diet is changed so that each week they consume 4 pounds of chicken and 1 pound of each other item. Assuming that the prices are those listed in the table in Example 20.3, calculate the weighted aggregate index for 1989, using 1988 as the base.

Solution. The weight assigned to each food item in each year is the percentage of the entire diet supplied by that item. The relevant weights are shown in the following table.

Item	July 1988 Price P_{0i}	July 1988 Quantity	July 1988 Weighting Q_{0i}	July 1989 Price P_{1i}	July 1989 Quantity	July 1989 Weighting Q_{1i}
Beef	5.50	2	.2	5.92	1	.125
Veal	7.48	2	.2	8.06	1	.125
Pork	4.80	0	0	5.05	1	.125
Chicken	3.62	0	0	3.45	4	.500
Fish	5.13	6	.6	6.25	1	.125
		10	1		8	1

The weighted aggregate index is

$$I_1 = \left[\frac{\sum_{i=1}^{5} P_{1i}Q_{1i}}{\sum_{i=1}^{5} P_{0i}Q_{0i}} \right] \cdot 100$$

$$= \left(\frac{5.92(.125) + 8.06(.125) + 5.05(.125) + 3.45(.500) + 6.25(.125)}{5.50(.2) + 7.48(.2) + 4.80(0) + 3.62(0) + 5.13(.6)} \right) 100$$

$$= 86.1$$

Thus there has been a decrease of 13.9% in this part of the family's food budget. The evident problem with this calculation, however, is that it does not really reflect the price changes that have taken place.

One way of correcting the weighted aggregate index is to substitute the weights in the base period for the weights in the current period. The result is the **Laspeyres index.**

Laspeyres Index

$$L_1 = \left[\frac{\sum_{i=1}^{n} P_{1i} \cdot Q_{0i}}{\sum_{i=1}^{n} P_{0i} \cdot Q_{0i}} \right] \cdot 100$$

By keeping the weights the same, the Laspeyres index more accurately measures the true price changes, as Example 20.5 illustrates.

EXAMPLE 20.5

Calculate the Laspeyres index for the family described in Example 20.4.

Solution

$$L_1 = \left[\frac{\sum_{i=1}^{5} P_{1i}Q_{0i}}{\sum_{i=1}^{5} P_{0i}Q_{0i}} \right] \cdot 100$$

$$= \left(\frac{5.92(.2) + 8.06(.2) + 5.05(0) + 3.45(0) + 6.25(.6)}{5.50(.2) + 7.48(.2) + 4.80(0) + 3.62(0) + 5.13(.6)} \right) 100 = 115.4$$

This number tells us that, if the 1989 diet had been the same as the 1988 diet, this part of the family budget would show a cost increase of 15.4%. Of course, since in 1989 the family no longer eats 6 pounds of fish, 2 pounds of beef, and 2 pounds of veal weekly, this figure is not accurate.

Another way of measuring the price increase is to use the current year's weighting. When this is done the result is the **Paasche index.**

Paasche Index

$$P_1 = \left[\frac{\sum_{i=1}^{n} P_{1i}Q_{1i}}{\sum_{i=1}^{n} P_{0i}Q_{1i}} \right] \cdot 100$$

■■■■■■■■■■ **EXAMPLE 20.6**

Calculate the Paasche index for the family in Exercise 20.4.

Solution

$$P_1 = \left[\frac{\sum_{i=1}^{5} P_{1i}Q_{1i}}{\sum_{i=1}^{5} P_{0i}Q_{1i}}\right] \cdot 100$$

$$= \left(\frac{5.92(.125) + 8.06(.125) + 5.05(.125) + 3.45(.500) + 6.25(.125)}{5.50(.125) + 7.48(.125) + 4.80(.125) + 3.62(.500) + 5.13(.125)}\right)100$$

$$= 104.5$$

Using the 1989 quantities, the aggregate price increase is 4.5%.

We now have three different indices based on the same data. The weighted aggregate index is

$$I_1 = 86.1$$

the Laspeyres index is

$$L_1 = 115.4$$

and the Paasche index is

$$P_1 = 104.5$$

Which index should we use to describe the price change? To answer this question, we must first address another question: what do you want to measure? Do you want to find out what actually happened to this family's food budget between 1988 and 1989? Then use $I_1 = 86.1$; the cost decreased by 13.9%. Do you want to know what happened to the prices, assuming that the 1988 diet remained unchanged? Then use $L_1 = 115.4$; prices increased by 15.4%. Do you want to know what happened to the prices, assuming that the 1989 diet was in effect in 1988? Then use $P_1 = 104.5$; prices increased by only 4.5%. Thus, your choice depends on what you wish to measure.

Governments in the United States, Canada, and other countries have chosen to use the Laspeyres index to measure how prices change monthly. The Consumer Price Index is an example of a Laspeyres index, and it is without doubt the most important measure of inflation in many countries. It is important for managers and economists to know more about this descriptive measurement.

CONSUMER PRICE INDEX

The Consumer Price Index works with a basket of some 300 goods and services in the United States (and a similar number in other countries), including such diverse things as food, housing, clothing, transportation, health, and recreation. Prices for each item in this basket are computed on a monthly basis, by city, state, and region, and the CPI is computed from these.

The basket is defined for the "typical" or "average" middle-income family, and the set of items and their weights are revised periodically (every 10 years in the United States, and every 7 years in Canada).

There are, of course, a number of problems associated with the construction and the continuing validity of such an index as the CPI. In constructing the index, we must perform the following steps:

1. Select the appropriate items for the basket.
2. Select the appropriate weights.
3. Select an appropriate base period.

For example, starting the index during a year of low prices or in the midst of a recession will cause a later economic recovery to appear to be imposing substantial increases on the price index.

To maintain the validity of the CPI over a number of years, the index's sponsors must deal with certain problems. Has the typical family changed from the currently used moderate-income urban couple? How much distortion occurs during the years between official revisions of the CPI (at which time new consumption patterns are incorporated into the new index)? Have definitional changes occurred with respect to such terms as "food away from home"? How important are qualitative changes, and does the revised CPI capture these differences? (For example, is the "movie camera, Super 8, zoom lens" the same quality or type of camera in 1989 as it was in 1967? If we are getting a better camera today, the price increase we have experienced may largely be attributable to the higher quality of the product, rather than to inflationary pressures.)

The CPI, despite never really being intended as the official measure of inflation, has come to be interpreted in this way by the general public. Pension-plan payments, old-age security, and many labor contracts are automatically linked to the CPI and automatically indexed (so it is claimed) to the level of inflation. However, if you are not the "typical American family," price changes may affect you quite differently from the way suggested by the CPI.

USING THE CONSUMER PRICE INDEX TO DEFLATE PRICES

Despite its flaws, the Consumer Price Index is used in numerous applications. One of these involves adjusting prices by removing the effect of inflation.

To do this, we first identify the CPI from 1967 to 1986 (see Table 20.1). Notice that the base year of the index is 1967, so its value that year by definition is 100. We can use this table to **deflate** the annual values of prices or wages. This removes the effect of inflation, making comparisons more realistic. For example, suppose that a worker in 1970 earned $3.25/hour and in 1983 earned $7.50/hour. To determine whether his purchasing power really increased, we deflate both figures by dividing by the CPI for each year and then multiplying by 100. Thus, we have the

TABLE 20.1   UNITED STATES CONSUMER PRICE INDEX, 1967–1986

Year	CPI	Year	CPI
1967	100	1977	181.5
1968	104.2	1978	195.4
1969	109.2	1979	217.4
1970	116.3	1980	246.8
1971	121.3	1981	272.4
1972	125.3	1982	289.1
1973	133.1	1983	298.4
1974	147.7	1984	311.1
1975	161.2	1985	322.2
1976	170.5	1986	328.4

SOURCE: U.S. Department of Commerce,
Bureau of the Census, *Statistical Abstract of
the United States: 1988.*

following figures:

Year	Wage	CPI	Deflated Wage
1970	$3.25	116.3	$2.79
1983	$7.50	298.4	$2.51

The deflated wages are now being measured in 1967 dollars. In 1967 dollars, the worker earns less in 1983 than he did in 1970.

Another way of making such comparisons is by dividing the 1983 wage by the 1983 CPI and then multiplying by the 1970 CPI.

Thus,

$$\left(\frac{7.50}{298.4}\right)116.3 = 2.92$$

This figure represents the worker's wages measured in 1970 dollars. Since in 1970 he actually earned $3.25, we can see that our earlier conclusion remains unchanged.

EXAMPLE 20.7

The gross national product (GNP) is often used as a measure of the economic growth of a country. The annual GNP of the United States for the years 1980–1986 is shown in the accompanying table. Use the CPI in Table 20.1 to deflate these figures to 1982 dollars.

Year	GNP ($billions)
1980	2,732.0
1981	3,052.6
1982	3,166.0
1983	3,405.7
1984	3,772.2
1985	4,010.3
1986	4,235.0

SOURCE: U.S. Department of
Commerce, Bureau of the Census,
*Statistical Abstract of the
United States: 1988.*

Solution.   To convert the GNP to 1982 (sometimes referred to as "constant 1982")
dollars, we will divide the GNP by its associated CPI and then multiply by the CPI
in 1982 (which is 289.1). The results are as follows.

Year	GNP ($billions) Current Dollars	CPI	GNP ($billions) 1982 Constant Dollars
1980	2,732.0	246.8	3,200.2
1981	3,052.6	272.4	3,239.7
1982	3,166.0	289.1	3,166.0
1983	3,405.7	298.4	3,299.6
1984	3,772.2	311.1	3,505.4
1985	4,010.3	322.2	3,598.3
1986	4,235.0	328.4	3,728.2

As you can see, the GNP in current dollars gives the impression that the economy
has grown rapidly in the period 1980–1986, whereas when measured in 1982
constant dollars the growth is quite modest. Our conclusion would not change if we
used some year other than 1982 as our basis.

SECTION 20.3   *SUMMARY*

We have looked at the basic concept of an index, and through successive examples
we have shown what they measure. In particular, we noted that **index numbers**
measure the changes over time of particular time-series data. **Simple indices** mea-

sure changes in only a single data series, while aggregate indices measure changes in several variables. We examined **simple aggregate indices** and **weighted aggregate indices.** Two specific examples of the latter are the **Laspeyres index** and the **Paasche index.** The most commonly used Laspeyres index is the **Consumer Price Index.** We discussed how the CPI is determined, and we showed how it could be used to deflate prices to facilitate comparisons.

EXERCISES

20.1 Taking 1972 as the base year, compute the simple index for the price of natural gas in 1965, 1975, and 1985, using the data in the accompanying table.

Year	Natural Gas Price (per 1,000 ft^3)
1965	$.16
1970	$.17
1971	$.18
1972	$.19
1973	$.22
1974	$.30
1975	$.45
1976	$.58
1977	$.79
1978	$.91
1979	$1.18
1980	$1.59
1981	$1.98
1982	$2.46
1983	$2.59
1984	$2.66
1985	$2.51

SOURCE: U.S. Department of Commerce, Bureau of the Census, *Statistical Abstract of the United States: 1988.*

20.2 Taking 1980 as the base year, calculate the simple index for the price of a short ton of coal in 1982, 1984, and 1986, using the data in the accompanying table.

Year	Coal Price (per short ton)
1980	$24.52
1981	$26.29
1982	$27.14
1983	$25.85
1984	$25.51
1985	$25.10
1986	$24.50

SOURCE: U.S. Department of Commerce, Bureau of the Census, *Statistical Abstract of the United States: 1988.*

20.3 Repeat Exercise 20.1, taking 1985 as the base year.

20.4 A cake recipe calls for the following ingredients.

Ingredient	Price 1980	Price 1989
Butter (per pound)	$1.27	$1.87
Sugar (per pound)	$.65	$.95
Flour (per pound)	$1.47	$1.89
Eggs (per dozen)	$.52	$.85

Compute a simple aggregate index, taking 1980 as the base year.

20.5 The hotel industry is very interested in understanding how tourists spend money. In order to measure the price changes in three important components of a tourist's budget, a statistician computed the average cost of a hotel room (one night), a meal, and a car rental (one day) in 1975 and in 1989. The results of these computations are shown in the following table. Compute a simple aggregate index, taking 1975 as the base year.

	Costs	
Component	**1975**	**1989**
Hotel (one night)	55.00	130.00
Meal	8.00	23.00
Car rental (one day)	17.50	40.00

20.6   Refer to Exercise 20.4. Suppose that the chef at Chez Henri's has decided to make his own improvements (adding more butter) to the cake recipe he used to use in 1980. The old and new quantities of ingredients are listed in Table E20.6. Compute a weighted aggregate index to measure the price increases.

20.7   Refer to Exercise 20.5. Suppose that in 1975 the average tourist stayed in the hotel for 6 days, ate 8 meals at the hotel, and rented a car for 2 days. In 1989 the average tourist stayed for 4 days, ate 6 meals at the hotel, and rented a car for 3 days. Calculate a weighted aggregate index.

20.8   For Exercise 20.7, compute the Laspeyres index.

20.9   For Exercise 20.7, compute the Paasche index.

20.10   For Exercise 20.6, calculate the Laspeyres index to measure the change in the costs of a cake's ingredients.

20.11   For Exercise 20.6, calculate the Paasche index to measure the change in the costs of a cake's ingredients.

20.12   What is being measured by each of the indices computed in Exercises 20.6, 20.10, and 20.11?

20.13   People continually look for investments that are inflation-proof. Particularly during periods of high and unexpected inflation, buying gold, silver, and even platinum as a hedge against inflation becomes attractive to some investors. Actual prices for these three precious metals are listed in Table E20.13. Compute the index for each metal for the years 1975, 1980, and 1985, taking 1970 as the base year.

20.14   For Exercise 20.13, calculate the aggregate index for all three metals for 1985, taking 1970 as the base year.

20.15   Suppose that an investor in 1970 owned 100 ounces of gold, 1,000 ounces of silver, and 50 ounces of platinum. By 1985, she had 500 ounces of gold, 1,500 ounces of silver, and 100 ounces of platinum. Construct a weighted aggregate index to measure how her investment's value changed between 1970 and 1985.

20.16   For Exercise 20.15, compute the Laspeyres index.

20.17   For Exercise 20.15, compute the Paasche index.

20.18   The annual price of a barrel of oil for the years 1975–1986 is shown in the table below. Calculate a simple index showing the price increases for 1980, 1983, and 1986. Use 1975 as the base year.

TABLE E20.6		1980		1989	
Ingredient	**Price**	**Quantity**	**Price**	**Quantity**
Butter	$1.27/lb	16 oz	$1.87/lb	20 oz
Sugar	$.65/lb	8 oz	$.95/lb	8 oz
Flour	$1.49/lb	18 oz	$1.89/lb	18 oz
Eggs	$.52/doz	3 eggs	$.85/doz	3 eggs

TABLE E20.13   *GOLD, SILVER, AND PLATINUM PRICES ($U.S.), 1970–1985*

Year	Gold Price (per fine oz)	Silver Price (per fine oz)	Platinum Price (per troy oz)
1970	$36	$1.77	$133
1971	$41	$1.55	$121
1972	$59	$1.69	$121
1973	$98	$2.56	$150
1974	$160	$4.71	$181
1975	$161	$4.42	$164
1976	$125	$4.35	$162
1977	$148	$4.62	$162
1978	$194	$5.40	$237
1979	$308	$11.09	$352
1980	$613	$20.63	$439
1981	$460	$10.52	$475
1982	$376	$7.95	$475
1983	$424	$11.44	$475
1984	$361	$8.14	$475
1985	$318	$6.14	$475

SOURCE: U.S. Department of Commerce, Bureau of the Census, *Statistical Abstract of the United States: 1988.*

Year	Price of Crude Petroleum (per barrel)
1975	$7.67
1976	$8.19
1977	$8.57
1978	$9.00
1979	$12.64
1980	$21.59
1981	$31.77
1982	$28.52
1983	$26.19
1984	$25.88

Year	Price of Crude Petroleum (per barrel)
1985	$24.09
1986	$12.66

20.19   Using Table 20.1, deflate the annual prices of crude petroleum in Exercise 20.18 so that they are measured in constant 1975 dollars.

Exercises 20.20 through 20.24 are based on the following problem.

A gasoline service station determined the price and the number of units sold per day of its four most popular items (after gasoline). These data were

TABLE E20.20

Item	1970 Price	1970 Quantity	1980 Price	1980 Quantity	1986 Price	1986 Quantity
Oil (quart)	$.65	23	$1.20	10	$1.85	5
Tire	$23	12	$55	15	$75	16
Antifreeze (quart)	$.80	7	$2.00	20	$2.50	14
Battery	$27	13	$45	22	$65	20

recorded for the years 1970, 1980, and 1986, as shown in Table E20.20.

20.20 Taking 1970 as the base year, calculate the simple aggregate index for 1980 and 1986.

20.21 Compute the weighted aggregate index for 1980 and 1986, taking 1970 as the base year.

20.22 Compute the Laspeyres index for 1980 and 1986.

20.23 Compute the Paasche index for 1980 and 1986.

20.24 Deflate (to 1970 constant dollars) each of the indices in Exercises 20.20 through 20.23, using the CPI in Table 20.1. What conclusions can you reach about these results?

20.25 Is real estate a good investment? In particular, will the price of a house keep up with inflation? To answer these questions, the median sales price of new privately owned one-family houses were recorded for 1970, 1975, 1980, and 1986. These data are shown next. Compute the prices in 1970 constant dollars, using the CPI in Table 20.1. What conclusions do these results lead to?

Year	Median Sales Price of New One-Family Houses
1970	$23,400
1975	$39,300
1980	$64,600
1986	$92,000

Source: U.S. Department of Commerce, Bureau of the Census, *Statistical Abstract of the United States: 1988.*

20.26 The median sales price of existing one-family homes is listed next. Repeat Exercise 20.25, using these data.

Year	Median Sales Price of Existing One-Family Houses
1970	$23,000
1975	$39,300
1980	$60,800
1986	$104,800

20.27 The table that follows lists the per capita gross national product. Convert these figures to constant 1975 dollars. What do these values tell you?

Year	Per Capita GNP
1975	$7,401
1980	$11,995
1981	$13,262
1982	$13,614
1983	$14,503
1984	$15,913
1985	$16,757
1986	$17,528

Source: U.S. Bureau of Economic Analysis, National Income and Products Accounts of the United States, July 1987.

20.28   The shellfish catch in the United States for 1980 and for 1990 is given in the accompanying table.

	Quantity (millions of pounds)		Price per Pound ($)	
	1980	1990	1980	1990
Clams	71	112	.24	1.26
Crabs	335	301	.09	.28
Lobsters	30	30	.73	1.63
Oysters	55	53	.51	.81
Scallops	23	13	.65	1.69
Shrimp	244	344	.34	.66

Compute the simple aggregate index to show how prices increased from 1980 to 1990.

20.29   Repeat Exercise 20.28, using the Laspeyres index.

20.30   Repeat Exercise 20.28, using the Paasche index.

20.31   What conclusions can you draw from the indices calculated in Exercises 20.28 through 20.30?

20.32   Unit energy-consumption costs and use patterns during the late 1970s are summarized in Table E20.32. Compute the simple aggregate index to measure the energy cost increases since 1975.

20.33   Repeat Exercise 20.32, using the weighted aggregate index.

20.34   Repeat Exercise 20.32, using the Laspeyres index.

20.35   Repeat Exercise 20.32, using the Paasche index.

20.36   Which of the indices computed in Exercises 20.32 through 20.35 most accurately measures the energy cost increases since 1975? Explain.

TABLE E20.32

	Unit Cost			Mean Monthly Consumption		
	1975	1977	1979	1975	1977	1979
Electricity (kw-hrs)	$.023	$.024	$.038	1,704	1,652	1,597
Oil (gallons)	$.44	$.48	$.82	257	260	230
Gas (millions ft^3)	$8.35	$9.46	$12.24	7.8	7.1	6.8

SOURCE: U.S. Department of Commerce, Bureau of Census, *Statistical Abstract of the United States: 1986.*

DECISION ANALYSIS

INTRODUCTION

In earlier chapters, we dealt with techniques for manipulating data in order to make decisions about population parameters and population characteristics. Our focus in this chapter is also on decision making, but the types of problems we will deal with here are quite different. First, the technique for hypothesis testing concludes with either rejecting or not rejecting some hypothesis concerning a dimension of a population. In decision analysis, we deal with the problem of selecting one alternative from a list of several possible decisions. Second, in hypothesis testing the decision is based on the statistical evidence available. In decision analysis, there may be no statistical data; or if there is, the decision may depend only partly on the data. Third, costs (and profits) are only indirectly considered (in the selection of a significance level) in the formulation of a hypothesis test. Decision analysis directly involves profits and losses. Because of these major differences, the only previously covered topics that are required for an understanding of decision analysis are Bayes' theorem and calculations of expected value.

DECISION PROBLEM

You would think that, by this point in the text, we would already have introduced all of the necessary concepts and terminology. Unfortunately, because this topic is so radically different from statistical inference, there are several more terms to learn. These will be introduced in the following example.

EXAMPLE 21.1

A man wishes to invest \$1 million for one year. After analyzing and eliminating numerous possibilities, he has narrowed his choice to one of three alternatives. These are referred to as **acts** and are denoted a_i:

a_1: Invest in a guaranteed income certificate paying 10%.

a_2: Invest in a bond with a coupon value of 8%.

a_3: Invest in a portfolio of banking institution stocks.

He believes that the payoffs associated with the last two acts depend on a number of factors, foremost among which is interest rates. He concludes that there are three possible **states of nature,** denoted s_j:

s_1: Interest rates increase.

TABLE 21.1   *PAYOFF TABLE FOR EXAMPLE 21.1*

	a_1 (GIC)	a_2 (Bond)	a_3 (Stocks)
s_1 (interest rates increase)	$100,000	− $50,000	$150,000
s_2 (interest rates stay the same)	$100,000	$80,000	$90,000
s_3 (interest rates decrease)	$100,000	$180,000	$40,000

s_2: Interest rates stay the same.

s_3: Interest rates decrease.

After further analysis, he determines the amount of profit he will make for each possible combination of one act and one state of nature. Of course, the payoff for the guaranteed income certificate will be $100,000, no matter which state of nature occurs. The profits from each alternative investment are summarized in Table 21.1, in what is called a **payoff table.** Notice that, when the decision is a_2 and the state of nature is s_1, the investor would suffer a $50,000 loss, which is represented by a − $50,000 payoff.

Another way of expressing the consequence of an act involves measuring the opportunity loss associated with each combination of one act and one state of nature. An **opportunity loss** is the difference between what the decision maker's profit for an act is and what the profit could have been had the best decision been made. For example, consider the first row of the payoff table. If s_1 is the state of nature that occurs and the investor chooses act a_1, he makes a profit of $100,000. However, had he chosen act a_3, he would have made a profit of $150,000. The difference between what he could have made ($150,000) and what he actually made ($100,000) is the opportunity loss. Thus, given that s_1 is the state of nature, the opportunity loss of act a_1 is $50,000. The opportunity loss of act a_2 is $200,000, which is the difference between $150,000 and − $50,000. The opportunity loss of act a_3 is 0, since there is no opportunity loss when the best alternative is chosen. In a similar manner we can compute the remaining opportunity losses for this example (see Table 21.2). Notice that we can never achieve a negative opportunity loss.

DECISION TREES

Most problems involving a simple choice of alternatives can readily be resolved by using the payoff table (or the opportunity loss table). In other situations, however,

TABLE 21.2   OPPORTUNITY LOSS TABLE FOR EXAMPLE 21.1

	a_1	a_2	a_3
s_1	$50,000	$200,000	0
s_2	0	$20,000	$10,000
s_3	$80,000	0	$140,000

FIGURE 21.1   DECISION TREE FOR EXAMPLE 21.1

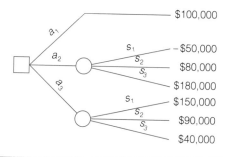

the decision maker must choose between sequences of acts. In Section 21.5, we will introduce one form of such questions. In these cases, a payoff table will not suffice to determine the solution; instead, we require a **decision tree.**

In Chapter 3, we suggested the probability tree as a useful device for computing probabilities. In this type of tree, all of the branches represent stages of events. In a decision tree, however, the branches represent both acts and events (states of nature). We distinguish between them in the following way: a point where a decision is to be made is represented by a square node; a point where a state of nature occurs is represented by a round node. Figure 21.1 depicts the decision tree for our example.

The tree in Figure 21.1 begins with a square node; that is, we begin by making a choice among a_1, a_2, and a_3. The branches emanating from the square node represent these alternatives. At the ends of branches a_2 and a_3, we reach round nodes representing the occurrence of some state of nature. These are depicted as branches representing s_1, s_2, and s_3. At the end of branch a_1, we don't really have a state of nature, since the payoff is fixed at $100,000, no matter what happens to interest rates.

At the ends of the branches, the payoffs are shown (alternatively, we could have worked with opportunity losses instead of with payoffs). These are, of course, the same values that appear in Table 21.1.

At this point, all we have done is set up the problem; we have not made any attempt to determine the decision. It should be noted that, in many real-life problems, determining the payoff table or decision tree can be a formidable task in itself. Many managers have observed that this task is often extremely helpful in making decisions.

▬▬▬ *EXERCISES*

LEARNING THE TECHNIQUES

21.1 Set up the opportunity loss table from the following payoff table.

	a_1	a_2
s_1	55	26
s_2	43	38
s_3	29	43
s_4	15	51

21.2 Given the following payoff table, draw the decision tree.

	a_1	a_2	a_3
s_1	20	5	-1
s_2	8	5	4
s_3	-10	5	10

21.3 Consider the following payoff table.

	a_1	a_2	a_3
s_1	-20	-30	-25
s_2	-10	-2	-5

a. Set up the opportunity loss table.

b. Draw the decision tree.

21.4 Set up the opportunity loss table from the following payoff table.

	a_1	a_2	a_3	a_4
s_1	200	100	110	80
s_2	75	120	110	90
s_3	50	150	110	200

21.5 Draw the decision tree for Exercise 21.4.

APPLYING THE TECHNIQUES

Self-Correcting Exercise (See Appendix 21.A for the solution.)

`RET` **21.6** A baker must decide how many specialty cakes to bake each morning. From past experience, he knows that the daily demand for cakes ranges from 0 to 3. If each cake costs $3.00 to produce and sells for $8.00, and if any unsold cakes are thrown into the garbage at the end of the day, set up a payoff table to help the baker decide how many cakes to bake.

`RET` **21.7** Set up the opportunity loss table for Exercise 21.6.

`RET` **21.8** Draw the decision tree for Exercise 21.6.

`GEN` **21.9** The manager of a large shopping center in Buffalo is in the process of deciding on the type of snow-clearing service to hire for his parking lot. Two services are available. The White Christmas Company will clear all snowfalls for a flat fee of $70,000 for the entire winter season. The Weplowem Company charges $18,000 for each snowfall they clear. Set up the payoff table to help the manager decide, assuming that the number of snowfalls per winter season is Poisson-distributed with $\mu = 3.0$.

GEN **21.10**   Draw the decision tree for Exercise 21.9.

RET **21.11**   The owner of a clothing store must decide how many men's shirts to order for the new season. For a particular type of shirt, she must order in quantities of 100 shirts. If she orders 100 shirts, her cost is $10 per shirt; if she orders 200 shirts, her cost is $9 per shirt; and if she orders 300 or more shirts, her cost is $8.50 per shirt. Her selling price for the shirt is $12, but any that remain unsold at the end of the season are sold at her famous "half-price, end-of-season sale." For the sake of simplicity, she is willing to assume that the demand for this type of shirt will be either 100, 150, 200, or 250 shirts. Of course, she cannot sell more shirts than she stocks. She is also willing to assume that she will suffer no loss of goodwill among her customers if she understocks and the customers cannot buy all the shirts they want. Furthermore, she must place her order today for the entire season; she cannot wait to see how the demand is running for this type of shirt. Construct the payoff table to help the owner decide how many shirts to order.

RET **21.12**   Set up the opportunity loss table for Exercise 21.11.

RET **21.13**   Draw the decision tree for Exercise 21.11.

RE **21.14**   A building contractor must decide how many mountain cabins to build in the ski resort area of Chick-oh-pee. He builds each cabin at a cost of $26,000 and sells each for $33,000. All cabins unsold after 10 months will be sold to a local investor for $20,000. The contractor believes that the demand for cabins follows a Poisson distribution, with a mean of .5. He assumes that any probability less than .01 can be treated as zero. Construct the payoff table and the opportunity loss table for this decision problem.

SECTION 21.3   *EXPECTED MONETARY VALUE DECISIONS*

In many decision problems, it is possible to assign probabilities to the states of nature. For example, if the decision involves trying to decide whether or not to draw to an inside straight in the game of poker, the probability of succeeding can easily be determined by using simple rules of probability. If we must decide whether or not to replace a machine that has broken down frequently in the past, we can assign probabilities on the basis of the relative frequency of the breakdowns. In many other instances, however, formal rules and techniques of probability cannot be applied. In Example 21.1, the historical relative frequencies of the ups and downs of interest rates will supply scant useful information to help the investor assign probabilities to the behavior of interest rates during the coming year. In such cases, the probabilities must be assigned subjectively. In other words, the determination of the probabilities must be based on the experience, knowledge, and (perhaps) guesswork of the decision maker.

If in Example 21.1 the investor has some knowledge about a number of economic variables, he might have a reasonable guess about what will happen to interest rates in the next year. Suppose, for example, that our investor believes that future interest rates are most likely to remain essentially the same as they are today, and that (of the remaining two states of nature) rates are more likely to decrease than to increase. He may then guess the following probabilities:

$$P(s_1) = .2$$
$$P(s_2) = .5$$
$$P(s_3) = .3$$

Because the probabilities are subjective, we would expect another decision maker to produce a completely different set of probabilities. In fact, if this were not true, we would rarely have buyers and sellers of stocks (or any other investment) since everyone would be a buyer (and there would be no sellers) or everyone would be a seller (with no buyers).

After determining the probabilities of the states of nature, we can address the expected monetary value (EMV) decision.

EMV DECISION

We now calculate what we expect will happen for each decision. Since we generally measure the consequences of each decision in monetary terms, we compute the **expected monetary value (EMV)** of each. Recall from Chapter 4 that we calculate expected values by multiplying the values of the random variables by their respective probabilities and then summing the products. Thus, in our example, the expected monetary value of alternative a_1 is

$$EMV(a_1) = .2(100,000) + .5(100,000) + .3(100,000) = \$100,000$$

The expected values of the other decisions follow in the same way:

$$EMV(a_2) = .2(-50,000) + .5(80,000) + .3(180,000) = \$84,000$$
$$EMV(a_3) = .2(150,000) + .5(90,000) + .3(40,000) = \$87,000$$

We choose the decision with the largest expected monetary value, which is a_1, and label its expected value EMV*. Hence, EMV* = \$100,000.

In general, the expected monetary values do not represent possible payoffs. For example, the expected monetary value of act a_2 is \$84,000, yet the payoff table indicates that the only possible payoffs from choosing a_2 are $-\$50,000$, \$80,000, or \$180,000. Of course, the expected monetary value of act a_1 (\$100,000) is possible, since that is the only payoff of the act.

What, then, does the expected monetary value represent? If the investment is made a large number of times, with exactly the same payoffs and probabilities, the expected monetary value is the average payoff per investment. That is, if the investment is repeated an infinite number of times with act a_2, 20% of the investments will result in a \$50,000 loss, 50% will result in an \$80,000 profit, and 30% will result in a \$180,000 profit. The average of all of these investments would be the expected monetary value, \$84,000. If act a_3 is chosen, the average payoff in the long run would be \$87,000.

An important point is raised by the question, how many investments are going to be made? The answer is one. Even if the investor intends to make the same type of investment annually, the payoffs and the probabilities of the states of nature will undoubtedly change from year to year. Hence, we are faced with having computed the expected monetary value decision on the basis of an infinite number of investments, when there will actually be only one investment. We can rationalize this apparent contradiction in two ways. First, the expected value decision is the only method that allows us to combine the two most important factors in the decision process—the payoffs and their probabilities. It seems inconceivable that, where both factors are known, the investor would want to ignore either one. (There are processes that make decisions on the basis of the payoffs alone; these, however, assume no knowledge of the probabilities, which is not the case with our example.) Second, typical decision makers make a large number of decisions over their lifetimes. By using the expected value decision, the decision maker should perform at least as well as anyone else. Thus, despite the problem of interpretation, we advocate the expected value decision.

EOL DECISION

We can also calculate the expected opportunity losses of each act. From the opportunity loss table, we get

$$\text{EOL}(a_1) = .2(50,000) + .5(0) + .3(80,000) = 34,000$$
$$\text{EOL}(a_2) = .2(200,000) + .5(20,000) + .3(0) = 50,000$$
$$\text{EOL}(a_3) = .2(0) + .5(10,000) + .3(140,000) = 47,000$$

Since we want to minimize losses, we choose the act that produces the smallest expected opportunity loss, which is a_1. We label its expected value EOL*.

Observe that the EMV decision is the same as the EOL decision. This is not a coincidence, since the opportunity loss table was produced directly from the payoff table.

ROLLBACK TECHNIQUE FOR DECISION TREES

Figure 21.2 presents the decision tree for Example 21.1, with the probabilities of the states of nature included. The process of determining the EMV decision is called the *rollback technique,* which operates as follows. Beginning at the end of the tree (right-hand side), we calculate the expected monetary value at each round node. The numbers above the round nodes in Figure 21.2 specify these expected monetary values. At each square node, we make a decision by choosing the branch with the largest EMV. In our example, there is only one square node. Our optimal decision is, of course, a_1.

FIGURE 21.2   ROLLBACK TECHNIQUE FOR EXAMPLE 21.1

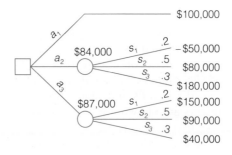

![] **EXERCISES**

LEARNING THE TECHNIQUES

21.15 Given the following payoff table and probabilities, determine the expected monetary values and the optimal act.

	a_1	a_2	a_3
s_1	10	5	13
s_2	20	25	13
s_3	15	12	15

$P(s_1) = .45$

$P(s_2) = .25$

$P(s_3) = .30$

21.16 Find the opportunity loss table from the following payoff table. Given these results and the accompanying probabilities, compute the expected opportunity loss for each act, and specify the optimal act.

	a_1	a_2	a_3	a_4
s_1	25	20	35	5
s_2	50	60	40	100

$P(s_1) = .7$

$P(s_2) = .3$

21.17 Use the rollback technique on the accompanying decision tree to determine the optimal act.

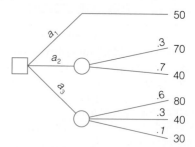

21.18 For the accompanying payoff table and probabilities, draw the decision tree; then use the rollback technique to determine the optimal act.

	a_1	a_2
s_1	-5	-12
s_2	3	-5
s_3	17	25
s_4	28	50

$P(s_1) = .10$

$P(s_2) = .20$

$P(s_3) = .45$

$P(s_4) = .25$

21.19 Refer to the accompanying payoff table and probabilities.

a. Calculate the optimal act, and determine EMV*.

b. Set up the opportunity loss table, and find EOL*.

	a_1	a_2	a_3
s_1	15	0	12
s_2	18	17	20
s_3	22	53	33

$P(s_1) = .6$

$P(s_2) = .3$

$P(s_3) = .1$

APPLYING THE TECHNIQUES

Self-Correcting Exercise (See Appendix 21.A for the solution.)

POM **21.20** The electric company is in the process of building a new power plant. There is some uncertainty regarding the size of the plant to be built. If the community that the plant will service attracts a large number of industries, the demand for electricity will be high. If commercial establishments (offices and retail stores) are attracted, demand will be moderate. If neither industries nor commercial stores locate in the community, the electricity demand will be low. The company can build a small, medium, or large plant; but if the plant is too small, the company will incur extra costs. The total costs of all options are shown in the accompanying table.

COST TABLE ($MILLIONS)

Demand for Electricity	Size of Plant		
	Small	Medium	Large
Low	220	300	350
Moderate	330	320	350
High	440	390	350

The following probabilities are assigned to the electricity demand.

Demand	P(Demand)
Low	.15
Moderate	.55
High	.30

a. Determine the act with the largest expected monetary value. (CAUTION: All of the values in the table are costs.)

b. Draw up an opportunity loss table.

c. Calculate the expected opportunity loss for each decision, and determine the optimal decision.

RET **21.21** A retailer buys bushels of mushrooms for $2 each and sells them for $5 each. The mushrooms begin to degenerate after the first day they are offered for sale; therefore, for him to sell the mushrooms for $5/bushel, he must sell them on the first day. Bushels not sold on the first day may be sold to a wholesaler who buys day-old mushrooms at the following rate.

Amount purchased (bushels)	1	2	3	4 or more
Price per bushel	$2.00	$1.75	$1.50	$1.25

A 90-day observation of past demand yields the following information.

Daily demand (bushels)	10	11	12	13
Number of days	9	18	36	27

a. Set up a payoff table that could be used by the retailer to decide how many bushels to buy.

b. Find the optimal number of bushels the retailer should buy in order to maximize the profit.

GEN **21.22** For Exercise 21.9, determine the act with the largest expected monetary value.

21.23 An international manufacturer of electronic products is contemplating introducing a new type of compact disk player. After some analysis of the market, the president of the company concludes that, within 2 years, the new product will have a market share of 5%, 10%, or 15%. He assesses the probabilities of these events as .15, .45, and .40, respectively. The vice-president of finance informs him that, if the product only captures a 5% market share, the company will lose $28 million. A 10% market share will produce a $2 million profit, and a 15% market share will produce an $8 million profit. If the company decides not to begin production of the new compact disk player,

there will be no profit or loss. Based on the expected value decision, what should the company do?

21.24 A retailer of microcomputers has an opportunity to buy a lot of 20 semiobsolete computers. She can purchase the entire lot for $30,000. The selling price she will be able to ask depends on whether a new line of computers is forthcoming in the next 3 months. If the new line is brought out, the 20 computers will be fully obsolete and she will be able to sell them for only $1,000 each. On the other hand, if the new line is delayed, she will be able to sell her computers for $2,200 each. If the probability that the new line is delayed is .40, should she purchase the lot?

SECTION 21.4   *EXPECTED VALUE OF PERFECT INFORMATION*

In Section 21.5, we discuss methods of introducing and incorporating additional information into the decision process. Such information generally has value, but it also has attendant costs; that is, we can acquire useful information in the form of consultants, surveys, or other experiments, but we usually must pay for this information. In this section, we calculate the maximum price that a decision maker should be willing to pay for any information, by determining the value of perfect information. We begin by calculating the **expected payoff with perfect information (EPPI).**

If we knew in advance which state of nature would occur, we would certainly make our decisions accordingly. For instance, if the investor in our initial example knew before investing his money what interest rates would do, he would choose the best act to suit that case. If he knew that s_1 was going to occur, he would choose act a_3; if s_2, he'd choose a_1; and if s_3, he'd choose a_2. Thus, in the long run, his expected payoff from perfect information would be

$$\text{EPPI} = .2(150,000) + .5(100,000) + .3(180,000) = \$134,000$$

Notice that we compute EPPI by multiplying the probability of each state of nature by the largest payoff associated with that state of nature, and then summing the products.

This figure, however, does not represent the maximum amount he'd be willing to pay for perfect information. Since the investor could make an expected profit of $\text{EMV}^* = \$100,000$ without perfect information, we subtract EMV^* from EPPI to determine the **expected value of perfect information (EVPI).** That is,

$$\text{EVPI} = \text{EPPI} - \text{EMV}^*$$
$$= \$134,000 - \$100,000$$
$$= \$34,000$$

This means that, if perfect information were available, the investor should be willing to pay up to $34,000 to acquire it.

You may have noticed that EVPI equals EOL*. Again, this is not a coincidence: it will always be the case. In future questions, if the opportunity loss table is determined, you need only calculate EOL* in order to know EVPI.

▬▬▬▬ EXERCISES

LEARNING THE TECHNIQUES

21.25 Find EPPI, EMV*, and EVPI for the accompanying payoff table and probabilities.

	a_1	a_2	a_3
s_1	60	110	75
s_2	40	110	150
s_3	220	120	85
s_4	250	120	130

$P(s_1) = .10$

$P(s_2) = .25$

$P(s_3) = .50$

$P(s_4) = .15$

21.26 For Exercise 21.25, determine the opportunity loss table, and compute EOL*. Confirm that EOL* = EVPI.

21.27 Given the following payoff table and probabilities, determine EVPI.

	a_1	a_2	a_3	a_4
s_1	65	20	45	30
s_2	70	110	80	95

$P(s_1) = .5$

$P(s_2) = .5$

21.28 Redo Exercise 21.27, changing the probabilities to.

a. $P(s_1) = .75$

$\quad P(s_2) = .25$

b. $P(s_1) = .95$

$\quad P(s_2) = .05$

21.29 What conclusion can you draw about the effect of the probabilities on EVPI from Exercises 21.27 and 21.28?

APPLYING THE TECHNIQUES

Self-Correcting Exercise (See Appendix 21.A for the solution.)

RET **21.30** A sporting-goods store owner has the opportunity to purchase a lot of 50,000 footballs for $100,000. She believes that she can sell some or all by taking out mail-order advertisements in a magazine. Each football will be sold for $6.00. The advertising cost is $25,000, and the mailing cost per football is $1.00. She believes that the demand distribution is as follows.

Demand	P(Demand)
10,000	.2
30,000	.5
50,000	.3

What is the maximum price the owner should pay for additional information about demand?

POM **21.31** Calculate the expected value of perfect information for the decision problem described in Exercise 21.20.

MKT **21.32** What is the maximum price the electronics product manufacturer should be willing to pay for perfect information regarding the market share in Exercise 21.23?

21.33   A radio station currently directing its programming toward middle-aged listeners is contemplating switching to rock-and-roll music. After analyzing advertising revenues and operating costs, the owner concludes that, for each percentage point of market share, revenues increase by $100,000 per year. Fixed annual operating costs are $700,000. The owner believes that, with the change, the station will get a 5, 10, or 20% market share, with probabilities .4, .4, and .2, respectively. The current annual profit is $285,000.

a. Set up the payoff table.

b. Determine the optimal act.

c. What is the most the owner should be willing to pay to acquire additional information about the market share?

21.34   What is the most the retailer in Exercise 21.24 should be willing to pay for any additional information?

SECTION 21.5   ## USING ADDITIONAL INFORMATION

Suppose that the investor in our continuing example wants to improve his decision-making capabilities. He learns about Investment Management Consultants (IMC), who, for a fee of $5,000, will analyze the economic conditions and forecast the behavior of interest rates over the next 12 months. The investor, who is quite shrewd (after all, he does have $1,000,000 to invest), asks for some measure of IMC's past successes. IMC has been forecasting interest rates for many years, and so provides him with various conditional probabilities (referred to as *likelihood probabilities*), as shown in Table 21.3.

Table 21.3 uses the following notation:

I_1: IMC predicts that interest rates will increase.

I_2: IMC predicts that interest rates will stay the same.

I_3: IMC predicts that interest rates will decrease.

The I_i terms are referred to as **experimental outcomes**, and the process by which we gather additional information is called the **experiment**.

Examine the first line of the table. When s_1 actually did occur in the past, IMC correctly predicted s_1 60% of the time; 30% of the time, it predicted s_2; and 10% of the time, it predicted s_3. The second row gives the conditional probabilities of I_1, I_2, and I_3 when s_2 actually occurred. The third row shows the conditional probabilities when s_3 actually occurred.

The question now arises, how is the investor going to use the forecast that IMC produces? One approach is simply to assume that whatever it forecasts will actually take place and to choose the act accordingly. There are several drawbacks to this approach. Foremost among these is that it puts the investor in the position of ignoring whatever knowledge (in the form of subjective probabilities) he had concerning the issue. The optimal way to use the forecast is to incorporate the investor's subjective probabilities with the consultant's forecast. The medium for doing this is Bayes' theorem (developed in Chapter 3).

Suppose for now that the investor pays IMC the $5,000 fee; IMC does its work and finally forecasts that s_1 will occur. We now want to determine, given that I_1 is the

TABLE 21.3   LIKELIHOOD PROBABILITIES $P(I_i \mid s_j)$

	I_1 (Predict s_1)	I_2 (Predict s_2)	I_3 (Predict s_3)
s_1	$P(I_1 \mid s_1) = .60$	$P(I_2 \mid s_1) = .30$	$P(I_3 \mid s_1) = .10$
s_2	$P(I_1 \mid s_2) = .10$	$P(I_2 \mid s_2) = .80$	$P(I_3 \mid s_2) = .10$
s_3	$P(I_1 \mid s_3) = .10$	$P(I_2 \mid s_3) = .20$	$P(I_3 \mid s_3) = .70$

outcome of the experiment, what the probabilities of the states of nature are. That is, what are $P(s_1 \mid I_1)$, $P(s_2 \mid I_1)$, and $P(s_3 \mid I_1)$? Before proceeding, let's develop some terminology.

The original subjective probabilities, $P(s_1)$, $P(s_2)$, and $P(s_3)$ are called **prior probabilities,** because they were determined prior to the acquisition of any additional information. In this example, they were based on the investor's experience. The set of probabilities that we wish to compute—$P(s_1 \mid I_1)$, $P(s_2 \mid I_1)$, and $P(s_3 \mid I_1)$—are called **posterior** or **revised probabilities.**

Now we will calculate the posterior probabilities, first by using a probability tree (as was done in Chapter 3), and then by applying a less time-consuming method. Figure 21.3 depicts the probability tree. We begin with the branches of the prior probabilities, which are followed by the likelihood probabilities.

Notice that we label only $P(I_1 \mid s_1)$, $P(I_1 \mid s_2)$, and $P(I_1 \mid s_3)$, since (at this point) we are assuming that I_1 is the experimental outcome. Thus,

$$P(s_1 \mid I_1) = \frac{P(s_1 \cap I_1)}{P(I_1)} = \frac{.12}{.20} = .60$$

FIGURE 21.3   PROBABILITY TREE TO COMPUTE POSTERIOR PROBABILITIES

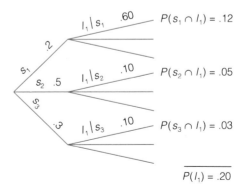

TABLE 21.4	*POSTERIOR PROBABILITIES FOR* I_1

s_j	$P(s_j)$	$P(I_1\|s_j)$	$P(s_j \cap I_1)$	$P(s_j\|I_1)$
s_1	.2	.60	.12	$.12/.20 = .60$
s_2	.5	.10	.05	$.05/.20 = .25$
s_3	.3	.10	.03	$.03/.20 = .15$
			$P(I_1) = .20$	

$$P(s_2 \mid I_1) = \frac{P(s_2 \cap I_1)}{P(I_1)} = \frac{.05}{.20} = .25$$

$$P(s_3 \mid I_1) = \frac{P(s_3 \cap I_1)}{P(I_1)} = \frac{.03}{.20} = .15$$

Instead of drawing the probability tree to compute the posterior probabilities, we can use Table 21.4, which performs exactly the same calculations.

For each state of nature s_j, we multiply the prior probability by the likelihood probability to produce the probability of the intersection. We then add these to determine $P(I_1)$, and we divide the probability of each intersection by $P(I_1)$ to compute the posterior probabilities.

Once the probabilities have been revised, we can use them in exactly the same way we used the prior probabilities. That is, we can calculate the expected monetary values of each act:

$$\text{EMV}(a_1) = .60(100{,}000) + .25(100{,}000) + .15(100{,}000) = \$100{,}000$$
$$\text{EMV}(a_2) = .60(-50{,}000) + .25(80{,}000) + .15(180{,}000) = \$17{,}000$$
$$\text{EMV}(a_3) = .60(150{,}000) + .25(90{,}000) + .15(40{,}000) = \$118{,}500$$

Thus, if IMC forecasts s_1, then the optimal act is a_3, and the expected monetary value of the decision is $118,500.

As further illustration, we now repeat the process for I_2 and I_3. If I_2 is the experimental outcome, we have the probabilities shown in Table 21.5. Applying these posterior probabilities to the payoff table, we find

$$\text{EMV}(a_1) = .115(100{,}000) + .770(100{,}000) + .115(100{,}000) = \$100{,}000$$
$$\text{EMV}(a_2) = .115(-50{,}000) + .770(80{,}000) + .115(180{,}000) = \$76{,}550$$
$$\text{EMV}(a_3) = .115(150{,}000) + .770(90{,}000) + .115(40{,}000) = \$91{,}150$$

As you can see, if IMC predicts that s_2 will occur, the optimal act is a_1, with an expected monetary value of $100,000.

TABLE 21.5   POSTERIOR PROBABILITIES FOR I_2

s_j	$P(s_j)$	$P(I_2 \mid s_j)$	$P(s_j \cap I_2)$	$P(s_j \mid I_2)$
s_1	.2	.30	.06	$.06/.52 = .115$
s_2	.5	.80	.40	$.40/.52 = .770$
s_3	.3	.20	.06	$.06/.52 = .115$
			$P(I_2) = .52$	

TABLE 21.6   POSTERIOR PROBABILITIES FOR I_3

s_j	$P(s_j)$	$P(I_3 \mid s_j)$	$P(s_j \cap I_3)$	$P(s_j \mid I_3)$
s_1	.2	.10	.02	$.02/.28 = .071$
s_2	.5	.10	.05	$.05/.28 = .179$
s_3	.3	.70	.21	$.21/.28 = .750$
			$P(I_3) = .28$	

If the experimental outcome is I_3, the posterior probabilities are as shown in Table 21.6. With this set of posterior probabilities, the expected monetary values are

$$\text{EMV}(a_1) = .071(100,000) + .179(100,000) + .750(100,000) = \$100,000$$
$$\text{EMV}(a_2) = .071(-50,000) + .179(80,000) + .750(180,000) = \$145,770$$
$$\text{EMV}(a_3) = .071(150,000) + .179(90,000) + .750(40,000) = \$56,760$$

As a result, if IMC predicts that s_3 will occur, the optimal act is a_2, with an expected monetary value of \$145,770.

At this point we know the following:

If IMC predicts s_1, then the optimal act is a_3.

If IMC predicts s_2, then the optimal act is a_1.

If IMC predicts s_3, then the optimal act is a_2.

Thus, even before IMC makes its forecast, we know which act is optimal for each of the three possible IMC forecasts. All of these calculations can be performed before paying IMC its \$5,000 fee. This leads to an extremely important calculation. By performing the computations just described, we can determine whether or not the investor should hire IMC. That is, we can determine whether or not the value of IMC's forecast exceeds the cost of its information. Such a determination is called a **preposterior analysis.**

PREPOSTERIOR ANALYSIS

The objective of a preposterior analysis is to determine whether the value of the prediction is greater or less than the cost of the information. The *posterior* refers to the revision of the probabilities, and the *pre* indicates that this calculation is performed before paying the $5,000 fee.

We begin by finding the expected monetary value of using the additional information. This value is denoted EMV', which is determined on the basis of the following analysis:

If IMC predicts s_1, then the optimal act is a_3, and the expected payoff is $118,500.

If IMC predicts s_2, then the optimal act is a_1, and the expected payoff is $100,000.

If IMC predicts s_3, then the optimal act is a_2, and the expected payoff is $145,770.

A useful by-product of calculating the posterior probabilities is the set of probabilities of I_1, I_2, and I_3:

$P(I_1) = .20$

$P(I_2) = .52$

$P(I_3) = .28$

(Notice that these probabilities sum to 1.) Now imagine that the investor seeks the advice of IMC an infinite number of times. (That is the basis for the expected value decision.) The set of probabilities of I_1, I_2, and I_3 indicates the following outcome distribution: 20% of the time, IMC will predict s_1 and the expected monetary value will be $118,500; 52% of the time, IMC will predict s_2 and the expected monetary value will be $100,000; and 28% of the time, IMC will predict s_3 and the expected monetary value will be $145,770.

The expected monetary value with additional information is the weighted average of the expected monetary values, where the weights are $P(I_1)$, $P(I_2)$, and $P(I_3)$. Hence,

$$EMV' = .20(118,500) + .52(100,000) + .28(145,770) = \$116,516$$

The value of IMC's forecast is the difference between the expected monetary value with additional information (EMV') and the expected monetary value without additional information (EMV*). This difference is called the **expected value of sample information** and is denoted EVSI. Thus,

$$EVSI = EMV' - EMV* = \$116,516 - \$100,000 = \$16,516$$

By using IMC's forecast, the investor can make an average additional profit of $16,516, in the long run. Since the cost of the forecast is only $5,000, the investor is advised to hire IMC.

If you review this problem, you'll see that the investor had to make two decisions. The first (chronologically) was whether or not to hire IMC, and the second was which type of investment to make. A decision tree is quite helpful in describing the acts and states of nature in this question. Figure 21.4 provides this tree diagram.

EXAMPLE 21.2

A factory produces a small but important component used in computers. The factory manufactures the component in 1,000-unit lots. Because of the relatively advanced technology, the manufacturing process results in a large proportion of defective units. In fact, the quality-control engineer has observed that the percentage of defective units per lot has been either 15% or 35%. In the past year, 60% of the lots have had 15% defectives and 40% have had 35% defectives. The present policy of the company is to send the lot to the customer, replace all defectives, and pay any additional costs. The total cost of replacing a defective unit that has been sent to the customer is $10/unit. Because of the high costs, the company management is considering inspecting all units and replacing the defective units before shipment. The sampling cost is $2/unit, and the replacement cost is $0.50/unit. Each unit sells for $5.

a. Based on the history of the past year, should the company adopt the 100% inspection plan?

b. Is it worthwhile to take a sample of size 2 from the lot before deciding to inspect 100% or not?

Solution, Part (a).   The two alternatives are

a_1: No inspection (the current policy)

a_2: 100% inspection

The two states of nature are

s_1: The lot contains 15% defectives.

s_2: The lot contains 35% defectives.

Based on the past year's historical record,

$P(s_1) = .60$

$P(s_2) = .40$

The payoff table is constructed as shown in Table 21.7. The expected monetary values are

$$\text{EMV}(a_1) = .60(3,500) + .40(1,500) = 2,700$$
$$\text{EMV}(a_2) = .60(2,925) + .40(2,825) = 2,885$$

The optimal act is a_2, with $\text{EMV}^* = 2,885$.

FIGURE 21.4   COMPLETE DECISION TREE OF EXAMPLE 21.1

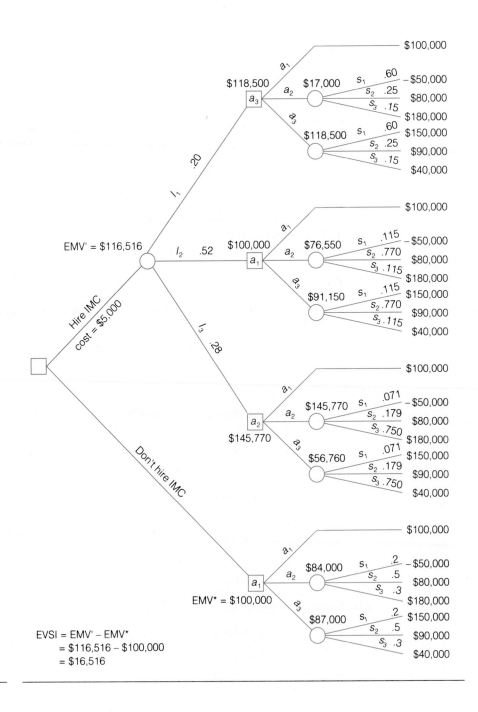

TABLE 21.7 PAYOFF TABLE FOR EXAMPLE 21.2

	a_1	a_2
s_1	$5(1,000) - .15(1,000)(10) = 3,500$	$5(1,000) - [(1,000)(2) + .15(1,000)(.50)] = 2,925$
s_2	$5(1,000) - .35(1,000)(10) = 1,500$	$5(1,000) - [(1,000)(2) + .35(1,000)(.50)] = 2,825$

Solution, Part (b).   The cost of the proposed sampling is $4. (The cost of inspecting a single unit is $2.) In order to determine whether we should sample, we need to calculate the expected value of sample information. That is, we need to perform the preposterior analysis.

The first step of the preposterior analysis is to calculate the likelihood probabilities. There are three possible sample outcomes:

I_0: No defectives in the sample

I_1: One defective in the sample

I_2: Two defectives in the sample

Since the sampling process is a binomial experiment, the likelihood probabilities are calculated by using the binomial probability distribution. (See Table 21.8.)

If I_0 is the sample outcome, the posterior probabilities are calculated as shown in Table 21.9. The expected monetary values in this case are

$$\text{EMV}(a_1) = .720(3,500) + .280(1,500) = \$2,940$$
$$\text{EMV}(a_2) = .720(2,925) + .280(2,825) = \$2,897$$

Therefore, the optimal act is a_1.

If I_1 is the sample outcome, the posterior probabilities are calculated as shown in Table 21.10. The expected monetary values in this case are

$$\text{EMV}(a_1) = .457(3,500) + .543(1,500) = \$2,414$$
$$\text{EMV}(a_2) = .457(2,925) + .543(2,825) = \$2,871$$

Therefore, the optimal act is a_2.

TABLE 21.8 LIKELIHOOD PROBABILITY TABLE

	$P(I_0\,|\,s_j)$	$P(I_1\,|\,s_j)$	$P(I_2\,|\,s_j)$
$s_1(p = .15)$	$P(I_0\,|\,s_1) = (.85)^2$	$P(I_1)\,|\,s_1) = 2(.15)(.85)$	$P(I_2\,|\,s_1) = (.15)^2$
	$= .7225$	$= .2550$	$= .0225$
$s_2(p = .35)$	$P(I_0\,|\,s_2) = (.65)^2$	$P(I_1)\,|\,s_2) = 2(.35)(.65)$	$P(I_2\,|\,s_2) = (.35)^2$
	$= .4225$	$= .4550$	$= .1225$

TABLE 21.9 POSTERIOR PROBABILITIES FOR I_0

s_j	$P(s_j)$	$P(I_0 \mid s_j)$	$P(s_j \cap I_0)$	$P(s_j \mid I_0)$
s_1	.60	.7225	.4335	.720
s_2	.40	.4225	.1690	.280
			$P(I_0) = .6025$	

TABLE 21.10 POSTERIOR PROBABILITIES FOR I_1

s_j	$P(s_j)$	$P(I_1 \mid s_j)$	$P(s_j \cap I_1)$	$P(s_j \mid I_1)$
s_1	.60	.2550	.153	.457
s_2	.40	.4550	.182	.543
			$P(I_1) = .3350$	

TABLE 21.11 POSTERIOR PROBABILITIES FOR I_2

s_j	$P(s_j)$	$P(I_2 \mid s_j)$	$P(s_j \cap I_2)$	$P(s_j \mid I_2)$
s_1	.60	.0225	.0135	.216
s_2	.40	.1225	.0490	.784
			$P(I_2) = .0625$	

TABLE 21.12 SUMMARY OF OPTIMAL ACTS

Sample Outcome	Probability	Optimal Act	Expected Monetary Value
I_0	.6025	a_1	$2,940
I_1	.3350	a_2	$2,871
I_2	.0625	a_2	$2,847

If I_2 is the sample outcome, the posterior probabilities are calculated as shown in Table 21.11. The expected monetary values in this case are

$$EMV(a_1) = .216(3,500) + .784(1,500) = \$1,932$$
$$EMV(a_2) = .216(2,925) + .784(2,825) = \$2,847$$

Therefore, the optimal act is a_2.

We can now summarize these results, as shown in Table 21.12. The expected monetary value with additional information is

$$EMV' = .6025(2,940) + .3350(2,871) + .0625(2,847) = \$2,911$$

The expected value of sample information is

$$EVSI = EMV' - EMV*$$
$$= 2,911 - 2,885$$
$$= \$26$$

Since the expected value of sample information is $26 and the sampling cost is $4, the company should take a sample of two units before deciding whether or not to inspect 100%. Figure 21.5 depicts the decision tree for this example. As you can see, the optimal sequence of decisions is as follows:

1. Take a sample of two units.
2. If neither sample unit is defective, continue the current policy of no inspection. If either one or two of the sample units are defective, perform a complete inspection of the lot.

EXERCISES

LEARNING THE TECHNIQUES

21.35 Determine the posterior probabilities, given the following prior and likelihood probabilities.

Prior Probabilities

$$P(s_1) = .25, \quad P(s_2) = .40, \quad P(s_3) = .35$$

Likelihood Probabilities

	I_1	I_2	I_3	I_4
s_1	.40	.30	.20	.10
s_2	.25	.25	.25	.25
s_3	0	.30	.40	.30

21.36 Calculate the posterior probabilities from the prior and likelihood probabilities that follow.

Prior Probabilities

$$P(s_1) = .5, \quad P(s_2) = .5$$

Likelihood Probabilities

	I_1	I_2
s_1	.98	.02
s_2	.05	.95

FIGURE 21.5   DECISION TREE FOR EXAMPLE 21.2

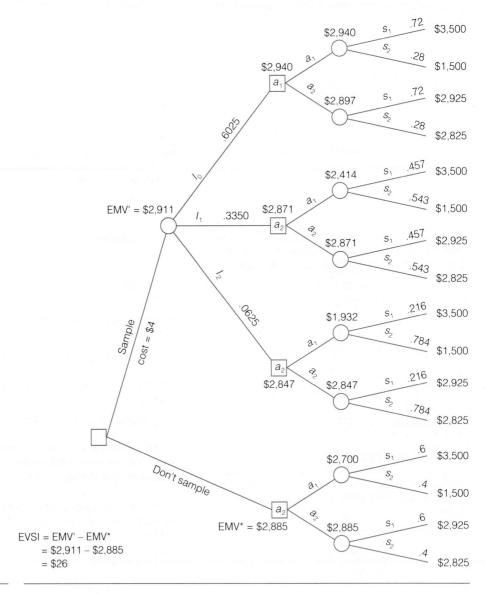

21.37 With the following payoff table and the prior and posterior probabilities computed in Exercise 21.36:

a. Calculate the optimal act for each experimental outcome.

b. Calculate EVSI.

PAYOFF TABLE

	a_1	a_2	a_3
s_1	10	18	23
s_2	22	19	15

21.38 Given the accompanying payoff table, prior probabilities, and likelihood probabilities, determine the optimal act for each experimental outcome.

PAYOFF TABLE

	a_1	a_2	a_3
s_1	15	17	25
s_2	20	17	10

Prior Probabilities

$P(s_1) = .75 \qquad P(s_2) = .25$

LIKELIHOOD PROBABILITIES

	I_1	I_2	I_3
s_1	.6	.3	.1
s_2	.1	.2	.7

21.39 Determine EVSI for Exercise 21.38.

21.40 Draw the decision tree for Exercise 21.38.

21.41 Given the following payoff table, prior probabilities, and likelihood probabilities, find EVSI.

PAYOFF TABLE

	a_1	a_2
s_1	60	90
s_2	90	90
s_3	150	90

Prior Probabilities

$P(s_1) = 1/3 \qquad P(s_2) = 1/3 \qquad P(s_3) = 1/3$

Likelihood Probabilities

	I_1	I_2
s_1	.7	.3
s_2	.5	.5
s_3	.2	.8

21.42 Repeat Exercise 21.41, with prior probabilities

$P(s_1) = .5, \quad P(s_2) = .4, \quad P(s_3) = .1$

21.43 Repeat Exercise 21.41, with prior probabilities

$P(s_1) = .90, \quad P(s_2) = .05, \quad P(s_3) = .05$

21.44 What conclusions can you draw about the effect of the prior probabilities on EVSI from Exercises 21.41 through 21.43?

21.45 For the following payoff table, prior probabilities, and likelihood probabilities, determine EVSI.

PAYOFF TABLE

	a_1	a_2
s_1	18	20
s_2	24	20

Prior Probabilities

$P(s_1) = .7, \quad P(s_2) = .3$

Likelihood Probabilities

	I_1	I_2
s_1	.8	.2
s_2	.3	.7

21.46 Draw the decision tree for Exercise 21.45.

21.47 Repeat Exercise 21.45, with the following likelihood probabilities.

	I_1	I_2
s_1	.96	.04
s_2	.02	.98

21.48 Repeat Exercise 21.45, with the following likelihood probabilities.

	I_1	I_2
s_1	.6	.4
s_2	.6	.4

21.49 What conclusions can you draw about the effect of the likelihood probabilities on EVSI from Exercises 21.45, 21.47, and 21.48?

Self-Correcting Exercise (See Appendix 21.A for the solution.)

21.50 FIN Mr. Jones is attempting to determine where he should invest his $100,000. There are three possible investments: a_1, a_2, and a_3. The events of interest are the various states of the economy. Table E21.50 shows the alternatives, the states of nature, and the payoffs.

The investor assigns the following probabilities:

$$P(s_1) = .2 \qquad P(s_2) = .5 \qquad P(s_3) = .3$$

Ace Economic Forecasters (AEF) will make a prediction on the state of the economy for $600. As a measure of its past reliability, AEF offered the accompanying set of likelihood probabilities.

LIKELIHOOD PROBABILITIES

	I_1 Predict Recession	I_2 Predict Stable Economy	I_3 Predict Upturn
s_1	.5	.5	0
s_2	.2	.7	.1
s_3	.1	.3	.6

Perform a preposterior analysis to determine whether AEF should be hired.

21.51 MKT In order to improve his decision-making capability, the electronics products manufacturer discussed in Exercise 21.23 performs a survey of potential buyers of compact disk players. He describes the product to 25 individuals, 3 of whom say they would buy it. Using this additional information (together with the prior probabilities), determine whether the new product should be produced.

21.52 MKT There is a garbage crisis in North America—too much garbage and no place to put it. As a consequence, the idea of recycling has become quite popular. A waste-management company in a large city is willing to begin recycling newspapers, aluminum cans, and plastic con-

TABLE E21.50		a_1	a_2	a_3
	s_1 (Recession)	$1,000	−$2,000	−$10,000
	s_2 (Stable economy)	$4,000	$7,000	$8,000
	s_3 (Economic upturn)	$8,000	$12,000	$15,000

TABLE E21.54   LIKELIHOOD PROBABILITIES

	I_1	I_2	I_3
	Predict Low Demand for Electricity	Predict Moderate Demand for Electricity	Predict High Demand for Electricity
s_1	.5	.3	.2
s_2	.3	.6	.1
s_3	.2	.2	.6

tainers. However, it is profitable to do so only if a sufficiently large proportion of households are willing to participate. In this city, 1 million households are potential recyclers. After some analysis it was determined that, for every 1,000 households that participate in the program, the contribution to profit is $500. It was also discovered that fixed costs are $55,000 per year. It is believed that 50,000, 100,000, 200,000, or 300,000 households will participate, with probabilities .5, .3, .1, and .1, respectively. A preliminary survey was performed wherein 25 households were asked if they would be willing to be part of this recycling program. If only 3 of the 25 respond affirmatively, incorporate this information into the decision-making process to decide whether the waste-management company should proceed with the recycling venture.

MKT **21.53**   Repeat Exercise 21.52, given that 12 out of 100 households respond affirmatively.

POM **21.54**   Suppose that in Exercise 21.20 a consultant offers to analyze the problem and predict the amount of electricity required by the new community. In order to induce the electric company to hire her, the consultant provides the set of likelihood probabilities given in Table E21.54. Perform a preposterior analysis to determine the expected value of the consultant's sample information.

MKT **21.55**   In Exercise 21.33, suppose that it is possible to do a survey of radio listeners to determine whether they would tune in to the station if the format changed to rock and roll. What would a survey of size 2 be worth?

MKT **21.56**   Suppose that in Exercise 21.55 a random sample of 25 radio listeners revealed that 2 people would be regular listeners of the station. What is the optimal decision now?

SECTION 21.6   ## SUMMARY

The objective of decision analysis is to select the optimal act from a list of **alternative acts.** We define the act with the largest **expected monetary value** or smallest **expected opportunity loss** as optimal. The expected values are calculated after assigning **prior probabilities** to the **states of nature.** The acts, states of nature, and their consequences may be presented in a **payoff table,** an **opportunity loss table,** or a **decision tree.**

We also discussed a method by which additional information in the form of an experiment may be incorporated in the analysis. This involves combining prior and **likelihood probabilities** to produce **posterior probabilities.** The **preposterior analysis** allows us to decide whether or not to pay for and acquire the experimental outcome. That decision is based on the **expected value of sample information** and on the sampling cost.

![SUPPLEMENTARY EXERCISES]

SUPPLEMENTARY EXERCISES

MKT **21.57** The MacTell toy company is considering producing a new toy—the R2-D2 robot. The company is considering four prototype designs for the robot. Each prototype represents a different technology for the moving parts, all of which are powered by a small electric motor using batteries.

The MacTell company is uncertain about the demand for the R2-D2 robot, but it feels that one of the following states of nature will occur:

> Light demand (25,000 units)
> Moderate demand (100,000 units)
> Heavy demand (150,000 units)

Using revenues, variable costs, and fixed costs, the MacTell company has calculated the payoffs shown in Table E21.57. After some consideration, the company president assigned the following probabilities to the states of nature:

> P(light demand) = .2
> P(moderate demand) = .6
> P(heavy demand) = .2

Based on the expected monetary value, which design should be selected?

RET **21.58** A pottery maker hand-makes beautiful vases. The materials for each vase cost her $3. By market-testing the vases at different prices, she obtained the frequency estimates of daily demand given in Table E21.58. Which price should she charge, based on the expected monetary value decision? (HINT: Draw a decision tree.)

MKT **21.59** The president of an automobile battery company must decide which one of three new types of batteries to produce. The fixed and variable costs of each battery are shown in the accompanying table.

Battery	Fixed Cost	Variable Cost (per unit)
1	$900,000	$20
2	$1,150,000	$17
3	$1,400,000	$15

TABLE E21.57 *POTENTIAL PAYOFFS, BY DESIGN ($1,000s)*

States of Nature	Design 1	Design 2	Design 3	Design 4
Light demand	30	0	− 100	− 300
Moderate demand	400	450	400	300
Heavy demand	600	750	800	700

TABLE E21.58

Demand (at $6)	Probability	Demand (at $7)	Probability
7	.15	5	.10
8	.25	6	.20
9	.40	7	.30
10	.20	8	.40

The president believes that demand will be 50,000, 100,000, or 150,000 batteries, with probabilities .3, .3, and .4, respectively. The selling price of the battery will be $40.

a. Determine the payoff table.

b. Determine the opportunity loss table.

c. Find the expected monetary value for each act, and select the optimal one.

d. What is the most the president should be willing to pay for additional information about demand?

MKT **21.60** Credibility is often the most effective feature of an advertising campaign. Suppose that, for a particular advertisement, 32% of people surveyed currently believe what the ad claims. A marketing manager believes that for each 1-point increase in that percentage, annual sales will increase by $1 million. For each 1-point decrease, annual sales will also decrease by $1 million. The manager believes that a change in the advertising approach can influence the ad's credibility. The probability distribution of the potential changes are listed next. If for each dollar of sales the profit contribution is 10 cents and the overall cost of changing the ad is $58,000, should the ad be changed?

Percentage Change	Probability
−2	.1
−1	.1
0	.2
+1	.3
+2	.3

MKT **21.61** Suppose that in Exercise 21.60 it is possible to perform a survey to determine the percentage of people who believe the ad. What would a sample of size 1 be worth?

MKT **21.62** Suppose that in Exercise 21.61 a sample of size 5 showed that only 1 person believes the new ad. In light of this additional information, what should the manager do?

GEN **21.63** After the first 78 games of an 80-game hockey season, Wayne Grootsky has scored 98 goals. As an additional incentive, the owner of his team (the LA Filter Kings) has offered him his choice of one of the following bonus plans:

1. $100,000 for each additional goal up to a maximum of 2

2. $50,000 for each additional goal

3. nothing for his 99th goal but $300,000 if he scores at least 2 more goals

Lately he has suffered a scoring slump, averaging only .9 goals per game. However, his goal scoring remains random, and the goals he scores are independent of one another.

Identify the acts from which Wayne must choose and the events that would affect the outcome, and construct the payoff table. (Treat probabilities of less than .01 as being equal to zero.)

GEN **21.64** Max the bookie is trying to decide how many telephones to install in his new bookmaking operation. Because of heavy police activity, he cannot increase or decrease the number of telephones once he sets up his operation. He has narrowed the possible choices to three: he can install 25, 50, or 100 telephones. His profit for one year (the usual length of time he can remain in business before the police close him down) depends on the average number of calls he receives. (Calls occur randomly and independently of one another.) After some deliberation, he concludes that the average number of calls per minute can be .5, 1.0, or 1.5, with probabilities of .50, .25, and .25, respectively. Max then produces the payoffs given in Table E21.64. Max's assistant, Lefty (who actually attended a business school for 2 years), points out that Max may be able to get more information by observing a competitor's similar operation. However, he will only be able to watch for ten minutes, and doing so will cost him $4,000. Max determines that if he counts fewer than 8 calls, that would be a low number; at least 8 but fewer than 17 would be a medium number; and at least 17 would be a large number of calls. Max also decides that, if the experiment is run, he will only record whether there is a small, medium, or large number of calls. Help Max by performing a preposterior

TABLE E21.64   *PAYOFF TABLE ($1,000s)*

	a_1 25 telephones	a_2 50 telephones	a_3 100 telephones
$s_1(\mu = .5)$	50	30	20
$s_2(\mu = 1.0)$	50	60	40
$s_3(\mu = 1.5)$	50	60	80

analysis to determine whether the sample should be taken. Conclude by specifying clearly what the optimal strategy is. (HINT: The number of telephone calls is Poisson-distributed.)

21.65 The Megabuck Computer Company is thinking of introducing two new products. The first, Model 101, is a small computer designed specifically for children between the ages of 8 and 16. The second, Model 202, is a medium-sized computer suitable for managers. Because of limited production capacity, Megabuck has decided to produce only one of the products.

The profitability of each model depends on the proportion of the potential market that would actually buy the computer. For Model 101, the size of the market is estimated at 10 million; while for Model 202, the estimate is 3 million.

After careful analysis, the management of Megabuck has concluded that the percentage of buyers of Model 101 is 5, 10, or 15%. The respective profits are given in the accompanying table.

Percentage Who Buy Model 101	Net Profits ($millions)
5%	20
10	100
15	210

An expert in probability from the local university estimated the probability of each of the percentages as Prob(5%) = .2, Prob(10%) = .4, and Prob(15%) = .4.

A similar analysis for Model 202 produced the following table.

Percentage Who Buy Model 202	Net Profits ($millions)
30%	70
40	100
50	150

For this model, the expert estimated the probabilities as Prob(30%) = .1, Prob(40%) = .4, and Prob(50%) = .5

a. Based on this information, and with the objective of maximizing expected profit, which model should Megabuck produce?

b. In order to make a better decision, Megabuck sampled 10 potential buyers of Model 101 and 20 potential buyers of Model 202. Only 1 of the 10 wished to purchase the Model 101, while 9 of the 20 indicated that they would buy Model 202. With this information, revise the prior probabilities and determine which model should be produced.

21.66 A major movie studio has just completed its latest epic, a musical comedy about the life of Atilla the Hun. Because the movie is different (no sex or violence), the studio is uncertain about how to distribute it. The studio executives must decide whether to release the movie to North American audiences or to sell it to a European distributor and realize a profit of $12 million. If the movie is shown in North America, the studio profit depends on its level of success, which can be classified as excellent, good, or fair. The payoffs and the prior subjective probabilities of the success levels are shown in the accompanying table.

Success Level	Payoff	Probability
Excellent	$33 million	.5
Good	$12 million	.3
Fair	−$15 million	.2

Another possibility is to have the movie shown to a random sample of North Americans and use their collective judgment to help make a decision. These judgments are categorized as "rave review," "lukewarm response," or "poor response." The cost of the sample is $100,000.

The sampling process has been used several times in the past. The likelihood probabilities relating the audience judgments and the movie's success level are shown in Table E21.66. Perform a preposterior analysis to determine what the studio executives should do.

MKT **21.67** Laurier Industries is considering whether or not to launch a new product. Its experience indicates that any new product has a 5% chance of being a "great success," a 20% chance of being a "moderate success," a 30% chance of being a "poor success," and a 45% chance of being an "outright failure."

In keeping with the firm's usual practice, a market study was carried out for the new product. This market study indicated that the product

would be a "moderate success." Based on past results, management would expect 30% of all "great success" products, 45% of all "moderate success" products, 20% of all "poor success" products, and 10% of all "outright failure" products to yield a market study result indicating "moderate success."

Management's criterion for launching the product is that the probability that the product will be a moderate or great success must be greater than .45. If the probability of failure is greater than .5, the new product will be dropped. Otherwise, another market study will be initiated.

What should be done with the new product? Justify your answer.

POM **21.68** A manufacturer of microcomputers is in the process of deciding whether or not to purchase a lot of 1 million monitors at $65 each. The current policy is to manufacture the monitors at a cost of $70. When the microcomputer manufacturer produces his own monitors, however, the defective rate is known to be 6%. The defective rate of the supplier's monitors is unknown, but the distribution of percent defectives shown in the accompanying table has been estimated.

Percent Defective	Probability
5%	.1
10	.2
15	.4
20	.3

TABLE E21.66   *LIKELIHOOD PROBABILITIES*

	Judgments		
Success Level	Rave Review	Lukewarm Response	Poor Response
Excellent	.8	.1	.1
Good	.5	.3	.2
Fair	.4	.3	.3

The cost to the microcomputer manufacturer of replacing a defective monitor is $50. Should the manufacturer purchase the 1 million monitors or produce them himself?

POM **21.69**   In Exercise 21.68, suppose that it is possible to take a random sample of monitors from the lot of 1 million to determine how many are defective.

a. What would a sample of size 1 be worth?

b. What would a sample of size 2 be worth?

POM **21.70**   In Exercise 21.68, suppose that a sample of 20 monitors was selected from the lot and that 4 were found to be defective. Should the manufacturer purchase the 1 million monitors or produce them himself?

SOLUTIONS TO SELF-CORRECTING EXERCISES

21.6 Let a_0 = Bake 0 cakes
a_1 = Bake 1 cake
a_2 = Bake 2 cakes
a_3 = Bake 3 cakes
s_0 = Demand for 0 cakes
s_1 = Demand for 1 cake
s_2 = Demand for 2 cakes
s_3 = Demand for 3 cakes

PAYOFF TABLE

States of Nature	Acts			
	a_0	a_1	a_2	a_3
s_0	0	-3	-6	-9
s_1	0	5	2	-1
s_2	0	5	10	7
s_3	0	5	10	15

21.20 a. Expected Cost (build small plant)
= .15(220) + .55(330) + .30(440) = 346.5

Expected Cost (build medium plant)
= .15(300) + .55(320) + .30(390) = 338

Expected Cost (build large plant) = 350

The act with the largest expected monetary value is the act with the smallest expected cost. Thus, the act with the largest expected monetary value is to build a medium plant.

b. OPPORTUNITY LOSS TABLE

States of Nature	Acts		
	a_1	a_2	a_3
s_1	0	80	130
s_2	10	0	30
s_3	90	40	0

c. $EOL(a_1)$ = .15(0) + .55(10) + .30(90) = 32.5
$EOL(a_2)$ = .15(80) + .55(0) + .30(40) = 24
$EOL(a_3)$ = .15(130) + .55(30) + .30(0) = 36

Optimal act is a_2 (build medium plant)

21.30 Let a_1 = Buy footballs
a_2 = Don't buy footballs
s_1 = Demand of 10,000
s_2 = Demand of 30,000
s_3 = Demand of 50,000

PAYOFF TABLE ($1,000s)

States of Nature	Acts a_1	a_2
s_1	-75	0
s_2	25	0
s_3	125	0

$\text{EMV}(a_1) = .2(-75) + .5(25) + .3(125) = 35$

$\text{EMV}(a_2) = 0$

$\text{EMV}^* = 35$

$\text{EPPI} = .2(0) + .5(25) + .3(125) = 50$

$\text{EVPI} = 50 - 35 = 15$

21.50   Based on prior probabilities,

$\text{EMV}(a_1) = .2(1,000) + .5(4,000) + .3(8,000)$
$= 4,600$

$\text{EMV}(a_2) = .2(-2,000) + .5(7,000) + .3(12,000)$
$= 6,700$

$\text{EMV}(a_3) = .2(-10,000) + .5(8,000) + .3(15,000)$
$= 6,500$

Optimal act is a_2. $\text{EMV}^* = 6,700$.
If prediction is I_1:

s_j	$P(s_j)$	$P(I_1 \mid s_j)$	$P(I_1 \cap s_j)$	$P(s_j \mid I_1)$
s_1	.2	.5	.10	.435
s_2	.5	.2	.10	.435
s_3	.3	.1	.03	.130
			$P(I_1) = .23$	

$\text{EMV}(a_1) = .435(1,000) + .435(4,000)$
$+ .130(8,000) = 3,215$

$\text{EMV}(a_2) = .435(-2,000) + .435(7,000)$
$+ .130(12,000) = 3,735$

$\text{EMV}(a_3) = .435(-10,000) + .435(8,000)$
$+ .130(15,000) = 1,080$

Optimal act is a_2.
If prediction is I_2:

s_j	$P(s_j)$	$P(I_2 \mid s_j)$	$P(I_2 \cap s_j)$	$P(s_j \mid I_2)$
s_1	.2	.5	.10	.185
s_2	.5	.7	.35	.648
s_3	.3	.3	.09	.167
			$P(I_2) = .54$	

$\text{EMV}(a_1) = .185(1,000) + .648(4,000)$
$+ .167(8,000) = 4,113$

$\text{EMV}(a_2) = .185(-2,000) + .648(7,000)$
$+ .167(12,000) = 6,170$

$\text{EMV}(a_3) = .185(-10,000) + .648(8,000)$
$+ .167(15,000) = 5,839$

Optimal act is a_2.
If prediction is I_3:

s_j	$P(s_j)$	$P(I_3 \mid s_j)$	$P(I_3 \cap s_j)$	$P(s_j \mid I_3)$
s_1	.2	0	0	0
s_2	.5	.1	.05	.217
s_3	.3	.6	.18	.783
			$P(I_3) = .23$	

$\text{EMV}(a_1) = 0(1,000) + .217(4,000) + .783(8,000)$
$= 7,132$

$\text{EMV}(a_2) = 0(-2,000) + .217(7,000)$
$+ .783(12,000) = 10,915$

$\text{EMV}(a_3) = 0(-10,000) + .217(8,000)$
$+ .783(15,000) = 13,481$

Optimal act is a_3.

$\text{EMV}' = .23(3,735) + .54(6,170) + .23(13,481)$
$= 7,291.48$

$\text{EVSI} = 7,291.48 - 6,700 = 591.48$

Since cost of additional information is $600, AEF
should not be hired.

ANSWERS TO SELECTED EVEN-NUMBERED EXERCISES

CHAPTER 2

2.2 b. .533; .467

2.4 b. .52; .48

2.6 c. 41.2% d. $23,577

2.8 c. .188

2.10 a. interval b. nominal c. ordinal d. interval

2.20 Shift 1: 22; Shift 2: 17.4

2.22 mode

2.26 1.4; 1; 1

2.28 a. 293,400
b. 1974: 16.28; 1984: 19.63
c. 1–3: 15.17; 4–6: 22.89

2.30 19; 35.56; 5.96

2.32 a. 9; 12.5; 3.54
b. 0; 4.67; 2.16
c. 6; 5.33; 2.31
d. 5; 0; 0

2.34 lower quartile: median; upper quartile

2.36 median; interquartile range

2.38 a. 5.67%; 277.16(%)^2; 16.65%
b. 70%; 5%; −7.5%; 8%

2.40 a. 10.2; −4.5; 13.65; 4.75; 30.7; 34.1; 21.3; 7.95; .9; 20.95
b. 14% c. 12.63%
d. Fund A, Portfolio, Fund B (lowest return and risk)

2.42 a. Mattel: 1263.57; Tonka: 1085.91; industry: 668.15; statement supported
b. Mattel: 4.21; Tonka: 6.31; industry: 1.59; statement supported

2.44 approx. 340; approx. 475; almost all 500

2.46 approx. 680; approx. 950; almost all 1,000

2.48 a. approx. 68%; approx. 100%
b. approx. 5%
c. approx. 2.5%

2.50 a. 16.98; 11.08
b. 17.75; 16.24

2.52 a. 32.8; 230.34 b. 256

2.54 a. 21.33; 163.77 b. 100

2.56 35.56; 4.68

2.58 48.08; 47; 5.93

2.62 a. 100% b. yes

2.66 a. 47.6 b. 115.42
c. 10.74

2.68 b. 47.8; 121

2.72 c. symmetric: Business Forms; positively skewed: Soft Drinks, Mobile Homes; negatively skewed: Manufactured Ice, Cutlery, Pottery Products
d. greater than 17.31%

2.74 a. (8.9, 32.9); yes
b. (14.9, 26.9)
c. not normal

2.76 b. 12.76; 1.84   c. 12.5
   d. approx. 12.81;
      approx. 2.01

2.78 b. 2.12%; 1.23%
   c. 2.6%
   d. bank yields are more
      concentrated
   e. bank yields are more
      concentrated

2.D.2 15

CHAPTER 3

3.4 a. $s = \{www, \bar{w}ww, w\bar{w}w,$
      $ww\bar{w}, \bar{w}\bar{w}w, \bar{w}w\bar{w}, w\bar{w}\bar{w},$
      $\bar{w}\bar{w}\bar{w}\}$
   b. $\{www, \bar{w}\bar{w}\bar{w}\}$

3.6 a. $A \cup B = \{2, 3, 6\}$
   b. $A \cap B = \{3, 5\}$
   c. $\bar{A} = \{1, 6\}$
   d. $A = \{3\}$ is a simple
      event
   e. yes

3.8 b. $A \cup B = \{O1, O2, O3,$
      $C2\}$
   c. $A \cap B = \{O2\}$
   d. $\bar{B} = \{O1, O3, C1, C3\}$
   e. no

3.10 a. .65   b. .60   c. .85
   d. 0

3.12 a. $S = \{HH, HT, TH, TT\}$
   b. $P\{HH\} = P\{HT\} =$
      $P\{TH\} = P\{TT\} = 1/4$
   c. 1/2   d. 3/4

3.14 b. $S = \{0, 1, 2, 3, 4\}$
   c. $P\{0\} = 36/80; P\{1\} =$
      $28/80; P\{2\} = 12/80;$
      $P\{3\} = P\{4\} = 2/80$
   d. relative frequency
   e. .05

3.16 a. .90   b. .595   c. .09
   d. .495

3.18 a. 49/75   b. 17/25
   c. 3/25   d. 32/75

3.20 a. 1   b. 6/7   c. 2/5
   d. 2/7   e. 1/5   f. 1/6

3.22 a. independent
   b. independent
   c. dependent

3.24 a. 1/13   b. 1/13   c. yes

3.26 .20

3.28 a. 67/125   b. 41/125
   c. no   d. no

3.30 12/44

3.32 a. .88543; .58259   b. .658
   c. .745

3.34 $P(A \cap B) = .1; P(B|A) = .5$

3.36 .22

3.38 .42

3.40 a. .25   b. .60   c. .15
   d. .70

3.42 a. .15   b. .4   c. .06
   d. .49

3.44 a. .2   b. .7

3.46 a. 39%   b. 100%

3.48 a. .25   b. .33   c. 1
   d. .42   e. .63   f. .56

3.50 a. approx. .63
   b. approx. .30
   c. approx. .26

3.52 b. $P(A \cap B) = .06;$
      $P(\bar{B}) = .66$

3.54 b. .84; .24

3.56 42/90

3.58 a. .7   b. .18

3.60 a. 3,600   b. .41   c. .34
   d. .805

3.62 .28

3.64 .5; .63

3.66 .125; 1/3

3.68 .5

3.70 .73

3.72 a. .997   b. .1

3.74 a. $S = \{HHH, HHT,$
      $HTH, HTT, THH,$
      $THT, TTH, TTT\}$
   b. 1/8 to each   c. 4/8
   d. 5/8   e. 0   f. 3/8

   g. 3/4   h. no
   i. A and C; B and C

3.76 a. 2/36   b. 10/36
   c. 6/36   d. 5/36
   e. 18/36   f. 5/18

3.78 a. .71   b. .16   c. 55/80

3.80 a. .78   b. .22   c. .35
   d. 21/78   e. 14/22
   f. 8/22   g. 8/65   h. 0
   i. 1   j. .57

3.82 .3

3.84 a. .19   b. .61

3.86 a. approx. 82   b. .164

3.88 a. .412   b. .206   c. 383

3.90 a. $S = \{HH, HT, TH, TT\}$
   b. $P\{HH\} = 4/9;$
      $P\{HT\} = P\{TH\} =$
      $2/9; P\{TT\} = 1/9$
   c. 4/9

3.92 .73

3.94 2/3

CHAPTER 4

4.2 a. 1   b. .9   c. .5
   d. .4   e. 0

4.4 a.

x	1	2	3	4	5	6
$p(x)$	1/6	1/6	1/6	1/6	1/6	1/6

4.6 b. positively skewed
   c. 0   d. .10

4.8 b. positively skewed
   c. .870   d. .97

4.10 a. 2.0; 1.0   b. yes

4.12 a. 15.75; 33.1875
   b. 60; 531

4.14 a. 8.5; 6.73   b. 117.5
   c. 587.5

4.16 a. up to $18   b. $55.46

4.18 $500 in cash

4.24 a.

x	0	1	2	3	4
p(x)	.0256	.1536	.3456	.3456	.1296

   b. .5248   c. 2.4; .96

4.26 .149; .246; .315

4.28 .051; .324; .311

4.30 a. .034   b. .922
   c. .161   d. .152
   e. .065

4.32 a. .018   b. 3

4.34 a. (i) .967; (ii) .006;
   (iii) .120
   b. 100 minutes

4.36 a. .015   b. .558
   c. .594

4.38 a. .616   b. .176
   c. .238

4.42 a. .277; .365; .231
   b. .287; .358; .235

4.44 .036

4.46 a. .265   b. .456
   c. .125

4.48 a. .122   b. .687

4.50 a. .004   b. claim is false

4.52 c. .8   d. 0

4.54 a. .25   b. 7:30 A.M.
   c. .58

4.56 a. .0446   b. .8289
   c. .025   d. .9925
   e. .0823   f. .8037

4.58 a. 2.575   b. 2.33
   c. 1.645

4.60 a. .25   b. −1.25
   c. −1.875   d. 1.75
   e. −2.25   f. −1.625

4.62 a. .0918   b. .9962
   c. .9082   d. .0918
   e. .8854

4.64 a. .0475   b. .3830
   c. .9901   d. $2,902,000

4.66 a. .9544   b. .1587

4.68 a. 10   b. 7,796

4.70 a. .0465   b. approx. 1.0
   c. 36

4.72 a. 20; 3.46   b. .0968
   c. .9429

4.76 a. .0025   b. .999994
   c. .0497   d. 0

4.78 a. .8892   b. yes

4.80 b. .865; .982   c. .05
   d. .05

4.82 a. .6703   b. .3679
   c. .8647

4.84 a. 4.4; 2.42   b. 25.2
   c. 95.8   d. 20.2; 7.25

4.86 a. $85,000   b. $629,504

4.88 a. 16%; 6.73%
   b. stock portfolio,
   combination, real-
   estate venture

4.90 a. .016   b. .012
   c. .874   d. .245
   e. .545   f. .505

4.92 a. .677   b. .165
   c. .323   d. .866

4.94 a. .096   b. .994

4.96 $89.20

4.98 a. .837   b. .999   c. .45

4.100 a. .163   b. .181
   c. .180

4.102 a. .0505   b. .1059
   c. .6985   d. .7439

4.104 6.082 ounces

4.106 .2912

4.108 .2703

CHAPTER 5

5.4 a. nominal   b. nominal
   c. interval   d. interval
   e. ordinal

5.6 a. analysis of the
   relationship between
   two variables

   b. comparison of two or
   more populations
   c. description of a single
   population
   d. comparison of two or
   more populations
   e. comparison of two
   populations
   f. analysis of the
   relationship among two
   or more variables
   g. comparison of two
   populations
   h. description of a single
   population
   i. comparison of two
   populations

CHAPTER 6

6.2 a. .0062   b. .0228   c. 0

6.4 a. .0089   b. .7270

6.6 a. .0150   b. .6907

6.8 c.

$\bar{x}$	$P(\bar{x})$
1.5	2/30
2.0	2/30
2.5	4/30
3.0	4/30
3.5	6/30
4.0	4/30
4.5	4/30
5.0	2/30
5.5	2/30

6.10 c.

$\bar{x}$	$P(\bar{x})$
1.5	2/12
2.0	2/12
2.5	4/12
3.0	2/12
3.5	2/12

6.12

$\hat{p}$	$P(\hat{p})$
0	25/36
.5	10/36
1	1/36

6.16 .6687

6.18 a. .0038
  b. 0; the manufacturer is probably wrong

6.20 .1056

CHAPTER 7

7.2 a. widens   b. widens
  c. widens

7.4 $1,500 \pm 7.40$

7.6 22.5 ± 5.82

7.8 7.2 ± 2.47

7.10 $4.3 \pm .28$

7.12 14.3 ± 1.23

7.14 a. $|z| > 1.96$ b. $z > 2.33$
  c. $z < -1.28$

7.16 $z = -1.41$; do not reject H_0

7.18 a. $\bar{x} > 505.13$
  b. $\bar{x} > 20.23$, $\bar{x} < 19.77$
  c. $\bar{x} > 1,022.92$, $\bar{x} < 977.08$

7.20 $z = 2.5$; reject H_0

7.22 $z = 0$; do not reject H_0

7.24 $z = 28$; yes

7.26 $z = -1.7$; yes

7.28 .0793

7.30 .0233

7.32 there is a lot of statistical evidence to allow us to reject H_0 in favor of H_A

7.34 150 ± 5.54

7.36 $t = -5.89$; reject H_0

7.38 $t = 2.77$; reject H_0

7.40 $t = -2.45$;

p-value $= .0071$; reject H_0

7.42 $t = 4.82$; yes

7.44 $t = -.56$; no

7.46 a. $t = 2.18$; yes
  b. $10.52 \pm .49$

7.48 a. (49.17, 377.94)
  b. $\chi^2 = 15.4$; do not reject H_0

7.50 a. $s^2 > 158.65$
  b. $s^2 < 306.6$
  c. $s^2 < 11.42$, $s^2 > 32.44$

7.52 $\chi^2 = 20.77$; reject H_0

7.54 $\chi^2 = 48.0$; yes

7.56 (304.85, 967.66)

7.58 a. $\chi^2 = 120.5$; yes
  b. (138.78, 334.22)

7.60 .0012; .1492; .83; .83; .1492; .0012

7.64 .0268

7.66 385

7.68 1,041

7.70 1,705

7.72 a. $t = 1.67$; no
  b. $1.1 \pm .17$
  c. (.05, .17)
  d. assume that the times are normally distributed

7.74 a. $z = -1.67$; yes
  b. .0475
  c. assume that σ is unchanged

7.76 1,041

7.78 a. $t = 5.89$; yes
  b. type I error: build on an unacceptable site; type II error: don't build on an acceptable site; the type I error is more expensive.
  c. small α
  d. no, it's better to control (through α) the more expensive error

7.80 $4.3 \pm .30$

7.82 a. number of cars: $t = .46$; no; number of hours parked: $t = 6.27$; yes
  b. type I error: accuse the employee of stealing when he's innocent; type II error: exonerate employee when he's guilty
  c. ignoring the possibility of a wrongful dismissal suit, the owner wants a large α
  d. small α

7.84 a. 33.06 ± 2.81
  b. no, just second-year business students
  c. assume that incomes are normally distributed

7.86 a. $27,500 \pm 832$
  b. (i) widens; (ii) narrows; (iii) no change in interval width

7.88 a. $z = -1.18$; no
  b. .3192

CHAPTER 8

8.2 $z = 1.4$; no

8.4 a. .83   b. .6103
  c. .0262

8.6 $z = 1.48$; no

8.8 .9319

8.12 $z = 2.36$; yes

8.14 $z = 4.0$; yes

8.16 0

8.18 $z = 1.48$; no

8.20 $.84 \pm .025$

8.22 $.245 \pm .080$

8.24 $.2 \pm .039$

8.26 $.5 \pm .098$

8.28 3,458

8.30 $.08 \pm .017$

8.32 $.44 \pm .028$

8.34 $.30 \pm .031$

8.36 $.253 \pm .075$

8.38 $z = 1.20$; no

8.40 $z = 2.64$; yes;
p-value $= .0041$

8.42 a. $z = 2.90$; yes   b. $.0019$

8.44 a. $.41 \pm .053$
b. $.42 \pm .053$
no, the two polls do not
contradict each other

8.46 4,161

8.48 $.33 \pm .11$

CHAPTER 9

9.2 a. $z = 2.78$; yes   b. $.0027$
c. 15 ± 12.58

9.4 $.0274$

9.6 $z = -2.62$; reject H_0

9.8 -3.2 ± 2.39

9.10 13,531

9.12 $z = -2.93$; yes;
p-value $= .0034$

9.14 $z = -1.05$; no

9.16 333

9.18 a. $t = 1.76$; reject H_0
b. $z = 10.95$; reject H_0

9.20 a. $t = -3.16$; yes
b. -15 ± 12.25

9.22 2.3 ± 6.10

9.24 4.1 ± 4.31

9.30 -23.0 ± 8.48

9.32 a. $t = 2.21$; yes
b. 5.8 ± 4.89
c. assume that weights are
normally distributed

9.34 $5,000 \pm 5,189$

9.36 0

9.38 3.8 ± 3.86

9.40 a. 2 ± 2.215
b. -8 ± 5.54

9.42 -4 ± 2.90

9.48 8.63 ± 11.33

9.50 $t = -1.83$; yes

9.52 $t = 4.84$; yes

9.54 $t = 2.03$; yes

9.56 a. $t = -1.646$; no
b. -2.3 ± 2.56

9.58 a. $(.401, 4.71)$
b. $(.810, 15.23)$

9.60 $(.203, .981)$

9.62 $(.022, 3.95)$

9.64 a. $F = .155$; yes
b. assume that returns are
normally distributed
c. $(.023, .870)$

9.66 $(.125, 2.038)$

9.68 $(.253, 1.79)$

9.70 a. $t = 2.49$; yes
b. assume that percentage
weight gains are
normally distributed
c. type I error: conclude
that the scheme works
when it doesn't; type II
error: conclude that the
scheme doesn't work
when it does; type II
error is more damaging;
select $\alpha = .10$
d. $F = 1.24$; no
e. 10.5 ± 12.15

9.72 $t = -2.19$; yes

9.74 a. $t = -3.64$; yes
b. $t = -2.43$; yes

9.76 623

9.78 $z = 4.04$; yes

9.80 $t = 1.35$; no

CHAPTER 10

10.2 a. $.1188$ b. 0

10.4 $z = -2.12$; do not reject
H_0

10.6 $z = -.73$; no

10.8 $-.05 \pm .052$

10.10 $.0764$

10.12 $z = -4.32$; yes

10.14 508

10.16 $.1 \pm .061$

10.18 a. $z = .93$; no   b. $.3524$
c. $.07 \pm .195$

10.20 a. $z = -3.16$; yes   b. 0
c. large α

10.22 $z = 1.30$; no

10.24 in the past six months,
there has been little or no
decrease in the politician's
popularity

10.26 a. $z = -5.02$; yes
b. $z = -2.39$; no;
because the sample
sizes are smaller, the
amount of statistical
evidence is not great
enough to allow us to
draw the same
conclusion

10.28 a. $z = -1.03$; no
b. $z = -0.50$; no
c. $z = -1.06$; no

10.30 $z = 2.33$; yes

10.32 a. $z = 1.01$; no
b. $-.053 \pm .092$

10.34 a. $z = 6.49$; yes
b. $z = 1.97$; yes
c. $-.038 \pm .042$

CHAPTER 11

11.2 a. $t = 2.68$; no
b. 1.4 ± 1.18

11.4 $t = 2.15$; yes

11.6 $t = -1.69$; no

11.8 $.5596$

11.10 $F = 3.0$; no

11.12 $t = 1.68$; yes

11.14 1,083

11.16 $t = -2.16$; yes

11.18 a. $t = -.44$; no
  b. $z = .71$; no
  c. $.24 \pm .20$
  d. $F = .833$; there is not enough evidence to allow us to conclude that the requirement is not satisfied

11.20 $z = -1.88$; yes

11.22 $-.03 \pm .049$

11.24 4.6 ± 9.94

11.26 .7422

11.28 $F = .550$; no

11.30 $z = .98$; no

11.32 684

11.34 a. 41 ± 1.87
  b. $t = 3.14$; yes

CHAPTER 12

12.6 $F = 52.74$, reject H_0

12.8 $F = 16.69$; reject H_0

12.10 $F = 1.26$; do not reject H_0

12.12 $F = 3.72$; yes

12.14 -2.150 ± 6.38;
  5.147 ± 5.39; 6.021 ± 5.82

12.16 a. 23.714 ± 1.932
  b. 31.000 ± 1.932
  c. -6.0 ± 2.733
  d. -1.286 ± 2.733

12.18 a. 8.75 ± 4.265
  b. -7.45 ± 5.722

12.22 a. 38.5 ± 6.324
  b. 34.286 ± 6.854
  c. -1.486 ± 9.536
  d. 15.5 ± 8.412

12.24 $F = 8.797$; yes

12.26 $F = 1.18$; no

12.28 $F = 3.47$; management should tailor its advertising toward the industry that uses the computer most frequently

12.30 a. 44.5 ± 3.778
  b. 13.5 ± 4.877

12.32 $F = 6.06$; yes

12.34 a. 8.36 ± 1.578
  b. $.14 \pm 2.232$

12.40 $F = 1.37$; do not reject H_0

12.42 $F = 2.18$; yes

12.44 a. 23.5 ± 3.52
  b. -2.25 ± 4.99
  c. 20.0 ± 4.07
  d. 2.33 ± 5.76

12.46 $F = 2.60$; yes

12.48 $F = 59.48$; the means differ

12.50 $F = 4.46$; no

12.52 $F = 2.39$; no

12.54 a. $9.64 \pm .832$
  b. $.38 \pm 1.18$
  c. $8.83 \pm .932$

12.56 a. 25.33 ± 2.00
  b. 19.33 ± 2.82
  c. 1.67 ± 2.82
  d. -1.67 ± 3.99

12.58 a. $F = 3.00$; yes
  b. $F = .76$; there is not enough evidence to indicate that the judges differ

12.60 $\omega = 9.11$; μ_2 and μ_3 differ

12.62 a. $F = 6.23$; yes
  b. $\omega = 15.56$; μ_1 and μ_3 differ

12.64 $\omega = 2.19$; μ_2 differs from μ_3 and μ_4

12.66 a. $F = 6.42$; yes
  b. $\omega = 9.51$; μ_1 differs from μ_2 and μ_3

12.68 a. 20.4 ± 1.93
  b. -5.2 ± 2.73

12.70 a. $F = 65.11$; yes
  b. $F = 16.15$; yes

12.72 $\omega = 6.82$; all means differ

12.74 $F = .20$; Henry should go to U. of A.

12.76 $F = 1.71$; do not change the print type

12.78 $F = 58.08$; yes

12.80 $F = 1.696$; no

12.82 a. 48.333 ± 8.58
  b. 7.166 ± 12.13

12.84 $F = 7.967$; yes

CHAPTER 13

13.4 a. at least one p_i is not equal to its specified value
  b. $\chi^2 = 3.88$; do not reject H_0

13.6 $\chi^2 = 9.96$; reject H_0

13.8 $\chi^2 = 5.70$; no

13.10 $\chi^2 = 14.07$; yes

13.12 $\chi^2 = 19.22$; distribution differs

13.14 a. $\chi^2 > 13.2767$
  b. $\chi^2 > 24.9958$

13.16 $\chi^2 = 16.57$; L and M are dependent

13.18 $\chi^2 = 2.27$; no

13.20 U.S.A.: $\chi^2 = 16.51$; reject H_0
  Mexico: $\chi^2 = 3.57$; do not reject H_0
  Austr.: $\chi^2 = 7.63$; do not reject H_0

13.22 $\chi^2 = 3.34$; no

13.24 $\chi^2 = 7.61$; yes

13.26 $\chi^2 = .70$; no

13.28 $\chi^2 = 3.08$; do not reject H_0

13.30 $\chi^2 = 1.68$; yes

13.32 $\chi^2 = 16.85$; no

13.34 $\chi^2 = 3.2$; no

13.36 $\chi^2 = 4.77$; no

13.38 $\chi^2 = 3.20$; no differences

13.40 $\chi^2 = 16.09$; yes

13.42 a. $\chi^2 = 1.73$; no differences

13.44 $\chi^2 = 20.69$; the two classifications are independent

13.46 $\chi^2 = 15.18$; reject H_0

13.48 $\chi^2 = 10.0$; reject H_0

13.50 b. $\chi^2 = 9.38$; reject H_0
c. $\chi^2 = 1.37$; do not reject H_0

13.52 a. $\chi^2 = 121.64$; yes
b. $\chi^2 = 19.93$; yes
c. $\chi^2 = 36.65$; yes

CHAPTER 14

14.2 $T = 19$; yes

14.4 $T = 64.5$; yes

14.6 $z = 1.15$; no

14.8 $T = 67$; yes

14.10 $T = 35.5$; no

14.12 $T = 81$; no

14.14 $z = 2.85$; yes

14.16 $z = -2.14$; yes

14.18 $z = 3.64$; yes

14.20 a. test statistic: $T = T^+$; rejection region: $T \leq 6$
b. test statistic: $T = $ smaller of T^+ or T^-; rejection region: $T \leq 37$
c. test statistic: $T = T^-$; rejection region: $T \leq 11$

14.22 $z = -.81$; no

14.24 $z = -.74$; no

14.26 $T = 6$; yes

14.28 $T = 6.5$; no

14.30 $T = 27$; enlarge the tennis department

14.32 $H = 0$; no

14.34 $H = .67$; no

14.36 $H = 17.03$; yes

14.38 $H = 7.46$; yes

14.40 $H = 9.98$; yes

14.42 $F_r = 6.93$; no

14.44 $F_r = 15.27$; yes

14.46 $F_r = 7.00$; yes

14.48 $F_r = 2.85$; Chuck should not make any changes

14.50 a. reject H_0
b. do not reject H_0
c. reject H_0

14.52 $D = .3620$; there is sufficient evidence to indicate that the data are not normally distributed, with $\mu = 10$ and $\sigma = 2$

14.54 $D = .1950$; the assumption is reasonable

14.56 $T = 120.5$; no

14.58 $H = 2.58$; no

14.60 $F_r = 12.15$; yes

14.62 $H = .51$; no

14.64 $D = .0823$; the assumption is reasonable

14.66 $H = 6.64$; no

14.68 $z = -2.92$; yes

14.70 $z = -1.24$; no

14.72 $T = 3.5$; purchase machine A

14.74 $H = 13.10$; yes

14.76 $z = 3.04$; yes

14.78 $z = -2.12$; yes

CHAPTER 15

15.4 $\hat{y} = 8.24 - 1.07x$

15.6 $\hat{y} = 24.56 - 6.73x$

15.8 a. $\hat{y} = 14.77 + 2.13x$

15.10 a. $\hat{y} = 6.86 + .54x$

15.12 a. $\hat{y} = -644.95 + 195.07x$

15.14 6.429

15.16 SSE $= 320,807.89$; $s_\varepsilon = 157.09$

15.20 2.05

15.22 1.50

15.24 73.52

15.26 1.48 ± 2.73

15.28 a. $t = 2.30$; no
b. 3.18 ± 4.37

15.30 $t = 3.418$; more hours of study results in higher exam scores

15.32 $t = 16.91$; advertising and sales are positively linearly related

15.34 $t = 2.55$; yes

15.36 .964

15.38 a. $t = 1.33$; do not reject H_0
b. $t = -.82$; do not reject H_0
c. $t = 2.19$; reject H_0

15.42 $r = .770$; $r^2 = .593$; 59.3% of the variation in y is explained by the variation in x

15.44 a. $\hat{y} = 102.94 + 44.71x$
c. SSE $= 43,247.06$; $s_\varepsilon = 73.52$
d. $t = 4.82$; yes
e. $r^2 = .745$; 74.5% of the variation in y is explained by the variation in x

15.46 $r^2 = .908$; 90.8% of the variation in y is explained by the variation in x

15.48 a. -37.5 ± 9.11
b. -47.5 ± 3.97

15.52 330.4 ± 136.3

15.54 83.92 ± 26.09

15.58 43.86 ± 5.19

15.60 .943

15.62 a. $r_s = .482$; do not reject H_0
b. $r_s = .413$; reject H_0
c. $r_s = -.588$; reject H_0

15.64 $z = 2.04$; do not reject H_0

15.66 $r_s = .823$; yes

15.68 $r_s = .405$; no

15.70 a. $\hat{y} = .378 + 5.76x$
b. $t = 15.67$; yes
c. $r^2 = .947$
d. 29.18 ± 11.35

15.72 $r_s = -.614$; yes

15.74 a. $t = 17.3$; yes
b. 268.31 ± 16.10
c. 119.39 ± 74.46

15.76 a. $t = 1.99$; yes
b. $.553 \pm .138$

15.78 a. $\hat{y} = 163.33 + 5.00x$
b. $t = 2.37$; yes
c. 213.33 ± 19.07
d. 208.33 ± 10.89

15.80 $r_s = -.993$; there is evidence of a linear relationship

CHAPTER 16

16.4 a. $t = 3.15$; yes
b. $t = -3.81$; yes

16.6 a. $t = 3.0$; reject H_0
b. $t = 1.67$; do not reject H_0

16.8 a. $t = 2.60$; yes
b. $t = -1.16$; no
c. $t = 1.23$; no

16.10 b. Permits: $t = 2.067$; yes;
Rates: $t = -1.839$; no;
GNP: $t = 4.400$; yes

16.12 b. $t = 2.125$; yes
c. $t = -3.161$; yes

16.14 visits: $t = 2.57$; yes
density: $t = 2.50$; yes

16.16 a. 4.36   b. .239
c. 2.38

16.18 a. 62.2   b. 2.35
c. .194   d. .159
e. $F = 5.64$; the model is useful

16.20 a. $r^2 = 12.7\%$; 12.7% of the variation in sales volume is explained by the variation in the independent variables
b. $F = 4.28$; the model is useful

16.22 a. $s_\varepsilon = 1.47985$; the model fits quite well
b. $r^2 = .9586$; the proportion of unexplained variability is 4.14%
c. $F = 69.503$; yes

16.24 a. $F = 7.44$; the model is useful
b. $t = -.53$; no

16.26 a. $d = 1.38$; there is evidence of positive first-order autocorrelation
b. $d = 1.60$; there is not enough evidence to indicate first-order autocorrelation
c. $d = 1.63$; there is evidence of negative first-order autocorrelation

16.46 $d = 2.15$; there is evidence of first-order autocorrelation

16.48 a. $F = 9.01$; reject H_0
b. $F = 4.93$; reject H_0

16.50 a. $\hat{y} = 239.5 + 7.380x_1 + 10.181x_2 + 17.309x_3$
c. $r^2 = .9233$; 92.33% of the variation in y is explained by the variation in the independent variables

16.16
d. $F = 88.256$; the model is useful

16.56 a. $\hat{y} = 12,432.1171 + 11.6432x_1 + 6.1135x_2$
b. $t = 4.1763$; yes
c. $t = 3.8942$; yes
d. $F = 8.49$; the model is useful
e. $r^2 = .6069$; 60.69% of the variation in y is explained by the variation in the independent variables
f. $s_\varepsilon = 8.5776$ indicates that the model fits well

16.58 b. $x_1: t = 2.82$; yes;
$x_2: t = 1.24$; no

16.72 a. $F = 21.2959$; yes
b. $t = -1.516$; no
c. $t = 1.184$; no

16.78 a. $F = 77.20$; yes
b. $t = 1.212$; no

CHAPTER 17

17.6 a. $F = 30.66$; the model is useful
b. $t = 3.90$; yes

17.10 a. interaction exists
b. interaction does not exist
c. interaction exists

17.12 a. $F = 14.17$; yes
b. $t = 1.48$; no

17.14 a. $F = 4.92$; yes
b. x_1 and x_1x_2 are linearly related to y

17.16 a. $F = 12.33$; yes
b. x_1, x_2 and x_1x_2 are linearly related to y
c. 39.6% of the variation in y is explained by the model

17.18 a. Apple
b. IBM
c. some other computer

17.20 a. $F = 9.328$; the model is useful
 b. (i) $t = .993$; no;
 (ii) $t - 2.747$; yes;
 (iii) $t = .121$; no

17.22 a. $F = 3.56$; reject H_0
 b. $F = 6.32$; reject H_0
 c. $F = 2.64$; do not reject H_0

17.24 a. $\hat{y} = -3.5521 + .0211x - .000131x^2$ b. yes

17.26 a. $F = 287.19771$; the model is useful
 b. $t = 4.720$; we cannot eliminate interaction term

17.28 $F = 33.76$; yes

17.30 a. $t = .253$; no
 b. very little change

17.32 c. $t = -2.5415$; yes

CHAPTER 18

18.2 $z = -2.24$; yes

18.4 a. $F = 9.32$; yes
 b. $H = 10.82$; yes

18.6 a. $t = -3.16$; yes
 b. $T = 3$; yes

18.8 a. $4.1 \pm .27$
 b. 47,875 to 54,625; yes

18.10 $t = -2.28$; yes

18.12 Table 1: $z = 4.32$; there is evidence that graduates have higher average entrance exam scores
 Table 2: $\chi^2 = 11.37$; there is evidence that the undergraduate degree is a factor

18.14 a. $t = -1.40$; no
 b. -4.98 ± 7.66
 c. $T = 62$; no

18.16 b. DE

18.18 $z = 1.84$; yes

18.20 a. $z = .71$; no

 b. $\chi^2 = 11.90$; yes
 c. $\chi^2 = 53.5$; yes

18.22 $\chi^2 = 1.24$; no

CHAPTER 19

19.2

Period	Moving Average
1	——
2	——
3	38.8
4	35.4
5	35.8
6	38.8
7	44.4
8	46.8
9	48.8
10	46.2
11	——
12	——

19.4

Period	Moving Average
1	——
2	——
3	50.500
4	55.750
5	60.000
6	60.875
7	——
8	——

19.6

Period	S_t
1	12.00
2	16.80
3	16.16
4	22.43
5	18.09
6	16.42
7	23.28
8	21.46
9	22.69
10	15.74

19.8 b.

Period	Moving Average
1	——
2	36.7
3	30.7
4	26.0
5	35.7
6	41.0
7	43.0
8	33.3
9	28.0
10	29.0
11	40.7
12	42.3
13	40.0
14	33.3
15	44.7
16	53.0
17	51.7
18	43.0
19	32.0
20	——

19.10

Period	Moving Average
1	——
2	——
3	29.750
4	28.625
5	28.375
6	28.750
7	28.375
8	31.250
9	34.500
10	37.875
11	40.750
12	39.750
13	36.375
14	33.625
15	——
16	——

19.14 $\hat{y} = 63.9 - 3.94t$

19.16 linear trend: $r^2 = .942$; logarithmic trend: $r^2 = .877$

19.18 1986: $\hat{y} = 284.72$;
1987: $\hat{y} = 294.53$

19.20 1986: $\hat{y} = 287.67$;
1987: $\hat{y} = 298.95$

19.26 logarithmic model:
$\hat{y} = 207,612$;
polynomial model:
$\hat{y} = 225,848$

19.28 c.

Period	Percentage of Trend
1	37.2
2	67.2
3	126.5
4	101.0
5	158.2
6	132.9
7	114.0
8	123.8
9	100.0
10	93.2
11	65.0
12	80.2

19.30 b.

Period	Percentage of Trend
1	115.7
2	105.6
3	95.9
4	92.1
5	87.7
6	94.0
7	95.0
8	100.7
9	108.5
10	117.9
11	103.2
12	96.1
13	94.9
14	104.8
15	103.6
16	95.1
17	87.2
18	91.5
19	97.5
20	116.8

19.32 Monday .671;
Tuesday .865;
Wednesday .855;
Thursday 1.260;
Friday 1.349;

19.34 Monday .675;
Tuesday .893;
Wednesday .863;
Thursday 1.212;
Friday 1.357

19.36 1: .839; 2: 1.057; 3: 1.275;
4: .829

19.38 b.

Period	Four-quarter Centered Moving Average
1	——
2	——
3	177.375
4	179.750
5	184.250
6	188.625
7	191.750
8	194.375
9	197.250
10	202.875
11	210.375
12	217.625
13	222.375
14	229.125
15	240.000
16	250.750
17	264.000
18	278.250
19	——
20	——

19.40 1: 1.055; 2: .962; 3: .928;
4: 1.055

19.42 1: 1.094; 2: .958; 3: .688;
4: 1.260

19.44 model 1: 1.225;
model 2: .625

19.46 MAD = .96; SSE = 5.52

19.48 23.1

19.50 $w = .3$: 115.5;

$w = .6$: 117.4;
$w = .7$: 117.2

19.52 123.0

19.54 40.1

19.56 1: 191.1; 2: 331.2; 3: 418.5;
4: 169.2

19.58 540.5

19.60 Monday 66,730;
Tuesday 67,010;
Wednesday 67,270;
Thursday 67,550;
Friday 67,750

19.62 Monday 16.528;
Tuesday 22.193;
Wednesday 21.763;
Thursday 31.008;
Friday 35.214

19.64 1: 297.05; 2: 283.82;
3: 283.83; 4: 320.24

19.66

Month	Seasonal Index	Forecast
January	.842	23,136
February	.862	23,826
March	1.027	28,553
April	1.030	28,803
May	1.063	29,898
June	1.078	30,494
July	1.034	29,417
August	1.044	29,871
September	.962	27,681
October	1.021	29,544
November	.981	28,545
December	1.052	30,782

19.68 Sunday 258.04;
Monday 99.54;
Tuesday 98.03;
Wednesday 122.04;
Thursday 139.45;
Friday 236.69;
Saturday 439.71

19.70 b.

Period	Percentage of Trend
1	197.7
2	140.7
3	115.9
4	100.3
5	92.7
6	89.6
7	88.1
8	87.3
9	86.7
10	88.2
11	92.4
12	97.6
13	101.1
14	103.0
15	104.6
16	105.4
17	106.9

19.72 13.92

19.76 1: .636; 2: 1.041; 3: 1.398; 4: .925

19.78 1: 22.980; 2: 37.938; 3: 52.036; 4: 34.142

19.80 there is evidence of first-order autocorrelation

19.82 seasonal index model forecast: SSE = 56.450; multiple regression model forecast: SSE = 128.820

19.84 January 1.154; February 1.125; March 1.135; April 1.080; May .968; June .929; July .894; August .891; September .929; October .915; November .965; December 1.015

19.86 January 9.286; February 8.890; March 8.884; April 8.288; May 7.142; June 6.666; July 6.240; August 6.114; September 6.418; October 6.212; November 6.586; December 6.940

19.88 seasonal index model forecast: MAD = .608; multiple regression model forecast: MAD = .578; autoregressive model forecast: MAD = 1.052

CHAPTER 20

20.2 1982: 110.7; 1984: 104.0; 1986: 99.9

20.4 142.2

20.6 139.0

20.8 243.4

20.10 137.4

20.14 468.0

20.16 513.3

20.18 1980: 281.5; 1983: 341.5; 1986: 165.1

20.20 1980: 200.6; 1986: 280.6

20.22 1980: 198.7; 1986: 278.8

20.24

DEFLATED INDICES

Year	1970	1980	1986
Aggregate	100	94.5	99.4
Weighted Aggregate	100	111.5	139.2
Laspeyres	100	93.6	98.7
Paasche	100	91.5	97.7

20.26 1970: $23,000; 1975: $28,354; 1980: $28,651; 1986: $37,114

20.28 247.3

20.30 248.0

20.32 1977: 113.1; 1979: 148.6

20.34 1977: 109.5; 1979: 170.7

CHAPTER 21

21.4

	a_1	a_2	a_3	a_4
s_1	0	100	90	120
s_2	45	0	10	30
s_3	150	50	90	0

21.6

	a_0	a_1	a_2	a_3
s_0	0	-3	-6	-9
s_1	0	5	2	-1
s_2	0	5	10	7
s_3	0	5	10	15

21.12

	a_1	a_2	a_3
s_1	0	200	350
s_2	100	0	150
s_3	400	0	150
s_4	550	150	0

21.14

PAYOFF TABLE

	a_0	a_1	a_2	a_3
s_0	0	$-6,000$	$-12,000$	$-18,000$
s_1	0	7,000	1,000	$-5,000$
s_2	0	7,000	14,000	8,000
s_3	0	7,000	14,000	21,000

OPPORTUNITY LOSS TABLE

	a_0	a_1	a_2	a_3
s_0	0	6,000	12,000	18,000
s_1	7,000	0	6,000	12,000
s_2	14,000	7,000	0	6,000
s_3	21,000	14,000	7,000	0

21.16 a_3; EOL* = 18

21.20 a. build medium plant;
    expected cost = 338

b.

	a_1	a_2	a_3
s_1	0	80	130
s_2	10	0	30
s_3	90	40	0

c. EOL* = 24

21.22 hire Weplowem;
    EMV* = −54

21.24 don't buy the lot;
    EMV* = 0

21.26

	a_1	a_2	a_3
s_1	50	0	35
s_2	110	40	0
s_3	0	100	135
s_4	0	130	120

EOL* = 32.5

21.28 a. 10.0   b. 2.0

21.30 $15,000

21.32 $4.1 million

21.34 $5,600

21.36
$P(s_1|I_1) = .95$ $P(s_2|I_1) = .05$
$P(s_1|I_2) = .02$ $P(s_2|I_2) = .98$

21.38 $I_1: a_3$ (EMV = 24.25)
    $I_2: a_3$ (EMV = 22.3)
    $I_3: a_1$ (EMV = 18.5)

21.42 .30

21.48 0

21.50 EVSI = $591.48;
    AEF should not be hired

21.52 don't recycle (EMV = 0)

21.54 $5.4 million

21.56 don't change (EMV = 285)

21.58 Price at $7

21.60 change advertisement
    (EMV = $2,000)

21.62 don't change (EMV = 0)

21.64 sample should be taken

(EVSI = $4,710);
if small number of calls,
install 25 telephones;
if medium number of
calls, install 50
telephones;
if large number of calls,
install 100 telephones

21.66 sample should be taken
(EVSI = $1.14 million);
if rave review, release to
North American
audiences;
if lukewarm or poor
response, sell to European
distributor

21.68 purchase the monitors
(expected cost =
$72.25 million)

21.70 produce the monitors
(expected cost =
$73 million)

APPENDIX B

TABLES

TABLE 1 BINOMIAL PROBABILITIES

Tabulated values are $P(x \le k) = \sum_{x=0}^{k} p(x)$. (Values are rounded to three decimal places.)

n = 5

k	.01	.05	.10	.20	.25	.30	.40	.50	.60	.70	.75	.80	.90	.95	.99
0	.951	.774	.590	.328	.237	.168	.078	.031	.010	.002	.001	.000	.000	.000	.000
1	.999	.977	.919	.737	.633	.528	.337	.187	.087	.031	.016	.007	.000	.000	.000
2	1.000	.999	.991	.942	.896	.837	.683	.500	.317	.163	.104	.058	.009	.001	.000
3	1.000	1.000	1.000	.993	.984	.969	.913	.812	.663	.472	.367	.263	.081	.023	.001
4	1.000	1.000	1.000	1.000	.999	.998	.990	.969	.922	.832	.763	.672	.410	.226	.049

n = 6

k	.01	.05	.10	.20	.25	.30	.40	.50	.60	.70	.75	.80	.90	.95	.99
0	.941	.735	.531	.262	.178	.118	.047	.016	.004	.001	.000	.000	.000	.000	.000
1	.999	.967	.886	.655	.534	.420	.233	.109	.041	.011	.005	.002	.000	.000	.000
2	1.000	.998	.984	.901	.831	.744	.544	.344	.179	.070	.038	.017	.001	.000	.000
3	1.000	1.000	.999	.983	.962	.930	.821	.656	.456	.256	.169	.099	.016	.002	.000
4	1.000	1.000	1.000	.998	.995	.989	.959	.891	.767	.580	.466	.345	.114	.033	.001
5	1.000	1.000	1.000	1.000	1.000	.999	.996	.984	.953	.882	.822	.738	.469	.265	.059

$n = 7$

k	.01	.05	.10	.20	.25	.30	.40	p .50	.60	.70	.75	.80	.90	.95	.99
0	.932	.698	.478	.210	.133	.082	.028	.008	.002	.000	.000	.000	.000	.000	.000
1	.998	.956	.850	.577	.445	.329	.159	.063	.019	.004	.001	.000	.000	.000	.000
2	1.000	.996	.974	.852	.756	.647	.420	.227	.096	.029	.013	.005	.000	.000	.000
3	1.000	1.000	.997	.967	.929	.874	.710	.500	.290	.126	.071	.033	.003	.000	.000
4	1.000	1.000	1.000	.995	.987	.971	.904	.773	.580	.353	.244	.148	.026	.004	.000
5	1.000	1.000	1.000	1.000	.999	.996	.981	.937	.841	.671	.555	.423	.150	.044	.002
6	1.000	1.000	1.000	1.000	1.000	1.000	.998	.992	.972	.918	.867	.790	.522	.302	.068

$n = 8$

k	.01	.05	.10	.20	.25	.30	.40	p .50	.60	.70	.75	.80	.90	.95	.99
0	.923	.663	.430	.168	.100	.058	.017	.004	.001	.000	.000	.000	.000	.000	.000
1	.997	.943	.813	.503	.367	.255	.106	.035	.009	.001	.000	.000	.000	.000	.000
2	1.000	.994	.962	.797	.679	.552	.315	.145	.050	.011	.004	.001	.000	.000	.000
3	1.000	1.000	.995	.944	.886	.806	.594	.363	.174	.058	.027	.010	.000	.000	.000
4	1.000	1.000	1.000	.990	.973	.942	.826	.637	.406	.194	.114	.056	.005	.000	.000
5	1.000	1.000	1.000	.999	.996	.989	.950	.855	.685	.448	.321	.203	.038	.006	.000
6	1.000	1.000	1.000	1.000	1.000	.999	.991	.965	.894	.745	.633	.497	.187	.057	.003
7	1.000	1.000	1.000	1.000	1.000	1.000	.999	.996	.983	.942	.900	.832	.570	.337	.077

TABLE 1 BINOMIAL PROBABILITIES (continued)

n = 9

k	.01	.05	.10	.20	.25	.30	.40	.50	.60	.70	.75	.80	.90	.95	.99
								p							
0	.914	.630	.387	.134	.075	.040	.010	.002	.000	.000	.000	.000	.000	.000	.000
1	.997	.929	.775	.436	.300	.196	.071	.020	.004	.000	.000	.000	.000	.000	.000
2	1.000	.992	.947	.738	.601	.463	.232	.090	.025	.004	.001	.000	.000	.000	.000
3	1.000	.999	.992	.914	.834	.730	.483	.254	.099	.025	.010	.003	.000	.000	.000
4	1.000	1.000	.999	.980	.951	.901	.733	.500	.267	.099	.049	.020	.001	.000	.000
5	1.000	1.000	1.000	.997	.990	.975	.901	.746	.517	.270	.166	.086	.008	.001	.000
6	1.000	1.000	1.000	1.000	.999	.996	.975	.910	.768	.537	.399	.262	.053	.008	.000
7	1.000	1.000	1.000	1.000	1.000	1.000	.996	.980	.929	.804	.700	.564	.225	.071	.003
8	1.000	1.000	1.000	1.000	1.000	1.000	1.000	.998	.990	.960	.925	.866	.613	.370	.086

n = 10

k	.01	.05	.10	.20	.25	.30	.40	.50	.60	.70	.75	.80	.90	.95	.99
								p							
0	.904	.599	.349	.107	.056	.028	.006	.001	.000	.000	.000	.000	.000	.000	.000
1	.996	.914	.736	.376	.244	.149	.046	.011	.002	.000	.000	.000	.000	.000	.000
2	1.000	.988	.930	.678	.526	.383	.167	.055	.012	.002	.000	.000	.000	.000	.000
3	1.000	.999	.987	.879	.776	.650	.382	.172	.055	.011	.004	.001	.000	.000	.000
4	1.000	1.000	.998	.967	.922	.850	.633	.377	.166	.047	.020	.006	.000	.000	.000
5	1.000	1.000	1.000	.994	.980	.953	.834	.623	.367	.150	.078	.033	.002	.000	.000
6	1.000	1.000	1.000	.999	.996	.989	.945	.828	.618	.350	.224	.121	.013	.001	.000
7	1.000	1.000	1.000	1.000	1.000	.998	.988	.945	.833	.617	.474	.322	.070	.012	.000
8	1.000	1.000	1.000	1.000	1.000	1.000	.998	.989	.954	.851	.756	.624	.264	.086	.004
9	1.000	1.000	1.000	1.000	1.000	1.000	1.000	.999	.994	.972	.944	.893	.651	.401	.096

$n = 15$

p

k	.01	.05	.10	.20	.25	.30	.40	.50	.60	.70	.75	.80	.90	.95	.99
0	.860	.463	.206	.035	.013	.005	.000	.000	.000	.000	.000	.000	.000	.000	.000
1	.990	.829	.549	.167	.080	.035	.005	.000	.000	.000	.000	.000	.000	.000	.000
2	1.000	.964	.816	.398	.236	.127	.027	.004	.000	.000	.000	.000	.000	.000	.000
3	1.000	.995	.944	.648	.461	.297	.091	.018	.002	.000	.000	.000	.000	.000	.000
4	1.000	.999	.987	.836	.686	.515	.217	.059	.009	.001	.000	.000	.000	.000	.000
5	1.000	1.000	.998	.939	.852	.722	.403	.151	.034	.004	.001	.000	.000	.000	.000
6	1.000	1.000	1.000	.982	.943	.869	.610	.304	.095	.015	.004	.001	.000	.000	.000
7	1.000	1.000	1.000	.996	.983	.950	.787	.500	.213	.050	.017	.004	.000	.000	.000
8	1.000	1.000	1.000	.999	.996	.985	.905	.696	.390	.131	.057	.018	.000	.000	.000
9	1.000	1.000	1.000	1.000	.999	.996	.966	.849	.597	.278	.148	.061	.002	.000	.000
10	1.000	1.000	1.000	1.000	1.000	.999	.991	.941	.783	.485	.314	.164	.013	.001	.000
11	1.000	1.000	1.000	1.000	1.000	1.000	.998	.982	.909	.703	.539	.352	.056	.005	.000
12	1.000	1.000	1.000	1.000	1.000	1.000	1.000	.996	.973	.873	.764	.602	.184	.036	.000
13	1.000	1.000	1.000	1.000	1.000	1.000	1.000	1.000	.995	.965	.920	.833	.451	.171	.010
14	1.000	1.000	1.000	1.000	1.000	1.000	1.000	1.000	1.000	.995	.987	.965	.794	.537	.140

TABLE 1   BINOMIAL PROBABILITIES *(continued)*

n = 20

k	.01	.05	.10	.20	.25	.30	.40	.50	.60	.70	.75	.80	.90	.95	.99
0	.818	.358	.122	.012	.003	.001	.000	.000	.000	.000	.000	.000	.000	.000	.000
1	.983	.736	.392	.069	.024	.008	.001	.000	.000	.000	.000	.000	.000	.000	.000
2	.999	.925	.677	.206	.091	.035	.004	.000	.000	.000	.000	.000	.000	.000	.000
3	1.000	.984	.867	.411	.225	.107	.016	.001	.000	.000	.000	.000	.000	.000	.000
4	1.000	.997	.957	.630	.415	.238	.051	.006	.000	.000	.000	.000	.000	.000	.000
5	1.000	1.000	.989	.804	.617	.416	.126	.021	.002	.000	.000	.000	.000	.000	.000
6	1.000	1.000	.998	.913	.786	.608	.250	.058	.006	.000	.000	.000	.000	.000	.000
7	1.000	1.000	1.000	.968	.898	.772	.416	.132	.021	.001	.000	.000	.000	.000	.000
8	1.000	1.000	1.000	.990	.959	.887	.596	.252	.057	.005	.001	.000	.000	.000	.000
9	1.000	1.000	1.000	.997	.986	.952	.755	.412	.128	.017	.004	.001	.000	.000	.000
10	1.000	1.000	1.000	.999	.996	.983	.872	.588	.245	.048	.014	.003	.000	.000	.000
11	1.000	1.000	1.000	1.000	.999	.995	.943	.748	.404	.113	.041	.010	.000	.000	.000
12	1.000	1.000	1.000	1.000	1.000	.999	.979	.868	.584	.228	.102	.032	.000	.000	.000
13	1.000	1.000	1.000	1.000	1.000	1.000	.994	.942	.750	.392	.214	.087	.002	.000	.000
14	1.000	1.000	1.000	1.000	1.000	1.000	.998	.979	.874	.584	.383	.196	.011	.000	.000
15	1.000	1.000	1.000	1.000	1.000	1.000	1.000	.994	.949	.762	.585	.370	.043	.003	.000
16	1.000	1.000	1.000	1.000	1.000	1.000	1.000	.999	.984	.893	.775	.589	.133	.016	.000
17	1.000	1.000	1.000	1.000	1.000	1.000	1.000	1.000	.996	.965	.909	.794	.323	.075	.001
18	1.000	1.000	1.000	1.000	1.000	1.000	1.000	1.000	.999	.992	.976	.931	.608	.264	.017
19	1.000	1.000	1.000	1.000	1.000	1.000	1.000	1.000	1.000	.999	.997	.988	.878	.642	.182

$n = 25$

								p							
k	.01	.05	.10	.20	.25	.30	.40	.50	.60	.70	.75	.80	.90	.95	.99
0	.778	.277	.072	.004	.001	.000	.000	.000	.000	.000	.000	.000	.000	.000	.000
1	.974	.642	.271	.027	.007	.002	.000	.000	.000	.000	.000	.000	.000	.000	.000
2	.998	.873	.537	.098	.032	.009	.000	.000	.000	.000	.000	.000	.000	.000	.000
3	1.000	.966	.764	.234	.096	.033	.002	.000	.000	.000	.000	.000	.000	.000	.000
4	1.000	.993	.902	.421	.214	.090	.009	.002	.000	.000	.000	.000	.000	.000	.000
5	1.000	.999	.967	.617	.378	.193	.029	.007	.000	.000	.000	.000	.000	.000	.000
6	1.000	1.000	.991	.780	.561	.341	.074	.022	.001	.000	.000	.000	.000	.000	.000
7	1.000	1.000	.998	.891	.727	.512	.154	.054	.004	.000	.000	.000	.000	.000	.000
8	1.000	1.000	1.000	.953	.851	.677	.274	.115	.013	.000	.000	.000	.000	.000	.000
9	1.000	1.000	1.000	.983	.929	.811	.425	.212	.034	.002	.000	.000	.000	.000	.000
10	1.000	1.000	1.000	.994	.970	.902	.586	.345	.078	.006	.000	.000	.000	.000	.000
11	1.000	1.000	1.000	.998	.989	.956	.732	.500	.154	.017	.001	.000	.000	.000	.000
12	1.000	1.000	1.000	1.000	.997	.983	.846	.655	.268	.044	.003	.000	.000	.000	.000
13	1.000	1.000	1.000	1.000	.999	.994	.922	.788	.414	.098	.011	.002	.000	.000	.000
14	1.000	1.000	1.000	1.000	1.000	.998	.966	.885	.575	.189	.030	.006	.000	.000	.000
15	1.000	1.000	1.000	1.000	1.000	1.000	.987	.946	.726	.323	.071	.017	.000	.000	.000
16	1.000	1.000	1.000	1.000	1.000	1.000	.996	.978	.846	.488	.149	.047	.000	.000	.000
17	1.000	1.000	1.000	1.000	1.000	1.000	.999	.993	.926	.659	.273	.109	.002	.000	.000
18	1.000	1.000	1.000	1.000	1.000	1.000	1.000	.998	.971	.807	.439	.220	.009	.000	.000
19	1.000	1.000	1.000	1.000	1.000	1.000	1.000	1.000	.991	.910	.622	.383	.033	.001	.000
20	1.000	1.000	1.000	1.000	1.000	1.000	1.000	1.000	.998	.967	.786	.579	.098	.007	.000
21	1.000	1.000	1.000	1.000	1.000	1.000	1.000	1.000	1.000	.991	.904	.766	.236	.034	.000
22	1.000	1.000	1.000	1.000	1.000	1.000	1.000	1.000	1.000	.998	.968	.902	.463	.127	.002
23	1.000	1.000	1.000	1.000	1.000	1.000	1.000	1.000	1.000	.999	.993	.973	.729	.358	.026
24	1.000	1.000	1.000	1.000	1.000	1.000	1.000	1.000	1.000	1.000	.999	.996	.928	.723	.222

TABLE 2 POISSON PROBABILITIES

Tabulated values are $P(x \le k) = \sum_{x=0}^{k} p(x)$. (Values are rounded to three decimal places.)

μ

k	.10	.20	.30	.40	.50	1.0	1.5	2.0	2.5	3.0	3.5	4.0	4.5	5.0	5.5	6.0
0	.905	.819	.741	.670	.607	.368	.223	.135	.082	.050	.030	.018	.011	.007	.004	.002
1	.995	.982	.963	.938	.910	.736	.558	.406	.287	.199	.136	.092	.061	.040	.027	.017
2	1.000	.999	.996	.992	.986	.920	.809	.677	.544	.423	.321	.238	.174	.125	.088	.062
3		1.000	1.000	.999	.998	.981	.934	.857	.758	.647	.537	.433	.342	.265	.202	.151
4				1.000	1.000	.996	.981	.947	.891	.815	.725	.629	.532	.440	.358	.285
5						.999	.996	.983	.958	.916	.858	.785	.703	.616	.529	.446
6						1.000	.999	.995	.986	.966	.935	.889	.831	.762	.686	.606
7							1.000	.999	.996	.988	.973	.949	.913	.867	.809	.744
8								1.000	.999	.996	.990	.979	.960	.932	.894	.847
9									1.000	.999	.997	.992	.983	.968	.946	.916
10										1.000	.999	.997	.993	.986	.975	.957
11											1.000	.999	.998	.995	.989	.980
12												1.000	.999	.998	.996	.991
13													1.000	.999	.998	.996
14														1.000	.999	.999
15															1.000	.999
16																1.000
17																
18																
19																
20																

$\mu = \lambda = 5$

$P(x=4 \text{ or } x=5)$

$P(x \le 4) - P(x \le 3) = .105$

$P(x \le 5) - P(x \le 4) = .196$

$.195 + .196 = .351 \ (35.1\%)$

$M = \dfrac{d+c}{2} = .5$

$6 = \dfrac{d-e}{\sqrt{12}} = .0115$

$.95 = 1.96$

k								μ					
	6.5	7.0	7.5	8.0	8.5	9.0	9.5	10	11	12	13	14	15
0	.002	.001	.001	.000	.000	.000	.000	.000	.000	.000	.000	.000	.000
1	.011	.007	.005	.003	.002	.001	.001	.000	.000	.000	.000	.000	.000
2	.043	.030	.020	.014	.009	.006	.004	.003	.001	.001	.000	.000	.000
3	.112	.082	.059	.042	.030	.021	.015	.010	.005	.002	.001	.000	.000
4	.224	.173	.132	.100	.074	.055	.040	.029	.015	.008	.004	.002	.001
5	.369	.301	.241	.191	.150	.116	.089	.067	.038	.020	.011	.006	.003
6	.527	.450	.378	.313	.256	.207	.165	.130	.079	.046	.026	.014	.008
7	.673	.599	.525	.453	.386	.324	.269	.220	.143	.090	.054	.032	.018
8	.792	.729	.662	.593	.523	.456	.392	.333	.232	.155	.100	.062	.037
9	.877	.830	.776	.717	.653	.587	.522	.458	.341	.242	.166	.109	.070
10	.933	.901	.862	.816	.763	.706	.645	.583	.460	.347	.252	.176	.118
11	.966	.947	.921	.888	.849	.803	.752	.697	.579	.462	.353	.260	.185
12	.984	.973	.957	.936	.909	.876	.836	.792	.689	.576	.463	.358	.268
13	.993	.987	.978	.966	.949	.926	.898	.864	.781	.682	.573	.464	.363
14	.997	.994	.990	.983	.973	.959	.940	.917	.854	.772	.675	.570	.466
15	.999	.998	.995	.992	.986	.978	.967	.951	.907	.844	.764	.669	.568
16	1.000	.999	.998	.996	.993	.989	.982	.973	.944	.899	.835	.756	.664
17		1.000	.999	.998	.997	.995	.991	.986	.968	.937	.890	.827	.749
18			1.000	.999	.999	.998	.996	.993	.982	.963	.930	.883	.819
19				1.000	.999	.999	.998	.997	.991	.979	.957	.923	.875
20					1.000	1.000	.999	.998	.995	.988	.975	.952	.917
21							1.000	.999	.998	.994	.986	.971	.947
22								1.000	.999	.997	.992	.983	.967
23									1.000	.999	.996	.991	.981
24										.999	.998	.995	.989
25										1.000	.999	.997	.994
26											1.000	.999	.997
27												.999	.998
28												1.000	.999
29													1.000

TABLE 3 NORMAL CURVE AREAS

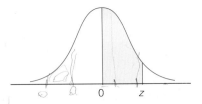

z	.00	.01	.02	.03	.04	.05	.06	.07	.08	.09
0.0	.0000	.0040	.0080	.0120	.0160	.0199	.0239	.0279	.0319	.0359
0.1	.0398	.0438	.0478	.0517	.0557	.0596	.0636	.0675	.0714	.0753
0.2	.0793	.0832	.0871	.0910	.0948	.0987	.1026	.1064	.1103	.1141
0.3	.1179	.1217	.1255	.1293	.1331	.1368	.1406	.1443	.1480	.1517
0.4	.1554	.1591	.1628	.1664	.1700	.1736	.1772	.1808	.1844	.1879
0.5	.1915	.1950	.1985	.2019	.2054	.2088	.2123	.2157	.2190	.2224
0.6	.2257	.2291	.2324	.2357	.2389	.2422	.2454	.2486	.2517	.2549
0.7	.2580	.2611	.2642	.2673	.2704	.2734	.2764	.2794	.2823	.2852
0.8	.2881	.2910	.2939	.2967	.2995	.3023	.3051	.3078	.3106	.3133
0.9	.3159	.3186	.3212	.3238	.3264	.3289	.3315	.3340	.3365	.3389
1.0	.3413	.3438	.3461	.3485	.3508	.3531	.3554	.3577	.3599	.3621
1.1	.3643	.3665	.3686	.3708	.3729	.3749	.3770	.3790	.3810	.3830
1.2	.3849	.3869	.3888	.3907	.3925	.3944	.3962	.3980	.3997	.4015
1.3	.4032	.4049	.4066	.4082	.4099	.4115	.4131	.4147	.4162	.4177
1.4	.4192	.4207	.4222	.4236	.4251	.4265	.4279	.4292	.4306	.4319
1.5	.4332	.4345	.4357	.4370	.4382	.4394	.4406	.4418	.4429	.4441
1.6	.4452	.4463	.4474	.4484	.4495	.4505	.4515	.4525	.4535	.4545
1.7	.4554	.4564	.4573	.4582	.4591	.4599	.4608	.4616	.4625	.4633
1.8	.4641	.4649	.4656	.4664	.4671	.4678	.4686	.4693	.4699	.4706
1.9	.4713	.4719	.4726	.4732	.4738	.4744	.4750	.4756	.4761	.4767
2.0	.4772	.4778	.4783	.4788	.4793	.4798	.4803	.4808	.4812	.4817
2.1	.4821	.4826	.4830	.4834	.4838	.4842	.4846	.4850	.4854	.4857
2.2	.4861	.4864	.4868	.4871	.4875	.4878	.4881	.4884	.4887	.4890
2.3	.4893	.4896	.4898	.4901	.4904	.4906	.4909	.4911	.4913	.4916
2.4	.4918	.4920	.4922	.4925	.4927	.4929	.4931	.4932	.4934	.4936
2.5	.4938	.4940	.4941	.4943	.4945	.4946	.4948	.4949	.4951	.4952
2.6	.4953	.4955	.4956	.4957	.4959	.4960	.4961	.4962	.4963	.4964
2.7	.4965	.4966	.4967	.4968	.4969	.4970	.4971	.4972	.4973	.4974
2.8	.4974	.4975	.4976	.4977	.4977	.4978	.4979	.4979	.4980	.4981
2.9	.4981	.4982	.4982	.4983	.4984	.4984	.4985	.4985	.4986	.4986
3.0	.4987	.4987	.4987	.4988	.4988	.4989	.4989	.4989	.4990	.4990

SOURCE: Abridged from Table I of A. Hald, *Statistical Tables and Formulas* (New York: John Wiley & Sons, Inc.), 1952. Reproduced by permission of A. Hald and the publisher, John Wiley & Sons, Inc.

Handwritten notes:

$\mu = 85,000$ Sample $\mu = \bar{x} = 85,000$
$6 = 8,000$ $Sd = \dfrac{8000}{\sqrt{40}} = 1264.9$
$n = 40$

$P(\bar{x} > 86,000) = 0.79 \ (21.48\%)$
$P(82,000 < \bar{x} < 86,000) \quad (77.63\%)$

$u = 11.5$ $\alpha = .05 \ (1.96)$
$n = 81$ $z = 1.49$
$\bar{x} = 11.54$ (Accept?)
$s = .25$
$\alpha = .05$
$H_0 \ u = 11.5$
$H_A \ u \neq 11.5$

$n = 50 \quad n_2 = 50$
$x = 25.4 \quad \bar{x}_2 = 27.3$
$S_1 = 3.1 \quad s_2 = 3.7$
a) $H_0: \bar{x}_1 - \bar{x}_2 \geq 0 \quad z = -1.64$
$H_A: \bar{x}_1 - \bar{x}_2 < 0 \quad z = z.78$
Reject. Yes it is less
b) $P(z \leq -2.78) = .0026$

TABLE 4   *CRITICAL VALUES OF t*

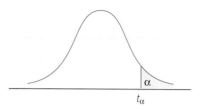

Degrees of Freedom	$t_{.100}$	$t_{.050}$	$t_{.025}$	$t_{.010}$	$t_{.005}$
1	3.078	6.314	12.706	31.821	63.657
2	1.886	2.920	4.303	6.965	9.925
3	1.638	2.353	3.182	4.541	5.841
4	1.533	2.132	2.776	3.747	4.604
5	1.476	2.015	2.571	3.365	4.032
6	1.440	1.943	2.447	3.143	3.707
7	1.415	1.895	2.365	2.998	3.499
8	1.397	1.860	2.306	2.896	3.355
9	1.383	1.833	2.262	2.821	3.250
10	1.372	1.812	2.228	2.764	3.169
11	1.363	1.796	2.201	2.718	3.106
12	1.356	1.782	2.179	2.681	3.055
13	1.350	1.771	2.160	2.650	3.012
14	1.345	1.761	2.145	2.624	2.977
15	1.341	1.753	2.131	2.602	2.947
16	1.337	1.746	2.120	2.583	2.921
17	1.333	1.740	2.110	2.567	2.898
18	1.330	1.734	2.101	2.552	2.878
19	1.328	1.729	2.093	2.539	2.861
20	1.325	1.725	2.086	2.528	2.845
21	1.323	1.721	2.080	2.518	2.831
22	1.321	1.717	2.074	2.508	2.819
23	1.319	1.714	2.069	2.500	2.807
24	1.318	1.711	2.064	2.492	2.797
25	1.316	1.708	2.060	2.485	2.787
26	1.315	1.706	2.056	2.479	2.779
27	1.314	1.703	2.052	2.473	2.771
28	1.313	1.701	2.048	2.467	2.763
29	1.311	1.699	2.045	2.462	2.756
∞	1.282	1.645	1.960	2.326	2.576

SOURCE: From M. Merrington, "Table of Percentage Points of the *t*-Distribution," *Biometrika* 32 (1941): 300. Reproduced by permission of the Biometrika Trustees.

$\mu = 250$ $t_{0.005, 19} (2.861)$
$n = 20$ $t = -2.72$
$\bar{X} = 236$ (Accept H_0)
$S = 23$ C: 99% CI
$H_0: \mu = 250$ $221.79446 \sim 250.10554$
$H_A: \mu \ne 250$

TABLE 5 CRITICAL VALUES OF χ^2

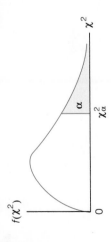

$f(\chi^2)$

χ^2_α

χ^2

Degrees of Freedom	$\chi^2_{.995}$	$\chi^2_{.990}$	$\chi^2_{.975}$	$\chi^2_{.950}$	$\chi^2_{.900}$	$\chi^2_{.100}$	$\chi^2_{.050}$	$\chi^2_{.025}$	$\chi^2_{.010}$	$\chi^2_{.005}$
1	0.0000393	0.0001571	0.0009821	0.0039321	0.0157908	2.70554	3.84146	5.02389	6.63490	7.87944
2	0.0100251	0.0201007	0.0506356	0.102587	0.210720	4.60517	5.99147	7.37776	9.21034	10.5966
3	0.0717212	0.114832	0.215795	0.351846	0.584375	6.25139	7.81473	9.34840	11.3449	12.8381
4	0.206990	0.297110	0.484419	0.710721	1.063623	7.77944	9.48773	11.1433	13.2767	14.8602
5	0.411740	0.554300	0.831211	1.145476	1.61031	9.23635	11.0705	12.8325	15.0863	16.7496
6	0.675727	0.872085	1.237347	1.63539	2.20413	10.6446	12.5916	14.4494	16.8119	18.5476
7	0.989265	1.239043	1.68987	2.16735	2.83311	12.0170	14.0671	16.0128	18.4753	20.2777
8	1.344419	1.646482	2.17973	2.73264	3.48954	13.3616	15.5073	17.5346	20.0902	21.9550
9	1.734926	2.087912	2.70039	3.32511	4.16816	14.6837	16.9190	19.0228	21.6660	23.5893
10	2.15585	2.55821	3.24697	3.94030	4.86518	15.9871	18.3070	20.4831	23.2093	25.1882
11	2.60321	3.05347	3.81575	4.57481	5.57779	17.2750	19.6751	21.9200	24.7250	26.7569
12	3.07382	3.57056	4.40379	5.22603	6.30380	18.5494	21.0261	23.3367	26.2170	28.2995
13	3.56503	4.10691	5.00874	5.89186	7.04150	19.8119	22.3621	24.7356	27.6883	29.8194
14	4.07468	4.66043	5.62872	6.57063	7.78953	21.0642	23.6848	26.1190	29.1413	31.3193
15	4.60094	5.22935	6.26214	7.26094	8.54675	22.3072	24.9958	27.4884	30.5779	32.8013
16	5.14224	5.81221	6.90766	7.96164	9.31223	23.5418	26.2962	28.8454	31.9999	34.2672
17	5.69724	6.40776	7.56418	8.67176	10.0852	24.7690	27.5871	30.1910	33.4087	35.7185
18	6.26481	7.01491	8.23075	9.39046	10.8649	25.9894	28.8693	31.5264	34.8053	37.1564
19	6.84398	7.63273	8.90655	10.1170	11.6509	27.2036	30.1435	32.8523	36.1908	38.5822
20	7.43386	8.26040	9.59083	10.8508	12.4426	28.4120	31.4104	34.1696	37.5662	39.9968
21	8.03366	8.89720	10.28293	11.5913	13.2396	29.6151	32.6705	35.4789	38.9321	41.4010
22	8.64272	9.54249	10.9823	12.3380	14.0415	30.8133	33.9244	36.7807	40.2894	42.7956
23	9.26042	10.19567	11.6885	13.0905	14.8479	32.0069	35.1725	38.0757	41.6384	44.1813
24	9.88623	10.8564	12.4011	13.8484	15.6587	33.1963	36.4151	39.3641	42.9798	45.5585
25	10.5197	11.5240	13.1197	14.6114	16.4734	34.3816	37.6525	40.6465	44.3141	46.9278

26	11.1603	12.1981	13.8439	15.3791	17.2919	35.5631	38.8852	41.9232	45.6417	48.2899
27	11.8076	12.8786	14.5733	16.1513	18.1138	36.7412	40.1133	43.1944	46.9630	49.6449
28	12.4613	13.5648	15.3079	16.9279	18.9392	37.9159	41.3372	44.4607	48.2782	50.9933
29	13.1211	14.2565	16.0471	17.7083	19.7677	39.0875	42.5569	45.7222	49.5879	52.3356
30	13.7867	14.9535	16.7908	18.4926	20.5992	40.2560	43.7729	46.9792	50.8922	53.6720
40	20.7065	22.1643	24.4331	26.5093	29.0505	51.8050	55.7585	59.3417	63.6907	66.7659
50	27.9907	29.7067	32.3574	34.7642	37.6886	63.1671	67.5048	71.4202	76.1539	79.4900
60	35.5346	37.4848	40.4817	43.1879	46.4589	74.3970	79.0819	83.2976	88.3794	91.9517
70	43.2752	45.4418	48.7576	51.7393	55.3290	85.5271	90.5312	95.0231	100.425	104.215
80	51.1720	53.5400	57.1532	60.3915	64.2778	96.5782	101.879	106.629	112.329	116.321
90	59.1963	61.7541	65.6466	69.1260	73.2912	107.565	113.145	118.136	124.116	128.299
100	67.3276	70.0648	74.2219	77.9295	82.3581	118.498	124.342	129.561	135.807	140.169

SOURCE: From C. M. Thompson, "Tables of the Percentage Points of the χ^2-Distribution," *Biometrika* 32 (1941): 188–89. Reproduced by permission of the Biometrika Trustees.

TABLE 6(a)   PERCENTAGE POINTS OF THE F DISTRIBUTION, $\alpha = .10$

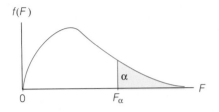

v_2	Numerator Degrees of Freedom								
	1	**2**	**3**	**4**	**5**	**6**	**7**	**8**	**9**
1	39.86	49.50	53.59	55.83	57.24	58.20	58.91	59.44	59.86
2	8.53	9.00	9.16	9.24	9.29	9.33	9.35	9.37	9.38
3	5.54	5.46	5.39	5.34	5.31	5.28	5.27	5.25	5.24
4	4.54	4.32	4.19	4.11	4.05	4.01	3.98	3.95	3.94
5	4.06	3.78	3.62	3.52	3.45	3.40	3.37	3.34	3.32
6	3.78	3.46	3.29	3.18	3.11	3.05	3.01	2.98	2.96
7	3.59	3.26	3.07	2.96	2.88	2.83	2.78	2.75	2.72
8	3.46	3.11	2.92	2.81	2.73	2.67	2.62	2.59	2.56
9	3.36	3.01	2.81	2.69	2.61	2.55	2.51	2.47	2.44
10	3.29	2.92	2.73	2.61	2.52	2.46	2.41	2.38	2.35
11	3.23	2.86	2.66	2.54	2.45	2.39	2.34	2.30	2.27
12	3.18	2.81	2.61	2.48	2.39	2.33	2.28	2.24	2.21
13	3.14	2.76	2.56	2.43	2.35	2.28	2.23	2.20	2.16
14	3.10	2.73	2.52	2.39	2.31	2.24	2.19	2.15	2.12
15	3.07	2.70	2.49	2.36	2.27	2.21	2.16	2.12	2.09
16	3.05	2.67	2.46	2.33	2.24	2.18	2.13	2.09	2.06
17	3.03	2.64	2.44	2.31	2.22	2.15	2.10	2.06	2.03
18	3.01	2.62	2.42	2.29	2.20	2.13	2.08	2.04	2.00
19	2.99	2.61	2.40	2.27	2.18	2.11	2.06	2.02	1.98
20	2.97	2.59	2.38	2.25	2.16	2.09	2.04	2.00	1.96
21	2.96	2.57	2.36	2.23	2.14	2.08	2.02	1.98	1.95
22	2.95	2.56	2.35	2.22	2.13	2.06	2.01	1.97	1.93
23	2.94	2.55	2.34	2.21	2.11	2.05	1.99	1.95	1.92
24	2.93	2.54	2.33	2.19	2.10	2.04	1.98	1.94	1.91
25	2.92	2.53	2.32	2.18	2.09	2.02	1.97	1.93	1.89
26	2.91	2.52	2.31	2.17	2.08	2.01	1.96	1.92	1.88
27	2.90	2.51	2.30	2.17	2.07	2.00	1.95	1.91	1.87
28	2.89	2.50	2.29	2.16	2.06	2.00	1.94	1.90	1.87
29	2.89	2.50	2.28	2.15	2.06	1.99	1.93	1.89	1.86
30	2.88	2.49	2.28	2.14	2.05	1.98	1.93	1.88	1.85
40	2.84	2.44	2.23	2.09	2.00	1.93	1.87	1.83	1.79
60	2.79	2.39	2.18	2.04	1.95	1.87	1.82	1.77	1.74
120	2.75	2.35	2.13	1.99	1.90	1.82	1.77	1.72	1.68
∞	2.71	2.30	2.08	1.94	1.85	1.77	1.72	1.67	1.63

v_1

Denominator Degrees of Freedom

SOURCE: From M. Merrington and C. M. Thompson, "Tables of Percentage Points of the Inverted Beta (F)-Distribution," *Biometrika* 33 (1943): 73–88. Reproduced by permission of the *Biometrika* Trustees.

TABLE 6(a)   (continued)

v_2 \ v_1	Numerator Degrees of Freedom									
	10	**12**	**15**	**20**	**24**	**30**	**40**	**60**	**120**	**∞**
1	60.19	60.71	61.22	61.74	62.00	62.26	62.53	62.79	63.06	63.33
2	9.39	9.41	9.42	9.44	9.45	9.46	9.47	9.47	9.48	9.49
3	5.23	5.22	5.20	5.18	5.18	5.17	5.16	5.15	5.14	5.13
4	3.92	3.90	3.87	3.84	3.83	3.82	3.80	3.79	3.78	3.76
5	3.30	3.27	3.24	3.21	3.19	3.17	3.16	3.14	3.12	3.10
6	2.94	2.90	2.87	2.84	2.82	2.80	2.78	2.76	2.74	2.72
7	2.70	2.67	2.63	2.59	2.58	2.56	2.54	2.51	2.49	2.47
8	2.54	2.50	2.46	2.42	2.40	2.38	2.36	2.34	2.32	2.29
9	2.42	2.38	2.34	2.30	2.28	2.25	2.23	2.21	2.18	2.16
10	2.32	2.28	2.24	2.20	2.18	2.16	2.13	2.11	2.08	2.06
11	2.25	2.21	2.17	2.12	2.10	2.08	2.05	2.03	2.00	1.97
12	2.19	2.15	2.10	2.06	2.04	2.01	1.99	1.96	1.93	1.90
13	2.14	2.10	2.05	2.01	1.98	1.96	1.93	1.90	1.88	1.85
14	2.10	2.05	2.01	1.96	1.94	1.91	1.89	1.86	1.83	1.80
15	2.06	2.02	1.97	1.92	1.90	1.87	1.85	1.82	1.79	1.76
16	2.03	1.99	1.94	1.89	1.87	1.84	1.81	1.78	1.75	1.72
17	2.00	1.96	1.91	1.86	1.84	1.81	1.78	1.75	1.72	1.69
18	1.98	1.93	1.89	1.84	1.81	1.78	1.75	1.72	1.69	1.66
19	1.96	1.91	1.86	1.81	1.79	1.76	1.73	1.70	1.67	1.63
20	1.94	1.89	1.84	1.79	1.77	1.74	1.71	1.68	1.64	1.61
21	1.92	1.87	1.83	1.78	1.75	1.72	1.69	1.66	1.62	1.59
22	1.90	1.86	1.81	1.76	1.73	1.70	1.67	1.64	1.60	1.57
23	1.89	1.84	1.80	1.74	1.72	1.69	1.66	1.62	1.59	1.55
24	1.88	1.83	1.78	1.73	1.70	1.67	1.64	1.61	1.57	1.53
25	1.87	1.82	1.77	1.72	1.69	1.66	1.63	1.59	1.56	1.52
26	1.86	1.81	1.76	1.71	1.68	1.65	1.61	1.58	1.54	1.50
27	1.85	1.80	1.75	1.70	1.67	1.64	1.60	1.57	1.53	1.49
28	1.84	1.79	1.74	1.69	1.66	1.63	1.59	1.56	1.52	1.48
29	1.83	1.78	1.73	1.68	1.65	1.62	1.58	1.55	1.51	1.47
30	1.82	1.77	1.72	1.67	1.64	1.61	1.57	1.54	1.50	1.46
40	1.76	1.71	1.66	1.61	1.57	1.54	1.51	1.47	1.42	1.38
60	1.71	1.66	1.60	1.54	1.51	1.48	1.44	1.40	1.35	1.29
120	1.65	1.60	1.55	1.48	1.45	1.41	1.37	1.32	1.26	1.19
∞	1.60	1.55	1.49	1.42	1.38	1.34	1.30	1.24	1.17	1.00

Denominator Degrees of Freedom

TABLE 6(b) PERCENTAGE POINTS OF THE F DISTRIBUTION, $\alpha = .05$

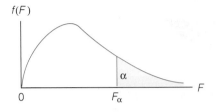

v_1	Numerator Degrees of Freedom								
v_2	1	2	3	4	5	6	7	8	9
1	161.4	199.5	215.7	224.6	230.2	234.0	236.8	238.9	240.5
2	18.51	19.00	19.16	19.25	19.30	19.33	19.35	19.37	19.38
3	10.13	9.55	9.28	9.12	9.01	8.94	8.89	8.85	8.81
4	7.71	6.94	6.59	6.39	6.26	6.16	6.09	6.04	6.00
5	6.61	5.79	5.41	5.19	5.05	4.95	4.88	4.82	4.77
6	5.99	5.14	4.76	4.53	4.39	4.28	4.21	4.15	4.10
7	5.59	4.74	4.35	4.12	3.97	3.87	3.79	3.73	3.68
8	5.32	4.46	4.07	3.84	3.69	3.58	3.50	3.44	3.39
9	5.12	4.26	3.86	3.63	3.48	3.37	3.29	3.23	3.18
10	4.96	4.10	3.71	3.48	3.33	3.22	3.14	3.07	3.02
11	4.84	3.98	3.59	3.36	3.20	3.09	3.01	2.95	2.90
12	4.75	3.89	3.49	3.26	3.11	3.00	2.91	2.85	2.80
13	4.67	3.81	3.41	3.18	3.03	2.92	2.83	2.77	2.71
14	4.60	3.74	3.34	3.11	2.96	2.85	2.76	2.70	2.65
15	4.54	3.68	3.29	3.06	2.90	2.79	2.71	2.64	2.59
16	4.49	3.63	3.24	3.01	2.85	2.74	2.66	2.59	2.54
17	4.45	3.59	3.20	2.96	2.81	2.70	2.61	2.55	2.49
18	4.41	3.55	3.16	2.93	2.77	2.66	2.58	2.51	2.46
19	4.38	3.52	3.13	2.90	2.74	2.63	2.54	2.48	2.42
20	4.35	3.49	3.10	2.87	2.71	2.60	2.51	2.45	2.39
21	4.32	3.47	3.07	2.84	2.68	2.57	2.49	2.42	2.37
22	4.30	3.44	3.05	2.82	2.66	2.55	2.46	2.40	2.34
23	4.28	3.42	3.03	2.80	2.64	2.53	2.44	2.37	2.32
24	4.26	3.40	3.01	2.78	2.62	2.51	2.42	2.36	2.30
25	4.24	3.39	2.99	2.76	2.60	2.49	2.40	2.34	2.28
26	4.23	3.37	2.98	2.74	2.59	2.47	2.39	2.32	2.27
27	4.21	3.35	2.96	2.73	2.57	2.46	2.37	2.31	2.25
28	4.20	3.34	2.95	2.71	2.56	2.45	2.36	2.29	2.24
29	4.18	3.33	2.93	2.70	2.55	2.43	2.35	2.28	2.22
30	4.17	3.32	2.92	2.69	2.53	2.42	2.33	2.27	2.21
40	4.08	3.23	2.84	2.61	2.45	2.34	2.25	2.18	2.12
60	4.00	3.15	2.76	2.53	2.37	2.25	2.17	2.10	2.04
120	3.92	3.07	2.68	2.45	2.29	2.17	2.09	2.02	1.96
∞	3.84	3.00	2.60	2.37	2.21	2.10	2.01	1.94	1.88

Denominator Degrees of Freedom

SOURCE: From M. Merrington and C. M. Thompson, "Tables of Percentage Points of the Inverted Beta (F)-Distribution," *Biometrika* 33 (1943): 73–88. Reproduced by permission of the Biometrika Trustees.

TABLE 6(b) *(continued)*

v_2 \ v_1	Numerator Degrees of Freedom									
	10	12	15	20	24	30	40	60	120	∞
1	241.9	243.9	245.9	248.0	249.1	250.1	251.1	252.2	253.3	254.3
2	19.40	19.41	19.43	19.45	19.45	19.46	19.47	19.48	19.49	19.50
3	8.79	8.74	8.70	8.66	8.64	8.62	8.59	8.57	8.55	8.53
4	5.96	5.91	5.86	5.80	5.77	5.75	5.72	5.69	5.66	5.63
5	4.74	4.68	4.62	4.56	4.53	4.50	4.46	4.43	4.40	4.36
6	4.06	4.00	3.94	3.87	3.84	3.81	3.77	3.74	3.70	3.67
7	3.64	3.57	3.51	3.44	3.41	3.38	3.34	3.30	3.27	3.23
8	3.35	3.28	3.22	3.15	3.12	3.08	3.04	3.01	2.97	2.93
9	3.14	3.07	3.01	2.94	2.90	2.86	2.83	2.79	2.75	2.71
10	2.98	2.91	2.85	2.77	2.74	2.70	2.66	2.62	2.58	2.54
11	2.85	2.79	2.72	2.65	2.61	2.57	2.53	2.49	2.45	2.40
12	2.75	2.69	2.62	2.54	2.51	2.47	2.43	2.38	2.34	2.30
13	2.67	2.60	2.53	2.46	2.42	2.38	2.34	2.30	2.25	2.21
14	2.60	2.53	2.46	2.39	2.35	2.31	2.27	2.22	2.18	2.13
15	2.54	2.48	2.40	2.33	2.29	2.25	2.20	2.16	2.11	2.07
16	2.49	2.42	2.35	2.28	2.24	2.19	2.15	2.11	2.06	2.01
17	2.45	2.38	2.31	2.23	2.19	2.15	2.10	2.06	2.01	1.96
18	2.41	2.34	2.27	2.19	2.15	2.11	2.06	2.02	1.97	1.92
19	2.38	2.31	2.23	2.16	2.11	2.07	2.03	1.98	1.93	1.88
20	2.35	2.28	2.20	2.12	2.08	2.04	1.99	1.95	1.90	1.84
21	2.32	2.25	2.18	2.10	2.05	2.01	1.96	1.92	1.87	1.81
22	2.30	2.23	2.15	2.07	2.03	1.98	1.94	1.89	1.84	1.78
23	2.27	2.20	2.13	2.05	2.01	1.96	1.91	1.86	1.81	1.76
24	2.25	2.18	2.11	2.03	1.98	1.94	1.89	1.84	1.79	1.73
25	2.24	2.16	2.09	2.01	1.96	1.92	1.87	1.82	1.77	1.71
26	2.22	2.15	2.07	1.99	1.95	1.90	1.85	1.80	1.75	1.69
27	2.20	2.13	2.06	1.97	1.93	1.88	1.84	1.79	1.73	1.67
28	2.19	2.12	2.04	1.96	1.91	1.87	1.82	1.77	1.71	1.65
29	2.18	2.10	2.03	1.94	1.90	1.85	1.81	1.75	1.70	1.64
30	2.16	2.09	2.01	1.93	1.89	1.84	1.79	1.74	1.68	1.62
40	2.08	2.00	1.92	1.84	1.79	1.74	1.69	1.64	1.58	1.51
60	1.99	1.92	1.84	1.75	1.70	1.65	1.59	1.53	1.47	1.39
120	1.91	1.83	1.75	1.66	1.61	1.55	1.50	1.43	1.35	1.25
∞	1.83	1.75	1.67	1.57	1.52	1.46	1.39	1.32	1.22	1.00

Denominator Degrees of Freedom

TABLE 6(c) *PERCENTAGE POINTS OF THE F DISTRIBUTION,* $\alpha = .025$

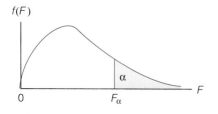

v_2 \ v_1	Numerator Degrees of Freedom								
	1	2	3	4	5	6	7	8	9
1	647.8	799.5	864.2	899.6	921.8	937.1	948.2	956.7	963.3
2	38.51	39.00	39.17	39.25	39.30	39.33	39.36	39.37	39.39
3	17.44	16.04	15.44	15.10	14.88	14.73	14.62	14.54	14.47
4	12.22	10.65	9.98	9.60	9.36	9.20	9.07	8.98	8.90
5	10.01	8.43	7.76	7.39	7.15	6.98	6.85	6.76	6.68
6	8.81	7.26	6.60	6.23	5.99	5.82	5.70	5.60	5.52
7	8.07	6.54	5.89	5.52	5.29	5.12	4.99	4.90	4.82
8	7.57	6.06	5.42	5.05	4.82	4.65	4.53	4.43	4.36
9	7.21	5.71	5.08	4.72	4.48	4.32	4.20	4.10	4.03
10	6.94	5.46	4.83	4.47	4.24	4.07	3.95	3.85	3.78
11	6.72	5.26	4.63	4.28	4.04	3.88	3.76	3.66	3.59
12	6.55	5.10	4.47	4.12	3.89	3.73	3.61	3.51	3.44
13	6.41	4.97	4.35	4.00	3.77	3.60	3.48	3.39	3.31
14	6.30	4.86	4.24	3.89	3.66	3.50	3.38	3.29	3.21
15	6.20	4.77	4.15	3.80	3.58	3.41	3.29	3.20	3.12
16	6.12	4.69	4.08	3.73	3.50	3.34	3.22	3.12	3.05
17	6.04	4.62	4.01	3.66	3.44	3.28	3.16	3.06	2.98
18	5.98	4.56	3.95	3.61	3.38	3.22	3.10	3.01	2.93
19	5.92	4.51	3.90	3.56	3.33	3.17	3.05	2.96	2.88
20	5.87	4.46	3.86	3.51	3.29	3.13	3.01	2.91	2.84
21	5.83	4.42	3.82	3.48	3.25	3.09	2.97	2.87	2.80
22	5.79	4.38	3.78	3.44	3.22	3.05	2.93	2.84	2.76
23	5.75	4.35	3.75	3.41	3.18	3.02	2.90	2.81	2.73
24	5.72	4.32	3.72	3.38	3.15	2.99	2.87	2.78	2.70
25	5.69	4.29	3.69	3.35	3.13	2.97	2.85	2.75	2.68
26	5.66	4.27	3.67	3.33	3.10	2.94	2.82	2.73	2.65
27	5.63	4.24	3.65	3.31	3.08	2.92	2.80	2.71	2.63
28	5.61	4.22	3.63	3.29	3.06	2.90	2.78	2.69	2.61
29	5.59	4.20	3.61	3.27	3.04	2.88	2.76	2.67	2.59
30	5.57	4.18	3.59	3.25	3.03	2.87	2.75	2.65	2.57
40	5.42	4.05	3.46	3.13	2.90	2.74	2.62	2.53	2.45
60	5.29	3.93	3.34	3.01	2.79	2.63	2.51	2.41	2.33
120	5.15	3.80	3.23	2.89	2.67	2.52	2.39	2.30	2.22
∞	5.02	3.69	3.12	2.79	2.57	2.41	2.29	2.19	2.11

Denominator Degrees of Freedom

SOURCE: From M. Merrington and C. M. Thompson, "Tables of Percentage Points of the Inverted Beta (*F*)-Distribution," *Biometrika* 33 (1943): 73–88. Reproduced by permission of the Biometrika Trustees.

TABLE 6(c) *(continued)*

v_2	\ v_1									
	Numerator Degrees of Freedom									
	10	12	15	20	24	30	40	60	120	∞
1	968.6	976.7	984.9	993.1	997.2	1001	1006	1010	1014	1018
2	39.40	39.41	39.43	39.45	39.46	39.46	39.47	39.48	39.49	39.50
3	14.42	14.34	14.25	14.17	14.12	14.08	14.04	13.99	13.95	13.90
4	8.84	8.75	8.66	8.56	8.51	8.46	8.41	8.36	8.31	8.26
5	6.62	6.52	6.43	6.33	6.28	6.23	6.18	6.12	6.07	6.02
6	5.46	5.37	5.27	5.17	5.12	5.07	5.01	4.96	4.90	4.85
7	4.76	4.67	4.57	4.47	4.42	4.36	4.31	4.25	4.20	4.14
8	4.30	4.20	4.10	4.00	3.95	3.89	3.84	3.78	3.73	3.67
9	3.96	3.87	3.77	3.67	3.61	3.56	3.51	3.45	3.39	3.33
10	3.72	3.62	3.52	3.42	3.37	3.31	3.26	3.20	3.14	3.08
11	3.53	3.43	3.33	3.23	3.17	3.12	3.06	3.00	2.94	2.88
12	3.37	3.28	3.18	3.07	3.02	2.96	2.91	2.85	2.79	2.72
13	3.25	3.15	3.05	2.95	2.89	2.84	2.78	2.72	2.66	2.60
14	3.15	3.05	2.95	2.84	2.79	2.73	2.67	2.61	2.55	2.49
15	3.06	2.96	2.86	2.76	2.70	2.64	2.59	2.52	2.46	2.40
16	2.99	2.89	2.79	2.68	2.63	2.57	2.51	2.45	2.38	2.32
17	2.92	2.82	2.72	2.62	2.56	2.50	2.44	2.38	2.32	2.25
18	2.87	2.77	2.67	2.56	2.50	2.44	2.38	2.32	2.26	2.19
19	2.82	2.72	2.62	2.51	2.45	2.39	2.33	2.27	2.20	2.13
20	2.77	2.68	2.57	2.46	2.41	2.35	2.29	2.22	2.16	2.09
21	2.73	2.64	2.53	2.42	2.37	2.31	2.25	2.18	2.11	2.04
22	2.70	2.60	2.50	2.39	2.33	2.27	2.21	2.14	2.08	2.00
23	2.67	2.57	2.47	2.36	2.30	2.24	2.18	2.11	2.04	1.97
24	2.64	2.54	2.44	2.33	2.27	2.21	2.15	2.08	2.01	1.94
25	2.61	2.51	2.41	2.30	2.24	2.18	2.12	2.05	1.98	1.91
26	2.59	2.49	2.39	2.28	2.22	2.16	2.09	2.03	1.95	1.88
27	2.57	2.47	2.36	2.25	2.19	2.13	2.07	2.00	1.93	1.85
28	2.55	2.45	2.34	2.23	2.17	2.11	2.05	1.98	1.91	1.83
29	2.53	2.43	2.32	2.21	2.15	2.09	2.03	1.96	1.89	1.81
30	2.51	2.41	2.31	2.20	2.14	2.07	2.01	1.94	1.87	1.79
40	2.39	2.29	2.18	2.07	2.01	1.94	1.88	1.80	1.72	1.64
60	2.27	2.17	2.06	1.94	1.88	1.82	1.74	1.67	1.58	1.48
120	2.16	2.05	1.94	1.82	1.76	1.69	1.61	1.53	1.43	1.31
∞	2.05	1.94	1.83	1.71	1.64	1.57	1.48	1.39	1.27	1.00

Denominator Degrees of Freedom

TABLE 6(d) PERCENTAGE POINTS OF THE F DISTRIBUTION, $\alpha = .01$

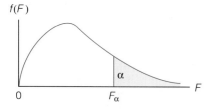

	v_1	Numerator Degrees of Freedom								
v_2		1	2	3	4	5	6	7	8	9
	1	4,052	4,999.5	5,403	5,625	5,764	5,859	5,928	5,982	6,022
	2	98.50	99.00	99.17	99.25	99.30	99.33	99.36	99.37	99.39
	3	34.12	30.82	29.46	28.71	28.24	27.91	27.67	27.49	27.35
	4	21.20	18.00	16.69	15.98	15.52	15.21	14.98	14.80	14.66
	5	16.26	13.27	12.06	11.39	10.97	10.67	10.46	10.29	10.16
	6	13.75	10.92	9.78	9.15	8.75	8.47	8.26	8.10	7.98
	7	12.25	9.55	8.45	7.85	7.46	7.19	6.99	6.84	6.72
	8	11.26	8.65	7.59	7.01	6.63	6.37	6.18	6.03	5.91
	9	10.56	8.02	6.99	6.42	6.06	5.80	5.61	5.47	5.35
	10	10.04	7.56	6.55	5.99	5.64	5.39	5.20	5.06	4.94
	11	9.65	7.21	6.22	5.67	5.32	5.07	4.89	4.74	4.63
	12	9.33	6.93	5.95	5.41	5.06	4.82	4.64	4.50	4.39
	13	9.07	6.70	5.74	5.21	4.86	4.62	4.44	4.30	4.19
	14	8.86	6.51	5.56	5.04	4.69	4.46	4.28	4.14	4.03
	15	8.68	6.36	5.42	4.89	4.56	4.32	4.14	4.00	3.89
	16	8.53	6.23	5.29	4.77	4.44	4.20	4.03	3.89	3.78
	17	8.40	6.11	5.18	4.67	4.34	4.10	3.93	3.79	3.68
	18	8.29	6.01	5.09	4.58	4.25	4.01	3.84	3.71	3.60
	19	8.18	5.93	5.01	4.50	4.17	3.94	3.77	3.63	3.52
	20	8.10	5.85	4.94	4.43	4.10	3.87	3.70	3.56	3.46
	21	8.02	5.78	4.87	4.37	4.04	3.81	3.64	3.51	3.40
	22	7.95	5.72	4.82	4.31	3.99	3.76	3.59	3.45	3.35
	23	7.88	5.66	4.76	4.26	3.94	3.71	3.54	3.41	3.30
	24	7.82	5.61	4.72	4.22	3.90	3.67	3.50	3.36	3.26
	25	7.77	5.57	4.68	4.18	3.85	3.63	3.46	3.32	3.22
	26	7.72	5.53	4.64	4.14	3.82	3.59	3.42	3.29	3.18
	27	7.68	5.49	4.60	4.11	3.78	3.56	3.39	3.26	3.15
	28	7.64	5.45	4.57	4.07	3.75	3.53	3.36	3.23	3.12
	29	7.60	5.42	4.54	4.04	3.73	3.50	3.33	3.20	3.09
	30	7.56	5.39	4.51	4.02	3.70	3.47	3.30	3.17	3.07
	40	7.31	5.18	4.31	3.83	3.51	3.29	3.12	2.99	2.89
	60	7.08	4.98	4.13	3.65	3.34	3.12	2.95	2.82	2.72
	120	6.85	4.79	3.95	3.48	3.17	2.96	2.79	2.66	2.56
	∞	6.63	4.61	3.78	3.32	3.02	2.80	2.64	2.51	2.41

Denominator Degrees of Freedom

SOURCE: From M. Merrington and C. M. Thompson, "Tables of Percentage Points of the Inverted Beta (F)-Distribution," *Biometrika* 33 (1943): 73–88. Reproduced by permission of the Biometrika Trustees.

$\alpha = .02 \qquad df = \frac{(8-1)}{(4-1)} = \frac{1}{3}$

rejection Region $F > F_{\alpha/2} = F_{.01} = 27.67$

$P(F > 27.67)$

$H_0 = \frac{\sigma_1^2}{\sigma_2^2} = 1 \quad H_A \frac{\sigma_1^2}{\sigma_2^2} \neq 1$

$F = \frac{(S_1)^2}{(S_2)^2} = \frac{(29)^2}{(23)^2} = 1.59 \qquad 1.59 < 27.67$

$v_1 = 24 \quad v_2 = 10$

$P(F \leq z.18) = F_{.10} \quad (z.18)$

$P(F \leq z.18)$

$\therefore 1 - .10 = .90 \quad \therefore 90\%$

TABLE 6(d) (continued)

v_2 \ v_1	10	12	15	20	24	30	40	60	120	∞
1	6,056	6,106	6,157	6,209	6,235	6,261	6,287	6,313	6,339	6,366
2	99.40	99.42	99.43	99.45	99.46	99.47	99.47	99.48	99.49	99.50
3	27.23	27.05	26.87	26.69	26.60	26.50	26.41	26.32	26.22	26.13
4	14.55	14.37	14.20	14.02	13.93	13.84	13.75	13.65	13.56	13.46
5	10.05	9.89	9.72	9.55	9.47	9.38	9.29	9.20	9.11	9.02
6	7.87	7.72	7.56	7.40	7.31	7.23	7.14	7.06	6.97	6.88
7	6.62	6.47	6.31	6.16	6.07	5.99	5.91	5.82	5.74	5.65
8	5.81	5.67	5.52	5.36	5.28	5.20	5.12	5.03	4.95	4.86
9	5.26	5.11	4.96	4.81	4.73	4.65	4.57	4.48	4.40	4.31
10	4.85	4.71	4.56	4.41	4.33	4.25	4.17	4.08	4.00	3.91
11	4.54	4.40	4.25	4.10	4.02	3.94	3.86	3.78	3.69	3.60
12	4.30	4.16	4.01	3.86	3.78	3.70	3.62	3.54	3.45	3.36
13	4.10	3.96	3.82	3.66	3.59	3.51	3.43	3.34	3.25	3.17
14	3.94	3.80	3.66	3.51	3.43	3.35	3.27	3.18	3.09	3.00
15	3.80	3.67	3.52	3.37	3.29	3.21	3.13	3.05	2.96	2.87
16	3.69	3.55	3.41	3.26	3.18	3.10	3.02	2.93	2.84	2.75
17	3.59	3.46	3.31	3.16	3.08	3.00	2.92	2.83	2.75	2.65
18	3.51	3.37	3.23	3.08	3.00	2.92	2.84	2.75	2.66	2.57
19	3.43	3.30	3.15	3.00	2.92	2.84	2.76	2.67	2.58	2.49
20	3.37	3.23	3.09	2.94	2.86	2.78	2.69	2.61	2.52	2.42
21	3.31	3.17	3.03	2.88	2.80	2.72	2.64	2.55	2.46	2.36
22	3.26	3.12	2.98	2.83	2.75	2.67	2.58	2.50	2.40	2.31
23	3.21	3.07	2.93	2.78	2.70	2.62	2.54	2.45	2.35	2.26
24	3.17	3.03	2.89	2.74	2.66	2.58	2.49	2.40	2.31	2.21
25	3.13	2.99	2.85	2.70	2.62	2.54	2.45	2.36	2.27	2.17
26	3.09	2.96	2.81	2.66	2.58	2.50	2.42	2.33	2.23	2.13
27	3.06	2.93	2.78	2.63	2.55	2.47	2.38	2.29	2.20	2.10
28	3.03	2.90	2.75	2.60	2.52	2.44	2.35	2.26	2.17	2.06
29	3.00	2.87	2.73	2.57	2.49	2.41	2.33	2.23	2.14	2.03
30	2.98	2.84	2.70	2.55	2.47	2.39	2.30	2.21	2.11	2.01
40	2.80	2.66	2.52	2.37	2.29	2.20	2.11	2.02	1.92	1.80
60	2.63	2.50	2.35	2.20	2.12	2.03	1.94	1.84	1.73	1.60
120	2.47	2.34	2.19	2.03	1.95	1.86	1.76	1.66	1.53	1.38
∞	2.32	2.18	2.04	1.88	1.79	1.70	1.59	1.47	1.32	1.00

Numerator Degrees of Freedom (v_1)

Denominator Degrees of Freedom (v_2)

TABLE 7 PERCENTAGE POINTS OF THE STUDENTIZED RANGE $q_\alpha(k, v)$

(a) $\alpha = .05$

k

v	2	3	4	5	6	7	8	9	10	11	12	13	14	15	16	17	18	19	20
1	18.0	27.0	32.8	37.1	40.4	43.1	45.4	47.4	49.1	50.6	52.0	53.2	54.3	55.4	56.3	57.2	58.0	58.8	59.6
2	6.08	8.33	9.80	10.9	11.7	12.4	13.0	13.5	14.0	14.4	14.7	15.1	15.4	15.7	15.9	16.1	16.4	16.6	16.8
3	4.50	5.91	6.82	7.50	8.04	8.48	8.85	9.18	9.46	9.72	9.95	10.2	10.3	10.5	10.7	10.8	11.0	11.1	11.2
4	3.93	5.04	5.76	6.29	6.71	7.05	7.35	7.60	7.83	8.03	8.21	8.37	8.52	8.66	8.79	8.91	9.03	9.13	9.23
5	3.64	4.60	5.22	5.67	6.03	6.33	6.58	6.80	6.99	7.17	7.32	7.47	7.60	7.72	7.83	7.93	8.03	8.12	8.21
6	3.46	4.34	4.90	5.30	5.63	5.90	6.12	6.32	6.49	6.65	6.79	6.92	7.03	7.14	7.24	7.34	7.43	7.51	7.59
7	3.34	4.16	4.68	5.06	5.36	5.61	5.82	6.00	6.16	6.30	6.43	6.55	6.66	6.76	6.85	6.94	7.02	7.10	7.17
8	3.26	4.04	4.53	4.89	5.17	5.40	5.60	5.77	5.92	6.05	6.18	6.29	6.39	6.48	6.57	6.65	6.73	6.80	6.87
9	3.20	3.95	4.41	4.76	5.02	5.24	5.43	5.59	5.74	5.87	5.98	6.09	6.19	6.28	6.36	6.44	6.51	6.58	6.64
10	3.15	3.88	4.33	4.65	4.91	5.12	5.30	5.46	5.60	5.72	5.83	5.93	6.03	6.11	6.19	6.27	6.34	6.40	6.47
11	3.11	3.82	4.26	4.57	4.82	5.03	5.20	5.35	5.49	5.61	5.71	5.81	5.90	5.98	6.06	6.13	6.20	6.27	6.33
12	3.08	3.77	4.20	4.51	4.75	4.95	5.12	5.27	5.39	5.51	5.61	5.71	5.80	5.88	5.95	6.02	6.09	6.15	6.21
13	3.06	3.73	4.15	4.45	4.69	4.88	5.05	5.19	5.32	5.43	5.53	5.63	5.71	5.79	5.86	5.93	5.99	6.05	6.11
14	3.03	3.70	4.11	4.41	4.64	4.83	4.99	5.13	5.25	5.36	5.46	5.55	5.64	5.71	5.79	5.85	5.91	5.97	6.03
15	3.01	3.67	4.08	4.37	4.59	4.78	4.94	5.08	5.20	5.31	5.40	5.49	5.57	5.65	5.72	5.78	5.85	5.90	5.96
16	3.00	3.65	4.05	4.33	4.56	4.74	4.90	5.03	5.15	5.26	5.35	5.44	5.52	5.59	5.66	5.73	5.79	5.84	5.90
17	2.98	3.63	4.02	4.30	4.52	4.70	4.86	4.99	5.11	5.21	5.31	5.39	5.47	5.54	5.61	5.67	5.73	5.79	5.84
18	2.97	3.61	4.00	4.28	4.49	4.67	4.82	4.96	5.07	5.17	5.27	5.35	5.43	5.50	5.57	5.63	5.69	5.74	5.79
19	2.96	3.59	3.98	4.25	4.47	4.65	4.79	4.92	5.04	5.14	5.23	5.31	5.39	5.46	5.53	5.59	5.65	5.70	5.75
20	2.95	3.58	3.96	4.23	4.45	4.62	4.77	4.90	5.01	5.11	5.20	5.28	5.36	5.43	5.49	5.55	5.61	5.66	5.71
24	2.92	3.53	3.90	4.17	4.37	4.54	4.68	4.81	4.92	5.01	5.10	5.18	5.25	5.32	5.38	5.44	5.49	5.55	5.59
30	2.89	3.49	3.85	4.10	4.30	4.46	4.60	4.72	4.82	4.92	5.00	5.08	5.15	5.21	5.27	5.33	5.38	5.43	5.47
40	2.86	3.44	3.79	4.04	4.23	4.39	4.52	4.63	4.73	4.82	4.90	4.98	5.04	5.11	5.16	5.22	5.27	5.31	5.36
60	2.83	3.40	3.74	3.98	4.16	4.31	4.44	4.55	4.65	4.73	4.81	4.88	4.94	5.00	5.06	5.11	5.15	5.20	5.24
120	2.80	3.36	3.68	3.92	4.10	4.24	4.36	4.47	4.56	4.64	4.71	4.78	4.84	4.90	4.95	5.00	5.04	5.09	5.13
∞	2.77	3.31	3.63	3.86	4.03	4.17	4.29	4.39	4.47	4.55	4.62	4.68	4.74	4.80	4.85	4.89	4.93	4.97	5.01

(b) $\alpha = .01$

k

ν	2	3	4	5	6	7	8	9	10	11	12	13	14	15	16	17	18	19	20
1	90.0	135	164	186	202	216	227	237	246	253	260	266	272	277	282	286	290	294	298
2	14.0	19.0	22.3	24.7	26.6	28.2	29.5	30.7	31.7	32.6	33.4	34.1	34.8	35.4	36.0	36.5	37.0	37.5	37.9
3	8.26	10.6	12.2	13.3	14.2	15.0	15.6	16.2	16.7	17.1	17.5	17.9	18.2	18.5	18.8	19.1	19.3	19.5	19.8
4	6.51	8.12	9.17	9.96	10.6	11.1	11.5	11.9	12.3	12.6	12.8	13.1	13.3	13.5	13.7	13.9	14.1	14.2	14.4
5	5.70	6.97	7.80	8.42	8.91	9.32	9.67	9.97	10.2	10.5	10.7	10.9	11.1	11.2	11.4	11.6	11.7	11.8	11.9
6	5.24	6.33	7.03	7.56	7.97	8.32	8.61	8.87	9.10	9.30	9.49	9.65	9.81	9.95	10.1	10.2	10.3	10.4	10.5
7	4.95	5.92	6.54	7.01	7.37	7.68	7.94	8.17	8.37	8.55	8.71	8.86	9.00	9.12	9.24	9.35	9.46	9.55	9.65
8	4.74	5.63	6.20	6.63	6.96	7.24	7.47	7.68	7.87	8.03	8.18	8.31	8.44	8.55	8.66	8.76	8.85	8.94	9.03
9	4.60	5.43	5.96	6.35	6.66	6.91	7.13	7.32	7.49	7.65	7.78	7.91	8.03	8.13	8.23	8.32	8.41	8.49	8.57
10	4.48	5.27	5.77	6.14	6.43	6.67	6.87	7.05	7.21	7.36	7.48	7.60	7.71	7.81	7.91	7.99	8.07	8.15	8.22
11	4.39	5.14	5.62	5.97	6.25	6.48	6.67	6.84	6.99	7.13	7.25	7.36	7.46	7.56	7.65	7.73	7.81	7.88	7.95
12	4.32	5.04	5.50	5.84	6.10	6.32	6.51	6.67	6.81	6.94	7.06	7.17	7.26	7.36	7.44	7.52	7.59	7.66	7.73
13	4.26	4.96	5.40	5.73	5.98	6.19	6.37	6.53	6.67	6.79	6.90	7.01	7.10	7.19	7.27	7.34	7.42	7.48	7.55
14	4.21	4.89	5.32	5.63	5.88	6.08	6.26	6.41	6.54	6.66	6.77	6.87	6.96	7.05	7.12	7.20	7.27	7.33	7.39
15	4.17	4.83	5.25	5.56	5.80	5.99	6.16	6.31	6.44	6.55	6.66	6.76	6.84	6.93	7.00	7.07	7.14	7.20	7.26
16	4.13	4.78	5.19	5.49	5.72	5.92	6.08	6.22	6.35	6.46	6.56	6.66	6.74	6.82	6.90	6.97	7.03	7.09	7.15
17	4.10	4.74	5.14	5.43	5.66	5.85	6.01	6.15	6.27	6.38	6.48	6.57	6.66	6.73	6.80	6.87	6.94	7.00	7.05
18	4.07	4.70	5.09	5.38	5.60	5.79	5.94	6.08	6.20	6.31	6.41	6.50	6.58	6.65	6.72	6.79	6.85	6.91	6.96
19	4.05	4.67	5.05	5.33	5.55	5.73	5.89	6.02	6.14	6.25	6.34	6.43	6.51	6.58	6.65	6.72	6.78	6.84	6.89
20	4.02	4.64	5.02	5.29	5.51	5.69	5.84	5.97	6.09	6.19	6.29	6.37	6.45	6.52	6.59	6.65	6.71	6.76	6.82
24	3.96	4.54	4.91	5.17	5.37	5.54	5.69	5.81	5.92	6.02	6.11	6.19	6.26	6.33	6.39	6.45	6.51	6.56	6.61
30	3.89	4.45	4.80	5.05	5.24	5.40	5.54	5.65	5.76	5.85	5.93	6.01	6.08	6.14	6.20	6.26	6.31	6.36	6.41
40	3.82	4.37	4.70	4.93	5.11	5.27	5.39	5.50	5.60	5.69	5.77	5.84	5.90	5.96	6.02	6.07	6.12	6.17	6.21
60	3.76	4.28	4.60	4.82	4.99	5.13	5.25	5.36	5.45	5.53	5.60	5.67	5.73	5.79	5.84	5.89	5.93	5.98	6.02
120	3.70	4.20	4.50	4.71	4.87	5.01	5.12	5.21	5.30	5.38	5.44	5.51	5.56	5.61	5.66	5.71	5.75	5.79	5.83
∞	3.64	4.12	4.40	4.60	4.76	4.88	4.99	5.08	5.16	5.23	5.29	5.35	5.40	5.45	5.49	5.54	5.57	5.61	5.65

SOURCE: From E. S. Pearson and H. O. Hartley, *Biometrika Tables for Statisticians* Vol. 1, pp. 176–77. Reproduced by permission of the Biometrika Trustees.

TABLE 8   CRITICAL VALUES OF THE WILCOXON RANK SUM TEST FOR INDEPENDENT SAMPLES

Test statistic is $T = T_A$, where T_A is the rank sum of the sample with the smaller sample size.

(a) $\alpha = .025$ one-tailed; $\alpha = .05$ two-tailed

n_2 \ n_1	3		4		5		6		7		8		9		10	
	T_L	T_U	T_L	T_U	T_L	T_U	T_L	T_U	T_L	T_U	T_L	T_U	T_L	T_U	T_L	T_U
3	5	16														
4	6	18	11	25												
5	6	21	12	28	18	37										
6	7	23	12	32	19	41	26	52								
7	7	26	13	35	20	45	28	56	37	68						
8	8	28	14	38	21	49	29	61	39	73	49	87				
9	8	31	15	41	22	53	31	65	41	78	51	93	63	108		
10	9	33	16	44	24	56	32	70	43	83	54	98	66	114	79	131

(b) $\alpha = .05$ one-tailed; $\alpha = .10$ two-tailed

n_2 \ n_1	3		4		5		6		7		8		9		10	
	T_L	T_U	T_L	T_U	T_L	T_U	T_L	T_U	T_L	T_U	T_L	T_U	T_L	T_U	T_L	T_U
3	6	15														
4	7	17	12	24												
5	7	20	13	27	19	36										
6	8	22	14	30	20	40	28	50								
7	9	24	15	33	22	43	30	54	39	66						
8	9	27	16	36	24	46	32	58	41	71	52	84				
9	10	29	17	39	25	50	33	63	43	76	54	90	66	105		
10	11	31	18	42	26	54	35	67	46	80	57	95	69	111	83	127

SOURCE: From F. Wilcoxon and R. A. Wilcox, "Some Rapid Approximate Statistical Procedures" (1964), p. 28. Reproduced with the permission of American Cyanamid Company.

TABLE 9   CRITICAL VALUES OF T_L IN THE WILCOXON SIGNED RANK SUM TEST FOR THE MATCHED PAIRS EXPERIMENT

n	$P(T \le T_L) = .05$	.025	.01	.005	n	$P(T \le T_L) = .05$	.025	.01	.005
	T_L	T_L	T_L	T_L		T_L	T_L	T_L	T_L
5	1	—	—	—	28	130	117	102	92
6	2	1	—	—	29	141	127	111	100
7	4	2	0	—	30	152	137	120	109
8	6	4	2	0	31	163	148	130	118
9	8	6	3	2	32	175	159	141	128
10	11	8	5	3	33	188	171	151	138
11	14	11	7	5	34	201	183	162	149
12	17	14	10	7	35	214	195	174	160
13	21	17	13	10	36	228	208	186	171
14	26	21	16	13	37	242	222	198	183
15	30	25	20	16	38	256	235	211	195
16	36	30	24	19	39	271	250	224	208
17	41	35	28	23	40	287	264	238	221
18	47	40	33	28	41	303	279	252	234
19	54	46	38	32	42	319	295	267	248
20	60	52	43	37	43	336	311	281	262
21	68	59	49	43	44	353	327	297	277
22	75	66	56	49	45	371	344	313	292
23	83	73	62	55	46	389	361	329	307
24	92	81	69	61	47	408	379	345	323
25	101	90	77	68	48	427	397	362	339
26	110	98	85	76	49	446	415	380	356
27	120	107	93	84	50	466	434	398	373

SOURCE: From F. Wilcoxon and R. A. Wilcox, "Some Rapid Approximate Statistical Procedures" (1964), p. 28. Reproduced with the permission of American Cyanamid Company.

TABLE 10 *CRITICAL VALUES OF THE KOLMOGOROV–SMIRNOV TEST*

Sample Size n	Significance Level α				
	.20	.10	.05	.02	.01
1	.900	.950	.975	.990	.995
2	.684	.776	.842	.900	.929
3	.565	.636	.708	.785	.829
4	.493	.565	.624	.689	.734
5	.447	.509	.563	.627	.669
6	.410	.468	.519	.577	.617
7	.381	.436	.483	.538	.576
8	.358	.410	.454	.507	.542
9	.339	.387	.430	.480	.513
10	.323	.369	.409	.457	.489
11	.308	.352	.391	.437	.468
12	.296	.338	.375	.419	.449
13	.285	.325	.361	.404	.432
14	.275	.314	.349	.390	.418
15	.266	.304	.338	.377	.404
16	.258	.295	.327	.366	.392
17	.250	.286	.318	.355	.381
18	.244	.279	.309	.346	.371
19	.237	.271	.301	.337	.361
20	.232	.265	.294	.329	.352
21	.226	.259	.287	.321	.344
22	.221	.253	.281	.314	.337
23	.216	.247	.275	.307	.330
24	.212	.242	.269	.301	.323
25	.208	.238	.264	.295	.317
26	.204	.233	.259	.290	.311
27	.200	.229	.254	.284	.305
28	.197	.225	.250	.279	.300
29	.193	.221	.246	.275	.295
30	.190	.218	.242	.270	.290
31	.187	.214	.238	.266	.285
32	.184	.211	.234	.262	.281

TABLE 10   *(continued)*

Sample Size n	Significance Level α				
	.20	.10	.05	.02	.01
33	.182	.208	.231	.258	.277
34	.179	.205	.227	.254	.273
35	.177	.202	.224	.251	.269
36	.174	.199	.221	.247	.265
37	.172	.196	.218	.244	.262
38	.170	.194	.215	.241	.258
39	.168	.191	.213	.238	.255
40	.165	.189	.210	.235	.252
Over 40	$\dfrac{1.07}{\sqrt{n}}$	$\dfrac{1.22}{\sqrt{n}}$	$\dfrac{1.36}{\sqrt{n}}$	$\dfrac{1.52}{\sqrt{n}}$	$\dfrac{1.63}{\sqrt{n}}$

SOURCE: From L. H. Miller, "Tables of Percentage Points of the Kolmogorov Statistics," *Journal of the American Statistical Association* 51 (1956): 111–21. As adapted by Conover, *Practical Nonparametric Statistics* (New York: John Wiley, 1971), p. 397. Reprinted by permission of John Wiley & Sons, Inc., and the American Statistical Association.

TABLE 11 *CRITICAL VALUES OF THE LILLIEFORS TEST*

Sample Size n	Significance Level α				
	.20	.15	.10	.05	.01
4	.300	.319	.352	.381	.417
5	.285	.299	.315	.337	.405
6	.265	.277	.294	.319	.364
7	.247	.258	.276	.300	.348
8	.233	.244	.261	.285	.331
9	.223	.233	.249	.271	.311
10	.215	.224	.239	.258	.294
11	.206	.217	.230	.249	.284
12	.199	.212	.223	.242	.275
13	.190	.202	.214	.234	.268
14	.183	.194	.207	.227	.261
15	.177	.187	.201	.220	.257
16	.173	.182	.195	.213	.250
17	.169	.177	.189	.206	.245
18	.166	.173	.184	.200	.239
19	.163	.169	.179	.195	.235
20	.160	.166	.174	.190	.231
25	.142	.147	.158	.173	.200
30	.131	.136	.144	.161	.187
Over 30	$\dfrac{.736}{\sqrt{n}}$	$\dfrac{.768}{\sqrt{n}}$	$\dfrac{.805}{\sqrt{n}}$	$\dfrac{.886}{\sqrt{n}}$	$\dfrac{.1031}{\sqrt{n}}$

SOURCE: From H. W. Lilliefors, "On the Kolmogorov–Smirnov Test for Normality with Mean and Variance Unknown," *Journal of the American Statistical Association* 62 (1967): 399–402. As adapted by Conover, *Practical Nonparametric Statistics* (New York: John Wiley, 1971), p. 398. Reprinted by permission of John Wiley & Sons, Inc., and the American Statistical Association.

TABLE 12 *CRITICAL VALUES OF THE SPEARMAN RANK CORRELATION COEFFICIENT*

The α values correspond to a one-tail test of H_0: $\rho_s = 0$. The value should be doubled for two-tail tests.

n	$\alpha = .05$	$\alpha = .025$	$\alpha = .01$	$\alpha = .005$
5	.900	—	—	—
6	.829	.886	.943	—
7	.714	.786	.893	—
8	.643	.738	.833	.881
9	.600	.683	.783	.833
10	.564	.648	.745	.794
11	.523	.623	.736	.818
12	.497	.591	.703	.780
13	.475	.566	.673	.745
14	.457	.545	.646	.716
15	.441	.525	.623	.689
16	.425	.507	.601	.666
17	.412	.490	.582	.645
18	.399	.476	.564	.625
19	.388	.462	.549	.608
20	.377	.450	.534	.591
21	.368	.438	.521	.576
22	.359	.428	.508	.562
23	.351	.418	.496	.549
24	.343	.409	.485	.537
25	.336	.400	.475	.526
26	.329	.392	.465	.515
27	.323	.385	.456	.505
28	.317	.377	.448	.496
29	.311	.370	.440	.487
30	.305	.364	.432	.478

SOURCE: From E. G. Olds, "Distribution of Sums of Squares of Rank Differences for Small Samples," *Annals of Mathematical Statistics* 9 (1938). Reproduced with the permission of the Institute of Mathematical Statistics.

TABLE 13(a) *CRITICAL VALUES FOR THE DURBIN–WATSON d STATISTIC, $\alpha = .05$*

n	k = 1 d_L	k = 1 d_U	k = 2 d_L	k = 2 d_U	k = 3 d_L	k = 3 d_U	k = 4 d_L	k = 4 d_U	k = 5 d_L	k = 5 d_U
15	1.08	1.36	.95	1.54	.82	1.75	.69	1.97	.56	2.21
16	1.10	1.37	.98	1.54	.86	1.73	.74	1.93	.62	2.15
17	1.13	1.38	1.02	1.54	.90	1.71	.78	1.90	.67	2.10
18	1.16	1.39	1.05	1.53	.93	1.69	.82	1.87	.71	2.06
19	1.18	1.40	1.08	1.53	.97	1.68	.86	1.85	.75	2.02
20	1.20	1.41	1.10	1.54	1.00	1.68	.90	1.83	.79	1.99
21	1.22	1.42	1.13	1.54	1.03	1.67	.93	1.81	.83	1.96
22	1.24	1.43	1.15	1.54	1.05	1.66	.96	1.80	.86	1.94
23	1.26	1.44	1.17	1.54	1.08	1.66	.99	1.79	.90	1.92
24	1.27	1.45	1.19	1.55	1.10	1.66	1.01	1.78	.93	1.90
25	1.29	1.45	1.21	1.55	1.12	1.66	1.04	1.77	.95	1.89
26	1.30	1.46	1.22	1.55	1.14	1.65	1.06	1.76	.98	1.88
27	1.32	1.47	1.24	1.56	1.16	1.65	1.08	1.76	1.01	1.86
28	1.33	1.48	1.26	1.56	1.18	1.65	1.10	1.75	1.03	1.85
29	1.34	1.48	1.27	1.56	1.20	1.65	1.12	1.74	1.05	1.84
30	1.35	1.49	1.28	1.57	1.21	1.65	1.14	1.74	1.07	1.83
31	1.36	1.50	1.30	1.57	1.23	1.65	1.16	1.74	1.09	1.83
32	1.37	1.50	1.31	1.57	1.24	1.65	1.18	1.73	1.11	1.82
33	1.38	1.51	1.32	1.58	1.26	1.65	1.19	1.73	1.13	1.81
34	1.39	1.51	1.33	1.58	1.27	1.65	1.21	1.73	1.15	1.81
35	1.40	1.52	1.34	1.58	1.28	1.65	1.22	1.73	1.16	1.80
36	1.41	1.52	1.35	1.59	1.29	1.65	1.24	1.73	1.18	1.80
37	1.42	1.53	1.36	1.59	1.31	1.66	1.25	1.72	1.19	1.80
38	1.43	1.54	1.37	1.59	1.32	1.66	1.26	1.72	1.21	1.79
39	1.43	1.54	1.38	1.60	1.33	1.66	1.27	1.72	1.22	1.79
40	1.44	1.54	1.39	1.60	1.34	1.66	1.29	1.72	1.23	1.79
45	1.48	1.57	1.43	1.62	1.38	1.67	1.34	1.72	1.29	1.78
50	1.50	1.59	1.46	1.63	1.42	1.67	1.38	1.72	1.34	1.77
55	1.53	1.60	1.49	1.64	1.45	1.68	1.41	1.72	1.38	1.77
60	1.55	1.62	1.51	1.65	1.48	1.69	1.44	1.73	1.41	1.77
65	1.57	1.63	1.54	1.66	1.50	1.70	1.47	1.73	1.44	1.77
70	1.58	1.64	1.55	1.67	1.52	1.70	1.49	1.74	1.46	1.77
75	1.60	1.65	1.57	1.68	1.54	1.71	1.51	1.74	1.49	1.77
80	1.61	1.66	1.59	1.69	1.56	1.72	1.53	1.74	1.51	1.77
85	1.62	1.67	1.60	1.70	1.57	1.72	1.55	1.75	1.52	1.77
90	1.63	1.68	1.61	1.70	1.59	1.73	1.57	1.75	1.54	1.78
95	1.64	1.69	1.62	1.71	1.60	1.73	1.58	1.75	1.56	1.78
100	1.65	1.69	1.63	1.72	1.61	1.74	1.59	1.76	1.57	1.78

TABLE 13(b) *CRITICAL VALUES FOR THE DURBIN–WATSON d STATISTIC, $\alpha = .01$*

n	$k = 1$ d_L	d_U	$k = 2$ d_L	d_U	$k = 3$ d_L	d_U	$k = 4$ d_L	d_U	$k = 5$ d_L	d_U
15	.81	1.07	.70	1.25	.59	1.46	.49	1.70	.39	1.96
16	.84	1.09	.74	1.25	.63	1.44	.53	1.66	.44	1.90
17	.87	1.10	.77	1.25	.67	1.43	.57	1.63	.48	1.85
18	.90	1.12	.80	1.26	.71	1.42	.61	1.60	.52	1.80
19	.93	1.13	.83	1.26	.74	1.41	.65	1.58	.56	1.77
20	.95	1.15	.86	1.27	.77	1.41	.68	1.57	.60	1.74
21	.97	1.16	.89	1.27	.80	1.41	.72	1.55	.63	1.71
22	1.00	1.17	.91	1.28	.83	1.40	.75	1.54	.66	1.69
23	1.02	1.19	.94	1.29	.86	1.40	.77	1.53	.70	1.67
24	1.04	1.20	.96	1.30	.88	1.41	.80	1.53	.72	1.66
25	1.05	1.21	.98	1.30	.90	1.41	.83	1.52	.75	1.65
26	1.07	1.22	1.00	1.31	.93	1.41	.85	1.52	.78	1.64
27	1.09	1.23	1.02	1.32	.95	1.41	.88	1.51	.81	1.63
28	1.10	1.24	1.04	1.32	.97	1.41	.90	1.51	.83	1.62
29	1.12	1.25	1.05	1.33	.99	1.42	.92	1.51	.85	1.61
30	1.13	1.26	1.07	1.34	1.01	1.42	.94	1.51	.88	1.61
31	1.15	1.27	1.08	1.34	1.02	1.42	.96	1.51	.90	1.60
32	1.16	1.28	1.10	1.35	1.04	1.43	.98	1.51	.92	1.60
33	1.17	1.29	1.11	1.36	1.05	1.43	1.00	1.51	.94	1.59
34	1.18	1.30	1.13	1.36	1.07	1.43	1.01	1.51	.95	1.59
35	1.19	1.31	1.14	1.37	1.08	1.44	1.03	1.51	.97	1.59
36	1.21	1.32	1.15	1.38	1.10	1.44	1.04	1.51	.99	1.59
37	1.22	1.32	1.16	1.38	1.11	1.45	1.06	1.51	1.00	1.59
38	1.23	1.33	1.18	1.39	1.12	1.45	1.07	1.52	1.02	1.58
39	1.24	1.34	1.19	1.39	1.14	1.45	1.09	1.52	1.03	1.58
40	1.25	1.34	1.20	1.40	1.15	1.46	1.10	1.52	1.05	1.58
45	1.29	1.38	1.24	1.42	1.20	1.48	1.16	1.53	1.11	1.58
50	1.32	1.40	1.28	1.45	1.24	1.49	1.20	1.54	1.16	1.59
55	1.36	1.43	1.32	1.47	1.28	1.51	1.25	1.55	1.21	1.59
60	1.38	1.45	1.35	1.48	1.32	1.52	1.28	1.56	1.25	1.60
65	1.41	1.47	1.38	1.50	1.35	1.53	1.31	1.57	1.28	1.61
70	1.43	1.49	1.40	1.52	1.37	1.55	1.34	1.58	1.31	1.61
75	1.45	1.50	1.42	1.53	1.39	1.56	1.37	1.59	1.34	1.62
80	1.47	1.52	1.44	1.54	1.42	1.57	1.39	1.60	1.36	1.62
85	1.48	1.53	1.46	1.55	1.43	1.58	1.41	1.60	1.39	1.63
90	1.50	1.54	1.47	1.56	1.45	1.59	1.43	1.61	1.41	1.64
95	1.51	1.55	1.49	1.57	1.47	1.60	1.45	1.62	1.42	1.64
100	1.52	1.56	1.50	1.58	1.48	1.60	1.46	1.63	1.44	1.65

SOURCE: From J. Durbin and G. S. Watson, "Testing for Serial Correlation in Least Squares Regression, II," *Biometrika* 30 (1951): 159–78. Reproduced by permission of the Biometrika Trustees.

TABLE 14 RANDOM NUMBERS

Row	1	2	3	4	5	6	7	8	9	10	11	12	13	14
1	13284	16834	74151	92027	24670	36665	00770	22878	02179	51602	07270	76517	97275	45960
2	21224	00370	30420	03883	96648	89428	41583	17564	27395	63904	41548	49197	82277	24120
3	99052	47887	81085	64933	66279	80432	65793	83287	34142	13241	30590	97760	35848	91983
4	00199	50993	98603	38452	87890	94624	69721	57484	67501	77638	44331	11257	71131	11059
5	60578	06483	28733	37867	07936	98710	98539	27186	31237	80612	44488	97819	70401	95419
6	91240	18312	17441	01929	18163	69201	31211	54288	39296	37318	65724	90401	79017	62077
7	97458	14229	12063	59611	32249	90466	33216	19358	02591	54263	88449	01912	07436	50813
8	35249	38646	34475	72417	60514	69257	12489	51924	86871	92446	36607	11458	30440	52639
9	38980	46600	11759	11900	46743	27860	77940	39298	97838	95145	32378	68038	89351	37005
10	10750	52745	38749	87365	58959	53731	89295	59062	39404	13198	59960	70408	29812	83126
11	36247	27850	73958	20673	37800	63835	71051	84724	52492	22342	78071	17456	96104	18327
12	70994	66986	99744	72438	01174	42159	11392	20724	54322	36923	70009	23233	65438	59685
13	99638	94702	11463	18148	81386	80431	90628	52506	02016	85151	88598	47821	00265	82525
14	72055	15774	43857	99805	10419	76939	25993	03544	21560	83471	43989	90770	22965	44247
15	24038	65541	85788	55835	38835	59399	13790	35112	01324	39520	76210	22467	83275	32286
16	74976	14631	35908	28221	39470	91548	12854	30166	09073	75887	36782	00268	97121	57676
17	35553	71628	70189	26436	63407	91178	90348	55359	80392	41012	36270	77786	89578	21059
18	35676	12797	51434	82976	42010	26344	92920	92155	58807	54644	58581	95331	78629	73344
19	74815	67523	72985	23183	02446	63594	98924	20633	58842	85961	07648	70164	34994	67662
20	45246	88048	65173	50989	91060	89894	36063	32819	68559	99221	49475	50558	34698	71800
21	76509	47069	86378	41797	11910	49672	88575	97966	32466	10083	54728	81972	58975	30761
22	19689	90332	04315	21358	97248	11188	39062	63312	52496	07349	79178	33692	57352	72862
23	42751	35318	97513	61537	54955	08159	00337	80778	27507	95478	21252	12746	37554	97775
24	11946	22681	45045	13964	57517	59419	58045	44067	58716	58840	45557	96345	33271	53464
25	96518	48688	20996	11090	48396	57177	83867	86464	14342	21545	46717	72364	86954	55580

Column

26	35726 58643 76869 84622 39098 36083 72505 92265 23107 60278 05822 46760 44294 07672
27	39737 42750 48968 70536 84864 64952 38404 94317 65402 13589 01055 79044 19308 83623
28	97025 66492 56177 04049 80312 48028 26408 43591 75528 65341 49044 95495 81256 53214
29	62814 08075 09788 56350 76787 51591 54509 49295 85830 59860 30883 89660 96142 18354
30	25578 22950 15227 83291 41737 79599 96191 71845 86899 70694 24290 01551 80092 82118
31	68763 69576 88991 49662 46704 63362 56625 00481 73323 91427 15264 06969 57048 54149
32	17900 00813 64361 60725 88974 61005 99709 30666 26451 11528 44323 34778 60342 60388
33	71944 60227 63551 71109 05624 43836 58254 26160 32116 63403 35404 57146 10909 07346
34	54684 93691 85132 64399 29182 44324 14491 55226 78793 34107 30374 48429 51376 09559
35	25946 27623 11258 65204 52832 50880 22273 05554 99521 73791 85744 29276 70326 60251
36	01353 39318 44961 44972 91766 90262 56073 06606 51826 18893 83448 31915 97764 75091
37	99083 88191 27662 99113 57174 35571 99884 13951 71057 53961 61448 74909 07322 80960
38	52021 45406 37945 75234 24327 86978 22644 87779 23753 99926 63898 54886 18051 96314
39	78755 47744 43776 83098 03225 14281 83637 55984 13300 52212 58781 14905 46502 04472
40	25282 69106 59180 16257 22810 43609 12224 25643 89884 31149 85423 32581 34374 70873
41	11959 94202 02743 86847 79725 51811 12998 76844 05320 54236 53891 70226 38632 84776
42	11644 13792 98190 01424 30078 28197 55583 05197 47714 68440 22016 79204 06862 94451
43	06307 97912 68110 59812 95448 43244 31262 88880 13040 16458 43813 89416 42482 33939
44	76285 75714 89585 99296 52640 46518 55486 90754 88932 19937 57119 23251 55619 23679
45	55322 07589 39600 60866 63007 20007 66819 84164 61131 81429 60676 42807 78286 29015
46	78017 90928 90220 92503 83375 26986 74399 30885 88567 29169 72816 53357 15428 86932
47	44768 43342 20696 26331 43140 69744 82928 24988 94237 46138 77426 39039 55596 12655
48	25100 19336 14605 86603 51680 97678 24261 02464 86563 74812 60069 71674 15478 47642
49	83612 46623 62876 85197 07824 91392 58317 37726 84628 42221 10268 20692 15699 29167
50	41347 81666 82961 60413 71020 83658 02415 33322 66036 98712 46795 16308 28413 05417

SOURCE: Abridged from W. H. Beyer, ed., *CRC Standard Mathematical Tables*, 26th ed. (Boca Raton: CRC Press, 1981). Reproduced by permission of the publisher. Copyright CRC Press, Inc., Boca Raton, Florida.

INDEX

NORMAL CURVE AREAS

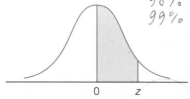

z	.00	.01	.02	.03	.04	.05	.06	.07	.08	.09
0.0	.0000	.0040	.0080	.0120	.0160	.0199	.0239	.0279	.0319	.0359
0.1	.0398	.0438	.0478	.0517	.0557	.0596	.0636	.0675	.0714	.0753
0.2	.0793	.0832	.0871	.0910	.0948	.0987	.1026	.1064	.1103	.1141
0.3	.1179	.1217	.1255	.1293	.1331	.1368	.1406	.1443	.1480	.1517
0.4	.1554	.1591	.1628	.1664	.1700	.1736	.1772	.1808	.1844	.1879
0.5	.1915	.1950	.1985	.2019	.2054	.2088	.2123	.2157	.2190	.2224
0.6	.2257	.2291	.2324	.2357	.2389	.2422	.2454	.2486	.2517	.2549
0.7	.2580	.2611	.2642	.2673	.2704	.2734	.2764	.2794	.2823	.2852
0.8	.2881	.2910	.2939	.2967	.2995	.3023	.3051	.3078	.3106	.3133
0.9	.3159	.3186	.3212	.3238	.3264	.3289	.3315	.3340	.3365	.3389
1.0	.3413	.3438	.3461	.3485	.3508	.3531	.3554	.3577	.3599	.3621
1.1	.3643	.3665	.3686	.3708	.3729	.3749	.3770	.3790	.3810	.3830
1.2	.3849	.3869	.3888	.3907	.3925	.3944	.3962	.3980	.3997	.4015
1.3	.4032	.4049	.4066	.4082	.4099	.4115	.4131	.4147	.4162	.4177
1.4	.4192	.4207	.4222	.4236	.4251	.4265	.4279	.4292	.4306	.4319
1.5	.4332	.4345	.4357	.4370	.4382	.4394	.4406	.4418	.4429	.4441
1.6	.4452	.4463	.4474	.4484	.4495	.4505	.4515	.4525	.4535	.4545
1.7	.4554	.4564	.4573	.4582	.4591	.4599	.4608	.4616	.4625	.4633
1.8	.4641	.4649	.4656	.4664	.4671	.4678	.4686	.4693	.4699	.4706
1.9	.4713	.4719	.4726	.4732	.4738	.4744	.4750	.4756	.4761	.4767
2.0	.4772	.4778	.4783	.4788	.4793	.4798	.4803	.4808	.4812	.4817
2.1	.4821	.4826	.4830	.4834	.4838	.4842	.4846	.4850	.4854	.4857
2.2	.4861	.4864	.4868	.4871	.4875	.4878	.4881	.4884	.4887	.4890
2.3	.4893	.4896	.4898	.4901	.4904	.4906	.4909	.4911	.4913	.4916
2.4	.4918	.4920	.4922	.4925	.4927	.4929	.4931	.4932	.4934	.4936
2.5	.4938	.4940	.4941	.4943	.4945	.4946	.4948	.4949	.4951	.4952
2.6	.4953	.4955	.4956	.4957	.4959	.4960	.4961	.4962	.4963	.4964
2.7	.4965	.4966	.4967	.4968	.4969	.4970	.4971	.4972	.4973	.4974
2.8	.4974	.4975	.4976	.4977	.4977	.4978	.4979	.4979	.4980	.4981
2.9	.4981	.4982	.4982	.4983	.4984	.4984	.4985	.4985	.4986	.4986
3.0	.4987	.4987	.4987	.4988	.4988	.4989	.4989	.4989	.4990	.4990

Source: Abridged from Table I of A. Hald, *Statistical Tables and Formulas* (New York: John Wiley & Sons, Inc.), 1952. Reproduced by permission of A. Hald and the publisher, John Wiley & Sons, Inc.